MASTER VISUALLY™

Dreamweaver® 4 and Flash™ 5

MASTER VISUALLY™

Dreamweaver® 4 and Flash™ 5

By Sherry Kinkoph, Mike Wooldridge, and Brock Bigard
Contributions by Ben Brock, Joseph S. Morse, and Jon Rohan

From

maranGraphics®

&

Best Selling Books • Digital Downloads • e-Books • Answer Networks • e-Newsletters • Branded Web Sites • e-Learning

New York, NY • Cleveland, OH • Indianapolis, IN

Master VISUALLY™ Dreamweaver® 4 and Flash™ 5

Published by
Hungry Minds, Inc.
909 Third Avenue
New York, NY 10022

maranGraphics, Inc.
5755 Coopers Avenue
Mississauga, Ontario, Canada
L4Z 1R9

Library of Congress Control Number: 2001089360
ISBN: 0-7645-0855-5
Printed in the United States of America
10 9 8 7 6 5 4 3 2 1

1V/RQ/QX/QR/IN

Distributed in the United States by Hungry Minds, Inc.

Distributed by CDG Books Canada Inc. for Canada; by Transworld Publishers Limited in the United Kingdom; by IDG Norge Books for Norway; by IDG Sweden Books for Sweden; by IDG Books Australia Publishing Corporation Pty. Ltd. for Australia and New Zealand; by TransQuest Publishers Pte Ltd. for Singapore, Malaysia, Thailand, Indonesia, and Hong Kong; by Gotop Information Inc. for Taiwan; by ICG Muse, Inc. for Japan; by Intersoft for South Africa; by Eyrolles for France; by International Thomson Publishing for Germany, Austria and Switzerland; by Distribuidora Cuspide for Argentina; by LR International for Brazil; by Galileo Libros for Chile; by Ediciones ZETA S.C.R. Ltda. for Peru; by WS Computer Publishing Corporation, Inc., for the Philippines; by Contemporanea de Ediciones for Venezuela; by Express Computer Distributors for the Caribbean and West Indies; by Micronesia Media Distributor, Inc. for Micronesia; by Chips Computadoras S.A. de C.V. for Mexico; by Editorial Norma de Panama S.A. for Panama; by American Bookshops for Finland.

For corporate orders, please call maranGraphics at 800-469-6616 or

fax 905-890-9434.

For general information on Hungry Minds' products and services please contact our Customer Care Department within the U.S. at 800-762-2974, outside the U.S. at 317-572-3993 or fax 317-572-4002.

For sales inquiries and reseller information, including discounts, premium and bulk quantity sales, and foreign-language translations, please contact our Customer Care Department at 800-434-3422, fax 317-572-4002, or write to Hungry Minds, Inc., Attn: Customer Care Department, 10475 Crosspoint Boulevard, Indianapolis, IN 46256.

For information on licensing foreign or domestic rights, please contact our Sub-Rights Customer Care Department at 212-884-5000.

For information on using Hungry Minds' products and services in the classroom or for ordering examination copies, please contact our Educational Sales Department at 800-434-2086 or fax 317-572-4005.

Please contact our Public Relations Department at 317-572-3168 for press review copies or 317-572-3168 for author interviews and other publicity information or fax 317-572-4168.

For authorization to photocopy items for corporate, personal, or educational use, please contact Copyright Clearance Center, 222 Rosewood Drive, Danvers, MA 01923, or fax 978-750-4470.

Screen shots displayed in this book are based on pre-released software and are subject to change.

Trademark Acknowledgments

Permissions

maranGraphics

Certain text and illustrations by maranGraphics, Inc., used with maranGraphics' permission.

Sunkist Growers

U.S. Corporate Sales
Contact maranGraphics
at (800) 469-6616 or
fax (905) 890-9434.

U.S. Trade Sales
Contact Hungry Minds
at (800) 434-3422
or (317) 572-4002.

Praise for Visual books...

"If you have to see it to believe it, this is the book for you!"

–PC World

"I would like to take this time to compliment maranGraphics on creating such great books. I work for a leading manufacturer of office products, and sometimes they tend to NOT give you the meat and potatoes of certain subjects, which causes great confusion. Thank you for making it clear. Keep up the good work."

–Kirk Santoro (Burbank, CA)

"I write to extend my thanks and appreciation for your books. They are clear, easy to follow, and straight to the point. Keep up the good work! I bought several of your books and they are just right! No regrets! I will always buy your books because they are the best."

–Seward Kollie (Dakar, Senegal)

"What fantastic teaching books you have produced! Congratulations to you and your staff."

–Bruno Tonon (Melbourne, Australia)

"Compliments To The Chef!! Your books are extraordinary! Or, simply put, Extra-Ordinary, meaning way above the rest! THANKYOUTHANKYOU THANKYOU! for creating these. They have saved me from serious mistakes, and showed me a right and simple way to do things. I buy them for friends, family, and colleagues."

–Christine J. Manfrin (Castle Rock, CO)

"A master tutorial/reference — from the leaders in visual learning!"

–Infoworld

"Your books are superior! An avid reader since childhood, I've consumed literally tens of thousands of books, a significant quantity in the learning/teaching category. Your series is the most precise, visually appealing and compelling to peruse. Kudos!"

–Margaret Rose Chmilar (Edmonton, Alberta, Canada)

"You're marvelous! I am greatly in your debt."

–Patrick Baird (Lacey, WA)

"Just wanted to say THANK YOU to your company for providing books which make learning fast, easy, and exciting! I learn visually so your books have helped me greatly – from Windows instruction to Web page development. I'm looking forward to using more of your Master Books series in the future as I am now a computer support specialist. Best wishes for continued success."

–Angela J. Barker (Springfield, MO)

"A publishing concept whose time has come!"

–The Globe and Mail

"I have over the last 10-15 years purchased $1000's worth of computer books but find your books the most easily read, best set out and most helpful and easily understood books on software and computers I have ever read. You produce the best computer books money can buy. Please keep up the good work."

–John Gatt (Adamstown Heights, Australia)

"The Greatest. This whole series is the best computer learning tool of any kind I've ever seen."

–Joe Orr (Brooklyn, NY)

maranGraphics is a family-run business located near Toronto, Canada.

At maranGraphics, we believe in producing great computer books — one book at a time.

maranGraphics has been producing high-technology products for over 25 years, which enables us to offer the computer book community a unique communication process.

Our computer books use an integrated communication process, which is very different from the approach used in other computer books. Each spread is, in essence, a flow chart — the text and screen shots are totally incorporated into the layout of the spread. Introductory text and helpful tips complete the learning experience.

maranGraphics' approach encourages the left and right sides of the brain to work together — resulting in faster orientation and greater memory retention.

Above all, we are very proud of the handcrafted nature of our books. Our carefully-chosen writers are experts in their fields, and spend countless hours researching and organizing the content for each topic. Our artists rebuild every screen shot to provide the best clarity possible, making our screen shots the most precise and easiest to read in the industry. We strive for perfection, and believe that the time spent handcrafting each element results in the best computer books money can buy.

Thank you for purchasing this book. We hope you enjoy it!

Sincerely,

Robert Maran
President
maranGraphics

Rob@maran.com

www.maran.com

www.hungryminds.com/visual

CREDITS

Acquisitions, Editorial, and Media Development

Project Editors
Dana Rhodes Lesh
Maureen Spears
Ted Cains

Acquisitions Editors
Martine Edwards
Jen Dorsey

Product Development Supervisor
Lindsay Sandman

Copy Editors
Jill Mazurczyk
Timothy J. Borek

Technical Editors
Kyle Bowen
James Marchetti

Senior Permissions Editor
Carmen Krikorian

Media Development Specialist
Angela Denny

Media Development Coordinator
Marisa Pearman

Editorial Manager
Rev Mengle

Media Development Manager
Laura VanWinkle

Editorial Assistant
Amanda Foxworth

Production

Book Design
maranGraphics®

Project Coordinator
Dale White

Layout
Adam Mancilla
Kristin Pickett
Brian Torwelle
Erin Zeltner

Graphics
Barry Offringa
Betty Schulte

Screen Artists
Mark Harris
Jill A. Proll

Illustrators
David E. Gregory
Ronda David-Burroughs

Proofreaders
Laura Albert
Joel K. Draper
Susan Moritz
Marianne Santy

Indexer
TECHBOOKS Production Services

Special Help
Angela Langford

GENERAL AND ADMINISTRATIVE

Hungry Minds, Inc.: John Kilcullen, CEO; Bill Barry, President and COO; John Ball, Executive VP, Operations & Administration; John Harris, CFO

Hungry Minds Technology Publishing Group: Richard Swadley, Senior Vice President and Publisher; Mary Bednarek, Vice President and Publisher; Walter R. Bruce III, Vice President and Publisher; Joseph Wikert, Vice President and Publisher; Mary C. Corder, Editorial Director; Andy Cummings, Publishing Director, General User Group; Barry Pruett, Publishing Director, Visual Group

Hungry Minds Manufacturing: Ivor Parker, Vice President, Manufacturing

Hungry Minds Marketing: John Helmus, Assistant Vice President, Director of Marketing

Hungry Minds Production for Branded Press: Debbie Stailey, Production Director

Hungry Minds Sales: Roland Elgey, Senior Vice President, Sales and Marketing; Michael Violano, Vice President, International Sales and Sub Rights

The publisher would like to give special thanks to Patrick J. McGovern, without whom this book would not have been possible.

ABOUT THE AUTHORS

Sherry Willard Kinkoph has written more than 40 books over the past nine years, covering a variety of computer topics ranging from software to hardware, from Microsoft Office programs to the Internet. Sherry's ongoing quest is to help users of all levels master the ever-changing computer technologies. No matter how many times they — the software giants and hardware conglomerates — throw out a new version or upgrade, Sherry vows to be there to make sense of it all and help computer users get the most out of their machines.

Mike Wooldridge is a Web developer in the San Francisco Bay Area. He has authored several other Visual™ books, including *Teach Yourself VISUALLY Dreamweaver 4* and *Teach Yourself VISUALLY Photoshop 6*. For more information about Dreamweaver, see his Web site at www.mediacosm.com/dreamweaver.

Brock Bigard is a Multimedia Development Specialist for Hungry Minds, Inc., where he creates interfaces for the CD-ROMs that accompany the publisher's books. He is a first-time author who studied computer science at Indiana University. He also develops promotional CD-ROMs for Hungry Minds and other companies.

AUTHORS' ACKNOWLEDGMENTS

From Sherry: Special thanks go out to project editor Maureen Spears, for keeping me on track with both material and time.

From Mike: Thanks to project editor Ted Cains and everyone else at Hungry Minds who worked on this book. Also thanks to Linda Comer, Asha Dornfest, and Jesse Reklaw (www.slowwave.com).

From Brock: There are several people I would like to thank for their participation in this project. First, I would like to thank Sherry Kinkoph for helping me and guiding me during my first authoring experience. Thanks to Brooke, for putting up with me being on the computer until the wee hours of the night. I would like to thank everybody on the Visual team who helped this book become a better book.

From all: Thanks to publishing director Barry Pruett, for having the vision to combine coverage of Dreamweaver and Flash in one book; to project editors Dana Lesh and Rev Mengle; to copy editors Jill Mazurczyk and Tim Borek, for ensuring that all the i's were dotted and t's were crossed; to acquisitions editors Martine Edwards and Jen Dorsey, for allowing us the opportunity to work on this project; and finally, to technical editors James Marchetti and Kyle Bowen, for checking everything over for accuracy.

To my dad, Dave Willard, for passing along his love of graphics and computers. — Sherry Willard Kinkoph

To Griffin, my two-year-old son who really likes to open and close the CD-ROM tray. — Mike Wooldridge

To my fiancée, Brooke, and my family. — Brock Bigard

DREAMWEAVER® 4 AND FLASH® 5

I USING DREAMWEAVER

1) Getting Started with Dreamweaver
2) Dreamweaver Basics
3) Working with HTML
4) Setting Up Your Web Site
5) Formatting Text
6) Working with Images and Graphics
7) Creating Hyperlinks
8) Creating Tables
9) Creating Forms
10) Designing with Frames
11) Using Library Items and Templates
12) Implementing Style Sheets and Layers
13) Implementing Behaviors
14) Implementing Timelines
15) Publishing a Web Site
16) Site Maintenance

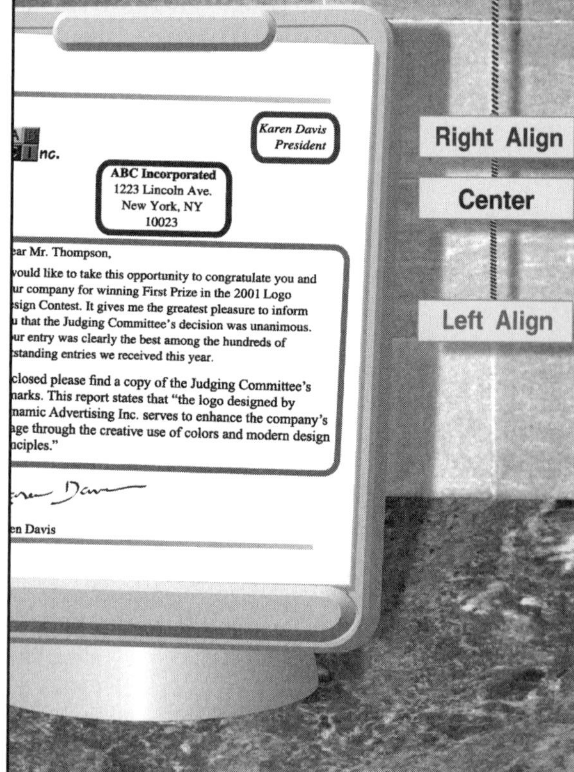

WHAT'S INSIDE

II USING FLASH

17) Getting Started with Flash
18) Drawing and Painting Objects
19) Enhancing and Editing Objects
20) Working with Text
21) Working with Layers
22) Working with Flash Symbols and Instances
23) Working with Imported Graphics
24) Animation Techniques
25) Animating with Tweening
26) Creating Interactive Buttons
27) Adding Sounds
28) Adding Flash Actions
29) Using Advanced Interactive Features
30) Distributing Flash Movies

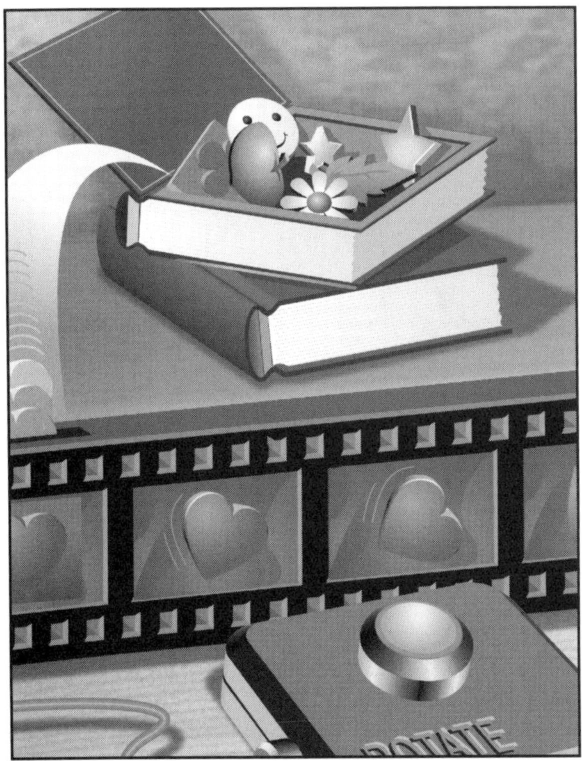

III BUILDING A WEB SITE WITH DREAMWEAVER AND FLASH

31) Building A Web Site
32) Building Web Site Forms with Flash
33) Enhancing the Web Site

IV ADVANCED FLASH TECHNIQUES

34) Building Interface Controls with Flash
35) Enhancing Interactivity with Flash
36) Creating Special Effects in Flash

Appendix

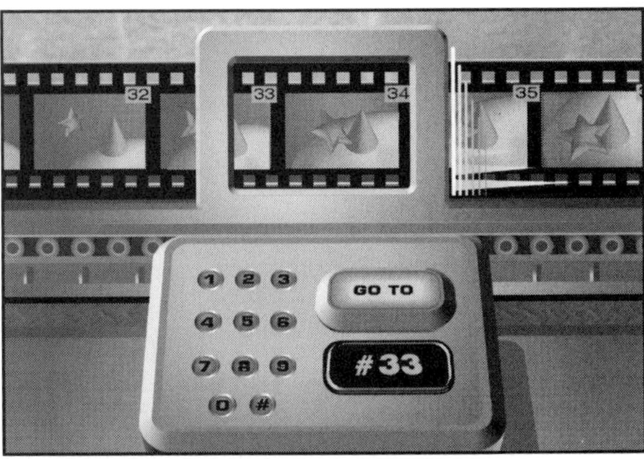

1 USING DREAMWEAVER

1) GETTING STARTED WITH DREAMWEAVER

An Introduction to the World Wide Web 4
The Parts of a Web Page 6
Plan Your Web Site 8
The Dreamweaver Interface on a Windows PC ..10
The Dreamweaver Interface on a Macintosh 11
Start Dreamweaver on a PC 12
Start Dreamweaver on a Macintosh 13
Get Help 14

2) DREAMWEAVER BASICS

Open and Close Windows, Panels, and Inspectors ..16
Using the Document Window 18
Using the Property Inspector 20
Using the Objects Panel 21
Undo Commands with the History Panel 22
Combine Panels 23
Create a Command with the History Panel 24
Create a Keyboard Shortcut 26
Set Preferences 28

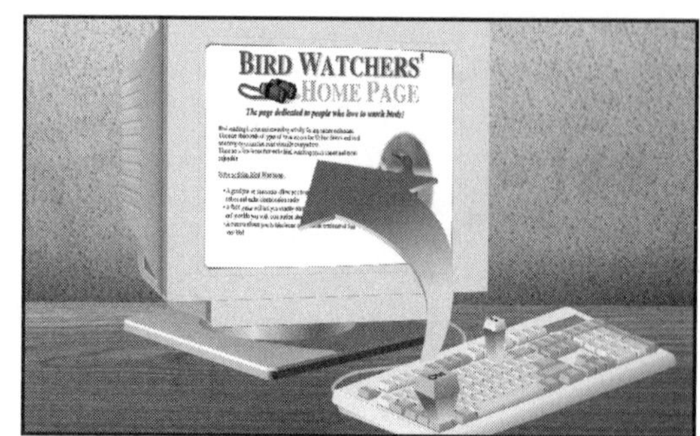

3) WORKING WITH HTML

An Introduction to HTML 30
View and Edit the Source Code 32
Clean Up Your HTML 34
Using the Quick Tag Editor 36
View and Edit Head Content 38
Using the Reference Panel 40

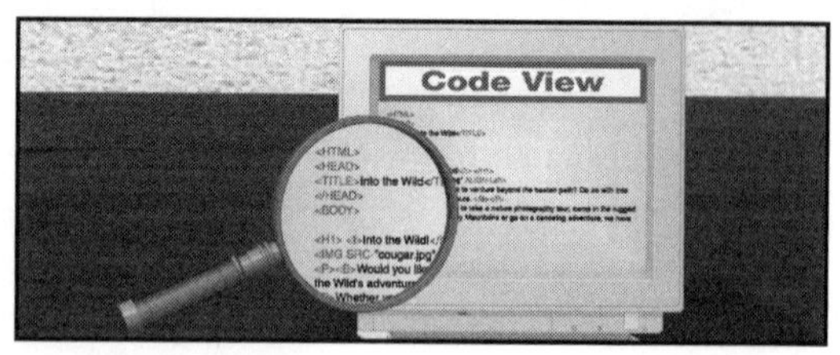

TABLE OF CONTENTS

4) SETTING UP YOUR WEB SITE

Set Up a Local Site 42
Open a Web Page 44
Create a New Web Page 46
Add a Title to a Web Page 47
Save a Web Page 48
Preview a Web Page in a Browser 50

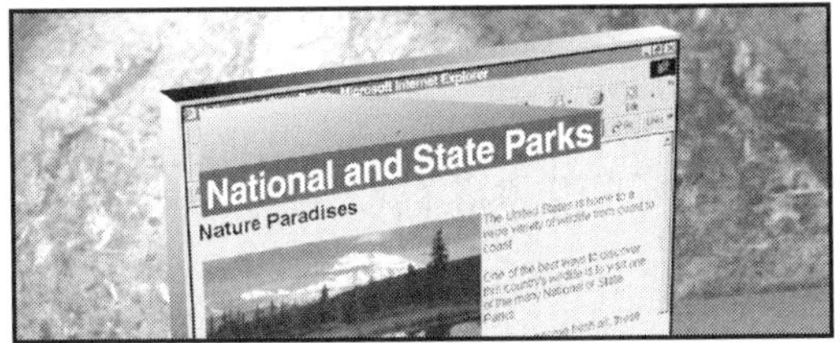

5) FORMATTING TEXT

Create Paragraphs 52
Create a Heading 54
Create Line Breaks 56
Add Extra Blank Space 57
Create Unordered Lists 58
Create Ordered Lists 60
Insert Special Characters 62
Change a Font 64
Format Text as Bold or Italic 66
Change Font Size 68
Change Font Color 70
Apply HTML Styles 72
Create a New HTML Style 73

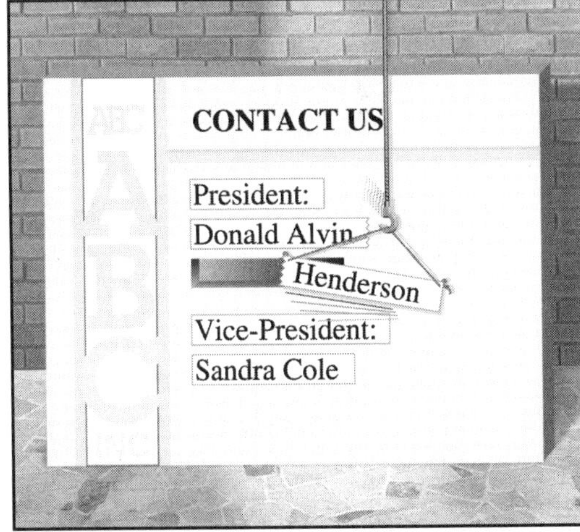

6) WORKING WITH IMAGES AND GRAPHICS

Incorporating Images and Graphics 74
Insert an Image into Your Web Page 76
Wrap Text around an Image 78
Center an Image 79
Change the Size of an Image 80
Add Space Around an Image 82
Add a Horizontal Rule 83
Add a Background Image 84
Change the Background Color 86
Add Alternate Text 87
Insert Multimedia 88

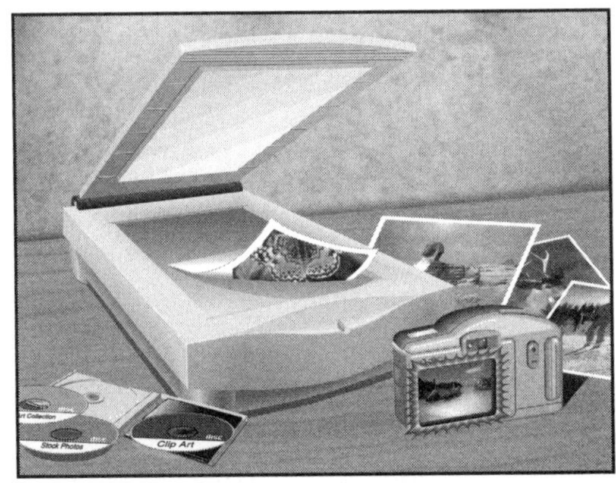

7) CREATING HYPERLINKS

Creating Hyperlinks 90
Hyperlink to Another Page in Your Site 92
Hyperlink to Another Web Site 94
Create Image Hyperlinks 96
Hyperlink to Information on the Same Page 98
Hyperlink to Other Files 100
Create Multiple Hyperlinks within an Image 102
Create a Hyperlink That Opens a New Window 104
Hyperlink by Using the Site Window 105
Change the Color of Hyperlinks 106
Create an E-mail Hyperlink 108
Check Hyperlinks 109

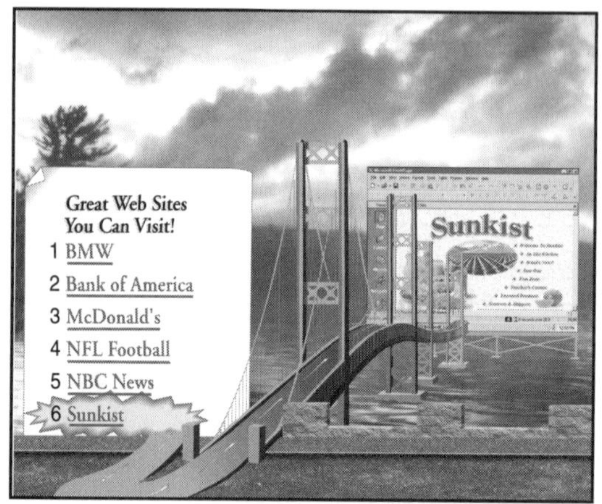

8) CREATING TABLES

Insert a Table into Your Web Page 110
Insert Content into a Table 112
Change the Background of a Table 114
Change the Cell Spacing or Padding in a Table 116
Change the Alignment of Table Content 117
Insert or Delete a Row or Column 118
Split or Merge Table Cells 120
Change the Dimensions of a Table 122
Create a Layout Table 124
Rearrange a Layout Table 126
Adjust the Width of a Layout Table 128

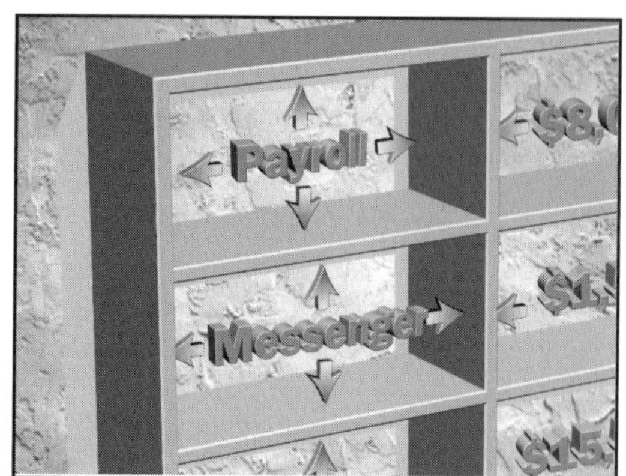

9) CREATING FORMS

An Introduction to Forms 130
Set Up a Form 131
Add a Text Field to a Form 132
Add a Multiline Text Field to a Form 134
Add a Password Field to a Form 136
Add Check Boxes to a Form 138

TABLE OF CONTENTS

Add Radio Buttons to a Form 140
Add a Menu or List to a Form 142
Create a Jump Menu 144
Add File Uploading to a Form 146
Add Hidden Information to a Form 147
Add a Submit Button to a Form 148
Add a Reset Button to a Form 149

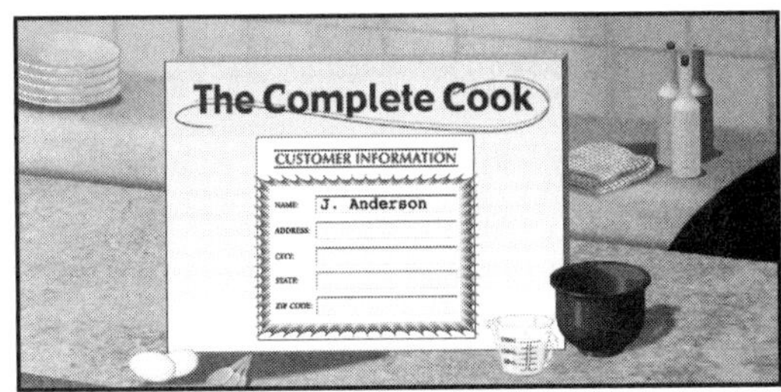

10) DESIGNING WITH FRAMES

An Introduction to Frames 150
Divide a Page into Frames 151
Insert a Predefined Frameset 152
Nest Frames 153
Add Content to a Frame 154
Save a Framed Site 156
Delete a Frame 158
Name a Frame 159
Hyperlink to a Frame 160
Change the Dimensions of a Frame 162
Format Frame Borders 164
Control Scroll Bars in Frames 166
Control Resizing in Frames 167

11) USING LIBRARY ITEMS AND TEMPLATES

An Introduction to Library Items and Templates ..168
View Library Items and Templates 169
Create a Library Item 170
Insert a Library Item 172
Edit a Library Item and Update Your Web Site ..174
Detach Library Content for Editing 176
Create a Template 178
Set a Template's Editable Regions 180
Create a Page Using a Template 182
Edit a Template and Update Your Web Site 184

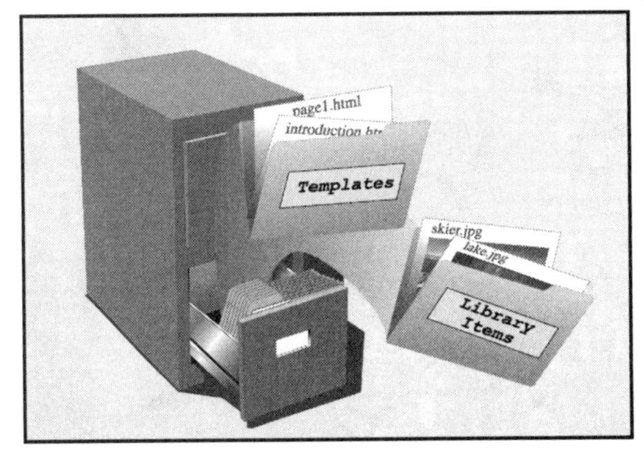

12) IMPLEMENTING STYLE SHEETS AND LAYERS

An Introduction to Style Sheets 186
Customize an HTML Tag 188
Create a Class 190
Apply a Class 192
Edit a Style Sheet Class 194
Using CSS Selectors to Modify Links 196
Create and Attach an External Style Sheet 198
Create a Layer 200
Resize and Reposition Layers 202
Add a Background Color to a Layer 204
Change the Stacking Order of Layers 205

13) IMPLEMENTING BEHAVIORS

An Introduction to Behaviors.............................206
Create a Rollover Image 208
Create a Status Bar Message 210
Validate a Form 212
Open a Customized Browser Window 214
Check a User's Browser 216
Debug JavaScript 218

14) IMPLEMENTING TIMELINES

An Introduction to Timelines.............................220
Using the Timelines Inspector 221
Create a Straight-Line Animation 222
Create an Animation by Dragging a Path 224
Change Other Layer Properties in Timelines 226
Change Animation Speed 228
Trigger an Animation with a Behavior 230

15) PUBLISHING A WEB SITE

Publish Your Web Site 232
Using the Site Window 233
Organize Files and Folders 234

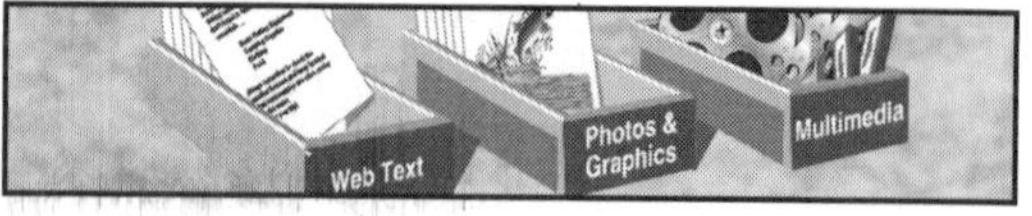

TABLE OF CONTENTS

Set Up a Remote Site 236
Connect to a Remote Site 238
Upload and Download Files 240
Synchronize Your Local and Remote Sites 242

16) SITE MAINTENANCE

Using the Site Map 244
Manage Site Assets 246
Add Content by Using the Assets Panel 248
Specify Favorite Assets 250
Check a Page In or Out 252
Make Design Notes 254
Run a Site Report 256
Change a Link Sitewide 257
Find and Replace Text 258
Search for Patterns of Text 260

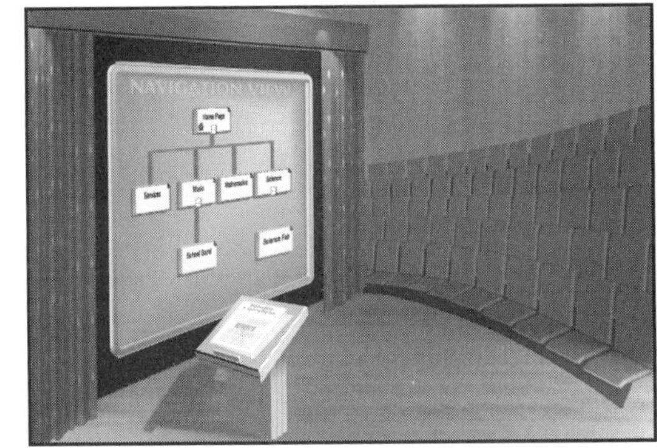

2 *USING FLASH*

17) GETTING STARTED WITH FLASH

An Introduction to Flash 264
Navigate the Flash Window 266
Open a Flash File 270
Save and Close a Flash File 272
Understand the Flash Timeline 274
Move and Dock the Timeline Window 276
Change the Stage Size 278
Find Help with Flash 280

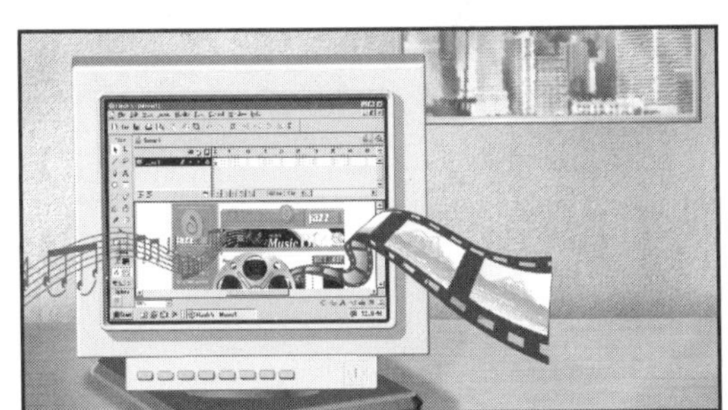

18) DRAWING AND PAINTING OBJECTS

An Introduction to Flash Objects 282
Using the Drawing Toolbar 284
Draw Line Segments 286
Format Line Segments 288

Draw a Custom Line 290
Draw Curves with the Pen Tool 292
Smooth or Straighten Line Segments 294
Draw Oval and Rectangle Shapes 296
Draw Objects with the Brush Tool 298
Fill Objects with the Paint Bucket Tool 300

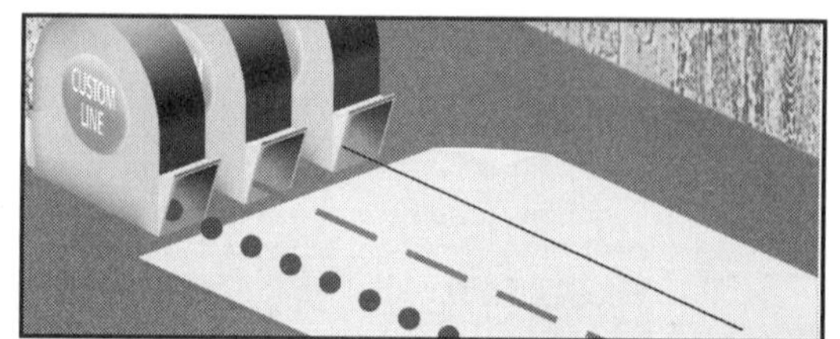

19) ENHANCING AND EDITING OBJECTS

Select Objects 302
Move and Copy Objects 306
Edit Line Segments 308
Edit Fills 310
Resize Objects 312
Add Strokes to Shapes 314
Rotate and Flip Objects 316
Using the Eraser Tool 318
Work with Gradient Effects 320
Edit a Color Set 324
Copy Attributes 326
Group Objects 328
Stack Objects 330
Align Objects 332

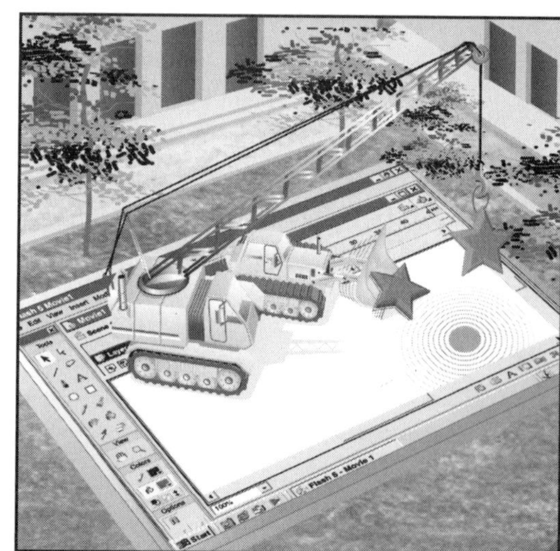

20) WORKING WITH TEXT

Add Text with the Text Tool 334
Format Text 336
Align and Kern Text 338
Set Text Box Margins and Indents 340
Move and Resize Text Boxes 342

21) WORKING WITH LAYERS

Understand Layers 344
Add and Delete Layers 346
Set Layer Properties 348
Work with Layers in the Timeline 350

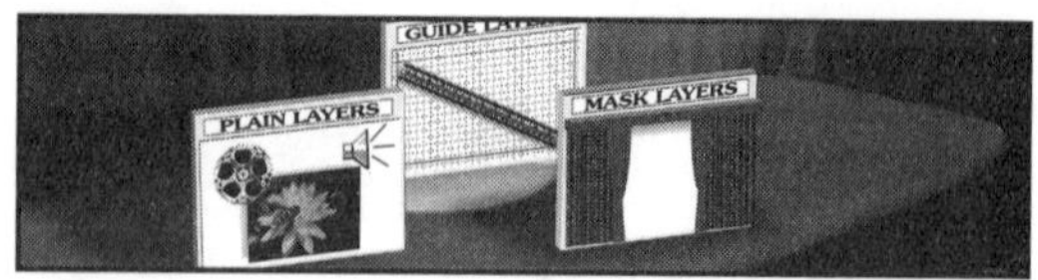

TABLE OF CONTENTS

Stack Layers 352
Add a Plain or Motion Guide Layer 354
Add a Mask Layers and Create a Mask 356

22) WORKING WITH FLASH SYMBOLS AND INSTANCES

Understand Symbols and Instances 358
Types of Symbols 359
Using the Flash Library 360
Create Symbols 364
Insert an Instance 366
Modify an Instance 368
Edit Symbols 370

23) WORKING WITH IMPORTED GRAPHICS

Understanding Vector and Bitmap Images 372
Import Graphics 374
Make Bitmaps into Vector Graphics 376
Turn Bitmaps into Fills 378

24) ANIMATION TECHNIQUES

An Introduction to Animation 380
Understanding Frames 382
Set Movie Dimensions and Speed 384
Add Frames 386
Select Frames 390
Modify Frame Properties 391
Delete or Change the Status of Frames 392
Create Frame-by-Frame Animation 394
Onion-Skinning an Animation 398
Preview a Flash Animation 402
Adjust the Animation Speed 403
Move and Copy Frames 404
Create Scenes 406
Save an Animation as a Movie Clip 408
Use the Movie Explorer 410

25) ANIMATING WITH TWEENING

Create a Motion Tween 412
Stop a Motion Tween 416
Add a Keyframe to a Motion Tween 417
Animate by Rotating a Symbol 418
Animate by Spinning a Symbol 422
Animate by Changing Symbol Size 426
Animate Symbols Along a Path 430
Set Tween Speed 434
Create a Shape Tween 436
Using Shape Hints 440
Using Reverse Frames 444

26) CREATING INTERACTIVE BUTTONS

Understanding Flash Buttons 446
Create a Button Symbol 448
Create Shape-Changing Buttons 452
Create an Animated Button 456
Assign a Button Action 460

27) ADDING SOUNDS

An Introduction to Flash Sounds 464
Import a Sound Clip 466
Add a Sound Layer 468
Assign Sound to a Frame 470
Assign Sounds to Buttons 472
Create Event Sounds 474
Assign Start Sounds 476
Assign Stop Sounds 478
Assign Streaming Sounds 480
Loop a Sound 482
Edit Sounds 484
Set Audio Output for Export 486

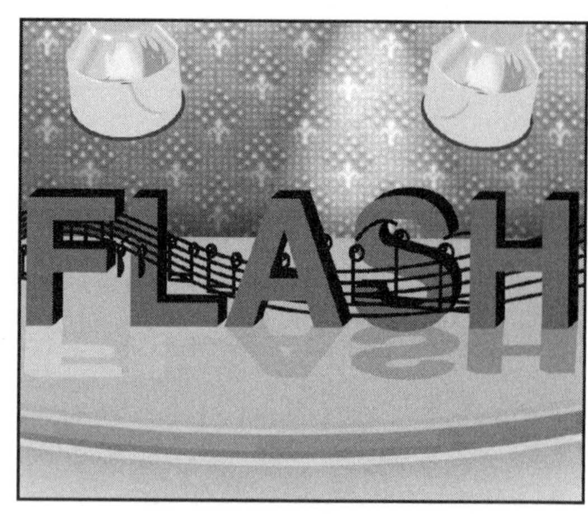

28) ADDING FLASH ACTIONS

An Introduction to Flash Actions 488
Add Actions to Frames 490
Assign Go To Actions 492
Assign Stop and Play Actions 496
Load a New Movie 500
Change Action Order 502
Assign Frame Labels 504

29) USING ADVANCED INTERACTIVE FEATURES

Understand Complex Actions 506
Add a Variable Text Field 508
Assign an If Frame Is Loaded Action 510
Using the Get URL Action 514
Using the Tell Target Action 516
Control the Flash Player with the FS Command ..518

30) DISTRIBUTING FLASH MOVIES

Understand Distribution Methods 520
Play a Flash Movie in Flash 522
Play a Flash Movie in a Browser 524
Test Movie Bandwidth 526
Publish a Movie 530
Publish a Movie in HTML Format 532
Create a Flash Projector 536
Export to Another Format 538
Print Movie Frames 540

3 *BUILDING A WEB SITE WITH DREAMWEAVER AND FLASH*

31) BUILDING A WEB SITE

Combine Dreamweaver and Flash 544
Sample Site Planning Considerations 546
Create a Sample Flash Interface 547

Create a Simple Preloader 548
Add a Skip Intro Button 550
Create an Intro Text Effect 552
Create a Laser-Writing Animation Effect 554
Create a Welcome Page 560
Add Hot Buttons 562
Create a Drop-Down Menu 564
Use the Root Property Action Statement 570
Enable Testing Options 571
Create Button Animations 572
Create a ToolTip 574
Create a Chat Feature 576

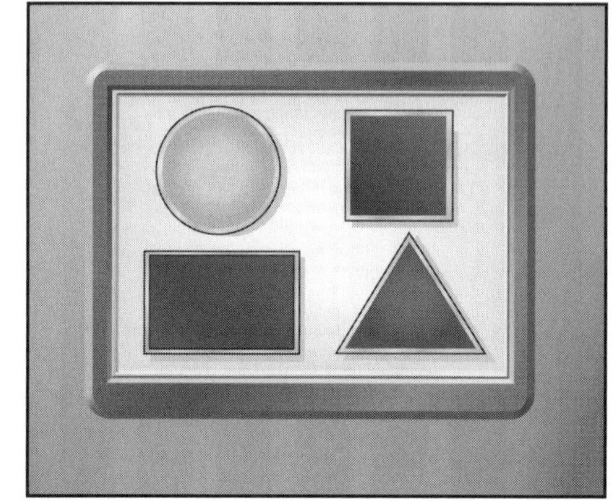

32) BUILDING WEB SITE FORMS WITH FLASH

Create a Simple Flash Form 582
Create a Clear Button 584
Create a Submit Button 586
Create a Scrolling Text Box 588
Edit a User Profile 590
Create a User Login Screen 592
Create a User Log Out Option 596
Use the MailTo Command 598
Add a Search Tool 600

33) ENHANCING THE WEB SITE

Integrate a Flash Banner 606
Create a Link with the Get URL Action 608
Call a Server-Side Script 610
Control Windows with Get URL Options 612
Control Windows with JavaScript 614
Make Your Files Downloadable 616
Compress Web Site Graphics 618
Reduce Download Time for a Large Movie 620
Flag a User Error 622

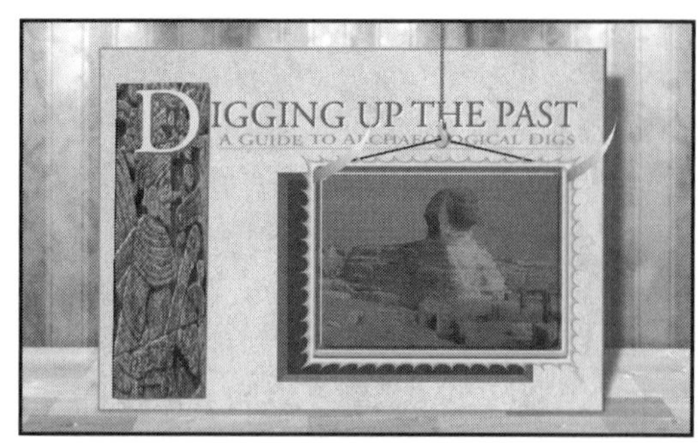

TABLE OF CONTENTS

4 ADVANCED FLASH TECHNIQUES

34) BUILDING INTERFACE CONTROLS WITH FLASH

Create an Animated Menu 626
Adjust Sound Clip Volume 632
Create an Advanced Preloader 638
Set Property of a Movie Clip 644
Track Cursor Position 648
Create a Window Hierarchy 652

35) ENHANCING INTERACTIVITY WITH FLASH

Create a Password Identification Box 656
Park a Movie Clip 660
Emulate an Array 664
Combine Strings Given by a User 668
Replicate a Movie Randomly or by Command 672
Send a Form Using a CGI Script 676
Make a Movie Clip Act Like a Button 680

36) CREATING SPECIAL EFFECTS IN FLASH

Create a Gravity Effect 682
Create a Magnifying Glass Effect 686
Create a Dragable Menu 692
Create a Filmstrip Effect 696

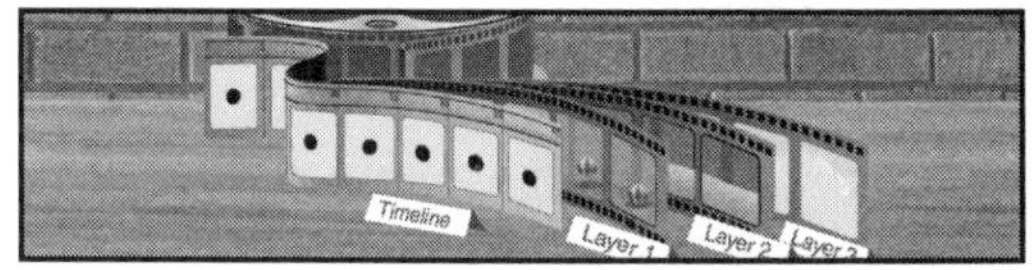

APPENDIX

What's on the CD-ROM 700
Master VISUALLY Dreamweaver 4 & Flash 5 on the CD-ROM 702

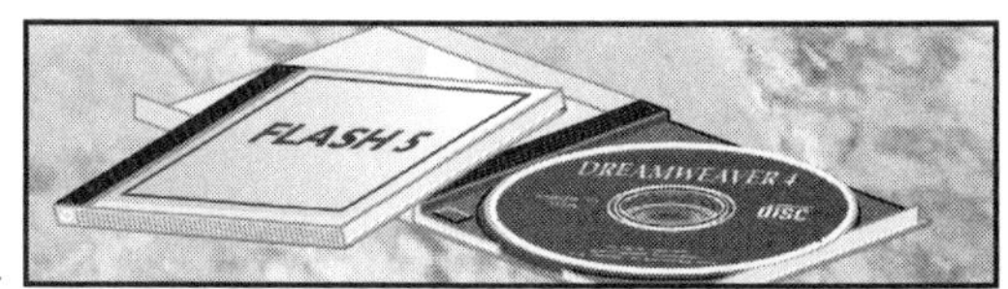

DREAMWEAVER® 4 AND FLASH™ 5

Master VISUALLY Dreamweaver 4 and Flash 5 is a visual reference for professionals and hobbyists who want to learn how to use two of today's leading programs to create dynamic, exciting Web pages. The book contains straightforward examples to teach you how to use Dreamweaver and Flash.

The Organization of the Book

This book is designed to give a reader quick access to topics related to Dreamweaver and Flash. You can simply look up a subject within the Table of Contents or Index and go immediately to the task of concern. A *task* is a self-contained unit that walks you through a computer operation step-by-step. That is, with rare exception, all the information you need regarding an area of interest is contained within a task.

Each task contains an introduction, a set of screen shots, and, if the task goes beyond one page, a set of tips. The introduction tells why you want to perform the task, the advantages and disadvantages of performing the task, a general explanation of task procedures, and references to other related tasks in the book. The screen shots, located on the bottom half of each page, show the steps required to complete a given task. The tip section gives you an opportunity to further understand the task at hand, to learn about other related tasks in other areas of the book, or to find out how to apply more complicated or alternative methods.

In addition to the task descriptions, some chapters also include an illustrated introduction that gives an overview of the information covered in a chapter.

The Parts and Chapters in This Book

Master VISUALLY Dreamweaver 4 and Flash 5 has 36 chapters and an appendix divided into four parts. You do not have to read the chapters in order; if you are new to Dreamweaver, however, we recommend that you read Part I. If you are new to Flash, we recommend that you read Part II. Otherwise, you can simply look up a topic that interests you and dive right in.

Part I, "Using Dreamweaver," contains 16 chapters, starting with an introduction to Dreamweaver, running through how to create tables, forms, and hyperlinks, all the way through publishing and maintaining a finished Web site.

Part II, "Using Flash," begins with how to get started with that program, then takes you through the basics of drawing and painting, on to animation and sounds, and finally putting together Flash movies.

Part III, "Building a Web Site with Dreamweaver and Flash," pulls both programs together. We have built an actual Web site and provided the files for you on the book's CD-ROM. Part III shows you step-by-step how the site was built, drawing on the Dreamweaver and Flash basics described in Parts I and II.

Part IV, "Advanced Flash Techniques," contains exciting examples of what you can do with Flash, some of which were inspired by real Web examples, and some of which were created especially for this book. Those Flash files can also be found on the CD-ROM, which is the topic of the appendix.

System Requirements

To perform the tasks in this book and use the contents of the CD-ROM, your computer must be equipped with the following hardware and software:

- A PC with a Pentium or faster processor; or a Mac OS computer with a 68040 or faster processor, and at least 32MB of RAM. For best performance, we recommend at least 64MB.
- Microsoft Windows 95 or later, or Mac OS system software 7.6.1 or later.
- Dreamweaver 4 and Flash 5.
- A CD-ROM drive.
- A sound card for PCs.
- A monitor capable of displaying at least 256 colors or grayscale.
- A modem with a speed of at least 14,400 bps.

Note: Some Part III example files make use of server-side scripting, meaning that you must have a Web server program such as Microsoft Personal Web Server or Microsoft Internet Information Server to run the files.

The Conventions in This Book

This book uses the following conventions to describe the actions you perform when using the mouse:

- **Click**: Press and release the left mouse button. You use a click to select an item on the screen.
- **Double-click**: Quickly press and release the left mouse button twice. You use a double-click to open a document or start a program.
- **Right-click**: Press and release the right mouse button. You use a right-click to display a shortcut menu, a list of commands specifically related to the selected item.
- **Click and Drag, and Release the Mouse**: Position the mouse pointer over an item on the screen and then press and hold down the left mouse button. While holding down the button, move the mouse to where you want to place the item and then release the button. Clicking and dragging lets you easily move an item to a new location.

A number of typographic and layout styles have been used throughout *Master VISUALLY Dreamweaver 4 and Flash 5* to distinguish different types of information.

- **Bold** indicates the information that you must type into a dialog box.
- *Italics* indicates a new term being introduced.
- Numbered steps indicate that you must perform these steps in order to successfully perform the task.
- Bulleted steps give you alternative methods, explain various options, or present what a program will do in response to the numbered steps.
- Notes in the steps give you additional information to help you complete a task. The purpose of a note is three-fold: It can explain special conditions that may occur during the course of the task, warn you of potentially dangerous situations, or refer you to tasks in the same, or a different chapter. References to tasks within the chapter are indicated by the phrase "See the section . . ." followed by the name of the task. References to tasks in other chapters are indicated by "See Chapter . . ." followed by the chapter number.
- Icons in the steps indicate a button that you must press.

This book also makes two other assumptions:

- When you display a menu, a short version of the menu, with the most recently-used commands, may appear. You can click the down arrows, displayed at the bottom of the menu, to display the complete list of commands. This book assumes that you are using full menus. If you do not see a particular command when following the steps in a task, click the arrows to list all commands.
- This book assumes the default toolbars settings unless otherwise indicated.

SECTION I

1) GETTING STARTED WITH DREAMWEAVER 4

2) DREAMWEAVER BASICS 16

3) WORKING WITH HTML 30

4) SETTING UP YOUR WEB SITE . . . 42

5) FORMATTING TEXT 52

6) WORKING WITH IMAGES AND GRAPHICS 74

7) CREATING HYPERLINKS 90

8) CREATING TABLES 110

USING DREAMWEAVER

9) CREATING FORMS 130

10) DESIGNING WITH FRAMES ...150

11) USING LIBRARY ITEMS AND TEMPLATES 168

12) IMPLEMENTING STYLE SHEETS AND LAYERS 186

13) IMPLEMENTING BEHAVIORS 206

14) IMPLEMENTING TIMELINES ...220

15) PUBLISHING A WEB SITE 232

16) SITE MAINTENANCE 244

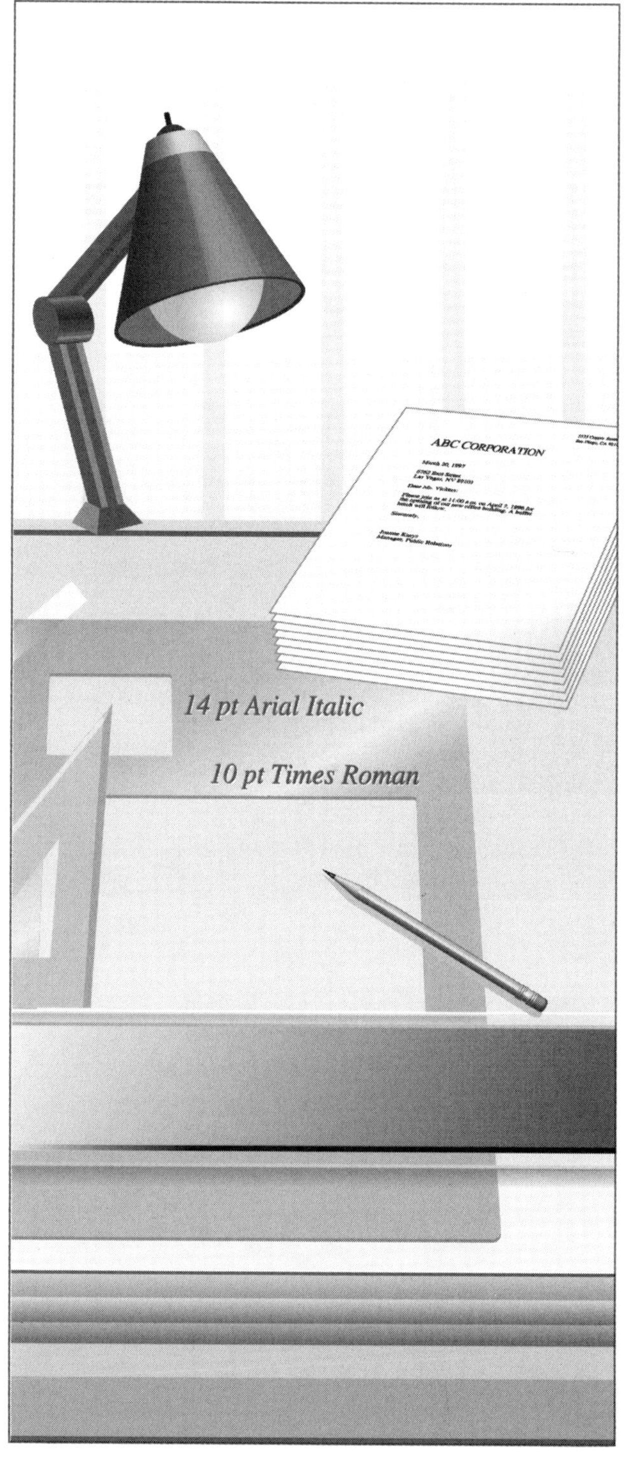

AN INTRODUCTION TO THE WORLD WIDE WEB

The World Wide Web, or Web, is a global collection of documents located on Internet-connected computers that you can access by using a Web browser. You usually view these documents in the form of Web pages, which are connected to one another by clickable hyperlinks.

Dreamweaver and the Web

Dreamweaver is a program that enables you to build and create Web pages that feature text, images, and multimedia. Dreamweaver provides an environment in which to organize your Web pages and link them together. Dreamweaver also includes tools that let you transfer the finished files to a Web server where others can view them.

What is HTML?

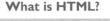

HTML, or HyperText Markup Language, is the formatting language you use to create Web pages. Every Web page you see has an associated page of HTML that gives it its structure. You can use Dreamweaver to create Web pages without knowing HTML, because Dreamweaver writes the HTML for you behind the scenes. For more about HTML, see Chapter 3.

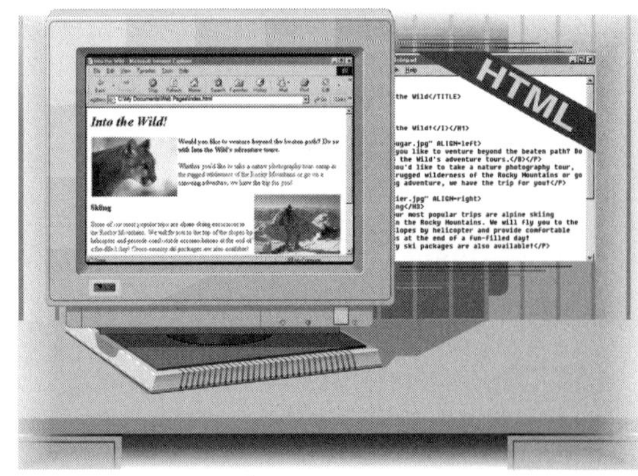

What is a Web Browser?

A Web browser is a program that downloads Web documents from the Internet, interprets their HTML, and then displays the Web page text and any associated images and multimedia as a Web page. Two popular Web browsers are Microsoft Internet Explorer and Netscape Navigator.

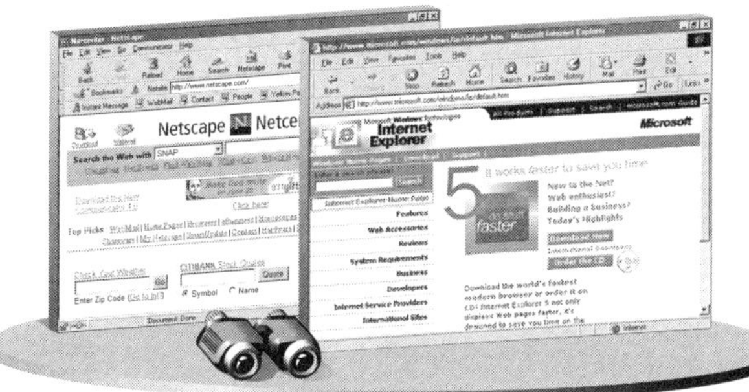

What is a Web Server?

A Web server is an Internet-connected computer that makes Web documents available to Web browsers. Each Web page that you view on the World Wide Web comes from a Web server somewhere on the Internet. When you are ready to publish your pages on the Web, Dreamweaver can connect to a Web server and transfer your files to it. Chapter 15 talks about this.

What is a Web site?

A Web site is a collection of linked Web pages stored on a Web server. Most Web sites have a *home page* that describes the information located on the Web site and provides a place where people can start their exploration of the site. The pages of a good Web site are intuitively organized and have a common theme. To learn about how to set up a Web site, see Chapter 4.

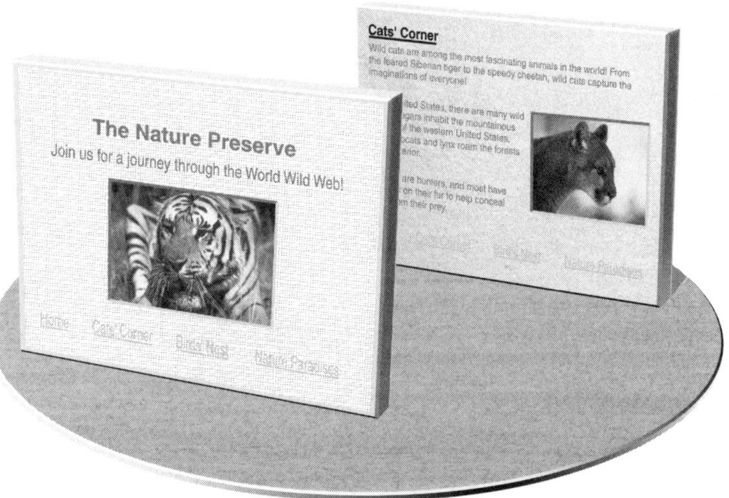

THE PARTS OF A WEB PAGE

You can communicate your message on the Web in a variety of ways. The following are some of the common elements found on Web pages.

Text

Text is the simplest type of content you can publish on the Web. Perhaps the best things about text is that practically everyone can view it, no matter what type of browser or Internet connection they have, and it downloads very quickly. Dreamweaver lets you change the size, color, and font of Web-page text and organize it into paragraphs, headings, and lists. Chapter 5 shows you how to use Dreamweaver's many text capabilities.

Images

You can digitize photographs, drawings, and logos using a digital camera or scanner and then save them for the Web in image editing programs such as Adobe Photoshop and Macromedia Fireworks. You can then place the images on your Web pages with Dreamweaver. Images are a must if you want your pages to stand out visually; complementing your text information with images can help you inform, educate, and entertain with your site. See Chapter 6 for more information.

Hyperlinks

Often simply called a *link*, a *hyperlink* is text or an image that you associate with another file. You can access the other file by clicking the hyperlink. Hyperlinks usually link to other Web pages, but they can also link to other locations on the same page or to other types of files. Text hyperlinks are usually colored and underlined. You can design image hyperlinks in an image editor so that they look like pushable buttons.

Tables

Tables organize information in columns and rows on your Web page. You can use tables to organize text, images, forms, and other page elements. By turning off a table's borders and setting it to span an entire page, you can use a table to invisibly organize the layout of a page. Dreamweaver's commands give you an easy way to create complex tables. See Chapter 8 for more on tables.

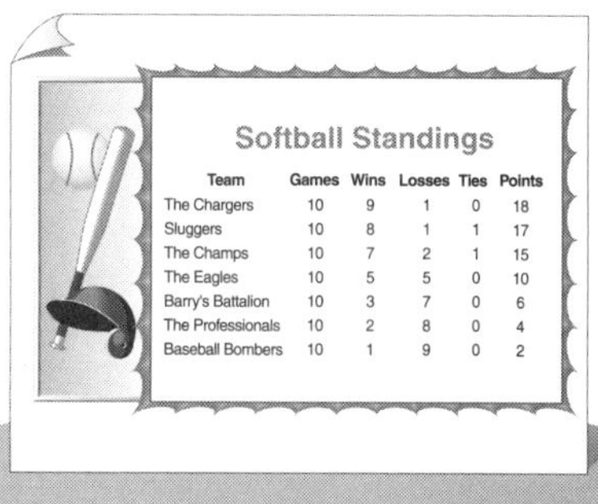

Softball Standings

Team	Games	Wins	Losses	Ties	Points
The Chargers	10	9	1	0	18
Sluggers	10	8	1	1	17
The Champs	10	7	2	1	15
The Eagles	10	5	5	0	10
Barry's Battalion	10	3	7	0	6
The Professionals	10	2	8	0	4
Baseball Bombers	10	1	9	0	2

Forms

Forms reverse the information flow on Web sites — they enable your site's visitors to send information back to you. This information can then be processed using programs called form handlers, which can forward the information to an e-mail address, insert it into a database, or use it in other ways. Dreamweaver lets you create forms that include text fields, drop-down menus, radio buttons, and other elements. See Chapter 9 for more information on forms.

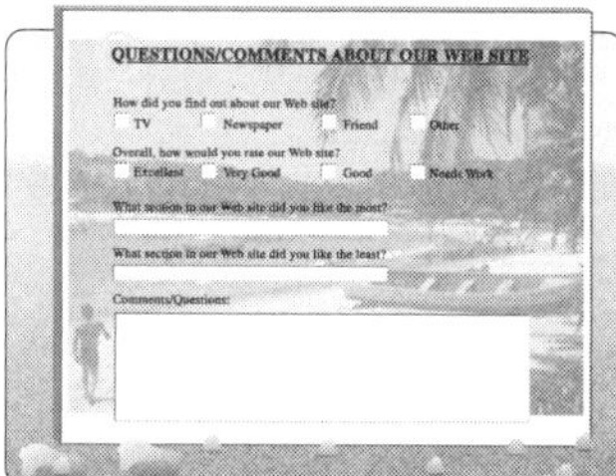

Frames

In a framed Web site, the browser window is divided into several rectangular frames, and a different Web page is loaded into each frame. Users can scroll through content in each frame independently of the content in the other frames. You can create hyperlinks that open up pages in other frames. Dreamweaver offers visual tools for building frame-based Web sites. You can learn about those tools in Chapter 10.

Advanced Features

Dreamweaver offers tools that enable you to integrate a variety of advanced Dreamweaver Web technologies on your pages. You can apply style sheets, which enable you to customize Web-page text. You can use layers to precisely position and overlap content on a page. You can use JavaScript programming, which can add interactivity to a site. Dreamweaver also has tools for inserting video, sound clips, and Flash animation into Web pages. See Chapter 12 for more on style sheets and layers, Chapter 13 for more on Java programming and Part II for more on Flash animation.

PLAN YOUR WEB SITE

No one would consider building a house without first drawing up blueprints, sourcing construction materials, and making other preparations. Similarly, doing some offline work on your Web site before you start opening pages, laying out text, and inserting images in Dreamweaver is a very good idea. This helps ensure that your finished Web site looks good and is well organized, and that you have a place to put the Web site online when you are finished building it.

Organize Your Ideas

Build your site on paper before you start building it in Dreamweaver. Make a list of the topics that you want to cover in your site, and try to organize those topics into categories that you can then assign to Web pages. Sketching out a site map, with rectangles representing Web pages and arrows representing hyperlinks, helps you visualize the size and scope of your project.

Gather Your Content

After you decide what types of Web pages you want to create, you have to generate content to appear on them. This process may involve writing text, shooting and scanning photos, and designing graphics. It may also involve producing multimedia content such as audio and video files. Having lots of content to choose from makes it easier to create pages that are interesting to read and look at.

Define Your Audience

Carefully defining your audience helps you decide what kind of content to offer on your Web site. Some advanced Dreamweaver features — such as Cascading Style Sheets and layers — can only be viewed using the most recent versions of Web browsers. Some multimedia content involves files that are too large for users on dial-up modems. Knowing how technologically advanced your audience is can help you decide whether to include more advanced features on your pages.

Host Your Finished Web Site

For users to access your finished site on the Web, you need to store, or *host,* the site on a Web server. Most people host their Web sites on a Web server at a commercial *Internet service provider* (ISP) or at their company. Most ISPs charge a monthly fee for a set amount of storage space on their Web servers. Other ISPs offer free hosting to customers in exchange for the ability to place advertising on the Web pages that they serve.

THE DREAMWEAVER INTERFACE ON A WINDOWS PC

You build Web pages in Dreamweaver on a Windows PC using various windows, panels, and inspectors. You build a page by inserting and arranging elements in the main Document window. Other accessory windows allow you to format and stylize those elements.

THE DREAMWEAVER INTERFACE ON A PC

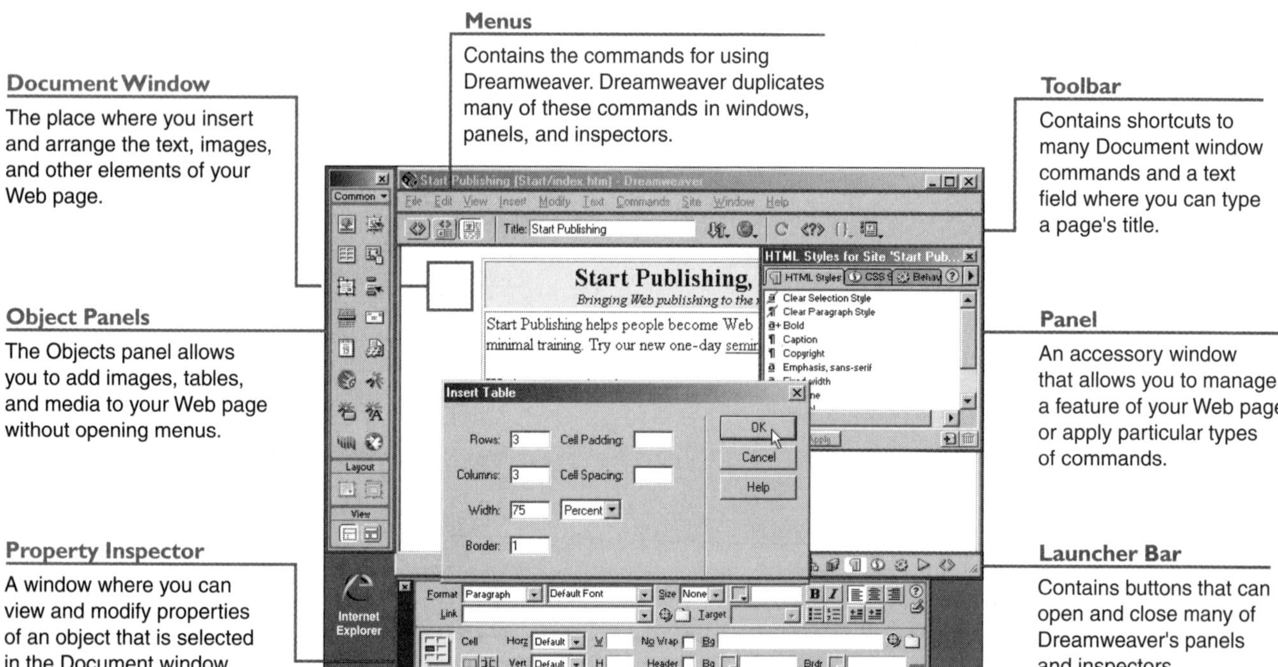
Menus
Contains the commands for using Dreamweaver. Dreamweaver duplicates many of these commands in windows, panels, and inspectors.
Document Window
The place where you insert and arrange the text, images, and other elements of your Web page.
Toolbar
Contains shortcuts to many Document window commands and a text field where you can type a page's title.
Object Panels
The Objects panel allows you to add images, tables, and media to your Web page without opening menus.
Panel
An accessory window that allows you to manage a feature of your Web page or apply particular types of commands.
Property Inspector
A window where you can view and modify properties of an object that is selected in the Document window.
Launcher Bar
Contains buttons that can open and close many of Dreamweaver's panels and inspectors.
Start Publishing
Insert Table
Rows:
Columns:
Width:
Border:
Cell Padding:
Cell Spacing:
Percent
OK
Cancel
Help

THE DREAMWEAVER INTERFACE ON A MACINTOSH

You build Web pages in Dreamweaver on a Macintosh using various windows, panels, and inspectors. You build a page by inserting and arranging elements in the main Document window. Other accessory windows allow you to format and stylize those elements.

THE DREAMWEAVER INTERFACE ON A MACINTOSH

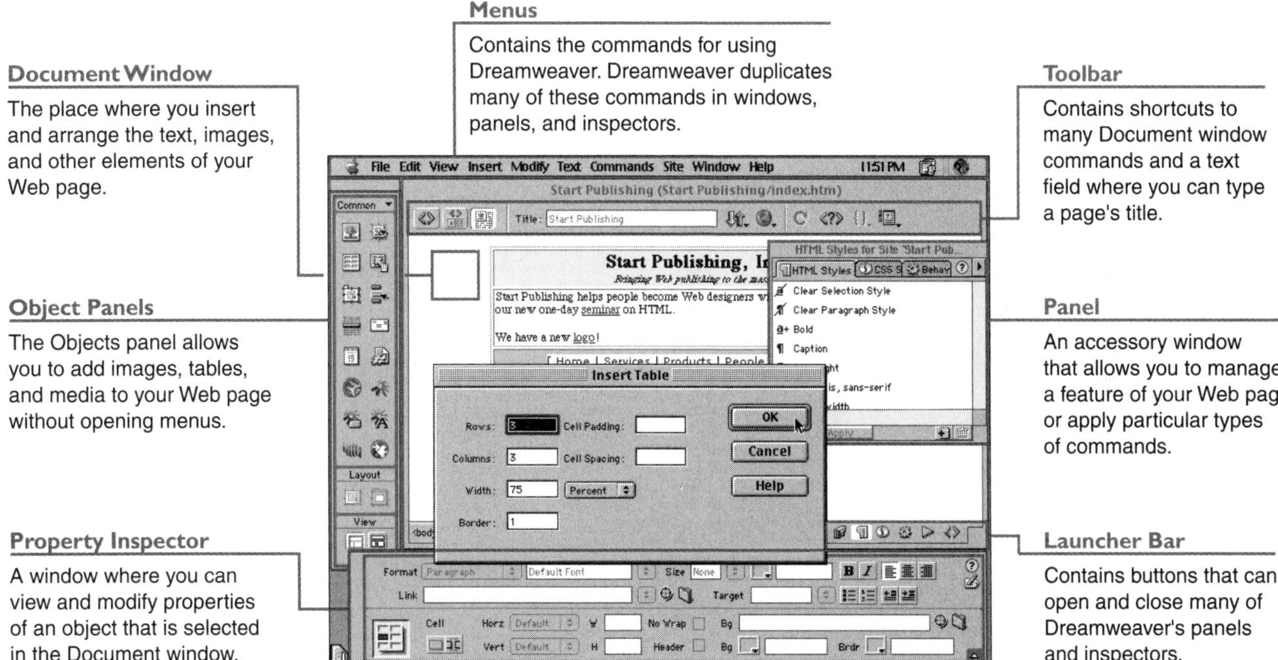

Menus

Contains the commands for using Dreamweaver. Dreamweaver duplicates many of these commands in windows, panels, and inspectors.

Document Window

The place where you insert and arrange the text, images, and other elements of your Web page.

Toolbar

Contains shortcuts to many Document window commands and a text field where you can type a page's title.

Object Panels

The Objects panel allows you to add images, tables, and media to your Web page without opening menus.

Panel

An accessory window that allows you to manage a feature of your Web page or apply particular types of commands.

Property Inspector

A window where you can view and modify properties of an object that is selected in the Document window.

Launcher Bar

Contains buttons that can open and close many of Dreamweaver's panels and inspectors.

START DREAMWEAVER ON A PC

You can start Dreamweaver on a PC and begin creating documents that you can publish on the Web. If you installed Dreamweaver's files in the default locations, you should be able to access the program in the Macromedia Dreamweaver 4 folder under the Programs folder in the Start menu.

Starting Dreamweaver opens a blank Document window, which serves as a blank canvas on which you can add text, images and other elements for your Web page. Accessory windows, know as panels and inspectors, can be accessed under the Window menu.

If you have 64MB or less of RAM installed on your computer, you may have trouble starting Dreamweaver when other programs are running because Dreamweaver needs a lot of available memory to run. You can close other programs to free memory to start Dreamweaver. Closing other programs can also improve Dreamweaver's performance.

START DREAMWEAVER ON A PC

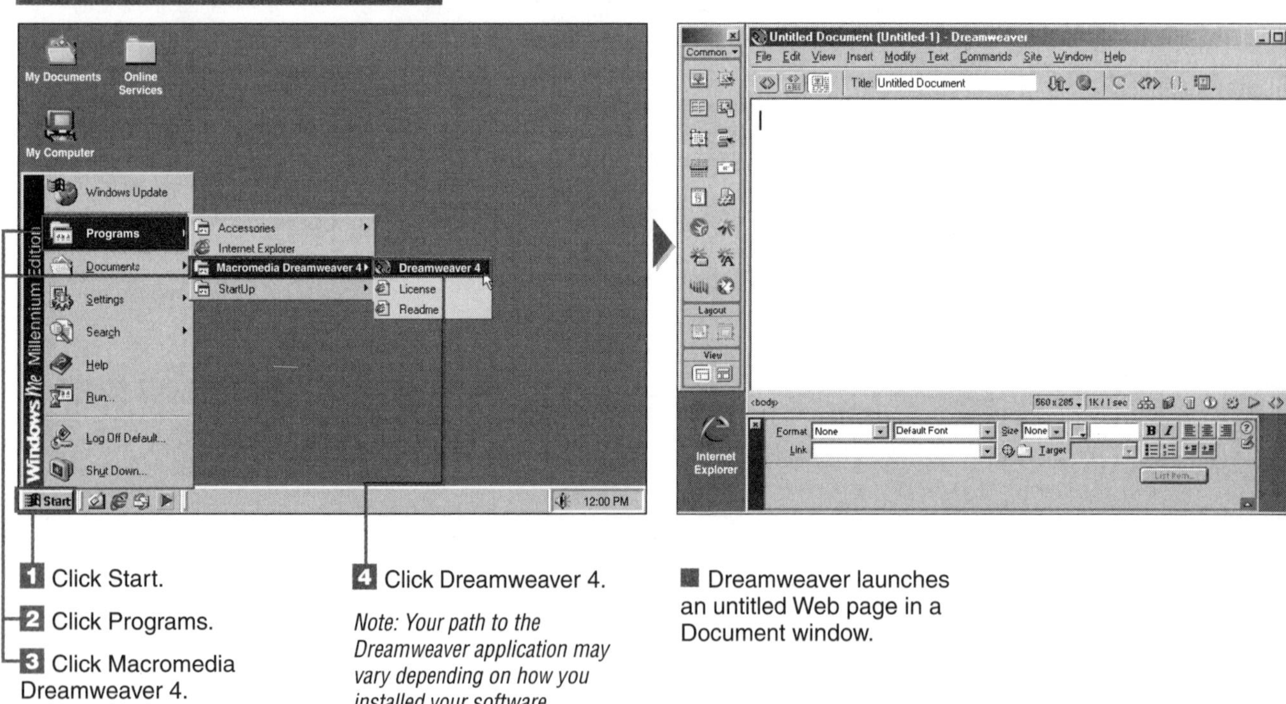

1 Click Start.

2 Click Programs.

3 Click Macromedia Dreamweaver 4.

4 Click Dreamweaver 4.

Note: Your path to the Dreamweaver application may vary depending on how you installed your software.

■ Dreamweaver launches an untitled Web page in a Document window.

START DREAMWEAVER ON A MACINTOSH

You can start Dreamweaver on a Macintosh and begin creating documents that you can publish on the Web. The default place to install Dreamweaver on a Macintosh is in the root folder of your computer's startup hard drive.

Starting Dreamweaver opens a blank Document window, which serves as a blank canvas on which you can add text, images and other elements for your Web page. You can access accessory windows, known as panels and inspectors, under the Windows menu.

If you have 64MB or less of RAM installed on your computer, you may have trouble starting Dreamweaver when other programs are running because Dreamweaver needs a lot of available memory to run. You can close other programs to free up memory so Dreamweaver can start up. Closing other programs can also improve Dreamweaver's performance.

START DREAMWEAVER ON A MACINTOSH

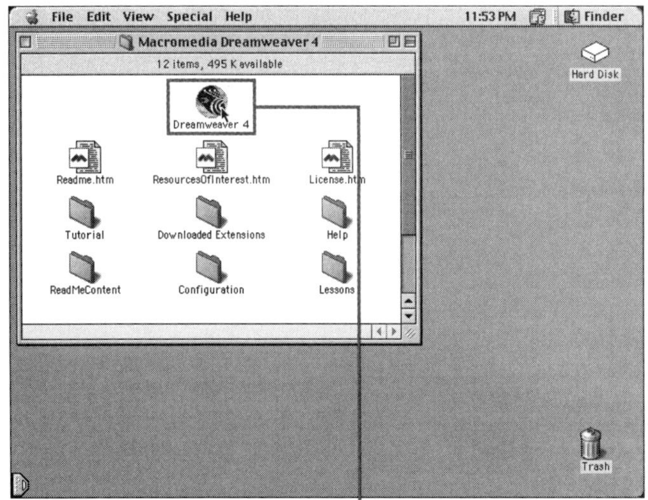

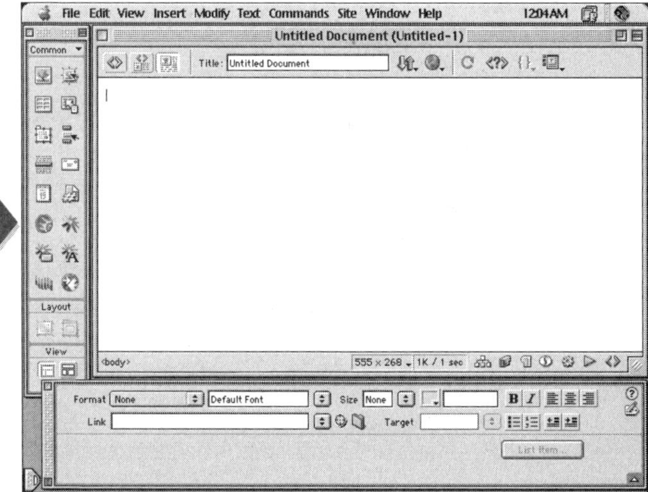

1 Open the Macromedia Dreamweaver 4 folder on your hard drive.

2 Double-click the Dreamweaver 4 icon.

Note: The location of the Dreamweaver folder depends on how you installed your software.

■ Dreamweaver launches an untitled Web page in a Document window.

GET HELP

Dreamweaver comes with extensive help documentation that is installed along with the application and that you can view in a Web browser. By opening the help documentation in a Web browser, you can switch back and forth between Dreamweaver and your browser to answer questions you may have, learn new functions, and solve many of the problems that may arise when you are using the application.

The help documentation is tightly integrated into the Dreamweaver application. Clicking the Help buttons in dialog boxes or the Help icons in the program's panels opens up information specific to that dialog box or panel.

In addition to the help documentation, Guided Tour movies offer an animated overview of many useful Dreamweaver topics, including using the application workspace, managing site content, and adding interactivity to your site. Click Help and then Guided Tour to access the movies.

You can also hone your Web-building skills with Lessons, which take you step-by-step through common tasks you may encounter when building a Web site. Click Help and then Lessons to access them.

GET HELP

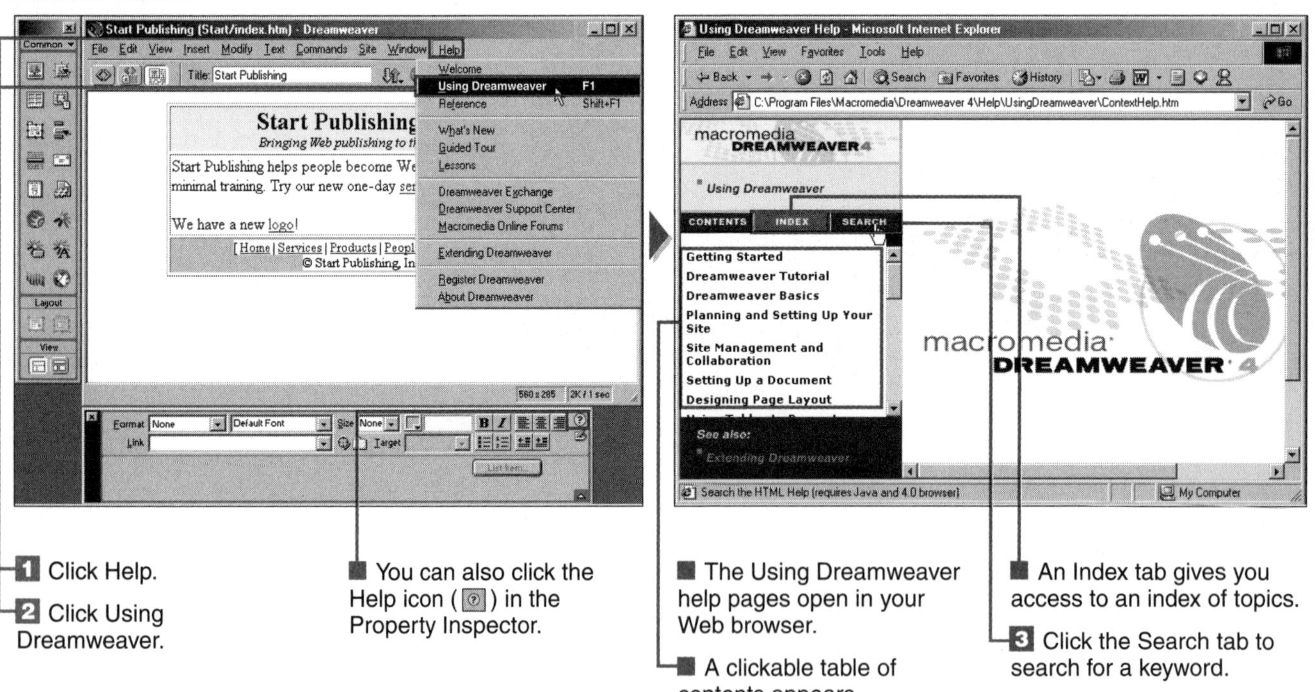

1 Click Help.

2 Click Using Dreamweaver.

■ You can also click the Help icon (?) in the Property Inspector.

■ The Using Dreamweaver help pages open in your Web browser.

■ A clickable table of contents appears.

■ An Index tab gives you access to an index of topics.

3 Click the Search tab to search for a keyword.

How can I receive a printed copy of Dreamweaver's help documentation?

✔ The boxed version of Dreamweaver comes with a *Using Dreamweaver 4* user's manual. This features a printed version of most of the information you find in the electronic help pages. The printed copy, however, does not have all the information — the electronic documentation is more extensive. If you downloaded your copy of Dreamweaver, you can obtain a printable copy of the user's manual at www.macromedia.com/support/dreamweaver/documentation.html.

How can I find help online?

✔ Visiting Macromedia's Web site is the best way to get the most up-to-date information about Dreamweaver support as well as reports of any bugs that may exist in the program. You can click Help and then Dreamweaver Support Center to view online help.

How can I learn about extending Dreamweaver's capabilities?

✔ Users who know how to program in JavaScript or C can create custom objects, commands, and other features in Dreamweaver. Click Help and then Extending Dreamweaver to learn more. You can also obtain add-ons that other programmers have written for Dreamweaver at Macromedia's Dreamweaver Exchange. You can access this by clicking Help and then Dreamweaver Exchange.

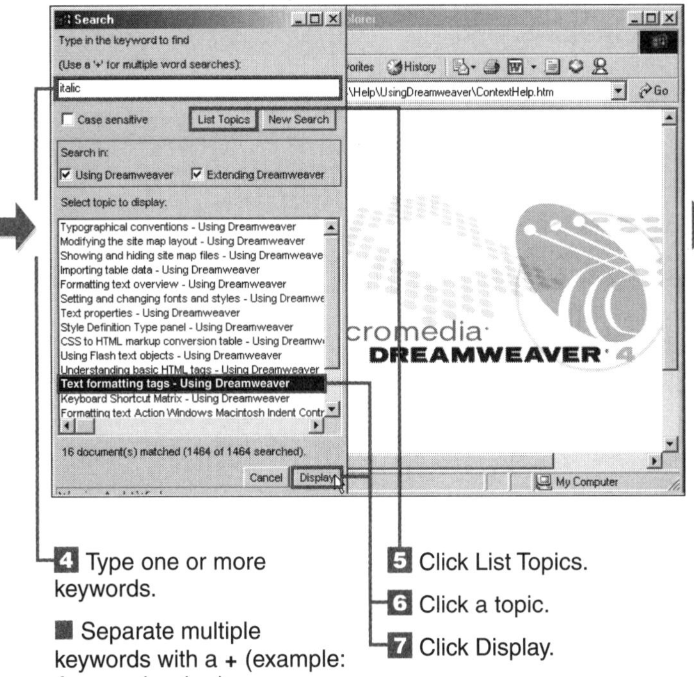

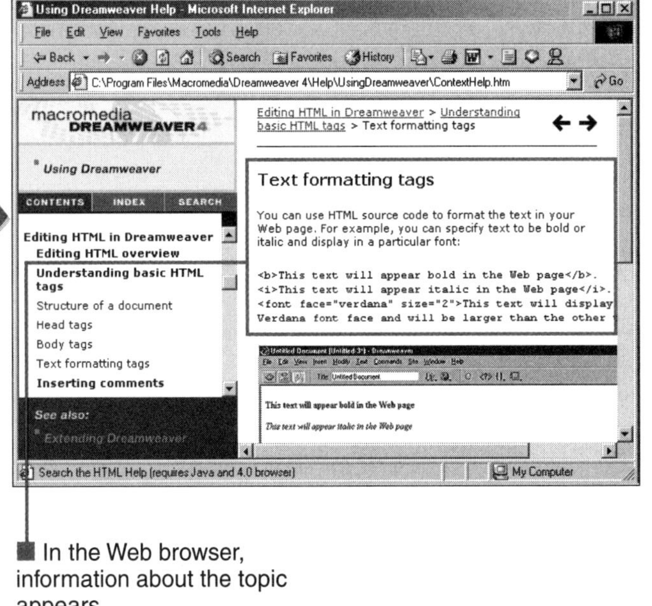

4 Type one or more keywords.

■ Separate multiple keywords with a + (example: *frame + borders*).

5 Click List Topics.

6 Click a topic.

7 Click Display.

■ In the Web browser, information about the topic appears.

OPEN AND CLOSE WINDOWS, PANELS, AND INSPECTORS

You work in a variety of windows when building Web pages in Dreamweaver. The main window is the Document window, where you insert and arrange the different elements of your Web pages. Dreamweaver also has accessory windows, called *inspectors* and *panels*, that display information and hold commands specific to different elements on your Web page.

When you are designing a page, you generally keep the Document window open at all times and open and close the inspectors and panels as you need them. Dreamweaver has commands for opening and closing all the inspectors and panels under the Window menu. You can also open and close these windows by clicking icons on the right side of the Document window status bar, an area called the *Launcher Bar*.

Dreamweaver also has a free-floating version of the Launcher Bar called simply the *Launcher*. You can change the icons that appear in the Launcher Bar and Launcher in the Panels category in Preferences. See the section "Set Preferences."

OPEN AND CLOSE WINDOWS, PANELS, AND INSPECTORS

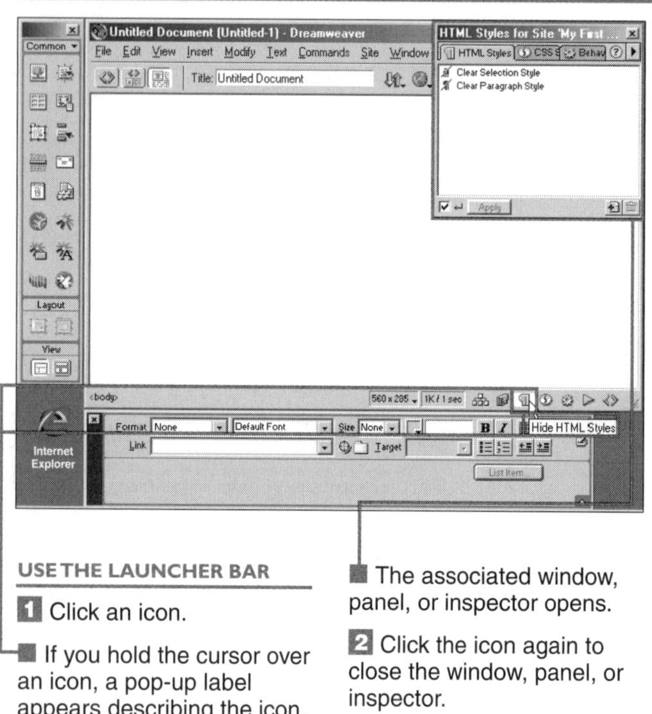

USE THE LAUNCHER BAR

1 Click an icon.

- If you hold the cursor over an icon, a pop-up label appears describing the icon.

- The associated window, panel, or inspector opens.

2 Click the icon again to close the window, panel, or inspector.

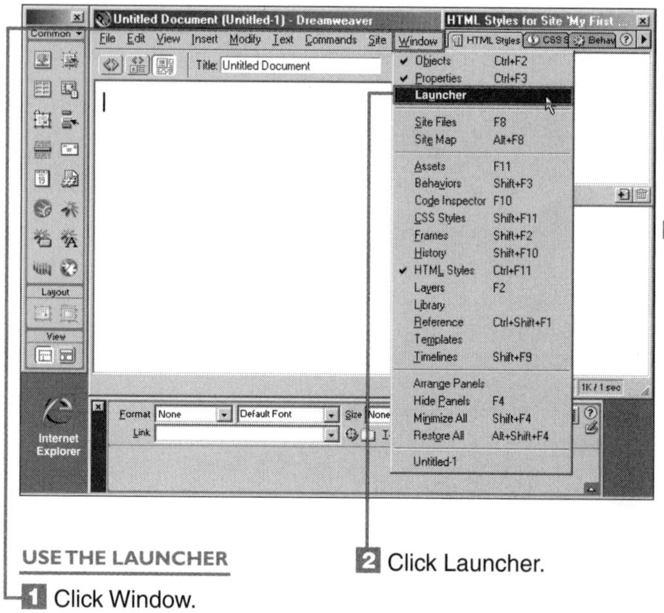

USE THE LAUNCHER

1 Click Window.

2 Click Launcher.

How do I change the orientation of the Launcher?

✔ Click the icon in the lower-right corner of the Launcher to toggle the window between its horizontal orientation and vertical orientation.

Can I remove the Launcher Bar from the bottom of the Document window?

✔ Yes. Under the Status Bar category in the Preferences dialog box, Dreamweaver has a check box that enables you to control whether to display the Launcher Bar. For more about Dreamweaver Preferences, see the "Set Preferences" section.

How do I move or resize windows, panels, and inspectors?

✔ You can move windows, panels, and inspectors by clicking and dragging their title bars. You can resize them by clicking and dragging their edges.

Are the icons in the Launcher and the Launcher Bar always the same?

✔ Yes. If you rearrange the Launcher icons, which you can do under the Panels category in Preferences, the Launcher Bar icons change in the same way.

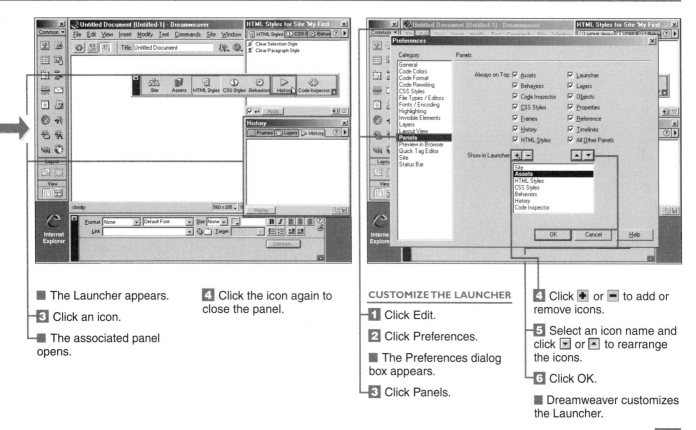

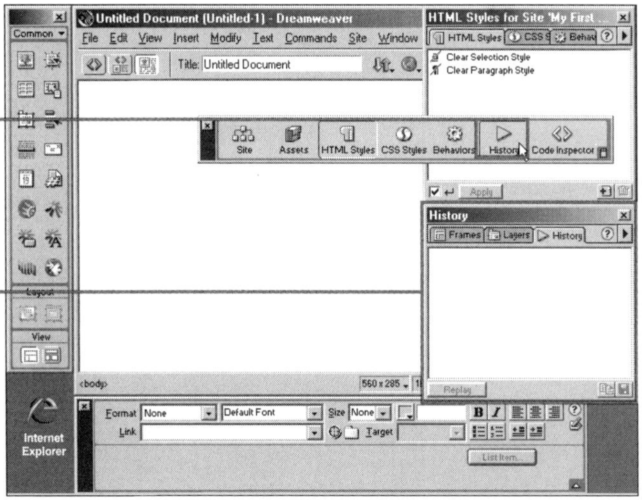

- The Launcher appears.

3 Click an icon.

- The associated panel opens.

4 Click the icon again to close the panel.

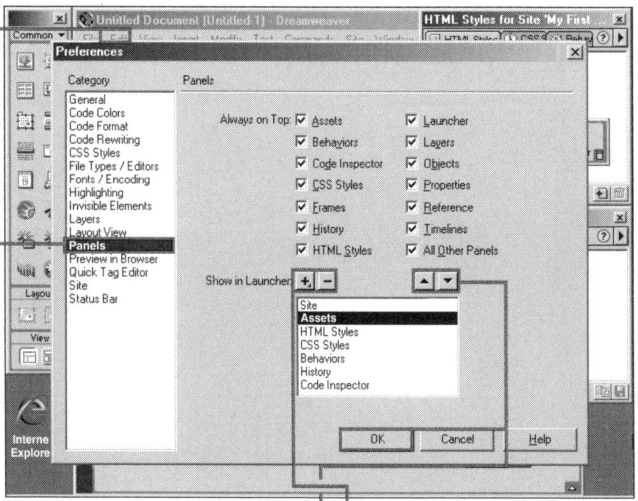

CUSTOMIZE THE LAUNCHER

1 Click Edit.

2 Click Preferences.

- The Preferences dialog box appears.

3 Click Panels.

4 Click + or − to add or remove icons.

5 Select an icon name and click ▼ or ▲ to rearrange the icons.

6 Click OK.

- Dreamweaver customizes the Launcher.

USING THE DOCUMENT WINDOW

The Document window is the main workspace in Dreamweaver, where you insert and arrange the text, images, and other elements of your Web page. For every page you open in Dreamweaver, you have a Document window.

The Document window has two views. You do most of your work in Design view where the Document window displays a WYSIWYG — "What Your See Is What You Get" — version of your Web page. You can work with your page in approximately the form it takes when you display it in the browser. You can also switch to Code view, where you can view and work with raw HTML in the Document window. Dreamweaver also has a Code and Design view, where you see both the Design view and Code view at the same time. Learn more about the different views in Chapter 3.

Dreamweaver also has two different subviews available in Design view: Standard view and Layout view. Standard view approximates what you see when you open the page in a browser. Layout view adds additional information to help you lay out the information in your page using tables. See Chapter 8 for more information.

USING THE DOCUMENT WINDOW

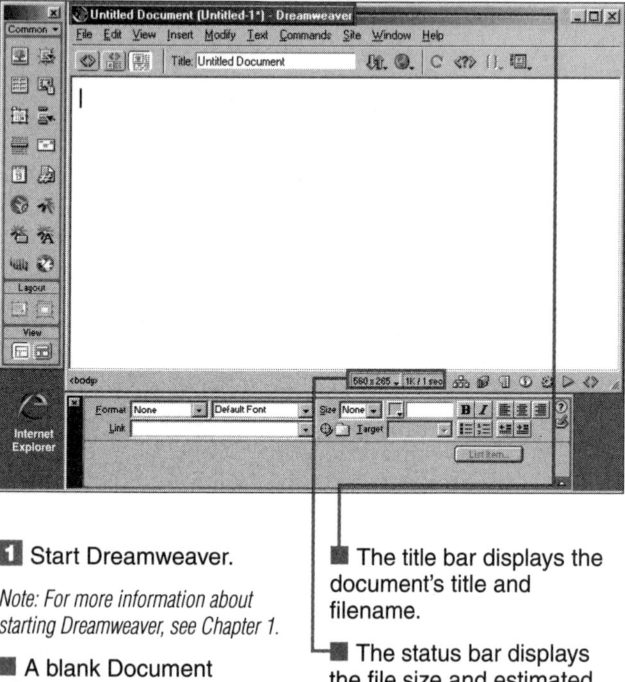

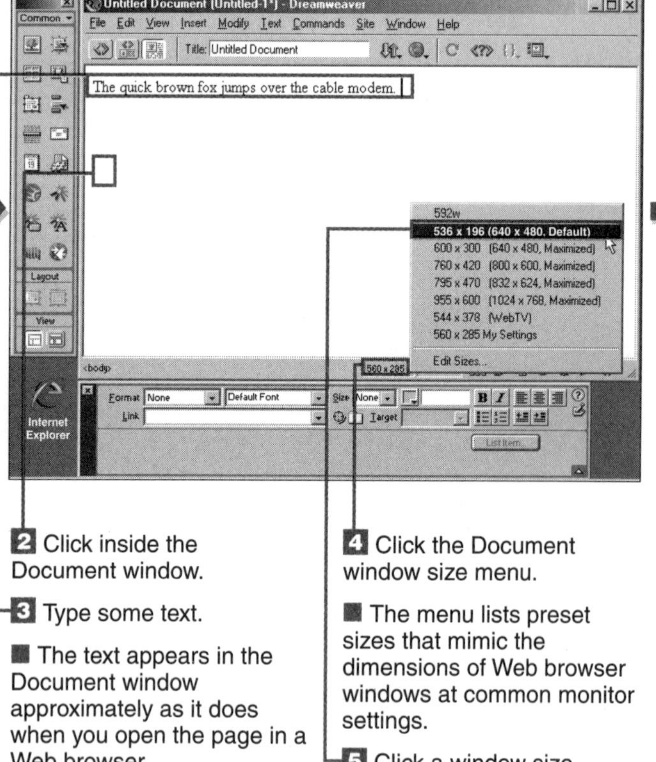

1 Start Dreamweaver.

Note: For more information about starting Dreamweaver, see Chapter 1.

■ A blank Document window opens.

■ The title bar displays the document's title and filename.

■ The status bar displays the file size and estimated download time for the page.

2 Click inside the Document window.

3 Type some text.

■ The text appears in the Document window approximately as it does when you open the page in a Web browser.

4 Click the Document window size menu.

■ The menu lists preset sizes that mimic the dimensions of Web browser windows at common monitor settings.

5 Click a window size.

What are some of the Web-page features that do not appear in Dreamweaver as they do in a Web browser window?

✔ Some of the features that do not appear as they do in a browser include behaviors, images that are referenced on an external Web server, and some style-sheet rules. Hyperlinks appear colored and underlined in the Document window but are not clickable. To view and test these features, preview your page in a Web browser. See Chapter 4 for more information.

How can I customize my view of the Document window?

✔ In addition to using the commands found in the Toolbar, you can use various commands in the View menu. For example, commands in the Visual Aids submenu let you turn on and off table, layer, and frame borders; image-map information; and invisible elements such as named anchors and layer icons. Commands under the Tracing Image submenu enable you to position an image beneath your page content to serve as a layout guide. This lets you design a page mock-up in an image editor and then use it as a guide for your Dreamweaver design.

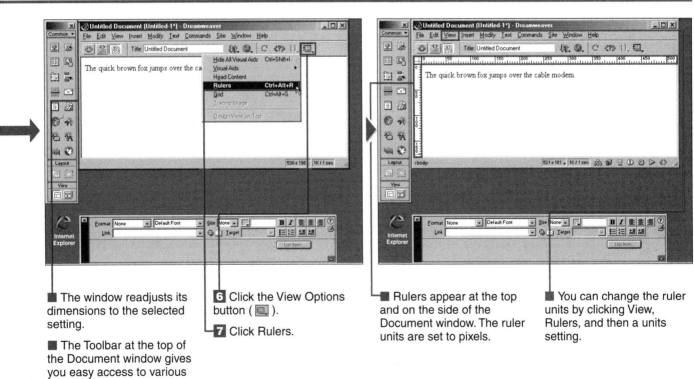

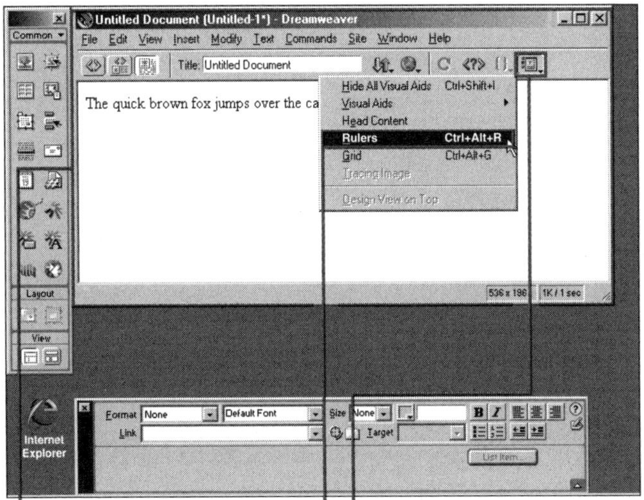

■ The window readjusts its dimensions to the selected setting.

■ The Toolbar at the top of the Document window gives you easy access to various commands.

6 Click the View Options button ( ).

7 Click Rulers.

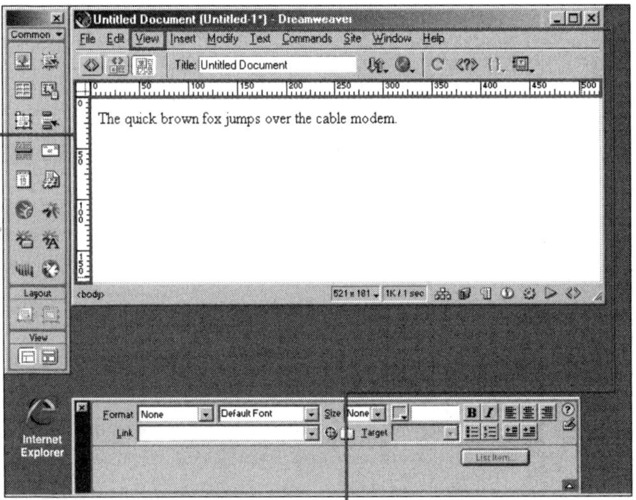

■ Rulers appear at the top and on the side of the Document window. The ruler units are set to pixels.

■ You can change the ruler units by clicking View, Rulers, and then a units setting.

USING THE PROPERTY INSPECTOR

The Property Inspector lets you view the properties associated with the object or text currently selected in the Document window. Text fields, drop-down menus, buttons, and other tools in the Property Inspector enable you to modify these properties.

The appearance of the Property Inspector changes as you select different elements of your page, because different elements have different properties. For example, text elements have different properties than image elements.

The Property Inspector has two modes: standard and expanded. The standard mode shows only the most commonly used properties for a selected element. In most cases, the expanded version shows all of an element's properties. This book shows the Property Inspector in expanded mode.

How do I access help in the Property Inspector?

✔ For more information about different properties, you can use the Question Mark (?) in the inspector to open the help documentation for Dreamweaver.

How do I switch between the standard and expanded mode?

✔ You can click ▾ to switch between standard and expanded mode.

USING THE PROPERTY INSPECTOR

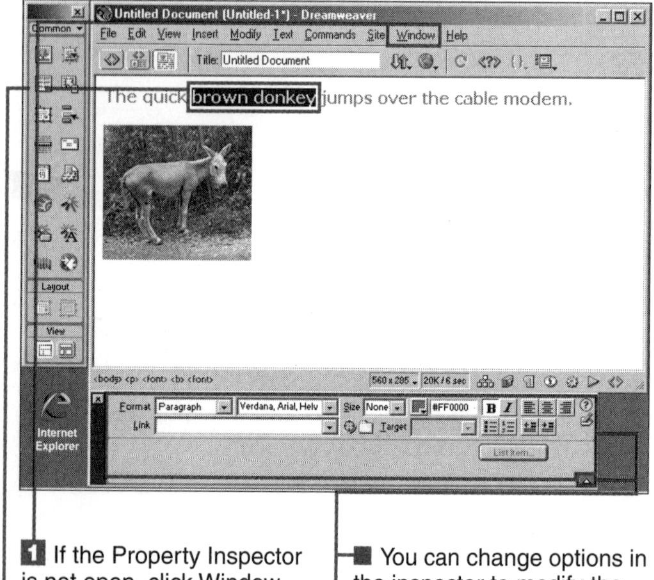

1 If the Property Inspector is not open, click Window and then Properties.

2 Select some text.

■ Text properties such as format, size, and alignment appear.

■ You can change options in the inspector to modify the text.

■ Clicking ▲ allows you to switch between standard and expanded modes of the inspector.

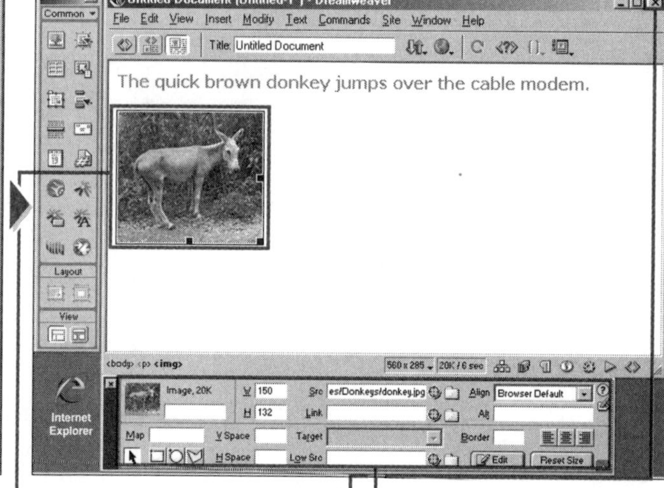

3 Click an image.

■ Image properties such as dimensions, filename, and alignment appear.

■ You can change options in the inspector to modify the image.

4 Click the Close button (☒) in the upper-left corner of the Property Inspector to close it.

USING THE OBJECTS PANEL

The Objects panel lets you create objects such as images, tables, and layers and insert them into the Document window. The panel has a drop-down menu at the top enabling you to view different sets of object-insertion buttons.

Dreamweaver has seven Menu categories: Common, for inserting images, tables, and other common objects; Characters, for inserting special symbols such as international characters; Forms, for inserting form objects; Frames, for inserting predefined frameset designs; Head, for inserting special HTML into the head section of your page; Invisibles, for inserting certain objects that do not appear in the browser window; and Special, for inserting multimedia objects.

Most of the time, a dialog box appears after you click an Objects panel button enabling you to specify the characteristics of the object that you are inserting.

Can I bypass the dialog box that appears when I click an Objects panel button?

✓ You can bypass the dialog box and insert a generic object by pressing the Control key (Windows) or the Option key (Mac) when you click the panel button. This works for some, but not all, objects.

USING THE OBJECTS PANEL

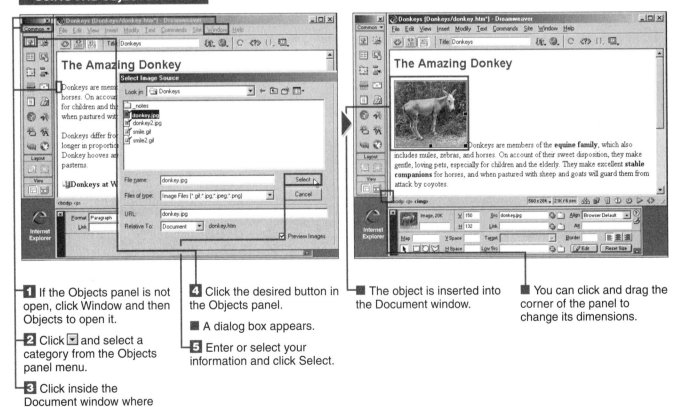

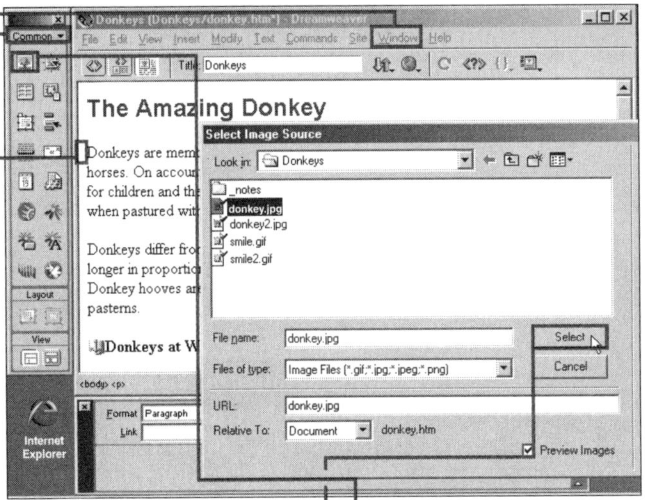

1 If the Objects panel is not open, click Window and then Objects to open it.

2 Click ▾ and select a category from the Objects panel menu.

3 Click inside the Document window where you want to insert an object.

4 Click the desired button in the Objects panel.

■ A dialog box appears.

5 Enter or select your information and click Select.

■ The object is inserted into the Document window.

■ You can click and drag the corner of the panel to change its dimensions.

UNDO COMMANDS WITH THE HISTORY PANEL

The History panel keeps track of the commands you perform in Dreamweaver and allows you to return your page to a previous state by backtracking through those commands. The History panel gives you a convenient way to correct errors or to revert your page to an earlier version if you do not like the modifications you have made.

The maximum number of steps that the History panel remembers is adjustable in Preferences — see the "Set Preferences" section for more information.

When you backtrack to undo several steps in the History panel, the content in the Document window reverts to the state it was prior to performing the steps. The steps that are undone are grayed out in the History panel list. You can redo the steps if necessary. If you perform new commands, any grayed-out commands are erased.

You can select a sequence of commands in the History panel and turn them into a custom command. See the "Create a Command with the History Panel" section for more information.

UNDO COMMANDS WITH THE HISTORY PANEL

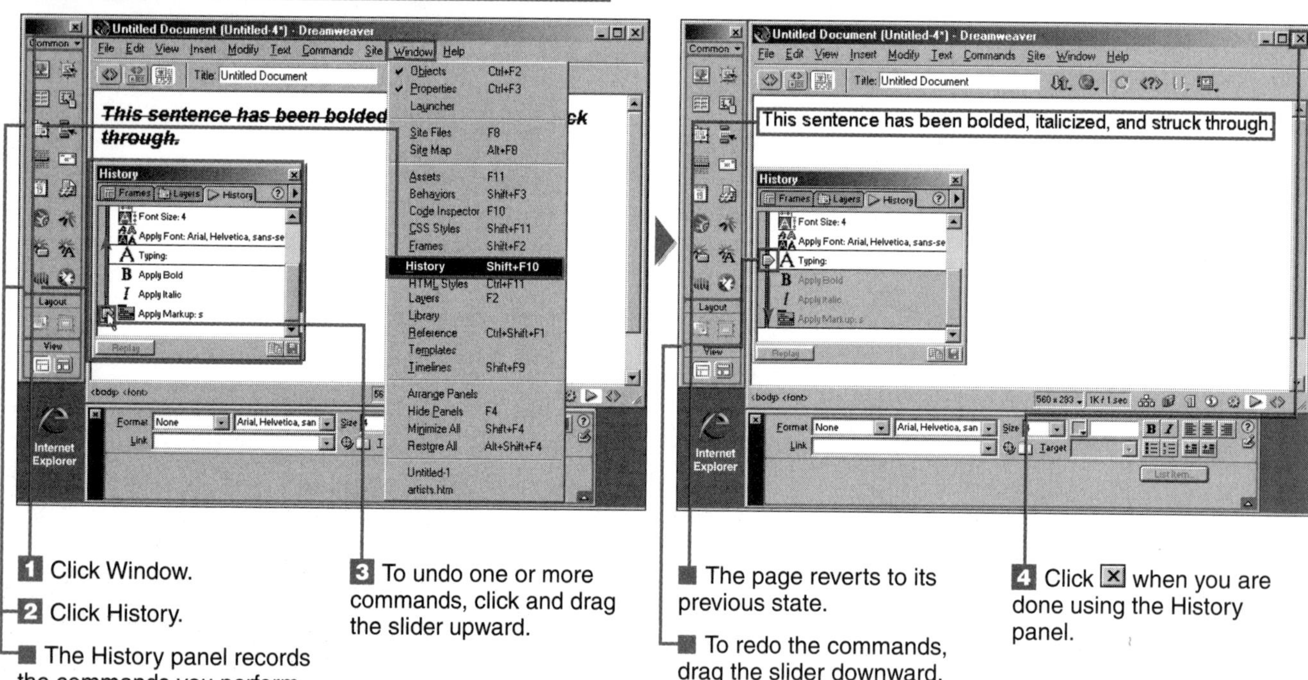

1 Click Window.

2 Click History.

■ The History panel records the commands you perform in Dreamweaver.

3 To undo one or more commands, click and drag the slider upward.

■ The page reverts to its previous state.

■ To redo the commands, drag the slider downward.

4 Click ☒ when you are done using the History panel.

COMBINE PANELS

Dreamweaver has more than a dozen panels and inspectors that you can use to build Web pages and to manage your Web site. To keep your on-screen workspace from getting cluttered, you can combine, or *dock*, most of these windows to create multi-tabbed windows. You can then click the tabs to switch between different tools.

Dreamweaver comes with some of the panels already in tabbed groups. For example, the History panel shares a window with the Frames and Layers panels. You can modify these arrangements by clicking and dragging tabs between windows to regroup the tools in ways that work best for you.

In addition to the docking feature, the different windows in Dreamweaver snap to the sides of one another and also to the edges of your screen. This makes it easy to arrange windows efficiently in your workspace. You can also automatically rearrange open panels and inspectors with the Arrange Panels command under the Windows menu.

COMBINE PANELS

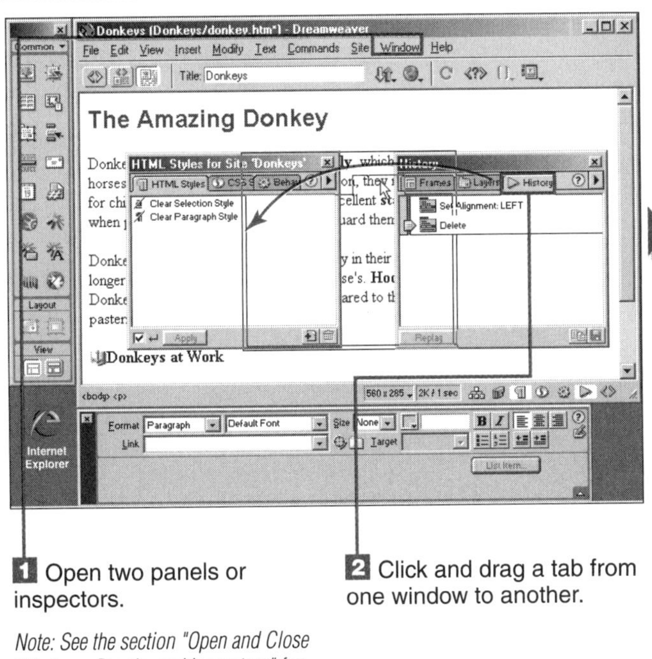

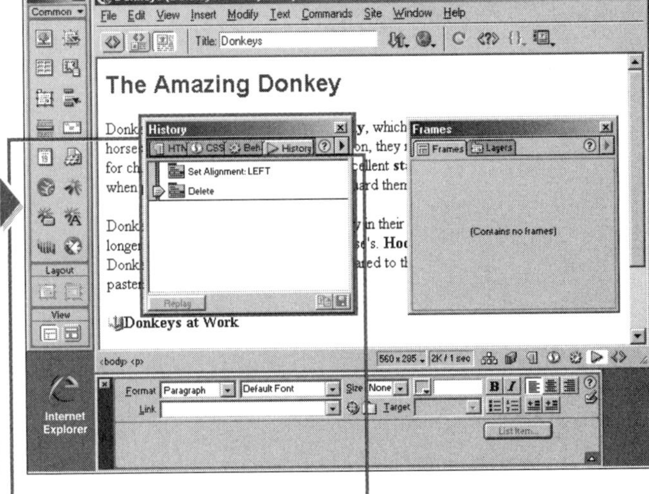

1 Open two panels or inspectors.

Note: See the section "Open and Close Windows, Panels, and Inspectors" for more on opening panels.

2 Click and drag a tab from one window to another.

■ The first window is docked with the second.

Note: You cannot combine the Property Inspector, Site window, or Launcher with other windows.

■ You can select among the different panels in the window by clicking the tabs.

■ You can undock a panel by clicking and dragging a tab outside the window.

CREATE A COMMAND WITH THE HISTORY PANEL

You can select a sequence of commands that the History panel has recorded and save that sequence as a custom command. The new command appears under the Commands menu.

You should consider saving any sequence of commands that you plan to perform over and over on your Web site as a custom command. This saves you time and physical effort, and ensures that the settings you apply are identical each time.

Dreamweaver stores saved commands as a JavaScript or HTML file in the Commands folder, which you find in the Dreamweaver application's Configuration folder.

Note that the commands that you see in the History panel are specific to the current Document window. If you switch to a different Document window, a different history list appears in the panel.

CREATE A COMMAND WITH THE HISTORY PANEL

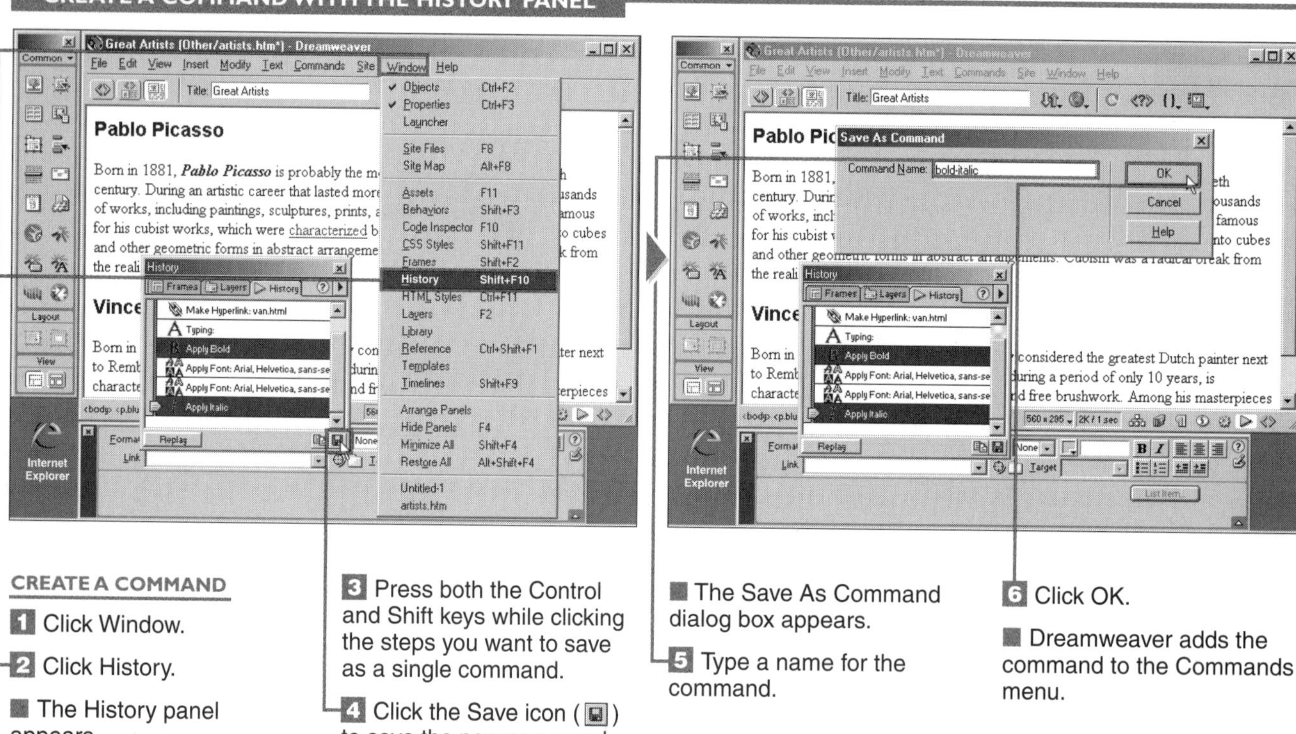

CREATE A COMMAND

1 Click Window.

2 Click History.

■ The History panel appears.

3 Press both the Control and Shift keys while clicking the steps you want to save as a single command.

4 Click the Save icon (💾) to save the new command.

■ The Save As Command dialog box appears.

5 Type a name for the command.

6 Click OK.

■ Dreamweaver adds the command to the Commands menu.

Can I rearrange the steps that appear in the History panel?

✔ No, you cannot rearrange the steps in the History panel. Dreamweaver lets you go back in history, but it does not let you rewrite it!

Why would I want to reduce the number of steps recorded by the History panel?

✔ Reducing the maximum number of steps you record, which you can do in Preferences, reduces the amount of memory Dreamweaver uses. Reducing the steps may also improve Dreamweaver's performance, especially if you do not have a lot of RAM installed on your computer.

What happens to the History panel when I close a document?

✔ Dreamweaver erases the history list for that document. Commands created from the History panel, however, are not erased.

Can I copy History information between Document windows?

✔ Yes. You can press Shift and then click to select the steps and use the Copy Steps command in the History panel menu. Then you can paste the commands into another Document window's History. You can also paste the steps into a text editor and view the JavaScript that defines them.

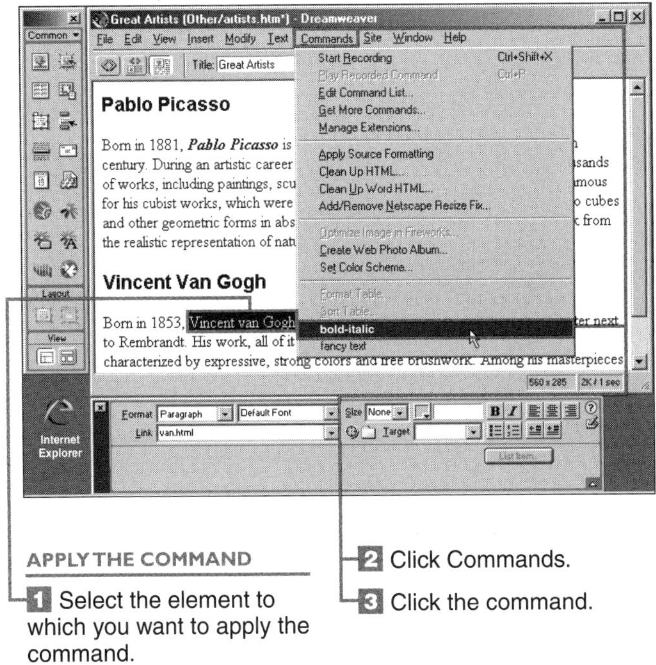

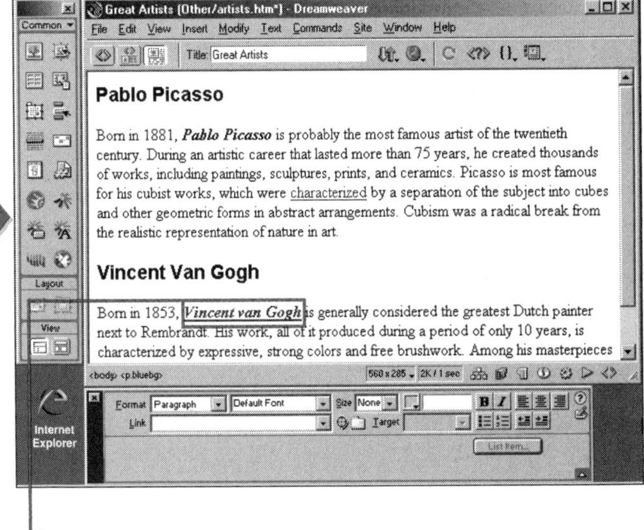

APPLY THE COMMAND

1 Select the element to which you want to apply the command.

2 Click Commands.

3 Click the command.

■ Dreamweaver applies the command to the selection.

CREATE A KEYBOARD SHORTCUT

You can use the Keyboard Shortcut Editor to define your own shortcut commands or edit existing shortcuts. This allows you to assign easy-to-remember keyboard combinations to commands that you use often in Dreamweaver.

To start defining your own keyboard shortcuts in Dreamweaver, you first have to create your own custom set of shortcuts, which you can do by duplicating an existing set.

The Keyboard Shortcuts Editor includes several predefined sets, which are complete collections of keyboard combinations mapped to Dreamweaver's commands. The default set is Macromedia Standard, which is the standard set of shortcuts for Dreamweaver 4. If you are more familiar with the previous version of Dreamweaver, you can load the set of shortcuts from Dreamweaver 3 with the editor and use the application with those.

You can also load sets from other Web editors, including HomeSite, a PC-based editor, and BBEdit, a Macintosh-based editor. These sets map shortcuts from the other applications to equivalent Dreamweaver commands. Where there are no equivalents (such as where Dreamweaver has commands that the other applications do not), Dreamweaver uses the Macromedia Standard shortcuts.

CREATE A KEYBOARD SHORTCUT

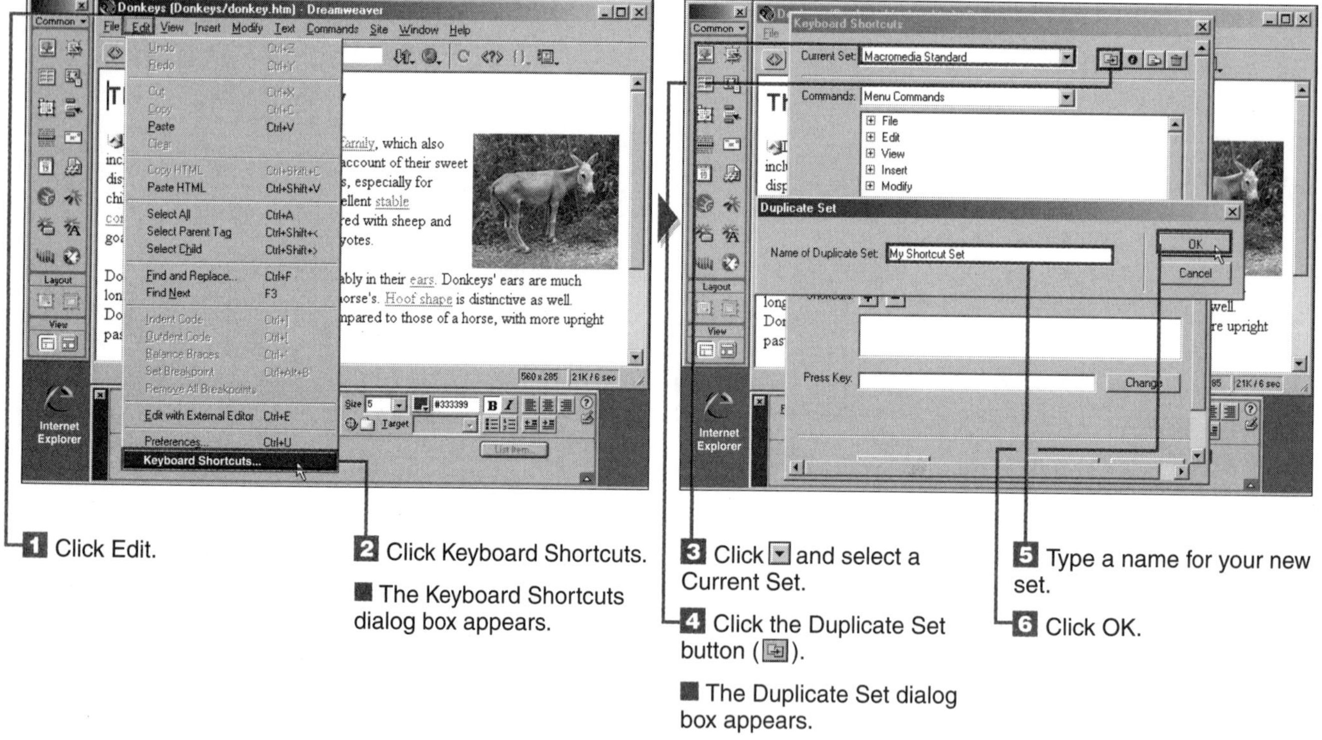

1 Click Edit.

2 Click Keyboard Shortcuts.

■ The Keyboard Shortcuts dialog box appears.

3 Click ▾ and select a Current Set.

4 Click the Duplicate Set button (⧉).

■ The Duplicate Set dialog box appears.

5 Type a name for your new set.

6 Click OK.

Can I edit the keyboard shortcut sets that come preinstalled — the sets for Dreamweaver 3, HomeSite, and so on?

✔ No. This is why you need to duplicate an existing shortcut set before you create any new shortcuts or make any modifications to existing shortcuts. Keeping the installed sets intact enables you to revert back to them if needed.

Can I reassign a keyboard shortcut?

✔ Yes. Dreamweaver warns you the keyboard shortcut already being used, but you can dismiss the warning and reassign the shortcut.

How can I print out a list of the assigned shortcuts of a set for reference?

✔ Click Export Set as HTML button in the Keyboard Shortcuts dialog box.

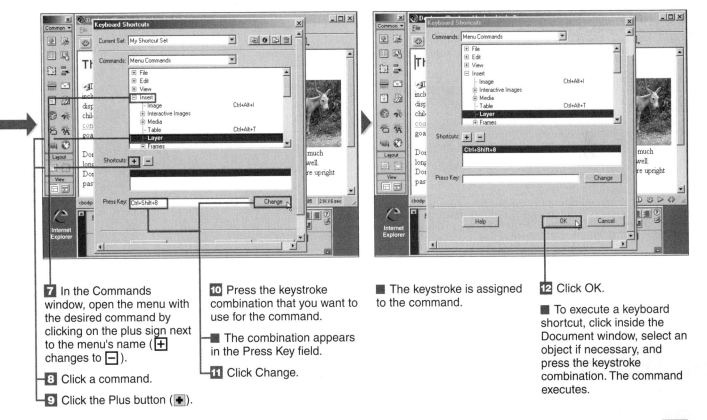

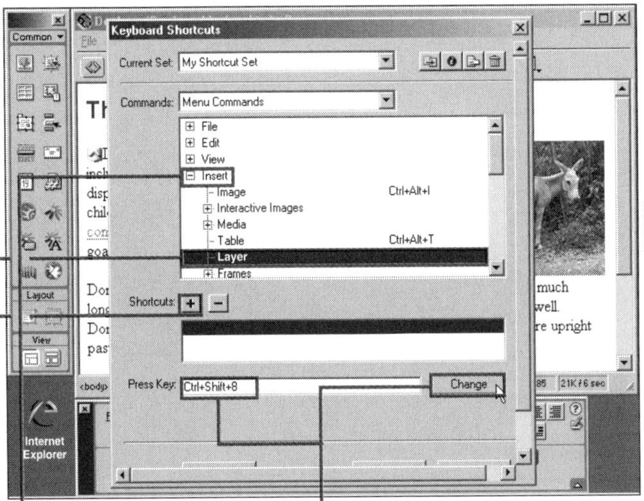

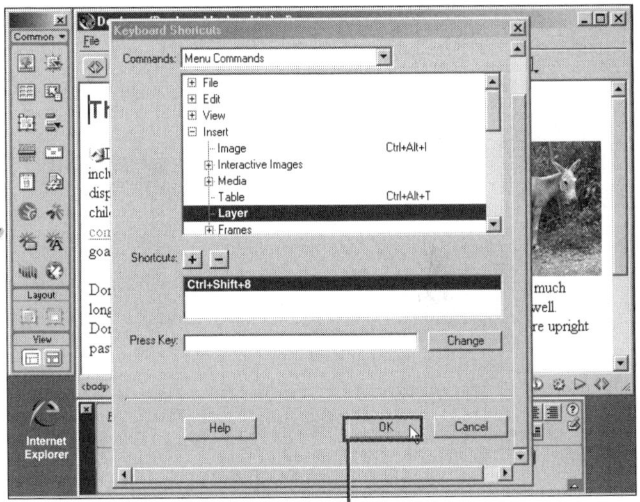

7 In the Commands window, open the menu with the desired command by clicking on the plus sign next to the menu's (⊞ changes to ⊟).

8 Click a command.

9 Click the Plus button (+).

10 Press the keystroke combination that you want to use for the command.

■ The combination appears in the Press Key field.

11 Click Change.

■ The keystroke is assigned to the command.

12 Click OK.

■ To execute a keyboard shortcut, click inside the Document window, select an object if necessary, and press the keystroke combination. The command executes.

SET PREFERENCES

You can easily change the default appearance and behavior of Dreamweaver by specifying settings in the Preferences dialog box. Preferences let you modify the user interface of Dreamweaver to better suit how you like to work. You can also use Preferences to change the way Dreamweaver writes HTML, how it generates page elements such as style sheets and layers, and a wide variety of other features.

The Preferences dialog box consists of a list of categories on the left side, and configurable menus, text fields, check boxes, and other elements on the right. The options available on the right change depending on the category selected on the left. For help in configuring a particular set of preferences, you can click the Help button at the bottom of the box to open Dreamweaver's help documentation.

When you change a preference in Dreamweaver, the program's behavior changes immediately after you click OK in the Preferences dialog box.

SET PREFERENCES

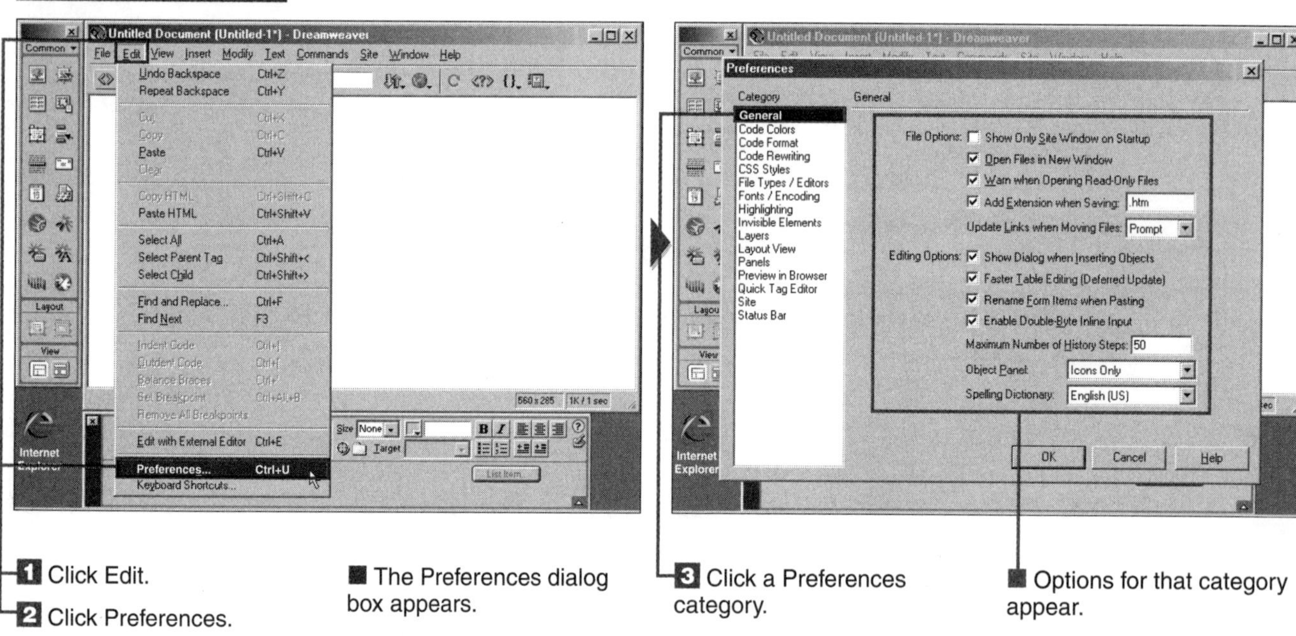

1 Click Edit.

2 Click Preferences.

■ The Preferences dialog box appears.

3 Click a Preferences category.

■ Options for that category appear.

How do I ensure that Dreamweaver does not rewrite my HTML or other code?

✔ You can select options under the Code Rewriting category in Preferences to ensure that Dreamweaver does not automatically correct or modify your code. You can turn off its error-correcting functions, specify files that that you do not want Dreamweaver to rewrite based on file extension, or disable its character-encoding features.

How do I customize the information available in the Document window's status bar?

✔ By selecting options under the Status Bar category in Preferences, you can add window sizes to the drop-down menu on the status bar and specify the connection speed it uses to determine the displayed download speed.

Can I change the default font styles and size for Dreamweaver's Design and Code views?

✔ Yes. Click the Fonts/Encoding category in Preferences to display the options. You can further customize the look and formatting of the text in Code view under the Code Color and Code Format categories.

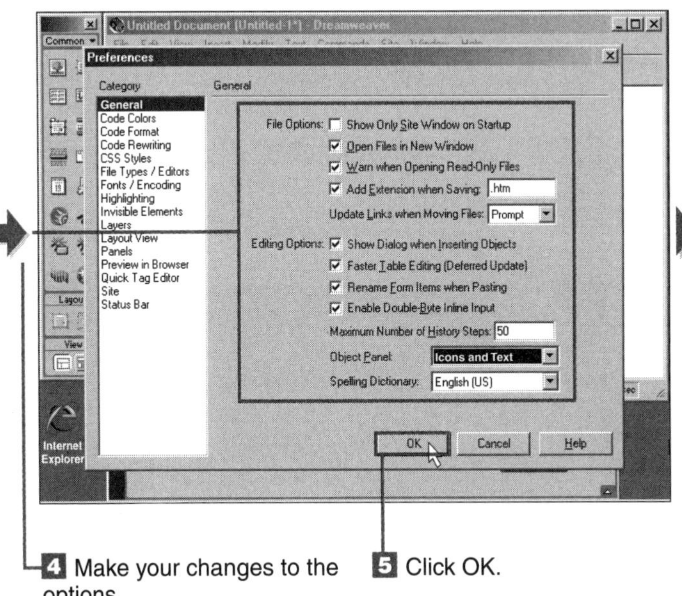

4 Make your changes to the options.

■ In this example, the Objects panel is set to display both icons and text descriptions.

5 Click OK.

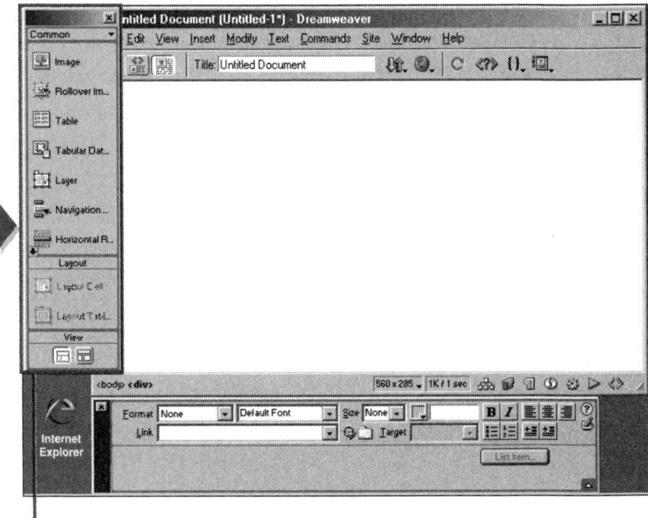

■ The preference changes take effect.

AN INTRODUCTION TO HTML

HTML

HyperText Markup Language, or HTML, is the formatting language that you use to create Web pages. When you open a Web page in a browser, its HTML code tells the browser how to display the text, images, and other content on the page. At its most basic level, Dreamweaver is an HTML-writing application, although it can do many other things as well.

The Official Standard

The World Wide Web Consortium, or W3C — an international body with members from industry, academia, and government — maintains the official HTML standard. The consortium makes recommendations as to what new HTML features should be adopted. Developers of browsers, servers, and HTML editors can then follow these guidelines when building their products. As of this writing, the current HTML standard is Version 4.01, which you can view at www.w3c.org.

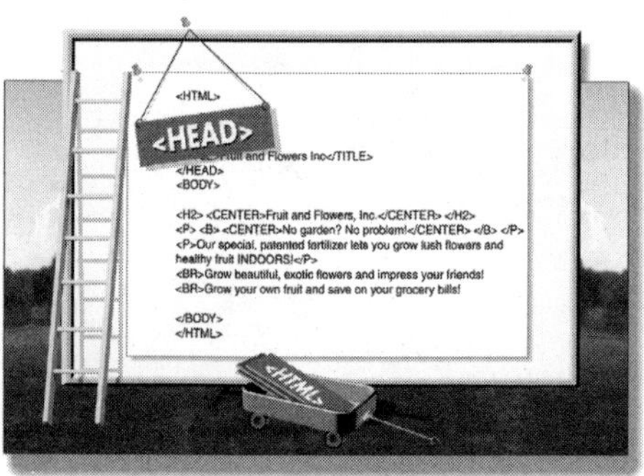

HTML Tags

The basic unit of HTML is a ***tag***. You can recognize HTML tags by their angle brackets:

```
<p>Today the weather was
<b>nice</b>.<br>

Tomorrow it may <i>rain</i>.</p>
```

Some HTML tags work in twos: Opening and closing tags surround content in a document and control the formatting of the content. For example, the `<b>` tags in the preceding code line cause text to be bold. Closing tags are distinguished by a forward slash (/). Other tags can stand alone. For example, the `<br>` tag adds a line break. HTML tags are not case sensitive; they can be uppercase, lowercase, or mixed case.

HTML Attributes

You can modify the effect of an HTML tag by adding extra information known as attributes. ***Attributes*** are name/value pairs such as `align="right"` that live inside the HTML angle brackets to the right of the tag name. For example, you can add the `align` attribute to a paragraph tag, `<p>`, to align a paragraph in various ways:

```
<p align="right">I think I will
go for a walk today instead of
typing on the computer. The sun
is shining and there is a warm
breeze.</p>
```

The preceding line of HTML causes the two-sentence paragraph to be aligned to the right side of the Web browser window.

HTML Documents

Because HTML documents are plain text files, you can open and edit them with any text editor. In fact, in the early days of the Web, most people created their pages with simple editors such as Window's Notepad and Macintosh's SimpleText. But writing HTML by hand can be a slow, tedious process, especially when creating advanced HTML elements such as tables, forms, and frames.

Create Web Pages without Knowing Code

Dreamweaver streamlines the process of creating Web pages by giving you an easy-to-use, visual interface with which to generate HTML. You specify formatting with menu commands and button clicks, and Dreamweaver takes care of writing the HTML code behind the scenes. When you build a Web page in the Document window, you see your page as it appears in a Web browser, instead of as HTML.

Direct Access to the Code

Dreamweaver gives you direct access to the raw HTML code if you want it. This can be an advantage for people who know HTML and want to do some formatting of their page by typing tags. The Code View mode, Code Inspector, and Quick Tag Editor in Dreamweaver enable you to edit your page by adding HTML information manually. Access to the code also means that you can add HTML features that Dreamweaver does not yet support, such as newly approved HTML tags.

Other Types of Code: Style Sheets

Although HTML provides the nuts and bolts that give a Web page its primary structure, there are also other types of code that play a part in making a Web page what it is. ***Style sheets***, also known as Cascading Style Sheets or CSS, enable you to specify how text and other elements appear visually on a Web page. Here is some style-sheet code:

```
h1 {font-style: italic; color:
red}
```

Style sheets allow you to implement much more elaborate formatting than you can with HTML. For more information about style sheets, see Chapter 12.

Other Types of Code: JavaScript

Another type code you find in Web pages is ***JavaScript***, which allows you to add interactive features to your Web page such as image rollovers, form validation, and pop-up windows. Dreamweaver allows you to add JavaScript features to Web pages by applying behaviors. For more information, see Chapter 13. Unlike HTML and style sheets, which are formatting languages, JavaScript is a programming language similar to C and Java. Here is some JavaScript code:

```
window.open(theURL,winName,
features);
```

You may see style sheets and JavaScript interspersed with HTML when you examine the code of a Web page.

VIEW AND EDIT THE SOURCE CODE

For Web developers who like to build their Web site the old-fashioned way — by writing HTML by hand — Dreamweaver offers several ways to edit a page's source code. You can open up a document's code in a separate window called the Code Inspector. Or you can switch to Code View mode in the Document window, which replaces Dreamweaver's "what you see is what you get" (WYSIWYG) Design View with the current page's raw HTML. Dreamweaver also allows you to split the Document window in two, and view a page's Design View and Code View simultaneously.

As you make changes in Code View or in the Code Inspector, a page's Design View changes in concert. The synchronization between the views makes Dreamweaver a useful environment for learning HTML. You can switch between views to see what tags do what. Dreamweaver also color codes the different HTML tags for easy reading and highlights HTML mistakes.

VIEW AND EDIT THE SOURCE CODE

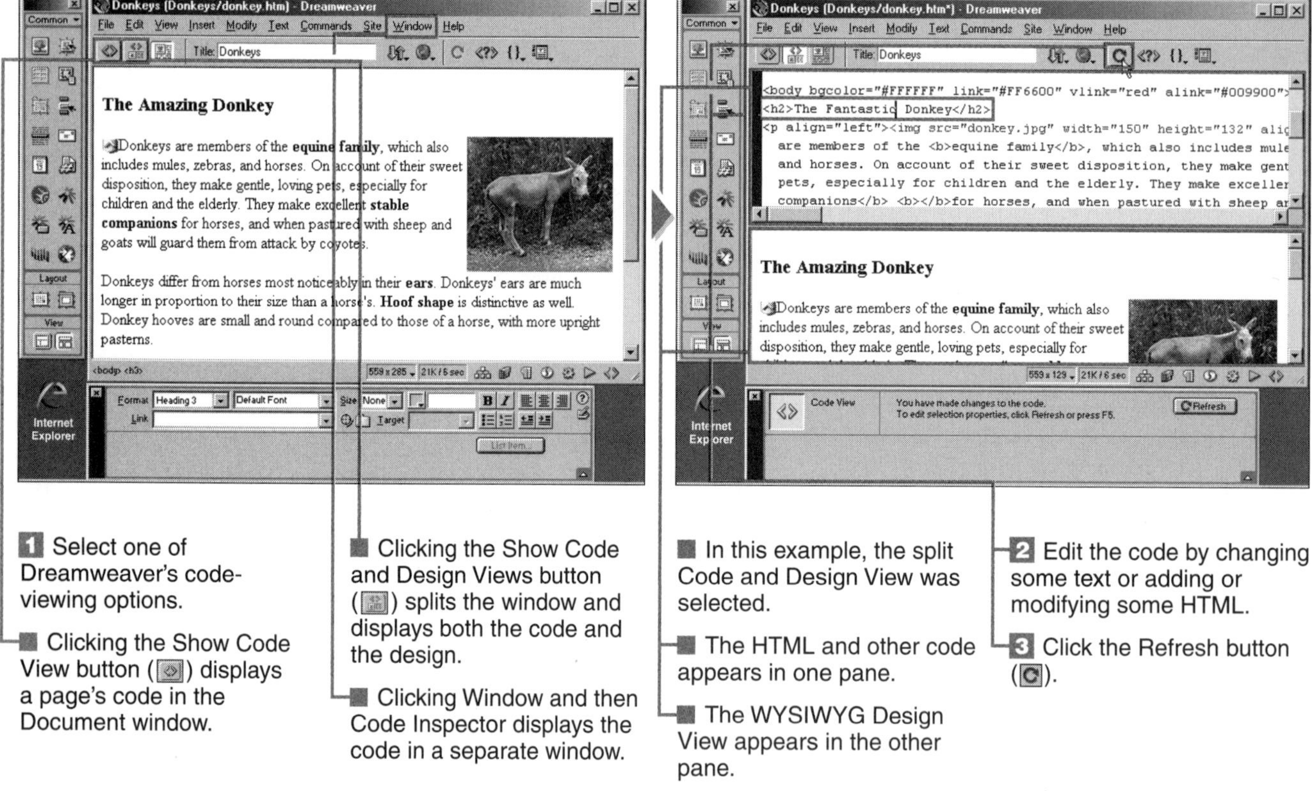

1 Select one of Dreamweaver's code-viewing options.

■ Clicking the Show Code View button (<>) displays a page's code in the Document window.

■ Clicking the Show Code and Design Views button splits the window and displays both the code and the design.

■ Clicking Window and then Code Inspector displays the code in a separate window.

■ In this example, the split Code and Design View was selected.

■ The HTML and other code appears in one pane.

■ The WYSIWYG Design View appears in the other pane.

2 Edit the code by changing some text or adding or modifying some HTML.

3 Click the Refresh button (C).

How do I make code wrap at the right edge of the window?

✔ To make the code wrap on the right in Code View, click the View Options button ( ) at the top of Document window and then click Word Wrap.

How does Dreamweaver display errors in my HTML?

✔ Dreamweaver displays suspected HTML errors in yellow highlighting in the Document window. Errors Dreamweaver flags include orphaned closing tags and opening and closing tags that do not match. Note that Dreamweaver *does not* flag HTML tags that it does not recognize, because these could be valid new tags that it simply is not aware of.

Can I write style-sheet and JavaScript code in Code View or in the Code Inspector?

✔ Yes. In fact, using the Code View is the only way to add many custom JavaScript features, other than the ones provided as Dreamweaver behaviors.

How do I change the color coding of my HTML?

✔ Click Edit and then Preferences. In the Preferences dialog box, click the category Code Colors. From there, you can change how Dreamweaver colors your HTML.

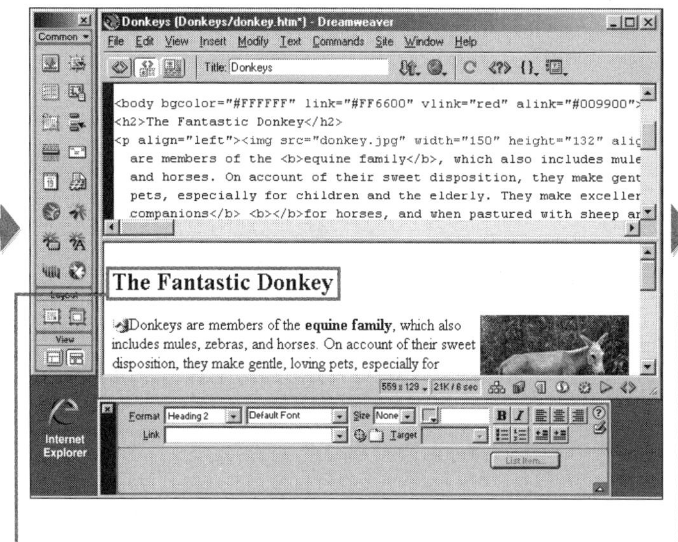

■ The content in the Design View is updated to reflect the code changes.

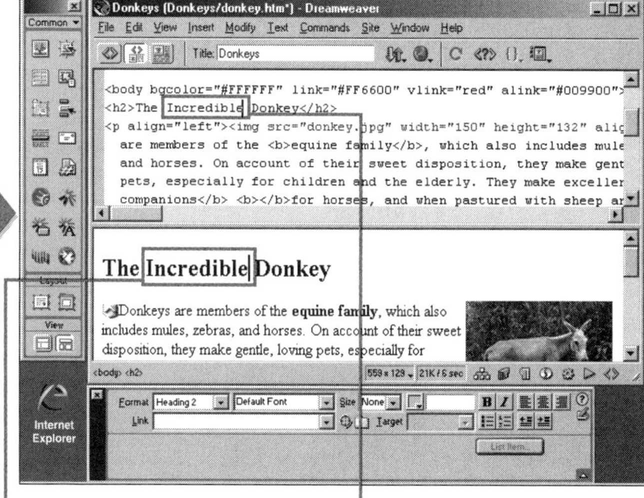

4 Make some changes to the content in the Design View.

■ The text in the Code View updates dynamically as you make your changes.

CLEAN UP YOUR HTML

Dreamweaver offers commands that optimize the HTML in your Web page by deleting extraneous or nonfunctional tags. This can decrease a page's file size and make the source code easier to read in Code View.

You can use the Clean Up HTML command to remove empty and redundant HTML tags as well as HTML comments. You can specify that Dreamweaver-generated comments be ignored; this ensures that template information and library items — which depend on special comments in the code — remain intact. The command also lets you automatically remove particular HTML tags in your code.

It is useful to clean up your HTML as a final step before uploading your pages to a remote Web server. It can also be useful when editing files originally built in other Web editors, which can sometimes write inefficient code and add their own proprietary tags.

CLEAN UP YOUR HTML

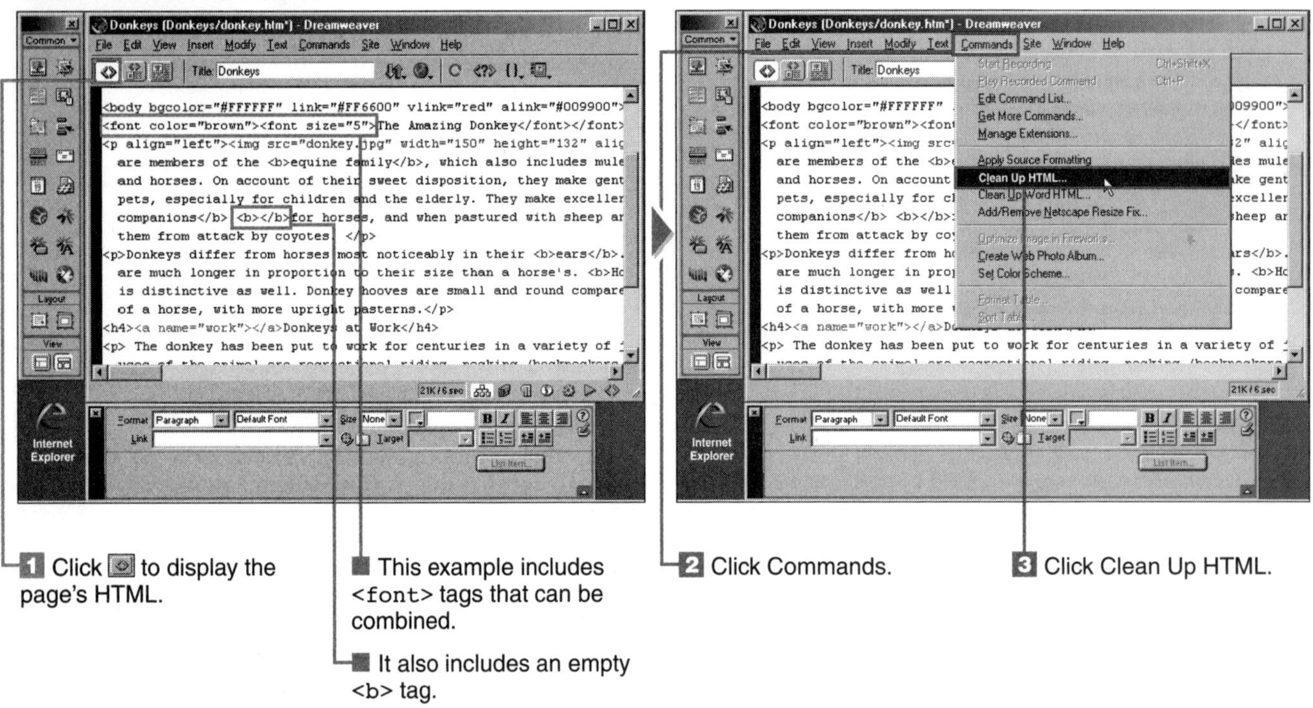

1 Click [icon] to display the page's HTML.

■ This example includes <font> tags that can be combined.

■ It also includes an empty <b> tag.

2 Click Commands.

3 Click Clean Up HTML.

How do empty tags end up appearing in Dreamweaver's HTML?

✔ Sometimes if you heavily edit Web-page text in the Document window — such as cutting and pasting sentences, and reformatting words, for example — Dreamweaver inadvertently removes text from inside tags without removing the tags themselves.

What does the Clean Up Word HTML command do?

✔ This command, which is also under the Commands menu, removes the extra head information, style-sheet rules, and XML tags that Microsoft Word adds when saving a document as a Web page. Most of these tags are added so that the HTML document can be displayed correctly in Word itself.

What does it mean to combine nested <font> tags?

✔ Dreamweaver can combine several nested instances of a `<font>` tag into one to save space.

Before:

```
<font color="red">
    <font size="4">
    Some text
    </font></font>
```

After:

```
<font color="red"size="4">
    Some text</font>
```

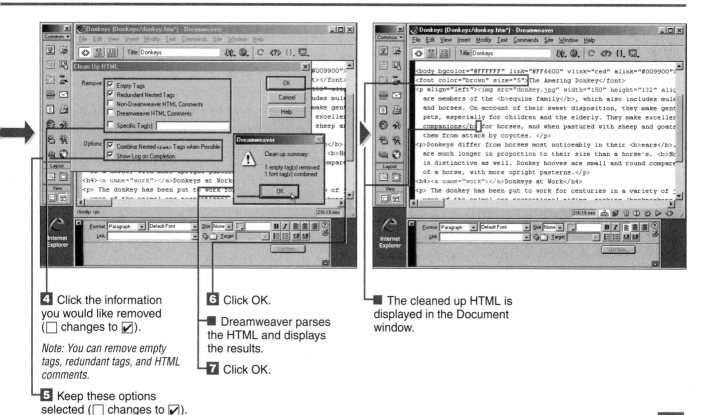

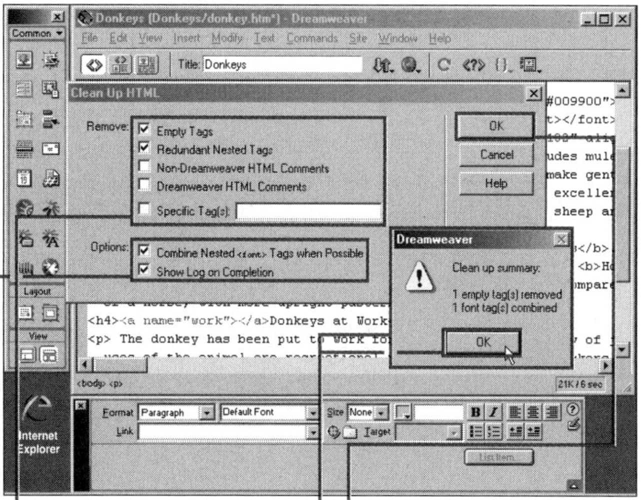

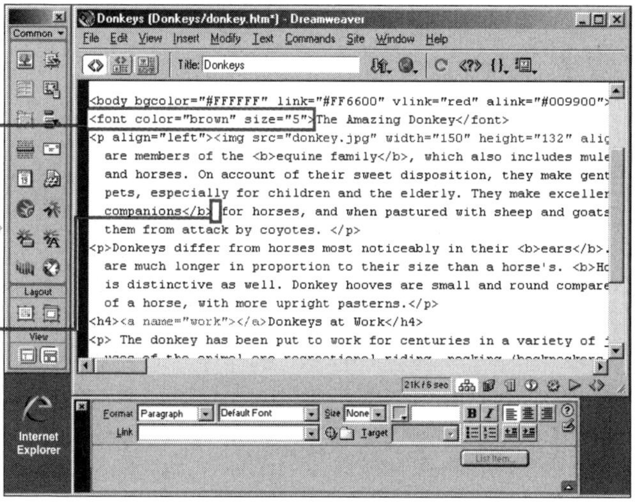

4 Click the information you would like removed (☐ changes to ☑).

Note: You can remove empty tags, redundant tags, and HTML comments.

5 Keep these options selected (☐ changes to ☑).

6 Click OK.

■ Dreamweaver parses the HTML and displays the results.

7 Click OK.

■ The cleaned up HTML is displayed in the Document window.

USING THE QUICK TAG EDITOR

Dreamweaver's Quick Tag Editor gives you easy access to HTML code without having to open the Code Inspector or switch to Code View. You can open it when you are working inside the Document window and use it to add or modify HTML tags.

The Quick Tag Editor can work in one of three modes: Edit Tag, Wrap Tag, or Insert HTML. Edit Tag lets you modify existing tags, Wrap Tag lets you wrap new tags around existing page content, and Insert Tag lets you add new tags. Which mode the Quick Tag Editor opens in depends on what you select in the Document window. For example, if you select an existing HTML tag in Code View, the Editor opens in Edit Tag mode. If you select plain text in Design View, it opens in Wrap Tag mode. If you do not select anything, the cursor appears between page elements and the Editor opens in Insert Tag mode.

The Quick Tag Editor includes a "help" feature for those who are not familiar with all the available HTML tags and their attributes. If you pause after opening the editor, it displays a drop-down list with all the available HTML tags. After you select a tag, the Quick Tag Editor displays a list of the attributes available for that tag.

USING THE QUICK TAG EDITOR

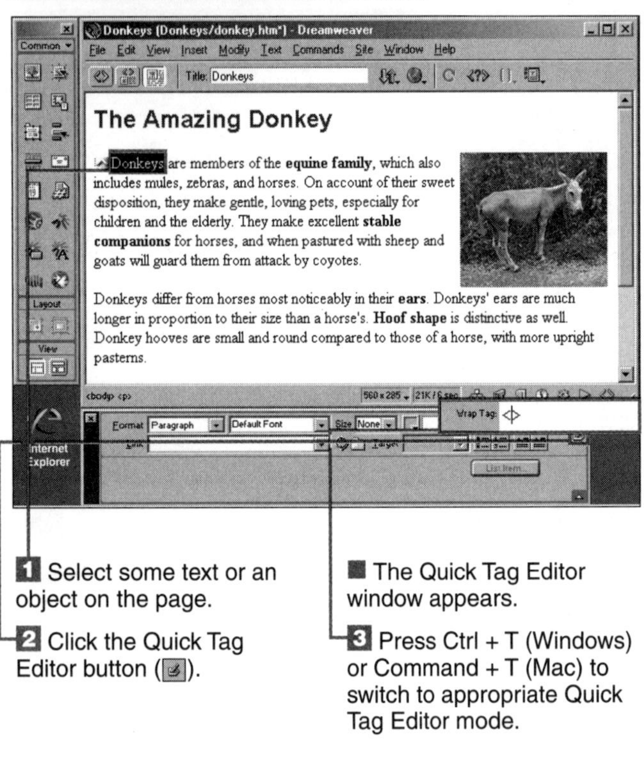

1 Select some text or an object on the page.

2 Click the Quick Tag Editor button (button icon).

■ The Quick Tag Editor window appears.

3 Press Ctrl + T (Windows) or Command + T (Mac) to switch to appropriate Quick Tag Editor mode.

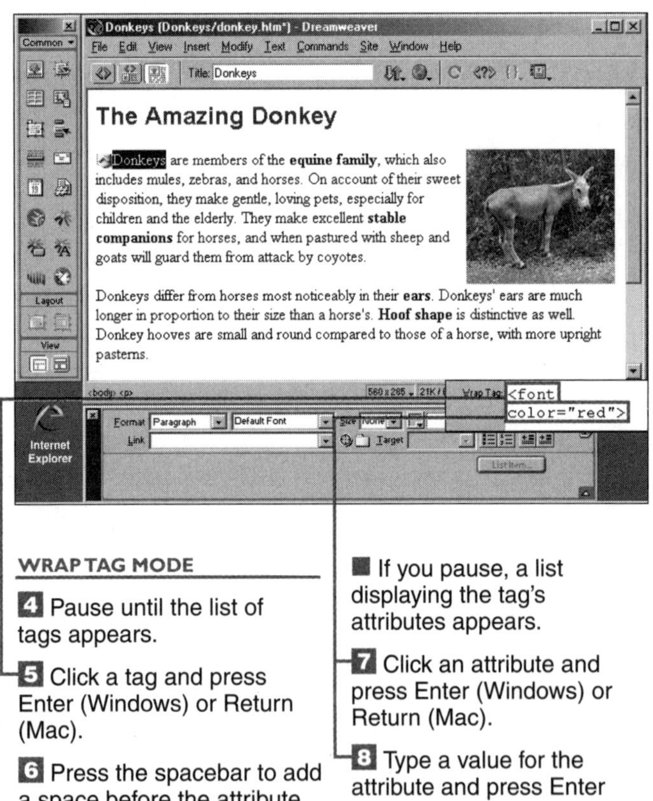

WRAP TAG MODE

4 Pause until the list of tags appears.

5 Click a tag and press Enter (Windows) or Return (Mac).

6 Press the spacebar to add a space before the attribute.

■ If you pause, a list displaying the tag's attributes appears.

7 Click an attribute and press Enter (Windows) or Return (Mac).

8 Type a value for the attribute and press Enter (Windows) or Return (Mac).

How can I customize the Quick Tag Editor?

✔ Click Edit and then Preferences. In the Preferences dialog box, click the Quick Tag Editor category. Here you can choose whether the tag information that you enter in the editor is applied immediately as you type it. You can also specify how long it takes for the drop-down "help" list to appear.

How do I exit the Editor without applying changes?

✔ You can press Esc to exit without applying changes.

Does the Quick Tag Editor allow me to enter incorrect HTML?

✔ Although the Quick Tag Editor can help you create well-formed HTML by adding the appropriate closing tags and quoted attributes, it does not try to correct HTML tags or attributes that it does not understand. Because HTML is an evolving language, Dreamweaver assumes that it may not know all the HTML tags that are currently being used.

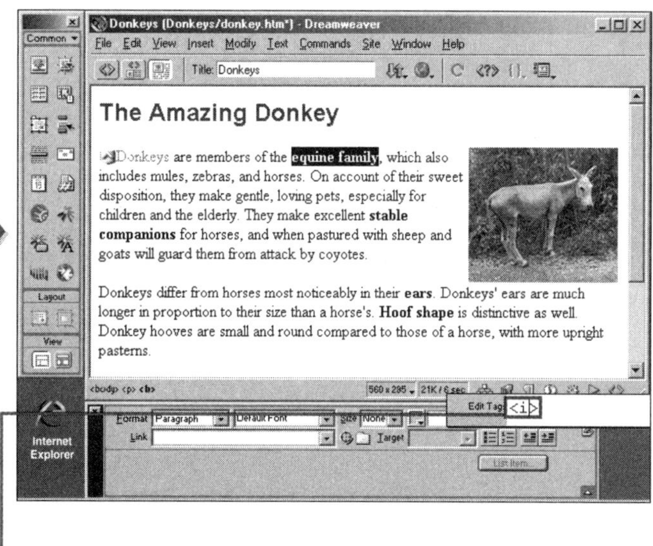

EDIT TAG MODE

■ Dreamweaver displays the HTML tag enclosing the selected object.

9 Edit the HTML tag.

■ If you pause, a list may appear.

■ To add a list item, you can select it and press Enter (Windows) or Return (Mac).

10 Type any attributes for the tag.

11 Press Enter (Windows) or Return (Mac).

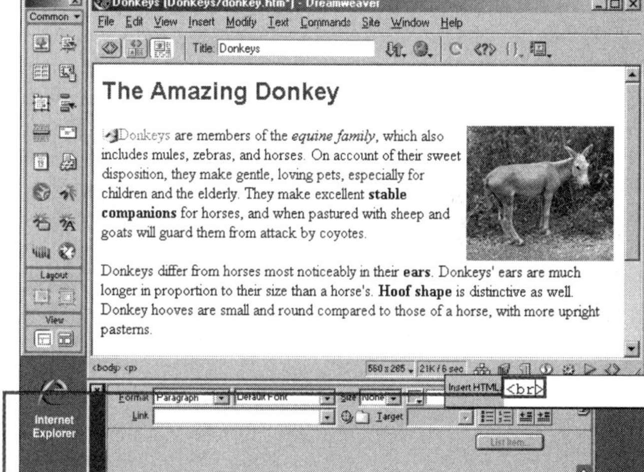

INSERT HTML MODE

12 Dreamweaver displays empty HTML brackets.

13 Type an HTML tag.

■ If you pause, a list may appear.

■ To add a list item, you can select it and press Enter (Windows) or Return (Mac).

14 Type any attributes for the tag.

15 Press Enter (Windows) or Return (Mac).

VIEW AND EDIT HEAD CONTENT

Near the beginning of every HTML document is a section of head content, defined by opening and closing <head> tags, where special information related to the Web page is stored. Dreamweaver gives you various ways to view, add to, and edit this information.

Information in a document's head includes the page title see Chapter 4, JavaScript variables and functions, and style-sheet rules. The head also can include optional "meta" information that describes the page to Web browsers and search engines.

When you create a new page in Dreamweaver, a <meta> tag is automatically added that specifies the type of content in your document — namely, text/html. Other types of information that you can add to a page using meta tags include a description, keywords, and code that automatically refreshes the page or forwards the user to a new address.

Dreamweaver gives you an easy way to add head information through buttons in the Object Panel. You can also add head information by hand via the Code View or in the Code Inspector.

VIEW AND EDIT HEAD CONTENT

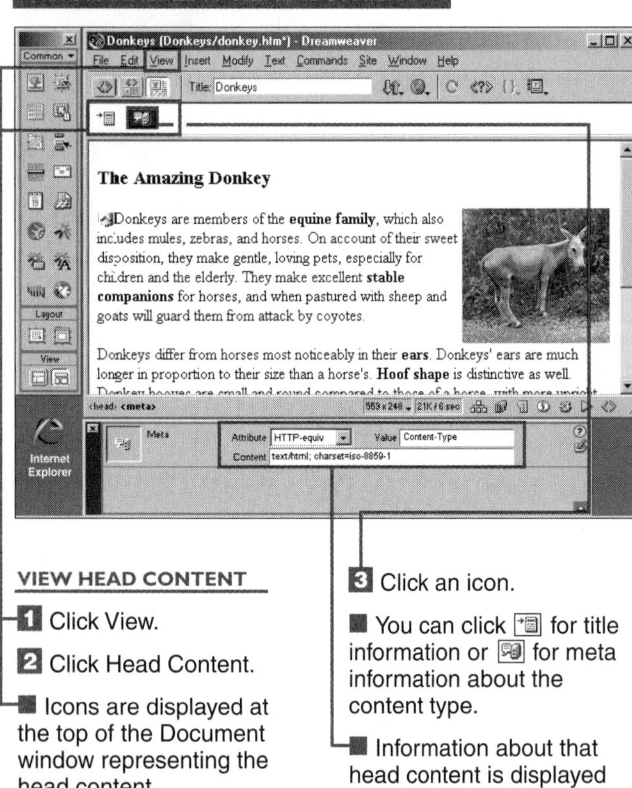

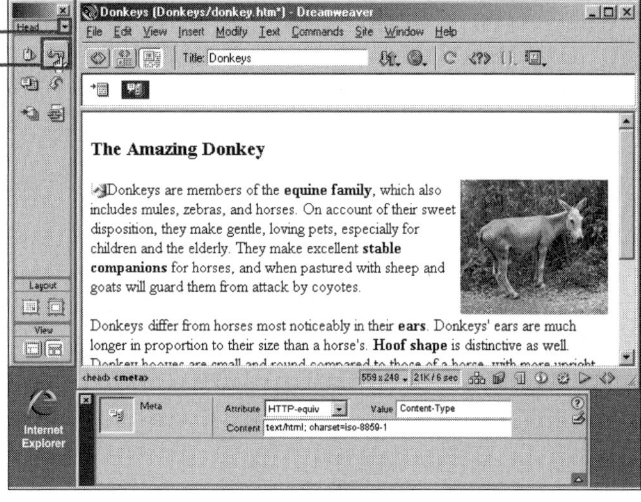

VIEW HEAD CONTENT

1 Click View.

2 Click Head Content.

■ Icons are displayed at the top of the Document window representing the head content.

3 Click an icon.

■ You can click for title information or for meta information about the content type.

■ Information about that head content is displayed in the Property Inspector.

INSERT HEAD CONTENT

1 Click the Object Panel and click Head in the menu that appears.

2 Click the button for the type of content that you want to insert.

■ You can click
to add meta information,
to add a meta description,
to specify a base URL,
to add meta keywords,
to specify a reload time, or
to specify a relationship to another file.

For what purpose is the description and keyword information I include in the head content used?

✓ When cataloging information from Web pages, many search engines give greater importance to the optional description and keyword information that can be added to the head content of HTML documents. You can influence how search engines rank your pages by making sure that you add concise descriptions and relevant keywords to the head content of each page you create.

How do I make a page automatically refresh, or reload, after a certain length of time?

✓ Add refresh instructions to the page using [icon] in the Objects Panel under the Head menu item. If you want, you can instruct the page to forward to a different Web address when it refreshes. Refreshing is useful if you move your content to a different Web site and want to redirect visitors there.

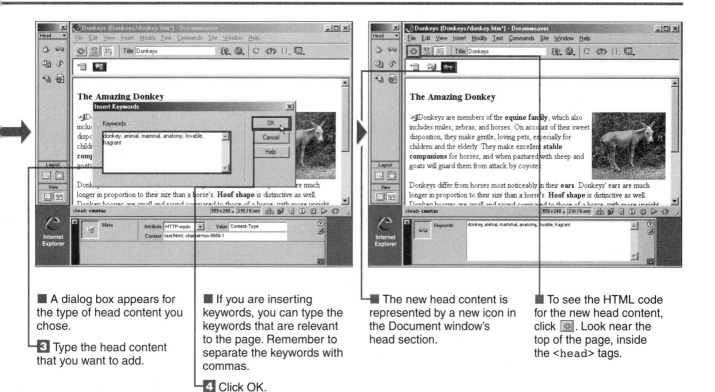

■ A dialog box appears for the type of head content you chose.

3 Type the head content that you want to add.

■ If you are inserting keywords, you can type the keywords that are relevant to the page. Remember to separate the keywords with commas.

4 Click OK.

■ The new head content is represented by a new icon in the Document window's head section.

■ To see the HTML code for the new head content, click [icon]. Look near the top of the page, inside the <head> tags.

USING THE REFERENCE PANEL

You can get quick access to reference information about HTML tags and their attributes via the drop-down lists at the top of the Reference panel. For each HTML tag, the Reference panel provides a basic definition, information about appropriate usage, and some sample code.

The Reference panel tells you which browser versions support each HTML tag. In the panel, NN represents Netscape Navigator and IE represents Microsoft Internet Explorer. This can help you decide whether to avoid certain features if your audience tends to use older browsers.

You can also use the Reference panel to look up information about style sheets and JavaScript. The style sheet information includes many examples of style rules that you can insert into your page if you are familiar with coding style sheets by hand. The JavaScript material is more technical and offers insight into how JavaScript objects work and how the language is organized.

USING THE REFERENCE PANEL

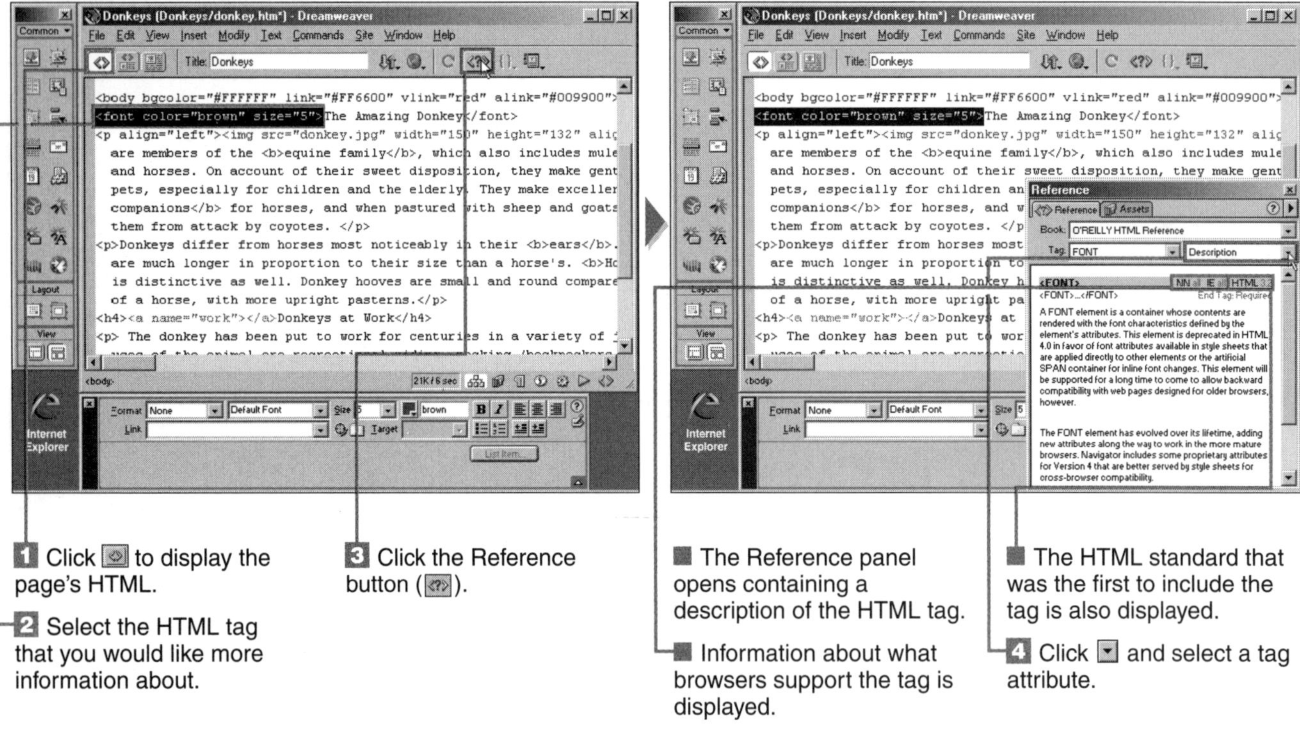

1 Click [icon] to display the page's HTML.

2 Select the HTML tag that you would like more information about.

3 Click the Reference button ([icon]).

■ The Reference panel opens containing a description of the HTML tag.

■ Information about what browsers support the tag is displayed.

■ The HTML standard that was the first to include the tag is also displayed.

4 Click [icon] and select a tag attribute.

What does it mean when the Reference panel says an HTML tag is deprecated?

✔ This means that the World Wide Web Consortium, or W3C — the organization that maintains the official HTML standard — recommends that you no longer use the tag. The W3C usually recommends using a different tag or a different coding method, such as style sheets, instead. `<center>` is an example of a deprecated tag. The W3C recommends you use the `<div>` tag instead. Although most deprecated tags are still supported by current browsers, there may eventually come a day when they are not.

Does Dreamweaver have commands for creating all the tags listed in the Reference panel?

✔ Dreamweaver's commands allow you to integrate *most* of the tags listed in the Reference panel, in particular the most widely used tags. But there are tags listed that Dreamweaver does not offer commands for. For example, you cannot insert the `<thead>` tag with any of Dreamweaver's table commands. Tags that Dreamweaver does not support with commands can be inserted by hand in the Code View mode or in the Code Inspector.

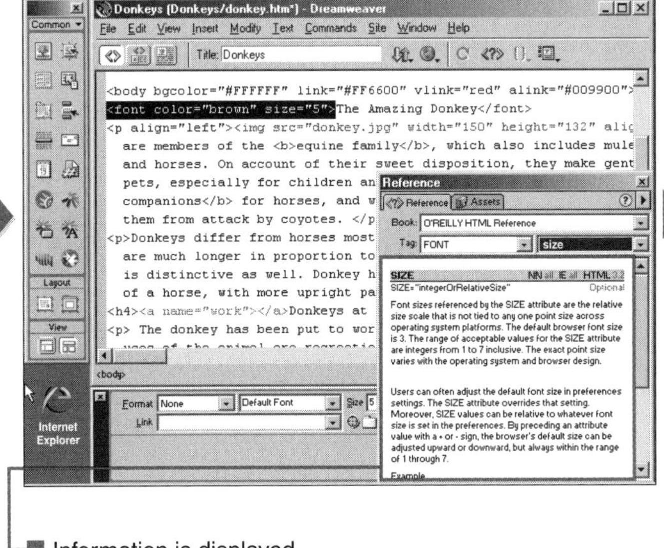

■ Information is displayed about the attribute.

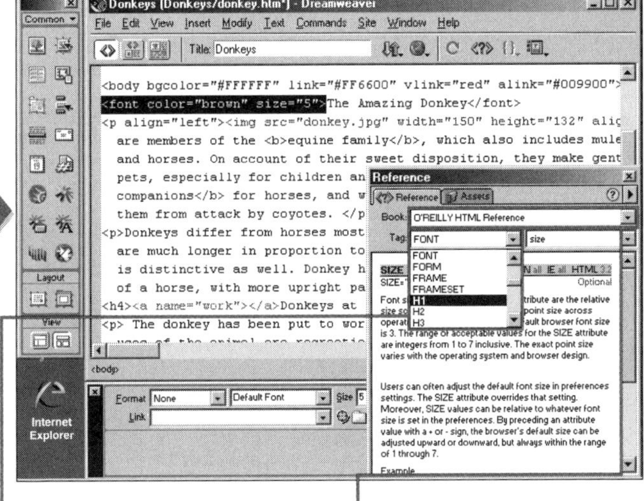

■ To look up a different HTML tag, click ▼ and select that tag.

■ To get information about JavaScript objects or style sheet rules, click the Book ▼ and click O'REILLY JavaScript Reference or O'REILLY CSS Reference.

SET UP A LOCAL SITE

Before creating your site's pages, you need to define a local site to tell Dreamweaver where to store the site's information, such as your HTML documents and image files. Dreamweaver then knows where to store certain accessory files — such as templates and library items — that help you maintain your pages efficiently.

After defining your local site, you can manage your site's files in the Site window (see Chapter 15).

You need to set up a different local site for each Web site you build in Dreamweaver. You may want to create a folder named "Sites" somewhere on your hard drive and create a subfolder for each Dreamweaver site that you create.

After you have created the Web pages for your local site, you can transfer those files to your remote site, where they can then be viewed by the rest of the world. The remote site usually exists on a Web server maintained by your Internet service provider. For details about setting up a remote site, see Chapter 15.

SET UP A LOCAL SITE

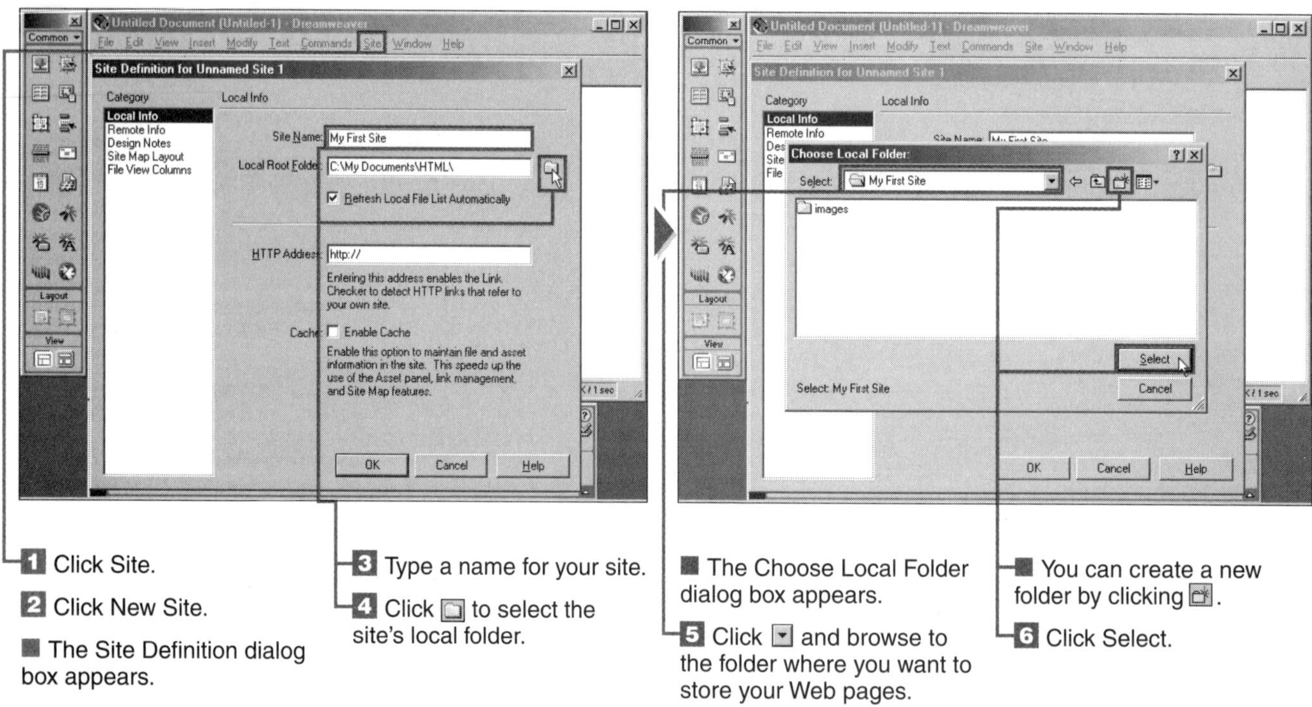

1 Click Site.

2 Click New Site.

■ The Site Definition dialog box appears.

3 Type a name for your site.

4 Click [folder icon] to select the site's local folder.

■ The Choose Local Folder dialog box appears.

5 Click [▼] and browse to the folder where you want to store your Web pages.

■ You can create a new folder by clicking [new folder icon].

6 Click Select.

Why is it important to keep all my Web site's files in a single folder on my computer?

✔ Keeping everything in the same folder enables you to easily transfer your site files to the Web server without changing their organization. If you do not organize your site files on the Web server the same way they appear on your local computer, hyperlinks will not work and images will not display properly.

Does the name that I give my local site appear anywhere on my finished Web site?

✔ No. The name is used only for keeping track of different sites in Dreamweaver. It appears in the Site drop-down list at the top of the Site window.

What happens when I create a local site cache?

✔ Dreamweaver creates a text file in its SiteCache folder that lists hyperlink and other information for the files that make up the site. The cache file helps Dreamweaver quickly update links when you move, rename, or delete a page.

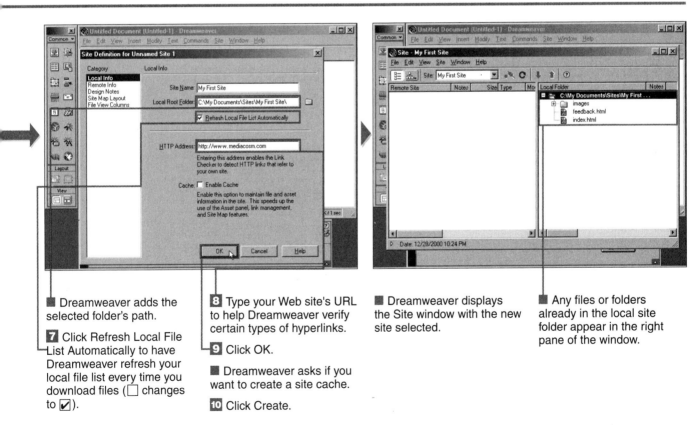

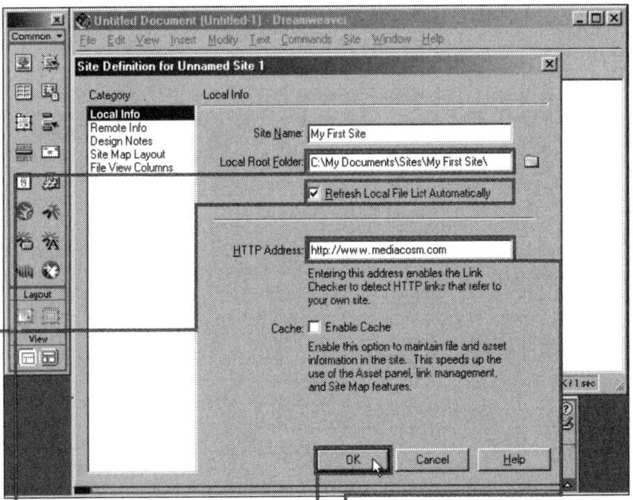

■ Dreamweaver adds the selected folder's path.

7 Click Refresh Local File List Automatically to have Dreamweaver refresh your local file list every time you download files (☐ changes to ☑).

8 Type your Web site's URL to help Dreamweaver verify certain types of hyperlinks.

9 Click OK.

■ Dreamweaver asks if you want to create a site cache.

10 Click Create.

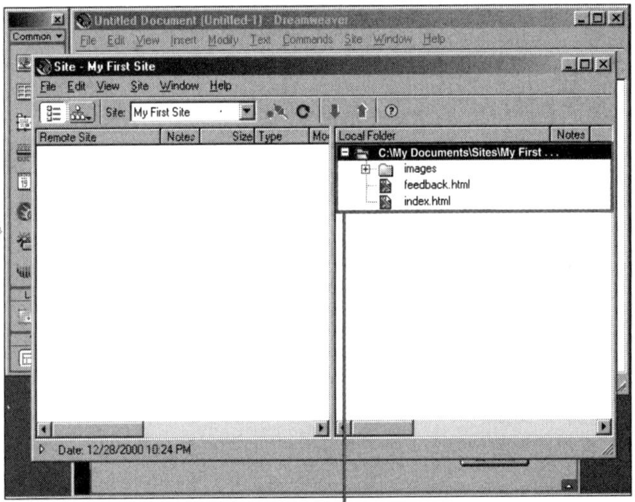

■ Dreamweaver displays the Site window with the new site selected.

■ Any files or folders already in the local site folder appear in the right pane of the window.

OPEN A WEB PAGE

You can open an existing Web page in Dreamweaver to view its structure and modify it. To do this, you open the document containing the HTML code that defines the page. For more about HTML, see Chapter 3.

When you open a page, Dreamweaver displays the text content, tables, forms, and other HTML features of the page in the Document window. Dreamweaver also displays any images that have been inserted into the page, as long as the image files are part of the local site. Dreamweaver does not display any images that have remote addresses. To see these, you have to preview the page in a Web browser.

You can have multiple Web pages open at once in Dreamweaver and even drag and drop content between open pages.

To open a Web page based on a template, see Chapter 11.

OPEN A WEB PAGE

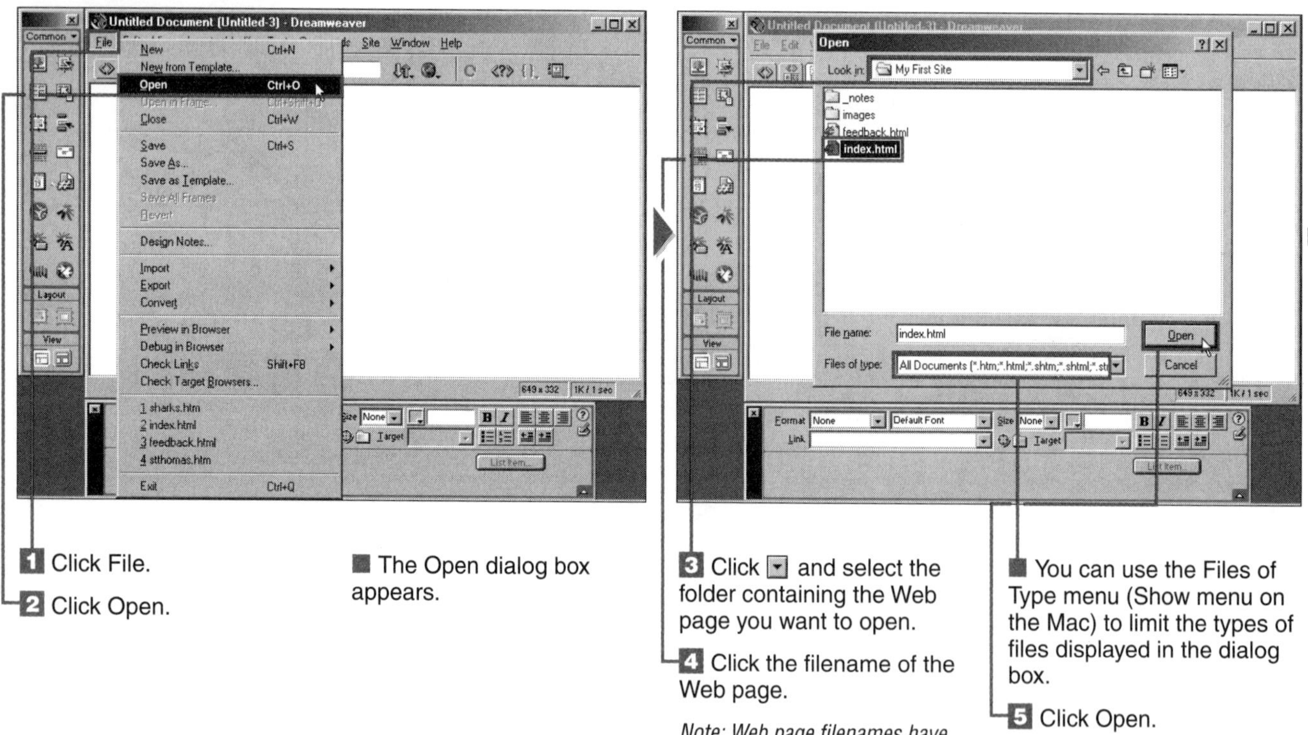

1 Click File.

2 Click Open.

■ The Open dialog box appears.

3 Click ▾ and select the folder containing the Web page you want to open.

4 Click the filename of the Web page.

Note: Web page filenames have .htm or .html file extensions.

■ You can use the Files of Type menu (Show menu on the Mac) to limit the types of files displayed in the dialog box.

5 Click Open.

Can I open Web pages created in other HTML editors?

✔ Yes. Dreamweaver can open any HTML file, no matter where it was created. It can also open non-HTML text files. However, the layout of such pages may look haphazard in Dreamweaver because they do not include HTML formatting.

How can I keep multiple Document windows from opening?

✔ Click Edit and then Preferences; then make sure that the General category is highlighted. Click Open Files in New Window (☑ changes to ☐) and then click OK. Any new page you open now appears in the current Document window. The current page open in the window closes. Setting this preference can help keep your workspace from getting cluttered.

How do I open a page that I find on the Web in Dreamweaver?

✔ You can open any page on the Web in Dreamweaver by first saving that page's HTML source code as a local file. You can do this by opening the page in a Web browser and using the browser's Save command. Then open the saved page as described in this section.

■ Dreamweaver opens the file in a Document window.

■ You can switch between open Web pages by clicking Window and then the filename that you want.

■ Open files also appear on the Windows taskbar.

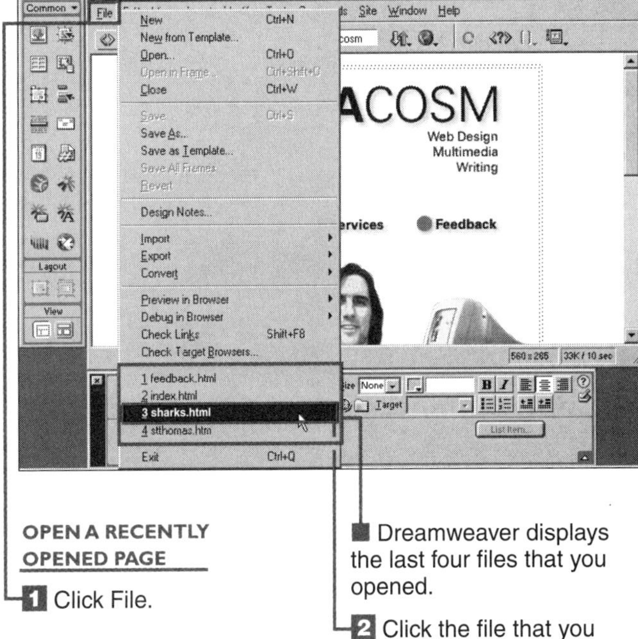

OPEN A RECENTLY OPENED PAGE

1 Click File.

■ Dreamweaver displays the last four files that you opened.

2 Click the file that you want to open.

CREATE A NEW WEB PAGE

You can open a new, blank page in Dreamweaver and then add text, images, and other elements to create a new Web page design. This is an alternative to opening up an existing Web page and using it as a starting point — see "Open a Web Page." You can also use Dreamweaver's template feature to start your new pages — see Chapter 11.

From an HTML standpoint, a blank page is not completely empty. If you click Window and then Code Inspector with a blank page open, you see a few rudimentary HTML tags. These include the `<html>`, `<head>`, `<title>`, and `<body>` tags, which almost all HTML pages include.

You can also create a blank page by simply starting the Dreamweaver application. A blank page appears automatically at startup.

CREATE A NEW WEB PAGE

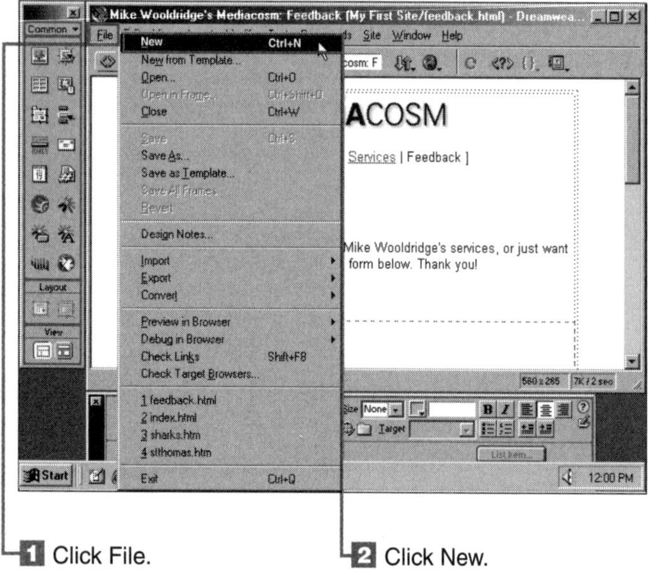

1 Click File.

2 Click New.

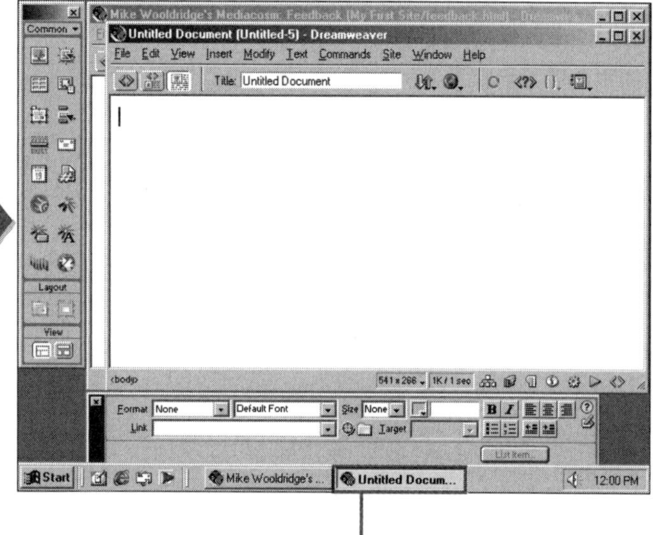

■ Dreamweaver opens an empty Document window. The filename remains untitled until you save the page (see "Save a Web Page" in this chapter).

■ The file appears on the Windows taskbar.

ADD A TITLE TO A WEB PAGE

A Web page's title appears in the title bar when the page is opened in a Web browser. Also, when a viewer adds a Web page to a browser's Bookmarks (in Netscape Navigator) or Favorites list (in Microsoft Internet Explorer), the title of the page appears as the placeholder in the list. It also appears in a browser's History list.

Some search engines give greater weight to the information in the title when indexing a Web page. If you are interested in getting your pages top placement on search engines, it is important to include titles on your pages that are descriptive and that include keywords that are the most relevant to your pages.

The Document window includes a text field for you to define a page's title. You can also define the title in the Page Properties dialog box, accessible under the Modify menu.

ADD A TITLE TO A WEB PAGE

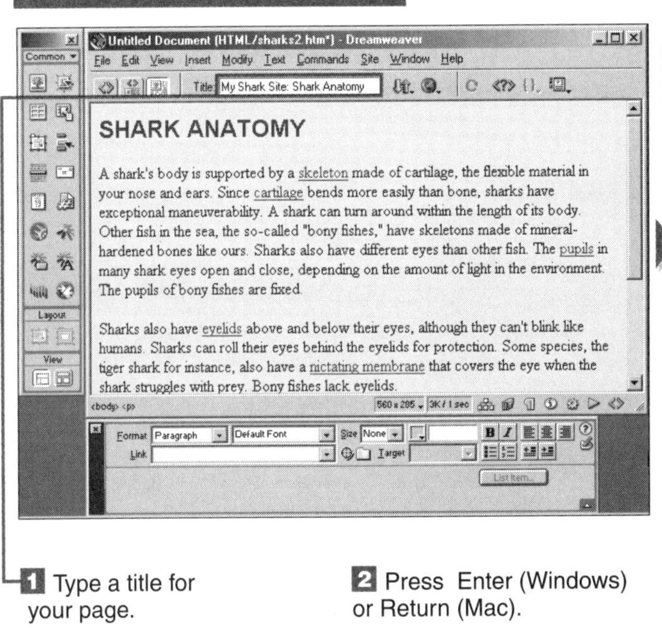

1 Type a title for your page.

2 Press Enter (Windows) or Return (Mac).

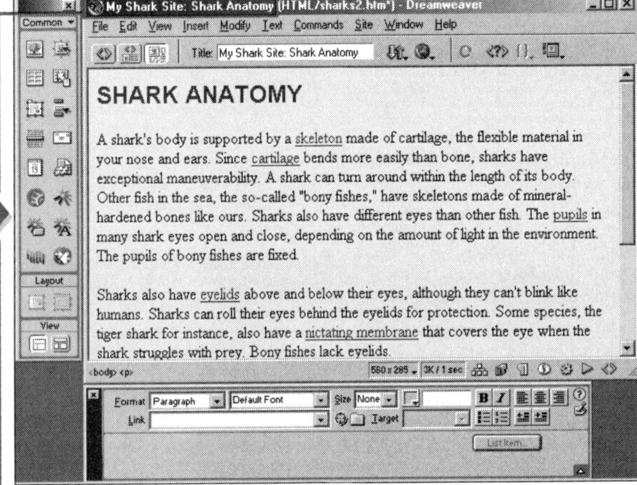

■ The title appears in the title bar of the Document window.

SAVE A WEB PAGE

Before closing your Web page files or transferring those files to your remote site (see Chapter 15), you should save them. It is also a good idea to save all your files frequently to prevent work from being lost due to power outages or system failures.

When you save a document for the first time, Dreamweaver displays a dialog box that allows you to name the file and choose its location. It is best to limit yourself to letters, numbers, hyphens, and underscores when naming your Web page files. Avoid using spaces, special characters such as é, ç, or ¥, and punctuation such as colons, slashes, or periods. Many servers convert these characters during upload, which can cause links to the files to break.

If you try to exit Dreamweaver and have unsaved documents open, you are asked whether you want to save them.

SAVE A WEB PAGE

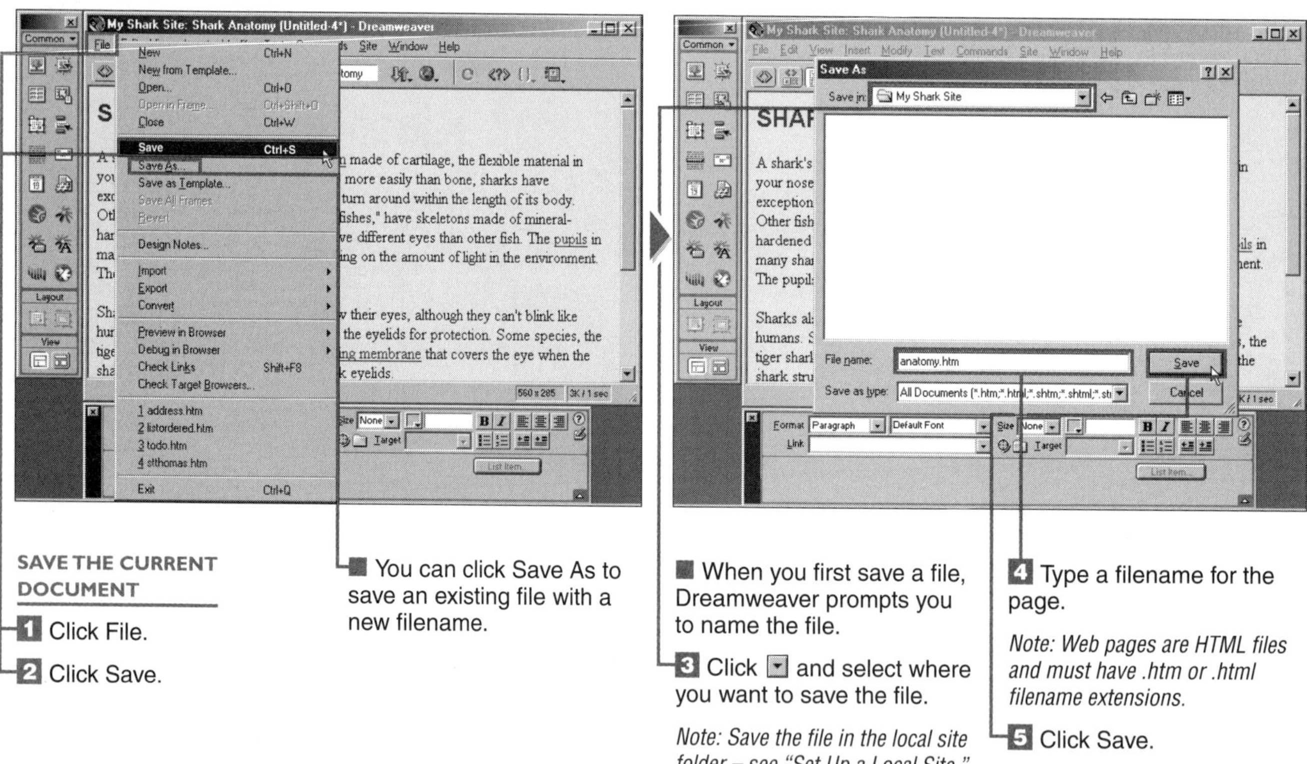

SAVE THE CURRENT DOCUMENT

1 Click File.

2 Click Save.

■ You can click Save As to save an existing file with a new filename.

■ When you first save a file, Dreamweaver prompts you to name the file.

3 Click ▾ and select where you want to save the file.

Note: Save the file in the local site folder – see "Set Up a Local Site."

4 Type a filename for the page.

Note: Web pages are HTML files and must have .htm or .html filename extensions.

5 Click Save.

How should I organize the saved files for my Web site on my computer?

✔ You should save all the files for your Web site in the folder that you defined as the local root folder — see "Set Up a Local Site" for more information. Keeping all the site's files in this folder makes it easier to hyperlink between local files and transfer those files to a remote Web server.

What is the keyboard shortcut for saving a page?

✔ You can save the current page by pressing Ctrl+S.

How can I make a duplicate of the current page?

✔ Make sure that the current page is saved. Then save it again by clicking File and then Save As and giving the file a different filename.

Does Dreamweaver have an auto-save feature?

✔ No. You need to save your files using the menu commands or keyboard shortcuts.

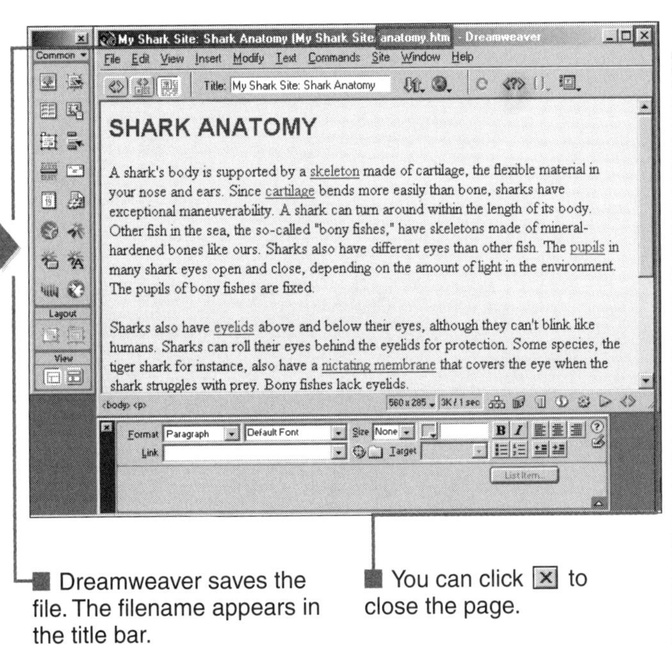

■ Dreamweaver saves the file. The filename appears in the title bar.

Note: After you have saved and named your page, you can save any subsequent changes by performing steps 1 and 2.

■ You can click ☒ to close the page.

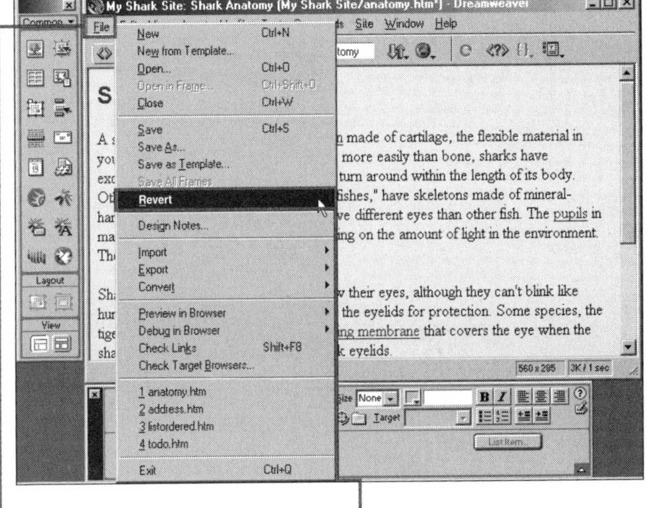

REVERT A PAGE TO THE LAST SAVED VERSION

1 Click File.

2 Click Revert.

■ Dreamweaver reverts the page to the previously saved version. All the changes made since you last saved are lost.

PREVIEW A WEB PAGE IN A BROWSER

You can see how your page looks online by previewing it in a Web browser. Dreamweaver's Preview in Browser command works with the Web browsers already installed on your computer. Dreamweaver does not come with browser software.

Previewing your pages before uploading them is important because some of Dreamweaver's features cannot actually be experienced when you create them in the Document window. These features include Dreamweaver's behaviors (such as rollover image effects and form validation — see Chapter 13), some style sheet commands (such as text spacing and border styles — see Chapter 12), and hyperlinks. You can see how these features behave when you open the pages in a browser.

You benefit from previewing your pages in several different browser types and versions before posting the pages live. This can help you catch features that Netscape Navigator and Microsoft Internet Explorer display differently or that one browser supports and the other does not. There are also features that are supported in newer browsers but not in older browsers, such as style sheets, Timeline animations, and layers.

PREVIEW A WEB PAGE IN A BROWSER

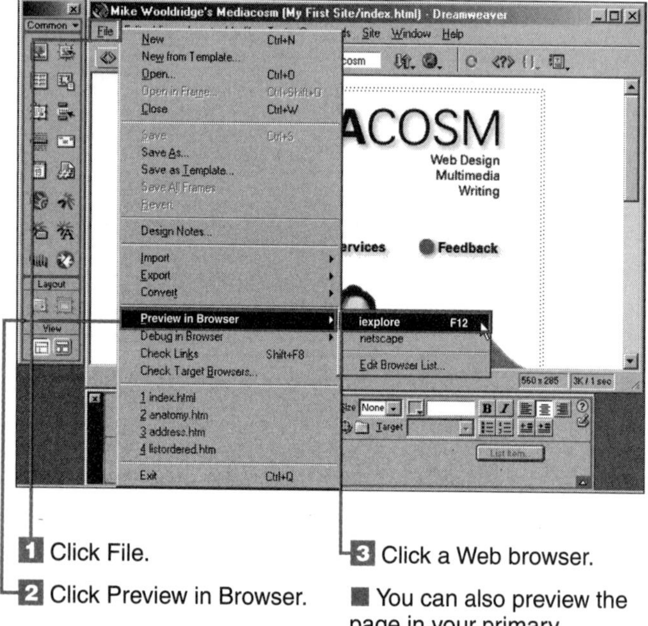

1 Click File.

2 Click Preview in Browser.

3 Click a Web browser.

■ You can also preview the page in your primary browser by pressing F12.

■ Dreamweaver launches the Web browser and opens the current page inside it.

■ The file is given a temporary filename for viewing in the browser.

Why does the browser open a temporary file — not the original file — when I preview my page?

✔ Dreamweaver usually needs to modify your page so that the content appears correctly in the browser. For example, if you define your images using root-relative paths, Dreamweaver changes those paths to document-relative paths for previewing. The modified page is stored as a temporary file, which the browser can then open.

How do I define which browser is considered primary?

✔ Click File, Preview in Browser, and then Edit Browser List. Select the browser you want to define as primary, and click Primary Browser (❑ changes to ☑).

How do I make my pages appear consistently in all browsers?

✔ Building a page compatible with *every* browser is probably unfeasible, given the multitude of browsers and browser versions in use on the Web. But if you want to achieve consistency in *most* browsers, it is a good idea to avoid advanced features such as behaviors, Timeline animations, style sheets, and layers.

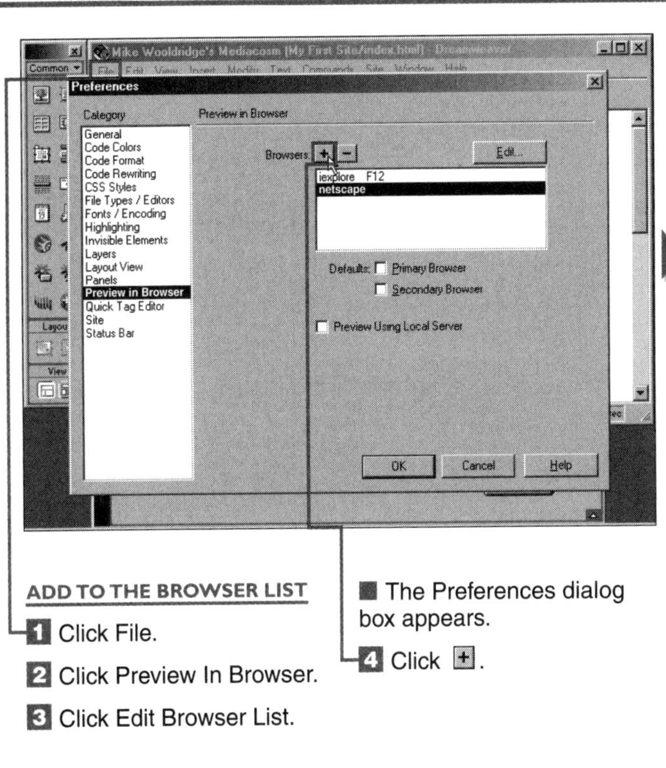

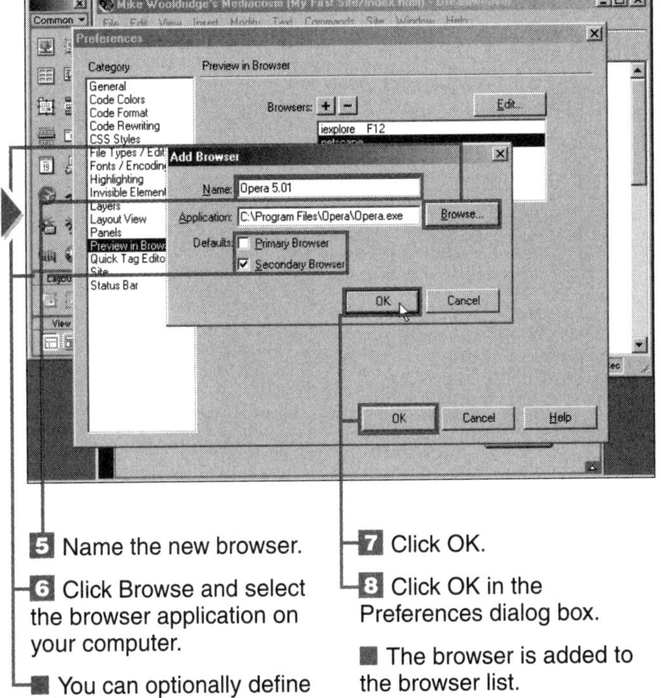

ADD TO THE BROWSER LIST

1 Click File.

2 Click Preview In Browser.

3 Click Edit Browser List.

■ The Preferences dialog box appears.

4 Click ⊞.

5 Name the new browser.

6 Click Browse and select the browser application on your computer.

■ You can optionally define the browser as primary or secondary.

7 Click OK.

8 Click OK in the Preferences dialog box.

■ The browser is added to the browser list.

CREATE PARAGRAPHS

You can organize text on your Web page by creating and aligning paragraphs. When you place text into its own paragraph, Dreamweaver separates the text from the content above and below it with space.

You can align a paragraph by clicking one of Dreamweaver's alignment buttons in the Property Inspector. Equivalent commands exist in the Text menu under the Alignment submenu.

You can add more elaborate formatting to your paragraphs — for example, different line spacing or complex indentations — by applying style sheet rules. See Chapter 12 for more information on style sheets.

To create a new line in the flow of your text without adding paragraph spacing, see "Create Line Breaks."

CREATE PARAGRAPHS

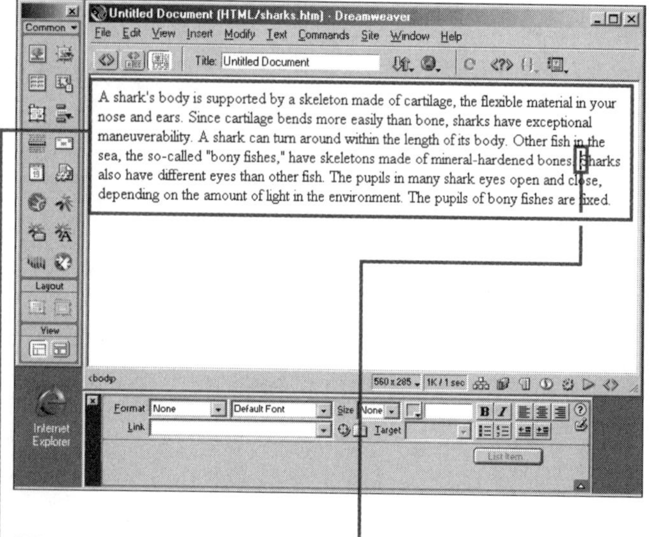

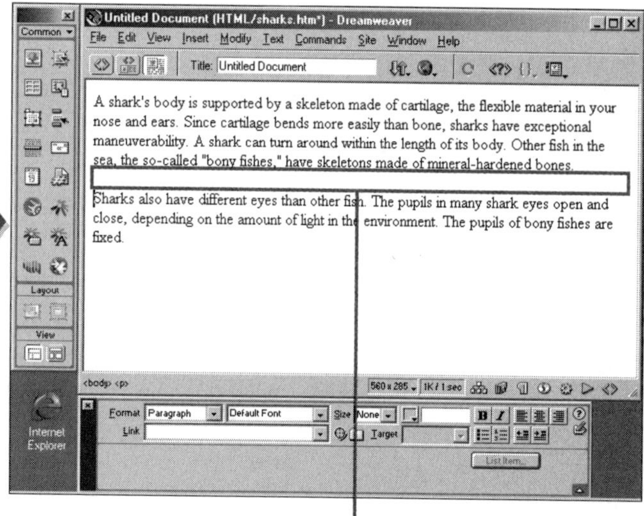

1 Type the text of your Web page into the Document window.

2 Place the cursor where you want a paragraph break.

3 Press Enter (Windows) or Return (Mac).

■ A blank line appears between the blocks of text, separating them into paragraphs.

What controls the width of the paragraphs on my Web page?

✔ The width of your paragraphs depends on the width of the Web browser window. When a user changes the size of the browser window, the width of the paragraphs also changes.

Can I give my paragraph a fixed width?

✔ You can fix a paragraph's width, so that it does not change with a change in the size of the browser window, by placing it inside a fixed-width table. See Chapter 8 for more information on creating and formatting tables.

Can I place an image inside a paragraph by itself?

✔ Yes, you can place an image inside a paragraph by pressing Enter (Window) or Return (Mac) before and after the image on you page. Then you can align the image using the paragraph alignment commands. You can also mix images and text in the same paragraph. See Chapter 6 for information about inserting images.

How do I remove paragraph formatting?

✔ To remove paragraph formatting, right-click the paragraph and select Remove Tag <p> from the menu that appears.

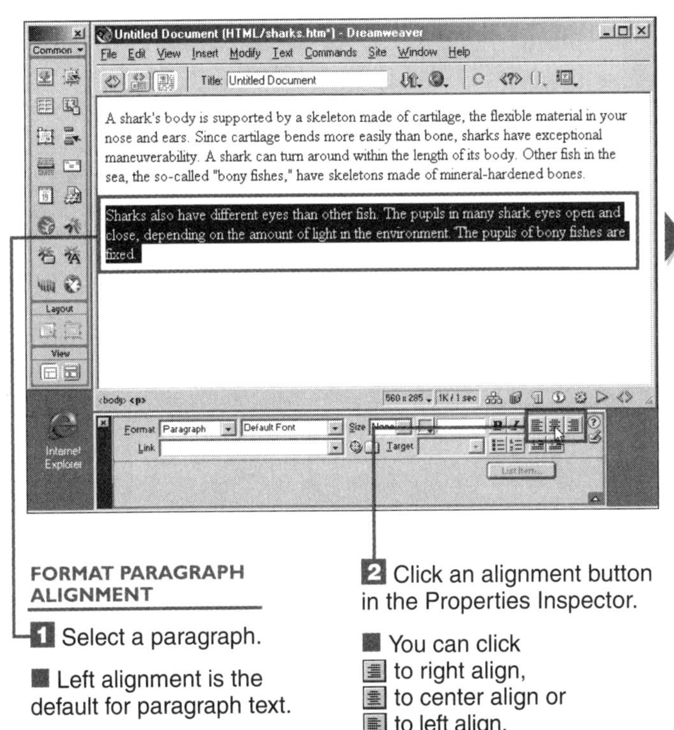

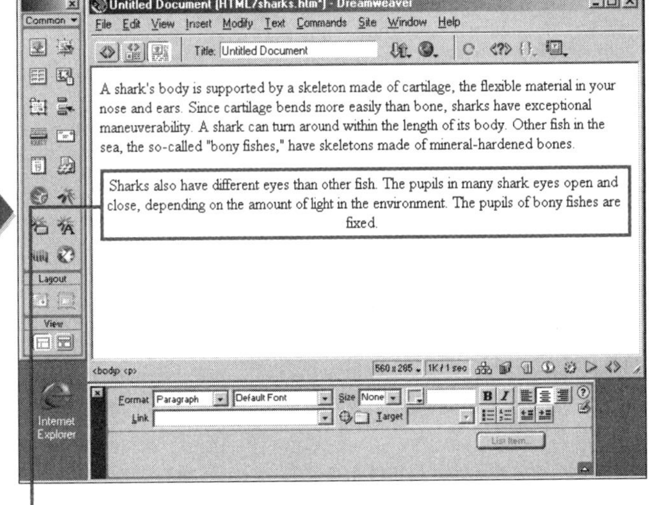

FORMAT PARAGRAPH ALIGNMENT

1 Select a paragraph.

■ Left alignment is the default for paragraph text.

2 Click an alignment button in the Properties Inspector.

■ You can click
[icon] to right align,
[icon] to center align or
[icon] to left align.

■ The paragraph's alignment changes.

CREATE A HEADING

You can define text on your Web page as a heading to give it emphasis and to set it off from other text.

You can define six different levels of headings. *Heading 1* creates the largest heading and *Heading 6* creates the smallest. The text in all six levels has a bold style.

Headings enable you to organize the information on your Web page hierarchically, with level-1 headings defining the initial headline text and other levels defining the different levels of subheadings.

You align a heading choosing from one Dreamweaver's alignment buttons in the Property Inspector.

As part of the earliest HTML specifications, headings used to be one of the only ways to give your text customized formatting. Nowadays, Web page authors can style their text in a variety of ways using various font commands as well as style sheets.

CREATE A HEADING

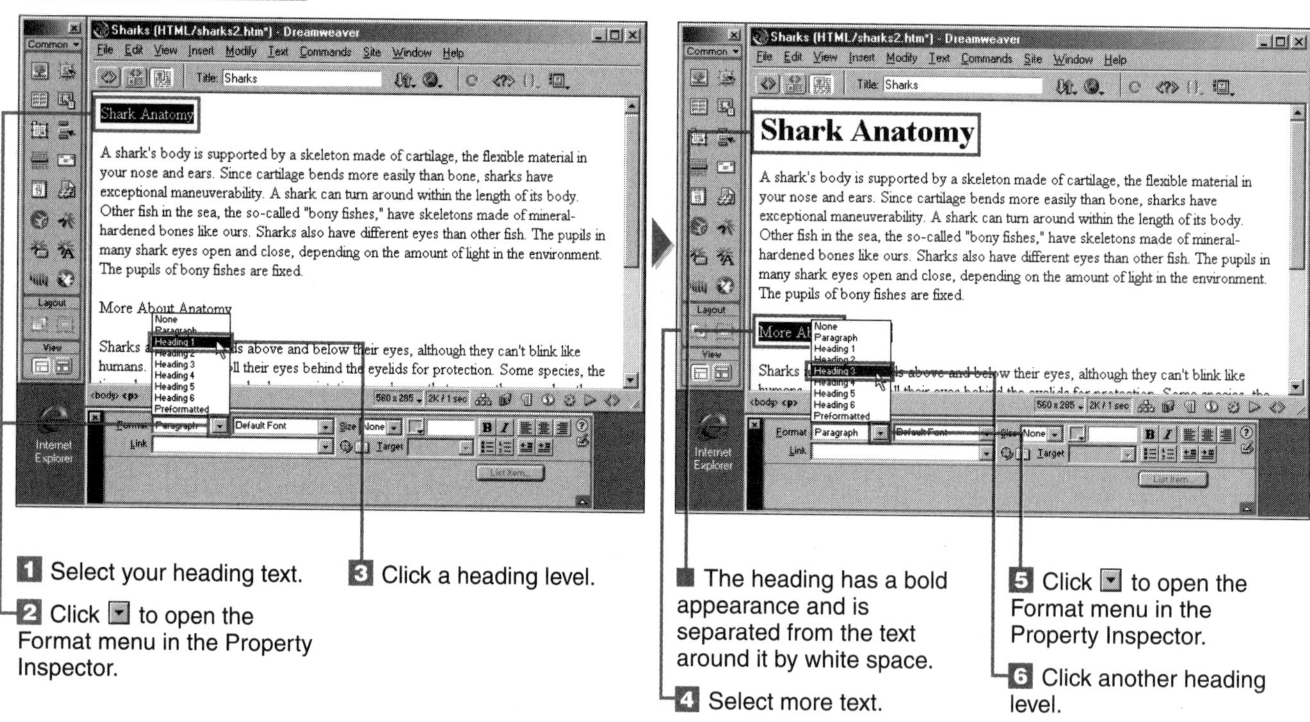

1 Select your heading text.

2 Click ▾ to open the Format menu in the Property Inspector.

3 Click a heading level.

■ The heading has a bold appearance and is separated from the text around it by white space.

4 Select more text.

5 Click ▾ to open the Format menu in the Property Inspector.

6 Click another heading level.

Can I make my headings a different font or color?

✔ Yes. You can customize your headings the same way you would customize regular text. See the sections "Change a Font" and "Change Font Color."

How do the sizes of headings compare to paragraph text?

✔ Most browsers display level-4 headings the same size as regular bolded paragraph text. Consequently, levels 1, 2, and 3 create larger-than-default bolded text, and levels 5 and 6 create smaller-than-default bolded text.

Do larger headings take longer to download than smaller headings?

✔ No. The same amount of HTML code is required to create headings, regardless of the heading level. So downloading text takes the same amount of time whether you format it as a large level-1 heading or as a small level-6 heading.

What are some common uses for level-5 and level-6 headings?

✔ You can use these heading styles to set copyright and disclaimer information apart from the rest of the page content.

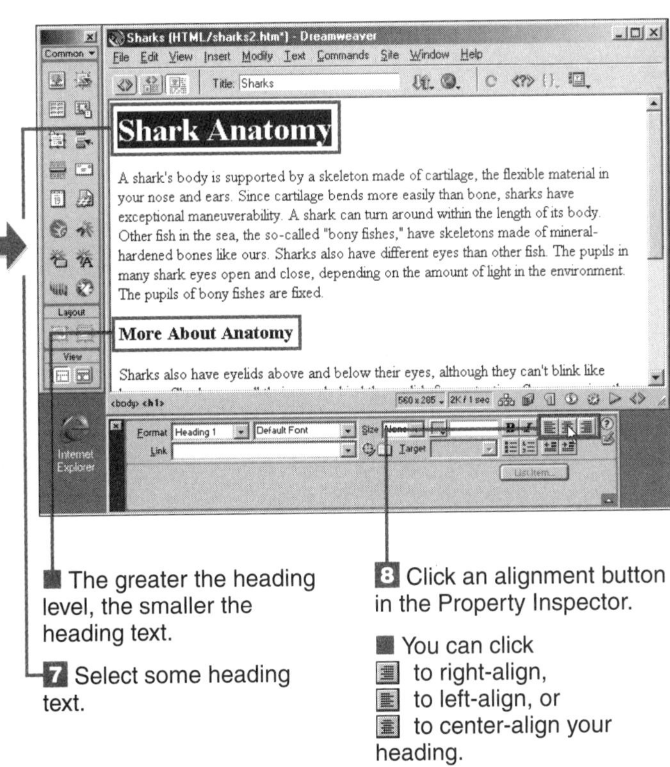

■ The greater the heading level, the smaller the heading text.

7 Select some heading text.

8 Click an alignment button in the Property Inspector.

■ You can click to right-align, to left-align, or to center-align your heading.

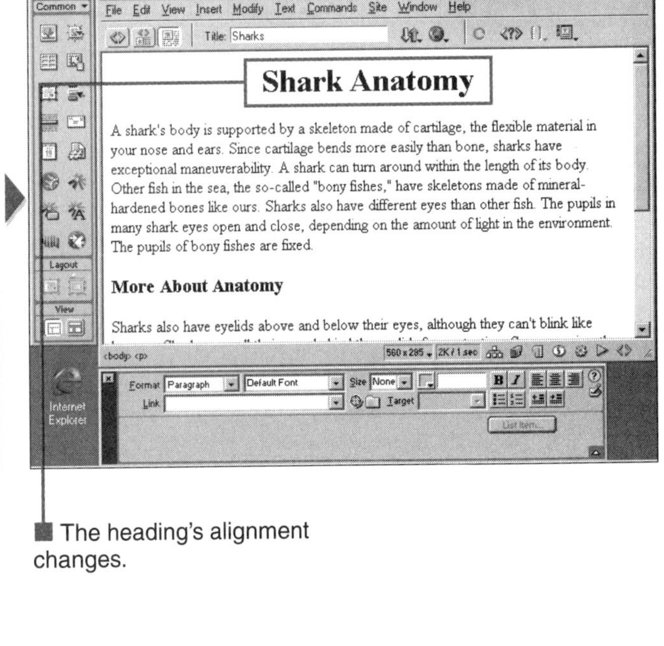

■ The heading's alignment changes.

CREATE LINE BREAKS

Adding line breaks to your page enables you to keep adjacent lines of related text close together. *Line breaks* are an alternative to paragraph breaks, which add more space between lines of text You can use line breaks when you are displaying content such as addresses and poetry. See the section "Create Paragraphs" for more information on paragraph breaks.

You can use line breaks with non-text elements as well. Placing a line break between images, tables, or form fields can ensure that the elements stay close together, which can help you fit more information onto a Web page.

Inserting line breaks inside a paragraph does not affect the alignment of the text inside the paragraph. For example, if you right align the paragraph text and add a new line break, the text before and after the break stays right-aligned.

You can easily add vertical space on your page by adding multiple line breaks.

CREATE LINE BREAKS

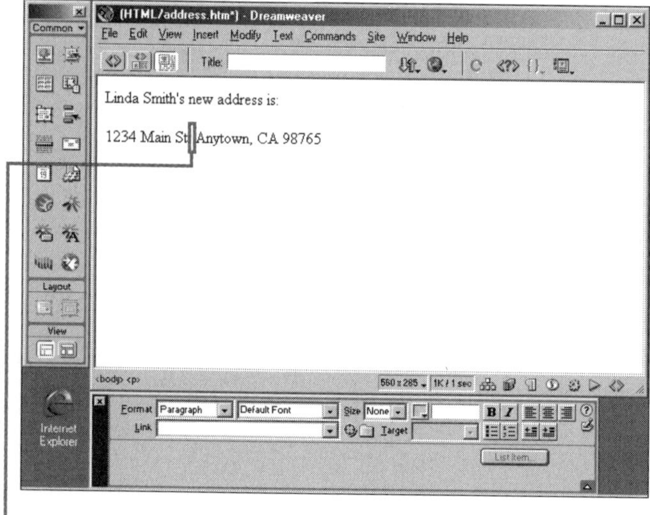

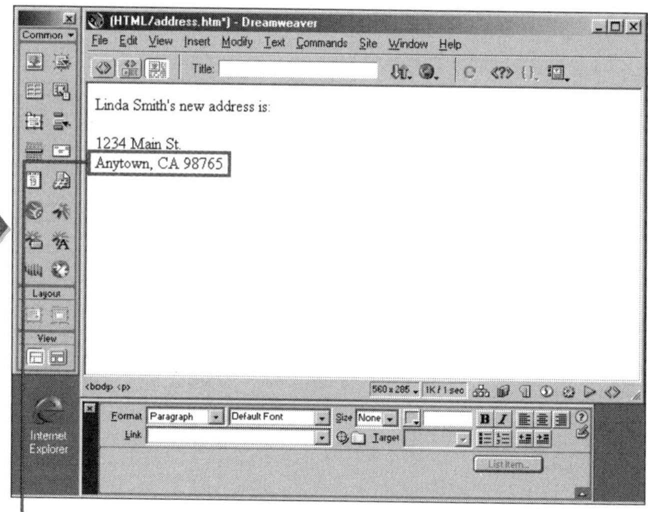

1 Place your cursor where you want the line to break.

2 Press Shift + Enter (Windows) or Shift + Return (Mac).

■ Dreamweaver adds a line break.

ADD EXTRA BLANK SPACE

You can insert more than one blank space between characters by using a special command. Dreamweaver ignores extra blank space in HTML code, which means you can usually insert only one space between the characters on your page using the space bar.

The character that you add with the special command is called a *nonbreaking space*. Nonbreaking means if you place more than one of these spaces in a row, they wrap as a single unit when they reach the right edge of a browser window, just like characters in a word do.

You can use extra spaces to indent the first line at the beginning of your paragraphs; you can also use them for artistic purposes, such as spreading words and letters at uneven horizontal intervals on your page.

You can achieve a similar effect with style sheets, which let you precisely define the spacing between the letters of your text. See Chapter 12 for more information on style sheets.

ADD EXTRA BLANK SPACE

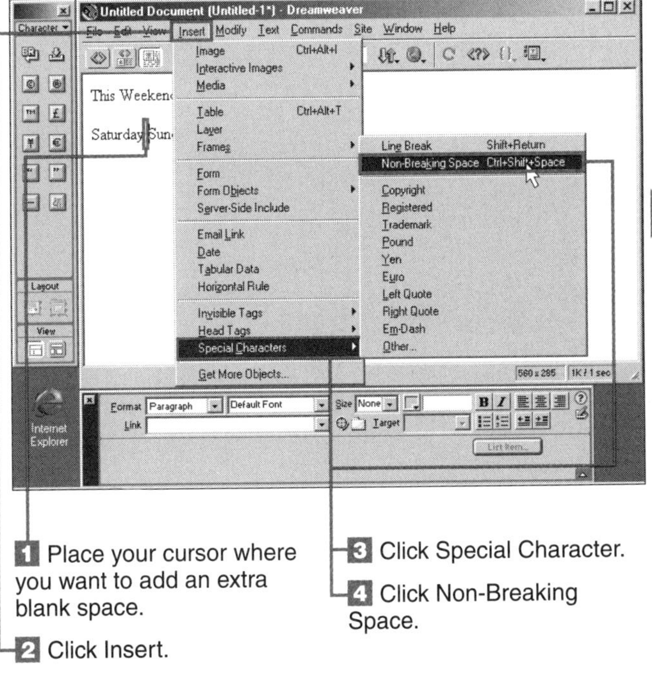

1 Place your cursor where you want to add an extra blank space.

2 Click Insert.

3 Click Special Character.

4 Click Non-Breaking Space.

■ You can repeat step 3 to add additional spaces.

■ You can also add an extra blank space by pressing Ctrl + Alt + Spacebar, (Windows) or Shift + Command + Spacebar (Mac).

■ Dreamweaver adds additional space between the characters.

CREATE UNORDERED LISTS

You can organize text items on your Web page into *unordered lists*, which display the items indented and bulleted. To create numbered lists, see the section "Create Ordered Lists."

Unordered lists are useful for organizing elements that you want to group in no particular order.

There is no limit to the size of each item in an unordered list: Items can be single words or long paragraphs.

You can *nest* unordered lists, which means you can have a list inside another list. In such a case, Dreamweaver further indents the inside list and gives it differently styled bullets. Dreamweaver uses hollow circles for the secondary list, and solid squares for any lists nested inside that.

Unordered lists are created in HTML with the `<ul>` and `<li>` tags. See Chapter 3 for information on viewing a page's HTML.

CREATE UNORDERED LISTS

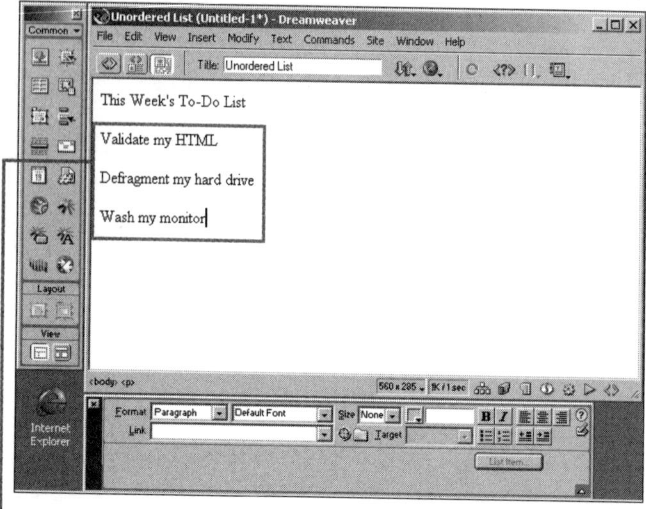

1 Type your list items into the Document window.

2 Make each item a separate paragraph by pressing Enter (Windows) or Return (Mac) between the items.

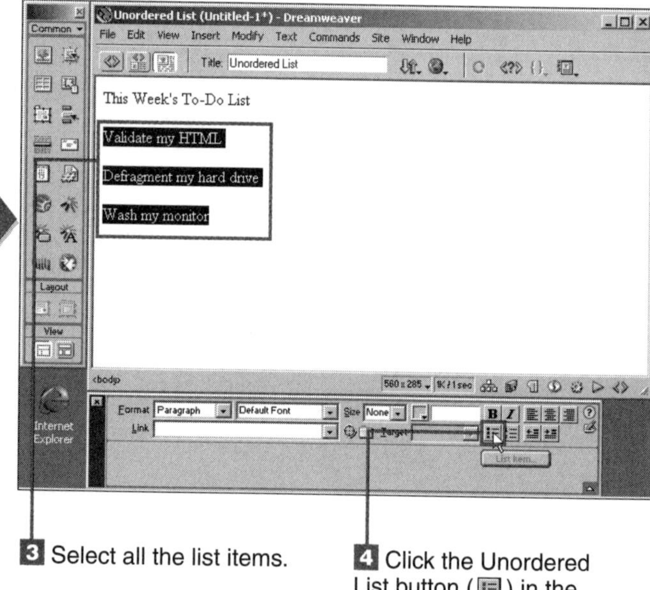

3 Select all the list items.

4 Click the Unordered List button (☰) in the Property Inspector.

How do I modify the bullets in my unordered list?

✔ You can modify the style of a bullet by highlighting an item in the list and clicking Text, List, and then Properties. A dialog box enables you to select different bullet styles for your unordered list.

How do I add extra space between my list items?

✔ By default, Dreamweaver single-spaces your list items. To add more space, insert line breaks by pressing Shift + Enter (Windows) or Shift + Return (Mac) at the end of each item.

How do I create different colored bullets?

✔ When you create your list using Dreamweaver commands, you can not change the color of the bullets — you are stuck with black. But you can create custom images to serve as bullets in an image editor and then insert them as Web-page images. See Chapter 6 for information on inserting images.

How do I indent content on my page without bulleting it as a list?

✔ Select the text and click [indent icon] in the Property Inspector. The [outdent icon] reverses the effect.

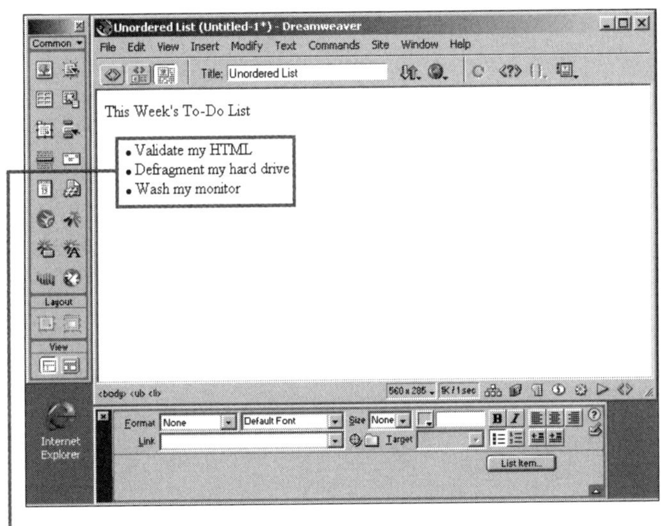

■ The items appear indented and bulleted.

■ You can add another item to the list by placing your cursor where you want to add the item and pressing Enter (Windows) or Return (Mac).

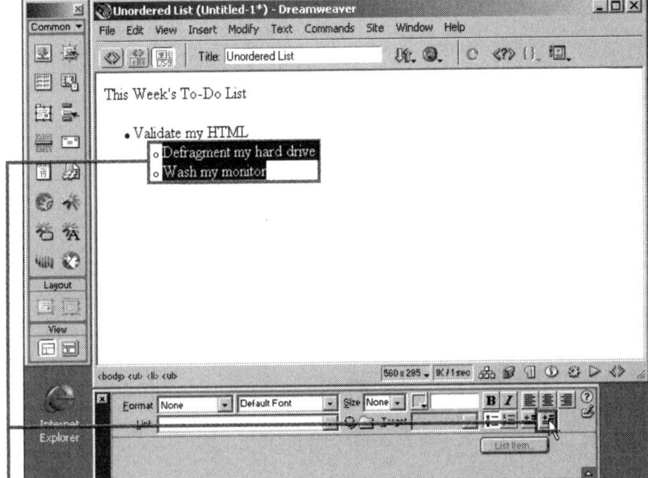

CREATE A NESTED UNORDERED LIST

1. Select the list items you want to nest.
2. Click the Indent button ([indent icon]).

■ Dreamweaver indents the text once again, with differently styled bullets.

CREATE ORDERED LISTS

You can display step-by-step instructions on your Web page by organizing text items into an ordered list. *Ordered lists* have items that are indented and numbered. To create lists that are bulleted, see the section "Create Unordered Lists."

Ordered lists are useful for displaying driving directions, test questions, or recipes on your Web pages. There is no limit to the size of each item in an ordered list: Items can be single words or long paragraphs.

You can *nest* ordered lists, which mean you place a list inside another list. In such cases, Dreamweaver indents the inside list and restarts its numbers at 1.

Ordered lists are created in HTML with the `<ol>` and `<li>` tags. See Chapter 3 for information on viewing a page's HTML.

CREATE ORDERED LISTS

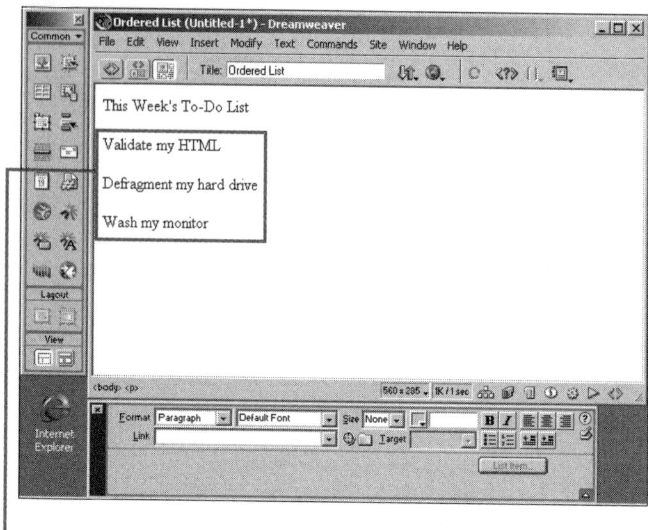

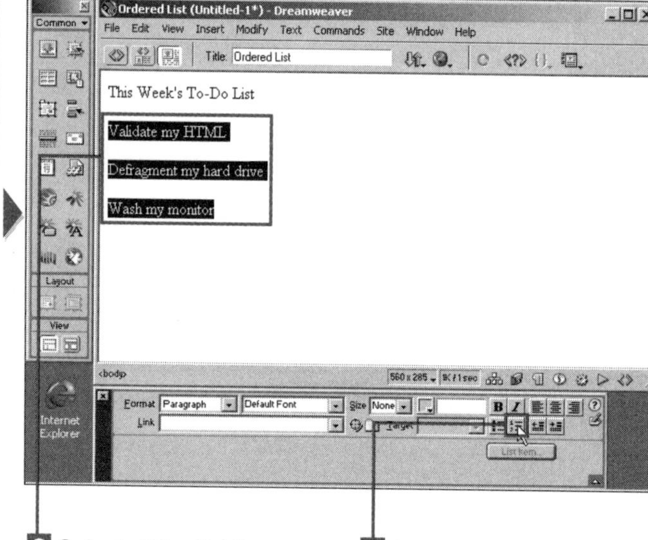

1 Type your list items into the Document window.

2 Make each item a separate paragraph by pressing Enter (Windows) or Return (Mac) between the items.

3 Select all the list items.

4 Click the Ordered List button (☰) in the Property Inspector.

How do I modify the numerals in my ordered list?

✔ You can modify the numerals by highlighting an item in the list and selecting Text, List, and then Properties. A dialog box enables you to select different numbering schemes, including Roman numerals (upper and lower case) and alphabetical styles. It also lets you begin a list with a number other than 1, which is the default, or reset the count in the middle of the list.

Can I bold or italicize the numerals in my list?

✔ Not when you create your list using Dreamweaver commands — you are stuck with the default text style. For fancier numbering, you have to create your lists from scratch on your pages, using regular text for numbering. You can then style the numbers all you want.

How do I align my list?

✔ Select some or all of your list items, and then click [icon], [icon], or [icon] in the Property Inspector. The selected items are aligned.

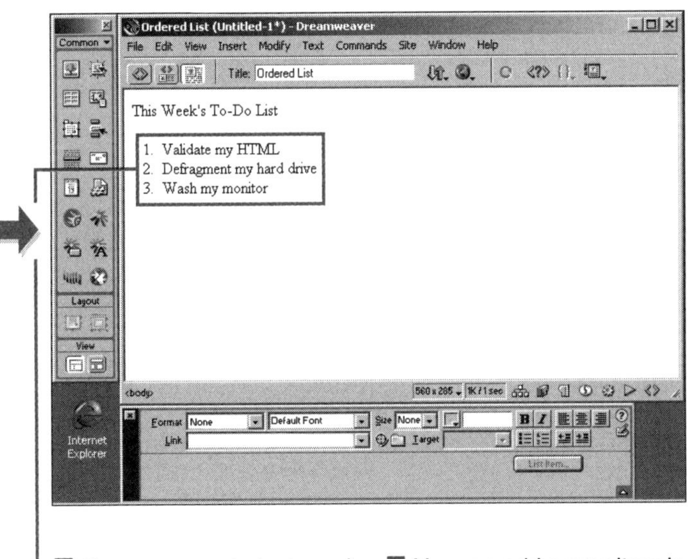

■ Dreamweaver indents and numbers the items.

■ You can add a new item in the list by placing your cursor where you want the item and pressing Enter (Windows) or Return (Mac).

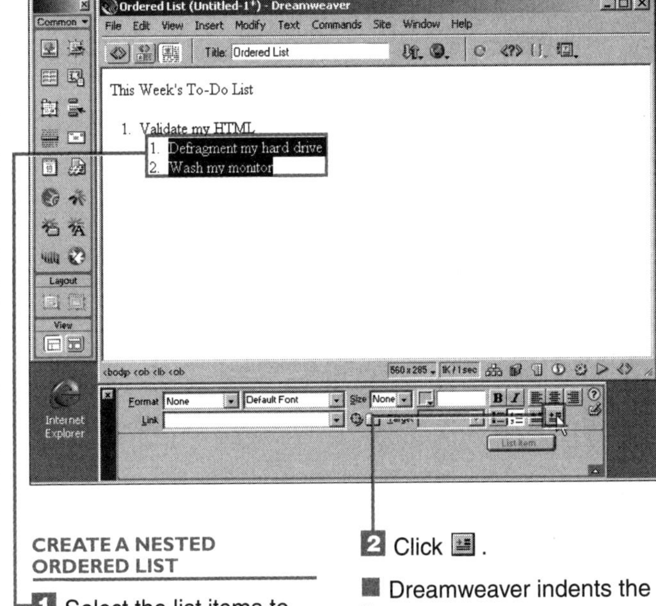

CREATE A NESTED ORDERED LIST

1 Select the list items to nest.

2 Click [icon].

■ Dreamweaver indents the list.

INSERT SPECIAL CHARACTERS

You can insert special characters that do not appear on your keyboard by using buttons from the Objects panel. Characters available in the panel include currency symbols, trademark and copyright symbols, non-English language characters, and mathematical symbols.

Dreamweaver adds the characters to your page by inserting special codes, also known as *entities*, into the HTML of the page. All the special codes begin with an `&` and end with a `;`. In between the `&` and `;` are a set of either letters or numbers. For the copyright symbol and trademark symbols, for example, Dreamweaver inserts `©` and `&153;` respectively.

You can see the special codes after you insert the characters by viewing a page's HTML. See Chapter 2 for more on HTML code.

When you copy and paste text that contains special characters from another text application, Dreamweaver inserts the special codes automatically.

INSERT SPECIAL CHARACTERS

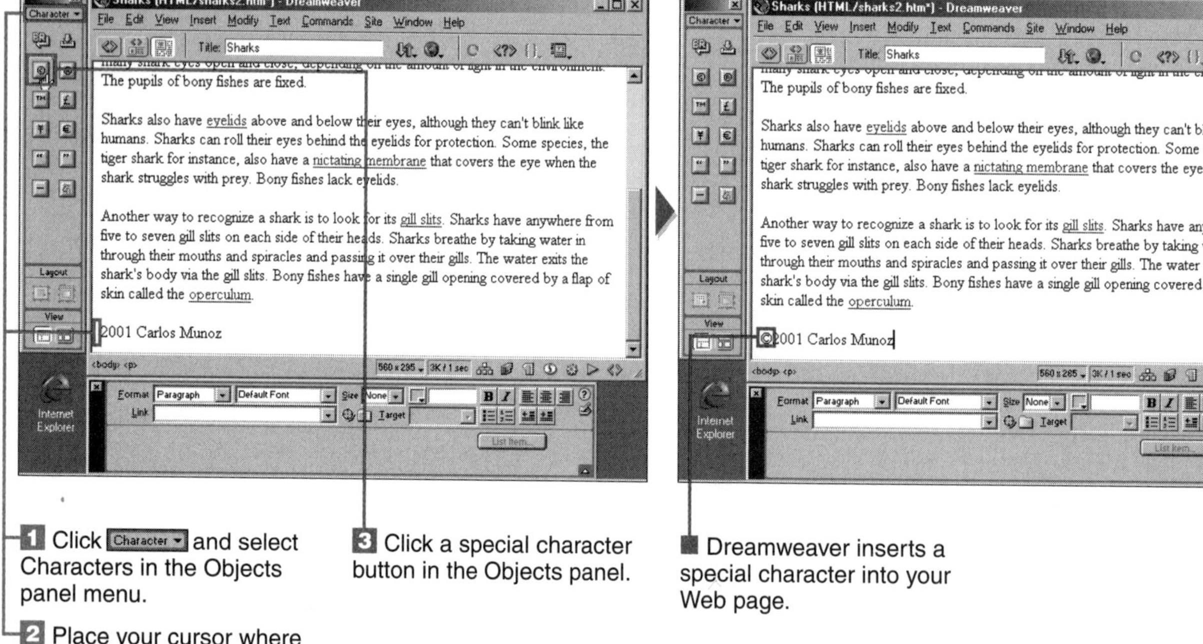

1 Click Character and select Characters in the Objects panel menu.

2 Place your cursor where you want to insert the special character.

3 Click a special character button in the Objects panel.

■ Dreamweaver inserts a special character into your Web page.

How can I make HTML tags display in the text of my Web page?

✔ HTML tags have to be coded differently if they are to be displayed on a Web page. This is because when a browser encounters an HTML tag in a page's code — for example a <P>, which codes for a paragraph tag — it interprets it as a formatting command and not something it should display for the viewer. So the viewer never sees it.

To actually display HTML tags on a Web page, you need to use special character codes for the angle brackets (< and >). To display a paragraph tag, you must code the tag as `<P>` in your HTML. (The `<` and `>` are the special codes for displaying angle brackets.)

How do I insert an en dash (–) or em dash (—) into my page text?

✔ The Insert Other Characters dialog box lets you insert both characters. You can also insert them by typing `&150;` or `&151;` into your HTML code.

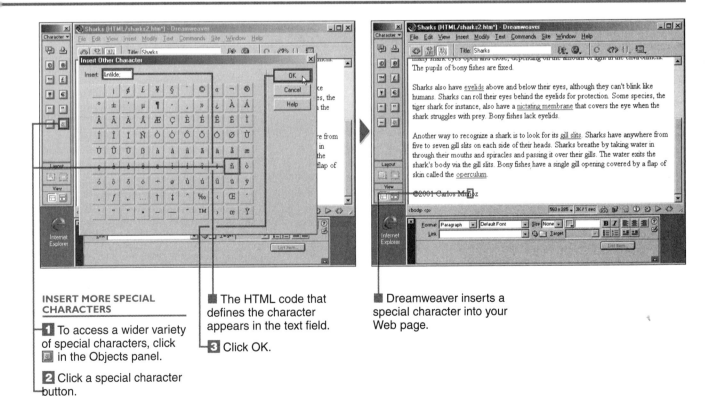

INSERT MORE SPECIAL CHARACTERS

1 To access a wider variety of special characters, click ▣ in the Objects panel.

2 Click a special character button.

■ The HTML code that defines the character appears in the text field.

3 Click OK.

■ Dreamweaver inserts a special character into your Web page.

CHANGE A FONT

You can make the text on your Web page look more interesting by changing its font. If you do not specify a particular font, most browsers display text on your Web page in Times New Roman (Windows) or Times (Macintosh).

You can specify any style of font that you want in Dreamweaver; however, Web browsers can only display the fonts installed on a user's computer. Because of this, it is a good idea to limit your font choices to the more popular ones, such as Arial, Verdana, Georgia, Comic Sans, and Courier.

To ensure that a user sees the style of text that you want them to see, you can specify more than one font choice for your text. If your first choice is available on the user's computer, the Web browser displays text using that font. If your first choice is not available and you have specified a second choice, the browser tries to display it using that font, and so on.

You can also change your text's font using style sheets. See Chapter 12 for information on style sheets.

CHANGE A FONT

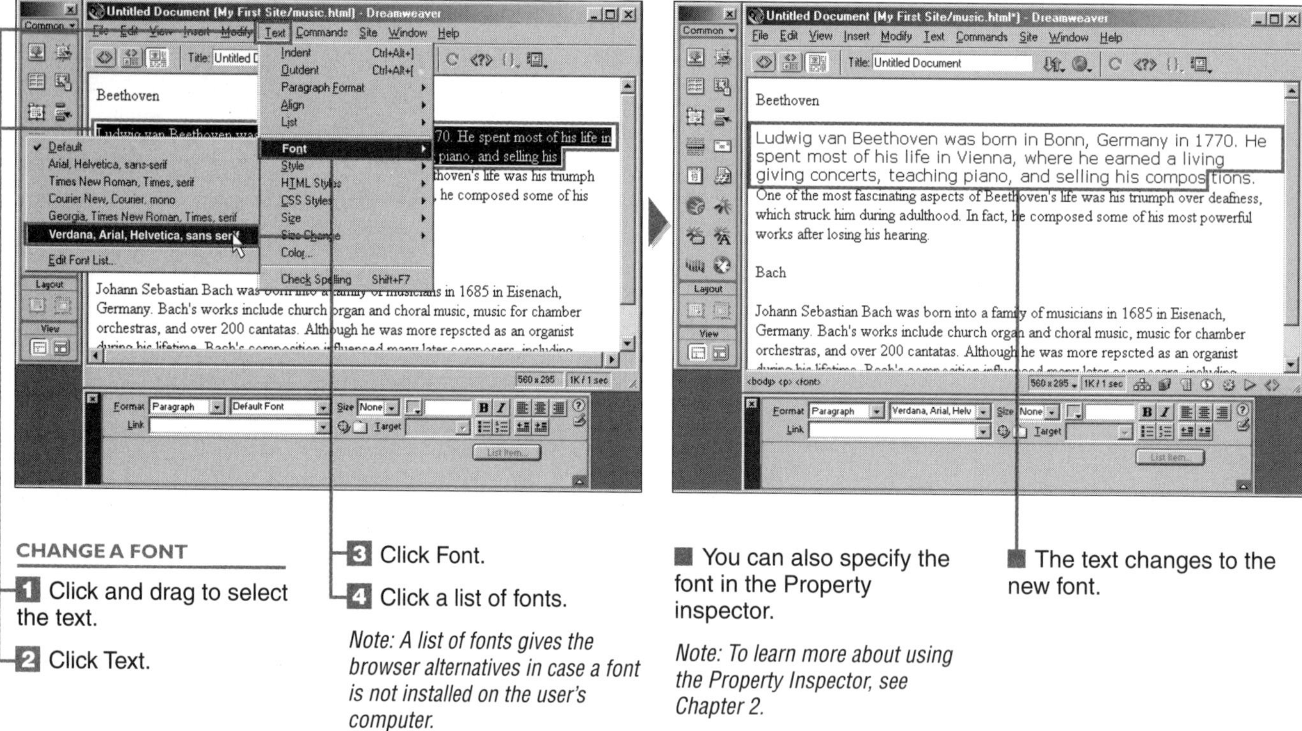

CHANGE A FONT

1. Click and drag to select the text.
2. Click Text.
3. Click Font.
4. Click a list of fonts.

Note: A list of fonts gives the browser alternatives in case a font is not installed on the user's computer.

■ You can also specify the font in the Property inspector.

Note: To learn more about using the Property Inspector, see Chapter 2.

■ The text changes to the new font.

What are serif and sans serif?

✔ *Serif* and *sans serif* are common font classifications. Serifs are the tiny decorations that appear on the ends of many traditional fonts such as Times New Roman, Georgia, Palatino, and the text you are reading now. Sans serif means "without serifs;" fonts in this category include Arial, Verdana, and Helvetica.

How do I create text that looks like typewriter text on my Web page?

✔ Use a monospaced font style such as Courier. *Monospaced* means that each letter in the font style has the same width, similar to typewriter text.

Can I specify a font category instead of a specific font name?

✔ Yes. Most browsers recognize "serif," "sans-serif" — hyphen required — and "mono," for monospaced, and some also recognize "cursive" and "fantasy." When you specify a font category, the browser displays the default font for that category. For example, the default sans-serif font for Windows is Arial; for Macintosh, it is Helvetica.

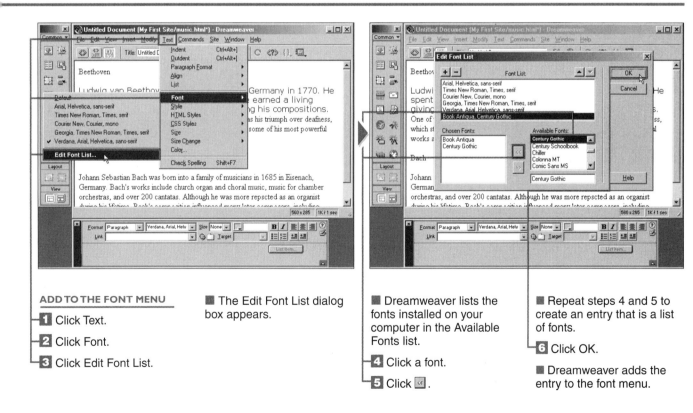

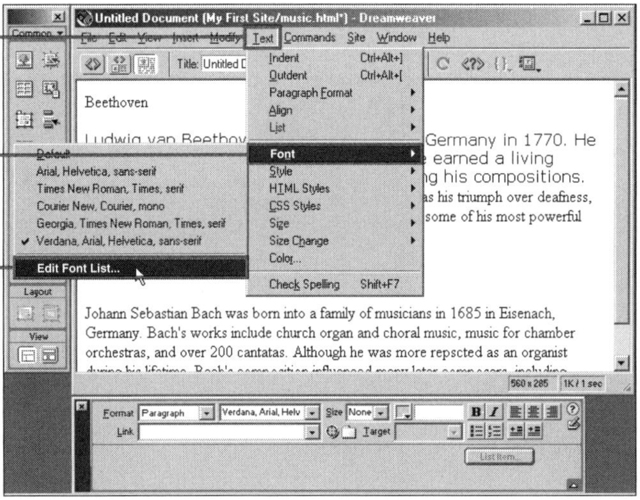

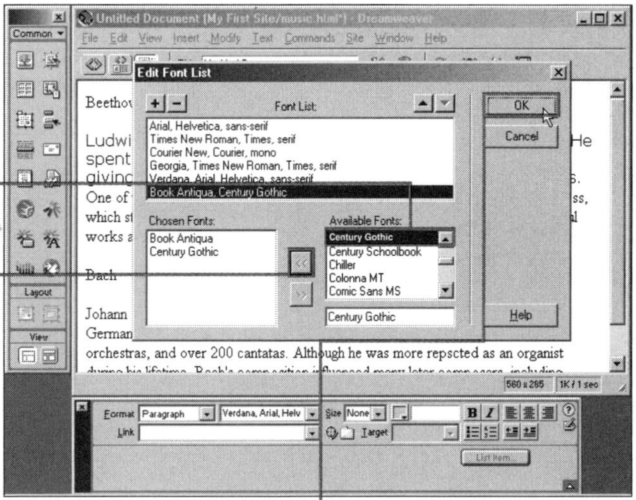

ADD TO THE FONT MENU

1 Click Text.

2 Click Font.

3 Click Edit Font List.

■ The Edit Font List dialog box appears.

■ Dreamweaver lists the fonts installed on your computer in the Available Fonts list.

4 Click a font.

5 Click «.

■ Repeat steps 4 and 5 to create an entry that is a list of fonts.

6 Click OK.

■ Dreamweaver adds the entry to the font menu.

FORMAT TEXT AS BOLD OR ITALIC

You can emphasize text on your Web page with a number of HTML-based style commands. You can access two of the most commonly used commands — Bold and Italic — via the Property Inspector.

You can find other styles in the Text menu under the Style submenu. The Strong and Emphasis styles have the same visual effect as the Bold and Italic styles, respectively. The Teletype style displays text in a typewriter-like font. Underline does just what you would expect, while Strikethrough crosses out text on your page.

You can combine text styles to create more complicated effects. For example, you can apply the bold, italic, and underline styles to a line of text all at once. If you use certain style combinations often, you can create shortcuts for them in the HTML Styles panel. See the section "Create a New HTML Style" for more information.

If you want to go beyond what is offered via HTML-based styles, consider using style sheets on your pages. You can learn more about style sheets in Chapter 12.

FORMAT TEXT AS BOLD OR ITALIC

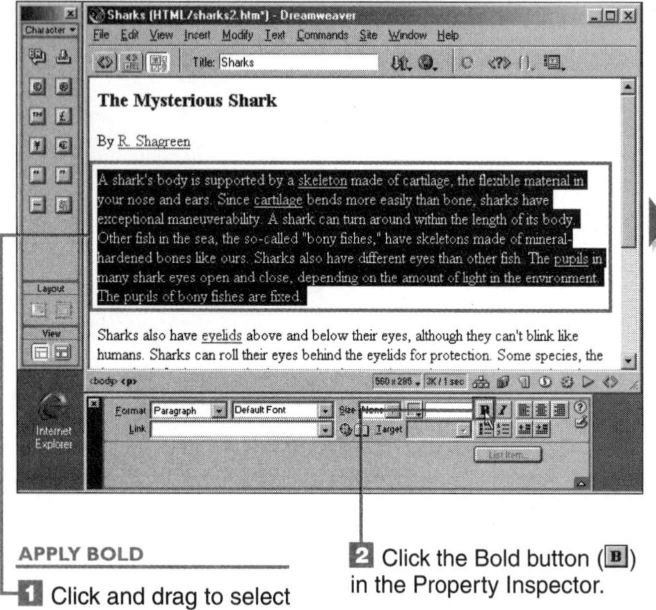

APPLY BOLD

1 Click and drag to select the text.

2 Click the Bold button (B) in the Property Inspector.

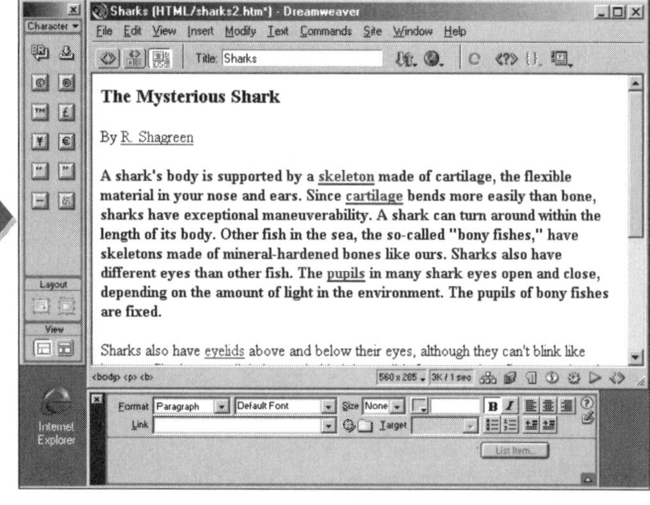

■ The text appears in a heavier weight.

If Italic and Emphasis produce the same visual effect on my page, which command should I use to produce italic text?

✔ A technical difference exists between the two commands: HTML tags such as <I> (which is the result of the Italic command) are known as physical appearance tags. Tags such as <EM> (which is the result of the Emphasis command) are known as structural meaning tags. Structural meaning commands tend to be preferred by HTML purists because physical appearance tags may be ignored by nonvisual Web browsers.

Is it better to use bold or italic formatting to emphasize words in my page?

✔ Some fonts are more legible in bold, others in italics. The font size and platform on which you are viewing can also make a difference — for example, the default Times font on Macintosh browsers can be very hard to read when italicized. You should test your completed pages in several different Web browsers to see what your audience will see.

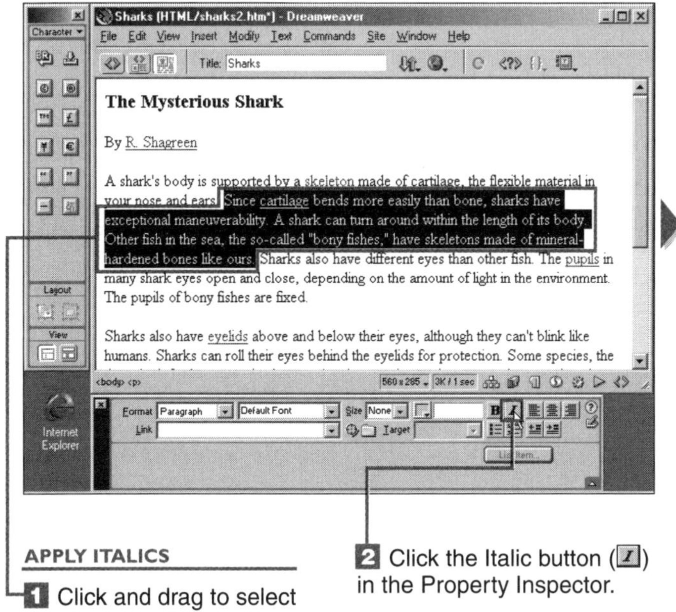

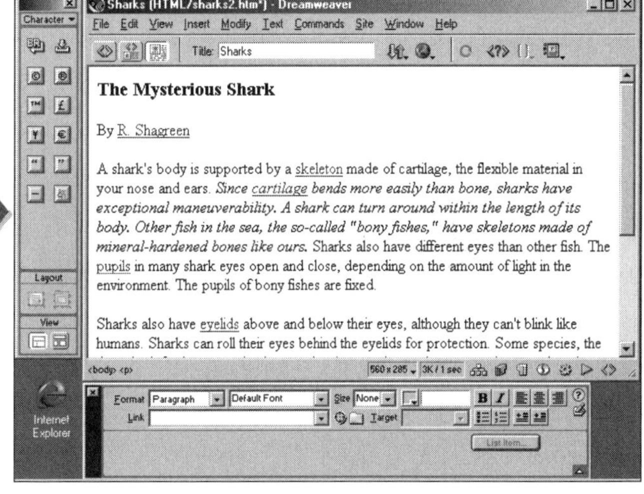

APPLY ITALICS

1 Click and drag to select the text.

2 Click the Italic button (*I*) in the Property Inspector.

■ The selected text is italicized.

CHANGE FONT SIZE

You can change the size of the font on your Web page to emphasize or de-emphasize sections of text. You can specify an absolute size from 1 to 7 for your font (3 is equivalent to the default text size). You can also specify a relative size, such as +1 or –2, and the font will increase or decrease relative to its current size.

You can use sizes 5 and 6 for titles and headlines; you can use size 1 for copyright and disclaimer text. Sans-serif type (Arial, Helvetica, Verdana) is relatively easy to read at small sizes and can usually be used as body text at size 2. This can help you fit more words in a browser window.

Note that the numeric value bears no relation to actual physical units of measurement such as picas, points, inches, and so on. To size your text using physical units, you can use style sheets. To learn more about style sheets, see Chapter 12.

CHANGE FONT SIZE

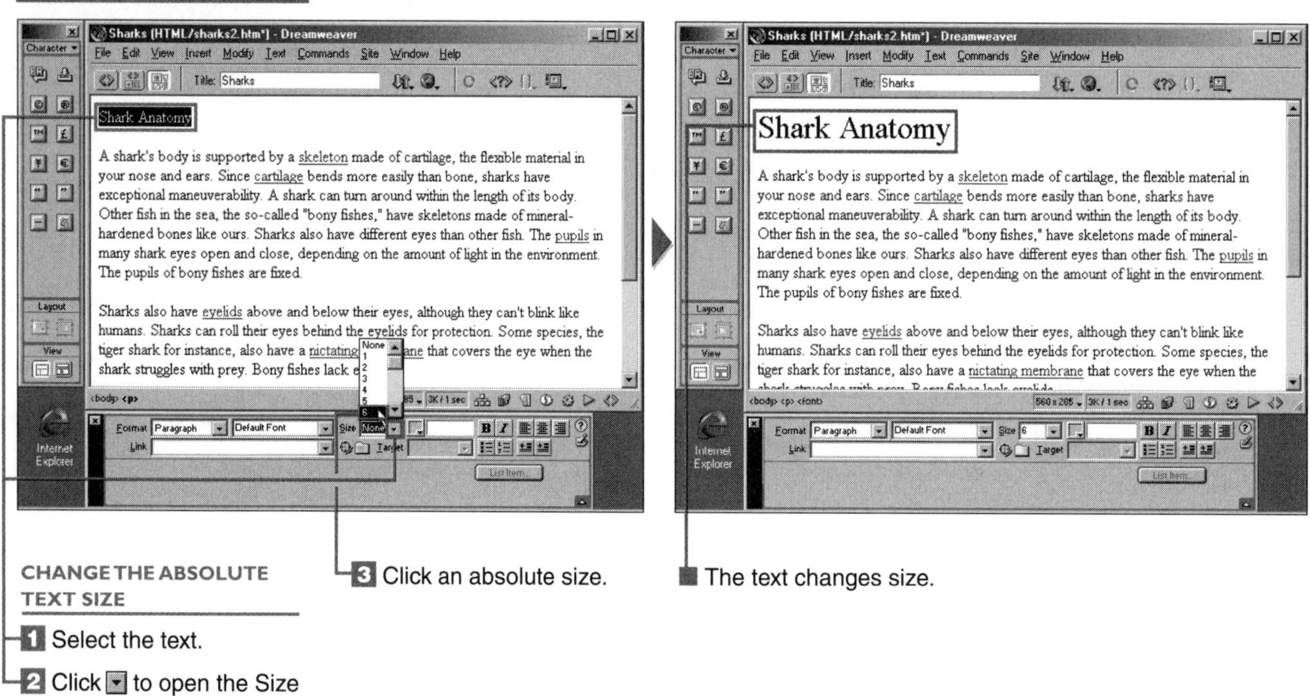

CHANGE THE ABSOLUTE TEXT SIZE

1 Select the text.

2 Click ▾ to open the Size drop-down list.

3 Click an absolute size.

■ The text changes size.

Should I use a larger font size or a heading to create the headlines on my page?

✔ It is up to you. Creating a level-1 or level-2 heading produces relatively large text, but also gives text a bold appearance and adds space above and below it. Experimenting with different font sizes as well as different headings can give you a variety of looks. For more information on headings, see the section "Create a Heading."

Can I change the size of individual characters?

✔ Yes. Simply select the character and follow the steps in this section. Increasing the size of the character that begins a passage can give a page a traditional feel.

How do I create text that is bigger than size 7 or smaller than size 1?

✔ One way is to format your text using style sheets, which give you an almost unlimited range of sizes when formatting text. You can also create the text in an image editor and then add it to your Web page as an image. See Chapter 6 to do so.

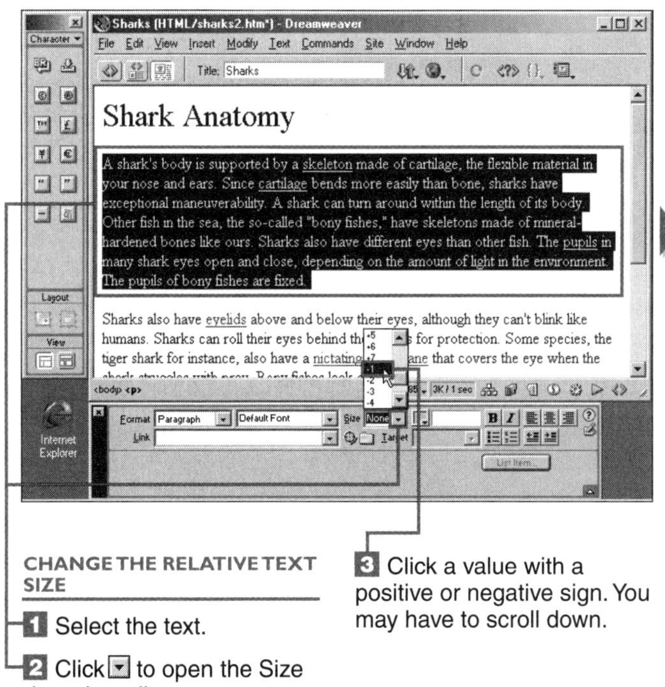

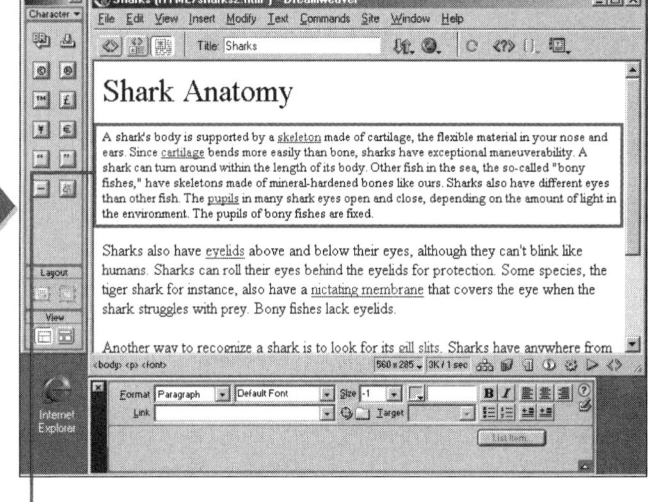

CHANGE THE RELATIVE TEXT SIZE

1 Select the text.

2 Click ▾ to open the Size drop-down list.

3 Click a value with a positive or negative sign. You may have to scroll down.

■ The text changes size.

Note: Another way to adjust text size is by creating a heading. See the section "Create a Heading."

CHANGE FONT COLOR

You can change the color of text on all or part of your Web page to make it more visually interesting. The default color for text is black.

Dreamweaver provides an easy-to-access palette of Web-safe colors that you can apply in the Property Inspector. *Web-safe* means the colors display accurately no matter what browser, platform, and monitor setting the user uses.

You can also choose the color of your text by accessing a standard color-picker dialog box, or by typing the color's common name or hexadecimal code. Hexadecimal codes are six-digit combinations of letters and numbers that define the amount of red, blue, and green mixed to produce a color.

To ensure that the text is readable, make sure its color contrasts with the background color or background image of your Web page. To adjust the background color or background image of your Web page, see Chapter 6.

CHANGE FONT COLOR

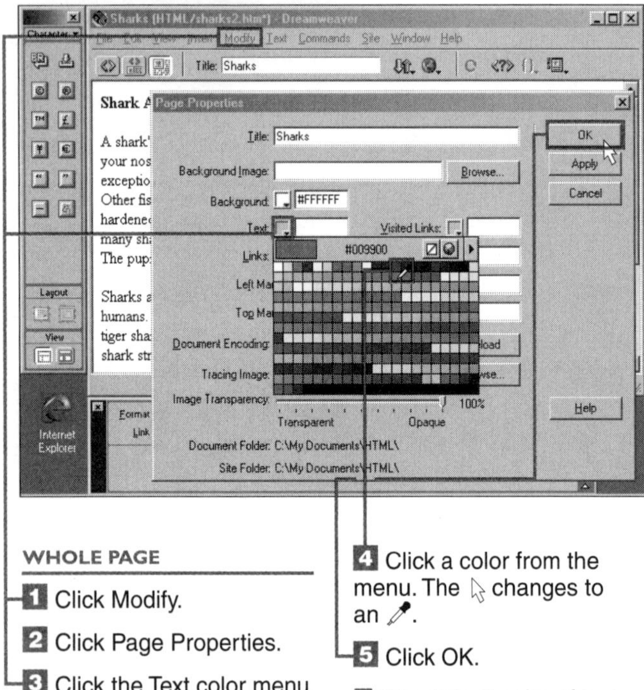

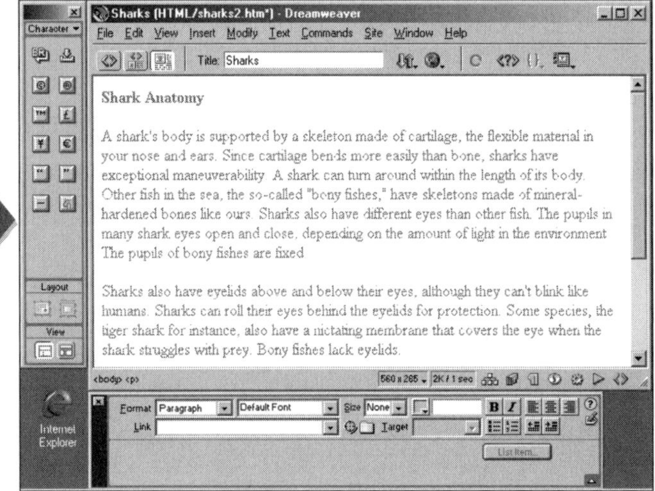

WHOLE PAGE

1 Click Modify.

2 Click Page Properties.

3 Click the Text color menu.

4 Click a color from the menu. The pointer changes to an eyedropper.

5 Click OK.

■ The default color of text on a Web page is black.

■ All the text on your Web page displays in the new color.

What are the letter and number combinations that show up in Dreamweaver's color fields when I define a color?

✔ HTML defines colors using six-digit codes called *hexadecimal codes,* which show up in the color field when you select from Dreamweaver's color menu. Hex codes are preceded by a pound sign (#). Instead of ranging from 0 through 9, hex-code digits range from 0 through F, with A equal to 10, B equal to 11, and so on through F, which is equal to 15. This special numbering scheme lets a pair of digits define 255 values, instead of the 99 available with decimal numbering. The first two digits in a hex code specify the amount of red in the selected color, the second two digits specify the amount of green, and the third two digits specify the amount of blue.

What are some examples of hex codes and the colors they stand for?

✔ #000000 represents black. #FFFFFF represents white. Using six of the same digits between 0 and F (such as #666666) produces a shade of gray. The primary colors — red, green, and blue — are represented by #FF0000, #00FF00, and #0000FF, respectively.

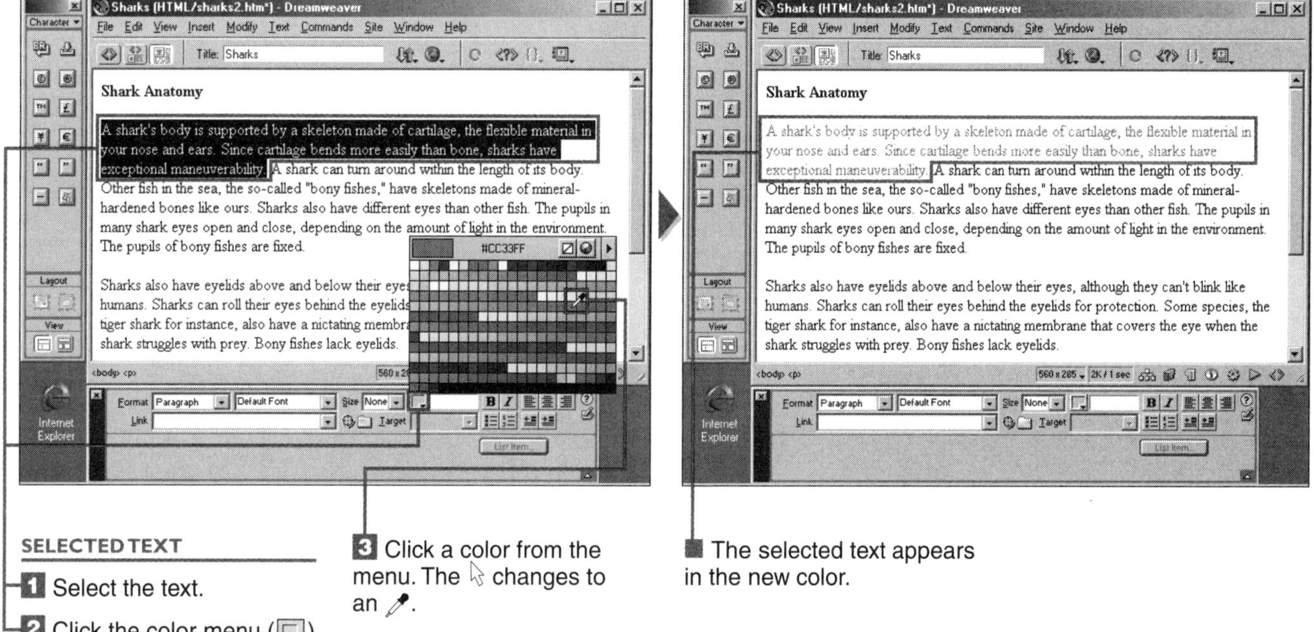

SELECTED TEXT

1 Select the text.

2 Click the color menu (▭) in the Properties window.

3 Click a color from the menu. The ↖ changes to an ✎.

■ The selected text appears in the new color.

APPLY HTML STYLES

You can format text using the HTML Styles panel, which enables you to apply complicated styles with a single click. The panel can be a timesaver when you need to apply styles that appear many times on a page or throughout a site.

Style definitions can involve text-level definitions (such as size, color, and boldness) as well paragraph-level definitions (such as heading level and alignment).

Dreamweaver comes with several predefined styles, including the following:

Caption: produces italicized, bold text in a sans-serif font

Copyright: produces tiny, italicized text in a serif font, centered on the page

Fixed-width: produces text in a typewriter-style font

Headline: produces large, bold text in a sans-serif font

Normal: produces text slightly larger than the default size in a serif font

To define your own custom styles, see "Create a New HTML Style."

You can define more complicated styles for use on your page using style sheets. See Chapter 12 to learn more about style sheets.

APPLY HTML STYLES

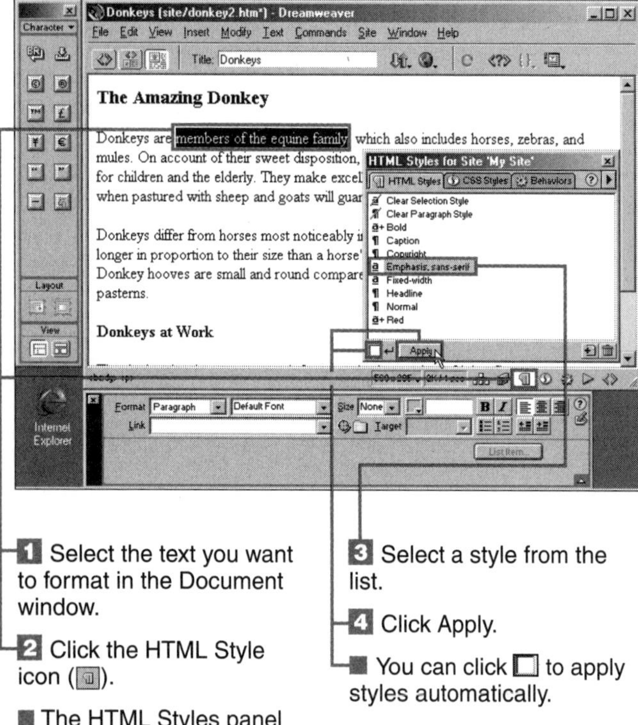

1 Select the text you want to format in the Document window.

2 Click the HTML Style icon (▣).

■ The HTML Styles panel appears.

3 Select a style from the list.

4 Click Apply.

■ You can click ☐ to apply styles automatically.

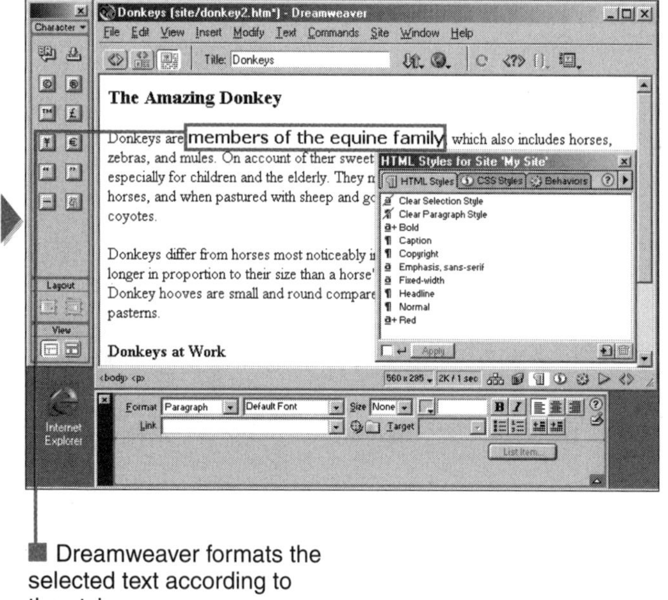

■ Dreamweaver formats the selected text according to the style.

CREATE A NEW HTML STYLE

You can save time by creating complicated text styles and adding them to the HTML Styles panel. From the panel, you can apply the styles to content in your page quickly and easily.

Style definitions can work at the text or paragraph level. When you define a new style, you specify whether you want to apply it to just selected text or to the entire paragraph. You also specify whether you want the style to replace any current styles or whether you want to add it to any current styles.

Note that if you decide to redefine a style in the HTML Styles panel, Dreamweaver does not apply the new definition to places where you have previously applied the style. This is in contrast to style sheets, which enable you to make changes to style definitions and then have previously styled text updated. See Chapter 12 for more information on style sheets.

CREATE A NEW HTML STYLE

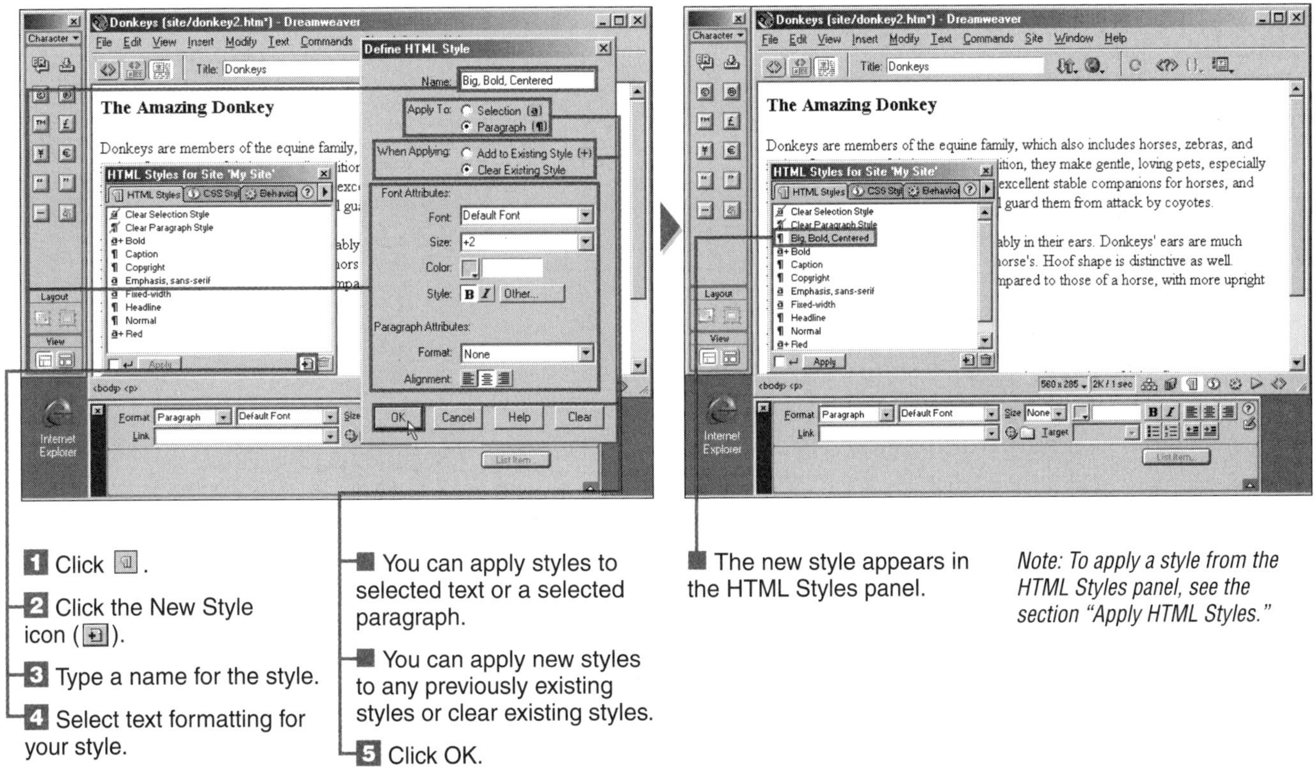

1 Click [icon].

2 Click the New Style icon ([icon]).

3 Type a name for the style.

4 Select text formatting for your style.

■ You can apply styles to selected text or a selected paragraph.

■ You can apply new styles to any previously existing styles or clear existing styles.

5 Click OK.

■ The new style appears in the HTML Styles panel.

Note: To apply a style from the HTML Styles panel, see the section "Apply HTML Styles."

INCORPORATING IMAGES AND GRAPHICS

Adding images and graphics to your pages is a great way to add color to your site and complement text and other non-graphical elements. Dreamweaver's commands let you insert images, align them on your page, add borders, and turn them into clickable hyperlinks. For an image to be viewable on a Web page, it has to be in a format that Web browsers can display. All the popular Web browsers can display JPEG and GIF images, and some can also display PNG images. Dreamweaver does not have image-editing capabilities, so if you want to customize the images that you use on your Web pages, you need an image editing program such as Macromedia Fireworks (included on the CD-ROM) or Adobe Photoshop.

Getting Images

You can get images for your Web pages from a variety of sources: A flat-bed scanner lets you digitize hand-drawn illustrations, photographic prints, and other paper-based content. Digital cameras let you skip the scanning step and shoot digital photos for your pages directly. You can also get a variety of images and graphics from clip art collections, which are available online and in computer stores. If the images you scan, shoot, or buy are not in a format appropriate for the Web (JPEG, GIF, or PNG), you have to convert them in an image editor before placing them on your pages in Dreamweaver.

GIF Images

GIF, which stands for Graphics Interchange Format, is the preferred Web image format for illustrations and other images that contain a lot of solid color. GIF images can only contain up to 256 colors, which is why the format is less suitable for photographic images. Saving your GIF images using a minimum number of colors can help keep your file sizes small. GIF is a *lossless* image format, which means quality doesn't degrade when you save as GIF. GIF files have a .gif extension.

JPEG Images

JPEG, which stands for Joint Photographic Experts Group, is the preferred Web image format for photos and other images that contain a broad range of colors. This is because JPEG files support 16.7 million colors in a single image (many more colors than GIF). When you save images as JPEGs, you specify the amount of JPEG compression to be applied. The more compression you apply, the smaller the resulting file size, but the lower the quality of the resulting image. JPEG is a *lossy* image format, which means some quality is lost when you save as JPEG. JPEG files have a .jpg or .jpeg extension.

PNG Images

PNG, which stands for Portable Network Graphics, is a relatively new Web image format. This format combines some of the advantages of JPEG (it supports 16.7 million colors) and other advantages of GIF (it is a lossless format). However, because many older Web browsers do not support PNG, the format is still much less popular than GIF and JPEG.

Download Time

One potential drawback to inserting images in your Web pages is that they can add to the total file size of a page, making it slower to download. That is why it is important to optimize your images to make them as small as possible before placing them on your page. Image-editing programs such as Macromedia Fireworks have special tools to help you create very compact GIF, JPEG, and PNG images. To see how images are affecting the file size of you page, you can look at the status bar of the Document window in Dreamweaver, which tells you the total size of your Web page. As a rule, it is a good idea to keep your Web pages below 50K if you are designing your pages for an audience using 56 Kbps modems. You may have to remove images, or split one page into several pages, to keep page sizes low.

INSERT AN IMAGE INTO YOUR WEB PAGE

You can insert different types of images, including clip art, digital camera images, and scanned photos, into your Web page. Adding images can complement your text and make your Web page more visually interesting. But images can also significantly increase a page's download time.

When you add an image to a page, Dreamweaver creates a reference to the image file in the HTML code — it does not actually insert image file's information into the HTML. When a browser accesses a Web page that includes images, it must download a separate file for each image on the page.

Dreamweaver lets you add borders to your images. You specify the size of the border in pixels, and the border appears around the image in the same color as the default text color on the page. You can change the color of the image border by changing the default text color for a page in the Page Properties dialog box. See Chapter 5 for more information.

INSERT AN IMAGE INTO YOUR WEB PAGE

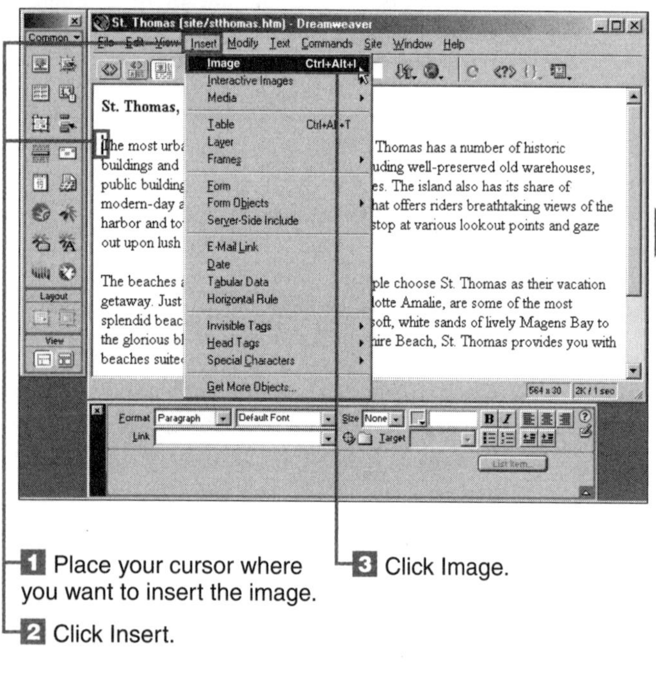

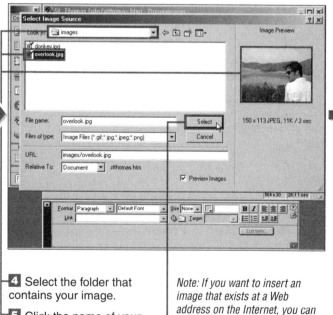

1 Place your cursor where you want to insert the image.

2 Click Insert.

3 Click Image.

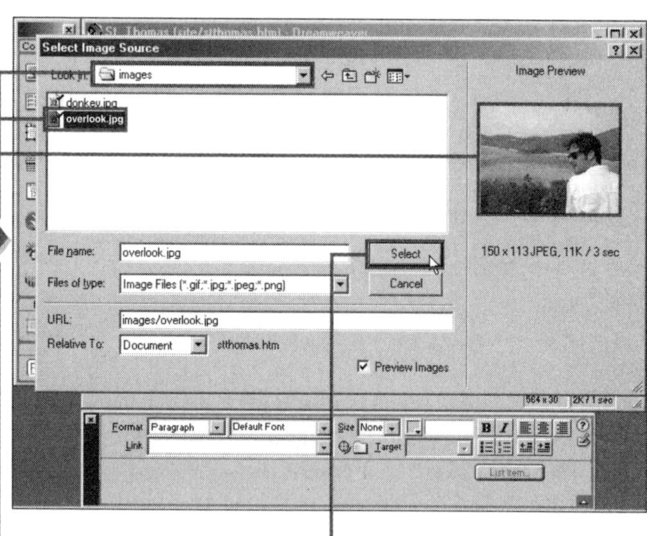

4 Select the folder that contains your image.

5 Click the name of your image file.

■ A preview of the image appears.

Note: If you want to insert an image that exists at a Web address on the Internet, you can type the image's address into the URL field.

6 Click Select.

Where should I store images that I want to use on my Web pages?

✔ You should store your images in the same folder as your HTML files. When your site consists of many files, you may find it more convenient to keep images in a subdirectory called images. Keeping your HTML files and image files in the same folder ensures that your Web site works correctly when you transfer it to a live Web server.

How do I delete an image?

✔ To delete an image that is in a Web page, click the image and press Delete. To delete an image file from a site entirely, open the Site window (see Chapter 16), click the image file in the local site list, and press Delete. Dreamweaver warns you if any of your Web pages reference the image file. If you delete an image that is referenced on a page, that page will display a broken image icon.

How can I tell how much space my images and text take up on my Web page?

✔ Dreamweaver displays your page's total size in kilobytes (K) on the status bar. This total includes the size of your HTML file, the size of your images, plus the size of anything else on the page. Next to the size is the estimated download time for the page. You can configure the connection speed used to determine this estimate in your Preferences. See Chapter 2 for more information.

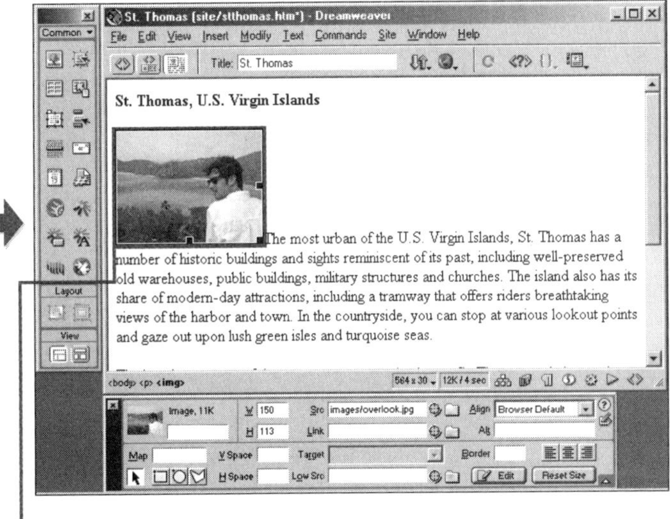

■ The new image appears on the Web page.

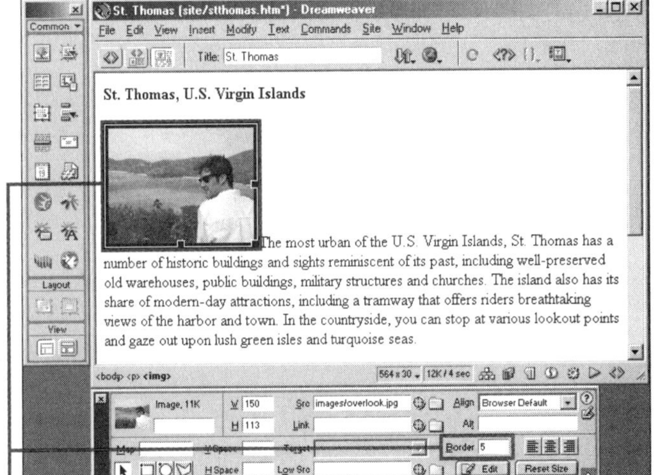

ADD A BORDER TO AN IMAGE

1 Click the image to select it.

2 Type a width (in pixels) into the Border field.

3 Press Enter (Windows) or Return (Mac).

■ A border appears around the image. The color of the border is the same as your page's default text.

WRAP TEXT AROUND AN IMAGE

You can wrap text around an image to fit more information inside the browser window and give your Web pages a more professional look.

You wrap text around an image by adjusting the image's alignment. Specifying Left alignment moves the image to the left of the page and wraps any following text around the right side of the image.

Right alignment moves the image to the right of the page and wraps any following text around the image's left side.

Dreamweaver offers several other alignment options that specify how the preceding or following text abuts the inserted image. Middle, for example, aligns the baseline of the text with the middle of the image. These other settings are typically less useful than the Right and Left settings.

Dreamweaver does not provide a simple alignment setting that wraps text around both sides of an image. To put text to the left and right of an image, you can insert a three-column table (see Chapter 8), place the image in the center cell, and place text in the neighboring cells.

WRAP TEXT AROUND AN IMAGE

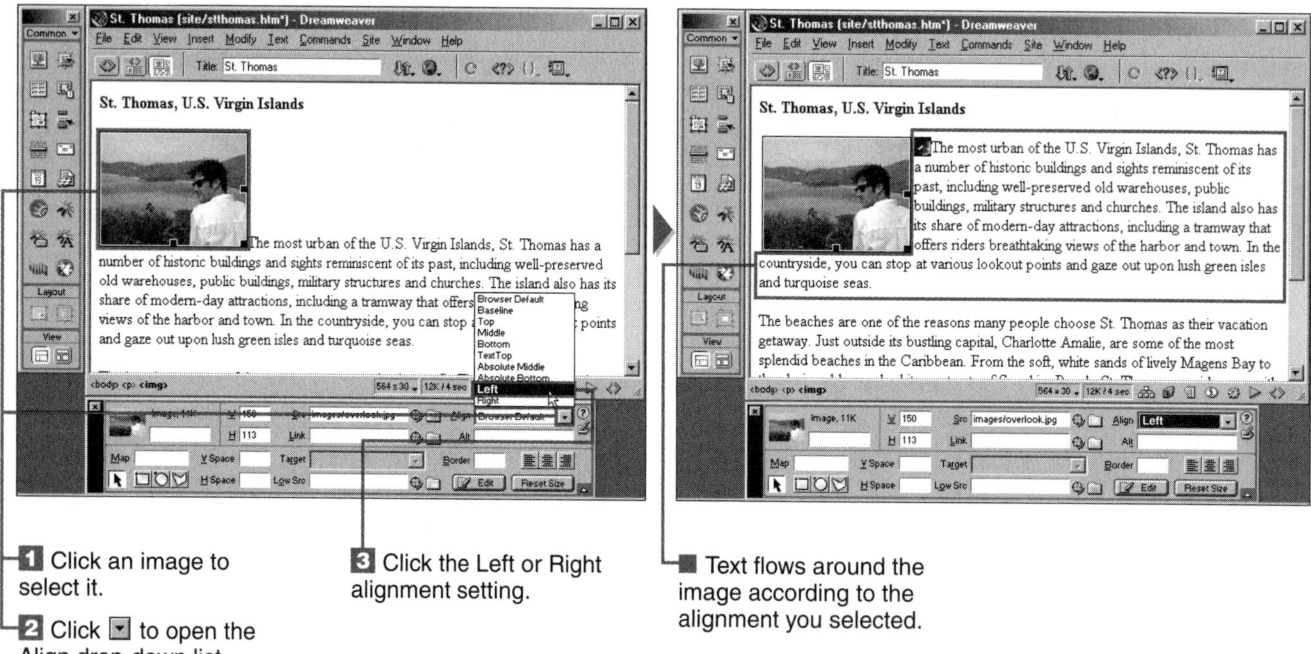

1 Click an image to select it.

2 Click ▾ to open the Align drop-down list.

3 Click the Left or Right alignment setting.

■ Text flows around the image according to the alignment you selected.

CENTER AN IMAGE

Centering an image can give a photo or banner prominence on your page. Dreamweaver makes centering an image easy — you select the image and click a center-align button.

No "center" alignment attribute exists for the HTML image tag, which is why you do not see a Center option in the Align drop-down menu. When you click the center-align button in the Property Inspector, Dreamweaver does one of three things: If the image is inside a paragraph, Dreamweaver aligns the entire paragraph to the center. If the image is not in a paragraph, Dreamweaver either adds a `<DIV ALIGN="CENTER">` tag or a `<CENTER>` tag around the image HTML. You can specify which in the Code Format category in your Preferences. The `<DIV>` option is recommended in newer HTML specifications.

Another way to align images and other content on your pages is by using styles sheets. See Chapter 12 for more information.

CENTER AN IMAGE

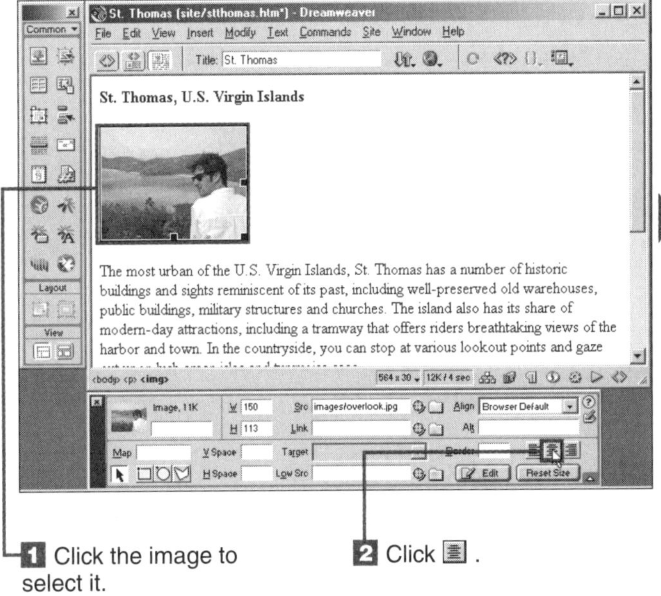

1 Click the image to select it.

2 Click (center-align button).

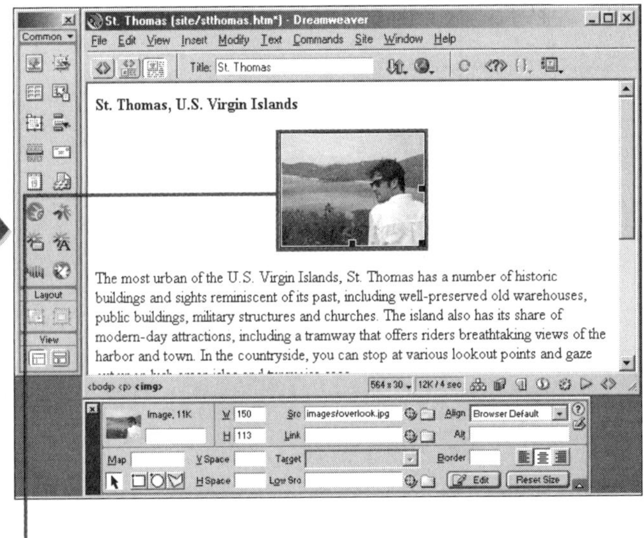

■ The image is centered on the page.

CHANGE THE SIZE OF AN IMAGE

Dreamweaver enables you to change an image's size in several ways. You can change the pixel dimensions either by entering new values in height and width fields or by clicking and dragging the corner of the image. You can also define the image as a percentage of the browser window, so that it expands and contracts as the user resizes the browser.

None of these techniques changes the size of the image in the actual image file. Instead, resizing in Dreamweaver simply changes how the image is presented on your Web page. For instance, you can insert a 10 x 10 pixel image into your page in Dreamweaver and specify that it display at 20 x 20 pixels (or at 5 x 30 pixels). The image will be stretched (or shrunken) for display on the page, but the actual image file will still be 10 x 10 pixels.

Enlarging an image in Dreamweaver can decrease the quality of the image. Shrinking an image in Dreamweaver means that your viewers will be downloading an image file that is larger than it needs to be. For both these reasons, it is usually best to change the size of your images in an image editor.

CHANGE THE SIZE OF AN IMAGE

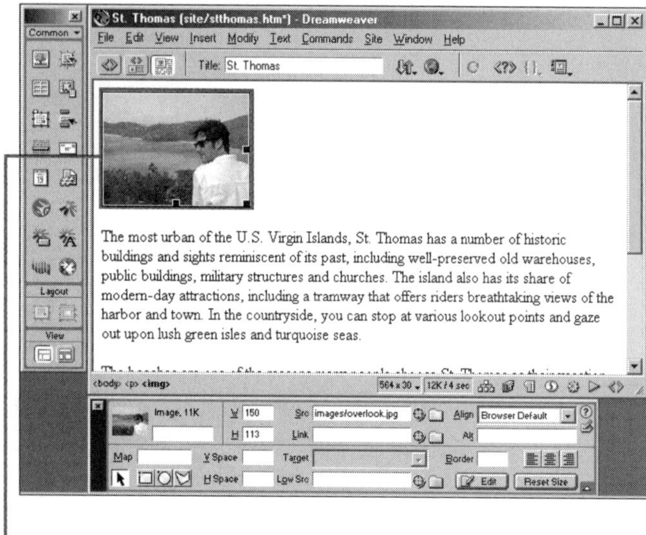

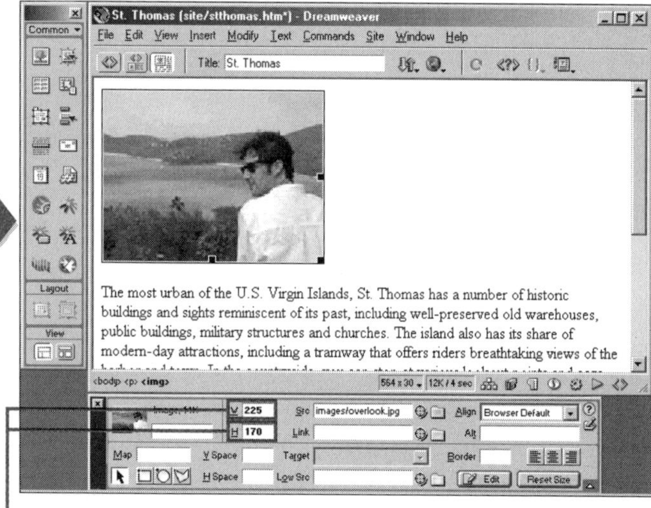

1 Click the image.

Note: When you insert an image, Dreamweaver automatically enters its real dimensions into the Property Inspector.

2 Type the desired width (in pixels) of the image.

3 Press Enter (Windows) or Return (Mac).

4 Type the desired height (in pixels) of the image.

5 Press Enter (Windows) or Return (Mac).

■ The image displays with its new pixel dimensions.

Is there a limit to how small I can make an image on my page?

✔ Using the handles on the image edges to resize, you can shrink an image to no smaller than 8 x 8 pixels. To decrease the size down to the real minimum of 1 x 1 pixel, you need to enter values in the W and H fields of the Property Inspector.

After resizing, how do I return an image to its original dimensions?

✔ These are the actual image file dimensions, which Dreamweaver automatically inserts into the H and W fields which you first add an image to a page.

How do I make an image take up the entire browser window?

✔ Set the W and H fields in the Property Inspector both to 100%. The image stretches to fill the entire window. This can distort an image if it was originally too small.

CLICK AND DRAG THE IMAGE

1 Click the image.

2 Drag the handles at the edges of the image. To retain the image's proportions, hold down the Shift key as you drag a corner.

■ The image expands or contracts to its new dimensions.

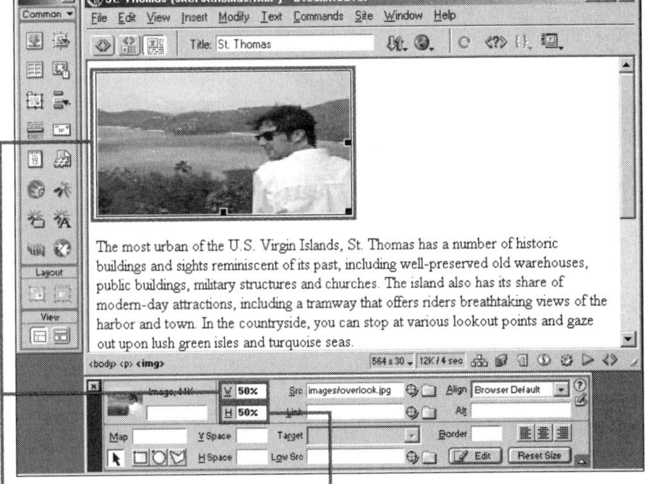

CHANGE THE PROPORTIONAL SIZE

1 Click the image.

2 Type the desired percentage of the width.

3 Press Enter (Windows) or Return (Mac).

4 Type the desired percentage of the height.

5 Press Enter (Windows) or Return (Mac).

■ The image displays as a percentage of the browser window (not as a percentage of the original image size).

ADD SPACE AROUND AN IMAGE

Adding space around an image can distinguish it from the text and other images on your Web page. You may want to add space if you are wrapping text around an image (see "Wrap Text around an Image" earlier in this chapter), or placing several images beside one another.

The techniques described here only let you add a fixed amount to the top and bottom (the V Space, or vertical space), and a fixed amount to the left and right sides (the H Space, or horizontal space). To add a fixed amount of space to just one side of an image, or to different combinations of sides, you can use style sheets. See Chapter 12 for more information on style sheets.

You can also add space to the sides of your images using an image editor. Just make sure the space you add is transparent or the same color as your page background (or else you will end up with an image border).

ADD SPACE AROUND AN IMAGE

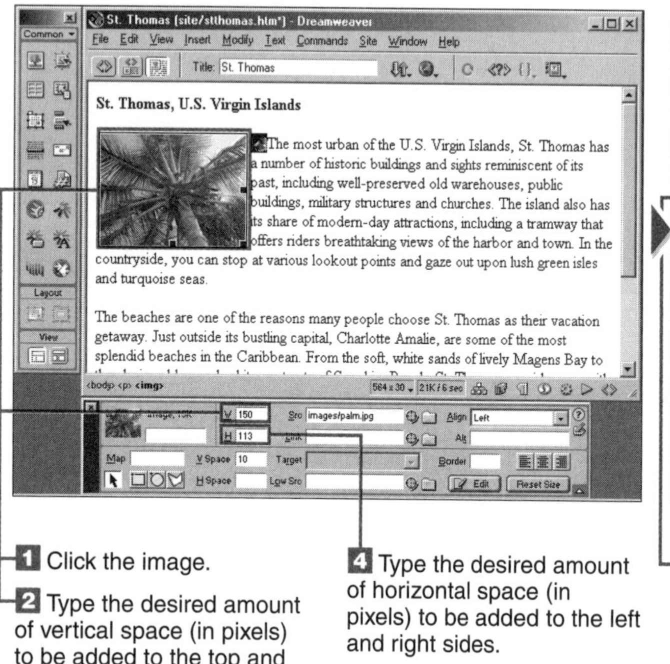

1 Click the image.

2 Type the desired amount of vertical space (in pixels) to be added to the top and bottom.

3 Press Enter (Windows) or Return (Mac).

4 Type the desired amount of horizontal space (in pixels) to be added to the left and right sides.

5 Press Enter (Windows) or Return (Mac).

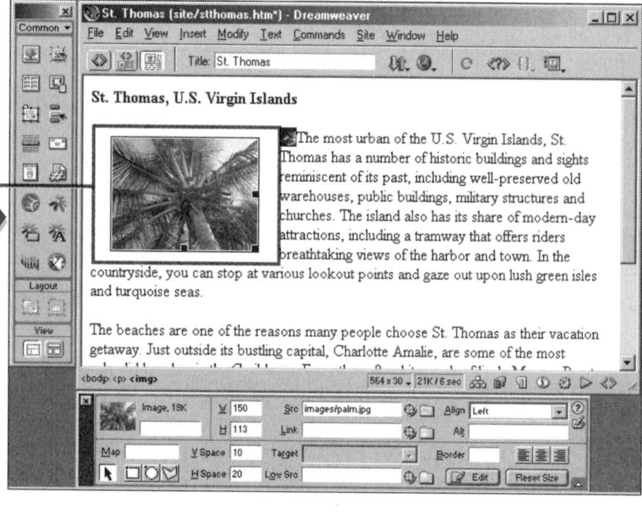

■ Extra space appears around the image.

ADD A HORIZONTAL RULE

You can use thin lines known as *horizontal rules* to your Web page to separate sections of content. It is the Web browser that produces the rules when a page loads; the rules are not separate image files. As a result, horizontal rules may appear slightly different in different types of browsers.

You can customize a horizontal rule in various ways. The default horizontal rule stretches to fill the entire width of the page. Alternatively, you can express the width as an absolute pixel value or a percentage of the browser window. You can also adjust the thickness of your rules.

Rules can have shading turned on, which gives them a 3D look. Rules without shading are solid gray.

If you are not pleased with the horizontal rules that Dreamweaver gives you, you can always use an image editor to create your own wavy rules, multicolored rules, or dashed rules and insert them as images. See "Insert an Image" earlier in this chapter.

ADD A HORIZONTAL RULE

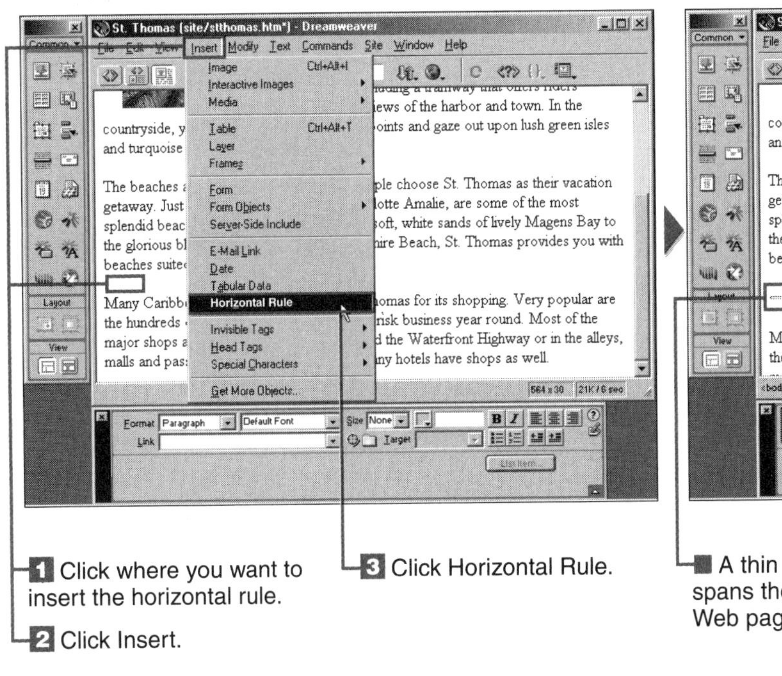

1 Click where you want to insert the horizontal rule.

2 Click Insert.

3 Click Horizontal Rule.

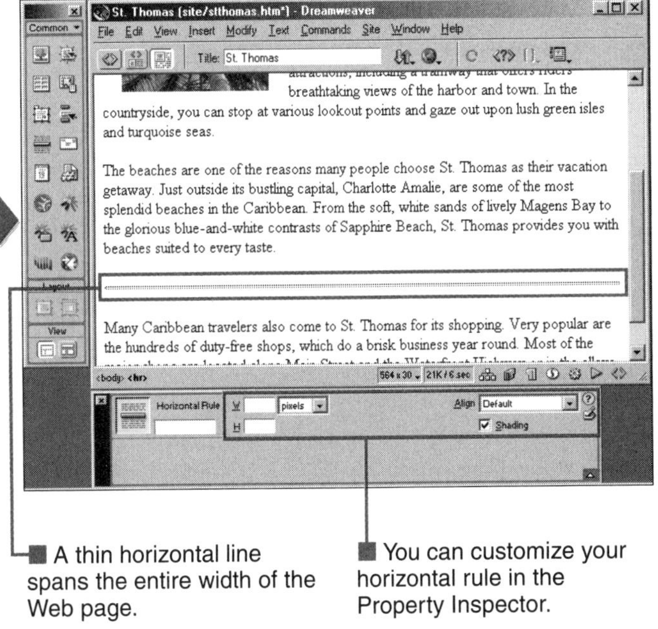

■ A thin horizontal line spans the entire width of the Web page.

■ You can customize your horizontal rule in the Property Inspector.

ADD A BACKGROUND IMAGE

You can add a background image to your Web page to complement the page's theme or to make the page more colorful. You can also design backgrounds that work with elements in the foreground of your pages. For example, you can make a background that has columns of color that underlay similarly arranged columns of text.

Unless the background image is larger than the browser window, the image will repeat horizontally and vertically to fill the entire window. This is an important design consideration, because viewers with different monitor settings can have browser windows with very different sizes. For example, a background that takes up the entire window on a browser running on a monitor set to 640 x 480 pixels (a common setting for older systems) may end up repeating on a browser running on a 1024 x 768 screen.

Another consideration when creating a background image is to make sure it does not overwhelm content in the foreground. A rainbow-colored background may call attention to a page, but it may also make it impossible to read the words displayed over it.

ADD A BACKGROUND IMAGE

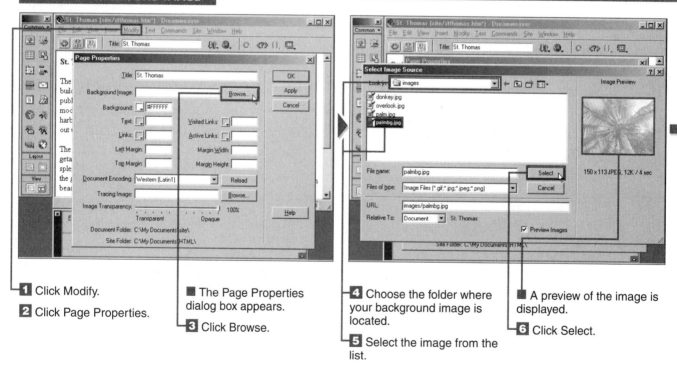

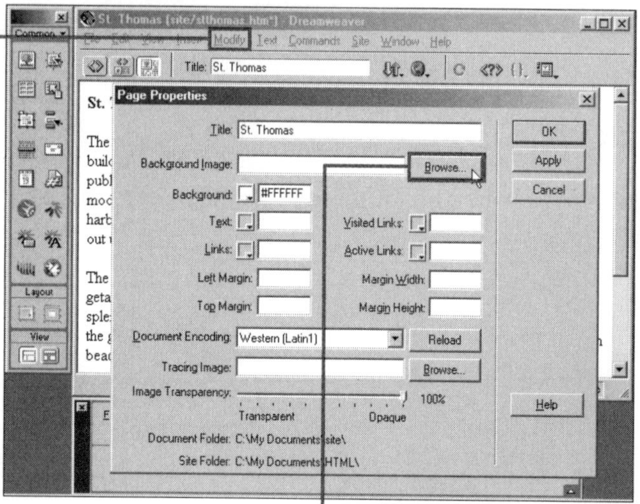

1 Click Modify.

2 Click Page Properties.

■ The Page Properties dialog box appears.

3 Click Browse.

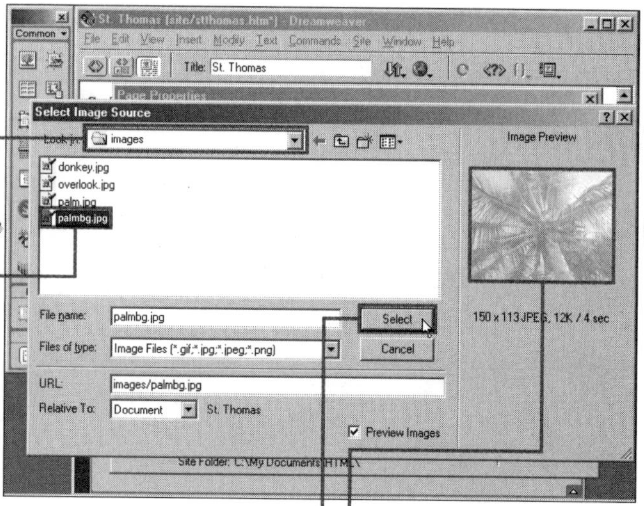

4 Choose the folder where your background image is located.

5 Select the image from the list.

■ A preview of the image is displayed.

6 Click Select.

How do I create a background image that repeats seamlessly?

✔ You can use an image editor, such as Adobe Photoshop or Macromedia Fireworks, to eliminate the seams that can appear when an image repeats. The trick involves offsetting the image horizontally and vertically, then cleaning up the seams with editing tools. Many books on Web graphics show you how to create seamless background images.

How do I estimate the browser sizes for monitors at different settings?

✔ Dreamweaver comes with several predefined window settings that mimic what a user sees at different monitor settings. To choose a setting, click the Dimensions menu on the status bar.

How do I keep my background images from taking up a lot of file space?

✔ Keeping your background image file sizes small is important if you want your pages to download quickly. For GIF backgrounds, try to keep the number of colors in the image to a minimum. For JPEG images, try to increase the amount of compression applied when you save your images.

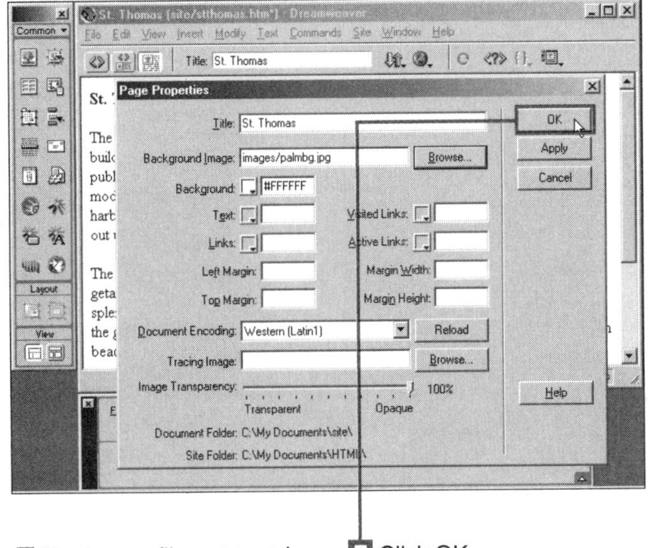

■ The image filename and path appear in the Background Image field.

7 Click OK.

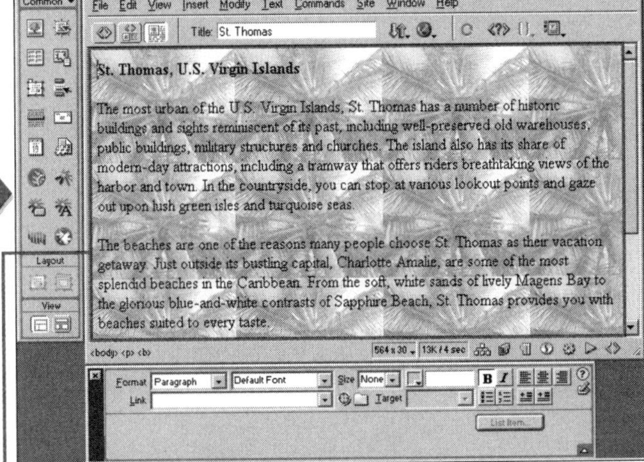

■ The image appears as a background on your Web page. If necessary, it repeats horizontally and vertically to fill the entire window.

CHANGE THE BACKGROUND COLOR

You can give your page a visually striking appearance by changing the background color. A background color also enables you to make your pages more consistent with your company's or organization's identity.

White is the default background color for Web pages created in Dreamweaver. You can choose a different color from a palette of Web-safe colors accessible from the Page Properties dialog box (*Web-safe* means that the colors display accurately on different platforms and monitor settings). You can also specify a background color by name ("red" or "green") or with a hex code definition.

Setting a background color has advantages over adding a background image (see "Add a Background Image"). For example, defining a color uses up practically zero file space whereas adding an image adds that image's file size to your page.

If you set both a background image and background color for your page, the image takes precedence.

CHANGE THE BACKGROUND COLOR

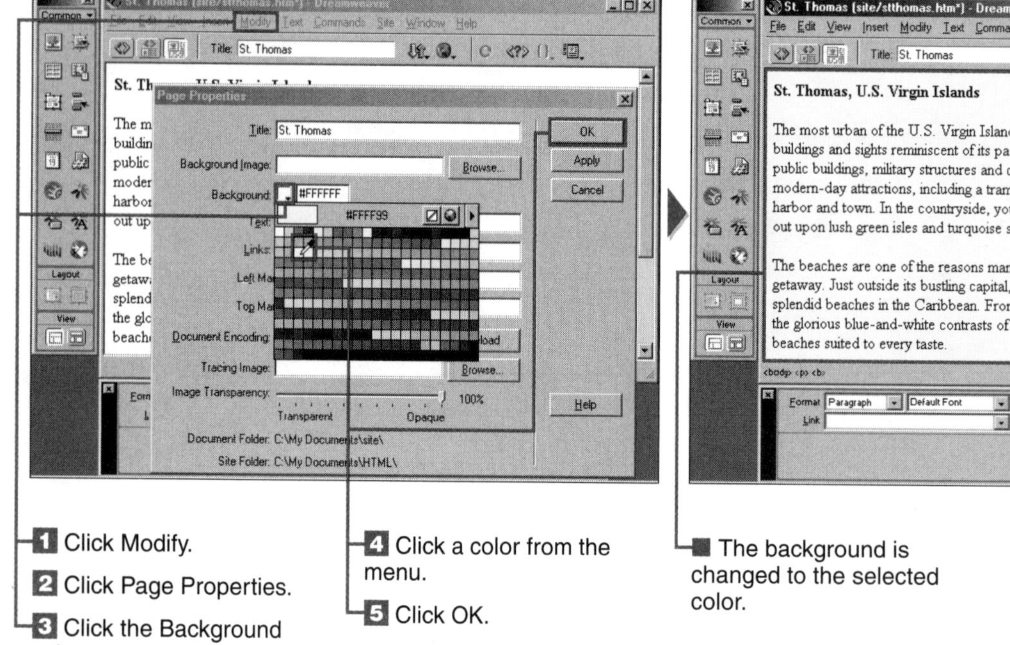

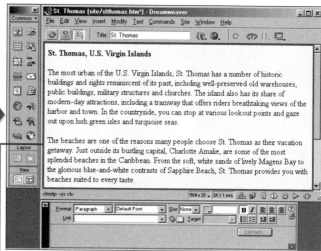

1 Click Modify.

2 Click Page Properties.

3 Click the Background color menu.

4 Click a color from the menu.

5 Click OK.

■ The background is changed to the selected color.

ADD ALTERNATE TEXT

You can add alternate, or alt, text that will display in the place of images for viewers using text-based or non-visual browsers. Alt text is also displayed in the place of images when a page is viewed with images turned off.

For photographs or illustrations, you usually want the alt information to describe the image being displayed ("Adorable kitten with ball of string"). For button graphics, you usually want the alt text to be the same as the label that is on the button ("Home" or "Contact Us").

Some newer browsers such as Internet Explorer 5 display the alt text temporarily when you roll your cursor over an image on a Web page.

Alt text is optional — your Web pages still load normally if you do not add it to your Web images.

Some search engine spiders index the alt text of Web pages. Adding important key words to your alt information could potentially help your pages score higher in search results.

ADD ALTERNATE TEXT

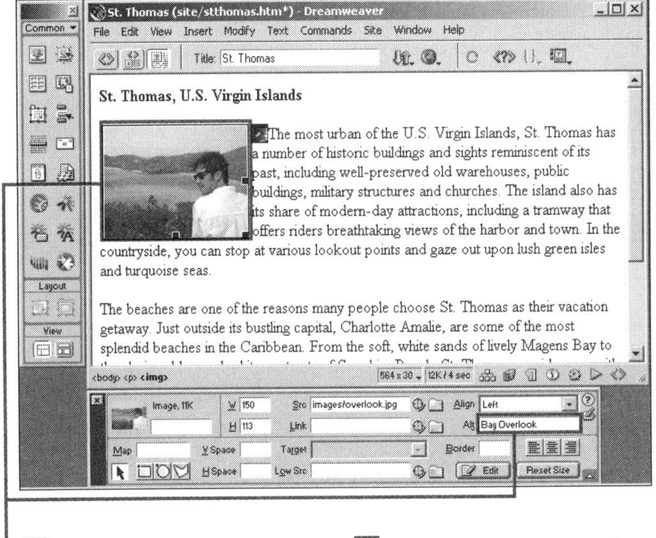

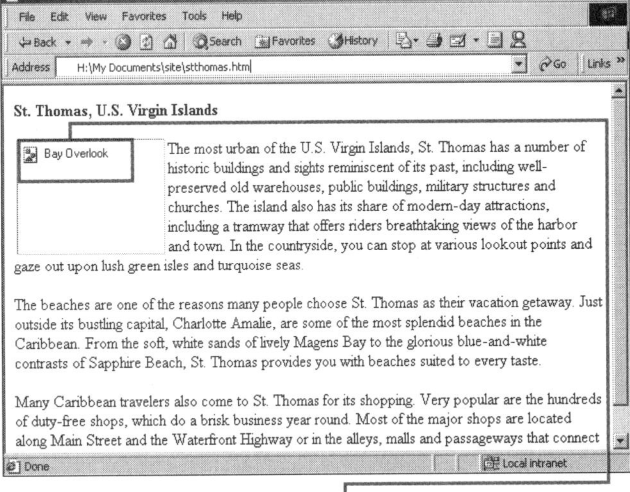

1 Click an image.

2 Type the desired alternate text in the Alt field.

3 Press Enter (Windows) or Return (Mac).

4 Preview your page in a Web browser.

Note: See Chapter 4 for details on previewing pages in your browser.

■ The alternate text displays when image loading is turned off in the browser.

INSERT MULTIMEDIA

Inserting video clips and other multimedia can jazz up your Web page. You can embed video clips into your page just like images. You can also add interactive controls that enable users to play sound. To integrate Flash into your Web pages, see Part III.

Until recently, there have been lots of reasons *not* to integrate multimedia into your pages. For one, users had to download and install extra *plug-in software* to be able to view it. Additionally, users with modems rarely had the patience to download the large files involved — a 10-second video can easily take more than two minutes to download over a 56 Kbps modem.

Today, most browsers come with plug-ins already installed for viewing common multimedia standards, such as QuickTime, MPEG, MP3, Flash, and Shockwave. The rise of cable modems and DSL has also made Web-based multimedia more accessible for the average user.

INSERT MULTIMEDIA

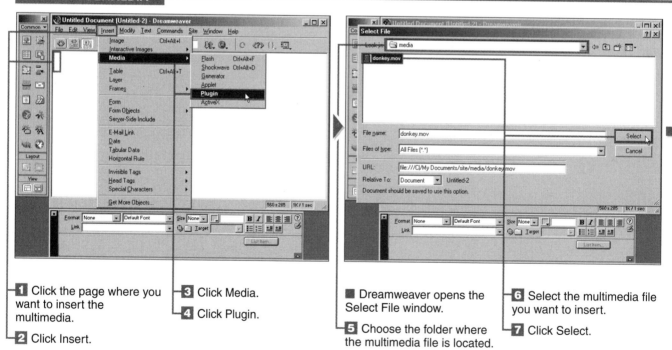

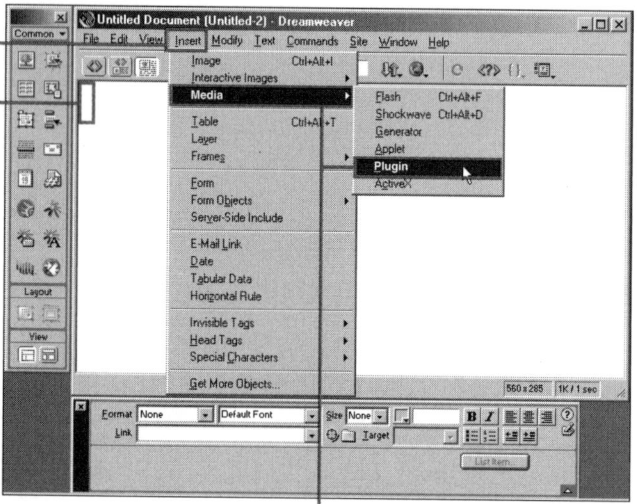

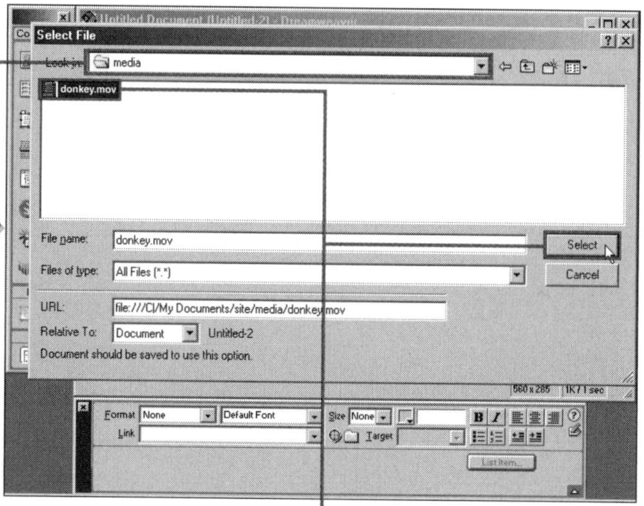

1 Click the page where you want to insert the multimedia.

2 Click Insert.

3 Click Media.

4 Click Plugin.

■ Dreamweaver opens the Select File window.

5 Choose the folder where the multimedia file is located.

6 Select the multimedia file you want to insert.

7 Click Select.

How do I insert a sound file?

✔ You can add sounds to your page the same way you add video clips. Just select a sound file instead of a video file in the Select File dialog box (see step 6 below). Common sound file formats include MP3, WAV, and AIFF.

How do I give users a choice of downloading a large multimedia file?

✔ Instead of embedding the multimedia in a page, you can create a text hyperlink to the multimedia file. The text can describe the file and the file size. If users want to view the multimedia, they can click the link. See Chapter 7 for more information on links.

How do I customize the multimedia on my page?

✔ Dreamweaver offers some customization — for example, the dimensions of the embedded media — through the Property Inspector. You can add advanced features for a particular media by clicking the Parameters button and adding parameters and values. For example, you can add an "autoplay" parameter (with a "true" or "false" value) to a QuickTime movie to specify whether the movie plays automatically after it loads.

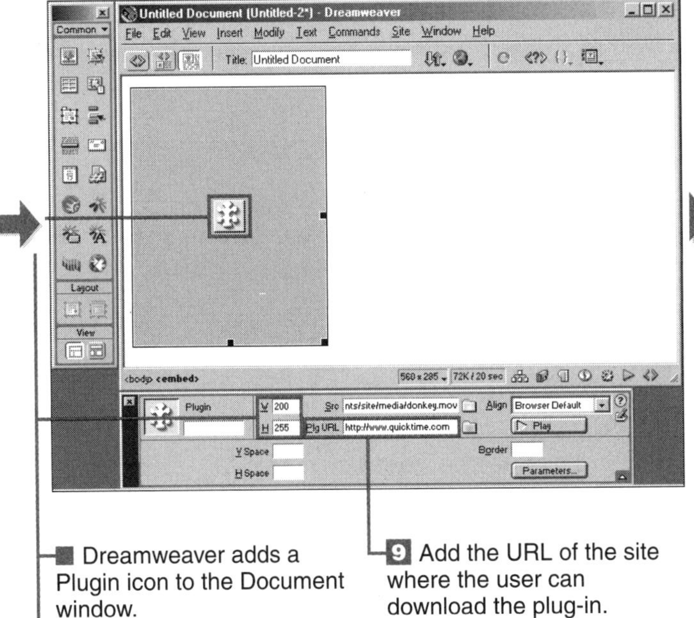

■ Dreamweaver adds a Plugin icon to the Document window.

8 Type the dimensions of the file (in pixels).

9 Add the URL of the site where the user can download the plug-in.

■ If the plug-in is not installed on a user's browser, the browser asks if the user wants to visit the site to download it.

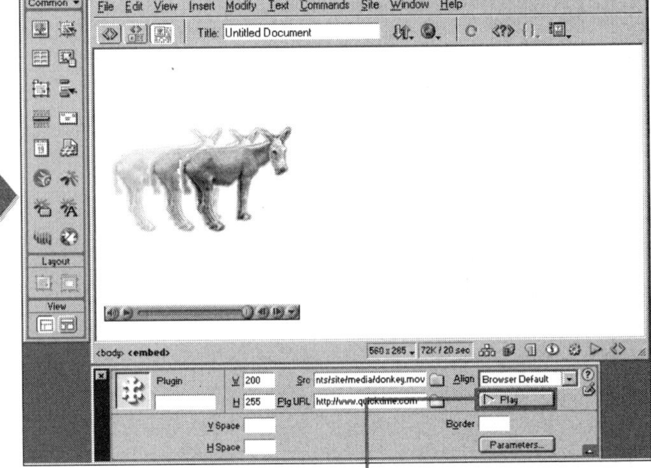

■ Some multimedia files, such as QuickTime movies, can be tested directly in the Dreamweaver Document window.

10 Click Play to test a multimedia file.

CREATING HYPERLINKS

Hyperlinks (also simply called links) are the clickable elements on a Web page that transfer a user to another Web page or file. Creating a link in Dreamweaver is as easy as selecting a piece of text or an image on your Web page and then specifying a destination page or other file.

Text links are distinguished on a Web page by underlining and color. Image hyperlinks can be outlined with color by turning on the image's Border property. Most browsers also change the appearance of the cursor when it is placed over a link.

Hyperlink Code

In HTML, hyperlinks are created with an <A> tag combined with an HREF attribute, which tells a browser where the link should lead. To view a link's HTML in Dreamweaver, you can select the link in the Document window and then open the Code Inspector. Here is an example of HTML code that turns the text "My page" into a link:

```
<A HREF="mypage.html">My page</A>
```

What the HREF value looks like can vary, depending on the type of addressing used. The three types of addressing, each of which you can use in Dreamweaver, are relative addressing, root-relative addressing, and absolute addressing.

Relative Addressing

Relative addressing defines the destination page relative to the page that contains the link. This type of addressing leaves off the Web server information in the HTML, since it is assumed that both files are on the same Web server. In HTML, relative addressing looks like this:

```
HREF="folder/file.htm"
```

Relative links allow a Web site to be portable. You can move a site from one server to another and not have relative links break, since their references are independent of the actual server where files are hosted.

Root-Relative Addressing

Root-relative addressing defines a destination page relative to the Web server's root folder. This root folder is represented by a leading "/" in the address path. Similar to relative addressing, root-relative addressing leaves off the Web server information, since it is assumed that both files are on the same Web server. In HTML, root-relative addressing looks like this:

```
HREF="/folder/file.htm"
```

Root-relative links allow individual files within a Web site to be portable. You can move a file that contains root-relative addressing to another folder in a site and root-relative links will not break. This is because the root folder does not change.

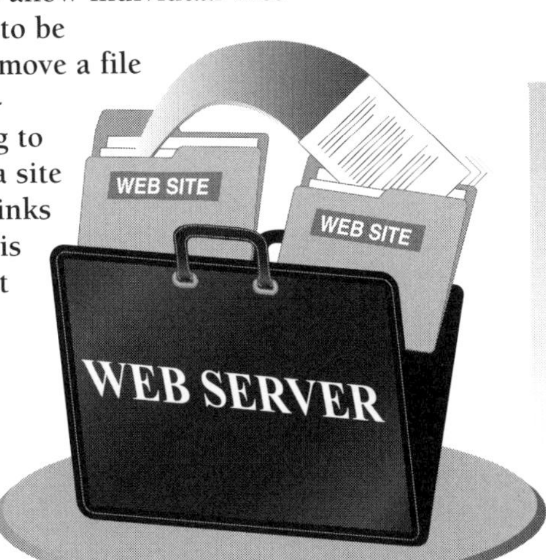

Absolute Addressing

Links can also be defined absolutely, which means a complete URL is used to define the destination page or file. In HTML, absolute addressing looks like this:

```
HREF="http://www.webserver.com/
folder/file.htm"
```

Absolute links are necessary when you are linking to content on other Web sites, because these pages exist on different Web servers.

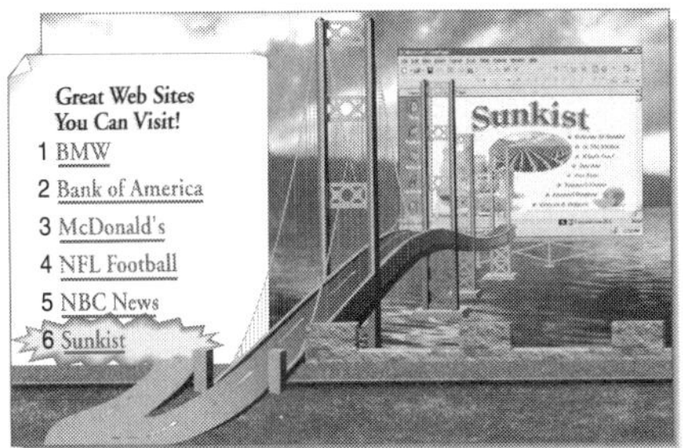

Frame Links

Creating links in a framed Web site is slightly more complicated than creating regular links. This is because for links in a framed site, you need to define not just the destination file but also into which frame you want that file to open. You can make a link open content in a particular frame by specifying the frame's name as a *target* for the link. See Chapter 10 for more information.

HYPERLINK TO ANOTHER PAGE IN YOUR SITE

You can create clickable *hyperlinks* (also simply called *links*) on your site's Web pages that lead to related information on other pages on your site. Well-placed links within your site can help users find the information they need quickly. You create links by selecting text or an image in the Document window and then selecting a destination page from your local site folder.

For navigation purposes, you can insert a set of links that lead to the main areas of your site in the same place on every page. It is common practice to place such navigation links along the side or at the bottom of your pages.

Most of the time when you create links to other pages on your Web site, you will want to use relative addressing (see the chapter introduction for more information on different types of addressing). You can specify the type of addressing that Dreamweaver uses for a link in the Select File dialog box that appears when you define the link's destination page.

HYPERLINK TO ANOTHER PAGE IN YOUR SITE

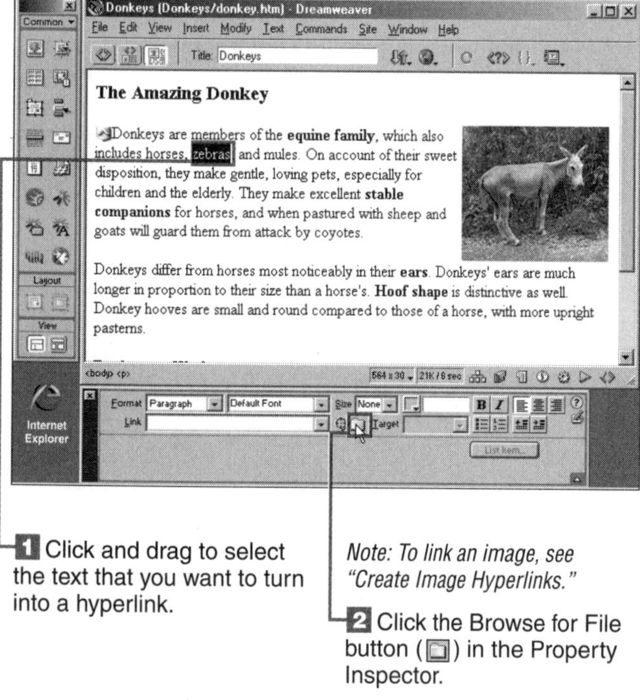

1 Click and drag to select the text that you want to turn into a hyperlink.

Note: To link an image, see "Create Image Hyperlinks."

2 Click the Browse for File button (▢) in the Property Inspector.

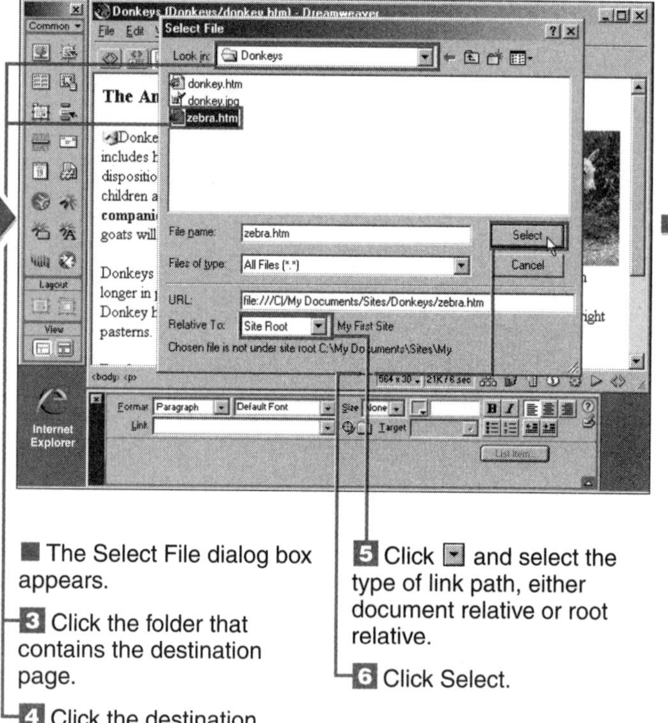

■ The Select File dialog box appears.

3 Click the folder that contains the destination page.

4 Click the destination page's HTML file.

5 Click ▾ and select the type of link path, either document relative or root relative.

6 Click Select.

If I rename a page in my site, what happens to hyperlinks that point to that page?

✔ Normally the links will break. If you rename the page using the Site window (see Chapter 15 for more information), however, Dreamweaver checks if there are links to that page and, if there are, gives you the opportunity to automatically update them.

How do I distinguish a row of text hyperlinks?

✔ It is a common convention to distinguish a row of hyperlinks with pipe symbols ("|") and brackets. This makes text links look more like buttons:

[Home | Products | Feedback]

(You can find the pipe symbol below the Backspace key on your keyboard.)

How do I organize hyperlinks down the left side of my Web page?

✔ This is a common way to organize a site's navigation. Create a two-column table that fills the entire page (see Chapter 8) with the left column narrower than the right. Then organize the hyperlinks as a list in the left column. If you are going to use the same navigation links on every page, it is a good idea to make the list a library item (see Chapter 11).

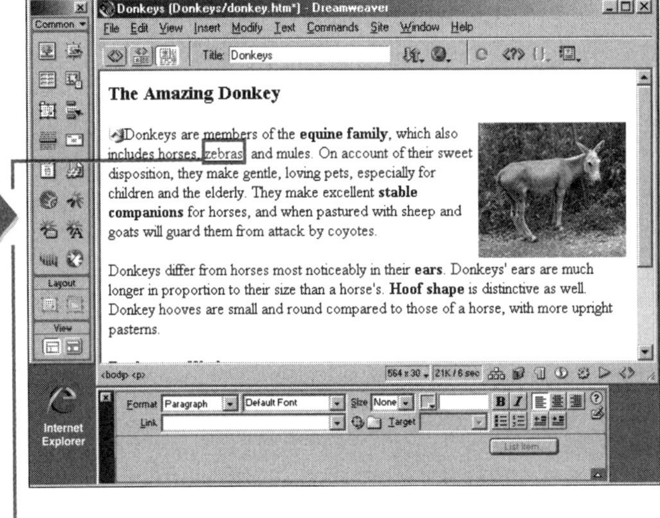

■ The new hyperlink appears colored and underlined.

Note: Hyperlinks are not clickable in the Document window. See Chapter 4 to learn how to test the link by previewing the page in a Web browser.

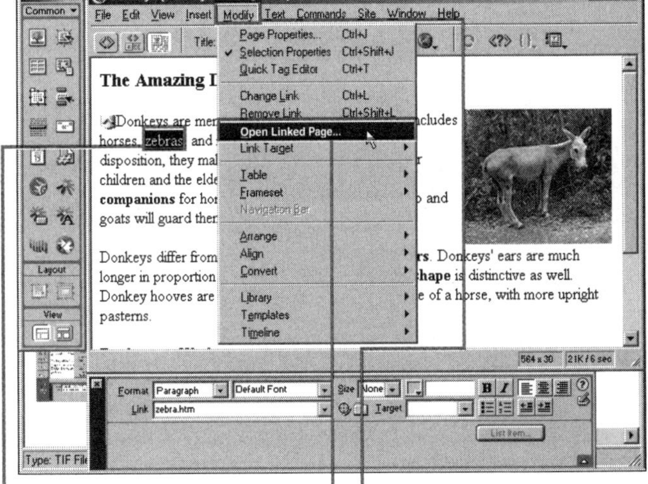

OPEN THE LINKED PAGE

1 Click and drag to select the text of the hyperlink whose destination you want to open.

2 Click Modify.

3 Click Open Linked Page.

■ The link destination opens in a Document window.

HYPERLINK TO ANOTHER WEB SITE

You can create clickable hyperlinks (also simply called *links*) from your site's pages to external pages elsewhere on the Web. You create such links by selecting text or an image in the Document window and then specifying the destination page's complete Web address (also known as a *Uniform Resource Locator*, or URL).

Links that reference a page using a complete Web address are known as absolute links, because those links contain all the information needed to locate the page from anywhere on the Internet. For more information on absolute links, see the chapter introduction.

You can link to any other page on the Web as long as you know its address. You can get an external Web page's address by opening the page in your Web browser and copying the text that appears in the browser's address field. While no one can stop a person from linking to a Web page, access to a page can be blocked by adding password protection. Password protecting pages is usually performed on the Web server; you can not add it using Dreamweaver.

As a service to their visitors, many Web developers include a list of links to sites that contain information similar to what is on their sites. These lists are simply collections of external links.

HYPERLINK TO ANOTHER WEB SITE

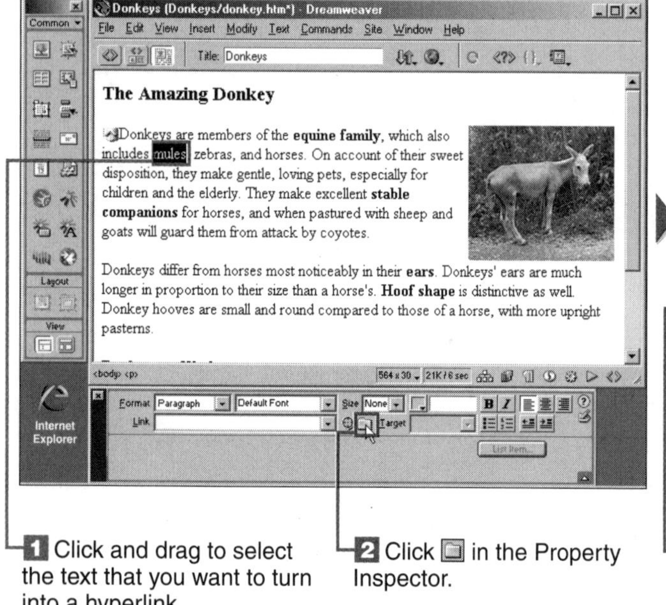

1 Click and drag to select the text that you want to turn into a hyperlink.

2 Click ▢ in the Property Inspector.

3 Type the Web address (URL) of the destination page (include the **http://**).

■ You can also visit the site in your Web browser and copy and paste the URL from the browser's address bar.

4 Click Select.

What happens when an external page is deleted or renamed?

✔ If you have linked to the page, that link breaks. This means a user clicking the link receives an error specifying that the page could not be found. This is one of the challenges of including external links on your site. Ultimately, you do not have control over whether they work. This makes testing your site's external links on a regular basis important.

How can I automatically test the external links in my site?

✔ Dreamweaver can not test external links in your site (it can only check links to pages within your site; see "Check Hyperlinks"), but other programs can test them. For a list of link checkers, see www.mediacosm.com/dreamweaver.

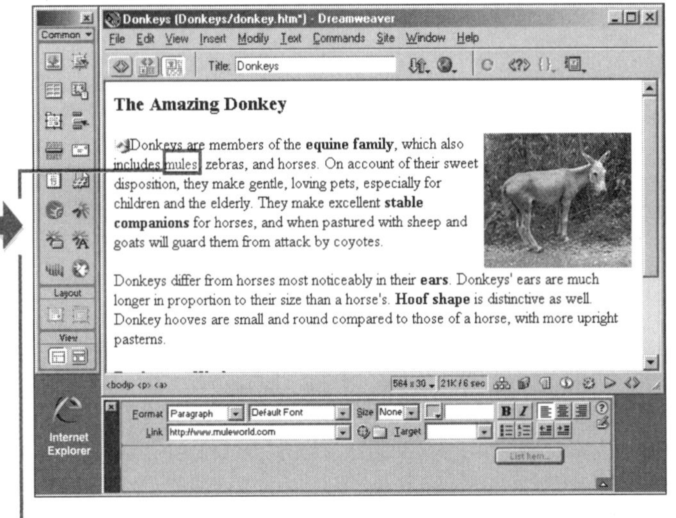

■ The new hyperlink appears colored and underlined.

Note: Hyperlinks are not clickable in the Document window. See Chapter 4 to learn how to test the link by previewing the page in a Web browser.

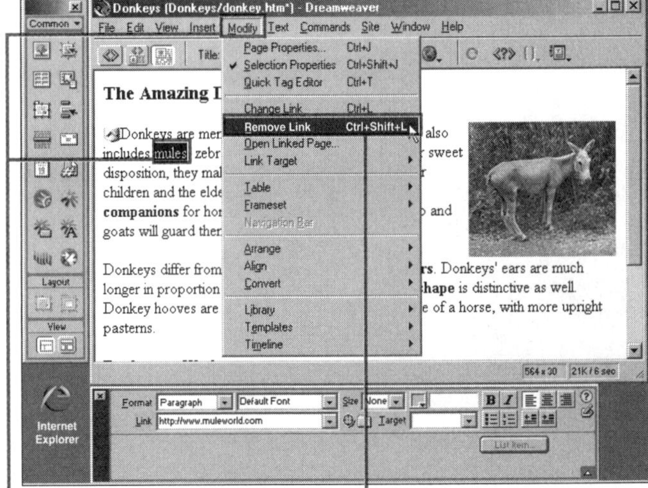

REMOVE AN EXTERNAL HYPERLINK

1 Click and drag to select the text of the hyperlink that you want to remove.

2 Click Modify.

3 Click Remove Link.

■ Dreamweaver removes the link.

■ These steps also work for links to pages within the site.

CREATE IMAGE HYPERLINKS

You can create image hyperlinks that lead to other pages when the user clicks them. You create such links by selecting an image in the Document window and then selecting the destination page from your local site folder.

If you pass your cursor over a hyperlinked image in a Web browser, the cursor changes shape. This is one way that hyperlinked images are distinguished from regular images on a Web page.

The stylized navigation buttons you see on many Web pages are usually image files that have been hyperlinked to other pages on the site. You can build such buttons in an image editor such as Adobe Photoshop or Macromedia Fireworks, and then insert them into your page and define them as hyperlinks.

Image hyperlinks can be useful when you want to display very large images on your site. You can make small versions of your image files (called *thumbnails*), which download quickly and give viewers a hint of what the image consists of. You can then hyperlink those thumbnails to the large versions of the image files.

CREATE IMAGE HYPERLINKS

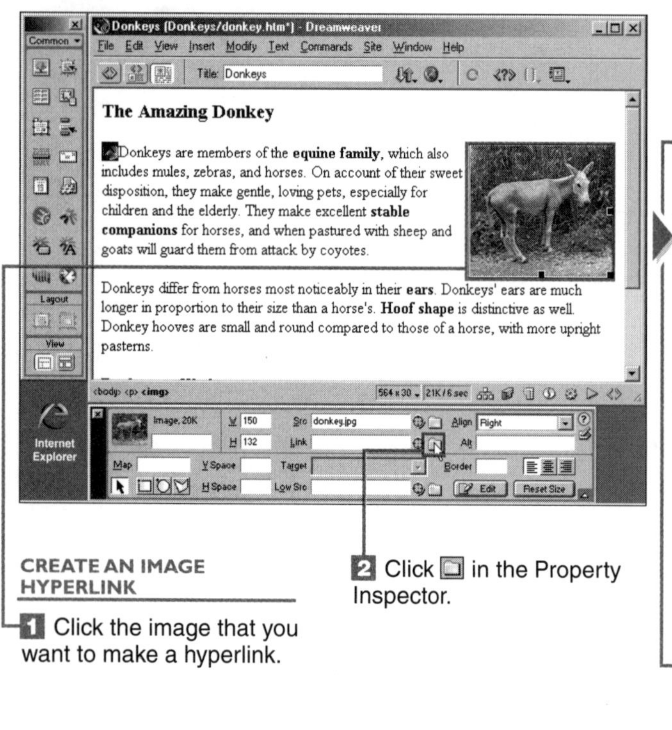

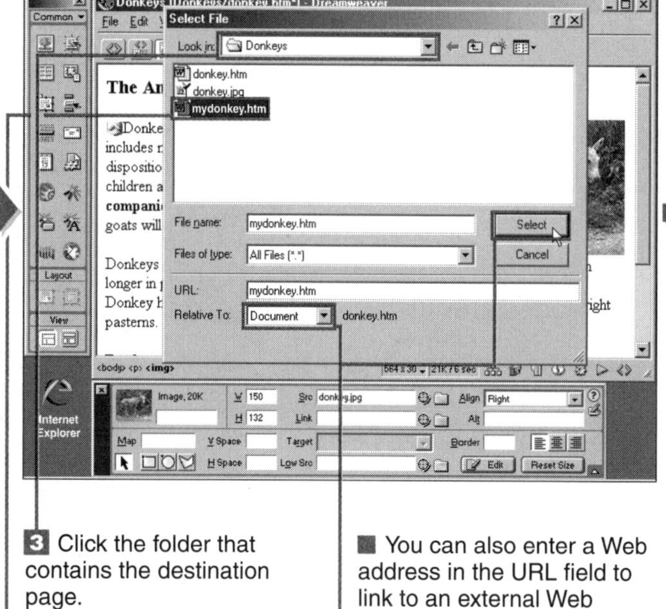

CREATE AN IMAGE HYPERLINK

1 Click the image that you want to make a hyperlink.

2 Click ▢ in the Property Inspector.

3 Click the folder that contains the destination page.

4 From the list menu, click the HTML file to which you want to link.

■ You can also enter a Web address in the URL field to link to an external Web page.

5 Click ▾ and select the type of link path, either document relative or root relative.

6 Click Select.

How do I add a colored border to my hyperlinked images?

✔ When you create an image hyperlink, Dreamweaver automatically sets the image border to 0, so the border is turned off. To make a border appear, set the Border field in the Property Inspector to a positive number, which defines the width of the border in pixels. The color of the border is the same as the text hyperlinks on the page. Turning on borders for hyperlinked images is a useful way to indicate that the images are clickable.

How can I obtain navigational buttons and other images that I can use on my Web pages?

✔ You can make them from scratch in an image editor such as Macromedia Fireworks (see the CD-ROM) or Adobe Photoshop, get them out of clip-art collections that you can purchase at a computer store or online, or download public-domain art from one of the many Web sites that offer it. For a list of some good free-image resources on the Web, visit www.mediacosm.com/dreamweaver.

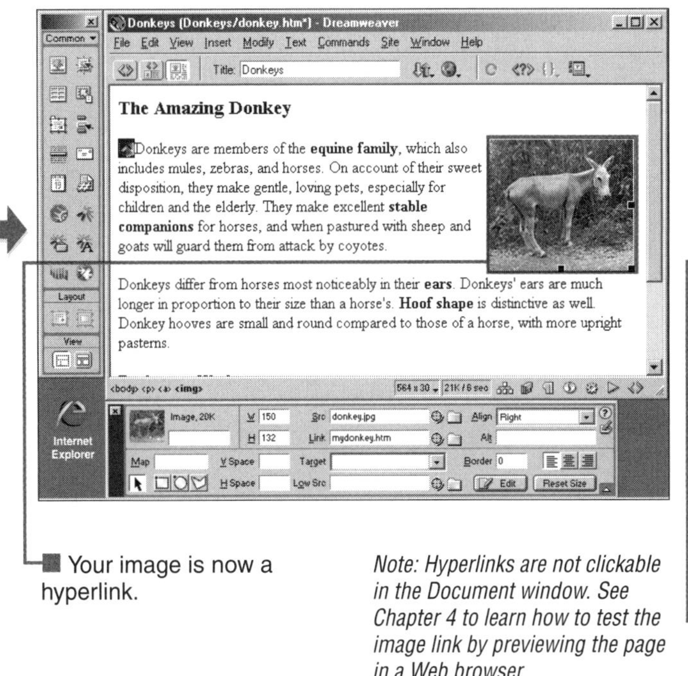

■ Your image is now a hyperlink.

Note: Hyperlinks are not clickable in the Document window. See Chapter 4 to learn how to test the image link by previewing the page in a Web browser.

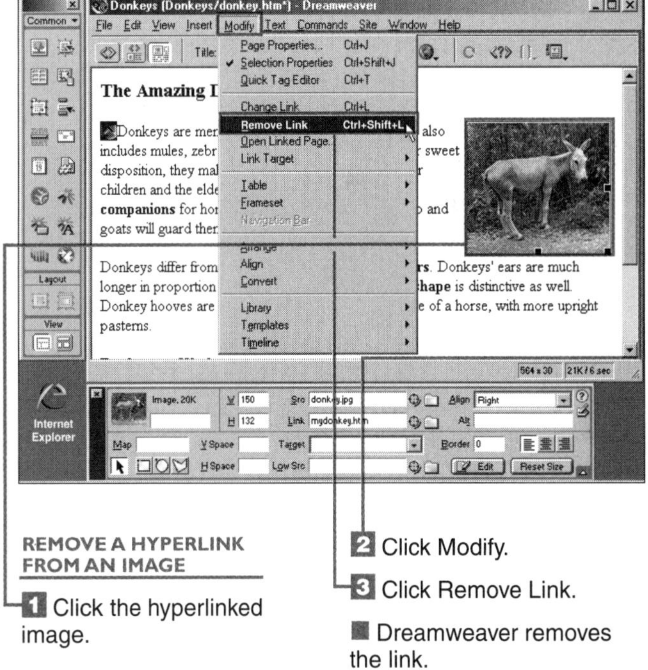

REMOVE A HYPERLINK FROM AN IMAGE

1 Click the hyperlinked image.

2 Click Modify.

3 Click Remove Link.

■ Dreamweaver removes the link.

HYPERLINK TO INFORMATION ON THE SAME PAGE

You can create a clickable hyperlink on a Web page that leads to information on the same page. This type of link can be useful for pages that are extremely long. It saves viewers from having to scroll to find the information in which they are interested.

Creating a same-page link is a two-step process. First, you create a *named anchor* at the place on the page that will be linked to (the link destination). Then you create a hyperlink that references that anchor. An anchor hyperlink is distinguished from a regular hyperlink in HTML by a # sign preceding the name of the anchor, for example `#myanchor`.

Many times when you create a long page with many anchor links, you will want to also create links that send a user back to the top of the page. You can do this by creating an anchor at the very top of the page and referencing it with your links.

HYPERLINK TO INFORMATION ON THE SAME PAGE

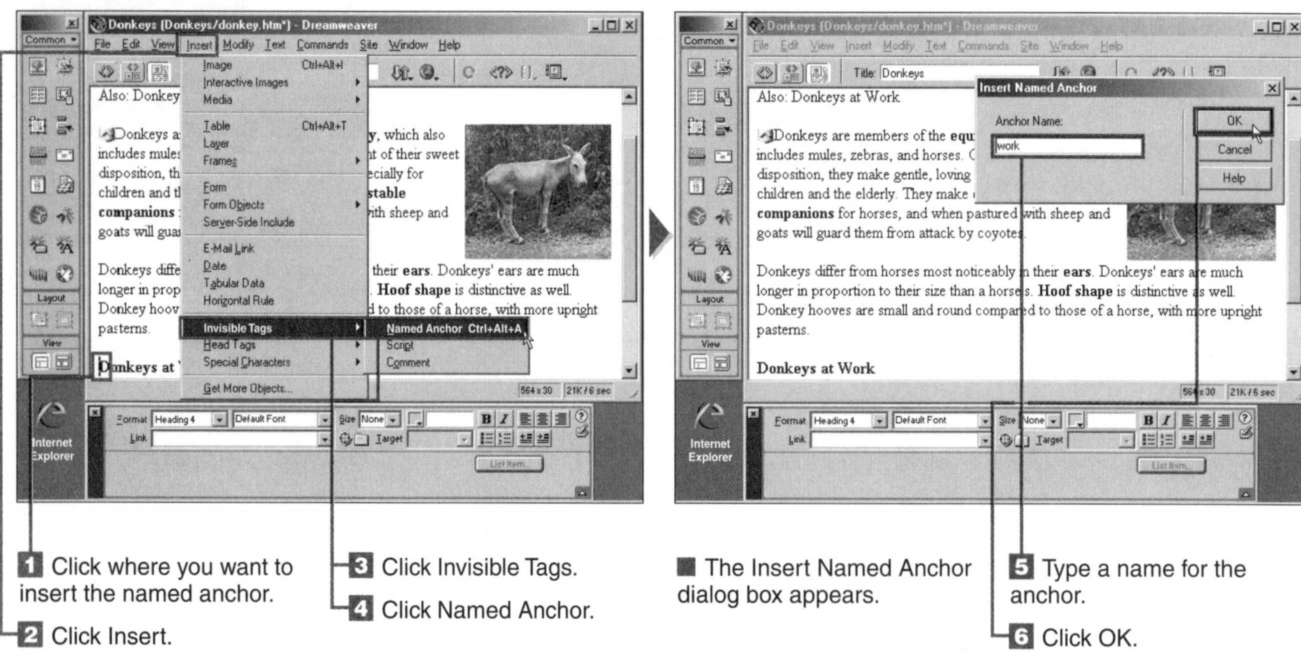

1 Click where you want to insert the named anchor.

2 Click Insert.

3 Click Invisible Tags.

4 Click Named Anchor.

■ The Insert Named Anchor dialog box appears.

5 Type a name for the anchor.

6 Click OK.

How can I use named anchors to make navigating a long page easier?

✔ At the top, you can create a table of contents for the page that consists of named anchor links. The links can take the user to the different sections of the page further down. This can be a good strategy for creating navigation for glossary pages, where named anchor links can take the user to different sections of the alphabet.

How do I link to an anchor using the ⊕?

✔ Select the text or image that you want to be the link. Then click and drag the ⊕, located in the Properties inspector, to the anchor icon in the Document window. (You may have to turn on anchor viewing by selecting Invisible Elements under the View menu.)

Can I link to an anchor that is defined in *another* page?

✔ Yes. First link to the page as you normally would. Then, in the Link field in the Property Inspector, type a # sign and the named anchor after the link code:

```
folder/page.html#anchorname
```

When the link is clicked in a browser, the destination page will open and then scroll to the position of the anchor.

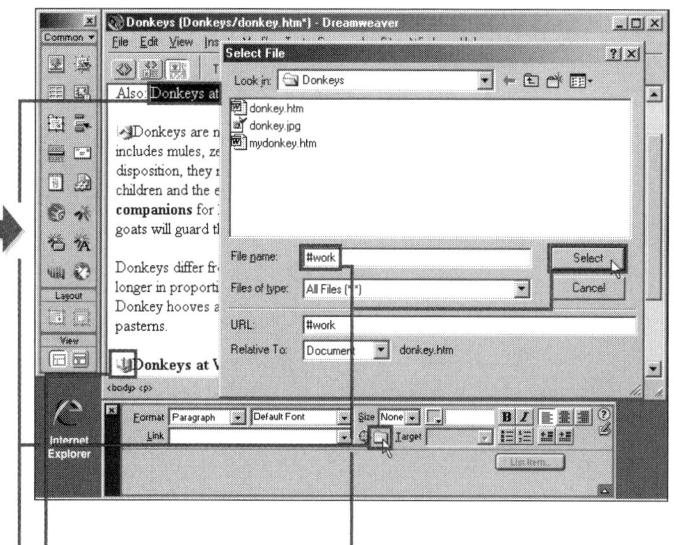

■ An anchor icon (⚓) appears in the Document window.

7 Click and drag to select the text that you want to turn into the hyperlink.

8 Click ▭ in the Property Inspector.

■ The Select File dialog box appears.

9 Type a pound sign (#) followed by the name of the anchor from step 5.

10 Click Select.

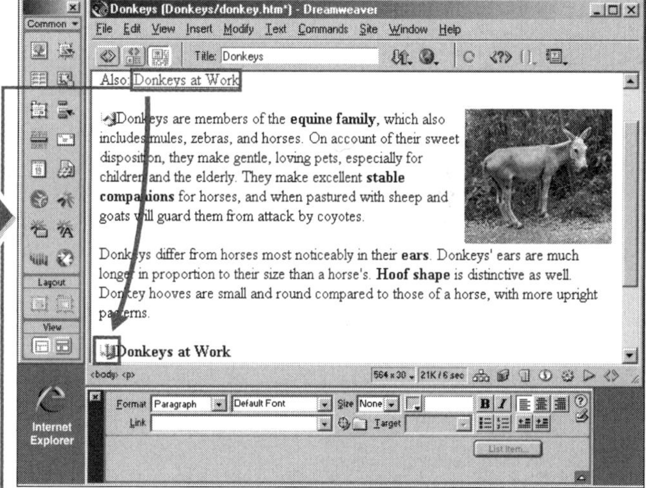

■ The new hyperlink is linked to the named anchor.

Note: The new hyperlink is not clickable in the Document window. See Chapter 4 to learn how to test the link by previewing the page in a Web browser.

HYPERLINK TO OTHER FILES

You can create clickable hyperlinks from your site's Web pages to non-HTML documents. You create such links by selecting text or an image in the Document window and then defining the destination file's location in the local site folder or its external address on the Web. You can link to any other type of file, including word-processing documents, PDF files, multimedia files, and image files.

What you need to remember about non-HTML documents is that users who click the links need to have the software necessary to view the files installed on their computers. Image files are usually not a problem, because practically all Web browsers can interpret JPEG and GIF files (the most common image files on the Web), and some can even read other image formats such as TIFF and PNG. Multimedia files, such as Flash and QuickTime movies, require that a user has add-on features known as plug-ins installed in their browsers. Other types of files — such as Microsoft Word documents — require that specific standalone applications are installed.

HYPERLINK TO OTHER FILES

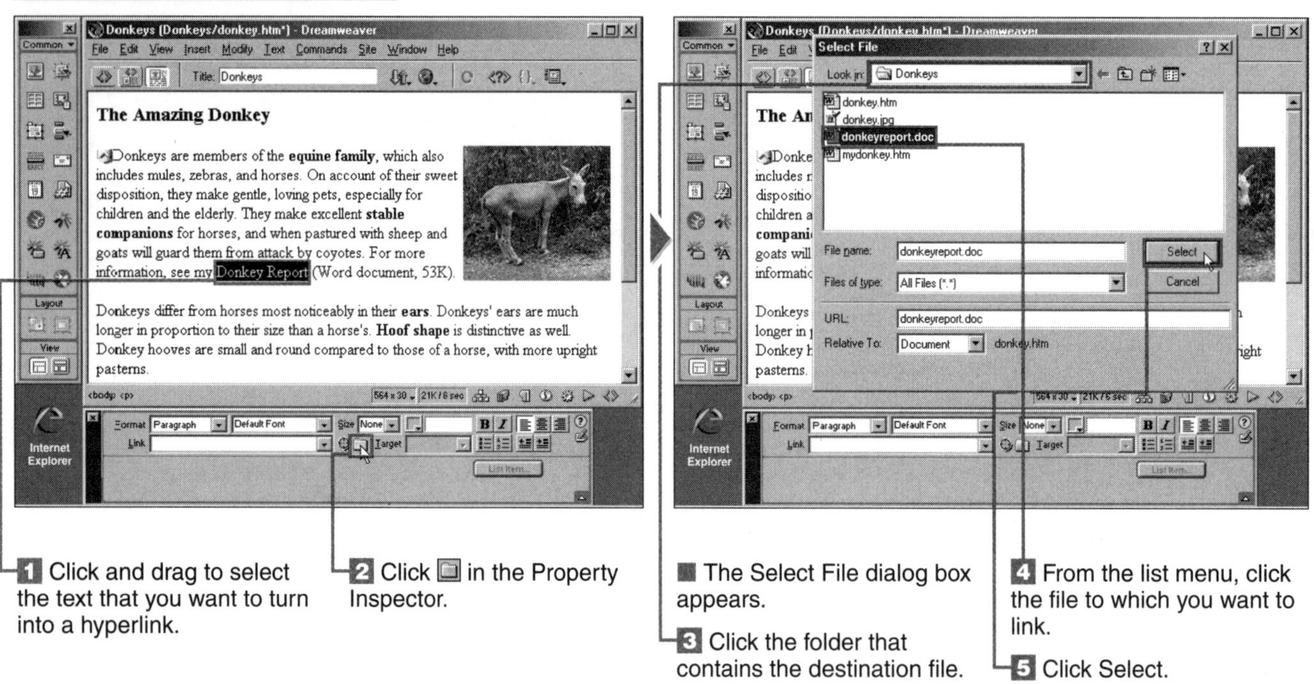

1 Click and drag to select the text that you want to turn into a hyperlink.

2 Click 🗀 in the Property Inspector.

■ The Select File dialog box appears.

3 Click the folder that contains the destination file.

4 From the list menu, click the file to which you want to link.

5 Click Select.

What happens if a user does not have the required software to view a hyperlinked file?

✔ Usually, the browser presents the user with several options, including saving the file to the computer (so the user can view the file later when the required software has been installed), visiting a Web site where the user can download the required software, or canceling the download altogether.

How can I ensure that my viewers are able to view the non-HTML files that I link to my site?

✔ Try to present content in file formats that are popular. This way, there is a good chance that viewers have the necessary software installed. For example, if you want to provide users with text in a page-layout form that they can print, it is probably a good idea to present it as a PDF file or as a Microsoft Word document. If you want to make your content *really* accessible, provide it in several different formats (for example, in both PDF *and* Word form). Then the user can click the link that is best for them.

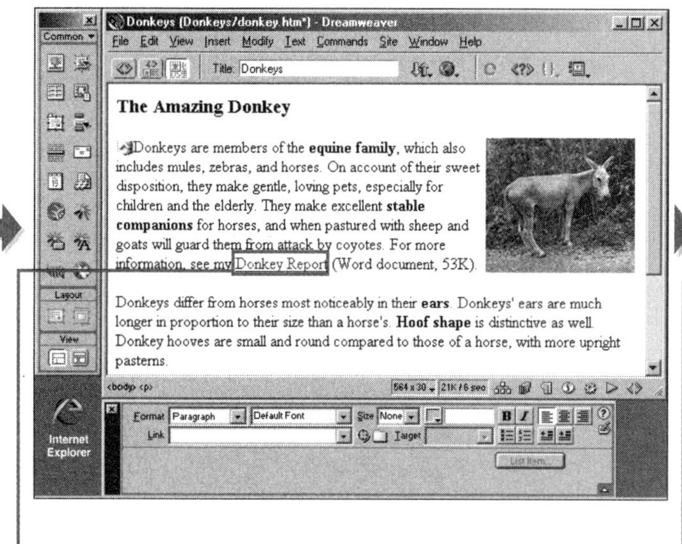

■ The new hyperlink appears colored and underlined.

Note: Hyperlinks are not clickable in the Document window. See Chapter 4 to learn how to test the link by previewing the page in a Web browser.

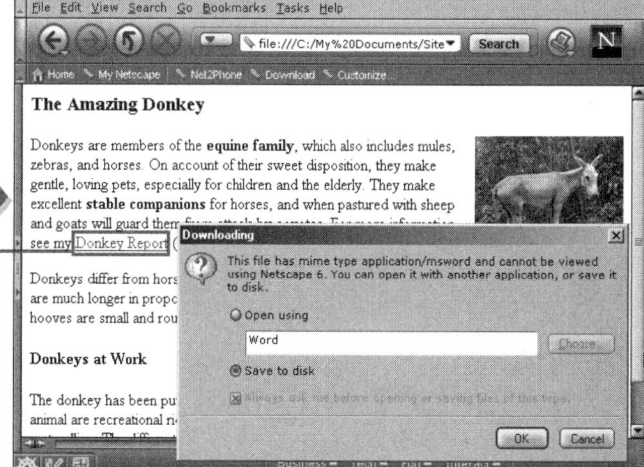

6 Click File, Preview in Browser, and then a browser to preview your page.

7 Click the link to test it.

Note: If a user clicks a link that points to a type of file that a browser cannot display, the browser will usually ask whether the user wants to open the file with another application or save it.

CREATE MULTIPLE HYPERLINKS WITHIN AN IMAGE

You can assign different hyperlinks to different parts of an image using Dreamweaver's image-mapping tools. This enables you to make a large image on your home page serve as a navigational jumping-off point for the rest of your Web site. You can also take a complicated image (such as a geography map) and link different parts of the image to different pages describing each part.

On an HTML level, mapping hyperlinks to specific areas of an image can be complicated. First you have to determine the mathematical coordinates that define the different areas (also called *hotspots*) in the image, and then you have to integrate those coordinates into the HTML.

Dreamweaver makes the process easy. First you click and drag with different shape-making tools to define the different hotspots on your image. Dreamweaver then determines the coordinates for those hotspots for you and writes them into the HTML.

One drawback to creating image maps is that viewers who do not have image-viewing capability will not be able to access the different hyperlinks (unless those hyperlinks are also defined elsewhere on the page).

CREATE MULTIPLE HYPERLINKS WITHIN AN IMAGE

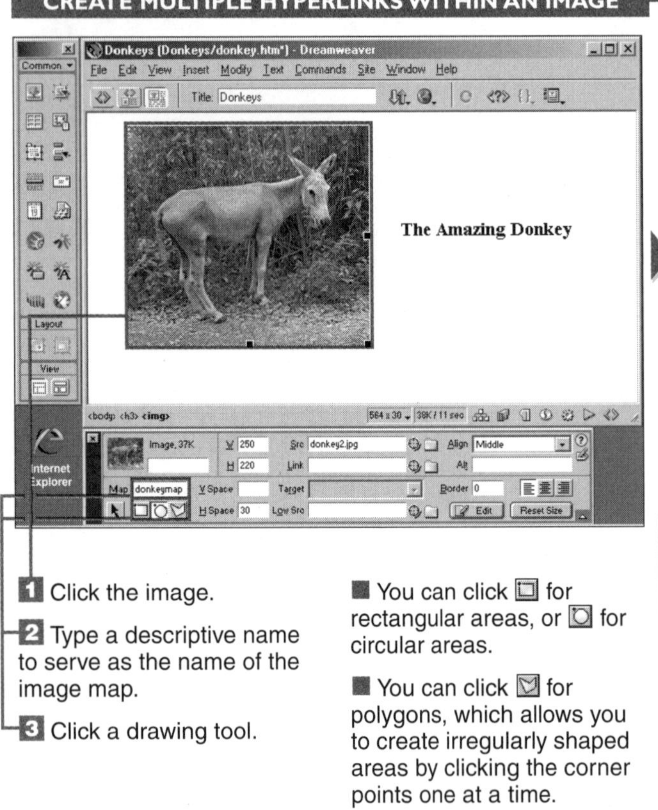

1 Click the image.

2 Type a descriptive name to serve as the name of the image map.

3 Click a drawing tool.

■ You can click for rectangular areas, or for circular areas.

■ You can click for polygons, which allows you to create irregularly shaped areas by clicking the corner points one at a time.

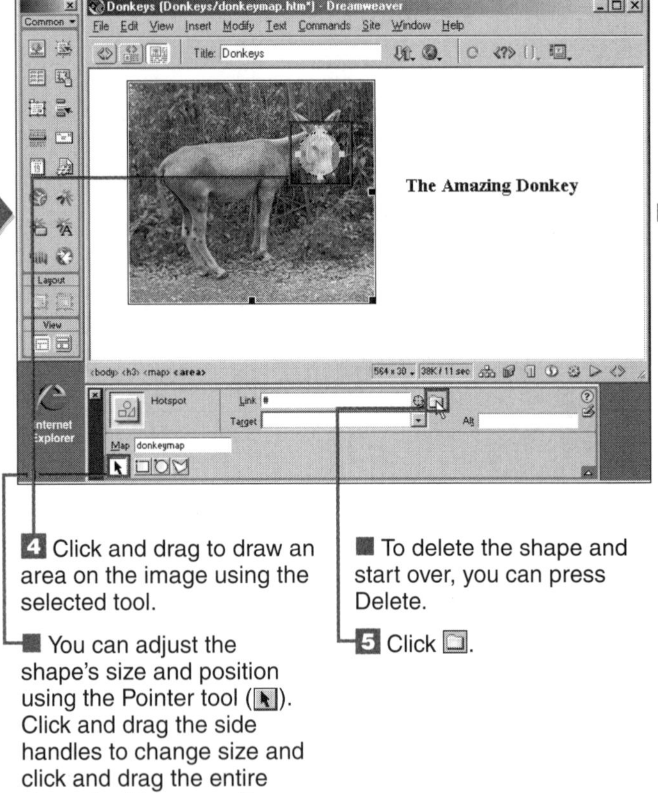

4 Click and drag to draw an area on the image using the selected tool.

■ You can adjust the shape's size and position using the Pointer tool. Click and drag the side handles to change size and click and drag the entire shape to change position.

■ To delete the shape and start over, you can press Delete.

5 Click .

How can I create an interactive map of the United States with each state having a different hyperlink?

✔ Add a map of the U.S. to your Web page and define a hotspot over each state. (You will probably want to use the polygon tool to draw around the states.) Then assign a different hyperlink to each state.

How can I create an image map and still accommodate viewers who can not view images?

✔ Duplicate the links defined in your image map as text hyperlinks elsewhere on the page. For example, if you created an interactive map of the U.S., you can also repeat the text hyperlinks for the states below the map image.

Where is the information about an image map stored?

✔ Dreamweaver stores the information about image maps inside a <MAP> tag in the page's HTML. This type of image map is known as a client-side image map, because the coordinate information is read and interpreted by the browser (also known as the client).

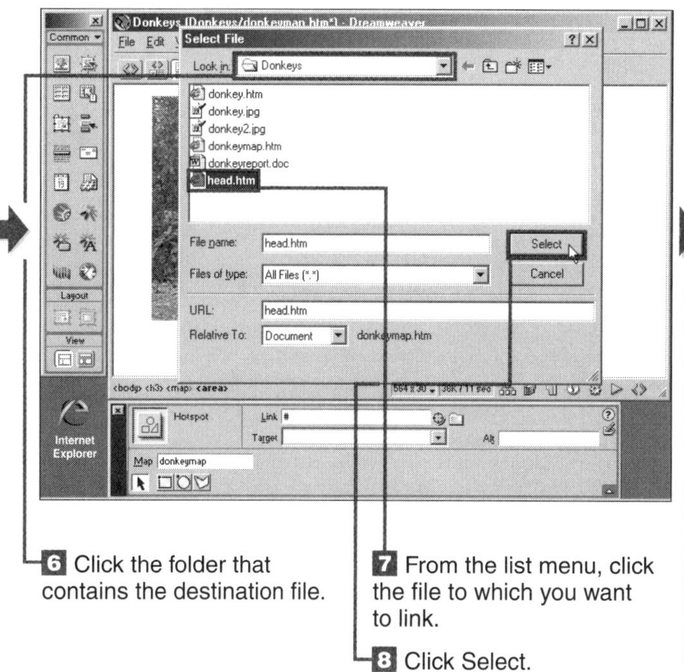

6 Click the folder that contains the destination file.

7 From the list menu, click the file to which you want to link.

8 Click Select.

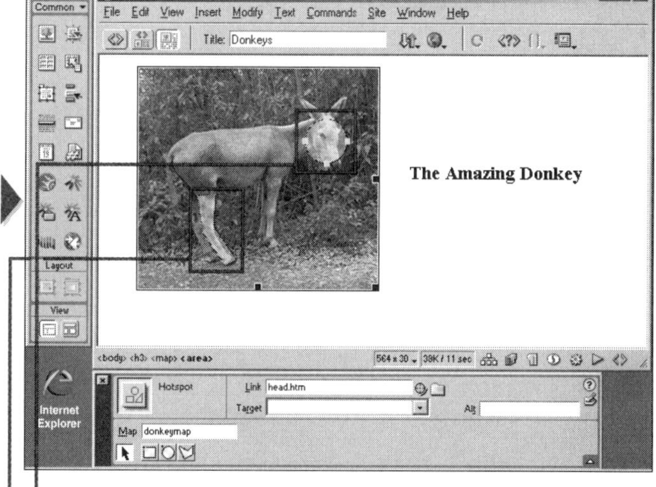

■ The area defined by the shape becomes a hyperlink to the selected file.

■ You can repeat steps 3 through 8 to add other linked areas to your image.

Note: The image-map shapes do not appear when you open the page in a Web browser. See Chapter 4 to learn how to test the links by previewing the page in a Web browser.

CREATE A HYPERLINK THAT OPENS A NEW WINDOW

You can create a hyperlink that opens a new browser window when clicked. The destination specified for the link then opens in the new window. Opening a new browser window involves specifying a target value for the link, in this case a value of `_blank`. (A link's target also comes into play when creating frames-based sites, because it is necessary to target links to particular frames in the window. For more information about frames, see Chapter 10.)

Opening a new browser window can be useful when linking to pages that exist on external Web sites. Creating a new window means your site's page in the old window remains open on the user's computer, making it easy for the user to return to your site later. Opening new windows can, however, lead to clutter on a user's desktop.

CREATE A HYPERLINK THAT OPENS A NEW WINDOW

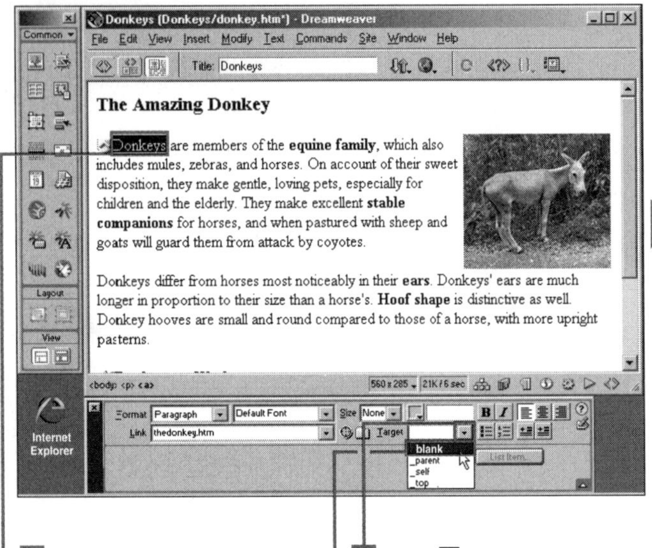

1 Click and drag to select the hyperlink that you want to open in a new window.

Note: To create a hyperlink, see the section "Hyperlink to Another Page in Your Site."

2 Click ▾ to open the Target menu.

3 Click _blank.

■ For information about other options in the Target menu, see Chapter 10.

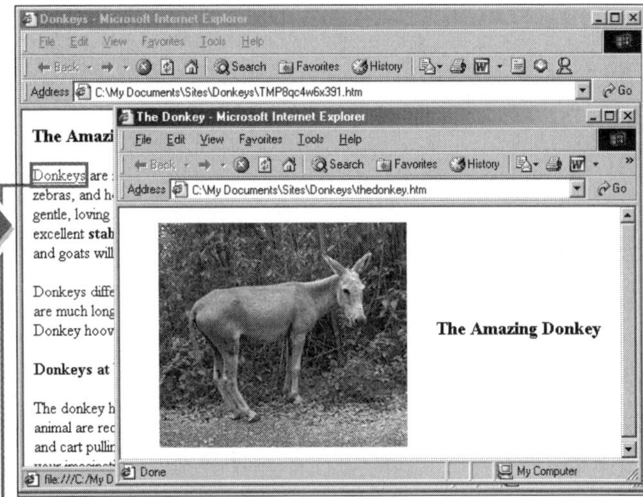

4 Preview the page in a Web browser and click the hyperlink.

Note: See Chapter 4 to learn how to preview a page in a Web browser.

■ Dreamweaver displays the hyperlink destination in a new window.

■ To create a link that opens a browser window with a predefined size and toolbar configuration, see Chapter 13.

HYPERLINK BY USING THE SITE WINDOW

A quick and easy way to create hyperlinks between pages in your Web site is by clicking and dragging to the Site window. The technique involves selecting the text or image that you want to define as a link, and then clicking and dragging the from the Properties inspector to the destination file in the Site window. This technique works best on large monitors where you can have many windows and palettes open and visible at once.

You can create links this way with the Site window in either Site Files or Site Map mode. The Site Map mode provides an additional advantage in that you can create links to external Web addresses if those addresses already exist in the Site Map structure.

The is also available next to the Image Source field in the Property Inspector when an image is selected in the Document window. With it, you can similarly specify the source file for an image.

HYPERLINK BY USING THE SITE WINDOW

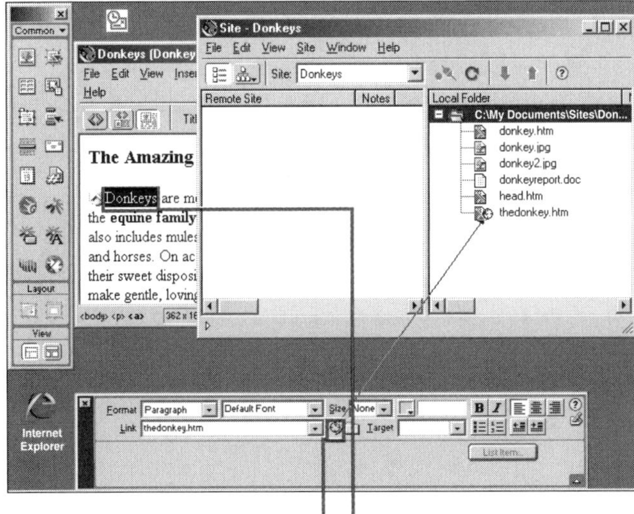

1 Arrange your workspace such that the Document and Site windows are visible.

■ See Chapter 15 for information about opening the Site window.

2 Click and drag to select text that you want to turn into a hyperlink.

■ Or, select an image to create an image hyperlink.

3 Click and drag the to the destination file listed in the Site window.

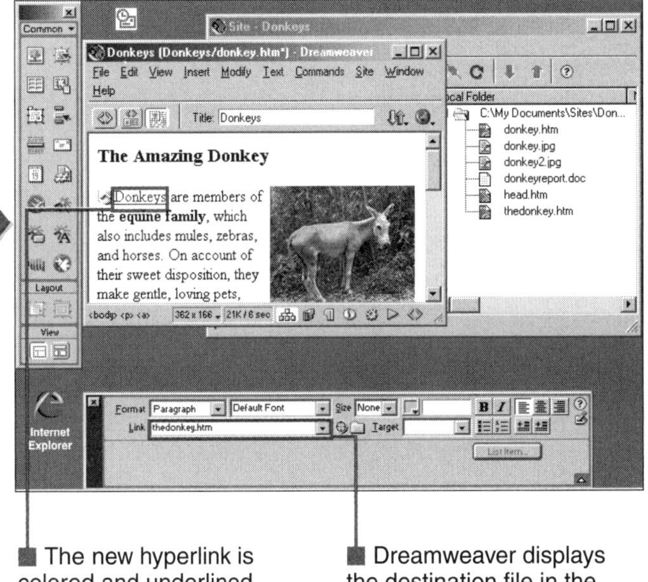

■ The new hyperlink is colored and underlined.

■ Dreamweaver displays the destination file in the Property Inspector.

CHANGE THE COLOR OF HYPERLINKS

You can change the color of the hyperlinks on your Web page to make them match the visual style of the text and images on your page. You can select a link color by choosing from a palette of colors, specifying a color by name (for example, "red" or "green"), or by specifying a color with a hexadecimal code.

Dreamweaver lets you specify the color of three different types of hyperlinks: unvisited links, visited links, and active links. Which links are defined as visited on a Web page is determined by the Web pages in the browser's history cache. A link turns the active color when the cursor clicks on it.

As a rule, it is good to choose link colors that are distinct from the color of the page's regular text so a viewer can pick out the links at a glance. For more information about defining colors, see "Change Font Color" in Chapter 5.

CHANGE THE COLOR OF HYPERLINKS

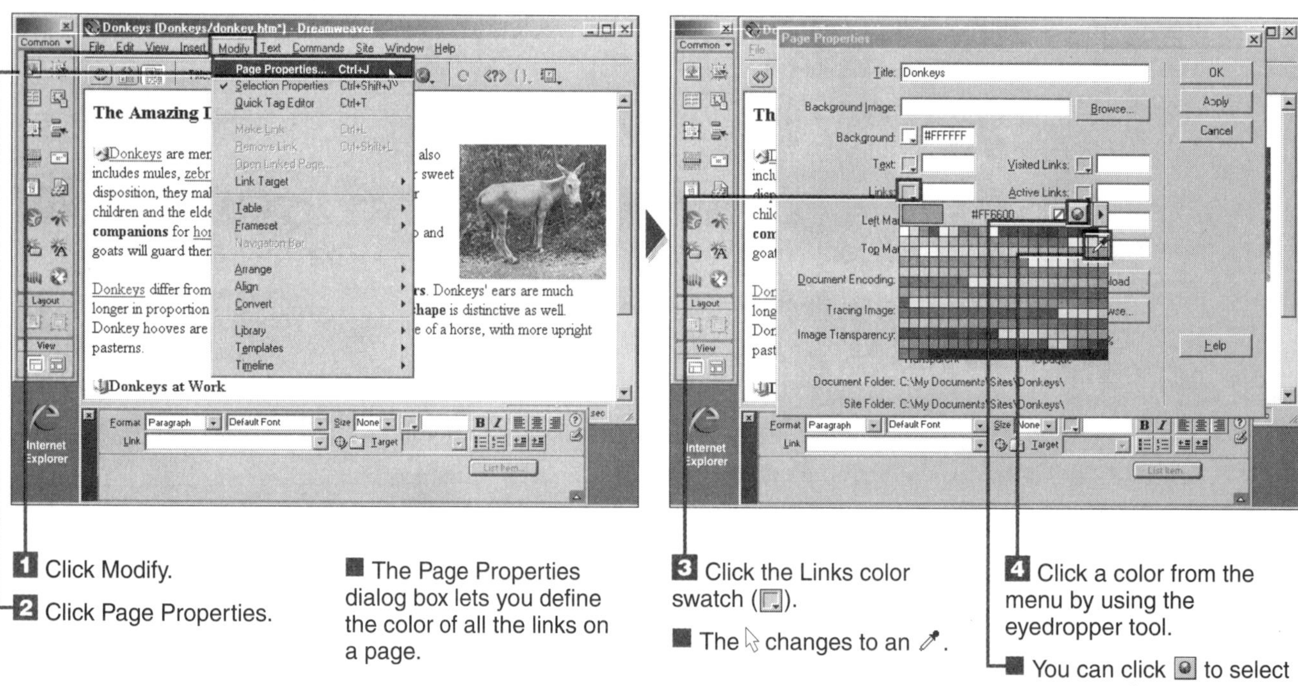

1 Click Modify.

2 Click Page Properties.

■ The Page Properties dialog box lets you define the color of all the links on a page.

3 Click the Links color swatch (□).

■ The ↖ changes to an eyedropper.

4 Click a color from the menu by using the eyedropper tool.

■ You can click ● to select a custom color.

What color do my links appear if I do not specifically define them in Dreamweaver?

✔ In the Dreamweaver Document window, blue is the default link color. What viewers see when the page is opened in a browser depends on the browser settings. By default, most browsers display unvisited links as blue, visited links as purple, and active links as red. (Users can override these settings in their browser options.)

How do I get rid of the underlining on my hyperlinks?

✔ You can specify that links not be underlined by using style sheets (see "Using CSS Selectors to Modify Links" in Chapter 12). However, doing this may confuse some users, since underlining is such a universal way to distinguish links from regular text.

How can I make my links disappear when they are clicked?

✔ If you set the active color to the same color as the page background, the link disappears when it is clicked. (The link reappears when the mouse button is released.)

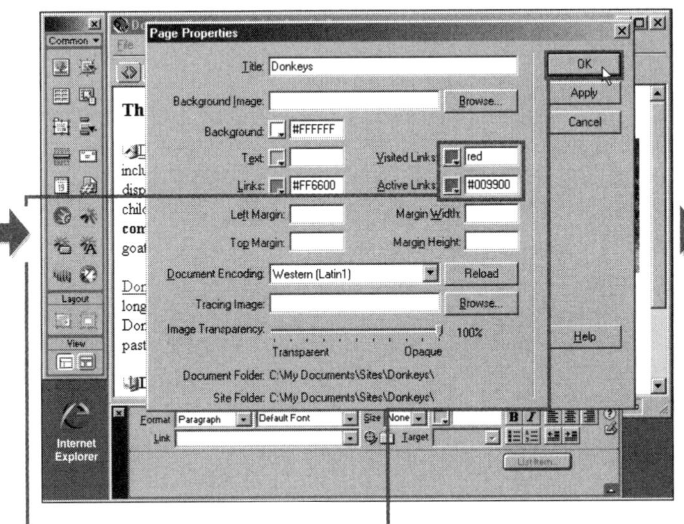

5 Click the ▢ for Visited Links and Active Links to define their colors.

6 Click OK.

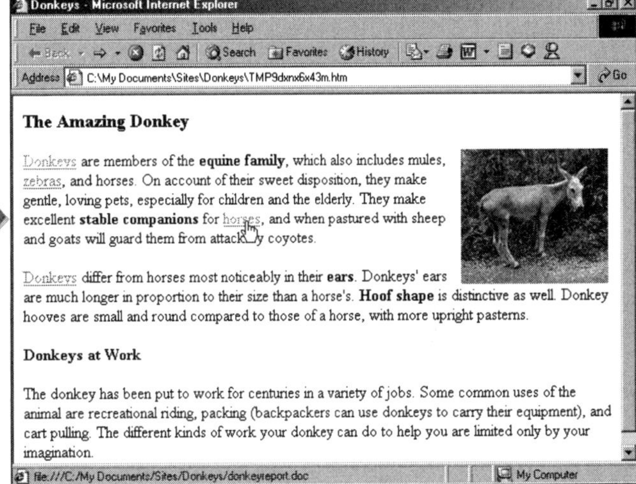

7 Preview the page in a Web browser.

Note: See Chapter 4 to learn how to preview a page in a Web browser.

■ The hyperlinks display in the defined colors.

CREATE AN E-MAIL HYPERLINK

You can create hyperlinks that launch an e-mail composition window when clicked. These are useful when you want to give your viewers a way to send you feedback about your site or request more information about your products or services.

When you define an e-mail link, you specify the e-mail address of the intended recipient (for example, webmaster@mysite.com). This address is automatically placed in the To: field when the e-mail composition window opens.

An e-mail hyperlink is a simpler alternative to a form, which you can also use to enable visitors to send you feedback or other information. (To use a form, you must install a form handler on your Web server that processes the entered information. For more information about forms, see Chapter 9.)

One drawback to e-mail hyperlinks is that some users may not be using browsers that have e-mail capability installed or configured. In such cases, the user may get no response when the link is clicked. But you probably do not need to worry about this too much — both Netscape Navigator and Microsoft Internet Explorer (used by most Web surfers) support e-mail links.

CREATE AN E-MAIL HYPERLINK

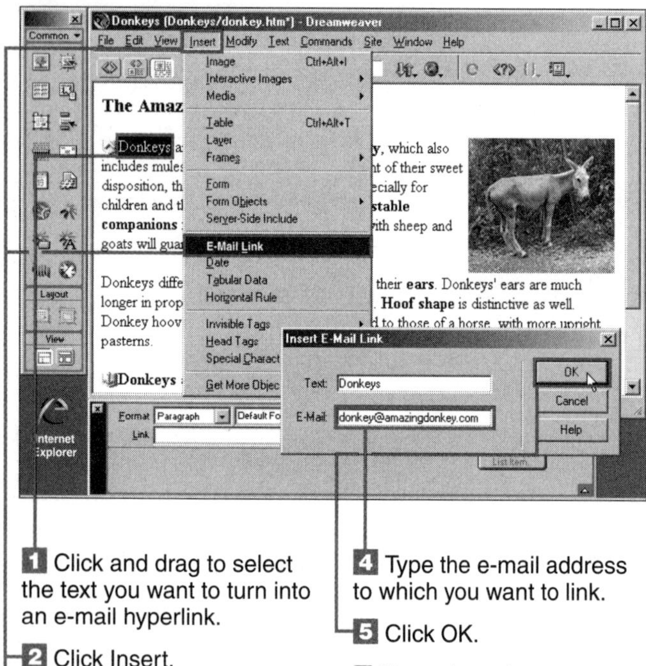

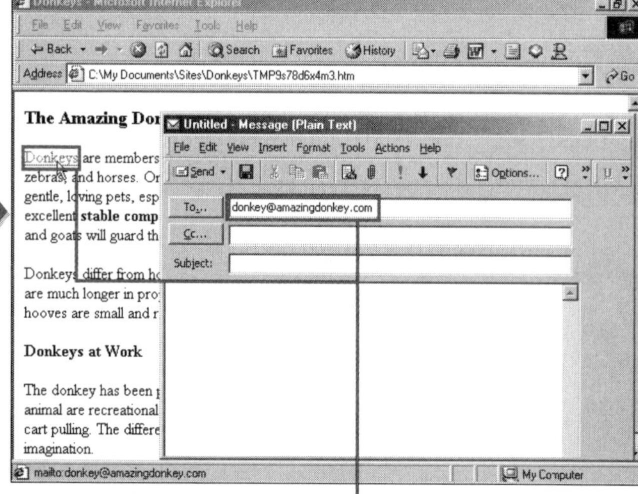

1 Click and drag to select the text you want to turn into an e-mail hyperlink.

2 Click Insert.

3 Click E-Mail Link.

■ The selected text appears in the Text field of the Insert E-Mail Link dialog box.

4 Type the e-mail address to which you want to link.

5 Click OK.

■ The selected text appears underlined and in color.

6 To test the link, preview the page in a browser

Note: See Chapter 4 to learn how to preview the page in a Web browser.

■ In Web browsers that support e-mail, clicking the hyperlink launches an e-mail composition window.

■ If the browser does not have e-mail capability, clicking the link has no effect.

CHECK HYPERLINKS

Dreamweaver can automatically check all the links among the pages of your Web site and report whether any are broken. This feature is especially useful for large sites, which may contain hundreds or thousands of hyperlinks.

Dreamweaver cannot check hyperlinks to files on external Web sites. For these, you have to check them by hand with a Web browser or use a third-party link checker (for a list of link checkers, see www.mediacosm.com/dreamweaver). Dreamweaver also cannot check e-mail links.

Different things can cause hyperlinks to break. A filename may be misspelled in the HTML, or the destination file may have been renamed or deleted. You can fix broken links inside the Link Checker dialog box by updating the spelling of the filename or reselecting the destination file.

CHECK HYPERLINKS

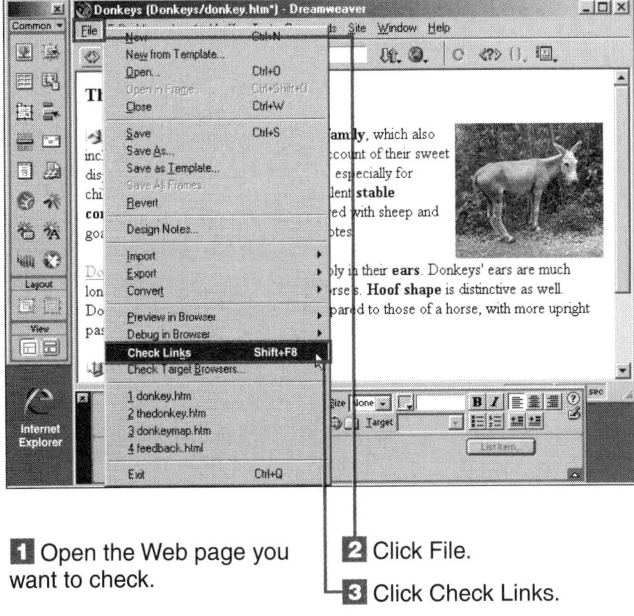

1 Open the Web page you want to check.

2 Click File.

3 Click Check Links.

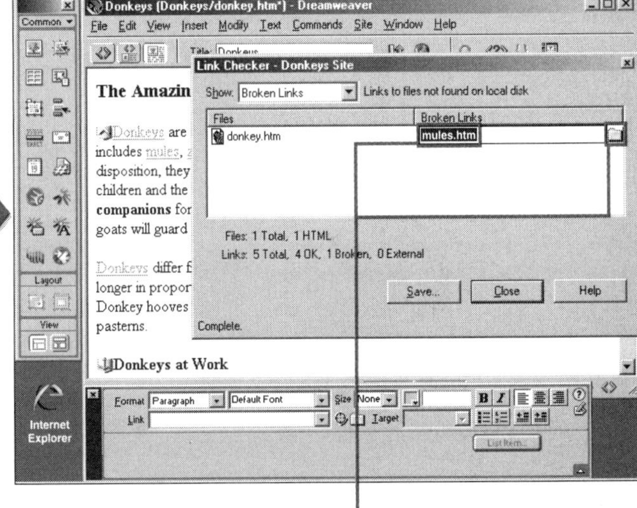

■ Dreamweaver checks the local hyperlinks and lists any broken links it finds.

■ You can edit a broken destination file by selecting it and editing the Broken Links field. You can also click ▢ to select a new destination for the link.

INSERT A TABLE INTO YOUR WEB PAGE

HTML tables offer you a flexible tool for organizing and positioning information on your Web page. You can use Dreamweaver to create HTML tables to organize text, images, and other information into regular rows and columns on your page.

You can also use tables to determine the overall layout of a page's content. For example, you can use a table to create a narrow side column, where you can organize navigation links, next to a larger area where you can put the page's main content. (Frames — discussed in Chapter 10 — are another way to organize the layout of your page.)

You define a table in Dreamweaver by specifying its number of rows and columns, size, and border characteristics. After you insert a table, you can further customize its structure by merging and splitting its cells — the rectangular containers that make up a table — or inserting another table inside a cell of an existing table.

You can turn on a table's borders to distinguish the individual cells that divide the content. Or you can keep the borders turned off to make the structure invisible to the viewer.

INSERT A TABLE INTO YOUR WEB PAGE

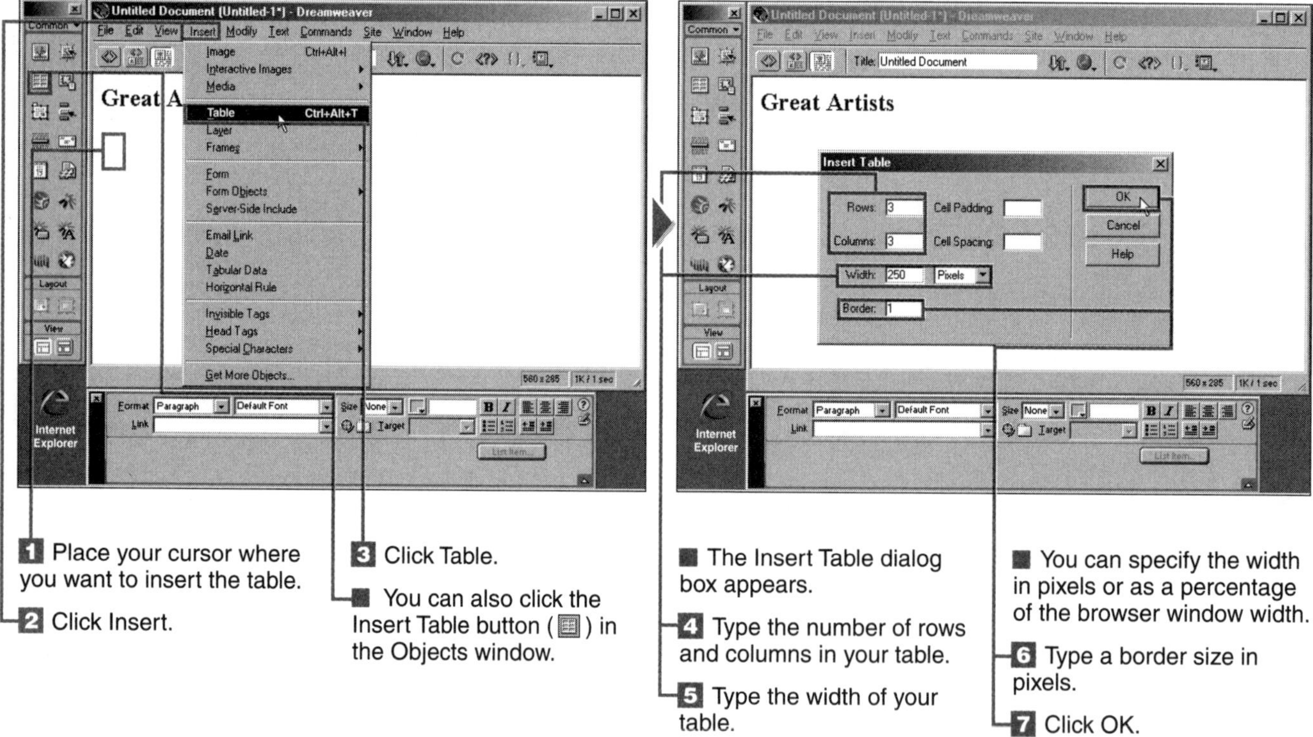

1 Place your cursor where you want to insert the table.

2 Click Insert.

3 Click Table.

■ You can also click the Insert Table button (▦) in the Objects window.

■ The Insert Table dialog box appears.

4 Type the number of rows and columns in your table.

5 Type the width of your table.

■ You can specify the width in pixels or as a percentage of the browser window width.

6 Type a border size in pixels.

7 Click OK.

How do I align a table on a Web page?

✔ Aligning a table is similar to aligning an image (see Chapter 6 for more information). You select the table in Dreamweaver by clicking its upper-left corner. Then, you choose an alignment from the Align menu in the Property Inspector. A left or right alignment wraps other content on the page around the table.

How can I duplicate a table on my Web page?

✔ First, you need to select the table by clicking its upper-left corner. Then use the Copy and Paste commands under the Edit menu to copy it and paste it elsewhere.

What are the HTML tags that define a table?

✔ The `<table>` tag defines where the table begins and ends in your HTML code, `<tr>` tags define the table rows, and `<td>` tags define the cells within each row. The content displayed in a table sits inside the `<td>` tags.

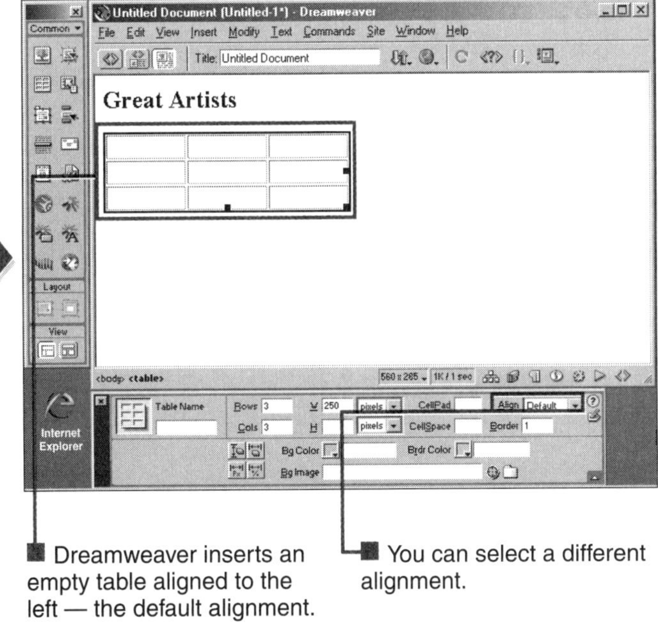

■ Dreamweaver inserts an empty table aligned to the left — the default alignment.

■ You can select a different alignment.

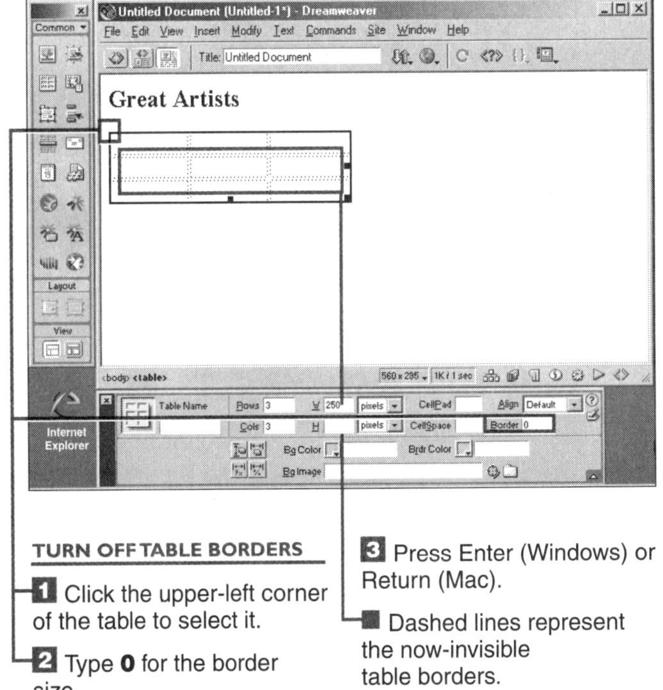

TURN OFF TABLE BORDERS

1 Click the upper-left corner of the table to select it.

2 Type **0** for the border size.

3 Press Enter (Windows) or Return (Mac).

■ Dashed lines represent the now-invisible table borders.

INSERT CONTENT INTO A TABLE

After you insert a table into your Web page, you can fill the table cells with text, images, form elements, and even other tables. Tables are useful for placing Web-page elements side by side (in table rows) or on top of one another (in table columns).

The cells of a table expand to accommodate whatever content you insert into it. After you insert content, you can adjust the content alignment or add space around the content. See the section "Change the Alignment of Table Content" and "Change the Cell Spacing or Padding in a Table" for more information.

You can place entire passages of text inside fixed-width tables to keep the text from rewrapping when a viewer adjusts the browser window size. To create a fixed-width table, see the section "Change the Dimensions of a Table." Tables are also useful for displaying grids of images in photo-gallery sites.

INSERT CONTENT INTO A TABLE

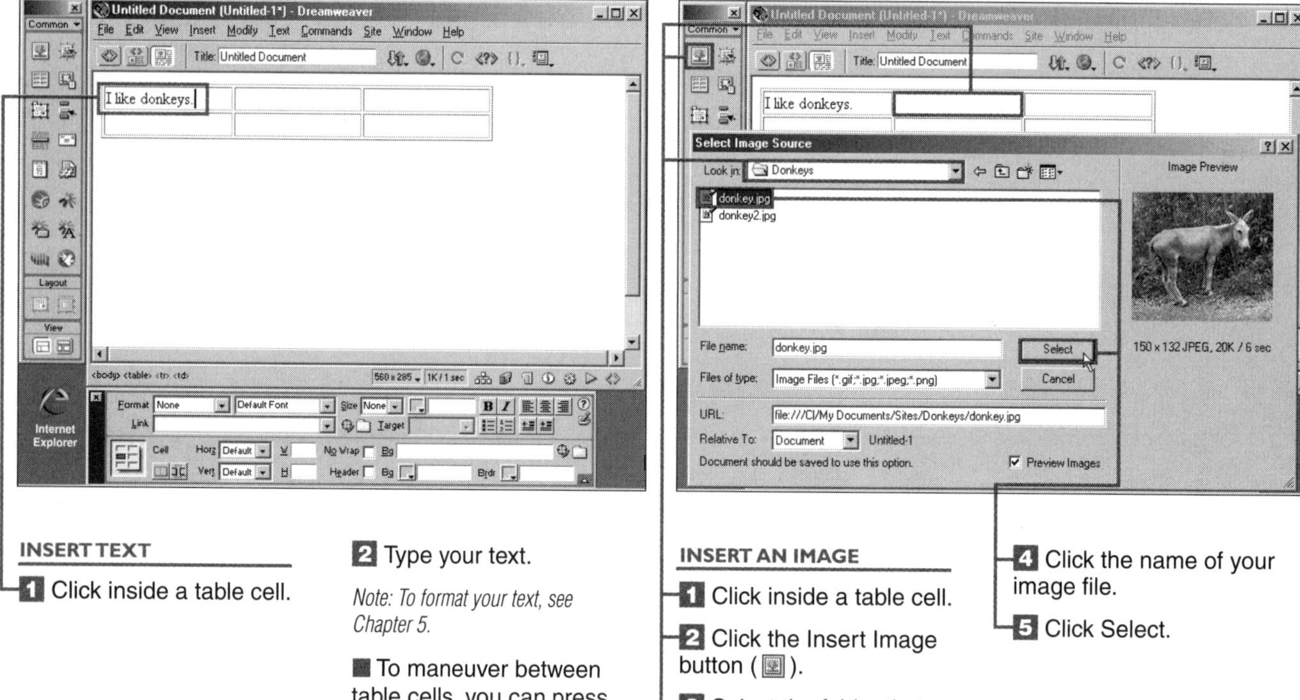

INSERT TEXT

1 Click inside a table cell.

2 Type your text.

Note: To format your text, see Chapter 5.

■ To maneuver between table cells, you can press Tab (Windows) or Shift + Tab (Mac).

INSERT AN IMAGE

1 Click inside a table cell.

2 Click the Insert Image button ( ).

3 Select the folder that contains your image.

4 Click the name of your image file.

5 Click Select.

How can I add captions to images on my Web page?

✔ The best way to add a caption to the top, bottom, or side of an image is with a two-celled table. Insert the table and place the image in one cell and the caption in the other. You can adjust the table's alignment to fit the captioned image in with the rest of your page's content.

How can I use a table to organize my forms?

✔ If you create a form on your page, you may want the text fields, drop-down menus, and other elements neatly aligned in one column on the page, and the labels for the elements aligned next to them. You can do this by inserting a two-column table and putting a label and a form element into the cells of each row. Table borders can be turned on or off, depending on your style preference.

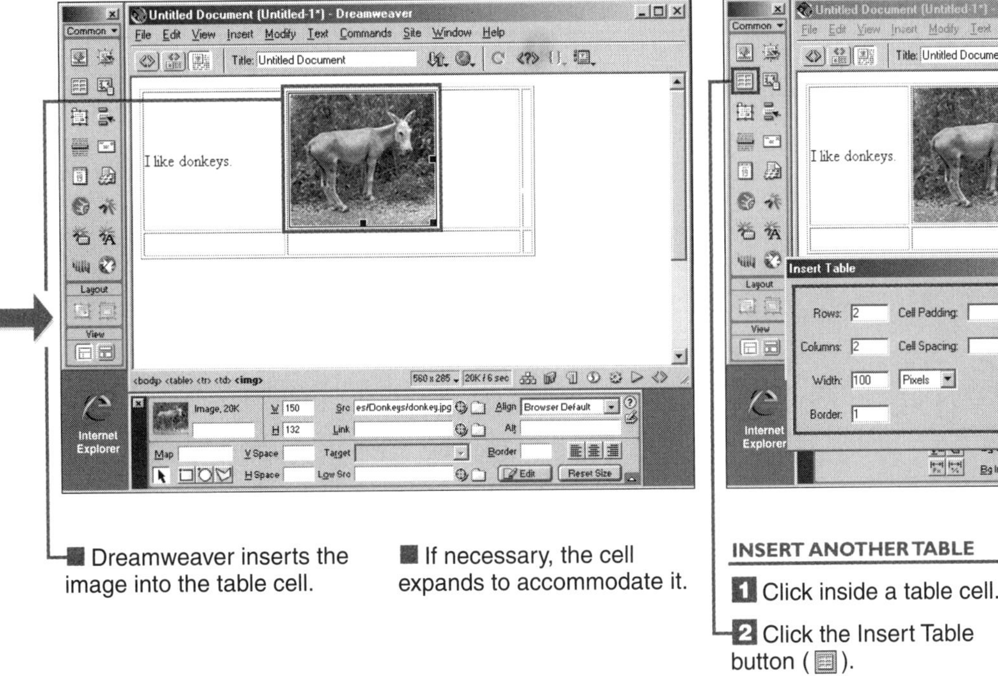

■ Dreamweaver inserts the image into the table cell.

■ If necessary, the cell expands to accommodate it.

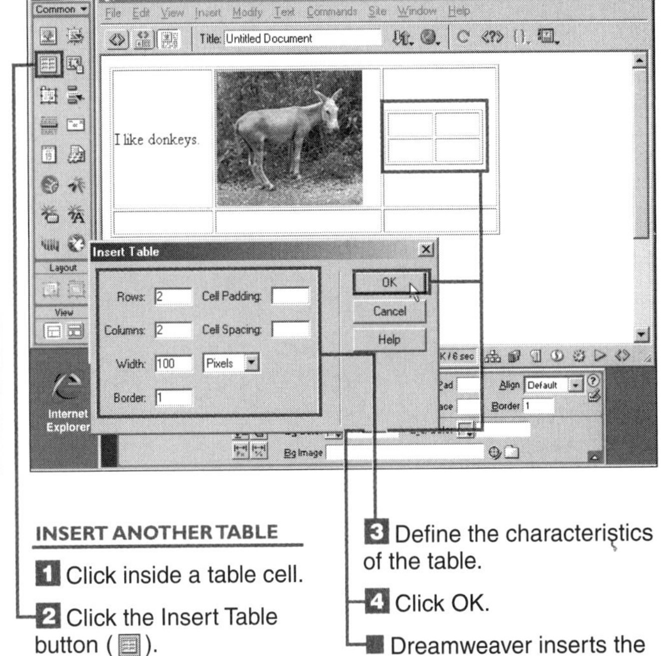

INSERT ANOTHER TABLE

1 Click inside a table cell.

2 Click the Insert Table button ( ).

3 Define the characteristics of the table.

4 Click OK.

■ Dreamweaver inserts the table into the table cell.

CHANGE THE BACKGROUND OF A TABLE

You can change the background of a table to make it complement the style of the rest of your Web page. You can change the color of a table's background or specify an image with which you want the table background filled.

To change the background, you can select the table in the Document window and then select a color from a palette in the Property Inspector. You can also specify a color by typing a color name or by specifying a color's hexadecimal code. (For more information about Web colors, see Chapter 5.)

In addition to changing the background of the entire table, you can also change just the background of a row, column, or cell. Alternating the colors of rows or columns can help viewers better distinguish related values in a large table.

CHANGE THE BACKGROUND OF A TABLE

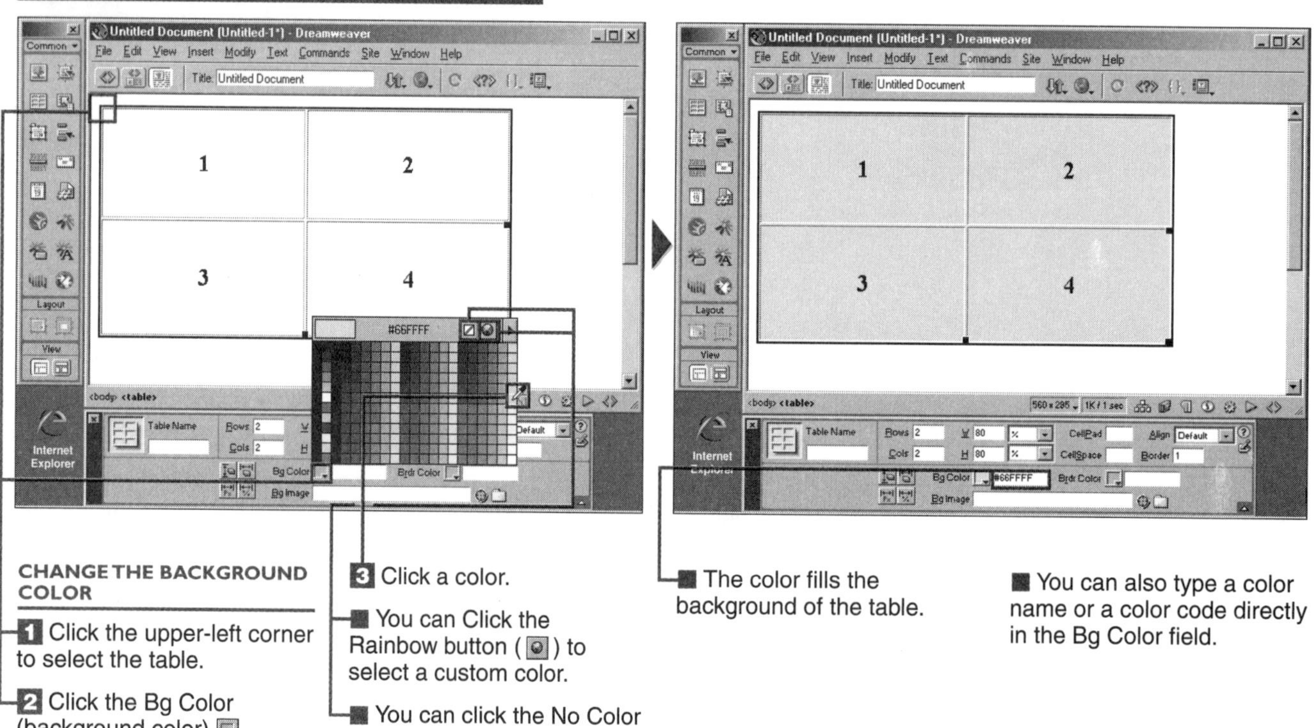

CHANGE THE BACKGROUND COLOR

1. Click the upper-left corner to select the table.
2. Click the Bg Color (background color) .
3. Click a color.

- You can Click the Rainbow button ( ) to select a custom color.
- You can click the No Color button ( ) to specify no color.
- The color fills the background of the table.
- You can also type a color name or a color code directly in the Bg Color field.

How do I change the color of a single table row or column?

✔ First, click the side edge of the row or top of the column to select it. You can also select a row or column by shift-clicking each component cell. Then, click the Bg color swatch in the Property Inspector to select the color for the row or column.

How can I quickly apply an interesting background color scheme to my table?

✔ Select the table by clicking its upper-left corner. Click Commands and Format Table. This opens a dialog box that enables you to quickly format your table with a number of preset color schemes. It also lets you format your table's alignment and border.

How do I change the color of the borders of my table?

✔ After selecting your table, you can adjust the border colors using the Brdr, Light Brdr, and Dark Brdr fields in the Property Inspector. You may want to test such effects in different browsers. Some versions of Netscape Navigator and Microsoft Internet Explorer differ in how they apply border colors.

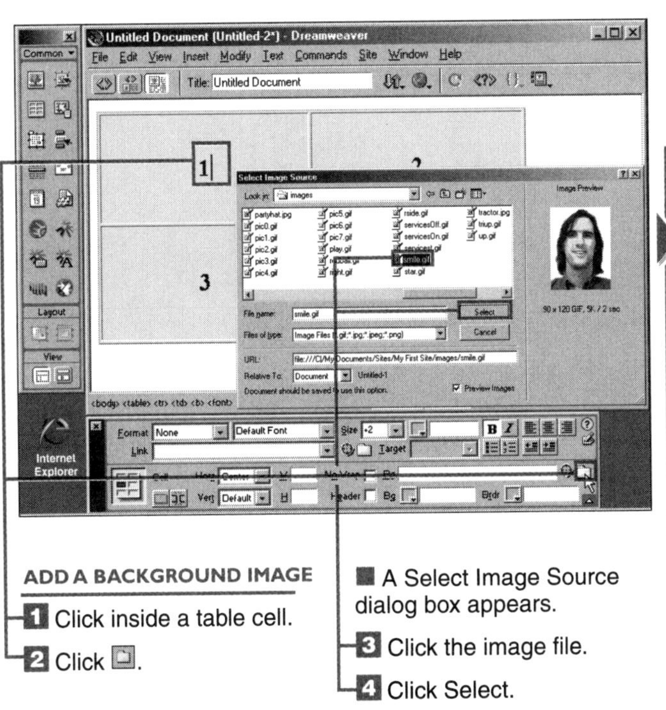

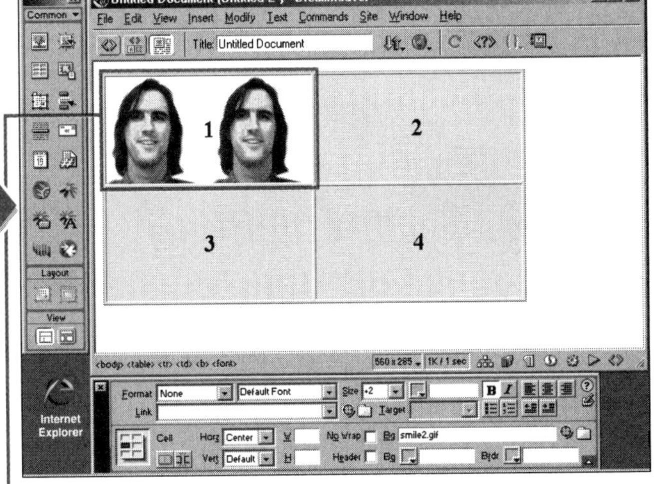

ADD A BACKGROUND IMAGE

1 Click inside a table cell.

2 Click 🗀.

■ A Select Image Source dialog box appears.

3 Click the image file.

4 Click Select.

■ The cell background fills with the image.

■ If necessary, the image tiles to fill the entire cell.

CHANGE THE CELL SPACING OR PADDING IN A TABLE

You can emphasize the borders in a table by adjusting the spacing between its different cells. You can also present a table's cell content more attractively by changing the spacing between the cell content and the cell borders, also known as its padding.

You define these settings in the CellSpace and CellPad fields in the Property Inspector. To see the difference between cell spacing versus cell padding, turn on a table's borders.

You may want to add some padding to a table to keep the table content from being squished against the table borders. When you do not assign specific values for cell spacing and cell padding, Dreamweaver, Netscape Navigator, and Microsoft Internet Explorer all display a table as if cell spacing were set to 2 and cell padding were set to 1.

CHANGE THE CELL SPACING OR PADDING IN A TABLE

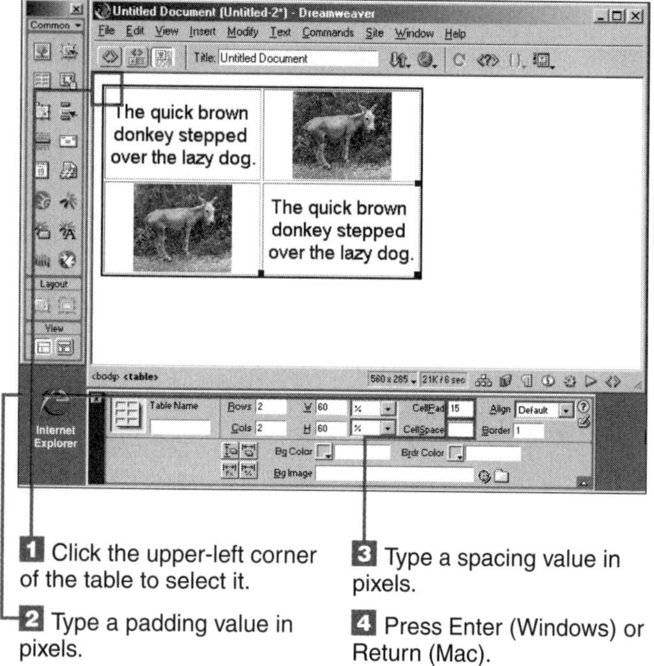

1 Click the upper-left corner of the table to select it.

2 Type a padding value in pixels.

3 Type a spacing value in pixels.

4 Press Enter (Windows) or Return (Mac).

■ Dreamweaver adds padding and spacing to all the table cells.

■ Padding affects the space between the content and the border.

■ Spacing affects the size of the border itself.

Note: You cannot define padding or spacing for just a few of a table's cells. It is all or nothing.

CHANGE THE ALIGNMENT OF TABLE CONTENT

You can change the horizontal and vertical alignment in table cells to clearly present the text, images, and other content inside them.

The default alignment for table cells is left horizontal alignment and middle vertical alignment. To set a different alignment, you must select the cells to define and then select alignments in the Horz and Vert menus in the Property Inspector.

You can set the alignment for a table's different cells independently of one another. For example, you can have content in the top row of a table center aligned, while the rest of the table is still set to the default left alignment.

When you use a table for layout purposes, you may want to change the vertical alignment in the cells to top, so that text content in the cell begins at the upper-left corner of the cell.

CHANGE THE ALIGNMENT OF TABLE CONTENT

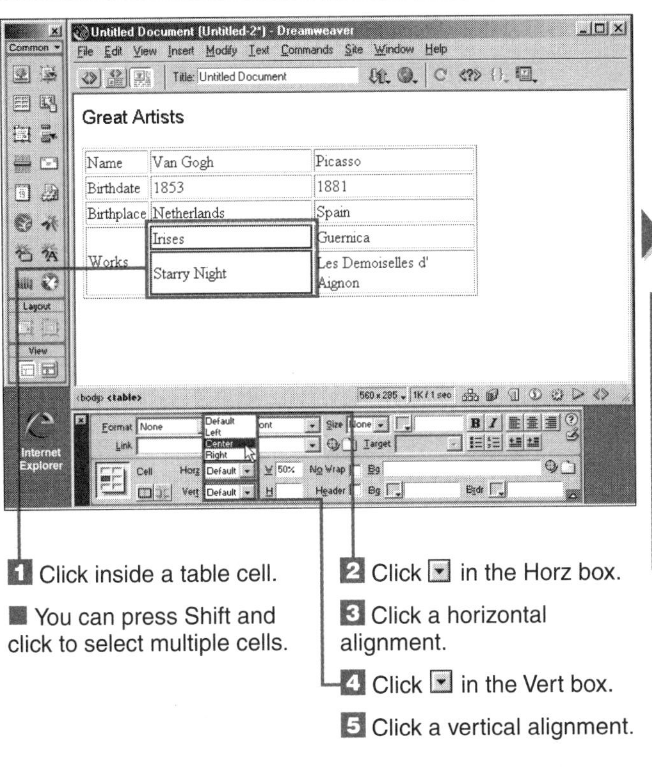

1 Click inside a table cell.

■ You can press Shift and click to select multiple cells.

2 Click ▼ in the Horz box.

3 Click a horizontal alignment.

4 Click ▼ in the Vert box.

5 Click a vertical alignment.

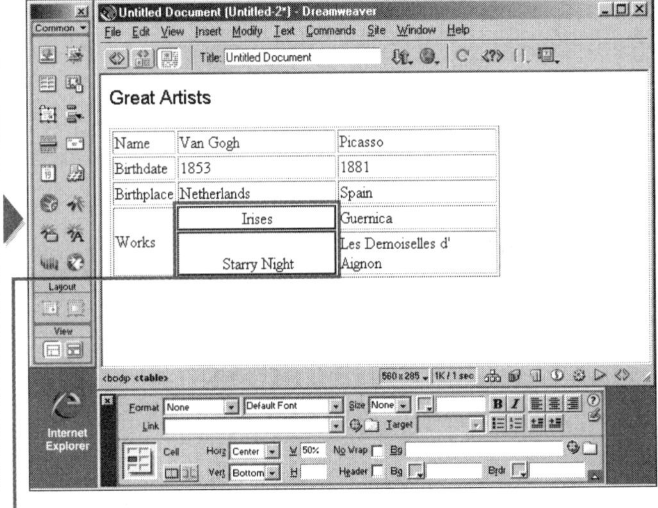

■ Dreamweaver aligns the content inside the cell (or cells).

INSERT OR DELETE A ROW OR COLUMN

You can add cells to or delete cells from your table a row or column at a time. Inserting cells into your table enables you to add additional content, while deleting lets you get rid of empty areas of a table.

You can add or remove rows and columns several ways: You can select a cell and then select one of the Insert or Delete commands under the Modify menu and Table submenu. You can select the entire table, by clicking its upper-left corner, and then change the Rows or Cols value in the Property Inspector. Or you can right-click (Windows) or Option-click (Mac) a table cell and select one of the Insert or Delete commands from the Table menu that appears.

The Insert Rows or Columns command, which is under the Modify menu and Table submenu, is useful in that it lets you add multiple rows or columns to a table all at once. The command also lets you specify whether to add the rows or columns before or after the current selection.

INSERT OR DELETE A ROW OR COLUMN

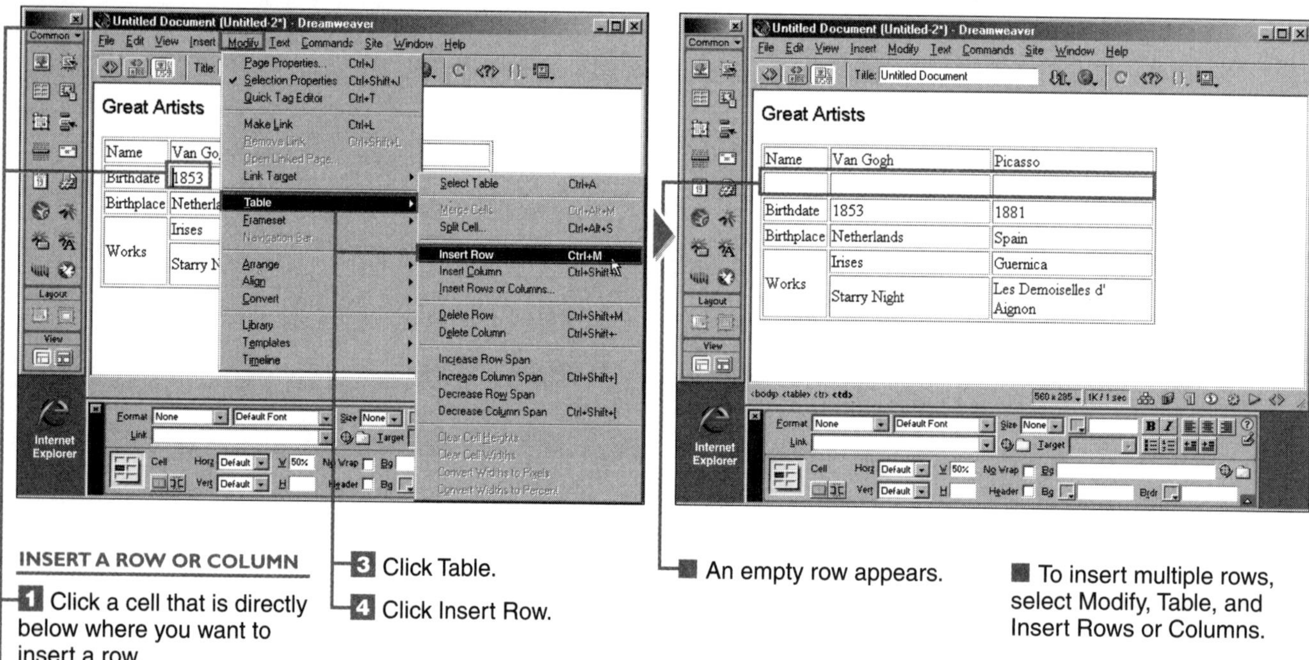

INSERT A ROW OR COLUMN

1 Click a cell that is directly below where you want to insert a row.

2 Click Modify.

3 Click Table.

4 Click Insert Row.

■ An empty row appears.

■ To insert multiple rows, select Modify, Table, and Insert Rows or Columns.

What happens to the content of a deleted cell?

✔ It is deleted as well. Dreamweaver does not warn you if the cells you are deleting contain content. If you accidentally remove content when deleting rows or columns, you can select Edit and then Undo to undo the last command.

How do I save a copy of the content in a row or column before I delete it?

✔ You can make a copy of the row or column elsewhere on the page. First select the row by clicking its side edge, or the column by clicking its top edge. Select Copy under the Edit menu. Then, click somewhere outside the table and select Paste under the Edit menu to duplicate the content.

How large are new rows or columns after I insert them?

✔ The size of the new row or column depends on how you have defined the dimensions of your table and what content is in the existing cells. If you need to, you can resize your table after you have added your rows or columns See the section "Change the Dimensions of a Table" for more information.

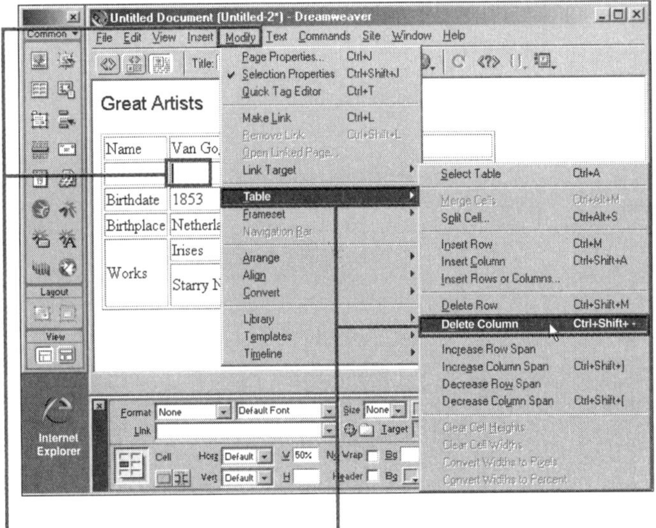

DELETE A TABLE COLUMN

1 Click a cell that is part of the column you want to delete.

2 Click Modify.

3 Click Table.

4 Click Delete Column.

■ The column disappears.

SPLIT OR MERGE TABLE CELLS

You can create a more elaborate arrangement of cells in a table by splitting or merging its cells.

You can split a cell by using the Split Cell command. This brings up a dialog box allowing you to specify whether you want to split the cell into rows or columns, and how many rows or columns. You can also right-click (Windows) or Control-click (Mac) a cell and select Table and Split Cell or click the Split Cell button (▦) in the Property Inspector. This brings up the same dialog box.

To merge cells, first select the cells to be merged by shift-clicking them. Then, you can either click Modify, Table, and Merge Cells; right-click (Option-click) the cells and select Table and then Merge Cells; or click the Merge Cells button (▣) in the Property Inspector.

When you split cells, any content in the cell moves to the topmost or rightmost cell. When you merge cells, all content is combined into the merged cell. No content is lost when you split or merge table cells.

SPLIT OR MERGE TABLE CELLS

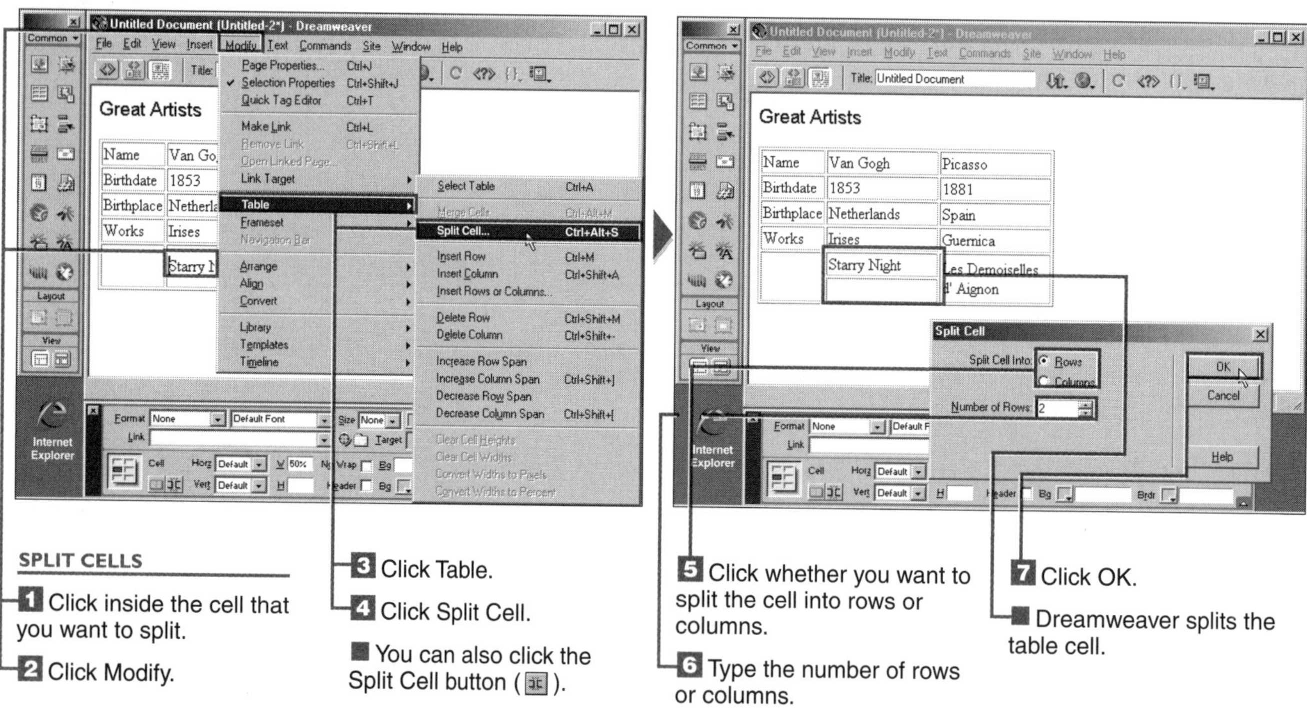

SPLIT CELLS

1 Click inside the cell that you want to split.

2 Click Modify.

3 Click Table.

4 Click Split Cell.

■ You can also click the Split Cell button (▦).

5 Click whether you want to split the cell into rows or columns.

6 Type the number of rows or columns.

7 Click OK.

■ Dreamweaver splits the table cell.

Can I merge any combination of table cells?

✔ No. The cells must have a rectangular arrangement. For example, you can merge all the cells in a two-row-by-two-column table. But you cannot select three cells that form an L shape and merge them into one.

What happens in the HTML code when you split or merge table cells?

✔ When you split or merge table cells, Dreamweaver adds or removes the necessary `<td>` tags, and then it adds `colspan` or `rowspan` attributes to cells that end up spanning more than one neighboring cell after the split or merge.

Can I merge an entire row or column of cells?

✔ Yes. Just click on the side of the row or top of the column to select it, and then select a Merge Cells command or click the Merge Cells button (▣) in the Property Inspector. You can conveniently add a title to your table by merging the cells in a table's first row, typing the title into the row, and then center-aligning the title.

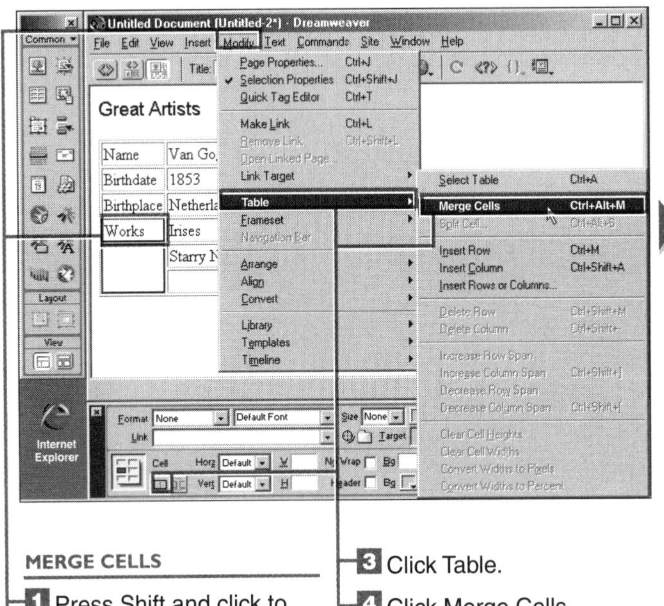

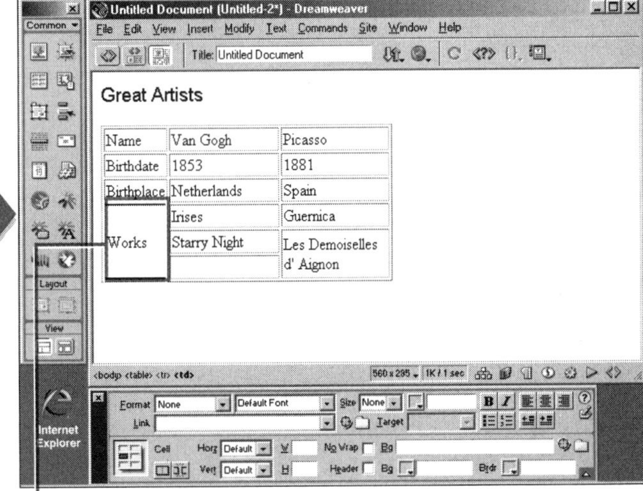

MERGE CELLS

1. Press Shift and click to select the cells that you want to merge.
2. Click Modify.
3. Click Table.
4. Click Merge Cells.

■ You can also click the Merge Cells button (▣).

■ Dreamweaver merges the table cells into one.

CHANGE THE DIMENSIONS OF A TABLE

You can change the dimensions of an HTML table in two ways: You can change the dimensions of individual cells, which enables you to allocate different amounts of space to different parts of a table. Or you can also change the dimensions of the entire table, which lets you best fit a table into the confines of the Web page.

To adjust the dimensions of individual cells, select one or more of the cells. You can define the W and H values in pixels (for example, 50) or a percentage (for example, 50%). A percentage specifies the width or height relative to the size of the entire table.

To change the dimensions of a table, select the table by clicking its upper-left corner. Then enter the desired dimensions of the table in the W and H fields. Drop-down menus enable you to specify a pixel or percentage value for the dimensions. A percentage specifies the width or height relative to the dimensions of the browser window.

If you are specifying dimensions of a table for layout purposes, you may want to design your table in layout mode. See "Create a Layout Table" for more information.

CHANGE THE DIMENSIONS OF A TABLE

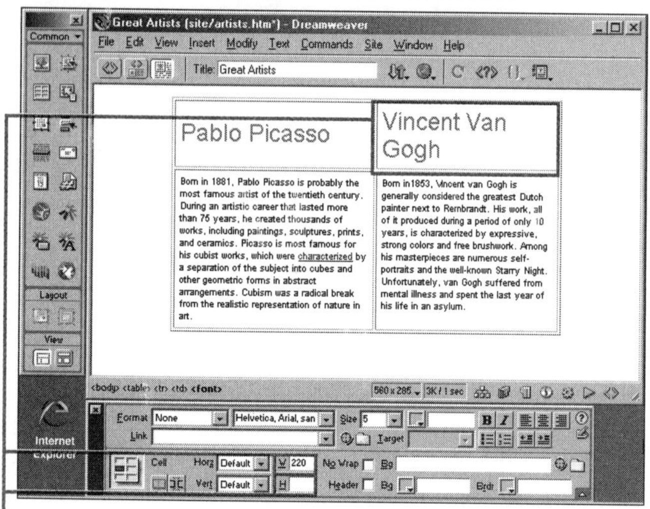

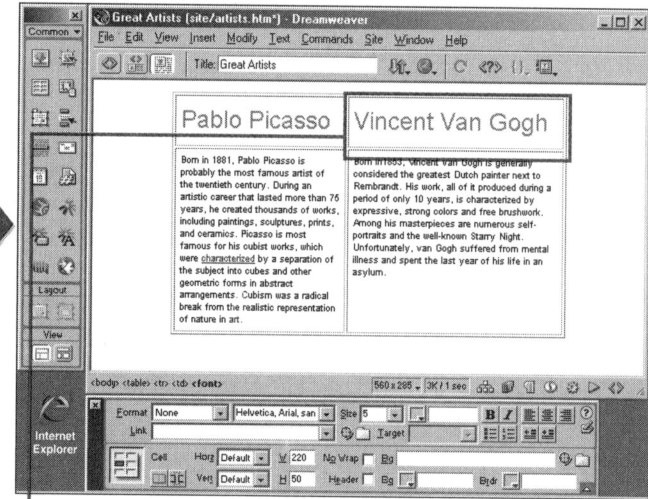

CHANGE CELL DIMENSIONS

1 Click inside the cell whose dimensions you want to adjust.

2 Type the width in pixels.

3 Type the height in pixels.

■ To specify a proportion of the entire table, type percentages for the dimensions.

4 Press Enter (Windows) or Return (Mac).

■ The dimensions of the cell change.

■ The dimensions of cells next to it change as well.

Note: A cell will not shrink to less than the size of the content inside it.

How do I make a table span the entire browser window?

✔ Select the table and specify a width (W) of 100% in the Property Inspector. To make it also span the page from top to bottom, specify a height (H) of 100%. Such a table fills the entire page, no matter what the browser window size.

How do I change the dimensions of a row or column?

✔ Select a row or column in a table by clicking the side edge of the row or top edge of the column. Then, change the dimensions as you would a cell — with the W and H fields in the Property Inspector.

Can I use a shortcut for changing cell and table dimensions?

✔ Yes. To change cell dimensions, you can place the cursor over the table borders. When the cursor changes shape, you can click and drag to change cell dimensions. To change a table's dimensions, you can select the table and then click and drag the square handles that appear on the table's edges. Clicking and dragging to resize causes the W and H fields in the Property Inspector to change dynamically.

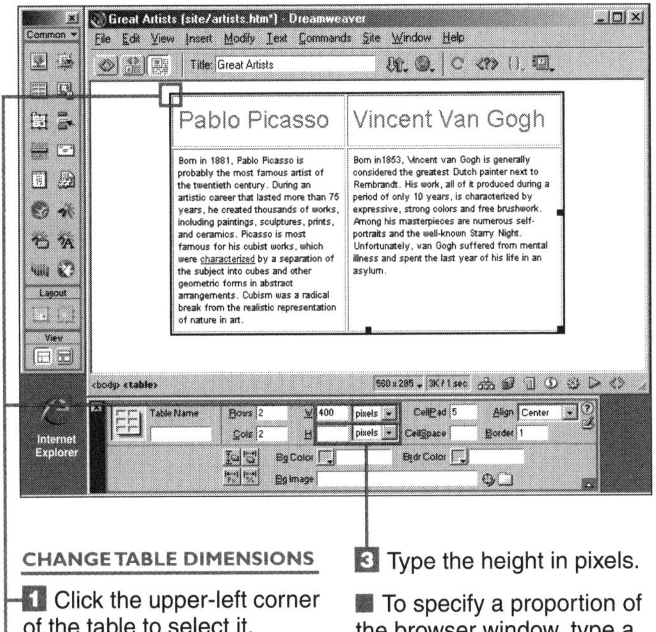

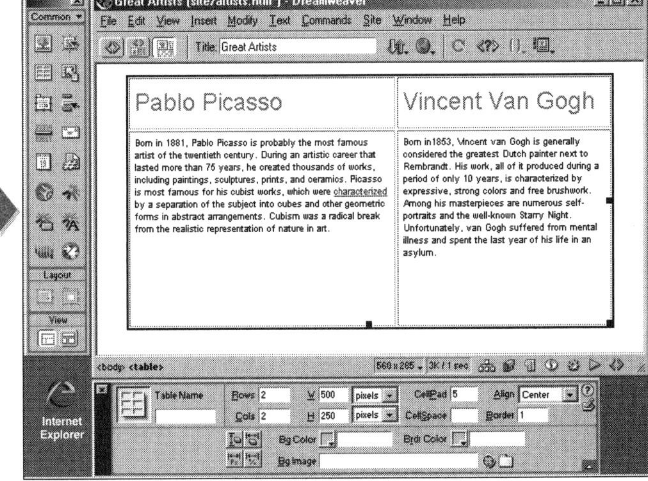

CHANGE TABLE DIMENSIONS

1 Click the upper-left corner of the table to select it.

2 Type the width in pixels.

3 Type the height in pixels.

■ To specify a proportion of the browser window, type a percentage for the dimensions.

4 Press Enter (Windows) or Return (Mac).

■ The dimensions of the table change.

CREATE A LAYOUT TABLE

A popular method for organizing the layout of information on a Web page is using tables that have their borders turned off. Dreamweaver offers a special Layout View in which you can create such tables and easily format their cells for layout purposes.

From a code standpoint, tables created in Layout View are no different from the tables created in Standard View. Layout View simply enables you to define page layout more efficiently using a table. When you draw new cells inside a table in Layout View, Dreamweaver automatically resizes the cells around them to keep the table structure valid. Layout View also lets you fix the width of some table cells and format others to stretch and contract depending on the size of the browser window (See "Adjust the Width of a Layout Table" later in this chapter).

You can switch out of Layout View at any time and continue to format and add content to the tables you created in the Standard View.

CREATE A LAYOUT TABLE

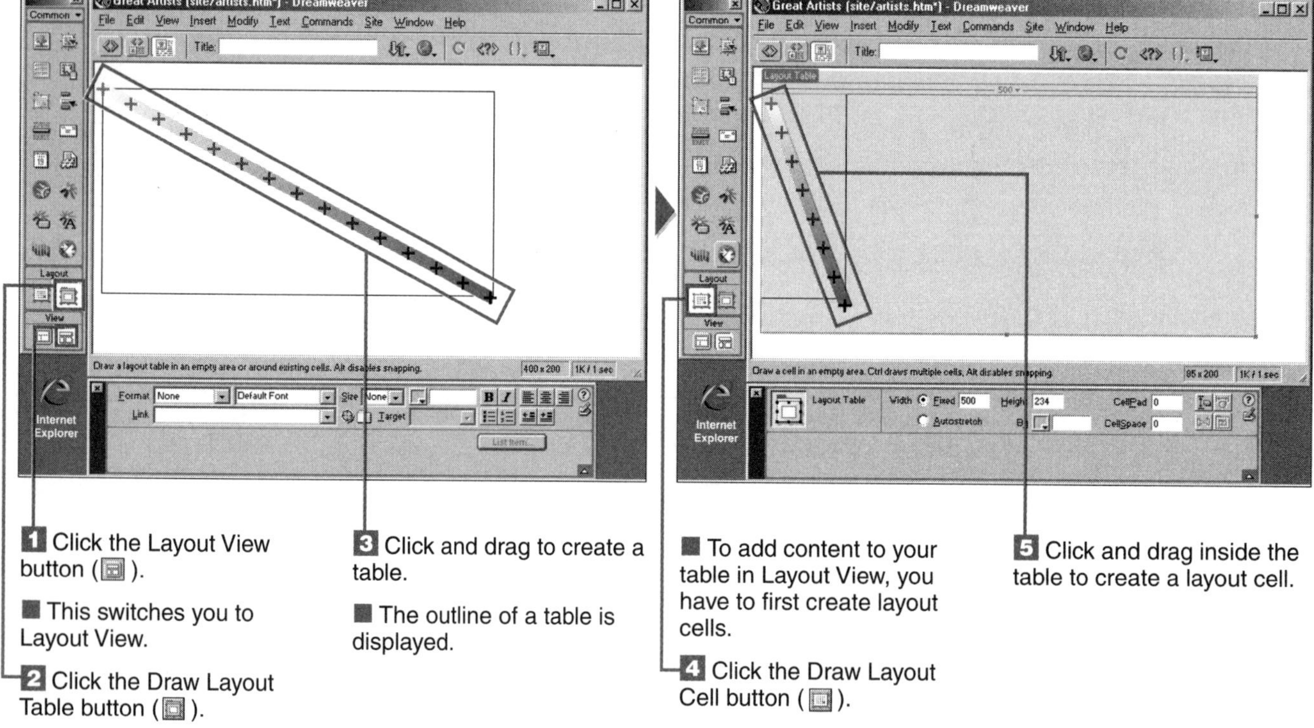

1 Click the Layout View button ( ).

■ This switches you to Layout View.

2 Click the Draw Layout Table button ( ).

■ In the Document window, the cursor changes to +.

3 Click and drag to create a table.

■ The outline of a table is displayed.

■ To add content to your table in Layout View, you have to first create layout cells.

4 Click the Draw Layout Cell button ( ).

5 Click and drag inside the table to create a layout cell.

Can I turn on the grid in the Document window to help me size my layout tables and table cells?

✔ Yes. This is one of the best uses of Dreamweaver's grid feature. You can turn it on by clicking View, Grid, and then Show Grid. To customize the grid, select Edit Grid under the Grid submenu. Options include changing the grid square size and specifying that table and cell edges snap to the grid edges when they are near them.

Can I use a shortcut to create cells in a layout table?

✔ To create a new cell in your layout table without having to click the layout cell button each time, press Control (Command) while you click and drag.

How do I disable the snap-to feature when I am drawing a cell?

✔ To temporarily disable snapping when you get near a table edge, another cell, or a grid line, press Alt (Windows) or Opton (Mac).

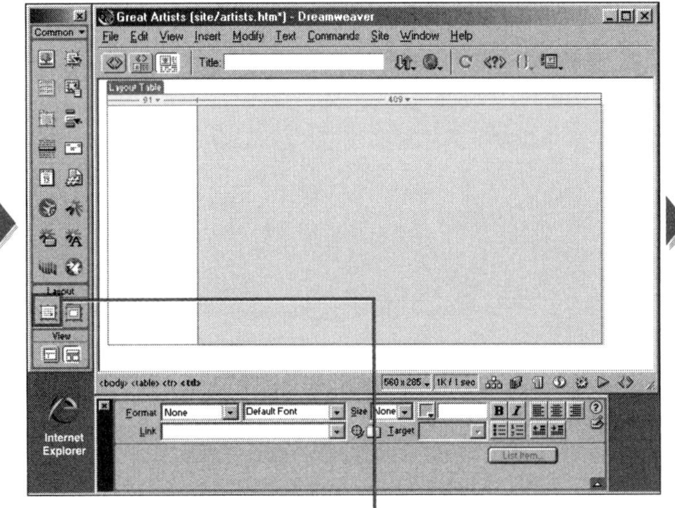

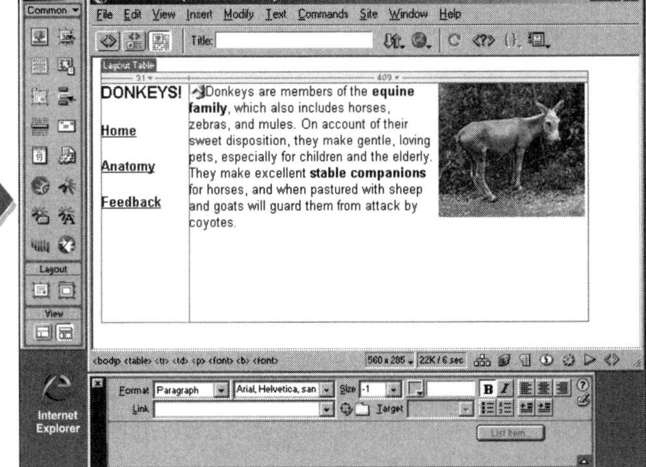

■ You can adjust the size and position of a cell by clicking its edge.

Note: See the section "Rearrange a Layout Table" to learn how to adjust size and position.

6 Click again to draw more cells.

7 Insert content into your cells.

Note: See the section "Insert Content into a Table" to learn how to insert content.

■ To change the properties of a table cell, click its edge and edit the values in the Property Inspector.

■ Dreamweaver displays the modified table cell.

REARRANGE A LAYOUT TABLE

One of the benefits of creating tables in Layout View is the ease at which you can rearrange and change the size of the component table cells.

To change a cell's size in Layout View, click on its edge, which causes handles to appear on the corners and sides of the cell. You can then click and drag the handles to change the size. To move a cell, click the cell's edge and then click and drag the edge. As you resize a cell, Dreamweaver resizes the other undefined cells in the table automatically.

You may run into some limitations with regard to resizing and moving cells: You cannot overlap other cells that you have defined, which means that you may have to resize other cells as you work. Also, a layout cell needs to be at least as large as the content it contains.

To resize or move an entire layout table, click the table's tab, which makes handles appear on the edges. Then, you click and drag the handles to resize the table, or drag the edge to move the table altogether.

REARRANGE A LAYOUT TABLE

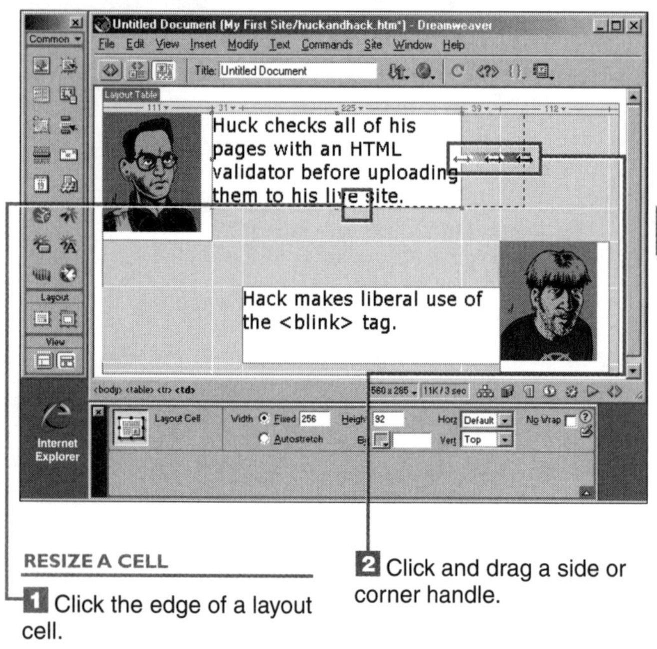

RESIZE A CELL

1 Click the edge of a layout cell.

2 Click and drag a side or corner handle.

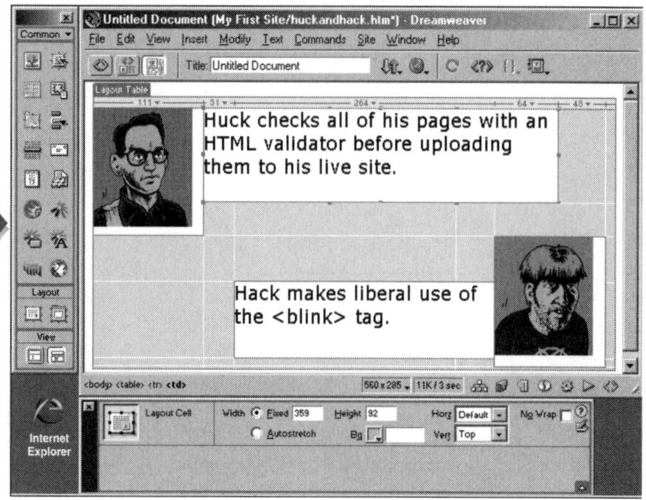

■ The layout cell resizes.

■ Dreamweaver does not let you overlap other layout cells that you have defined.

How do I add content to a layout table?

✔ You add content just like you do to a table in Standard View. However, you can add content only to cells you have defined using the layout cell tool. You cannot add content to the gray cells in a layout table; you must turn them into layout cells first with the layout cell tool.

How do I format a layout cell or table?

✔ To format a layout cell, click the outside edge of the cell. You can then adjust the cell's properties, such as its dimensions, alignment, and background color, in the Property Inspector. To format a table, click the Table tab and adjust the properties in the Property Inspector.

How do I delete a layout cell or table?

✔ Select the cell by clicking its edge, and then press Delete. Dreamweaver replaces the space with gray, noneditable cells. Similarly, you can delete a layout table by clicking the table's top tab and pressing Delete.

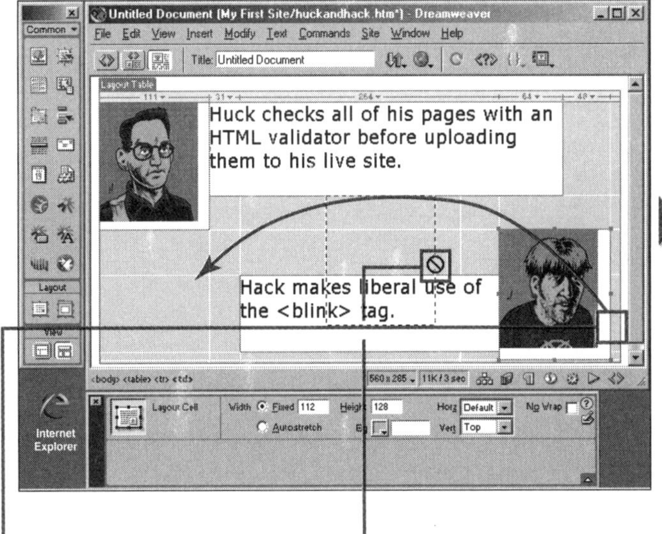

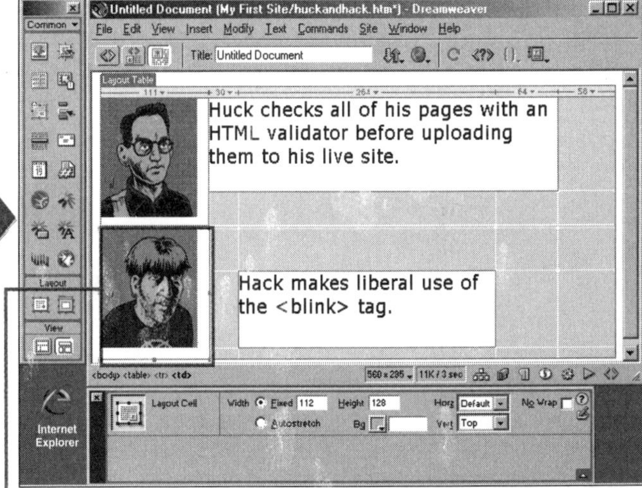

MOVE A CELL

1 Click the edge of a layout cell.

2 Click and drag the edge of the cell. Do not click and drag a handle.

■ A ⃠ symbol appears when you drag over other layout cells, because you cannot overlap cells.

3 Place the layout cell in its new position.

■ Undefined cells in the table adjust their sizes to make room for the cell's new position.

ADJUST THE WIDTH OF A LAYOUT TABLE

In the Layout View, you can specify how a table behaves when the user resizes the browser window. You can define the width of the columns of a layout table as either fixed or autostretch. You define a column as fixed by clicking its drop-down menu and selecting Add Spacer Image. You define a column as autostretch by selecting the Make Column Autostretch command in the menu.

Columns with fixed widths are kept that way with spacers — transparent images of a fixed width that Dreamweaver inserts into a table's cells. Autostretch columns lack spacers in their cells. They have their widths defined in the HTML as 100% so that they stretch to take up any available space on the page. Only one column in a layout table can be set to autostretch.

You can then define the widths as fixed or change them to autostretch by clicking the column heading to open a drop-down menu.

ADJUST THE WIDTH OF A LAYOUT TABLE

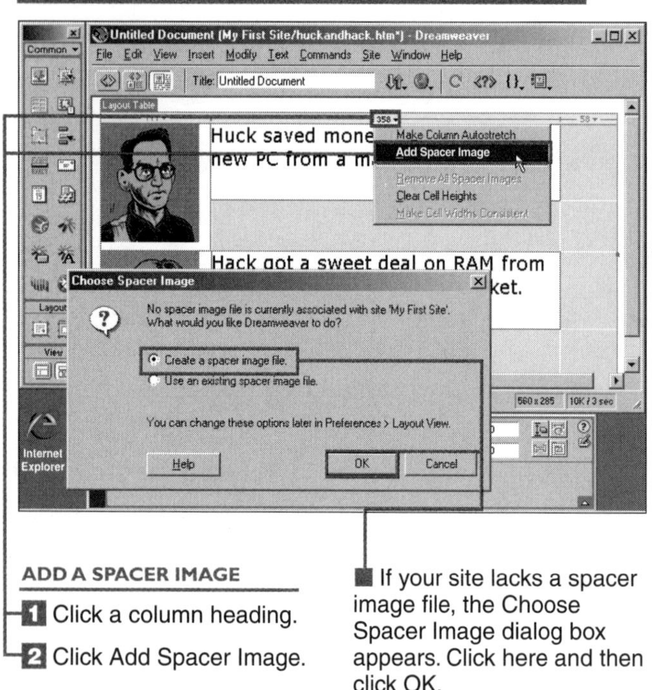

ADD A SPACER IMAGE

1 Click a column heading.

2 Click Add Spacer Image.

■ If your site lacks a spacer image file, the Choose Spacer Image dialog box appears. Click here and then click OK.

■ A spacer image appears in your local site folder.

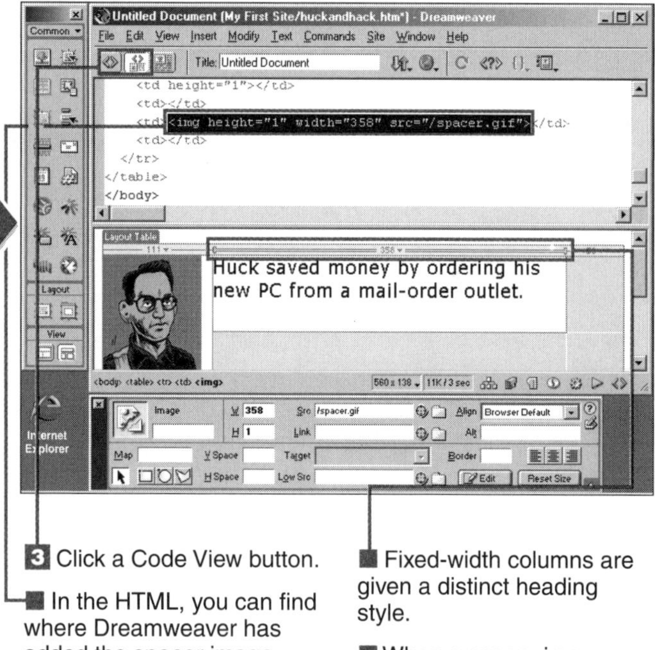

3 Click a Code View button.

■ In the HTML, you can find where Dreamweaver has added the spacer image.

■ Fixed-width columns are given a distinct heading style.

■ When a spacer image has been created for a site, Dreamweaver can use that image with any table in that site.

What is a spacer image?

✔ A spacer image is a transparent GIF image file that is one pixel by one pixel in size. Dreamweaver inserts these into tables and then uses HTML code to stretch the images to specific sizes to keep table cells at fixed widths. Because Dreamweaver can stretch a spacer image to any height or width, you only need one such image in your site folder.

What does it mean to "make cell widths consistent?"

✔ When objects in table cells are larger than the width defined by the HTML, table columns display at a width different from the HTML-defined width. You can rectify such conflicts by selecting Make Cell Widths Consistent in a table's column header menu.

What happens if spacers are removed from layout table cells?

✔ If a column in a table is set to autostretch, and other columns do not have spacers, those columns may change size when the browser is resized, or even disappear completely if they lack content. This is why spacers are important to keep widths in your layout tables fixed.

AUTOSTRETCH A COLUMN

1 Click a column heading.

2 Click Make Column Autostretch.

■ Dreamweaver writes HTML code that will stretch the column to take up any available horizontal space in the browser window.

3 Preview the page in a Web browser.

Note: To learn how to preview a page in a Web browser see Chapter 4.

■ To see the autostretch effect, you can resize the browser window.

AN INTRODUCTION TO FORMS

Adding forms to your Web site makes it more interactive, enabling viewers to type and submit information to you through your Web pages. Every form works in conjunction with a separate program called a *form handler,* which processes the form information.

Creating a Form

You can construct a form by inserting text fields, pull-down menus, check boxes, and other interactive elements into your page. You can also assign the Web address of a form handler to the form so that the information can be processed. Visitors to your Web page fill out the form and send the information to the form handler by clicking a Submit button.

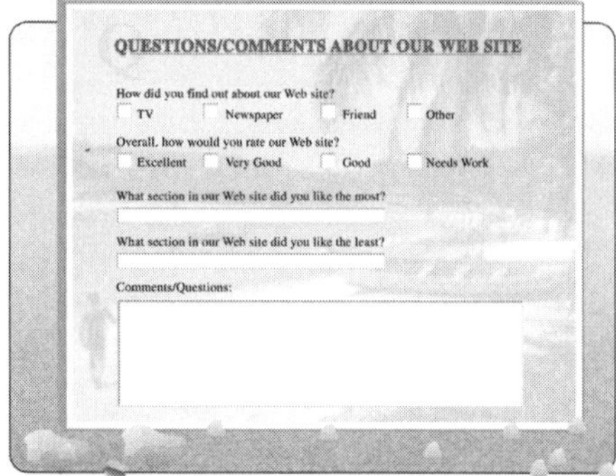

Choosing Your Form Elements

Creating a useful form requires you to think about the information you want to collect as well as how you want to collect it. You can use a variety of input elements to capture the information that you are interested in. Think about whether you want users to send you information in a free-form manner, such as typing into text fields, or in a more controlled manner, such as using menus or check boxes that you prepopulate with information.

Designing for the User

Think about your audience when creating your form. Make sure that you present the form clearly, with instructions at the beginning and intuitive labels on all the form elements. Also, make sure the form is not too long; not very many people take the time to fill out a long form.

Processing the Form Information

The form handler (also known as a *CGI script*) is the program that processes the form information and does something useful with it, such as forwarding the information to an e-mail address or entering it into a database. You cannot create form handlers with Dreamweaver; form handlers are often written in programming languages, such as Perl and C. However, you can find many ready-made form handlers free on the Web. Your Internet service provider may also have form handlers available for you to use with your site.

Handling the Form Data

The form handler receives the form information as a series of name/value pairs sent by the browser. Each name corresponds to an element in the form — for example, a text field, or menu. You define these names when you insert your form elements. The values correspond to the information that the user types into or selects with the form element.

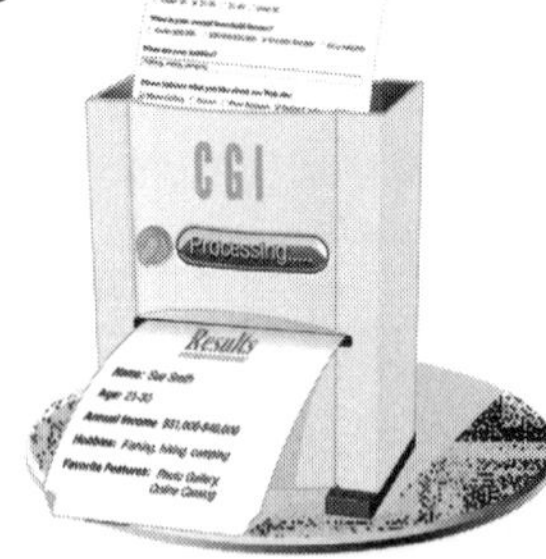

SET UP A FORM

You set up a form on your Web page by first creating a container that will hold the text fields, menus, and other form elements. You assign this container the Web address of the form handler — the program that processes the submitted form.

The form container is defined in HTML code with the opening and closing <form> tags. This container appears as a dashed red box in Dreamweaver so that you can tell where you need to insert the form elements. See the rest of the sections of this chapter to add elements.

If you try to add form elements to a page that does not have a form container, Dreamweaver displays an alert box asking if you want to insert one. Sometimes you do not need to insert a form container into your page if your form elements are interacting with JavaScript code rather than an external form handler.

SET UP A FORM

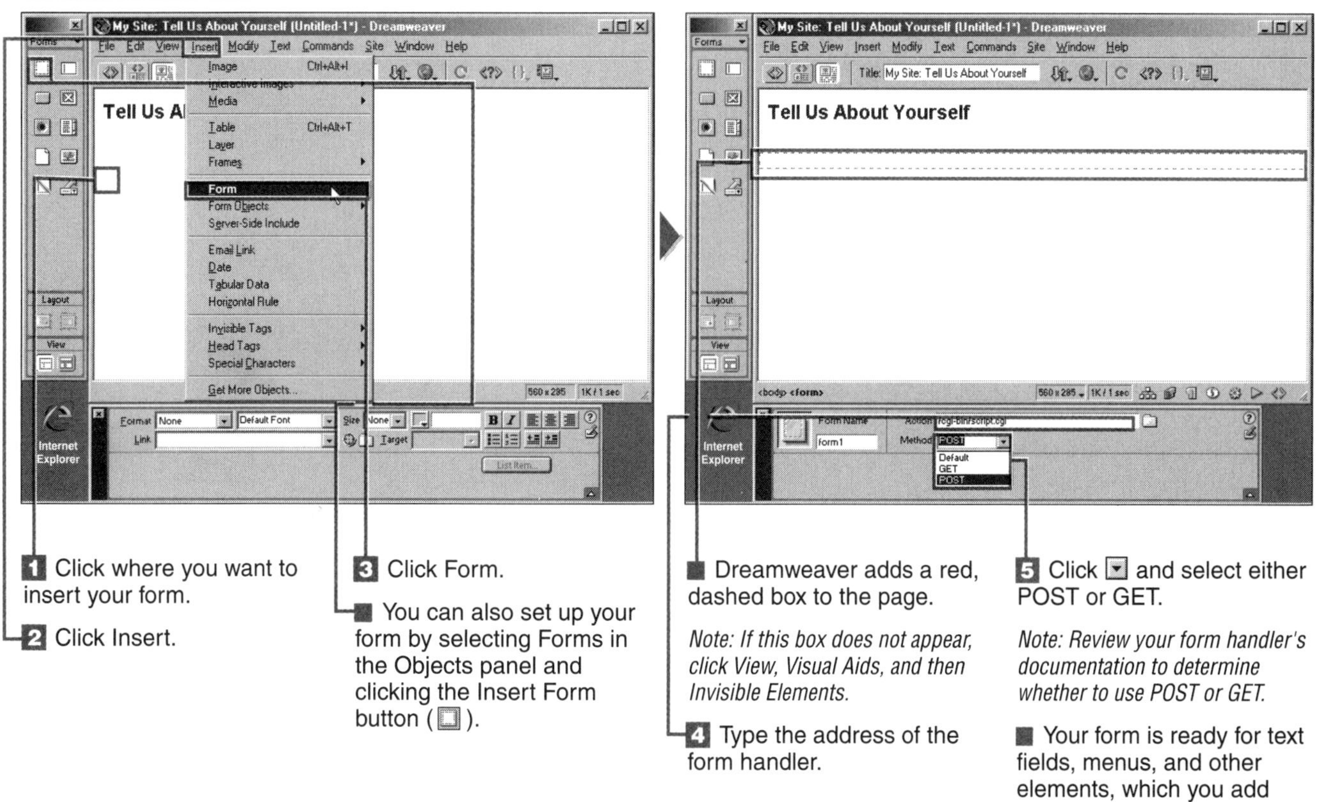

1 Click where you want to insert your form.

2 Click Insert.

3 Click Form.

■ You can also set up your form by selecting Forms in the Objects panel and clicking the Insert Form button (▢).

■ Dreamweaver adds a red, dashed box to the page.

Note: If this box does not appear, click View, Visual Aids, and then Invisible Elements.

4 Type the address of the form handler.

5 Click ▾ and select either POST or GET.

Note: Review your form handler's documentation to determine whether to use POST or GET.

■ Your form is ready for text fields, menus, and other elements, which you add inside the red box.

ADD A TEXT FIELD TO A FORM

You can add a *text field* to enable viewers to submit text through your form. Text fields are probably the most common form elements — they enable users to type names, addresses, brief answers to questions, and other short pieces of text.

You can customize your text field in various ways, such as defining the size of the field or limiting the number of characters it can contain. Assigning a character limit can sometimes keep users from typing erroneous information. For example, if your form handler can process only five-number postal codes, you may want to limit your form's postal-code text field to a maximum of five characters. To learn more about making sure a form's input is valid, see Chapter 13.

To give your users the opportunity to type longer text responses in a form, see the section "Add a Multiline Text Field to a Form."

ADD A TEXT FIELD TO A FORM

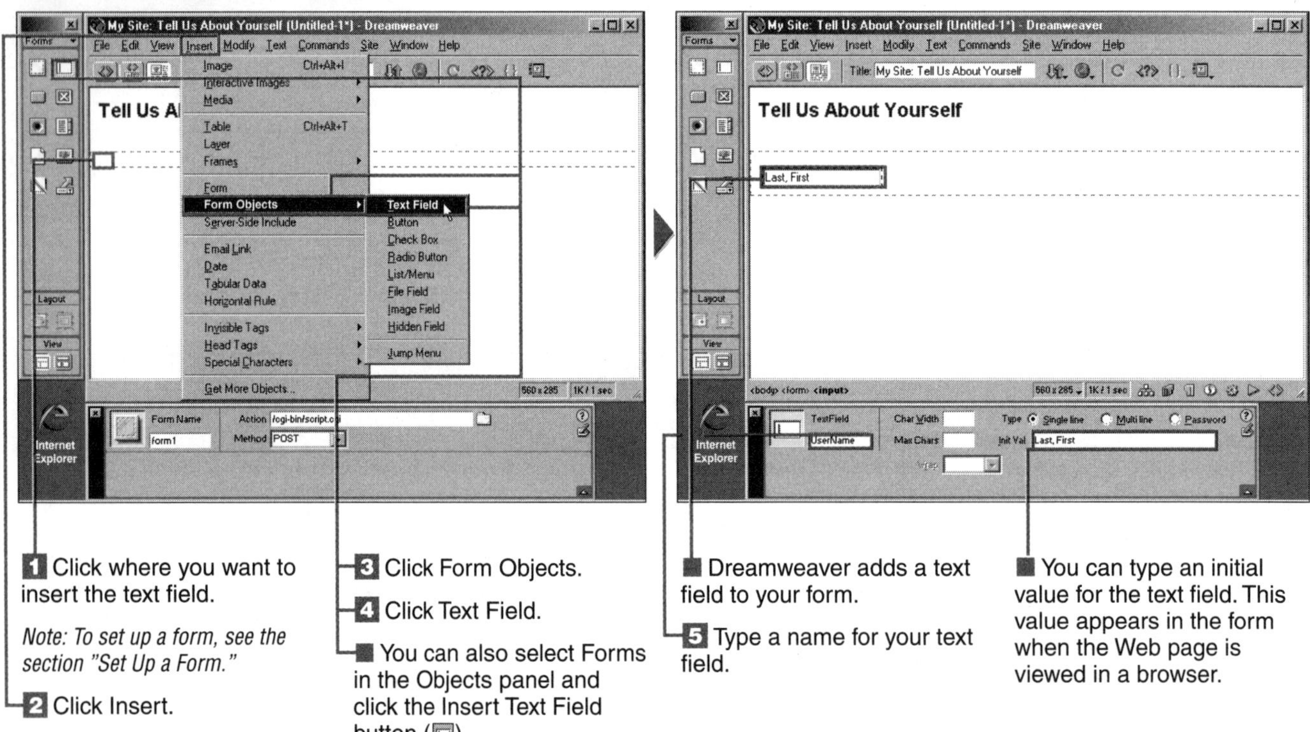

1 Click where you want to insert the text field.

Note: To set up a form, see the section "Set Up a Form."

2 Click Insert.

3 Click Form Objects.

4 Click Text Field.

■ You can also select Forms in the Objects panel and click the Insert Text Field button (▢).

■ Dreamweaver adds a text field to your form.

5 Type a name for your text field.

■ You can type an initial value for the text field. This value appears in the form when the Web page is viewed in a browser.

What is sent to the form handler from a text field?

✔ When a user submits a form, the browser sends the text field's name and the information typed into the field by the user. The form handler distinguishes one text field from another by their unique names, so be sure to give your text fields different names.

What happens if I do not specify an initial value, width, or maximum characters to my text field?

✔ The text field is blank when it appears in the browser, it displays at a default width — usually about 24 characters — and there is no limit as to how much text a user can type.

Can I define the style of text that appears in the text field?

✔ No. The browser determines what style of text appears in the form fields. But you can customize the style of the text labels that you put beside the text fields, just like you can any Web page text.

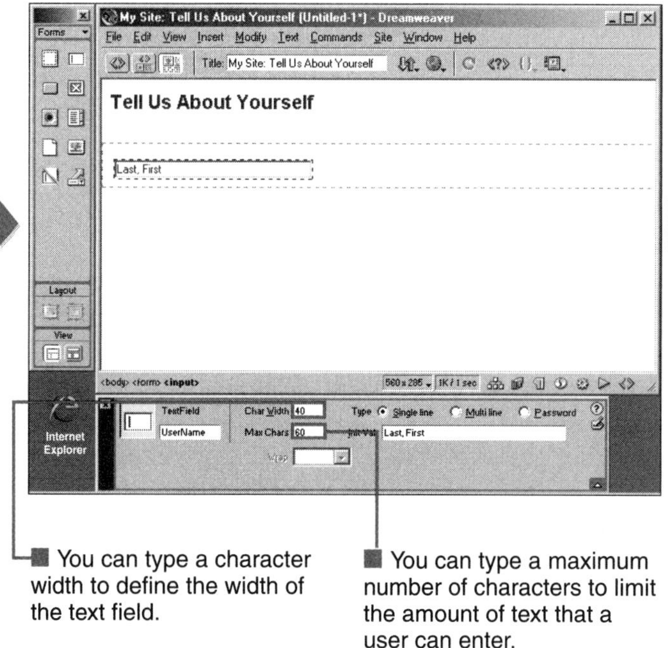

■ You can type a character width to define the width of the text field.

■ You can type a maximum number of characters to limit the amount of text that a user can enter.

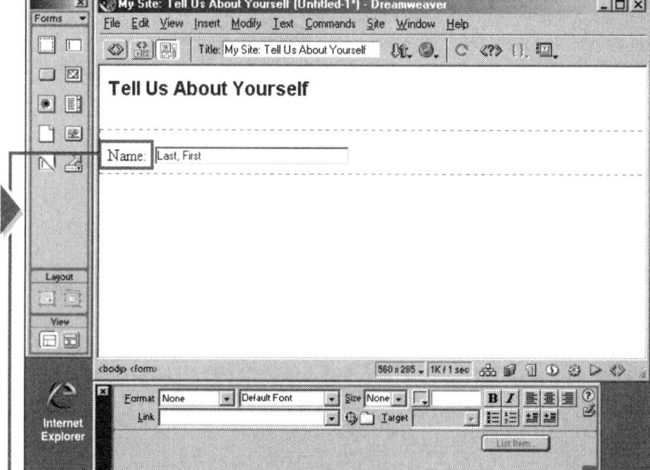

6 Type a label for the text field so that users know what kind of information to enter.

■ The text field is complete.

ADD A MULTILINE TEXT FIELD TO A FORM

Multiline text fields enable users to submit large amounts of text in a form. These fields are useful when you want viewers to send you lengthy feedback about your site or cut and paste large amounts of text — for example, a resume — into a form.

You define the size of the multiline text field by specifying the number of rows and columns you want to display. If the user adds more information than the text field allows, scroll bars appear on the edges of the text field for viewing all the entered text. Unlike single-line text fields, you cannot define a maximum character value for multiline text fields.

Dreamweaver enables you to specify a wrap value for multiline text fields. Doing so tells the browser what should happen when entered text hits the right side of the text-field window.

ADD A MULTILINE TEXT FIELD TO A FORM

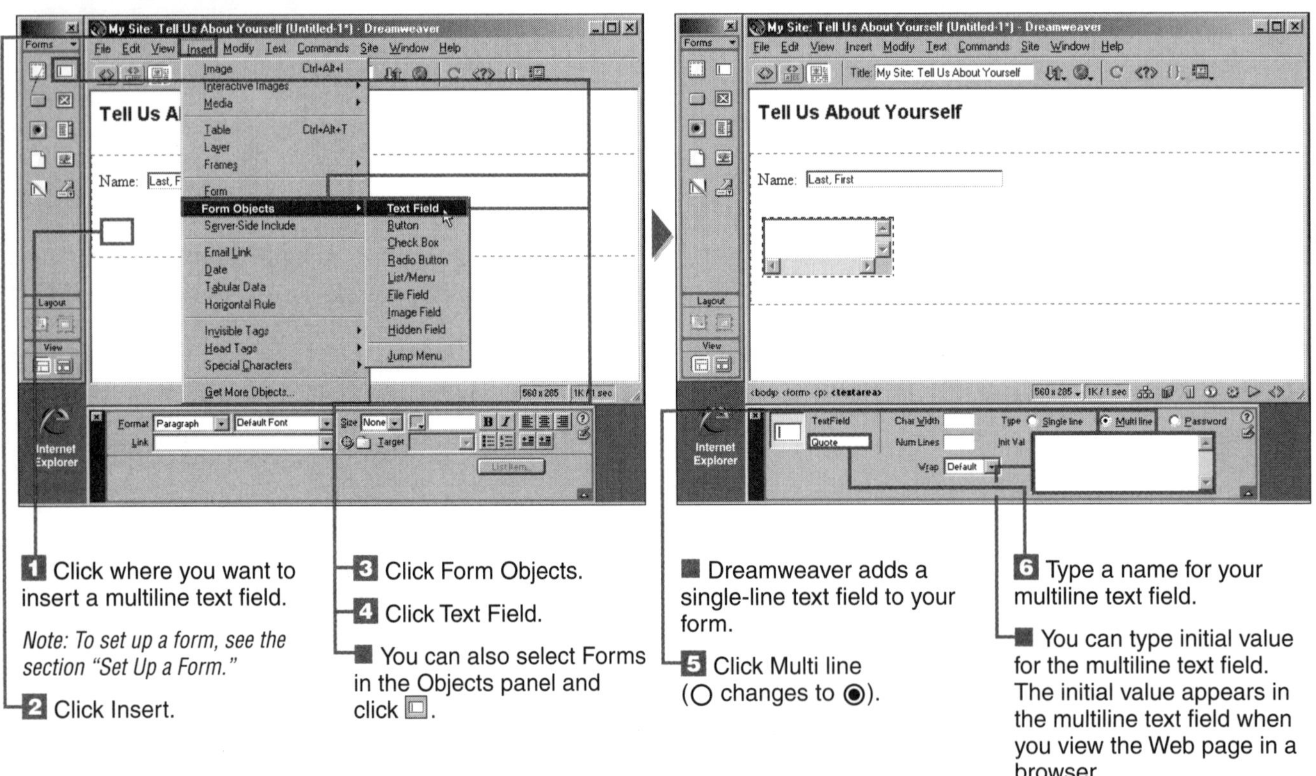

1 Click where you want to insert a multiline text field.

Note: To set up a form, see the section "Set Up a Form."

2 Click Insert.

3 Click Form Objects.

4 Click Text Field.

■ You can also select Forms in the Objects panel and click ▢.

■ Dreamweaver adds a single-line text field to your form.

5 Click Multi line (○ changes to ◉).

6 Type a name for your multiline text field.

■ You can type initial value for the multiline text field. The initial value appears in the multiline text field when you view the Web page in a browser.

Why should I define the wrap attribute of a multiline text field?

✔ In some Web browsers, text typed into a multiline text field does not automatically wrap when it reaches the right edge of the field, which may annoy the user. Selecting Virtual or Physical in the Wrap menu ensures that text automatically wraps in a multiline text field.

What is the difference between the wrap values?

✔ Setting wrap to Off turns off word wrapping. Users must add line breaks by pressing the Enter button (Windows) or the Return button (Mac) to wrap the text. The Virtual option automatically wraps the text in the text-field window, but the information is sent to the form handler without line breaks at those places. The Physical option wraps the lines and also sends line-break commands to the form handler. If you specify Default, the user's browser determines the wrapping behavior.

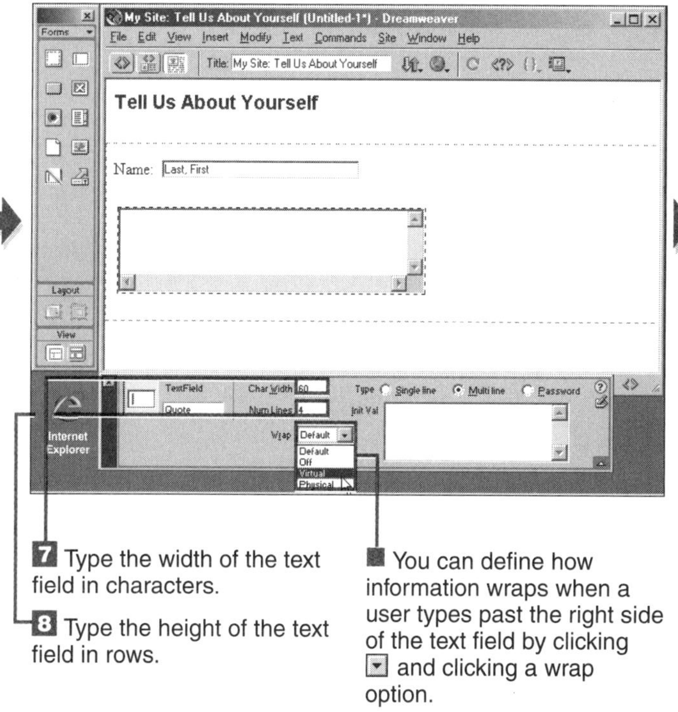

7 Type the width of the text field in characters.

8 Type the height of the text field in rows.

■ You can define how information wraps when a user types past the right side of the text field by clicking ▾ and clicking a wrap option.

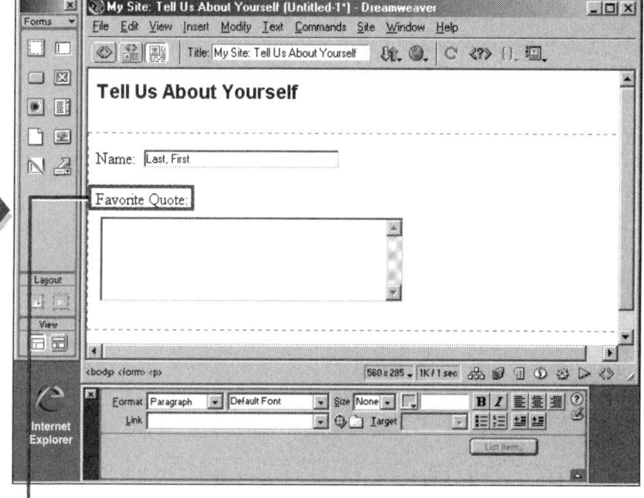

9 Type a label for the multiline text field so that users know what kind of information to enter.

■ The multiline text field is complete.

ADD A PASSWORD FIELD TO A FORM

A *password field* is similar to a text field, except that the text in the field is hidden as the user types it. The characters display as asterisks or bullets, depending on the type of operating system used to view the page. Password fields are useful for letting users type passwords or other secure pieces of text.

Just like regular text fields, you can set the length of a password field as well as the maximum characters that a user can type into the field. You can also type an initial value for the password field.

Often in account-setup forms, a user must choose a password and type it in two different password fields. The two fields allow a form handler to compare the two entries and make sure that users do not make mistakes when typing their password information.

ADD A PASSWORD FIELD TO A FORM

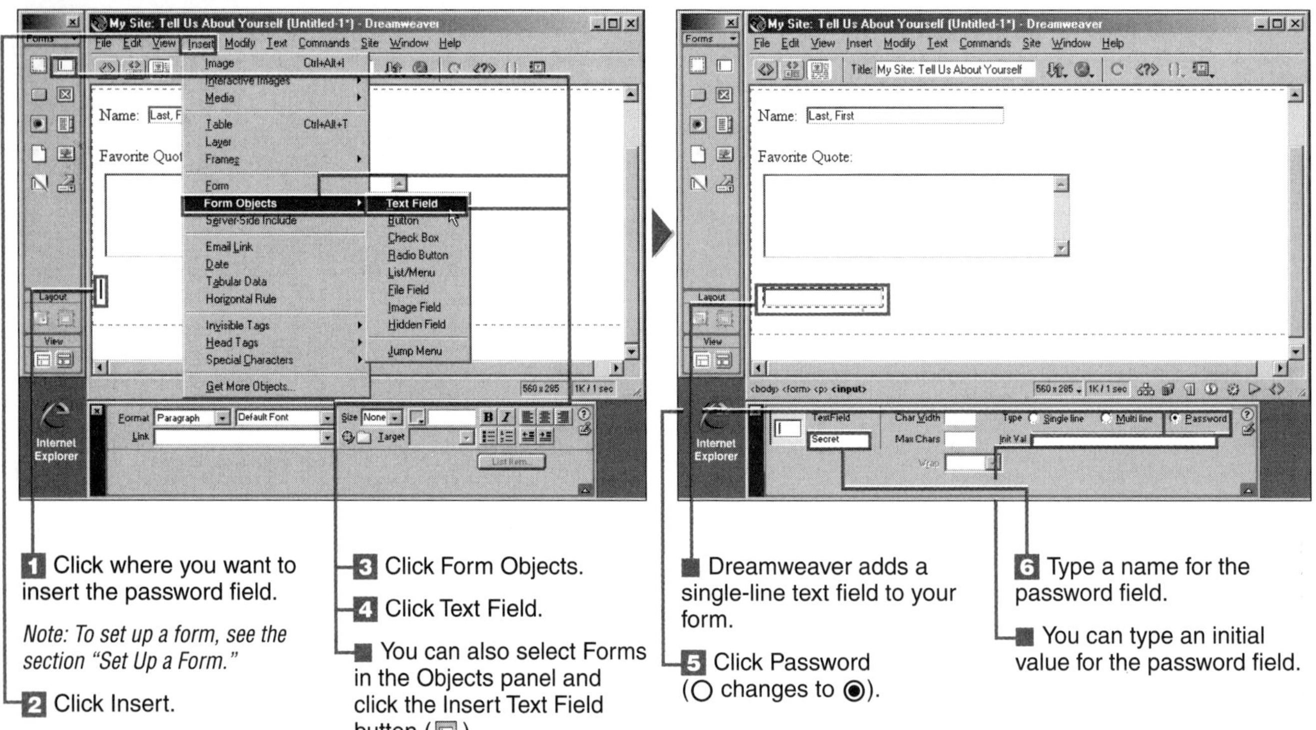

1 Click where you want to insert the password field.

Note: To set up a form, see the section "Set Up a Form."

2 Click Insert.

3 Click Form Objects.

4 Click Text Field.

■ You can also select Forms in the Objects panel and click the Insert Text Field button (▭).

■ Dreamweaver adds a single-line text field to your form.

5 Click Password (○ changes to ◉).

6 Type a name for the password field.

■ You can type an initial value for the password field.

Does the password field protect the user information as it travels over the Internet?

✔ No. The browser sends the password field information to the form handler as plain text, just like it does everything else in the form. The password field does *not* protect your information from someone intercepting it as it travels between the user's computer and the form handler. To protect your form information during transmittal, you can host your site on a secure Web server, which enables you to encrypt information passed from a user's browser to the server.

Can I specify the character that appears in the password field when the user types information?

✔ No. Dreamweaver does not let you specify the character that appears. What character appears depends on the operating system the viewer uses.

What is the difference between a password field and hidden field?

✔ Password fields allow viewers to type information into a form, but disguise that information so that onlookers cannot see it. Hidden fields let the Web designer add information to a form that does not appear in the browser window. For more information, see the section "Add Hidden Information to a Form."

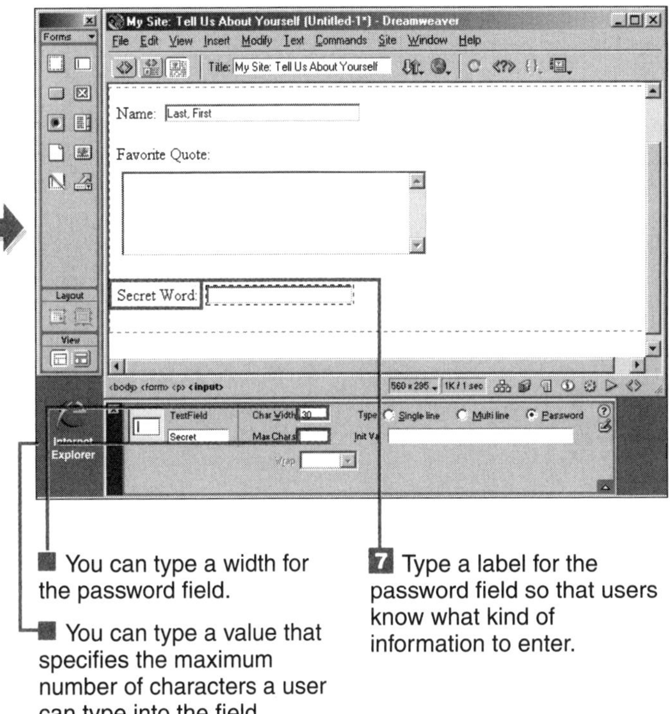

■ You can type a width for the password field.

■ You can type a value that specifies the maximum number of characters a user can type into the field.

7 Type a label for the password field so that users know what kind of information to enter.

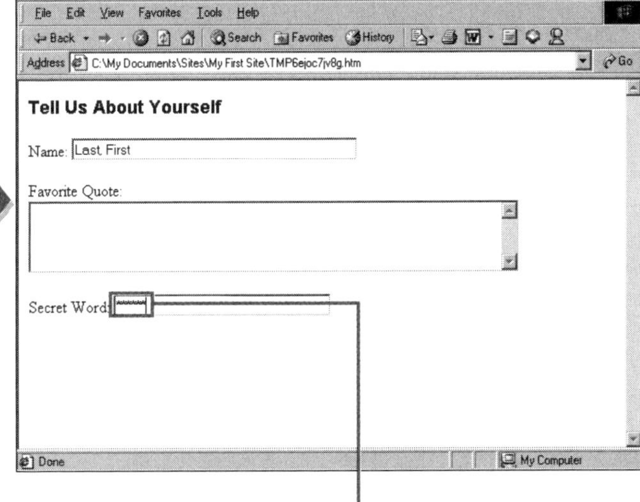

8 Preview the page in a browser.

Note: To preview a page in a browser, see Chapter 4.

■ When entering text in the password field, asterisks or bullets appear instead of the text.

ADD CHECK BOXES TO A FORM

Check boxes enable you to present multiple options in a form and allow users to select one, several, or none of the options. Check boxes usually appear in a group, with a label next to each check box.

Each check box in a form has a name and a checked value associated with it. You must assign a name and a checked value to each check box in a form. The name of each check box should be unique to the form. The checked value should be something similar to "checked," "selected," or "yes" to tell the form handler that the check box was indeed selected. (A form handler may need a particular check value to function correctly.)

If you want the user to select only a single choice from a group of choices, present the choices as radio buttons or in a menu instead of as check boxes. For more information, see the section "Add Radio Buttons to a Form" or "Add a Menu or List to a Form."

ADD CHECK BOXES TO A FORM

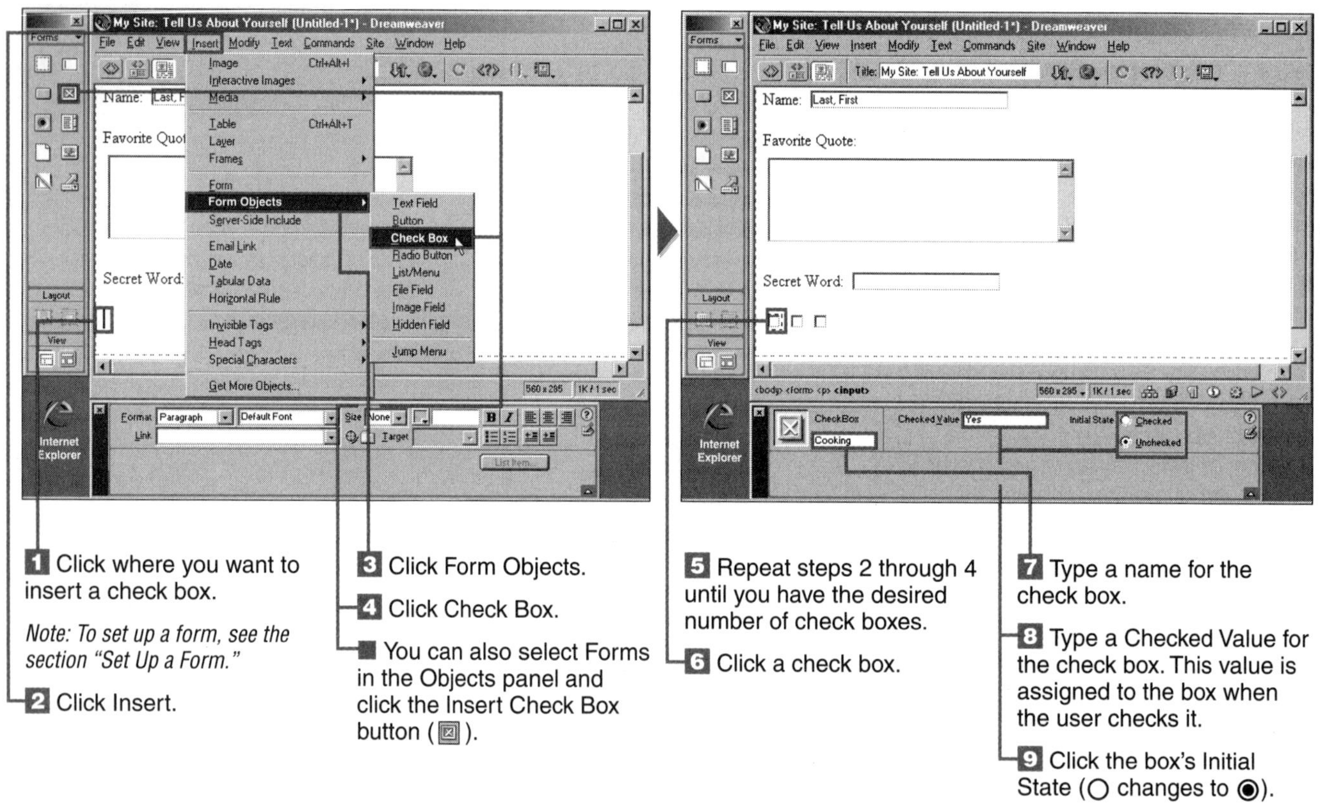

1 Click where you want to insert a check box.

Note: To set up a form, see the section "Set Up a Form."

2 Click Insert.

3 Click Form Objects.

4 Click Check Box.

■ You can also select Forms in the Objects panel and click the Insert Check Box button (☒).

5 Repeat steps 2 through 4 until you have the desired number of check boxes.

6 Click a check box.

7 Type a name for the check box.

8 Type a Checked Value for the check box. This value is assigned to the box when the user checks it.

9 Click the box's Initial State (○ changes to ◉).

What does the browser send to the form handler from a set of check boxes?

✔ When the user submits a form, the browser sends a name and value for each selected check box to the form handler. It does not send information for check boxes that the user did not select.

Can I use the same checked value for all my check boxes?

✔ Yes. This is probably a good idea, so that the information that is sent to the form handler is consistent. Remember that the *name* given to each check box should be unique.

Can I have several different groups of check boxes in the same form?

✔ Yes. How you organize the check boxes in a form — in one group, several groups, or each one by itself — is up to you. Because each box has a unique name, how you visually organize the boxes does not matter to the form handler.

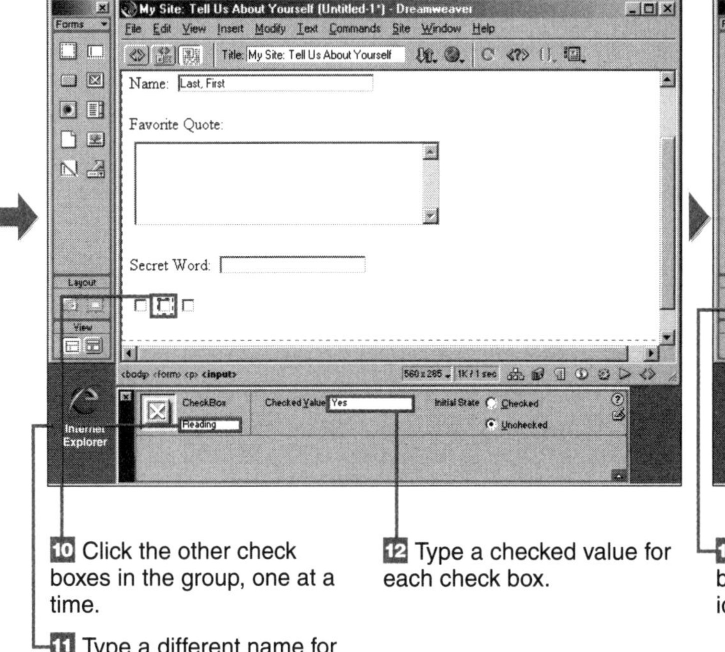

10 Click the other check boxes in the group, one at a time.

11 Type a different name for each check box.

12 Type a checked value for each check box.

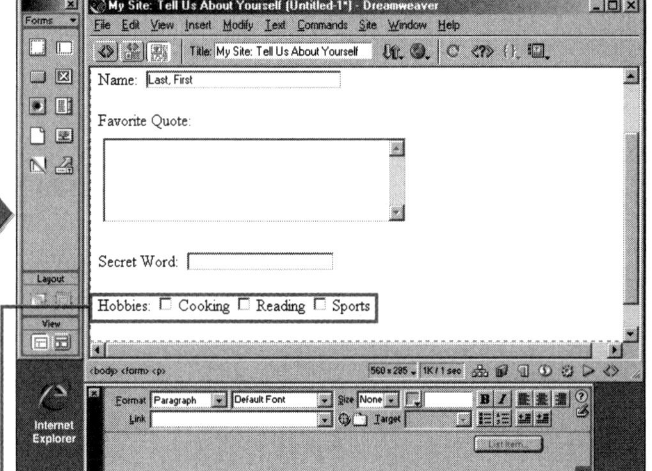

13 Type labels for the check boxes so that users can identify what to check.

ADD RADIO BUTTONS TO A FORM

You can let users select one option from a set of several options by adding a set of *radio buttons* to your form. With radio buttons, a user cannot select more that one option from a set.

Radio buttons get their name from the buttons on old car radios, where pushing in one button would cause the one that was currently selected to pop out.

Each radio button in a form has a name and a checked value associated with it. You should name all the radio buttons in a set the same name, while making the checked value for each button unique. This is in contrast to check boxes, where the names are unique and the checked values are the same.

If you want to allow the user to select more than one option from a group of options, you should present the options as check boxes. See the section "Add Check Boxes to a Form."

ADD RADIO BUTTONS TO A FORM

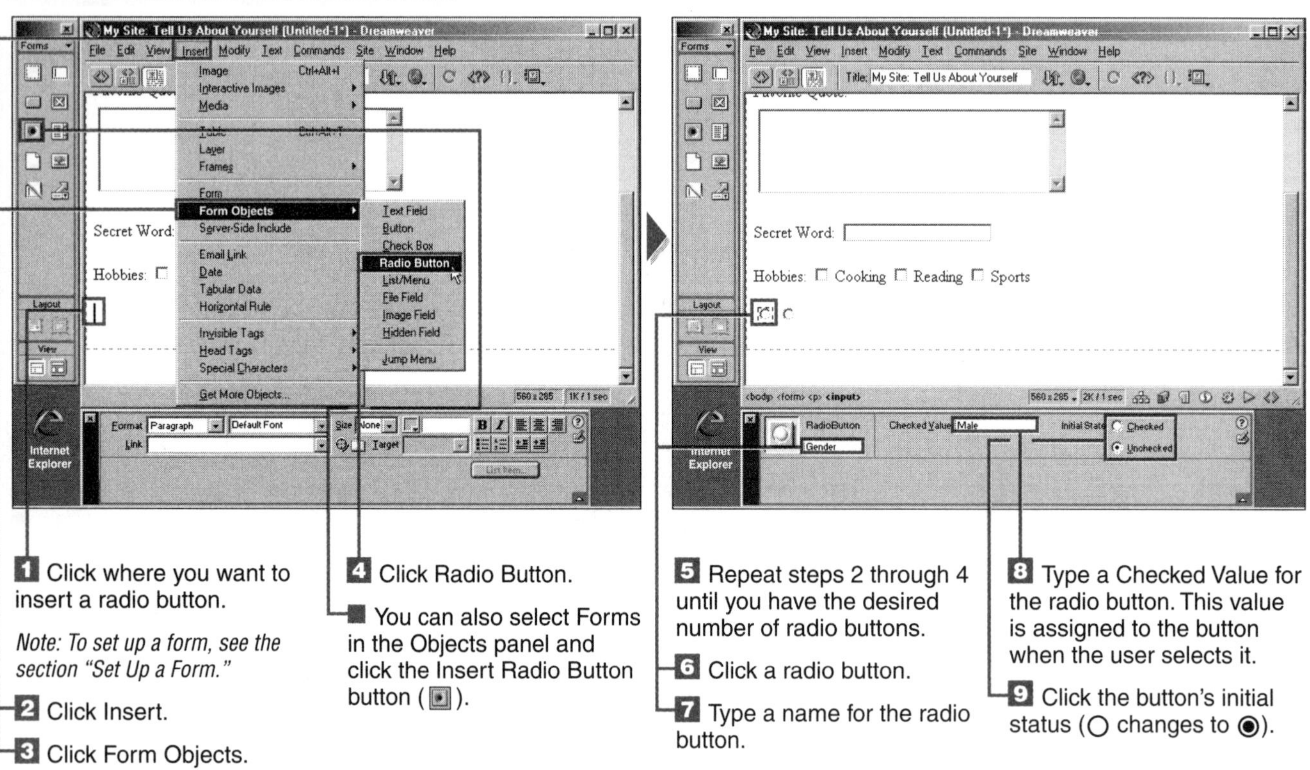

1 Click where you want to insert a radio button.

Note: To set up a form, see the section "Set Up a Form."

2 Click Insert.

3 Click Form Objects.

4 Click Radio Button.

■ You can also select Forms in the Objects panel and click the Insert Radio Button button (▣).

5 Repeat steps 2 through 4 until you have the desired number of radio buttons.

6 Click a radio button.

7 Type a name for the radio button.

8 Type a Checked Value for the radio button. This value is assigned to the button when the user selects it.

9 Click the button's initial status (○ changes to ◉).

What information does the browser send to the form handler from a set of radio buttons?

✔ When the user submits a form, the browser sends the name assigned to the set of buttons and the value of the selected radio button. It does not send information if the user did not select any buttons from the group.

What happens if I give each radio button in a set different names?

✔ If you do this, a user can select more than one button at a time, and after a button is selected, the user cannot deselect it. If the user submits the form, information from each selected button is sent to the form handler. This defeats the purpose of radio buttons.

Can I have more than one set of radio buttons in a form?

✔ Yes. Just make sure that each set uses a different name.

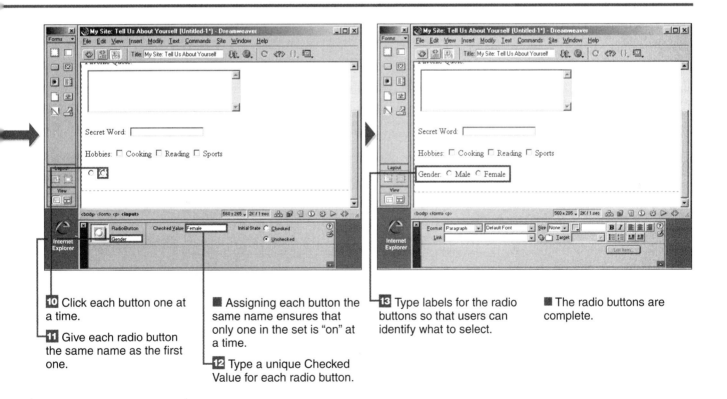

10 Click each button one at a time.

11 Give each radio button the same name as the first one.

■ Assigning each button the same name ensures that only one in the set is "on" at a time.

12 Type a unique Checked Value for each radio button.

13 Type labels for the radio buttons so that users can identify what to select.

■ The radio buttons are complete.

ADD A MENU OR LIST TO A FORM

Menus and *lists* are similar in that they both present users with a set of several options from which to choose. A menu allows users to choose one of the options, while a list allows users to choose several options. A user can select multiple items in a list by clicking the items while pressing the Ctrl button (Windows) or the Command button (Mac).

To view the options in a form menu, the user clicks the menu and the options appear in a drop-down arrangement. Items in a list are displayed in a window that a user can scroll through.

One advantage to using menus and lists in your forms is that they let you organize a lot of information in a small space. For example, a menu that allows users to select from a list of the 50 U.S. states only takes up one line in the browser window. Organizing this information using radio buttons requires you to display 50 different radio buttons in your form.

A separate Dreamweaver command enables you to create a special *jump menu* that lets a user navigate to other pages. See the section "Create a Jump Menu."

ADD A MENU OR LIST TO A FORM

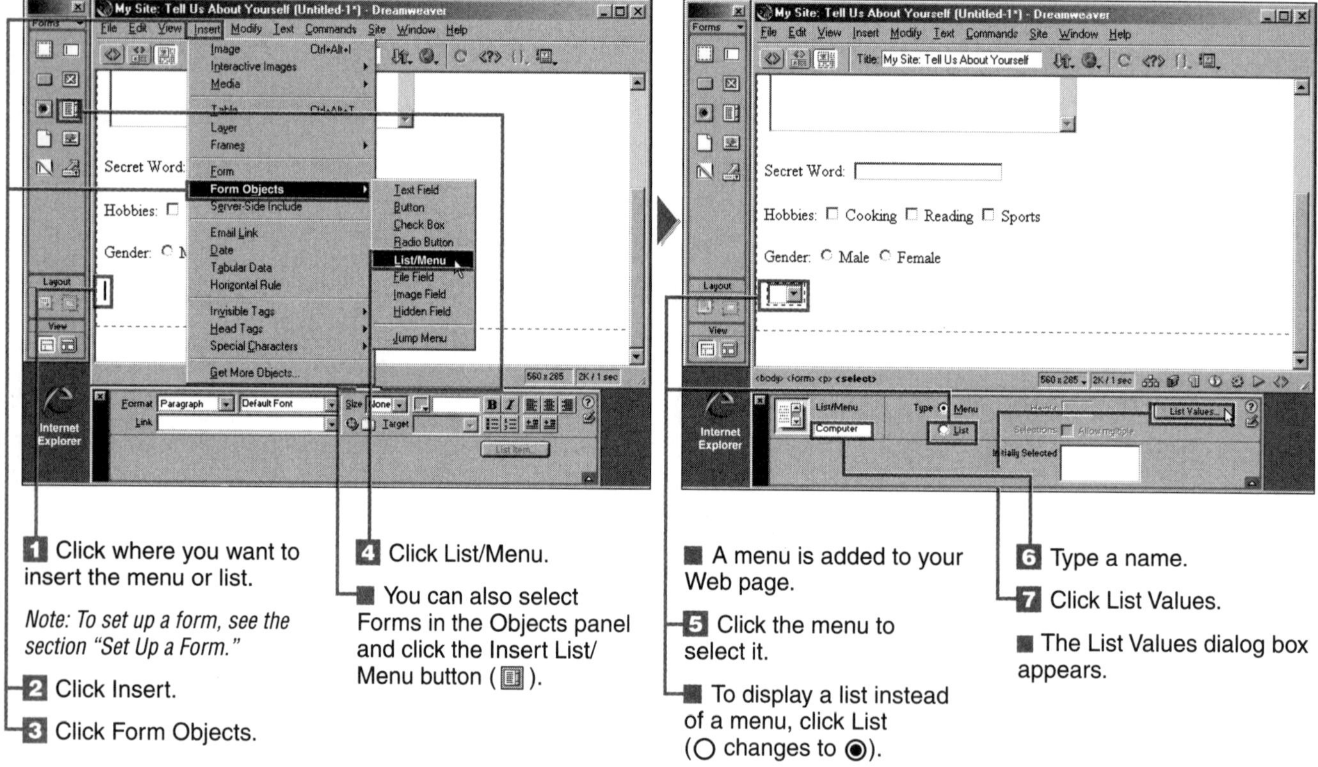

1 Click where you want to insert the menu or list.

Note: To set up a form, see the section "Set Up a Form."

2 Click Insert.

3 Click Form Objects.

4 Click List/Menu.

■ You can also select Forms in the Objects panel and click the Insert List/ Menu button ( ).

■ A menu is added to your Web page.

5 Click the menu to select it.

■ To display a list instead of a menu, click List (○ changes to ◉).

6 Type a name.

7 Click List Values.

■ The List Values dialog box appears.

What does the browser send to the form handler from a menu or list?

✔ When the user submits the form, the browser sends the name of the menu or list and the value of the option that the user selected. If a user selected multiple items in a list, the browser sends multiple name/value pairs.

Can I specify the width of a menu or list?

✔ No. The width of the menu or list is determined by its widest item. To change the width, you can make the items in the list shorter or longer.

When should I use a list instead of check boxes?

✔ Both elements let your viewers choose several options from a set of options in your form. Lists let you combine your set of options into a relatively small space; check boxes let your viewers have a clearer view of all the options that are available. The best choice probably depends on the type of information you are presenting and the space available.

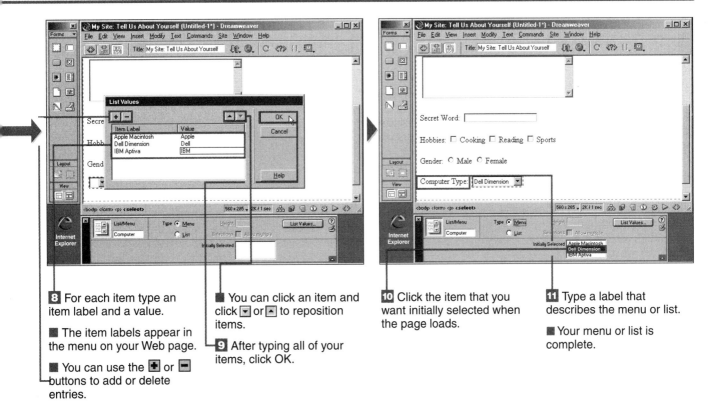

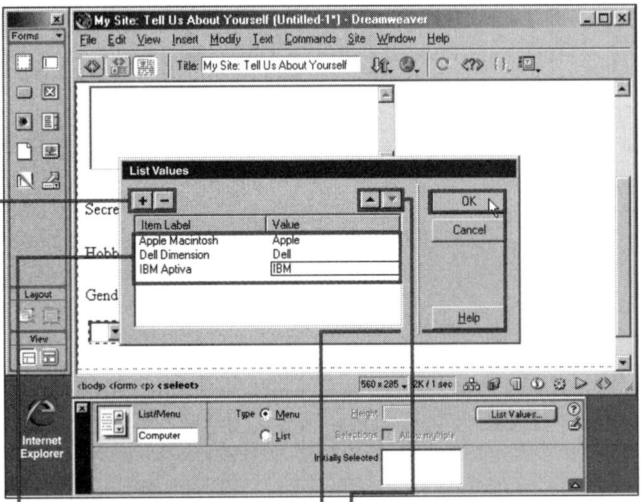

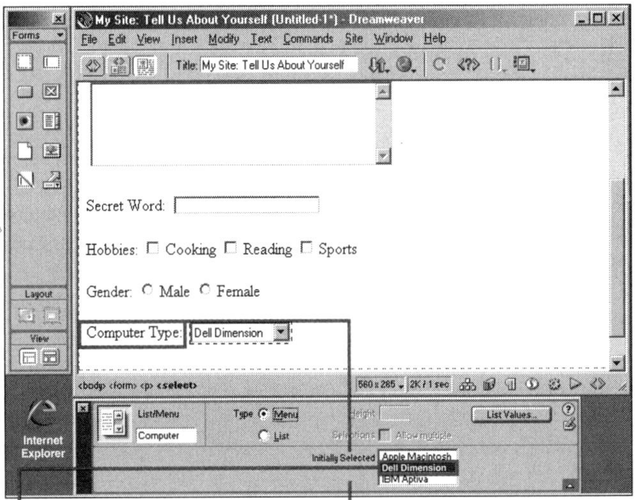

8 For each item type an item label and a value.

■ The item labels appear in the menu on your Web page.

■ You can use the + or − buttons to add or delete entries.

■ You can click an item and click ▼ or ▲ to reposition items.

9 After typing all of your items, click OK.

10 Click the item that you want initially selected when the page loads.

11 Type a label that describes the menu or list.

■ Your menu or list is complete.

CREATE A JUMP MENU

A *jump menu* lets users easily navigate to other Web pages using a form menu. You can also let users access non-HTML documents from a jump menu.

A jump menu uses the same HTML code as regular form menus (see "Add a Menu or List to a Form"), but combines that code with JavaScript. The JavaScript reads the selected menu item and then forwards the user to the requested URL.

You can use jump menus in addition to, or in place of, regular navigation links on your site. Because form menus enable you to hide a lot of information in a small amount of space, you can fit a lot more links in a jump menu than you can as regular text links on a page.

Jump menus can include an optional Go button that the user can click to visit the selected URL. If you do not include the Go button, users are forwarded to the new URL whenever they choose a new item in the menu.

CREATE A JUMP MENU

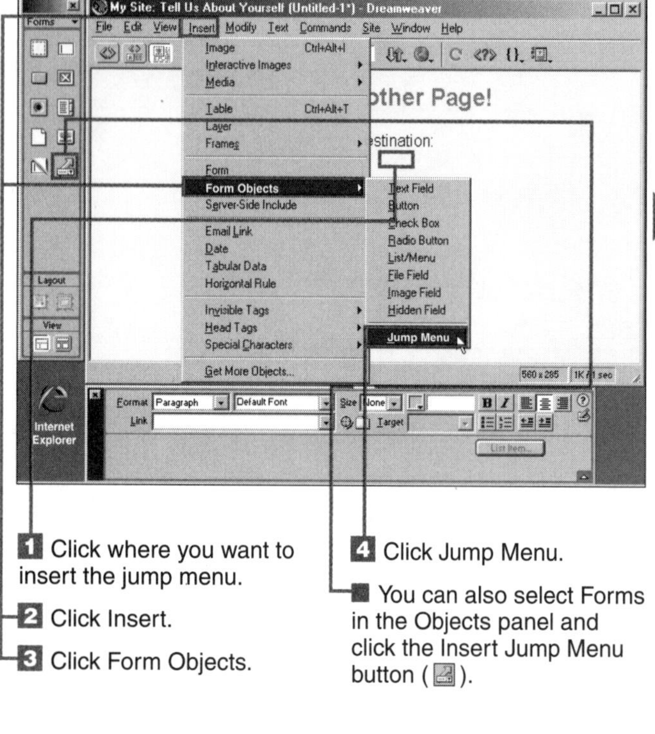

1 Click where you want to insert the jump menu.

2 Click Insert.

3 Click Form Objects.

4 Click Jump Menu.

■ You can also select Forms in the Objects panel and click the Insert Jump Menu button ( ).

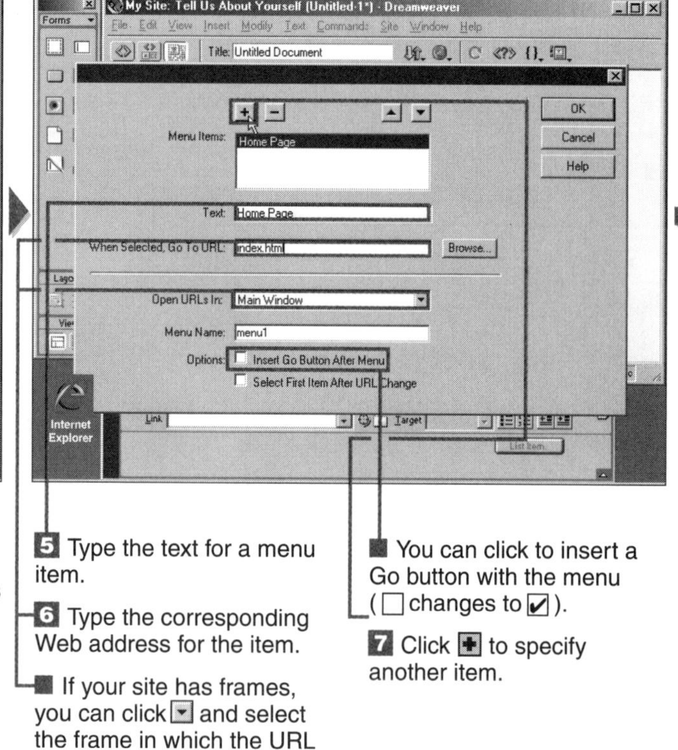

5 Type the text for a menu item.

6 Type the corresponding Web address for the item.

■ If your site has frames, you can click ▾ and select the frame in which the URL opens.

■ You can click to insert a Go button with the menu (☐ changes to ☑).

7 Click + to specify another item.

How do I edit the jump menu items after I have inserted the menu on the page?

✔ You can select the menu and click the List Values button in the Property Inspector. Doing this enables you to edit the menu items just as you would a regular form menu. You can also open the Behaviors panel and double-click the Jump Menu item. (Jump menus are listed in the Behaviors panel because their functionality requires JavaScript code.)

Does a jump menu require a form handler?

✔ No. A form handler does not process the jump menu information; JavaScript code does. If you view the code used to display a jump menu, you may notice that the `<form>` tag is missing the `action` attribute that usually specifies the form handler.

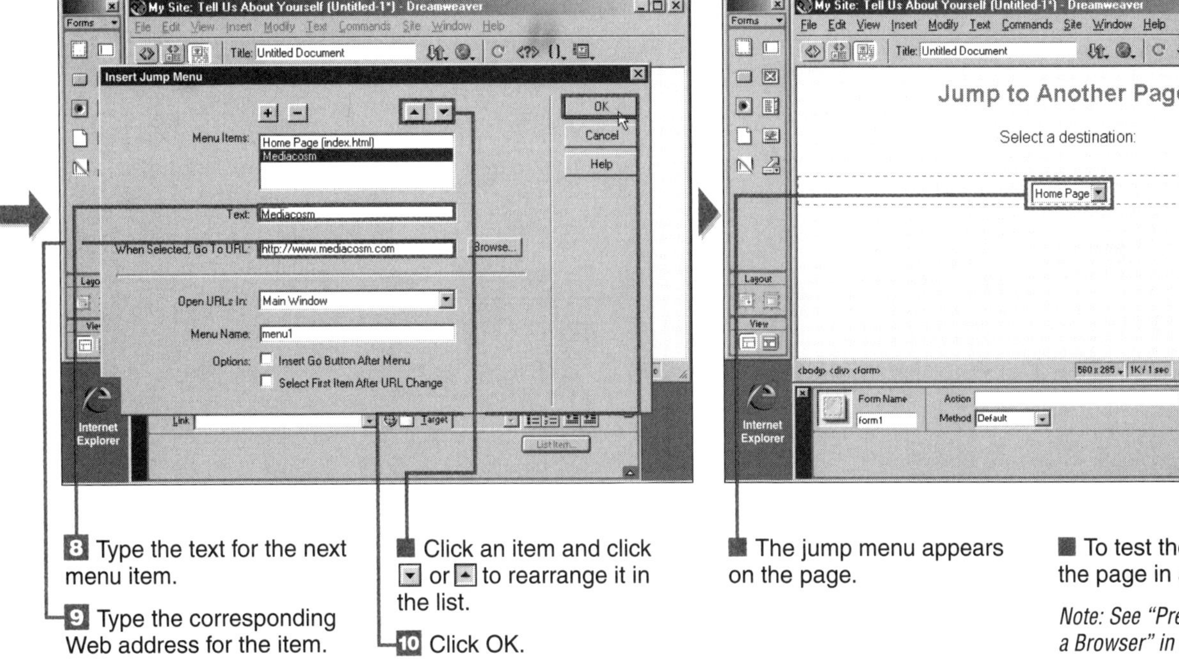

8 Type the text for the next menu item.

9 Type the corresponding Web address for the item.

■ Click an item and click ▼ or ▲ to rearrange it in the list.

10 Click OK.

■ The jump menu appears on the page.

■ To test the menu, preview the page in a Web browser.

Note: See "Preview a Web Page in a Browser" in Chapter 4.

ADD FILE UPLOADING TO A FORM

You can let users select files from their computer and upload them with the other form information that they submit. File uploading is a nice feature when you want users to send you a lot of information. For example, you can include a form element that allows users to send you their resumes through a form on a company's job-listing page. File uploading can also let people send you images and other information that you cannot send using other form elements.

The file-uploading feature inserts a text field and Browse button into the form container. The Browse button enables users to search their hard drives for the file that they want to send. After the user selects the file, the path to the file appears in the text field.

If you include a file-upload element in your form, you must set up your form to use the `post` method of sending its information to the form handler. For more information, see the section "Set Up a Form."

ADD FILE UPLOADING TO A FORM

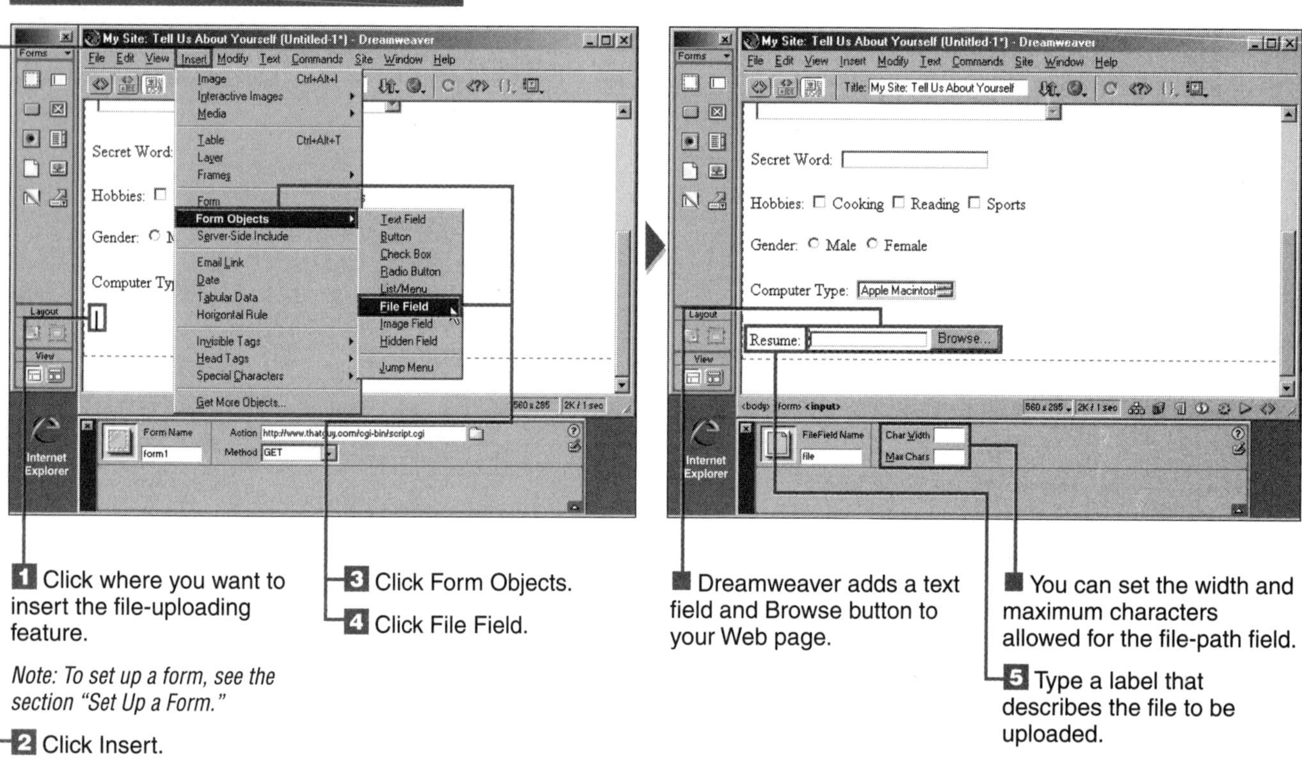

1 Click where you want to insert the file-uploading feature.

Note: To set up a form, see the section "Set Up a Form."

2 Click Insert.

3 Click Form Objects.

4 Click File Field.

■ Dreamweaver adds a text field and Browse button to your Web page.

■ You can set the width and maximum characters allowed for the file-path field.

5 Type a label that describes the file to be uploaded.

ADD HIDDEN INFORMATION TO A FORM

You can use hidden form fields to add information to your forms and not have that information displayed in the browser window. You may want to add hidden information in order to customize the form for use with a particular page or form handler.

For example, you may add a hidden field that tells the form handler what URL you want users forwarded to after they submit a form.

The information in a hidden field consists of a name/value pair, just as other form elements have names to distinguish them and values that represent the user-added information.

Dreamweaver denotes a hidden form field in the document window by a special icon. You need to turn on Dreamweaver's invisible elements to see the icon.

ADD HIDDEN INFORMATION TO A FORM

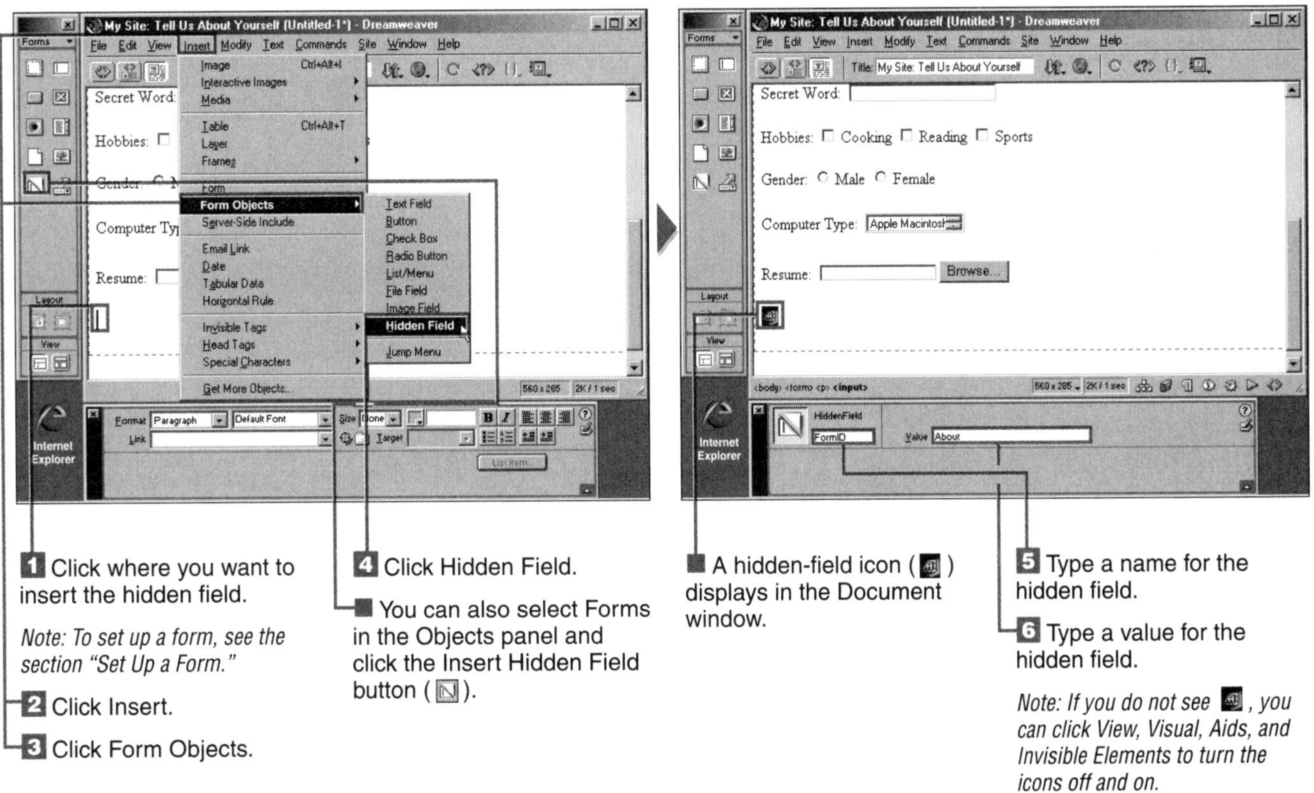

1 Click where you want to insert the hidden field.

Note: To set up a form, see the section "Set Up a Form."

2 Click Insert.

3 Click Form Objects.

4 Click Hidden Field.

■ You can also select Forms in the Objects panel and click the Insert Hidden Field button (▣).

■ A hidden-field icon (▣) displays in the Document window.

5 Type a name for the hidden field.

6 Type a value for the hidden field.

Note: If you do not see ▣, you can click View, Visual, Aids, and Invisible Elements to turn the icons off and on.

ADD A SUBMIT BUTTON TO A FORM

You can add a button that enables users to submit a form's information to the specified form handler. (To specify a form handler, see the section "Set Up a Form.")

You can specify the label for the Submit button in the Label field of the Property Inspector. The default label is Submit.

An alternative to the standard HTML button for the Submit button is a custom image button. You can create a custom button in an image editor, such as Macromedia Fireworks or Adobe Photoshop.

How do I add a custom image button to my form?

✔ You can add a custom image button to your form by selecting Forms in the Objects panel and clicking ▣. Make sure you insert it inside the red dashed box of your form. You must then change the Image Field information in the Property Inspector to "Submit" for that image. This causes Dreamweaver to use the image as a clickable Submit button.

ADD A SUBMIT BUTTON TO A FORM

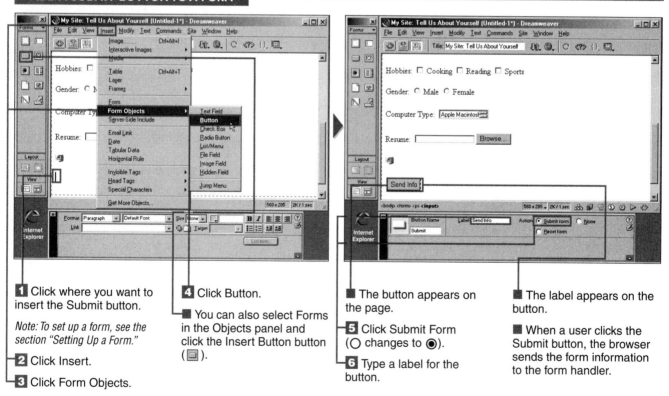

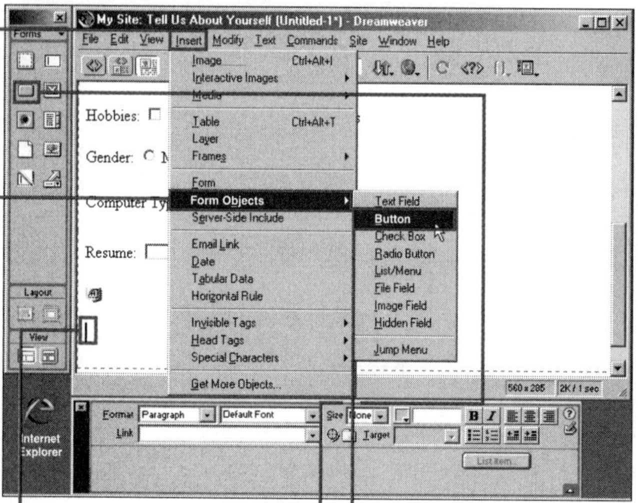

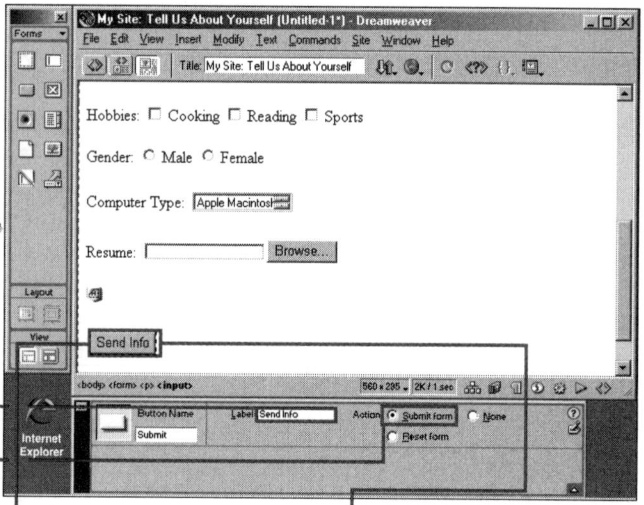

1 Click where you want to insert the Submit button.

Note: To set up a form, see the section "Setting Up a Form."

2 Click Insert.

3 Click Form Objects.

4 Click Button.

■ You can also select Forms in the Objects panel and click the Insert Button button (▭).

■ The button appears on the page.

5 Click Submit Form (○ changes to ◉).

6 Type a label for the button.

■ The label appears on the button.

■ When a user clicks the Submit button, the browser sends the form information to the form handler.

ADD A RESET BUTTON TO A FORM

You can add a button that enables users to reset all the elements of a form to their initial values. This Reset button enables users to quickly erase their form entries so that they can start over again.

You can specify the label that goes on the Reset button in the Label field of the Property Inspector. Reset is the default label.

An alternative to the standard HTML button for the Reset button is a custom image button. You can create a custom button in an image editor, such as Macromedia Fireworks or Adobe Photoshop.

How do I add a custom Reset button to my form?

✔ You can add a custom image button to your form by selecting Forms in the Objects panel and clicking the Insert Image Field button (▣). Make sure you insert it inside the red dashed box of your form. You must then change the Image Field information in the Property Inspector to "Reset" for that image. This causes Dreamweaver to use the image as a clickable Reset button.

ADD A RESET BUTTON TO A FORM

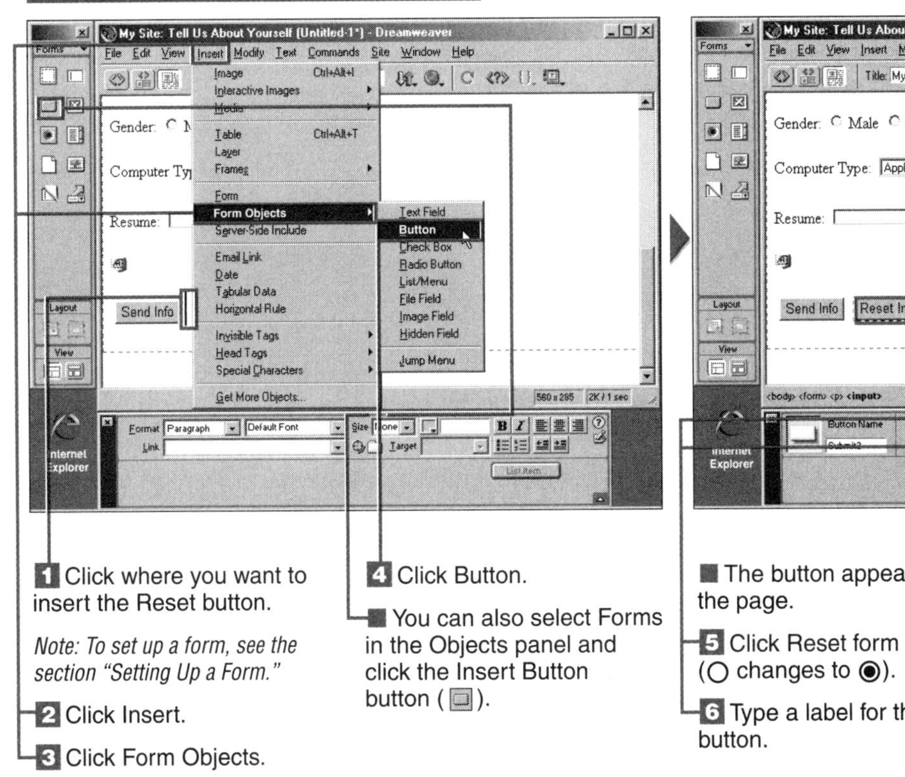

1 Click where you want to insert the Reset button.

Note: To set up a form, see the section "Setting Up a Form."

2 Click Insert.

3 Click Form Objects.

4 Click Button.

■ You can also select Forms in the Objects panel and click the Insert Button button (▢).

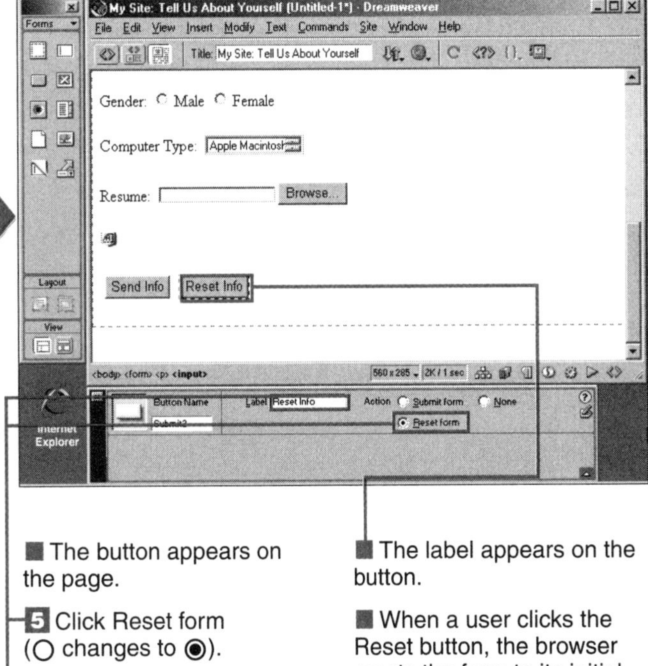

■ The button appears on the page.

5 Click Reset form (○ changes to ◉).

6 Type a label for the button.

■ The label appears on the button.

■ When a user clicks the Reset button, the browser resets the form to its initial values.

AN INTRODUCTION TO FRAMES

Frames enable you to divide your Web page into several smaller windows and then display a different Web page in each window. You commonly use frames to organize a site's navigational links. You can place a list of navigational links in one frame and have the destination pages open in a larger content area. Organizing your site this way means the browser does not need to reload the navigational links each time the user clicks a link. The user can always see the links, as well.

Issues to Consider When Using Frames

Frames can introduce some complications. Because frames split your site content into more pages, other Web designers may find it difficult to link to specific content on your site. Also, users with older browsers that are not frames-capable, or with small monitors that can not display a large window size, cannot always view framed pages. Additionally, frames mean more work for the designer, who has to keep track of how to organize content in the frameset.

Creating Frames

You create a framed Web site by dividing the Document window horizontally or vertically one or more times. You can also choose from one of several predefined frameset templates in Dreamweaver. You then load a Web page into each frame by specifying the page in the Property Inspector. You control the overall organization of frames in your site by a separate HTML document called a *frameset page*. You can manage the pages that make up your framed site using Dreamweaver's Frames panel.

Behavior of Framed Pages

Frames allow the pages that users view to operate independently of one another. As you scroll through the content of a frame, the content in other frames remains fixed. In one frame, you can create hyperlinks that open pages in other frames; you can either make the linked pages part of your site or external Web sites. You can also cause a linked Web page to open on top of any existing frames, thereby taking a user out of the framed version of your site.

DIVIDE A PAGE INTO FRAMES

The first step you perform to create a framed Web site is to divide the Document window into more than one frame. You can split the Document window horizontally to create a frameset with left and right frames, or you can split it vertically to create a frameset with top and bottom frames. An alternative to splitting the window by hand is choosing one of Dreamweaver's predefined framesets for your site. See the section "Insert a Predefined Frameset" for more information.

Many Web sites consist of a narrow left frame, containing navigation links, and a wide right frame, displaying the site's main content. Other site designs may split the window vertically and place the site's title and navigation links across a short top frame and the main content in a taller bottom frame. See the section "Change the Dimensions of a Frame" to learn how to resize frames.

For a more complicated framed site, you can continue to split your component frames to create a *nested* frameset. Nested framesets are useful if you have many different page elements, each of which needs to be placed in its own frame. See "Nest Frames" for more information.

DIVIDE A PAGE INTO FRAMES

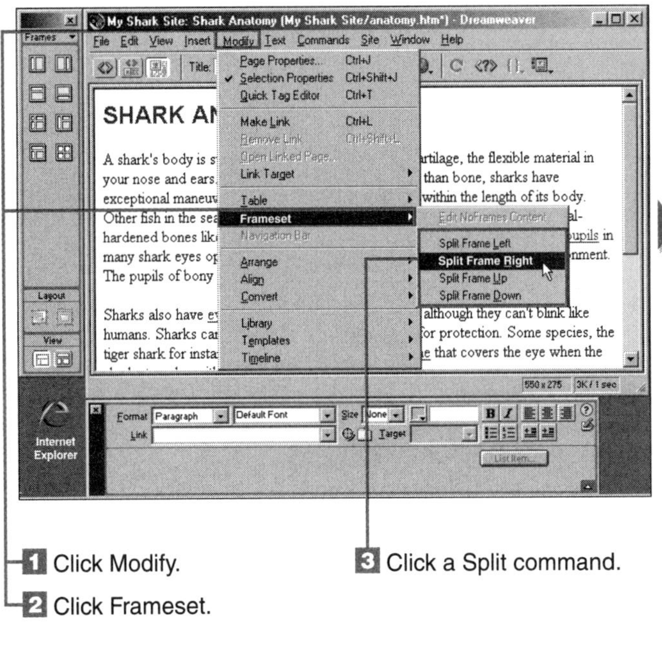

1 Click Modify.

2 Click Frameset.

3 Click a Split command.

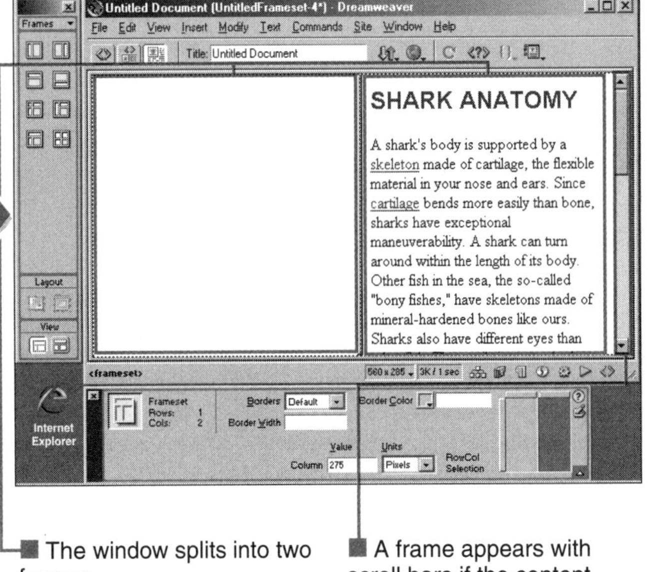

■ The window splits into two frames.

■ If content existed in the original page, it shifts to one of the new frames.

■ A frame appears with scroll bars if the content extends outside its borders.

INSERT A PREDEFINED FRAMESET

Dreamweaver makes it easy to create several popular frameset styles with its predefined framesets, which you can find in the Objects panel. After choosing a frameset from the Objects panel, Dreamweaver applies the frameset to the current page and moves any existing content into one of the new frames.

When you apply a predefined frameset to a page, Dreamweaver automatically gives your frames generic names, such as topFrame, leftFrame, and mainFrame. If you prefer, you can rename your frames to reflect the type of content that is inside them. For more information, see the section, "Name a Frame."

Most of the predefined page designs lend themselves to a particular site-navigation scheme. For example, you can place a list of navigational links in the narrow side frame and the main site content in one of the larger frames.

To create Web pages after you insert a frameset, see the section "Add Content to a Frame."

INSERT A PREDEFINED FRAMESET

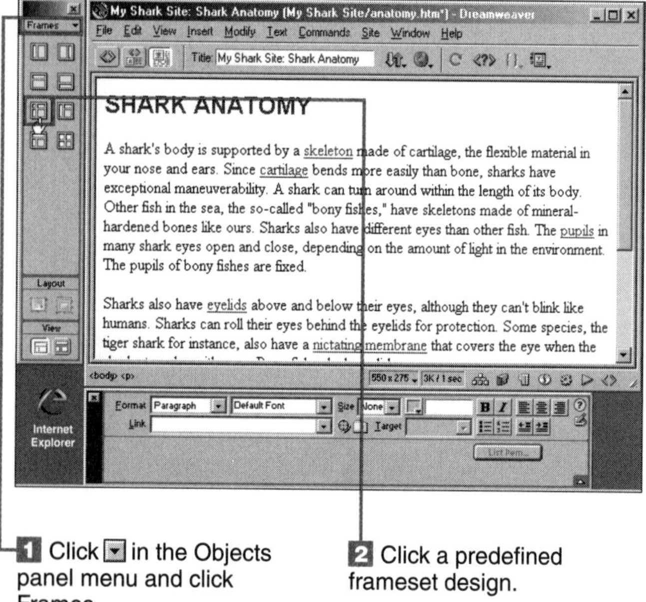

1 Click ▼ in the Objects panel menu and click Frames.

2 Click a predefined frameset design.

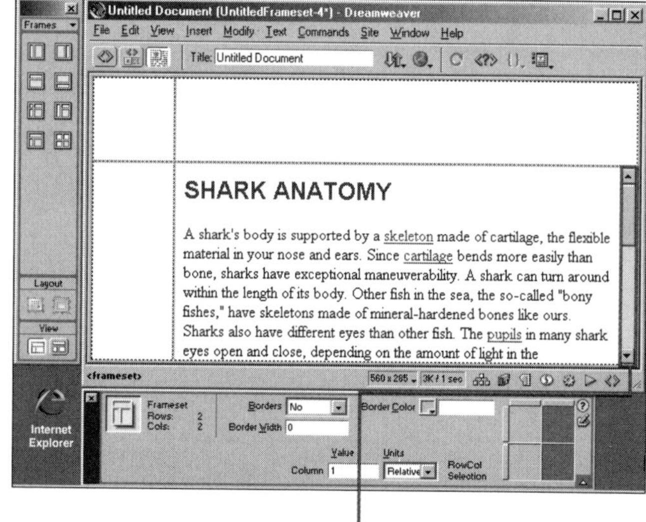

■ Dreamweaver applies the frameset to your page.

■ If content exists in the original page, it shifts to one of the new frames.

■ A frame appears with scroll bars if the content extends outside its borders.

NEST FRAMES

Dreamweaver's frame commands make creating and managing nested frames easy. Nesting frames involves subdividing the frames of an existing frameset. Nested frames give your site a more complex organization and more options regarding where you can insert your page information.

To nest frames, you click inside an existing frame and then subdivide that frame horizontally or vertically. See the section "Divide a Page into Frames" for more information. Some of the predefined framesets in the Objects panel are nested frameset designs. See the section "Insert a Predefined Frameset" to see what designs are available.

You add content to your nested frames the same way you do regular frames. See the section "Add Content to a Frame" for more information.

Can I nest frames using HTML code?

✔ Yes. You may find nested framesets hard to create using HTML. To see the code for a frameset, select the frameset by clicking on a frame border, and click the Show Code View button on the top of the Document window. You create nested framesets with nesting groups of `<frameset>` and `<frame>` tags.

NEST FRAMES

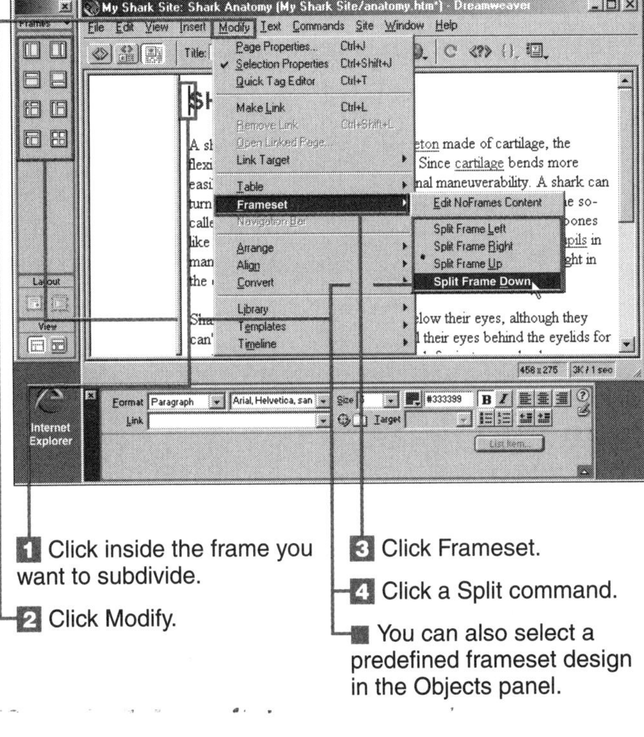

1 Click inside the frame you want to subdivide.

2 Click Modify.

3 Click Frameset.

4 Click a Split command.

■ You can also select a predefined frameset design in the Objects panel.

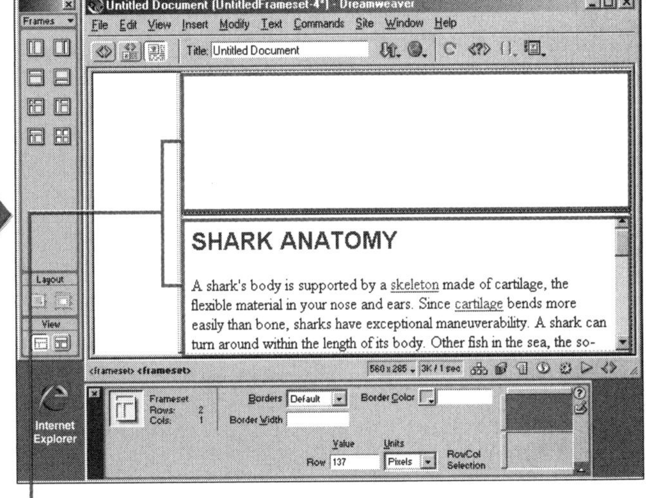

■ Dreamweaver splits the selected frame into two frames. You now have a frameset inside a frameset.

■ You can add content to the empty frame.

Note: See the section "Adding Content to a Frame" for more information.

■ You can continue to split your frames into more frames.

ADD CONTENT TO A FRAME

You can add content to a frame by opening up an existing HTML document in the frame. You can also add content by typing text or inserting elements, such as images and tables, just as you do with an unframed page.

Content in a frame behaves just as it does in a normal Document window. Scroll bars appear on the frame if the content extends outside its boundaries. To turn the scroll bars off, see the section "Control Scroll Bars in Frames." Text also wraps at the edge of a frame, unless you enclose the text in a fixed-width table.

When you design the layout of the content in your framesets, think about how your audience views your site. A user may see a framed site differently depending on the monitors and the resolution setting. You may want to test your finished framed site at different browser size settings to make sure all the content appears correctly.

ADD CONTENT TO A FRAME

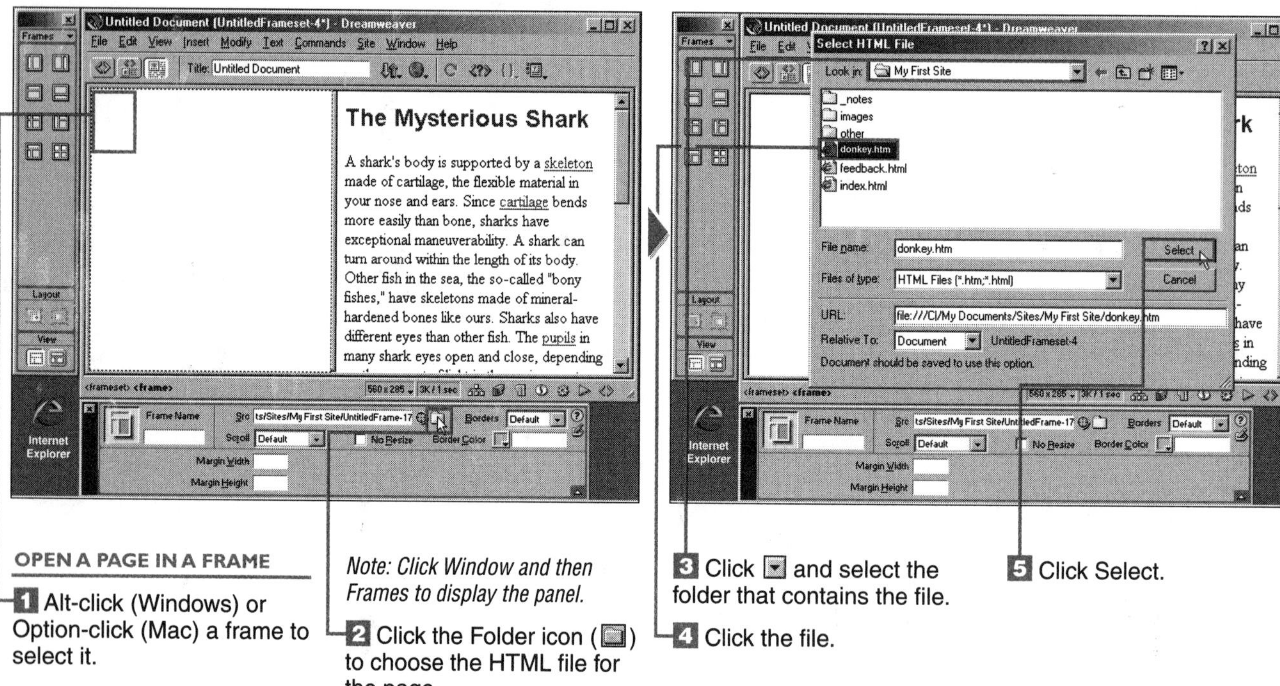

OPEN A PAGE IN A FRAME

1 Alt-click (Windows) or Option-click (Mac) a frame to select it.

■ You can also select your frames by clicking inside the Frames panel.

Note: Click Window and then Frames to display the panel.

2 Click the Folder icon (📁) to choose the HTML file for the page.

3 Click ▾ and select the folder that contains the file.

4 Click the file.

5 Click Select.

Can I load an image into an empty frame?

✔ Yes. An alternative to loading HTML pages into your frames is loading GIF or JPEG images. If the image is smaller than the size of the frame, blank space appears around the image. An image in a frame will not tile to fill the entire frame like a background image will.

What are the HTML tags that define a page's frames?

✔ The `<frameset>` tag defines the dimensions and organization of the frames of your site. The `<frameset>` tag encloses `<frame>` tags, which define what content fills the different frames. The `<frameset>` and `<frame>` tags also define the physical characteristics of frames, such as whether they have scroll bars, or whether you can resize them. To see the code that defines your frames, select the frameset by clicking the frame border, and click the Show Code View button on the top of the Document window.

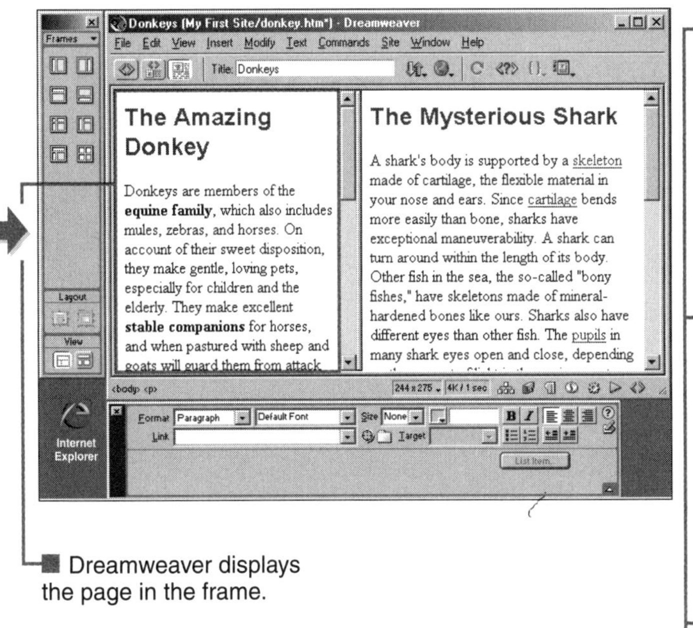

■ Dreamweaver displays the page in the frame.

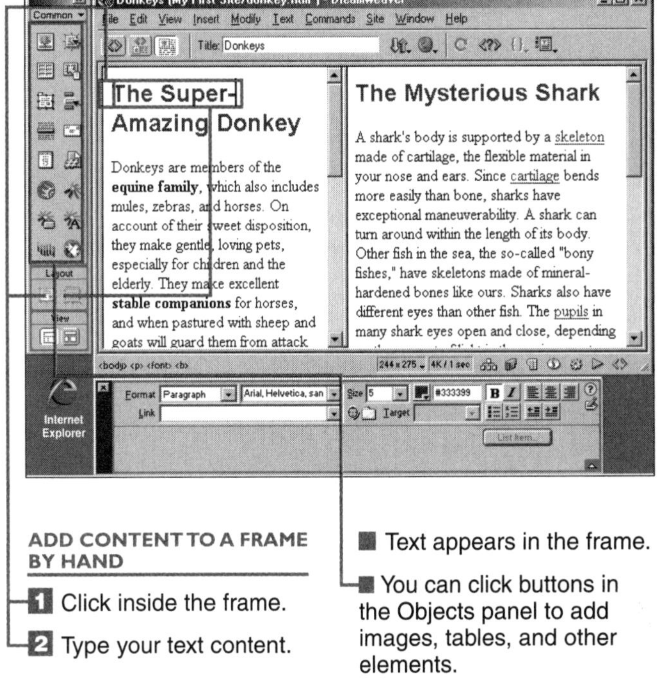

ADD CONTENT TO A FRAME BY HAND

1 Click inside the frame.

2 Type your text content.

■ Text appears in the frame.

■ You can click buttons in the Objects panel to add images, tables, and other elements.

SAVE A FRAMED SITE

Saving a framed site is slightly more complicated than saving regular pages. That is because a framed site is made up of multiple HTML documents: one for each frame in the site, plus a frameset document that defines how Dreamweaver organizes the frames.

You save a framed page much like you do a regular page, except you first must select the framed page by clicking inside its frame. Saving a frameset requires you to select the frameset and then to use the Save Frameset menu command.

You can duplicate an already-saved frameset by selecting it and using the Save Frameset As command. Saving the frameset with a new name creates a duplicate. The duplicate has the same framed pages as the original.

You need to save all the framed pages and framesets before you can preview the framed site in a browser.

SAVE A FRAMED SITE

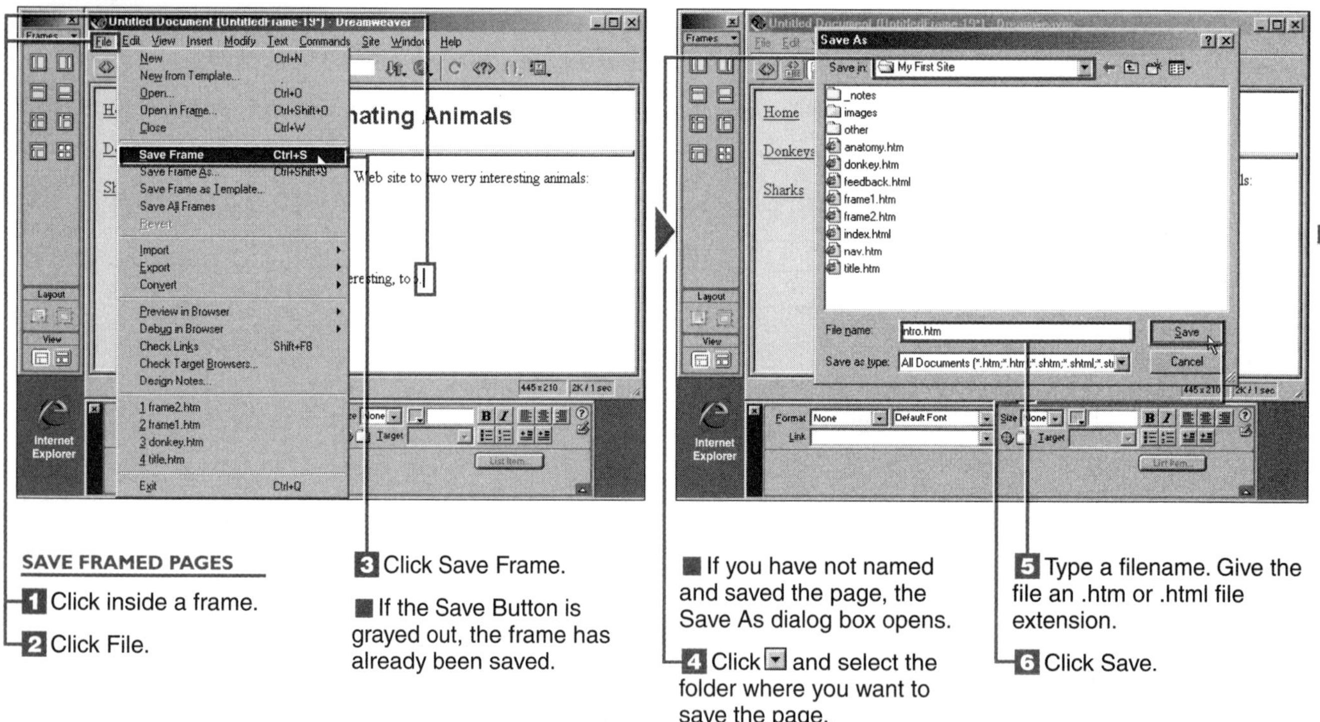

SAVE FRAMED PAGES

1 Click inside a frame.

2 Click File.

3 Click Save Frame.

■ If the Save Button is grayed out, the frame has already been saved.

■ If you have not named and saved the page, the Save As dialog box opens.

4 Click ▾ and select the folder where you want to save the page.

5 Type a filename. Give the file an .htm or .html file extension.

6 Click Save.

Is there a shortcut for saving all the documents of my framed site?

✔ Yes. You can select File and then Save All Frames. This option saves all the framed pages and framesets that make up your site. This is definitely a time saver!

Do I have to save framed pages in the same folder?

✔ You usually save frameset files and the pages that they hold in the same folder. But you do not have to do this. You can reference frame contents from the frameset page just like a hyperlink, which means they can exist in another folder or even on another Web site.

Do framed sites take up more space than non-framed sites?

✔ Typically not. If a framed site has the same content as its non-framed version, the sites take up close to the same amount of space. The fact that a framed site includes an extra frameset file is usually more than offset by a non-framed site having to repeat navigation information on every page.

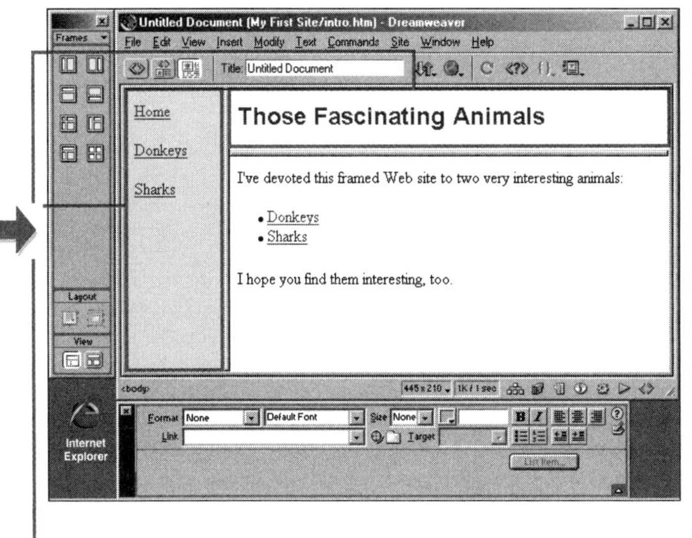

7 Repeat steps 1 through 6 for the other framed pages in your site.

■ Dreamweaver saves all of your framed pages.

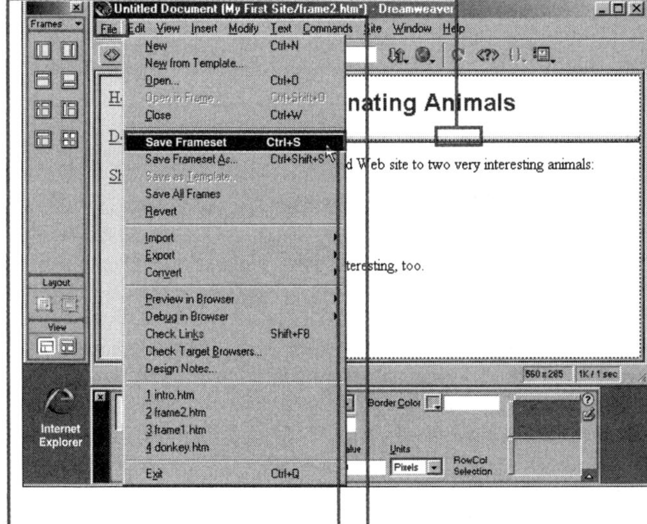

SAVE THE FRAMESET

1 Click the frame border to select the frameset.

■ You can also open the Frames panel and click the frameset border in the panel.

2 Click File.

3 Click Save Frameset.

4 Save the frameset as an .htm or .html file.

■ Dreamweaver saves the Frameset.

DELETE A FRAME

You can delete a frame in Dreamweaver by clicking and dragging the frame's border to the edge of the Document window. This can be convenient when you have a nested frameset that has become too complicated.

Deleting a frame does not delete the information that is currently open in it if that frame has already been saved. If you delete a frame that has not been saved or has unsaved changes, the content or changes will be lost.

If you delete a frame from a two-frame site, what is left is a frame inside a frameset. This is not the same as having the page open by itself, because a frameset still encloses the page. If you want to get rid of the frameset, you need to close the Document window and open the content in a regular, unframed window.

DELETE A FRAME

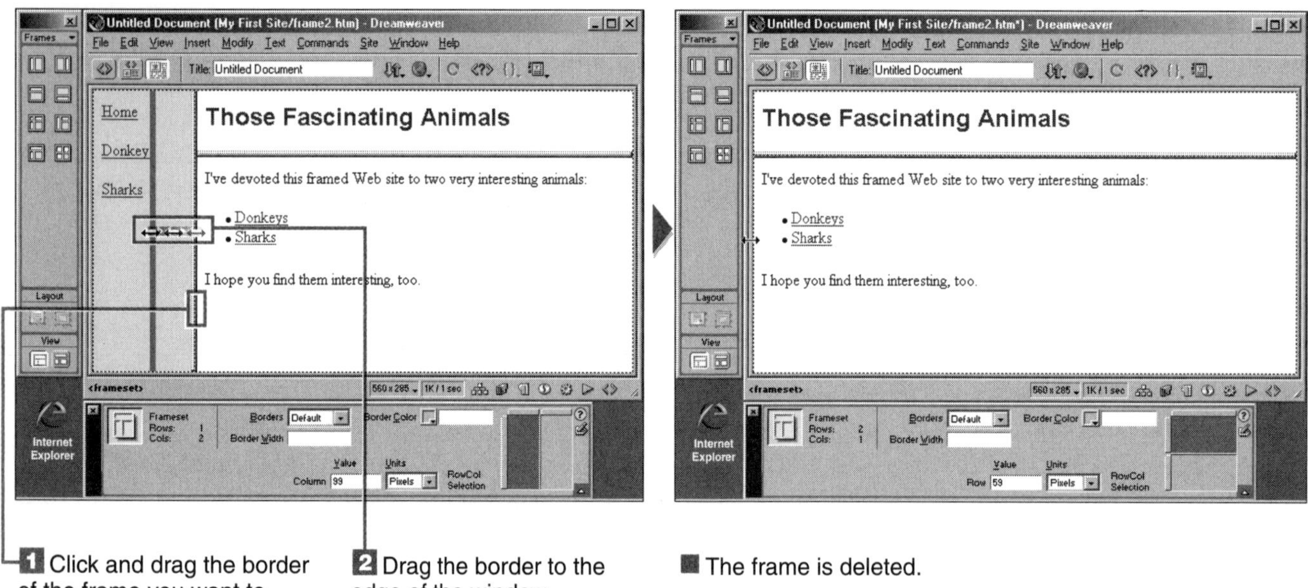

1 Click and drag the border of the frame you want to delete.

2 Drag the border to the edge of the window.

■ The frame is deleted.

NAME A FRAME

In order to create hyperlinks that can work between your frames, you need to give your frames names. The frame name is what you reference in a hyperlink's target; the hyperlink target tells a browser where the hyperlink destination should open.

When you create your frameset manually (see "Divide a Page into Frames" in this chapter), your frames are created without names. You have to name them before you can create hyperlinks that target other frames in the frameset.

When you create your frames using a predefined frameset, Dreamweaver automatically gives your frames generic names, such as topFrame, leftFrame, and mainFrame. If you prefer, you can rename your frames to reflect the type of content that is inside them. See the section "Insert a Predefined Frameset" for more information.

After you have named your frames, targeting your hyperlinks is easy. The frame names for the frameset appear in the Target drop-down menu in the Property Inspector. For more information about creating links, see the section "Hyperlink to a Frame."

NAME A FRAME

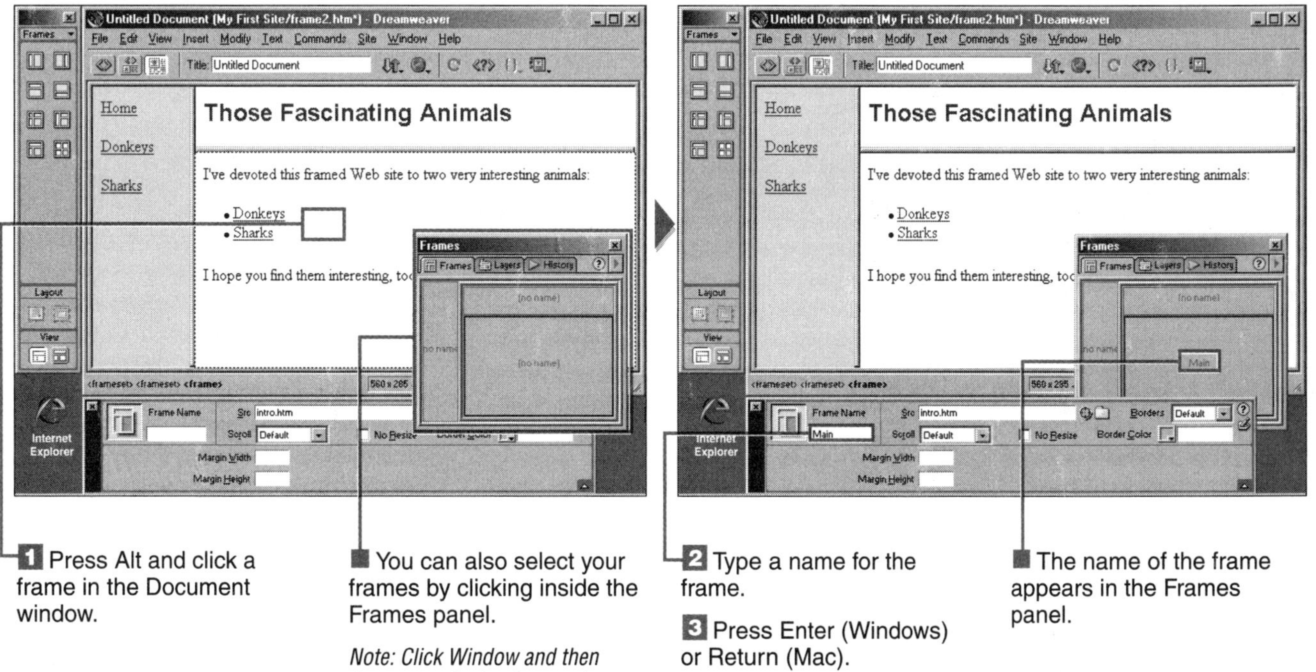

1 Press Alt and click a frame in the Document window.

■ You can also select your frames by clicking inside the Frames panel.

Note: Click Window and then Frames to display the panel.

2 Type a name for the frame.

3 Press Enter (Windows) or Return (Mac).

■ The name of the frame appears in the Frames panel.

HYPERLINK TO A FRAME

Hyperlinking from one frame in your site to another requires you to give the destination frame a name. After you name the frame, you can link to it by specifying the name as the hyperlink target. To name a frame, see the section "Name a Frame."

Including target information enables you to use frames for navigation. For example, you can create a list of hyperlinks in a left frame and have all the linked content open up in the right frame. This is a useful way to organize glossary or dictionary information on a Web site.

If you do not specify the target of a hyperlink in a framed site, the hyperlink destination opens in the same frame as the hyperlink.

You can also specify special keywords as hyperlink targets. These keywords enable you to open hyperlink destinations on top of existing frames. See the tips on the facing page for details.

For more information about hyperlinking, see Chapter 7.

HYPERLINK TO A FRAME

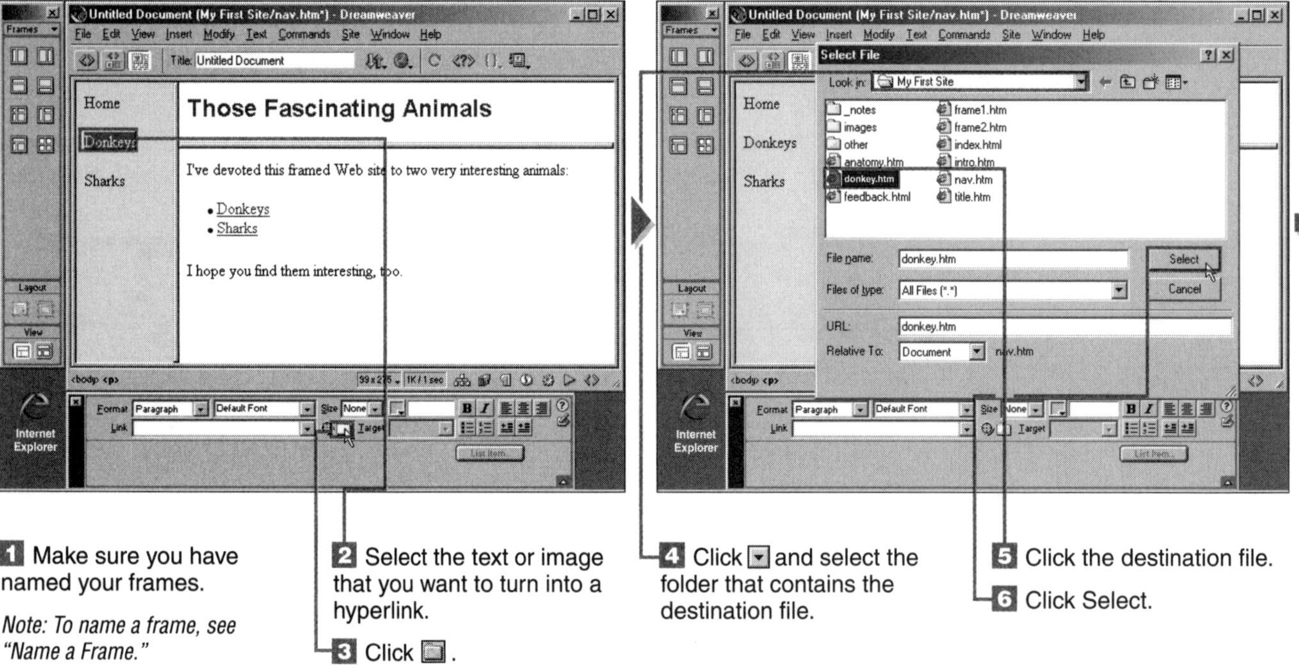

1 Make sure you have named your frames.

Note: To name a frame, see "Name a Frame."

2 Select the text or image that you want to turn into a hyperlink.

3 Click ▢.

4 Click ▾ and select the folder that contains the destination file.

5 Click the destination file.

6 Click Select.

What happens if I select _top for my hyperlink target?

✔ Selecting _top, instead of a frame name, opens the hyperlink destination on "top" of any existing framesets. This gets rid of a site's existing frameset.

What happens if I select _parent for my hyperlink target?

✔ Selecting _parent as the target opens the hyperlink destination over the current frame's "parent" frameset. A nested frameset has more than one parent. For a non-nested frameset, _parent has the same effect as _top.

What happens if I select _self for my hyperlink target?

✔ Selecting _self as the target opens the hyperlink destination in the same frame as the hyperlink. This is the default behavior for most browsers.

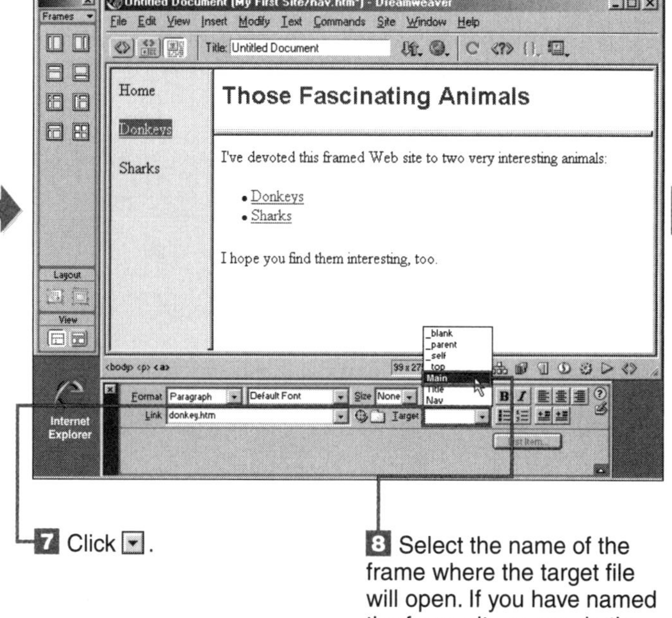

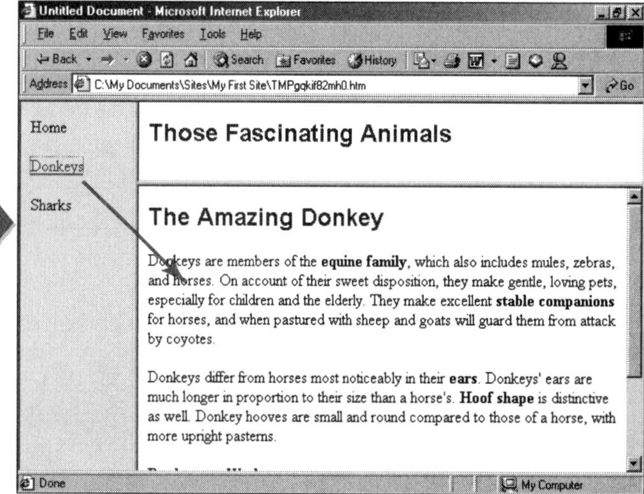

7 Click ▾.

8 Select the name of the frame where the target file will open. If you have named the frame, it appears in the menu.

9 Preview the page in a Web browser.

Note: See Chapter 4 for more about previewing pages in a Web browser.

■ When you open the framed page in a Web browser and click the hyperlink, the destination page opens inside the targeted frame.

CHANGE THE DIMENSIONS OF A FRAME

You can change the dimensions of a frame to attractively and efficiently display the information inside it.

You can define the dimensions of your frames in one of three ways. Defining it in *pixels* lets you specify the exact physical dimensions of a frame. Defining it as a *percentage* lets you specify the frame size as a proportion of the browser window. Giving the frame a *relative* value lets you specify the dimensions relative to the other frames in the frameset.

Different frames in a frameset can be defined using different types of units. In such cases, frames defined using pixels are sized first by the browser, followed by frames defined using percentages, followed by frames defined using relative values.

This precedence means you can create a frameset in which some frames are fixed and others automatically stretch to take up the rest of the available space. For example, for a two-column frame design, you can specify that the navigation frame on the left take up a fixed amount of space, such as 80 pixels, while the content frame on the right takes up the remaining area in the browser window — or 100 percent.

CHANGE THE DIMENSIONS OF A FRAME

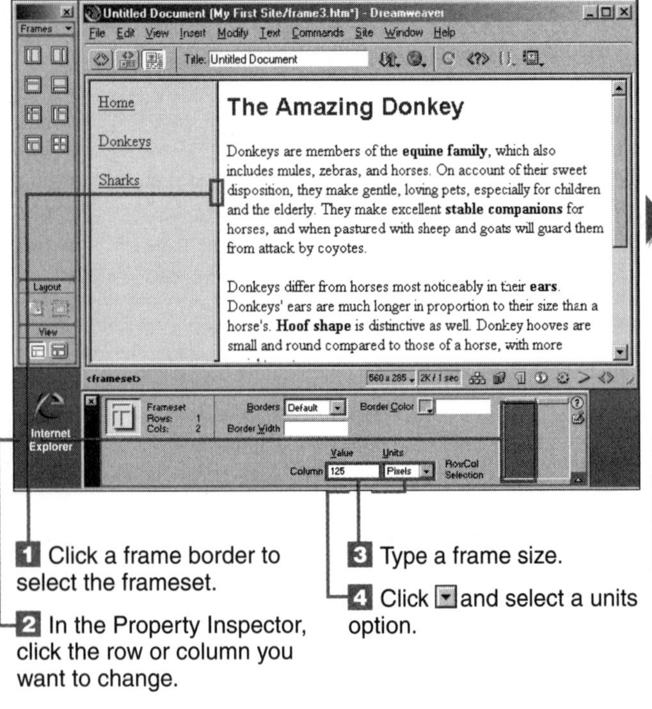

1 Click a frame border to select the frameset.

2 In the Property Inspector, click the row or column you want to change.

3 Type a frame size.

4 Click ▼ and select a units option.

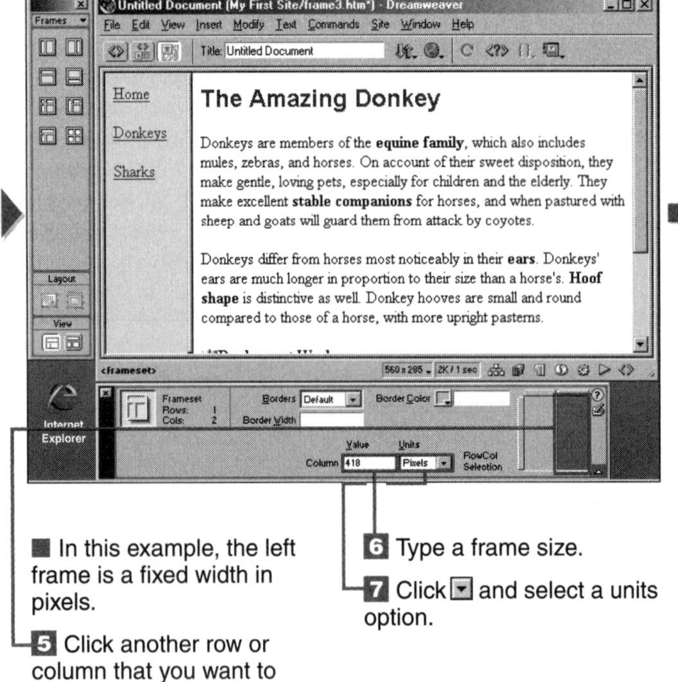

■ In this example, the left frame is a fixed width in pixels.

5 Click another row or column that you want to change.

6 Type a frame size.

7 Click ▼ and select a units option.

Is there a shortcut for changing the dimensions of frames?

✔ Yes. You can click and drag a frame border to quickly adjust the dimensions of a frameset. The values in the Property Inspector change as you drag.

Are viewers able to resize the frames in the browsers?

✔ Most browsers allow the user to resize frames, unless you add a "noresize" attribute to the frame's HTML. To control whether or not a user can resize your frames in browsers, see the section "Control Resizing in Frames."

What happens when I specify pixel sizes for my frames that add up to more than the size of the browser window?

✔ Browsers interpret the sizes as relative values. For example, if you define two frames in a frameset as 1,000 pixels and 2,000 pixels, the browser allocates them ⅓ and ⅔ of the browser space, respectively.

How can I create two frames that assume equal sizes on my page, no matter what size of the browser window?

✔ Set the size of each frame to 50% or a relative size of 1.

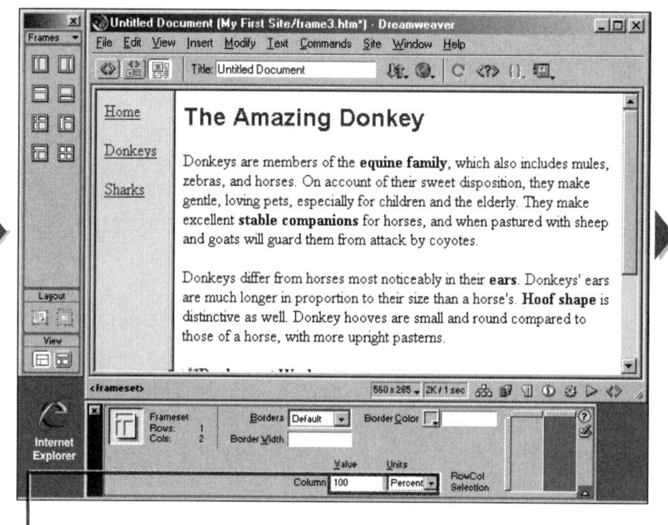

■ In this example, the right frame is defined as a percentage width.

■ Because its width has been defined as 100%, the right frame will take up the remaining space in the browser window.

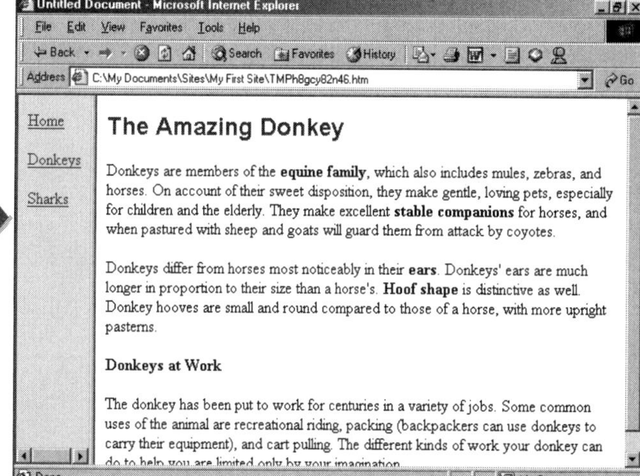

8 Preview the page in a Web browser.

Note: See Chapter 4 for more about previewing pages in Web browsers.

■ The frameset displays as you defined it in Dreamweaver.

FORMAT FRAME BORDERS

You can modify the appearance of your frame borders to make them complement the style of your Web-site content. You can specify that borders be turned on or off, and you can also set the color and width, in pixels, of your borders.

Turning borders off can disguise the fact that you are using frames in the first place. If you want to further disguise your frames, you can set the pages inside your frames to the same background color. See Chapter 6 for more information.

You specify the color of borders just like you do the color of Web page text or the page background — by selecting from a pop-up color palette or by specifying the color name or hex code. For more about Web color, see Chapter 5.

If the frame characteristics for your site are left unspecified, most browsers display frames as turned on, gray in color, and with a width of two pixels.

FORMAT FRAME BORDERS

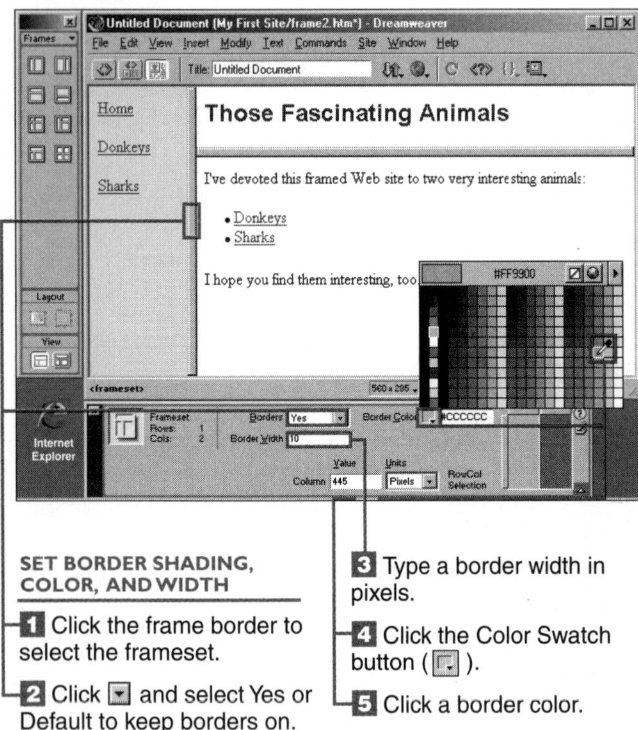

SET BORDER SHADING, COLOR, AND WIDTH

1 Click the frame border to select the frameset.

2 Click ▾ and select Yes or Default to keep borders on.

3 Type a border width in pixels.

4 Click the Color Swatch button ( ).

5 Click a border color.

■ The frame border is displayed at the specified settings.

■ Settings at the frameset level can be overridden at the frame level. You can press Alt and click (Windows) or Option and click (Mac) to select a frame and then specify formatting in the Property Inspector.

What happens if I set my frames and frameset to different border colors?

✔ In most browsers, border color set at the frame level overrides border color at the frameset level. But to make sure your borders appear how you expect them to, you should make your border-color settings consistent.

Can I change the spacing between my frame borders and the frame content?

✔ Yes. Select a frame by pressing Alt and clicking (Windows) or Option clicking (Mac), or by clicking in the Frames panel. Specify the spacing using the Margin Width for left and right margins, and Margin Height for top and bottom margins settings.

Is there an easy way to change the background color of a framed page?

✔ You can right-click (Windows) or Control and click (Mac) inside the frame and select Page Properties from the menu that appears. You can define the page background inside the dialog box.

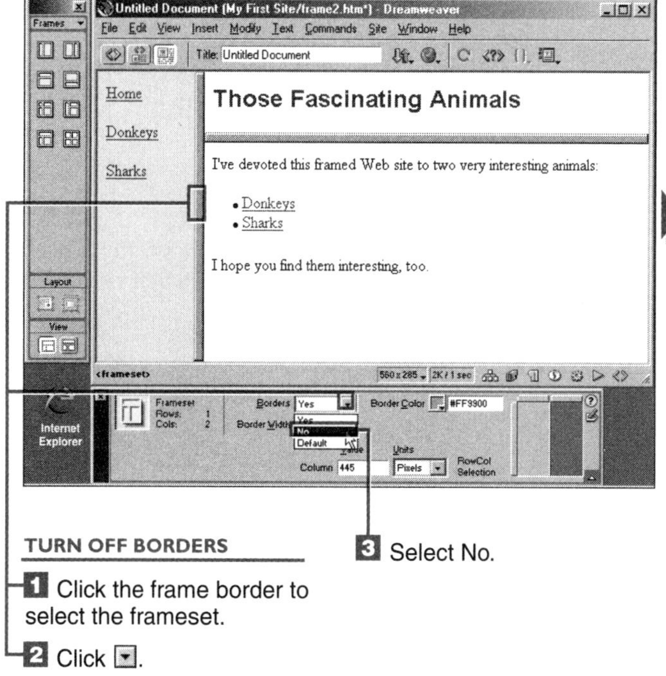

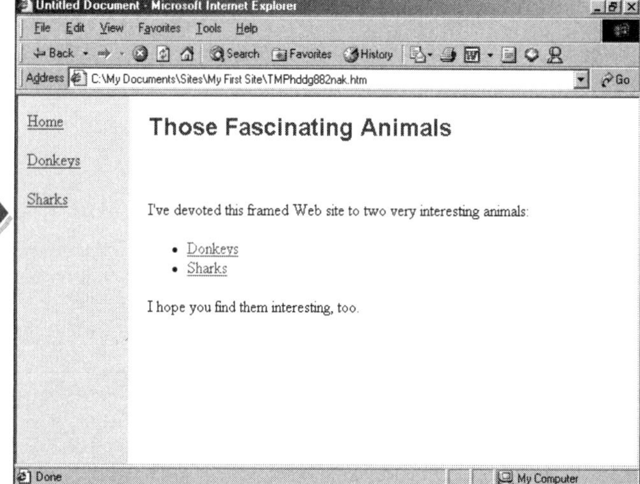

TURN OFF BORDERS

1 Click the frame border to select the frameset.

2 Click ▾.

3 Select No.

4 Preview the page in a Web browser.

Note: See Chapter 4 for more about previewing pages in Web browsers.

■ The frame border is not displayed.

■ Settings at the frameset level can be overridden at the frame level. You can press Alt and click (Windows) or Option and click (Mac) to select a frame and then specify formatting in the Property Inspector.

CONTROL SCROLL BARS IN FRAMES

A browser normally adds scroll bars to frames when the frame content extends outside the borders. A scroll bar on the bottom edge lets a user scroll horizontally, while a scroll bar on the right side lets a user scroll vertically. In Dreamweaver, you can adjust this default behavior so that scroll bars are always on or always off.

You may want to consider turning your scroll bars off if you are trying to disguise the presence of frames in your site — for example, if you have turned off borders. Even when you turn off borders, scroll bars can appear if content extends outside the frame, unless you explicitly turn off the scroll bars. See the section "Format Frame Borders" for more information.

CONTROL SCROLL BARS IN FRAMES

■ The default behavior in Dreamweaver shows scroll bars on when they are needed (left frame) and off when they are not (right frame).

1 Press Alt and click inside a frame to select it.

2 Click ▼.

3 Click a setting.

■ The frame is displayed with the new setting.

■ In this example, scroll bars have been turned off in the left frame. The user now has no way to access all of that frame's content.

CONTROL RESIZING IN FRAMES

The default behavior of most browsers lets users resize frames by clicking and dragging the frame borders. The shape of the cursor changes when you place it over a border and indicates that you can resize the frame. In Dreamweaver, you can adjust this default behavior so that users cannot resize frames.

Note that you can always change the dimensions of frames in Dreamweaver by clicking and dragging borders in the Document window. The resize setting affects the behavior only when a user opens the page in a browser. For more about changing frame dimensions, see the section "Change the Dimensions of a Frame."

You may want to turn resizing off if your page layout depends on the size of your frames. This can keep users from changing the dimensions of your frames and causing the content to become disorganized.

Note that, unless you disable resizing, a user can still resize borders even if you turn them off. In such a case, a user just needs to click and drag where the two frame edges meet. See the section "Format Frame Borders" for more information.

CONTROL RESIZING IN FRAMES

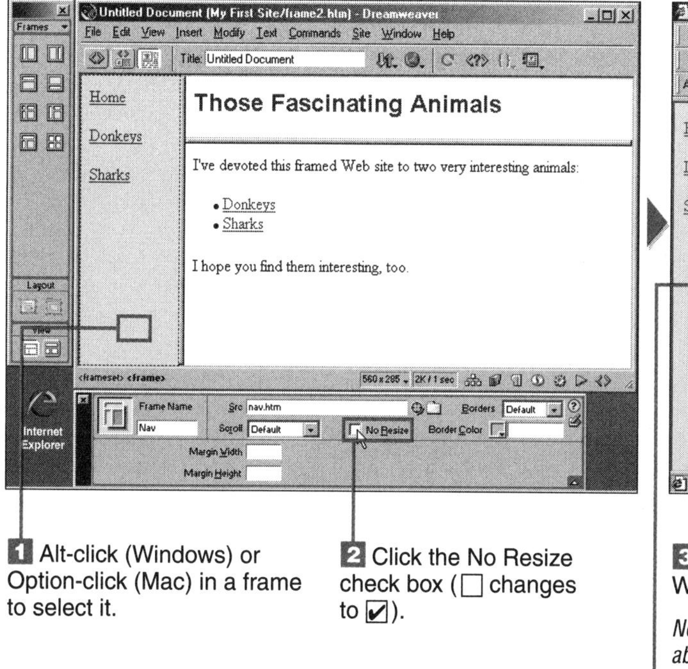

1 Alt-click (Windows) or Option-click (Mac) in a frame to select it.

2 Click the No Resize check box (☐ changes to ☑).

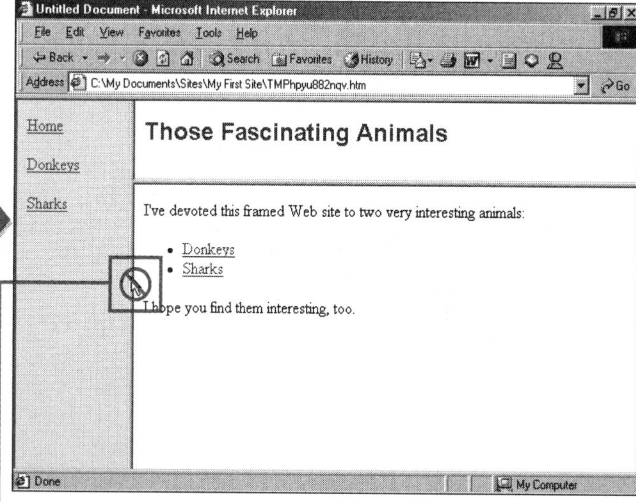

3 Preview the page in a Web browser.

Note: See Chapter 4 for more about Web browsers.

4 Click and drag the border.

■ The browser prevents you from resizing the frame.

AN INTRODUCTION TO LIBRARY ITEMS AND TEMPLATES

Timesaving Tools

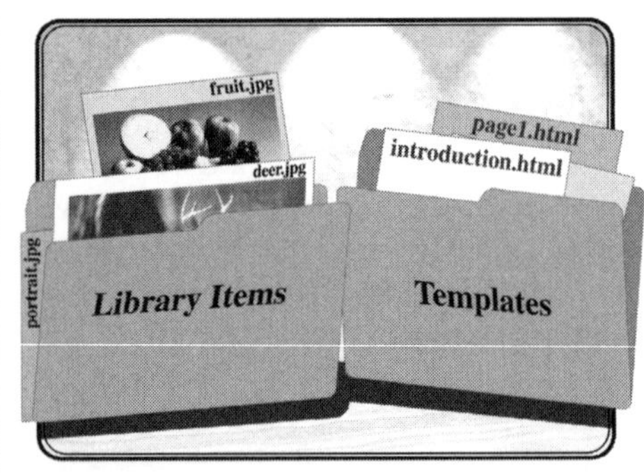

Library items and templates let you avoid repetitive work by storing copies of frequently used page elements and layouts. You can access the library items and templates that you create for your site through the Assets panel.

Templates

You can define commonly used Web page layouts as *templates* to save time as you build your pages. Templates can also help you maintain a consistent page design across a site. After you make changes to a template, Dreamweaver can automatically update all your site's pages that are based on that template. If you use just a few page layouts across all the pages in your site, you should consider defining those layouts as templates.

Library Items

You can define parts of your Web pages that are repeated in your site as *library items*, so you do not have to create them from scratch over and over. Each time you need a library item, you can just insert it from your library. If you ever make changes to a library item, Dreamweaver can automatically update all the instances of the item across your Web site. Good candidates for library items include advertising banners, company slogans, and any other features that appear many times across a site.

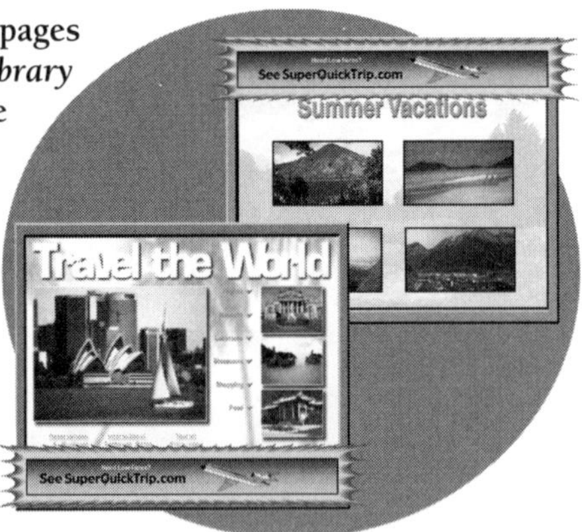

VIEW LIBRARY ITEMS AND TEMPLATES

You can access a site's library and templates with commands in the Window menu. You can also access them by opening the Assets panel and clicking (for templates) and (for the library) buttons. For more information about the Assets panel, see Chapter 16.

Dreamweaver does not include any default library items or templates, and both lists begin empty when you start creating a site. But you can copy library items and templates from one site to another using the Assets panel menu (click in the Assets panel).

Dreamweaver stores the files for a site's library items and templates in special folders in your local site folder (see Chapter 4) — library items in a folder called Library and templates in a folder called Templates. Dreamweaver automatically creates the folders.

VIEW LIBRARY ITEMS AND TEMPLATES

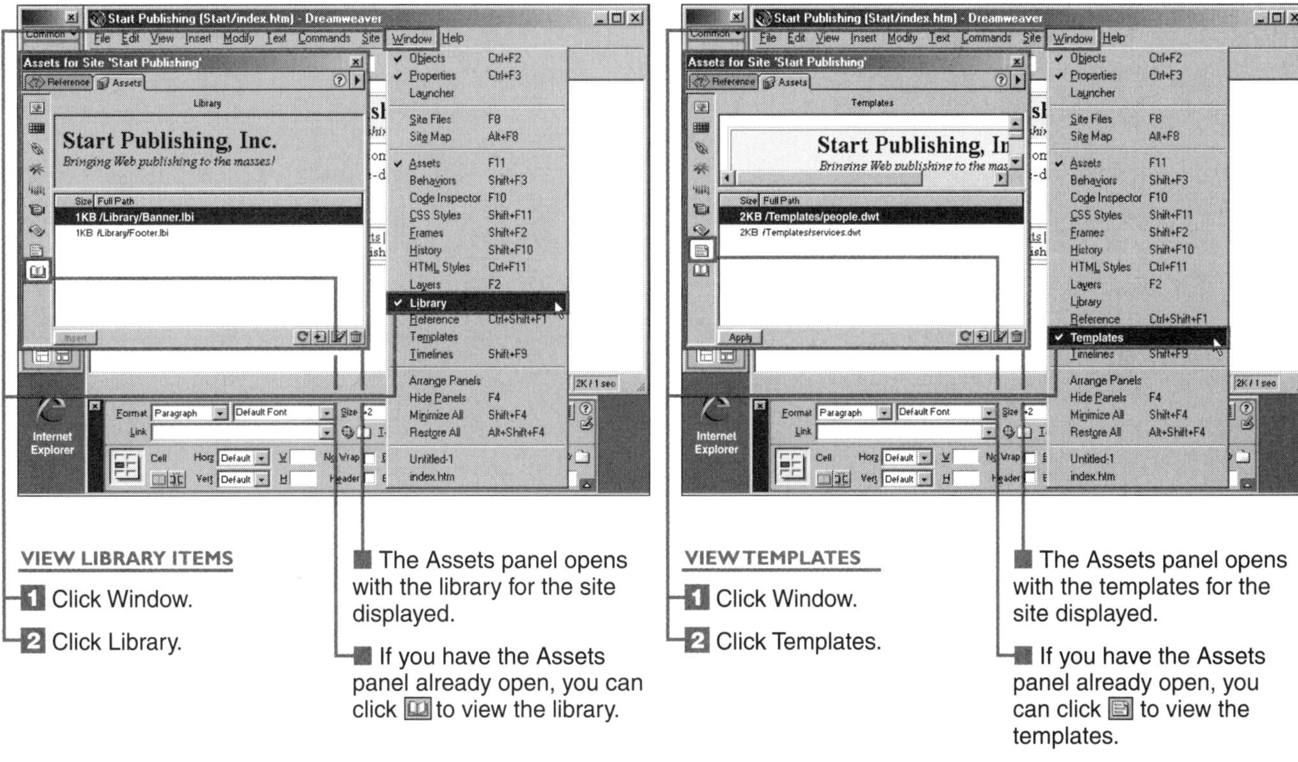

VIEW LIBRARY ITEMS

1 Click Window.

2 Click Library.

■ The Assets panel opens with the library for the site displayed.

■ If you have the Assets panel already open, you can click to view the library.

VIEW TEMPLATES

1 Click Window.

2 Click Templates.

■ The Assets panel opens with the templates for the site displayed.

■ If you have the Assets panel already open, you can click to view the templates.

CREATE A LIBRARY ITEM

You can define text, images, and other Dreamweaver objects that you want to appear frequently in your Web site as library items. Library items enable you to quickly insert such page elements without having to re-create them from scratch every time.

If you ever need to edit your library items, you can change the copies in your site library and have Dreamweaver automatically update the instances of each item across your site. This can save you a lot of time, especially if you maintain a large site that has hundreds of pages.

When you create a library item, Dreamweaver saves the item as a separate file with an .lbi extension. These files are stored in a Library folder inside your local site folder. (See Chapter 4 for information about setting up a local site.)

CREATE A LIBRARY ITEM

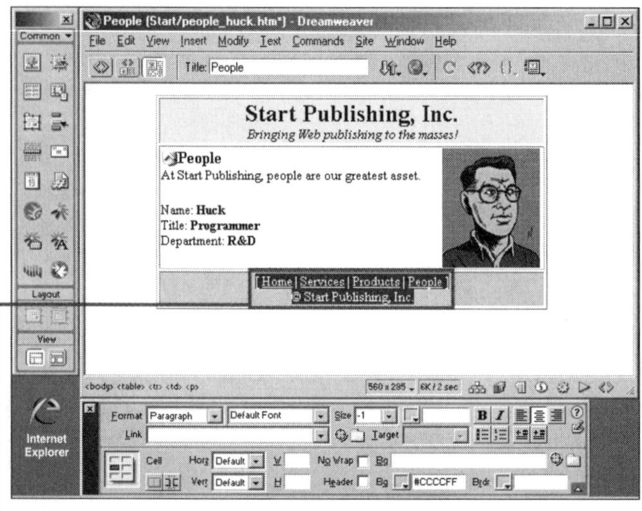

1 Select the part of your page that you want to define as a library item.

■ Library items can be created from any elements that appear in the body of an HTML document, including text, images, tables, forms, layers, and multimedia.

Note: To create library items for your Web pages, you must already have defined a local site. To set up a local site, see Chapter 4.

2 Click Modify.

3 Click Library.

4 Click Add Object To Library.

How do I delete a library item?

✓ The correct way to delete a library item is to select the item in the Assets panel and click [delete icon]. If you delete a library file directly from the Library folder, Dreamweaver does not have the opportunity to properly detach the file from the site, and the file still shows up in the Assets panel (although you can no longer use it). Note that deleting an item from the library does not delete instances of the item that you have already inserted into your pages.

How can I re-create a library item after I delete it?

✓ If you delete a library item from the Assets panel and later want to use it again, you can select an instance of the old item somewhere in the Document window and click the re-create button in the Property Inspector. The item is again available in the Assets panel.

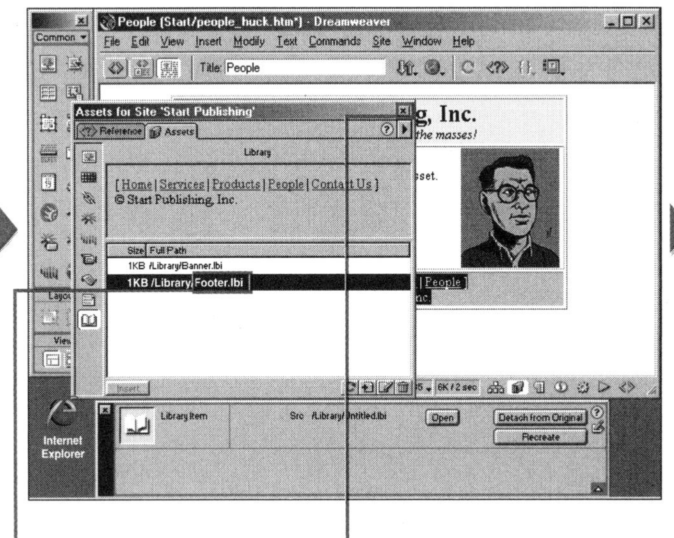

■ Dreamweaver opens the Library window for your site and creates a new, untitled library item.

5 Name the library item.

6 Press Enter (Windows) or Return (Mac).

7 Click the Close button ([close icon]) to close the Library window.

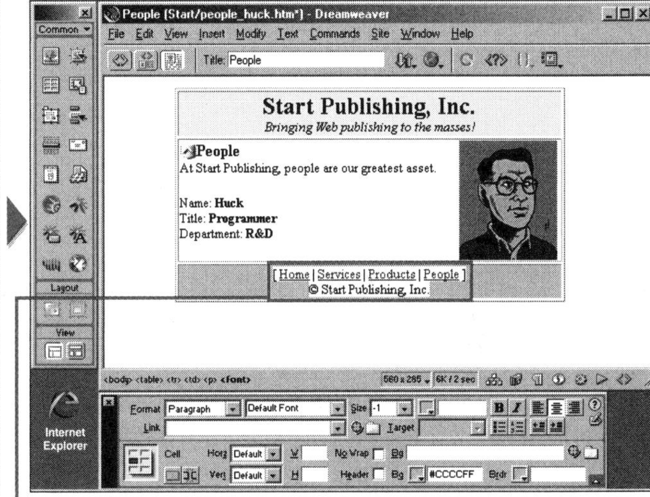

■ The new library item is highlighted in yellow.

■ You can change the highlighting color for library items in Preferences. See Chapter 2.

■ Defining an element as a library item prevents you from editing it in the Document window. To edit library items, see "Edit a Library Item and Update Your Web Site" later in this chapter.

INSERT A LIBRARY ITEM

Inserting an element onto your page from the library not only saves you from having to create it from scratch, but also ensures that its design is identical to other instances of that library item in your site. When you are ready to update the item later, you can edit the original in the site Library and have Dreamweaver automatically update all the instances on your pages.

When you insert a library item onto a page, Dreamweaver inserts the item's HTML along with some extra HTML comment information. You can identify HTML comments by their surrounding <!-- and --> characters. The comments identify the information as a library item and let Dreamweaver perform automatic updating in the future.

Instances of library items are highlighted in yellow in the Document window. (You can change the highlighting color in Preferences — see Chapter 2.) However, you cannot edit instances of library items without detaching them from the library. See "Detach Library Content for Editing" later in this chapter.

INSERT A LIBRARY ITEM

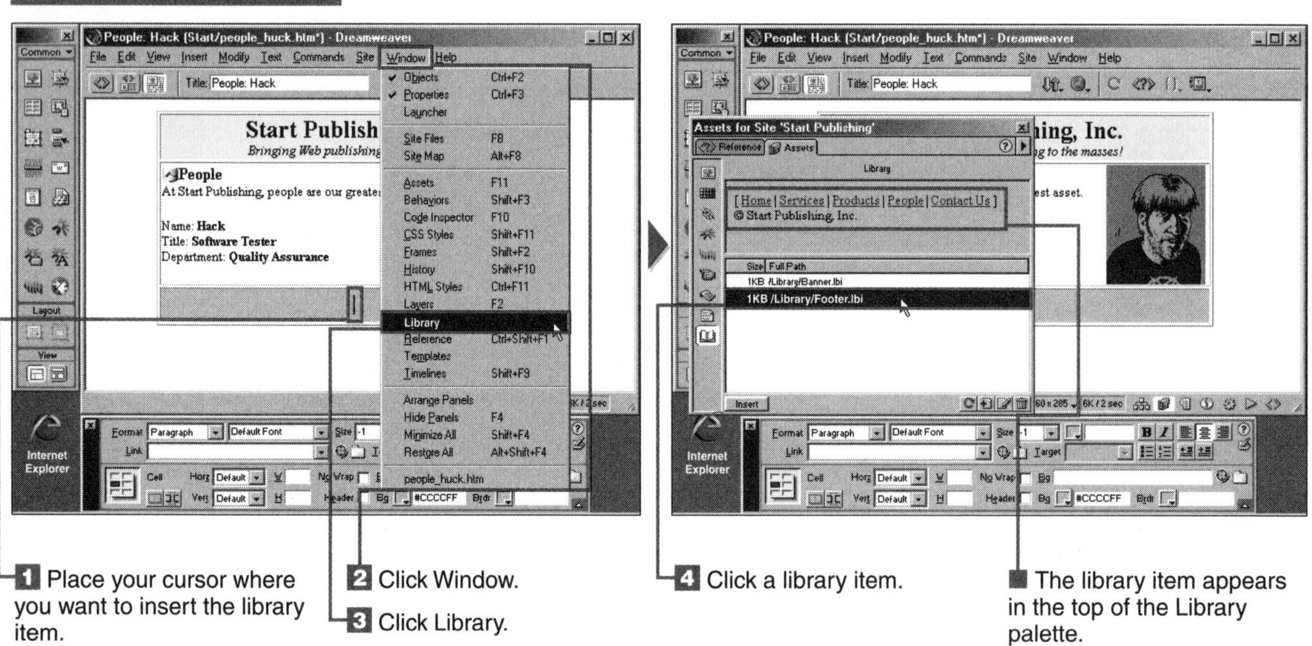

1 Place your cursor where you want to insert the library item.

2 Click Window.

3 Click Library.

4 Click a library item.

■ The library item appears in the top of the Library palette.

What kind of content cannot be defined as a library item?

✔ Most content that is defined in the head area of a page's HTML cannot be defined as a library item. This includes style-sheet rules and timelines. You *can* define elements that have behaviors attached to them as library items, even though some of the code for behaviors is stored in the head of a document. When you insert an item that includes a behavior into a page, Dreamweaver adds the necessary JavaScript code into the head to permit the behavior to work.

How can I quickly find the instances of a particular library item in my site?

✔ You can perform a search on the name of the library item file (for example, myitem.lbi) by clicking Edit and then Find and Replace. Be sure to search through the "Entire Local Site" and in each file's "Source Code." For more information on searching for text, see Chapter 16.

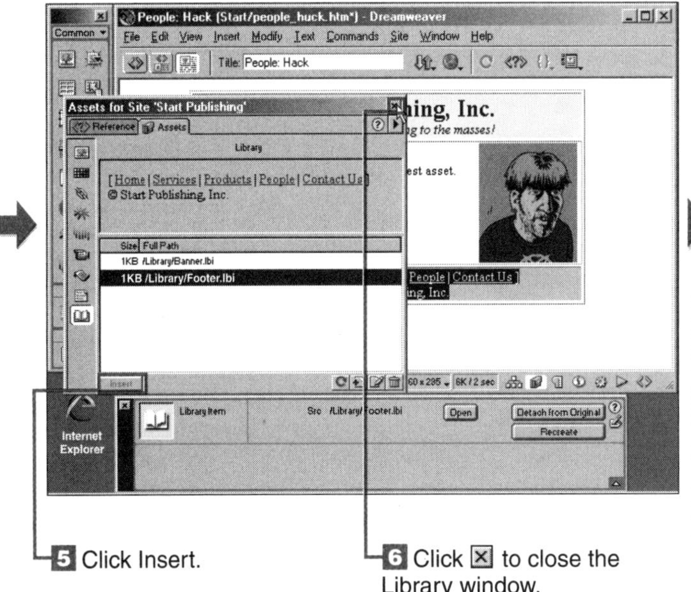

5 Click Insert.

6 Click ☒ to close the Library window.

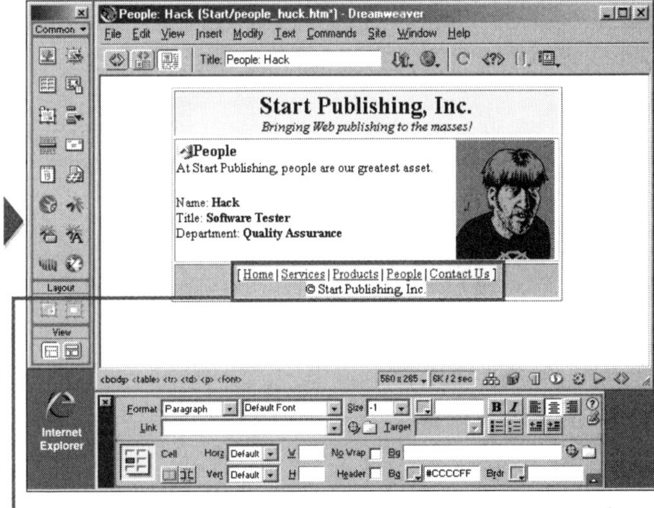

■ Dreamweaver inserts the library item, which is highlighted in yellow, in the Document window.

EDIT A LIBRARY ITEM AND UPDATE YOUR WEB SITE

Library items can take some of the effort out of maintaining large sites by streamlining the process of updating elements that appear on multiple pages. When you need to make a sitewide change to a repeating item — for example, incrementing the year in the copyright notice on all your pages — you can modify the library item for that element instead of modifying by hand the hundreds of pages that make up your site.

Whenever you modify a library item, Dreamweaver gives you the opportunity to immediately update the site wherever the item appears.

You can also make updates to library items manually, using commands under the Library submenu (located under the Modify menu). The Update Pages command brings up a dialog box that enables you to select which library items should get updated and on which pages.

EDIT A LIBRARY ITEM AND UPDATE YOUR WEB SITE

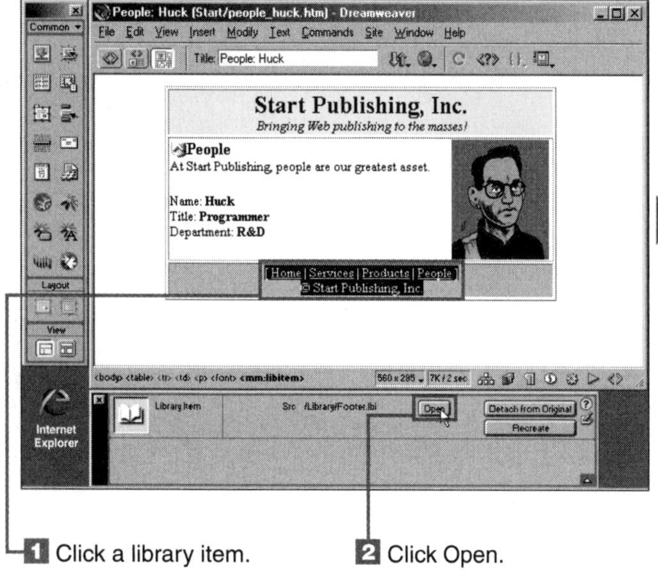

1 Click a library item.

2 Click Open.

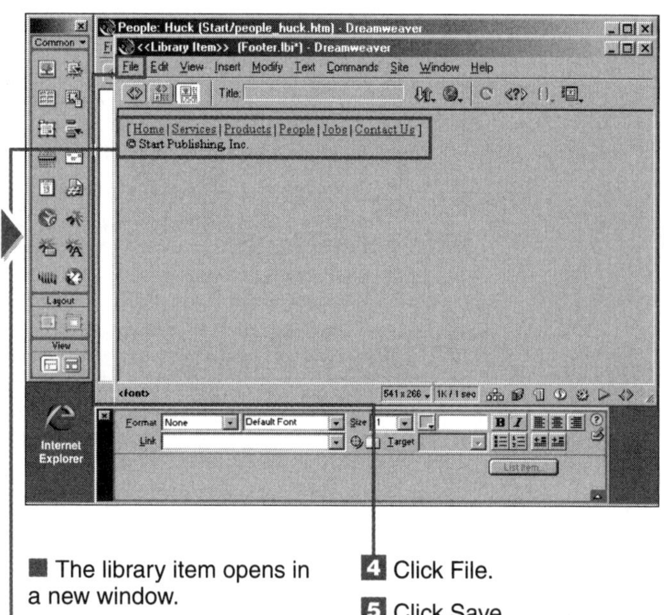

■ The library item opens in a new window.

3 Edit the library item.

4 Click File.

5 Click Save.

How do I keep particular instances of library items from being changed during the update process?

✔ If, for some reason, you no longer want a particular library item to be changed with all the others on your site (for example, you want the old content to remain on a certain page for archival purposes), you can detach it from the library. (See "Detach Library Content for Editing" later in this chapter.) If you want to just keep the item unchanged temporarily and still be able to update it later, you can perform updates for a library item one page at a time. Use the Update Current Page command under the Library submenu under the Modify menu.

What can make a library item in the site fail to be updated?

✔ If somehow the HTML comment code that surrounds and identifies a library item becomes corrupted, Dreamweaver may not be able to correctly update it. For this reason, you may not want to edit library items in Code view if you are unfamiliar with HTML.

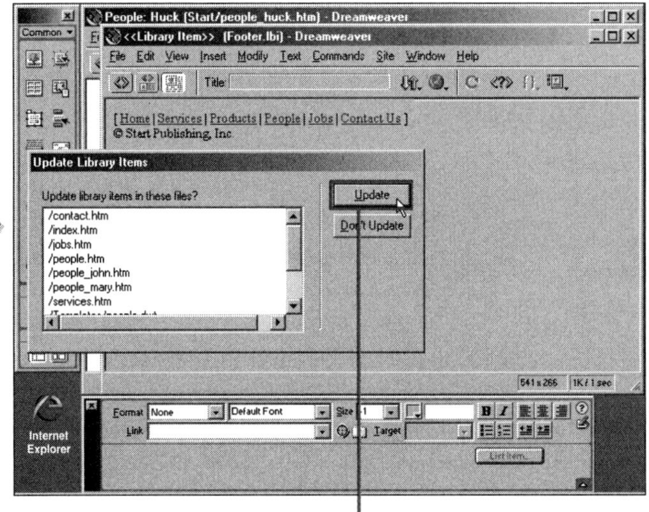

■ An alert box asks if you want to update all the instances of the library item in the site.

6 Click Update.

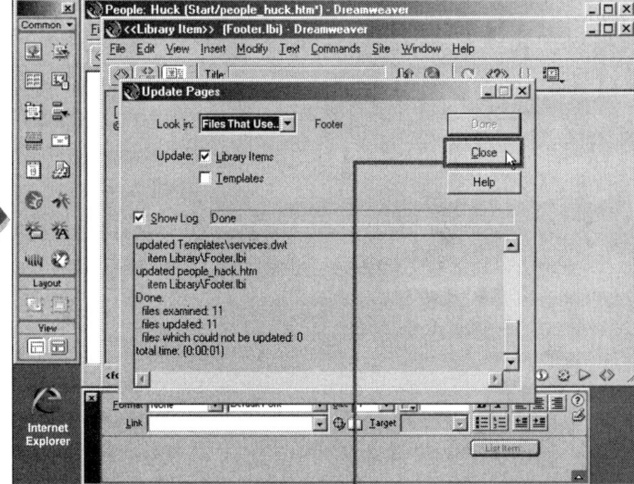

■ A dialog box shows the progress of the updates.

7 After Dreamweaver is finished updating the site, click Close.

DETACH LIBRARY CONTENT FOR EDITING

Unlike regular content, you cannot edit library items that you insert into your pages in the Document window. If you want to edit an instance of a library item in a page, you have to detach it from the library. The item is no longer associated with the original library item and is not updated when that original item is edited.

When you detach an instance of a library item, Dreamweaver removes the HTML comment information that defines it as such in the page. With that code gone, the yellow highlighting that denotes an element as a library item in the Document window disappears and you can change the item.

This command is useful if you need to make updates to site elements that diverge from the normal design. For example, if you are adding a holiday theme to your page, and you want the normal header library item on several pages to have an extra decorative graphic, you could detach the header on these pages from the library. When the season is over, you can reinsert the normal header library item.

DETACH LIBRARY CONTENT FOR EDITING

1 Click the library item.

2 Click Detach from Original.

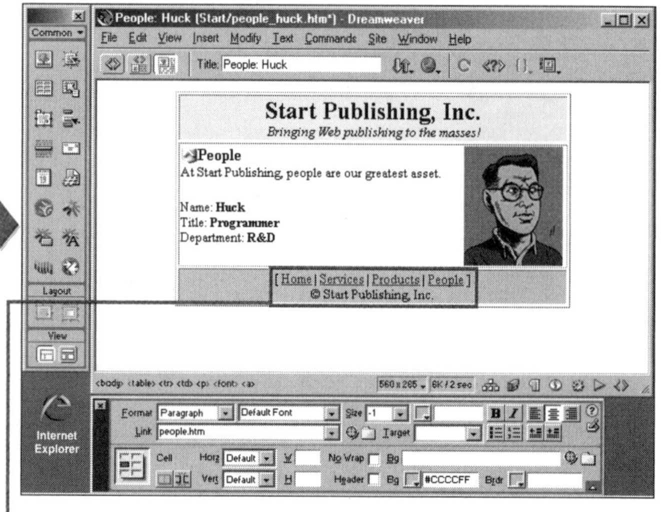

■ The element is no longer a library item and no longer has the distinctive highlighting.

How do I revert a detached library item back to its undetached state?

✔ While no specific command for doing this exists, you can use the Undo command (under the Edit menu) if you detached the item with your previous command. Or you can backtrack over several previous commands using the History panel. See Chapter 2 for more information about the History panel.

Why would I want to use the Detach from Original command on a regular basis?

✔ You may want to use this command a lot if you use library items as templates for specific design elements on your pages. For example, if you need numerous captioned images in your Web site, you can create a library item that has a two-cell table with a generic image and caption. To place an image and caption, you insert the library item and then detach the item from the library to make it editable. You can then replace the generic image and caption with appropriate content.

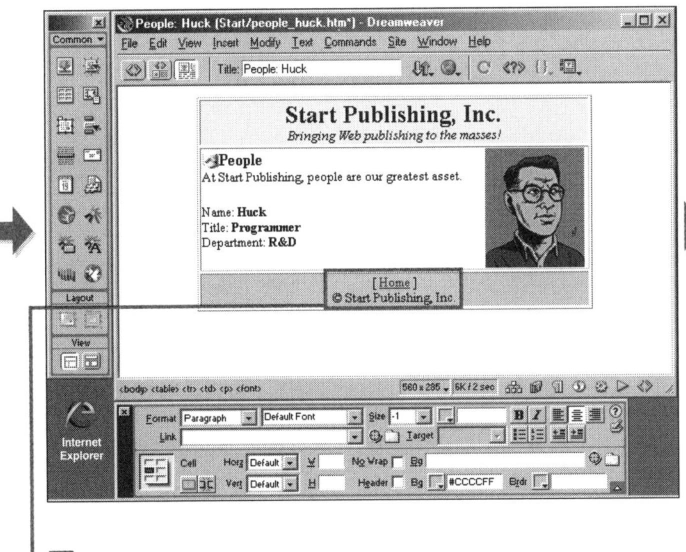

3 Edit the content.

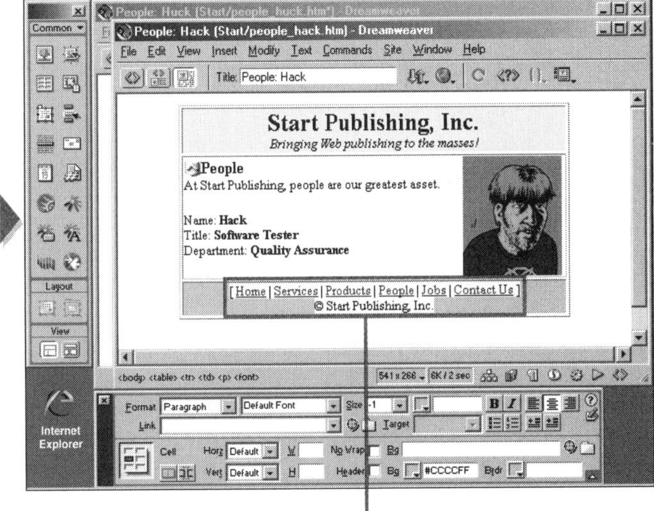

4 Open another page that has the library item.

■ As you can see, editing the detached library item has no effect on other library items.

CREATE A TEMPLATE

Most pages of a Web site share common design elements — such as navigation links, headers, and footers — so it often makes sense to use page templates when building sites to save time and help ensure consistency. Dreamweaver enables you to build such generic template pages, which you can use as starting points for new pages.

To make a Dreamweaver template functional, you must define which areas of the page you want to make editable. (See "Set a Template's Editable Regions" later in this chapter.) The rest of the page stays locked and can only be edited by editing the original template.

Similar to library items, when you later make changes to your original template, Dreamweaver can automatically update all the pages in your site that are based on the template. See "Edit a Template and Update Your Web Site" later in this chapter.

When you create and save a template, Dreamweaver stores the file in a Templates folder inside your local site folder. See Chapter 4 for information about setting up a local site. Templates have a .dwt

CREATE A TEMPLATE

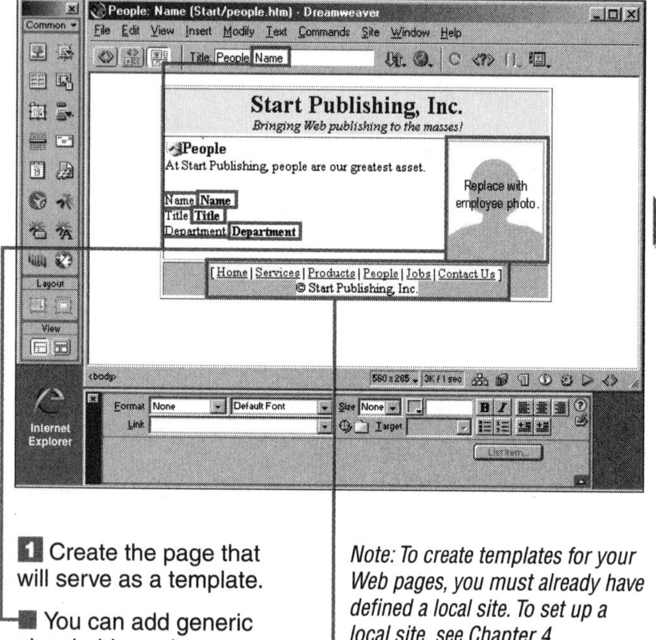

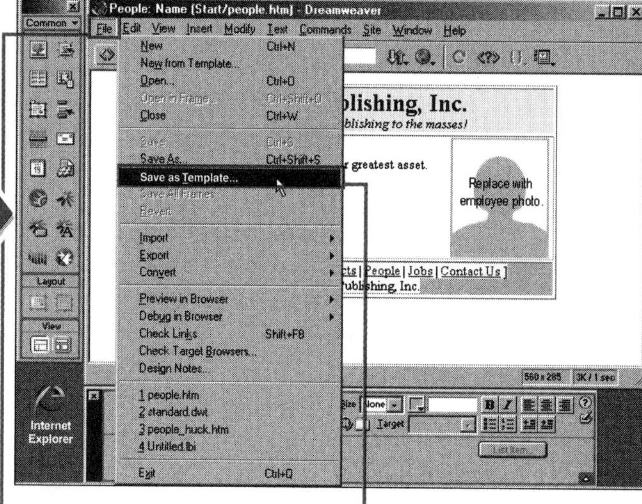

1 Create the page that will serve as a template.

■ You can add generic placeholders where information will change from page to page.

Note: To create templates for your Web pages, you must already have defined a local site. To set up a local site, see Chapter 4.

■ You can also include library items in the template.

2 Click File.

3 Click Save As Template.

How do I delete a template?

✔ The correct way to delete a template is to select it in the Assets panel and click 🗑. If you delete a template file directly from the Library folder, Dreamweaver does not have the opportunity to properly detach the file from the site. The file still shows up in the Assets panel, although you can no longer use it. Note that deleting a template does not delete pages that you have already built using that template.

How can I store notes about a template that other people using the template can access?

✔ You can attach information about a template — such as who created it, when it was created, and tips about using it — with Design Notes. See Chapter 16 for more information on Design Notes.

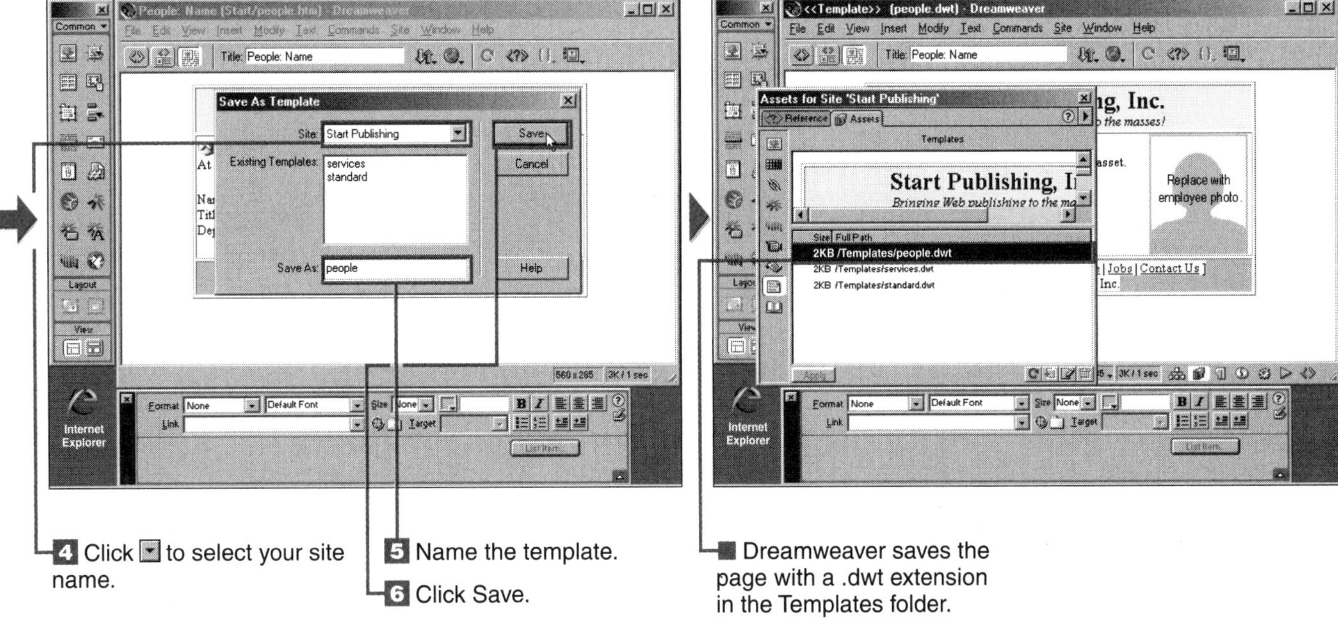

4 Click ▾ to select your site name.

5 Name the template.

6 Click Save.

■ Dreamweaver saves the page with a .dwt extension in the Templates folder.

SET A TEMPLATE'S EDITABLE REGIONS

Dreamweaver templates have two types of content: *locked* content, which you can edit only in the original template file, and *editable* content, which you can edit in the original template and in all the files you create based on the template.

After you save a page as a template (see "Create a Template" earlier in this chapter), you must define which areas of the page are editable. These editable regions appear highlighted in blue on pages that you create using the template. Areas that are not specifically defined as editable remain locked.

You typically define as editable the areas that contain the main content for a page, as well as areas that contain other variable content, such as page headlines and ad banners. Navigation areas, headers, and footers are usually left locked.

You can modify the editable and locked areas of a template further at any time, even after you begin creating pages with the template. See "Edit a Template and Update Your Web Site" later in this chapter for details.

SET A TEMPLATE'S EDITABLE REGIONS

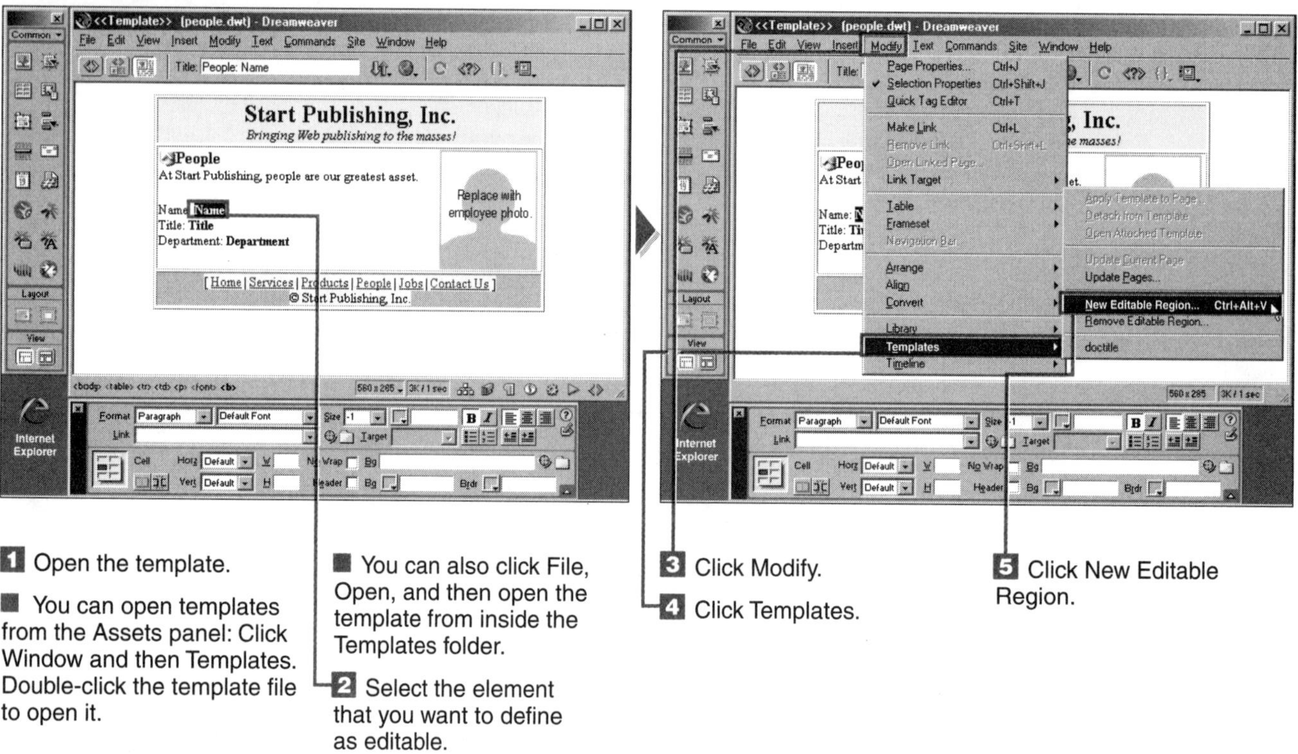

1 Open the template.

■ You can open templates from the Assets panel: Click Window and then Templates. Double-click the template file to open it.

■ You can also click File, Open, and then open the template from inside the Templates folder.

2 Select the element that you want to define as editable.

3 Click Modify.

4 Click Templates.

5 Click New Editable Region.

How do I define a table in my page as editable?

✔ You can define an individual cell of a table as an editable area. You can also define an entire table as an editable area, but you cannot select several cells of a table and define them as a single editable area. Such cells have to be defined as separate editable regions.

Can I make a layer editable?

✔ Yes, but you have to choose between making the entire layer (including its contents) editable and making just the layer contents editable. If you make just the contents editable, the layer's position in the Document window is locked. If you make the entire layer editable, you can move the layer wherever you want. To make the entire layer editable, click the icon associated with the layer in the Document window. To make just the contents editable, click inside the layer and click Edit, and then Select All.

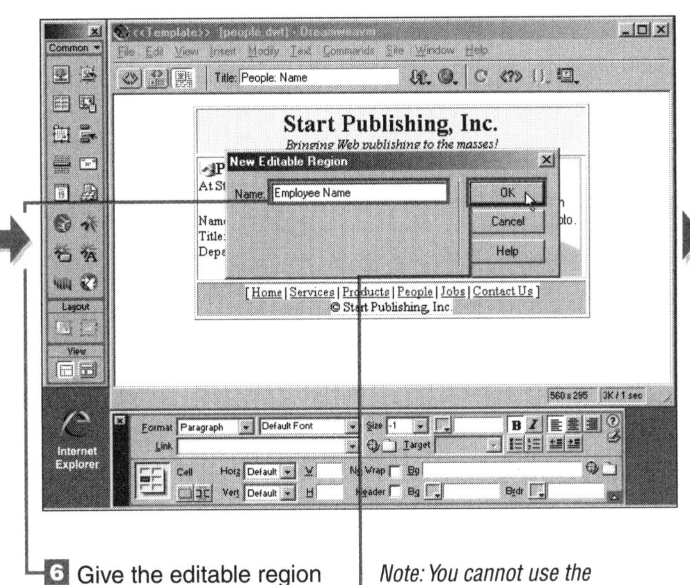

6 Give the editable region a name that distinguishes it from other editable regions on the page.

Note: You cannot use the characters &, ", ', <, or > in the name.

7 Click OK.

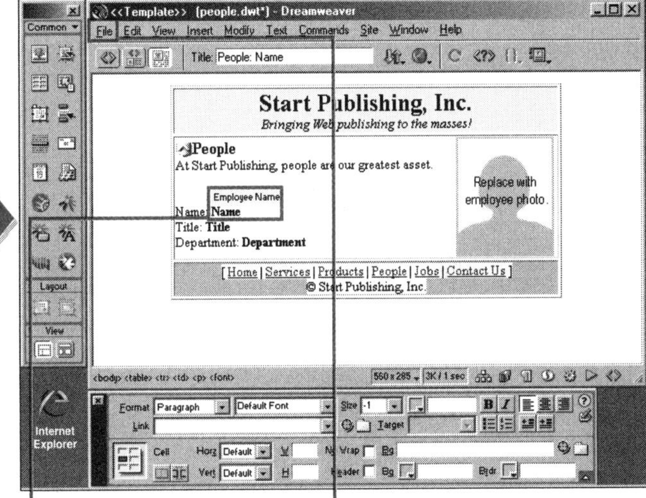

■ The editable region is highlighted in light blue on the page. A tab denotes its name.

■ You can change the highlighting color for editable text in Preferences. See Chapter 2.

8 Repeat steps 2 through 7 for all the regions on the page that you want to make editable in the template.

9 Click File.

10 Click Save.

CREATE A PAGE USING A TEMPLATE

Creating a page using a template saves you from having to build from scratch all the generic elements of the page — for example, elements that appear across many pages of your site, such as headers, footers, copyright information, and so on. Using a template also enables you to automatically update the design of the page, as well as other pages based on the template, by editing the original template.

You can create a page from one of the templates that you have already saved for your site (see "Create a Template" earlier in this chapter) with the New from Template command in the File menu. You can also open the Assets panel, where you can view a list of all your site's templates and select a template to start with (click ▸ to open the panel's menu commands). A third option is to apply a template to an existing Web page by selecting a template from the Assets panel and clicking the Apply button.

When you build a page from a template, you can modify only the areas of the page that you have specifically defined as editable. (See "Set a Template's Editable Regions" earlier in this chapter.) The editable areas are highlighted in blue in the Document window.

CREATE A PAGE BY USING A TEMPLATE

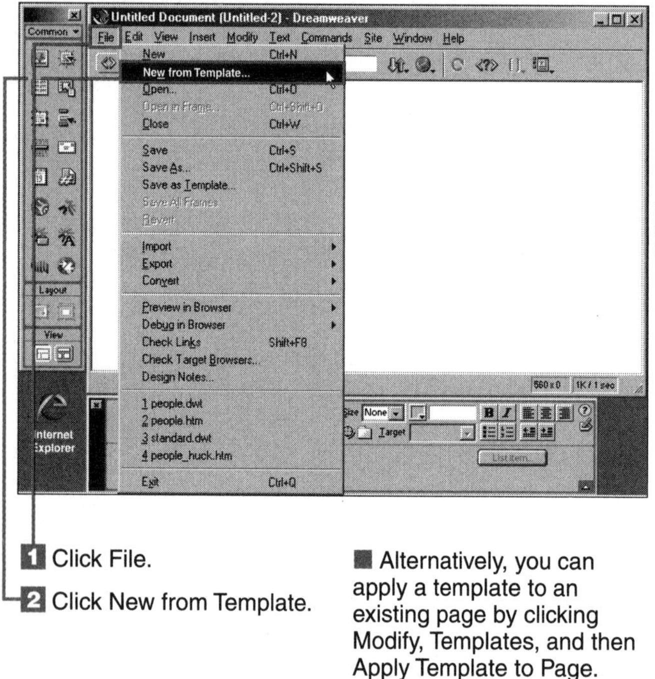

1 Click File.

2 Click New from Template.

■ Alternatively, you can apply a template to an existing page by clicking Modify, Templates, and then Apply Template to Page.

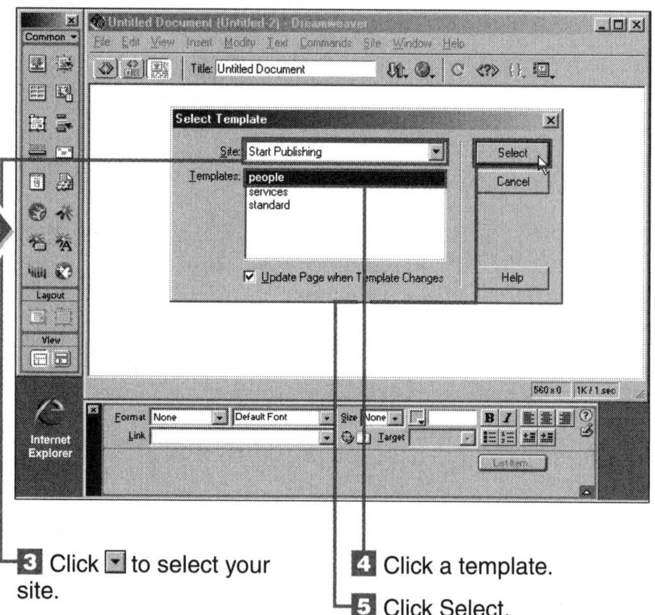

3 Click ▾ to select your site.

4 Click a template.

5 Click Select.

How do I detach a page from a template?

✔ Select the Detach from Template command located under the Templates submenu under the Modify menu. The page becomes a regular document, with its previously locked regions now fully editable. It will no longer be updated when the original template is updated.

Can I apply a template to a page that is already based on a different template?

✔ Yes. Open the page and click Modify, Templates, and then Apply Template to Page. Dreamweaver tries to match content in the original document with editable areas that have the same names in the new template. For content that it cannot match, Dreamweaver asks which editable area the content should be placed in.

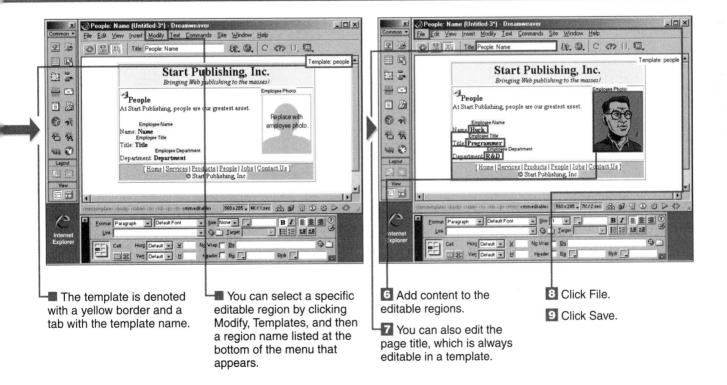

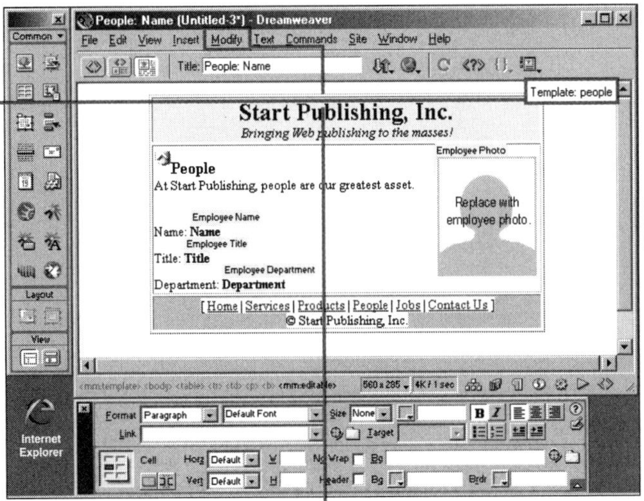

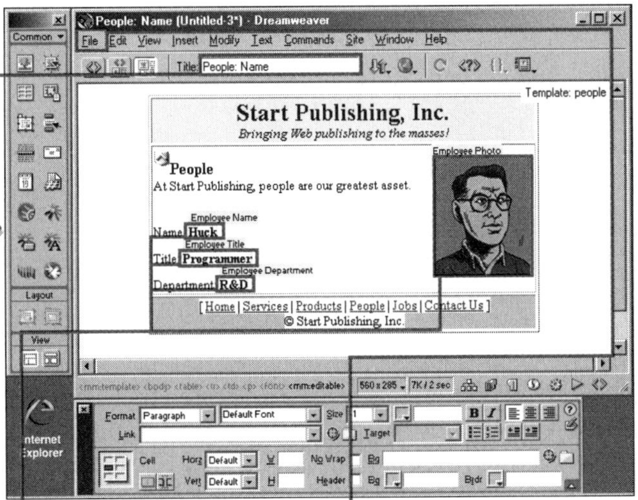

■ The template is denoted with a yellow border and a tab with the template name.

■ You can select a specific editable region by clicking Modify, Templates, and then a region name listed at the bottom of the menu that appears.

6 Add content to the editable regions.

7 You can also edit the page title, which is always editable in a template.

8 Click File.

9 Click Save.

EDIT A TEMPLATE AND UPDATE YOUR WEB SITE

Basing your site's pages on templates can be a tremendous timesaver when maintaining and evolving the design of your site pages. You can make changes to an original template file and then have Dreamweaver update other pages that you based on that template. You can easily make wholesale changes to your site's page design in a matter of seconds, instead of having to open and edit dozens or hundreds of pages one at a time.

In contrast to pages that are based on templates, which can have only their editable regions modified (see "Create a Page by Using a Template" earlier in the chapter), you can modify everything in the original template file. You can modify the locked regions inside the page body, body properties such as background and link colors, and head properties such as timelines and style sheets. When you save your changes, you can have Dreamweaver update all the files based on that template.

EDIT A TEMPLATE AND UPDATE YOUR WEB SITE

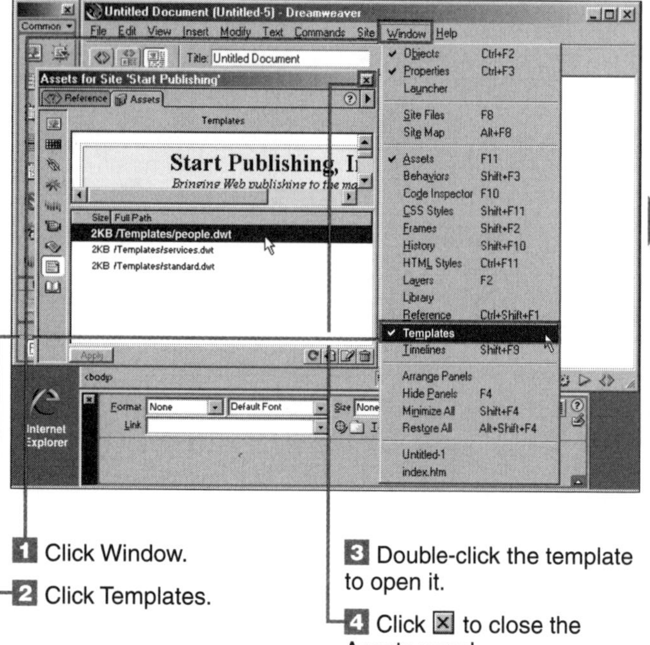

1 Click Window.

2 Click Templates.

3 Double-click the template to open it.

4 Click ☒ to close the Assets panel.

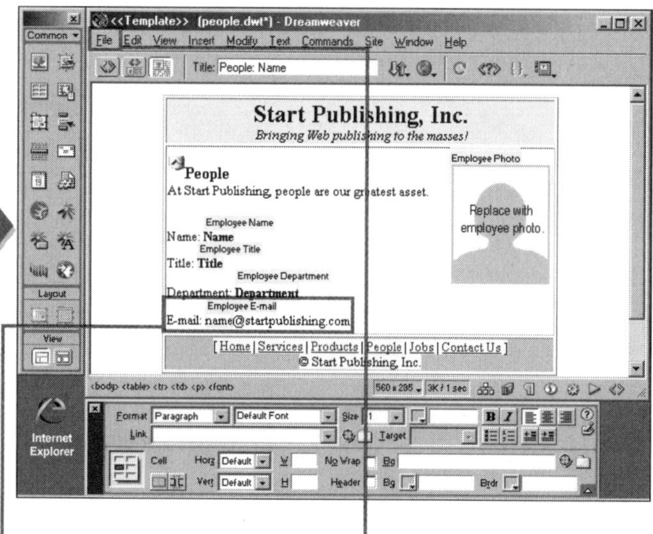

5 Edit the template.

■ You can add, modify, or delete editable or locked content in the page. See "Set a Template's Editable Regions" earlier in this chapter for details.

6 Click File.

7 Click Save.

How do I create new links in a template file?

✔ Creating links in an original template is a bit tricky, because template files are located in a subfolder (named Templates) inside the local site, and therefore must have relative links that are different from those in normal pages in the local site folder. You can avoid any problems by clicking the Link ▢ when you need to define your links to other pages in your site, instead of trying to define them in the Link text field by hand. Clicking ▢ allows Dreamweaver to build the correct path to the destination page for you.

Can I edit timelines and style sheets in pages based on templates?

✔ Unfortunately, no, because only body content in a document can be defined as editable in a template, and timelines and style sheets are located in a page's head area. To add or modify timelines or style sheets, you need to work with the original template file, or detach the template-based page from the template by clicking Modify, Templates, and then Detach from Template.

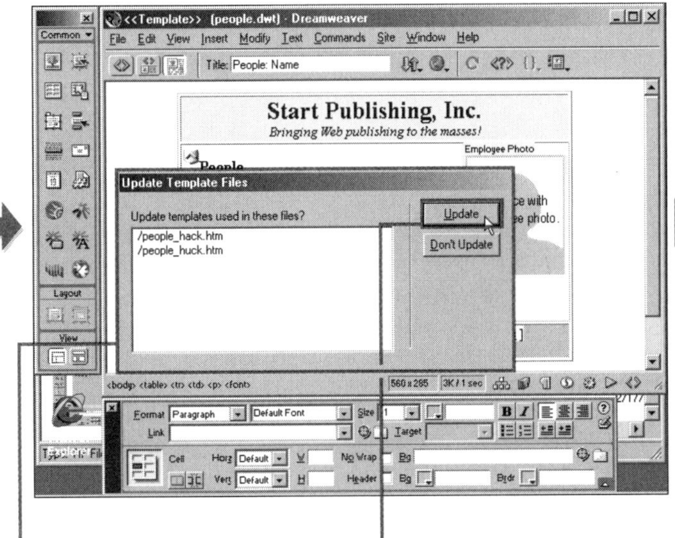

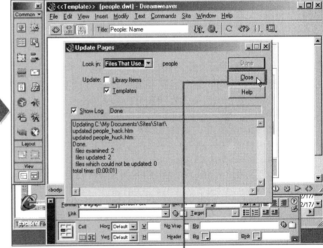

■ An alert box appears asking if you want to update all the pages that are based on the template.

8 Click Update.

■ A dialog box shows the progress of the updates.

9 After Dreamweaver is finished updating the site, click Close.

AN INTRODUCTION TO STYLE SHEETS

Style sheets (also called *Cascading Styles Sheets* or *CSS*) let you create complex formatting rules for your page that can be stored in the <head> area of a Web page or in a separate text file. Styles sheets offer designers much more power and precision in terms of styling their Web content compared to HTML. They also make maintaining a consistent style across a site easier, because many pages can link to a single set of style rules.

Format Text

A separate standard from HTML, style sheets let you format type (adjust character, paragraph, and margin spacing), choose different fonts, customize the look of hyperlinks, tailor the colors on your page, and more. You can apply this formatting by using style sheets to customize existing HTML tags or by creating style-sheet *classes* that you can add to your HTML.

Using Style Sheets Instead of HTML

You can perform many of the HTML-based formatting features discussed in Chapter 5 using style sheets. You can also use style sheets to apply more elaborate formatting to your pages than is possible with regular HTML. Because the World Wide Web Consortium — which sets Web publishing standards — favors the use of style sheets over many HTML style-related tags, you should see style sheets continue to increase in popularity.

Position Web Page Elements

You can use style sheets to position images, text, and other elements precisely on your Web page, something that is not possible with HTML. Dreamweaver's layer feature offers a user-friendly way to apply the positioning capabilities of style sheets.

Embedded Style Sheets

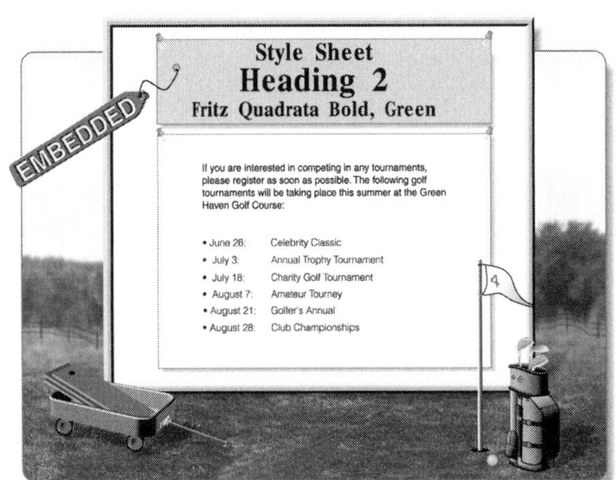

A style sheet that is saved inside a particular Web page is called an *embedded style sheet.* Embedded style sheet rules apply only to the page in which they are embedded.

External Style Sheets

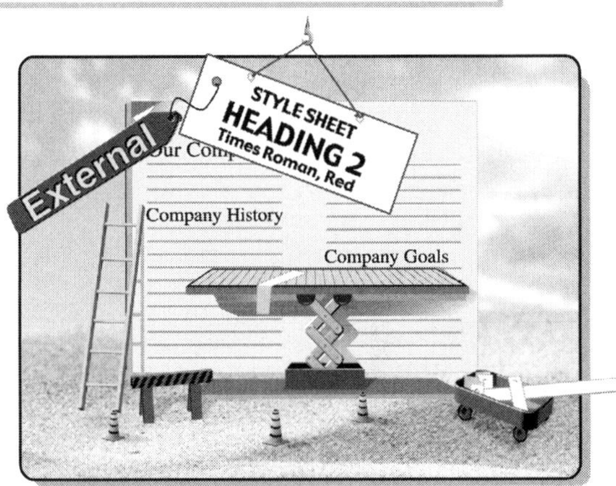

You can save style sheets as separate files; these external style sheets exist independently of your HTML pages. Different Web pages can access a common set of style rules by linking to the same external style sheet.

Style Sheets and Browsers

The first Web browsers to begin supporting style sheets were Microsoft Internet Explorer Version 3 and Netscape Navigator Version 4. However, these browsers supported the standard incompletely and interpreted some style sheet rules differently from one another. Newer browser versions support more style sheet features and support them more consistently. But you should still thoroughly test pages that use style sheets in both browsers before you put them live to ensure that the content displays correctly.

CUSTOMIZE AN HTML TAG

You can use style sheets to customize the style that is applied by an HTML tag. Doing this enables you to add color or font definitions to headings (by customizing the <h> tags), add backgrounds or borders to paragraphs (by customizing the <p> tag), or apply different margin settings to the page body (by customizing the <body> tag).

Designers used to be stuck with the relatively few style options that HTML offered and that browsers supported. Style sheets, in contrast, offer a wide variety of style options and let *you* determine how tags affect your content.

Style sheets also make updating customized tags easy. You can make style changes to the <h3> heading in the style sheet and have those changes instantly show up in all instances of the <h3> tag on your page or site, if you define the styles in an external style sheet. See "Create and Attach an External Style Sheet."

A drawback to customizing a tag is that a change affects all the instances of a tag whether you want it to or not. To apply style settings independently of particular HTML tags, see "Create a Class" and "Apply a Class."

CUSTOMIZE AN HTML TAG

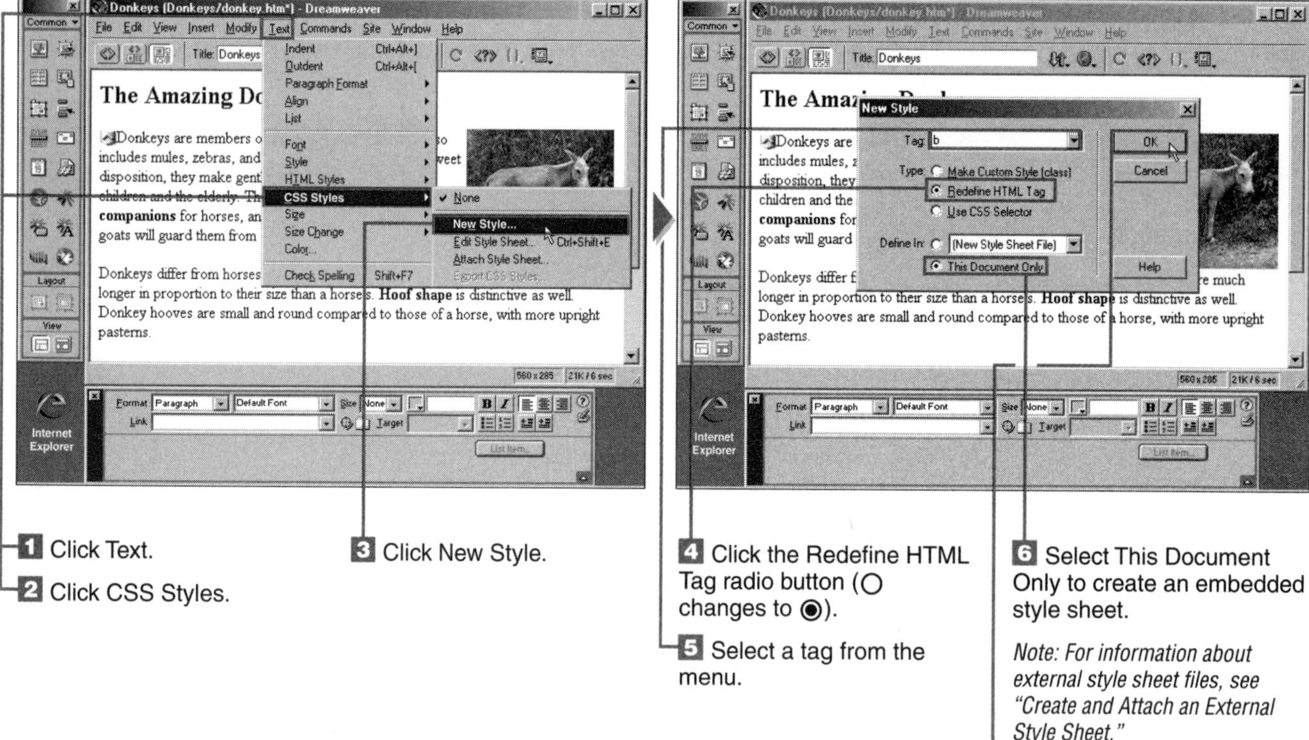

1 Click Text.

2 Click CSS Styles.

3 Click New Style.

4 Click the Redefine HTML Tag radio button (○ changes to ◉).

5 Select a tag from the menu.

6 Select This Document Only to create an embedded style sheet.

Note: For information about external style sheet files, see "Create and Attach an External Style Sheet."

7 Click OK.

Can I use style sheets to make one tag behave exactly like another?

✔ Yes. You can, for example, customize the <b> (bold) tag so that it applies an italic style and no change in weight, just like the <i> (italic) tag.

How do I keep a background image fixed in the browser while content scrolls?

✔ The Background category in the Style Definition dialog box enables you to set an Attachment value. To keep a background fixed, customize the <body> tag and set the Attachment to fixed.

How do I edit the style that I have applied to a tag?

✔ Click Text, CSS Styles, and then Edit Style Sheet. The dialog box that opens displays the current customized tags and style-sheet classes. Click the tag and then click Edit.

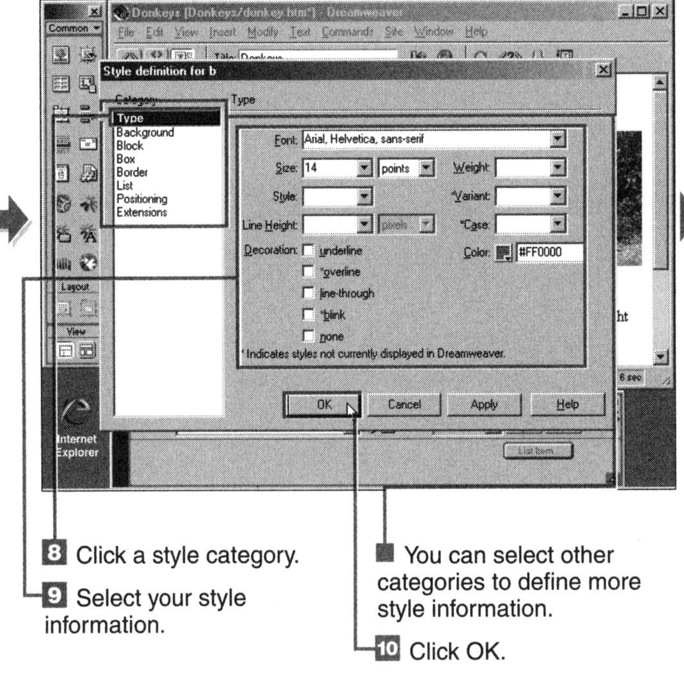

8 Click a style category.

9 Select your style information.

■ You can select other categories to define more style information.

10 Click OK.

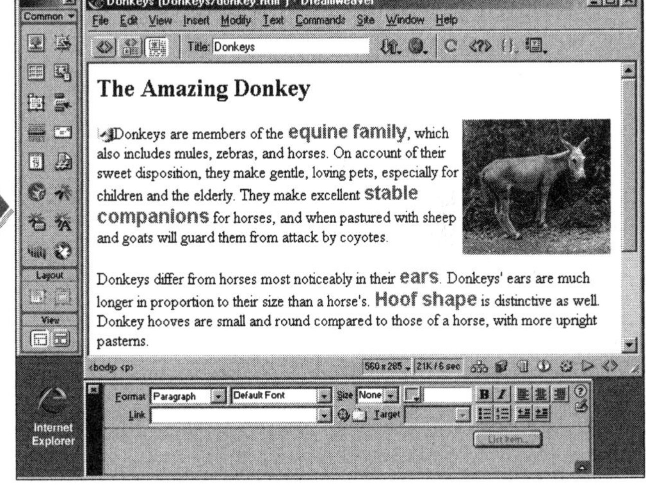

■ Dreamweaver adds the new style to any content formatted with the redefined tag (in this example, the <b> tag).

■ Formatting new content with the tag will apply the style as well.

CREATE A CLASS

Style sheet classes let you define custom style rules that you can apply to many different types of content on your page. For example, you can create a class that turns text blue and underlined. You can then apply the class to a paragraph, a heading, or a sentence on the same page.

Creating classes is an alternative to using style sheet rules to customize existing HTML tags. (See "Customize an HTML Tag" earlier in this chapter.) Classes exist independently of the HTML tags that they customize on a page.

You can view the classes that you create for your page in the CSS Styles panel (click Window and then CSS Styles). These include classes that you have embedded in your page (and are accessible only by that page) and classes that you have applied to the page via an external style sheet.

After you create and apply a class, you can edit it. When you save edits to a class, the changes are immediately applied to the instances of that class on your page. See "Edit a Style Sheet Class" later in this chapter.

CREATE A CLASS

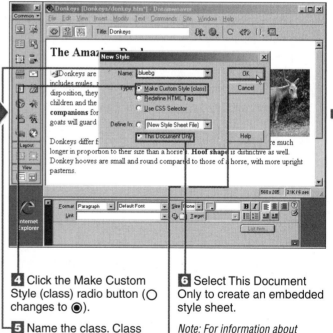

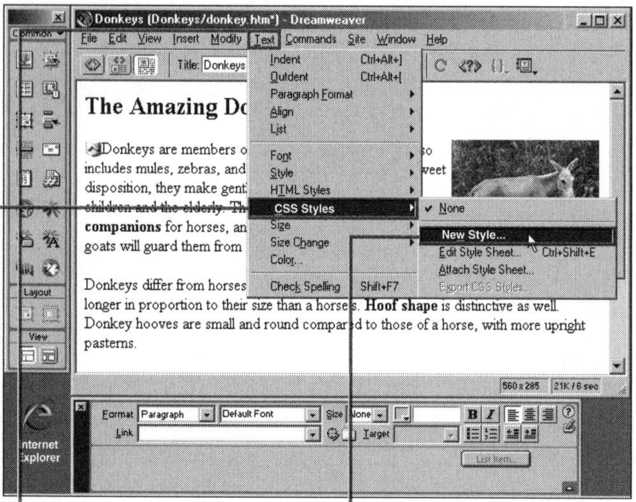

1 Click Text.

2 Click CSS Styles.

3 Click New Style.

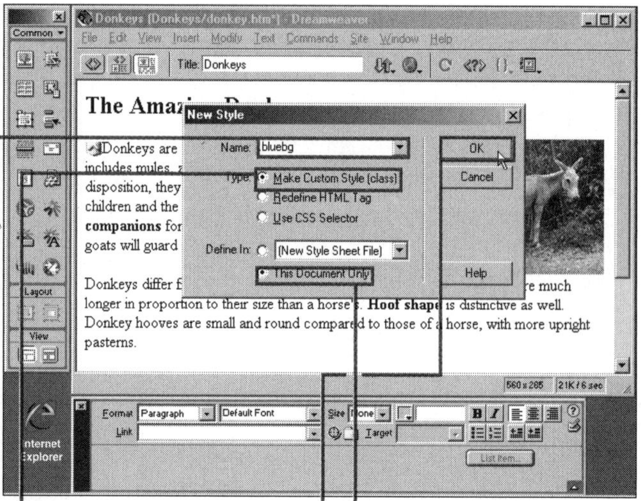

4 Click the Make Custom Style (class) radio button (○ changes to ◉).

5 Name the class. Class names must begin with a period (".").

6 Select This Document Only to create an embedded style sheet.

Note: For information about external style sheet files, see "Create and Attach an External Style Sheet" later in this chapter.

7 Click OK.

What does the code that defines a class look like?

✔ The code includes the name of the class (which must start with a "."), plus property/value pairs that determine the style of the class. Here is an example:

```
.myclass {font-weight: bold;
color: green}
```

The above code creates a class that turns text bold and green. Style sheet code is placed in the <head> area of an HTML document.

How can I find out about the styles that I can create with style sheets?

✔ You can look at the many options available in the Style Definition dialog box that appears when you create styles. You can also open the Dreamweaver Reference panel (click Window and then Reference) and look up style information there. You will need to select O'REILLY CSS Reference in the top menu.

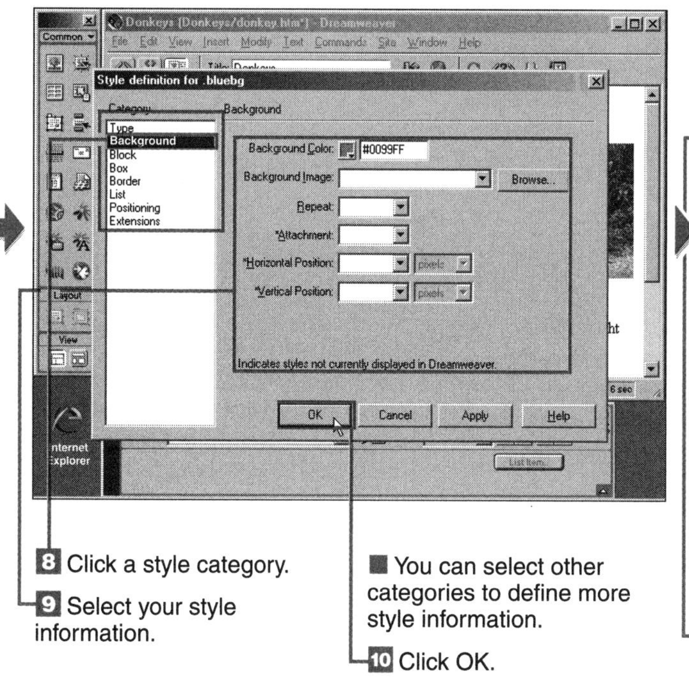

8 Click a style category.

9 Select your style information.

■ You can select other categories to define more style information.

10 Click OK.

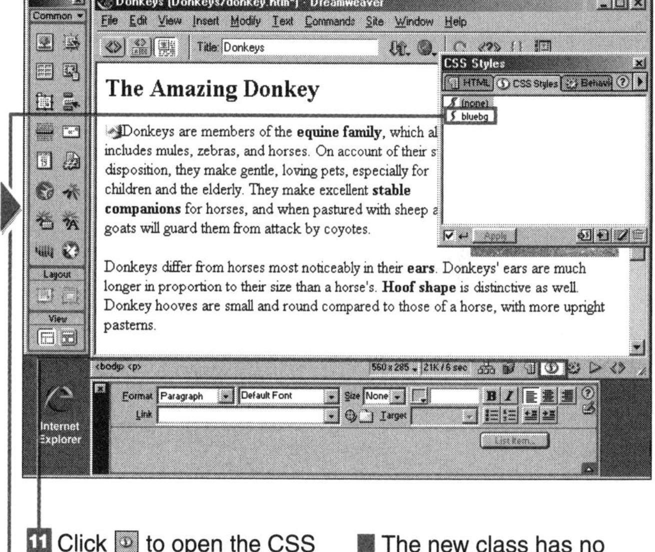

11 Click [icon] to open the CSS Styles panel.

■ The new class appears in the panel.

■ The new class has no effect on your content until you apply it.

Note: See "Apply a Class" later in this chapter.

APPLY A CLASS

Because classes are independent of the tags and other code that makes up your Web page, they need to be explicitly applied to have an effect. After you select an object in your page, you can apply a class to the object by clicking the class name in CSS Styles panel.

You can apply more than one class to an element on a page. What effect the combination of classes has depends on how you apply the information. If a conflict between classes exists, the style that is closest to the content in question wins out.

For example, if you give a paragraph a blue style and a sentence inside the paragraph a green style, the sentence appears green while the rest of the paragraph appears blue.

Many of the style rules that you can apply in Dreamweaver are specifically designed for text (which is why you access style sheet commands under the Text menu). But you can also create styles that apply to both text and other page elements. For example, you can create a border style that creates a blue, double-lined border

APPLY A CLASS

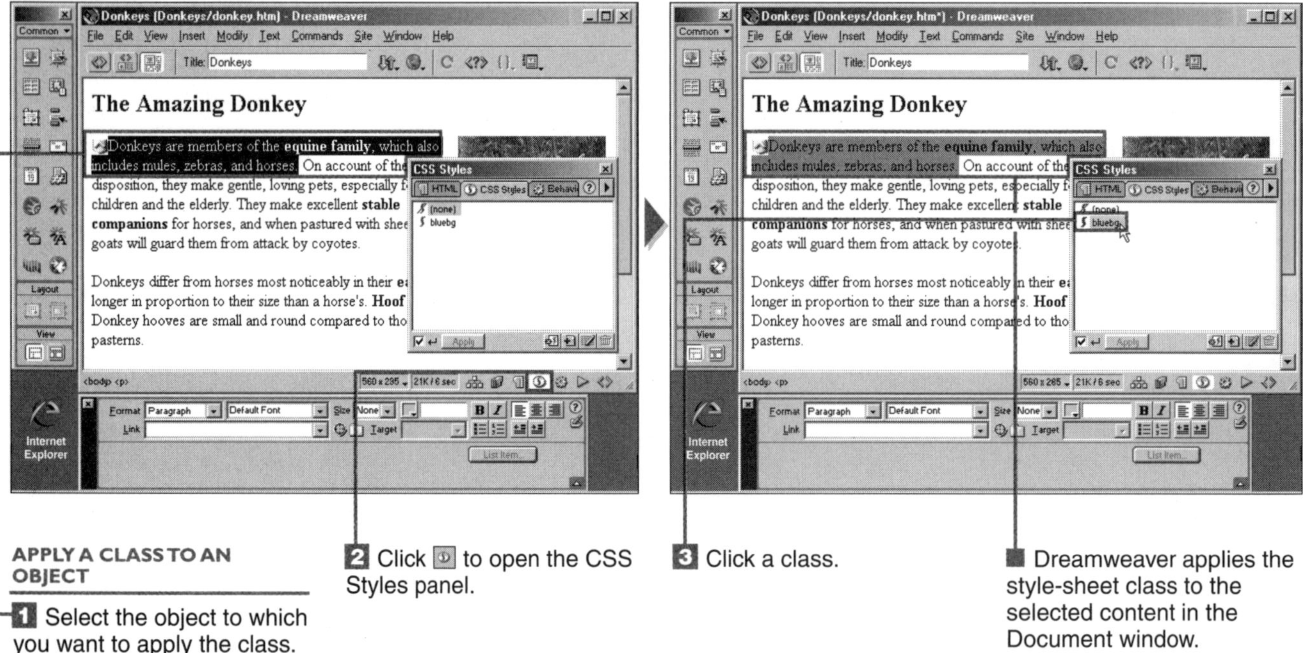

APPLY A CLASS TO AN OBJECT

1 Select the object to which you want to apply the class.

2 Click ⓘ to open the CSS Styles panel.

3 Click a class.

■ Dreamweaver applies the style-sheet class to the selected content in the Document window.

Does Dreamweaver display all the styles that I apply to my pages?

✔ Dreamweaver can display only a subset of the style rules that it lets you define. Style rules that are marked with an asterisk in the Style Definitions dialog box cannot be displayed. You need to open the page in a style sheet-capable browser to view these styles. Some of the styles that Dreamweaver cannot display include borders, word and letter spacing, and list characteristics.

How can I tell which styles have been applied to an element in my page?

✔ You can select the element and look at the tag selector at the bottom of the Document window. HTML tags and any associated classes are displayed. Applied classes are also highlighted in the CSS Styles panel and checked in the CSS Styles submenu under the Text menu.

How do I remove a style from an element in my page?

✔ Select the element and then click Text, CSS Styles, and None. You can also select the element and click None in the CSS Styles panel.

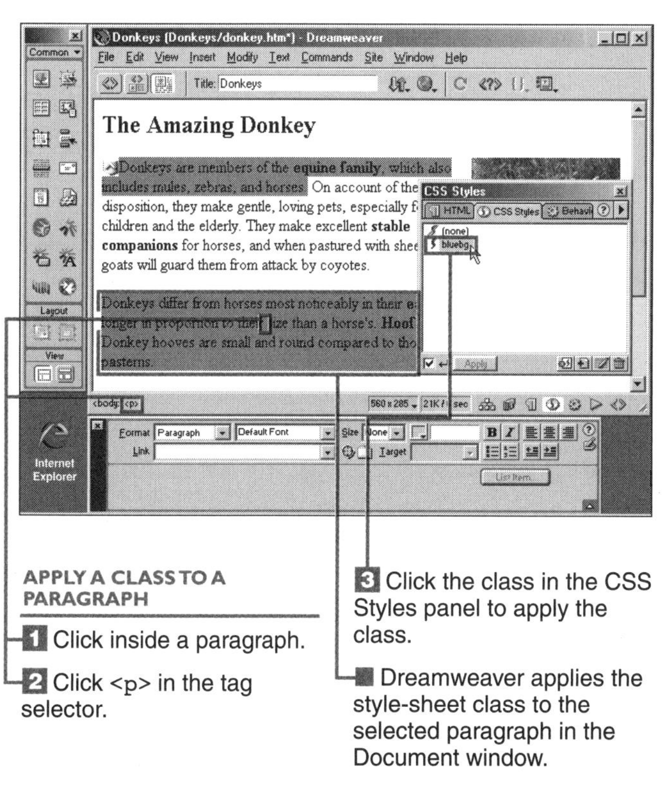

APPLY A CLASS TO A PARAGRAPH

1 Click inside a paragraph.

2 Click <p> in the tag selector.

3 Click the class in the CSS Styles panel to apply the class.

■ Dreamweaver applies the style-sheet class to the selected paragraph in the Document window.

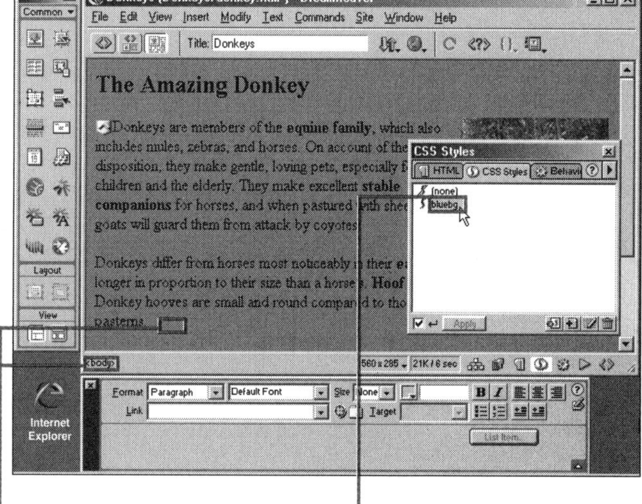

APPLY A CLASS TO THE ENTIRE BODY OF A PAGE

1 Click inside the Document window.

2 Click <body> in the tag selector.

3 Click the class in the CSS Styles panel to apply the class.

■ Dreamweaver applies the style-sheet class to the entire body of the page in the Document window.

EDIT A STYLE SHEET CLASS

Style sheet classes are powerful tools for maintaining the look and feel of a page or an entire site. Classes let you define a collection of style rules that control the formatting of body text, headings, subheadings, headers, and footers in one place. Changing the appearance of all those elements can then be as easy as editing the style sheet rules.

When you edit a style, the change takes effect immediately. You do not have to update your styles across your pages like you do library items and templates (see Chapter 11). Edits also have the same effect no matter when you apply them. The effects that styles have are always tied to the current style sheet rules, not what the rules happened to be when you applied them.

EDIT A STYLE SHEET CLASS

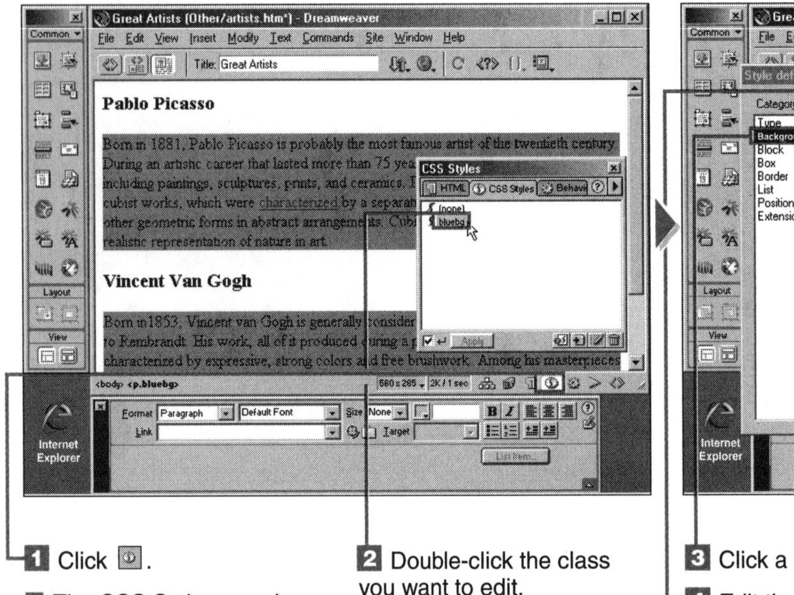

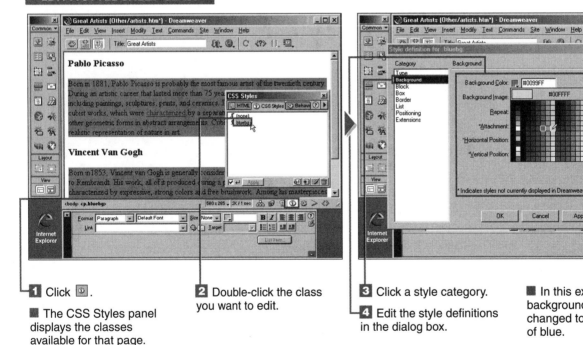

1 Click .

■ The CSS Styles panel displays the classes available for that page.

2 Double-click the class you want to edit.

3 Click a style category.

4 Edit the style definitions in the dialog box.

■ In this example, the background color has been changed to a different shade of blue.

What are some type-based features that I can apply with style sheets that I cannot apply with HTML?

✔ Style sheets let you specify a numeric value for font weight, enabling you to apply varying degrees of boldness, instead of just a single boldness setting as with HTML. Note that this works with only certain fonts. You can also define type size in absolute units (pixels, points, picas, inches, centimeters, millimeters) or relative units (ems, exes, percentage). HTML offers no such choices of units.

How do I indent the first line of my paragraphs?

✔ Create a class that applies a positive Indent value (using the options under the Block category in the Style Definitions dialog box). Then apply the class to the paragraphs that you want to indent. You can also use the setting customize the <p> tag to indent all the paragraphs on the page. A negative Indent value causes the first line of text to stick out into the margin, which can also provide an interesting effect.

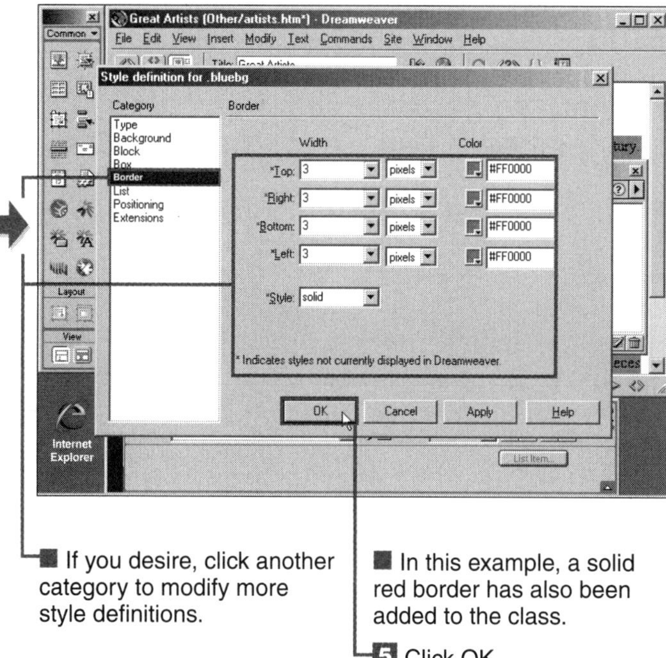

Great Artists - Microsoft Internet Explorer

Pablo Picasso

Born in 1881, Pablo Picasso is probably the most famous artist of the twentieth century. During an artistic career that lasted more than 75 years, he created thousands of works, including paintings, sculptures, prints, and ceramics. Picasso is most famous for his cubist works, which were characterized by a separation of the subject into cubes and other geometric forms in abstract arrangements. Cubism was a radical break from the realistic representation of nature in art.

Vincent Van Gogh

Born in1853, Vincent van Gogh is generally considered the greatest Dutch painter next to Rembrandt. His work, all of it produced during a period of only 10 years, is characterized by expressive, strong colors and free brushwork. Among his masterpieces are numerous self-portraits and the well-known Starry Night. Unfortunately, van Gogh suffered from mental illness and spent the last year of his life in an asylum.

■ If you desire, click another category to modify more style definitions.

■ In this example, a solid red border has also been added to the class.

5 Click OK.

6 Preview the page in a Web browser.

Note: For more information on Web browsers, see Chapter 4.

■ The page is displayed with the edited class.

Note: Dreamweaver cannot display some style definitions — for example, border styles — so sometimes you must open the page in a Web browser to see the full effect of your edits.

USING CSS SELECTORS TO MODIFY LINKS

Just as style sheets give you more options when styling regular text on a page, they also offer new ways to style hyperlinks. You can style your hyperlinks with CSS selectors.

Using regular HTML styles, you can customize only the color of links on a page (see "Change the Color of Hyperlinks" in Chapter 7). *CSS selectors* enable you to fully customize hyperlinks — you can specify weight, letter spacing, background color, border, and many other characteristics.

The CSS selectors Dreamweaver makes available are

- `a:active`, which lets you define the style of clicked links;
- `a:hover`, which lets you define the style of links when a cursor rolls over them;
- `a:link`, which lets you define the style of unvisited links;
- and `a:visited`, which lets you define the style of links that your browser has recently visited.

In contrast to the other selectors, the `a:hover` selector enables you to apply a dynamic effect to your links by making the link style change in response to the cursor in the browser window.

USING CSS SELECTORS TO MODIFY LINKS

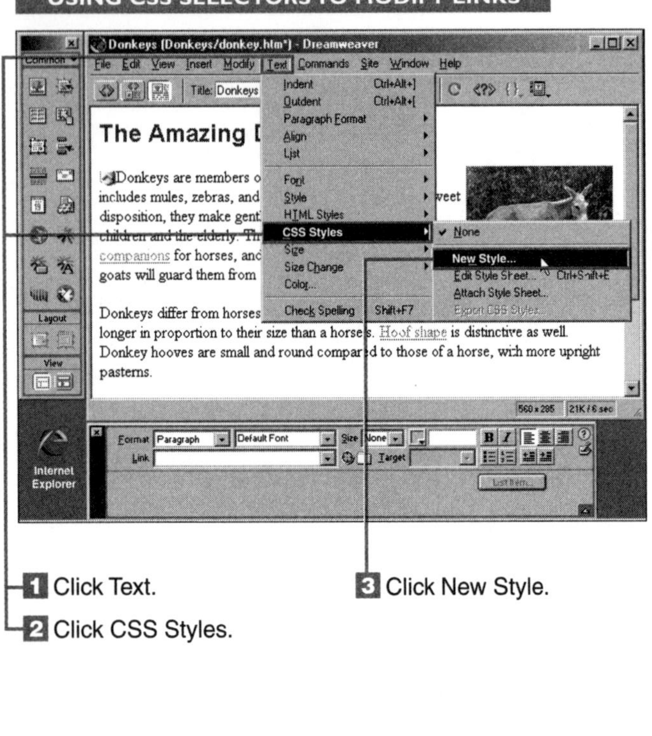

1 Click Text.

2 Click CSS Styles.

3 Click New Style.

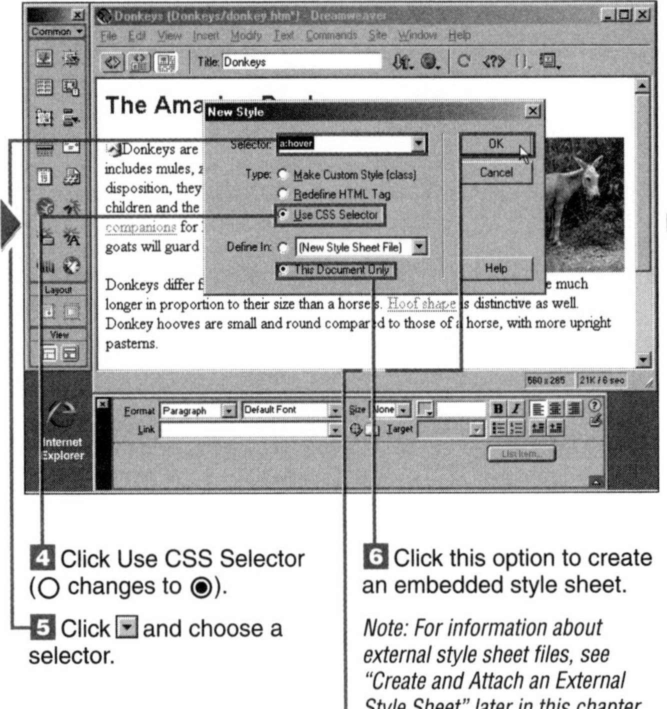

4 Click Use CSS Selector (○ changes to ◉).

5 Click ▾ and choose a selector.

6 Click this option to create an embedded style sheet.

Note: For information about external style sheet files, see "Create and Attach an External Style Sheet" later in this chapter.

7 Click OK.

Should I leave my links underlined?

✔ Underlining has long been a visual cue to signal a clickable hyperlink. If you remove the underlining, viewers skimming your page may not recognize all the links. Users on black-and-white systems, who can see underlining but not changes in color (which also accompanies hyperlinks), will be even worse off.

What is the overlining feature?

✔ The *overlining* applies a line across the top of your text. It is the stylistic opposite of underlining. The overline style is available under the Type category in the Style Definition dialog box. When used with CSS selectors, overline places a line across the top of your links.

How can I make my links look like they have been marked with highlighter pen?

✔ Define a bright background color for your links under the Background category in the Style Definition dialog box.

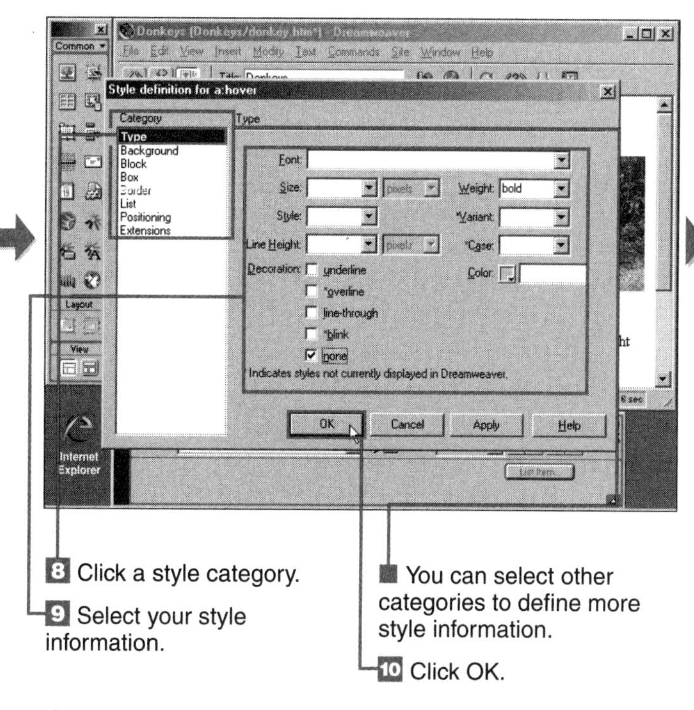

8 Click a style category.

9 Select your style information.

■ You can select other categories to define more style information.

10 Click OK.

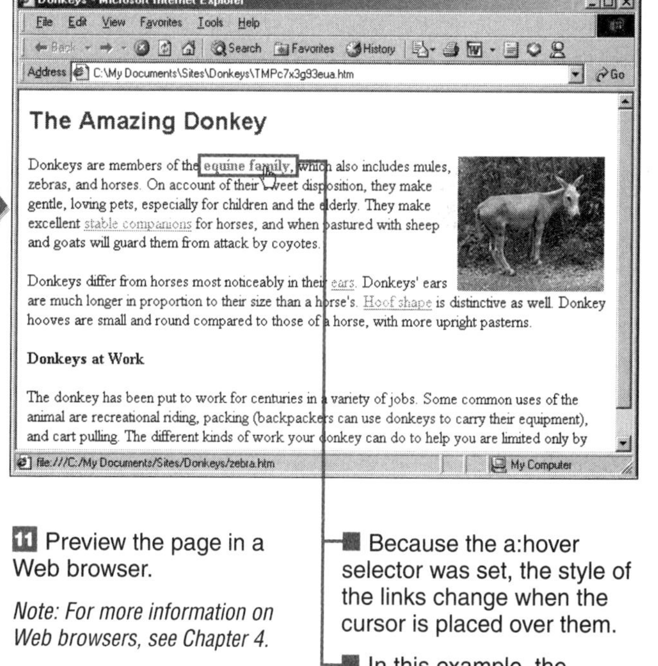

11 Preview the page in a Web browser.

Note: For more information on Web browsers, see Chapter 4.

■ Because the a:hover selector was set, the style of the links change when the cursor is placed over them.

■ In this example, the underlining disappears and the text becomes bold.

CREATE AND ATTACH AN EXTERNAL STYLE SHEET

External style sheets enable you to put a list of style sheet rules in a separate file. You can save this file in your local site folder, and all the pages of your site can access it.

Creating external style sheets offers a big advantage to designers who want to separate style rules for a site from its content. Placing style information in a separate file means that updating page content does not affect (or corrupt) the styles for that page. Storing style definitions centrally can also help ensure a consistent look and feel across all pages of a site.

The same code that is used to build embedded style sheets is used to create external style sheets. Instead of being in the <head> area of an HTML document, external style sheets have their rules listed without any surrounding HTML content. Embedded style sheets are described in "Customize an HTML Tag" and "Create a Class" earlier in this chapter.

CREATE AND ATTACH AN EXTERNAL STYLE SHEET

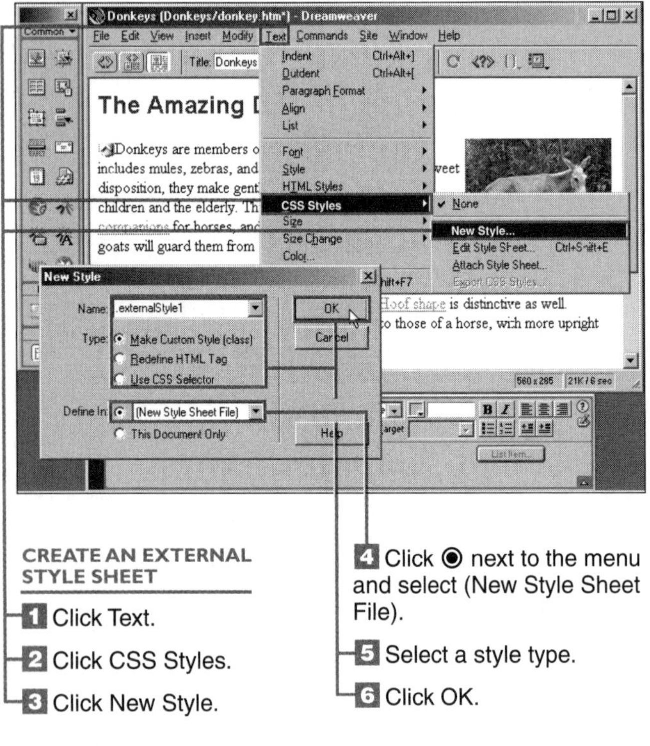

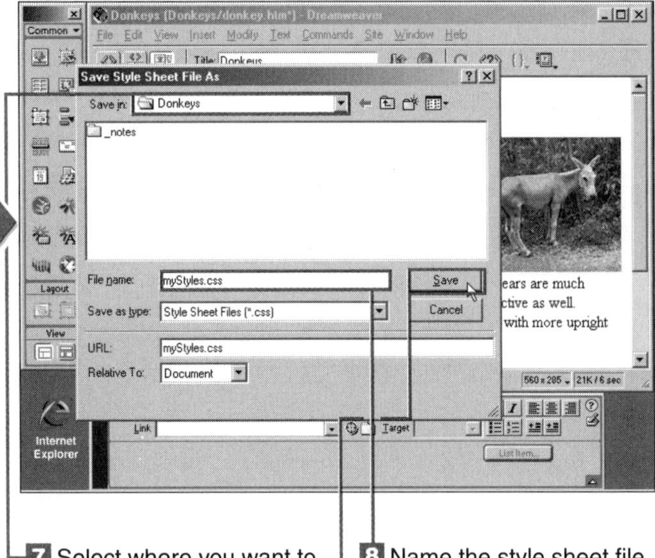

CREATE AN EXTERNAL STYLE SHEET

1 Click Text.

2 Click CSS Styles.

3 Click New Style.

4 Click ◉ next to the menu and select (New Style Sheet File).

5 Select a style type.

6 Click OK.

7 Select where you want to store the external style sheet. You should store it somewhere inside your local site folder.

Note: See Chapter 4 for more about defining a local site.

8 Name the style sheet file. Give it a **.css** extension.

9 Click Save.

How do I export a set of embedded styles to create an external style sheet?

✔ You can click File, Export, and then Export Styles. This enables you to name a new CSS file and specify where the file is stored. You can then link to the external file to use those styles in other documents.

What happens when I delete an external style sheet?

✔ All the files that link to the sheet lose the style information that was in the sheet. Before you delete an external style sheet, consider whether you or someone else could be relying on it to format pages.

Where can I see an example of an external style sheet?

✔ The Dreamweaver Help pages use a linked external style sheet called help.css located on your hard drive here:

```
Dreamweaver4/Help/
UsingDreamweaver/html/
help.css
```

You can open that file in a text editor to see an example of CSS code.

Can I reference an external style sheet stored on another Web site?

✔ When you attach a style sheet to a page in Dreamweaver, you can either browse for the file in your local site folder or enter a URL. The URL option lets you link to a style sheet on another Web site.

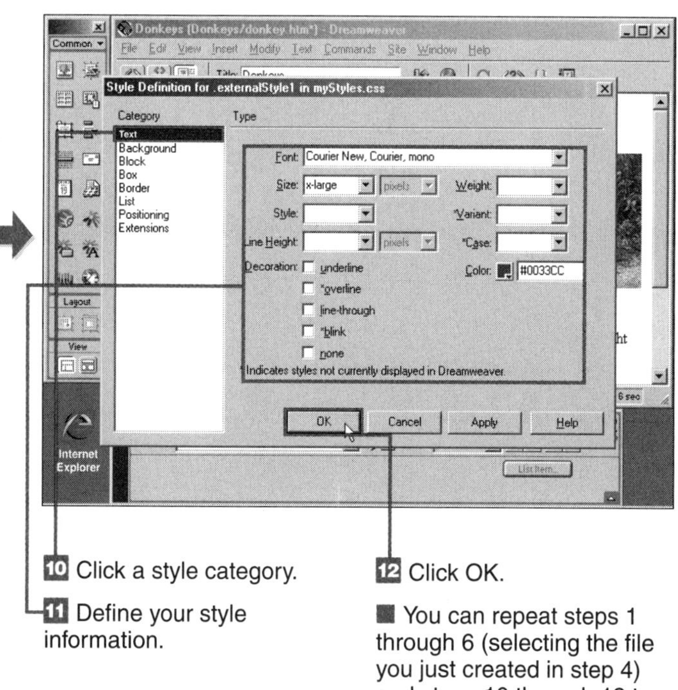

10 Click a style category.

11 Define your style information.

12 Click OK.

■ You can repeat steps 1 through 6 (selecting the file you just created in step 4) and steps 10 through 12 to add more style rules to the external style sheet.

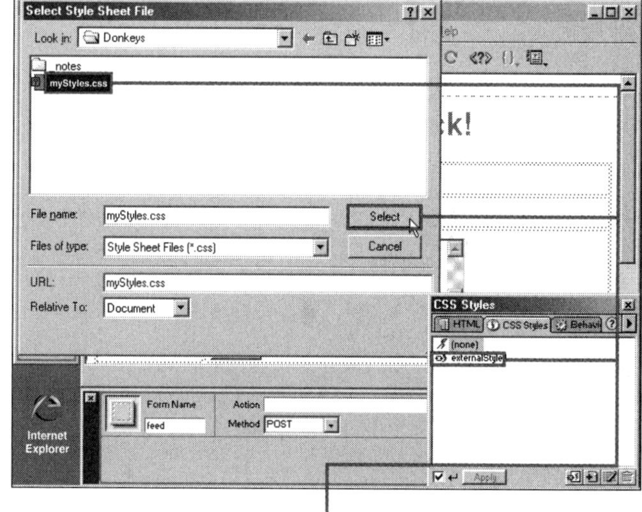

ATTACH AN EXTERNAL STYLE SHEET

1 Open the page to which you want to attach the style sheet.

2 Click Text.

3 Click CSS Styles.

4 Click Attach Style Sheet.

5 Select the external style sheet in the Select Style Sheet File dialog box.

6 Click Select.

■ The style(s) from the style sheet appear in the CSS Styles panel and are

CREATE A LAYER

Layers give you the option of creating rectangular areas that float above the other content on your page. You can fill these blocks with different types of content and position them precisely in the browser window.

Layers are actually a style sheet phenomenon — they are built using the positioning capabilities afforded by style sheets. When you create a layer in the Document window, Dreamweaver writes the style sheet code behind the scenes. The code specifies the positioning properties as well as the dimensions of the layer. You can change these properties interactively in the Document window or by typing new values in the Property Inspector. See "Resize and Reposition Layers" later in this chapter.

You can animate layered content using timelines. Animation involves changing the position of layers on a page over time. Chapter 14 covers timelines.

To view layers on a page with a browser, you need Version 4 or later of Microsoft Internet Explorer or Netscape Navigator.

CREATE A LAYER

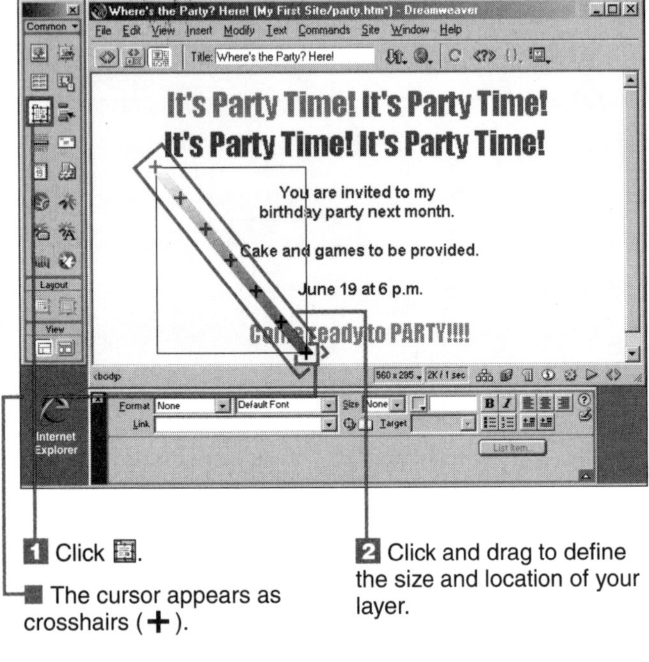

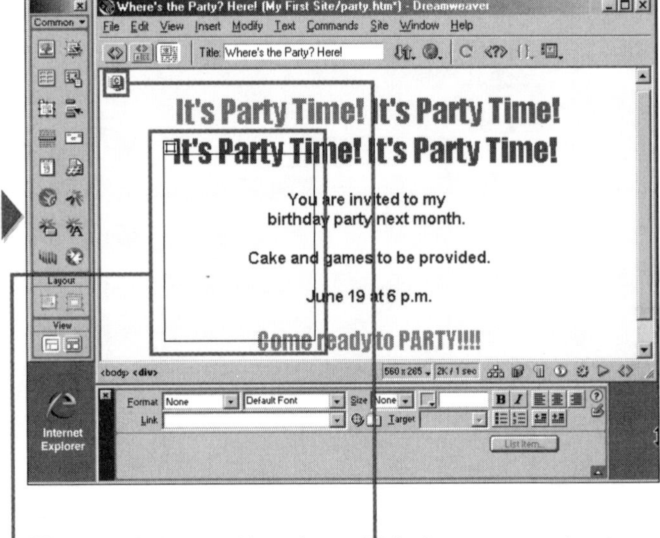

1 Click .

■ The cursor appears as crosshairs (+).

2 Click and drag to define the size and location of your layer.

■ A layer is inserted into the page. Layers are removed from the regular flow of content on the page, and can sit on top of other content.

■ An icon represents where you inserted the layer code. You can click the icon to select the layer.

Can I create layers without using style sheets?

✔ You can use an alternate method for creating layers that use `<layer>` or `<ilayer>` tags. But this method is supported only by Netscape Navigator Version 4 (support for the standard was discontinued in later versions). You can specify that Dreamweaver creates layers this way in Preferences (select the Layers category and select `<layer>` or `<ilayer>` in the drop-down menu) or in the Property Inspector. Just keep in mind that Microsoft Internet Explorer and Netscape Navigator 5 and above will not be able to display them.

How do I nest layers?

✔ Make sure the Nesting check box is selected in Preferences (under the Layers category). Click the Object panel layer button and then click and drag inside an existing layer. When you nest a layer inside another, the layer's icon appears inside the enclosing layer.

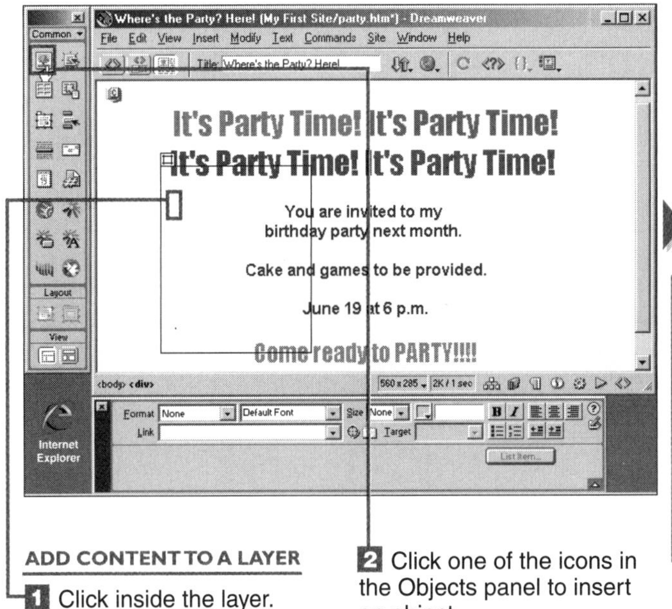

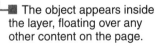

ADD CONTENT TO A LAYER

1 Click inside the layer.

2 Click one of the icons in the Objects panel to insert an object.

Note: See Chapter 2 for more information.

■ The object appears inside the layer, floating over any other content on the page.

■ To add text, you can also click inside the layer and type. You can also style the text in a layer.

RESIZE AND REPOSITION LAYERS

Every layer has specific position and dimension settings that define its place in the page. You can adjust these settings to make a layer fit attractively with the rest of the content on your page.

When you select the layer, its position coordinates, as well as its dimension values, appear in the Property Inspector. The default unit of measurement is pixels (px), but you can change this to inches (in), centimeters (cm), and even a percentage of the browser window (%). The position of a layer in Dreamweaver is measured from the top left of the browser window.

A useful way to control the position and size of your layers as you click and drag them in the Document window is to turn on the grid (click View, Grid, and Show Grid). Make sure that you set the page content to snap to the grid lines (click View, Grid, and Snap to Grid).

RESIZE AND REPOSITION LAYERS

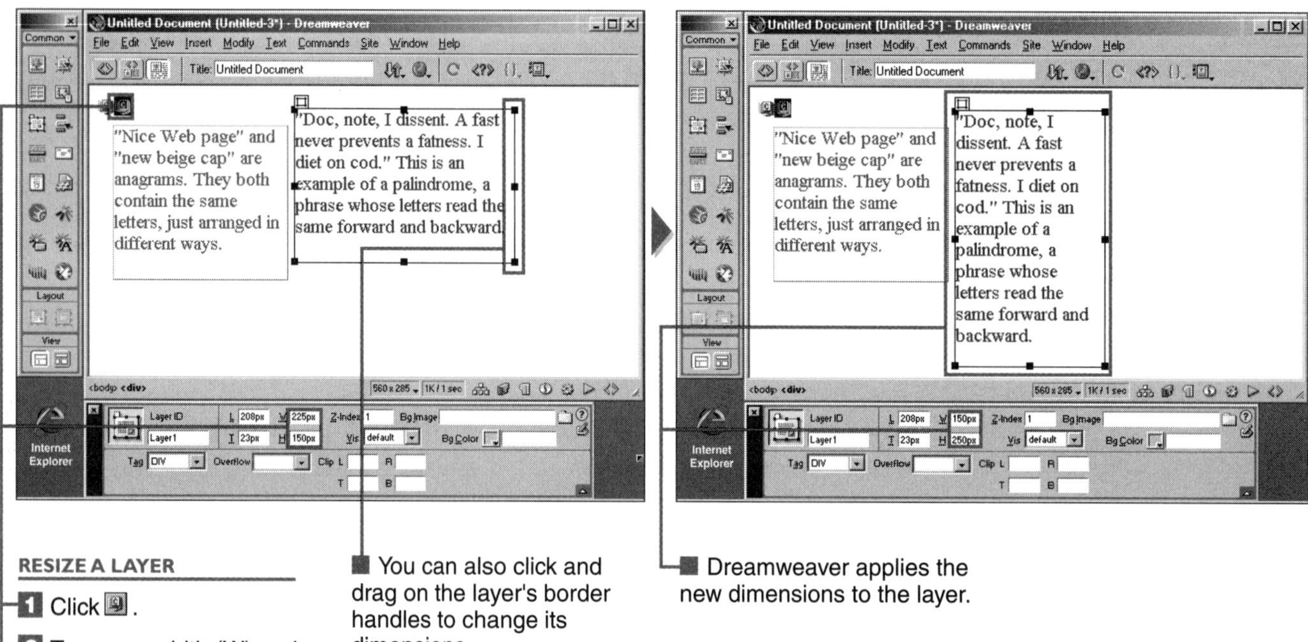

RESIZE A LAYER

1 Click [icon].

2 Type new width (W) and height (H) values, using px for pixels, in for inches, or cm for centimeters.

■ You can also click and drag on the layer's border handles to change its dimensions.

■ Dreamweaver applies the new dimensions to the layer.

How do I change the properties of several layers at once?

✔ Select more than one layer in the Document window by shift-clicking. Then change the properties of these layers by adjusting the values in the Property Inspector.

What limits the size of my layer?

✔ The content inside a layer may limit its size. For example, you cannot shrink a layer that contains an image to smaller than the size of the image.

What happens if the L (left) or T (top) values for a layer are larger than the dimensions of the browser window?

✔ The layer is positioned out of sight from your viewers. This is something you should consider if you think your site's visitors may be using small monitors.

How do I make a layer invisible?

✔ Adjust the Vis (Visibility) menu in the Property Inspector. The menu lets you make a layer visible, invisible, or have it inherit its characteristic from its parent (the enclosing layer).

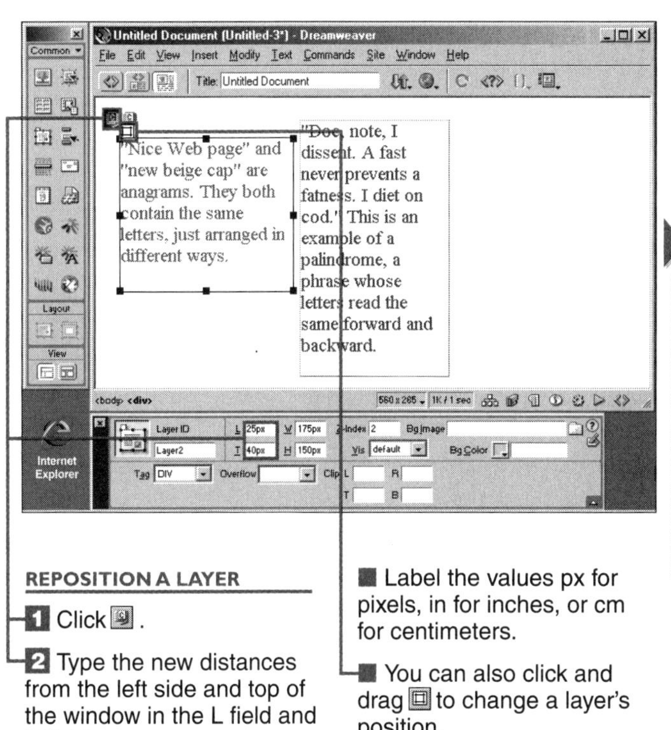

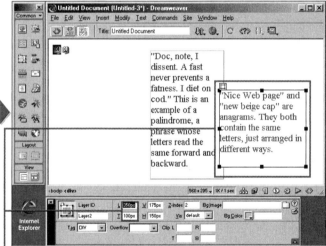

REPOSITION A LAYER

1 Click .

2 Type the new distances from the left side and top of the window in the L field and T field.

■ Label the values px for pixels, in for inches, or cm for centimeters.

■ You can also click and drag to change a layer's position.

■ Dreamweaver applies the new positioning to the layer.

ADD A BACKGROUND COLOR TO A LAYER

Just as you can set the background color of pages and tables, you can set the background color of a layer. Dreamweaver lets you define a layer's color by selecting from a pop-up color palette in the Property Inspector. You can also define the color by name or hexadecimal code.

Layer backgrounds can prove especially effective when several layers overlap one another on a page. When a background color is absent, the organization of the layers can be unclear, especially when text overlaps other text. Adding background color can make apparent the overlapping nature of the layers on the page.

You can also define a background image for a layer. Just as with pages and tables, background images in layers will tile horizontally and vertically to fill the entire dimensions of the layer.

With timelines (see Chapter 14), you can create a background color in a layer that changes over time. This can result in a colorful flashing effect.

ADD A BACKGROUND COLOR TO A LAYER

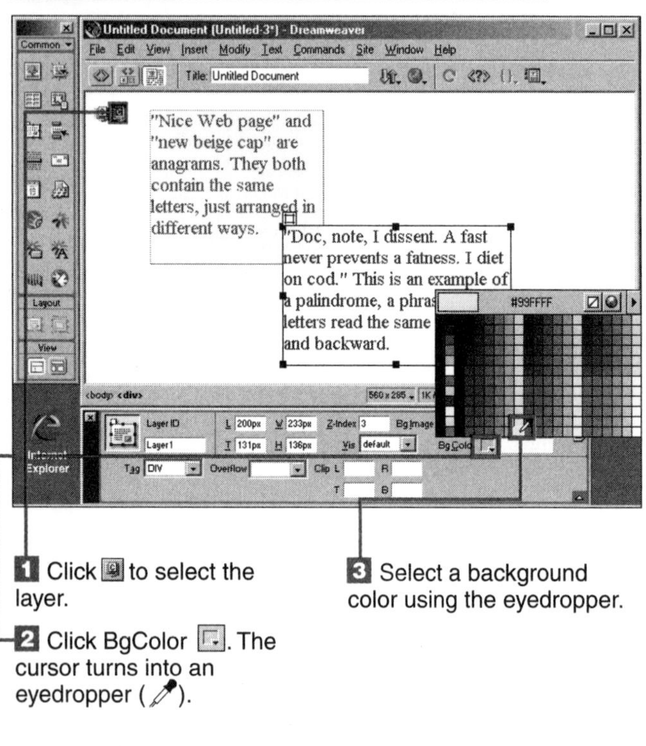

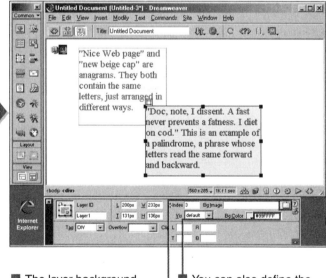

1 Click to select the layer.

2 Click BgColor. The cursor turns into an eyedropper ( ).

3 Select a background color using the eyedropper.

■ The layer background assumes the specified color.

■ In this example, the page background has one color, and the backgrounds of the two layers have two other colors.

■ You can also define the background color by typing a color name ("red") or hex code ("#FF0000") in the BgColor field in the Property Inspector.

■ Clicking lets you select a background image for the layer.

CHANGE THE STACKING ORDER OF LAYERS

Layers that float on top of one another in the Document window have a stacking order. This determines which layer displays on top, and on down through the stack to the bottom. Stacking order is determined by each layer's *z-index*. The greater the z-index relative to the other layers in a stack, the higher the layer is in the stack.

You can view the stacking order of a page's layers by opening the Layers panel (click Window and then Layers). Layers are ordered in the panel from top to bottom by their z-index. You can click and drag layers up and down in the panel, and Dreamweaver adjusts their z-indexes accordingly.

If you click Prevent Overlaps in the Layers panel, Dreamweaver prevents layers from overlapping as you arrange them in the Document window. This renders the z-index moot in a page.

CHANGE THE STACKING ORDER OF LAYERS

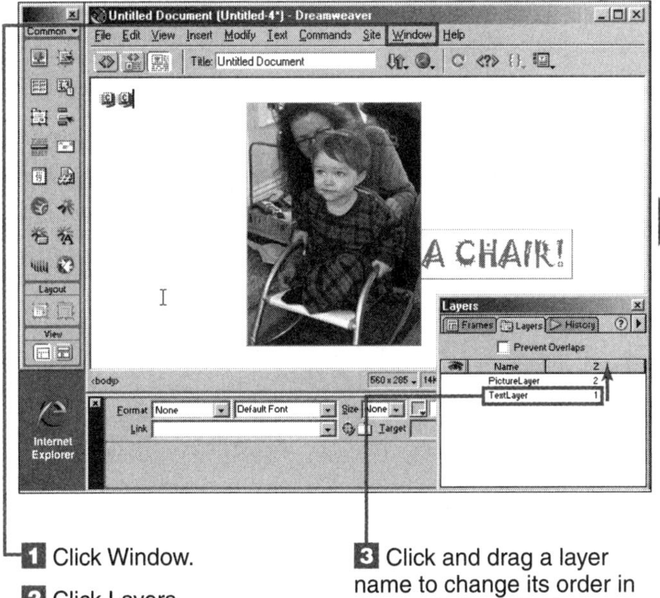

1 Click Window.

2 Click Layers.

■ The layers in the page appear in the Layers palette.

3 Click and drag a layer name to change its order in the stack. Drag the layer name up to move it higher in the stack; drag down to move it lower.

■ Dreamweaver changes the stacking order of the layers.

■ You can also select a layer in the Document window and change its z-index value in the Property Inspector.

AN INTRODUCTION TO BEHAVIORS

What Is a Behavior?

You can add interactivity to your Web pages with Dreamweaver's *behaviors*. A behavior is a cause-and-effect feature that you set up in your Web page. You specify a user event (such as a mouse click) and the resulting action (such as a pop-up window appearing) that should take place when that event occurs. Dreamweaver lets you create behaviors that produce image rollovers, validate forms, check browser versions, and more.

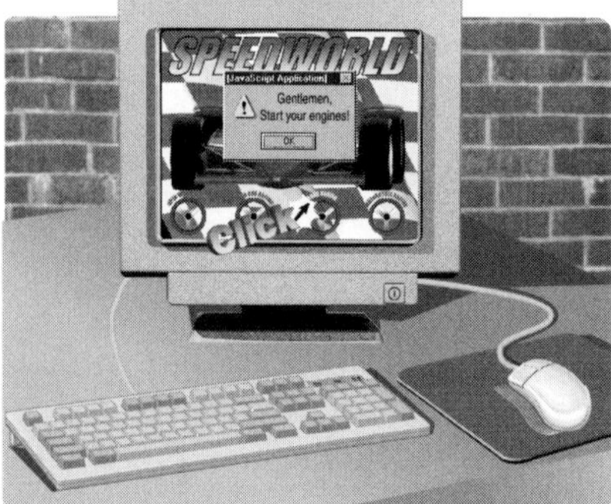

Behaviors Are Created with JavaScript

Dreamweaver builds behaviors with *JavaScript*, a popular programming language for adding dynamic features to Web sites. You apply behaviors to specific objects on your Web page using dialog boxes, and then Dreamweaver writes the JavaScript code behind the scenes to create the behaviors. The JavaScript that Dreamweaver writes coexists with your page's HTML code. You can view it by switching to Code view (see Chapter 3) and looking for text enclosed in opening and closing `<script>` tags.

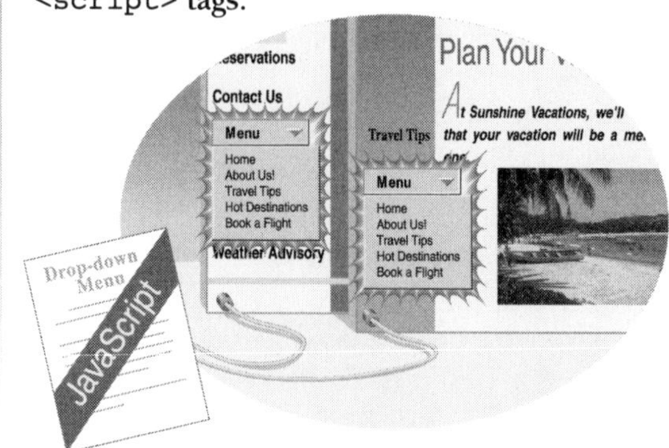

Behaviors and Browsers

Dreamweaver's standard behaviors all work in Version 4 or later of Microsoft Internet Explorer and Netscape Navigator. Some of the behaviors also work in earlier browsers. The behaviors are designed such that if they load into browsers that do not support them, they fail without error. (The page can still be viewed.) Because some browsers still do not

support certain JavaScript features and because some users surf the Web with JavaScript turned off, you probably should not make the use of a behavior a prerequisite for browsing your site. For example, you may not want to put critical text that your users need to see inside a pop-up message window that is generated by a behavior.

Creating Rollover Images

A *rollover* behavior replaces an image on your page with another in response to a cursor passing over it. You often see the rollover behavior applied to navigation buttons on Web pages. Rollovers can add pizzazz to your page and give users an extra visual cue that such buttons produce an effect when clicked.

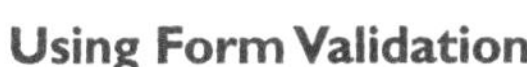

Using Form Validation

You can keep users from entering erroneous information into your forms by using a behavior to validate form fields. The behavior generates an alert if invalid data is submitted. Validating form information using behaviors is an alternative to validating it at the form handler (the program on the Web server that processes your form information).

Checking Browser Versions

Designing a page that works equally well in all browsers can be difficult, especially if you use advanced features such as style sheets and layers. You can use a behavior to check the brand of browser, such as Microsoft Internet Explorer or Netscape Navigator, as well as the version. The behavior can then forward a user to a page built specifically for that browser.

CREATE A ROLLOVER IMAGE

A *rollover* behavior replaces an image on your page with another in response to a cursor passing over it. You often apply rollover effects to navigation buttons, where passing your cursor over the button causes it to light up or appear depressed, like a real button. A rollover gives the viewer an extra visual cue that the button produces an effect when clicked.

For a rollover to look its best, you want the images involved to be the same size, because the replacement image appears in the space occupied by the original. If the images differ in size, the replacement image will need to be stretched or shrunk.

You can specify that the images involved in rollovers preload, which means the original and replacement images load into the browser when the page first appears. With preloading, the rollover effect can appear instantly when triggered. Without preloading, the browser has to load the replacement image off the Web — which can take several seconds — when the rollover event occurs.

CREATE A ROLLOVER IMAGE

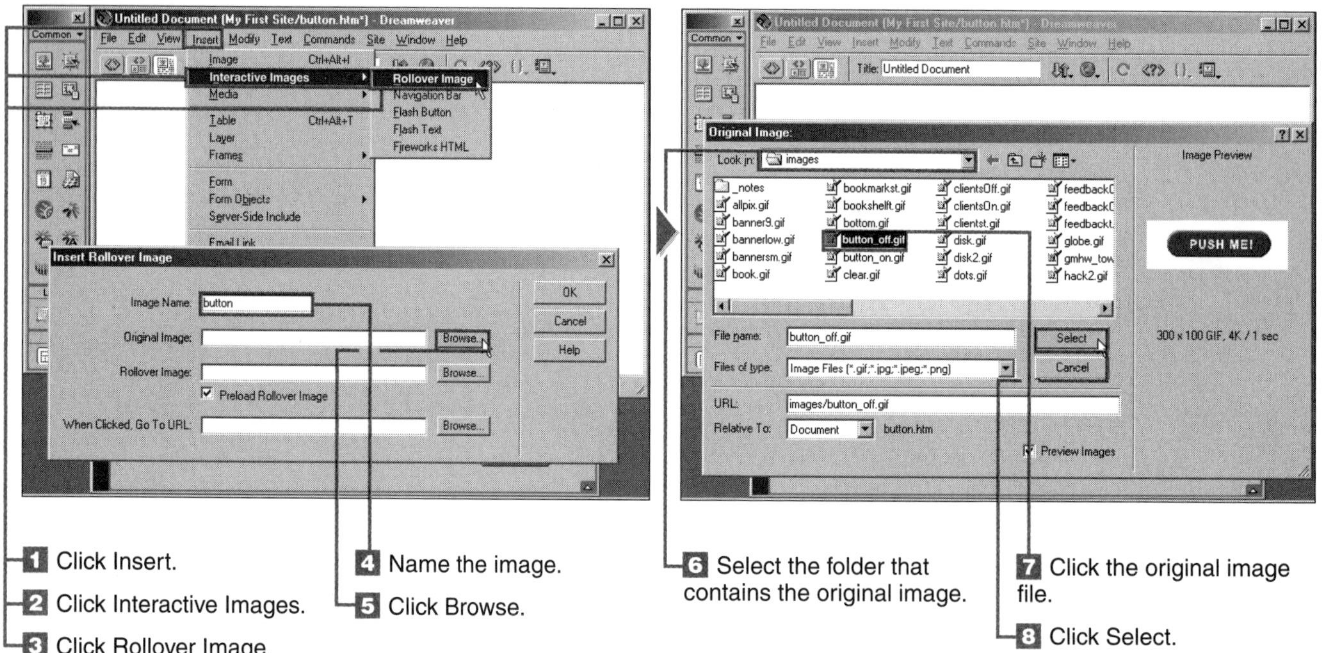

1 Click Insert.

2 Click Interactive Images.

3 Click Rollover Image.

4 Name the image.

5 Click Browse.

6 Select the folder that contains the original image.

7 Click the original image file.

8 Click Select.

How do I create interesting rollover buttons for my page navigation?

✔ You can create interesting buttons to use for navigation in an image editor, such as Adobe Photoshop or Macromedia Fireworks. Both programs include commands that let you easily create contoured or colorful shapes (buttons) that you can then label with text. Some common ways to create the replacement version of a rollover button are to reverse its colors, add a border, or shift the art slightly so it looks like the graphic has been pressed down.

Can I create a rollover using the Behaviors panel?

✔ Yes. The steps in this task show you how to create the behavior using the Rollover Image command. You can alternatively select an image in your page, open the Behaviors panel, and apply the Swap Image action to it. Note that unlike using the Rollover Image command, creating a rollover using the Behaviors panel lets you swap an image other than the image that is being rolled over.

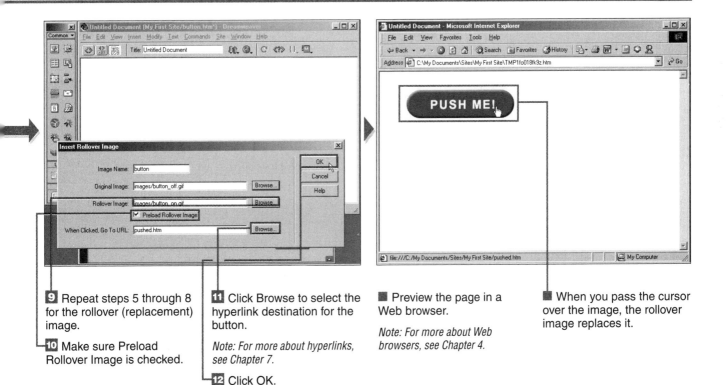

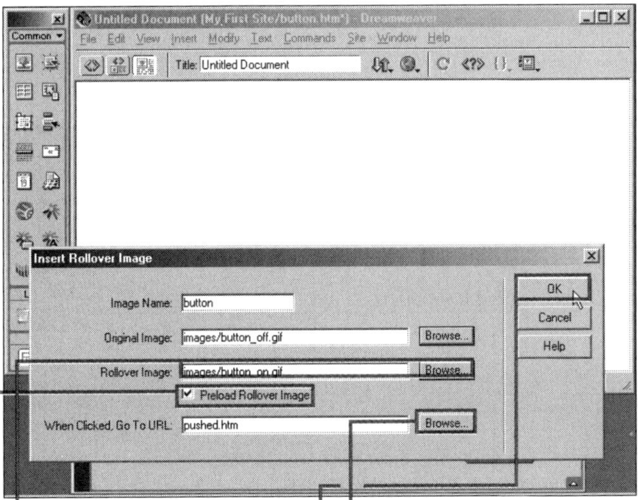

9 Repeat steps 5 through 8 for the rollover (replacement) image.

10 Make sure Preload Rollover Image is checked.

11 Click Browse to select the hyperlink destination for the button.

Note: For more about hyperlinks, see Chapter 7.

12 Click OK.

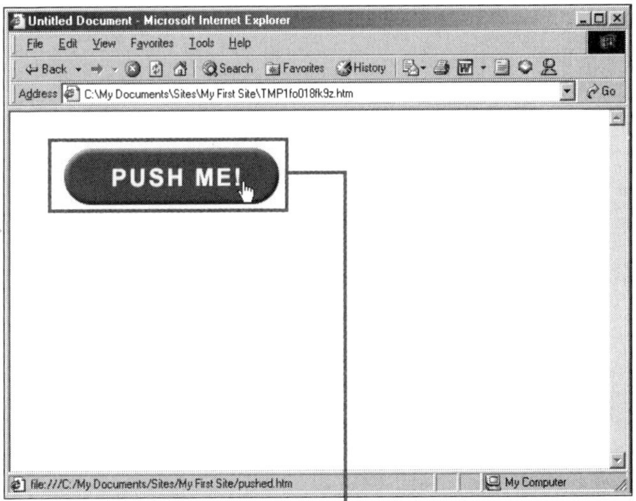

■ Preview the page in a Web browser.

Note: For more about Web browsers, see Chapter 4.

■ When you pass the cursor over the image, the rollover image replaces it.

CREATE A STATUS BAR MESSAGE

Usually when you pass your cursor over a hyperlink on a page, that hyperlink's destination URL appears in the Document window's status bar. You can use a Dreamweaver behavior to change that status bar message to one of your choosing. For example, you can display a message that describes where the hyperlink takes the user.

You can see an example of this effect in Dreamweaver's electronic help documentation, which uses status messages in its browser interface. Roll your cursor over the Contents, Index, or Search buttons to see the effect in action.

The disadvantage of displaying information in the status bar is that the area is relatively inconspicuous, and some users may overlook it. In some browsers, users can even hide the status bar.

CREATE A STATUS BAR MESSAGE

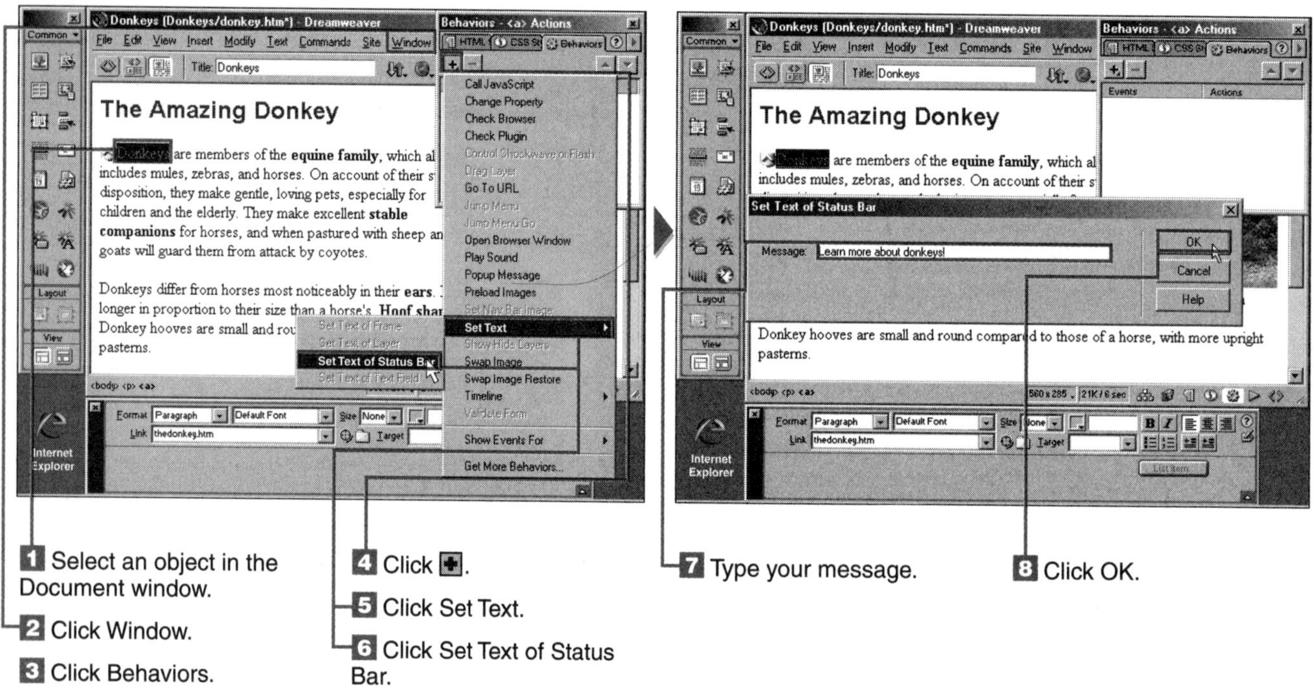

1 Select an object in the Document window.

2 Click Window.

3 Click Behaviors.

4 Click [+].

5 Click Set Text.

6 Click Set Text of Status Bar.

7 Type your message.

8 Click OK.

How do I cause the status bar message to disappear when I roll the cursor off my object?

✔ You need to define a complementary `onMouseOut` action for your object. Repeat the steps in this task, but specify a blank message and use the `onMouseOut` event. Doing this causes the message to disappear when you roll off the object.

Can I make special information appear in my status bar message?

✔ You can add special JavaScript code enclosed in braces to make certain information appear. For example, `{window.location}` causes the current page's URL to appear. `{new Date()}` displays the date.

What happens if my message is too long to fit in the browser's status bar?

✔ The message still appears, but most browsers cut it off on the right.

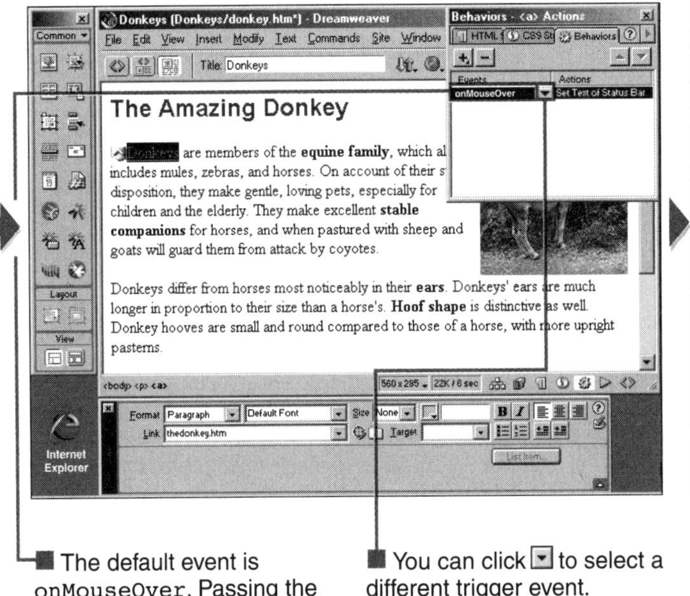

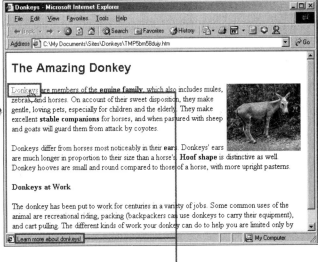

■ The default event is `onMouseOver`. Passing the cursor over the selected object triggers the message.

■ You can click ▾ to select a different trigger event.

■ Preview the page in a Web browser.

Note: For more about Web browsers, see Chapter 4.

■ When you pass the cursor over the page element, the message appears.

VALIDATE A FORM

Good form-building practices require that you validate the information the user submits before processing it. This validation can include checking that postal codes have the correct number of numeric characters and that e-mail addresses are in the correct format.

You can use a Dreamweaver behavior to check this kind of data submitted by a form and generate an alert if the data is not valid. The user can then re-enter the data and submit the form again.

This kind of form validation is known as *client-side validation*, because the check is done by the client (the user's browser). An alternative is to validate the form data at the form handler (*server-side validation*). This can be slower, because the form data needs to be sent to the Web server to be processed, and more difficult to implement, because form handlers can be a challenge to write and debug. On the other hand, browsers that do not have JavaScript capability cannot have their form information validated by the Dreamweaver features.

VALIDATE A FORM

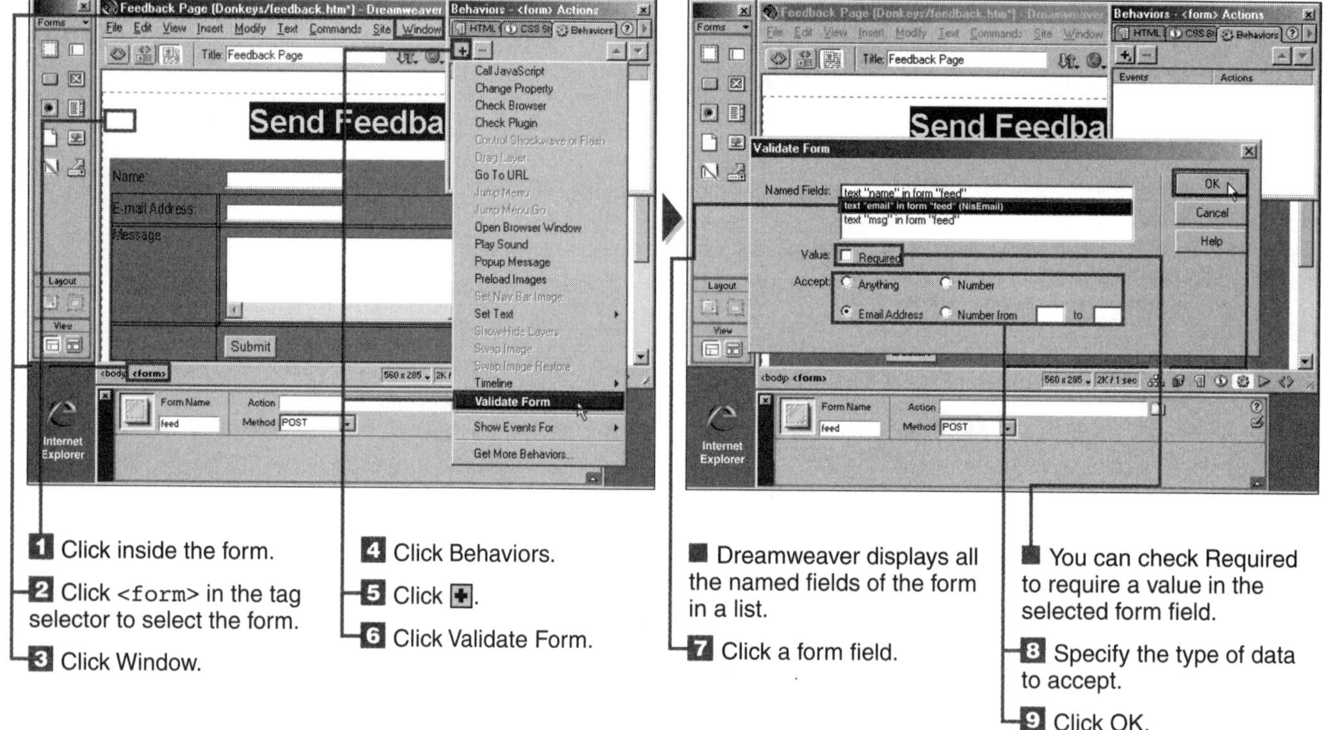

1 Click inside the form.

2 Click <form> in the tag selector to select the form.

3 Click Window.

4 Click Behaviors.

5 Click [+].

6 Click Validate Form.

■ Dreamweaver displays all the named fields of the form in a list.

7 Click a form field.

■ You can check Required to require a value in the selected form field.

8 Specify the type of data to accept.

9 Click OK.

What browser events can trigger validation?

✔ If you need to validate a single field in a form, you can use the `onBlur` event to trigger validation. In this case, the validation occurs when the user clicks away from the field. If you need to validate multiple fields, you can use `onSubmit` for the trigger. In this case, the validation occurs after the Submit button is clicked. Dreamweaver automatically applies `onBlur` for single-field validations and `onSubmit` for validation you apply to an entire form. You can change the trigger event in the Behaviors panel.

Why is the Anything option made available in the Validate Form dialog box?

✔ If you select Anything and check Required, Dreamweaver checks to make sure *something* is entered in the field — and alerts the user if that field is empty. Without Required selected, the Anything selection is meaningless.

How does Dreamweaver determine if a field contains a number or an e-mail address?

✔ Dreamweaver's criteria for determining this are rudimentary. If Number is selected, Dreamweaver checks for non-numeric characters (anything other than numbers and a single decimal point). E-mail addresses are validated by checking for an @ sign.

■ The default event when you apply validation to an entire form is `onSubmit`. When the user clicks the Submit button, the form is validated.

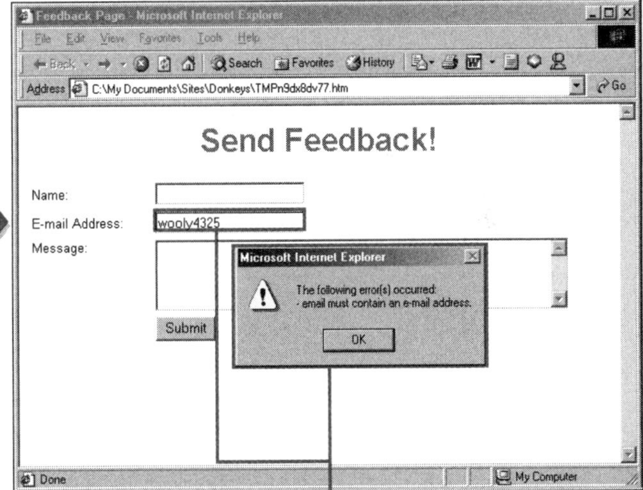

10 Preview the Web page in a browser.

Note: For more about Web browsers, see Chapter 4.

■ If you submit the form with invalid content in a field, the browser generates a pop-up alert.

■ In this example, an alert appears because an invalid e-mail address was entered.

OPEN A CUSTOMIZED BROWSER WINDOW

You can cause information to open into a new, customized browser window using a Dreamweaver behavior. You can set various properties of the new window, including its dimensions, whether it has a menu bar or scroll bars, its name, and other attributes. By leaving off the typical attributes that usually appear in browser windows, you can maximize the amount of space available for displaying content.

One useful way to use customized windows is to size them to the exact dimensions of the image, movie, or other content that will appear in the window. This way, the window can open over the existing page and act as a miniature console for viewing the content. The user can click the Close button on the window when they want to return to the original page.

The Open Browser Window behavior is similar to the feature described in "Create a Hyperlink That Opens a New Window" in Chapter 5. That feature uses the target hyperlink attribute rather than JavaScript to cause a hyperlink to open a new window.

OPEN A CUSTOMIZED BROWSER WINDOW

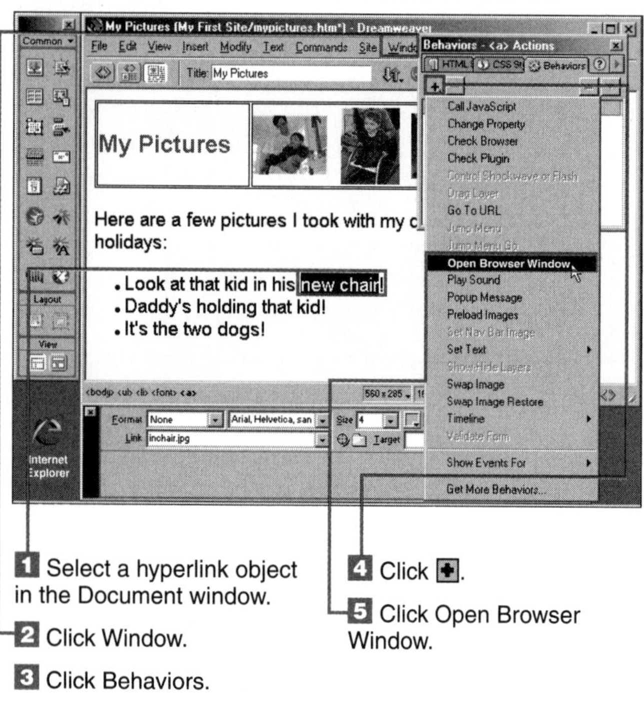

1 Select a hyperlink object in the Document window.

2 Click Window.

3 Click Behaviors.

4 Click +.

5 Click Open Browser Window.

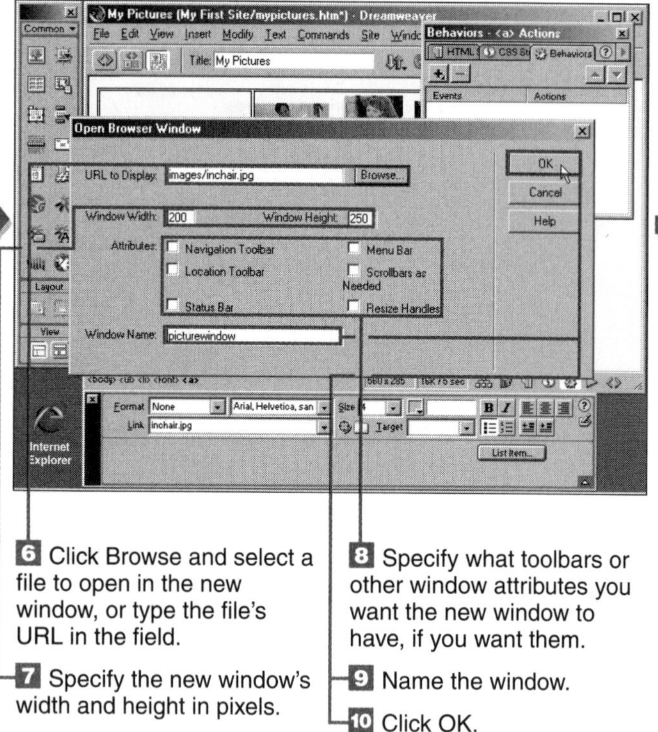

6 Click Browse and select a file to open in the new window, or type the file's URL in the field.

7 Specify the new window's width and height in pixels.

8 Specify what toolbars or other window attributes you want the new window to have, if you want them.

9 Name the window.

10 Click OK.

What happens if I do not specify any attributes of the window?

✔ If you do not specify *any* attributes, the new window opens at the size and with the attributes of the window that spawned it (the current window). If you specify *some* attributes, such as just the window dimensions, all the other attributes that are not explicitly turned on are disabled.

What happens if I leave resize handles off of my new window?

✔ The user cannot resize the new window by clicking and dragging the bottom-right corner or by clicking the maximize button on the title bar.

Why is naming the window useful?

✔ Naming the window enables you to target the window with other hyperlinks in your site. Similar to having a set of hyperlinks in one frame open all their destination content in another frame, you can have a set of links in one window open all their content in a another window.

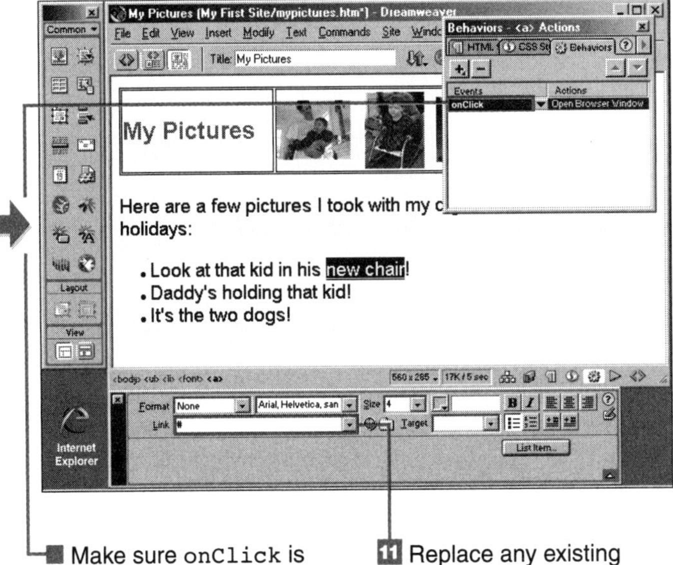

■ Make sure `onClick` is the trigger event. You may have to click ▾, click Show Events For, and then click 4.0 and Later Browsers to make it available.

11 Replace any existing hyperlink destination with a pound sign (#) to prevent pages from opening in the old window.

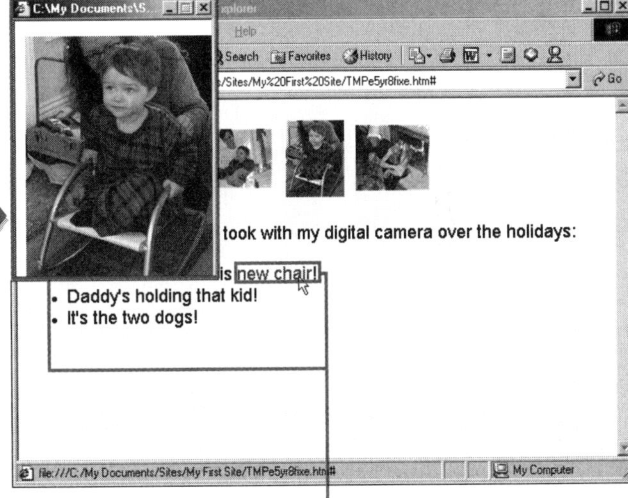

12 Preview the Web page in a browser.

Note: For more about Web browsers, see Chapter 4.

■ When you click the hyperlink, the new browser window appears with the specified file inside it.

CHECK A USER'S BROWSER

Designing a page that works equally well in all browsers can be difficult, especially if you use advanced features, such as style sheets and layers. To get around this, you can use a behavior to check the brand and version of a user's browser and then forward a user to a page built specifically for that browser.

Suppose that you want to feature layers-based content on your home page. But you also want to accommodate Version 3 browsers, which cannot display layers. A solution could be to create your home page without layers and put the layers version on a secondary page. Then you can have a behavior check the browser on the home page and forward users with Version 4 or better to the secondary page while keeping users with other browsers where they are.

You can also use the check-browser feature to forward users of Netscape Navigator and Microsoft Internet Explorer to different pages. This option can be useful if you want to apply design features that are specific to one or the other browser.

CHECK A USER'S BROWSER

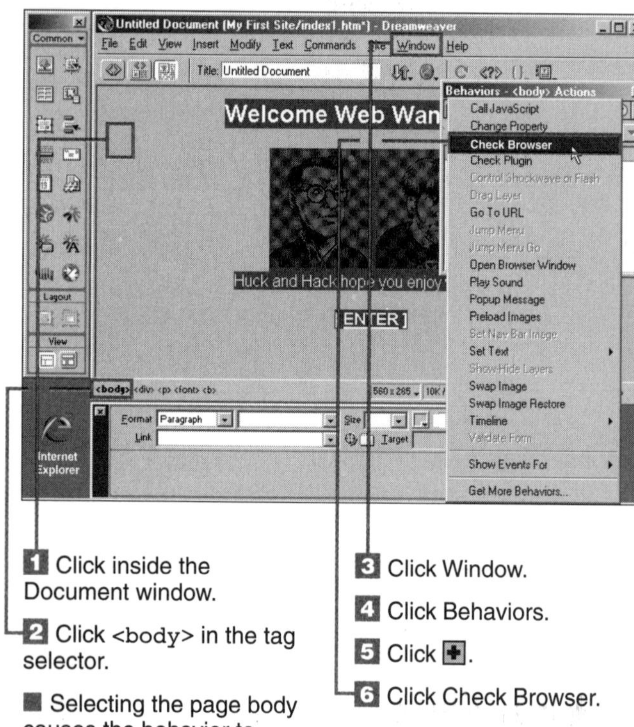

1 Click inside the Document window.

2 Click <body> in the tag selector.

■ Selecting the page body causes the behavior to execute when the page loads.

3 Click Window.

4 Click Behaviors.

5 Click [+].

6 Click Check Browser.

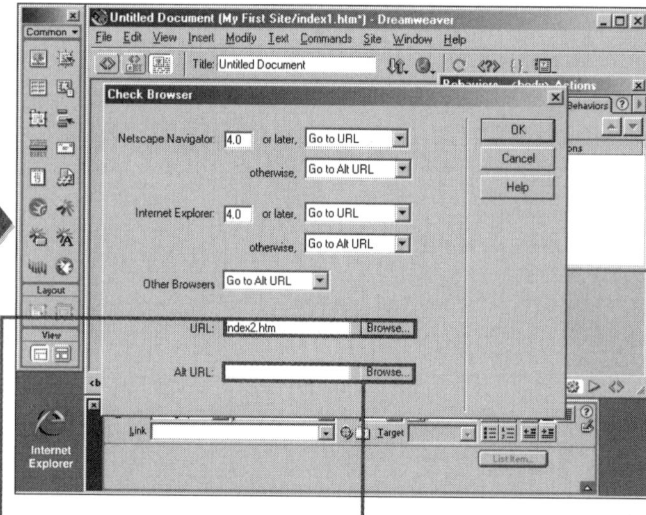

7 Click Browse to select a destination page on your site. You can also type an external URL.

■ If you want to send some users to a second page, click Browse to select the page. You can also type an external URL.

What other browsers are there besides Microsoft Internet Explorer and Netscape Navigator?

✔ Although the vast majority of Web users have one of the "big two" browsers, some may use America Online's browser (which is based on Internet Explorer), Opera (available for all platforms), Lynx (which is text-based, for Windows, UNIX, and DOS), iCab (for Macintosh), WebTV, and others.

Can I use a behavior to check a browser for plugins?

✔ Yes. Similar to Check Browser, you can use a Check Plugin behavior to check for multimedia plug-ins installed in a browser. The behavior lets you test for Flash, Shockwave, LiveAudio, Netscape Media Player, and QuickTime in Netscape Navigator. In Internet Explorer, only the Flash and Shockwave tests work. In the Behavior dialog box, a text box lets you specify other plug-in names to test for.

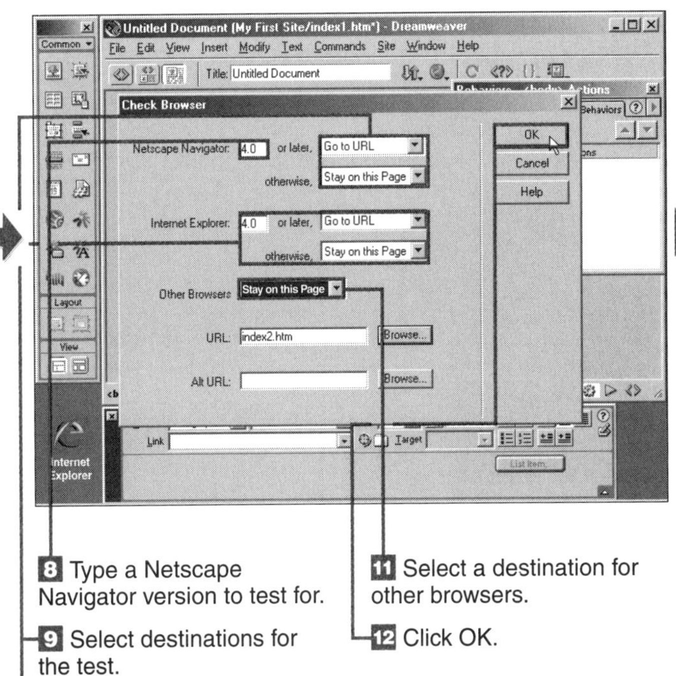

8 Type a Netscape Navigator version to test for.

9 Select destinations for the test.

10 Repeat steps 7 and 8 for Microsoft Internet Explorer.

11 Select a destination for other browsers.

12 Click OK.

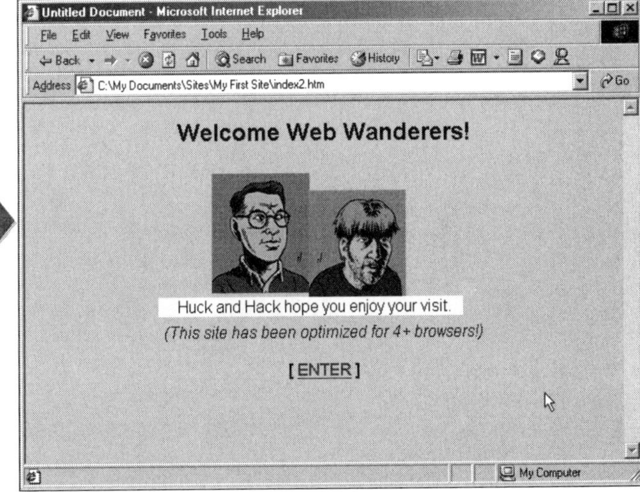

13 Preview the page in a Web browser.

Note: For more about Web browsers, see Chapter 4.

■ When the Web page opens in a Web browser, the page checks the browser's brand and version, and forwards the user to a new page if required.

DEBUG JAVASCRIPT

JavaScript is a programming language that you can use to add interactivity to your Web page. Unlike HTML, which is a *markup language* used for formatting Web pages, JavaScript is a full-fledged programming language that can be challenging to write and difficult to get working perfectly.

Dreamweaver provides a JavaScript debugger that helps you pinpoint errors in your JavaScript code. The debugger can also help you fix your JavaScript by letting you step through code line by line and examine the program's variables as it executes.

The debugger needs a browser running to operate. It can work with Netscape Navigator and Microsoft Internet Explorer on Windows, and Netscape Navigator on Macintosh. To debug your page, you view the page in a browser and the JavaSript code in a special Dreamweaver window.

Dreamweaver writes JavaScript code when you add behaviors to your page. You can use the debugger to analyze this code. You can also use the debugger to check any custom JavaScript that you have added to your page yourself.

DEBUG JAVASCRIPT

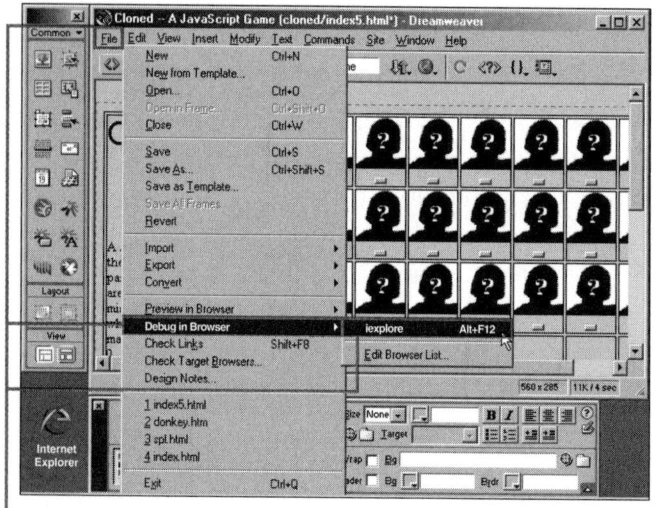

1 Open a file that contains JavaScript.

2 Click File.

3 Click Debug in Browser.

4 Click a browser.

Note: You may initially see dialog boxes asking if you want to grant Dreamweaver access to your browser. Click the buttons that give it access.

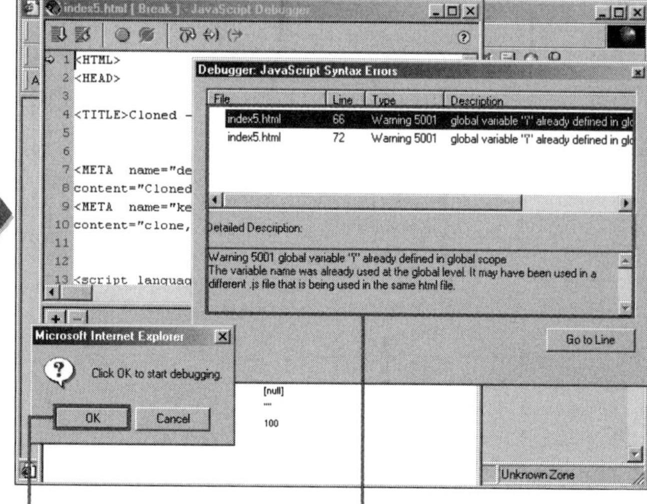

5 Click OK to start the debugger.

6 Click OK if Dreamweaver displays a dialog box asking you to set a breakpoint.

■ Dreamweaver checks the syntax of your JavaScript. It displays any errors that it finds in a separate window.

What are breakpoints?

✔ Breakpoints are "triggers" that you can set at specific lines of your JavaScript code. When the JavaScript debugger encounters a breakpoint, it pauses. Breakpoints let you examine variables at a point in time during the execution of your JavaScript.

How do I remove the breakpoints that I have defined in the debugger?

✔ You can click [icon] to delete all your breakpoints.

How do I step through my code one statement at a time?

✔ You can use the [icon] button to step through your code one statement at a time. When you hit a function call, you can click [icon] to step into (execute) the function and monitor how it runs. You can click [icon] to step out of (exit) a function.

How do I stop code execution in progress?

✔ You can click [icon] to stop your JavaScript from executing.

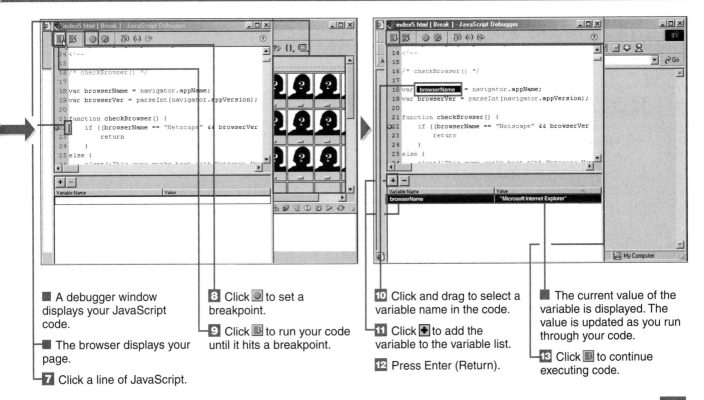

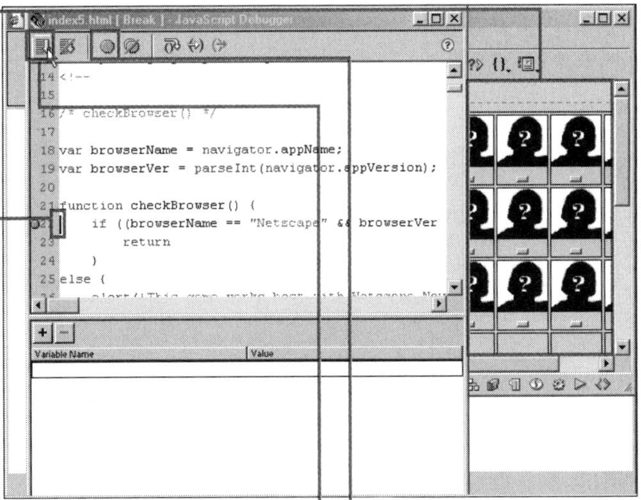

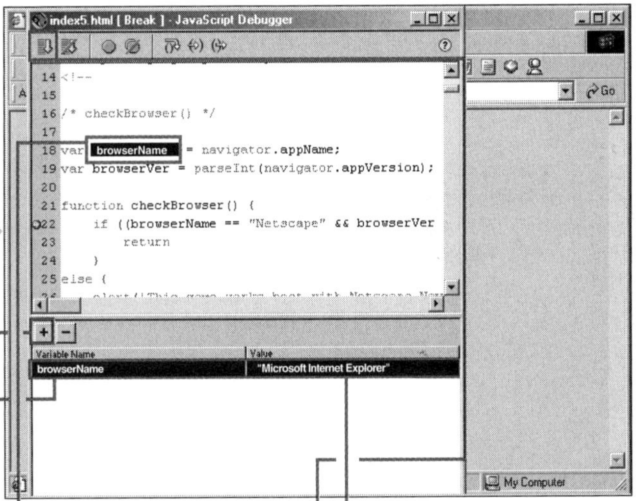

■ A debugger window displays your JavaScript code.

■ The browser displays your page.

7 Click a line of JavaScript.

8 Click [icon] to set a breakpoint.

9 Click [icon] to run your code until it hits a breakpoint.

10 Click and drag to select a variable name in the code.

11 Click [icon] to add the variable to the variable list.

12 Press Enter (Return).

■ The current value of the variable is displayed. The value is updated as you run through your code.

13 Click [icon] to continue executing code.

AN INTRODUCTION TO TIMELINES

Animating Your Pages

Timelines enable you to change the position, visibility, and other attributes of a Web page's layers over time. For an introduction to layers, see Chapter 12. You can use timelines to make images float across a page, cause overlapping layers of text to shuffle positions, or create tables that appear and disappear. Because timelines rely on layers, timeline animation works only in Version 4.0 or later browsers.

Timelines Combine HTML and JavaScript

Timeline animations are created with JavaScript, which can change the HTML and style-sheet properties of a page over time. (This combining of JavaScript, style sheets, and HTML is also known as Dynamic HTML.) You define the characteristics of a timeline using the Timelines inspector; Dreamweaver then writes the JavaScript code behind the scenes to create the animation.

Creating Timeline Frames

You define the action that occurs in a timeline animation as a sequence of frames. Typically, you have 10 to 15 frames for every second of animation. Each frame contains information about the layer being animated at a moment in time. Usually, you define just a few of the frames — the so-called *keyframes* — in a timeline yourself. Dreamweaver fills in the rest, basing the other frames off the keyframe information you provide.

USING THE TIMELINES INSPECTOR

The Timelines Inspector lets you create animations by specifying the position and other characteristics of layers on your page at different times. You can click Window and then Timelines to open the inspector.

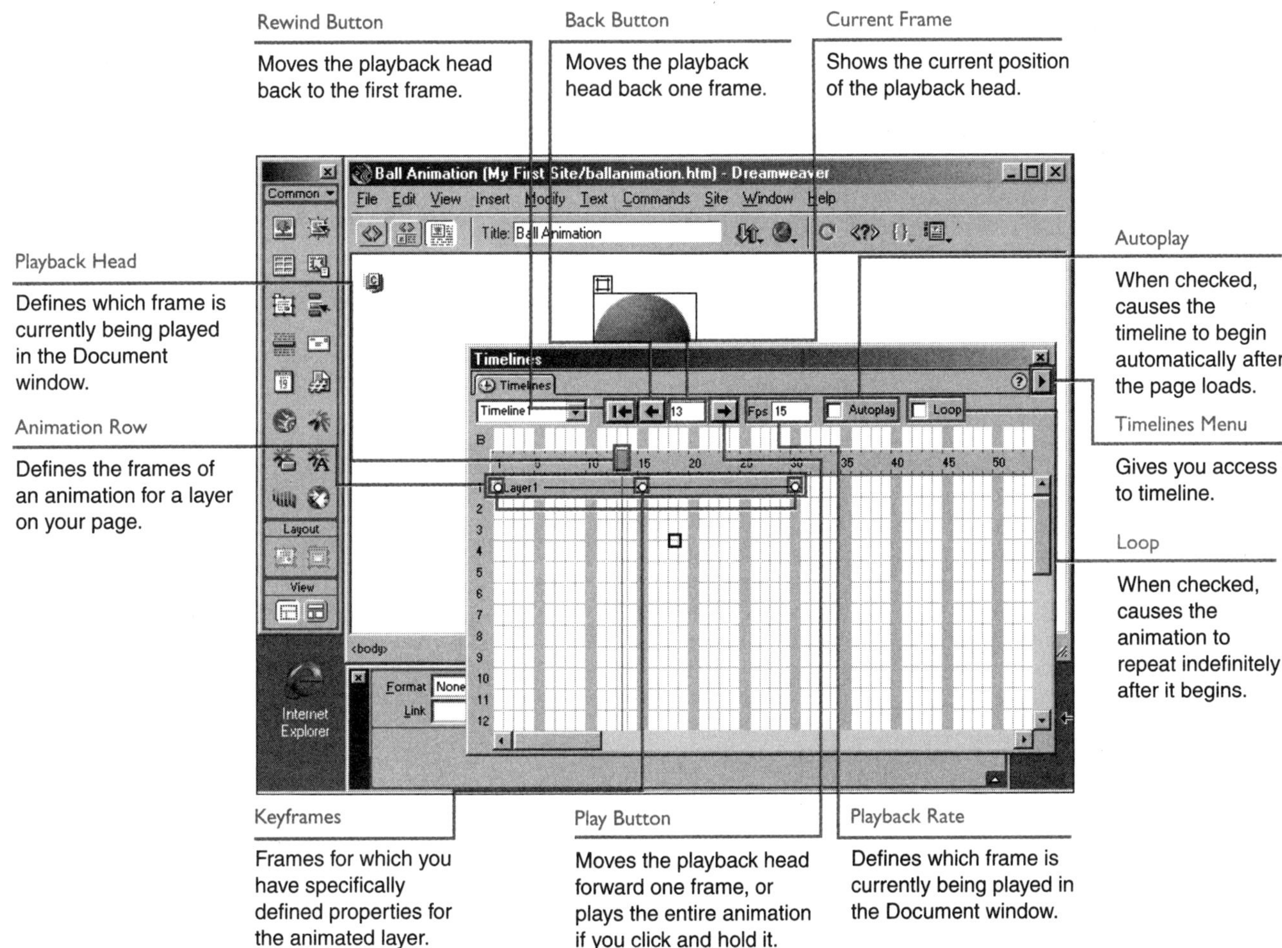
Rewind Button
Moves the playback head back to the first frame.
Back Button
Moves the playback head back one frame.
Current Frame
Shows the current position of the playback head.
Playback Head
Defines which frame is currently being played in the Document window.
Animation Row
Defines the frames of an animation for a layer on your page.
Autoplay
When checked, causes the timeline to begin automatically after the page loads.
Timelines Menu
Gives you access to timeline.
Loop
When checked, causes the animation to repeat indefinitely after it begins.
Keyframes
Frames for which you have specifically defined properties for the animated layer.
Play Button
Moves the playback head forward one frame, or plays the entire animation if you click and hold it.
Playback Rate
Defines which frame is currently being played in the Document window.
Ball Animation (My First Site/ballanimation.htm) - Dreamweaver
File Edit View Insert Modify Text Commands Site Window Help
Title: Ball Animation
Timelines
Timeline1
13
Fps 15
Autoplay
Loop
Layer1
Format None
Link
Internet Explorer

CREATE A STRAIGHT-LINE ANIMATION

You can create a timeline animation that moves a layer in a straight line on your page. A *straight-line animation* can be a quick and easy way to enliven a page that otherwise consists of static text and images.

Creating a straight-line animation involves defining two keyframes: one at the beginning of the timeline's animation bar, and one at the end. The beginning keyframe specifies the position of your layer at the start of the animation. The end keyframe frame specifies the position of the layer at the end of the animation. Dreamweaver fills in position information for the frames in between.

You can change the speed of the animation by adjusting the length of the animation bar or the timeline's frame rate. See "Change Animation Speed" for more information.

Because you can fill a layer with any type of page element — including text, images, tables, and multimedia — you can turn practically anything you can put on a Web page into an animation. To learn more about adding layers to your page and filling them with content, see Chapter 12.

CREATE A STRAIGHT-LINE ANIMATION

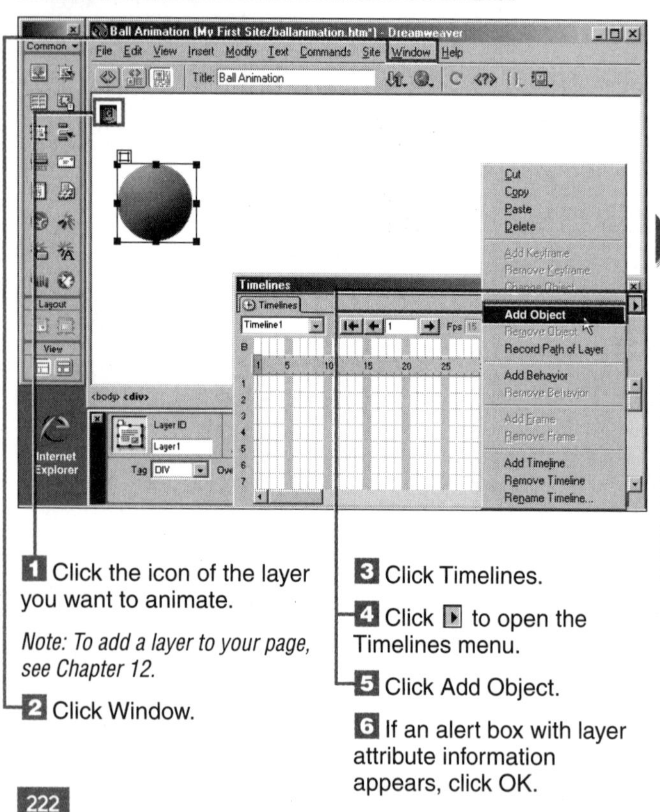

1 Click the icon of the layer you want to animate.

Note: To add a layer to your page, see Chapter 12.

2 Click Window.

3 Click Timelines.

4 Click ▶ to open the Timelines menu.

5 Click Add Object.

6 If an alert box with layer attribute information appears, click OK.

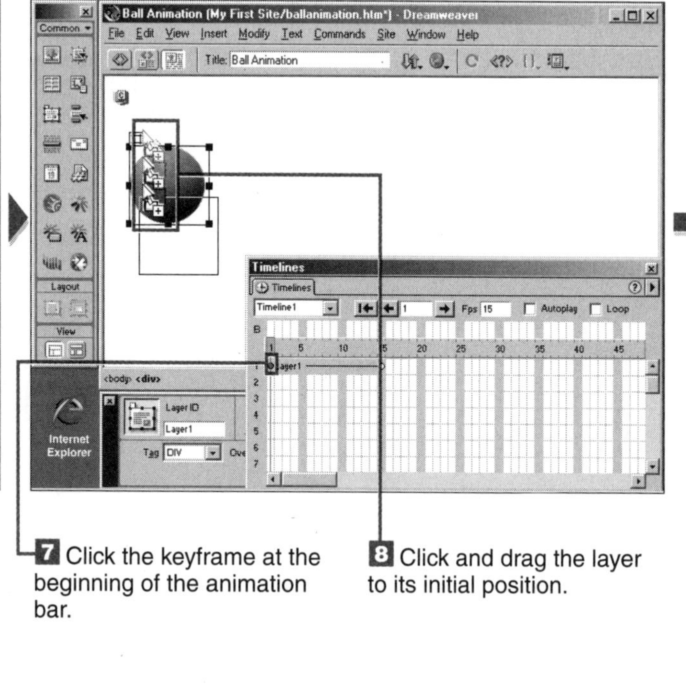

7 Click the keyframe at the beginning of the animation bar.

8 Click and drag the layer to its initial position.

Does the position of the animation on the page depend on the size of the browser window?

✔ You define timeline animations using absolute coordinates, which means that their positions do not change with changes in the size of the browser window. This means that if you place animations on the far right of your page, they could potentially not be visible to users viewing your site on smaller monitors.

Can I create several straight-line animations on a single Web page?

✔ Yes. Put each piece of content that you want to animate in its own layer and then define an animation bar in the Timelines Inspector for each layer. To add each additional animation bar to the Timelines Inspector, click a layer and use the Add Object command in the Timelines menu. You can place animation bars on different rows in the inspector, which allows the animations to play simultaneously on the page. You can also place the bars one after the other on the same row, which causes the animations to play sequentially. You can click and drag the animation bars in the inspector to change their positions.

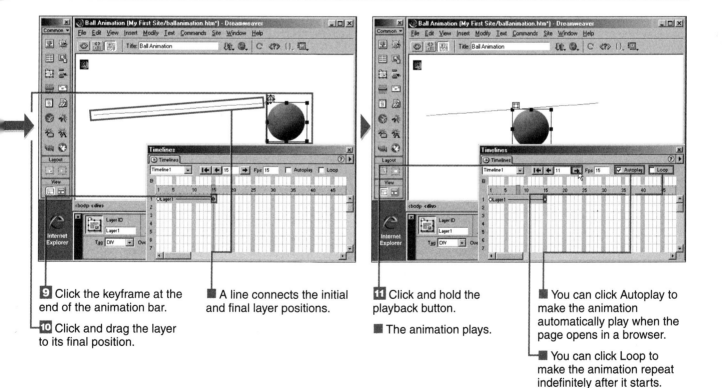

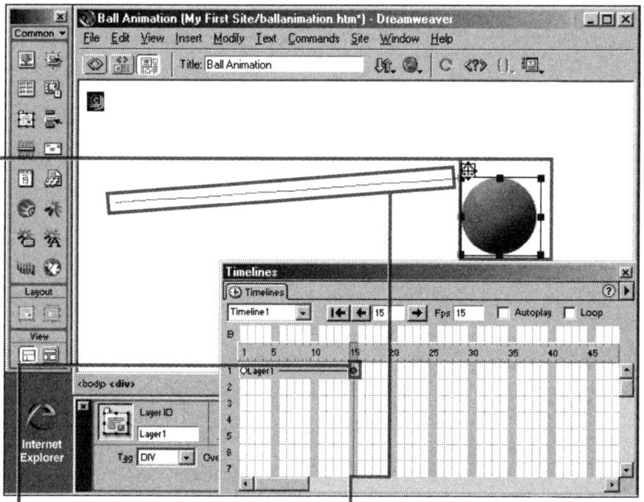

9 Click the keyframe at the end of the animation bar.

10 Click and drag the layer to its final position.

■ A line connects the initial and final layer positions.

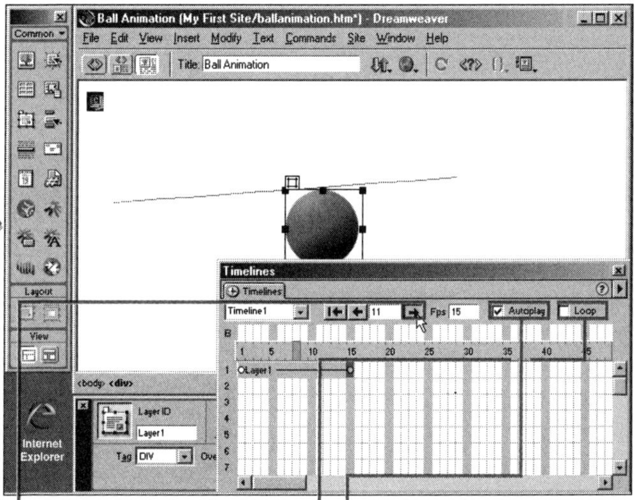

11 Click and hold the playback button.

■ The animation plays.

■ You can click Autoplay to make the animation automatically play when the page opens in a browser.

■ You can click Loop to make the animation repeat indefinitely after it starts.

CREATE AN ANIMATION BY DRAGGING A PATH

Although some of the animations you may want to create involve movement in straight lines, others may involve more complex paths that include loops and curves. To create these animations, you can drag a layer along the intended path and have Dreamweaver record the path as you go.

Dreamweaver creates the animation bar for you in the inspector, inserting the appropriate keyframes where the path changes direction. After you record your path, you can edit it by moving the playback head to a keyframe, and then repositioning the layer in the Document window.

Recording a path can be a great time saver, because describing an animation that includes loops or curves by hand can require you to insert many keyframes and carefully position your layer for each one.

Creating an acceptable recording by dragging can be a challenge, however, because Dreamweaver records not only the position of the layer as you drag but also the speed at which you move it. If you speed up and slow down as you move your layer, you can end up with a jerky animation that looks unnatural.

CREATE AN ANIMATION BY DRAGGING A PATH

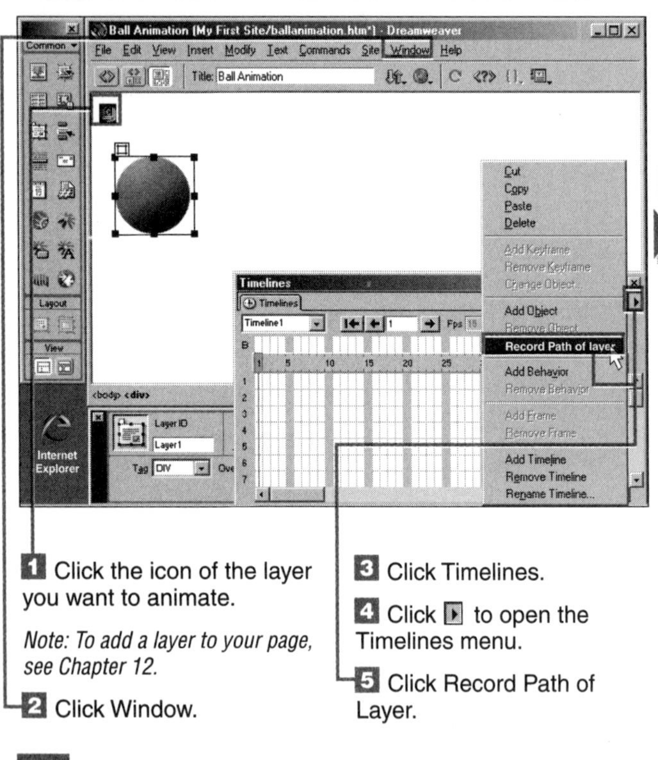

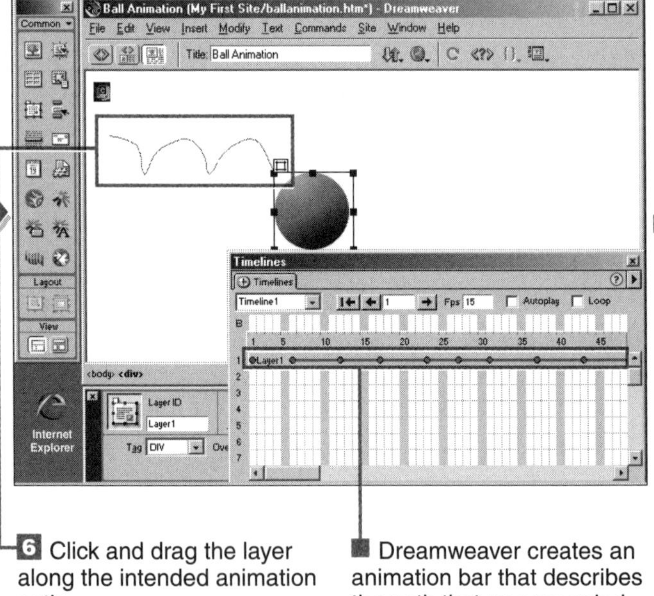

1 Click the icon of the layer you want to animate.

Note: To add a layer to your page, see Chapter 12.

2 Click Window.

3 Click Timelines.

4 Click ▶ to open the Timelines menu.

5 Click Record Path of Layer.

6 Click and drag the layer along the intended animation path.

7 If after dragging, an alert box with layer attribute information appears, click OK.

■ Dreamweaver creates an animation bar that describes the path that was recorded.

Can I cause a layer to rotate using timelines?

✔ While the path of a timeline animation can contain curves and loops, you can not use timelines to actually rotate the content that is inside a layer. The content in the layer that is being animated must stay perpendicular to the browser window as it moves. One way to put rotating content on your page is to create it as an animated GIF file. You can create animated GIFs in Macromedia Fireworks.

How can I change the speed of a recorded animation?

✔ If you want to slow down an animation, increase the length of the animation bar (click the last keyframe on the bar and drag right). If you want to speed it up, decrease the length of the animation bar (click the last keyframe on the bar and drag left). For more information, see "Change Animation Speed."

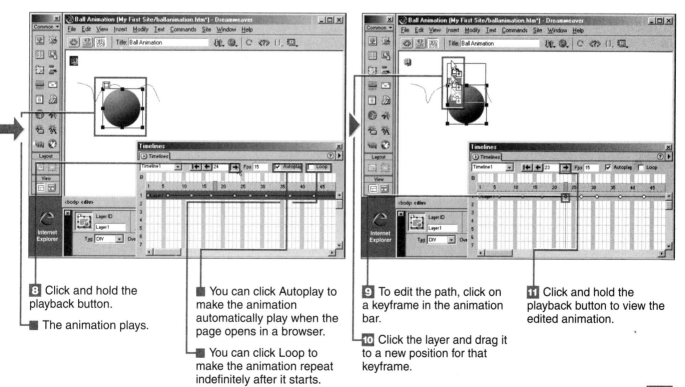

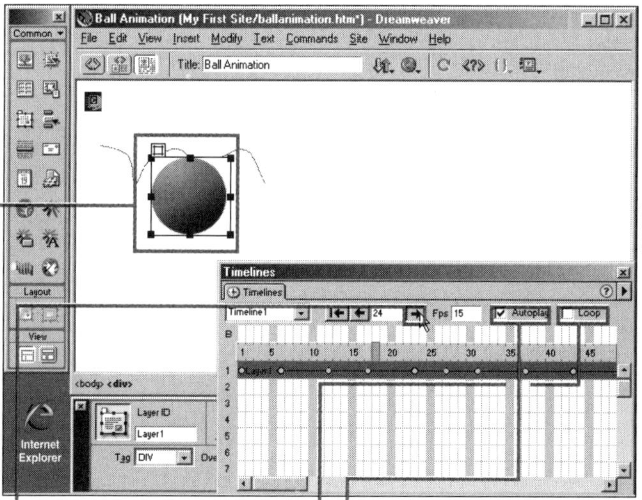

8 Click and hold the playback button.

■ The animation plays.

■ You can click Autoplay to make the animation automatically play when the page opens in a browser.

■ You can click Loop to make the animation repeat indefinitely after it starts.

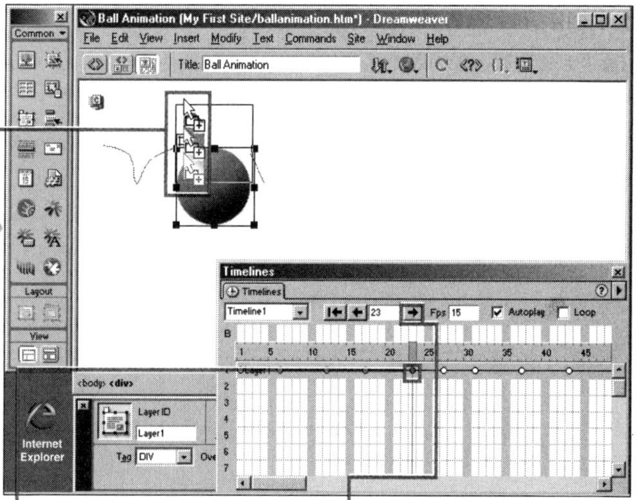

9 To edit the path, click on a keyframe in the animation bar.

10 Click the layer and drag it to a new position for that keyframe.

11 Click and hold the playback button to view the edited animation.

CHANGE OTHER LAYER PROPERTIES IN TIMELINES

In addition to changing the position of a layer along a timeline, you can also change other properties of a layer, including its visibility, dimensions, and Z-index.

Changing visibility enables you to make elements in your page appear or disappear at different times, or flash on and off repeatedly. You can combine changes of visibility with changes in position to create layered content that flashes as it moves across the page.

Changing dimensions of a layer in a timeline can make the layer gradually expand or shrink in size. If the Overflow value of a layer is set to hidden, shrinking a layer over time can cause content to gradually disappear as the layer closes around it. You can set a layer's Overflow value in the Property Inspector.

The *Z-index* refers to the relative position a layer assumes when it is stacked with other layers. The greater the Z-index, the higher the layer is in the stack. You can change the Z-index in a timeline to shuffle stacked layers on your page.

CHANGE OTHER LAYER PROPERTIES IN TIMELINES

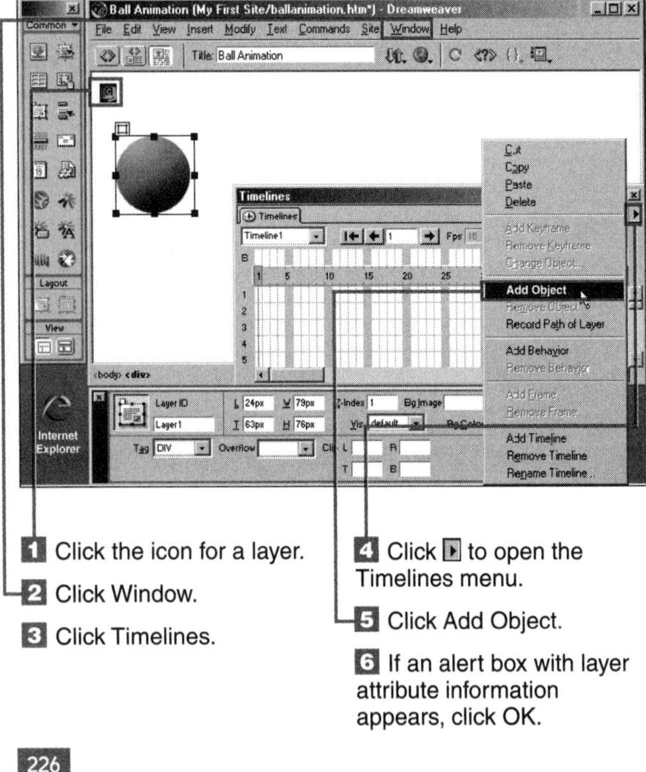

1 Click the icon for a layer.

2 Click Window.

3 Click Timelines.

4 Click ▶ to open the Timelines menu.

5 Click Add Object.

6 If an alert box with layer attribute information appears, click OK.

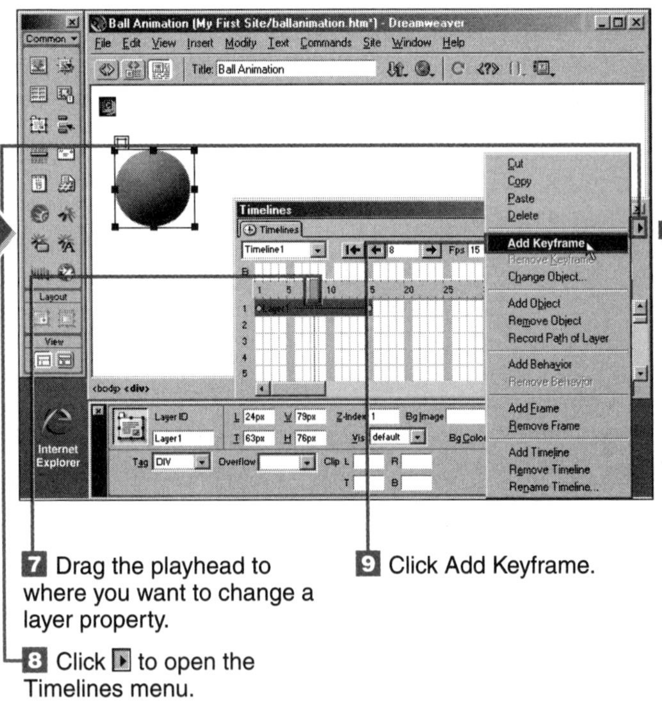

7 Drag the playhead to where you want to change a layer property.

8 Click ▶ to open the Timelines menu.

9 Click Add Keyframe.

How can I create labels that pop up when the user rolls the cursor over images on my page?

✔ You can create a pop-up label for an image by using a hidden layer, a timeline, and a behavior. First, create the label using a layer (for example, put text into a layer that has a background color) and set the visibility of the layer to hidden. Then create a timeline that turns the invisible layer visible. Finally, define a behavior that triggers the timeline when the cursor rolls over the image. For information about triggering timelines, see "Trigger an Animation with a Behavior."

What Z-index values should I use in my timelines?

✔ Z-indexes come into play only when layers overlap. When they do overlap, what matters is not the exact Z-index value, but what the value is relative to the Z-indexes of other layers. For example, if you want to use a timeline to move a layer whose Z-index is 1 beneath a layer with a Z-index of 5, you need to switch the Z-index of the first layer to something greater than 5. (6 and 60 have the same effect.)

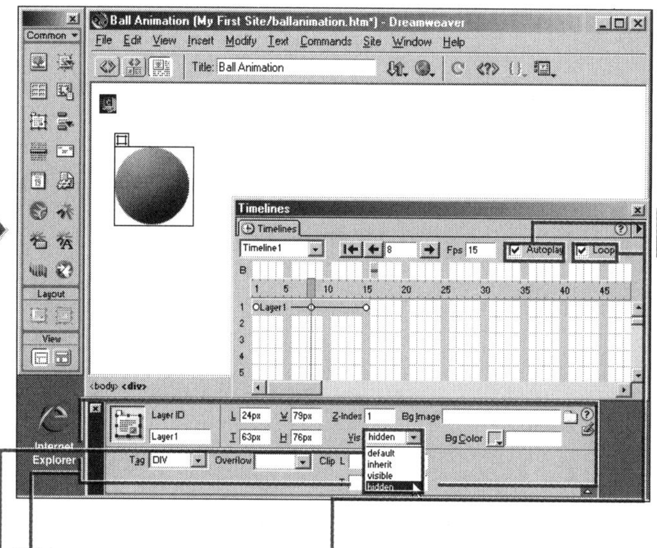

10 With the new keyframe selected, make changes to the layer in the Property Inspector.

■ In this example, the layer's visibility is turned off in the middle of the animation.

■ Autoplay is selected to start the animation when the page opens.

■ Loop is selected to make the animation repeat indefinitely.

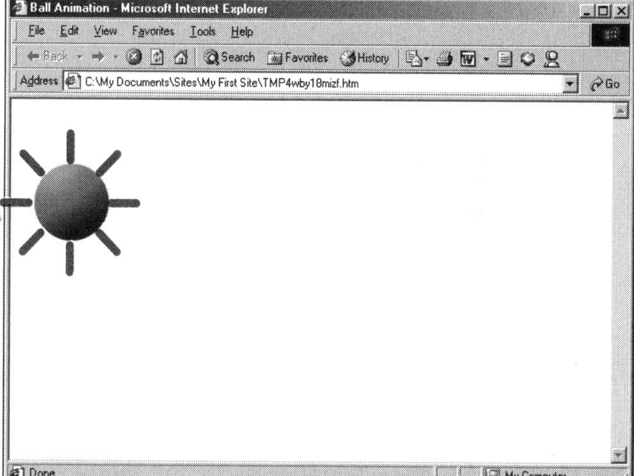

11 Preview the Web page in a browser.

Note: For more information on Web browsers, see Chapter 4.

■ In this example, the object flashes on and off indefinitely.

CHANGE ANIMATION SPEED

You can speed up or slow down a timeline animation by changing the frame rate of the animation or by adjusting the number of frames that make up the animation.

You can change the rate at which the frames are displayed in the Timelines Inspector. If the frame rate is increased and the number of frames of the animation stays the same, the animation runs faster. Conversely, if you decrease the frame rate, the animation slows down. The default animation speed in the Timelines Inspector is 15 frames per second (fps).

You can also change the number of frames in an animation by increasing or decreasing the length of its animation bar. Increasing the animation bar's size means the browser has to play more frames to display the same animation. If the frame rate stays the same, the animation runs slower. Decreasing the size of the animation bar has the opposite effect: Fewer frames are played and the animation speeds up.

CHANGE ANIMATION SPEED

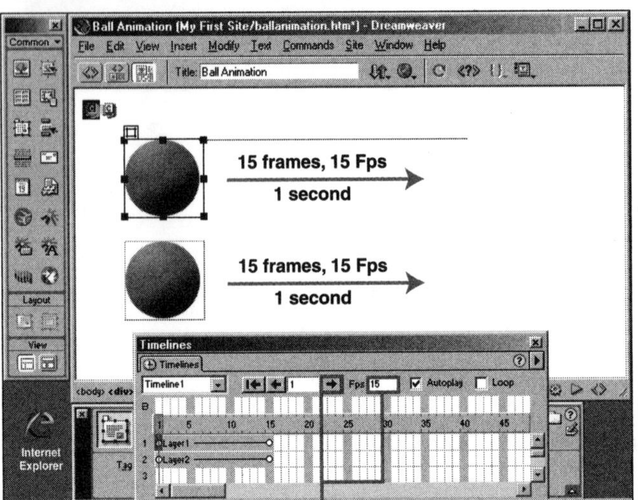

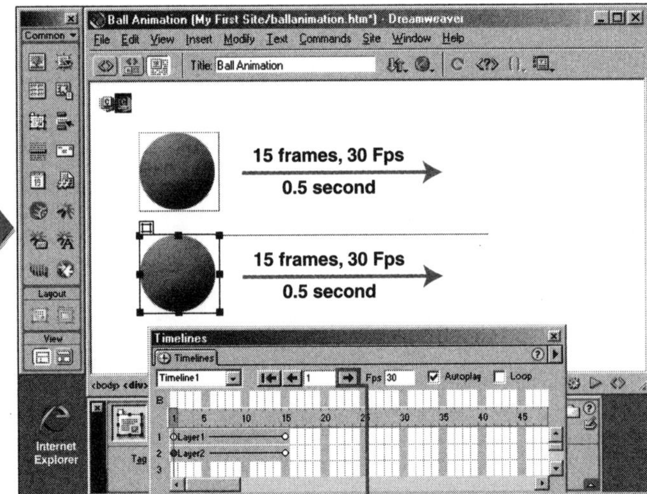

CHANGE FRAME RATE

1 Create two timeline animations on a page.

Note: See "Create a Straight-Line Animation" earlier in this chapter.

■ In this example, two layers have animation bars of equal lengths and move at 15 frames per second (fps).

2 Click and hold the playback button.

3 Type a new fps value for the animations.

■ A higher value increases their speed. A lower value decreases their speed.

■ The change in the fps rate affects all the animations in the timeline equally.

4 To preview the modified animations, click and hold the playback button.

How high should I set my frame rate for animations?

✔ Most browsers running on average computers systems cannot display animations at rates faster than 15 frames per second. Most likely, you will want to use this rate as your ceiling. If you are running many animations on a page and want to make sure all users can play them without having performance issues, you may want to decrease the frame rate to less than 15 fps. As a comparison, 30 fps is the standard frame rate for video, and 24 fps is standard for film.

What happens when a browser can not display an animation at the specified frame rate?

✔ The browser still plays all the frames in the animation, but it just plays them at a slower speed. It does not skip frames to make up for lost time.

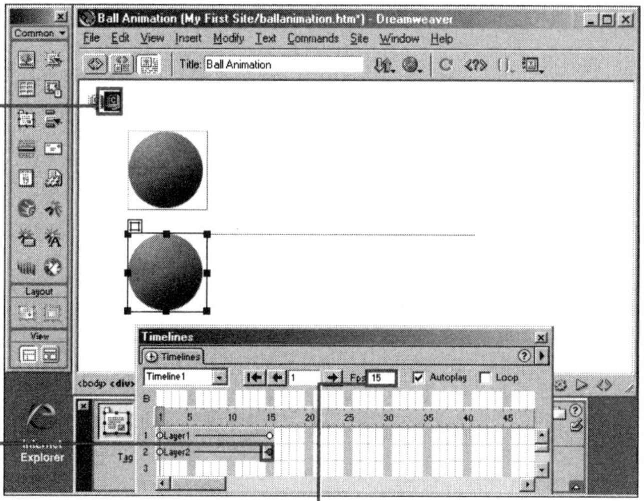

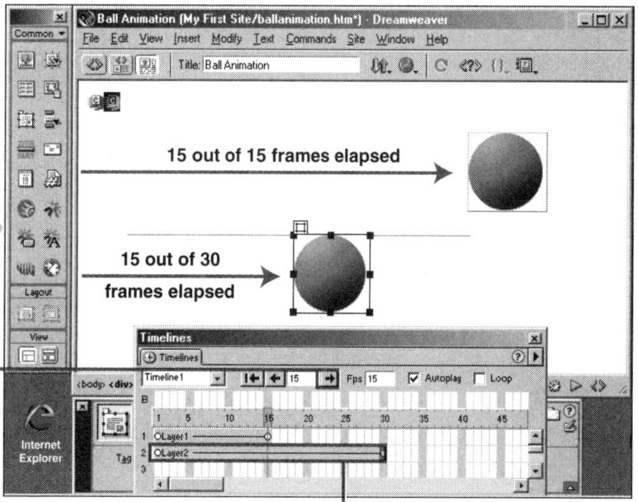

15 out of 15 frames elapsed

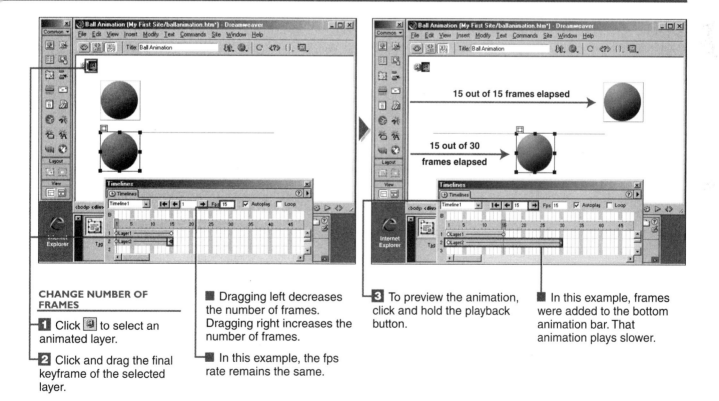

15 out of 30 frames elapsed

CHANGE NUMBER OF FRAMES

1 Click to select an animated layer.

2 Click and drag the final keyframe of the selected layer.

■ Dragging left decreases the number of frames. Dragging right increases the number of frames.

■ In this example, the fps rate remains the same.

3 To preview the animation, click and hold the playback button.

■ In this example, frames were added to the bottom animation bar. That animation plays slower.

TRIGGER AN ANIMATION WITH A BEHAVIOR

You can combine Dreamweaver behaviors and timelines so that clicking on an image or a hyperlink in your page starts an animation. This is an alternative to selecting Autoplay in the Timelines Inspector, which causes an animation to start automatically when a page loads.

To create a behavior-triggered animation, you first create your timeline. See "Create a Straight-Line Animation" or "Create an Animation by Dragging a Path" for more information. Then you add an image or text hyperlink to your page that serves as the trigger when clicked, and you assign the Start Timeline behavior for it.

A similar Stop Timeline behavior will stop a timeline animation in progress. This enables you to create a simple VCR-like interface for an animation on your page. Just associate the Start Timeline behavior with a "Start" hyperlink or image, and the Stop Timeline behavior with a "Stop" hyperlink or image.

TRIGGER AN ANIMATION WITH A BEHAVIOR

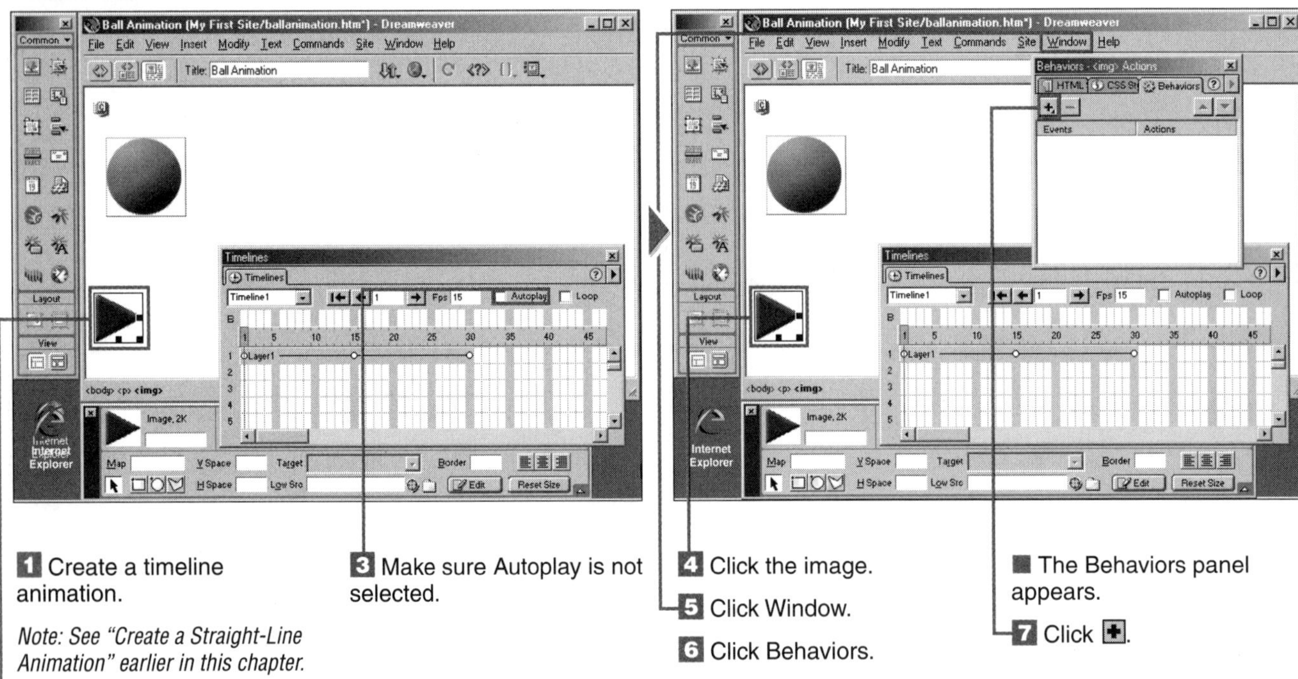

1 Create a timeline animation.

Note: See "Create a Straight-Line Animation" earlier in this chapter.

2 Insert an image to serve as a clickable trigger for the animation.

3 Make sure Autoplay is not selected.

4 Click the image.

5 Click Window.

6 Click Behaviors.

■ The Behaviors panel appears.

7 Click [+].

Can I make other events (other than a mouse click) start my animation?

✔ After you have defined the behavior that starts the animation, you can select from a variety of trigger events in the Behaviors inspector. Just click the behavior, and then click ▼ to select an event. For example, `onDblClick` makes double-clicking the object start the animation. `onMouseOver` starts the animation when the cursor rolls over the object.

How do I remove a trigger that has been applied to an animation?

✔ You can remove the trigger by selecting the object in the Document window that does the triggering, clicking the behavior in the Behaviors panel, and pressing Delete. You can then assign the triggering behavior to another object on the page or make the animation autoplay (click the animation bar and select the Autoplay in the Timelines Inspector).

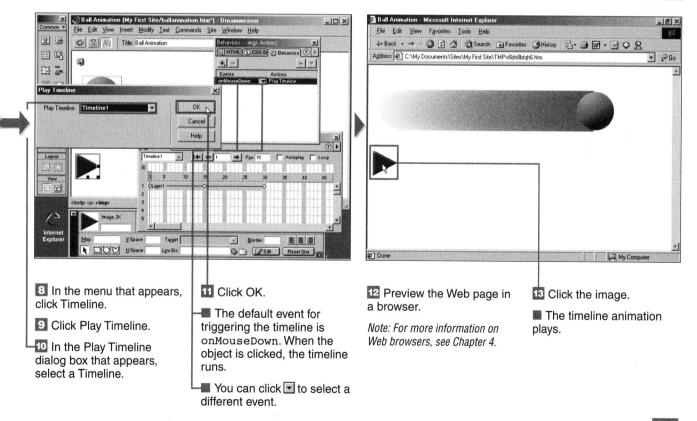

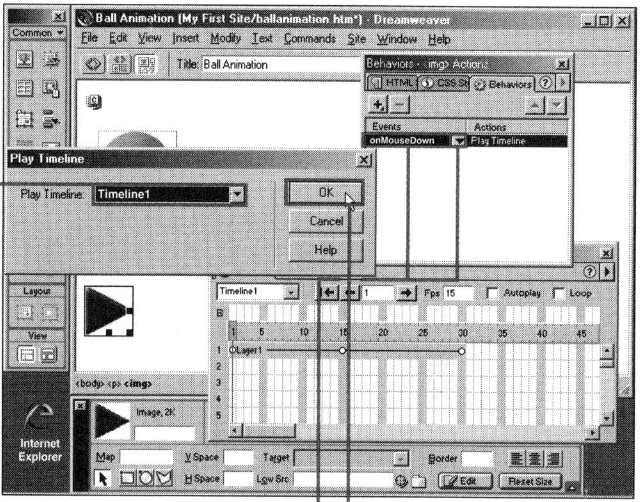

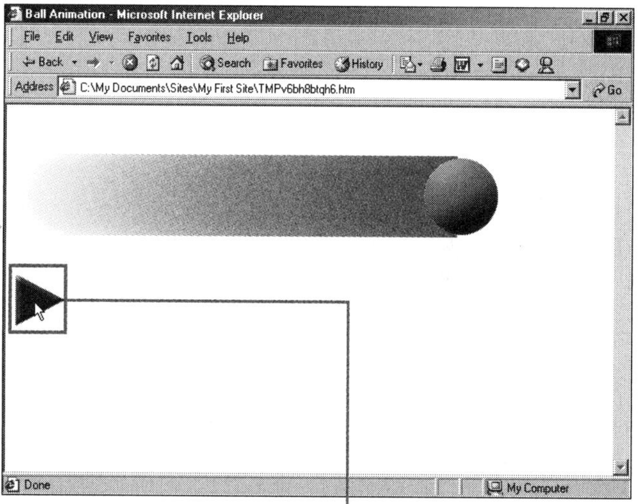

8 In the menu that appears, click Timeline.

9 Click Play Timeline.

10 In the Play Timeline dialog box that appears, select a Timeline.

11 Click OK.

■ The default event for triggering the timeline is `onMouseDown`. When the object is clicked, the timeline runs.

■ You can click ▼ to select a different event.

12 Preview the Web page in a browser.

Note: For more information on Web browsers, see Chapter 4.

13 Click the image.

■ The timeline animation plays.

PUBLISH YOUR WEB SITE

To make the pages that you have built in Dreamweaver accessible to other people on the Web, you must transfer them to a *Web server.* A Web server is an Internet-connected computer running special software that enables it to distribute files to Web browsers. Most people publish their Web pages on servers maintained by their *Internet service provider* (ISP) or by their company. Dreamweaver includes tools that enable you to connect to a Web server and transfer your Web documents to it.

Steps for Publishing Your Web Site

Publishing your site content using Dreamweaver involves the following steps:

1 Specify where on your computer the site files are kept. You do this by defining a local site, which is covered in Chapter 4.

2 Specify the Web server to which you want to publish your files. You do this by defining a remote site. See "Set Up a Remote Site" later in this chapter.

3 Connect to the Web server and transfer the files. The Dreamweaver Site window gives you a user-friendly interface for organizing your files and transferring them to the remote site.

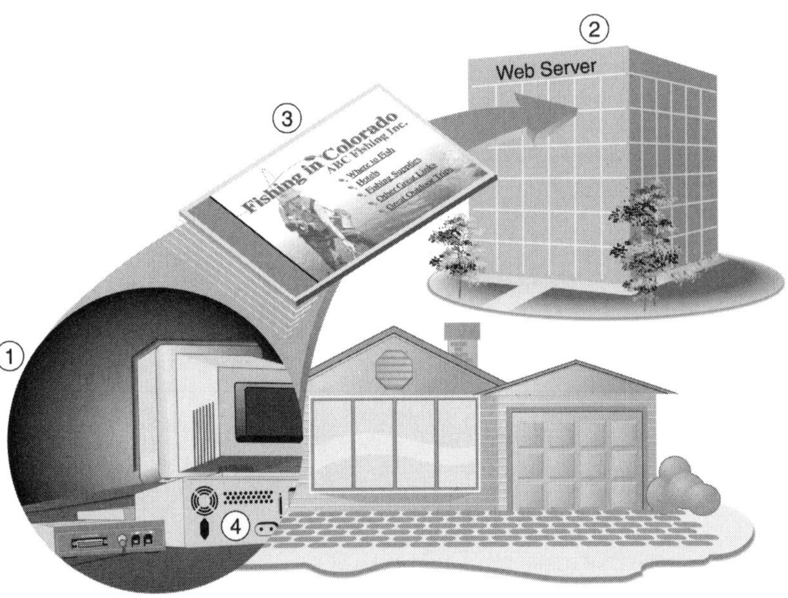

After uploading your site, you can update it by editing the copies of the site files on your computer (the local site) and then transferring those updated copies to the Web server (the remote site).

USING THE SITE WINDOW

The Site window lets you view the organization of all of the files in your site. It is also where you upload local files to the remote site and download remote files to the local site.

To open the Site window, click Window and then Site Files.

USING THE SITE WINDOW

SITE WINDOW

Site Menu

Here, you select from the different sites that you have defined in Dreamweaver.

Remote Site

The left pane displays the contents of your site as it exists on the remote Web server. To define a remote site, see the section "Set Up a Remote Site."

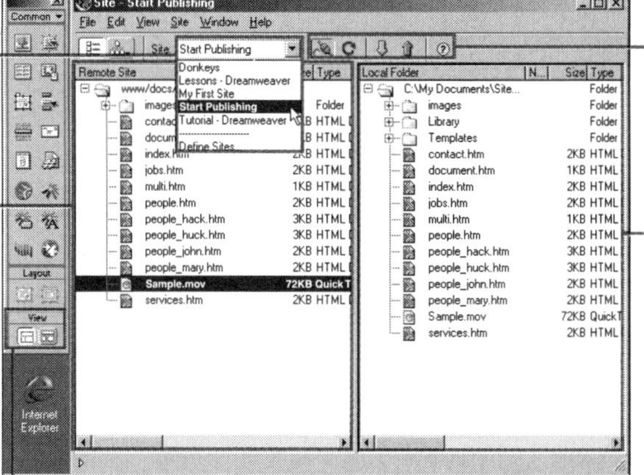

File Transfer

Buttons enable you to connect to your remote site, refresh the file lists, upload files to the remote server, and download files to the local site.

Local Site

The right pane displays the content of your site as it exists on your local computer. To define a local site, see Chapter 4.

Site Window Views

You can click and to switch between viewing your site as lists of files (shown here) or as a site map. See "Using the Site Map" in Chapter 16.

ORGANIZE FILES AND FOLDERS

You can use the Site window to organize the elements that make up your local and remote sites. The window lets you create and delete files and folders, as well as move files between folders. It also updates page references (links) in your HTML when you move a file.

Creating subfolders to organize files of a similar type can be useful if you have a large Web site. Most developers at a minimum create an "images" subfolder in which to store JPEG and GIF image files.

When you move files into and out of folders, the hyperlinks and image references on those pages will most likely need to be updated because document-relative references will no longer be valid. Dreamweaver keeps track of any affected code when you rearrange files, and updates it for you after you move a file. This file tracking is a key advantage to moving your HTML files in the Site window rather than through your computer's file-management system.

ORGANIZE FILES AND FOLDERS

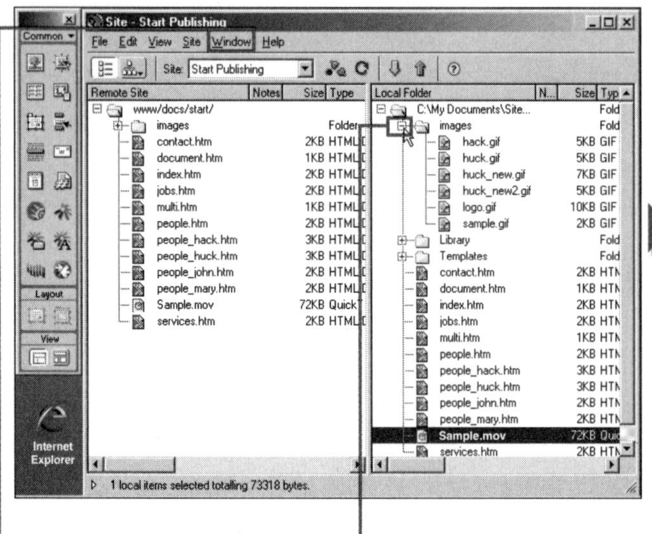

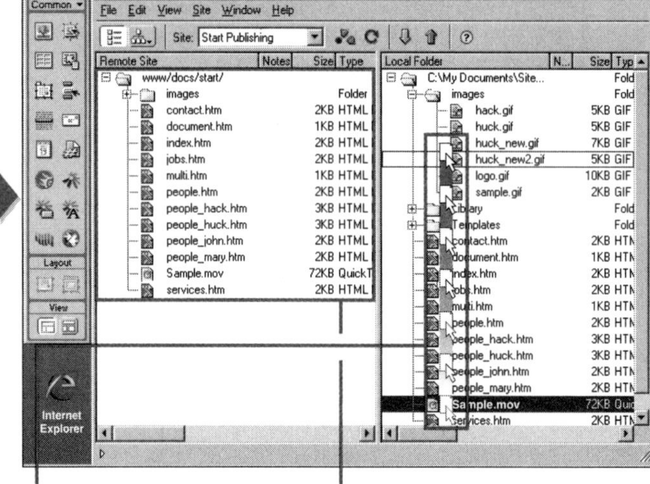

REARRANGE SITE FILES

1 Click Window.

2 Click Site Files to open the Site window.

3 Click ⊞ to view the files in a subfolder in your local site folder.

■ ⊞ turns to ⊟ and the folder contents are displayed. You can click ⊟ to close the subfolder.

4 Click and drag a file from the local site folder into a subfolder.

■ Dreamweaver reorganizes the files in your local site folder.

■ If any links need updates, Dreamweaver asks if it should update them. Click Update to update them.

■ You can rearrange files the same way in the remote site pane, but Dreamweaver cannot update these links.

How do I create a new file in the Site window?

✔ Click inside either the local or remote file list. Click File and then New File. Dreamweaver creates a new HTML file that has an empty body. You can also right-click a list and select New File from the contextual menu that appears.

How do I delete a file in the Site window?

✔ Click a file in either the local or remote file list. Click File and then Delete. An alert box asks you to confirm the deletion. You can also right-click a list and select Delete from the contextual menu that appears.

How do I open a file from the Site window?

✔ Double-click the file in the local or remote file lists. If you open a remote file and edit it, you can only save the modified file to the local site. (You cannot save directly to the remote site in Dreamweaver.)

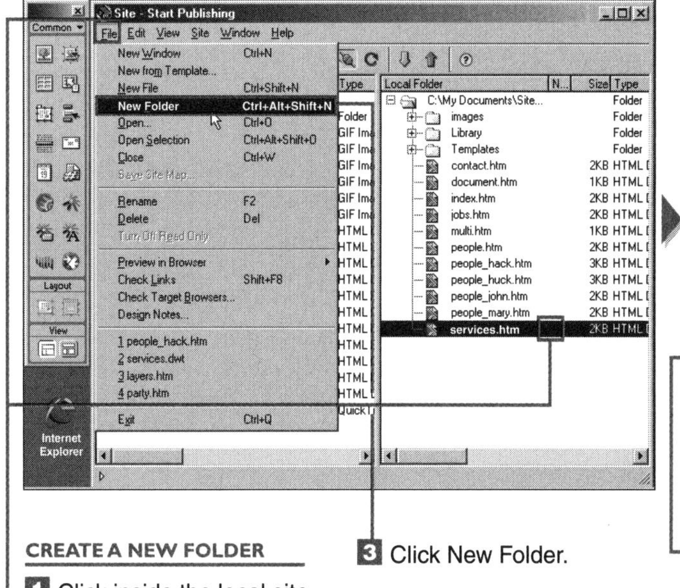

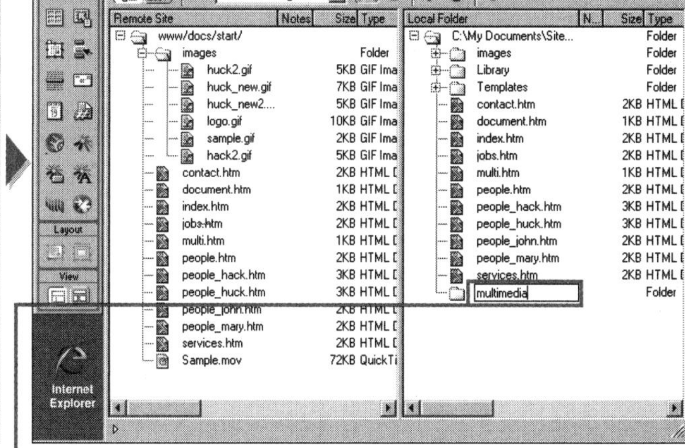

CREATE A NEW FOLDER

1 Click inside the local site pane.

2 Click File.

3 Click New Folder.

4 Type a name for the new folder.

■ To create a new folder on the remote site, click inside the remote site and perform steps 2 through 4.

SET UP A REMOTE SITE

The *remote site* is the place where your site's files are made available to the rest of the world. You set up a remote site by specifying a directory on a Web server where your site will be hosted. Most remote sites are located on a Web server maintained by your Internet service provider (ISP) or company.

Dreamweaver can connect to your remote site, transfer files there, and manage the files when you have to update them. To do these things, Dreamweaver needs certain technical information, including the name of the Web server (the host name), the user name and password for the Web server account, and the directory on the server where the files are to be stored. You enter this information in the Site Definition dialog box.

You can still build your local Web site without having set up a remote site. And while Dreamweaver's file-transfer capabilities are convenient, your can still upload Dreamweaver-built files to your server with a separate FTP program. See the CD-ROM for FTP resources.

SET UP A REMOTE SITE

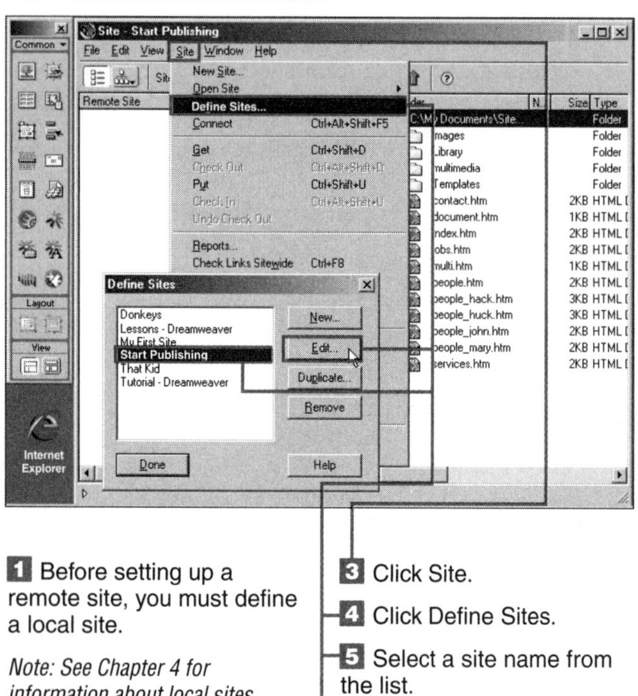

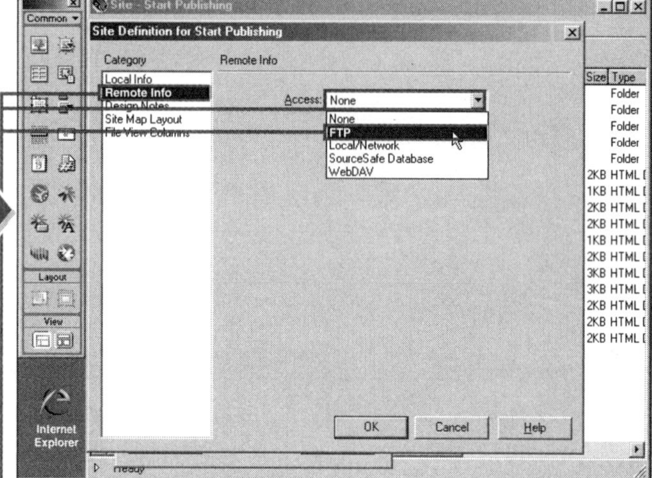

1 Before setting up a remote site, you must define a local site.

Note: See Chapter 4 for information about local sites.

2 Click Window and then Site Files to open the Site window.

3 Click Site.

4 Click Define Sites.

5 Select a site name from the list.

6 Click Edit.

■ The Site Definition dialog box appears.

7 Click Remote Info.

8 Click ▾ to view access options.

9 Click FTP.

■ If your Web server is mounted as a network drive (Windows) or as an AppleTalk or NFS server (Macintosh), or if you are running a Web server on your local machine, select Local/Network.

What should I do if the computer I build my site on is also my Web server?

✔ You should select Local/Network from the Access menu in the Site Definition dialog box. You can then specify the local folder where the live site files will be stored. In such a case, both your local and remote sites are on your local computer.

What are WebDAV and SourceSafe?

✔ WebDAV is an extension of the HTTP protocol that enables users to collaboratively edit files on remote Web servers. SourceSafe is a database application that offers similar capabilities. If you build sites using a WebDAV-enabled system or SourceSafe, you can have Dreamweaver connect to it when it needs to upload and download site files.

What is a firewall and how can it affect Dreamweaver?

✔ A *firewall* is a networking security system attached to a local-area network that controls information flowing in and out of the network. Sometimes a firewall can prevent Dreamweaver from connecting or transferring files to an external Web server. The Use Firewall and Passive FTP options in the Site Definition dialog box may remedy this.

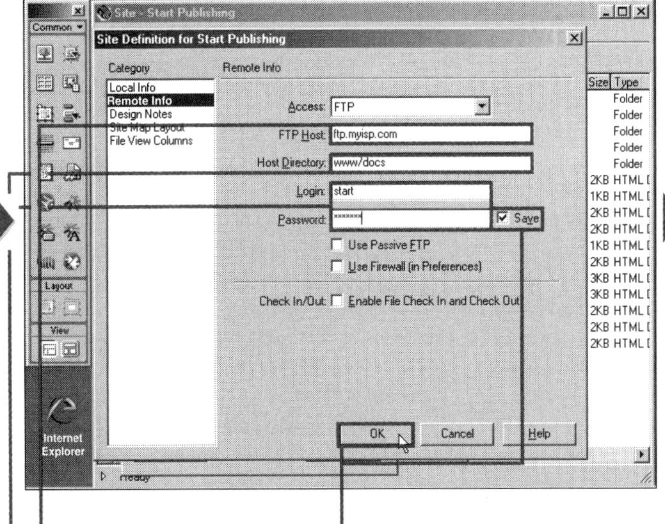

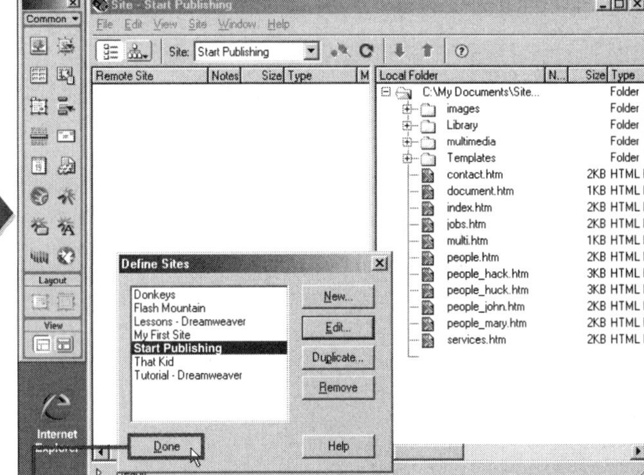

10 Type the name of the FTP host (Web server).

11 Type your site's directory path on the Web server.

12 Type your login name and password.

■ Check Save to have Dreamweaver save your password (☐ changes to ☑).

■ Enable Check In/Check Out if you plan to work on the site collaboratively.

13 Click OK.

14 Click Done to close the Define Sites dialog box.

Note: To access your remote site, see "Connect to a Remote Site."

CONNECT TO A REMOTE SITE

To transfer and manage files between your local and remote sites, Dreamweaver must connect to a Web server. This requires several things to happen: Dreamweaver must make contact with the server, log in using your user name and password, and then access the host directory.

If any of these steps fail — Dreamweaver cannot access the server, cannot log in, or cannot find the specified directory — Dreamweaver displays a warning message informing you of its failure to connect. Failure can be the fault of either parties. The remote Web server may be down or information that you typed for your remote site may be invalid.

Dreamweaver connects to the remote Web server using *File Transfer Protocol* (FTP), which is the common standard for moving files between Internet-connected computers. *HyperText Transfer Protocol*, or HTTP, which transmits information between Web browsers and servers, is a related standard.

CONNECT TO A REMOTE SITE

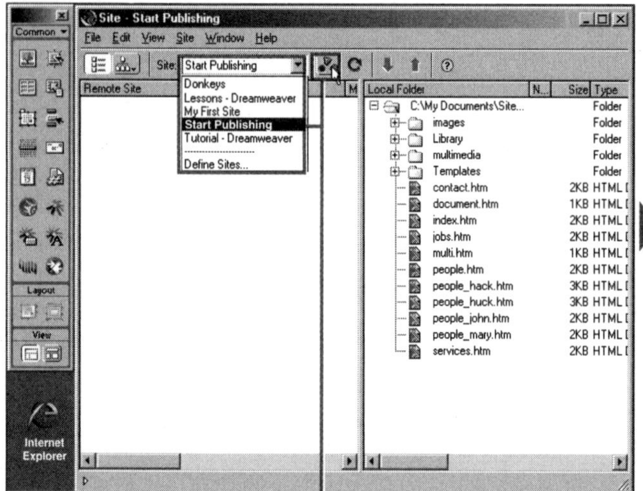

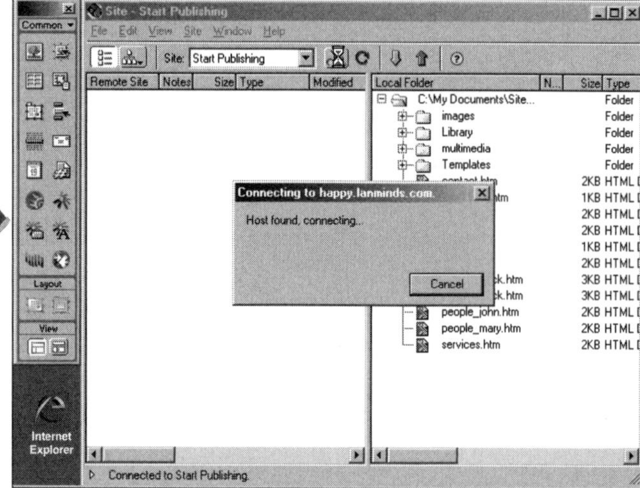

■ Before connecting, you must set up a local site and a remote site.

Note: See Chapter 4 for setting up a local site. See "Set Up a Remote Site" for setting up a remote site.

1 Click Window and then Site Files to open the Site window.

2 Click ▼ to select your Web site.

3 Click the connect button.

■ Dreamweaver attempts to connect to the remote site.

■ If it cannot connect to the site, Dreamweaver alerts you with a dialog box. If you have trouble connecting, double-check the host information you entered for the remote site.

Note: See "Set Up a Remote Site."

What if I do not know the host directory for my site?

✔ You can leave that field blank in the Site Definition dialog box (see "Set Up a Remote Site"). Dreamweaver opens the default folder on the server when it connects. This may or may not be the correct place to store your files. Most servers require you store your files inside a folder named public_html or www.

How do I keep Dreamweaver from disconnecting from the Web server prematurely?

✔ You can access Preferences under the Edit menu and select the Site category. There, you can adjust the time that Dreamweaver lets pass between commands before it logs you off of the server — the default is 30 minutes. Web servers also have a similar setting on their end, so the server, not Dreamweaver, may log you off.

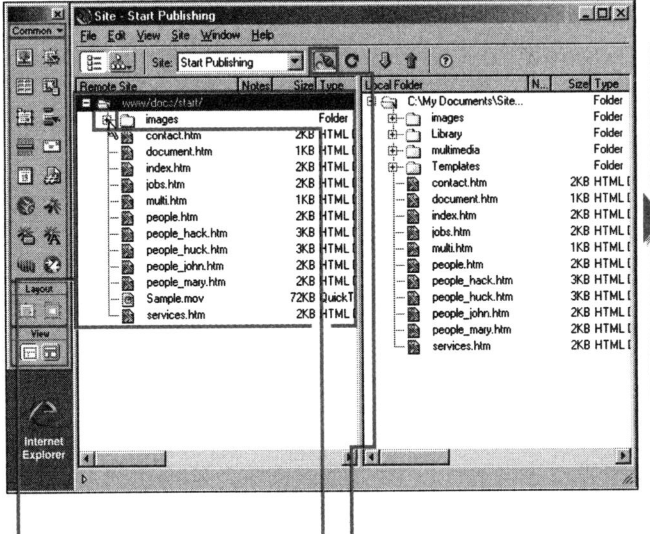

■ When you have connected, Dreamweaver displays the contents of the remote site's host directory, which you specified when you set up the remote site.

Note: See the section "Set Up a Remote Site."

■ The Connect button changes to a Disconnect button.

4 To open a directory's contents on the Web server, click ⊞.

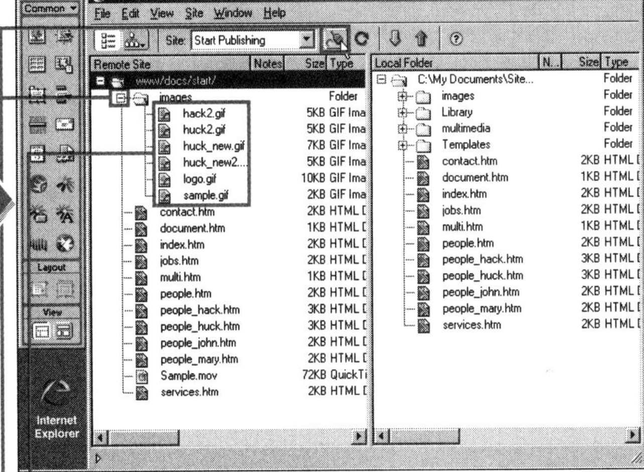

■ Dreamweaver displays the contents of the directory.

■ You can click ⊟ to close a directory.

5 Click [disconnect icon] to disconnect from the Web server.

■ Dreamweaver disconnects from a Web server if you do not transfer files for 30 minutes. You can change the disconnect period in Preferences under Site FTP.

Note: See Chapter 2 for more information.

UPLOAD AND DOWNLOAD FILES

The Dreamweaver Site window makes transferring files between your local and remote sites easy. Clicking local files in the right pane and then clicking uploads files to the remote Web server. Clicking remote files in the left pane and then clicking downloads files to your local computer.

If you try to upload a file that has unsaved changes, Dreamweaver displays an alert and enables you to save those changes first. Dreamweaver also offers to transfer dependent files when you upload a Web page. Dependent files can be images and framed pages that are referenced by the page's HTML. When you upload a page for the first time, you usually want to also upload dependent files.

Dreamweaver includes a Check In/Check Out feature that flags site files when they have been downloaded from the remote site for editing. This feature is convenient when many people are collaborating to build a site. See Chapter 16 for details about site management.

UPLOAD AND DOWNLOAD FILES

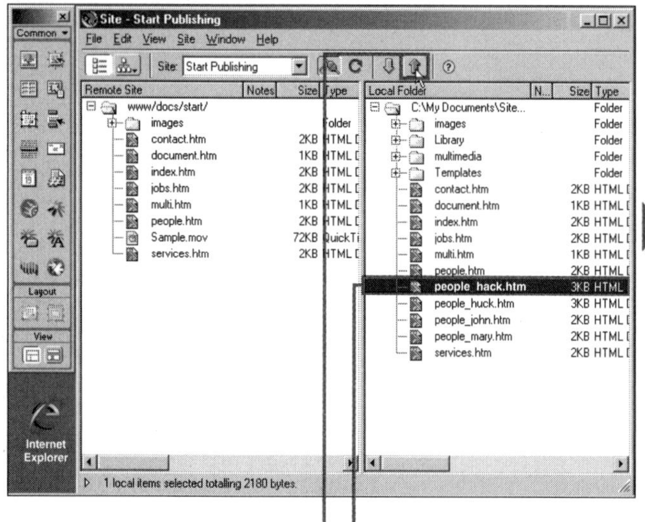

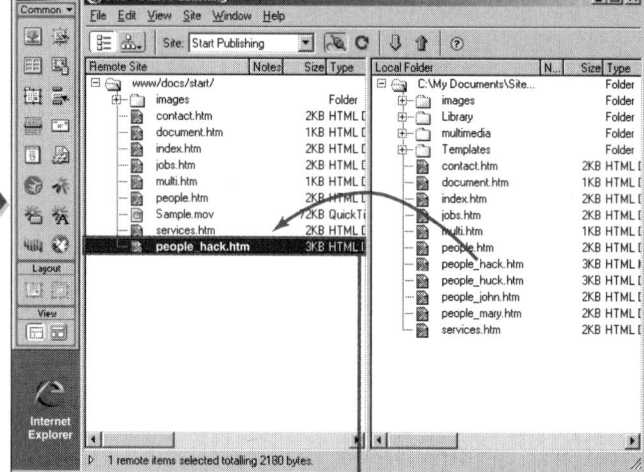

UPLOAD A FILE

1 Connect to the Web server by using the Site window.

Note: Refer to "Connect to a Remote Site" for details.

2 Click the file or folder you would like to upload.

■ You can Ctrl-click (Windows) or Shift-click (Mac) to select multiple items.

3 Click .

■ An alert may appear asking if you want to include dependent files. Dependent files are images and other files referenced in the page's HTML code. Click Yes if you would like to upload the dependent files.

■ Dreamweaver transfers the file or folder from your local site to the remote site (on the Web server).

How do I stop a file transfer in progress?

✔ You can click [icon], which appears at the bottom of the Document window while a transfer is in progress. You can also press Esc (Windows) or Command+. (Macintosh).

Where does Dreamweaver log errors that occur during transfer?

✔ Dreamweaver logs all transfer activity, including errors, in a file-transfer log. You can view it by clicking Window and then Site FTP log (Windows), or Site and then Site FTP log (Mac).

What happens if I change my Internet service provider and need to move my site to a different server?

✔ You will need to change your remote site settings to enable Dreamweaver to connect to the new service provider's server. Your local site settings can stay the same.

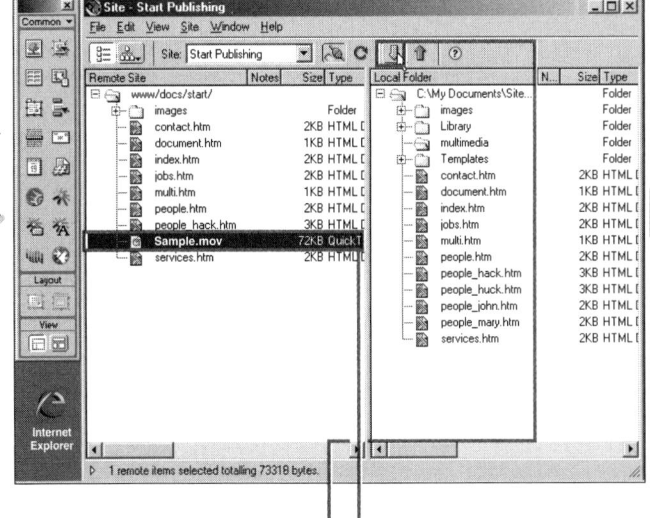

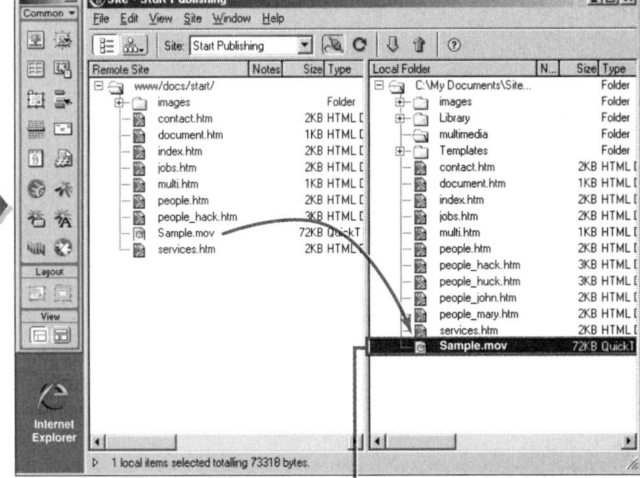

DOWNLOAD A FILE

1 Connect to the Web server by using the Site window.

Note: See the section "Connect to a Remote Site" for details.

2 Click the file or folder you would like to download.

■ You can Ctrl-click (Windows) or Shift-click (Mac) to select multiple items.

3 Click [icon].

■ Dreamweaver asks if you want to include dependent files. Dependent files are images and other files that are referenced in the page's HTML. Click Yes if you would like to download the dependent files.

■ Dreamweaver transfers the file or folder from the remote site (on the Web server) to the local site.

SYNCHRONIZE YOUR LOCAL AND REMOTE SITES

When you synchronize your local and remote sites, Dreamweaver transfers files between them so that both versions have a set of the most recent files. You can also optionally synchronize in one direction, uploading local files that are more recent to the remote site, or downloading remote files that are more recent to the local site.

The synchronizing commands keep you from having to figure out which have been updated and need to be uploaded each time you edit your local site. If you are working collaboratively (where several developers have their own local sites), it lets you automatically transfer the most recent files from the Web server when others have made changes.

When synchronizing, Dreamweaver examines the modified dates for the files on the local and remote sites. You can view this information in the Site window (under the Modified column).

SYNCHRONIZE YOUR LOCAL AND REMOTE SITES

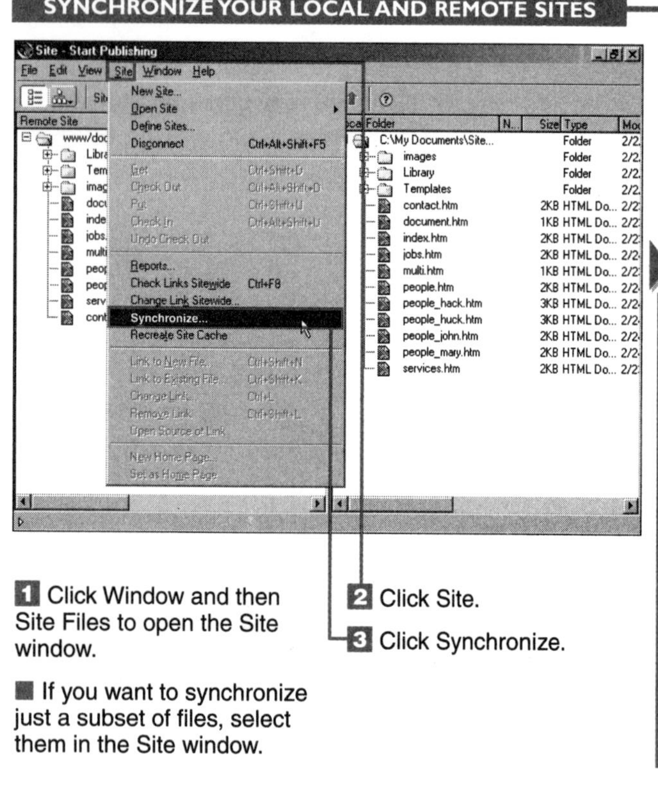

1 Click Window and then Site Files to open the Site window.

■ If you want to synchronize just a subset of files, select them in the Site window.

2 Click Site.

3 Click Synchronize.

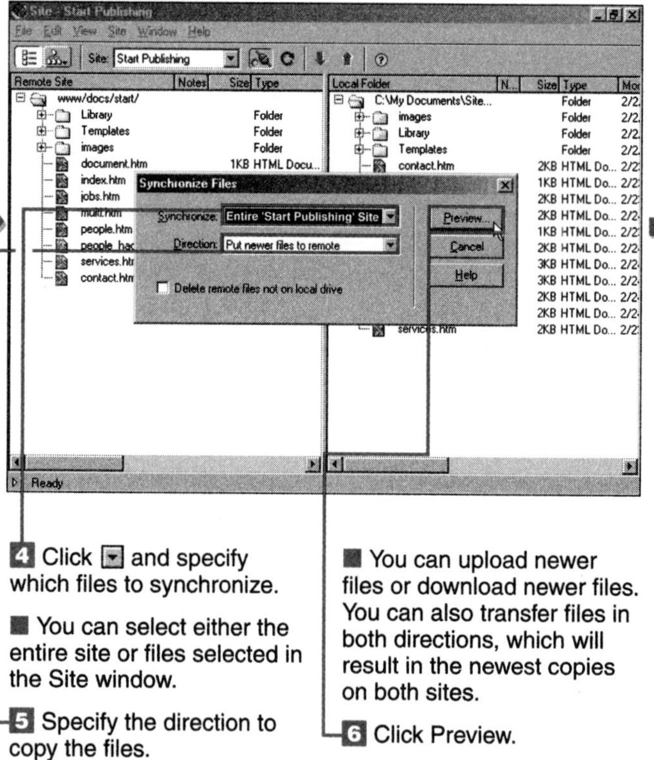

4 Click ▾ and specify which files to synchronize.

■ You can select either the entire site or files selected in the Site window.

5 Specify the direction to copy the files.

■ You can upload newer files or download newer files. You can also transfer files in both directions, which will result in the newest copies on both sites.

6 Click Preview.

How can I get rid of dead pages that are no longer used on the remote server?

✔ You can have those files deleted by selecting the Delete option in the Synchronize Files dialog box when performing a Put Newer Files to Remote synchronization.

How can I see which files are more recent on the local or remote site?

✔ In the Site window, click Edit and then Select Newer Local or Select Newer Remote. Dreamweaver compares the modified dates of the two sets of files and highlights the newer ones. On a Macintosh, you must click Site, Site Files, and then Select Newer Local or Select Newer Remote.

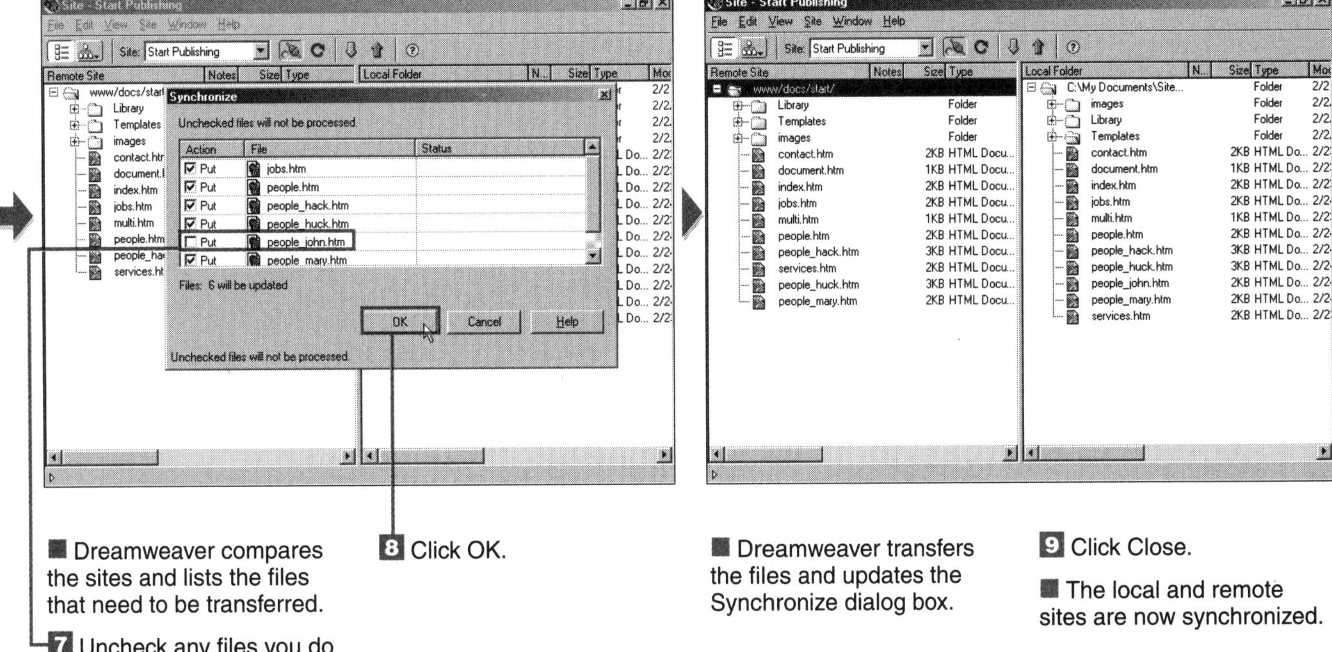

■ Dreamweaver compares the sites and lists the files that need to be transferred.

7 Uncheck any files you do not want transferred.

8 Click OK.

■ Dreamweaver transfers the files and updates the Synchronize dialog box.

9 Click Close.

■ The local and remote sites are now synchronized.

USING THE SITE MAP

For designers who want a visual representation of their site's structure, Dreamweaver's Site Map view lays out the different pages of a site in flowchart form, with arrows between them representing links. It also highlights pages that have broken internal links.

Dreamweaver gives you an option of saving the Site Map as a BMP file, which can be useful if you need to give a slide-show presentation about the site or document the site on paper.

Besides serving as a visual tool, you can also perform management duties via the Site Map view. Many of the tasks you can perform in the Site window (such as updating links — see "Change a Link Sitewide") can also be done when the Site Map is displayed.

You can also create links with the Site Map open. Just click and drag the point-to-file icon (⊕) from a file in the Site Map to a file in the local site list.

USING THE SITE MAP

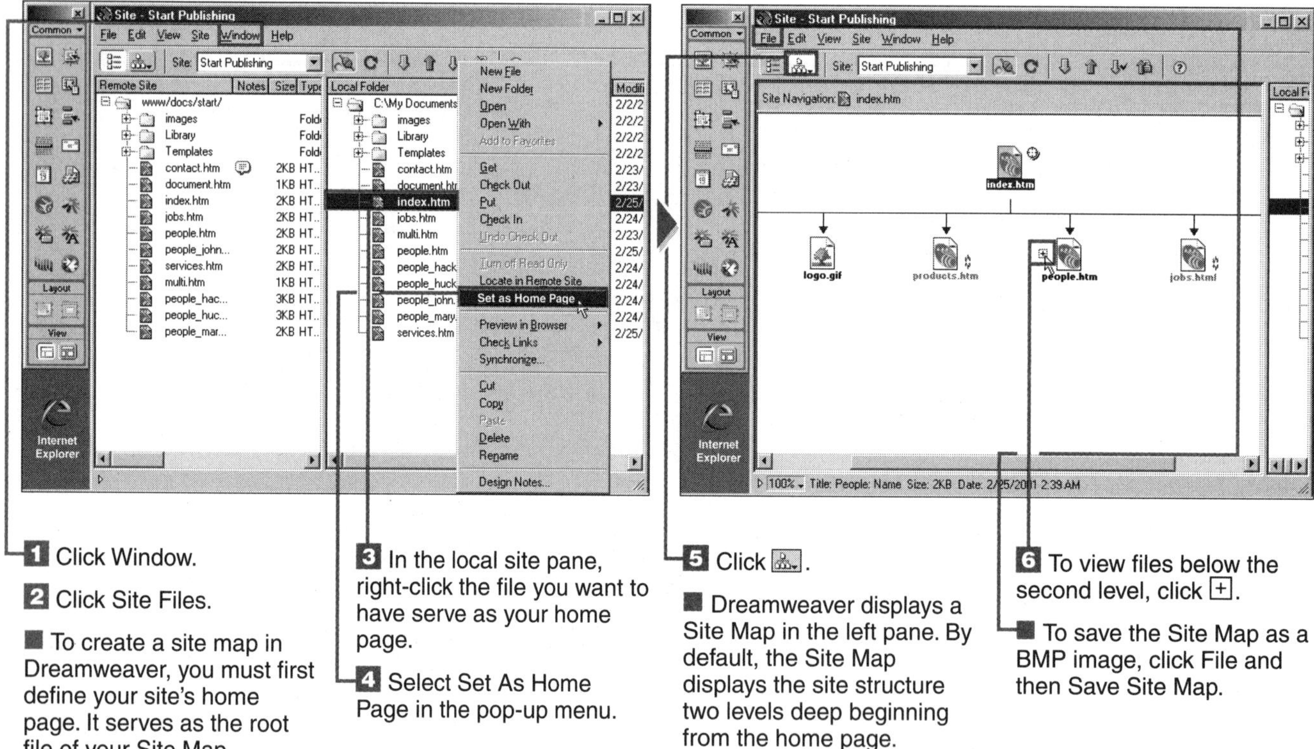

1 Click Window.

2 Click Site Files.

■ To create a site map in Dreamweaver, you must first define your site's home page. It serves as the root file of your Site Map.

3 In the local site pane, right-click the file you want to have serve as your home page.

4 Select Set As Home Page in the pop-up menu.

5 Click [site map icon].

■ Dreamweaver displays a Site Map in the left pane. By default, the Site Map displays the site structure two levels deep beginning from the home page.

6 To view files below the second level, click ⊞.

■ To save the Site Map as a BMP image, click File and then Save Site Map.

How can I view a subset of the Site Map, starting from a particular page?

✔ Click the page that you want to serve as the map root. Click View, and then View as Root (Windows). Or click Site, SiteMap View, and then View as Root (Mac). The Site Map redraws with the selected file at the top of the map.

How do I temporarily hide a part of my Site Map?

✔ You can hide files in your Site Map by clicking the files, and then clicking View, and then Show/Hide Link (Windows). Or click Site, Site Map View, and then Show/Hide Link (Mac).

How do I unhide files in my Site Map?

✔ First click View and then Show Files Marked as Hidden (Windows). Or click Site, Site Map View, and then Show Files Marked as Hidden (Mac). You can then select the hidden files (they appear with their filenames italicized) and use the Show/Hide Link command to hide them.

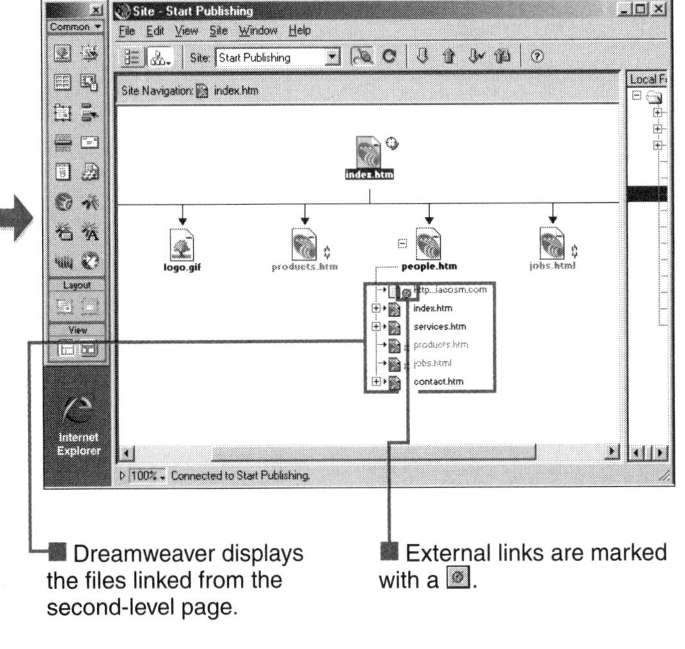

■ Dreamweaver displays the files linked from the second-level page.

■ External links are marked with a ◙.

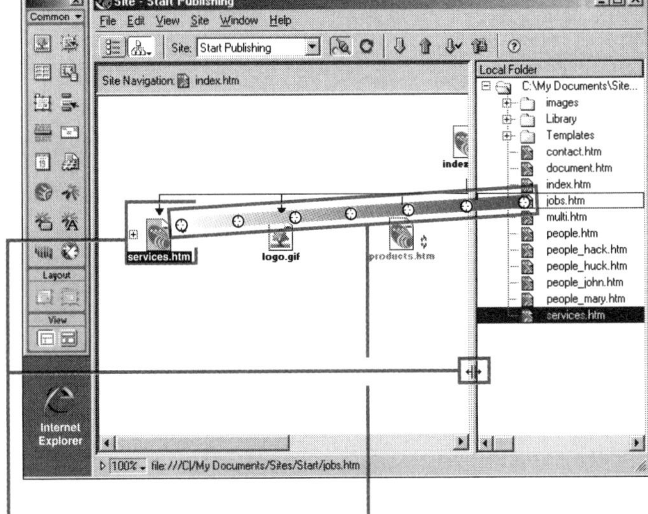

CREATE A LINK USING THE SITE MAP

1 Click and drag the Site window border to display both the Site Map and the local site.

2 Click a file in the Site Map. This page will contain the link.

3 Click and drag ⊕ to the destination file in the local site.

■ A new link is added to the top of the page selected in the Site Map. You can double-click the page to open it.

MANAGE SITE ASSETS

The Dreamweaver Assets panel provides a central place where you can view and manage important elements that appear in your site's pages. Items in the Assets panel are organized into categories:

Images: GIF, JPEG, and PNG images

Color: Text, background, and link colors; style-sheet colors

URLs: External Web addresses that are linked to your site

Flash Movies: Flash-based multimedia

Shockwave Movies: Shockwave-based multimedia

Movies: QuickTime and MPEG movies

Scripts: External JavaScript or VBScript files

Templates: Page layouts for your site

Library Items: Reusable page elements

You can further organize the items in the panel by defining often-used ones as Favorites. See "Specify Favorite Assets" for more information. These favorite items can be displayed separately in the panel.

Dreamweaver populates the Assets panel by searching through the files of a site for recognized file types and HTML code. It adds references to recognized items to the panel (files are not duplicated).

MANAGE SITE ASSETS

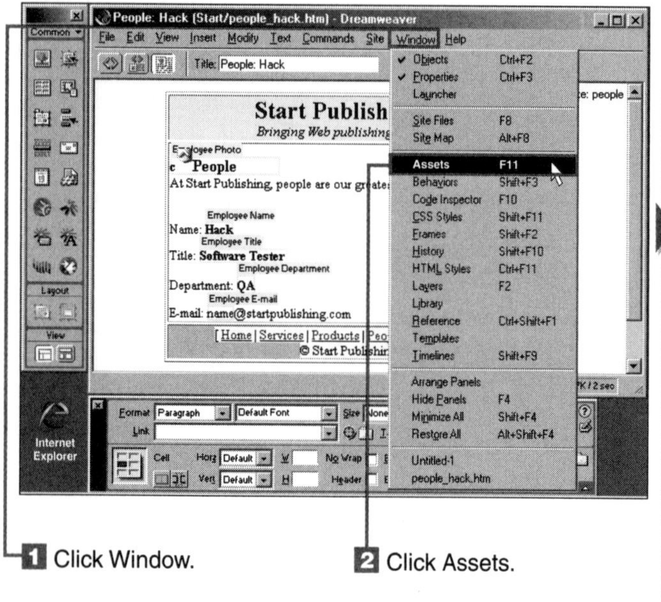

1 Click Window.

2 Click Assets.

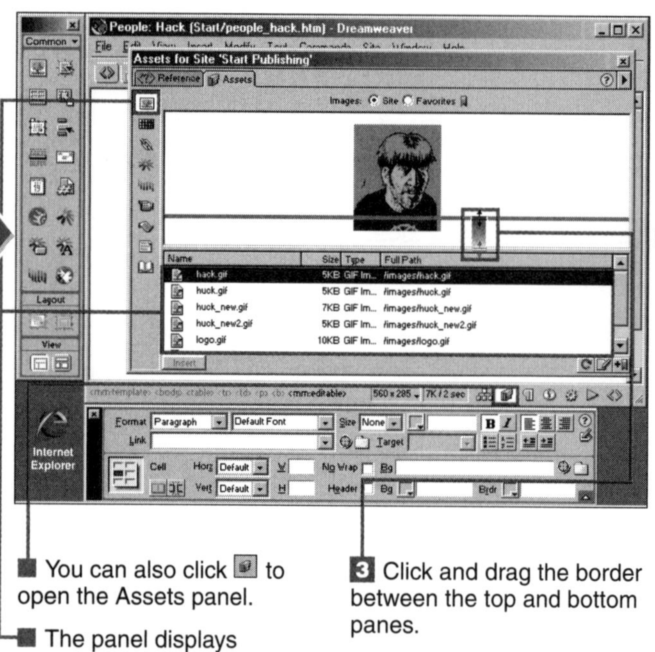

■ You can also click [icon] to open the Assets panel.

■ The panel displays objects from the selected category (in this example, Images).

3 Click and drag the border between the top and bottom panes.

How do I refresh the Assets panel lists?

✔ You can click the Refresh button (C) in the bottom right of the panel. This updates the panel and adds or removes assets that you have recently added or removed from your site. If items still do not display properly, you can Control-click (Windows) or Command-click (Mac) the C button and Dreamweaver rebuilds its site cache from scratch and refreshes the Assets panel.

How can I find out where an asset is in the site file structure?

✔ You can select the item in the Assets panel and select Locate in Site from the Assets panel menu. The Site window opens with the item highlighted.

Can I preview multimedia in the Assets panel?

✔ You can preview QuickTime movies. Click , select a QuickTime file, and click ▷.

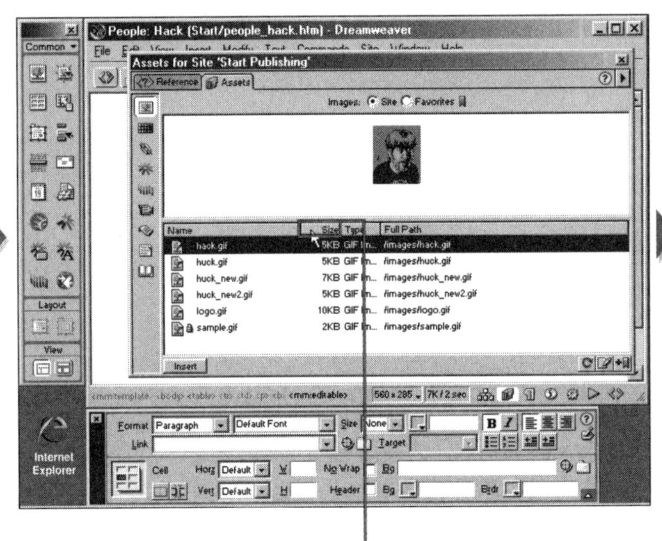

■ The panes assume the new dimensions.

4 Click a column heading.

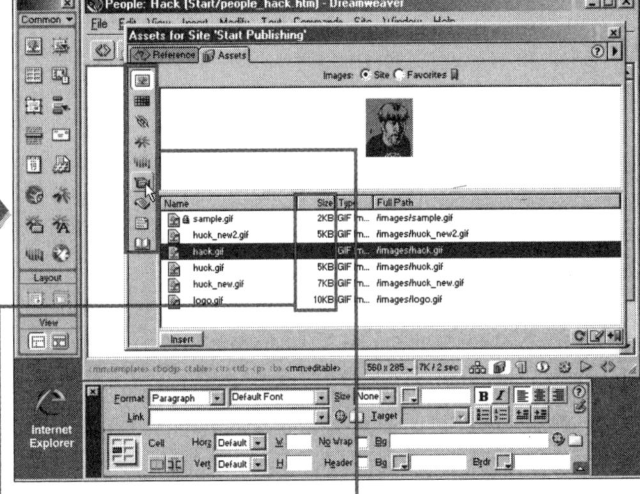

■ The assets are sorted by column, in ascending order. You can click the column again to sort in descending order.

■ To view other assets, click a different category.

ADD CONTENT BY USING THE ASSETS PANEL

In addition to providing an interface for viewing the important elements in your site pages, you can also add content to your site directly from the Assets panel.

This can be a more convenient way of adding objects such as images and multimedia files. These objects normally have to be added by selecting a command (or clicking a button in the Objects panel) and then searching through the file structure of your site. With the Assets panel, you can drag and drop the file from the panel, or select it in the list and click the Insert button.

The Assets panel features also let you apply colors to your page and create external links. You can select text in the Document window and drag and drop a color asset onto the text to change its color. Similarly, you can drag a URL from the Assets panel to a selected piece of text or image to create a new external hyperlink.

ADD CONTENT BY USING THE ASSETS PANEL

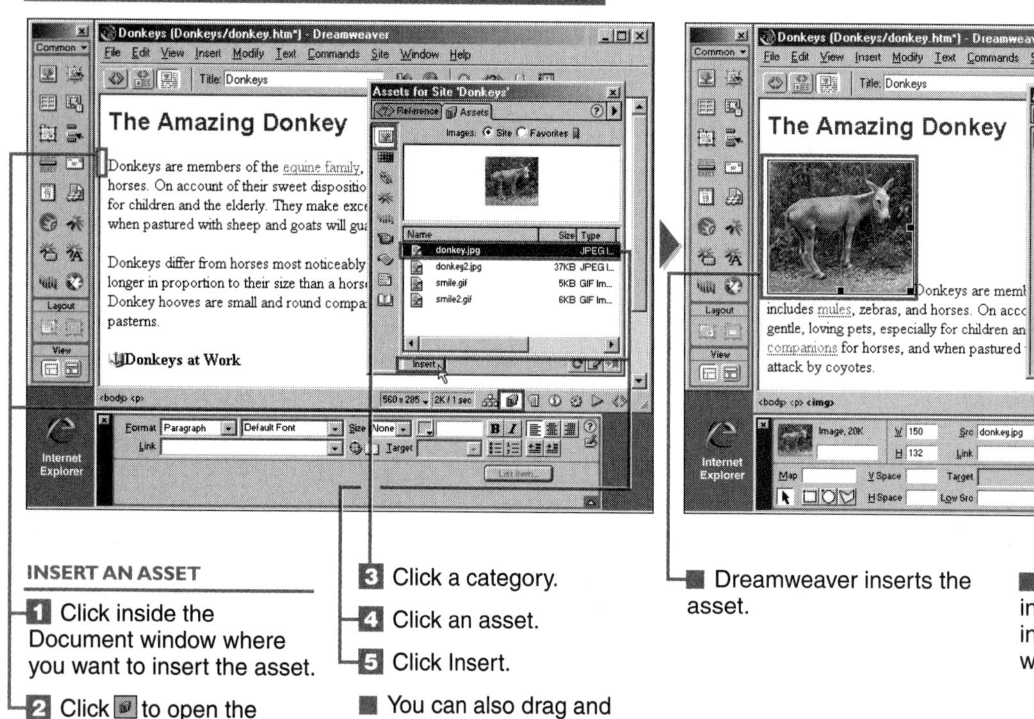

INSERT AN ASSET

1 Click inside the Document window where you want to insert the asset.

2 Click [icon] to open the Assets panel.

3 Click a category.

4 Click an asset.

5 Click Insert.

■ You can also drag and drop the asset from the panel to the Document window.

■ Dreamweaver inserts the asset.

■ In this example, an image in the Assets panel is inserted into the Document window.

How do I copy assets from one site to another?

✔ Select one or more items in the Assets panel, click Copy to Site in the Assets panel drop-down menu, and click a site to copy to. The assets appear in the Favorites list under the same category in the other site.

How can I edit an asset?

✔ You can double-click most assets in the Assets panel to edit them. For templates and library items, Dreamweaver opens a new Document window for editing the item. For items such as images and multimedia, Dreamweaver launches an external editing application, if one is available for the filetype. For example, double-clicking a GIF image opens the image in Macromedia Fireworks.

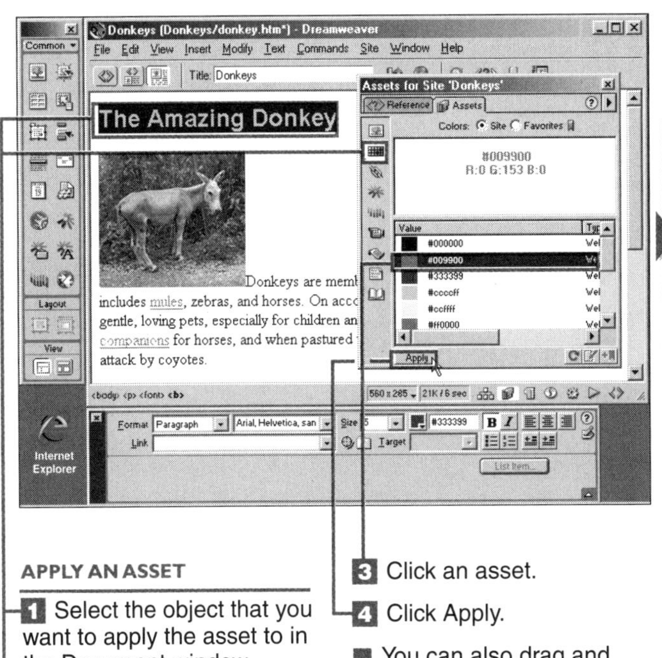

APPLY AN ASSET

1 Select the object that you want to apply the asset to in the Document window.

2 Click a category.

3 Click an asset.

4 Click Apply.

■ You can also drag and drop the asset from the panel onto the selected object in the Document window.

■ Dreamweaver applies the asset.

■ In this example, a color in the Assets panel was applied to text in the Document window.

SPECIFY FAVORITE ASSETS

For a large site that has lots of content and complicated page designs, the number of items that appear in the Assets panel can become cumbersome. To make the assets lists more manageable, you can segregate assets that you use often into a Favorites list inside a category. Then you have the option of viewing all the items in a category, or just a subset — your favorites. You choose between the two views by clicking the Site and Favorites radio buttons at the top of the Assets panel. Assets that are defined as a favorite show up in both views — Site and Favorites.

You can also give the assets in your Favorites folder nicknames by right-clicking (Windows) or Control-clicking (Mac) the name and selecting Edit Nickname. Nicknames can be useful for assets that normally have names that are not descriptive, such as colors defined using a hexadecimal code.

You can further group assets that are in a Favorites list by moving them into folders. To create a folder inside Favorites, open a Favorites list and then click the Favorites folder. You can add Favorites items to the folder by dragging and dropping them onto the folder.

SPECIFY FAVORITE ASSETS

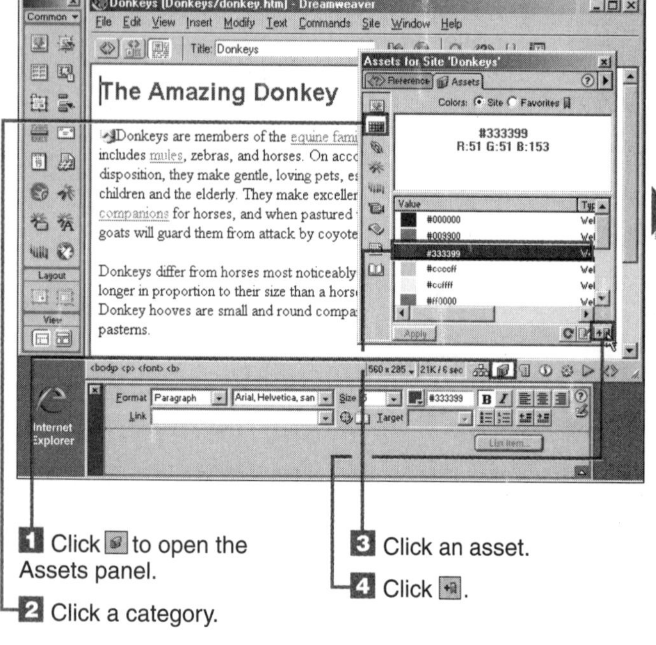

1 Click [icon] to open the Assets panel.

2 Click a category.

3 Click an asset.

4 Click [icon].

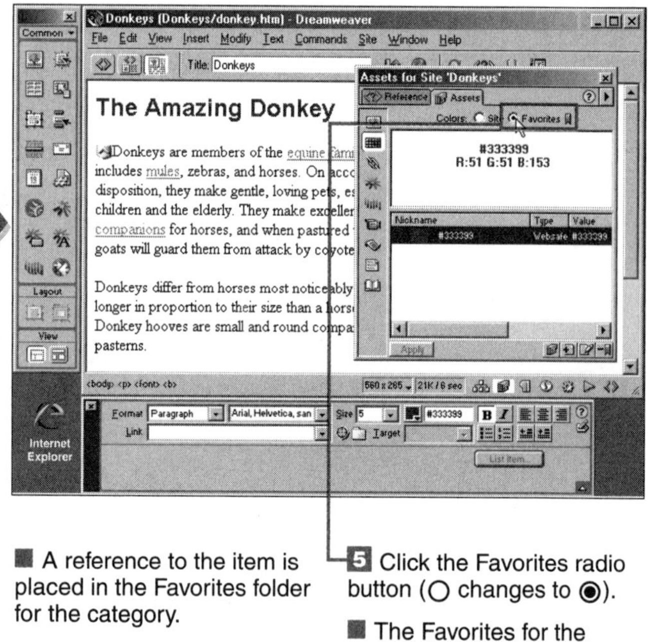

■ A reference to the item is placed in the Favorites folder for the category.

5 Click the Favorites radio button (○ changes to ◉).

■ The Favorites for the category are displayed.

Can I specify favorites for all of my assets?

✔ The Templates and Library categories cannot have Favorites. All the other categories of assets can.

How do I remove an asset from my Favorites?

✔ View your Favorites, select the asset, and click [icon] in the lower right of the panel.

How do I remove an item from the Assets panel entirely?

✔ You can not remove an asset while in the Assets panel itself. You need to open the Site window and delete the file from there. When you return to the Assets panel and click Refresh Site List in the Assets menu, the asset is gone.

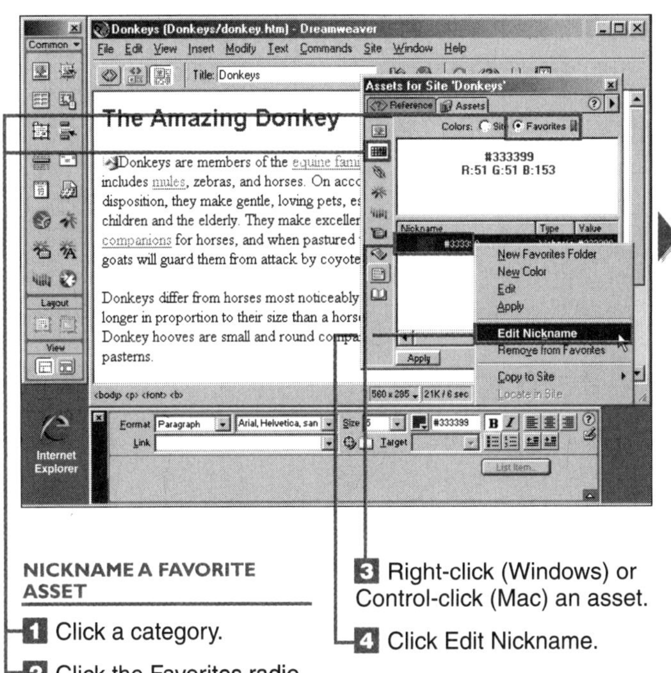

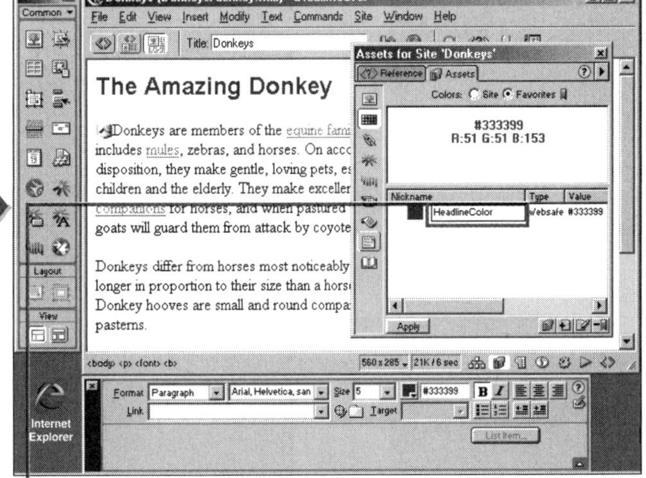

NICKNAME A FAVORITE ASSET

1 Click a category.

2 Click the Favorites radio button (○ changes to ◉).

3 Right-click (Windows) or Control-click (Mac) an asset.

4 Click Edit Nickname.

5 Type a nickname.

6 Press Enter (Windows) or Return (Mac).

■ The nickname appears in the Favorites list.

■ The item name in the Site list of the Assets panel does not change.

CHECK A PAGE IN OR OUT

Dreamweaver's Check In/Check Out system allows more than one designer to work collaboratively on a Web site. With the system turned on, Dreamweaver keeps track of which files in the site are being worked on and by whom. It also controls which files in your local site can be changed, depending on who has files checked out.

In the Site window, a checked out file has a check next to it. The check is green if the file was checked out by you. It is red if it was checked out by someone else. To edit a file, you need to check it out from the Site window. Otherwise, the file is read-only in your local site — meaning you can not change it.

You click a special button (![check out]) in the Site window to check out a file. You can also specify in the remote site settings that files are automatically checked out when they are double-clicked in the Site window. This can help keep people from unintentionally making edits to a file at the same time.

CHECK A PAGE IN OR OUT

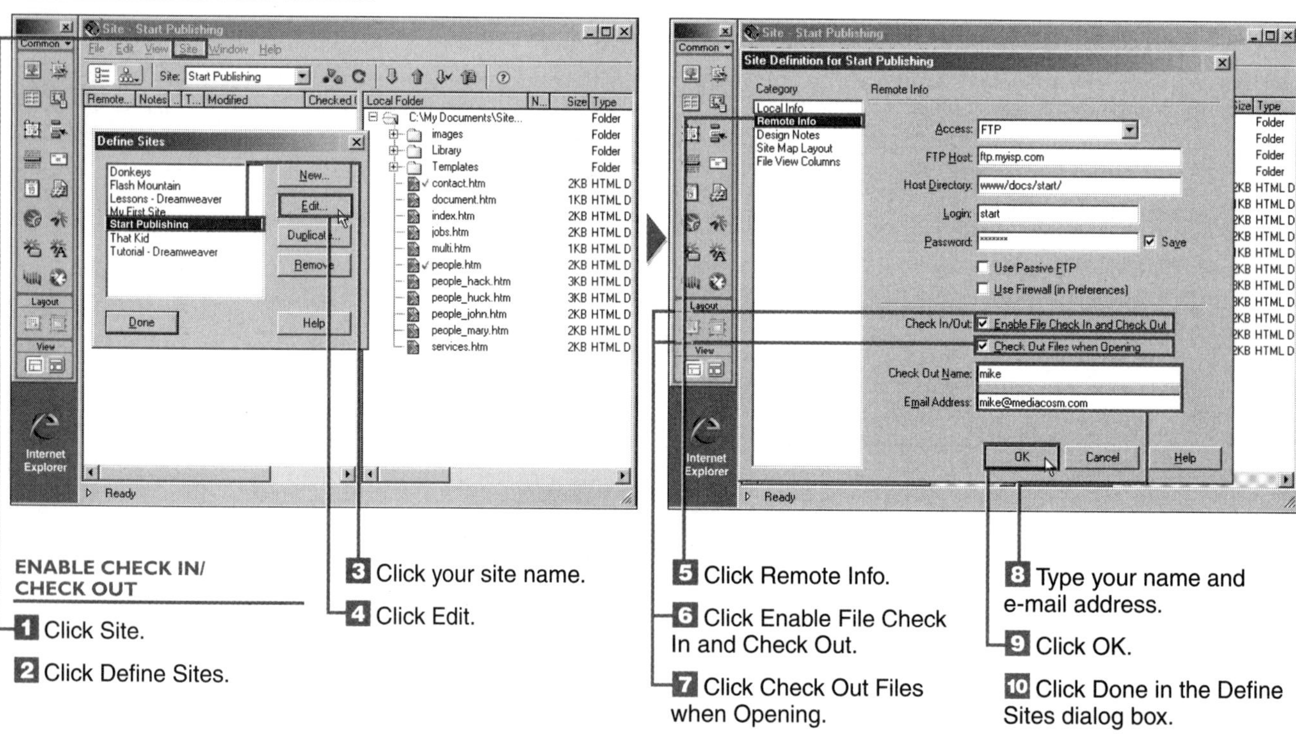

ENABLE CHECK IN/ CHECK OUT

1 Click Site.

2 Click Define Sites.

3 Click your site name.

4 Click Edit.

5 Click Remote Info.

6 Click Enable File Check In and Check Out.

7 Click Check Out Files when Opening.

8 Type your name and e-mail address.

9 Click OK.

10 Click Done in the Define Sites dialog box.

How does Dreamweaver lock a file on the remote server?

✔ When you check out a file, Dreamweaver creates a temporary LCK file that is stored in the remote folder while the page is checked out. The file contains information about who has checked the file out. Dreamweaver does not display the LCK files in the Site window, but you can see them if you access your remote site with an FTP program.

How do I contact the person who has checked out a file from a site?

✔ Each person working on a site can enter their name and e-mail address in the remote site information for that site. When a file is checked out, this information is displayed as a link next to the file in the Site window under the Checked Out By heading. Clicking the link opens an e-mail composition window with the name of the person who checked out the file in the To field.

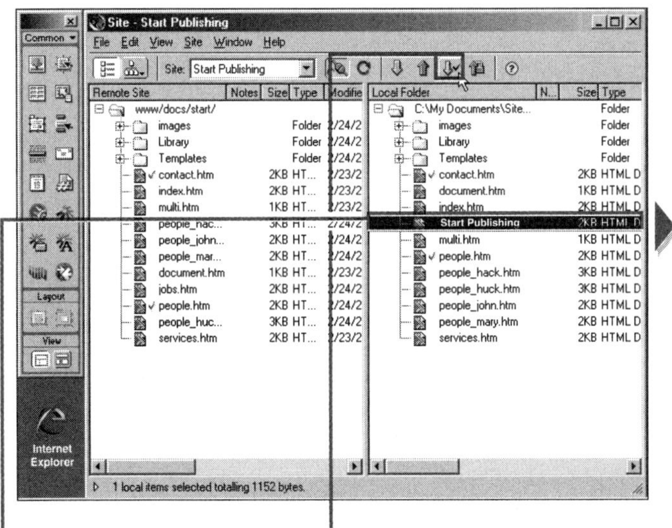

CHECK OUT A FILE

1 Click Window.

2 Click Site Files.

■ The Site window opens.

3 Click a file that is not checked out.

■ Checked out files have check marks next to them.

4 Click [icon].

■ You are asked if you want to include dependent files, which can include referenced images or frame files. Click Yes if you do.

■ A green check mark is placed next to the file.

■ Files checked out by others have a red check mark placed next to them.

CHECK IN A FILE

1 Click a file that is checked out by you.

2 Click [icon].

■ The green check mark turns into a lock. To edit the file, you need to check the file out again.

MAKE DESIGN NOTES

You can attach accessory information — such as editing history and author names — to your Web pages with Dreamweaver's Design Notes. Such notes can be especially useful if you are working on a site collaboratively, because they let you update the development status of a page every time you edit it. Other users can view a page's Design Notes by double-clicking an icon next to the page in the Site window.

Design Notes can also be useful if you are working alone to develop your site. For example, you can use them to specify where the original design specs for each page is stored on your hard drive.

Design Notes can be a more secure alternative to using HTML comments to add extra information to your Web page files. Although they do not show up in the browser window when a page is opened, HTML comments can still be viewed if the page's source code is examined. Design Notes are stored separately from the HTML files themselves.

MAKE DESIGN NOTES

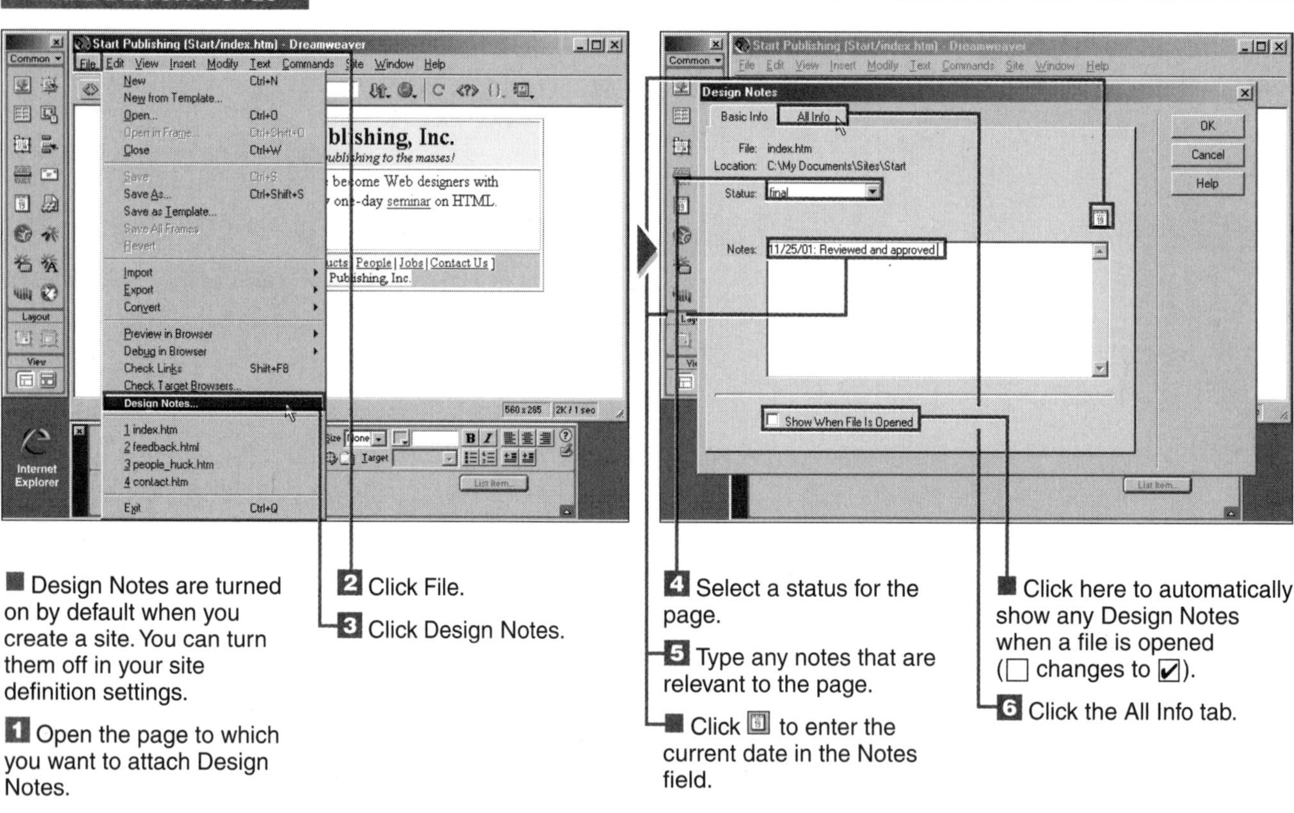

■ Design Notes are turned on by default when you create a site. You can turn them off in your site definition settings.

1 Open the page to which you want to attach Design Notes.

2 Click File.

3 Click Design Notes.

4 Select a status for the page.

5 Type any notes that are relevant to the page.

■ Click 📅 to enter the current date in the Notes field.

■ Click here to automatically show any Design Notes when a file is opened (☐ changes to ☑).

6 Click the All Info tab.

Can I specify that Design Notes not be uploaded to the remote site?

✔ If you want your Design Notes to be kept private (accessible only to you), you can keep them from being uploaded to the remote site. Open the Site Definition dialog box for your site (click Site, Define Sites, and then select your site and click Edit), click the Design Notes category, and then unclick Upload Design Notes for Sharing.

How do I add Design Notes to an object on my page?

✔ Right-click (Windows) or Control-click (Mac) the object in the Document window. In the contextual menu that appears, click Design Notes. You can then add notes to the object, just as you can to a page.

How are Design Notes stored in my site?

✔ Dreamweaver saves the information for Design Notes as XML files and stores them in a folder called `_notes` in your local site folder. The folder does not appear in the Site window.

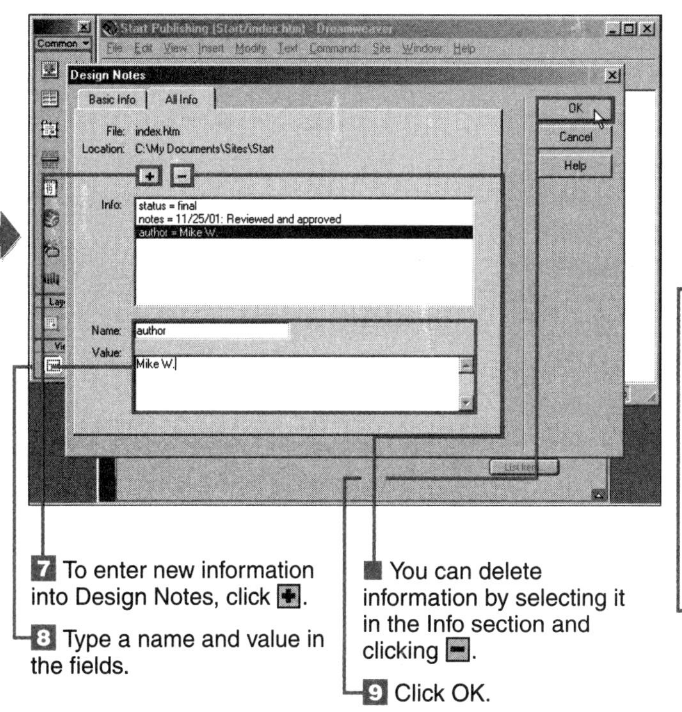

7 To enter new information into Design Notes, click ⊞.

8 Type a name and value in the fields.

■ You can delete information by selecting it in the Info section and clicking ⊟.

9 Click OK.

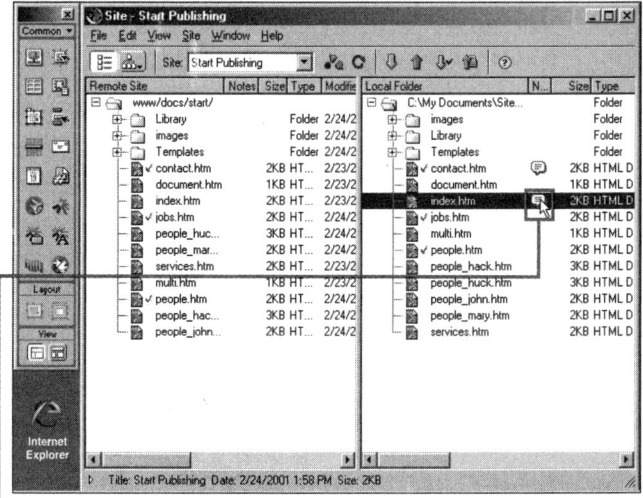

VIEW DESIGN NOTES

1 From the Site window, double-click 💬 next to a file.

■ The Design Notes for that file open.

■ You can also click File and then Design Notes when a page is open in the Document window.

RUN A SITE REPORT

Dreamweaver lets you generate reports on a page, several pages, or an entire site. The reports can tell you if there are HTML errors that need to be corrected and any pages lack descriptive information such as image "alt" text and page titles. The reports can also display checkout and Design Notes information for files.

Once a report has been run, you can save it as an XML file, which can be imported into a database or spreadsheet for further analysis.

After running a site report, you can use the Clean Up HTML command to fix the code errors that were found (see Chapter 3). You can also open files to add titles and alt text where these elements are missing. Adding descriptive titles and alt text to all your pages can potentially increase their visibility in search engines.

RUN A SITE REPORT

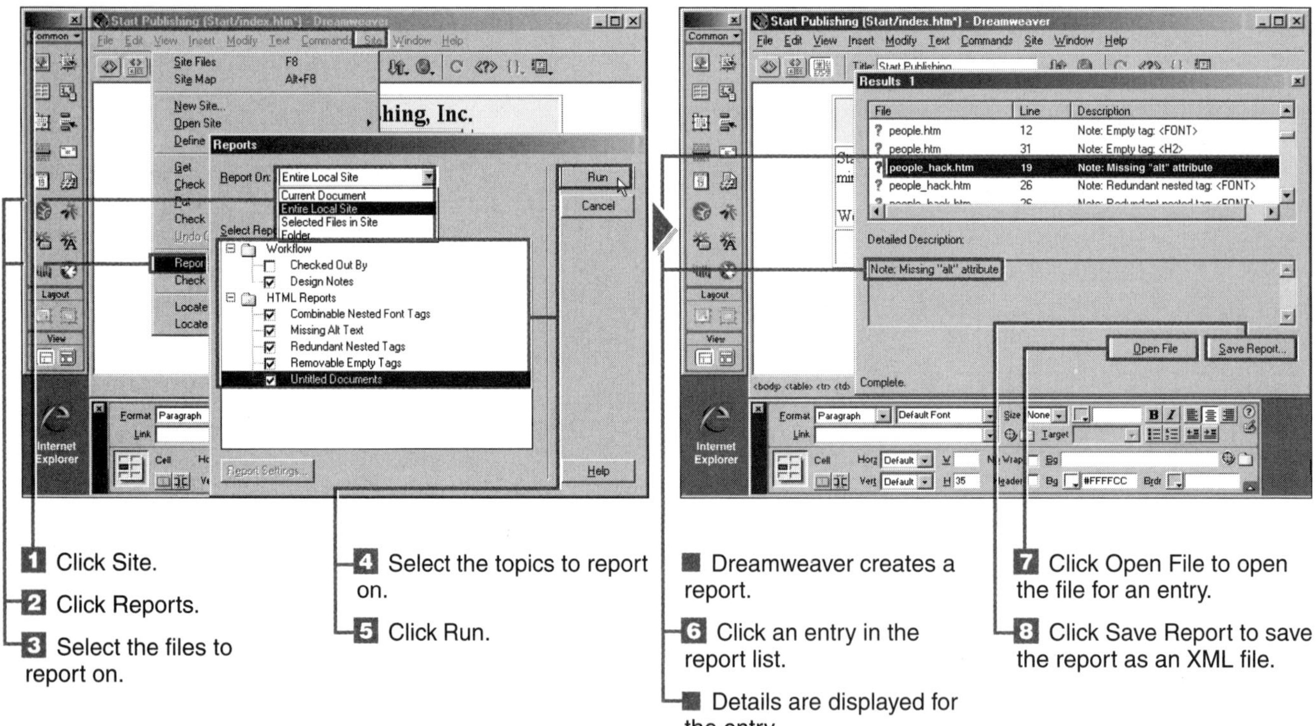

1 Click Site.

2 Click Reports.

3 Select the files to report on.

4 Select the topics to report on.

5 Click Run.

■ Dreamweaver creates a report.

6 Click an entry in the report list.

■ Details are displayed for the entry.

7 Click Open File to open the file for an entry.

8 Click Save Report to save the report as an XML file.

CHANGE A LINK SITEWIDE

An important task when maintaining a Web site is keeping all the hyperlinks working and up to date. The Change Link Sitewide command lets you search for and replace hyperlink references when those references need to be fixed or updated. Hyperlinks can break when you delete or rename files on your site, or when pages that you link to externally get deleted or renamed.

The Change Link Sitewide command is useful if you have content on your page that changes on a regular basis, such as a page that displays a monthly schedule. The Change Link Sitewide command can let you easily update links to a new schedule file each month.

This command is also useful if you point to an external Web page in several places on your site, and the address of that page changes. You can update the links to that page by entering full URLs into the Change Link Sitewide dialog box.

You can also use the command to change e-mail (mailto:) links. This can come in handy if a contact e-mail address for a site changes.

CHANGE A LINK SITEWIDE

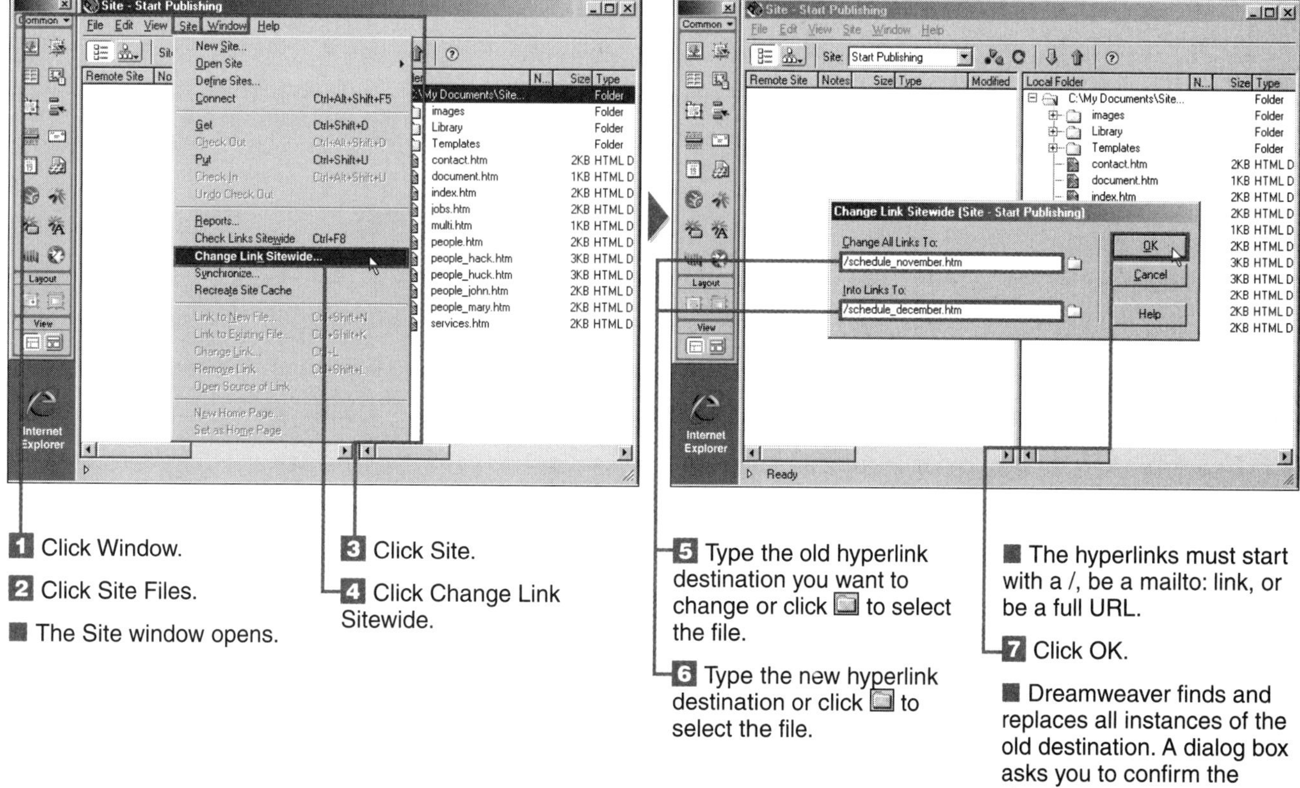

1 Click Window.

2 Click Site Files.

■ The Site window opens.

3 Click Site.

4 Click Change Link Sitewide.

5 Type the old hyperlink destination you want to change or click [folder icon] to select the file.

6 Type the new hyperlink destination or click [folder icon] to select the file.

■ The hyperlinks must start with a /, be a mailto: link, or be a full URL.

7 Click OK.

■ Dreamweaver finds and replaces all instances of the old destination. A dialog box asks you to confirm the changes.

FIND AND REPLACE TEXT

With Dreamweaver's Find and Replace feature, you can search for text on your Web page, text in your source code, or specific HTML tags in your pages. You can also perform searches across the current document, a set of selected documents, a folder, or the entire site. After searching, you can replace some or all of the instances where your search query was found.

The Find and Replace feature is a powerful tool for making changes to text elements that repeat across many pages. A search query can be something as small as a copyright date in a page footer or something as complex as a nested HTML table.

The HTML tag search enables you to specifically remove, replace, or edit the tags or attributes of tags in your pages. There is also an advanced text search that lets you find text only if it appears inside a specific HTML tag.

You can add even more power to your Find and Replace queries with Regular Expressions, which enable you to add wild card characters to your search queries. See "Search for Patterns of Text" for more information.

FIND AND REPLACE TEXT

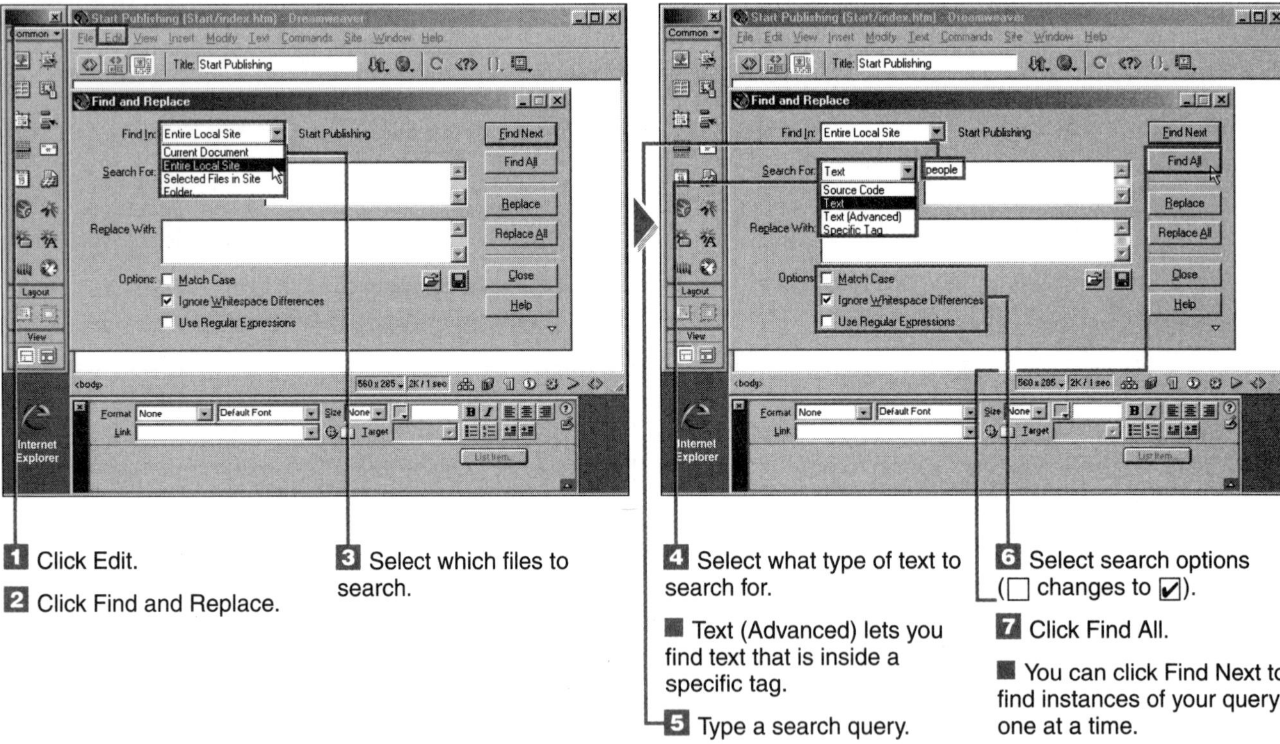

1 Click Edit.

2 Click Find and Replace.

3 Select which files to search.

4 Select what type of text to search for.

■ Text (Advanced) lets you find text that is inside a specific tag.

5 Type a search query.

6 Select search options (☐ changes to ☑).

7 Click Find All.

■ You can click Find Next to find instances of your query one at a time.

How do I search through a select group of files in my site?

✔ Control-click (Windows) or Shift-click (Mac) the files in the Site window before performing the Find and Replace. Be sure to choose Selected Files in Site in the Find In menu. Clicking Find All searches for text in only the files you selected.

Do searches of the source code find JavaScript and style-sheet code?

✔ Yes. It finds any text that is in a page's source code, which can include JavaScript and style-sheet code.

Why might I want to find and replace an HTML attribute?

✔ You can replace attributes to achieve many things. You can change the alignment of the contents of a table (change `align="center"` to `align="right"` in `<td>` tags), change the color of specific text in your page (change `color="red"` to `color="green"` in `<font>` tags), or change the page background color across your site (change `bgcolor="black"` to `bgcolor="white"` in `<body>` tags).

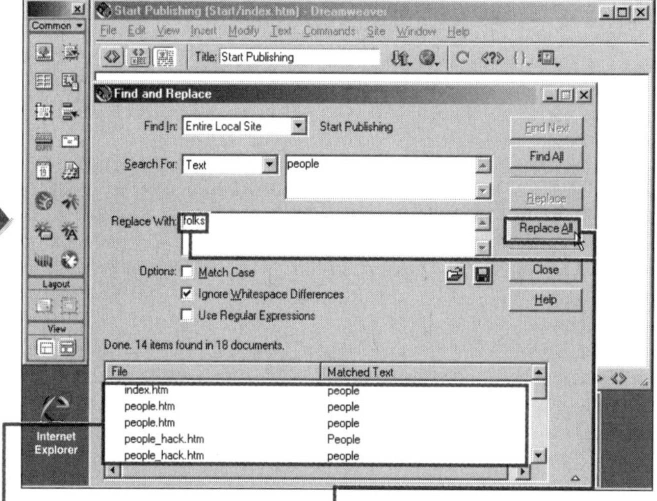

■ Dreamweaver displays an alert box telling you if it found anything.

8 Click OK to close the alert box.

■ The results of your search are displayed.

9 Type your replacement text.

10 Click Replace All.

■ You can also click to select items in the found list and then click Replace to replace them individually.

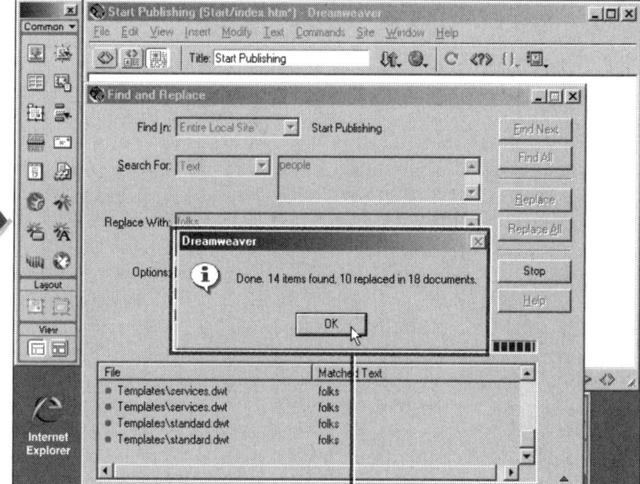

■ An alert box may appear asking if you want to replace text in documents that are not open. Click OK.

■ An alert box displays the results of the replace.

SEARCH FOR PATTERNS OF TEXT

There may be times when you want to search for a *pattern* of text in your pages rather than a specific string of letters. You can search for patterns in Dreamweaver by using regular expressions, which enable you to substitute special wild-card characters in your search queries. You turn on regular expressions in your queries by clicking a check box at the bottom of the Find and Replace dialog box.

Some common regular-expression symbols include the following:

* matches the character it follows 0 or more times.

+ matches the character it follows 1 or more times.

? matches the character it follows 0 or 1 time.

With regular expressions turned on, the query `eb*` matches "eb" in "web," "ebb" in "webby," and "e" in "went." The query `eb+` matches "eb" in "web" and "ebb" in "webby," but nothing in "went" (because for `eb+`, patterns must contain at least one "b").

Other special symbols include

^ matches the beginning of a line.

$ matches the end of a line.

. matches any single character except a newline.

`\w` matches any alphanumeric character, including underscore.

With regular expressions turned on, the query `^M.*` matches all the lines in a document that begin with "M."

For more information, see www.mediacosm.com/dreamweaver/.

SEARCH FOR PATTERNS OF TEXT

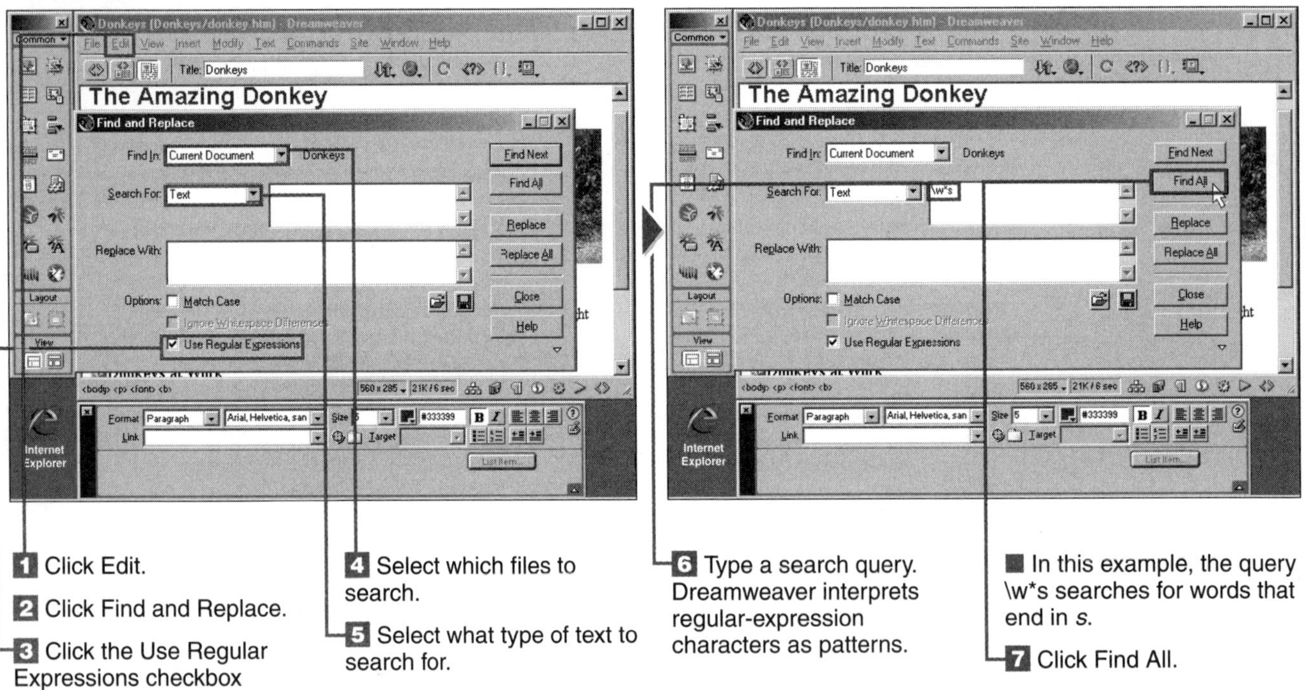

1 Click Edit.

2 Click Find and Replace.

3 Click the Use Regular Expressions checkbox (☐ changes to ☑).

4 Select which files to search.

5 Select what type of text to search for.

6 Type a search query. Dreamweaver interprets regular-expression characters as patterns.

■ In this example, the query \w*s searches for words that end in *s*.

7 Click Find All.

With regular expressions turned on, how do I search for characters in my code that have a special meaning (for example * or ?)?

✔ You must "escape" these characters with a preceding \ (for example, * or \?). A preceding backslash tells Dreamweaver that characters such as * and ? need to be treated as regular characters in a query.

How can I save my search patterns?

✔ You can save a search pattern by clicking 💾 in the Find and Replace dialog box. This can be handy if you have a complicated regular-expression search that you might want to use again. Clicking 📂 lets you access search patterns that you have saved.

How do I specify white space in a regular expression?

✔ There are various special characters that match different types of white space:

`\r` matches a carriage return

`\t` matches a tab

`\s` matches any single white-space character (space, carriage return, tab, and so on)

These special characters can be mixed with others. For example, `\s+` matches one or more white-space characters.

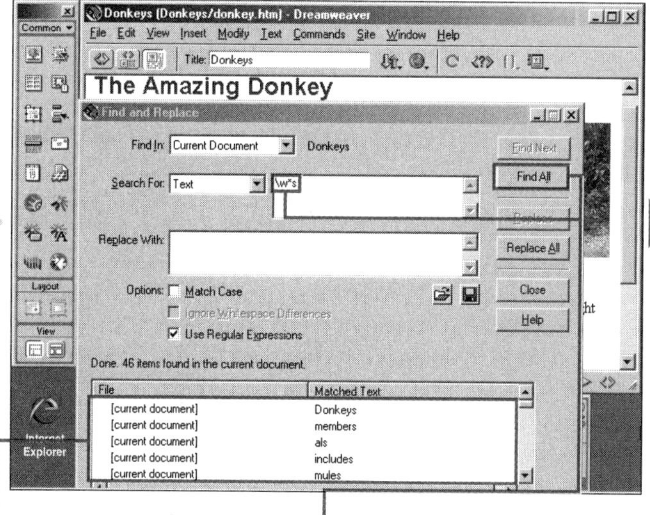

■ Dreamweaver displays an alert box telling you if it found anything.

8 Click OK to close the alert box.

■ The results of your search are displayed.

9 You can edit your search query to look for a different pattern.

■ With this second query, \w*es searches for words that end in *es*.

10 Click Find All.

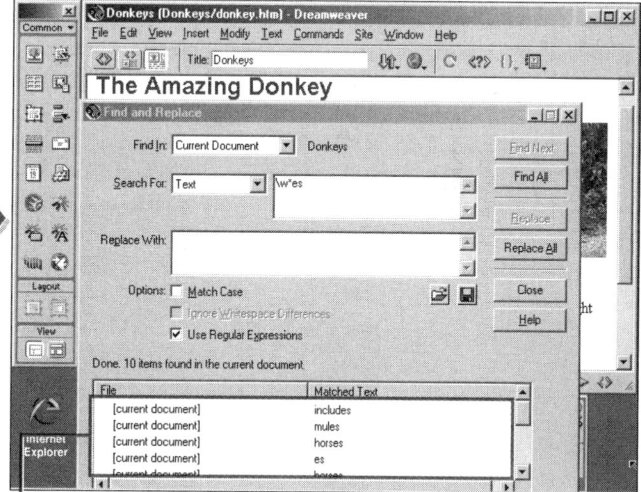

■ Dreamweaver displays a results list for the revised query.

SECTION II

17) GETTING STARTED WITH FLASH 264

18) DRAWING AND PAINTING OBJECTS 282

19) ENHANCING AND EDITING OBJECTS 302

20) WORKING WITH TEXT 334

21) WORKING WITH LAYERS 344

22) WORKING WITH FLASH SYMBOLS AND INSTANCES 358

23) WORKING WITH IMPORTED GRAPHICS 372

USING FLASH

24) ANIMATION TECHNIQUES 380

25) ANIMATING WITH TWEENING 412

26) CREATING INTERACTIVE BUTTONS 446

27) ADDING SOUNDS 464

28) ADDING FLASH ACTIONS 488

29) USING ADVANCED INTERACTIVE FEATURES 506

30) DISTRIBUTING FLASH MOVIES .520

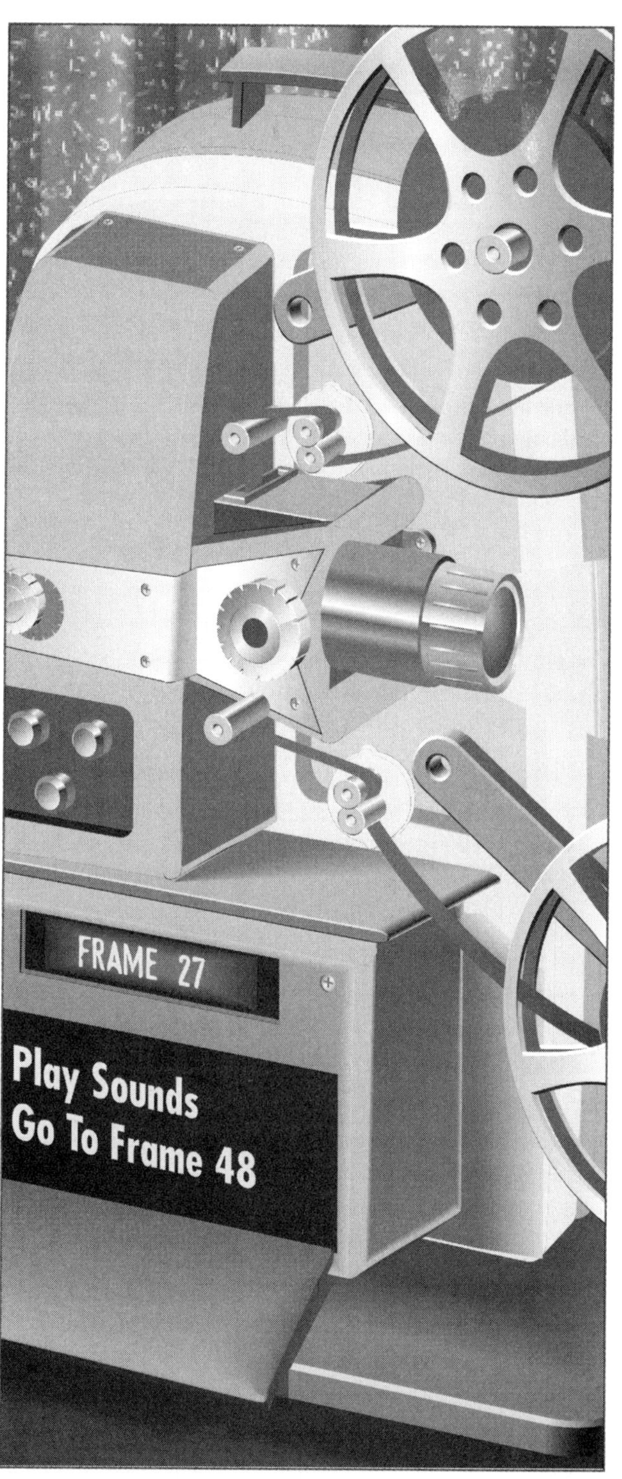

AN INTRODUCTION TO FLASH

Macromedia Flash has quickly become the standard for creating lively vector art and animation on the Web. Most browsers include a Flash player for displaying and playing Flash movies.

Flash is the perfect tool for both new and experienced Web page designers who want to create expressive, dynamic Web page elements. With Flash's many tools, you can add interactivity to page elements such as banner ads and navigation buttons, and you can animate graphic objects, create cartoons and movies, and coordinate accompanying sounds.

Flash humbly started out as another program. Originally called Future Splash Animator, the program was designed to help make and animate vector art. Macromedia purchased the program in 1997, changed its name to Flash, and marketed it for the Web. It has experienced phenomenal growth ever since.

Flash offers easy-to-use drawing tools as well as top-of-the-line animation features. The program includes a publishing feature that produces the necessary HTML code for displaying the animation effects in browsers. In addition to Web animation, Flash enables you to play movies on a local computer in the Flash Player format as well as alternative formats.

What Is So Special about Flash?

Flash is a versatile multimedia-authoring program. One component of this multifunctional program is its vector-based drawing tools for creating graphics for the Internet. Most graphics you encounter on the Web are *raster,* or *bitmap, graphics,* such as JPEGs and GIFs. Raster graphics consist of pixels in a grid with each pixel containing information on how to display the intensity and color of the image. Raster graphics, due to their size, take longer to display on a Web page. Every Web surfer has experienced the frustration of waiting for raster graphics to display.

Vector-based graphics, such as those you can create in Flash, are much smaller in file size. Rather than rely on pixels to define an image, vector-based graphics use mathematical coordinates to define an image. As such, the image is much easier to scale and incredibly compact in size. Vector graphics display much faster on a downloading Web page and are a much more efficient method of delivering images over the Internet.

After you draw a vector-based graphic in Flash, you can save the object in the file's library to be used throughout your project. You can also borrow graphics from other Flash movies.

If you are not too keen on drawing your own graphics, you can also import graphics from other programs. supports BMP, G JPEG, PICT, and PNG file types. You can also convert bitmap graphics into vector graphics or use other Flash tools to optimize the graphic's file size.

Animate with Flash

Another reason Flash is widely used is its animation tools. Flash frames let you animate graphics you create with Flash or any other graphic-editing program. You can easily animate graphic objects, buttons, and even text. You can create mini-movies that play on Web pages or as self-extracting files.

The animation techniques used in Flash are based on animation techniques employed by early cartoonists. Animators of yesteryear painstakingly drew graphic objects onto transparent cells and stacked the cells to create a single image for a single movie frame. They reused images that stayed the same throughout the animation, such as backgrounds, and added new images whenever there was a key change in the animation sequence. Flash works in a similar fashion, allowing you to layer objects to create backgrounds and reuse objects throughout a movie.

Add Interactivity

You can also create interactive Web page features using Flash, such as a button that performs an action as soon as the user moves the mouse pointer over it or a button that, when clicked, starts playing a Flash movie. You can use Flash to create interactive elements, such as forms or search engines, or complex interactive elements such as games. With a little imagination and Flash know-how, you can create all kinds of interactive elements using Flash.

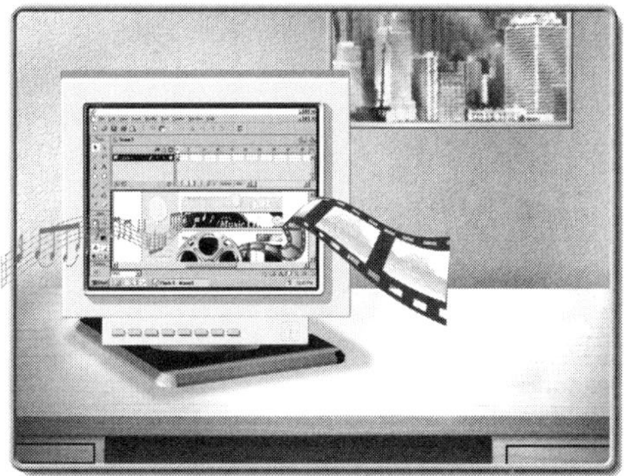

Add Sound

In addition to its graphics and animating features, Flash also has controls for adding and manipulating sound files. You can include sound effects or music files with animation for added pizzazz and interest. For example, you can add a background sound to play along with a movie or a narration that corresponds with several movie frames. You can also add sound effect clips to various parts of your animations or buttons, such as clicking noise the user hears when he clicks on a button in your movie.

NAVIGATE THE FLASH WINDOW

The Flash program window has several components for working with graphics and movies. Take time to familiarize yourself with the on-screen elements. The Flash program window varies slightly in appearance between the Windows version and the Mac version, but the features and tools all work the same.

Flash in the Windows Environment

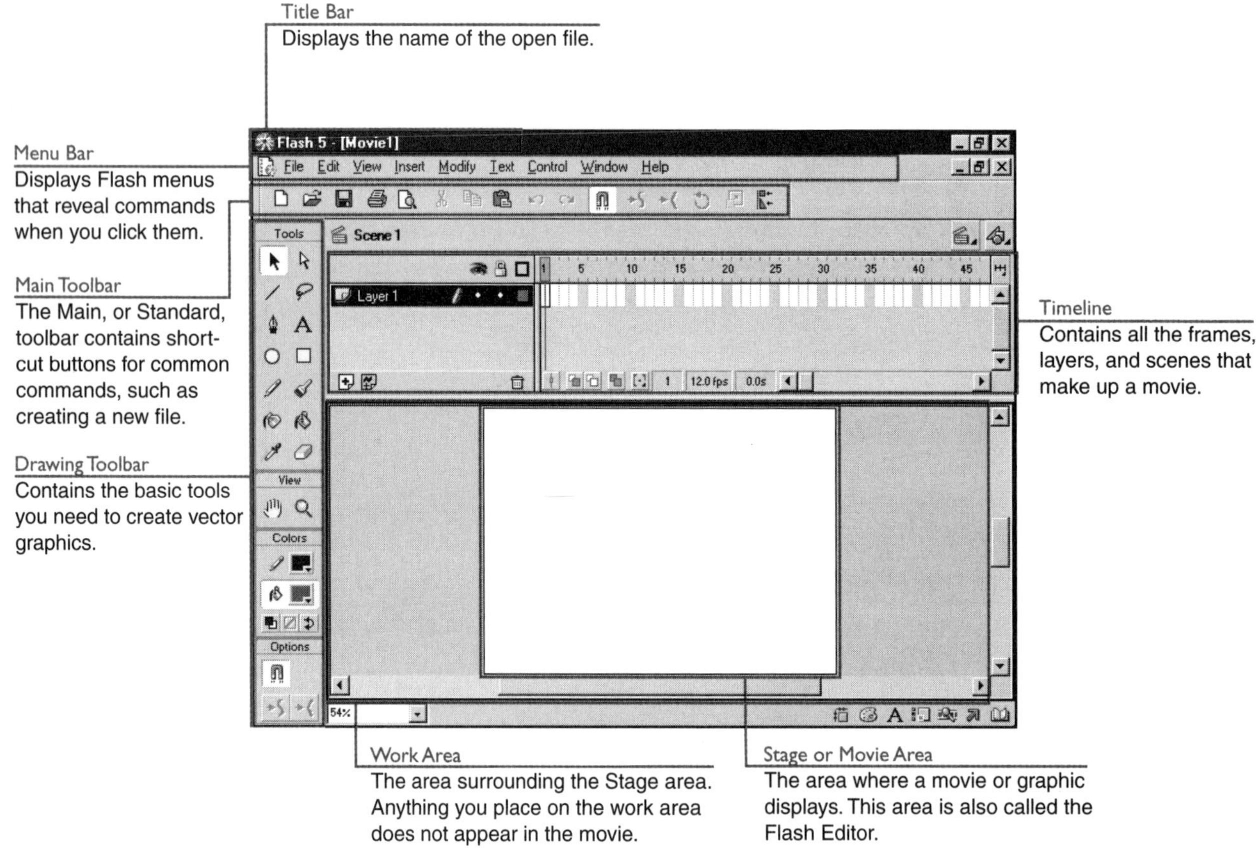
Title Bar
Displays the name of the open file.
Menu Bar
Displays Flash menus that reveal commands when you click them.
Main Toolbar
The Main, or Standard, toolbar contains shortcut buttons for common commands, such as creating a new file.
Drawing Toolbar
Contains the basic tools you need to create vector graphics.
Timeline
Contains all the frames, layers, and scenes that make up a movie.
Work Area
The area surrounding the Stage area. Anything you place on the work area does not appear in the movie.
Stage or Movie Area
The area where a movie or graphic displays. This area is also called the Flash Editor.
Flash 5 - [Movie1]
File Edit View Insert Modify Text Control Window Help
Tools
Scene 1
Layer 1
View
Colors
Options
12.0 fps
0.0s
54%

Flash on a Macintosh

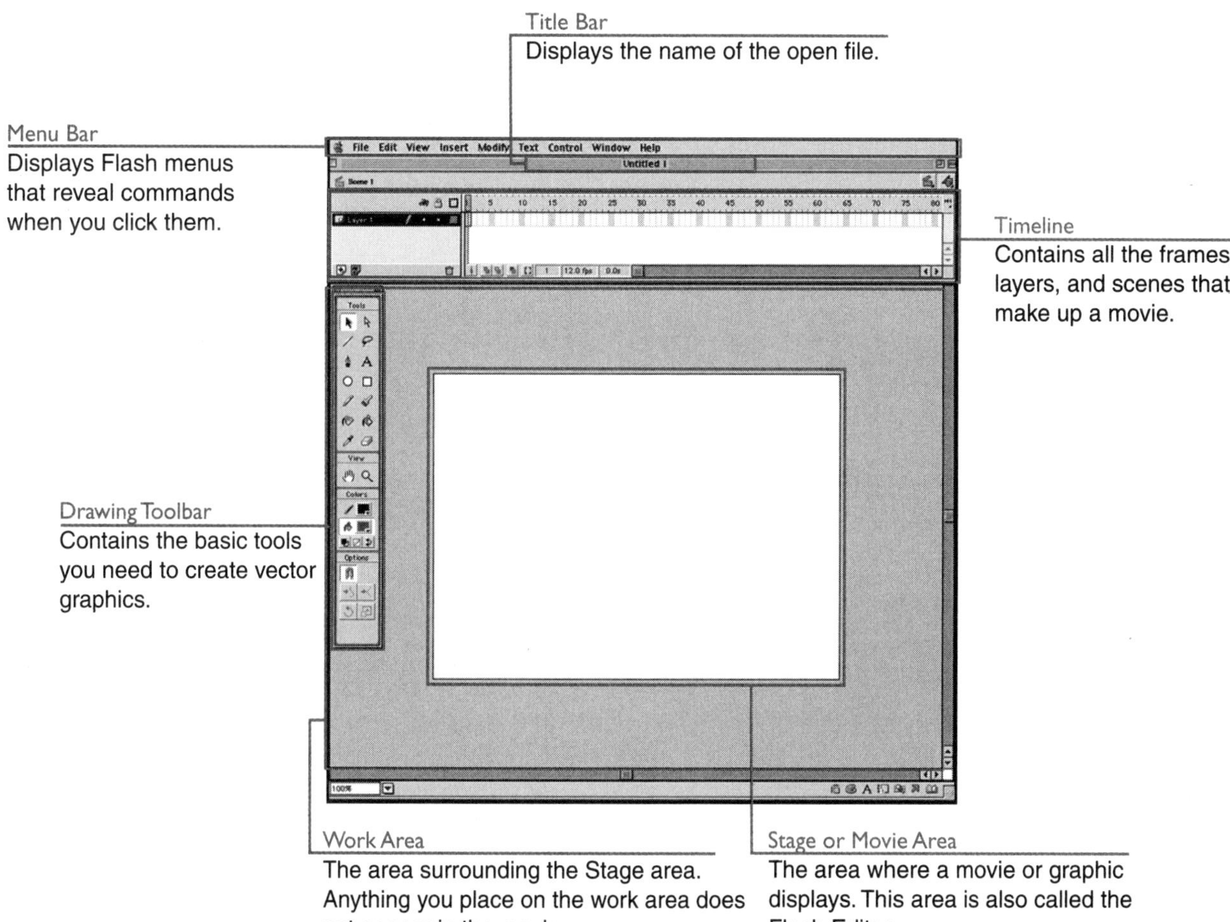
Title Bar
Displays the name of the open file.
Menu Bar
Displays Flash menus that reveal commands when you click them.
Timeline
Contains all the frames, layers, and scenes that make up a movie.
Drawing Toolbar
Contains the basic tools you need to create vector graphics.
Work Area
The area surrounding the Stage area. Anything you place on the work area does not appear in the movie.
Stage or Movie Area
The area where a movie or graphic displays. This area is also called the Flash Editor.

CONTINUED

NAVIGATE THE FLASH WINDOW (CONTINUED)

Navigate with the Mouse or Keyboard

Whether you are using a PC or a Mac, you can use the mouse to move around the Flash window, select tools, and activate menus. To activate a button or menu, move the mouse pointer over the item and click it.

There are also numerous shortcut menus you can activate with the mouse by right-clicking over the on-screen item on which you are working. A pop-up menu appears listing commands pertaining to the task.

You can also use the keyboard to select commands. For example, Windows users can display the Text menu by pressing and holding the Alt key and then pressing the letter T. To activate a command, press the corresponding underlined character.

You can find keyboard shortcut commands scattered throughout the menus. Keyboard shortcuts are listed beside menu commands, where applicable, for both the Mac and Windows versions of Flash.

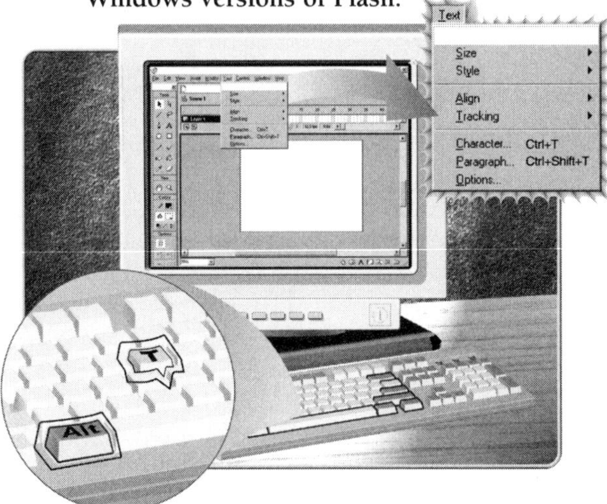

Navigate with the Scroll Bars

Depending on the size of your Flash project, you can use the scroll bars to move your view of the Stage area to see different portions of your drawing. Click the scroll arrow boxes to quickly move your view of the Stage up, down, right, or left. You can also click and drag the scroll boxes to move your view.

Navigate Component Windows

The first time you use Flash after installing the program, a number of mini-windows may appear open on-screen. These mini-windows act much like dialog boxes found in other programs and are called panels in Flash. They hold numerous options for controlling or editing your Flash projects.

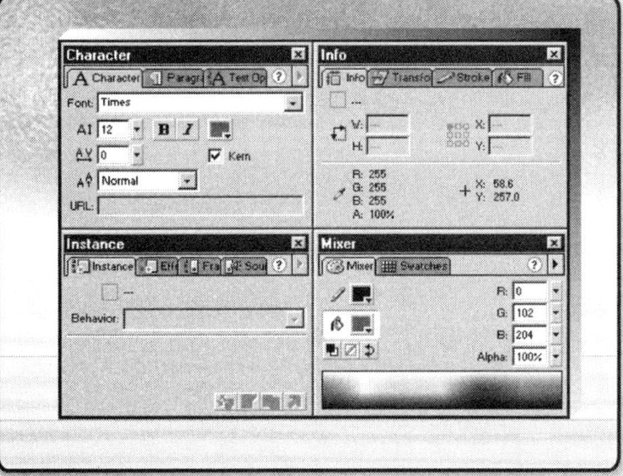

Related options within each mini-window are grouped into tabs. For example, you can find a variety of text formatting controls on the Character tab. When the Character options are displayed, the panel is called the Character panel. If you click the Paragraph tab, a different set of options is displayed, and the name in the panel's title bar changes to Paragraph.

With the default panel set open on-screen, much of the Stage area is covered up. Close the panels to free up on-screen workspace.

To close an open panel, simply click the panel's ⊠ button. Mac users can click the Mac Close box (▣).

As you begin to use Flash, you may decide to keep one or more features or panels open in order to quickly access commands pertinent to the task you are performing. For example, you may want to display both the Library window and the Sound panel on-screen as you work.

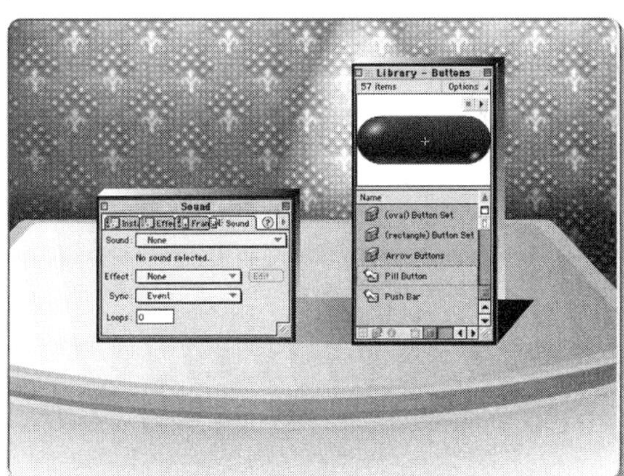

OPEN A FLASH FILE

Flash files are called *documents* or *movies*. When you save a file, you can open it and work on it again. Flash files can be as simple as a drawing you have created using the Flash drawing tools or as complex as an animation sequence consisting of scenes and interactive elements.

There are several ways to access Flash files you have previously saved. Flash keeps track of the last four files you have worked with and lists them at the bottom of the File menu. You can display the menu and select the file you want to open.

To open other Flash files, use the Open dialog box. The Open dialog box in Flash works similarly to the Open dialog box found in other programs. You can open Flash files of all types, including files created using older versions of Flash.

You can also start a new file whenever you want. Every new file you start in Flash uses a default Stage size. To learn more about setting the Stage dimensions, see the section "Change the Stage Size."

OPEN A FLASH FILE

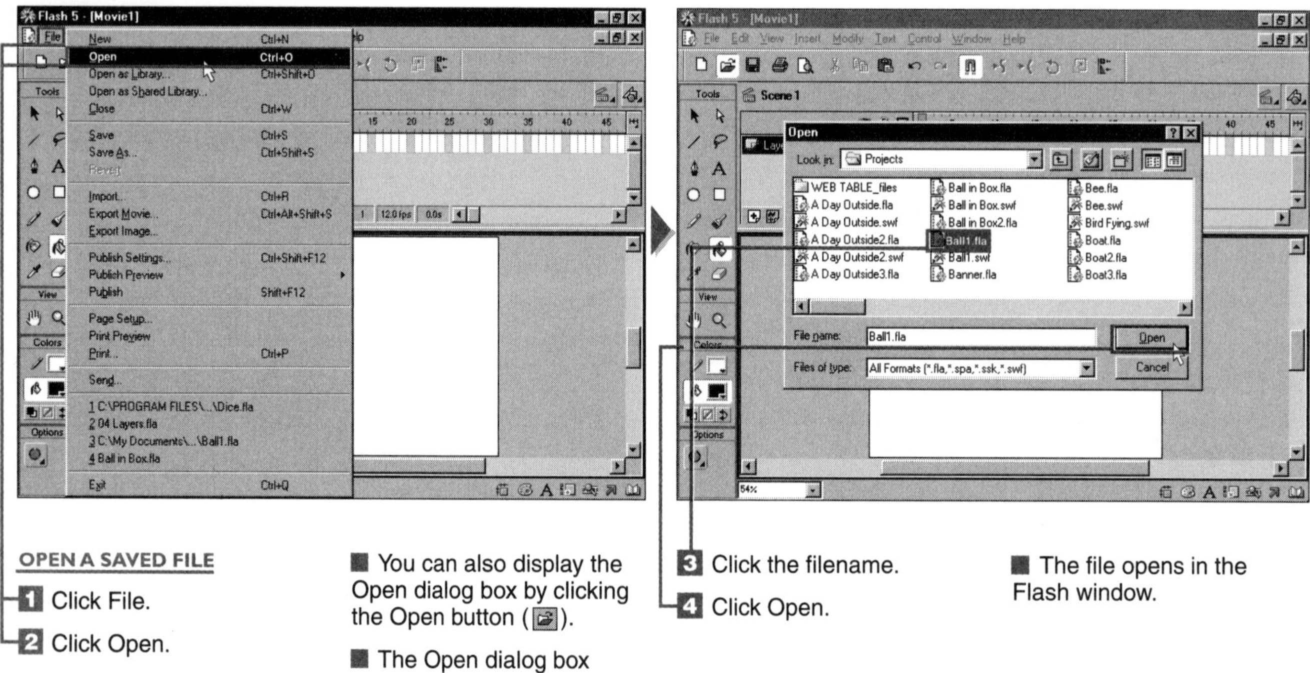

OPEN A SAVED FILE

1 Click File.

2 Click Open.

■ You can also display the Open dialog box by clicking the Open button (📂).

■ The Open dialog box appears.

3 Click the filename.

4 Click Open.

■ The file opens in the Flash window.

I cannot see my Main toolbar? Why?

✔ If you are looking for the Open or New buttons and cannot find them, the Main toolbar is not displayed. If you share your computer with other users, someone may have hidden the Main toolbar. To display the Main toolbar again, click Windows, Toolbar, and then Main.

Is there a limit to how many Flash files I can have open?

✔ No, there is no limit. However, keep in mind that the more files you open, the slower your computer becomes. Graphics files, such as those you author in Flash, can take up more processing power than other programs. Unless you are sharing data between the files, it is a good idea to close Flash files you are no longer using.

Can I open other file types besides Flash files?

✔ Yes. To open other file formats, such as QuickTime movies, use the Import command. Click File and then Import. This opens the Import dialog box, which looks just like the Open dialog box. From there, you can locate the file type and import it into Flash.

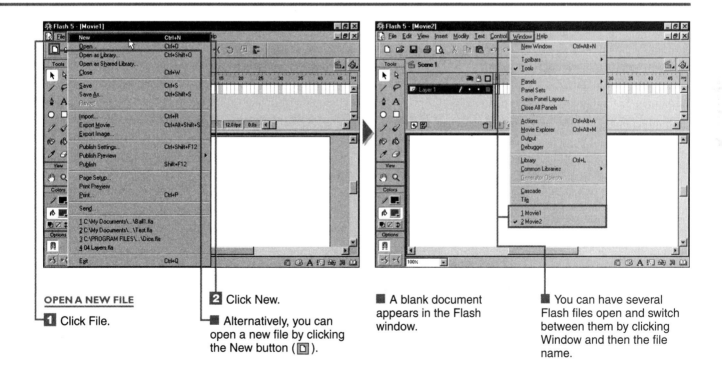

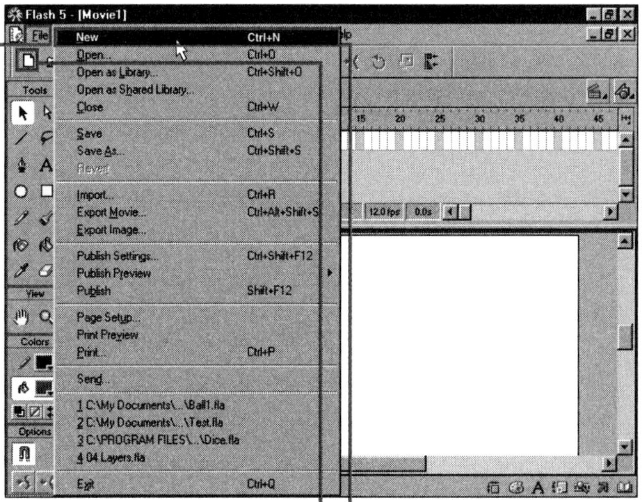

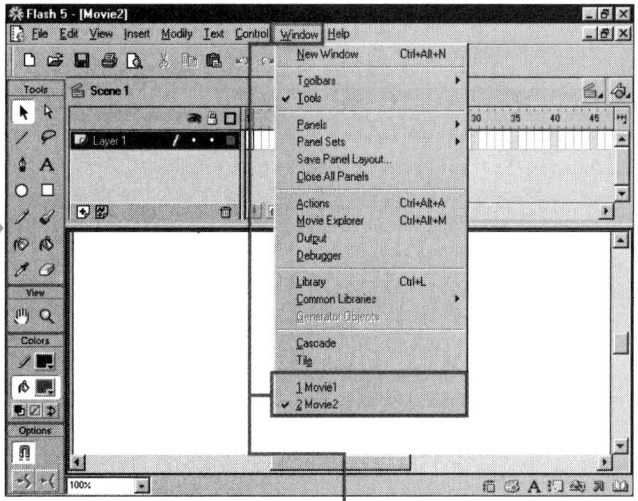

OPEN A NEW FILE

1 Click File.

2 Click New.

■ Alternatively, you can open a new file by clicking the New button ( ).

■ A blank document appears in the Flash window.

■ You can have several Flash files open and switch between them by clicking Window and then the file name.

SAVE AND CLOSE A FLASH FILE

As you create movies in Flash, you need to save them in order to work on them again. By default, Flash saves all files in the FLA file format. After you complete a Flash movie, you can publish it to a Web page or to a self-extracting file, both of which use another file format. To learn more about the Flash publishing options, turn to Chapter 30.

To perform a simple save, you can close just the file or close both the file and the Flash program. If you have not saved your changes, Flash prompts you to do so.

SAVE A FILE

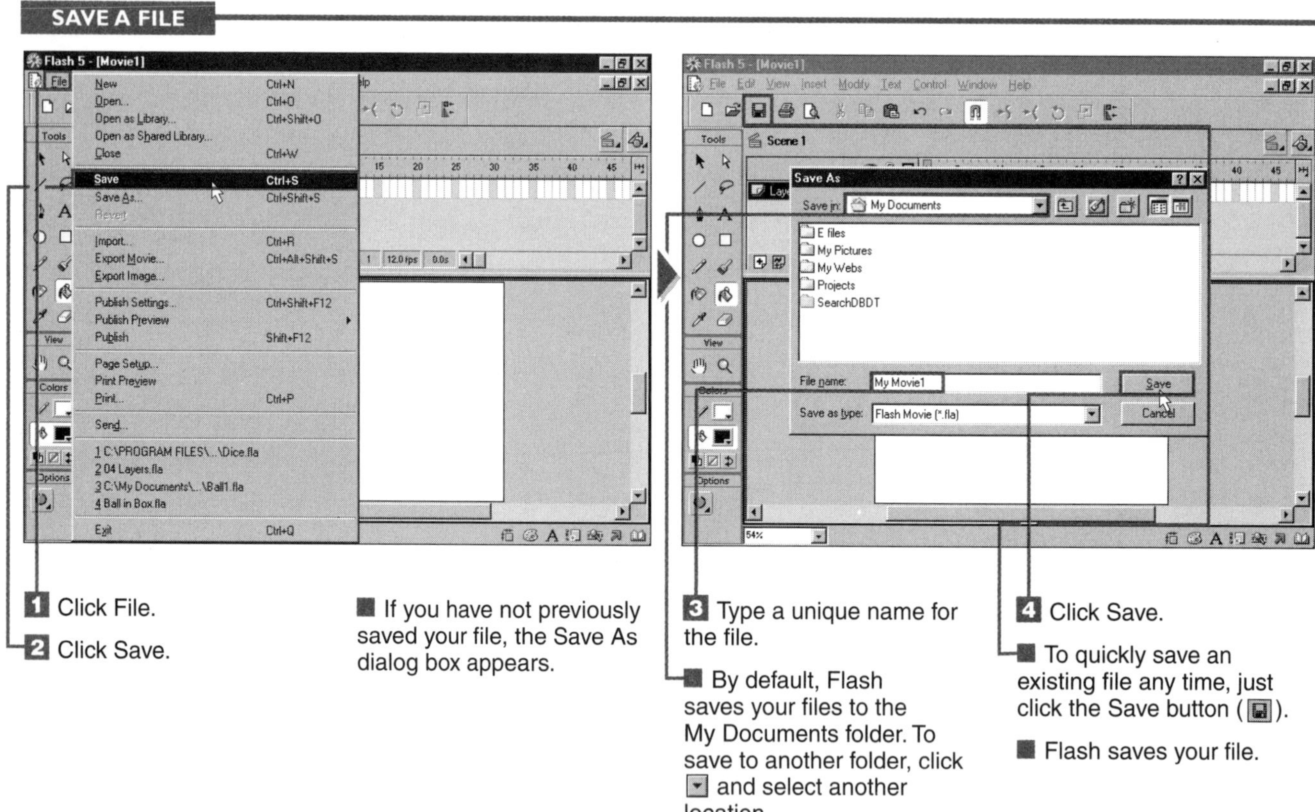

1 Click File.

2 Click Save.

■ If you have not previously saved your file, the Save As dialog box appears.

3 Type a unique name for the file.

■ By default, Flash saves your files to the My Documents folder. To save to another folder, click ▾ and select another location.

4 Click Save.

■ To quickly save an existing file any time, just click the Save button (💾).

■ Flash saves your file.

How do I save a previously saved file under a new name?

✔ You can copy a previously saved file and save it under a new filename. You can then make changes to the copied file without worrying about changing the original file. To do so, click File and then Save As. This opens the Save As dialog box. Enter a new name for the file and click Save.

Can I save a Flash file in another file format?

✔ Yes, but you cannot use the Save command to do so. Instead, you must use the Export Movie command. For example, if you prefer to save a file as a QuickTime movie or a Windows AVI file, click File and then Export Movie to open the Export dialog box. Click the Save as Type ▾ and select another file type from the list. Give the file a unique filename and click Save.

CLOSE A FILE

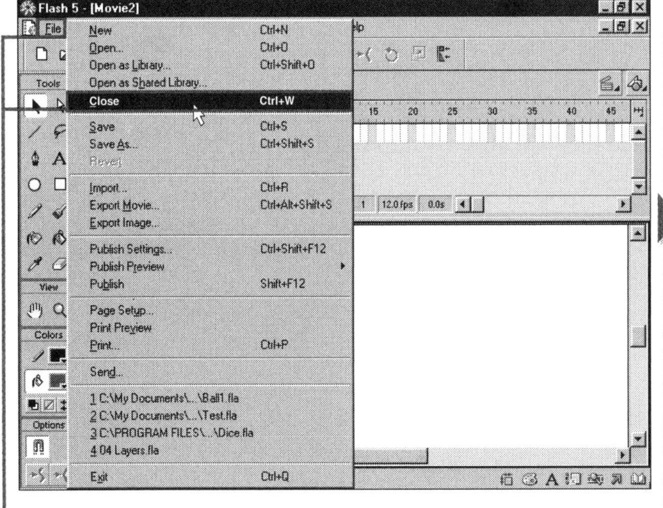

1 Save your file.

Note: See the subsection "Save a File."

2 Click File.

3 Click Close.

Note: If you have not saved your changes, Flash prompts you to do so with a dialog box. Click Yes.

■ Flash closes the file, but the program window remains open.

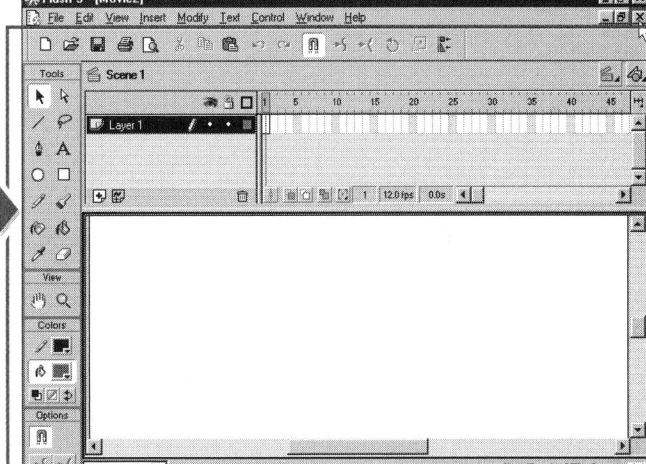

USING THE CLOSE BUTTON

1 Save your file.

Note: See the subsection "Save a File."

2 Click the file's Close button (☒).

Note: If you have not saved your changes, Flash prompts you to do so with a dialog box. Click Yes.

■ Flash closes the file.

Note: Clicking the program window's (☒) button closes the Flash application entirely and may result in lost files.

UNDERSTAND THE FLASH TIMELINE

The Flash Timeline contains the frames, layers, and scenes that make up a movie. You can use the Timeline to organize and control your movies.

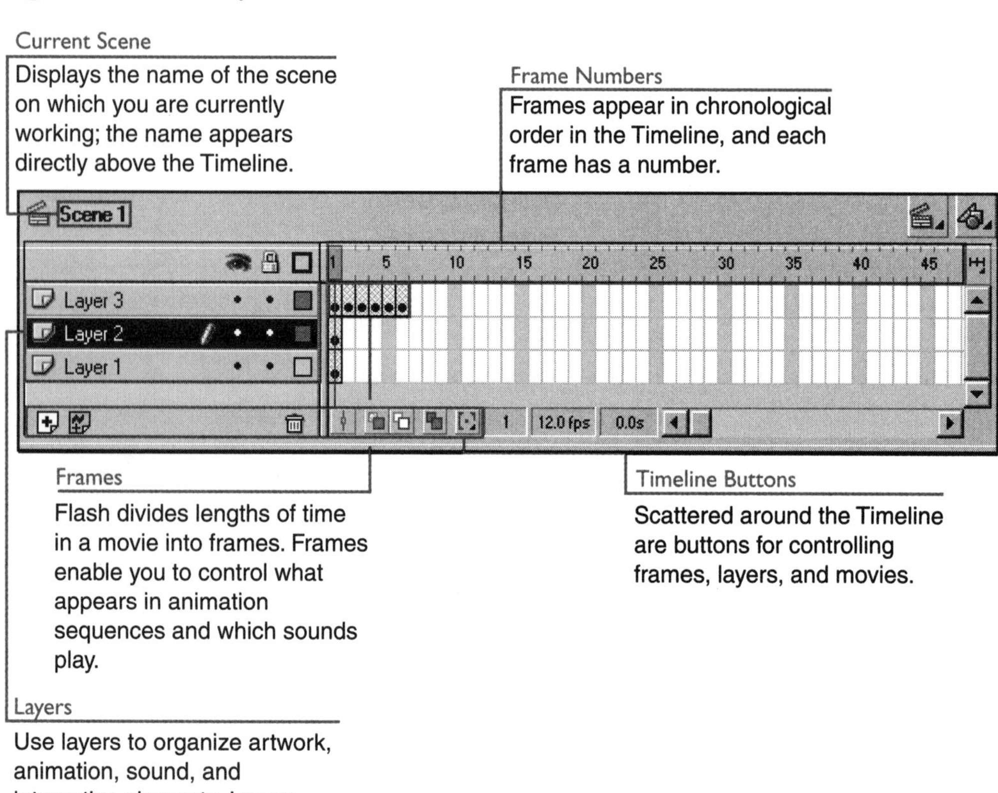

Current Scene

Displays the name of the scene on which you are currently working; the name appears directly above the Timeline.

Frame Numbers

Frames appear in chronological order in the Timeline, and each frame has a number.

Frames

Flash divides lengths of time in a movie into frames. Frames enable you to control what appears in animation sequences and which sounds play.

Timeline Buttons

Scattered around the Timeline are buttons for controlling frames, layers, and movies.

Layers

Use layers to organize artwork, animation, sound, and interactive elements. Layers enable you to keep pieces of artwork separate. Flash combines them to form a cohesive image. For example, a company logo may include a layer of text and another layer with a graphic shape.

Playhead and Frame Display

The Playhead, also called the Current Frame Indicator, marks the current frame displayed on the Stage.

Click a frame to display its contents on the Stage and move the Playhead. You can also drag the Playhead across the frames to simulate the animation on the Stage.

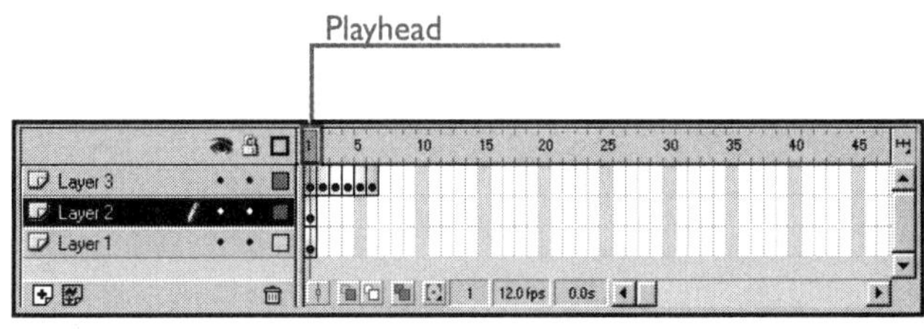

Layers and Layer Buttons

You can have numerous layers in a single frame. Newer layers are listed at the top of the layer stack. Layers help you to organize graphics as well as create backgrounds and masking effects.

Directly above the layer names are icons that represent the layer's status, such as whether a layer is hidden, locked, or outlined on the Flash Stage. Below the layers are buttons for adding and deleting layers. See Chapter 21 to learn more about working with the Timeline layers.

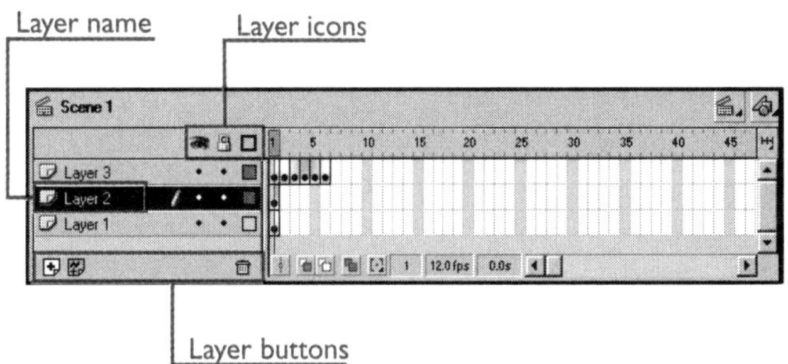

Timeline Controls

Click the Timeline button (▤) to display a drop-down menu of customizing options that control how Flash displays the frames. For example, you can enlarge or shrink the frame size. This is particularly helpful if you are having trouble seeing the individual frames on the Timeline.

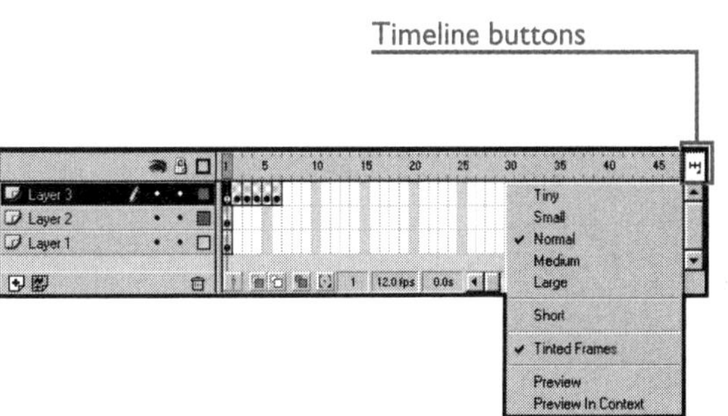

MOVE AND DOCK THE TIMELINE WINDOW

The Flash Timeline is an essential tool for animating graphics. By default, the Timeline appears at the top of the work area; however, you can move the Timeline around the program window or dock it to any side of the window.

You may prefer to move the Timeline out of the way when you are drawing on the Stage, thus giving you more room to draw. In this case, you can hide the Timeline and redisplay it when you need it.

Or you may prefer to dock the Timeline in another position. For example, a vertical docking enables you to see all the layers in the Timeline but decreases the number of frames visible.

When the Timeline is not docked, it appears to float as its own window. You can drag the Timeline's title bar to move the Timeline window around on-screen. You can click the window's ☒ button to close the floating Timeline.

MOVE THE TIMELINE

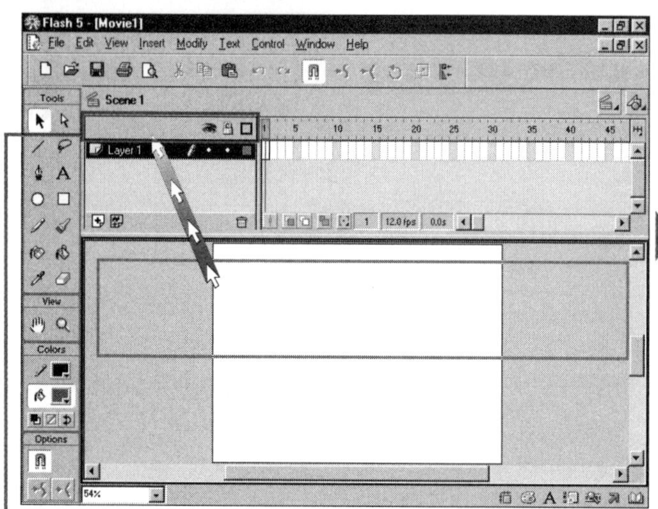

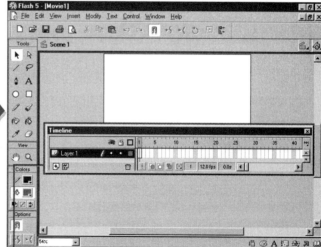

1 Click and drag the Timeline's gray bar area above the layer names.

■ As you drag, an outline of the Timeline moves away from its docked position.

2 Position the Timeline where you want it on-screen.

3 Release the mouse button.

■ Flash repositions the Timeline

Can I hide the Timeline?

✔ If you are drawing vector graphics, you can hide the Timeline to increase your drawing room. Click View and then Timeline. This turns off the Timeline display on-screen. You can also use the keyboard shortcuts Control+Alt+T (Windows) or Option+Command+T (Mac) to toggle the Timeline on or off.

Is there a faster way to dock the Timeline?

✔ You can double-click on the floating Timeline's title bar to quickly dock to the nearest side of the program window.

Can my Timeline be customized?

✔ Flash offers you several customization settings you can use to control the Timeline's appearance. For example, you can enlarge the size of the frames or shorten the layer/frame height. To do so, click to reveal a drop-down menu of Timeline controls and select the customizing feature you want to apply.

DOCK THE TIMELINE

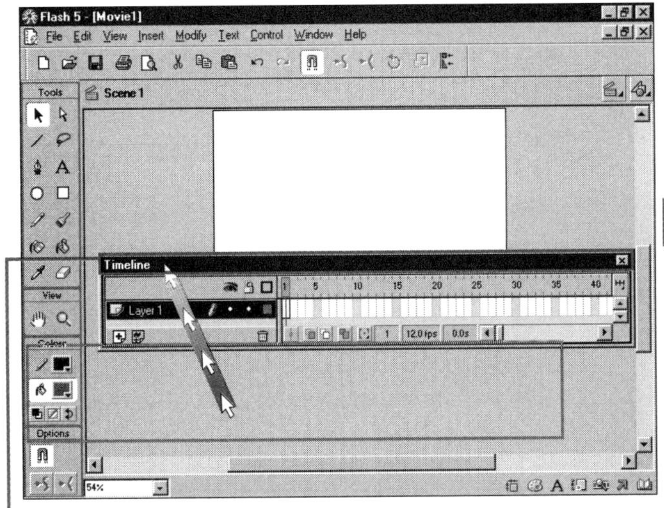

1 Click and drag the Timeline's title bar area to the window edge where you want to dock it.

■ As you drag, an outline of the Timeline moves with the mouse pointer.

2 Release the mouse button.

■ The Timeline docks and resizes to fit the horizontal or vertical space in the program window.

CHANGE THE STAGE SIZE

The Stage is the on-screen area where you can view the contents of a frame and draw graphic objects. You can control the size and appearance of the Stage.

The size of the Stage determines your Flash movie screen size, which you can specify along with the unit of measurement in the Movie Properties dialog box. By default, Flash sets the Stage size at 550 x 400 pixels for every movie file you create, but you can set your own dimensions with the very minimum size being 18x18 pixels, and the maximum being 2,880 x 2,880 pixels.

It is a good idea to set your movie Stage size before adding content to your frames. If you do not, you may have to reposition objects in your movie to fit the Stage size.

The Movie Properties dialog box offers two Match options you can use to determine Stage size: Match Printer or Match Contents. Use the Printer button to change the dimension settings to the maximum print area allowed on your printer. Use the Contents button to set the Stage dimensions to fit all the content with an equal amount of space all around.

CHANGE THE STAGE SIZE

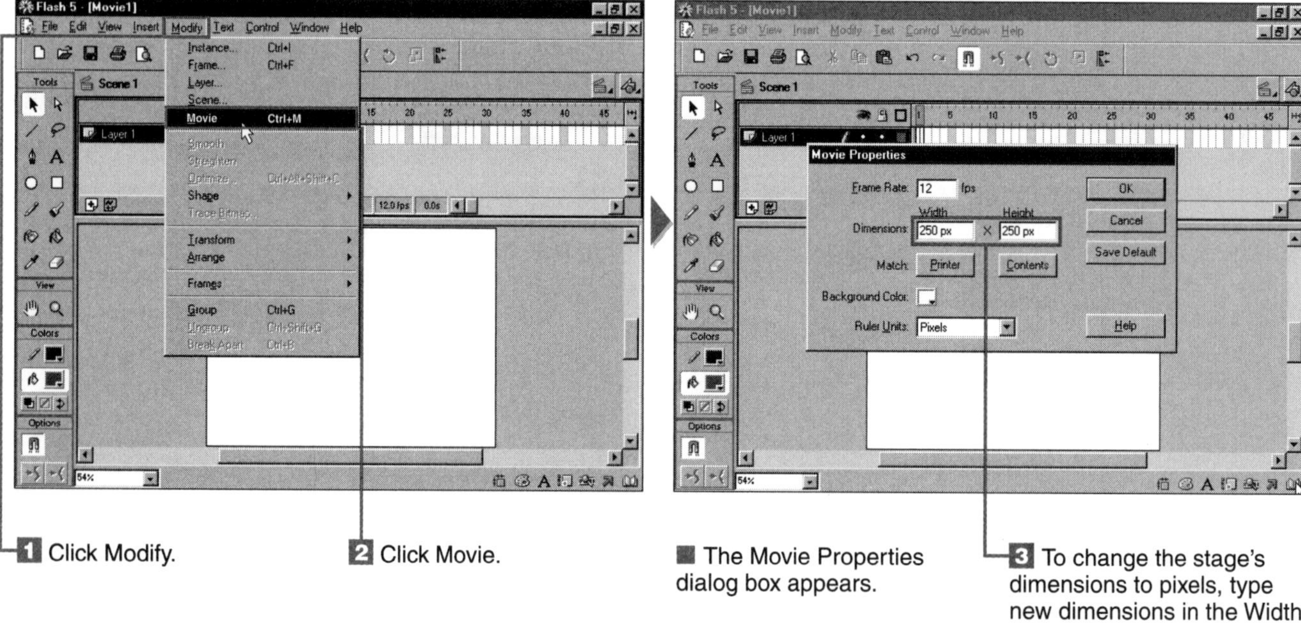

1 Click Modify.

2 Click Movie.

■ The Movie Properties dialog box appears.

3 To change the stage's dimensions to pixels, type new dimensions in the Width and Height boxes.

How do I specify different units of measurement for the Stage?

✔ From the Movie Properties dialog box, click the Ruler Units ▼ and then click on the unit of measurement you want to apply. The unit of measurement immediately changes in the Width and Height text boxes, and you can now set the appropriate measurements.

How can I save the Stage settings for future movies?

✔ Use the Save Default button to save your settings as the default Stage measurements for all Flash movies. Any new Flash project files you create will use the new measurements.

How do I set a new background color?

✔ By default, the Stage background color is set to white. To set another color as a background, click the Background Color button. A pop-up palette of color choices appears. Click the color you want to apply. Flash uses the color you choose throughout your movie as the Stage background color.

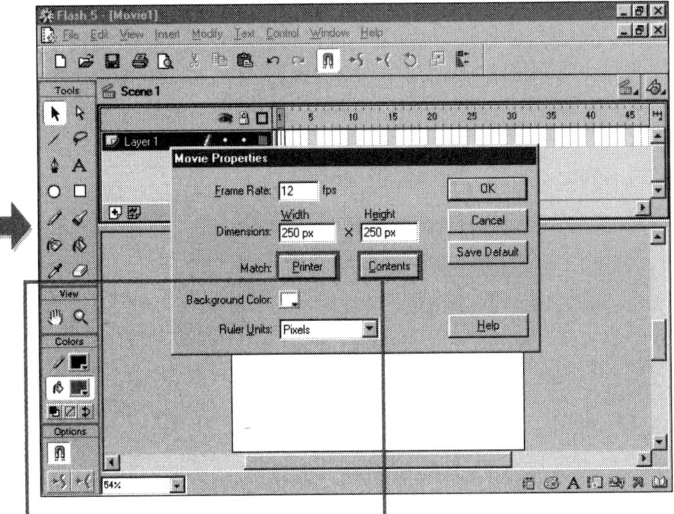

■ Click Printer if you want to match the Stage dimensions to the maximum available print area size used for your printer.

■ Click Contents to change the Stage dimensions to match the contents of your movie with equal spacing all around.

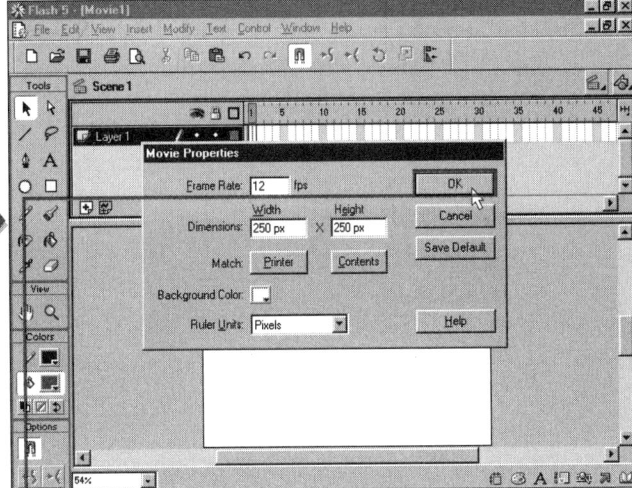

4 Click OK.

■ Flash resizes the Stage area according to your new settings.

FIND HELP WITH FLASH

When you run across a program feature or technique that you do not understand, consult the Flash Help system. The Flash help files offer a wide variety of topics ranging from basic Flash features, such as how to use on-screen buttons and drawing tools, to advance features, such as how to write scripts using ActionScript.

In order to fully utilize the Help features, you must have an Internet connection and access to a Web browser. For example, when you access the offline Help HTML page, your default browser window automatically opens and you can peruse a variety of Flash topics. Other features, like the Flash Support Center, require an Internet connection in order to log on to the Macromedia Web site.

When you install Flash, a number of lessons and sample Flash files are loaded onto your computer. You can use these features to help you learn the program.

FIND HELP WITH FLASH

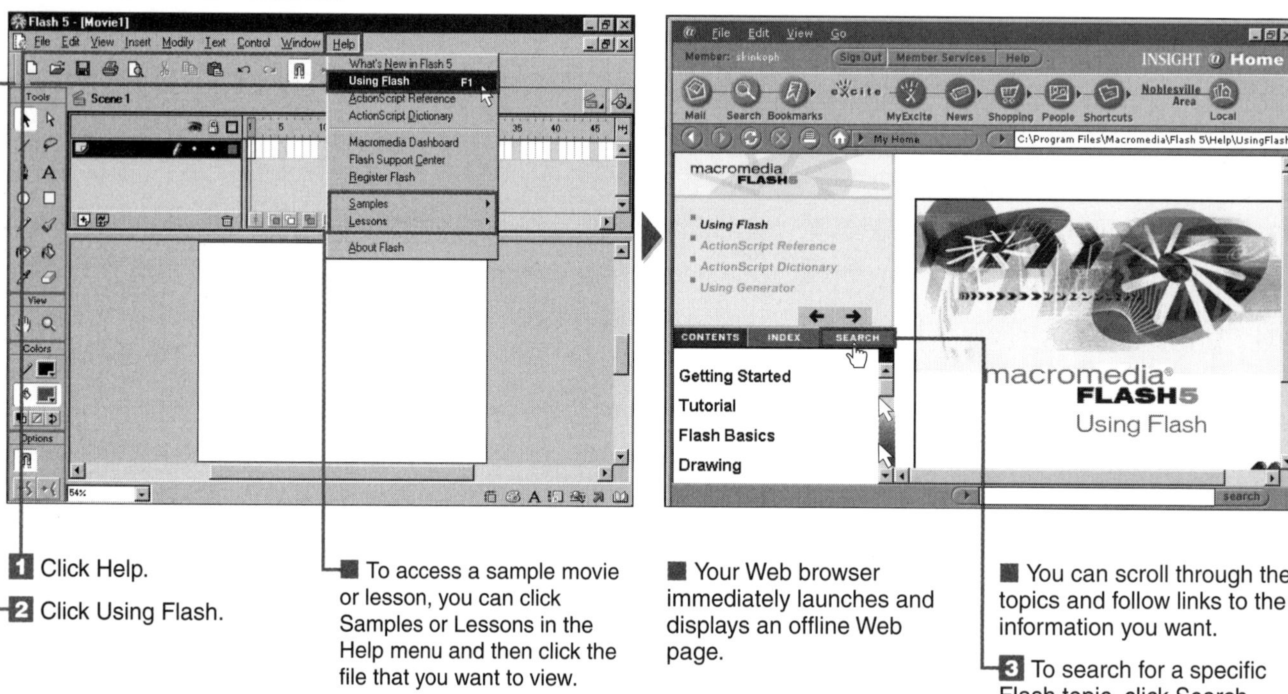

1 Click Help.

2 Click Using Flash.

■ To access a sample movie or lesson, you can click Samples or Lessons in the Help menu and then click the file that you want to view.

■ Your Web browser immediately launches and displays an offline Web page.

■ You can scroll through the topics and follow links to the information you want.

3 To search for a specific Flash topic, click Search.

Where else can I find Flash help?

✔ Macromedia's Web site, www.macromedia.com/support/flash/, is a good place to start if you are looking for additional information about the Flash program. You can also find numerous sites on the Internet dedicated to Flash users by performing a simple search for the keyword *Flash* using your favorite search engine.

How would I use the sample files?

✔ Flash ships with several sample movie files that you can study to help you learn how the program works as well as a variety of things you can do with it.

What does the Dashboard feature do?

✔ New to Flash 5, the Macromedia Dashboard is help-central for developers who want to explore what is available for Flash among third-party vendors, find technical notes concerning the Flash program, and download sample Flash movies. To access the Dashboard, click Help and then Macromedia Dashboard.

What do the Flash tutorials cover?

✔ Flash comes with a set of interactive tutorials you can view from the Flash program window. The tutorials cover a variety of topics, including drawing, layers, and animation.

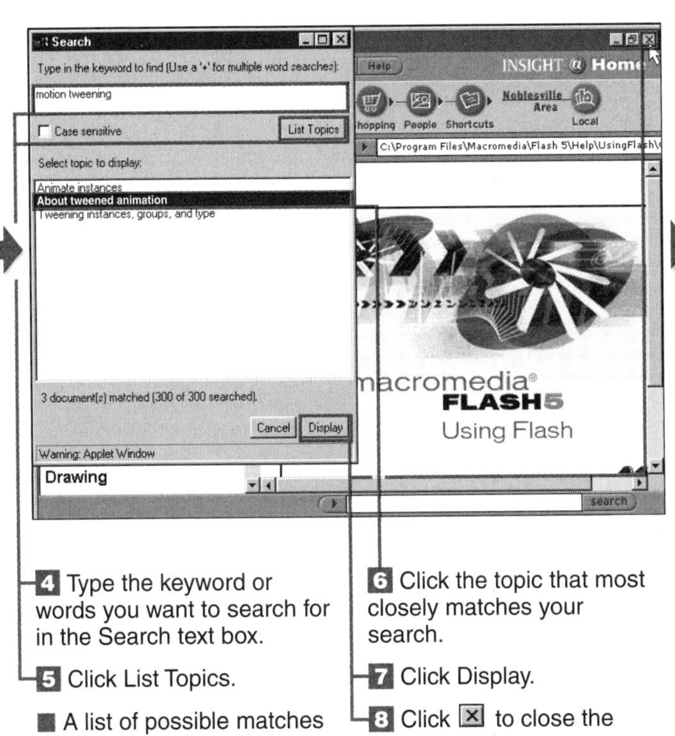

4 Type the keyword or words you want to search for in the Search text box.

5 Click List Topics.

■ A list of possible matches appears in the topic list box.

6 Click the topic that most closely matches your search.

7 Click Display.

8 Click ☒ to close the Search window.

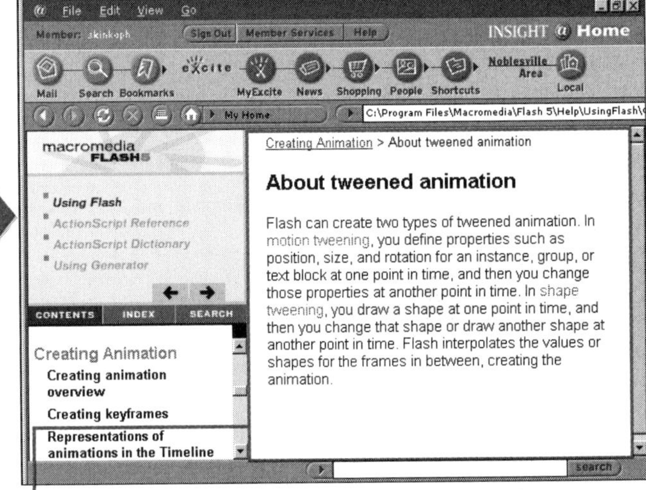

■ The results of your search appear in the browser window. You can now read about the topic or click links to view related topics.

AN INTRODUCTION TO FLASH OBJECTS

Drawings you create in Flash are composed of lines, called *strokes*, and *fills*, the solid colors that fill the interior of connected lines. An item you draw, such as a single square or a detailed scene of images, is called an *object*. With the tools found on the Drawing toolbar, you can create simple objects, such as shapes, or complex objects that involve layers, grouped elements, and more.

If you have worked with other drawing programs, such as Macromedia FreeHand, you will find the drawing features in Flash familiar. For example, you can use the Pencil tool to draw freeform lines or the Line tool to draw straight lines. You can combine simple objects to create more complex drawings or remove parts of shapes and lines to create new shapes. You can change an object's color, scale, and positioning.

Whether you are an experienced graphic designer or are just learning to create graphics with a computer, Flash drawing tools are completely adequate for making detailed drawings or simple objects.

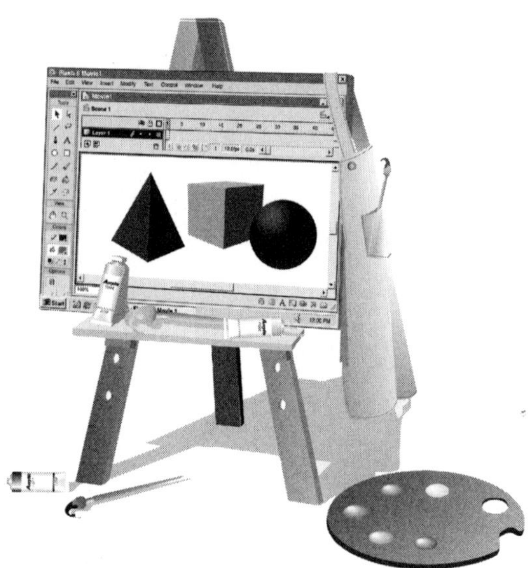

Shape Recognition

It is not always easy to draw with a mouse, but Flash makes it simpler with shape recognition. Draw a rough idea of a shape, and Flash automatically cleans it up for you.

Shape recognition is turned on by default, but you can turn the feature off if you do not want Flash to guess at what you are trying to draw on-screen.

Segments

When you draw overlapping lines or shapes, the areas that overlap divide the image into segments. For example, if you draw a straight line through the middle of an oval shape, the line is divided into three sections: the section that falls outside the left side of the oval, the section that goes through the middle of the oval, and the section that falls outside the right side of the oval. You can use the Arrow tool to manipulate any of the three line segments separately, if needed. If the oval shape includes a fill color in the middle, the fill is also divided into two segments by the line. You can edit each fill segment as well.

Import Graphics

You do not have to rely on your drawing skills to create objects for your movies. You can also import graphics from other programs and manipulate them with the Flash drawing tools. You can find out about importing graphic objects in Chapter 23.

Drawing Levels

When working with objects on the Flash Stage, there are two levels: the *stage* level and the *overlay* level. The stage level is the bottom level on the Stage, and any objects you place there can interact. For example, a line and a shape can connect. Stage-level objects include anything you draw with the drawing tools.

The overlay level is like a transparent sheet of paper on top of the stage level. Any object you place on the overlay level floats on top and will not interact with stage-level objects. Overlay-level objects include items you group together to act as a single unit, symbols you create for reuse throughout your movie, text blocks, and imported graphics.

As you work with objects in Flash, it is important to distinguish between the two levels. You may find yourself trying to make two objects interact that are actually located on two different levels.

You can make objects from different levels interact by using the Break Apart command. This command makes it easy to break apart overlay-level objects and turn them into stage-level objects that you can manipulate and edit. For example, you can turn text into graphic shapes that you can resize and rotate.

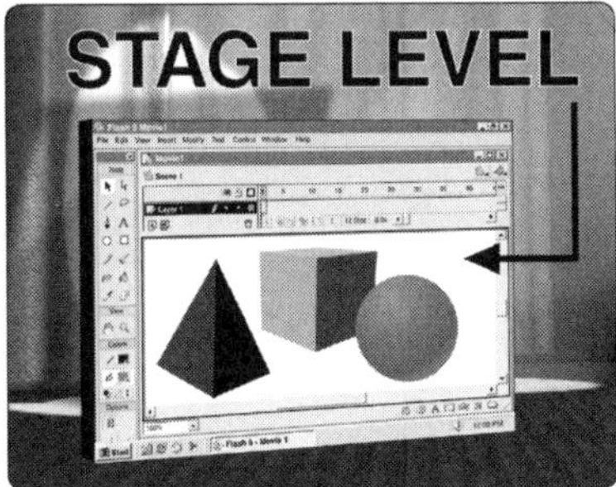

USING THE DRAWING TOOLBAR

The Drawing toolbar is packed with tools that you can use to create and work with text and graphic objects. By default, the Drawing toolbar is docked vertically on the far left side of the Flash program window, allowing you handy access to the many tools you will need for creating objects on the Stage.

Before you start using the tools, take a moment to acquaint yourself with each tool and its function.

To hide the Drawing toolbar at any time, click Window and then Tools.

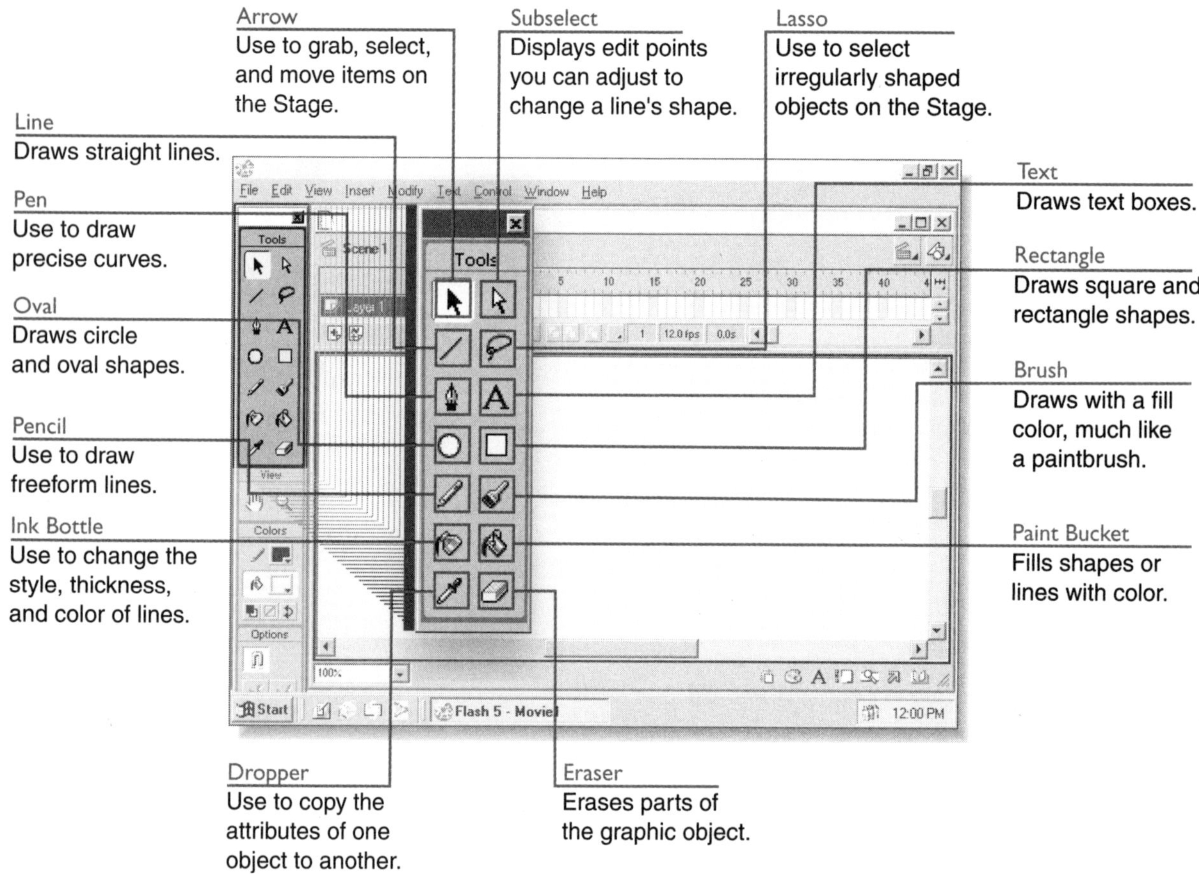
Arrow
Use to grab, select, and move items on the Stage.
Subselect
Displays edit points you can adjust to change a line's shape.
Lasso
Use to select irregularly shaped objects on the Stage.
Line
Draws straight lines.
Pen
Use to draw precise curves.
Oval
Draws circle and oval shapes.
Pencil
Use to draw freeform lines.
Ink Bottle
Use to change the style, thickness, and color of lines.
Text
Draws text boxes.
Rectangle
Draws square and rectangle shapes.
Brush
Draws with a fill color, much like a paintbrush.
Paint Bucket
Fills shapes or lines with color.
Dropper
Use to copy the attributes of one object to another.
Eraser
Erases parts of the graphic object.
Tools
Start
Flash 5 - Movie
12:00 PM

Using the View Tools

In addition to the various tools for drawing objects on the Stage, the Drawing toolbar also contains buttons for changing your view of the Stage area. For example, you can move your view of the objects on the Stage or in the work area by dragging the Hand tool (✋) on the Stage.

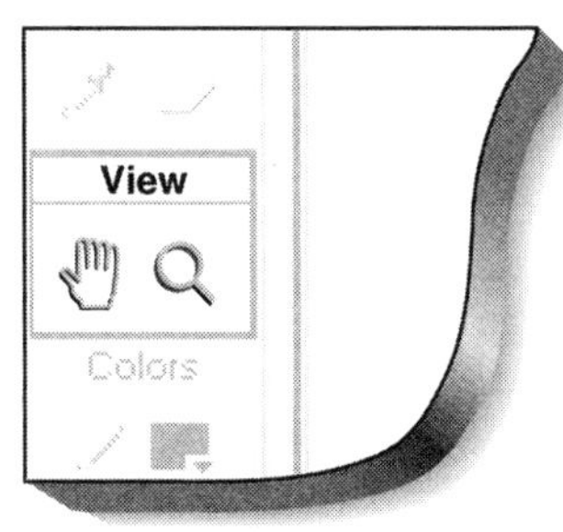

You can use the Zoom tool to magnify your view of an object on the Stage or zoom out for a bird's eye view. Simply click the Zoom tool button (🔍), click a view option from the Options tray (Enlarge or Reduce), and then click over the Stage. The more you click, the greater (or lesser) your magnification.

To zoom in or out by a magnification percentage, use the Zoom box at the bottom of the program window. Click ▼ and then click a zoom percentage. You can also type in an exact percentage for a zoom directly in the Zoom box.

You can also find additional zoom tools in the View menu. Click View and then click Zoom In and Zoom Out, or click View, click Magnification, and then select from the list of magnification levels.

Using the Color Tools

The Color tools are used to define line and fill colors for objects you draw on the Stage. For example, click and hold the Stroke Color button (■) to display a palette of colors for lines.

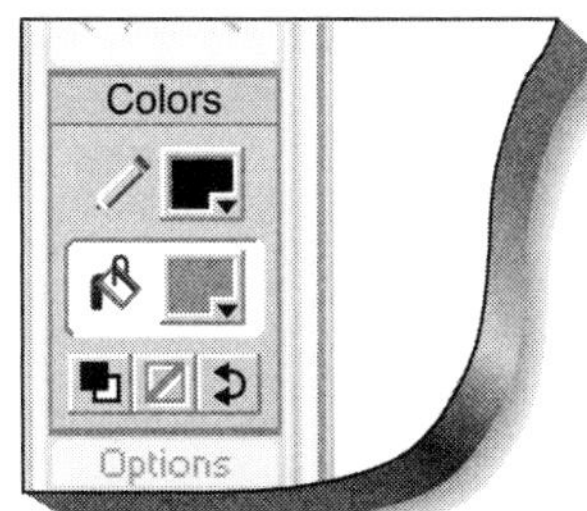

To select a color, drag the mouse pointer over your color choice and release the mouse button.

To choose a fill color, click and hold the Fill Color button (■), drag the mouse pointer over your color choice, and release the mouse button.

Use the buttons directly below the Stroke and Fill Color tools to quickly modify object color. Click the Default Colors button (■) to change the line color to black and the fill color to white. Click the No Color button (☒) to draw shapes without outlines or borders. Or click the Swap Colors button (⇅) to switch the line color to the fill color and vice versa.

Using the Option Tools

Some of the drawing tools you select may offer modifiers that enable you to set additional controls for the tool. Any modifiers associated with a tool will appear in the Options tray at the bottom of the toolbar. For example, if you click the Arrow tool (↖), additional option buttons will appear for snapping to objects, smoothing and straightening lines, and rotating and scaling objects.

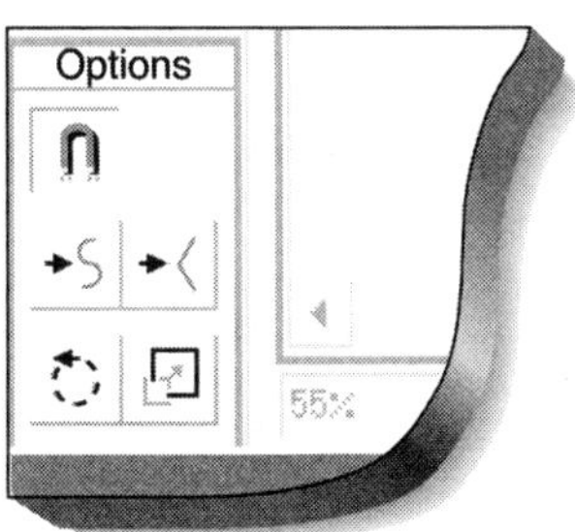

DRAW LINE SEGMENTS

You can draw all sorts of objects with lines. Lines, called *strokes* in Flash, can connect with other lines and shapes to create an image or shape.

The easiest way to draw straight lines in Flash is to use the Line tool. The Line tool draws perfectly straight lines. You control where the line starts and where the line stops.

To draw a freeform line, use the Pencil tool. The Pencil tool has three pencil modes that control how a line is drawn: Straighten, Smooth, or Ink.

If you select the Straighten mode, any line you draw on the Stage will straighten itself after you release the mouse button. If you choose the Smooth mode, your curved lines will be smoothed. If you choose the Ink mode, the line you draw will stay as is; no straightening or smoothing occurs.

DRAW A STRAIGHT LINE

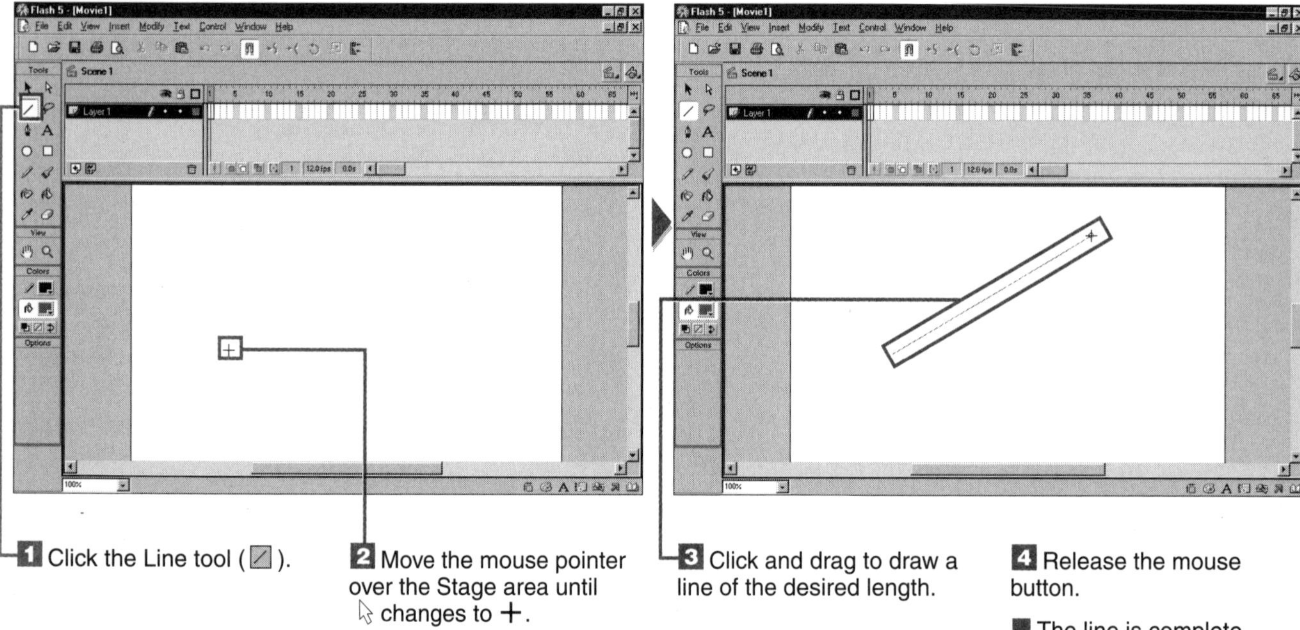

1 Click the Line tool ( ).

2 Move the mouse pointer over the Stage area until ↖ changes to +.

3 Click and drag to draw a line of the desired length.

4 Release the mouse button.

■ The line is complete.

How do I control the line thickness?

✔ You can set a line thickness before you start drawing the actual line segment. Click Window, Panels, and then Stroke or click ▣. This opens the Stroke panel, a box with options for controlling line thickness and color. To change the thickness, drag the thickness slider up or down. You can apply a new line thickness to an existing line by first selecting the line and then dragging the slider.

How do I keep a straight line vertical or horizontal?

✔ Using the Line tool, hold down Shift and draw a line that is pretty much vertical or horizontal. Flash will make the line perfectly vertical or horizontal. The Shift trick also works when drawing a 45-degree line.

Can I use a ruler to help draw my lines?

✔ Yes. Flash has two features to help you with objects you draw on the Stage: rulers and gridlines. To turn the rulers on, click View and then Rulers. Horizontal and vertical rulers appear around the work area. To turn on gridlines, click View, Grid, and then Show Grid.

DRAW A FREEFORM LINE

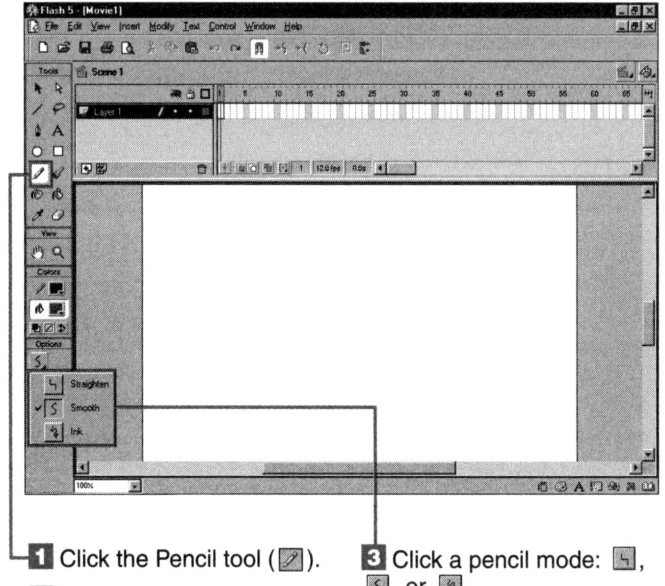

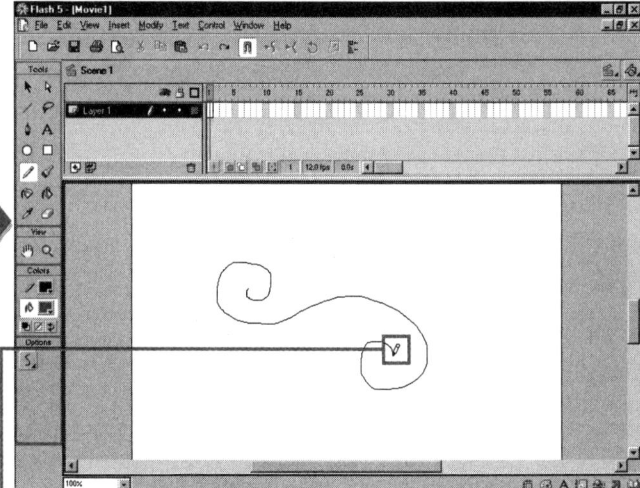

1 Click the Pencil tool (✎).

2 Click the Pencil Mode button (⌐).

3 Click a pencil mode: ⌐, S, or ✎.

Note: Use the Straighten mode to draw straight lines, the Smooth mode to draw curvy lines, and the Ink mode to draw freeform lines.

4 Click and drag the cursor on the Stage to draw the line (↖ changes to ✎).

5 Release the mouse button.

■ The line is complete. If you were using the Straighten or Smooth mode, the line becomes straight or smooth, respectively.

FORMAT LINE SEGMENTS

By default, lines you draw on the Stage are solid black and 1-point thick. You can control a line's thickness, style, and color by using the formatting controls found in the Stroke panel. You can set the formatting options before you draw a line, or you can assign them to an existing line. For example, you may want to change the formatting for a particular line segment in a drawing, or you may want to draw a new line that is precisely 5 points thick and dashed. Use the Stroke panel options to set the exact formatting you want.

You can use the options in the Stroke panel to set the formatting of lines drawn with the Line, Pen, or Pencil tool and any outlines drawn with the shape tools. See the section "Draw Line Segments" in this chapter to find out more about drawing lines on the Stage. See the section "Draw Oval and Rectangle Shapes," also in this chapter, to find out more about the shape tools.

FORMAT LINE SEGMENTS

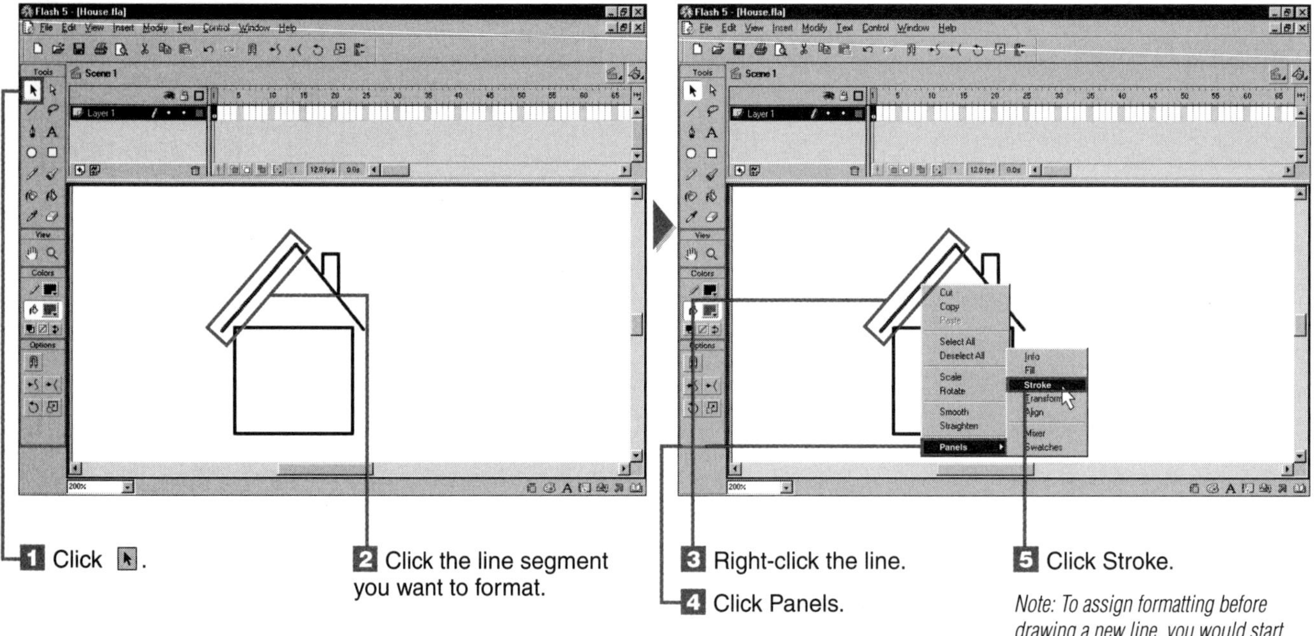

1 Click [arrow tool icon].

2 Click the line segment you want to format.

3 Right-click the line.

4 Click Panels.

5 Click Stroke.

Note: To assign formatting before drawing a new line, you would start with steps 4 through 6.

How do I change the line color?

✔ In the Stroke panel, click the Stroke Color box to display a palette of color choices. Then click the color you want to assign.

Are there ways other than using the right-click menu to display the Stroke panel?

✔ Yes. You can click ▤ at the bottom of the Flash program window to open the Info panel and then click the Stroke tab to display the line formatting options. You can also click Window, Panels, and then Stroke.

How do I straighten a curved line?

✔ First select the line segment you want to edit and then click Modify and Straighten. You may have to select this command several times to get the effect you want. You can also click ⋅(in the Options tray at the bottom of the Drawing toolbar. See the section "Smooth or Straighten Line Segments" for more information.

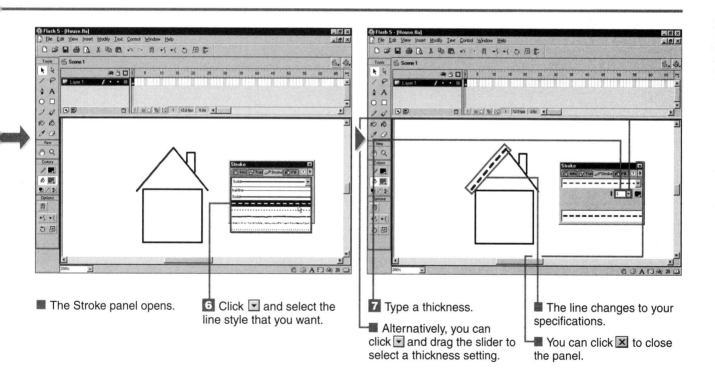

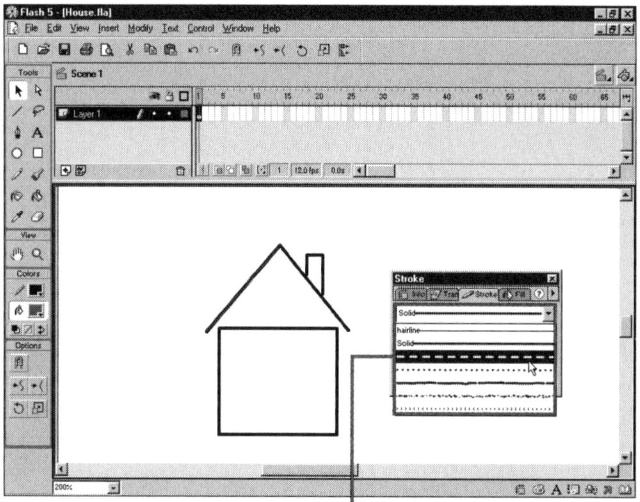

■ The Stroke panel opens.

6 Click ▼ and select the line style that you want.

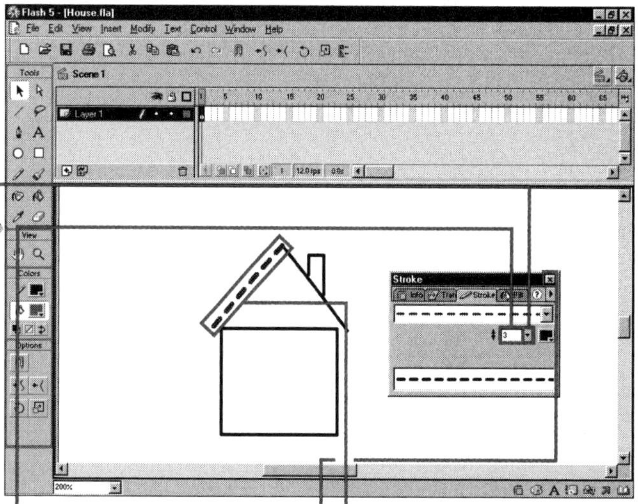

7 Type a thickness.

■ Alternatively, you can click ▼ and drag the slider to select a thickness setting.

■ The line changes to your specifications.

■ You can click ☒ to close the panel.

DRAW A CUSTOM LINE

You can select a line style and customize its appearance using the options in the Line Style dialog box. For example, you may want a dotted line with the dots spaced far apart or very tightly together.

You can use the Line Style dialog box when you want to create a unique or specialized line style. Depending on the style you select, such as Dotted or Ragged, additional customizing options appear in the Line Style dialog box. For example, if you choose a Ragged line style, you can additionally set the wave pattern, height, length, and thickness.

The preview area of the Line Style dialog box lets you see an example of what the selected options will look like when applied to a line. Experiment with the various dialog box settings to create just the right line style for your Flash drawing.

DRAW A CUSTOM LINE

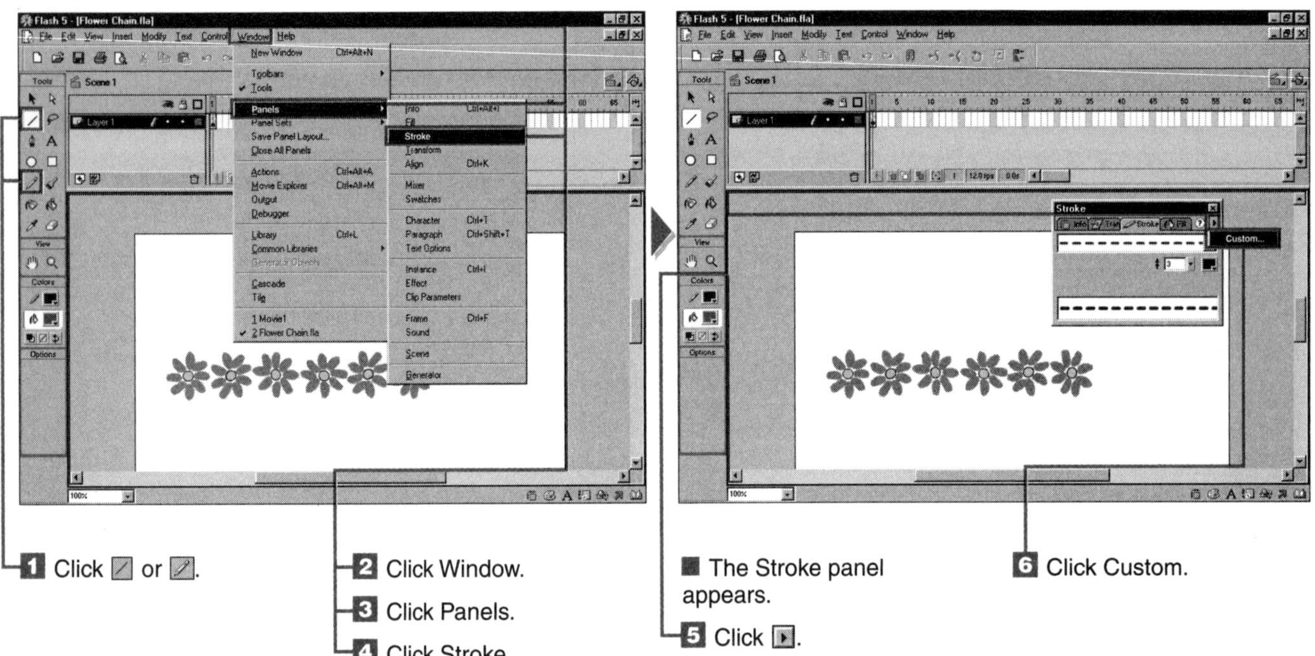

1 Click or .

2 Click Window.

3 Click Panels.

4 Click Stroke.

■ The Stroke panel appears.

5 Click .

6 Click Custom.

How do I fix a mistake?

✔ To undo your last action, such as drawing a line segment, just click [undo]. If you change your mind and want the action back, click [redo].

How do I smooth my line style?

✔ You can further customize your line segment by using the Arrow tool's Smooth feature in the Options tray on the Drawing toolbar. See the section "Smooth or Straighten Line Segments" for more information.

Can I turn off the shape recognition feature?

✔ Yes. By default, the Flash shape recognition feature tries to determine what sort of object you are drawing and completes the shape for you. If you draw an open-ended triangle using the Pencil tool, for example, Flash assumes that you want to draw a triangle and completes the shape. To keep the program from doing so, click Edit and then Preferences. This opens the Preferences dialog box. Click the Editing tab and then click the Recognize Shapes [▼] and select Off. Click OK to exit the dialog box.

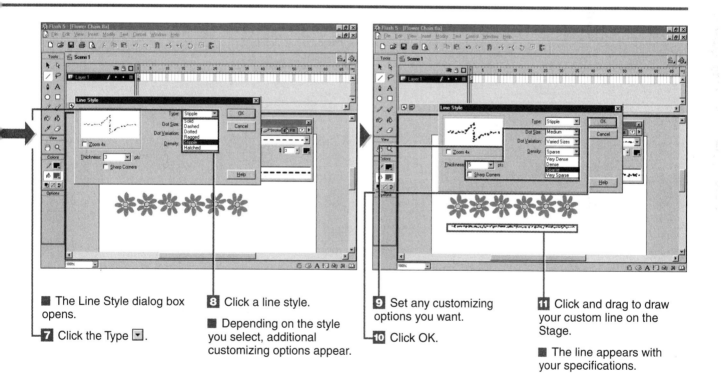

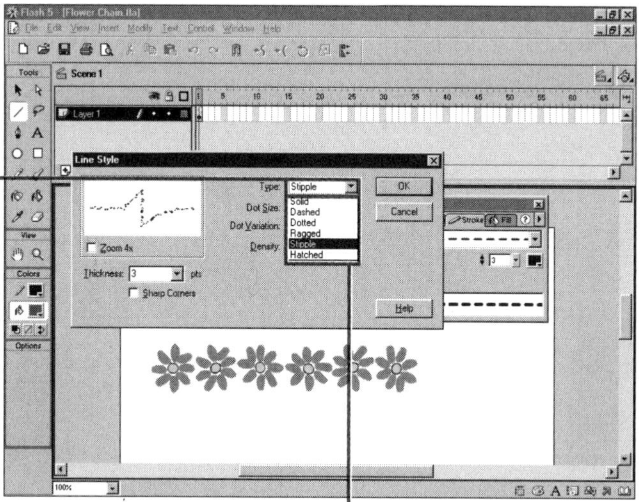

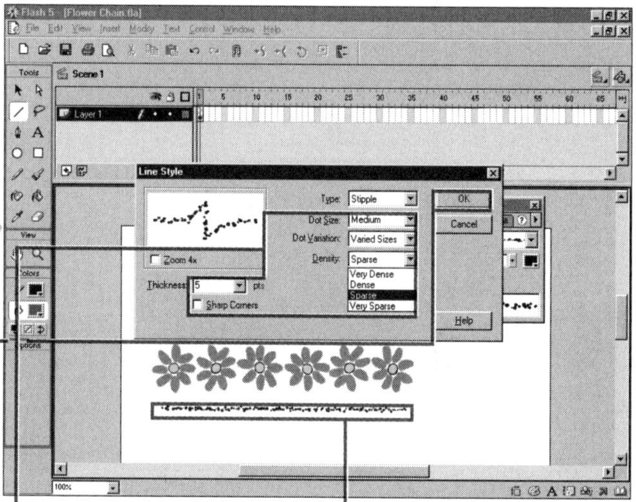

■ The Line Style dialog box opens.

7 Click the Type [▼].

8 Click a line style.

■ Depending on the style you select, additional customizing options appear.

9 Set any customizing options you want.

10 Click OK.

11 Click and drag to draw your custom line on the Stage.

■ The line appears with your specifications.

DRAW CURVES WITH THE PEN TOOL

You can draw precise lines and curves using the Pen tool. Using this tool takes some getting used to, but with a little practice, you can draw curves like a pro.

The quickest way to draw curved lines is to drag the Pen tool along with its curve bar on the Flash Stage. The *curve bar* is a straight line with two solid points at either end. You can rotate the curve bar to create different degrees of curvature for the line. The key to creating just the right curve is learning to drag the curve bar in the correct direction. This technique takes a bit of practice, so be sure to experiment in a new file to get the hang of it.

Lines created with the Pen tool are composed of points. The points appear as dots on the line segment and represent segments or changes in the line's curvature.

DRAW CURVES WITH THE PEN TOOL

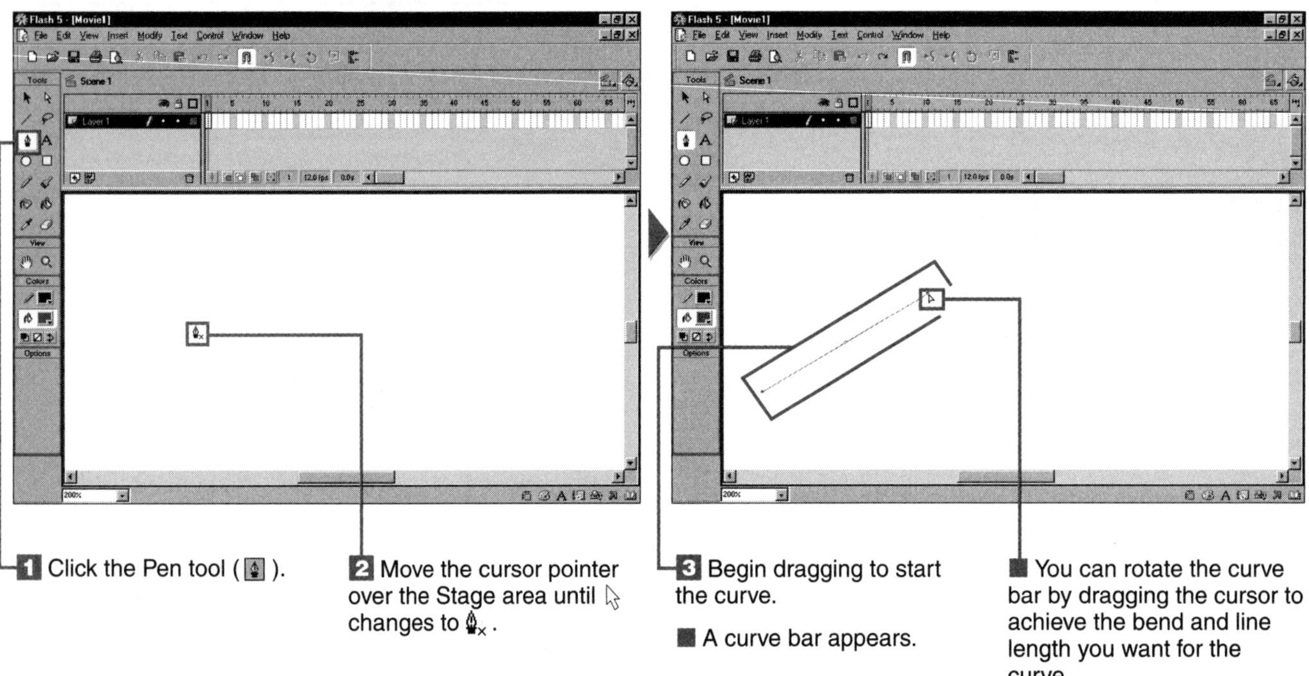

1 Click the Pen tool ( ).

2 Move the cursor pointer over the Stage area until changes to .

3 Begin dragging to start the curve.

■ A curve bar appears.

■ You can rotate the curve bar by dragging the cursor to achieve the bend and line length you want for the curve.

How can I edit points on a curved line?

✔ Use the Subselect tool to make changes to a curved line you have created using the Pen tool. Click ⬚ and move the cursor over an edit point on the line or at the end of the line. Drag to reposition and reshape the line or curve.

Can I constrain the degree of curvature?

✔ Yes. You can press and hold down Shift while dragging the Pen tool to keep the curves at 45-degree angles.

Can I customize the Pen tool?

✔ Yes. You can control how the tool's pointer appears on-screen, how you want the line's displayed, and more. Click Edit and then Preferences. Click the Editing tab. Click Show Pen Preview (☐ changes to ☑) if you want to see the resulting line segment as you draw. Click Show Solid Points (☐ changes to ☑) if you prefer to see line points as solid dots. Click Show Precise Cursors (☐ changes to ☑) to change the tool's pointer icon to a crosshair. Click OK to exit.

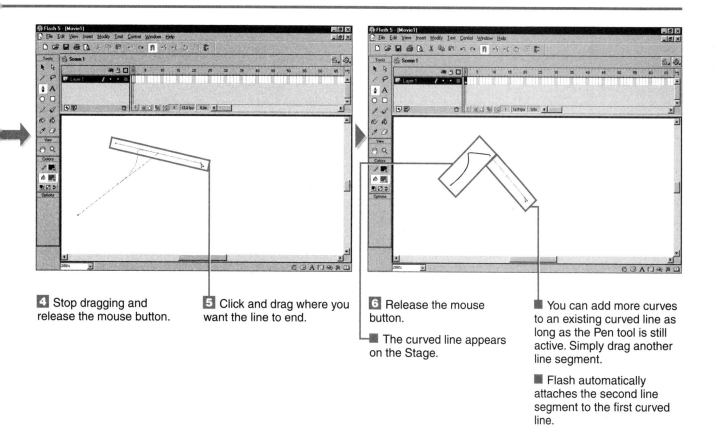

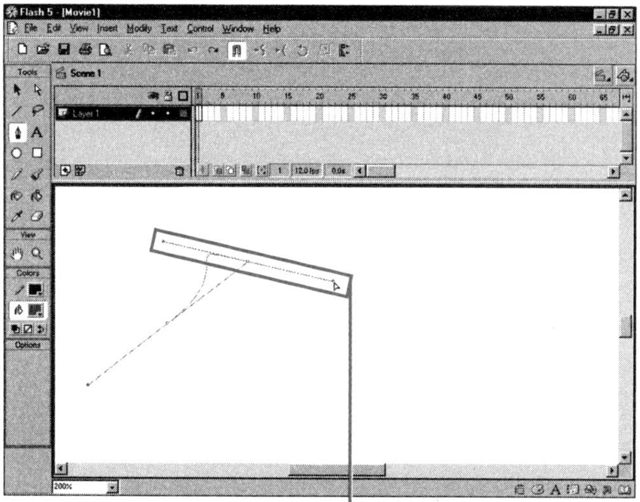

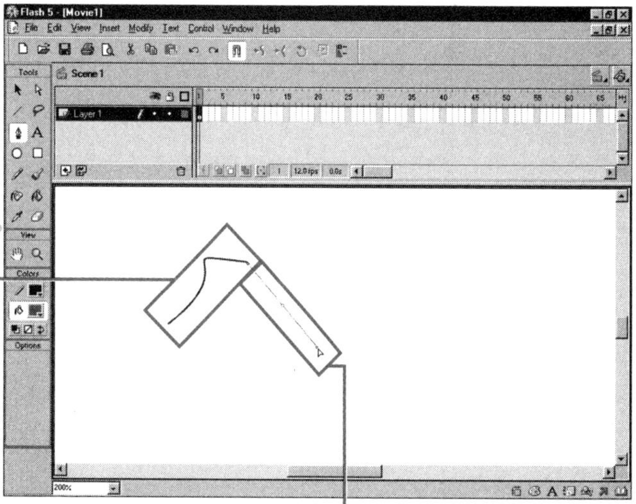

4 Stop dragging and release the mouse button.

5 Click and drag where you want the line to end.

6 Release the mouse button.

■ The curved line appears on the Stage.

■ You can add more curves to an existing curved line as long as the Pen tool is still active. Simply drag another line segment.

■ Flash automatically attaches the second line segment to the first curved line.

SMOOTH OR STRAIGHTEN LINE SEGMENTS

You can smooth or straighten the lines that you draw to create subtle or dramatic changes to your drawing. For example, perhaps you have painstakingly drawn a tree with several curving branches. You now decide a few of your branches need some modifications. You can use the Arrow tool's Smooth or Straighten option buttons on the Drawing toolbar to adjust your lines.

The Smooth feature can take a curved line and smoothen it as much or little as you need. Use the Smooth feature to smooth out rough corners or edges on a line or curve. The Straighten feature will turn a curvy line into a straight one. Like the Smooth feature, you can apply the Straighten feature as much as you need to get the desired effect. Keep in mind that you can straighten only rough and curved lines: Straightening an already straight line will have no effect.

SMOOTH A LINE

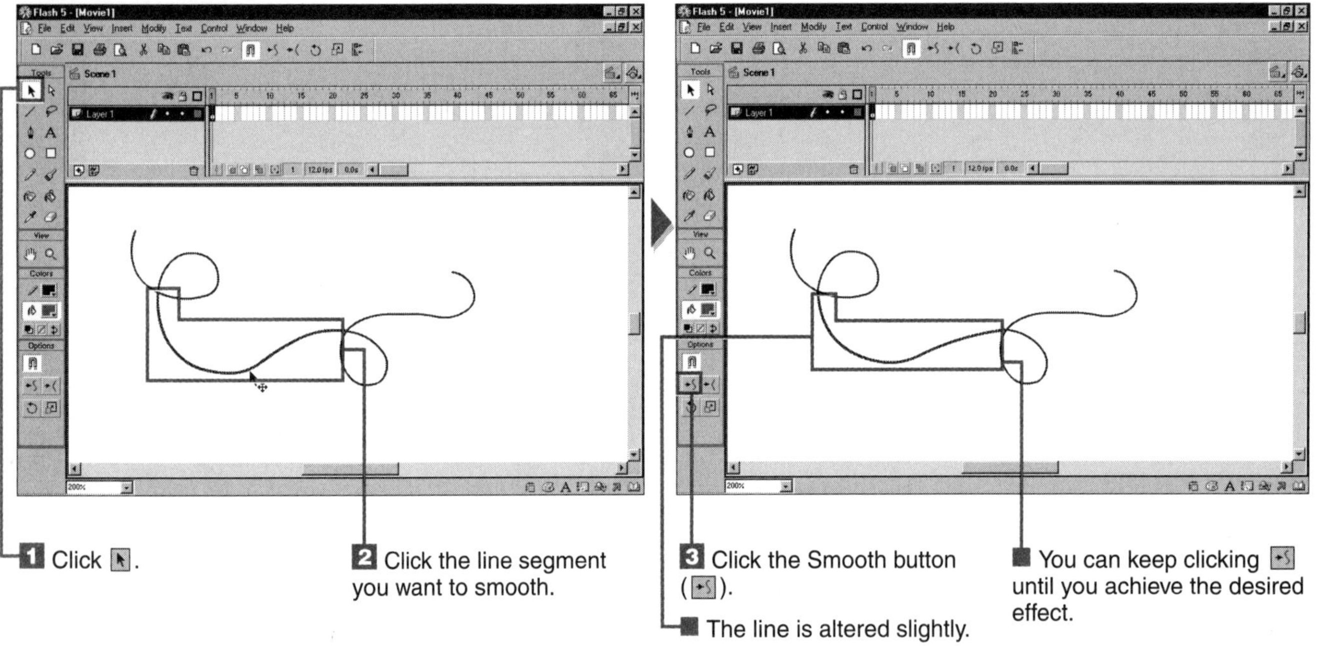

1 Click ▶.

2 Click the line segment you want to smooth.

3 Click the Smooth button (+S).

■ The line is altered slightly.

■ You can keep clicking +S until you achieve the desired effect.

Can I draw in Smooth or Straighten mode?

✔ Yes. When you draw lines with the Pencil tool, you can preselect the Smooth or Straighten mode. Refer to the section "Draw Line Segments," earlier in this chapter, for more information.

Which two Smooth buttons should I use, the set on the Drawing toolbar or the set on the Main toolbar?

✔ Both sets of buttons do the same thing. One set is located at the bottom of the Drawing toolbar in the Options tray. These buttons appear only when the Arrow tool is selected. Another set of Smooth and Straighten buttons appear on the main toolbar at the top of the program window. These buttons are always available, whether the Arrow tool is selected or not.

Why do my curved lines appear so rough?

✔ A previous user may have made some adjustments to the program's preferences. You can adjust settings for drawing lines and shapes through the Preferences dialog box. Click Edit and then Preferences. This opens the Preferences dialog box. Click the Editing tab; then click the Smooth Curves ▾ and select Normal. Click OK to exit the dialog box and apply the new setting.

STRAIGHTEN A LINE

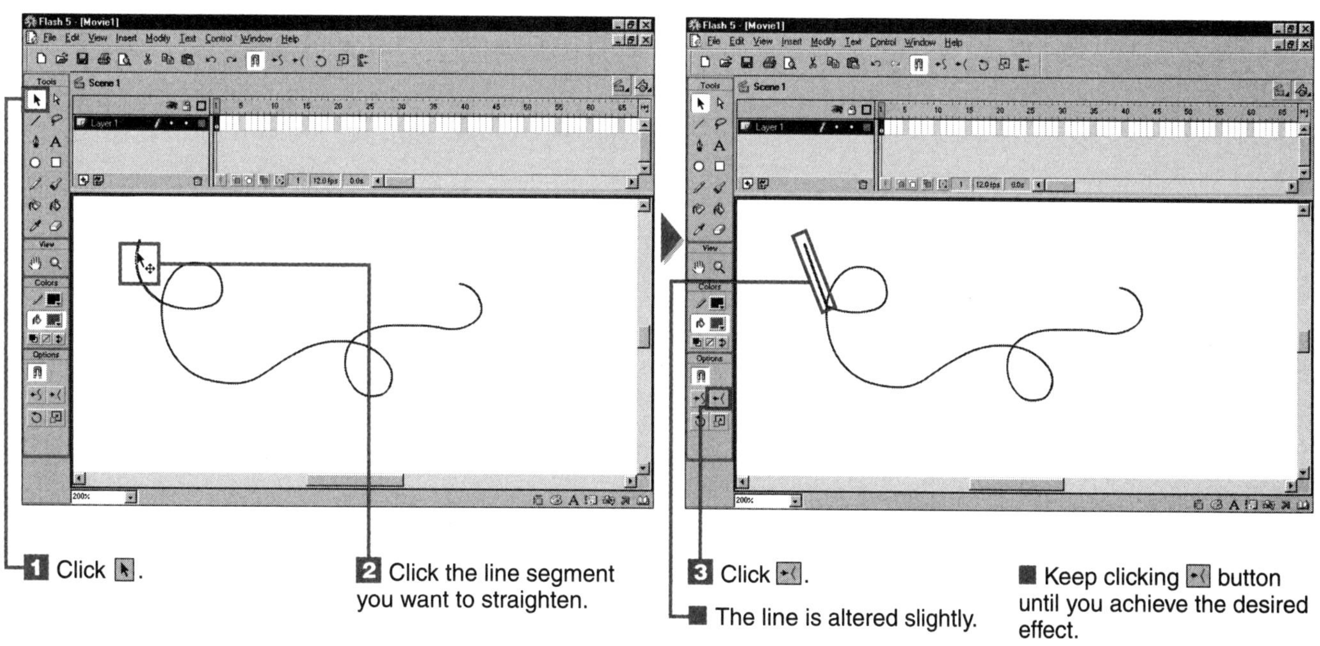

1 Click ↖.

2 Click the line segment you want to straighten.

3 Click ⁺(.

■ The line is altered slightly.

■ Keep clicking ⁺(button until you achieve the desired effect.

DRAW OVAL AND RECTANGLE SHAPES

You can create simple shapes in Flash and then fill them with a color or pattern or use them as part of a drawing. You can create shapes using many of the tools found on the Drawing toolbar, such as the Pencil or Line tool, just by connecting or closing the lines. For more uniform shapes, such as circles, ovals, squares, and rectangles, you can use the Oval or Rectangle tools.

The Oval tool can create all kinds of oval or circular shapes. You can overlap the shapes to create more shapes. The Rectangle tool is used to create all kinds of rectangular or square shapes. These, too, can be overlapped to make more shapes.

You can choose to draw an oval or rectangle shape with or without a fill. A *fill* is the color or pattern that fills up the inside of your shape. By default, the Fill color is selected. You can turn the Fill off or choose another color from the Fill Color palette. You can also change the fill later (see the section "Fill Objects with the Paint Bucket Tool" in this chapter).

DRAW AN OVAL OR RECTANGLE

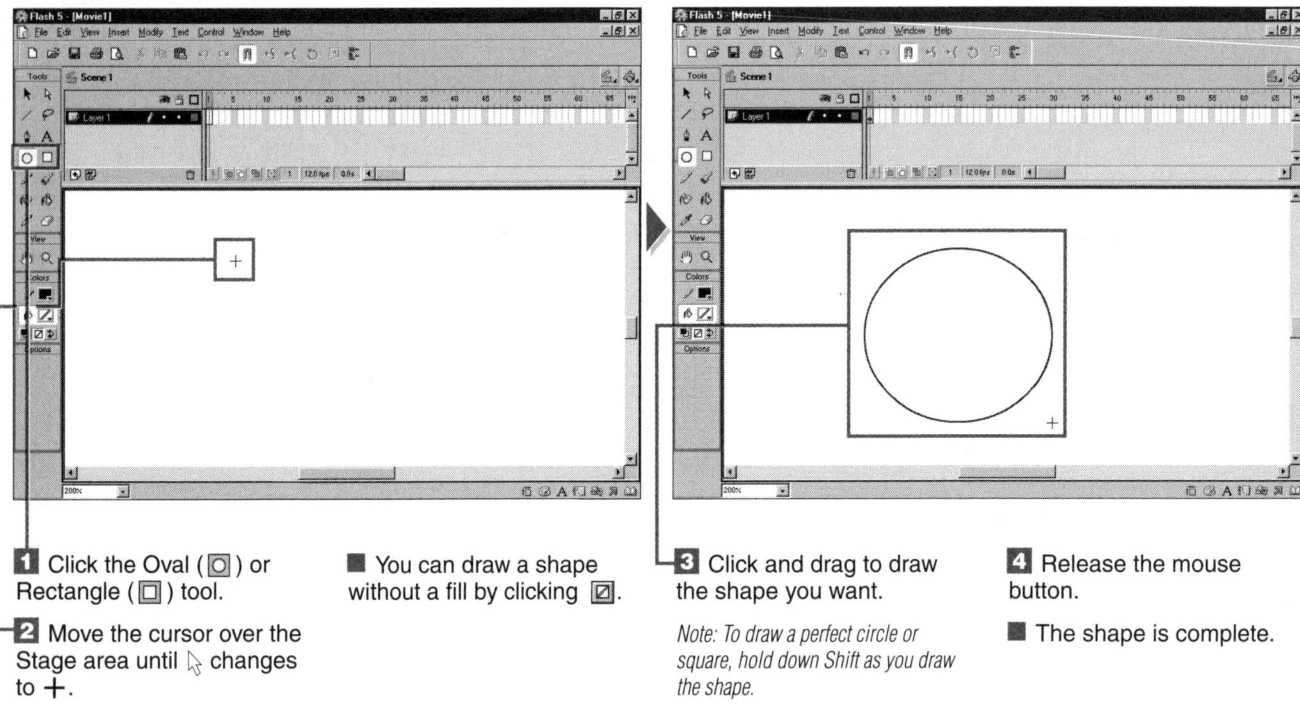

1 Click the Oval (○) or Rectangle (□) tool.

2 Move the cursor over the Stage area until ↖ changes to +.

■ You can draw a shape without a fill by clicking ▢.

3 Click and drag to draw the shape you want.

Note: To draw a perfect circle or square, hold down Shift as you draw the shape.

4 Release the mouse button.

■ The shape is complete.

How do I draw a rectangle with rounded corners?

✔ By default, all rectangular shapes you draw with the Rectangle tool have sharp corners. You can create rounded corners by using the Rectangle options. Click ▢ on the Drawing toolbar; then click ◰ in the Options area. The Rectangle Settings dialog box appears. Type a corner radius setting, such as 10 points. Click OK. Then draw your rectangle shape with rounded corners. To draw regular corners again, enter 0 as the radius setting.

Can I open a Fill Color dialog box?

✔ Yes. Double-click the Fill Color button on the Drawing toolbar to open the Color dialog box. You can then click a color to use as a fill and click OK.

Is there another way to assign a fill color?

✔ Yes. Open the Mixer panel (click ◉) to display the color palette and use the panel's Fill Color button to change fill colors. You can then leave the panel open and use it when you need it.

DRAW A SHAPE WITH A FILL COLOR

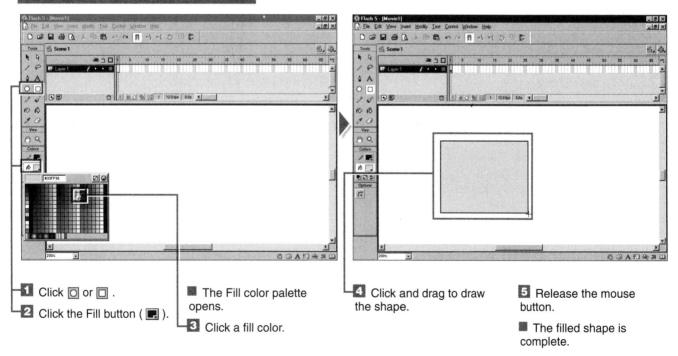

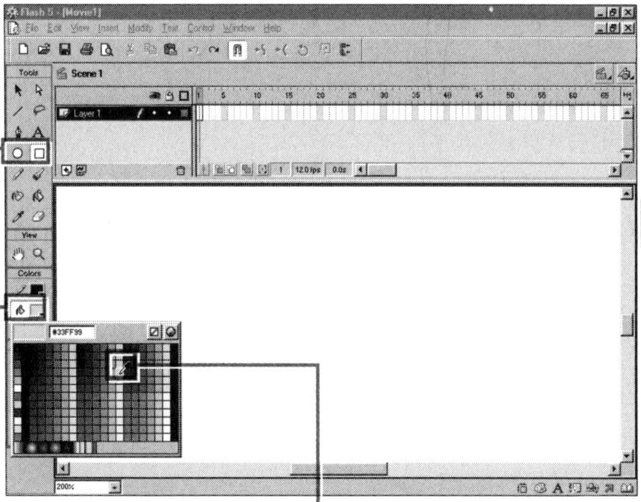

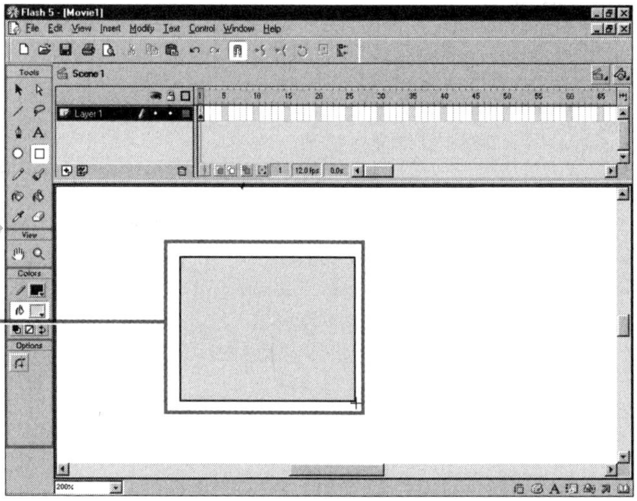

1 Click ○ or ▢ .

2 Click the Fill button (■).

■ The Fill color palette opens.

3 Click a fill color.

4 Click and drag to draw the shape.

5 Release the mouse button.

■ The filled shape is complete.

DRAW OBJECTS WITH THE BRUSH TOOL

You can use the Brush tool to draw with brush strokes, much like a paintbrush. You can control the size and shape of the brush as well as how the brush strokes appear on the Stage.

The Brush tool is handy when you want to draw varying sizes of freeform strokes on the Stage. You can choose a specific color to use with the Brush tool by first selecting a color from the Fill Color palette (see the section "Draw Oval and Rectangle Shapes" in this chapter to learn more about using the Fill Color palette).

After you select the Brush tool, several Brush modifiers appear in the Options tray at the bottom of the Drawing toolbar. You can use the modifiers to change the brush shape and size and how the brush strokes interact with objects on the Stage. For example, some of the brush shapes will allow you to create calligraphy effects.

DRAW OBJECTS WITH THE BRUSH TOOL

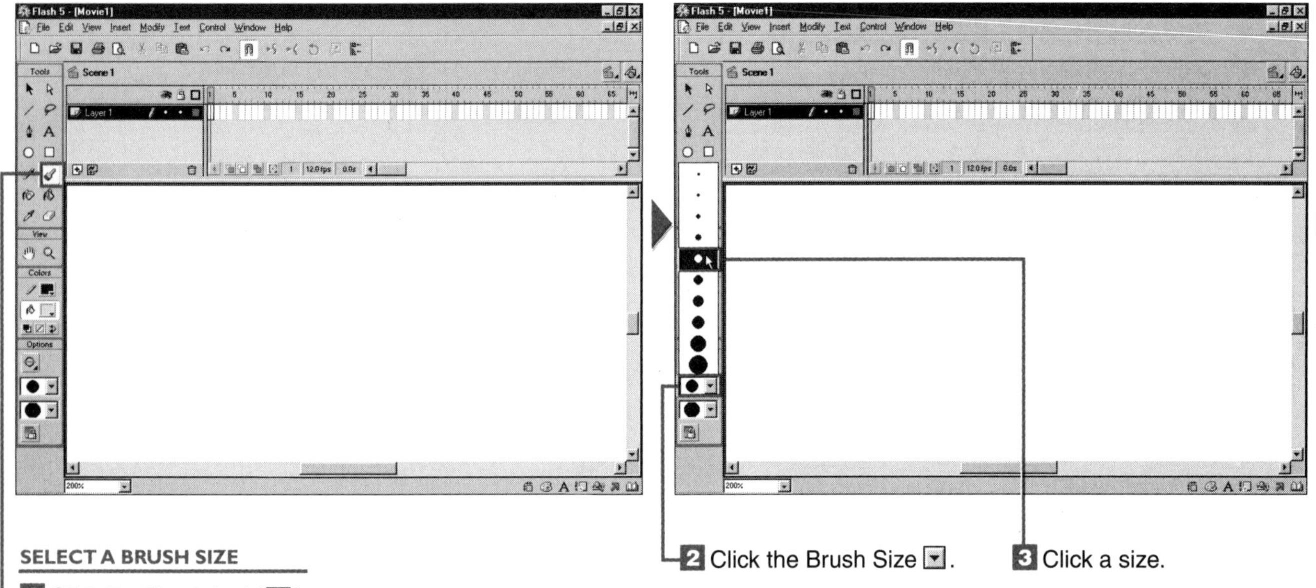

SELECT A BRUSH SIZE

1 Click the Brush tool (🖌).

2 Click the Brush Size ▾.

3 Click a size.

What do the Brush modes do?

✔ You find the five brush modes by clicking the Brush Mode button ( ) at the bottom of the Drawing toolbar. Paint Normal lets you paint over anything on the Stage. Paint Fills paints inside fills but not on lines. Paint Behind paints beneath any existing objects on the Stage. Paint Selection paints only inside the selected area. Paint Inside begins a brush stroke inside a fill area without affecting any lines.

How do I brush in just one direction?

✔ Yes. If you press and hold Shift while dragging the Brush tool on the Stage, the tool allows you to draw only in a horizontal or vertical direction.

How do I use the Brush tool with a pressure-sensitive tablet?

✔ If you use a pressure-sensitive tablet to draw, you will see an extra modifier for the Brush tool at the bottom of the Drawing toolbar. Use the Pressure modifier to activate a finer degree of sensitivity in the Brush tool when drawing. This feature toggles on or off.

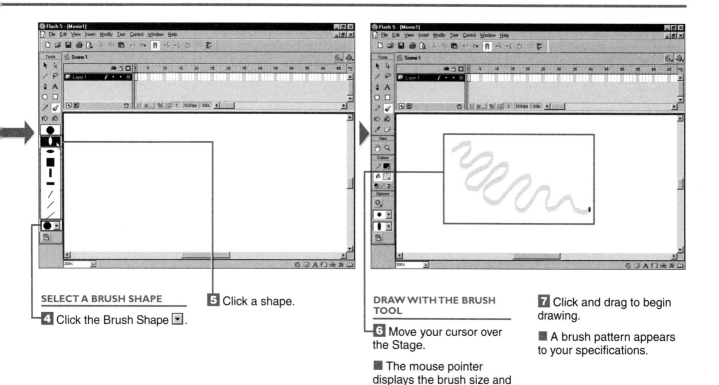

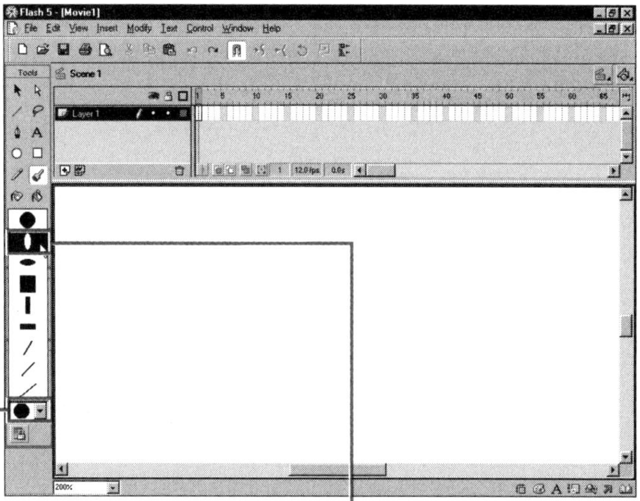

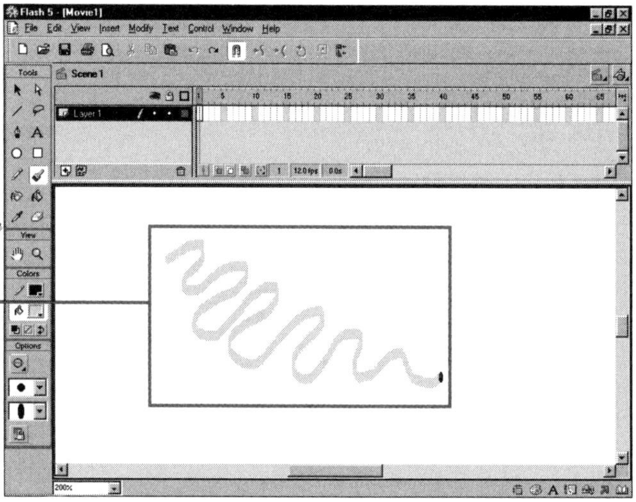

SELECT A BRUSH SHAPE

4 Click the Brush Shape .

5 Click a shape.

DRAW WITH THE BRUSH TOOL

6 Move your cursor over the Stage.

■ The mouse pointer displays the brush size and shape you selected.

7 Click and drag to begin drawing.

■ A brush pattern appears to your specifications.

FILL OBJECTS WITH THE PAINT BUCKET TOOL

You can use the Paint Bucket tool to quickly fill in objects, such as shapes. You can fill objects with a color, a gradient effect, or even a picture (see Chapter 23). The Flash color palette comes with numerous colors and shades, as well as several premade gradient effects to choose from.

The Paint Bucket tool uses the same Fill Color palette as the other drawing tools. The palette shows all the available colors plus some gradient effects. The Fill Color palette is a common feature among most drawing programs, so if you have used a color palette with other programs, you will find that the Flash color palette works the same way. When you select a color from the palette, you can then fill the inside of any closed shape with the selected color.

ADD A FILL

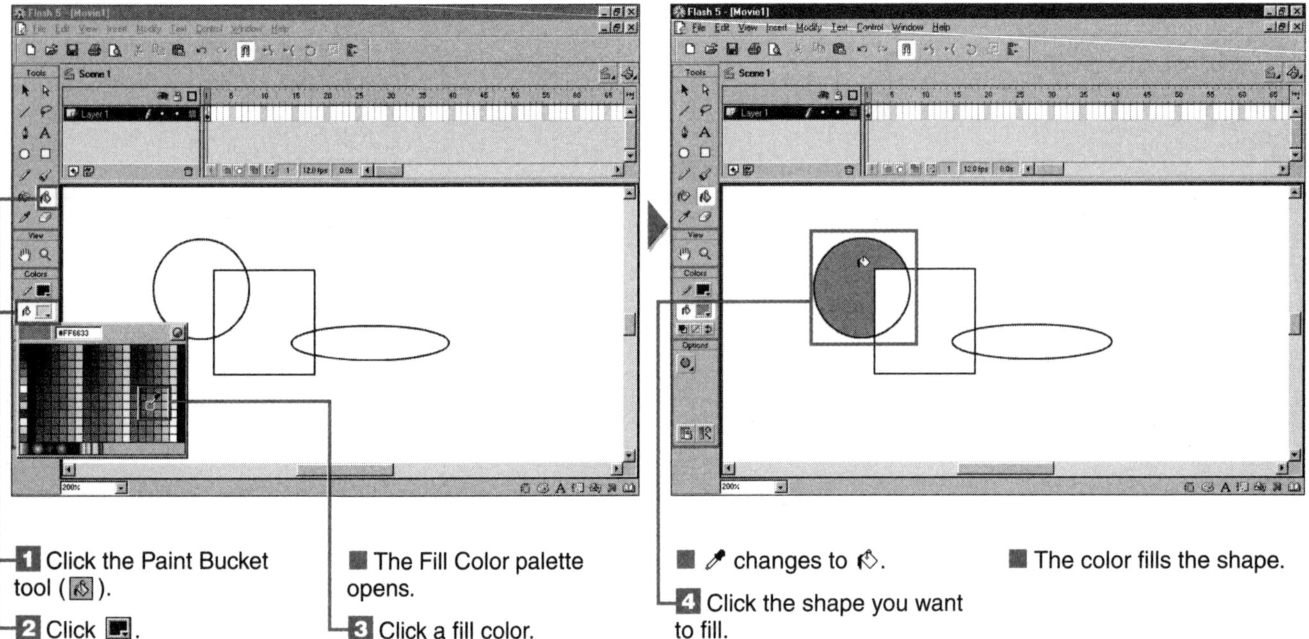

1 Click the Paint Bucket tool ( ).

2 Click .

■ The Fill Color palette opens.

3 Click a fill color.

■ changes to .

4 Click the shape you want to fill.

■ The color fills the shape.

What is a gradient effect?

✔ A *gradient effect* shows one or several colors of different intensities, creating a three-dimensional effect. With Flash, you can create a linear gradient effect that intensifies color shading from left to right or top to bottom or create a radial gradient effect that intensifies color shading from the middle to the outer edges or vice versa. To find out more about creating new gradient effects, see Chapter 19.

What does the Gap Size modifier do?

✔ When the Paint Bucket tool is selected, the Gap Size modifier (◙) appears in the Options tray at the bottom of the Drawing toolbar. Click ◙ to display a menu list of four settings. These settings determine how the Paint Bucket tool treats any gaps that appear in the shape you are trying to fill. *Note:* For very large gaps, you may need to close them yourself before applying the fill color.

ADD A GRADIENT FILL

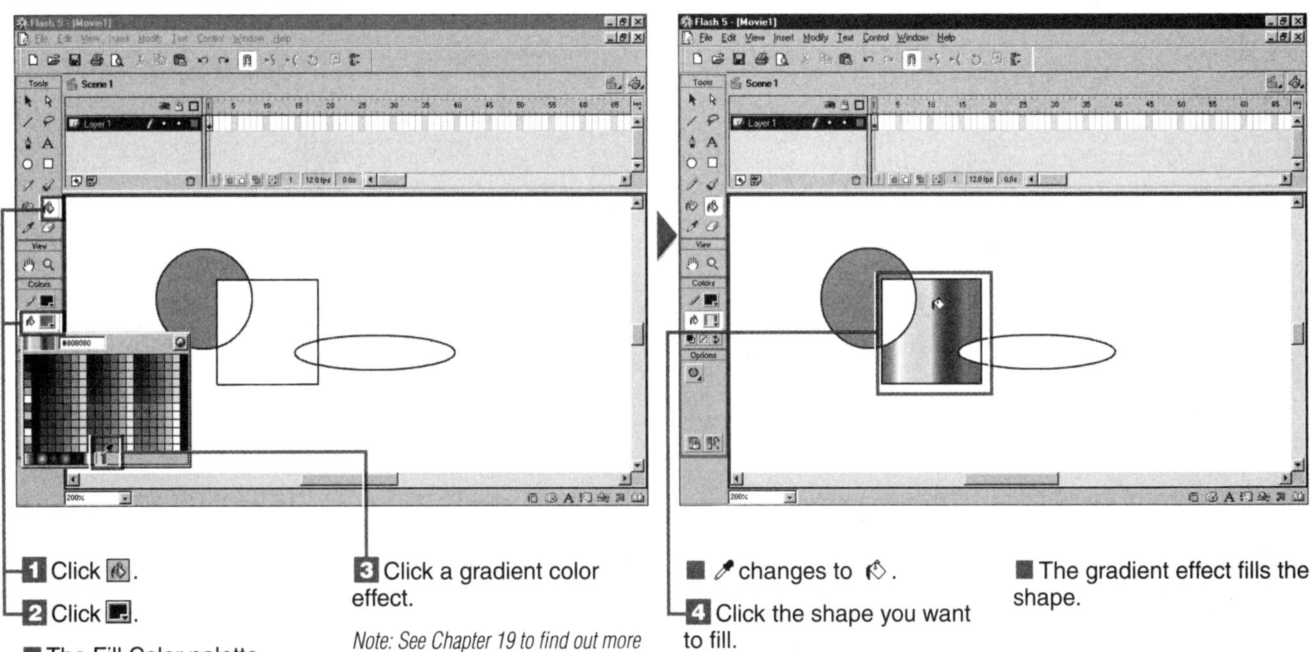

1 Click ◙.

2 Click ◙.

■ The Fill Color palette opens.

3 Click a gradient color effect.

Note: See Chapter 19 to find out more about creating new gradient effects.

■ ◙ changes to ◙.

4 Click the shape you want to fill.

■ The gradient effect fills the shape.

SELECT OBJECTS

To work with objects you draw or place on the Flash Stage, you must first select them. For example, you may want to change the color of a line outlining a shape, or modify the curve of a particular line segment. In order to do so, you must first select the line segment you want to edit. The more lines and shapes you place on the Stage, the trickier it is to select only the ones you want.

There are several techniques you can employ to select objects onscreen. You can use the Arrow tool to quickly select any single object, such as a line segment or fill. To select several objects, such as a couple of shapes or an entire drawing, you can drag a frame, also called a *marquee,* around the items. Flash selects anything inside the selection frame. Any edits you make effect all the items within the selection frame.

SELECT OBJECTS

CLICK TO SELECT OBJECTS

1 Click the Arrow button (↖).

2 Move the ↖ over the object you want to select, and then click.

■ You can select a fill and its surrounding line border by double-clicking the fill.

■ Selected objects appear highlighted with a pattern.

■ You can now edit the object.

How do I select multiple objects?

✔ Hold down the Shift key while clicking objects when you want to select more than one at a time. For example, if a line is comprised of several segments, you can select all of them for editing. Click the Arrow button (), then hold the Shift, and click each line segment you want to select.

How do I unselect a selected object?

✔ Just click anywhere outside the selected object. You can also press the Esc key on the keyboard.

Is there a fast way to select everything on the Stage?

✔ Yes. Click the Edit menu and click Select All. You can also press Ctrl+A (Windows) or Command+A (Mac) on the keyboard.

How do I select just a fill and not its border?

✔ Simply click the fill to select it. To select both the fill and the fill's border, double-click the fill.

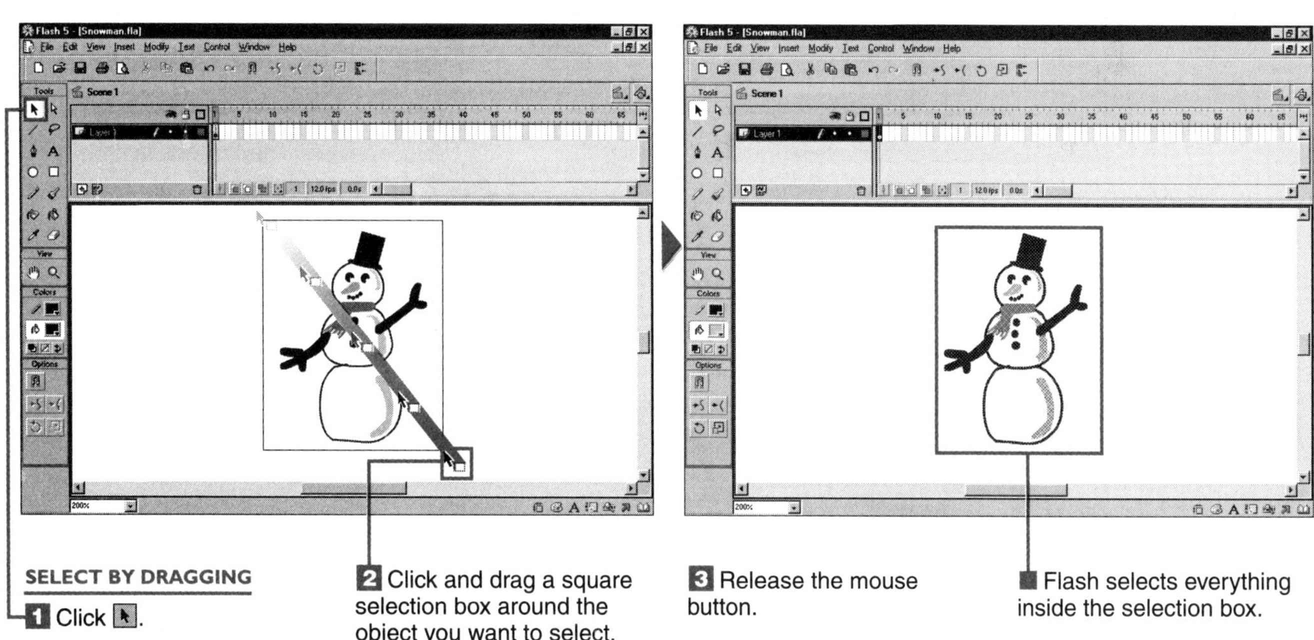

SELECT BY DRAGGING

1 Click .

2 Click and drag a square selection box around the object you want to select.

3 Release the mouse button.

■ Flash selects everything inside the selection box.

SELECT OBJECTS (CONTINUED)

If you are working with several irregularly shaped objects, it is not always easy to select a specific item. For example, you may have several circle shapes that overlap and need to select one section only, or perhaps you have several objects drawn closely together, but only want to select one object. You can use the Lasso tool to help you select irregular objects.

The Lasso tool draws a freehand "rope" around the item you want to select. This allows you to select an oddly shaped object or just a small portion of an object. You must drag the Lasso tool completely around the item you want to select. You drag the loop closed to complete the rope, so be sure to end the dragging procedure in the same place you started from. Flash selects anything inside the roped area. Using the Lasso tool takes a steady hand.

SELECT OBJECTS (CONTINUED)

LASSO AN OBJECT

1 To select an irregularly-shaped object, click the Lasso button (lasso icon).

■ When you move the pointer over the Stage area, it changes to a lasso.

2 Click and drag the lasso completely around the object until you reach the point where you started.

3 Release the mouse button.

■ Flash highlights anything inside the lasso shape.

How can I select complex shapes?

✔ You may find drawing around irregular items with the lasso difficult. You can use the Lasso tool's Polygon Mode modifier to help. Click , then click the Polygon mode tool ( ) in the Options tray. Click your way around the object you want to select. Every click creates a connected line to the last click. To turn off the Polygon Mode, double-click.

What does the Magic Wand modifier do?

✔ You use the Magic Wand modifier ( ), which appears in the Options tray when you select the , with broken apart bitmap images, to help you select areas within the image for modifications. See Chapter 23 to learn more about bitmap images in Flash.

Can I customize the Magic Wand settings?

✔ You can customize two Magic Wand modifier settings, the Threshold Setting and the Smoothing Setting, by clicking . Alter the Threshold Setting to define color values of adjacent colors to be included in the Lasso selection, and adjust the Smoothing Setting to specify the degree of smoothing (similar to antialiasing) of the edges of the selected area.

SELECT PART OF AN OBJECT

1 Click or .

■ You can click for simple shapes or lines.

■ You can click for irregularly-shaped objects.

2 Drag the pointer to surround the object part you want to select.

3 Release the mouse button.

■ Flash selects everything inside the area.

MOVE AND COPY OBJECTS

You can easily reposition objects on the Flash Stage. Flash lets you quickly move an object from one area to another, and you can make copies of the original object. Moving and copying in Flash works the same way as moving and copying items in other programs, using the Cut, Copy, and Paste commands. In Flash, the Cut, Copy, and Paste commands are available as toolbar buttons on the Main toolbar, or as menu commands on the Edit menu.

You can move an object by dragging it around the Stage using the mouse, or you can activate the standard Cut and Paste commands. Dragging an object is the quickest way to place it where you want it to go.

Copying an object places a duplicate of the selected object on the Stage. You need to move the duplicate to the desired location.

MOVE AN OBJECT

1 Click the arrow tool.

2 Click the object you want to move.

■ A move icon appears next to the arrow pointer.

3 Click and drag the object to a new position.

4 Release the mouse button.

■ Your object moves to the location you selected.

Can I precisely control where I position an object?

✔ For more precise positioning controls, open the Align panel. Press Ctrl+K (Windows) or Command+K (Mac), or click ▦ to open the Align panel where you can find a variety of controls for positioning an object precisely on the Stage. To learn more about using the alignment controls, see the section "Align Objects."

Are the Cut, Copy, and Paste keyboard shortcuts the same in Flash?

✔ Yes. Whether you are using Mac or Windows, the keyboard shortcuts work the same way in Flash as they do in other programs:

COPY AN OBJECT

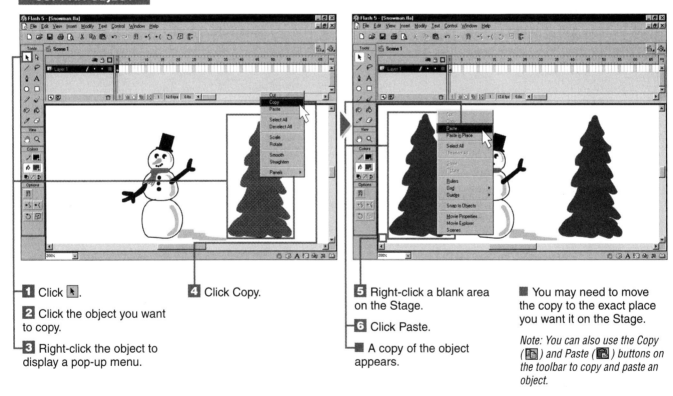

1 Click ↖.

2 Click the object you want to copy.

3 Right-click the object to display a pop-up menu.

4 Click Copy.

5 Right-click a blank area on the Stage.

6 Click Paste.

■ A copy of the object appears.

■ You may need to move the copy to the exact place you want it on the Stage.

Note: You can also use the Copy (▦) and Paste (▦) buttons on the toolbar to copy and paste an object.

EDIT LINE SEGMENTS

You can change a line by adjusting its length, or reshaping its curve. For example, you may want to change a line's angle, extend a curved line to make it appear longer, or just simply make the line curve more.

You can edit any line segment by altering its end points. Dragging an end point shortens or lengthens the line. Unlike other editing techniques, you do not need to first select the line in order to modify its end points.

You can edit a line's shape by dragging the area between the line's end points. Depending on the direction you drag, the line seemingly bends along with the pointer as you drag. When you release the mouse button, the line immediately takes on the new curvature. For example, if you move the middle of a line in an upward direction on the Stage, Flash creates a bulge or hill in the middle of the line. If you move the middle of the line in a downward direction, Flash creates a valley or dip in the middle of the line.

CHANGE A LINE SEGMENT LENGTH

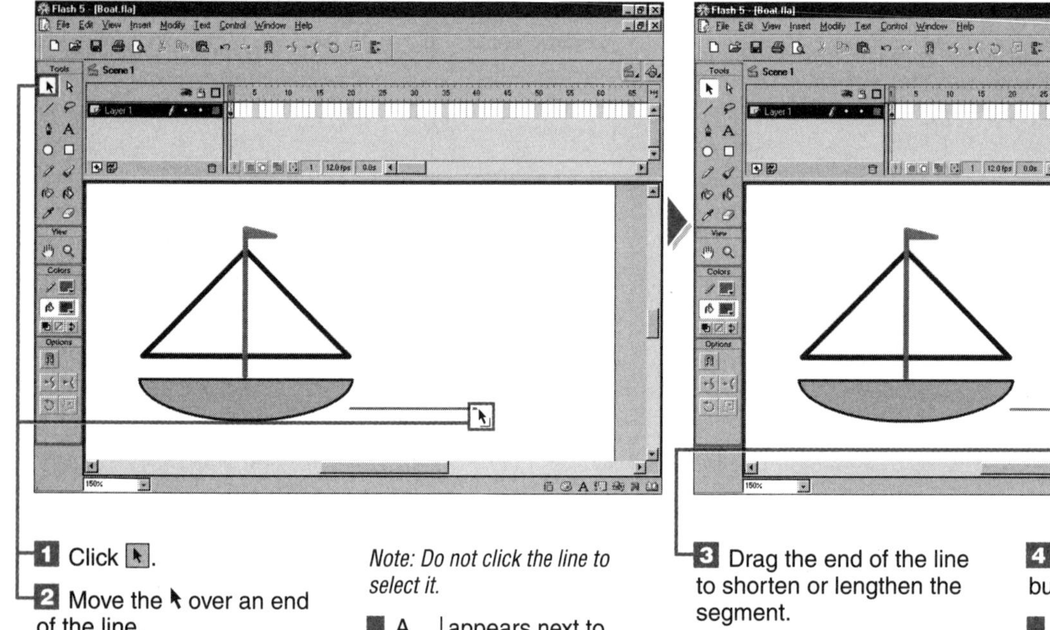

1 Click .

2 Move the over an end of the line.

Note: Do not click the line to select it.

■ A appears next to the .

3 Drag the end of the line to shorten or lengthen the segment.

■ As you drag the in any direction, you can change the line's angle.

4 Release the mouse button.

■ Flash resizes the line.

How do I draw perfectly vertical and horizontal lines?

✔ It is not always easy to hold a steady hand while you draw a line on the Stage. You can draw perfectly straight horizontal and vertical lines if you hold the Shift down while dragging the Line tool across the Stage.

Can I see precise edit points on a line?

✔ Yes. Click the Subselect button (↖) and then click the line. Edit points appear at either end of the line, and if the line consists of more than one segment, edit points also appear at each change of segment. You can drag any edit point to reshape the line.

How do I edit a line's color or thickness?

✔ Click the Window menu and click Panels, Stroke. This opens the Stroke panel where you can find settings for changing line color, thickness, and style. See Chapter 18 to learn more about assigning line-formatting attributes.

CHANGE A LINE SHAPE

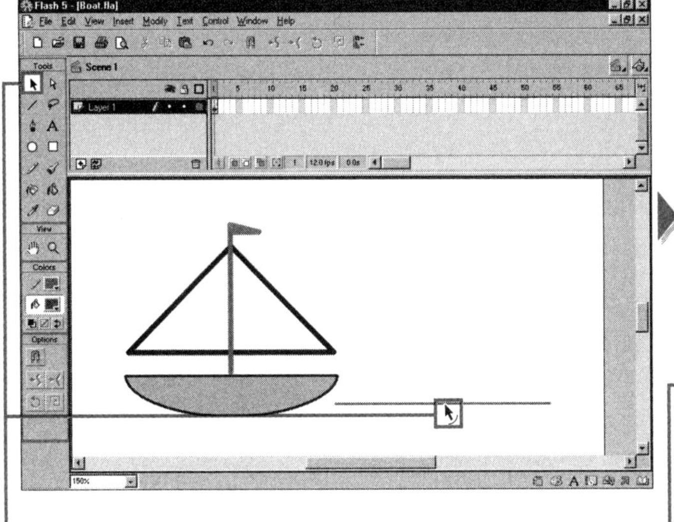

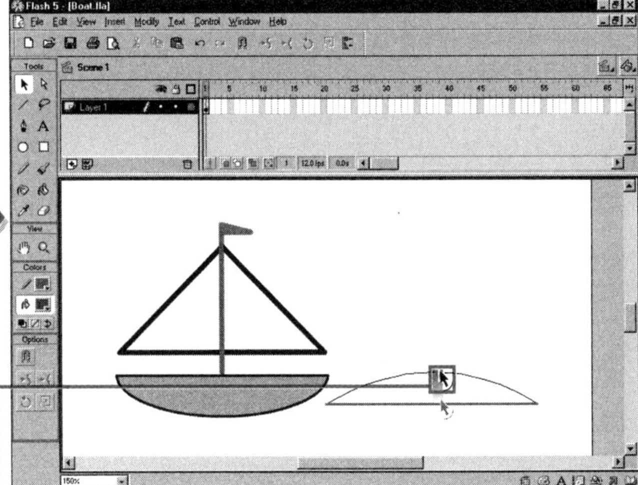

1 Click ↖.

2 Move the ↖ over the area of the line you want to curve.

Note: Do not click the line to select it.

■ A ⌒ appears next to the ↖.

3 Drag the line to add or reshape the curve.

4 Release the mouse button.

■ Flash reshapes the line.

EDIT FILLS

With Flash, you can change a fill shape by adjusting the sides of the fill. You can also change the fill color at any time.

You can easily adjust the edges of a fill to create new and unusual shapes. The fastest way to change a shape's edge is to drag it.

Depending on the direction you drag, the shape's edge may curve or straighten regardless of whether the shape uses an outline or not. You do not have to select the fill you want to edit in order to execute the edit.

In addition to changing the fill's edges, you can also change the color. Using the Fill Color palette, you can assign a new color or gradient effect. You must select, however, the fill first in order to apply a new color. As long as the fill is highlighted on the Stage, you can continue trying different colors from the Fill Color palette. Flash applies each color you select immediately to the fill.

EDIT FILLS

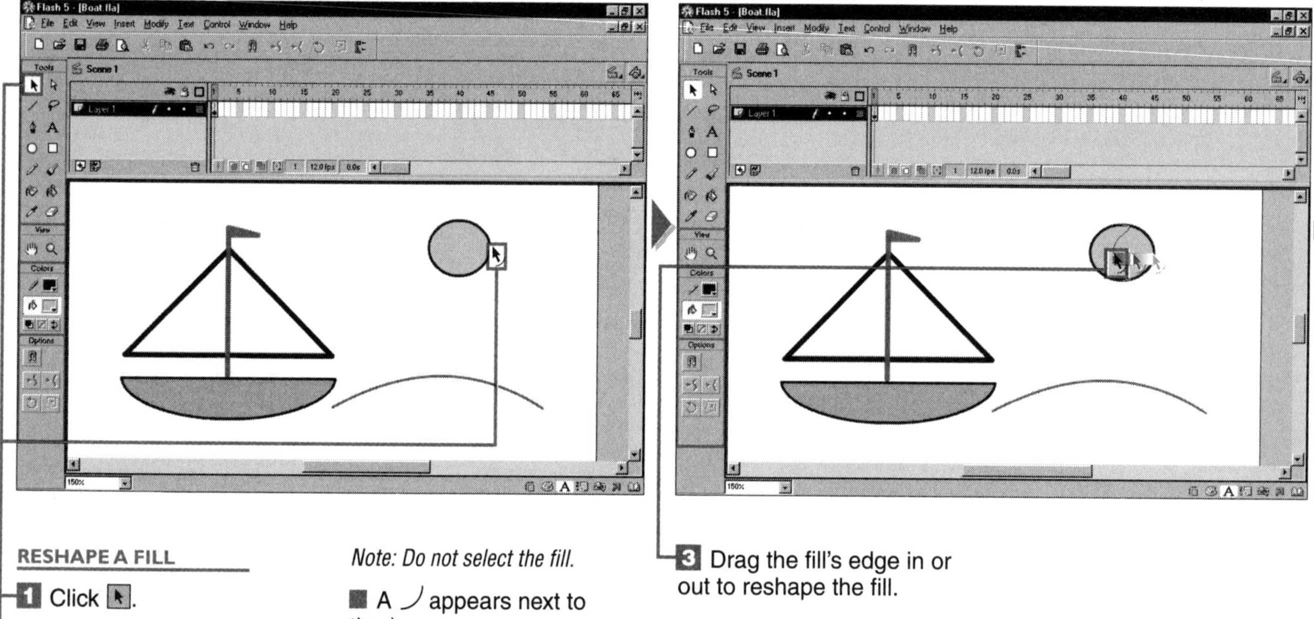

RESHAPE A FILL

1 Click the Arrow tool.

2 Move the arrow over the edge of the fill.

Note: Do not select the fill.

■ A curve symbol appears next to the arrow.

3 Drag the fill's edge in or out to reshape the fill.

Are there other ways to edit fill shapes?

✔ You can find additional Shape commands on the Modify menu that can help you edit fills. For example, to soften a fill's edges, select the fill, and then click Modify, Shape, and then Soften Fill Edges. From the Soften Edges dialog box, adjust the settings and click OK. Experiment with the settings to see what sort of effects you can create. See Chapter 18 to learn more about drawing shapes in Flash.

Can I adjust edit points on a fill outline?

✔ Yes. Click [icon], then click on the fill shape's outline. This displays edit points on the outline that surrounds the fill. You can then drag an edit point to change the shape of both the fill outline as well as the fill itself.

Flash does not let me edit my fill's edges. Why not?

✔ Make sure you have not selected the fill. If the fill appears in a highlighted pattern on the Stage, that indicates that you have selected the fill. You cannot edit the edges of a selected fill. Click outside the fill to deselect it and try editing the edges again.

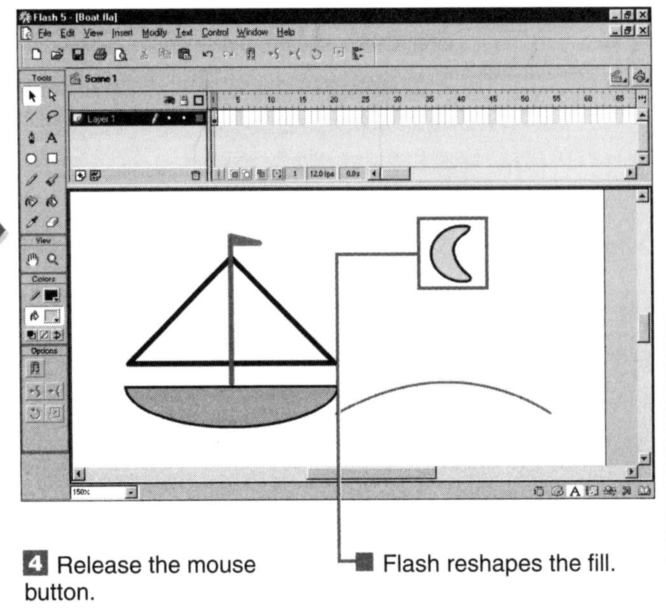

4 Release the mouse button.

■ Flash reshapes the fill.

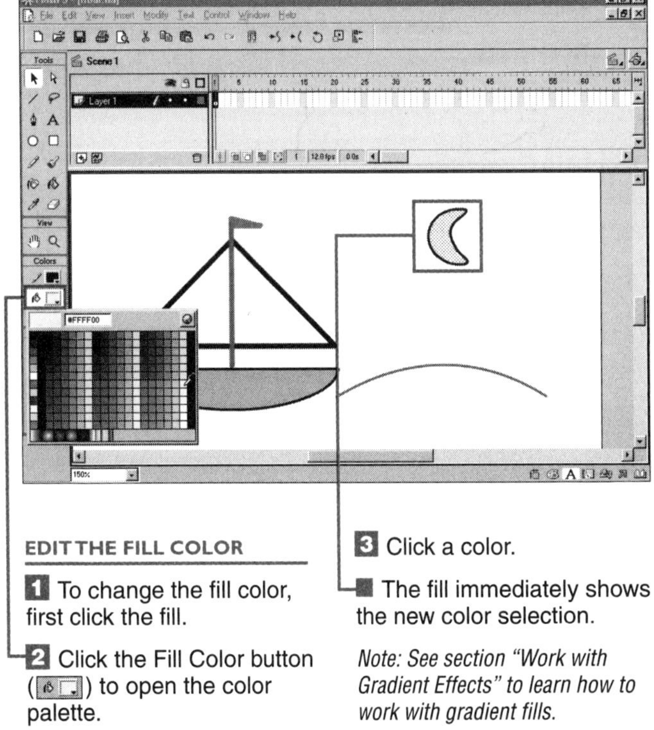

EDIT THE FILL COLOR

1 To change the fill color, first click the fill.

2 Click the Fill Color button ([icon]) to open the color palette.

3 Click a color.

■ The fill immediately shows the new color selection.

Note: See section "Work with Gradient Effects" to learn how to work with gradient fills.

RESIZE OBJECTS

You can scale objects in Flash to make them bigger or smaller than their original size using Flash's Scale feature. You can also use this feature to stretch or squish an object's proportions, altering the object's appearance from its original shape into a distorted shape.

The Scale command enables you to drag edit points — also called selection or resize handles — on the object to resize the object. The direction you drag a selection handle determines whether the object grows or shrinks in size, or whether the object's overall shape distorts. For example, if you drag any corner selection handle, Flash scales the object in proportion to its original size. If you drag a center selection handle on any side of the selected object, the object appears to be stretched or squished depending on which way you drag the mouse.

You can find the Scale button on the Main toolbar, or in the Options tray at the bottom of the Drawing toolbar when you select the Arrow tool.

RESIZE OBJECTS

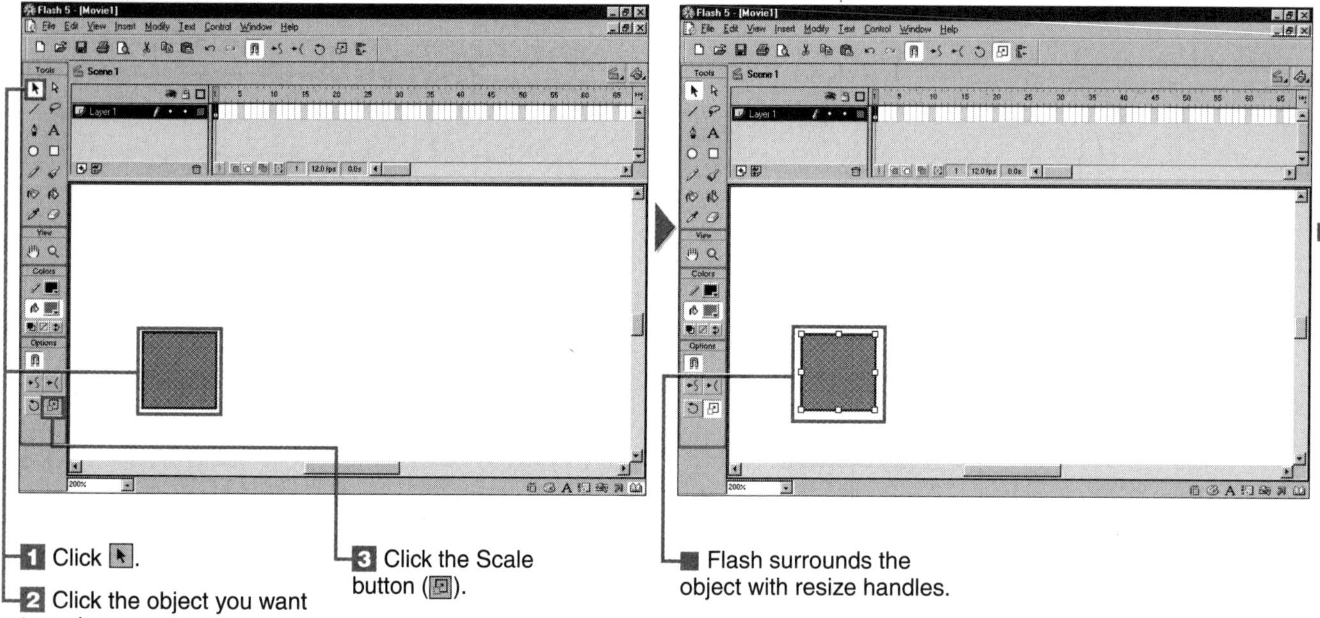

1 Click .

2 Click the object you want to resize.

3 Click the Scale button ().

■ Flash surrounds the object with resize handles.

How do I set a precise size?

✔ If you need to size an object to a precise measurement, use the Info panel. Select the object, then click the Info button (▣). This opens the Info panel. Here you can set a precise size for the object using the width (W) and height (H) text boxes. Simply type in the measurement you want, then click outside the panel to see the changes take effect.

What happens if I resize an item beyond the Stage?

✔ In some cases, the object you resize may reach beyond the Stage area. Not to worry, the object is still there. You may need to zoom out to see the object. You can move the item back onto the Stage or resize the Stage to fit the larger object. Any part of the object that hangs off the Stage is still considered in the work area; however, you may not see the part when you play your Flash movie. See Chapter 17 to learn more about resizing the Stage area.

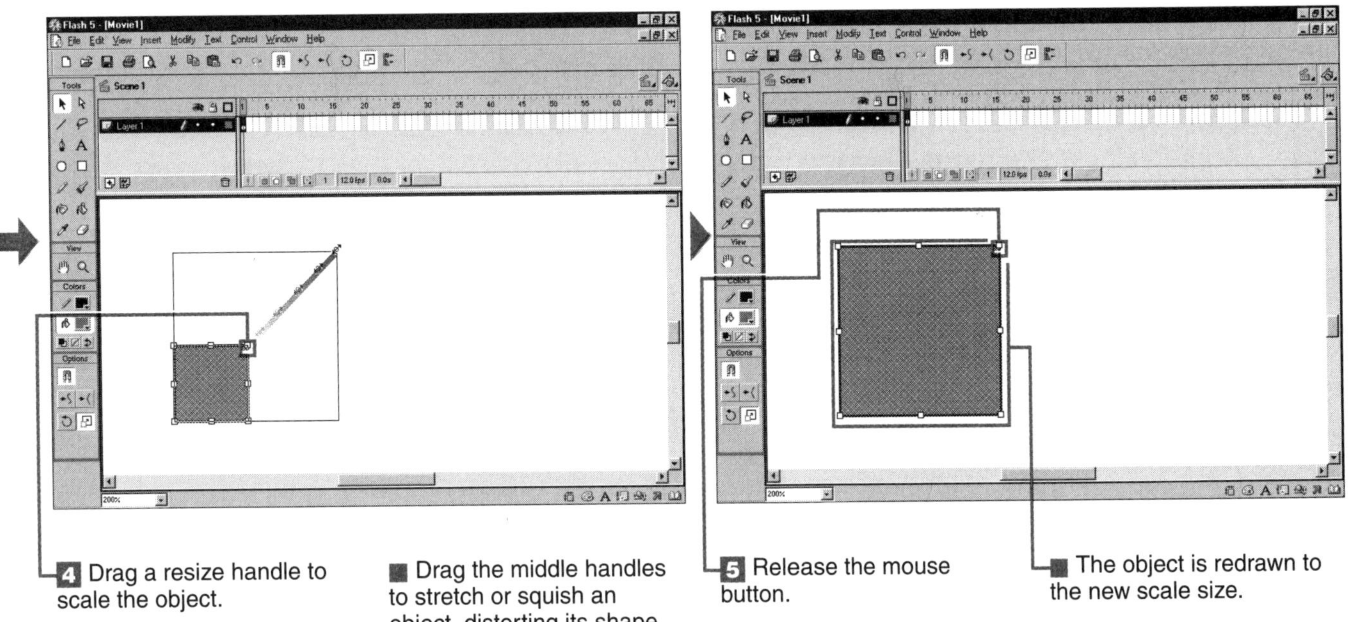

4 Drag a resize handle to scale the object.

■ Drag the corner handles to resize the object while keeping its proportions.

■ Drag the middle handles to stretch or squish an object, distorting its shape.

5 Release the mouse button.

■ The object is redrawn to the new scale size.

ADD STROKES TO SHAPES

The outline that surrounds a shape is called a *stroke* in Flash. When drawing shapes, you can choose to include an outline around the shape or not. If you choose the No Outline option, you draw a shape without an outline. You can apply an outline to the shape at any time using the Ink Bottle tool.

The Ink Bottle tool can quickly add outlines to fills or change existing outline strokes. You can control the stroke's thickness and color, and even add inside and outside strokes at the same time.

For example, you can create a unique shape using the Brush tool. You can easily add an outline to the shape with the help of the Ink Bottle tool. You can format the stroke to the exact line thickness and color you want. See Chapter 18 to learn more about creating shapes in Flash.

ADD STROKES TO SHAPES

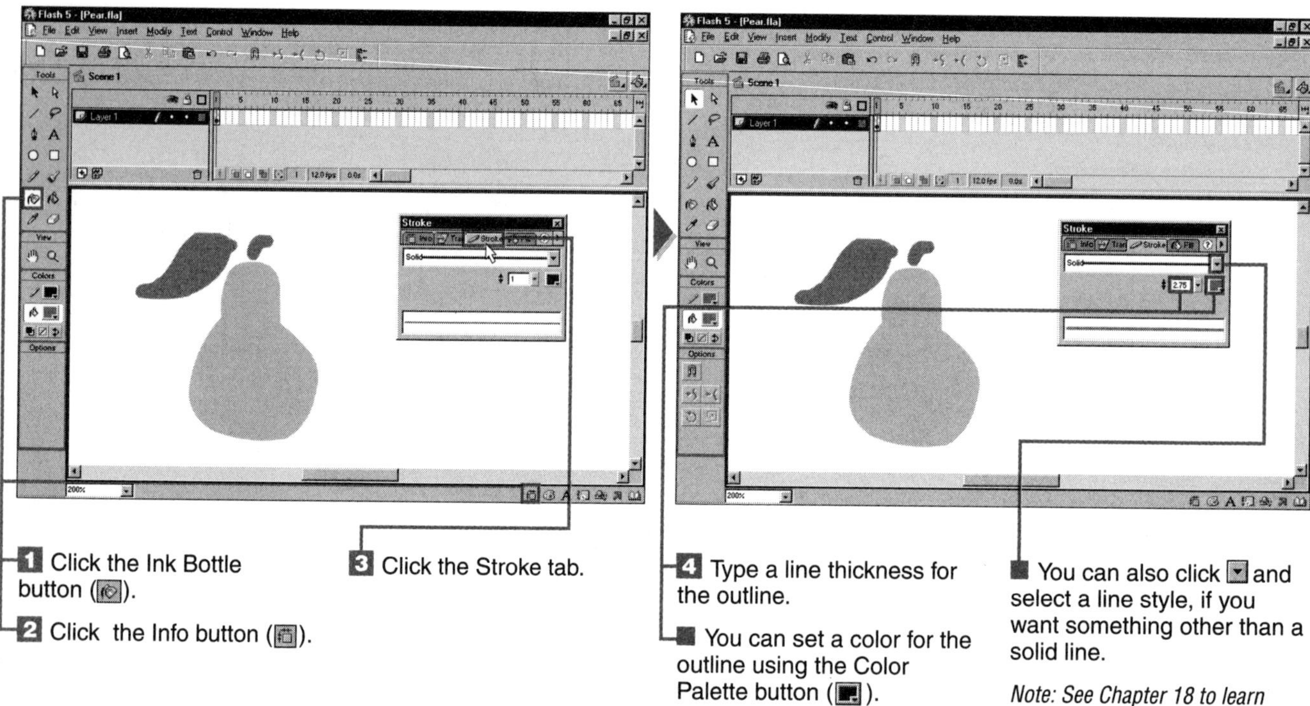

1 Click the Ink Bottle button (![]).

2 Click the Info button (![]).

3 Click the Stroke tab.

4 Type a line thickness for the outline.

■ You can set a color for the outline using the Color Palette button (![]).

■ You can also click ▾ and select a line style, if you want something other than a solid line.

Note: See Chapter 18 to learn more about formatting line segments using the Stroke panel.

Can I add multiple strokes?

✔ If your drawing has a shape inside a shape, you can add outlines to both at once. Click anywhere between the inside and outside shapes using the Ink Bottle tool (). Remember to set a line thickness, color, or style first unless you want to use the current stroke settings.

How do I delete an outline?

✔ Select the outline using the Arrow tool, then press Delete on your keyboard.

Can I add a stroke to a shape created with the Brush tool?

✔ Shapes you create using the Brush tool do not have outlines. However, you can add a stroke to the shape using the steps in this section.

How do I customize a stroke before I add it to a shape?

✔ Use the Line Style dialog box to customize an outline. From the Stroke panel, click and click Custom. The Line Style dialog box displays. You can choose a line style and select from the customizing settings associated with the style. To learn more about customizing strokes, see Chapter 18.

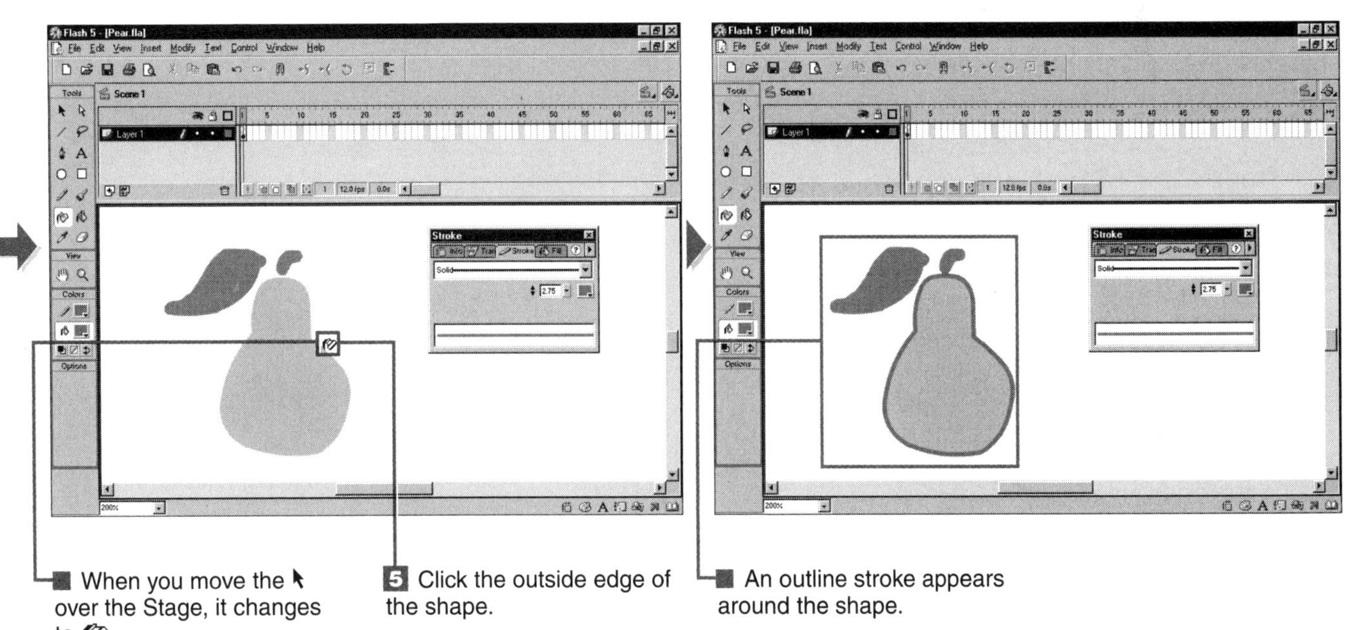

■ When you move the over the Stage, it changes to .

5 Click the outside edge of the shape.

■ An outline stroke appears around the shape.

ROTATE AND FLIP OBJECTS

Not every shape or line you draw has to remain as it is on the Stage. You can reorient objects to create different looks. You can spin an object based on its center point, or you can flip an object vertically or horizontally. Both actions enable you to quickly change an object's position in a drawing.

When you rotate an object on the Stage, you use the selection handles, also called rotation handles, to reorient the object. You can achieve different degrees of rotation depending on the direction in which you drag a handle on-screen.

When you flip an object, there are no selection handles. Flash automatically reorients the object in the position you indicate. You can flip an object horizontally or vertically. The Flip command flips an object 180 degrees. This example shows how to rotate and flip a selected object on the Stage.

ROTATE AN OBJECT

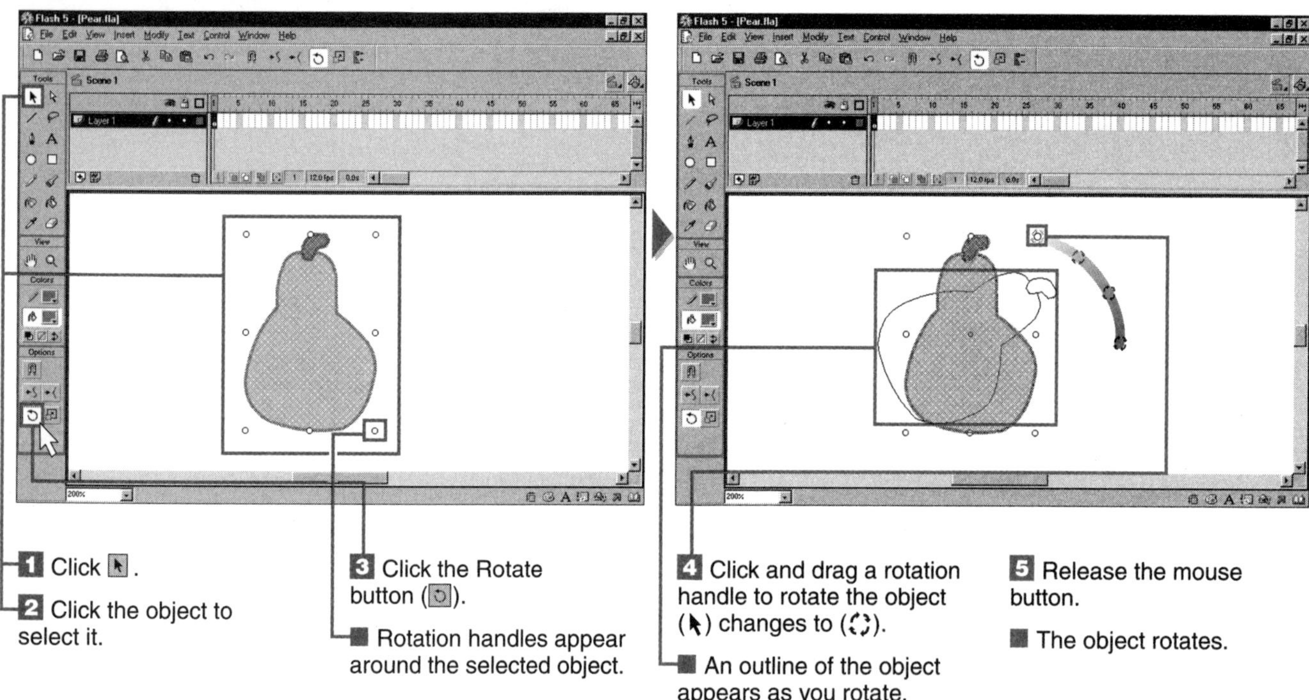

1 Click .

2 Click the object to select it.

3 Click the Rotate button ( ).

■ Rotation handles appear around the selected object.

4 Click and drag a rotation handle to rotate the object ( ) changes to ( ).

■ An outline of the object appears as you rotate.

5 Release the mouse button.

■ The object rotates.

Can I change an object's center point?

✔ For most objects, the center point is truly the object's center. But there are times when you want the center point to reference another part of the object. To change an object's center point, click Modify, Transform, Edit Center, and then drag the center point icon to a new location. This only works on overlay-level, not stage-level, objects.

Can I enter a precise degree of rotation?

✔ Yes. Select the object you want to rotate, then click the Info button (ⓘ) to open the Info panel. Click the Transform tab. Click the Rotate option and type a degree of rotation in the text box. Flash immediately rotates the object on the Stage.

How do I skew an object?

✔ You can both rotate and skew a flipped object using the Scale tool (⧉), which you find in the Main toolbar, or, when you click ↖, at the bottom of the Drawing toolbar. First rotate the object to the desired position, then click ⧉, and drag a selection handle to skew the object in the direction you want to shape it.

FLIP AN OBJECT

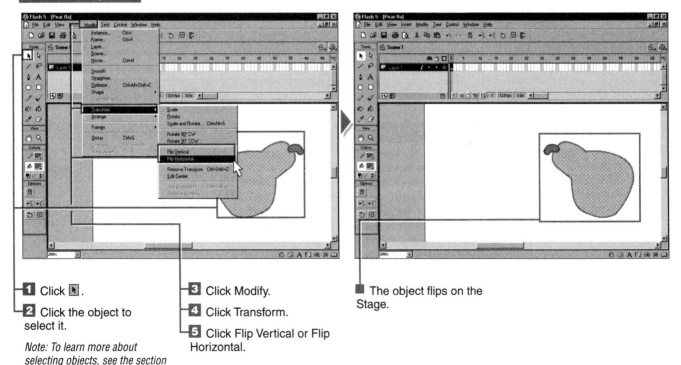

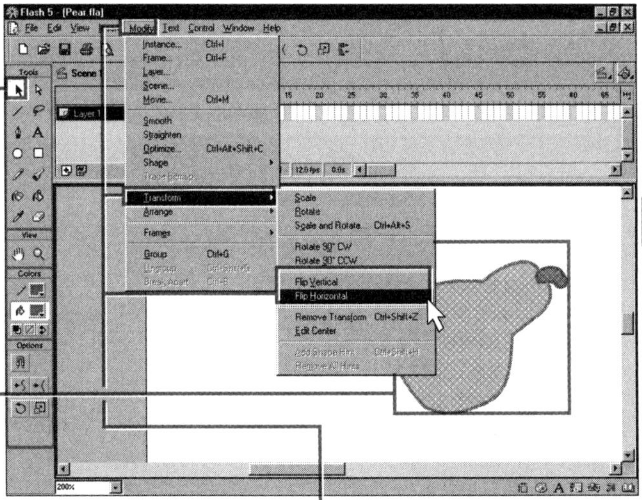

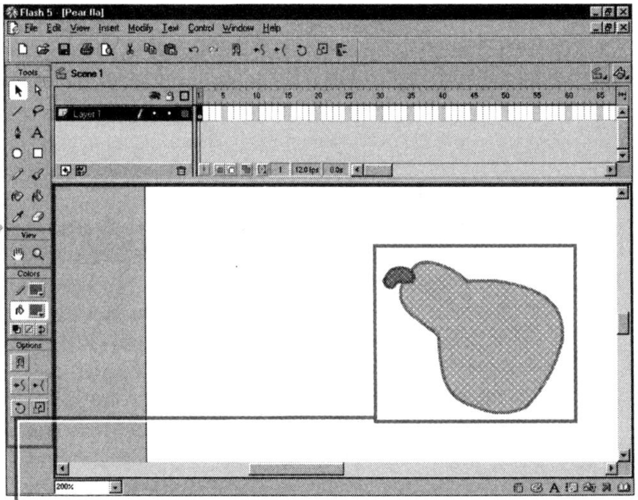

1 Click ↖.

2 Click the object to select it.

Note: To learn more about selecting objects, see the section "Select Objects" in this chapter.

3 Click Modify.

4 Click Transform.

5 Click Flip Vertical or Flip Horizontal.

■ The object flips on the Stage.

USING THE ERASER TOOL

You can use the Eraser tool to erase stray parts of a drawing or object, or you can use it to create new shapes within an object. The Eraser tool has several modifiers you can use to control how the tool works.

The Eraser tool does not really draw or paint, but rather it eliminates drawings or parts of drawings from the Stage. You can specify a shape for the Eraser as it moves around on the Stage. For example, perhaps you need to erase only a small piece of a line at the edge of a drawing. Such a task requires a small Eraser shape. A larger Eraser shape may end up erasing parts of your drawing that you do not want to erase.

Use the Eraser tool to erase strokes and fills on the stage level. You cannot erase grouped objects, symbols, or text blocks unless you apply the Break Apart command and make the items part of the stage level rather than the overlay level. See Chapter 18 to learn more about drawing levels in Flash.

USING THE ERASER TOOL

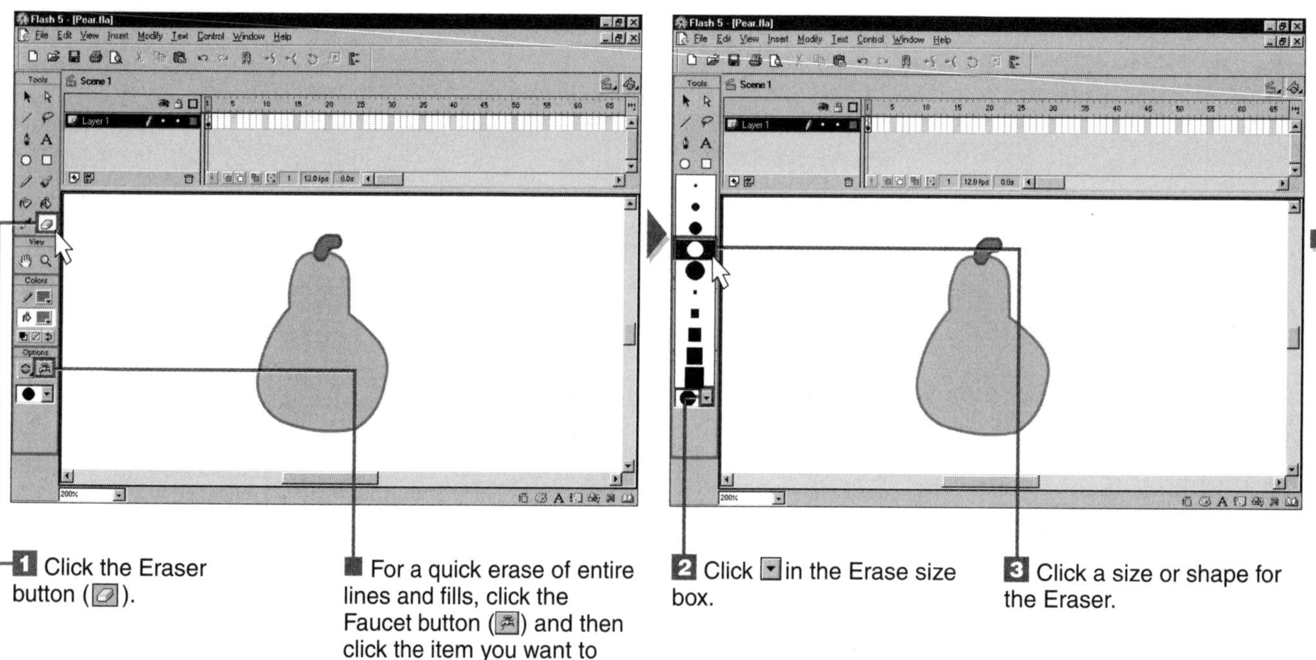

1 Click the Eraser button ( ).

■ For a quick erase of entire lines and fills, click the Faucet button ( ) and then click the item you want to erase.

2 Click ▼ in the Erase size box.

3 Click a size or shape for the Eraser.

How does the Eraser differ from a white fill?

✔ When you use the Eraser tool, you are literally erasing strokes and fills on the Stage. When you paint with the Brush tool using the white fill color, you are not erasing, but rather adding a shape to the Stage. Even if you cannot see the shape, because it is painted white and blends with the Stage background color, the shape is still there, and you can select and manipulate it. When you erase something on the Stage, it is permanently gone.

What do the Eraser modifiers do?

✔ You can use one of five modifiers with the Eraser tool. Click the Eraser Mode button (◻) in the Options tray at the bottom of the Drawing toolbar to view the five modifiers. Erase Normal lets you erase over anything on the Stage. Erase Fills erases inside fill areas but not lines. Erase Lines erases only lines. Erase Selected Fills does just that — erases only the selected fill. Erase Inside erases only inside the selected area.

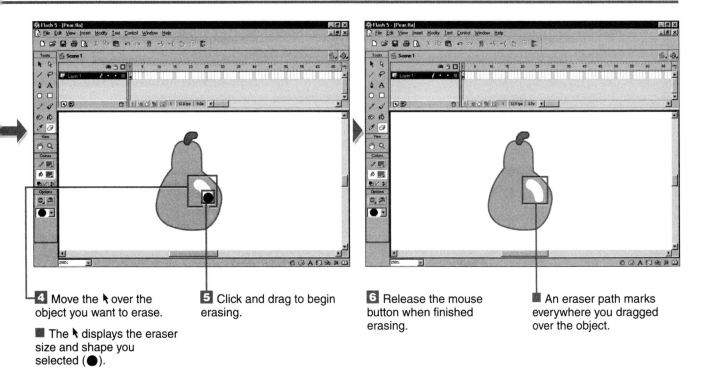

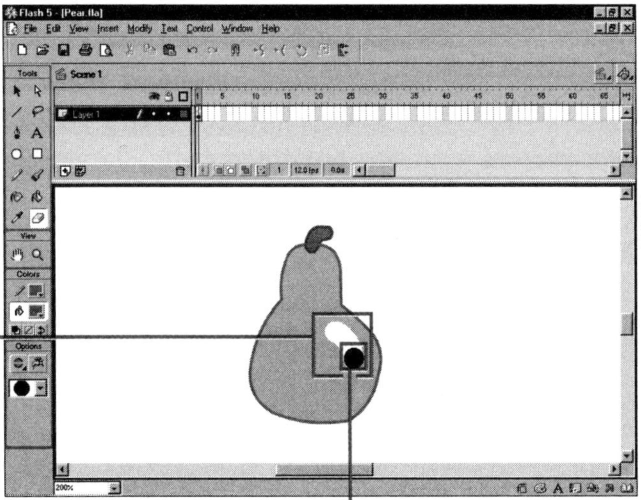

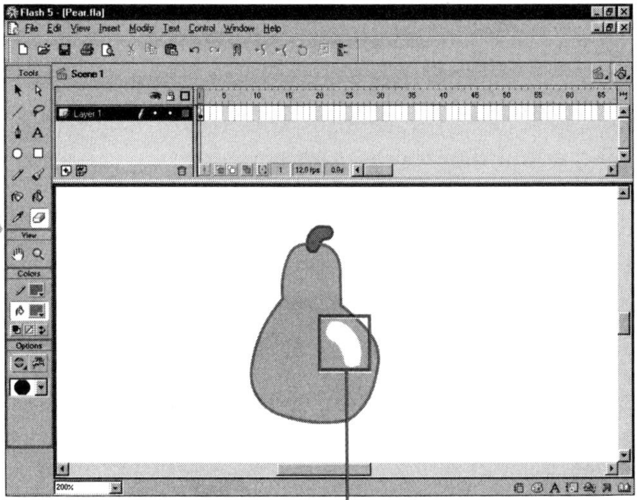

4 Move the ↖ over the object you want to erase.

■ The ↖ displays the eraser size and shape you selected (●).

5 Click and drag to begin erasing.

6 Release the mouse button when finished erasing.

■ An eraser path marks everywhere you dragged over the object.

WORK WITH GRADIENT EFFECTS

A *gradient* effect is a band of blended color or shading. Gradient effects can add depth and dimension to your Flash drawings. In Flash, you can apply a gradient effect as a fill to any shape.

By default, the Fill Color palette offers several gradient effects you can use. There are three vertical color bar effects, called *linear gradients*, and four circle gradient effects, called *radial gradients* that you can choose on the color palette. If you do not like the default choices, you can create your own linear or radial gradient effect.

You can save time if you plan out which colors you want to use in a gradient and decide which type of gradient you want to apply. For example, if you want to create an illusion of depth and apply it to an interactive button you have created, experiment with a radial gradient.

This example shows you how to assign a default gradient effect from the Fill Color palette as well as customize a new gradient. You can use the steps in the example to apply any gradient effect.

ASSIGN A GRADIENT EFFECT

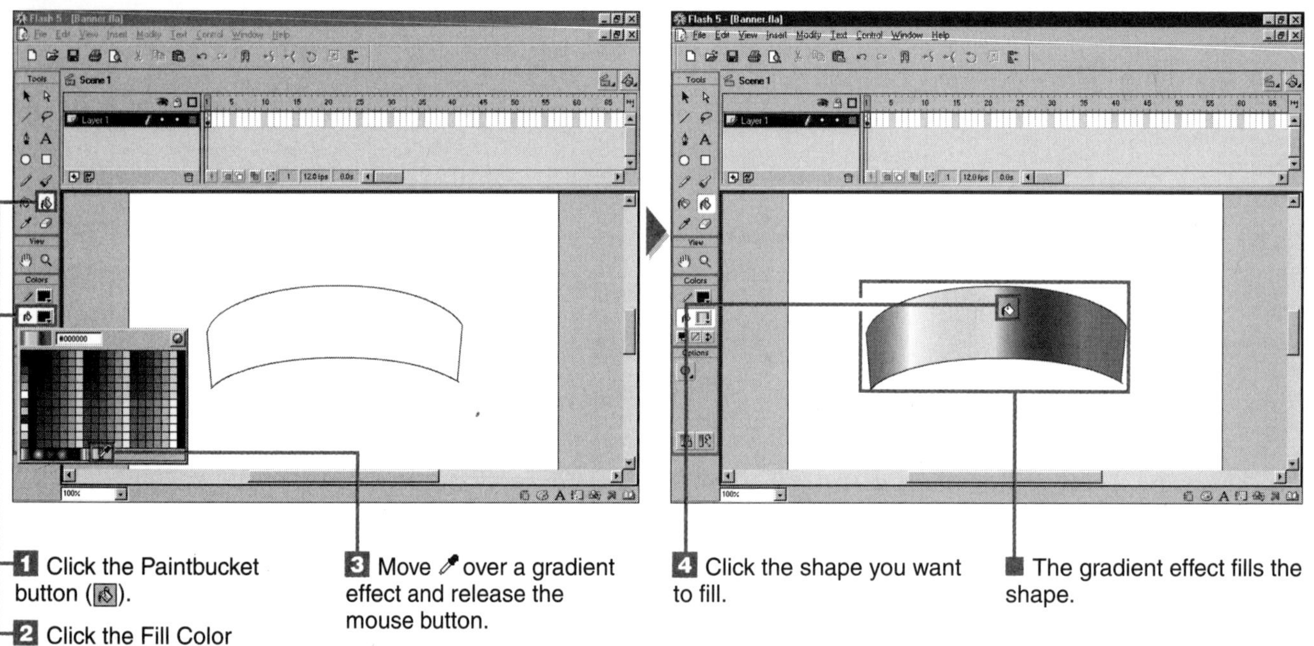

1 Click the Paintbucket button (🪣).

2 Click the Fill Color button (🪣■).

■ The ↖ changes to an 🖊.

3 Move 🖊 over a gradient effect and release the mouse button.

4 Click the shape you want to fill.

■ The gradient effect fills the shape.

What makes a gradient effect?

✔ The term *gradient* refers to an effect in which two or more colors graduate in color intensity from one color to another. For example, a two-color gradient effect can show the color red blending into yellow from the left to the right. The middle area of the effect shows the subtle blending of the two colors. You can create gradient effects in Flash that blend colors from left to right. Gradient effects can also create a three-dimensional appearance. You can create a radial effect that intensifies color from the middle to the outer edges, or from the outer edges to the middle.

Can I use a gradient as a Brush color?

✔ Yes. You can assign a gradient as the color you use with the Brush tool. You can specify a gradient effect from the Fill Color palette before you begin using the Brush tool, or you can use the Paint Bucket to fill the painted shape after you have drawn it on the Stage.

CREATE A NEW GRADIENT

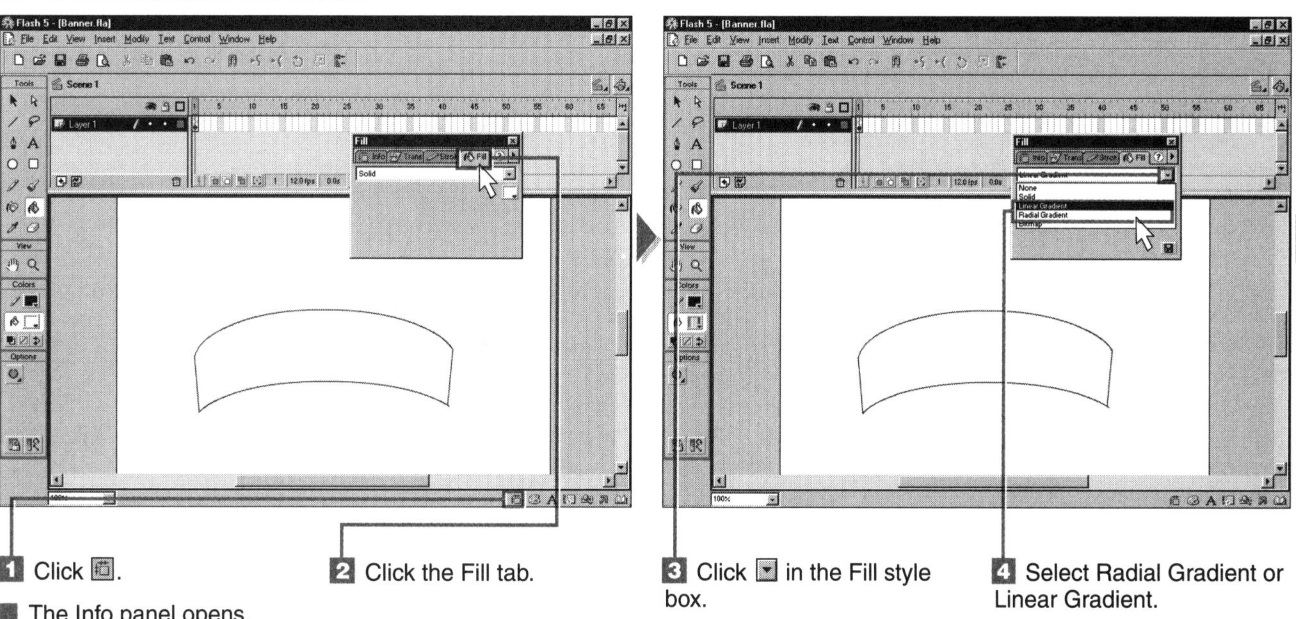

1 Click 🗔.

■ The Info panel opens.

2 Click the Fill tab.

3 Click ▾ in the Fill style box.

4 Select Radial Gradient or Linear Gradient.

CONTINUED

WORK WITH GRADIENT EFFECTS (CONTINUED)

Using the tools associated with the Fill panel, you can customize your own unique gradient effect. After you create the effect, Flash adds it to the Fill Color palette where you can access it again throughout your project.

You can change the properties of the your gradient by adjusting different colors and color markers, which create color intensity bandwidths. Color markers are the tiny icons beneath the gradient bar in the Fill panel. By dragging a marker on the gradient bar, you can create different areas of intensity in the gradient effect. To get a feel for how the customizing effect works, start with one color and adjust the marker left and right across the color bar in the Fill panel. Flash does not limit you to the number of colors you use in the gradient, and once you create the gradient just the way you want it, you can save it as a swatch in the color palette to reuse again.

CREATE A NEW GRADIENT (CONTINUED)

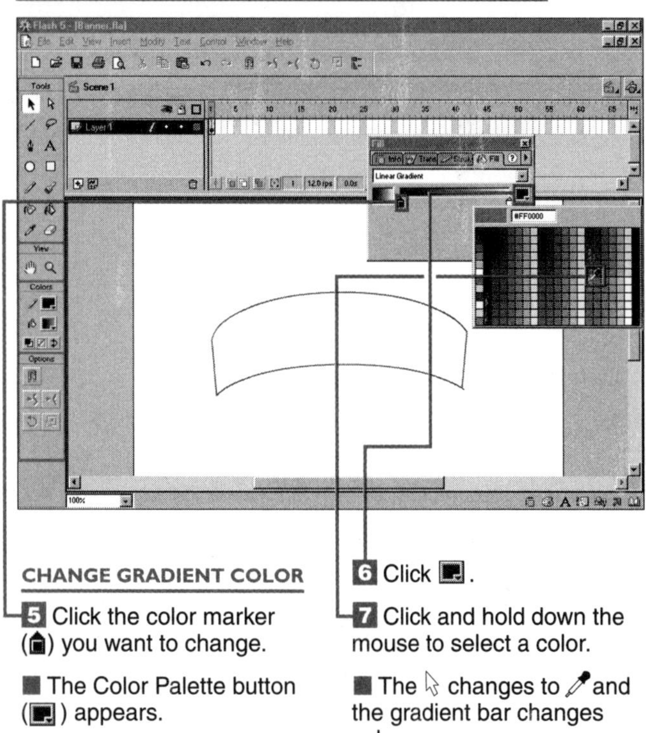

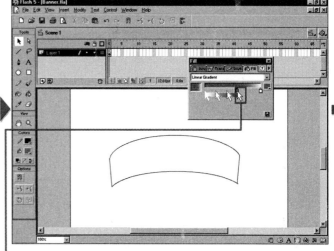

CHANGE GRADIENT COLOR

5 Click the color marker ( ) you want to change.

■ The Color Palette button ( ) appears.

6 Click .

7 Click and hold down the mouse to select a color.

■ The changes to and the gradient bar changes color.

ADJUST COLOR INTENSITY

8 Drag the left or right to adjust the color intensity bandwidth on the gradient.

■ To add another to the effect, click below the gradient bar.

■ To remove a , drag it off the panel.

■ You can continue creating the gradient effect by adding color markers, assigning colors, and dragging the markers to change the intensity.

Can I make changes to an existing gradient in the palette?

✔ Yes. You can select an existing gradient effect and make modifications as needed. From the Fill panel, click the Fill Color Palette button on the Drawing toolbar and click the gradient swatch you want to edit. The gradient appears in the Fill panel, with color markers for each color used in the effect. You can now make changes to the colors or intensities and save the edits as a new gradient color swatch.

Can I delete a customized gradient effect I no longer need?

✔ Yes. Click the Mixer button () to display the Mixer panel, and then click the Swatches tab. Click on the gradient effect swatch you want to delete. Click the button at the top of the panel to display a pop-up menu of related commands. Click Delete Swatch. Flash permanently deletes the gradient effect from all color palettes.

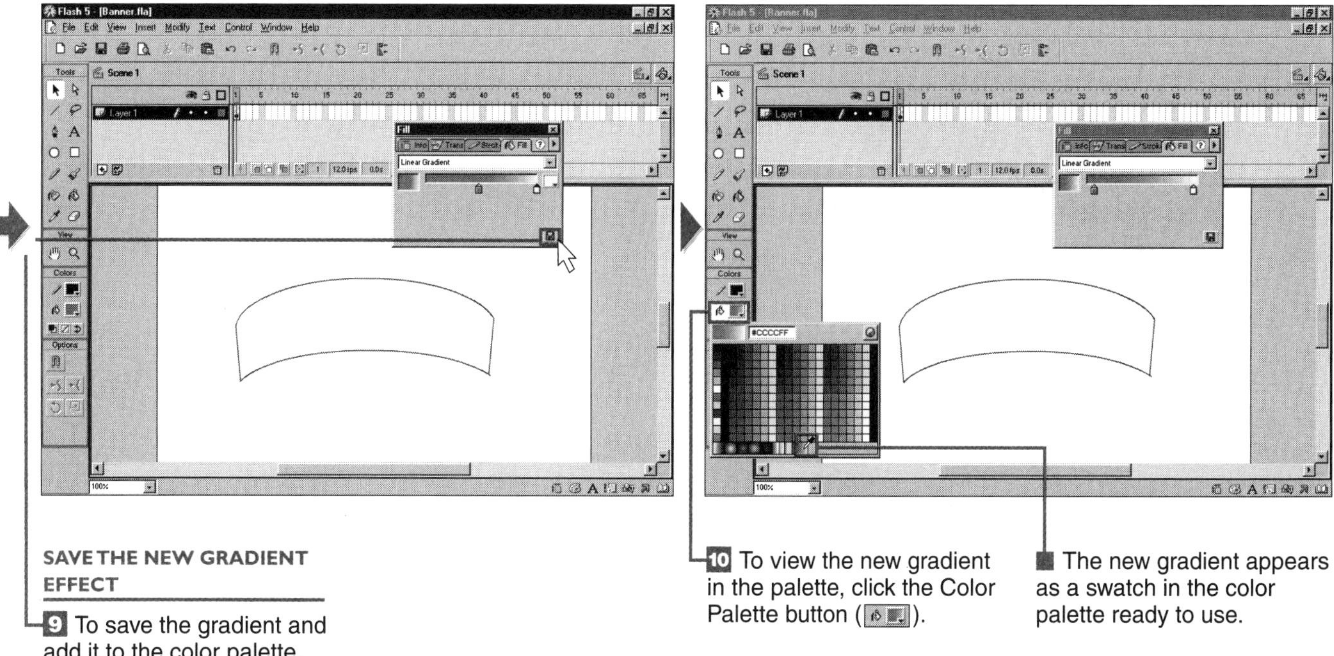

SAVE THE NEW GRADIENT EFFECT

9 To save the gradient and add it to the color palette, click the Save button ().

10 To view the new gradient in the palette, click the Color Palette button ().

■ The new gradient appears as a swatch in the color palette ready to use.

EDIT A COLOR SET

Color is an important part of the drawing portion of the Flash program, and you can customize colors to suit the projects you create. Flash comes with a default color set, but you can make new color sets based on the default set by removing colors you do not need for a particular project. You can then save the edited color set as a new color set for use in other Flash projects. You save color sets with the .clr file extension.

You can mix colors and edit color sets using the Mixer and Swatches panels. When working with colors, keep in mind that Flash handle colors differently across platforms (Windows and Mac). Computer systems and monitors also display colors differently, and older equipment is often incapable of displaying full color. Ultimately, this means that browsers may not always have the same colors available for Web page display as the colors you painstakingly choose for your Flash creations.

EDIT A COLOR SET

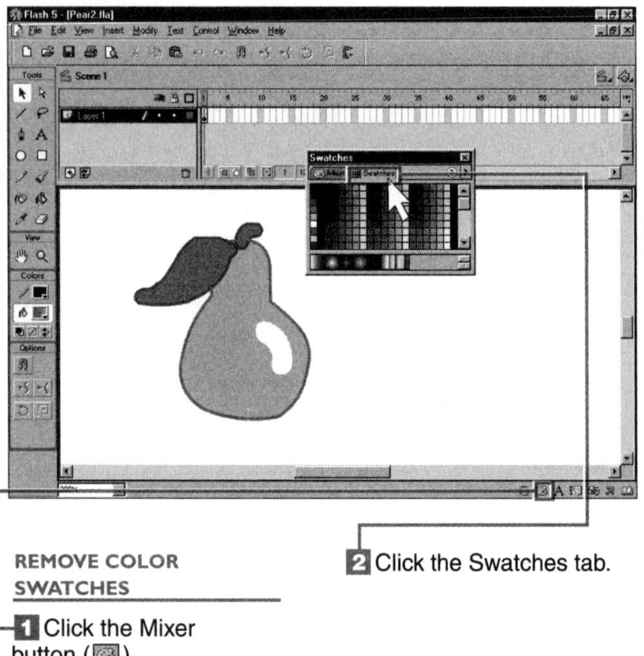

REMOVE COLOR SWATCHES

1 Click the Mixer button.

■ The Mixer panel opens.

2 Click the Swatches tab.

3 To remove a color swatch from the set, click the color.

4 Click the ▶ to display the pop-up menu.

5 Click Delete Swatch.

■ You can continue removing swatches you do not want as part of your color set.

How do I load a color set?

✔ After you create a color set, you can reuse it in any Flash file. Click [icon], and then click the Swatches tab. Click the [icon] and click Replace Colors. Locate the color set file you want to use, select it, and click Open.

Which colors should I use for Web page designs?

✔ Since different computers handle color differently, designers have come up with a Web Safe color palette. The Web Safe palette consists of 216 colors that Web designers find are consistent in both Windows and Mac platforms for all the major Web browser programs. To use the Web Safe palette in Flash, open the Swatches panel, click [icon] in the upper-right corner of the palette, and then click Web 216. Using the Web 216-color palette assures that your color selections are suitable for all browsers.

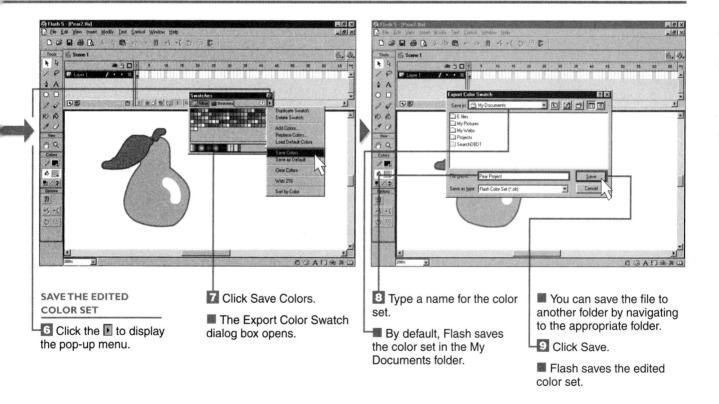

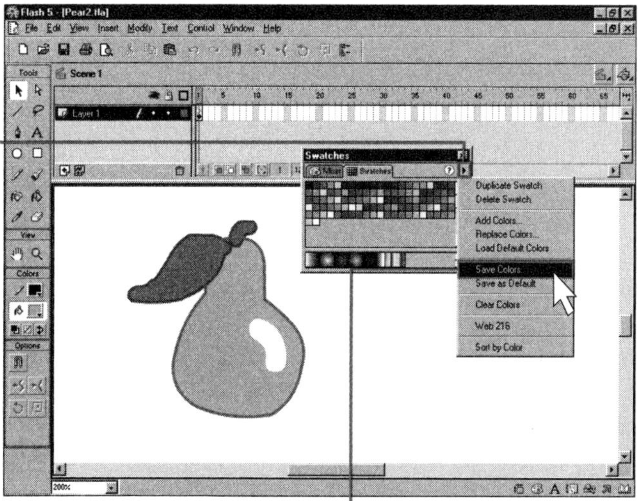

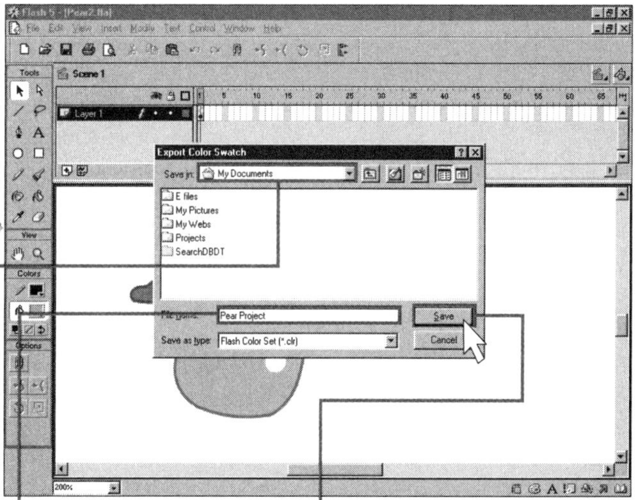

SAVE THE EDITED COLOR SET

6 Click the [icon] to display the pop-up menu.

7 Click Save Colors.

■ The Export Color Swatch dialog box opens.

8 Type a name for the color set.

■ By default, Flash saves the color set in the My Documents folder.

■ You can save the file to another folder by navigating to the appropriate folder.

9 Click Save.

■ Flash saves the edited color set.

COPY ATTRIBUTES

You can use the Dropper tool to quickly copy attributes from one object to another. The Dropper tool copies fill and line attributes and enables you to copy the same formatting to other fills and lines.

The Dropper tool is unique to Flash. Much like a real life eyedropper, the Dropper tool "absorbs" the formatting you apply to a particular line or shape. When it is not over a line or fill, the Dropper icon looks the same as the icon Flash uses to select a fill color. Move the Dropper over a line and a tiny pencil appears next to the dropper icon. The pencil icon lets you know you are hovering the Dropper over a stroke. When you click the Dropper, it absorbs the formatting applied to the stroke.

After picking up the attributes you want to copy, the Dropper becomes an ink bottle icon. You can then move the Dropper over the Stage and "drop" the same formatting onto another line.

COPY ATTRIBUTES

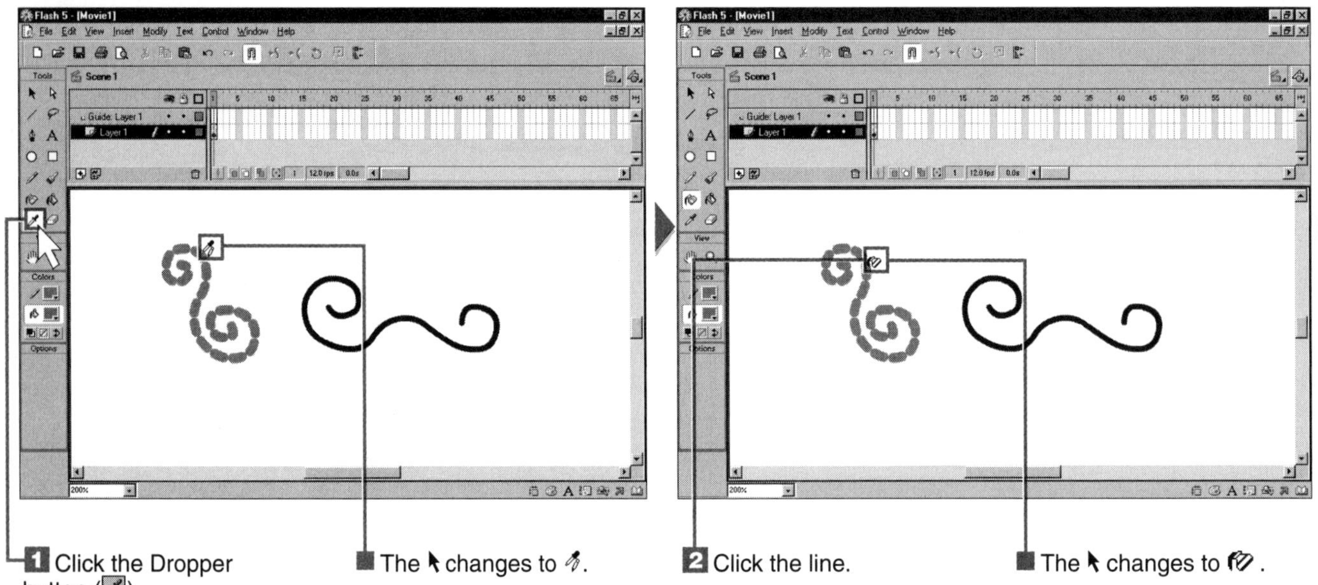

1 Click the Dropper button (✐).

■ The ↖ changes to ✐.

2 Click the line.

■ The ↖ changes to ✐.

Can I copy fill attributes, too?

✔ You can copy fill attributes just like you copy line attributes. When you move the Dropper tool (🖊) over a fill, a tiny ☑ appears next to it to show that youare over a fill. Click 🖊 to absorb the fill formatting. Move 🖊 over the fill you want to reformat, and click again. Flash immediately changes the second fill to match the first.

My Dropper tool does not work. Why not?

✔ When copying line attributes, you cannot use the 🖌 on grouped lines. Be sure to ungroup the lines first and then try copying the line attributes to each line. See the section "Group Objects" for more information.

Can I copy attributes before I draw another line or fill on the Stage?

✔ You can use the Dropper to copy the attributes of an existing line or fill, and the Line Color and Fill Color buttons change to reflect the formatting you assign to the object. You can then select a tool and draw on the Stage. The new object you draw has the same attributes as the original object.

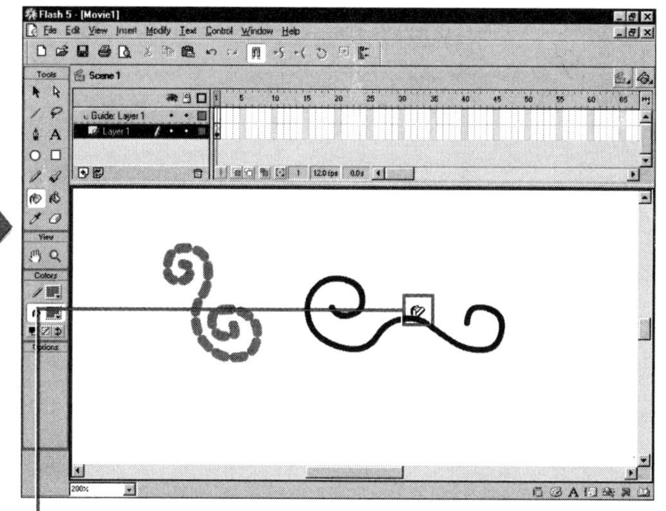

3 Click the line to which you want to copy.

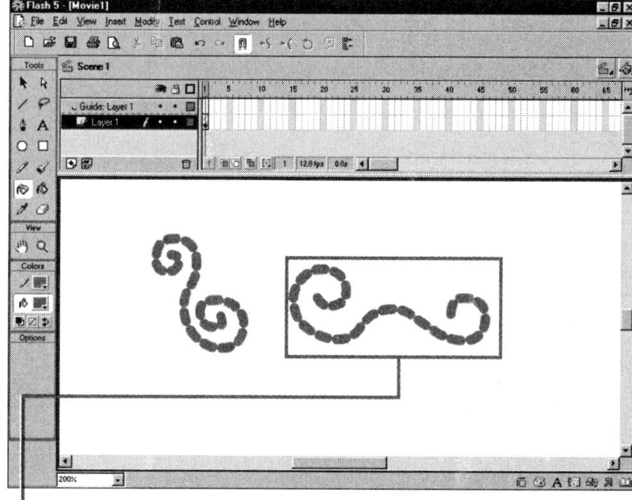

■ Flash immediately applies the line formatting.

GROUP OBJECTS

To work on multiple items at the same time, place them in a group. A group enables you to treat the items as a single unit. Any edits you make effect all items in the group.

You place grouped objects on the overlay drawing level in Flash. Grouped objects do not interact with objects on the stage level. See Chapter 18 to learn more about drawing levels.

One of the prime benefits of grouping several objects is that you can move them all at once on the Stage instead of moving one object at a time. Grouping is also helpful when you want to keep related objects together, such as the elements that create a logo. For example, your logo can include a background box, a text box, and several freeform lines. After you design or create the logo on the Flash Stage and layer the objects just the way you want them, turn the objects into a group. You can ungroup the objects again to edit them individually. See the section "Stack Objects" to learn about stacking layers.

GROUP OBJECTS

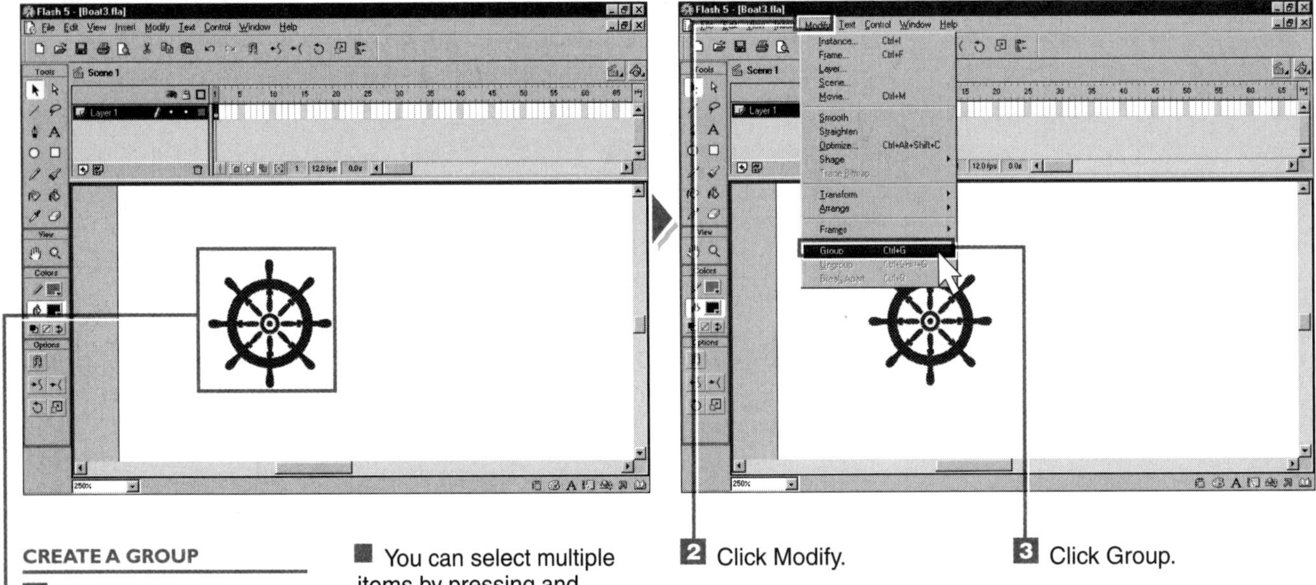

CREATE A GROUP

1 Select all the objects you want to include in a group.

Note: See the section "Select Objects" to learn more about selecting items on the Flash Stage.

■ You can select multiple items by pressing and holding Shift while clicking each item.

2 Click Modify.

3 Click Group.

How can I avoid accidentally changing a group?

✔ If you worry about accidentally moving or changing a group, you can lock it. Click Modify, Arrange, and then Lock. To unlock the group again, click Modify, Arrange, and then Unlock.

How is grouping different from stacking?

✔ Grouping sticks objects together so that they act as one object. Stacking allows you to move different grouped objects to the background or foreground, or somewhere in between.

Can I have a group of one?

✔ Yes. You can turn one object into a group to move it to the overlay level and keep it from interacting with other objects on the stage level.

How do I edit a group?

✔ Click [arrow icon], then double-click on the group you want to edit. Everything else on the Stage dims except for the items in the selected group. After editing the group, double-click anywhere outside the group.

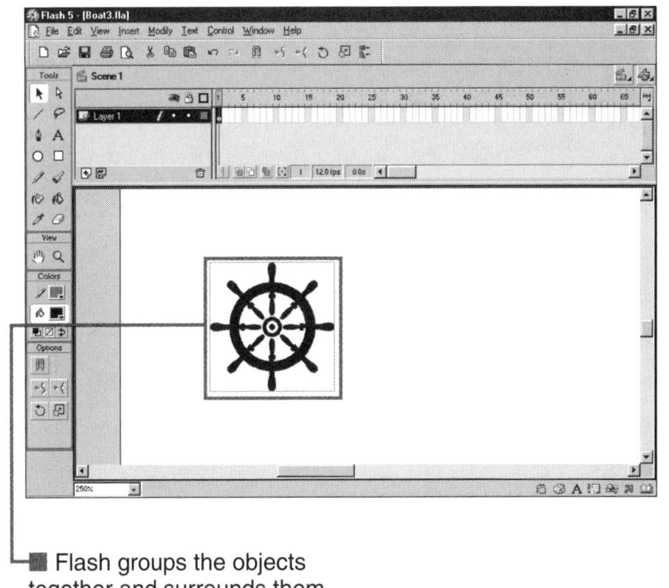

■ Flash groups the objects together and surrounds them with a blue box.

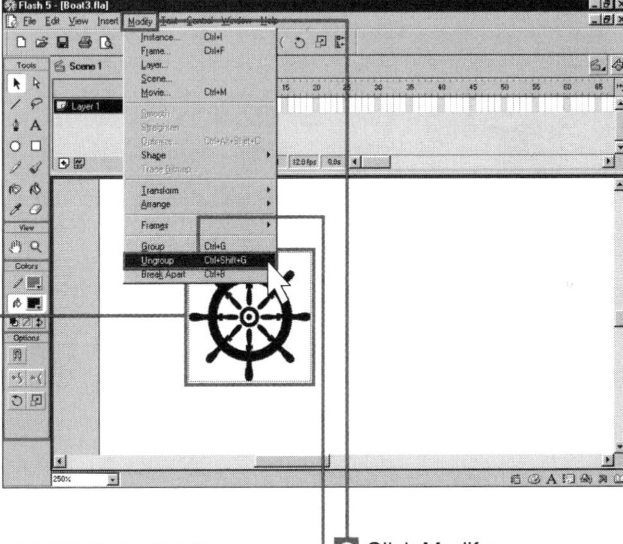

UNGROUP A GROUP

1 Select the group you want to ungroup.

Note: See the section "Select Objects" to learn more about selecting items on the Flash Stage.

2 Click Modify.

3 Click Ungroup.

■ Flash ungroups the objects.

STACK OBJECTS

When creating a drawing, you may need to move an object on top of another object. When placing objects over other objects, you can control exactly where an object appears in the stack. You can place an object at the very back of a stack, at the very front, or somewhere in-between.

Stacking only works with grouped objects. Flash places grouped objects — whether the group consists of several objects or just one — on the overlay level, which means that they always appear stacked on top of objects that are located on the stage level. When stacking grouped objects, you can move them to several different layers. These layers are invisible on the Flash Stage, but quickly become apparent when you move one group over another and reorder their placement in the stack. Stacking placement involves moving elements from the front of the stack to the very back, with several levels in between.

STACK OBJECTS

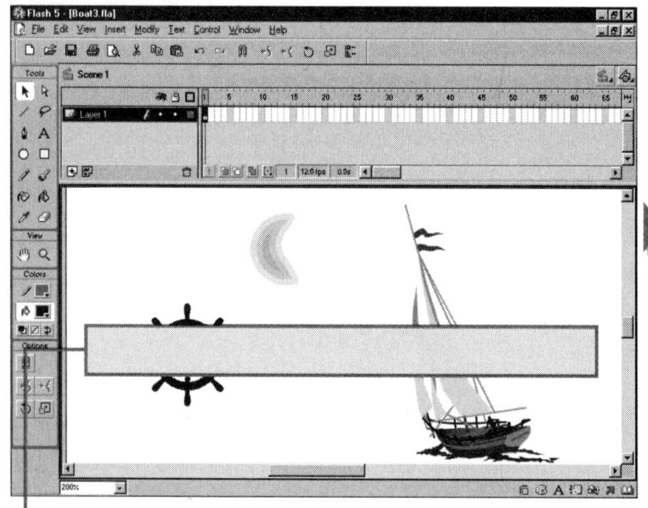

1 Select the object or group you want to reorder.

Note: See the section "Select Objects" to learn more about selecting items on the Flash Stage.

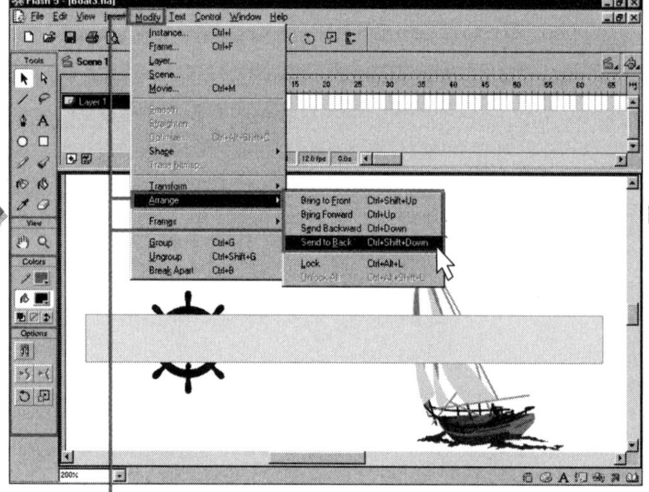

2 Click Modify.

3 Click Arrange.

4 Select whether you want to send the object to the front or back of the stack.

■ To send an object to the very back of the stack, click Send to Back.

■ To bring an object to the very front of the stack, click Bring to Front.

Is there a shortcut to moving an object up or back a layer in a stack?

✔ Yes. You can use keyboard shortcuts to quickly reposition an object in a stack:

Move the object up one layer	Press Ctrl+↑ (Windows) Press Command+↑ (Mac)
Move the object directly to the top of the stack	Press Ctrl+Shift+↑ (Windows) Press Command+Shift+↑ (Mac)
Move the object back a layer	Press Ctrl+↓ (Windows) Press Command+↓ (Mac).
Move the object directly to the back of the stack	Press Ctrl+Shift+↓ (Windows) Press Command+Shift+↓ (Mac)

Can I stack objects located on the stage level?

✔ No. You cannot apply the stacking commands to objects on the stage level; if you try, they do not work. Objects you place on the stage level interact, which means if you move a shape over a line, the line is covered. If you move the shape again, the line is no longer there; it has become a part of the shape. Stacking only works on objects you place on the overlay level.

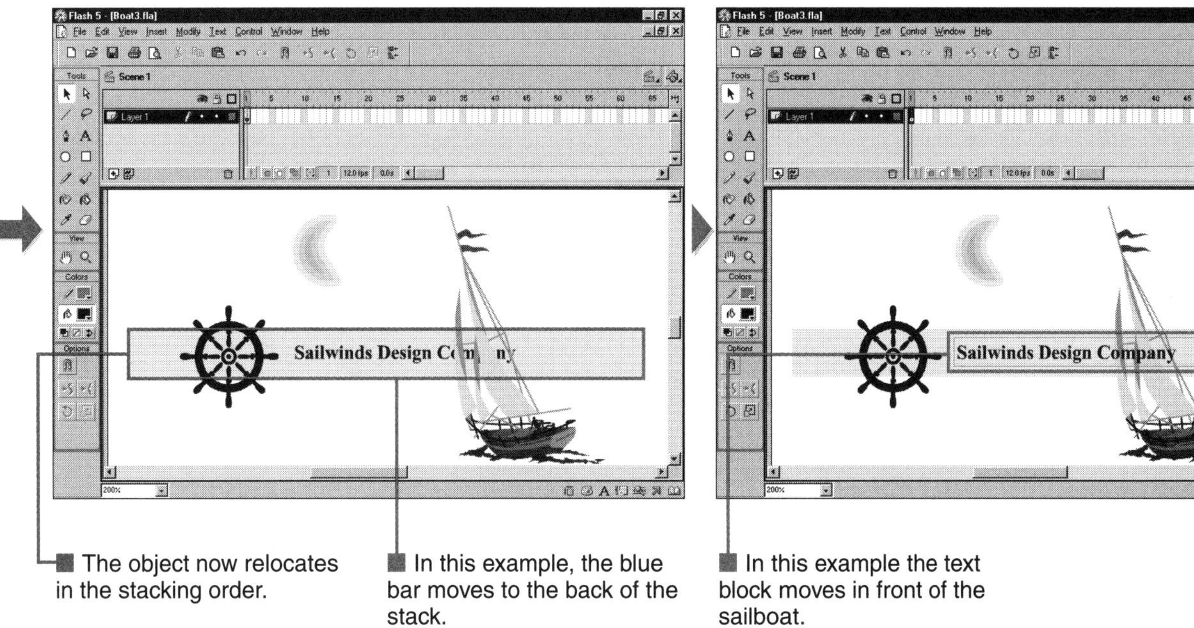

■ The object now relocates in the stacking order.

■ In this example, the blue bar moves to the back of the stack.

■ In this example the text block moves in front of the sailboat.

ALIGN OBJECTS

The Align panel has tools for controlling precisely where an object sits on the Stage. You can align objects vertically and horizontally by their edges or centers. You can align objects with other objects, with the edges of the Stage, or even control the amount of space between the objects.

The alignment commands come in handy when you are trying to position several objects on the Stage, and dragging them around manually does not seem to create the results you want. Although the Flash rulers and grid can help you line things up on the Stage, applying alignment options are much faster and easier.

You can find a variety of options just a quick click away in the Align panel. For example, the Align panel has a set of buttons for controlling horizontal alignment on the Stage and another set of buttons for controlling vertical alignment.

ALIGN OBJECTS WITH OTHER OBJECTS

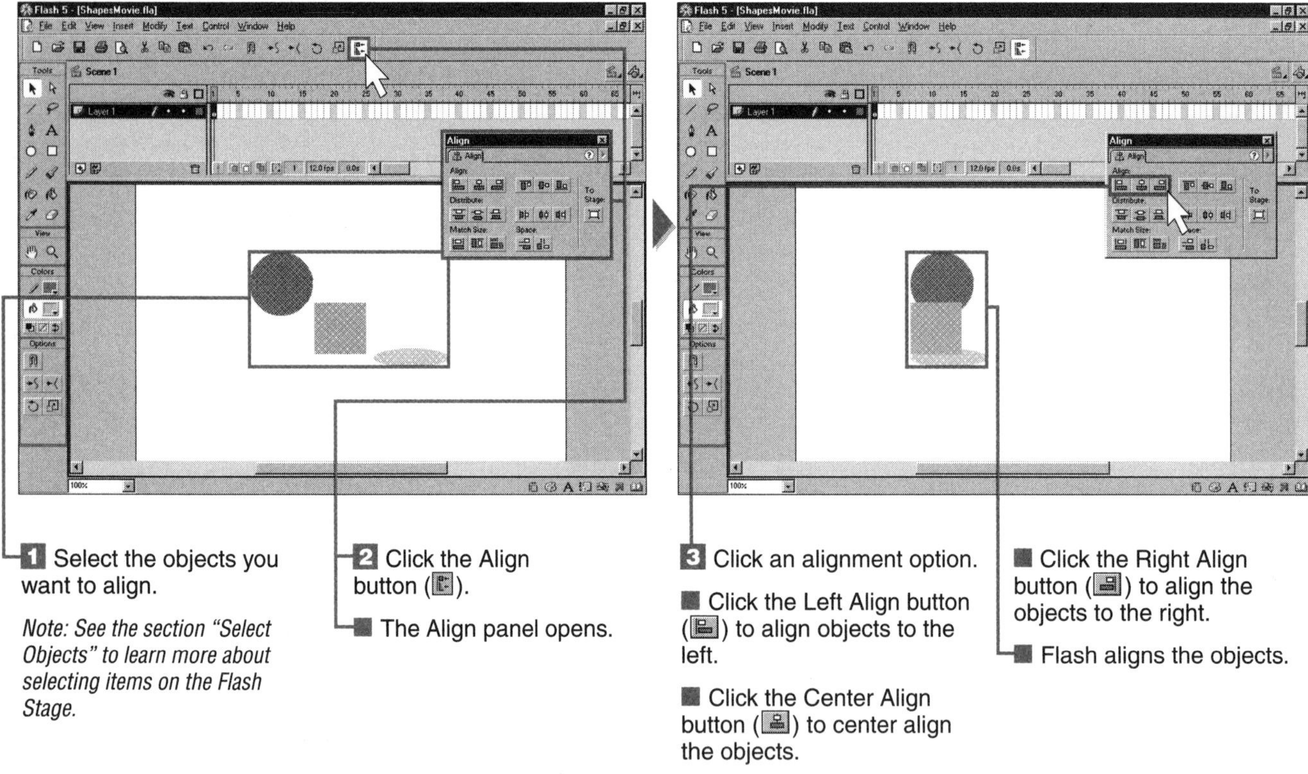

1 Select the objects you want to align.

Note: See the section "Select Objects" to learn more about selecting items on the Flash Stage.

2 Click the Align button ( ).

■ The Align panel opens.

3 Click an alignment option.

■ Click the Left Align button ( ) to align objects to the left.

■ Click the Center Align button ( ) to center align the objects.

■ Click the Right Align button ( ) to align the objects to the right.

■ Flash aligns the objects.

How can I align objects vertically?

✔ The Align panel has buttons for setting vertical alignments along with horizontal alignments. Each button in the Align panel has an image that shows how the objects align when you select that button. Click [icon] to align objects with the top-most object or the top of the Stage. Click [icon] to center objects evenly with each other, or between the top and bottom of the Stage. Click [icon] to align objects with the bottom-most object or to the bottom edge of the Stage.

Can I align multiple items at the same time?

✔ Yes. Hold down the Shift key while selecting each item, and then apply the alignment command you want to use.

ALIGN OBJECTS WITH THE STAGE

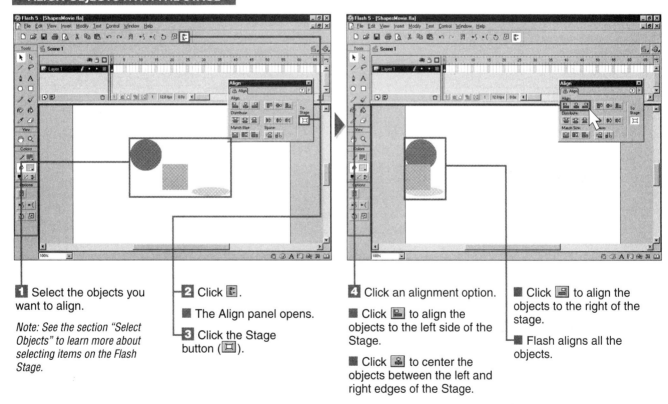

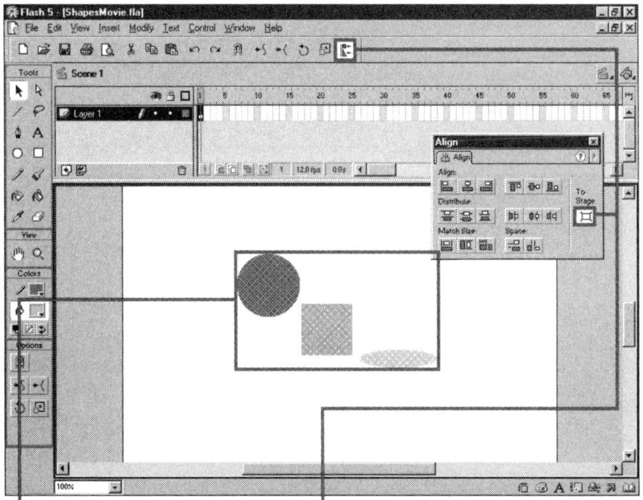

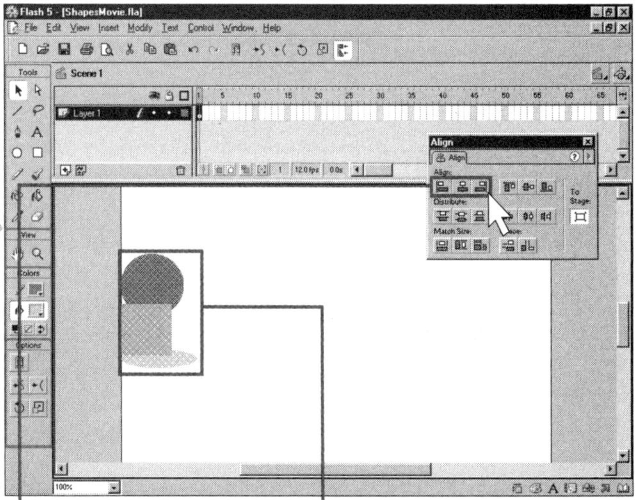

1 Select the objects you want to align.

Note: See the section "Select Objects" to learn more about selecting items on the Flash Stage.

2 Click [icon].

■ The Align panel opens.

3 Click the Stage button ([icon]).

4 Click an alignment option.

■ Click [icon] to align the objects to the left side of the Stage.

■ Click [icon] to center the objects between the left and right edges of the Stage.

■ Click [icon] to align the objects to the right of the stage.

■ Flash aligns all the objects.

ADD TEXT WITH THE TEXT TOOL

You can use the Text tool to add text to a movie or graphic. You can add a single word or several paragraphs to the Flash Stage and manipulate the text just as you would in a word processing program.

For example, you can add a company name to layer over a logo or explanatory text to an animation about company products or services. Like graphic objects you add to the Stage, you can animate text objects as well.

You add text to the Stage in text boxes, which you can easily reposition or resize as needed. You can insert label or block text boxes on the Stage area. With a label text box, you can click where you want the text to appear and start typing. With block text, you define the box size first by dragging its dimensions on the Stage.

You can control the type size and font before or after you add text to the Stage using the options in the Character panel. To learn more about formatting text in the next section, "Format Text."

ADD TEXT WITH THE TEXT TOOL

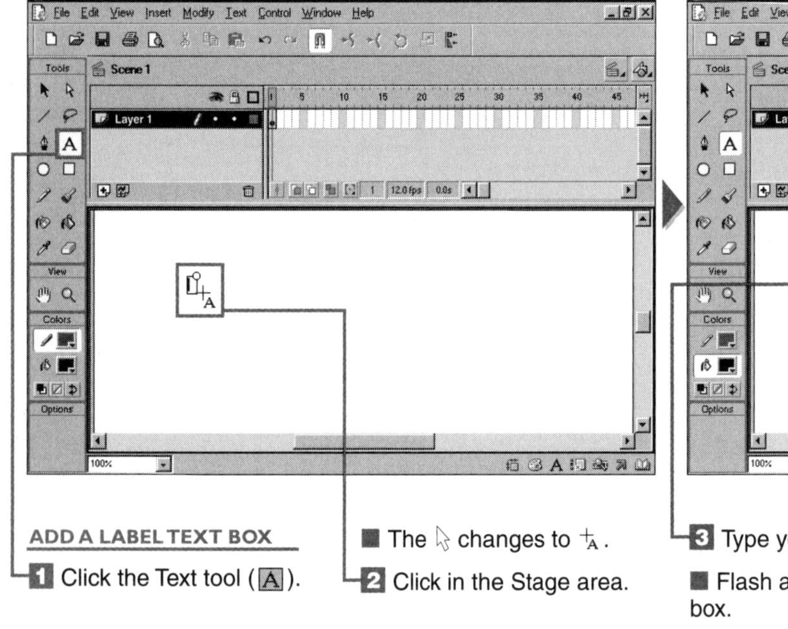

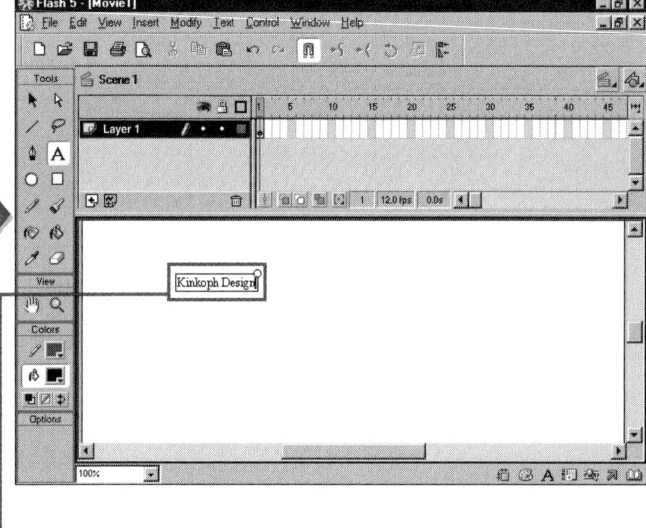

ADD A LABEL TEXT BOX

1 Click the Text tool (A).

■ The pointer changes to a text cursor.

2 Click in the Stage area.

3 Type your text.

■ Flash adds a Label text box.

Note: If you select the Arrow tool, you can double-click a text box to switch to edit mode and make changes to text. If you select the Text tool, you can click the text box and make edits.

What is the difference between labels and blocks?

✔ When you type text into a label text box, text does not wrap. The width of the text box keeps expanding as you type characters. With a block text box, you specify a width, and when the text you are typing reaches the end of the block, it wraps to start a new line, increasing the depth of the text box. To visually discern between labels and blocks, look at the icon in the upper-right corner of the text box. Label text boxes display a tiny circle icon, and block text boxes have a tiny square icon.

How do I turn a label text box into a block text box?

✔ Select the text box and move the ⇖ over ○ in the upper-right corner of the text box. Drag ⟷ to the right and release the mouse button. The label text box is now a block text box. You cannot turn block text boxes into label text boxes.

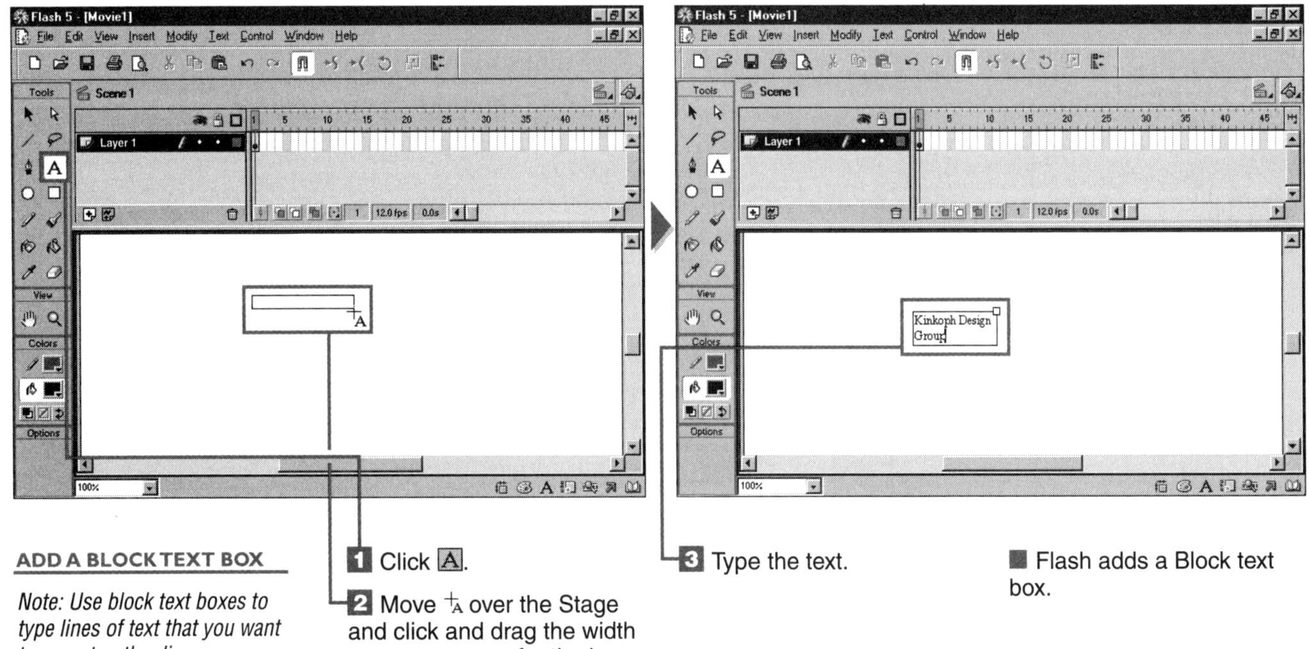

ADD A BLOCK TEXT BOX

Note: Use block text boxes to type lines of text that you want to wrap to other lines.

1 Click A.

2 Move ⁺A over the Stage and click and drag the width you want to use for the box.

3 Type the text.

■ Flash adds a Block text box.

FORMAT TEXT

You can easily format text by using the Character panel. It has all the controls for changing text attributes located in one convenient mini-window. You can quickly change the font, font size, font color, and spacing.

You can choose text attributes before you start typing in text or apply formatting to existing text. Leave the Character panel open on-screen to keep the formatting controls handy as you work with text on the Flash Stage.

The Character panel offers many of the same formatting controls you find in word processing programs. For example, you can click the Bold button to make your text boldface.

Regardless of which attributes you assign to your text, it is important that the text is legible. While animation effects can add pizzazz to any message, the effects should never take precedence over the readability of your text.

APPLY BOLD AND ITALICS

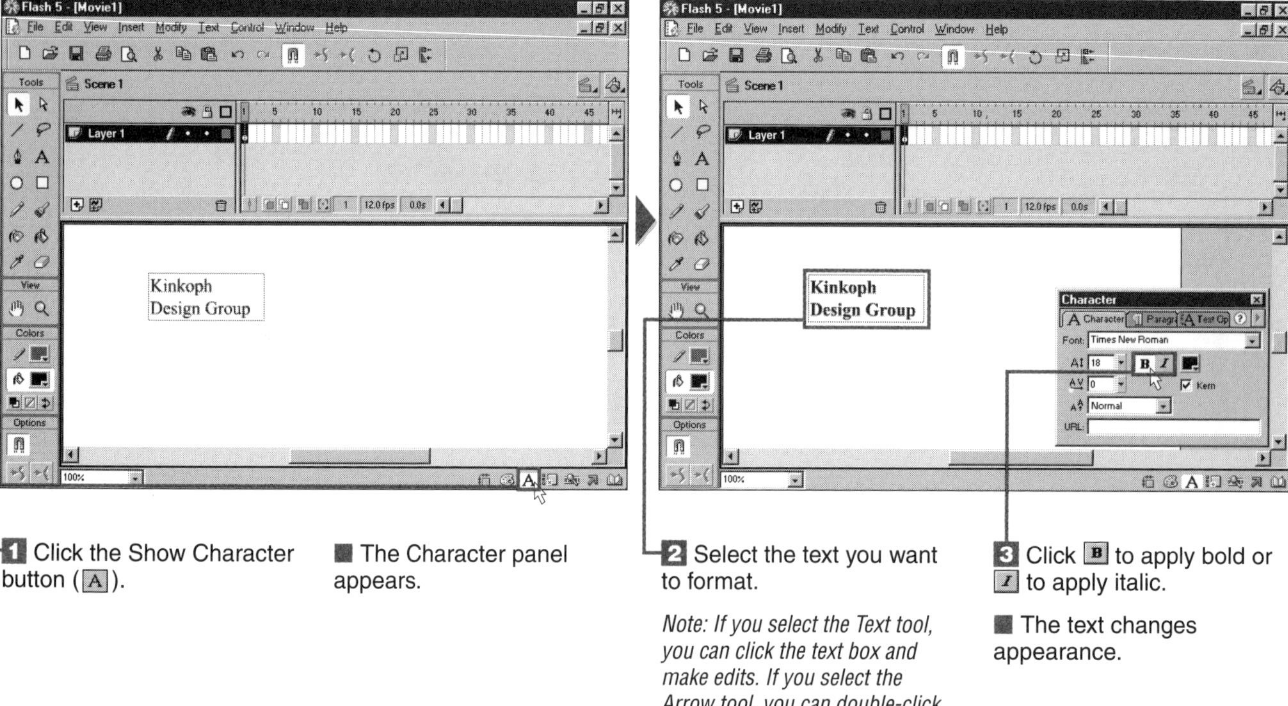

1 Click the Show Character button (A).

■ The Character panel appears.

2 Select the text you want to format.

Note: If you select the Text tool, you can click the text box and make edits. If you select the Arrow tool, you can double-click a text box and make edits.

3 Click **B** to apply bold or *I* to apply italic.

■ The text changes appearance.

Do I have to use the Character panel to format text?

✔ You can also find text formatting controls in the Text menu. For example, to change the font, click Text and then Font and then click a font from the menu list that appears.

Can I move the Character panel out of my way?

✔ Yes, all the Flash panels, windows, and dialog boxes are movable. You can click and drag the panel's title bar to move the panel out of your way. To close the feature entirely, click its ☒ button.

What types of fonts does Flash support?

✔ Flash supports TrueType and bitmap fonts and Type 1 PostScript fonts. Flash also includes device fonts — sans serif, serif, and typewriter — that, when exported, instruct the Flash Player to use equivalent fonts found on the target computer. Device fonts take up less movie size than other fonts because Flash does not have to embed information about each font when exporting. You can find device fonts at the top of the Font list.

CHANGE THE FONT AND SIZE

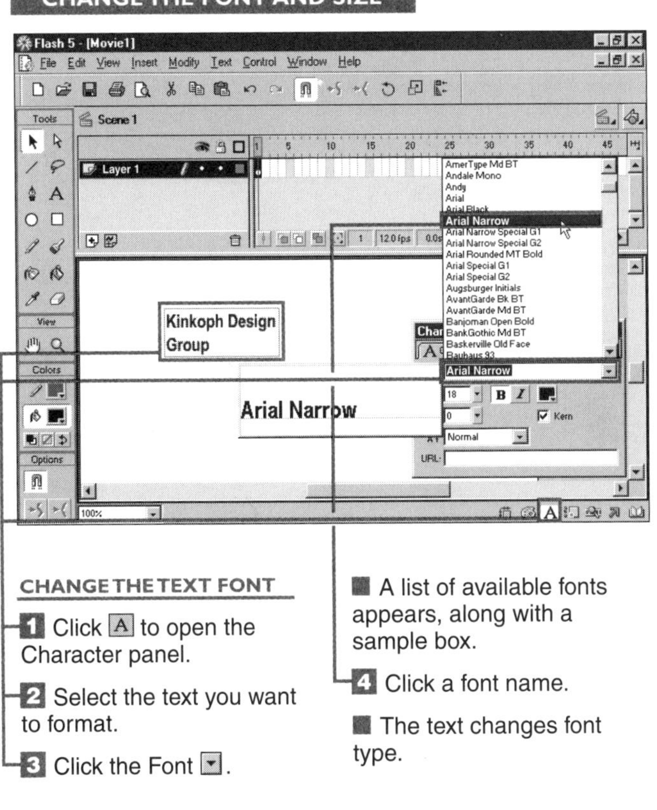

CHANGE THE TEXT FONT

1 Click A to open the Character panel.

2 Select the text you want to format.

3 Click the Font ▼.

■ A list of available fonts appears, along with a sample box.

4 Click a font name.

■ The text changes font type.

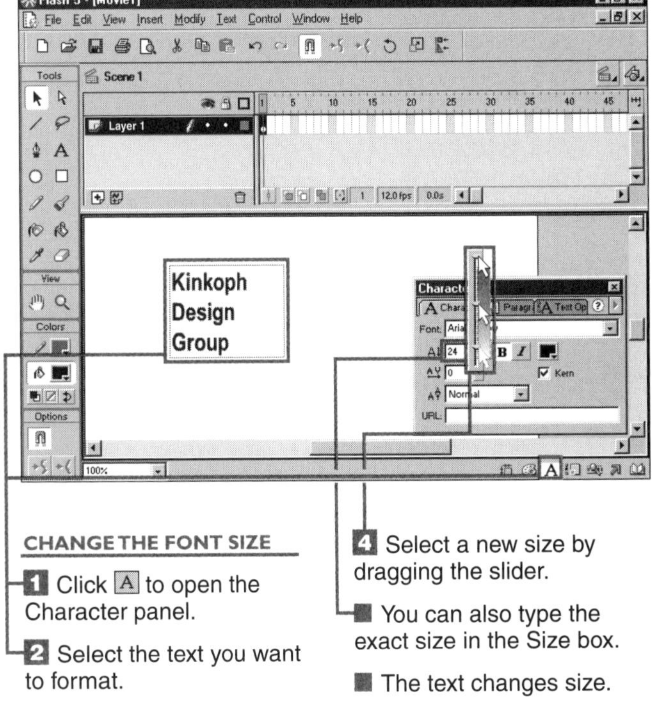

CHANGE THE FONT SIZE

1 Click A to open the Character panel.

2 Select the text you want to format.

3 Click the Size ▼.

4 Select a new size by dragging the slider.

■ You can also type the exact size in the Size box.

■ The text changes size.

ALIGN AND KERN TEXT

You can control the position of text within a text box using the alignment options you find in the Paragraph panel or on the Text menu. Alignment options include setting horizontal controls for the positioning of text, such as left, center, right, or fully justified.

Left alignment moves the text to the far left side of the text box. Right alignment moves the text to the right side. Center alignment centers the text between the left and right edges of the text box. Fully justified text spaces out the text evenly between the left and right edges so that both margins are flush with the edges of the text box. To learn how to set margins for text boxes, see the section "Set Text Box Margins and Indents."

Another way to control the positioning of text is with kerning. *Kerning* refers to the spacing of characters. By changing the kerning setting, you can create text effects such as word characters squished together or pulled apart. You can find kerning controls in the Character panel.

ALIGN TEXT

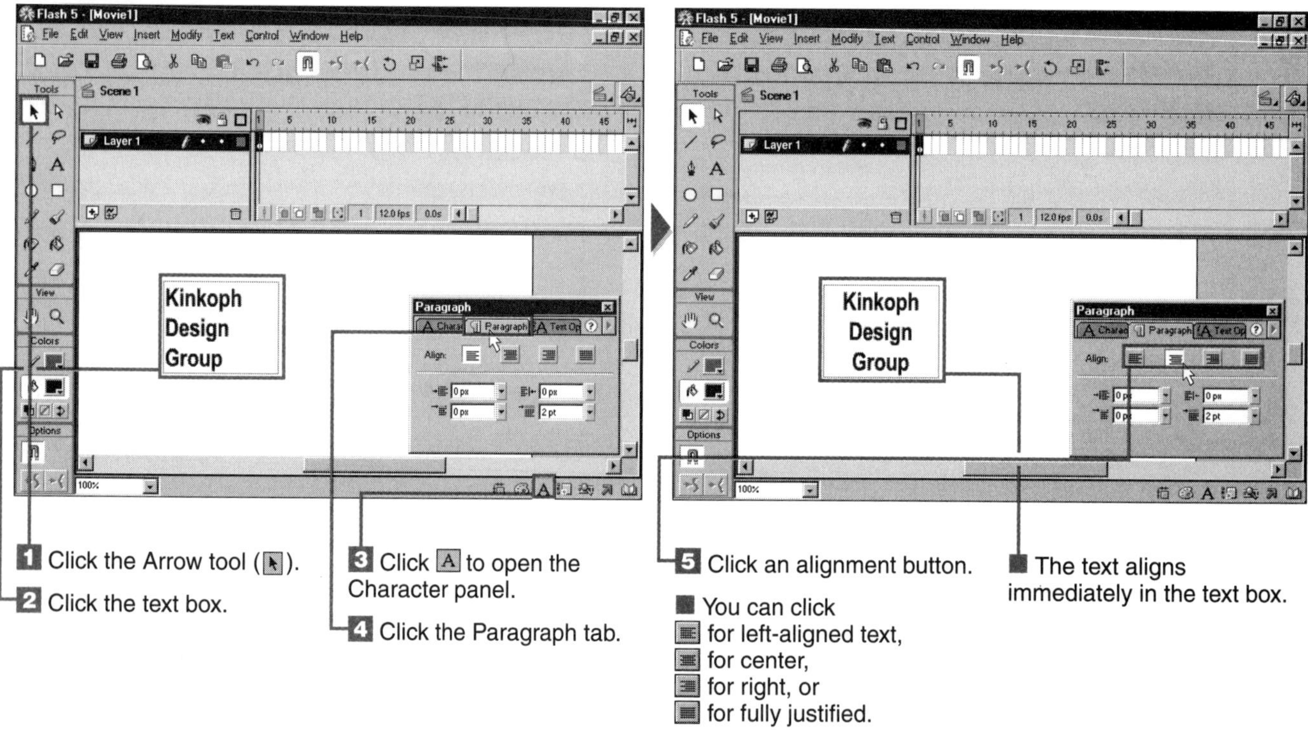

1 Click the Arrow tool (↖).

2 Click the text box.

3 Click A to open the Character panel.

4 Click the Paragraph tab.

5 Click an alignment button.

■ You can click ≡ for left-aligned text, ≡ for center, ≡ for right, or ≡ for fully justified.

■ The text aligns immediately in the text box.

Does the Character panel save my current formatting settings?

✔ The Character and Paragraph panels retain your last formatting settings as long as you have Flash opened. If you add another text box to the Stage, the text appears using the current attributes you previously assigned. The next time you open Flash and the panels again, the default settings are in effect until you change them.

How do I fix a formatting mistake?

✔ You can click the Undo button ( ) on the Main toolbar to quickly undo the last formatting command you applied.

How do I copy attributes from one text box to another?

✔ Click and then the text box containing the text to which you want to copy attributes. Click the Dropper tool ( ) on the Drawing toolbar and then click the text box containing the attributes you want to copy. The attributes are immediately copied.

Do I have to use the Character panel to align text?

✔ No, you can use the Text menu to align text. Click the Text menu, click Align, and then click the alignment you want to apply.

KERN TEXT

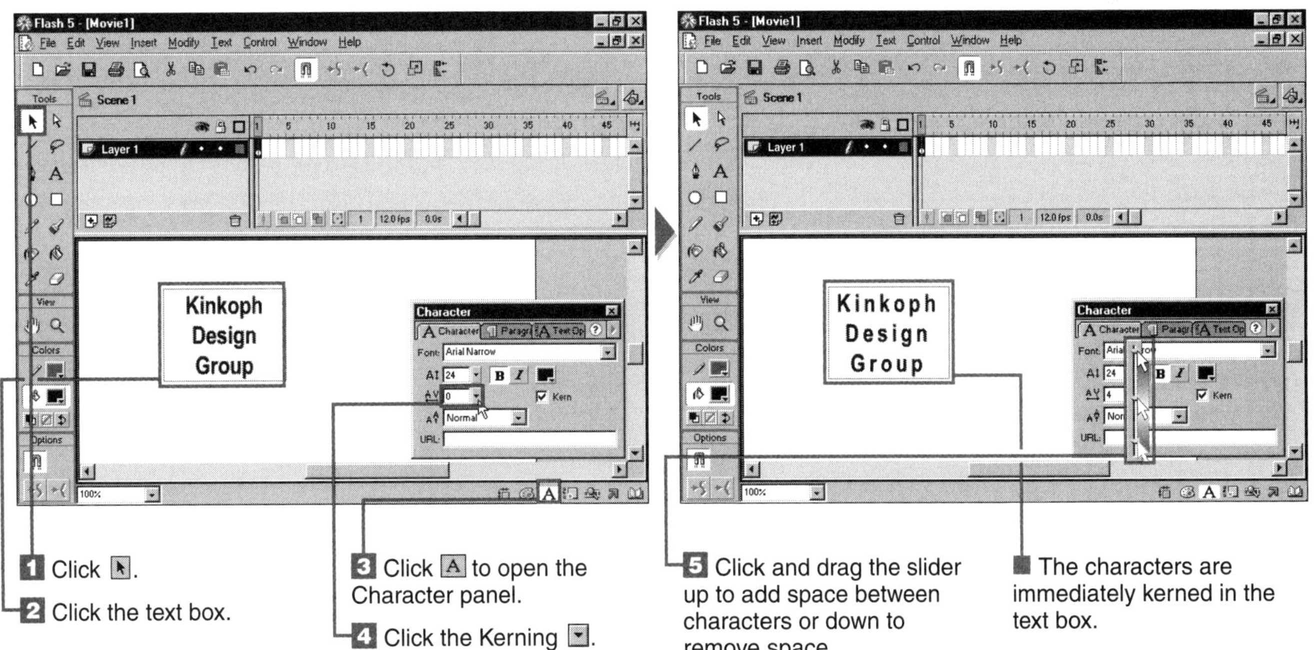

1 Click .

2 Click the text box.

3 Click to open the Character panel.

4 Click the Kerning .

5 Click and drag the slider up to add space between characters or down to remove space.

■ The characters are immediately kerned in the text box.

SET TEXT BOX MARGINS AND INDENTS

Set margins and indents within text boxes for greater control of text positioning. You can find margin and indent commands in the Paragraph panel or on the Text menu.

Margins define the distance between the edge of the text box and the text inside. You can define left and right margins in Flash, as well as top and bottom margins.

You use indents to control where a line of text sits within the margins. For example, you can choose to indent the first line in a paragraph by several pixels or points.

In addition to margin and indent controls, the Paragraph panel also has controls for line spacing. Line spacing is the distance between lines of text. Increase the line spacing to add space between lines or decrease the spacing to bring the lines closer together.

SET THE MARGINS

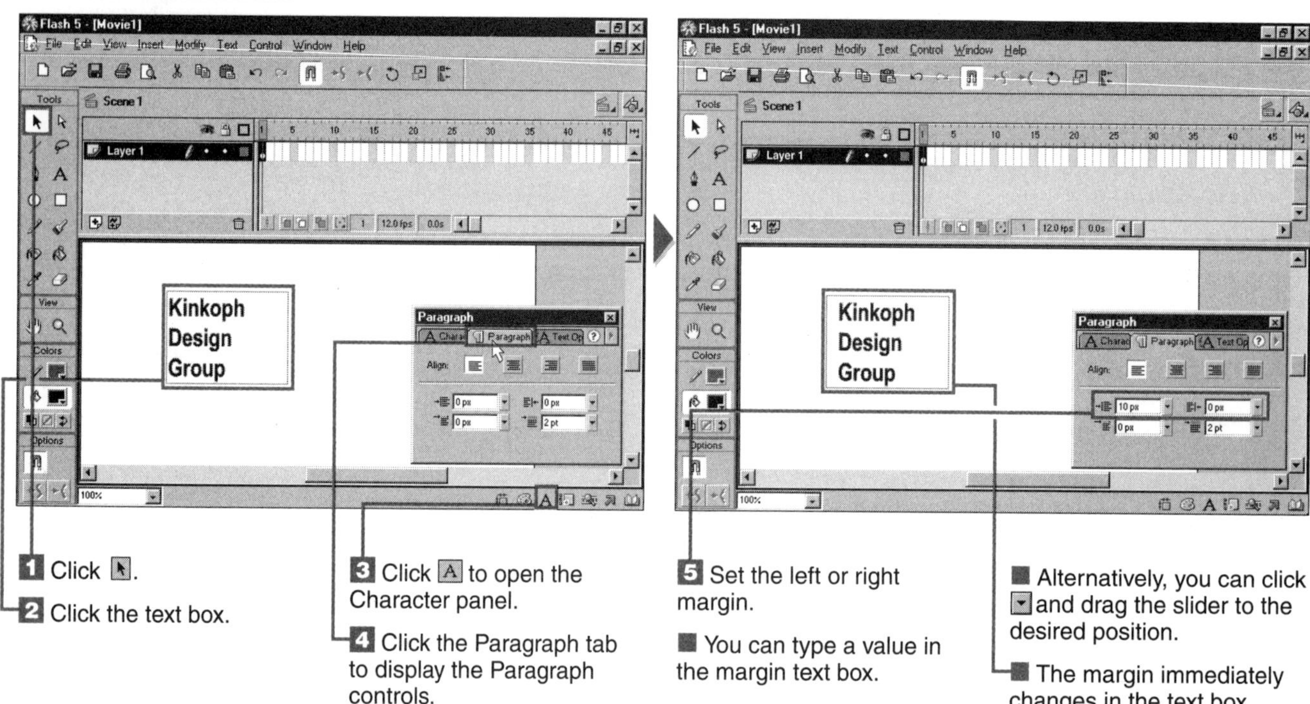

1 Click [arrow tool icon].

2 Click the text box.

3 Click [A icon] to open the Character panel.

4 Click the Paragraph tab to display the Paragraph controls.

5 Set the left or right margin.

■ You can type a value in the margin text box.

■ Alternatively, you can click [dropdown icon] and drag the slider to the desired position.

■ The margin immediately changes in the text box.

How do I change the margin's unit of measurement?

✔ By default, Flash assumes you want to work with pixels as your unit of measurement, but you can change it to the unit of your choice, such as points or inches. Click Modify and then Movie. This opens the Movie Properties dialog box. You can also press Ctrl + M in Windows or Command + M on the Mac to open the dialog box. Click ▾ of the Ruler Units box and select the appropriate units. Click OK to close the dialog box. When you open the Paragraph panel, the margin values reflect the unit of measurement you defined.

Would I use the Line Spacing slider to set superscript or subscript characters in Flash?

✔ No, the Line Spacing slider cannot be used on individual characters — only entire lines. Instead, to set superscript or subscript characters, first select the text. Next, display the Character panel by clicking A. Click the Character Position ▾. A list of choices appear. Click Superscript or Subscript, and the attribute is immediately applied.

SET AN INDENT

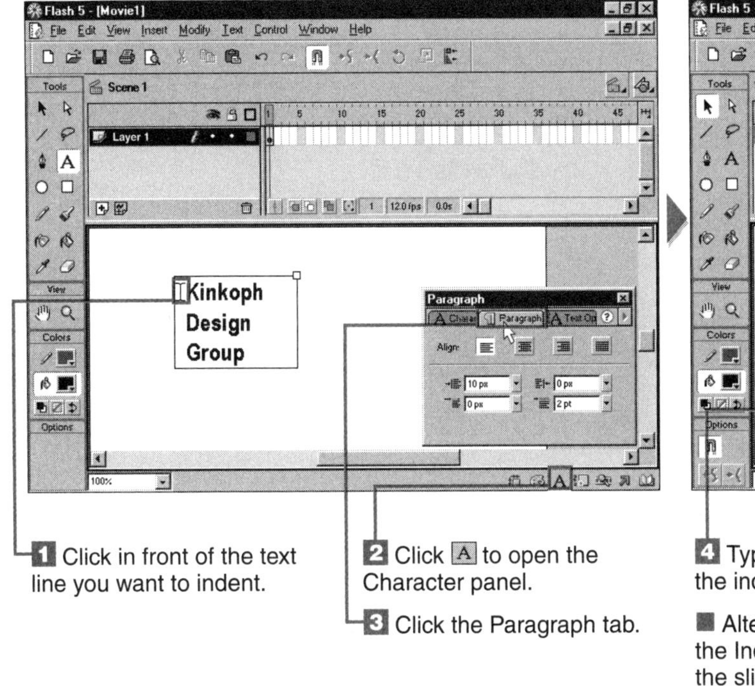

1 Click in front of the text line you want to indent.

2 Click A to open the Character panel.

3 Click the Paragraph tab.

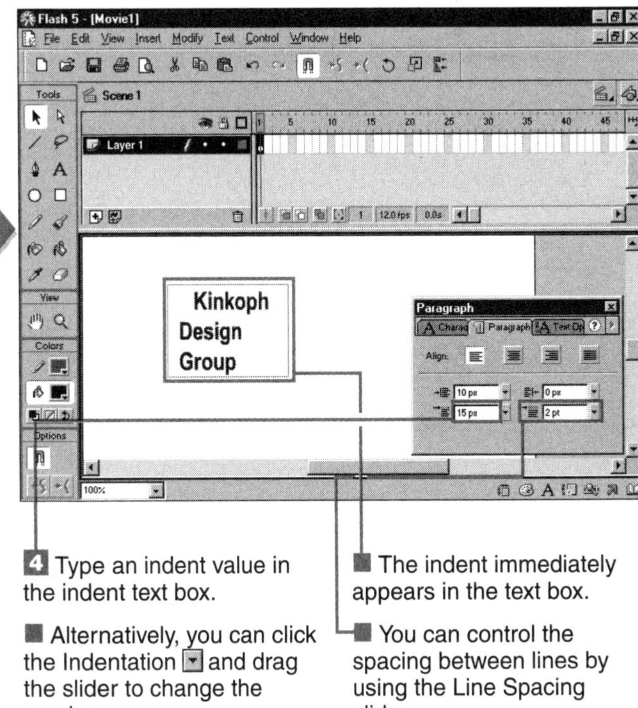

4 Type an indent value in the indent text box.

■ Alternatively, you can click the Indentation ▾ and drag the slider to change the number.

■ The indent immediately appears in the text box.

■ You can control the spacing between lines by using the Line Spacing slider.

MOVE AND RESIZE TEXT BOXES

You can move text boxes around on the Flash Stage or resize them as needed. Text boxes are as mobile and scalable as other objects you add to the Stage.

You can position a text box anywhere on Stage. Or you can move a text box off the Stage onto the work area, the gray area that surrounds the Stage. Anything you place in the work area does not appear in your Flash movie. However, you can move items to the work area and move them back onto the Stage when you need them, such as when you want to place an item into a particular Flash frame. See Chapter 24 to learn more about working with frames.

Flash resizes the text inside the box, depending on the direction you choose to scale the box, and overrides any font sizes for the text. If you want the text set at a certain size, you must manually change the font size again after you scale the text box.

MOVE A TEXT BOX

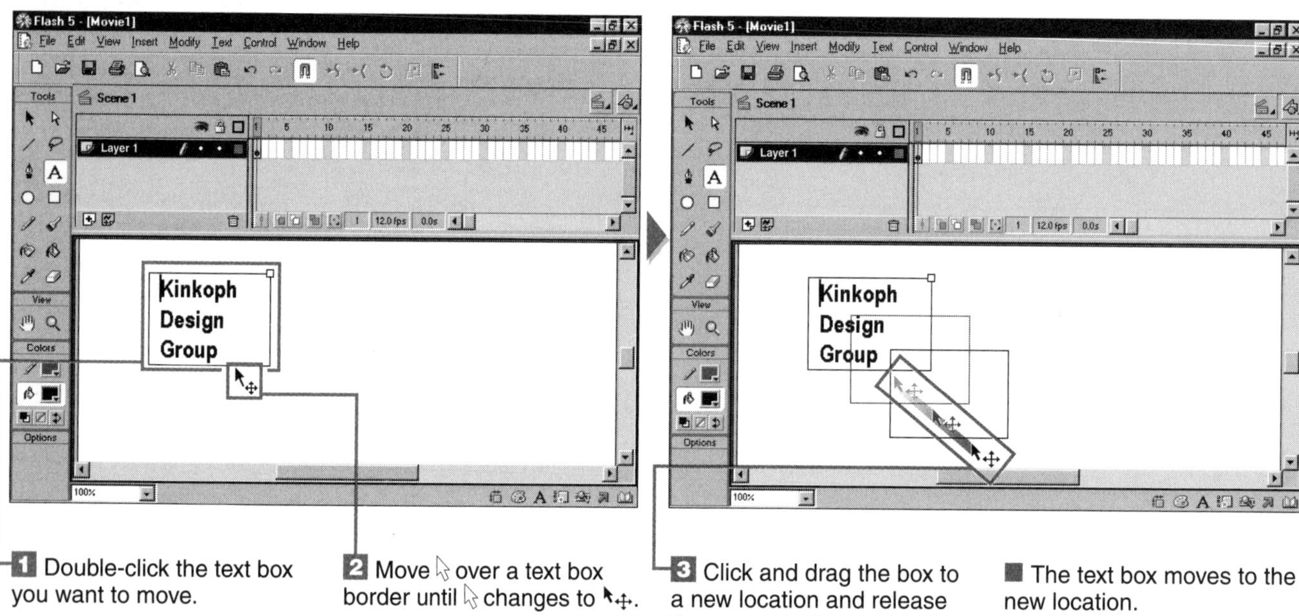

1 Double-click the text box you want to move.

2 Move ↖ over a text box border until ↖ changes to ↖✥.

3 Click and drag the box to a new location and release the mouse button.

■ The text box moves to the new location.

Can I rotate a text box?

✔ Yes. First select the text box and then click the Rotate button (⟲) on the Main toolbar. Flash surrounds the text box. Click and drag a handle to rotate the text box. Click ⟲ again to turn the feature off. You can find out more about rotating objects in Chapter 19.

How do I move a text box to a new position on the Stage?

✔ Click the ↖, then click and drag the text box to a new location.

Can I use the Scale command to resize a text box?

✔ Yes. Select the text box with the Arrow tool (↖) and then click the Scale button (⊡) on the Main toolbar or at the bottom of the Drawing toolbar. The text box is surrounded by resize handles. Click and drag a handle to resize the text box. Click ⊡ again to turn the feature off. Learn more about resizing objects Chapter 19.

RESIZE A TEXT BOX

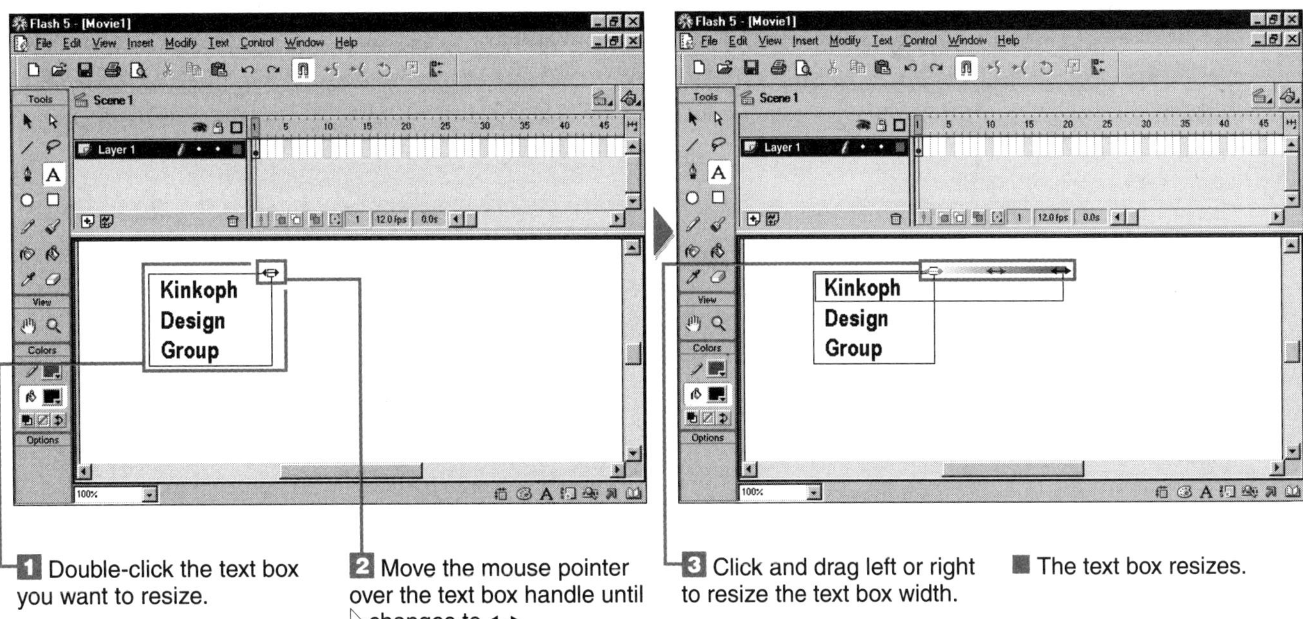

1 Double-click the text box you want to resize.

2 Move the mouse pointer over the text box handle until ↖ changes to ↔.

3 Click and drag left or right to resize the text box width.

■ The text box resizes.

UNDERSTAND LAYERS

The key to working with graphic objects and animation in Flash is *layers*. Layers can help you organize elements and add depth to your Flash projects. By default, every time you create a new Flash file, the Timeline starts out with one layer. The layer name appears on the left side of the Flash Timeline.

You can add new layers as needed and change their order around in the Timeline. Each layer has its own Timeline containing frames. See Chapter 17 to learn more about the Flash Timeline.

You can have as many layers as you need in Flash, but you can work on only one layer at a time. You can use layers to accomplish several different tasks.

Layers Can Organize

One important way you can use layers is to help you organize elements in your project. The bigger your project, the more elements it is likely to contain. Rather than placing all of these elements in a single layer, which makes them more difficult to locate and edit, you can insert them into separate layers and name each layer with a descriptive name for the layer. For example, you may have a very complex movie that uses sound, animation, a button, and actions. To help organize your movie, you can place the sound clip on a layer named "Sound." You can then create your animation effect in a layer named "MyMovie" or "Animation." When you add a button to the movie, place it in a new layer named "Button." You can keep any actions you assign to the button in yet another layer, named "Actions."

Layers can also help you keep track of the various pieces, such as related elements of an animation sequence. You can place related objects on a single layer to keep them together, making it easier to find them later. For example, if your Flash movie uses a company logo, you could place all the elements related to the logo on a single layer and name the layer "Logo."

You can edit objects in one layer without affecting objects on another layer. For example, if you place all the logo elements on a single layer, any edits you make to the logo elements do not affect objects on other layers. This keeps you from accidentally changing items you do not want to change. You can also lock a layer to make sure no edits occur to its contents.

Layers Add Depth

Layers act similarly to transparent sheets of paper or plastic when you stack one on top of another. Flash stacks layers from top to bottom. Each layer lets you see through to the layer below. As you add more layers to the Timeline, existing layers move down in the stack to appear behind new layers. Items you place on the top layer appear in front of items placed on a bottom layer. You can place a background on the bottom layer, and add other objects to subsequent layers to create a feeling of depth.

Flash makes it easy to rearrange layers in the Timeline. You can move a layer by dragging it to a new location in the Timeline and dropping it in place. For example, you can move a back layer to the top of the stack by dragging it from the bottom of the layer list to the top. Moving layers around does not effect the layer's contents, only the stacking order of the contents on the Stage.

Types of Layers

There are several different kinds of layers in Flash. A *plain layer* holds various elements such as graphics, sounds, and movie clips. Flash classifies plain layers as *normal* layer types, which are the most commonly used layers.

Guide layers are another type of layer. Guides can help you with the layout and positioning of objects on other layers. You most often use guides with motion tween animations, animation effects that follow a specified path in your Flash movie. See Chapter 25 to learn more about creating motion tween animations.

The third type of layer is a *mask layers*. Mask layers enable you to hide elements in underlying layers from view. You create a hole, as it were, in the mask layer that lets you view layers below. You can make the hole in the shape of a circle, square, or other type of outline. Any objects in the layers beneath the mask that fall into the shape of the hole appear. Flash masks anything lying outside the hole from view.

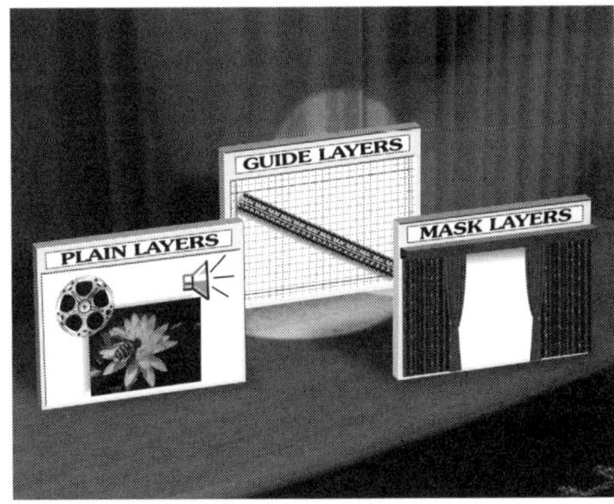

ADD AND DELETE LAYERS

When you create a new movie or scene, Flash starts you out with a single layer and timeline. You can add layers to the Timeline, or delete layers you no longer need. Additional layers do not affect the file size, so you can add and delete as many layers as your project requires. See Chapter 17 to learn more about the Flash Timeline.

You use layers to organize objects in your Flash project. For example, you can devote a layer to the background image that you require for your Flash movie. You can add another layer on top of the background layer that plays an animation sequence. You may then include another layer that holds all the sound clips related to your movie. You can add as many layers as your project requires.

Layers can help you keep track of related items in your movie. For example, you may want to place all the objects you use for a logo on a single layer and all the objects for a product illustration on another layer.

ADD A LAYER

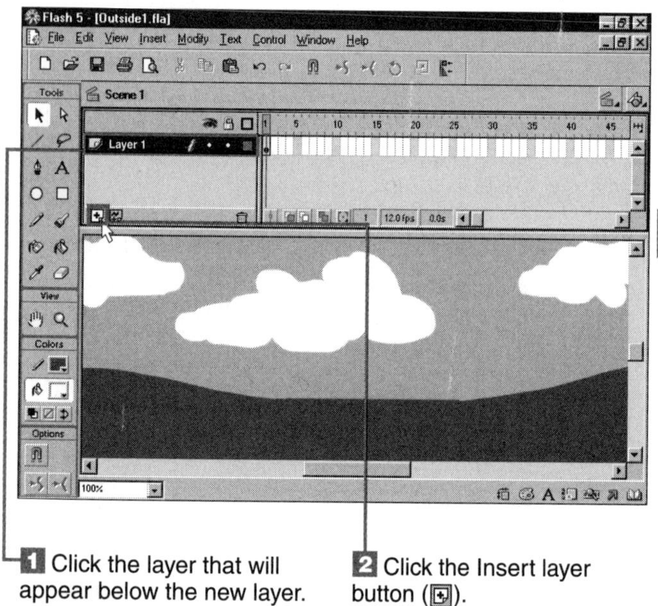

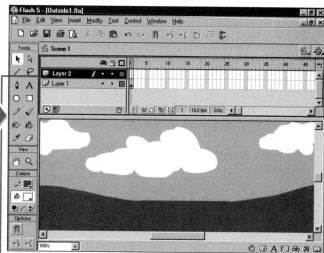

1 Click the layer that will appear below the new layer.

2 Click the Insert layer button (⊞).

■ A new layer immediately appears.

■ Flash adds the same amount of frames to the new layer to match the layer with the longest frame sequence.

Note: See Chapter 24 to learn more about frames.

Are there other ways to add layers?

✔ Yes. You can click the Insert menu and click Layer, or you can right-click a layer name (Windows users) and click Insert Layer from the pop-up menu. Remember, Flash adds a new layer directly above the active layer.

Can I drag a layer to the Trash button (🗑) to delete it?

✔ Yes. You can quickly drag any selected layer over the 🗑 on the Timeline and drop it to delete it. This method saves you a step because you do not have to first select the layer, then click the 🗑.

How do I hide a layer in Flash?

✔ You can hide a layer to move it out of view. Simply click on the tiny bullet (•) under the eye icon (👁) for the layer you want to hide. The • changes to a ✖, and Flash hides the layer from view on the Stage. Click ✖ to show the layer again.

DELETE A LAYER

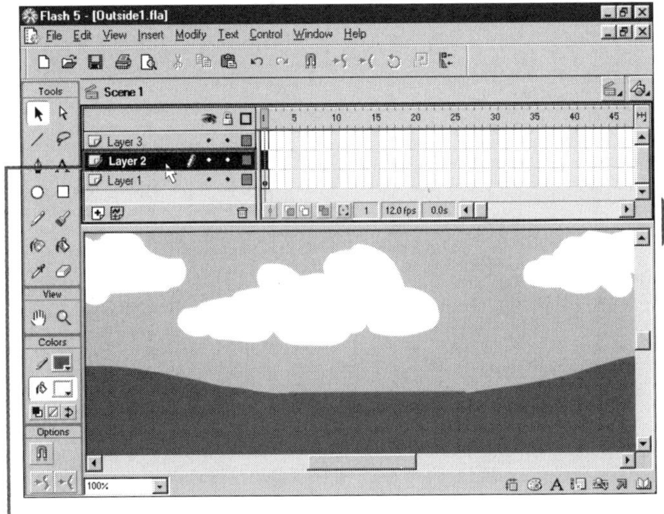

1 Click the layer you want to delete.

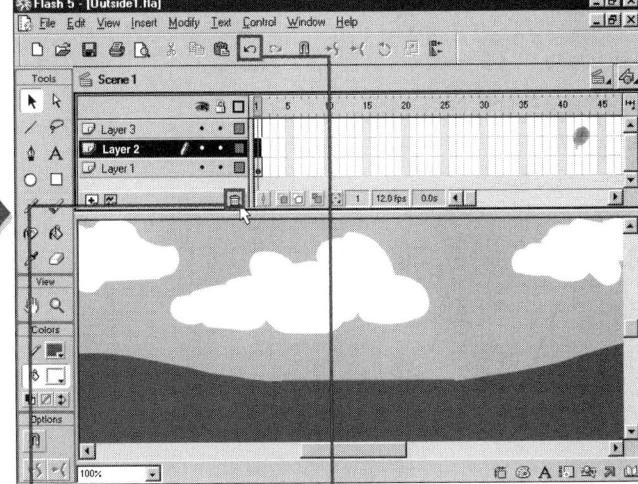

2 Click the Trash button (🗑).

■ You can delete more than one layer by clicking the first layer you want to remove, and then pressing Ctrl (Windows) or Command (Mac) while clicking other layers, then clicking 🗑.

■ The layer disappears from the Timeline.

■ If you accidentally delete the wrong layer, you can click the Undo button (↶) immediately.

SET LAYER PROPERTIES

You can define the aspects of any given layer through the Layer Properties dialog box, a one-stop shop for controlling a layer's name, function, and appearance. The more you work with layers in Flash, the more necessary it is to change layer properties. To learn more about layers, see the section "Add and Delete Layers."

You assign layer properties to the currently selected active layer in the Flash Timeline. An important option you can apply to a layer is to change its name. By naming different layers in your Timeline, you can more easily keep track of their contents and position. You also have the option of hiding the layer to get its contents out of the way. To keep the layer's contents safe from editing, you can lock the layer.

The Layer Properties dialog box also has options for changing the layer type, such as turning a normal layer into a guide layer. It also has options for changing how you view layers. You can view a layer's contents as colored outlines on the Stage, or change the height of the layer as it appears in the Timeline.

SET LAYER PROPERTIES

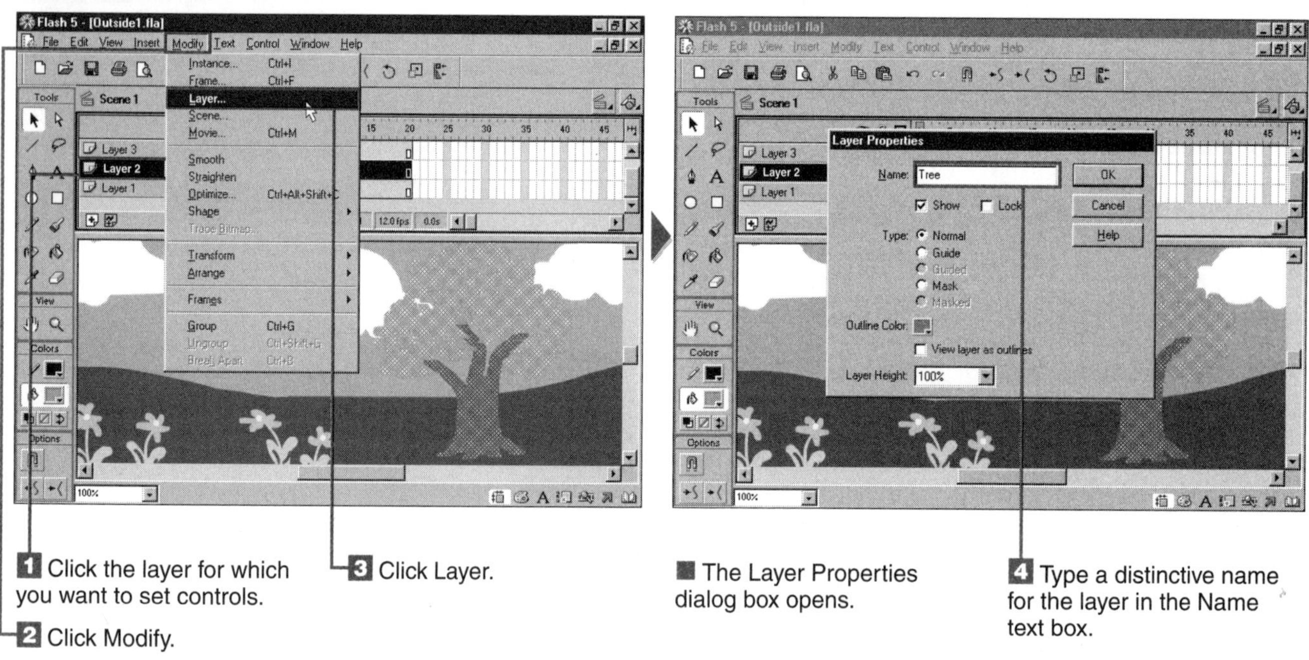

1 Click the layer for which you want to set controls.

2 Click Modify.

3 Click Layer.

■ The Layer Properties dialog box opens.

4 Type a distinctive name for the layer in the Name text box.

What are layer types?

✔ By default, all layers you add to the Timeline are *normal*, which means all the objects on the layer appear in the movie. Objects on guide layers do not appear in the movie. You can use a regular *guide* layer for reference points and alignment. A *guided layer* is a layer you link to a regular guide layer. A *mask* layer hides any layers you link to it. A *masked layer* links to the mask layer. To change the layer type, click a type in the Layer Properties dialog box.

Does Flash offer a shortcut to the Layer Properties dialog box?

✔ Yes. Right-click the layer name and click Properties from the pop-up menu.

What happens when I choose an outline color?

✔ The outlining feature helps you to assess exactly which objects on the Stage are on the current layer by assigning colors. From the Layer Properties dialog box, click the Outline Color button to display a palette of available colors. Click the color you want to use. Flash outlines all objects associated with the layer in that color.

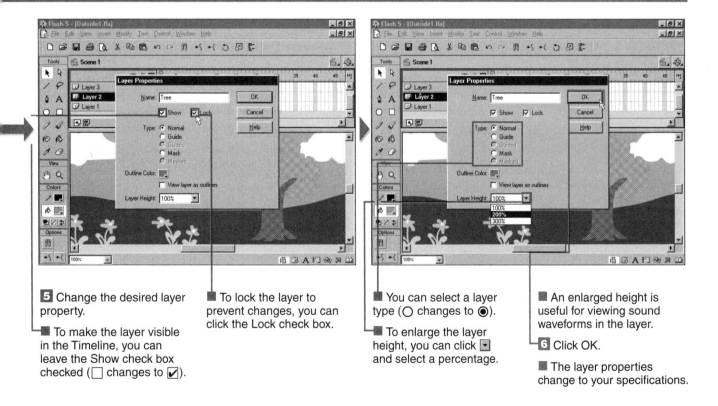

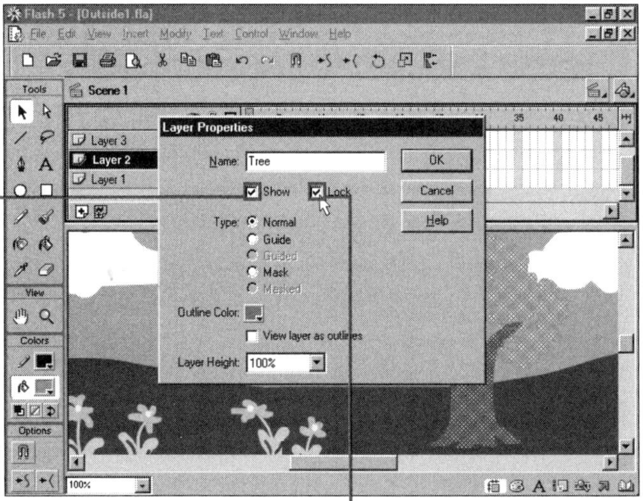

5 Change the desired layer property.

■ To make the layer visible in the Timeline, you can leave the Show check box checked (☐ changes to ☑).

■ To lock the layer to prevent changes, you can click the Lock check box.

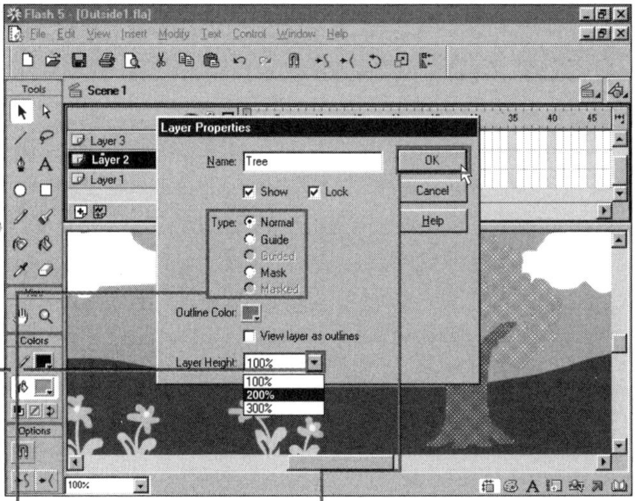

■ You can select a layer type (○ changes to ◉).

■ To enlarge the layer height, you can click ▾ and select a percentage.

■ An enlarged height is useful for viewing sound waveforms in the layer.

6 Click OK.

■ The layer properties change to your specifications.

WORK WITH LAYERS IN THE TIMELINE

Flash makes it easy to control layers in the Timeline. You can quickly rename a layer, hide a layer, or lock a layer to prevent unnecessary changes without having to open a separate dialog box. The Timeline has buttons and toggles that you can use to control a layer with a quick click.

The bar above the layer names list has three icons that help you discern each layer's status. Each icon indicates a specific status setting for the column below it. For example, the eye icon column indicates whether the layer is visible or not. The lock icon tells you whether the layer is locked or not. The outline icon enables you to view a layer's contents as outlines on the Flash Stage. You can toggle all three of the icon categories for each layer on or off.

In addition to controlling layer status, you can also quickly name layers in the Timeline by entering new labels directly on the layer name list. To create a layer, see the section "Add and Delete Layers."

WORK WITH LAYERS IN THE TIMELINE

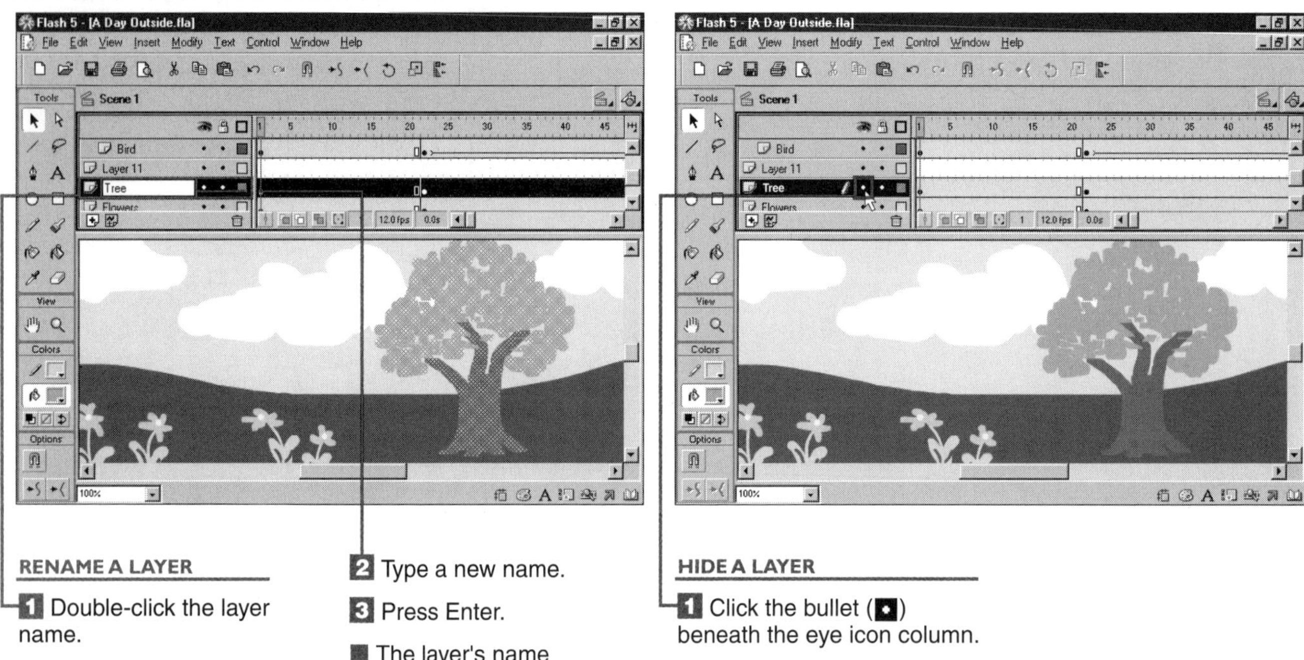

RENAME A LAYER

1 Double-click the layer name.

2 Type a new name.

3 Press Enter.

■ The layer's name changes.

HIDE A LAYER

1 Click the bullet (■) beneath the eye icon column.

How can I tell which objects are on which layer?

✔ You can choose to view layer contents as outlines, making it easy to distinguish the objects from other layers. Click the colored square ■ under the square icon column (■ changes to □). Flash outlines all objects on the layer in the same color as the square you clicked.

Can I lock multiple layers?

✔ Yes. Right-click the layer you want to remain unlocked. Click Lock Others from the pop-up menu.

How do I view a long list of layers?

✔ Use the scroll bar (▮) on the far right side of the Timeline to scroll through a long list of layer names and view their frames.

Can I enlarge the size of a layer?

✔ All layers you add to the Timeline use a default size; however, you can enlarge a layer to better view its contents. This is useful when a frame contains a sound clip. To enlarge the layer height, right-click the layer name and click Properties to open the Layer Properties dialog box. Click the Layer Height ▾ and choose a percentage. Click OK to apply the new size.

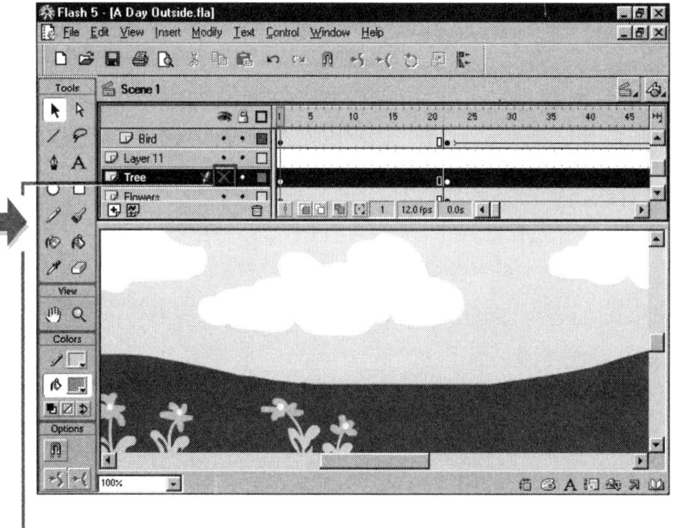

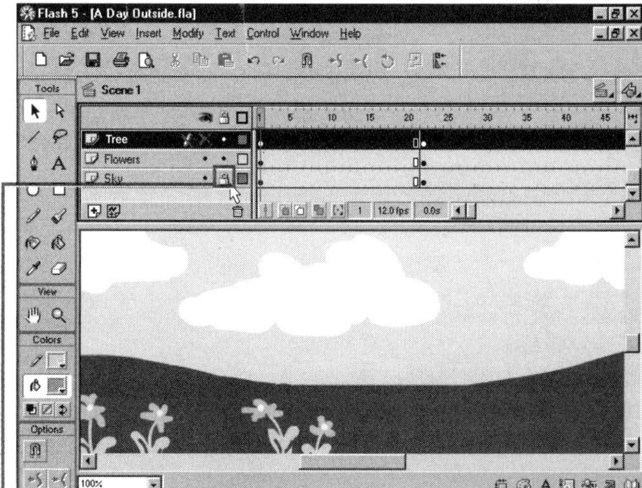

■ All the objects on the layer become invisible (• changes to ✕).

■ To make the layer objects visible again, you can click ✕ under the eye icon column (✕ changes to •).

LOCK A LAYER

1 Under the padlock icon column, click the layer's bullet (• changes to 🔒).

■ Flash locks the layer and you cannot edit the contents.

■ To unlock a layer, click the layer's padlock icon (🔒 changes to •).

STACK LAYERS

To rearrange how objects appear in your Flash project, you can stack Flash layers in a manner similar to how you stack objects in a drawing. Flash layers act like sheets of transparent plastic or film. Depending on the placement of the layers, objects can appear in front of or behind objects on other layers. For example, if you have a layer containing background elements, you can move it to the back of the layer stack. Any objects you insert onto layers that are stacked on top of the background layer appear on top of the background. Stacking layers in this manner creates the illusion of depth in your movie.

You can change the order of a layer by moving it up or down in placement in the layer list on the Flash Timeline. The layer at the top of the list appears at the top of the stack, while the layer at the bottom of the list appears at the bottom of the stack. To create a layer, see the section "Add and Delete Layers.

STACK LAYERS

1 Click the layer you want to move.

2 Drag the layer up or down to its new location in the stack.

■ An insertion point appears, showing where the dragged layer will rest.

I cannot see all my layers. Why?

✔ The more layers you add to the Timeline, the longer the list of layer names. Not all the layers stay in view. Use ⇕ at the far right end of the Timeline to scroll up and down the layer list and view other layers.

Can I copy a layer?

✔ Yes. First create a new layer per the steps in the section "Add and Delete Layers" and then click the layer you want to copy. Click ⎘ on the toolbar. Click the new layer, then click ⎘ on the toolbar. Flash copies the contents of the first layer and places them on the second layer, slightly offset.

How can I see more layers at a time in my Timeline?

✔ You can resize the Timeline to see more of your layers. Move the ↖ over the bottom border of the Timeline until the ↖ becomes ⟷. Click and drag the border down to increase the size of the Timeline. This should enable you to see more of the layers in the Timeline.

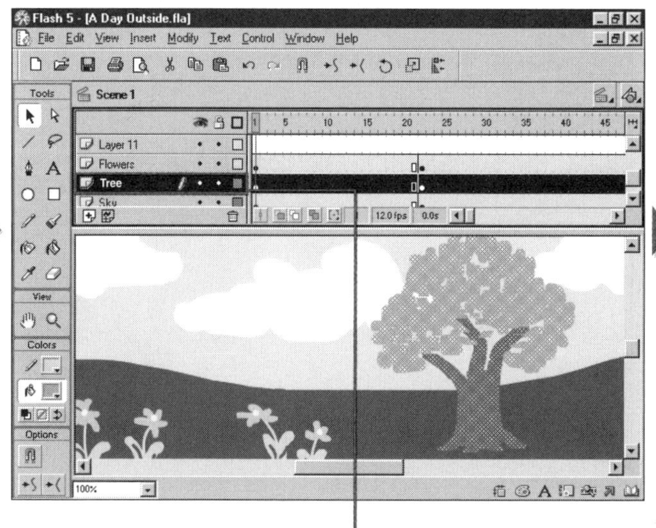

3 Release the mouse button.

■ The layer assumes its new position.

■ To move the layer back to its original position, click ↶.

ADD A PLAIN OR MOTION GUIDE LAYER

Guide layers help you position objects. There are two types of guide layers in Flash: *plain* and *motion*. A plain guide layer can help you position objects on the Stage, but it does not appear in your final movie. Use plain guide layers to keep your layout consistent, to trace objects you draw, or generally assist you in lining things up.

You use a motion guide layer to animate an object to a path on the Flash Stage. For example, you can create a motion guide layer that specifies a path of flight for a bee on another layer. A motion guide layer contains the animation path that links to an object on another layer. Flash exports motion guide layers with the movie, but the guide layers are not visible in the movie. Flash displays all guide layers in the Timeline with a unique icon. See Chapter 25 to learn more about creating a motion tween animation.

ADD A PLAIN GUIDE LAYER

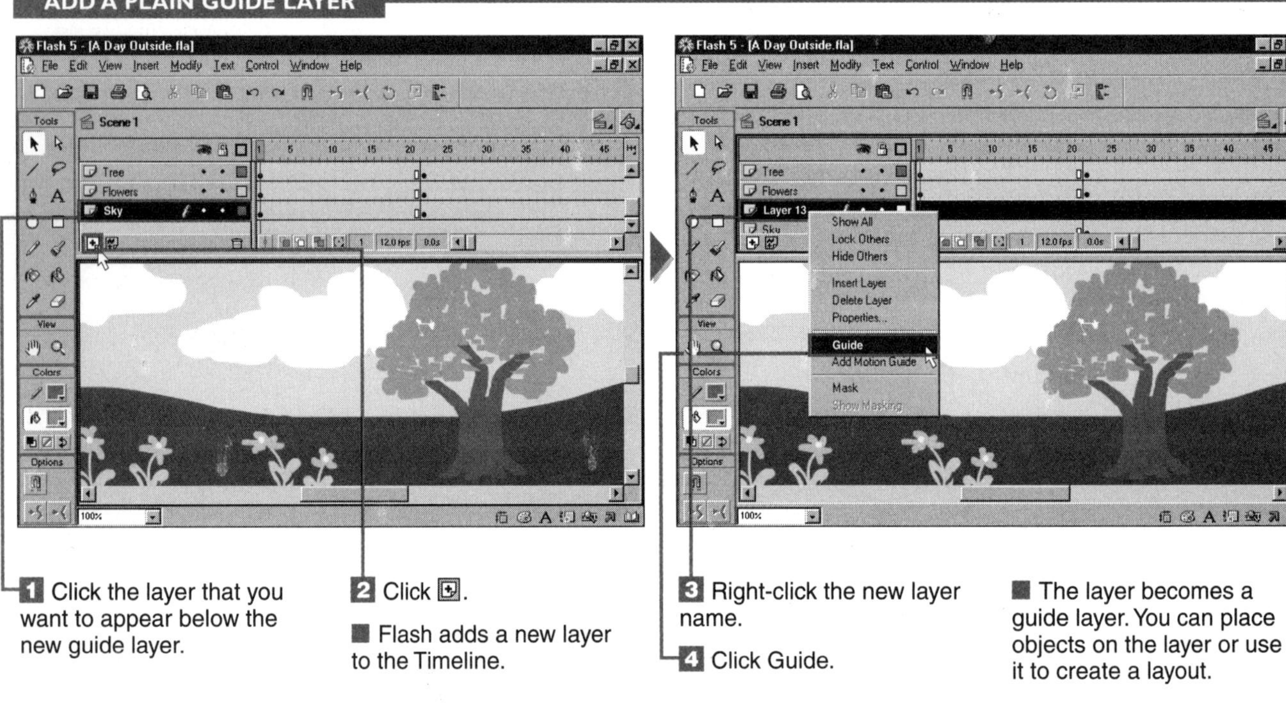

1 Click the layer that you want to appear below the new guide layer.

2 Click ⊞.

■ Flash adds a new layer to the Timeline.

3 Right-click the new layer name.

4 Click Guide.

■ The layer becomes a guide layer. You can place objects on the layer or use it to create a layout.

How exactly does a motion guide layer work?

✔ Flash links motion guide layers to layers containing objects you want to animate along a given path. The motion guide layer contains the path and you can link it to one or more layers. The motion guide layer always appears directly above the layer (or layers) to which it links. To learn more about animating in Flash, see Chapter 24.

Can I lock my guide layer in place?

✔ Yes. In fact, it is a good idea to always lock guide layers and motion guide layers in place so you do not accidentally move anything on them. To lock a layer, click the 🔒 on the Timeline. To unlock the layer again, click the 🔒 again. See the section "Work with Layers in the Timeline" to learn more about using the layer toggles.

ADD A MOTION GUIDE LAYER

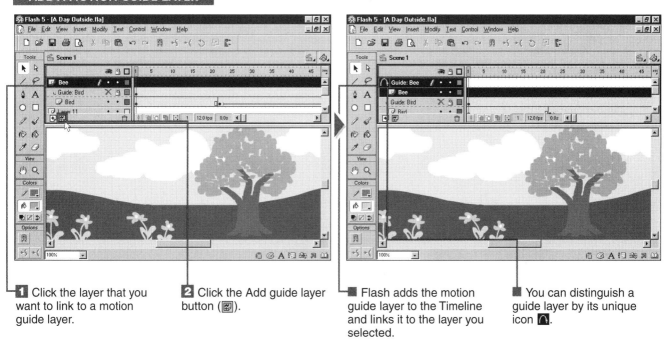

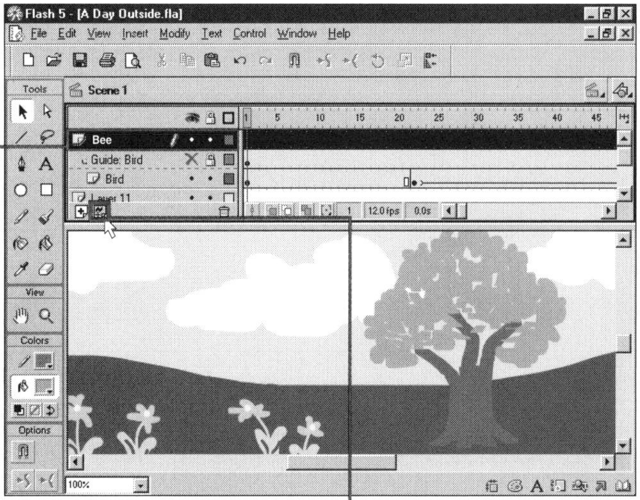

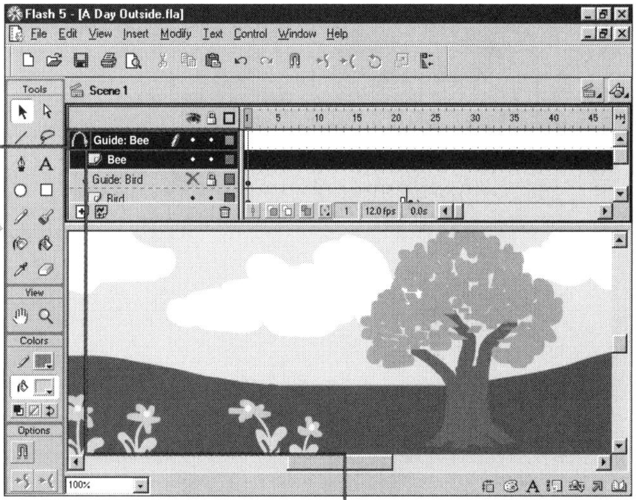

1 Click the layer that you want to link to a motion guide layer.

2 Click the Add guide layer button ( ).

■ Flash adds the motion guide layer to the Timeline and links it to the layer you selected.

■ You can distinguish a guide layer by its unique icon ( ).

ADD A MASK LAYERS AND CREATE A MASK

You can use mask layers to hide various elements on underlying layers. A mask is much like a stencil you tape to a wall. Only certain portions of the underlying layer appear through the mask design, while other parts of the layer are hidden, or *masked*. Flash links masked layers to layers and exports them in the final movie file.

You can create a mask layer, for example, that has a filled square shape in the middle that acts like a window to the layer below it. The "hole" or square shape lets you see anything directly beneath it, but the remainder of the mask layer hides anything that lies out of view of the "hole."

Mask layers appear with a unique icon on the Timeline. You can only link a mask layer to the layer directly below it. Mask layers can only contain one fill shape, symbol, or object to use as a window.

ADD A MASK LAYER

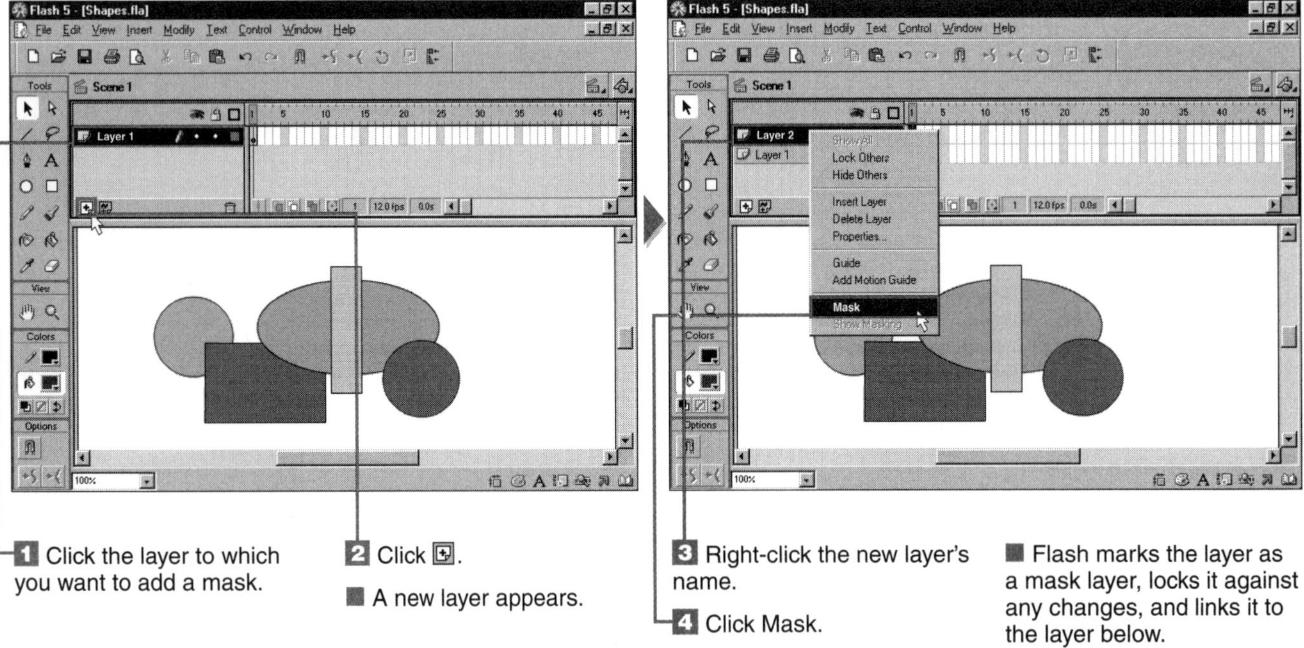

1 Click the layer to which you want to add a mask.

2 Click ⊞.

■ A new layer appears.

3 Right-click the new layer's name.

4 Click Mask.

■ Flash marks the layer as a mask layer, locks it against any changes, and links it to the layer below.

I cannot I see the mask effect. Why not?

✔ Probably because you unlocked the layer. You must first lock the mask layer in order to see the mask effect. You can also see the effect if you run the movie in test mode; click the Control menu and click Test Movie. The Flash Player window opens and runs the movie. Click the window's ☒ to return to the Flash program window.

What sort of fill should I draw for my mask shape?

✔ You can use any kind of fill color or pattern to create the mask shape. Regardless of what makes up your fill, Flash treats the shape as a window to the linked layer (or layers) below. For that reason, you might consider using a transparent fill rather than a solid so you can see through the fill to the layer below and position it correctly on the Stage.

CREATE A MASK

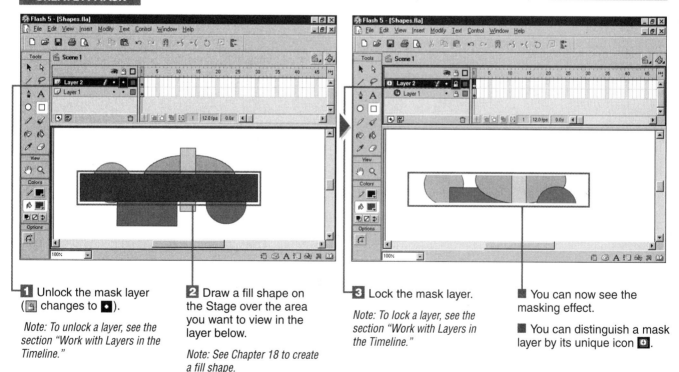

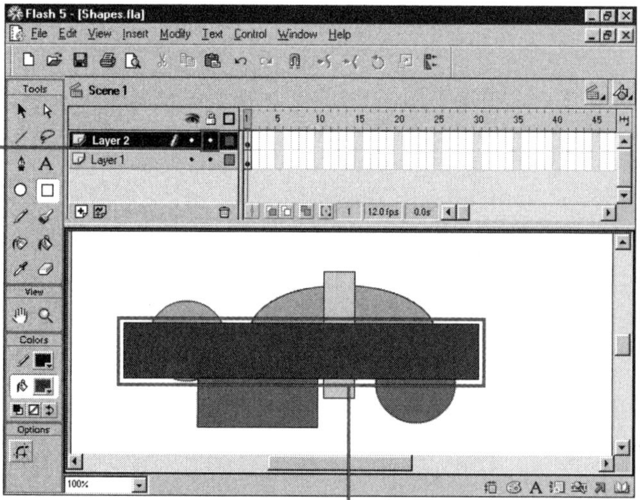

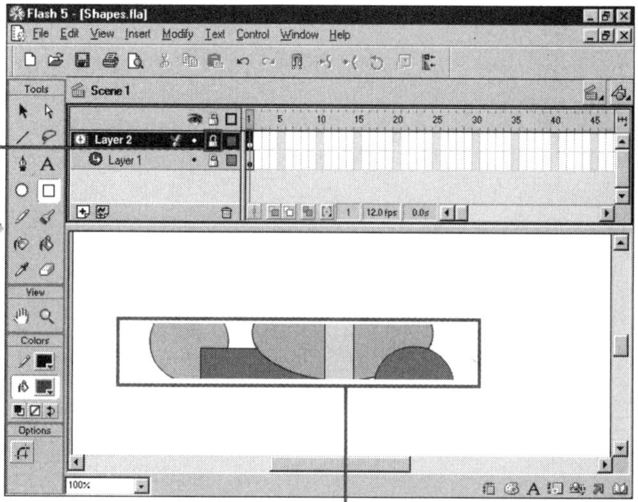

1 Unlock the mask layer (🔒 changes to •).

Note: To unlock a layer, see the section "Work with Layers in the Timeline."

2 Draw a fill shape on the Stage over the area you want to view in the layer below.

Note: See Chapter 18 to create a fill shape.

3 Lock the mask layer.

Note: To lock a layer, see the section "Work with Layers in the Timeline."

■ You can now see the masking effect.

■ You can distinguish a mask layer by its unique icon ◘.

UNDERSTAND SYMBOLS AND INSTANCES

To create animation sequences in Flash, you need to understand how the program handles graphics elements in your projects. In Flash terminology, a *symbol* is a reusable element you can store in the Flash Library. When you repeatedly use a symbol throughout your movie, Flash calls it an *instance*.

What Is a Library?

Every file you create in Flash has a *Library* where you store elements you want to reuse in your project. You can organize elements into related folders from the Library window, much like you organize files on your computer's hard drive.

The Library window is a separate mini-window inside the Flash program window that lists symbols alphabetically. You open this window to drag and drop symbols from the Library onto the Stage, or to add and delete symbols. See the section "Using the Flash Library" to learn more about this feature.

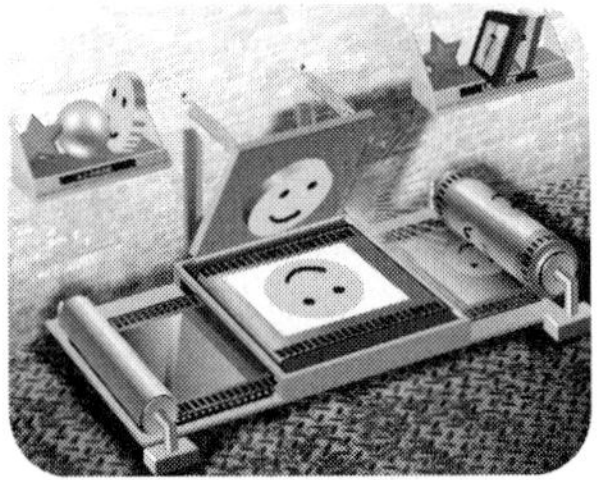

What are Flash Symbols?

Stored in the Flash Library, a *symbol* is a drawing you create with the Flash drawing tools, a graphic you create in another program, or a rollover button. Symbols are also sound clips, movie clips, or text you treat as symbols in your project. See Chapter 26 to learn more about button symbols.

When you import a graphic, Flash automatically classifies and adds it to the file's Library. To place graphics that you create from scratch in the file's Library, you must first define them as symbols. You can convert existing graphical elements into symbols using the Convert to Symbol command, or you can use the Symbol editor to create new symbols.

You edit symbols in Symbol-Edit mode. Flash reflects any edits in the Library window, and updates any instances in the Flash Timeline.

What is an Instance?

An *instance* is the copy of a symbol you insert into your project, which references the original, but which does not greatly affect file size. The original symbol stays in the Library, unaltered by edits you make to the instance. Edits to an instance are good only for that one occurrence in your movie.

You can use as many instances of a symbol in your project as you like. You can also use symbols from other Flash files.

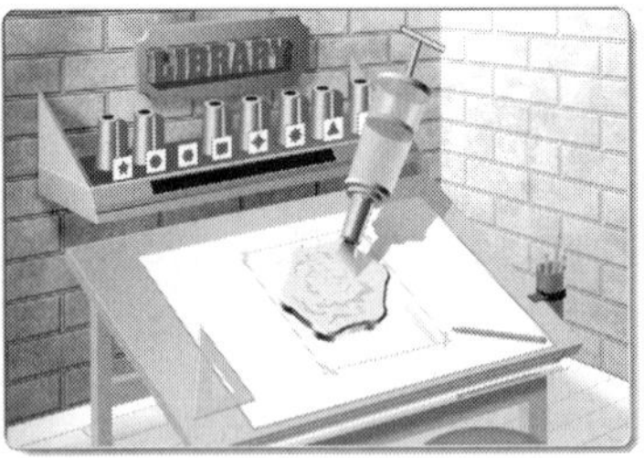

TYPES OF SYMBOLS

As you can reuse symbols to create animation in the Flash Timeline, you must specify how you want the symbol to behave. Flash classifies symbols, or *behaviors*, into three types: graphics, movie clips, or buttons.

Graphic Symbols

You can create *graphic symbols* with Flash drawing tools, or you can import graphics from other programs to use as graphics in Flash. You can make the graphic symbol a simple circle or square, or a highly detailed drawing. You can also turn text into graphic symbols that you manipulate and animate in your movies. For example, you can turn a company name into a rotating graphic symbol that plays at the beginning of a project. To learn more about drawing graphic objects in Flash, see Chapter 17. To learn how to create text in Flash, see Chapter 20.

Movie Clip Symbols

Independent of the main movie's timeline, *movie clip* symbols are mini-movies that reside inside the main Flash movie file and utilize timelines of their own. For example, instead of building a sequence into your main movie timeline, you can create a short animation, make a movie clip symbol of it, and reuse it in your movie. When you define a short animation sequence as a movie clip symbol, you can easily keep track of it, edit it separately from your main movie, and drop it into place whenever you want it to play. To learn more about creating animations in Flash, see Chapters 24 and 25.

Button Symbols

You can save interactive, or *rollover*, buttons as symbols and reuse them by associating different actions to the same button. You can use graphics or movie clips as buttons. You can make a button a simple shape or a complex graphic. You can also create hidden buttons, which look like the rest of the movie, but which the user must find and click to start another action. You can use just about anything as a button in Flash.

Button symbols react to mouse cursor movements in your Flash movies. Mouse cursor movements include rolling over the button, pressing the button, and releasing the button. By altering the button's state, you can clue users in to the button's presence. To learn more about creating buttons in Flash, see Chapter 26.

USING THE FLASH LIBRARY

A Flash project can contain hundreds of graphics, sounds, interactive buttons, and movie clips. The Flash Library can help you organize these elements. For example, you can store related symbols in the same folder, create new folders, or delete folders and symbols you no longer need. You can organize symbols in the Library much like you organize files on your computer.

Every time you import a graphic image into a Flash file, convert a graphic element into a symbol, or add a new sound to a frame, Flash adds it to the file's Library. In effect, the Library is a compendium of your movie's contents.

When you open the Library, it appears as a mini-window within the Flash program window. You can move the Library around on-screen, or hide it when you no longer need to use it. You can enlarge the Library window to view more details about its contents and use the scroll bars to view different symbols in the list. You can also preview what a symbol looks like before adding it to the Stage.

USING THE FLASH LIBRARY

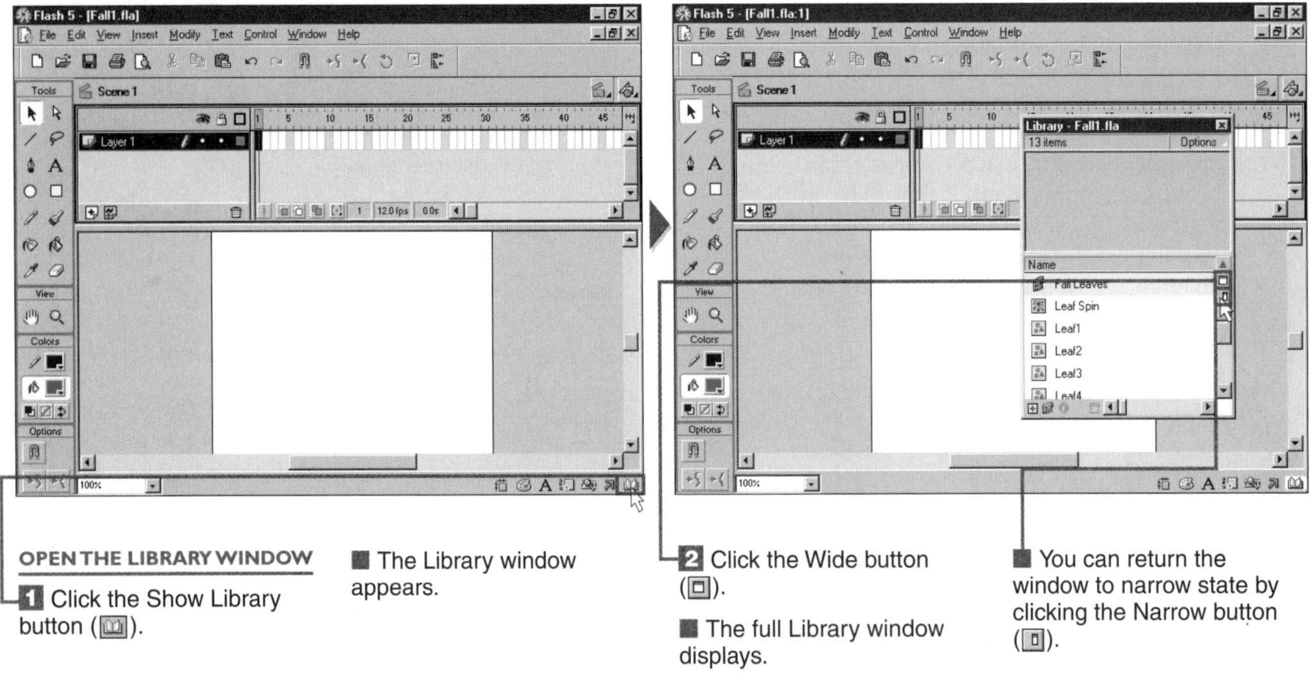

OPEN THE LIBRARY WINDOW

1 Click the Show Library button (📖).

■ The Library window appears.

2 Click the Wide button (▭).

■ The full Library window displays.

■ You can return the window to narrow state by clicking the Narrow button (▯).

Can I use symbols from another movie's Library?

✔ You can easily insert symbols into your current project from another file's library. Click the File menu and click Open as Library. The Open as Library dialog box appears. Click the filename, and then click Open. The Library window opens and lists the other file's symbols. Drag the symbol you want to use onto the Stage.

Does Flash offer another way to open the Library window?

✔ Yes. You can click the Window menu and then click Library to display the Library window. You can also press Control + L (Windows) or Command + L (Mac) on the keyboard to quickly summon the Library at any time.

How do I place a symbol from the Library onto the Stage?

✔ From the Library window, locate the symbol you want to use, and then drag it from the Library and drop it onto the Stage.

How do I close the Library window?

✔ You can leave the Library window open as long as you need it, or you can hide it again by clicking 📖 or by clicking the window's Close button (X).

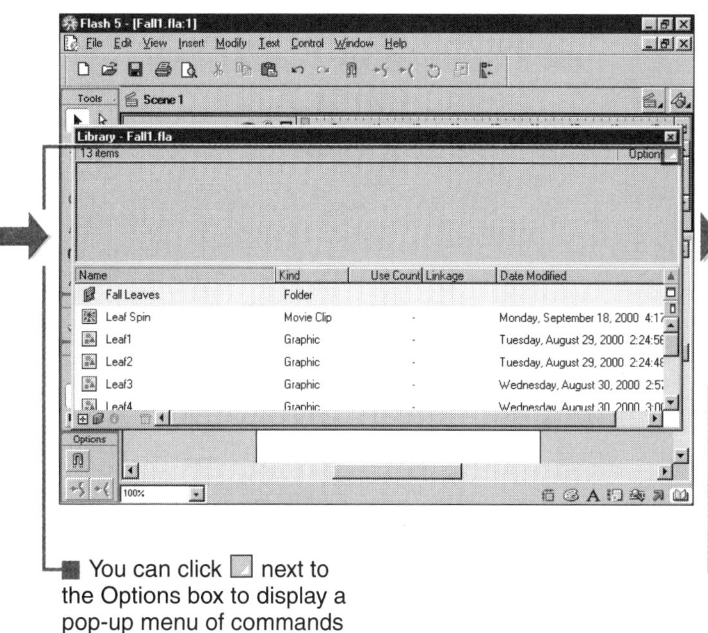

■ You can click ☐ next to the Options box to display a pop-up menu of commands related to Library tasks and items.

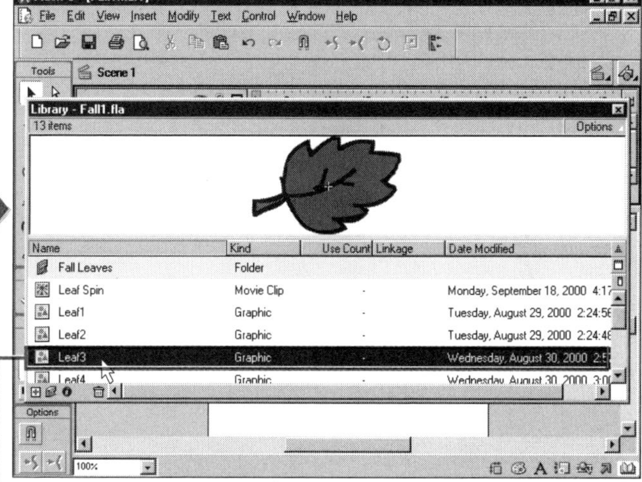

■ You can preview an item in the Library by clicking the item.

CONTINUED

USING THE FLASH LIBRARY (CONTINUED)

To organize all of your symbols, you can store them in folders. You may have a folder containing symbols you use in a company logo, and another folder containing symbols you use in an animation sequence. You can name and rename folders any way you like. You can add and delete folders and move symbols from one folder to another. You can also delete symbols from the Library that you no longer need.

The Library folders display like any other folder on your computer system. Open the folder to view its contents or hide the contents and view only the folder name. When you open a folder, you can see every symbol it contains. The icons next to the symbol name in the Library window indicate the symbol type. For example, a speaker icon indicates the symbol is a sound clip symbol while an icon with three tiny shapes indicates a graphic symbol.

USING THE FLASH LIBRARY (CONTINUED)

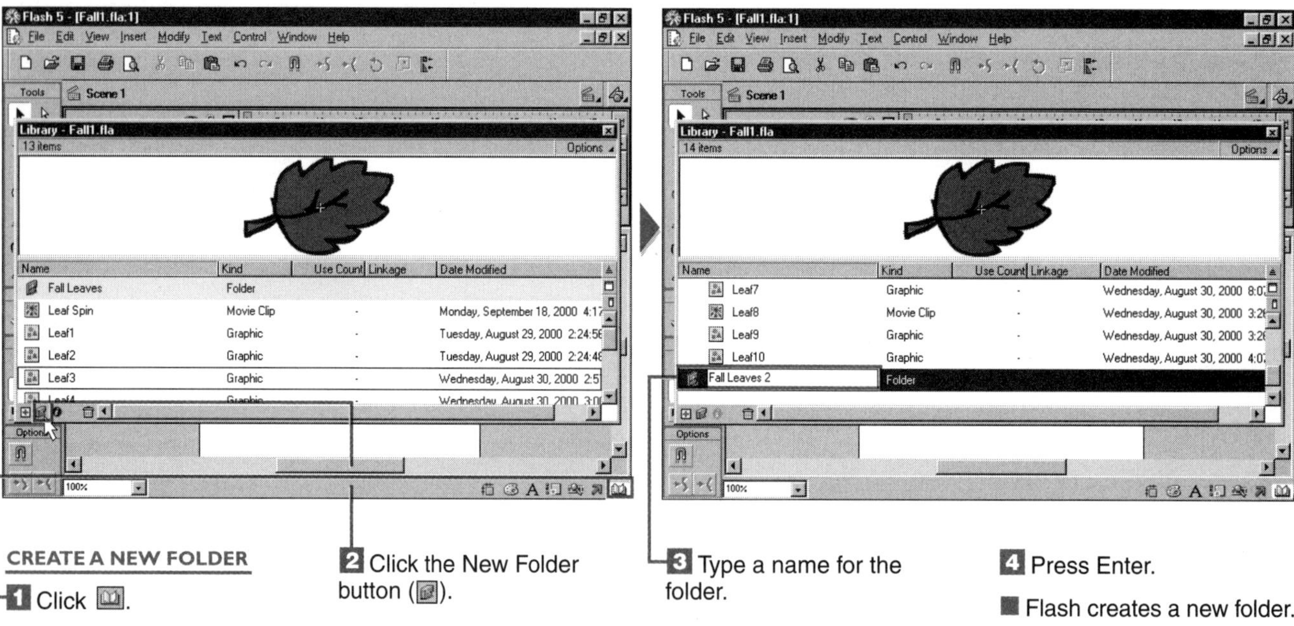

CREATE A NEW FOLDER

1 Click [icon].

2 Click the New Folder button ([icon]).

3 Type a name for the folder.

4 Press Enter.

■ Flash creates a new folder.

How do I rename a folder?

✔ Double-click the folder name in the Library window to highlight the folder name. Type a new name, press Enter and Flash applies the new name. You can use this technique to rename symbols in the Library window.

Do I have to widen the Library window?

✔ No. You only widen it if you want to see more content details. You may find it easier to leave the window narrow to easily see the Flash Stage contents, and to drag symbols from the window onto the Stage.

Can I delete a folder I no longer need?

✔ Yes, but make sure it does not contain any symbols you want to keep or are currently using in the Flash file. Once you delete a folder, Flash deletes its contents, along with any instances you use in your Flash animation. To delete a folder, click it, and then click Delete at the bottom of the Library window. Flash warns you that you are about to permanently delete the folder and its contents. Click Delete, and Flash removes the folder from the Library list.

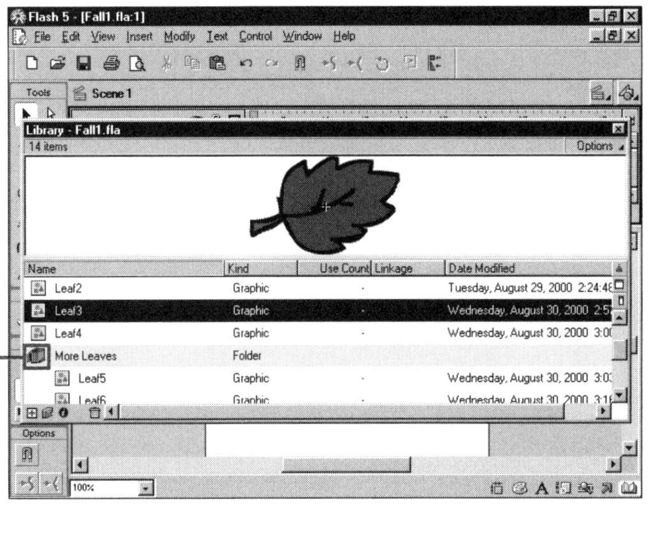

■ To view a folder's contents, you can double-click the Folder icon (📁).

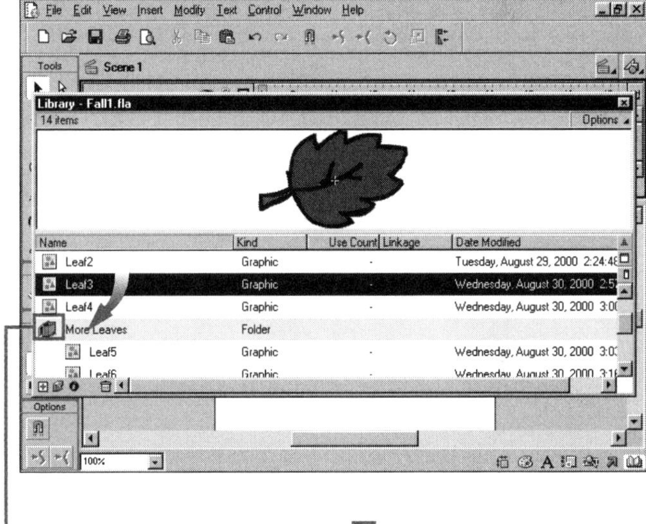

MOVE A SYMBOL TO ANOTHER FOLDER

1 Drag the symbol over 📁.

2 Release the mouse button.

■ The symbol moves into the folder.

CREATE SYMBOLS

You can easily turn any object you draw on the Flash Stage into a symbol, which you can reuse throughout your project. You can also convert any existing drawing or graphical element into a symbol. When you save an item as a symbol, Flash stores it in the file's Library. When you reuse the symbol, you are using an *instance* or copy of the original symbol.

There are three types of behaviors you can assign to a symbol: graphic, movie clip, or button. The behavior you assign depends on what you want to do with the symbol.

By turning graphical elements into symbols, you can considerably reduce the file's size. Converting an element into a symbol places it in the file's Library. Any time you want to use the symbol elsewhere in your Flash project, you can place an instance of the symbol onto the Stage. The instance contains information that references the original symbol. The referencing data takes up much less file size than a complete set of instructions for drawing the symbol each time you want it to appear in your project.

CREATE SYMBOLS

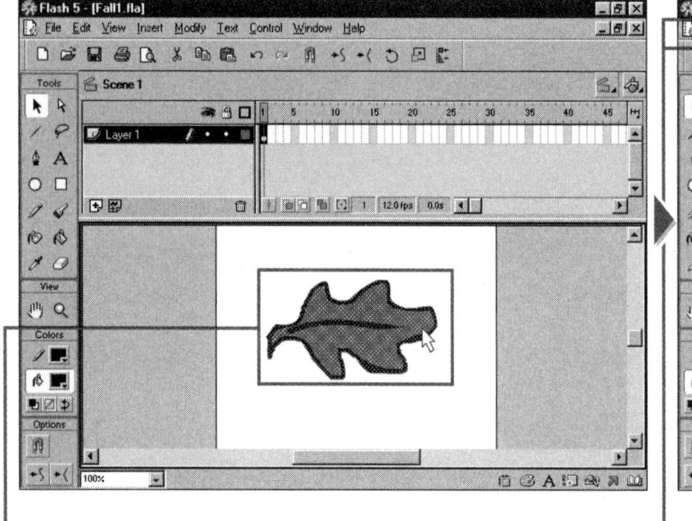

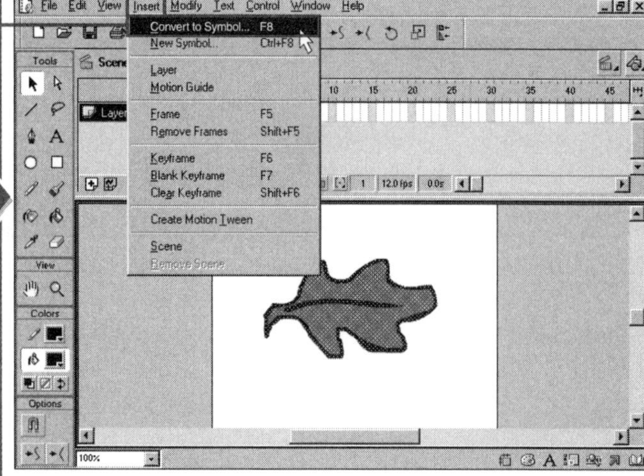

CONVERT AN OBJECT TO A SYMBOL

1 Click all the objects on the stage you want to convert into a symbol.

■ To select multiple objects, you can hold down Shift while clicking on each object.

2 Click Insert.

3 Click Convert to Symbol.

■ The Symbol Properties dialog box opens.

How do I create a symbol from scratch?

✔ Rather than converting an object into a symbol, you can switch to symbol-edit mode and create a new symbol. Click the Insert menu and click New Symbol. Type a name for the symbol and assign a behavior, such as Graphic, and then click OK. Flash immediately switches you to symbol-edit mode and you can use the drawing tools to create a new symbol. The symbol's name appears above the Timeline. To save the symbol and exit symbol-edit mode, click the Scene name link to the left of the symbol name.

Can I create a duplicate symbol?

✔ Yes. For example, you may want to copy a symbol and change it ever so slightly in one frame of your Flash movie. From the Library window, right-click the symbol you want to duplicate. Click Duplicate. Type a new name and assign a behavior. Click OK. Now you can edit the copy of the symbol without affecting the original.

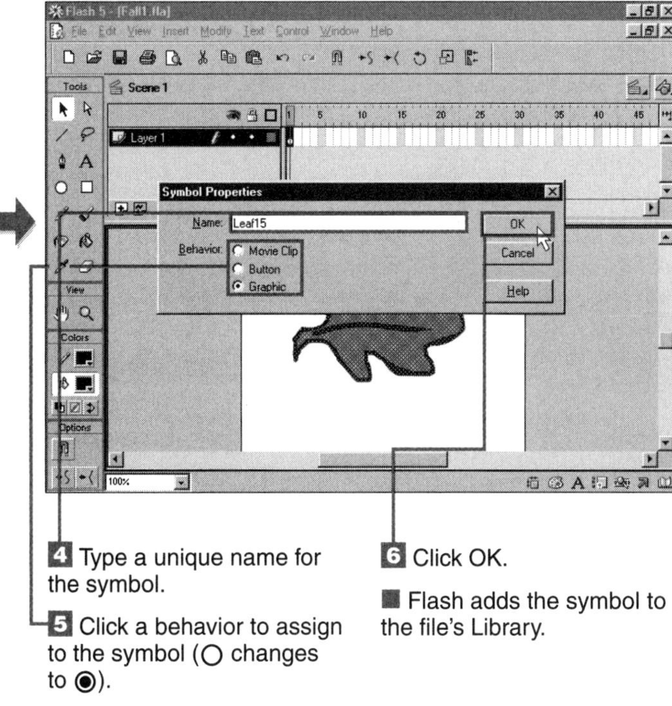

4 Type a unique name for the symbol.

5 Click a behavior to assign to the symbol (○ changes to ◉).

6 Click OK.

■ Flash adds the symbol to the file's Library.

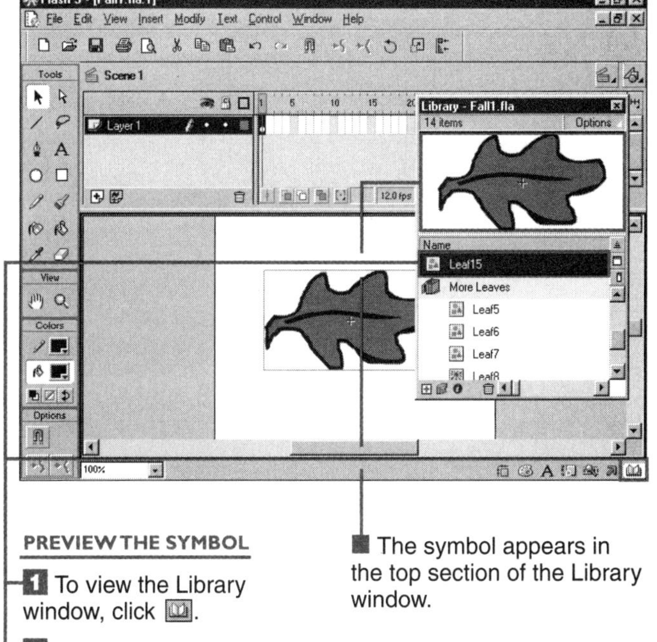

PREVIEW THE SYMBOL

1 To view the Library window, click 📖.

2 Click the symbol name.

■ The symbol appears in the top section of the Library window.

INSERT AN INSTANCE

To reuse a symbol in your Flash project, you can place an *instance* of it on the Stage. An instance is a copy of the original symbol. The copy references the original instead of redrawing the object completely. This method of referencing a vector object for reuse is much more efficient than copying an object over and over again in a file. To learn how to create an original symbol, see the section "Create a Symbol."

When copying an object, you are copying the entire set of instructions that tells the computer how to draw the object. With the Flash method, the symbol instance merely points to the original symbol without needing a complete set of instructions for recreating the object. This greatly decreases the movie's file size.

You can place as many instances as you like throughout your Flash movie or in a single frame. You can also make edits to an instance without affecting the original symbol. For example, you might want to change the object's appearance or shape. You can learn more about editing an instance in the section "Modify an Instance."

INSERT AN INSTANCE

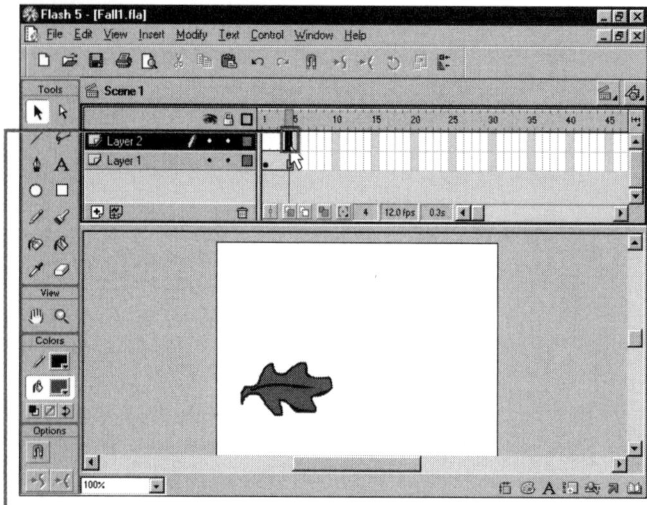

1 Click the frame and layer where you want to insert the instance.

Note: To learn more about frames, see Chapter 24. To learn more about layers, turn to Chapter 21.

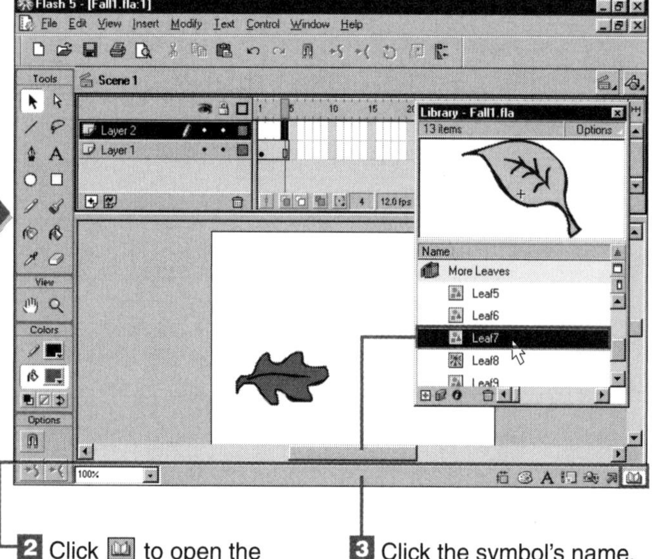

2 Click [icon] to open the Library window.

3 Click the symbol's name.

Can I replace one instance with another?

✔ Yes. First click the symbol you want to replace, and then click the Show Instance button ( ). This opens the Instance panel. From the Instance tab, click the Swap Symbol button ( ). Click the replacement symbol from the Swap Symbol dialog box. Click OK.

Flash does not let me place an instance in a regular frame. Why?

✔ You can only place an instance in a keyframe in the Flash Timeline. You are not allowed to place instances in regular frames. To learn more about how frames work in the Timeline, see Chapter 24.

I made a mistake. How do I remove an instance?

✔ If you change your mind about placing an instance on the Stage, you can undo your action with the Undo command. Click the Undo button ( ) to immediately reverse your last action in Flash. To redo the action again, click the Redo button ( ).

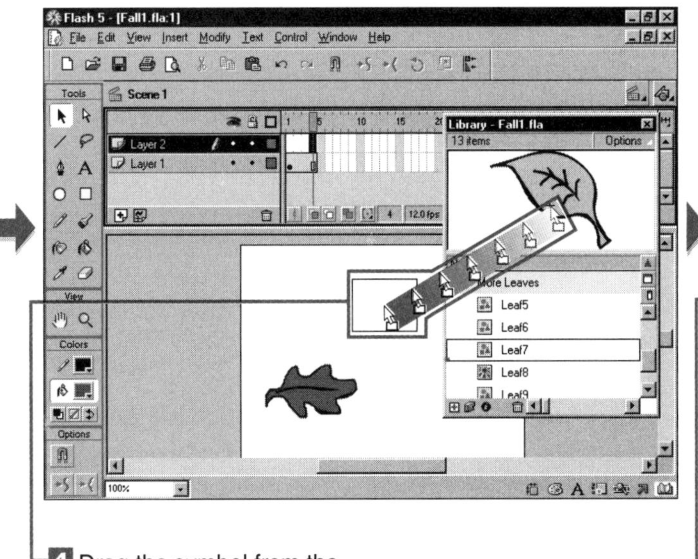

4 Drag the symbol from the Library window.

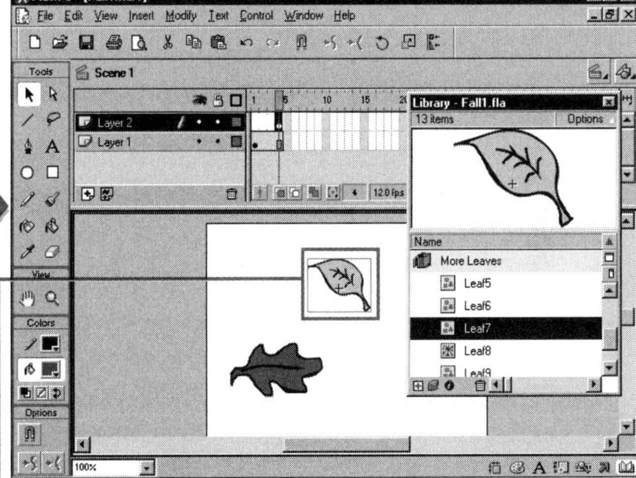

5 Drop the instance on the Stage.

■ An instance of the symbol now appears on the Stage.

MODIFY AN INSTANCE

After you place a symbol instance on the Stage, you can change the way it appears without changing the original symbol. For example, you can change its color or make it appear transparent.

When you make changes to an instance in the Instance Panel, you use several tools to modify its properties. For example, you can change the object's behavior by turning a graphic symbol into a movie clip, or into a button. You can also experiment by fine-tuning an instance's brightness, tint, or transparency, all of which are color effects.

The Brightness option enables you to adjust the brightness level of the instance, ranging from 100% dark (black) to 100% light (white).

You use the Tint option to change the hue of the instance. You can choose from a palette of colors or specify exact RGB values for red, green, and blue.

The Alpha option enables you to change the transparency of the instance to make it appear faded or transparent.

Use the Advanced option to modify both color and transparency settings in value.

MODIFY AN INSTANCE

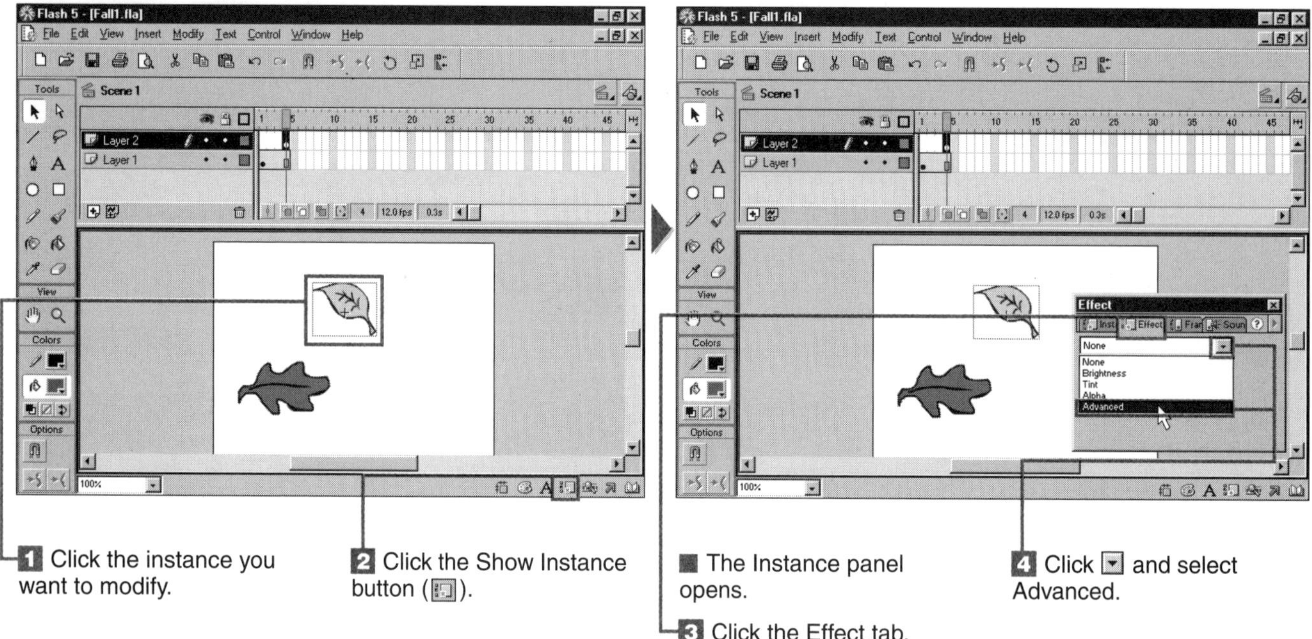

1 Click the instance you want to modify.

2 Click the Show Instance button ( ).

■ The Instance panel opens.

3 Click the Effect tab.

4 Click ▾ and select Advanced.

How do I make the instance transparent?

✔ To make an instance appear transparent, change its Alpha setting. Follow steps 1 through 3 in the section "Modify an Instance." Click ▼ in the Effects box and select Alpha. Click the Alpha slider ▼ and drag the slider to the transparency level you want to apply.

Can I test how my edits affect the movie?

✔ Yes. As you edit an instance, you may want to see the results of your edits before exiting symbol-edit mode. Click Control, Test Movie to run the movie and check the appearance of the instance.

Can I edit the symbol instead of just the instance?

✔ Yes. When you edit a symbol rather than an instance, Flash updates every appearance of the symbol throughout the entire movie. To learn more about editing symbols, see the task "Edit Symbols" in this chapter.

Can I name an instance?

✔ You can name a movie clip instance and use the name in your action variables. Click inside the Name text box in the Instance panel and type a name. This only works for movie clip instances. See Chapter 28 to learn more about Flash actions.

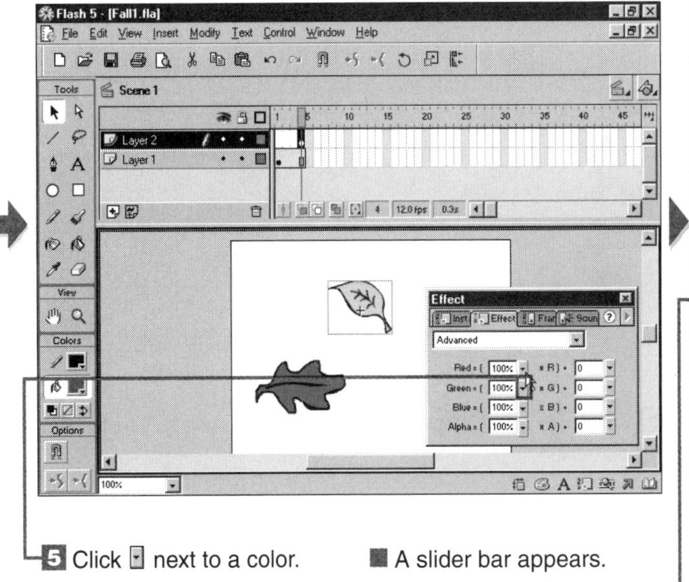

5 Click ▼ next to a color.

■ A slider bar appears.

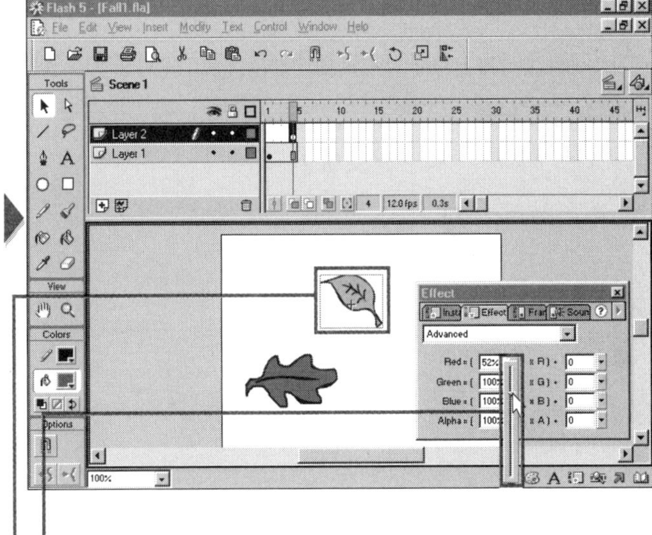

6 Drag the slider to a new color setting.

■ The selected object changes color as you drag the slider.

■ You might want to experiment with the various color settings to achieve the color effect you want.

EDIT SYMBOLS

You can edit symbols you have stored in the Library. For example, you may need to change a symbol slightly, such as adjusting a line or shape, or perhaps assigning another color. You can make changes to the original symbol and Flash automatically updates all instances of it in your movie. This can save you considerable time and effort.

You can edit symbols in symbol-edit mode. When in symbol-edit mode, Flash locks the other objects on the Stage to prevent accidental changes. This means you cannot edit other symbols or objects on the Stage area, only the selected symbol. It is not always easy to discern whether you are in symbol-edit mode or not. The easiest way to tell is to look for the symbol name at the top of the Timeline, to the right of the scene name.

EDIT SYMBOLS

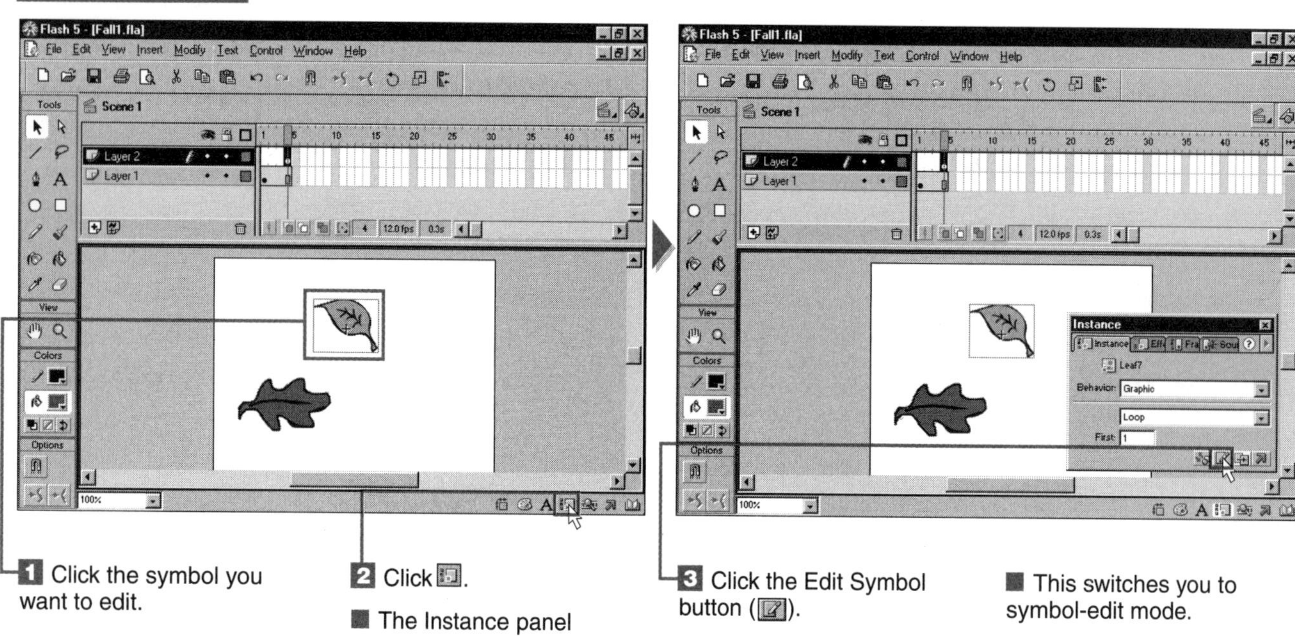

1 Click the symbol you want to edit.

2 Click .

■ The Instance panel opens.

3 Click the Edit Symbol button ().

■ This switches you to symbol-edit mode.

How do I remove a symbol I no longer want?

✔ First make sure you do not use the symbol anywhere in your Flash movie. When you delete a symbol, Flash removes any instances of the symbol. Click 📖 to open the Library window, and then select the symbol you want to remove. Click Delete. A warning prompt box appears asking you to confirm the deletion. Note that once you delete a symbol, you cannot undo the action. To continue, click Delete. Flash permanently removes the symbol from the file's Library.

Flash does not let me edit my symbol. Why?

✔ Depending on the complexity of the symbol, you may need to first apply the Break Apart or Ungroup command. The Break Apart command breaks the symbol down into its most basic construction — lines and fills. You can then edit a single line or fill. The Ungroup command ungroups a grouped object. You can find the Break Apart and Ungroup commands on the Modify menu. See Chapter 19 to learn more about using these commands.

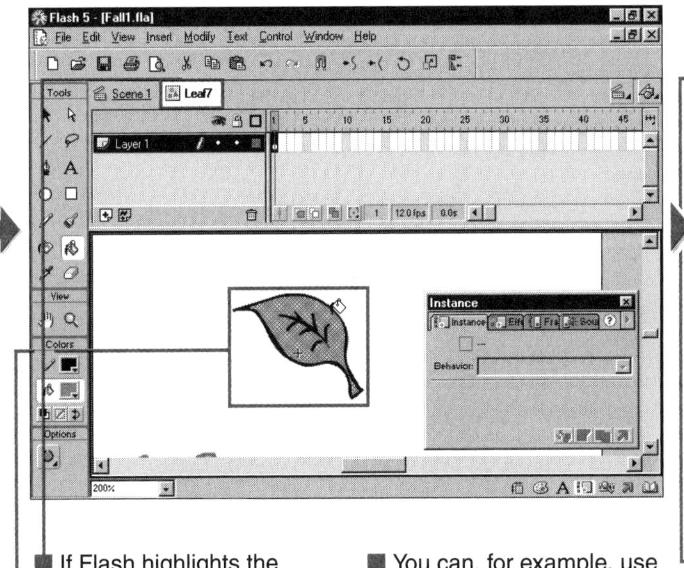

■ If Flash highlights the symbol name at the top of the Timeline, you know you are in symbol-edit mode.

4 Edit the symbol as you desire.

■ You can, for example, use the Flash drawing tools to make changes to the object, such as changing the fill color, or adjusting a line segment.

Note: See Chapter 19 to learn more about editing objects.

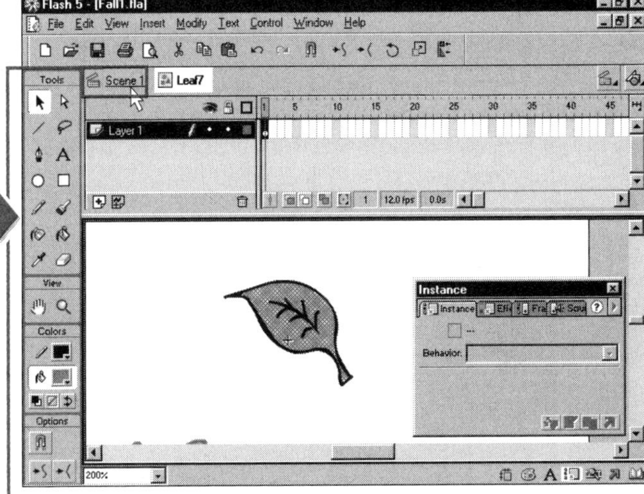

5 After editing the symbol, click the Scene button.

■ You are no longer in symbol-edit mode.

UNDERSTANDING VECTOR AND BITMAP IMAGES

You can create your own vector graphics in Flash, or import graphics from other sources for use in your movies. *Vector* graphics are Flash's native file type, so anything you draw using the Drawing tools is a vector graphic. You can also import vector graphics from other vector graphics programs, such as Macromedia Freehand or Adobe Illustrator, or vector graphics from earlier versions of Flash.

Flash does not limit you to just vector graphics. You can import other graphic types into Flash. For example, you can import GIF, PNG, JPEG, and BMP file formats. You can also import PICT, WMF, and EMF formats. These other graphic file types are known as *bitmap* images.

It is important to understand the basic differences between vector and bitmap file formats before you begin importing graphics from other programs.

A Word about Bitmap Graphics

Until recently, bitmap graphics — also called *raster* graphics — were the traditional way to illustrate Web pages. While bitmap images offer a great deal of detail, their file sizes are often large, requiring a lot of bandwidth when you transfer them across a network or the Internet.

Bitmaps and Pixels

To understand why bitmap images are so large, you must first understand what comprises a bitmap. Bitmap graphics are made up of square dots, called *pixels*. The dots are arranged in a grid pattern, and each dot includes information about its color and position. Most bitmap images use thousands of pixels. A single bitmap file must contain information that maps out each pixel's placement and color in order to redisplay the image. The resulting file size is extremely large.

To illustrate this concept, try drawing a simple yellow smiley face in a bitmap drawing program and save the file in the bitmap file format. The resulting file size is likely to consume well over 100,000 bytes or 100 kilobytes (K). If you draw the same smiley face in Flash and save it as a Flash movie, the file consumes only about 11K.

A Look at Vector Graphics

Vector graphics use mathematical equations, or *vectors*, to define an image's shape, color, position, and size. Vector instructions tell how to display an image based on lines and curves (or arcs). The use of equations instead of pixels makes the image file size the same, regardless of whether the image is large or small. The vector file need only contain the mathematical data that describes the line and curve properties. This data tells the computer how to display the lines and curves that make up an image, including colors and size.

Technically, bitmap images utilize mathematical data too, but the data includes instructions for each dot in the image, resulting in a much larger file size. The data that describes a vector graphic merely instructs how to display lines and arcs based on mathematical formulas. The data also provides coordinates to place lines and arcs. The result is a graphic file that is much more versatile.

You can easily scale vector graphics, unlike bitmap graphics. Because of their smaller file size, vector graphics download much more quickly onto Web pages. This is a big plus for Web page designers.

Importing Graphics

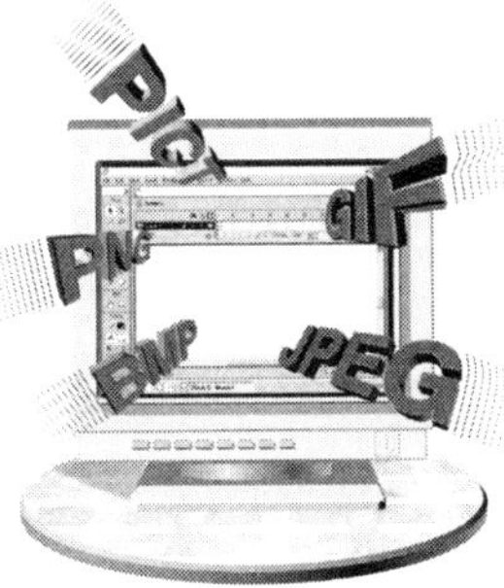

Flash supports a variety of graphic file formats, both bitmap and vector. Flash supports the following bitmap file types: Graphic Interchange Format (GIF), animated GIF, Joint Photographic Experts Group (JPEG), Portable Network Graphic (PNG), and Windows Bitmap (BMP, DIB). Flash supports the following vector file types: Adobe Illustrator AI or EPS, Metafile (WMF) and Enhanced Metafile (EMF), PICT, PCT, and Flash Player files SWF and SPL. Flash also supports multimedia and a few AutoCAD file formats, such as QuickTime Movie (MOV) and AutoCAD DXF (DXF).

Although you can certainly use bitmap graphics in your Flash projects, just remember that they are not as scalable, and increase file size. One way around these issues is to convert an imported bitmap graphic into a vector graphic, or utilize other Flash tools to optimize the graphic's file size.

There are several ways to import a graphic, whether it is a bitmap or vector image. If you are using Windows, you can copy and paste images using the Windows Clipboard. Another way to import graphics is to use the Import command. You can learn more about importing and working with non-Flash graphics in the remainder of this chapter.

IMPORT GRAPHICS

You can import graphics, including vector or bitmap graphics, from other sources to use in Flash. For example, you may create a company logo in Macromedia's Freehand program that you want to place in a Flash movie, or you may want to use a clipart image from the Web in a Flash drawing. You can manipulate imported images with Flash commands. See the section "Understand Vector and Bitmap Images" to learn more about vector and bitmap graphic types.

When you import a graphic, Flash immediately places it on the Stage in the current frame. Flash also automatically adds the graphic to the movie's Library. Flash treats imported graphics as a group. To edit an imported graphic, you need to break apart the image. See section "Turn Bitmaps into Fills" to learn how to break an image apart.

In addition to importing graphics, you can also use the Paste command to paste graphics you cut or copy from other programs. The Cut, Copy, and Paste commands work the same way in Flash that they do in other programs.

IMPORT GRAPHICS

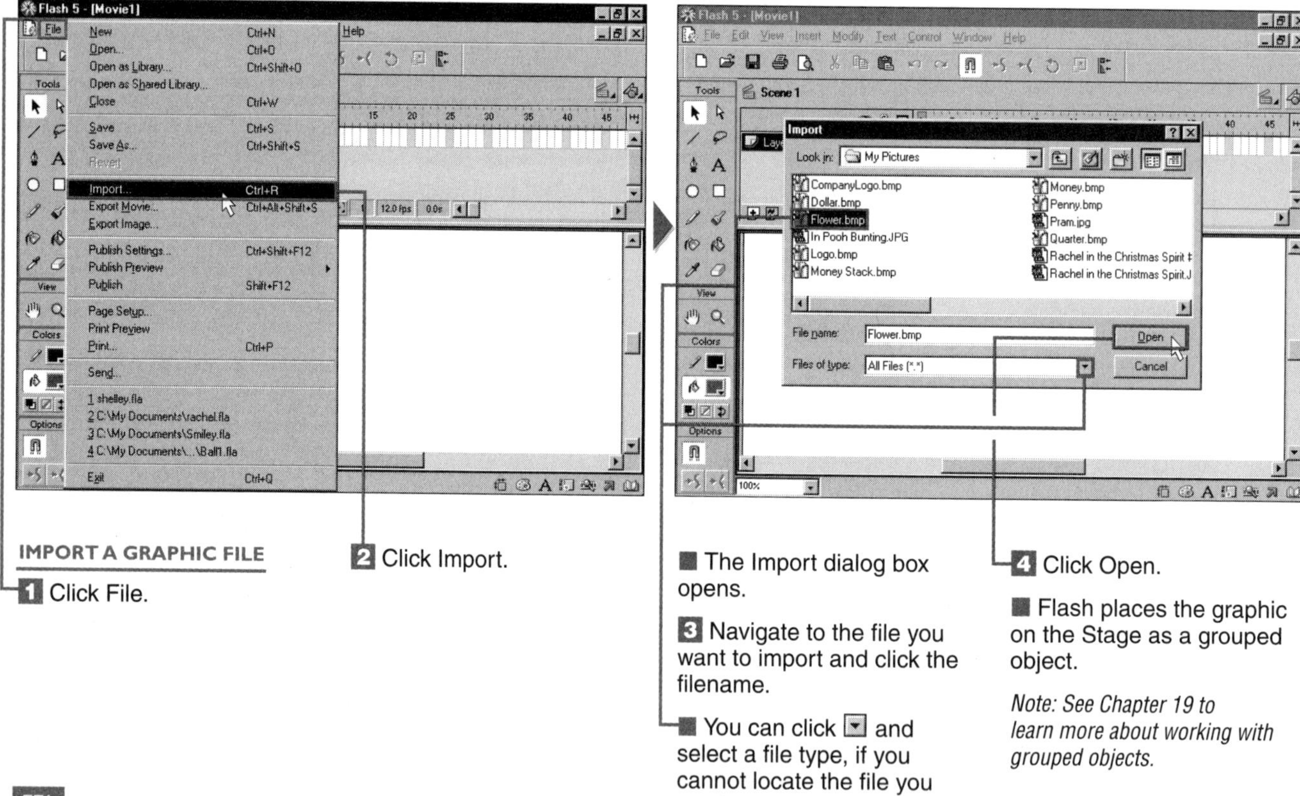

IMPORT A GRAPHIC FILE

1 Click File.

2 Click Import.

■ The Import dialog box opens.

3 Navigate to the file you want to import and click the filename.

■ You can click ▼ and select a file type, if you cannot locate the file you want.

4 Click Open.

■ Flash places the graphic on the Stage as a grouped object.

Note: See Chapter 19 to learn more about working with grouped objects.

What graphic file types does Flash support?

✔ Flash supports GIF, animated GIF, JPEG, PNG, BMP, DIB, TGA, TIF, QTIF, WMF, EMF, PICT, PCT, PNTG, Freehand, and Illustrator files, Photoshop files (PSD), and Flash Player files (SWF and SPL). Flash also supports QuickTime Movie (MOV) and AutoCAD (DXF) file types.

Can I reuse the same bitmap graphic without importing each time?

✔ Yes. You do not have to repeat the import procedure to reuse the same image. Any time you import a graphic, Flash immediately adds it to its library for use in other frames in your movie. To view the Library, click the Show Library button (📖). To learn more about using Library images, see Chapter 22.

Can I import a series of images?

✔ Yes. If you want to include a series of images in sequential keyframes, such as animation sequence in PICT format, you can easily import all the files at once. Flash recognizes sequentially numbered files in the Import dialog box and offers to import the entire sequence. Click Yes to do so or click No to import only the selected file.

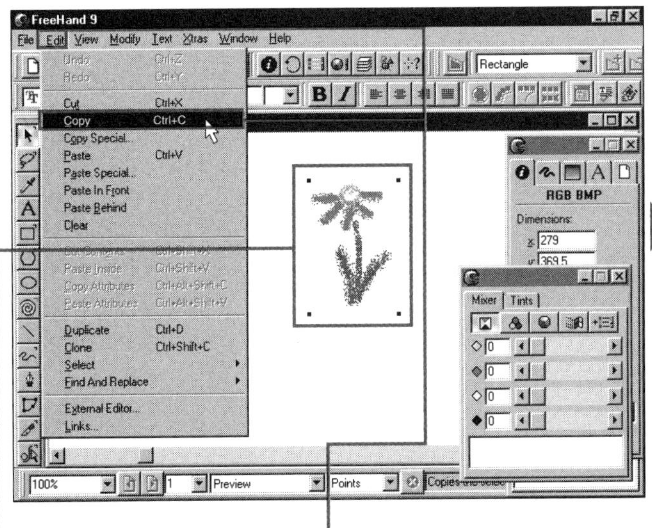

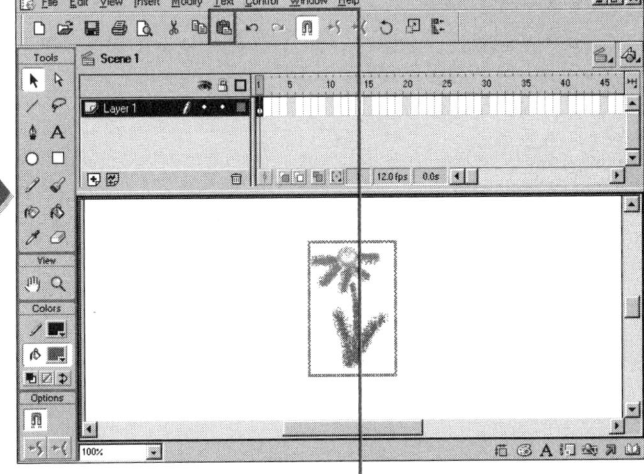

COPY AND PASTE A GRAPHIC

1 Open the program and file containing the graphic to copy.

2 Click the graphic.

■ In most programs, selection handles surround the selected object.

3 Click Edit.

4 Click Copy.

■ You can also click the Copy button (📋), if available.

5 Switch back to Flash. For example, if you are using Windows, click the Flash button on the Windows Taskbar.

6 Click the Paste button (📋).

■ Flash pastes the graphic onto the Stage area.

MAKE BITMAPS INTO VECTOR GRAPHICS

You can use the Trace Bitmap command to convert a bitmap graphic, which can minimize the file size and enable you to utilize the Flash tools to manipulate the graphic.

When you apply the Trace Bitmap command, you have an opportunity to adjust several parameters that define the rendering of the image, including how Flash handles the color variances, pixel size translation, and the smoothness of curves or sharpness of corners. These parameters can help you manage how closely the bitmap image matches the vector graphic image.

During conversion, Flash examines how the pixels in the bitmap relate to one another. You can specify a color threshold setting that instructs Flash how to treat bordering pixels of the same or similar colors. A higher color threshold setting groups subtle color changes into a single vector object, thus decreasing the number of overall colors in the image. A lower setting results in more vector objects, yet more colors display in the image.

For most images, the default settings work fine. You can experiment with the settings to create different looks. See the section "Import Graphics" to learn more about importing bitmaps.

MAKE BITMAPS INTO VECTOR GRAPHICS

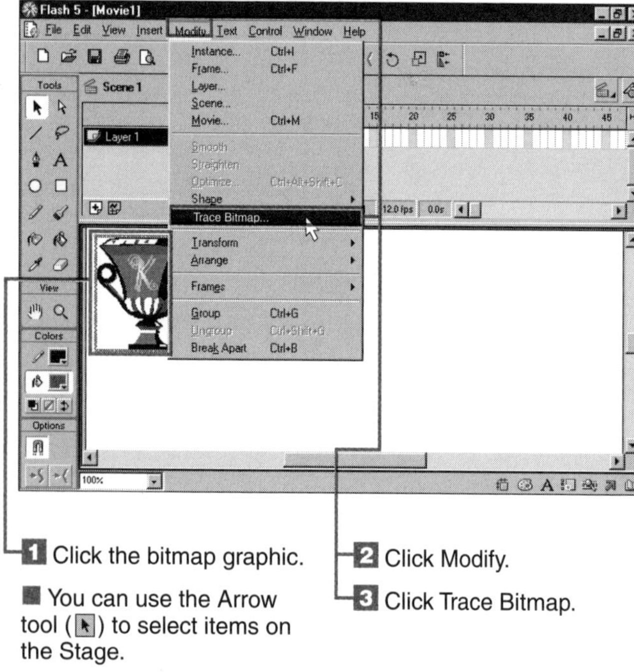

1 Click the bitmap graphic.

■ You can use the Arrow tool (↖) to select items on the Stage.

2 Click Modify.

3 Click Trace Bitmap.

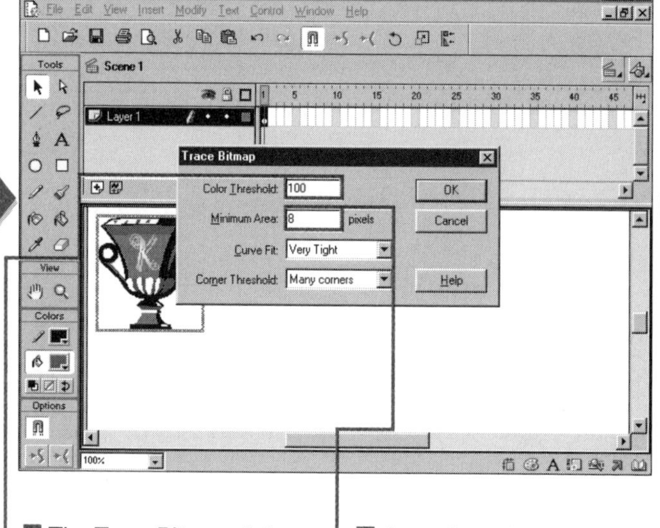

■ The Trace Bitmap dialog box opens.

4 Type a value that determines the amount of color variance between neighboring pixels.

■ A smaller value results in many vector shapes; a larger value results in fewer vectors.

5 Type a minimum pixel radius.

How does the Color Threshold setting work?

✔ It determines the number of colors converted into vectors. For example, perhaps your image is of a boat on water, and the water is made up of three shades of blue. A high color threshold setting may result in a single vector object for the water, or one shade of blue. If you set the color threshold too low, the color of the water displays as dozens of vector objects, one for each shade change in the image.

What if my graphic does not look quite like the original?

✔ When applying the Trace Bitmap controls, you might need to experiment with the settings in the Trace Bitmap dialog box to get the results you want. Start with the default settings. If those do not work, click [undo], and try again, making a few adjustments, such as changing color variance or pixel radius values.

Does the bitmap reduce its file size when Flash converts it?

✔ Yes, if you do not set the Trace Bitmap threshold settings too low. If the bitmap is a complex drawing with lots of colors and shapes, low threshold settings may result in a larger vector file size. Try to find a balance when adjusting the threshold settings.

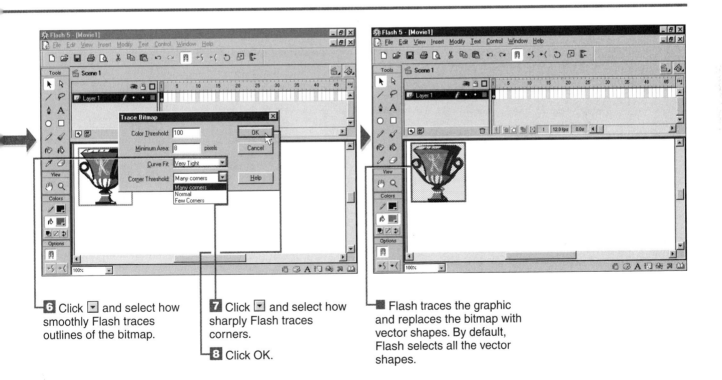

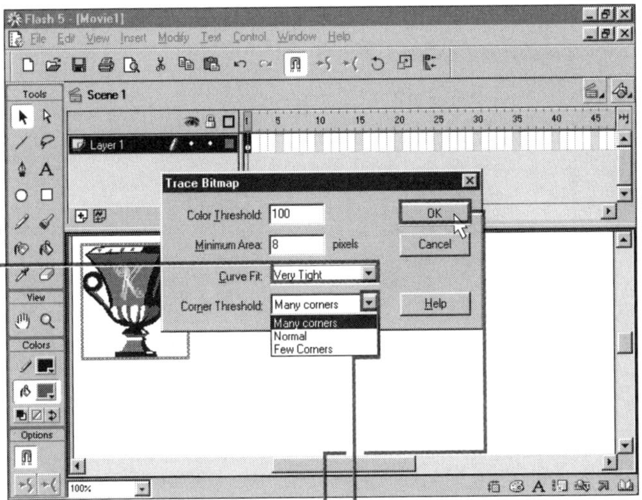

6 Click [▼] and select how smoothly Flash traces outlines of the bitmap.

7 Click [▼] and select how sharply Flash traces corners.

8 Click OK.

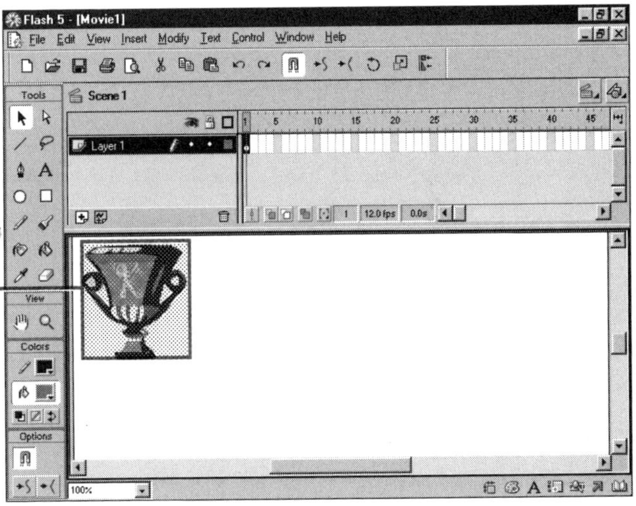

■ Flash traces the graphic and replaces the bitmap with vector shapes. By default, Flash selects all the vector shapes.

TURN BITMAPS INTO FILLS

You can turn a bitmap image into a fill for use with Flash drawing tools that use fills, such as the Oval, Rectangle, or Brush. Fills are solid colors or patterns that fill a shape. Conventional fills include colors and gradient effects. See Chapter 19 to learn more about working with fills and gradients. You can also use a bitmap image, such as a photo, as a fill. Depending on the size of the shape, Flash repeats the image within the shape.

Bitmap photos, for example, make good fills. You may have a photo of a face that you fill into an oval shape, or a photo that makes a good repeated background pattern.

To prepare a bitmap image as a fill, you must utilize the Break Apart command. This command converts the image into separate pieces. Once you separate the image, you can use the Dropper tool to duplicate the image as a fill.

It is a good idea to use layers in your Flash Timeline to organize different elements in your movie, such as bitmaps you turn into fills.

TURN BITMAPS INTO FILLS

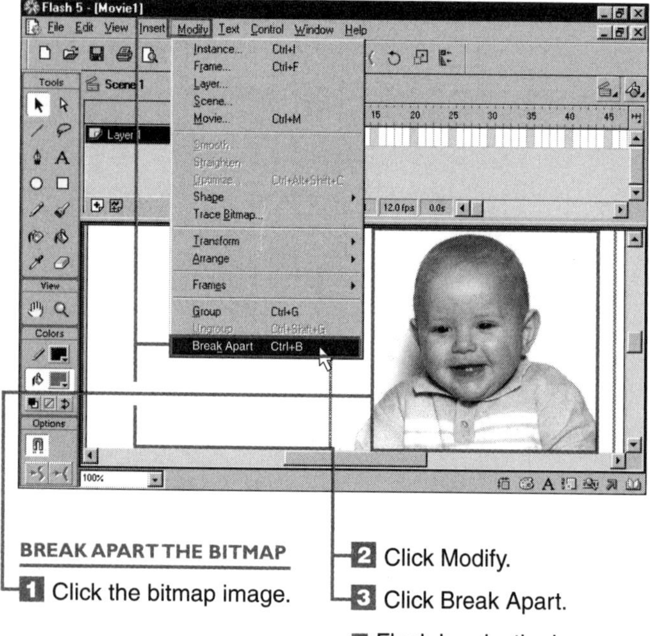

BREAK APART THE BITMAP

1 Click the bitmap image.

2 Click Modify.

3 Click Break Apart.

■ Flash breaks the image into individual elements that comprise the image.

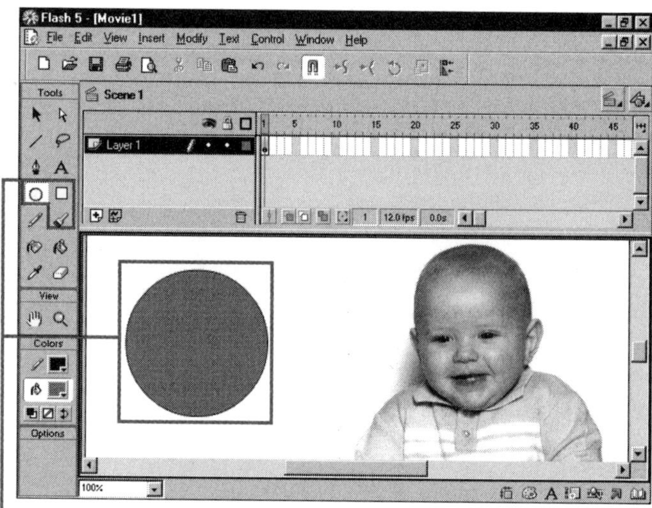

TURN A BITMAP INTO A FILL

1 Select the drawing tool of your choice to create a shape you want to fill.

■ This example uses the Circle tool (○).

■ You might want to place the new shape on another layer to help you keep objects organized.

Note: See Chapter 21 to learn more about Flash layers.

What types of edits can I perform on the bitmap fill?

✔ You can edit a bitmap fill just as you can any other fill, including rotating the image and scaling it to another size. See Chapter 19 to learn more about editing Flash fills.

How do I use a bitmap fill with the Brush tool?

✔ Turn the bitmap into a fill following the steps in this task. Click the Brush tool, select a brush size or shape, and then draw brush strokes on the Stage. Everywhere you draw, Flash uses the bitmap image as your "paint color." To learn more about the Brush tool and its options, see Chapter 18.

How do I use a bitmap image as a tiled pattern?

✔ Click the Show Information button (▣) to open the Info panel, and then click the Fill tab. Click the Fill Type ▾ and select Bitmap. Click the image you want to use, and then click the Paint Bucket tool. You can now fill any shape with a tiled pattern of the bitmap image.

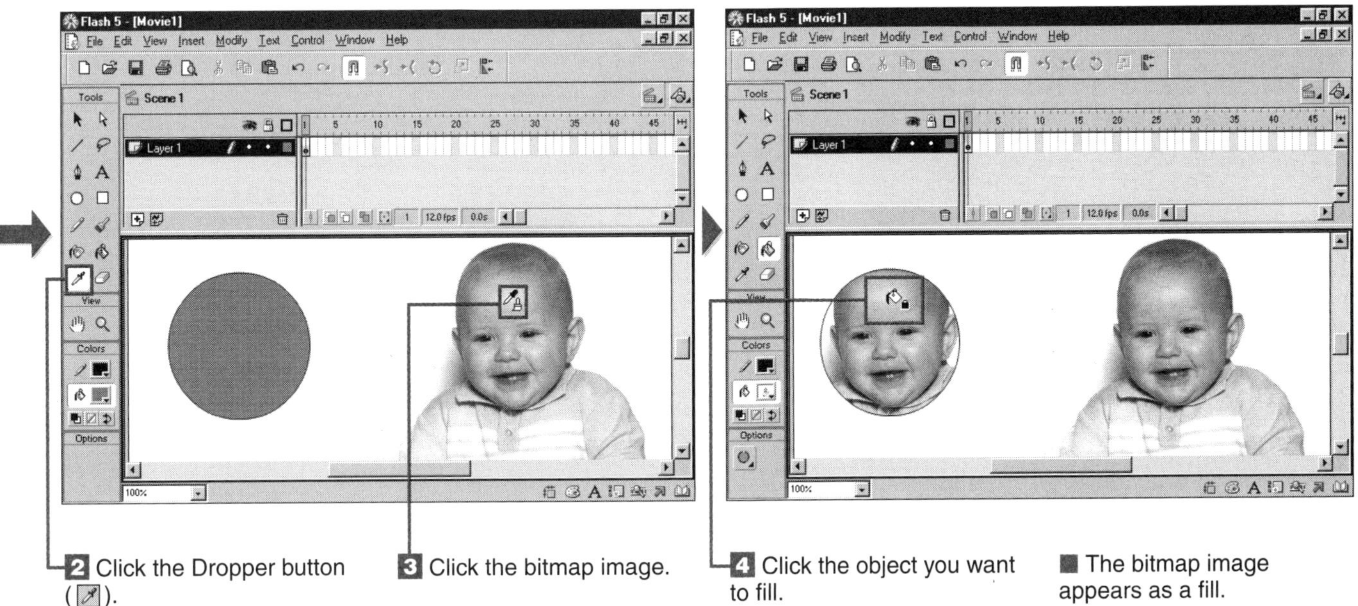

2 Click the Dropper button (✎).

3 Click the bitmap image.

4 Click the object you want to fill.

■ The bitmap image appears as a fill.

AN INTRODUCTION TO ANIMATION

One of the most exciting aspects of Flash is its animation features. You can animate objects, synchronize the animation with sounds, add backgrounds, animate buttons, and much more. After you complete a Flash project, you can place it on a Web page or distribute it for others to view.

How Do I Use Animations?

You can use Flash animations to present a lively message or to simply entertain. Animations you create in Flash can make a Web site come to life. For example, you can create a cartoon to play in your site's banner, or animate buttons for the user to click. You can make your company logo seem to grow in size, or make your company tagline seem to glow. You can create interactive presentations for employees to teach a workplace task, or make an online tutorial for clients that explains your latest product developments and applications.

You can create animation effects for all kinds of elements associated with Web pages, such as an animated preloader timer that displays how long it takes to complete a download or an animated cursor users can click to view different parts of your site. The various ways you can use animations are limitless, and with the Flash animation tools, you have complete control over your movies.

How Do Animations Work?

Animation is simply a change that occurs between two or more frames in a movie. The change can be the placement of an object that moves slightly from one area on the screen to another, or it can be a change in color, intensity, size, or shape of an object. Any change you make to an object makes the object appear to be animated during playback of your movie.

Animation effects use frames to hold illustrated scenes or objects. The scene or object changes slightly from frame to frame to create the illusion of movement. For example, you can have an animation of a ball bouncing. Each frame displays a "snapshot" of the ball in various bouncing positions. When you play the animation back, each frame appears very briefly before the next frame replaces it. The effect is a ball that seems to bounce.

Back in the early days of animating, cartoonists and other animators painted objects and scenery on transparent cels. The cels were stacked to create an image. A movie camera then took a snapshot of that image to create a single frame. The animators reused some of the cels for the next frame, such as backgrounds, and changed other cels to create an object's movement across the foreground. The end result was a strip of film that, when played back through a projector, created the illusion of movement.

Flash uses similar principles to create animations today. Instead of transparent cels, you add content to frames and layers, and then stack the layers to create depth. Anytime you want the content to change, you can add keyframes to the Timeline and vary the position or appearance of the content. When the animation, or movie, is played back, the content appears to move.

Instead of using a film projector for playback, Flash movies use a Flash Player application. The Flash Player is a special program designed to view Flash content.

Using frames and layers, you can create simple or sophisticated animation effects for your Web site or as Flash files to distribute to others. To learn more about distributing movies using the Flash Player, see Chapter 30.

Animation Types

You can apply animation a couple of ways in Flash: You can create animation manually frame-by-frame, or you can let Flash help you create the illusion of motion using tweening.

Frame-by-frame animation is just as its name implies, creating the effect of movement by subtly changing the content's appearance from frame to frame. This type of animation method gives you a great deal of control over how the content changes across the Flash Timeline. You determine how much of a change appears from one frame to the next, whether it be very subtle or very pronounced. Keep in mind when creating frame-by-frame animations that this type of animation increases the overall file size.

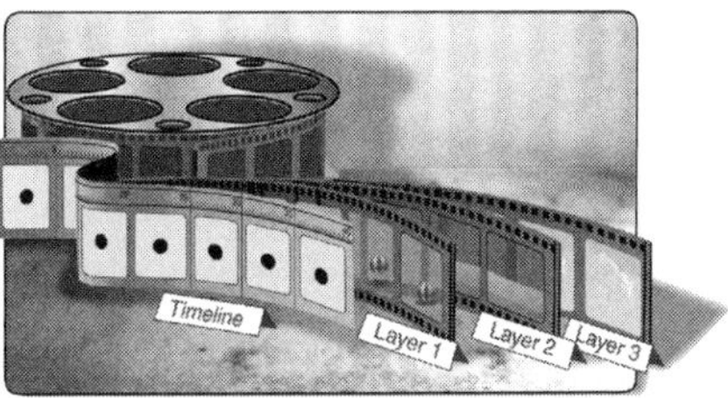

The other method of animating in Flash is called *tweened animation.* With tweened animation, you tell Flash to calculate the in-between frames from one keyframe to the content change in the next keyframe. Flash then draws the in-between phases of change to get from the first keyframe to the next. This in-between framing is where the term "tweened" comes from.

Tweened animation is faster, easier to edit, and consumes less file size. This is because Flash does all the hard work for you by describing the subtle changes between frames mathematically. The two types of tweening are motion tweening and shape tweening. Chapter 25 shows you how to create both types.

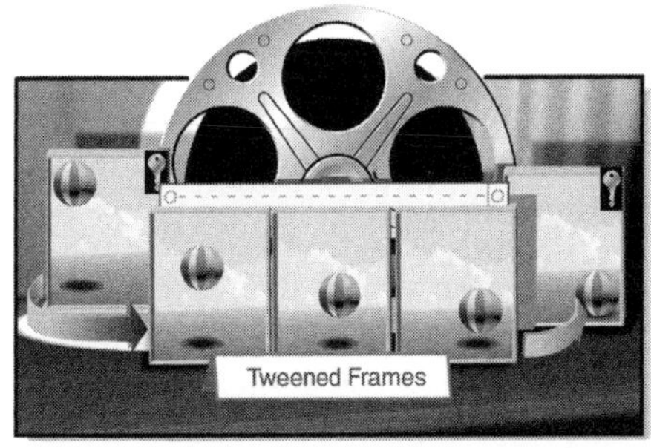

UNDERSTANDING FRAMES

Frames are the backbone of your animation effects. When you start a new Flash file, it opens with a single layer and hundreds of placeholder frames in the Timeline. Before you start animating objects, you need to understand how frames work.

Frames Control Time and Movement

The number of frames you use in your Flash movie combined with the speed at which they play determines the length of the movie. By default, new Flash files you create use a frame rate of 12 frames per second, or 12 fps. You can set a frame rate higher or lower than the default if needed.

Frame Types

Frames appear as tiny boxes in the Timeline. By default, the frames appear in Normal size; however, Normal can be a bit small when you are peering into your monitor screen for any length of time. You can use the Timeline menu button to change the size of the frames in your Timeline.

You can work with several different types of frames in the Flash Timeline: placeholder frames, keyframes, static frames, and tweened frames. A *placeholder frame* is merely an empty frame. It has no content. When your movie reaches an empty frame, it stops playing. With the exception of the first frame in a new layer (see Chapter 21 for more on layers), the remaining frames are all placeholders until you assign another frame type.

A *keyframe* defines a change in animation, such as an object moving or taking on a new appearance. Keyframes are crucial in creating your animation effects. By default, Flash inserts a blank keyframe for you in the first frame of every new layer you add to the Timeline. You can add and delete keyframes as needed. Keyframes are identified with black bullets in the Timeline.

When you add a keyframe, Flash duplicates the content from the previous keyframe and inserts it in the new keyframe. This technique makes it easy to tweak the contents slightly to create the illusion of movement between frames. If the content of the previous keyframe is blank, for example, the new keyframe shows nothing, but if the previous keyframe held an object, the new keyframe holds the same object. To create animation, move the second object slightly.

Keyframes can be added using the Insert menu, or by pressing a shortcut key on the keyboard. Pressing F6 inserts a keyframe, while pressing F7 inserts a blank keyframe. A blank keyframe does not duplicate the contents of the previous keyframe. Use blank keyframes to start a brand new animation sequence in your movie.

You can also delete keyframes. When you use the Clear Keyframe command to remove a keyframe, you are not removing the frame, but reassigning its status to a regular frame. If you want to completely remove a frame from your movie, use the Delete Frame command.

Another type of frame you use in Flash is the *static frame*. Static frames (or *regular frames*) display the same content as the previous frame in the Timeline. Static frames must be preceded by a keyframe. Static frames are used to hold content that you want to remain visible until you add another keyframe in the layer.

For example, if your movie has five static frames between two keyframes, all five frames between the two keyframes show the same content as the first keyframe. If you make a change to the content in the first keyframe, all the static frames that appear after it reflect the change as well.

Placing static frames between keyframes slows down the speed at which the animation plays in your movie. For example, if five static frames between two keyframes seems too fast during playback, you can add more static frames to the sequence to slow down the animation effect.

Animate with Tweened Frames

You can use tweened frames to create tweened animation effects in Flash. With tweening, Flash calculates the number of frames between two keyframes to create movement.

Tweened frames are marked with an arrow extending from the start of the first frame following the keyframe in the tween effect to the last frame before a new keyframe in the tween. In addition, all of the frames associated with a tween effect, including keyframes, are shaded in another tint. You can learn about creating tweened animation in Chapter 25.

SET MOVIE DIMENSIONS AND SPEED

Before you begin an animation project, take time to set up the size of your movie and the speed at which you want it to play. A movie's size is its dimensions — the vertical and horizontal size. You can control a movie's size and speed through the Movie Properties dialog box as outlined in the steps in this section. Taking time to set the movie dimensions and speed now saves you time and headaches later. If you resize the movie after you have created it, you may find yourself having to reposition elements on numerous layers to make things fit.

When defining your movie's size, you are specifying the size of the screen used to play the movie. For example, users may playback your movie in the Flash Player window. The size you set in the Movie Properties defines the size used in the player window. You can make your movie any size, but most users prefer to keep the size relative to the largest objects in the movie.

The movie's play speed determines the number of frames per second, or *fps*, that the animation occurs. By default, Flash assigns a frame rate of 12 fps, a good setting for animation delivered over the Web. You can set a faster rate, but set it too fast and the images blur. Set too slow of a rate and the user sees each individual frame image.

SET MOVIE DIMENSIONS AND SPEED

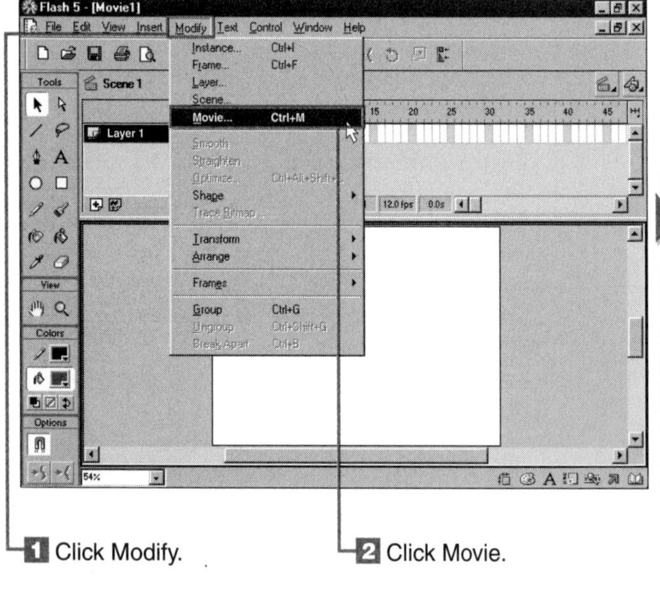

1 Click Modify.

2 Click Movie.

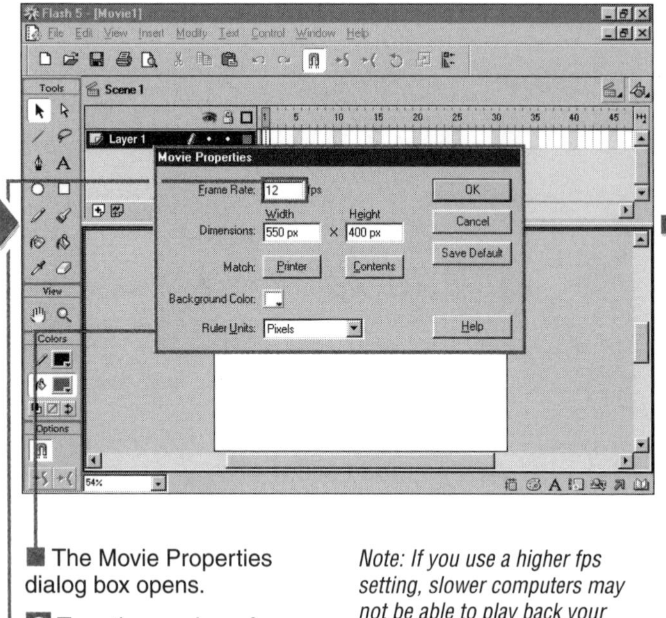

■ The Movie Properties dialog box opens.

3 Type the number of frames per second you want the movie to play in the Frame Rate text box.

Note: If you use a higher fps setting, slower computers may not be able to play back your movie properly.

What is a good frame rate for my movie?

✔ The default frame rate of 12 fps works well for most projects. The maximum rate you should set is 24 fps, unless you are exporting your movie as a QuickTime or Windows AVI video file (which can handle higher rates without consuming computer processor power). If you set a higher frame rate, slower computers struggle to play at such speeds. Most simply cannot, and a very high fps rate slows all but a supercomputer down.

Can I vary the frame rate throughout my movie?

✔ No. After you set a frame rate, that rate is in effect for the entire movie file. You can, however, vary the speed of animation sequences by adding or removing frames. For example, if a particular sequence seems to go too fast, you can add more regular frames between the two keyframes to slow the sequence down. See "Add Frames," next in this chapter.

Can I tell which frame rate is in effect without opening the Movie Properties dialog box?

✔ Yes. Look at the status bar at the bottom of the Timeline. The status bar displays the current frame number, frame rate, and elapsed time for the movie. You can quickly open the Movie Properties dialog box by double-clicking the frame rate number in the Timeline's status bar.

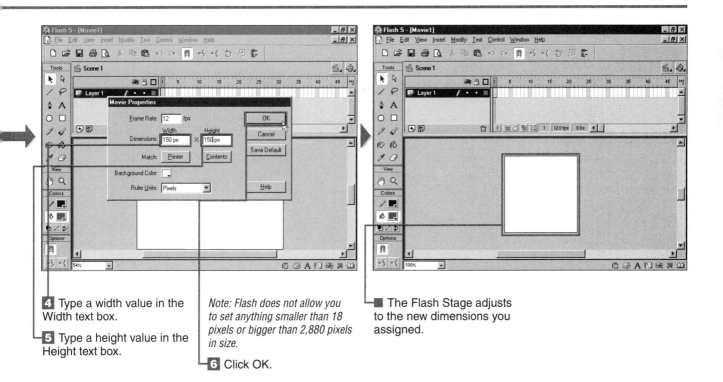

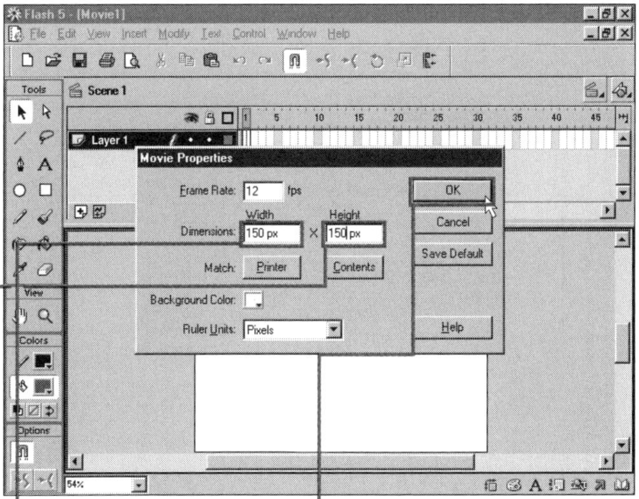

4 Type a width value in the Width text box.

5 Type a height value in the Height text box.

Note: Flash does not allow you to set anything smaller than 18 pixels or bigger than 2,880 pixels in size.

6 Click OK.

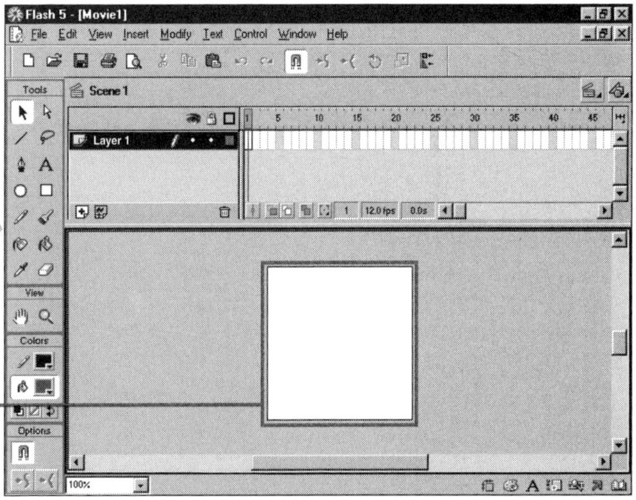

■ The Flash Stage adjusts to the new dimensions you assigned.

ADD FRAMES

When you add a new layer or start a new file, Flash starts you out with one keyframe in the Timeline and lots of placeholder frames. To add content and length to your movie, you must add frames to the Timeline.

Adding frames is as easy as adding pages to a document. Flash lets you specify exactly which kind of frame to add and how many. You can add regular frames, keyframes, blank keyframes, and you can add more than one at a time.

Add keyframes to define changes in the animation's appearance, such as changing the object's placement or color. When you add a keyframe, Flash copies the contents of the previous keyframe, which you can then edit to create a change in the animation sequence.

You also can add regular frames to repeat the content of the keyframe preceding them. Regular frames help extend the animation effect between keyframes.

You can also designate frames as tweened, a special animation effect you can learn more about in Chapter 25.

See the section "Understanding Frames" to learn more about how frames are used in Flash.

ADD FRAMES

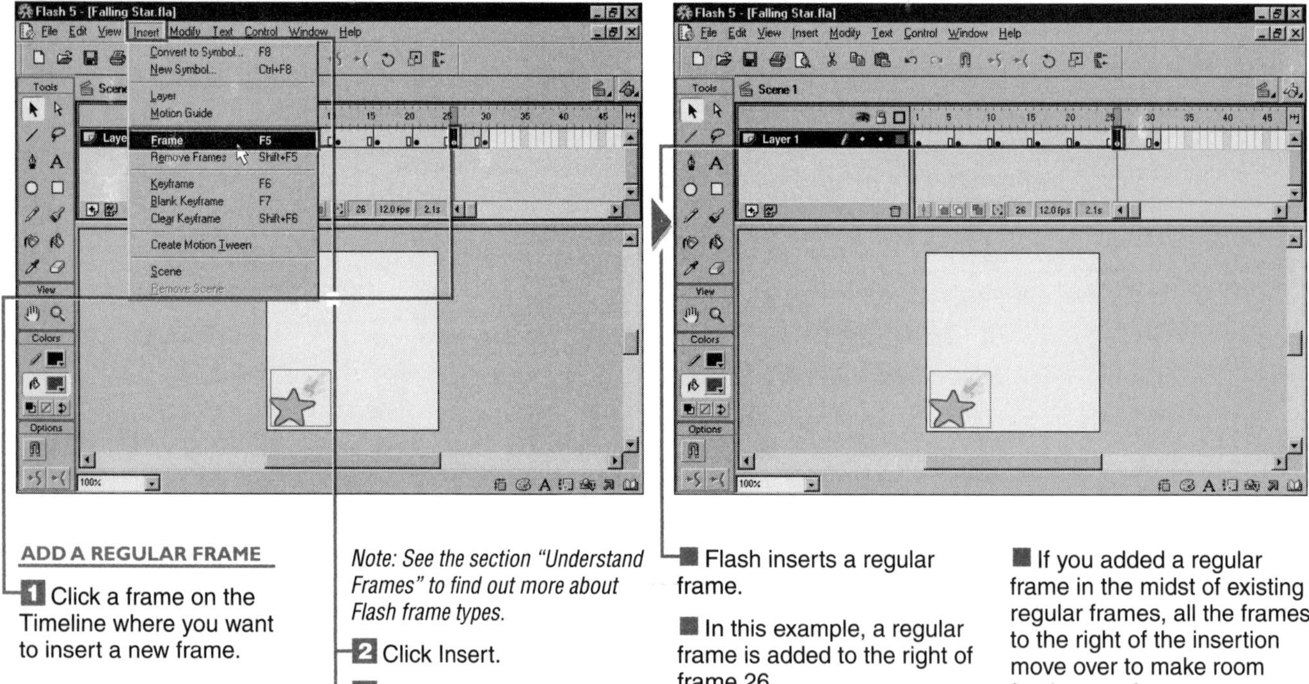

ADD A REGULAR FRAME

1 Click a frame on the Timeline where you want to insert a new frame.

Note: See the section "Understand Frames" to find out more about Flash frame types.

2 Click Insert.

3 Click Frame.

■ Flash inserts a regular frame.

■ In this example, a regular frame is added to the right of frame 26.

■ If you added a regular frame in the midst of existing regular frames, all the frames to the right of the insertion move over to make room for the new frame.

How can I tell which frames are which in the Timeline?

✔ You can identify Flash frames by the following characteristics:

- Keyframes with content appear with a solid bullet in the Timeline.
- Blank keyframes (keyframes which have no content added yet) appear as a hollow box in the preceding frame.
- In-between frames that contain content appear tinted or grayed on the Timeline.
- In-between frames without content appear as a block of white.
- Empty frames appear white.

What is the keyboard shortcut for adding frames?

✔ Press F6 to add a keyframe. Press F8 to add a blank keyframe. To add a regular frame, press F5.

Can I add frames to a motion tween?

✔ Yes. Tweened animation frames work the same way as frame-by-frame animation frames. You can add keyframes and regular frames as needed. See Chapter 25 for more about creating tweened animations.

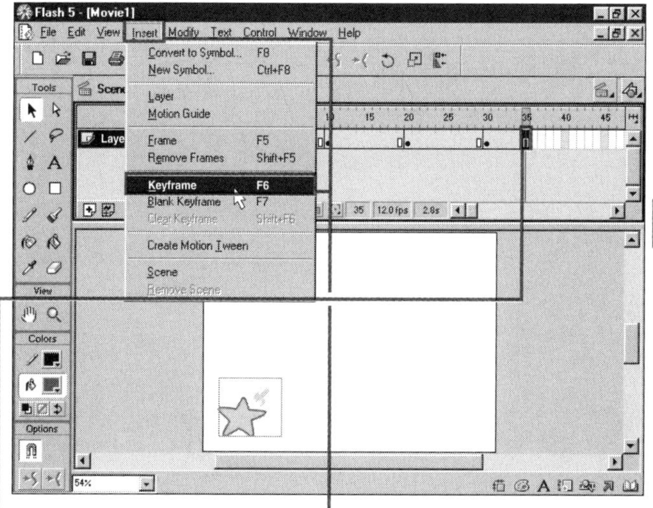

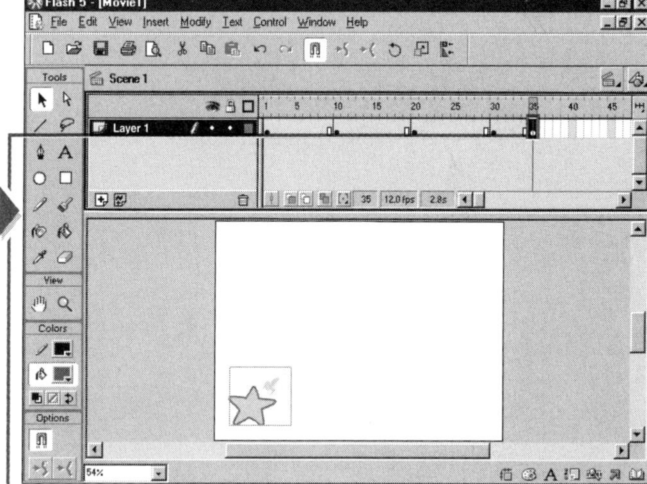

ADD A KEYFRAME

1 Click the frame on the Timeline which you want to turn into a keyframe.

Note: If you are having trouble selecting a single frame within a group of frames, press Ctrl (Windows) or Command (Mac) while clicking the frame.

2 Click Insert.

3 Click Keyframe.

■ Flash inserts a keyframe, marked by a solid bullet in the Timeline.

■ If the frame you selected in step 1 was a regular frame, Flash converts it to a keyframe.

■ If the frame was an empty frame, Flash inserts regular frames in between the last regular frame or keyframe up to the frame you clicked in step 1.

CONTINUED

ADD FRAMES (CONTINUED)

Each layer in your movie's Timeline has its own set of frames to work with. You can add different types of frames to each layer.

You can add a blank keyframe when you want to start brand new content in your movie. Unlike a default keyframe, which copies the content from the previous keyframe in the sequence, a blank keyframe is completely without content. You can insert a blank keyframe when you want to start a new segment in your movie.

You can also add multiple frames at a time in Flash. For example, perhaps you are creating an animation sequence that needs to be extended a bit in the Timeline in order to play more slowly in playback. Rather than insert one regular frame at a time, you can insert multiple frames, such as five frames at once.

You can also delete frames you no longer need or change a frame's status from a keyframe to a regular frame. See the section "Delete or Change the Status of Frames" to learn more.

ADD FRAMES (CONTINUED)

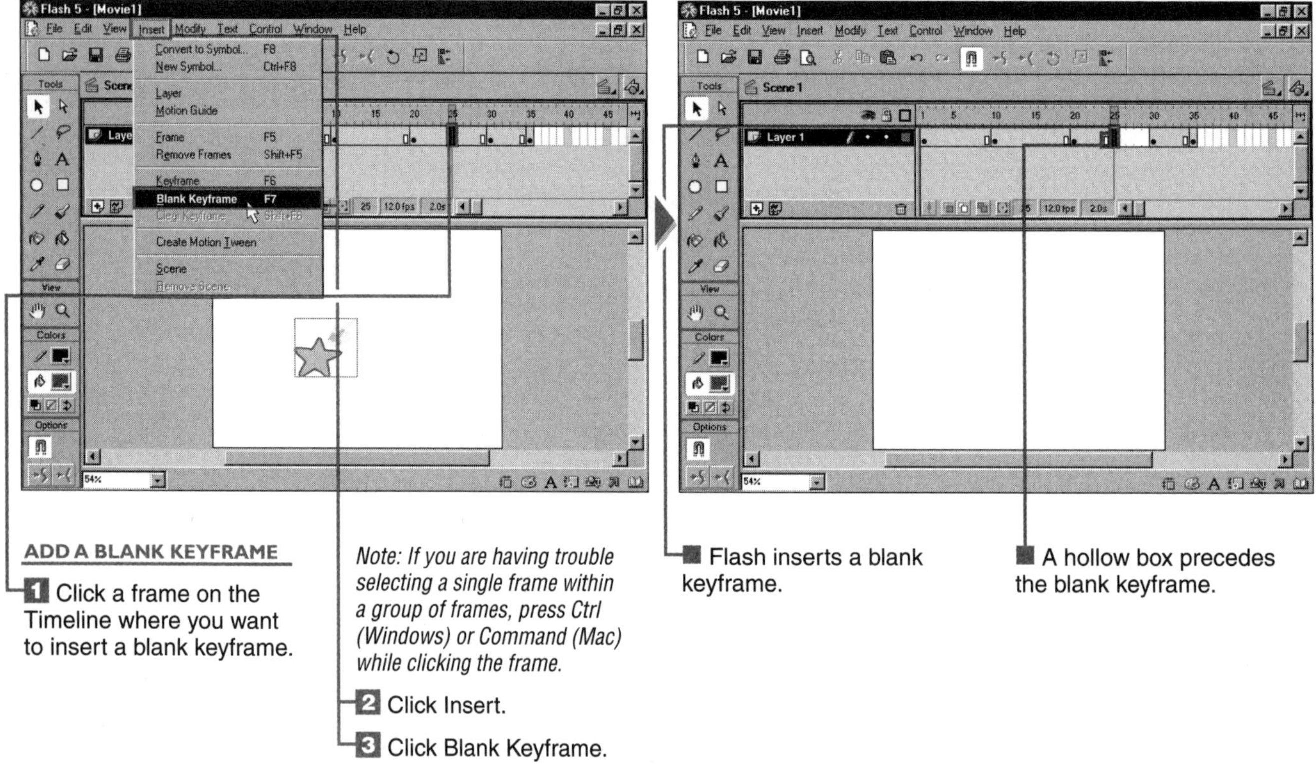

ADD A BLANK KEYFRAME

1 Click a frame on the Timeline where you want to insert a blank keyframe.

Note: If you are having trouble selecting a single frame within a group of frames, press Ctrl (Windows) or Command (Mac) while clicking the frame.

2 Click Insert.

3 Click Blank Keyframe.

■ Flash inserts a blank keyframe.

■ A hollow box precedes the blank keyframe.

Can I change the size of the Timeline frames?

✔ You can change the size of the frames in the Timeline using the Timeline menu. By default, the frames appear in Normal size. You can change them to Tiny or Small to fit more frames in the Timeline view, or try Medium or Large to make the frames easier to see. Click the Timeline menu button. Click the frame size you want to apply.

Is there another shortcut for adding frames?

✔ Yes. You can right-click a frame to view a pop-up list of commands related to frames, including the commands for inserting different types of frames. Simply make your selection from the shortcut menu and the frame is added.

Can I resize the Timeline to view more layers?

✔ Yes. You can drag the bottom border of the docked Timeline to increase its size. To learn more about using the Flash Timeline, see Chapter 1.

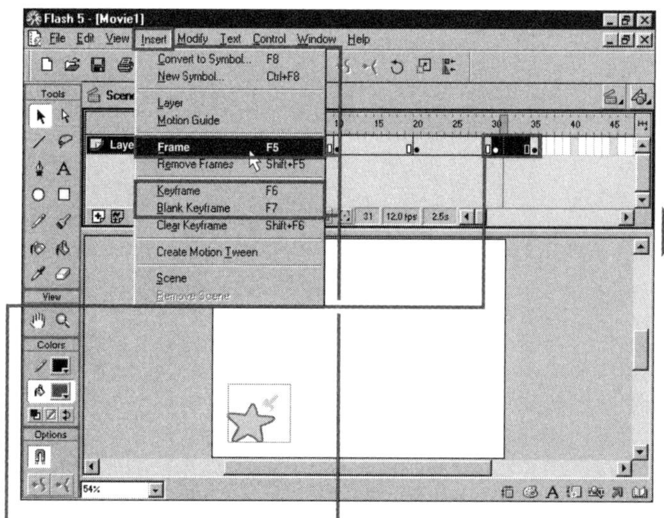

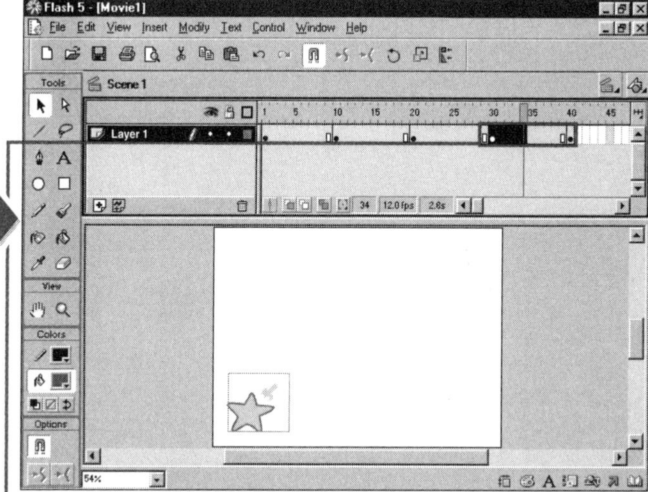

ADD MULTIPLE FRAMES

1 Select two or more frames by clicking them.

■ To select multiple frames, click the first frame in the range, press the Shift key, and click the last frame in the range.

Note: See the section "Select Frames" to find out more about selecting frames.

2 Click Insert.

3 Click Frame to insert regular frames, or click Keyframe or Blank Keyframe to make the new frames all keyframes.

■ Flash inserts the same number of new frames and lengthens the movie.

SELECT FRAMES

When you work with frames in the Flash Timeline, you must select the frame or frames you want to edit. You can use a couple of selection techniques when working with frames.

When you select a single frame, it appears highlighted in the Timeline and the frame number appears in the Timeline's status bar. The playhead also appears directly above the selected frame.

Selecting keyframes and placeholder frames that have no content is easy, but selecting in-between frames is a bit more difficult. Individual frames that are part of an animation sequence, such as a tweened animation, are not selected with a simple click. In fact, when you click an in-between frame, the surrounding range of frames are also selected. You can employ a couple of keyboard tricks to select a single frame from within a range of frames, as shown in the steps below.

See "Add Frames" and "Delete Frames" to find out more about adding and deleting frames from the Timeline.

SELECT FRAMES

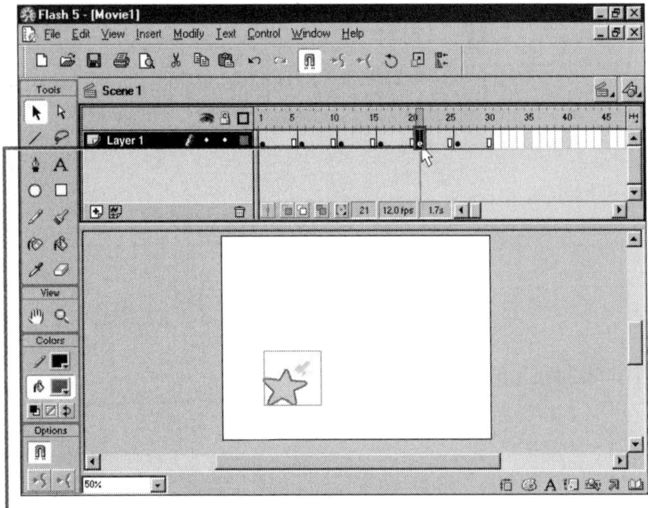

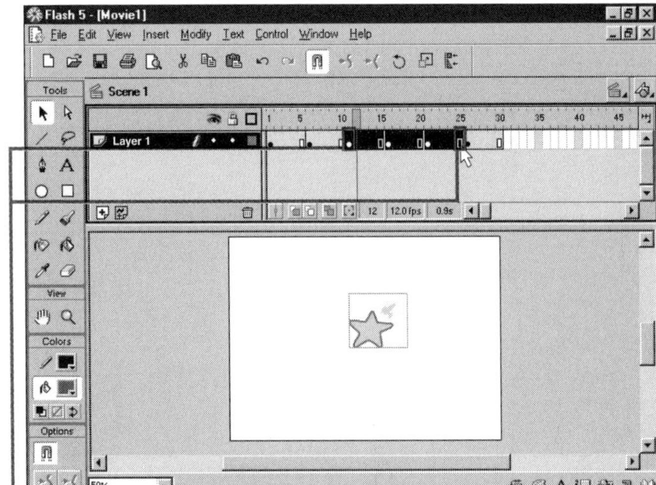

SELECT A SINGLE FRAME

1 Click the frame to select it.

■ Flash highlights the frame in the Timeline.

■ If you have difficulty selecting a frame between keyframes, hold down Ctrl (Windows) or Command (Mac), and then click the frame you want to select.

Note: See "Understand Frames" to find out more about frame types.

SELECT MULTIPLE FRAMES

1 Click the first frame in the range of frames you want to select.

2 Press and hold Shift and click the last frame in the range.

■ Flash selects all the frames in-between.

■ To select multiple frames between two keyframes, click anywhere between the two keyframes.

MODIFY FRAME PROPERTIES

You can use the Frame panel to define properties for frames, such as labels and tweening status. You can learn more about creating tweening effects in Chapter 25.

By default, a frame is recognized by its frame number. However, the longer and more complex your movie, the more you may need to identify frames by descriptive labels. A label can help you immediately recognize a frame's contents, while a frame number does not tell you anything about the frame other than its place in the Timeline.

You can use frame labels to organize frames with actions, frames with animation effects, frames with sounds, and so on. See the section "Understand Frames" to find out more about using frames in Flash.

When you select a tweening status, additional options appear in the Frame panel. See Chapter 25 to learn more about creating tweened animations.

MODIFY FRAME PROPERTIES

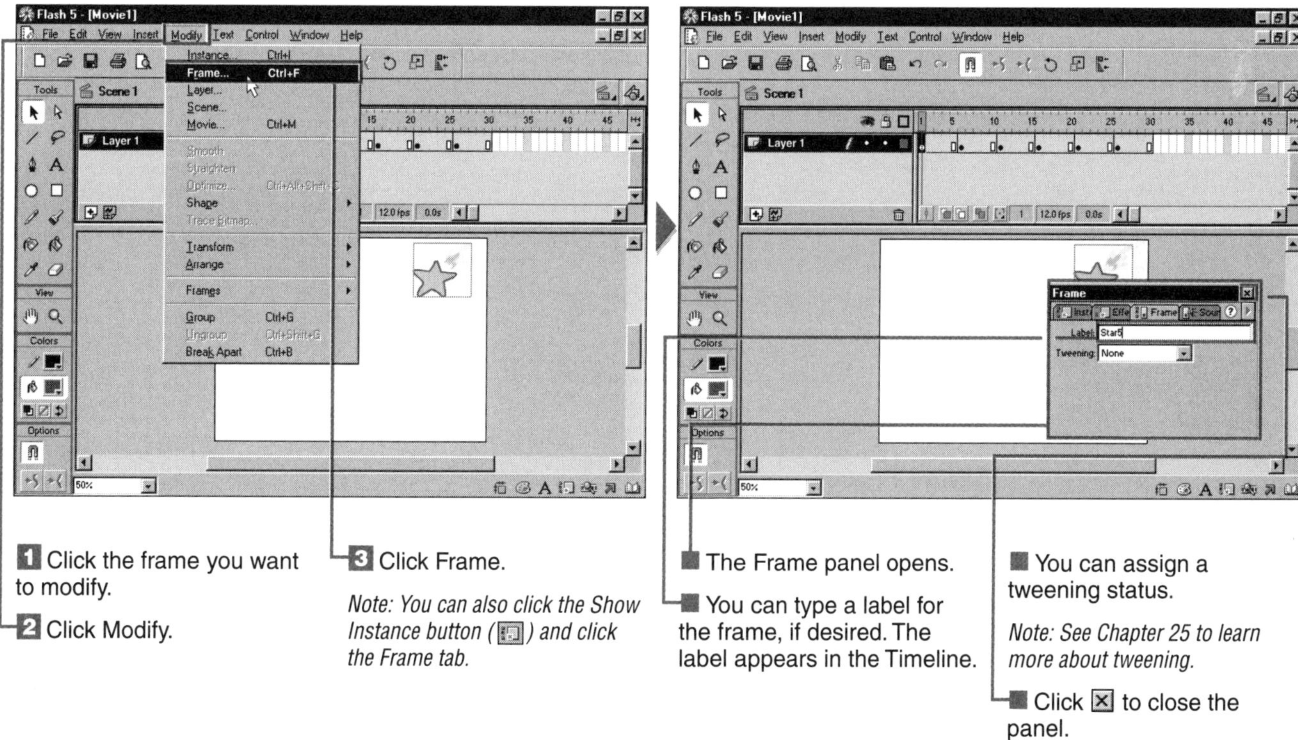

1 Click the frame you want to modify.

2 Click Modify.

3 Click Frame.

Note: You can also click the Show Instance button ( ) and click the Frame tab.

■ The Frame panel opens.

■ You can type a label for the frame, if desired. The label appears in the Timeline.

■ You can assign a tweening status.

Note: See Chapter 25 to learn more about tweening.

■ Click ☒ to close the panel.

DELETE OR CHANGE THE STATUS OF FRAMES

You can remove frames you no longer need or change them to a type of frame that you do need. For example, you may decide a particular animation sequence between two keyframes runs too slowly during playback. You can remove several regular frames to speed up the sequence. Or you can make a drastic change in your animation and decide you no longer need a particular keyframe in the sequence.

If you want to remove a frame or several frames completely from the Timeline, use the Remove Frames command. When you apply the Remove Frames command, the selected frames are permanently removed from the Timeline.

To remove a keyframe completely from the Timeline, you must select both the keyframe and all the in-between frames associated with it; otherwise, the Remove Frames command does not work properly to remove the keyframe.

Instead of removing a keyframe completely, however, you can turn it into a regular frame. Using the Clear Keyframe command you can remove the frame's keyframe status and demote it to a regular frame. If you change a keyframe's status, all in-between frames are altered as well.

See the section "Understanding Frames" to find out more about Flash frame types.

DELETE FRAMES

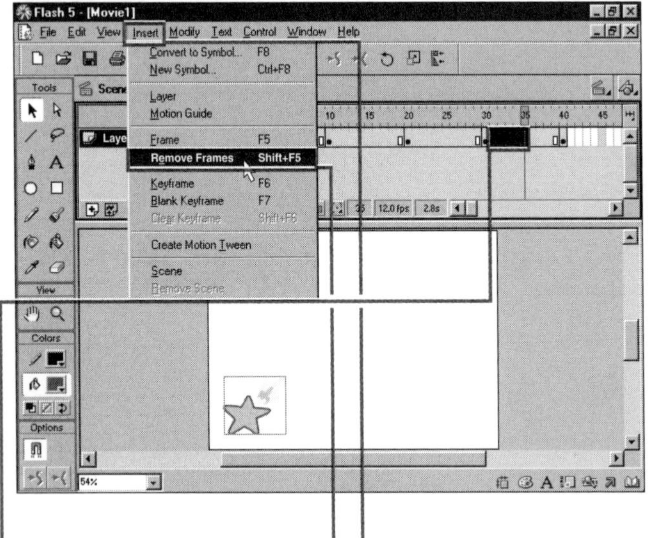

1 Click the frame, or range of frames, you want to delete.

■ To delete a range of frames, select the range first. See the section "Select Frames" to find out more about selecting frames.

2 Click Insert.

3 Click Remove Frames.

Note: To select a single frame within a group of frames, press Ctrl (Windows) or Command (Mac) while clicking the frame.

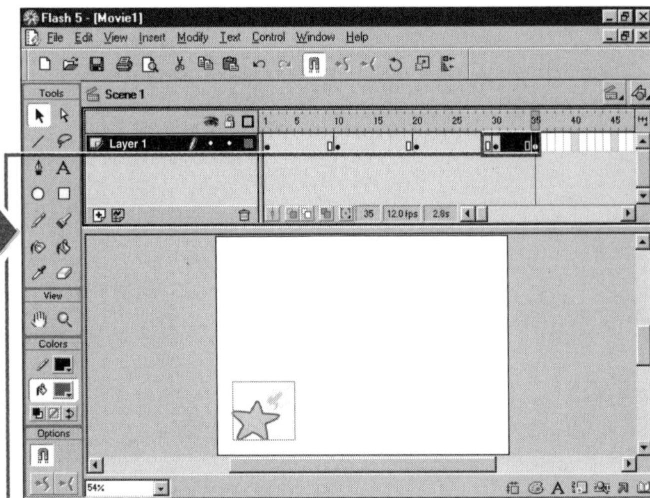

■ Flash removes the frame and any existing frames to the right move over to fill the void.

Note: To select multiple frames within a group of frames, press Ctrl + Shift (Windows) or Command + Shift (Mac) while clicking the frames.

Can I remove a range of frames?

✔ Yes. First select the range of frames you want to delete by clicking the first frame in the group, and then dragging to highlight the remaining frames. Once all the frames in the range are selected, you can apply the Remove Frames command. See the section "Select Frames" to learn more.

If I delete a frame, is the frame label removed as well?

✔ Yes. Any time you remove a frame from the Timeline, any associated frame labels are removed as well. See the section "Modify Frame Properties" to learn more about frame labels.

Can I reverse the order of a segment of frames?

✔ Yes. You can reverse frames to play in the opposite order. Learn how this command works in Chapter 25.

Can I undo a frame deletion?

✔ Yes. If you click the Undo button immediately after removing a frame, Flash undoes the action.

Why does Flash not let me click a frame?

✔ If you are trying to remove a regular frame between two keyframes, you may have difficulty selecting a single frame. Hold down Ctrl (Windows) or Command (Mac) and then click on the frame you want to remove.

DEMOTE A KEYFRAME

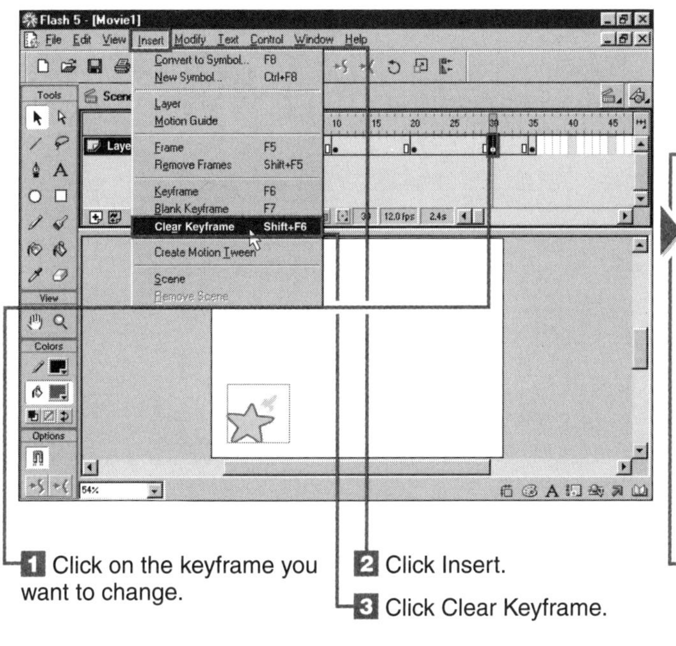

1 Click on the keyframe you want to change.

2 Click Insert.

3 Click Clear Keyframe.

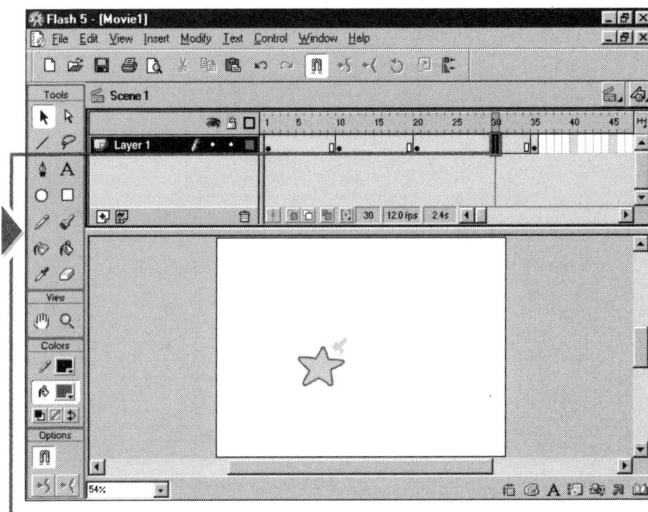

■ Flash converts the frame to a regular frame, and changes the frame to match the previous keyframe's contents.

Note: You cannot change the status of the first keyframe in a layer.

CREATE FRAME-BY-FRAME ANIMATION

You can create the illusion of movement in a Flash movie by changing the placement or appearance of the Stage content from keyframe to keyframe in the Flash Timeline. This type of animation is called, appropriately, *frame-by-frame animation.*

With frame-by-frame animation, you control exactly how your object (or objects) changes from one keyframe to the next. It is crucial that the object (or objects) experience some sort of change, whether that change involves changing color, size, or placement on the Stage. Without some sort of change, your animation sequence does not appear animated.

You can add an animation sequence to any layer in your movie, and you can use one sequence right after another. For example, you can start your movie with a fade-in animation of your company logo, then jump to a completely different animation detailing a new product or service.

See the section "An Introduction to Animation" to find out more about animating techniques you can use in Flash.

CREATE FRAME-BY-FRAME ANIMATION

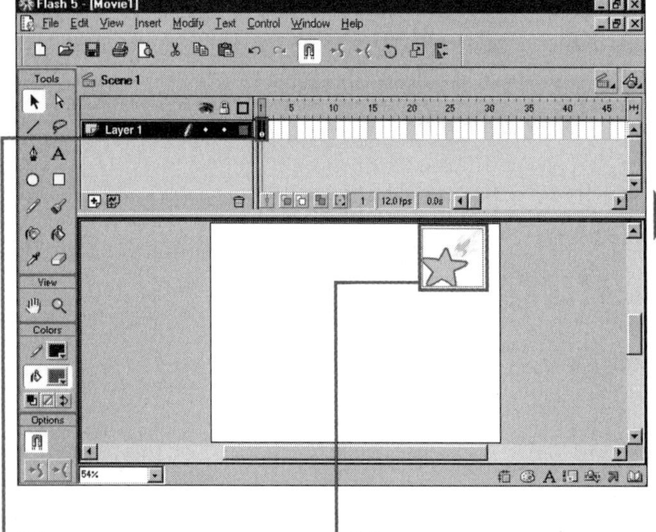

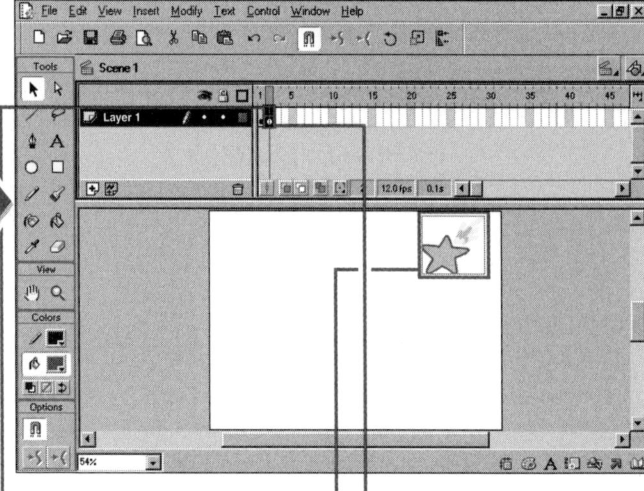

1 Click the first keyframe in the layer you want to animate.

Note: See the section "Understand Frames" to find out more about Flash frame types.

2 Place the object you want to animate on the Flash Stage.

■ For example, you can drag a symbol (Chapter 22) from the Flash Library onto the Stage, or use the drawing tools (Chapter 18) to create a new object.

3 Click the next frame in the Timeline where you want to continue the animation.

■ You can choose to continue the animation in the very next frame, or space the animation out with a few regular frames in between.

4 Add a keyframe.

Note: See "Add Frames" to find out how to add a keyframe to the Timeline.

■ Flash inserts a keyframe that duplicates the previous keyframe's contents.

Can I add in-between frames to the animation?

✔ To slow down the animation sequence, especially if the changes between keyframes are happening too fast to see very well, just add regular frames between keyframes in your frame-by-frame animation. To add in-between frames, first click a keyframe. Click the Insert menu, and then click Frame. Flash adds a regular frame behind the keyframe. You can keep adding more regular frames to achieve the effect you want. When you play back the movie, the animation appears to slow down a bit in its movement.

How do I edit a symbol as I create the animation?

✔ To make changes to a symbol you use in your movie, first select the keyframe where you want to introduce a change. To open the symbol in symbol-edit mode, double-click on the symbol. Make your edits, and then click the Scene name to return to movie-edit mode. You can switch back and forth between edit modes as needed when creating your animation sequence. You can also introduce new objects using the Drawing tools.

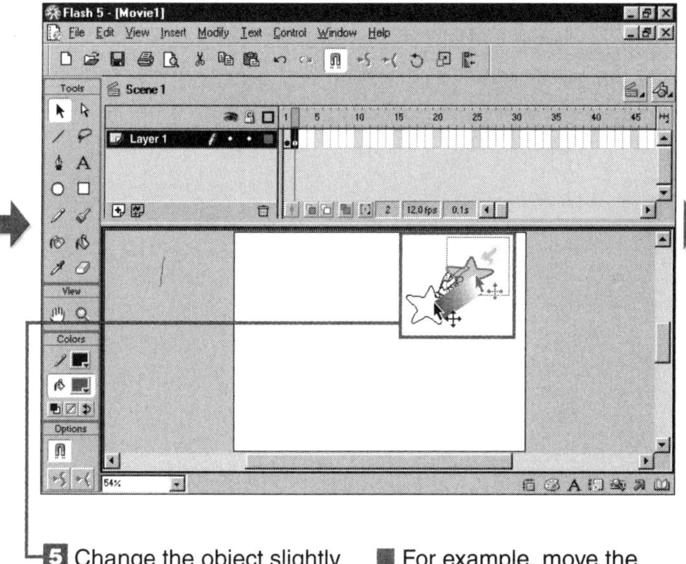

5 Change the object slightly to animate.

■ For example, move the object a bit on the Stage, or change the object's appearance (such as a different color or size).

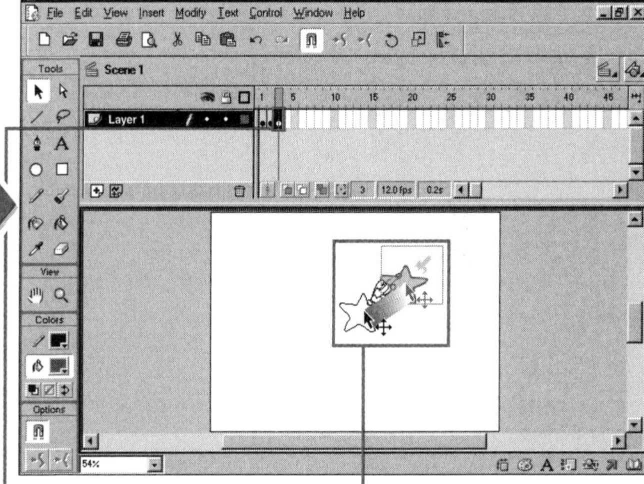

6 Click the next frame in the layer and add a keyframe.

■ Flash duplicates the previous keyframe's contents.

7 Change the object slightly again.

■ For example, move the object a bit more on the Stage, or change the object's appearance (such as a different color or size).

CONTINUED

CREATE FRAME-BY-FRAME ANIMATION (CONTINUED)

You can create all kinds of animation effects using frame-by-frame animation techniques. For example, a simple circle shape can become a bouncing ball if moved strategically around the Stage in each frame of the movie. A text box can glow if you change the text color and boldness from one keyframe to the next. A company logo may appear to grow in size by subtly enlarging it in each keyframe in the sequence.

If you are new to using Flash, you can quickly learn the principles of frame-by-frame animation by creating a simple animation sequence, such as making an object move across the Flash Stage. The example in this section shows how to create the illusion of a falling star by moving the star ever so slightly down the Stage in each keyframe. By the last keyframe, the star reaches the bottom. When the animation is played back, the star appears to drop from the top-right corner to the bottom-left corner.

CREATE FRAME-BY-FRAME ANIMATION (CONTINUED)

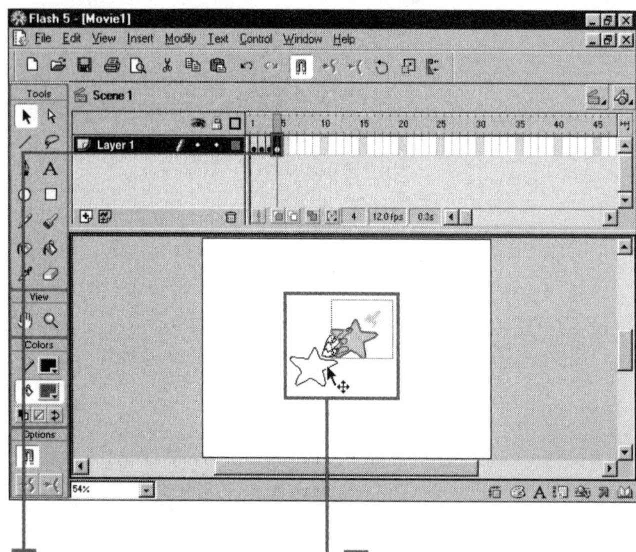

8 Click the next frame in the layer and add a keyframe.

■ Flash duplicates the previous keyframe's contents.

9 Change the object again.

■ For example, move the object a bit more on the Stage, or change the object's appearance (such as a different color or size).

10 Click the next frame in the layer and add a keyframe.

■ Flash duplicates the previous keyframe's contents.

11 Change the object again.

■ For example, move the object a bit more on the Stage, or change the object's appearance (such as a different color or size).

How do I know where to reposition an object on the Stage?

✔ To help you control how an object moves around the Stage, turn on the Flash gridlines by clicking the View menu, and then clicking Grid, Show Grid. Flash turns on the gridlines on the Stage area. With the grid turned on, you can more clearly see the placement of objects on the Stage. To turn off the grid marks again, click View, Grid, Show Grid.

What does the Snap To Objects feature do?

✔ When the Snap to Objects button ( ) is clicked, Flash automatically aligns objects to each other on the Stage. This feature is turned on by default; however, you can turn it off or on as needed as you move items around on the Stage area. When the feature is on and you turn on gridlines, you can quickly align objects on the Stage to the nearest gridline.

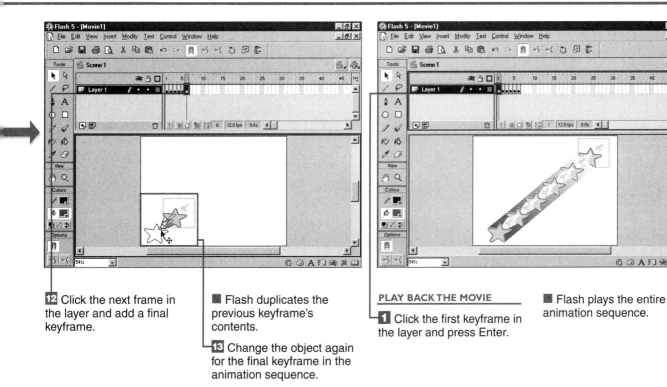

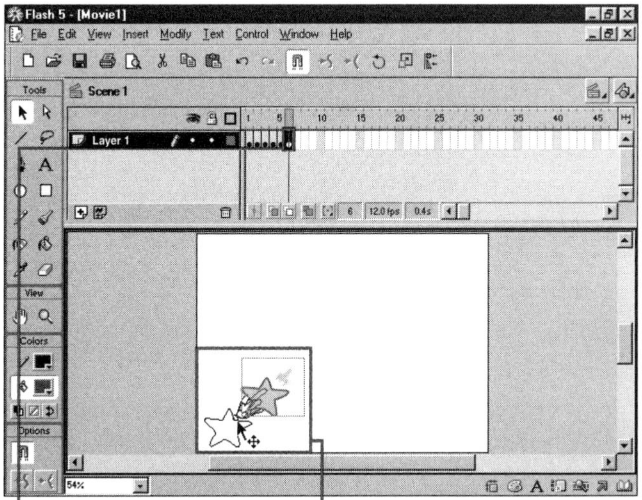

12 Click the next frame in the layer and add a final keyframe.

■ Flash duplicates the previous keyframe's contents.

13 Change the object again for the final keyframe in the animation sequence.

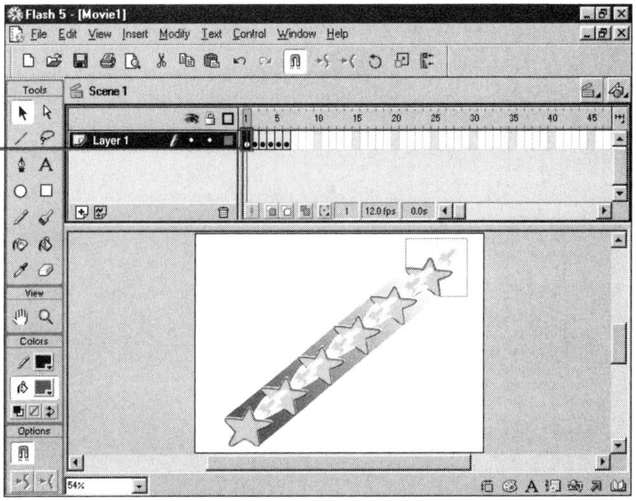

PLAY BACK THE MOVIE

1 Click the first keyframe in the layer and press Enter.

■ Flash plays the entire animation sequence.

ONION-SKINNING AN ANIMATION

You can use Flash's onion-skinning feature to quickly assess the positioning of objects in surrounding frames in your movie. By viewing the placement of objects in other frames, you can more clearly determine how you want to position the object in the frame in which you are working. This is particularly useful when creating an animation sequence in which object placement is crucial to the appearance of the animation.

The name *onion-skinning* refers to the effect of seeing the contents of other frames as shaded layers — like the translucent layers of an onion — in context to the current frame.

Onion-skinning offers two modes of display: dimmed content or outlined content. The objects in the frames surrounding the current frame are displayed as dimmed (the default option) or outlined objects. But regardless of the choice, the current frame's contents are fully displayed. This enables you to see multiple frames and how their movements relate to the current frame.

See the section "Understanding Frames" to find out more about Flash frame types.

ONION-SKINNING AN ANIMATION

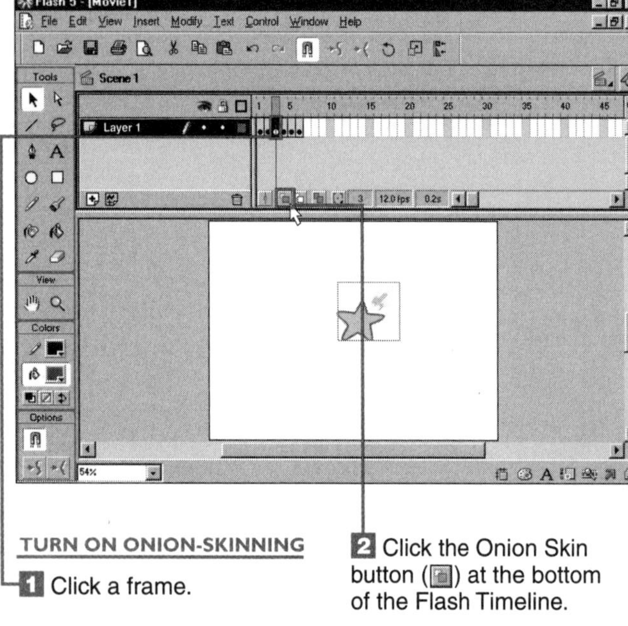

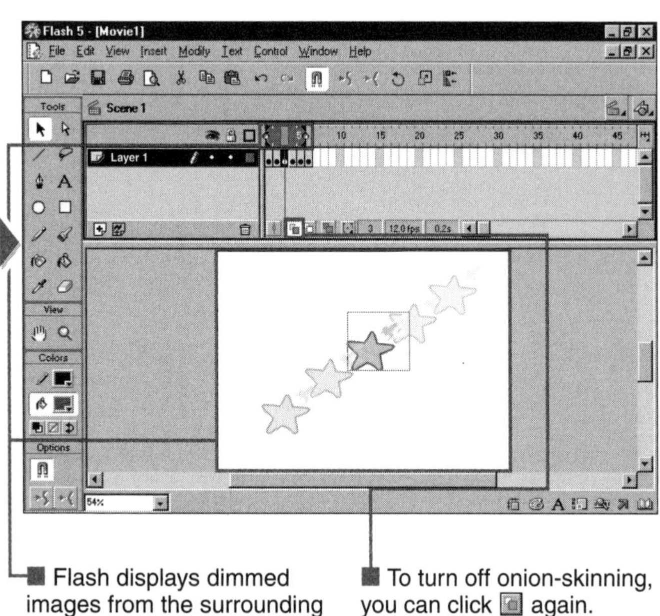

TURN ON ONION-SKINNING

1 Click a frame.

2 Click the Onion Skin button (▣) at the bottom of the Flash Timeline.

■ Flash displays dimmed images from the surrounding frames and places onion-skin markers at the top of the Timeline.

■ To turn off onion-skinning, you can click ▣ again.

Can I edit the onion-skinned frames?

✔ No. You cannot edit the onion-skin frames unless you click the Edit Multiple Frames button (▣). When you make the other frames editable, you can select and move the onion-skinned objects to fine-tune the animation sequence.

In what kinds of situations does onion skinning work best?

✔ If you need to track the positioning of an object as it moves across the Stage, onion-skinning will definitely assist you in showing the placement of the object in each frame of the sequence. However, if, for example, an object stays in one spot but changes in color, the onion-skinning feature is not a great benefit.

Can I play back my movie with the onion-skin feature on?

✔ Yes. However, the onion-skinning turns off while the movie plays. Click in the first frame of your movie and then press Enter. Flash plays the movie on the Stage. When it reaches the last frame, the onion-skin feature resumes its active state again.

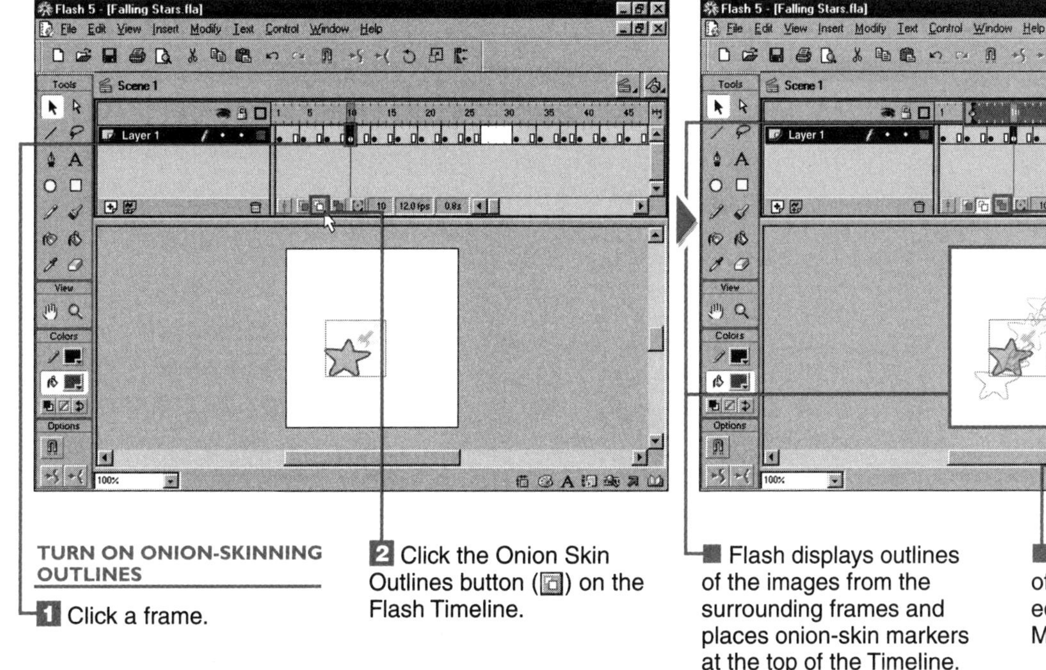

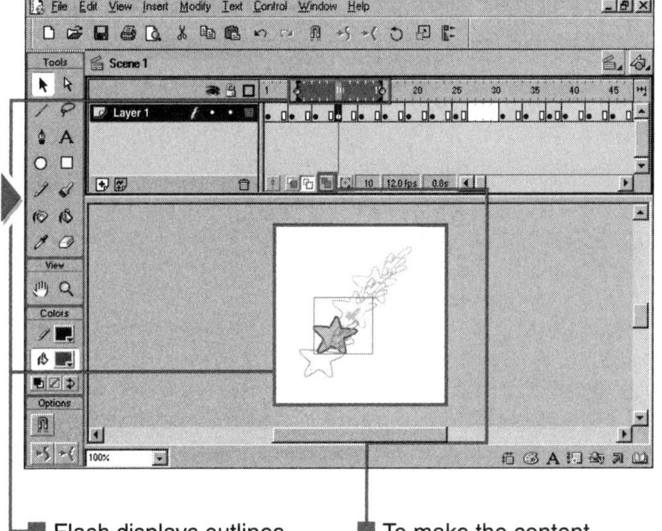

TURN ON ONION-SKINNING OUTLINES

1 Click a frame.

2 Click the Onion Skin Outlines button (▣) on the Flash Timeline.

■ Flash displays outlines of the images from the surrounding frames and places onion-skin markers at the top of the Timeline.

■ To make the content of the onion-skin frames editable, click the Edit Multiple Frames button (▣).

ONION-SKINNING AN ANIMATION (CONTINUED)

The onion-skinning features can help you better gauge the changes needed to create your animations. You can control which frames appear in onion-skin mode using the onion-skin markers that appear on the Timeline. You can also opt to control the markers using the Modify Onion Markers pop-up menu.

When you click the Modify Onion Markers button, the pop-up menu displays several choices for controlling markers on the Timeline:

- Click Always Show Markers to leave the markers on even when onion-skinning is turned off.
- Click Anchor Onion to lock the markers in place, even as you view frames at the other end of the Timeline.
- Click Onion 2 or Onion 5 to display the corresponding number of frames before and after the current frame.
- Click Onion All to onion-skin all the frames.

ONION-SKINNING AN ANIMATION (CONTINUED)

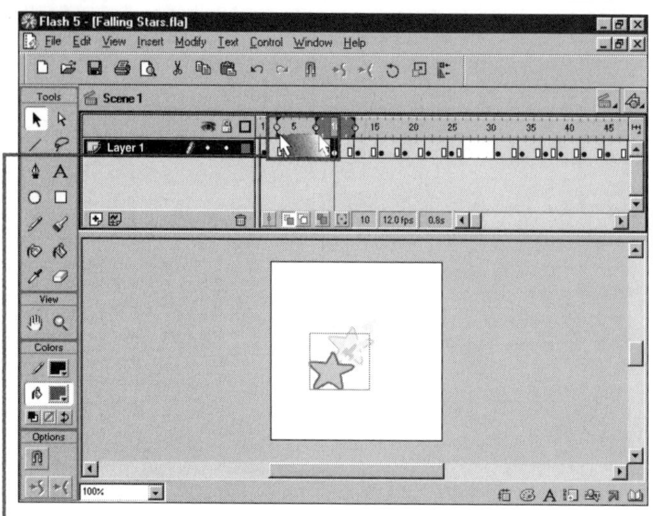

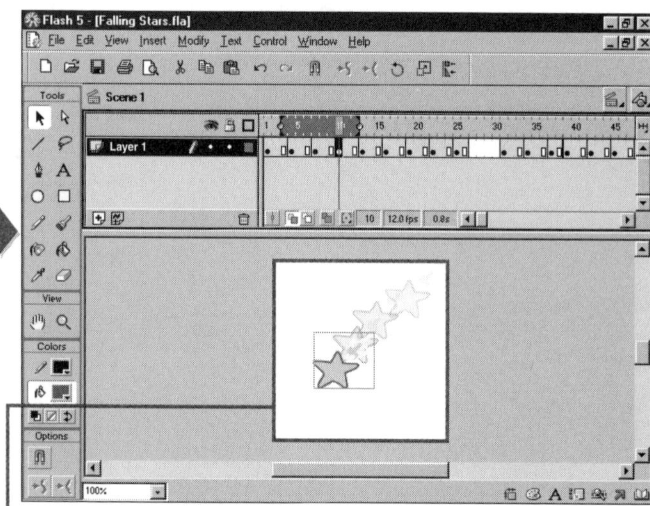

MOVE THE ONION-SKIN MARKERS

1 To view more or less frames with onion-skinning, you can click and drag an onion-skin marker left or right.

■ Flash adds or subtracts the additional frames from the view.

What should I keep in mind when adjusting the onion-skin markers?

✔ Remember that the greater the range of frames you onion-skin, the more difficult it may be to discern the image and which frame is associated with which onion-skin outline. This is particularly true of animation effects that do not involve a great deal of movement.

Can I apply onion-skinning to all the frames and layers in my movie?

✔ Yes. Click the ([icon]) button to display a pop-up menu of marker options. Click Onion All. This causes Flash to onion-skin all the frames in all the layers in your movie.

How do I make the onion-skin markers stay in place?

✔ If you click in another frame, the onion-skin markers move in position relative to the frame you are in. To keep them anchored in their original locations, click the Modify Onion Markers button ([icon]), and then click Anchor Onion. This command keeps the markers from adjusting when you click in different frames.

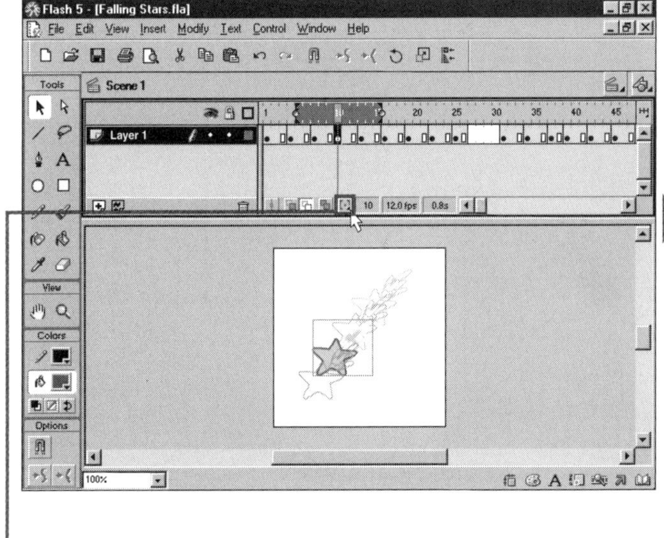

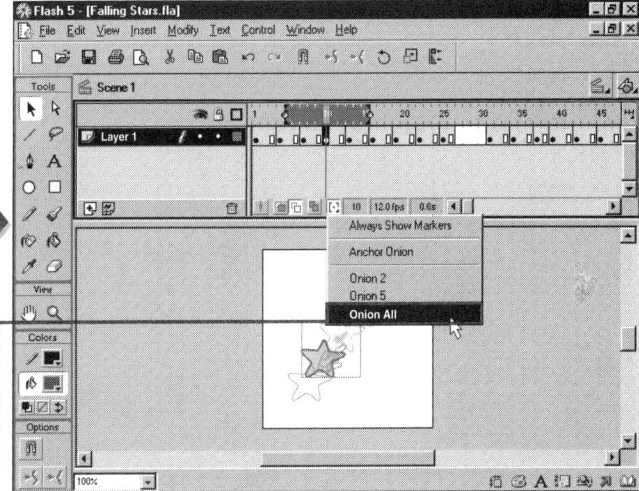

CHANGE THE MARKER DISPLAY

1 To change how the onion-skin markers appear on the Timeline, click the Modify Onion Markers button ([icon]).

■ The Modify menu appears with options for changing the marker display.

2 Click the marker setting you want to apply.

PREVIEW A FLASH ANIMATION

You can click an animation sequence one frame at a time to see each frame's contents, but a faster way to check the sequence is to play the movie. A quick way to test the movie is to move the playback head to the first frame and press the Enter key. Flash plays your movie on the Stage.

For other testing, however, you may prefer to see how your movie plays in the Flash Player window. Use the test movie mode to open the built-in Flash Player within the Flash program window. This option enables you to see the movie without all the surrounding Flash tools, such as the timelines, layers, and drawing tools. Test movie mode lets you see the movie as your audience sees it.

You can preview animation in the Flash Player window as many times as you like, and then exit the player and return to the Flash program window.

When using the built-in player, the regular Flash menu controls are not available. Instead, you see the Flash Player controls for testing and playing the movie.

PREVIEW A FLASH ANIMATION

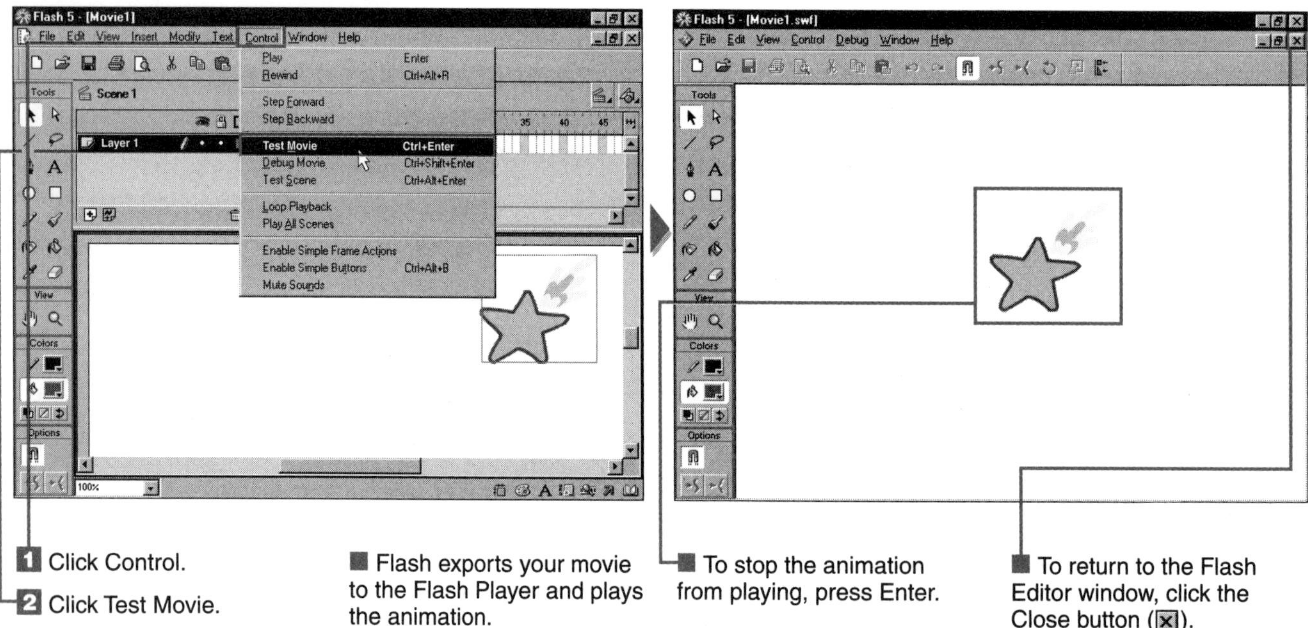

1 Click Control.

2 Click Test Movie.

■ Flash exports your movie to the Flash Player and plays the animation.

■ To stop the animation from playing, press Enter.

■ To return to the Flash Editor window, click the Close button (☒).

ADJUST THE ANIMATION SPEED

A Flash movie's frame rate is constant throughout the movie, but you can slow or speed up an animation by adding or subtracting frames in your movie. Adding regular frames to an animation sequence extends the length of time the sequence plays back.

For example, if a particular section of your animation seems to happen too quickly during playback, you can slow it down a bit if you insert regular frames between two keyframes. In the falling star animation sequence shown in the steps below, a regular frame is added immediately following a keyframe. By adding in-between frames rather than keyframes, you do not increase the movie's file size.

You may need to add several regular frames before you begin to notice the animation speed slowing. See "Set Movie Dimensions and Speed" to find out more about setting a movie's frame rate.

ADJUST THE ANIMATION SPEED

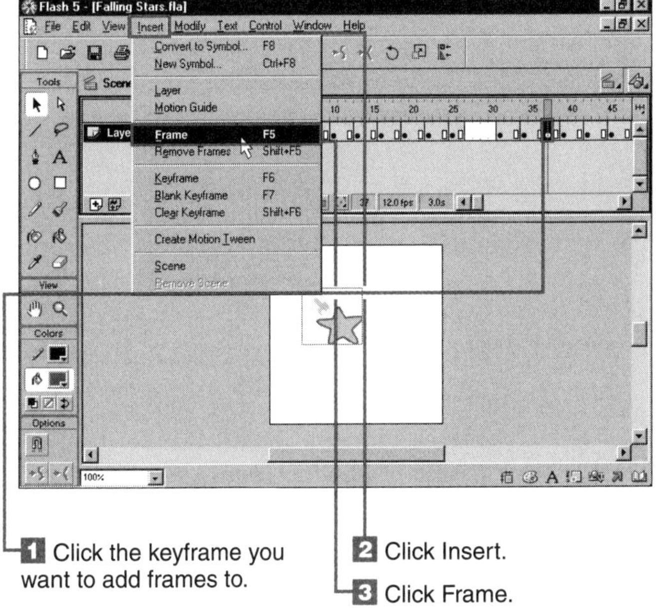

1 Click the keyframe you want to add frames to.

2 Click Insert.

3 Click Frame.

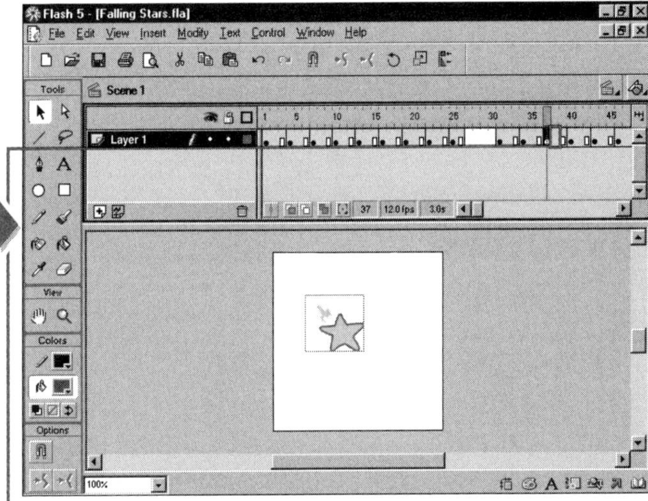

■ Flash adds a frame after the keyframe.

4 Because adding just one regular frame is not always enough, repeat steps 2 and 3 as needed to add more frames to the sequence.

■ To test the animation, click the first frame in the Timeline and press Enter.

MOVE AND COPY FRAMES

One way you can edit your Flash movie is to move or copy frames in the animation sequence. For example, you may want to move a keyframe up or back in the Timeline, or copy multiple regular frames to place between two keyframes. You cannot copy frames like you copy other objects in Flash; you must use the Copy Frames and Paste Frames commands found in the Edit menu. The standard Copy and Paste commands do not work.

You can drag frames around on the Timeline and drop them into new locations. You can also drag a frame to another layer. You can even select multiple frames and relocate them as a group. If you are familiar with using the drag-and-drop feature with other programs, it works the same way in Flash.

See the sections "Add Frames" and "Delete Frames" to find out more about adding and deleting frames from the Timeline.

MOVE AND COPY FRAMES

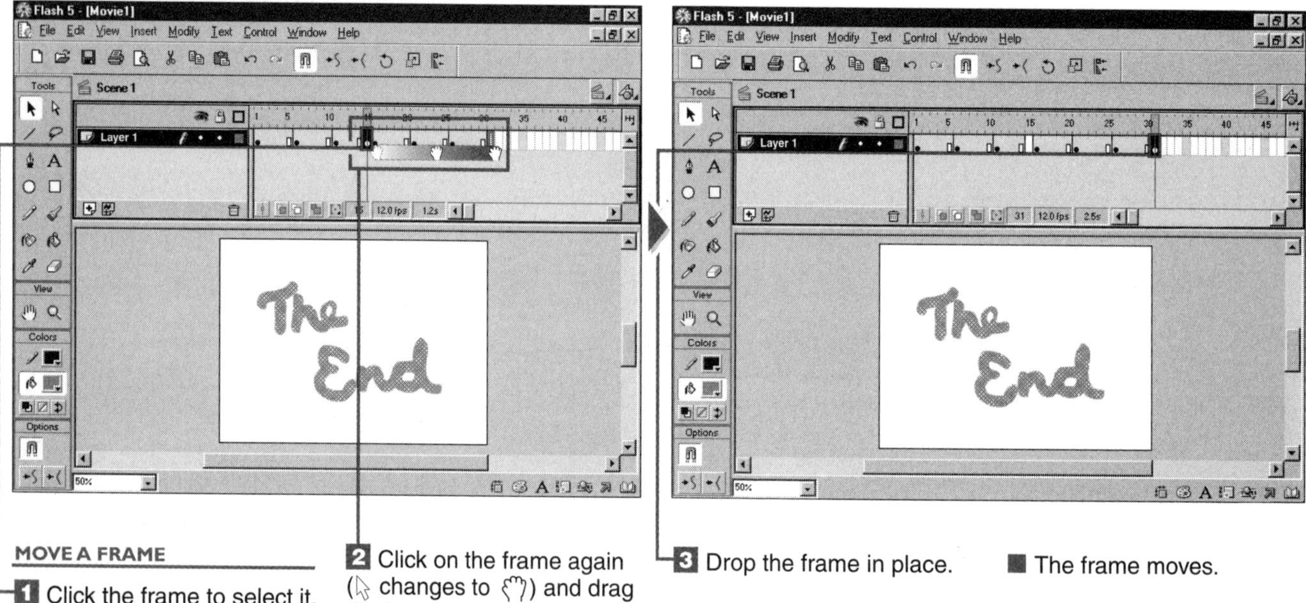

MOVE A FRAME

1 Click the frame to select it.

■ Flash highlights the frame in the Timeline.

2 Click on the frame again (↖ changes to ✋) and drag the frame to a new location in the Timeline.

3 Drop the frame in place.

■ The frame moves.

What do I do if I pasted a copy in the wrong place?

✔ Anytime you make a mistake in Flash, click the Undo button (↶) to undo your last action. This command only works if you click the button immediately after performing the action. If you perform another action before clicking ↶, Flash undoes the most recent action, and the previous action is lost.

Can I drag an end keyframe to extend an animation?

✔ Yes. Dragging an end keyframe in your animation sequence can quickly lengthen or shorten an animation, depending on which direction you drag. For example, you can drag a keyframe to the right a couple of frames and Flash automatically adds in-between frames for you. This extends your animation sequence.

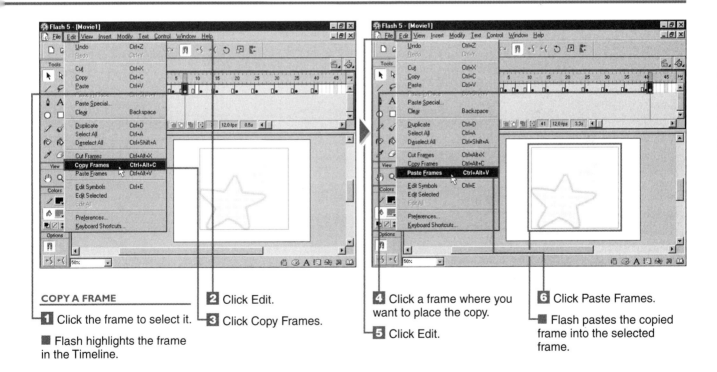

Can I use the drag-and-drop technique to copy frames?

✔ Yes. First select the frame or frames you want to copy. Press and hold Alt (Windows) or Option (Mac) and then drag the frame or frames and drop into the new location on the Timeline. Flash duplicates the frames.

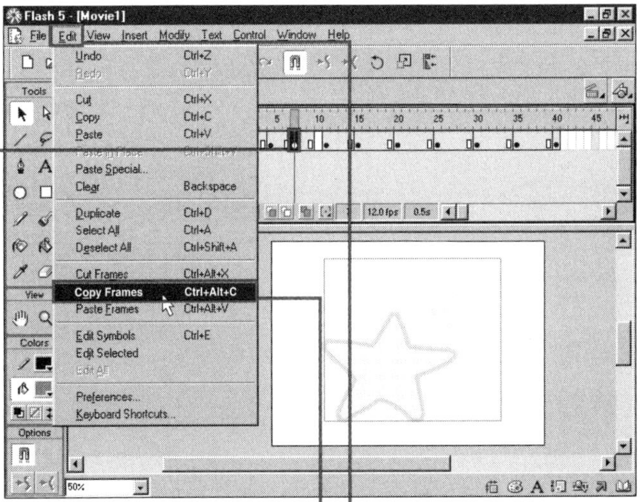

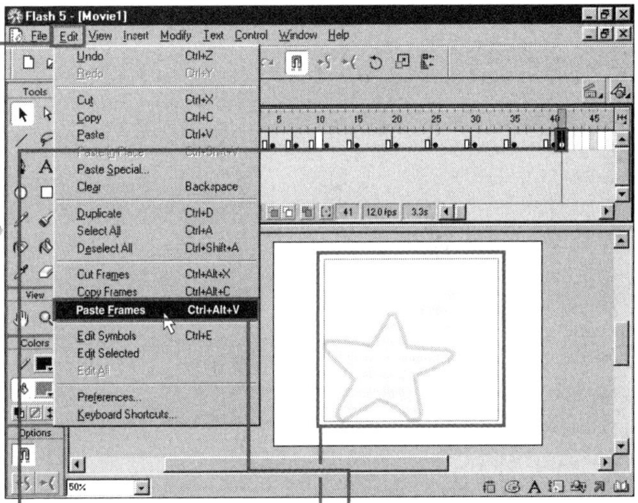

COPY A FRAME

1 Click the frame to select it.

■ Flash highlights the frame in the Timeline.

2 Click Edit.

3 Click Copy Frames.

4 Click a frame where you want to place the copy.

5 Click Edit.

6 Click Paste Frames.

■ Flash pastes the copied frame into the selected frame.

CREATE SCENES

To help you organize really long movies, you can break up your movie into scenes. Scenes are actually chunks of the animation frames turned into their own independent Timelines. Rather than scrolling around long Timelines and trying to keep track of where you are, you can break your movie into scenes that you can work with individually.

For example, one scene may include frames 1 through 50, and another scene may include frames 51 through 75. The scenes are still part of the overall movie, but handily organized into sections that you can label and rearrange as needed. You can even use Flash actions — see Chapter 28 — to jump to different scenes. By default, Flash starts you out with a scene, labeled Scene 1. You can rename the scene and add others.

The current scene's name appears at the top of the Timeline. During playback, the scenes are played in the order in which they are listed in the Scene panel.

CREATE SCENES

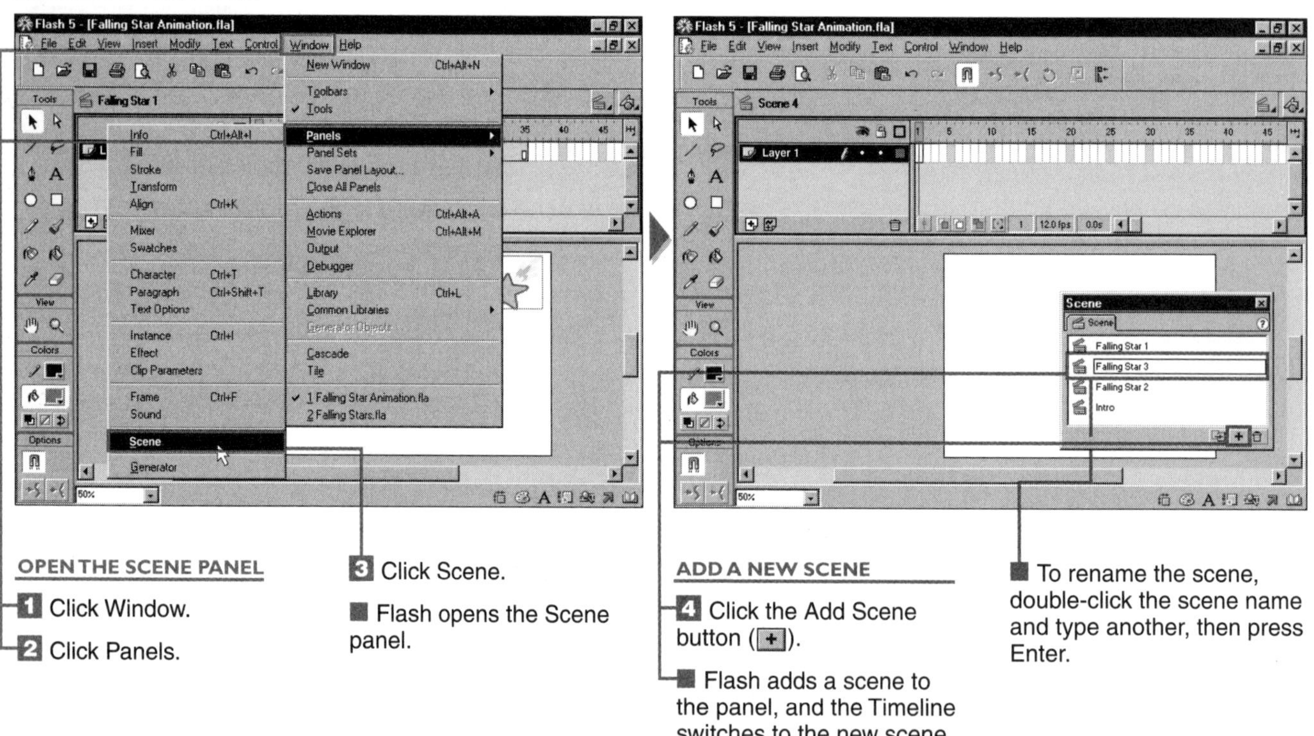

OPEN THE SCENE PANEL

1 Click Window.

2 Click Panels.

3 Click Scene.

■ Flash opens the Scene panel.

ADD A NEW SCENE

4 Click the Add Scene button (+).

■ Flash adds a scene to the panel, and the Timeline switches to the new scene.

■ To rename the scene, double-click the scene name and type another, then press Enter.

How do I rearrange the scene order?

✔ You can move scenes around using the Scene panel. Open the Scene panel to display a list of all the available scenes (steps 1 through 3 in this section). Click the scene you want to move. Click and drag the scene to a new location in the list. Release the mouse button and the scenes are reordered.

How do I delete a scene?

✔ You can delete scenes from the Scene panel. Select the scene you want to remove, then click the Delete button (🗑) at the bottom of the scene panel. If the Scene panel is not open, you can delete the current scene showing in the Timeline by clicking the Insert menu and selecting Remove Scene.

Can I tell Flash to stop the movie after a particular scene?

✔ Yes. You can assign Flash actions to your scenes just like you assign actions to frames (see Chapter 28 to learn more about using Flash actions). For example, you can add a Stop action to the last frame in a scene to stop the movie and any remaining scenes do not play.

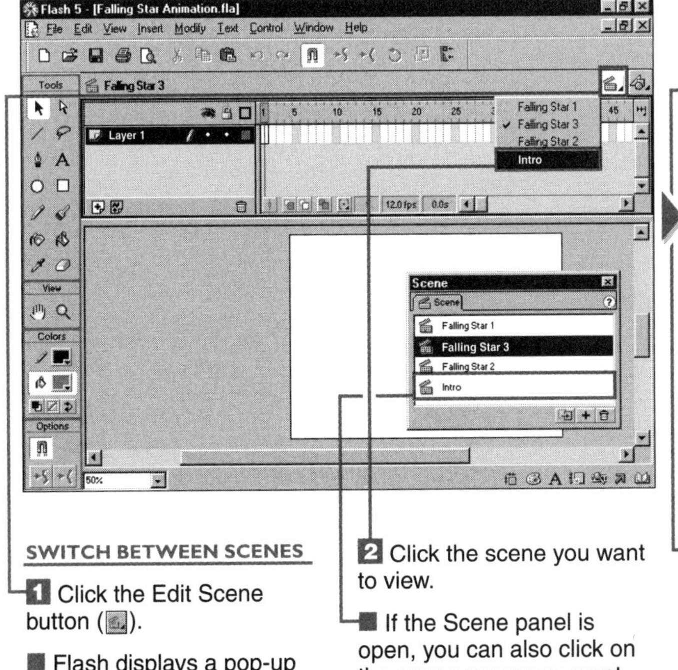

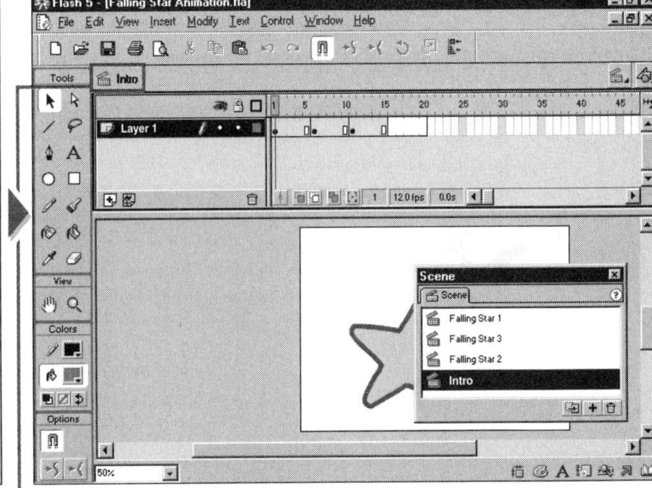

SWITCH BETWEEN SCENES

1 Click the Edit Scene button (🎬).

■ Flash displays a pop-up menu listing all the available scenes.

2 Click the scene you want to view.

■ If the Scene panel is open, you can also click on the scene name you want to view.

■ The Flash Timeline switches to the scene you selected.

SAVE AN ANIMATION AS A MOVIE CLIP

You can save an animation sequence as a movie clip that you can use again elsewhere in your movie. You can create three types of symbols in Flash: graphic symbols, button symbols, or movie clip symbols. Chapter 22 shows you how to create graphic symbols, and you can read about button symbols in Chapter 26. In this section, you learn how to create a movie clip symbol.

Like the other types of symbols, you can place a movie clip symbol on the Stage for any frame. When Flash reaches that frame during playback, it plays the movie clip animation.

You can assign a distinctive name to your movie clip so you can easily find it and use it again. As a symbol, the movie clip is added to the file's Library, a collection of all the symbols that are part of the project. See Chapter 22 to learn more about using the Library window.

SAVE AN ANIMATION AS A MOVIE CLIP

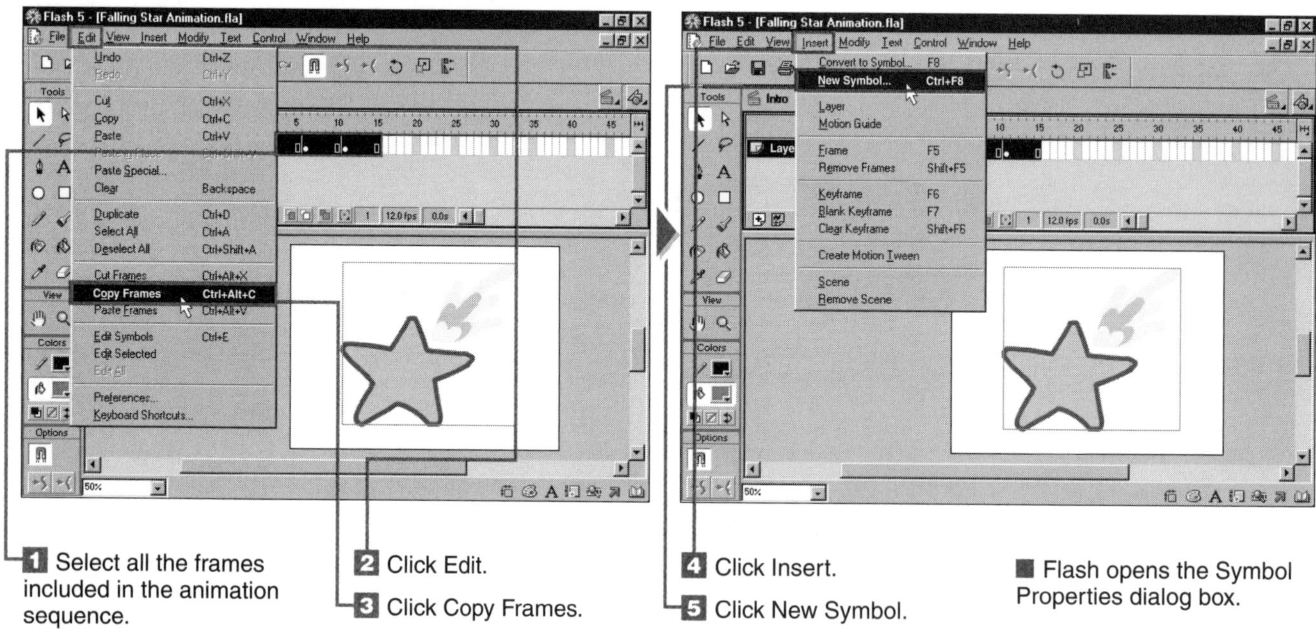

1 Select all the frames included in the animation sequence.

Note: See the section "Select Frames" to learn how to select frames in the Timeline.

2 Click Edit.

3 Click Copy Frames.

4 Click Insert.

5 Click New Symbol.

■ Flash opens the Symbol Properties dialog box.

How do I place a movie clip in my movie?

✔ You can place movie clips into your project just as you place any other item saved in the Flash Library: Click the frame where you want to insert the clip. Click the Show Library button (📖) to open the Library window and drag the movie clip onto the Stage. You can turn any animation effect, including frame-by-frame motion and shape tweens, into movie clips.

Does Flash have any premade clips I can study?

✔ Yes. Flash installs with a couple of movie clips you can use to help you learn how animation techniques work. To locate the clips, open the Window menu and click Common Libraries, Movie Clips. You can drag a premade movie clip onto the Stage to work with and study. The clips are available in any Flash file you open.

How do I save an existing clip as a new clip?

✔ You can use the Convert to Symbol command to save an existing movie clip as a new movie clip symbol. You may do this if you want to alter the clip slightly and use it again elsewhere in your movie. On the Flash Stage, select the clip you want to save, and then click the Insert menu and select Convert to Symbol. Type a new name for the clip and click OK. The clip is added to your movie's Library. You can now edit it and use it in your movie.

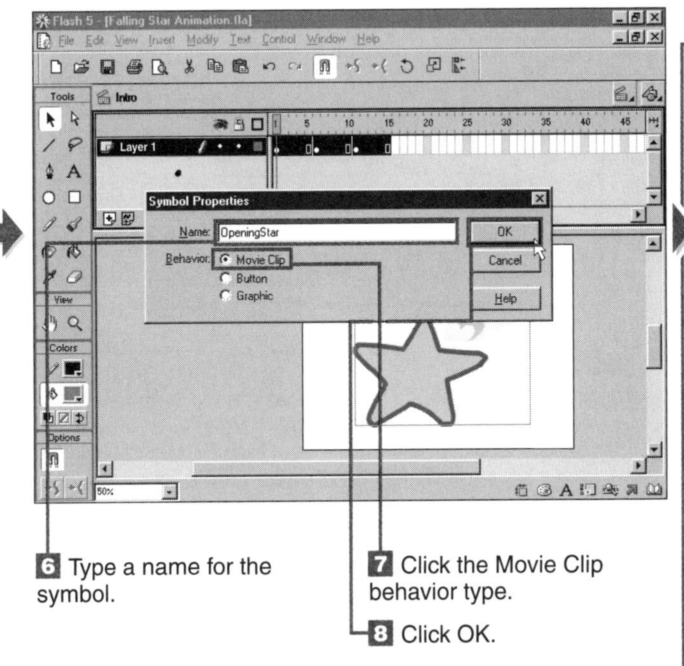

6 Type a name for the symbol.

7 Click the Movie Clip behavior type.

8 Click OK.

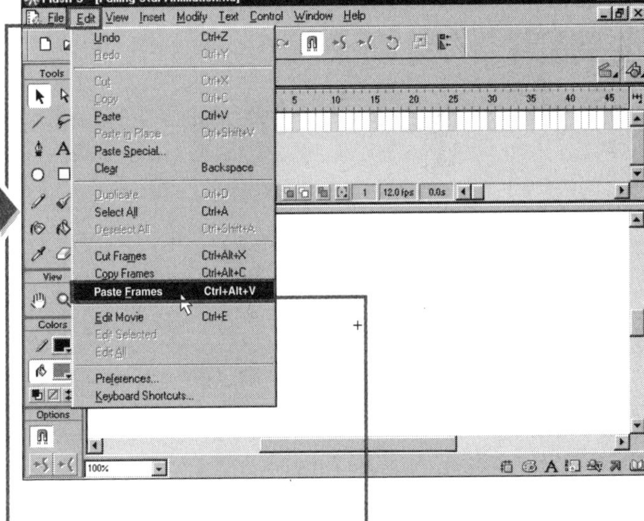

■ Flash switches you to symbol-edit mode.

9 Make sure frame 1 is selected.

10 Click Edit.

11 Click Paste Frames.

■ Flash copies the animation into the movie clip's Timeline. Flash saves the animation in the Flash Library as a movie clip.

USE THE MOVIE EXPLORER

To help you organize and view your movie's contents, use the Movie Explorer panel. This feature, like many of the other panels in Flash, offers you easy access to your movie's elements, such as symbols and clips. You can use the Movie Explorer panel to check which actions are assigned or search for a specific item in your movie.

All the elements associated with your Flash file are listed in a hierarchical manner in the Movie Explorer panel, much like your computer's files are listed in Windows Explorer or Mac's Finder.

You can search for a specific item in your movie using the Find field at the top of the panel.

You can also choose exactly which movie elements to view in the panel's list box using the Show buttons at the top of the panel window.

USE THE MOVIE EXPLORER

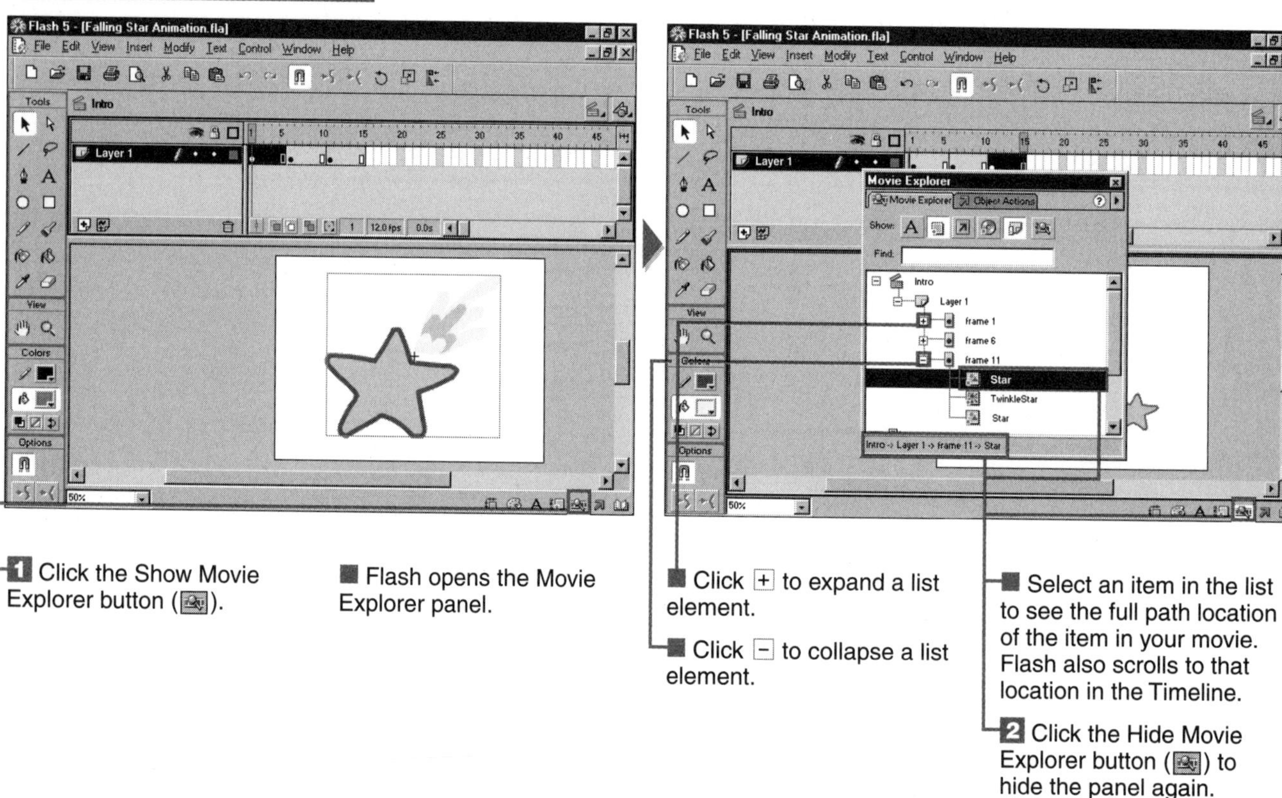

1 Click the Show Movie Explorer button ( ).

■ Flash opens the Movie Explorer panel.

■ Click ⊞ to expand a list element.

■ Click ⊟ to collapse a list element.

■ Select an item in the list to see the full path location of the item in your movie. Flash also scrolls to that location in the Timeline.

2 Click the Hide Movie Explorer button ( ) to hide the panel again.

Can I filter which items appear in the Movie Explorer list box?

✔ Yes. Click on any of the Show filter buttons at the top of the panel to show text, symbols, actions, sound, video and bitmaps, frames, and layers. For example, click the Show button (A) to display symbols used in your movie, including buttons, movie clips, and graphic symbols. Flash shows those items in the list box. You can expand and collapse the hierarchy as needed to help you view more items in the panel list box.

Can I customize my list view?

✔ Yes. Click the Customize button (▣) to open the Movie Explorer Settings dialog box. From here you can select which types of movie elements you want to view in the Movie Explorer panel's list box. Click OK to close the dialog box and apply the new settings.

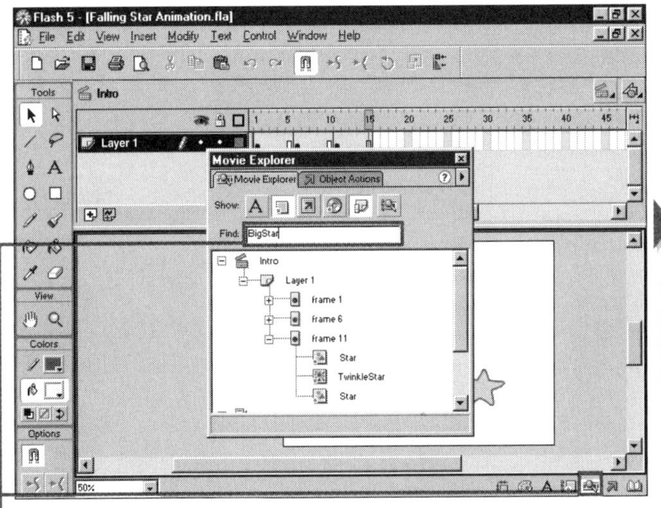

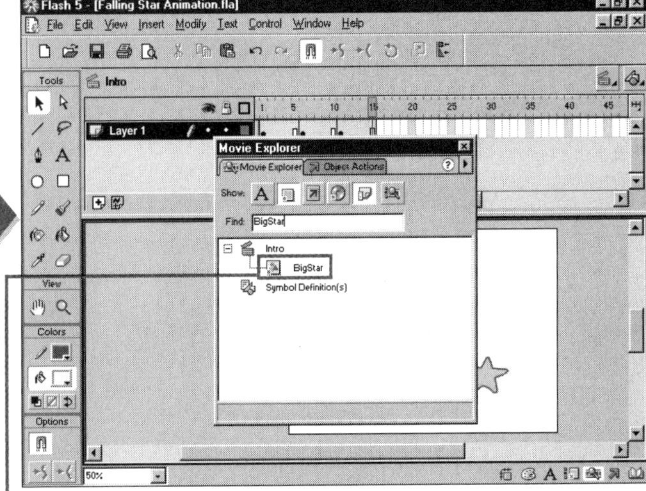

SEARCH FOR AN ITEM

1 Click ▣.

■ The Movie Explorer dialog box appears.

2 Click in the Find text field.

3 Enter the item name or description.

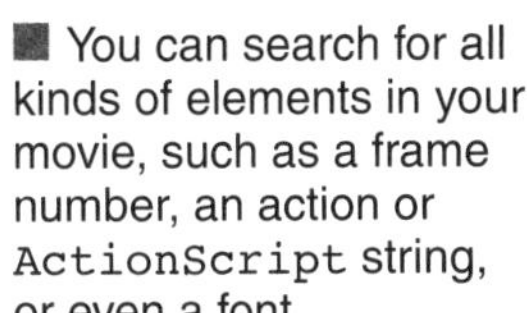

■ You can search for all kinds of elements in your movie, such as a frame number, an action or `ActionScript` string, or even a font.

Note: See Chapters 28 and 29 to learn more about actions.

■ Flash immediately performs a search for the item you entered and displays any matches in the list box.

CREATE A MOTION TWEEN

Flash can help you animate moving objects when you apply a motion tween. A *motion tween* occurs when you define two points of movement in the Timeline with two keyframes and then let Flash calculate all the in-between frames necessary to get from point A to point B. The term *tween* comes from the fact that Flash calculates the *in-between* frames.

Motion-tweened animations take up much less file space than frame-by-frame animations. Tweened animations are also much less labor-intensive than the frame-by-frame animation technique; you do not have to work so hard to make sure the object you are animating is placed just so for each frame in the animation sequence. Instead, tweened animation lets Flash do all the work regarding the placement of the object.

You can motion tween only symbols or grouped objects, and you can tween only one symbol per layer. You cannot create a motion tween using an object or objects you have just drawn on the Stage. You must save the object or objects as a symbol, or group the items together first.

CREATE A MOTION TWEEN

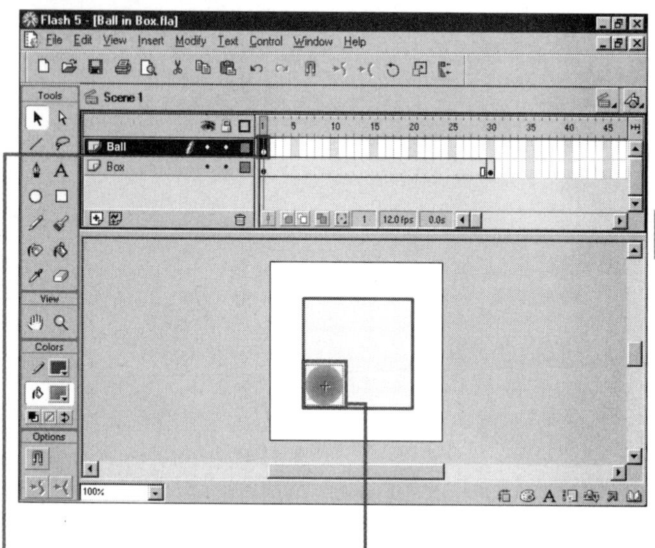

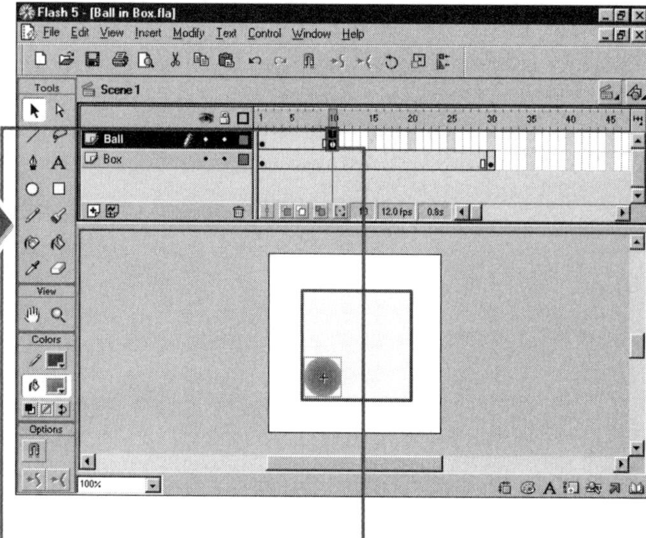

SELECT KEYFRAMES AND SYMBOL

1 Insert a keyframe where you want to start the motion tween.

Note: See Chapter 24 to learn about adding frames.

2 Place the symbol you want to animate on the Stage.

■ The symbol's position should be the animation's starting point.

Note: Chapter 22 explains how to work with symbols.

3 Click the last frame you want to include in the motion tween.

4 Insert a keyframe.

Note: See Chapter 24 to find out how to add keyframes.

When would I use a frame-by-frame animation as opposed to a motion tween animation?

✔ Use a motion tween animation when you want Flash to calculate the changes between frames. Use a frame-by-frame animation when you want complete control over the changes between keyframes. When you create a frame-by-frame animation, you manually input the changes made to each frame in the sequence. Just keep in mind that creating a manual animation sequence results in a larger file size than the same sequence calculated with a motion tween.

What is the difference between a shape tween and a motion tween?

✔ You can create two types of tweened animations in Flash: *motion tween* or *shape tween*. Use motion tweening to make Flash calculate the changes for an object moving around the Stage. Use shape tweening to make Flash calculate the changes between an object that morphs into another object.

Can I add frames to a motion tween?

✔ Yes. You can add or delete regular frames between two keyframes of a motion tween to shorten or lengthen the tween effect. The quickest way to add frames is to drag the end keyframe of the sequence right or left in the Timeline to lengthen or shorten the effect.

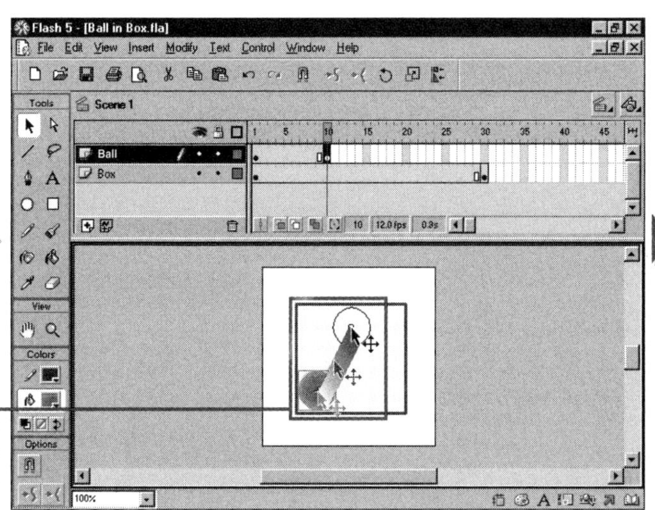

5 Move the symbol to the position on which you want the motion tween to end (for example, the other side of the Stage).

Note: See Chapter 19 to find out how to move objects on the Flash Stage.

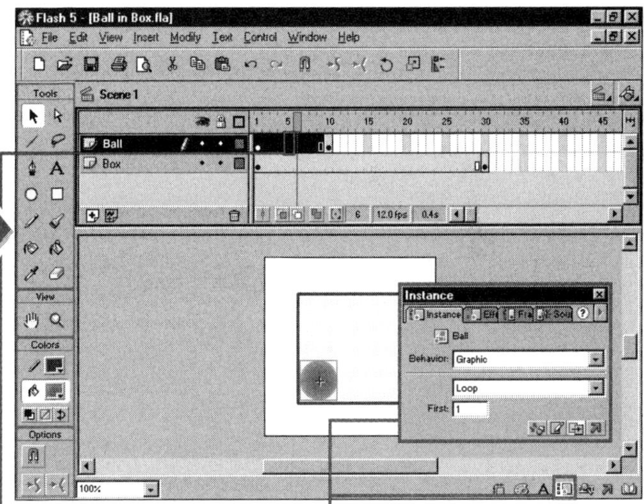

6 Click a frame between the two keyframes that make up your motion tween to select the frames.

Note: See Chapter 24 to find out how to select frames.

7 Click ▣.

■ Flash opens the Instance panel.

CONTINUED

CREATE A MOTION TWEEN (CONTINUED)

You can assign as many motion tween segments as you like throughout your movie, or you can make your animation one long motion tween.

Motion tweening works best for objects you want to move around the Flash Stage. For example, you can make a company logo seem to move across the top of the movie, or a cartoon character seem to walk around. In the movie demonstrated in the steps in this section, the animation focuses on a ball bouncing around inside a box. You can apply the same principles to a logo or product picture. You determine where the logo starts and where it finishes, and then Flash supplies the necessary frames containing incremental changes to make the object appear to move from one spot to another.

The number of in-between frames is determined by your placement of the second keyframe in the sequence. If you insert the second keyframe only a couple of frames away from the first keyframe, you do not see a very smooth motion tween. You should allow five or more frames between your reference keyframes to create a smooth motion tween effect.

CREATE A MOTION TWEEN (CONTINUED)

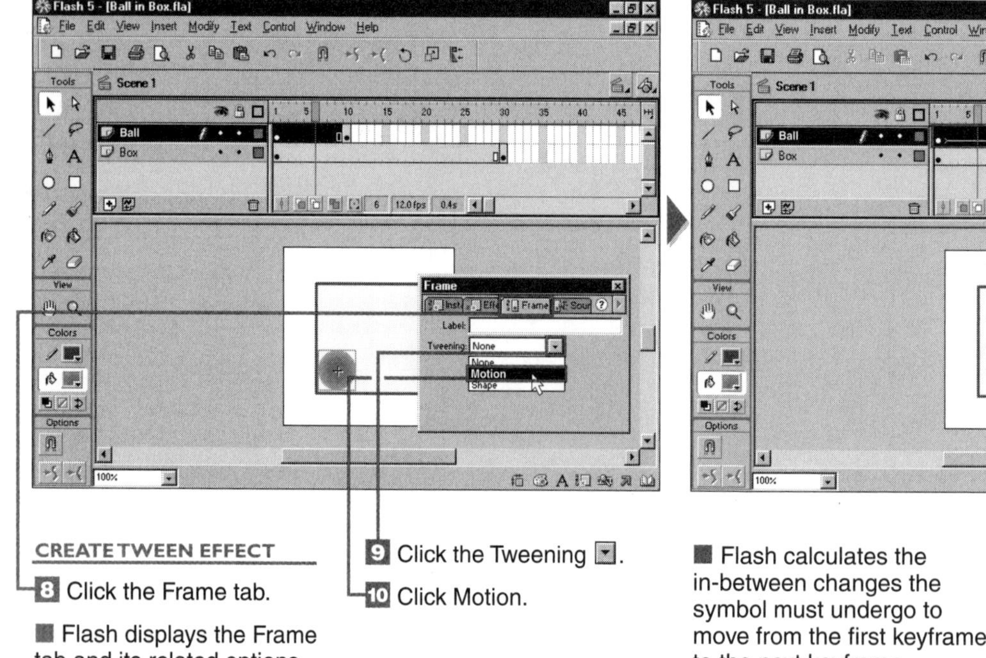

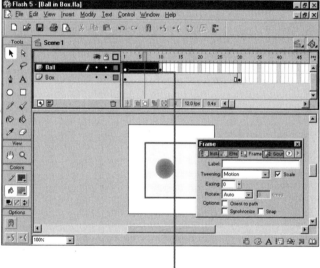

CREATE TWEEN EFFECT

8 Click the Frame tab.

■ Flash displays the Frame tab and its related options.

9 Click the Tweening ▼.

10 Click Motion.

■ Flash calculates the in-between changes the symbol must undergo to move from the first keyframe to the next keyframe.

■ Flash adds a motion tween arrow (⟶) from the first keyframe in the tween effect to the last keyframe in the tween effect.

Can I create a motion tween as I go?

✔ You can start a motion tween without defining the end keyframe in the sequence. To do so, start by adding a keyframe and placing the symbol you want to animate on the Stage. Click the Insert menu and click Create Motion Tween. Add as many frames as you like to the sequence. A dotted line appears in the frames, indicating a motion tween in the making, but not yet complete. In the final frame of the sequence, move the symbol on the Stage to where you want the animation to end. Flash automatically assigns keyframe status to the frame and marks the in-between frames with an arrow to show that the motion tween is complete.

Can I see the incremental changes on the between frames?

✔ Yes. If you turn on the onion-skinning feature, you can see the incremental changes in the frames surrounding the current frame. Click ▣ at the bottom of the Timeline to activate the feature. See Chapter 24 to learn more about using the onion-skinning feature.

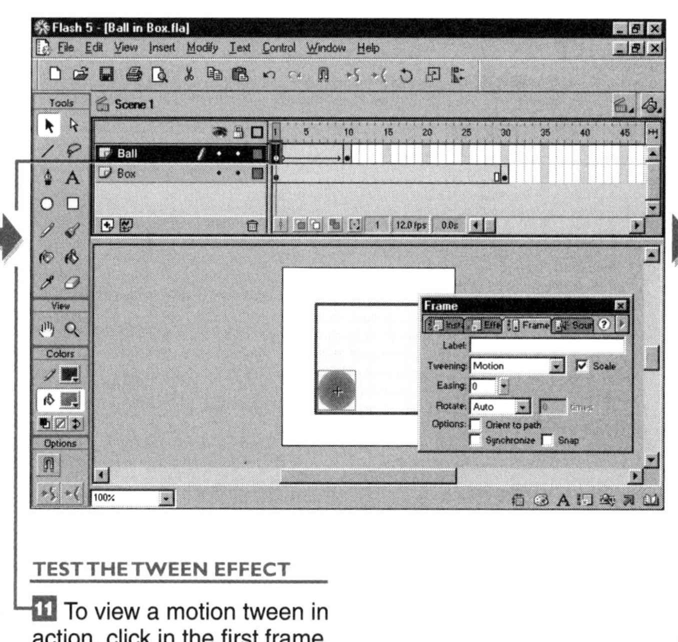

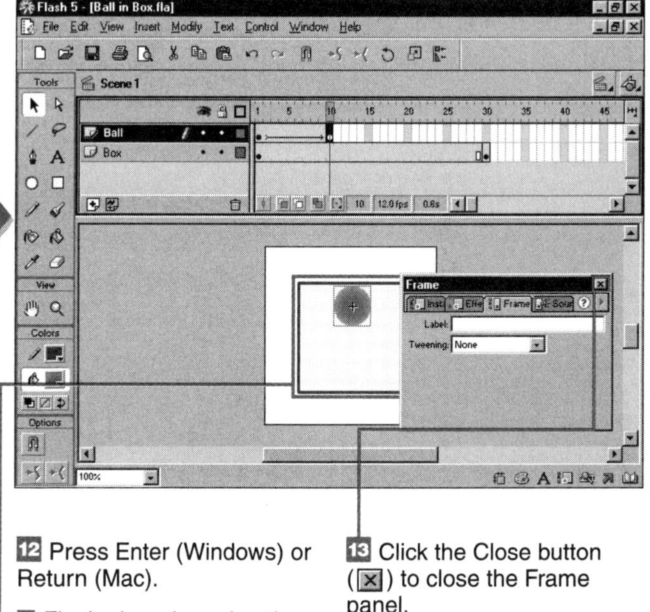

TEST THE TWEEN EFFECT

11 To view a motion tween in action, click in the first frame of the motion tween.

12 Press Enter (Windows) or Return (Mac).

■ Flash plays the animation sequence.

13 Click the Close button (☒) to close the Frame panel.

STOP A MOTION TWEEN

If your movie uses a motion tween, the tween is in effect until you tell it to stop. If you add additional frames to the end of the movie, Flash tries to create more motion tween effects, unless you turn off the motion tween property. See the previous section to learn how to create a motion tween.

You can control tween properties using the Frame panel. The Frame panel includes options for entering frame labels as well as defining tween properties. When Flash attempts to continue the tween effect, the tinted tween frames in the Timeline appear with a dashed line rather than the motion tween arrow. The dashed lines indicate that an end keyframe in the tween sequence has not been defined.

You can keep the Frame panel open on-screen as you work with your motion tween; that way, you have quick access to its controls. You can drag the panel around to keep it out of the way or close it when you are finished.

STOP A MOTION TWEEN

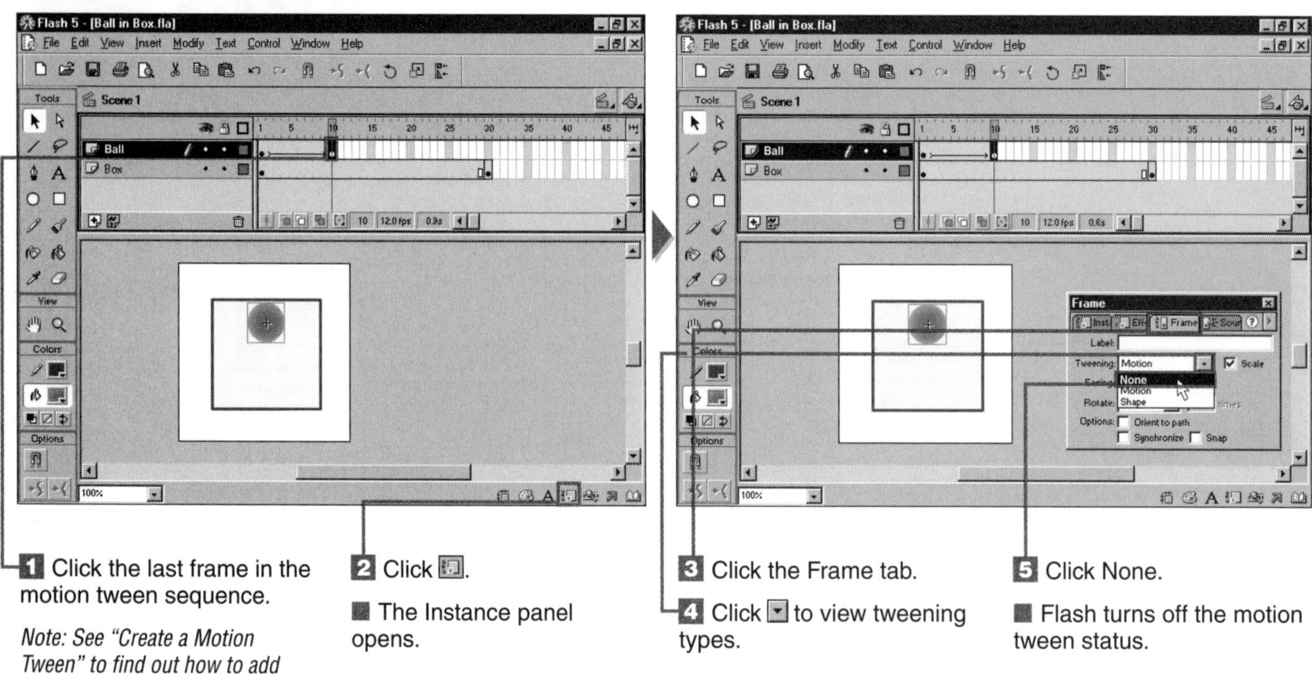

1 Click the last frame in the motion tween sequence.

Note: See "Create a Motion Tween" to find out how to add a tween effect to your movie.

2 Click .

■ The Instance panel opens.

3 Click the Frame tab.

4 Click to view tweening types.

5 Click None.

■ Flash turns off the motion tween status.

ADD A KEYFRAME TO A MOTION TWEEN

You can make changes to a motion tween by adding keyframes to the animation sequence. *Keyframes* are used to mark changes in your animation, such as adding a new object or changing object position. See Chapter 24 to learn more about frame types used in Flash.

For example, you may want to change the direction in which the object moves in a motion tween animation. If you add a keyframe to change the direction, Flash reconfigures the in-between frames to reflect changes in the new keyframe. In the bouncing ball animation demonstrated in this section, a new keyframe is added to create a change in the ball's position as it bounces around inside the box. A new keyframe is added every time the box bounces off the box wall in a new direction.

See "Create a Motion Tween" to find out how to animate with the motion tween feature.

ADD A KEYFRAME TO A MOTION TWEEN

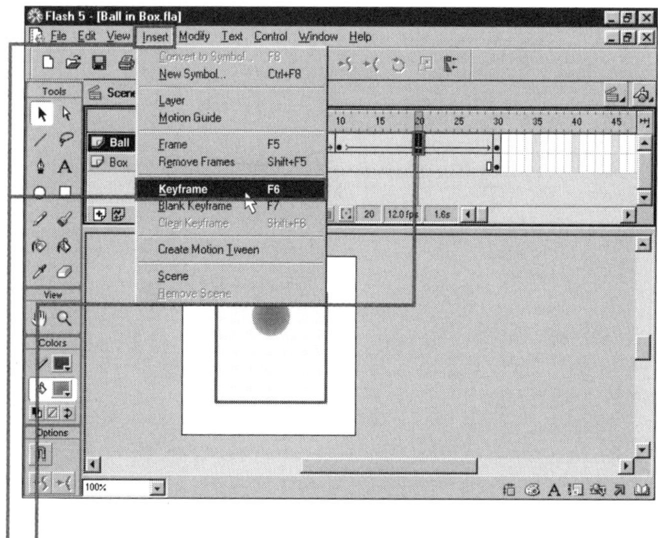

1 Click the Timeline where you want to insert a new keyframe.

2 Click Insert.

3 Click Keyframe.

■ Flash duplicates the previous keyframe in the animation.

Note: See Chapter 24 to learn how to work with Flash frames.

4 Change the symbol you are animating by moving it on the Stage or changing its appearance.

■ Flash recalculates the in-between frames to generate the animation.

Note: Flash cannot change the symbol in keyframes following the newly inserted keyframe. You must manually make changes to subsequent keyframes.

ANIMATE BY ROTATING A SYMBOL

You can turn a regular symbol from your Flash Library into an animated object that rotates in your movie. This method requires a series of keyframes in which you control how much rotation occurs in each keyframe. By assigning the animation sequence motion tween status, Flash calculates the in-between frames to create the rotation effect. The result is an animation in which the object appears to rotate.

In Flash, you can create many types of objects that make good rotating animation effects. Shapes, lines, and text boxes all make good candidates for rotating. For example, you can make your corporate logo rotate at the top of your movie screen, or you can make a text box seem to rotate upside-down and back. The steps in this section show how to rotate a text box, but you can apply the same steps to rotate any symbol on the Stage.

See "Create a Motion Tween" to find out more about the motion tween effect.

ANIMATE BY ROTATING A SYMBOL

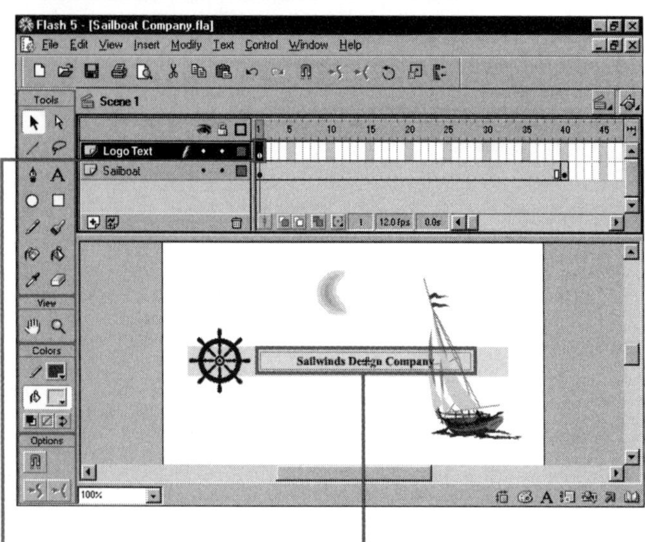

1 Insert a keyframe where you want to start the motion tween.

Note: See Chapter 24 to learn more about adding frames to the Timeline.

2 Place the symbol you want to animate on the Stage.

Note: Placing animations on a separate layer from your movie's background is a good idea. See Chapter 21 to learn more about working with layers.

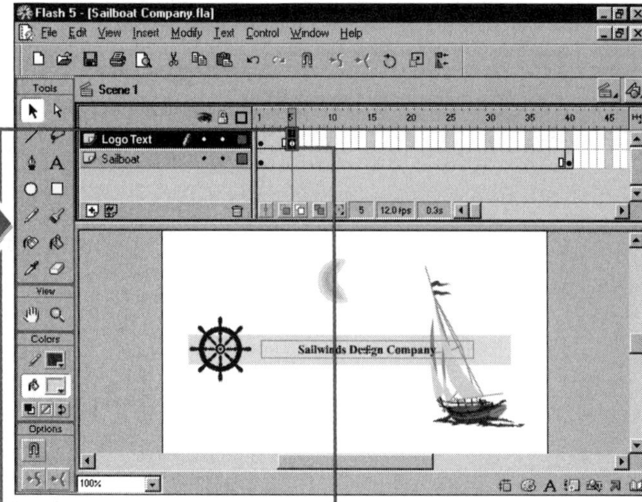

3 Click the next frame you want to include in the motion tween.

■ For example, you can start the rotation five frames later.

4 Insert a keyframe.

Can I rotate an object I draw on the Flash Stage?

✔ The Flash motion tween effect does not work with items you draw on the Stage. It does work with objects that you turn into symbols or that you group together. You can also motion tween text blocks. To find out more about using Flash symbols, see Chapter 22. To find out how to group objects, turn to Chapter 19.

How else can I access the Frame panel?

✔ Click the Modify menu and then click Frame to open the Frame panel directly.

Does it matter which direction I rotate the object?

✔ No. You can drag a rotation handle in any direction to start rotating the object. The direction you drag determines the direction of the rotation. For example, you may want your object to rotate counterclockwise. To do this, drag a rotation handle to the left. To rotate clockwise, drag the handle to the right. The rotation feature works best if you drag a corner handle versus a handle from the middle of the selected object.

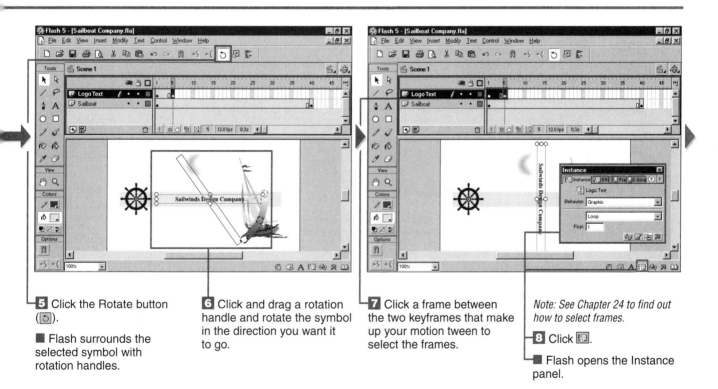

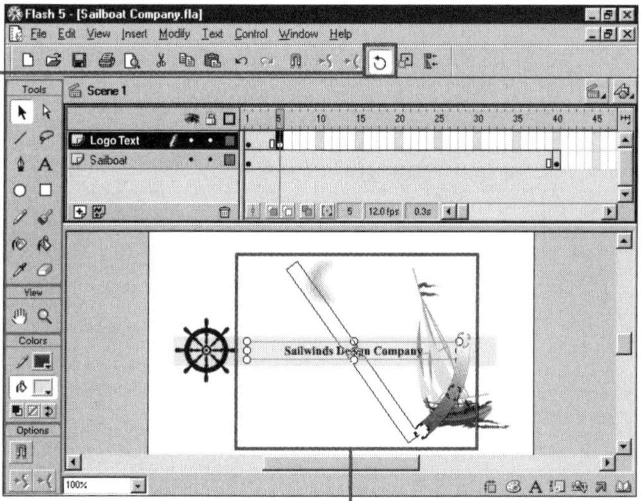

5 Click the Rotate button (↻).

■ Flash surrounds the selected symbol with rotation handles.

6 Click and drag a rotation handle and rotate the symbol in the direction you want it to go.

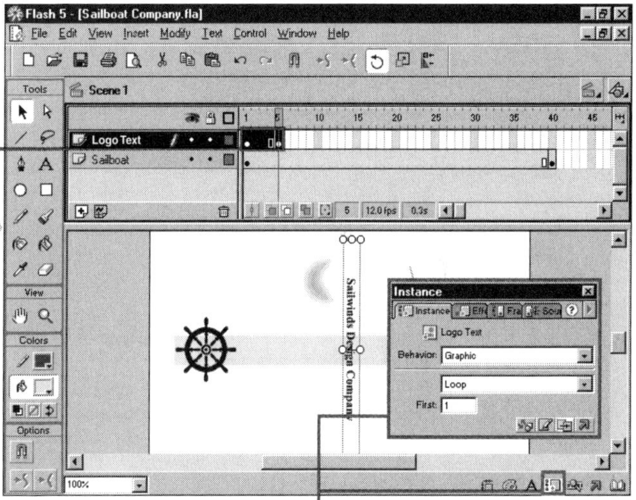

7 Click a frame between the two keyframes that make up your motion tween to select the frames.

Note: See Chapter 24 to find out how to select frames.

8 Click (Instance panel button).

■ Flash opens the Instance panel.

CONTINUED

ANIMATE BY ROTATING A SYMBOL (CONTINUED)

You can create keyframes at key points of the animation Timeline to rotate your symbol. For example, you can change the rotation's progress by stretching it out over four keyframes, rotating the symbol 90 degrees each time. Then, add regular frames between the keyframes to lengthen the animation time.

Creating a rotating motion tween requires more than two keyframes. Remember, you use keyframes to indicate a change in the animation, such as a position on the Stage. A rotation involves an object that faces different directions on the Stage. You need a keyframe for each major change in the rotation sequence. Flash cannot calculate the between frames without key spots that change the direction of the object in the rotation.

When rotating objects in Flash, you can choose to rotate clockwise or counterclockwise.

ANIMATE BY ROTATING A SYMBOL (CONTINUED)

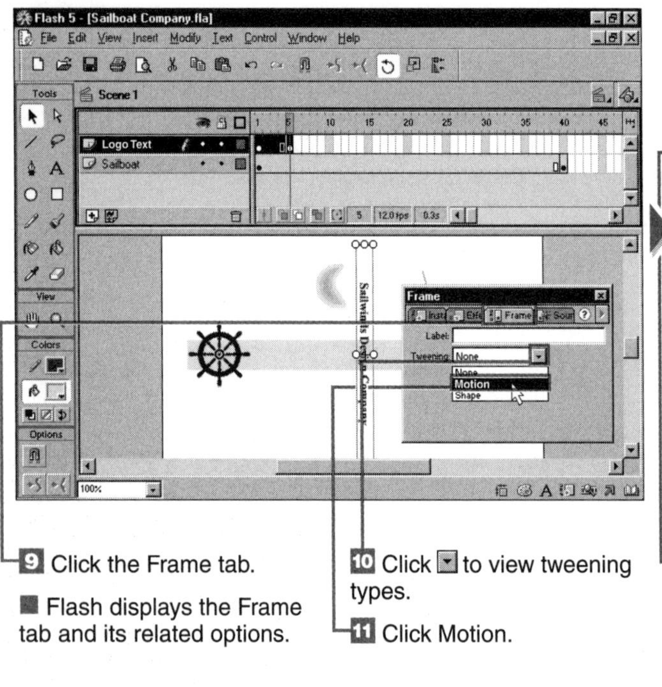

9 Click the Frame tab.

■ Flash displays the Frame tab and its related options.

10 Click ▾ to view tweening types.

11 Click Motion.

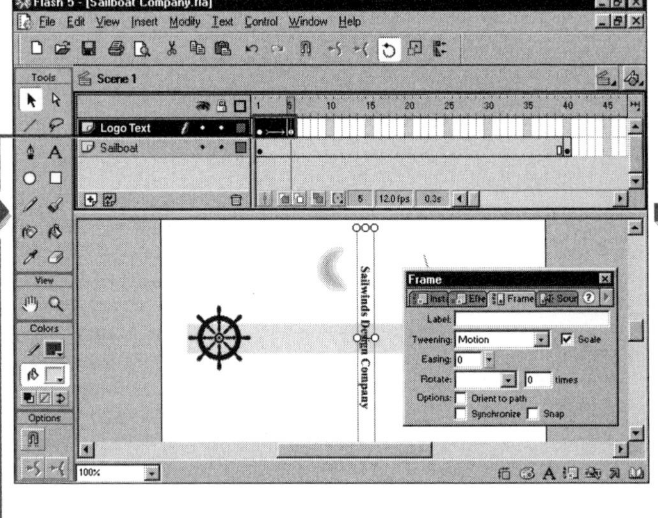

■ Flash calculates the in-between changes the symbol must undergo between keyframes. Flash also adds a ⟶ to the frames.

Can I tell Flash to rotate the symbol for me?

✔ Yes. Flash can help you with the rotation process if you prefer not to do it manually. From the Frame panel, click the Rotate box ▾ and then select a rotation direction. You can select CW for clockwise or CCW for counterclockwise. Next to the Rotate option, type the number of rotations you want to occur. Start with 1 to see whether you like the effect or not. When the movie plays, Flash rotates the symbol in the direction you specified.

How do I make the object seem to keep rotating?

✔ Repeat the animation sequence in your movie by copying the rotation sequence and adding it to the end of the movie as many times as needed, or set the sequence to loop with the Go To and Play actions. To learn more about assigning actions in Flash, see Chapter 28.

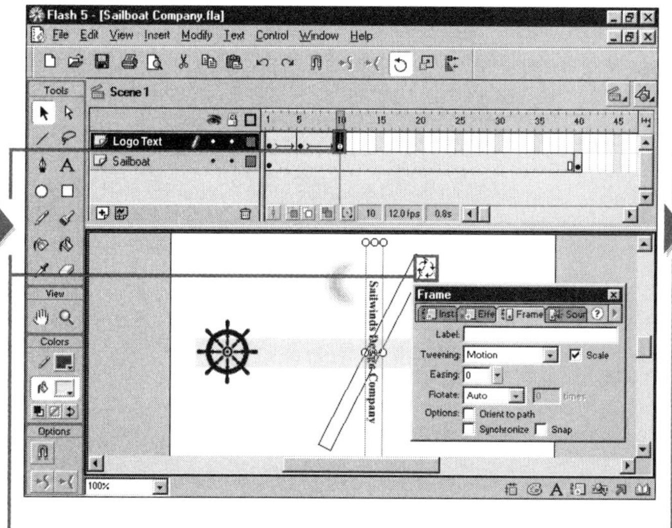

■ You can continue rotating the symbol by adding more keyframes and changing the rotation each time. For example, you can make the symbol complete a full rotation. The motion tween is in effect until you cancel it.

Note: See "Stop a Motion Tween" to find out how to cancel the motion tween effect.

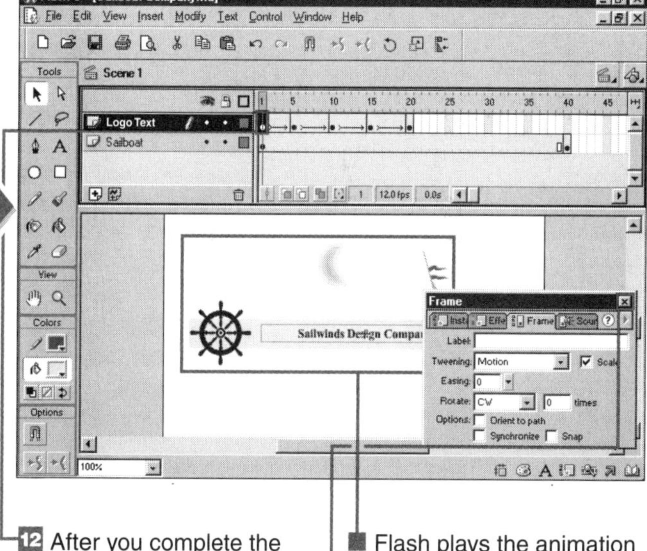

12 After you complete the motion tween you can test the sequence by clicking the first frame and pressing Enter (Windows) or Return (Mac).

■ Flash plays the animation sequence.

13 Click ☒ to close the Frame panel to free up onscreen workspace.

ANIMATE BY SPINNING A SYMBOL

You can create an animation effect that makes a symbol appear to spin in your Flash movie. Using two identical keyframes, you can tell Flash to rotate the symbol in the in-between frames to create a spinning effect during playback.

Because a spin is a 360-degree rotation, you do not have to alter the keyframe content. In other words, you do not require more than two keyframes to create the effect. The rotated object starts and ends up at the same spot, so the two keyframes that begin and end the effect remain the same. You just tell Flash which direction to spin the object. Flash then calculates all the incremental changes that must occur in the in-between frames to create the illusion of spinning.

See "Create a Motion Tween" earlier in this chapter to find out more about the motion tween effect. See "Animate by Rotating a Symbol" earlier in this chapter to learn more about rotating options available in Flash.

ANIMATE BY SPINNING A SYMBOL

CREATE THE TWEEN EFFECT

1 Insert a keyframe where you want to start the motion tween in your movie's Timeline.

Note: See Chapter 24 to learn about adding frames.

2 Place the symbol you want to animate on the Stage.

Note: Placing animations on a separate layer from your movie's background is a good idea. See Chapter 21 to learn about working with layers.

3 Click the end frame in which you want to conclude the motion tween.

■ For example, you can complete the spin effect 20 frames later.

4 Insert a keyframe.

Note: See Chapter 24 to learn more about adding frames to the Timeline.

Does it matter in which direction the symbol spins?

✔ You can set a rotation direction in the Frame panel, or you can tell Flash to set a direction for you. If you let Flash pick a direction, it chooses the rotation that involves the least amount of change from frame to frame. This method creates a smoother animation sequence. To instruct Flash to handle the rotation, leave the Auto option selected.

Why does Flash keep me from selecting all the frames?

✔ If you are having difficulty selecting the end keyframe, the start keyframe and all the regular frames in-between — particularly in step 5 of this section — try this trick: First, click the end keyframe in the range. Next, press and hold down the Shift key while clicking anywhere in the range to the left of the end keyframe. This should select all the frames in the motion tween.

My spinning effect happens too fast during playback. What can I do?

✔ You can add more regular frames between keyframes to extend the animation effect. Try adding 5 or more frames, and play the movie again. Adding regular frames makes the motion tween appear to happen more slowly.

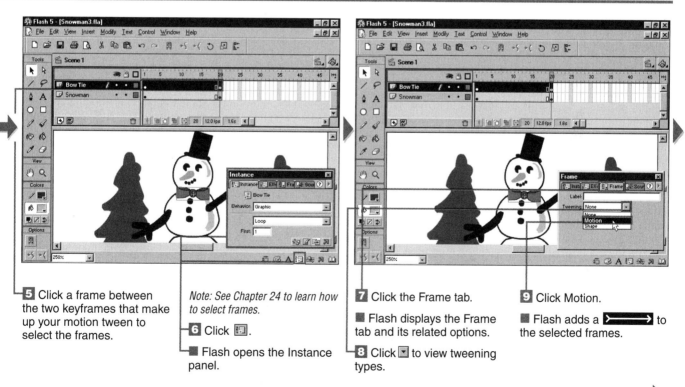

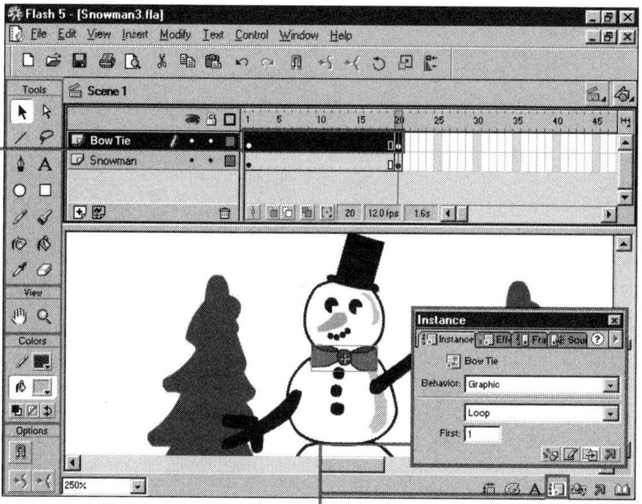

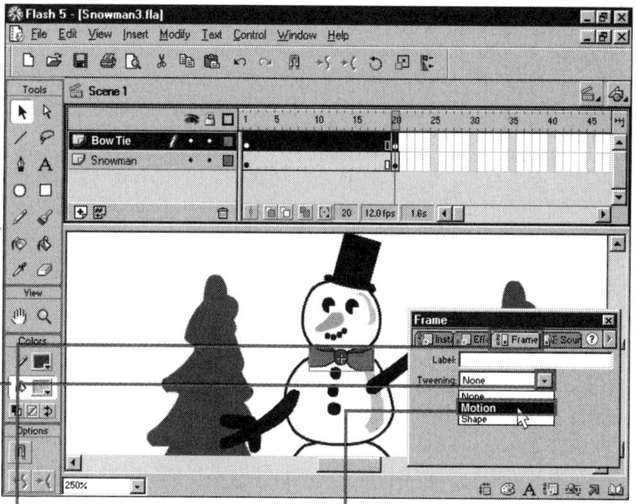

5 Click a frame between the two keyframes that make up your motion tween to select the frames.

Note: See Chapter 24 to learn how to select frames.

6 Click [icon].

■ Flash opens the Instance panel.

7 Click the Frame tab.

■ Flash displays the Frame tab and its related options.

8 Click [▼] to view tweening types.

9 Click Motion.

■ Flash adds a [arrow] to the selected frames.

CONTINUED

ANIMATE BY SPINNING A SYMBOL (CONTINUED)

You can use the Rotation controls to spin items such as corporate logos or text blocks. By assigning a motion tween effect, Flash takes care of the hard work of differing each frame in the sequence for you. You can specify how many times the symbol rotates between the two keyframes, and exactly which direction it goes.

The steps in this section show an example of a spinning object, the snowman's bowtie. You can apply the same principles to other objects you can create or add to the Flash Stage, such as a wheel, a button, or a star shape. You can also import artwork from another program and make it seem to spin in your Flash movie. See Chapter 23 to learn more about importing graphics into Flash.

ANIMATE BY SPINNING A SYMBOL (CONTINUED)

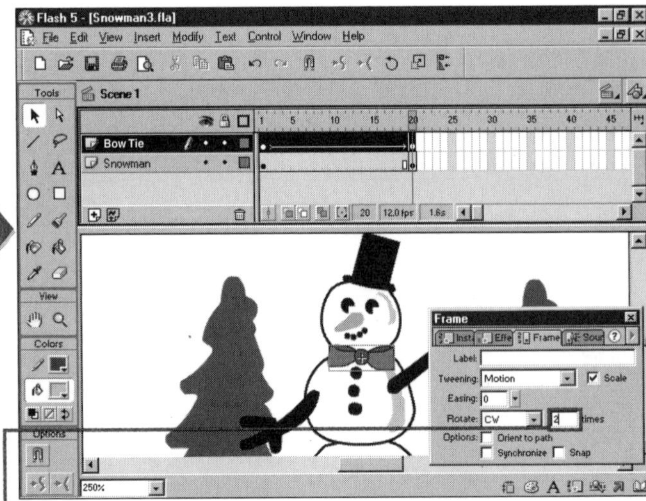

SELECT A SPIN ROTATION

10 Click the ▾ to view rotation types.

11 Click a rotation direction for the spin.

■ Choose CW to spin the symbol clockwise.

■ Choose CCW to spin the symbol counterclockwise.

12 Type the number of times you want the rotation to occur.

■ Flash calculates the in-between changes the symbol must undergo to move from the first keyframe to the next keyframe.

How can I see the spin effect play more than once?

✔ To really see how your animation looks, open the movie in Test Movie mode. Click the Control menu and click Test Movie. By default, the Flash Player is set to loop a movie within the Flash program window. To stop the animation at any time, press Enter.

What does the Auto rotate setting do?

✔ You can choose Auto from the Rotate menu in the Frame panel to have Flash determine the rotation for you. The Auto selection rotates the selected object in the direction using the least amount of motion.

Can I control how quickly the object starts spinning?

✔ Yes. Use the Ease setting in the Frame panel to speed up the start of your motion tween's spinning effect. You can drag the Ease slider up to accelerate the spin or down to slow it down.

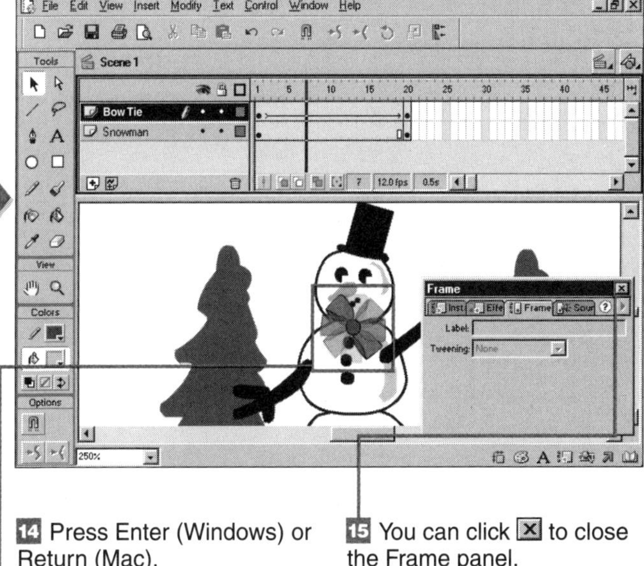

VIEW THE SPIN

13 To view a motion tween in action, click in the first frame of the motion tween.

14 Press Enter (Windows) or Return (Mac).

■ Flash plays the animation sequence.

15 You can click ☒ to close the Frame panel.

ANIMATE BY CHANGING SYMBOL SIZE

You can use the motion tween technique to create an animation that changes size. For example, you can make a symbol seem to grow or shrink in size. You define two keyframes, one of which includes the symbol scaled to a new size. With the motion tween effect applied, Flash fills in all the in-between frames with the incremental changes needed to create the illusion of growth or shrinkage.

You can use the same scaling feature from the Flash drawing tools to resize symbols for animation effects. The Scale command can be found as a button on the Main toolbar as well as a button at the bottom of the Drawing toolbar when the Arrow tool is selected.

To help keep your animations organized, consider placing them on a separate layer from the movie background layer in the Flash Timeline. By placing an animation sequence on a different layer, you can easily locate the animation sequence and make edits to it without accidentally changing other elements, such as background elements, in the movie. See Chapter 21 to learn more about Flash layers.

See "Create a Motion Tween" earlier in this chapter to find out more about the motion tween effect.

ANIMATE BY CHANGING SYMBOL SIZE

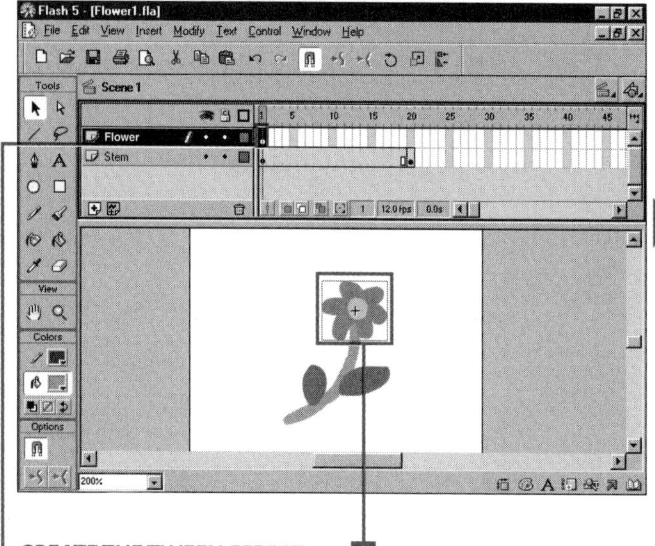

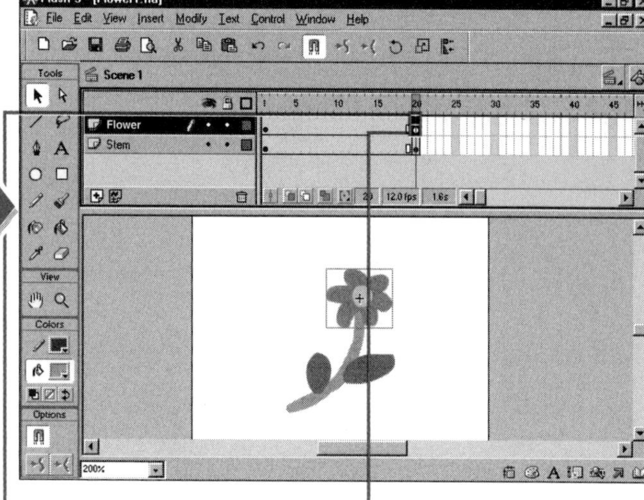

CREATE THE TWEEN EFFECT

1 Insert a keyframe where you want to start the motion tween.

Note: See Chapter 24 to learn more about adding frames.

2 Place the symbol you want to animate on the Stage.

Note: Placing animations on a separate layer from your movie's background is a good idea. See Chapter 21 to learn more about layers.

3 Click the end frame in which you want to conclude the motion tween.

■ In this example, the flower seems to grow in the course of 20 frames.

4 Insert a keyframe.

Note: See Chapter 24 to learn more about adding frames to the Timeline.

How does Flash break down my motion tween to get from one keyframe to the next?

✔ By default, Flash makes equal incremental changes to tween the object from the first keyframe in the sequence to the last keyframe. If few regular frames separate the two keyframes, the change in size is minimal and appears quickly during playback. Adding a few regular frames to extend the animation effect slows it down during playback. For help on adding frames, see Chapter 24.

How can I tell what size changes Flash makes in my motion tween?

✔ You can use the Onion Skin tool to see the changes in the frames that surround the current frame. To turn on the feature, click ▣ at the bottom of the Timeline. After you activate onion skinning, you can drag the onion skin markers left or right to include other frames in the view. See Chapter 24 to learn more about how to use this feature when animating.

Which Scale handle should I drag?

✔ When resizing an object on the Stage, you can use any of the selection handles to drag the object to a new size. Depending on the handle you drag, the object resizes in different directions. For best results, drag a corner handle. Dragging the corner handle away from the object makes the object larger dragging the corner handle toward the object to make the object smaller.

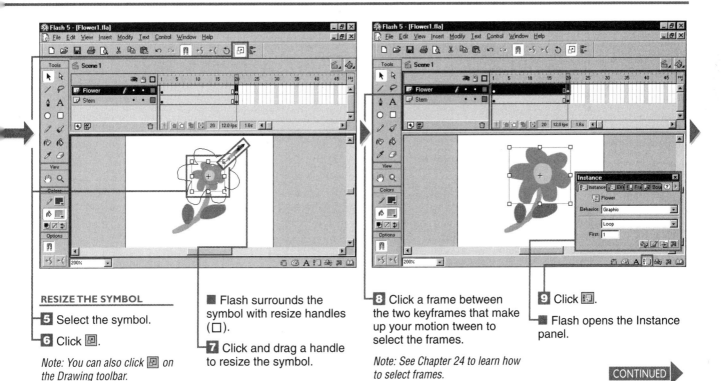

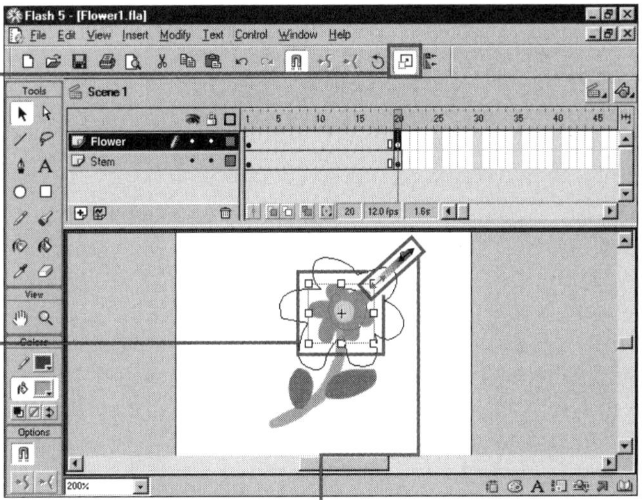

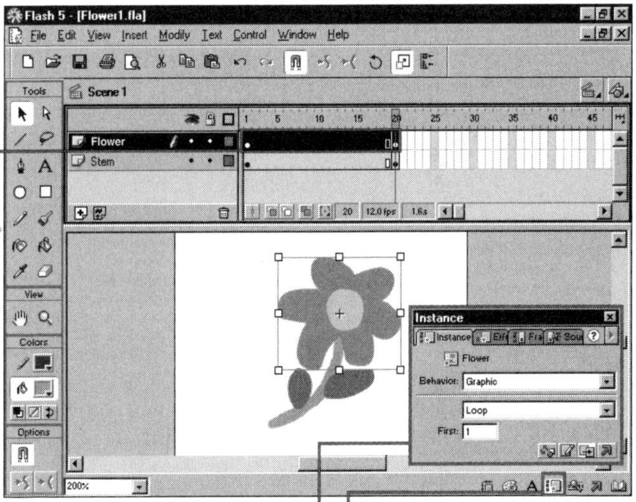

RESIZE THE SYMBOL

5 Select the symbol.

6 Click ▣.

Note: You can also click ▣ on the Drawing toolbar.

■ Flash surrounds the symbol with resize handles (□).

7 Click and drag a handle to resize the symbol.

8 Click a frame between the two keyframes that make up your motion tween to select the frames.

Note: See Chapter 24 to learn how to select frames.

9 Click ▣.

■ Flash opens the Instance panel.

CONTINUED

ANIMATE BY CHANGING SYMBOL SIZE (CONTINUED)

In addition to the Scale button you use to actually resize a symbol for your animation effect, you must also tell Flash the type of effect you want to create. You can do this by assigning the Scale option to your motion tween.

You can use the Scale option in the Frame panel to make symbols seem to grow or shrink. The speed at which this occurs depends on how many frames you insert between the two defining keyframes. You can experiment with the number of regular frames to create just the right animation speed. For example, if your motion tween uses five in-between frames, adding five more slows down the tween effect. The object seems to grow or shrink at a slower pace.

See Chapter 24 to learn more about adding frames to the Timeline.

ANIMATE BY CHANGING SYMBOL SIZE (CONTINUED)

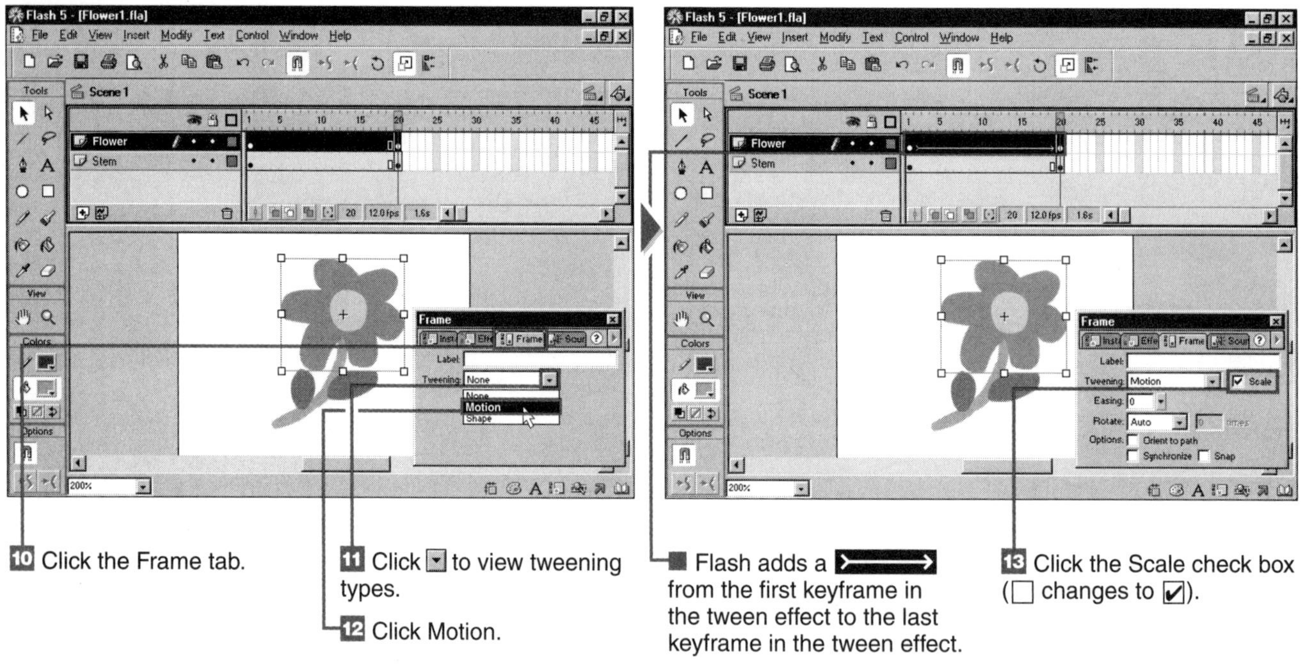

10 Click the Frame tab.

11 Click ▾ to view tweening types.

12 Click Motion.

■ Flash adds a ⟶ from the first keyframe in the tween effect to the last keyframe in the tween effect.

13 Click the Scale check box (☐ changes to ☑).

My symbol does not grow or shrink very much. Why not?

✔ For a maximum tween effect, you need to make the final symbol in the tween sequence much smaller or larger than the symbol shown in the first keyframe. You should also allow plenty of regular keyframes in between the two anchor keyframes. See Chapter 24 to learn more about adding frames to the Timeline.

How do I make my object shrink back again to its original size?

✔ You can copy the entire sequence and apply the Reverse Frames command to make the object seem to shrink again after growing. See "Using Reverse Frames" later in this chapter to learn how to apply this command to your motion tweens.

Can I both rotate and scale an object in a motion tween?

✔ Yes. To apply both rotation and scaling at the same time, click the Modify menu and click Transform, then click Scale and Rotate. This opens the Scale and Rotate dialog box. Enter values for both the percentage of scaling and the degree of rotation. Click OK, and Flash applies both types of changes at once to the selected object.

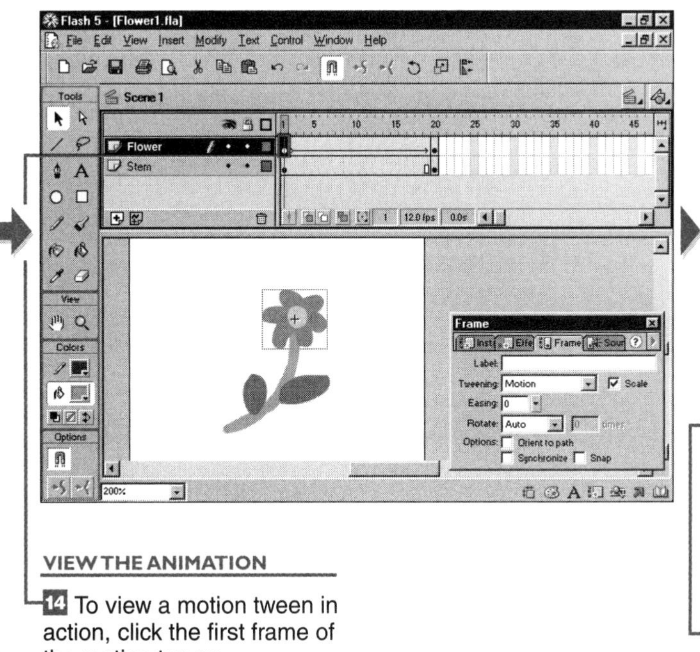

VIEW THE ANIMATION

14 To view a motion tween in action, click the first frame of the motion tween.

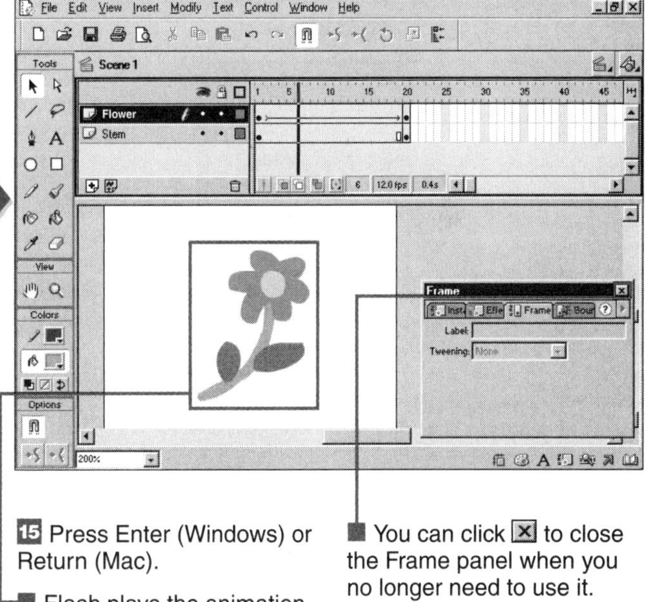

15 Press Enter (Windows) or Return (Mac).

■ Flash plays the animation sequence.

■ You can click ☒ to close the Frame panel when you no longer need to use it.

ANIMATE SYMBOLS ALONG A PATH

You can make a symbol follow a path in your Flash movie. Using the Flash motion tween technique and a *motion guide layer*, you define points A and B in the sequence, draw a line that tells Flash exactly where you want the symbol to move, and then Flash calculates all the in-between frames for you. The motion guide layer is not visible when you export the movie.

A *motion guide layer* is a special layer used to define the motion tween path. Using the drawing tools, such as the Pencil tool or the Brush tool, you draw on the Stage exactly where you want the symbol to go. The symbol follows the path you specify. In the example shown in the steps in this section, the motion guide layer is used to define a flight path for a bumblebee symbol.

See "Create a Motion Tween" earlier in this chapter to learn more about the motion tween effect. See Chapter 21 to learn more about layers.

ANIMATE SYMBOLS ALONG A PATH

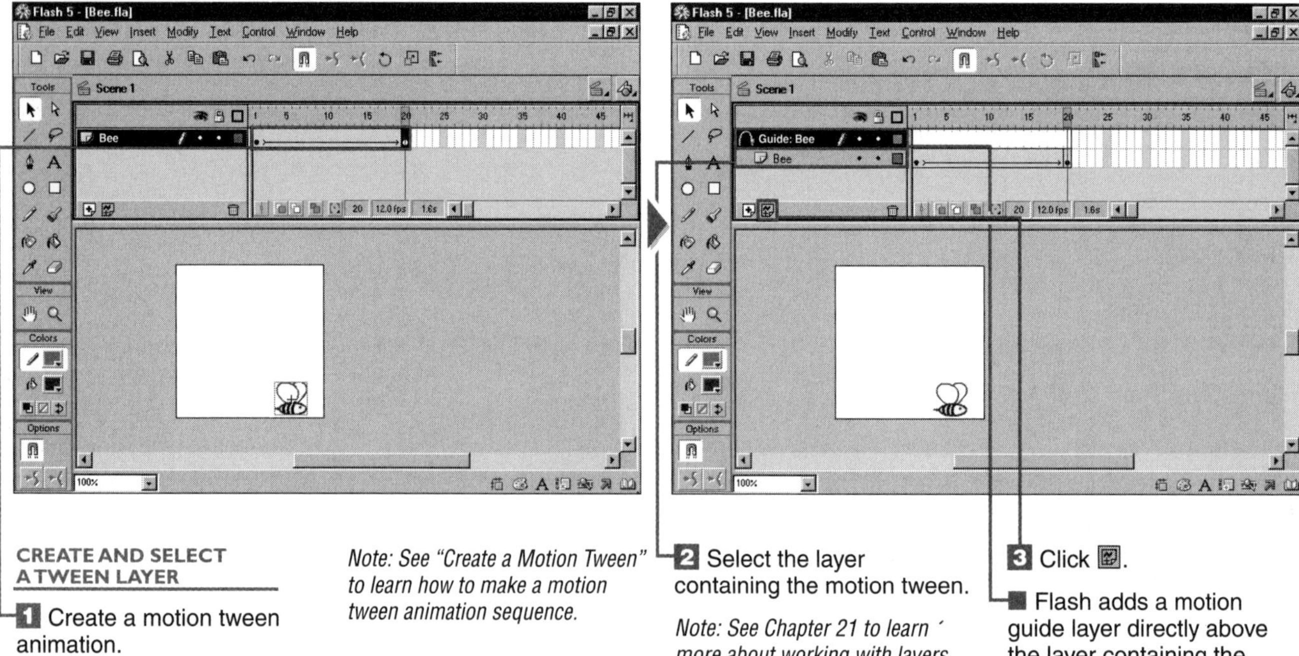

CREATE AND SELECT A TWEEN LAYER

1 Create a motion tween animation.

Note: See "Create a Motion Tween" to learn how to make a motion tween animation sequence.

2 Select the layer containing the motion tween.

Note: See Chapter 21 to learn more about working with layers.

3 Click [icon].

■ Flash adds a motion guide layer directly above the layer containing the motion tween.

Does it matter which line color or thickness I use to draw the motion path?

✔ You can use any line color or attributes you like for the motion path. To make the line easy to see, consider using a thicker line style in a bright color. Be sure to set the line attributes before you start drawing the motion path. Click [icon], click the Stroke tab, and then adjust the settings to your liking. See Chapter 18 to learn more about changing line attributes.

What Drawing tools can I use to define a path?

✔ You can use any of the following Drawing tools to add a path to the motion guide layer: Pencil, Brush, Line, Oval, or Rectangle. For example, to make a symbol follow a perfect loop around the Stage, use the Oval tool to draw the motion path, creating a large circular line for the path to follow. Make sure you turn off the Fill feature when drawing a path with the Oval or Rectangle tools.

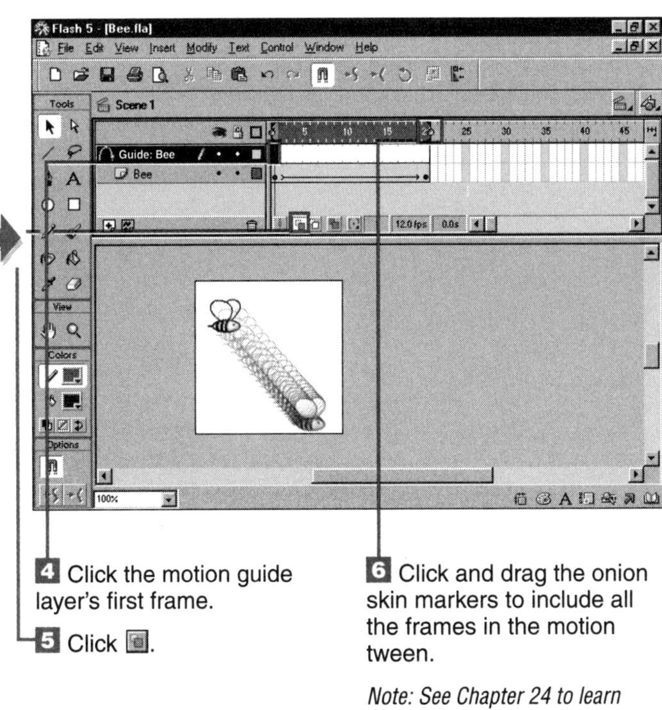

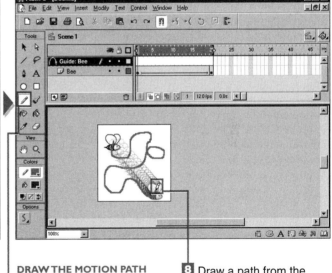

4 Click the motion guide layer's first frame.

5 Click [icon].

6 Click and drag the onion skin markers to include all the frames in the motion tween.

Note: See Chapter 24 to learn more about the onion-skinning feature.

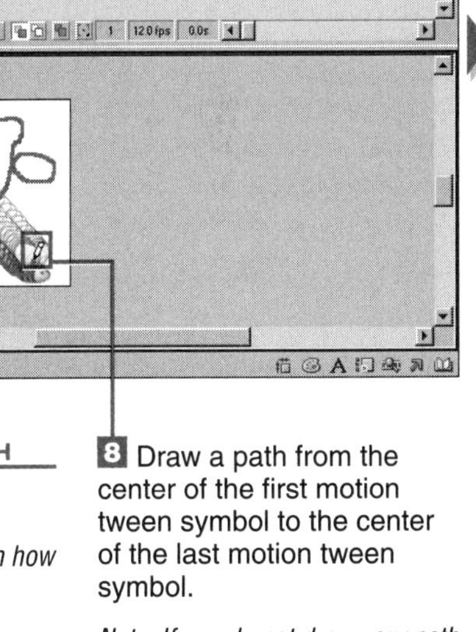

DRAW THE MOTION PATH

7 Click [icon].

Note: See Chapter 18 to learn how to draw with the Pencil tool.

8 Draw a path from the center of the first motion tween symbol to the center of the last motion tween symbol.

Note: If you do not draw your path from center to center, the symbol cannot follow the motion path.

CONTINUED

ANIMATE SYMBOLS ALONG A PATH (CONTINUED)

You can make your motion tween follow any type of path, whether it is extremely curvy, it loops back on itself, or even if it falls out of the movie area's boundaries. The motion guide path you create does not appear in your final movie. Instead, the symbol appears to move along a path on its own accord.

Starting and ending your path directly in the center of the symbol you are animating is very important. Do not stop your path line when you reach the edge of the object; continue it on to the middle of the object and then stop the path line.

In addition, you must also make sure that you select the Snap option in the Frame panel. This feature sticks the symbol to the path, much like a magnet. Without the Snap feature turned on, the symbol may not properly follow the path you have established.

ANIMATE SYMBOLS ALONG A PATH (CONTINUED)

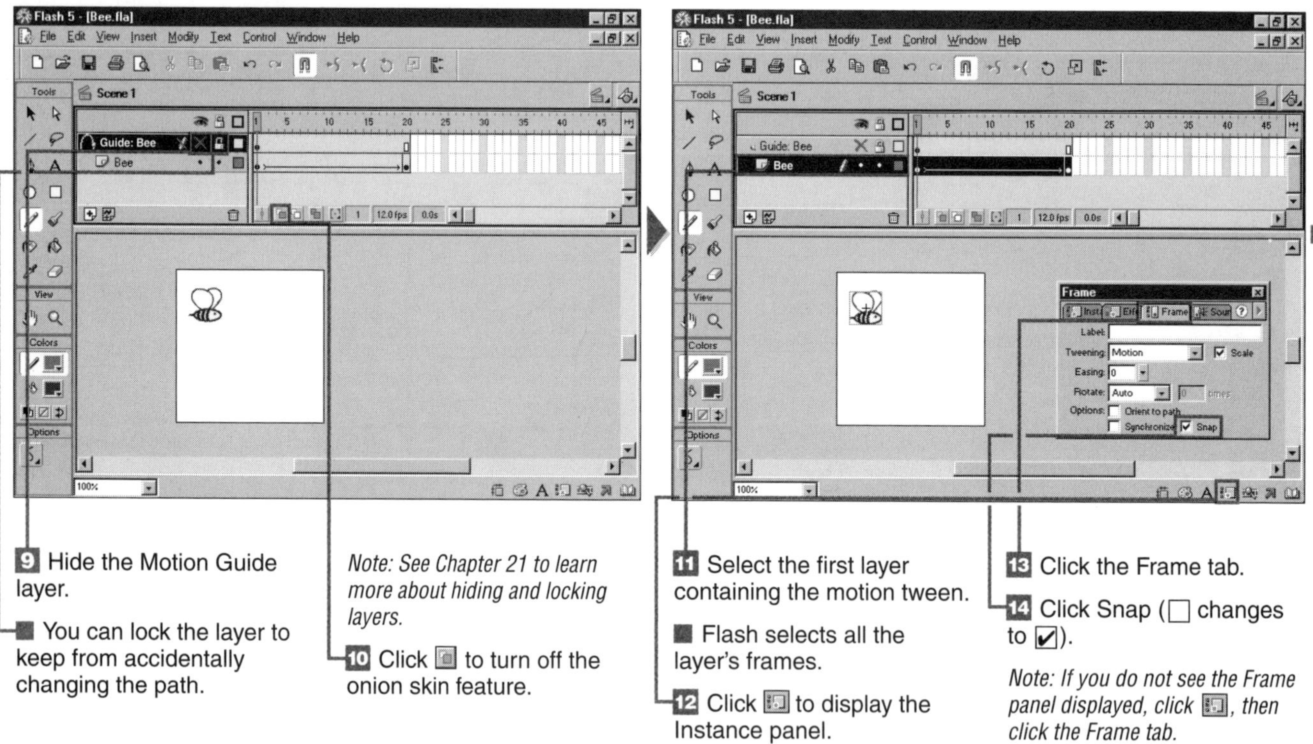

9 Hide the Motion Guide layer.

■ You can lock the layer to keep from accidentally changing the path.

Note: See Chapter 21 to learn more about hiding and locking layers.

10 Click ▣ to turn off the onion skin feature.

11 Select the first layer containing the motion tween.

■ Flash selects all the layer's frames.

12 Click ▣ to display the Instance panel.

13 Click the Frame tab.

14 Click Snap (☐ changes to ☑).

Note: If you do not see the Frame panel displayed, click ▣, then click the Frame tab.

What does the Orient to Path option do?

✔ To make your symbol orient itself to the motion path you have drawn, click the Orient to path check box. The Orient to path option aligns the symbol to the path, regardless of which direction it goes. Sometimes, the effect makes the symbol's movement seem unnatural. To remedy the situation, you can insert extra keyframes in the animation sequence and rotate the symbol to where you want it on the path. Flash recalculates the in-between frames for you. To learn more about rotating objects, see Chapter 19. To learn how to rotate animated symbols, see "Animate by Rotating a Symbol."

Can I make my motion tween speed up?

✔ Yes. You can use the Ease setting in the Frame panel to speed up the start of your motion tween as it follows the motion path. Drag the Ease slider up to start the object quickly along the motion path or drag the slider down to slow the object down.

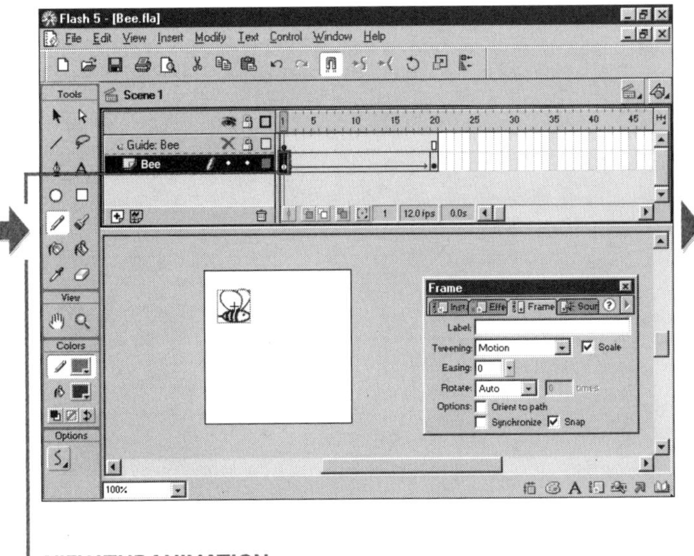

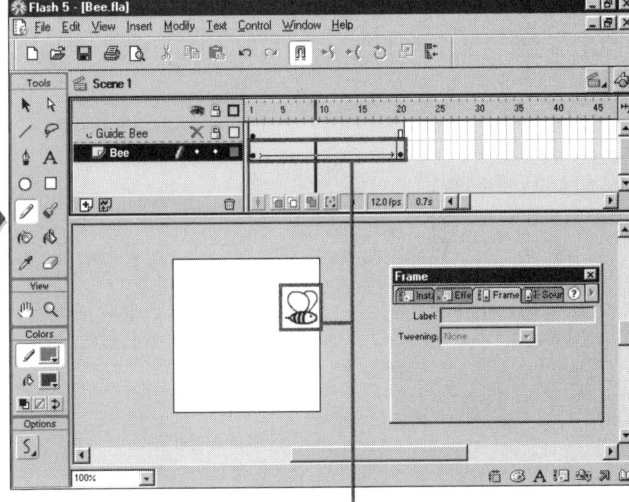

VIEW THE ANIMATION

15 Click in the first frame of the motion tween.

16 Press Enter (Windows) or Return (Mac).

■ Flash plays the animation sequence along the motion path.

SET TWEEN SPEED

You can control a tweened animation's speed by using the Flash Ease control. Found in the Frame panel, the Ease control enables you to speed up or slow down the tween effect.

You may have learned in some of the previous sections that you can slow down or speed up an animation sequence by subtracting or adding frames. The addition or subtraction of regular frames between two keyframes does not affect tween speed. With a motion tween, Flash distributes the incremental changes between the two keyframes evenly over the regular frames, regardless of how many frames are in between. However, you can control the effects of a tween sequence using the Ease control.

The Ease control enables you to slow down or speed up the beginning or end of your tween effect. For example, perhaps you have a bumblebee symbol that lands on a flower symbol in your movie. You may prefer the bee to fly quickly at the beginning of your motion tween, but slow down right before it lands on the flower symbol.

See "Create a Motion Tween" earlier in this chapter to learn more about the motion tween effect.

SET TWEEN SPEED

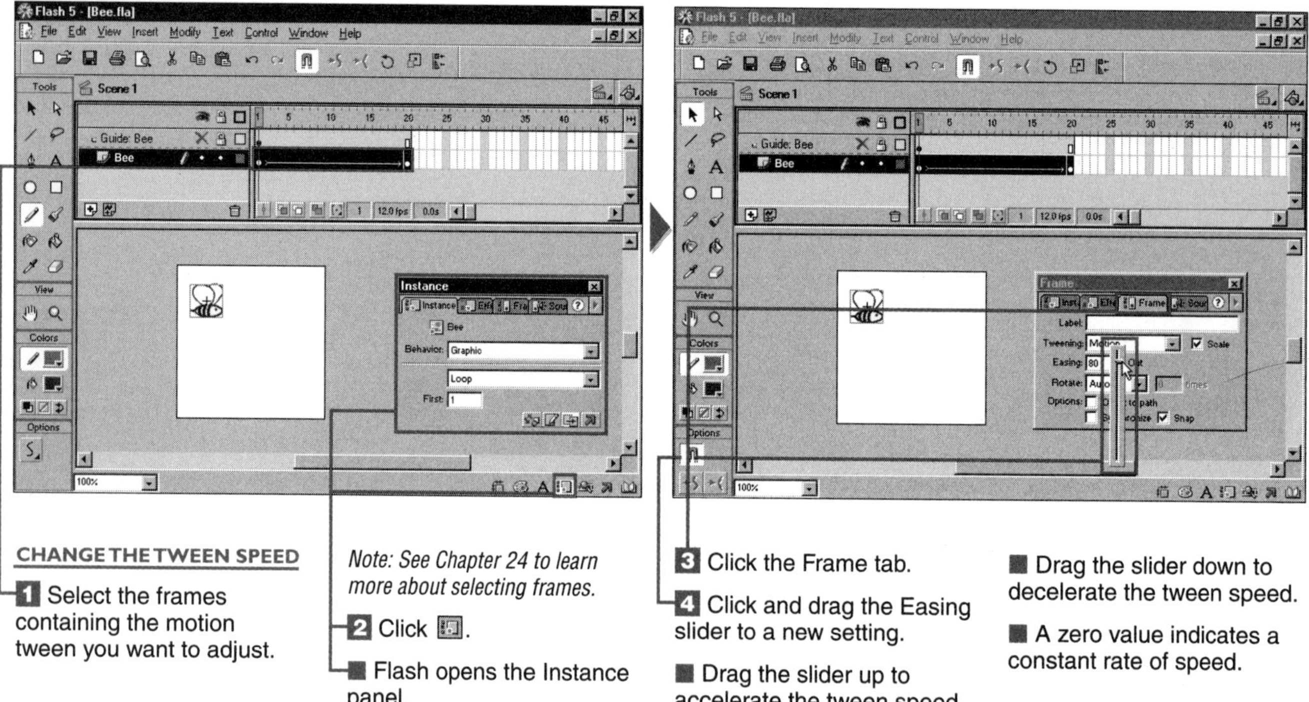

CHANGE THE TWEEN SPEED

1 Select the frames containing the motion tween you want to adjust.

Note: See Chapter 24 to learn more about selecting frames.

2 Click .

■ Flash opens the Instance panel.

3 Click the Frame tab.

4 Click and drag the Easing slider to a new setting.

■ Drag the slider up to accelerate the tween speed.

■ Drag the slider down to decelerate the tween speed.

■ A zero value indicates a constant rate of speed.

Does tween speed affect frames per second (fps)?

✔ No. Tweening distributes the animation evenly between the two keyframes. When you adjust the Ease control to a setting other than the default 0, it merely accelerates or decelerates the beginning or end of the tween. It does not affect the movie's frames per second rate.

Which direction do I drag the Ease control to slow down my effect?

✔ The Ease control slider drags up or down in the Frame panel. If you drag the slider up, the setting results in the animated object starting quickly and slowing down at the end of the sequence. If you drag the slider down, the animated object starts slowly and then speeds up at the end of the sequence.

Can I add a label to my tween effect?

✔ Yes. You can add frame labels to help you identify areas where you have applied a tween and designate exactly which tween it is. To add a frame label, click the keyframe that starts the tween effect, and then open the Frame panel. Click inside the Label text box and type a name for the tween. Press Enter and the label is assigned to the keyframe.

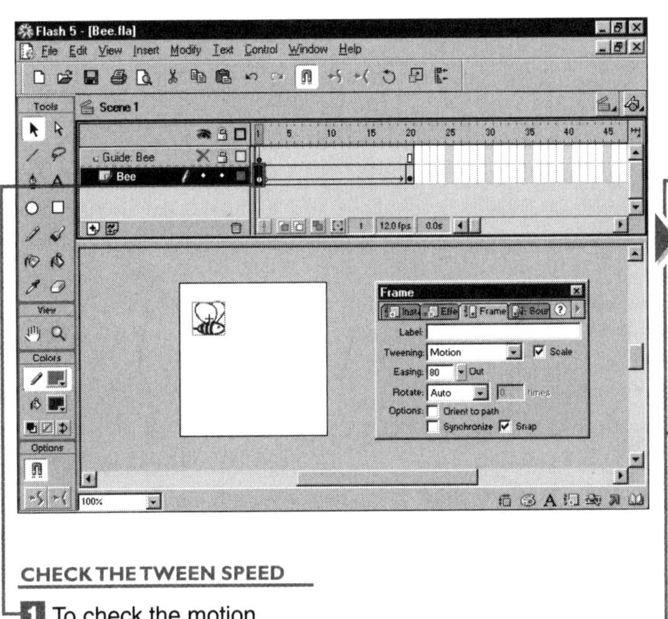

CHECK THE TWEEN SPEED

1 To check the motion tween speed, click in the first frame of the motion tween.

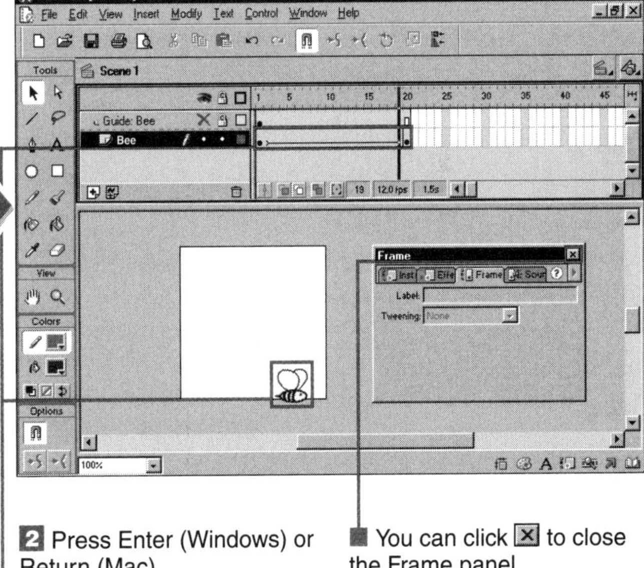

2 Press Enter (Windows) or Return (Mac).

■ Flash plays the animation sequence.

■ You can click ☒ to close the Frame panel.

CREATE A SHAPE TWEEN

You can create a shape tween to morph objects you draw on the Stage. For example, you can morph a circle shape into a square or turn your company logo into a graphic depicting a product. Unlike other animations you create in Flash, shape tweening does not require the use of symbols or groups. You can animate any object you draw with the Drawing tools using the shape tween effect.

Like the motion tween effect, you define two keyframes when applying a shape tween. The first keyframe shows the beginning state of the object you want to morph. The last keyframe in the sequence shows the end state of the shape tween, the object in its morphed state. When the shape tween is applied, Flash calculates all the necessary frames in between to create the morphing effect.

See "Create a Motion Tween" earlier in this chapter to learn more about the motion tween effect.

CREATE A SHAPE TWEEN

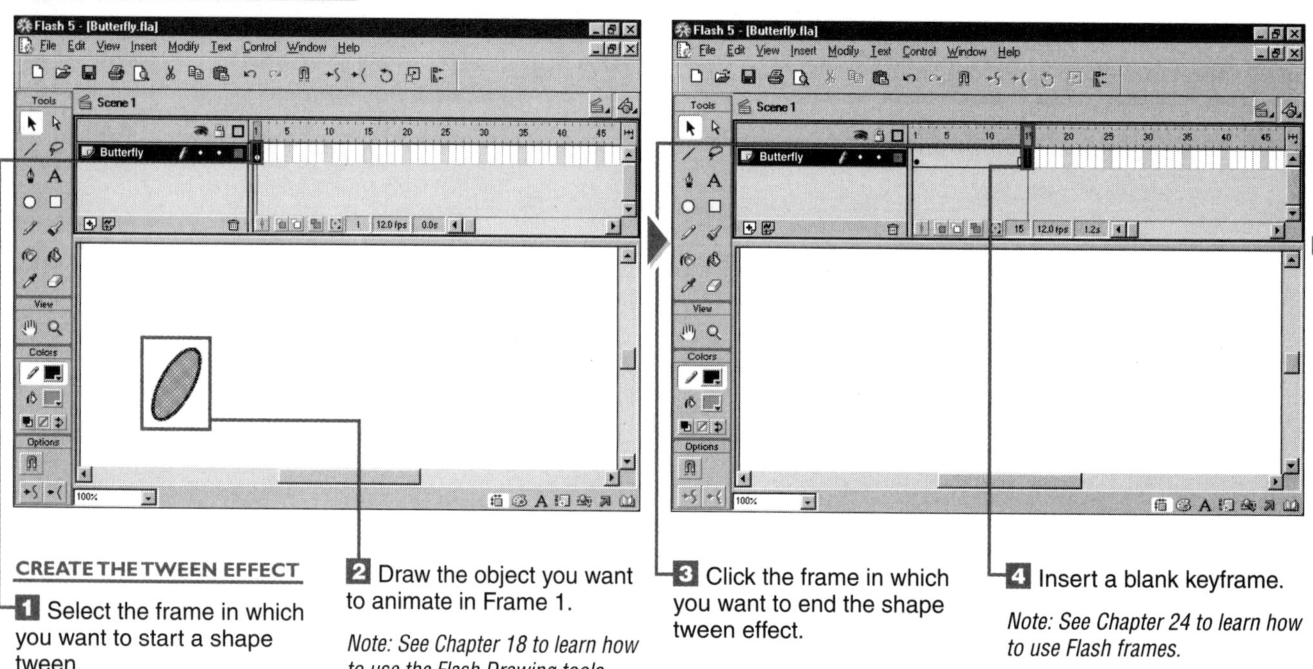

CREATE THE TWEEN EFFECT

1 Select the frame in which you want to start a shape tween.

2 Draw the object you want to animate in Frame 1.

Note: See Chapter 18 to learn how to use the Flash Drawing tools.

3 Click the frame in which you want to end the shape tween effect.

4 Insert a blank keyframe.

Note: See Chapter 24 to learn how to use Flash frames.

How is a shape tween different from a motion tween?

✔ With a motion tween, you can animate only symbols, grouped objects, or text blocks. With a shape tween, you can animate any object you draw on the Stage. You do not have to save it as a symbol first or group it in order for Flash to create in-between frames. You cannot shape tween a symbol or group. Although a motion tween is good for moving objects from one point to another, you should use a shape tween when you want to morph the object into another object entirely.

Can I control the speed of the shape tween?

✔ Yes. By default, Flash spreads out the incremental changes in the shape tween effect evenly among the in-between frames. By applying the Ease control, however, you can speed up or slow down the beginning or end of the shape tween. The Ease control works the same way for shape tween animations as it does for motion tween animations. You can find the Ease control in the Frame panel. For more information about how to apply the Ease feature, see "Set Tween Speed" earlier in this chapter.

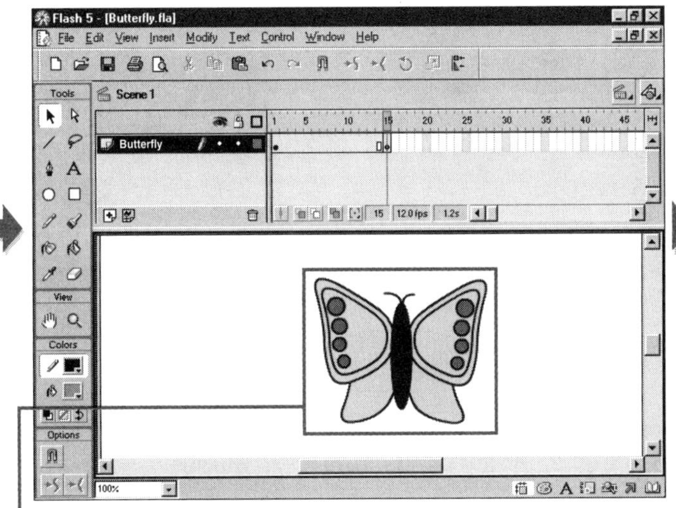

5 Draw the shape into which you want your image to morph, such as a variation of the first frame's shape, or an entirely different shape.

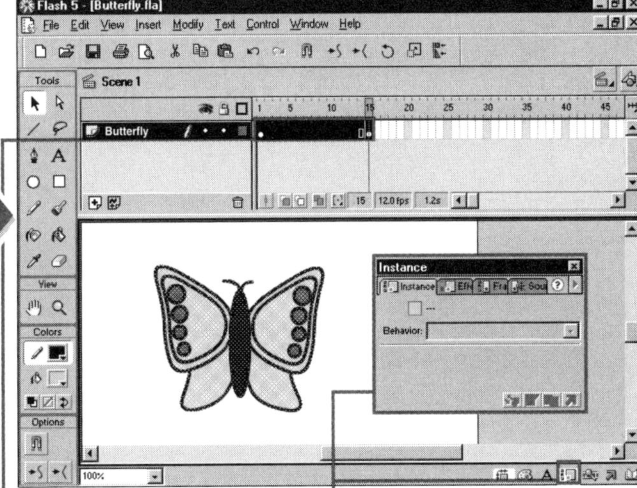

6 Click a frame between the two keyframes that make up your motion tween to select the frames that comprise the shape tween.

Note: See Chapter 24 to learn how to select frames.

7 Click [icon].

■ Flash opens the Instance panel.

CONTINUED

CREATE A SHAPE TWEEN (CONTINUED)

You can use shape tweens to morph between all kinds of objects you draw, including text that you turn into an object. You can use as many shape tweens as you like in an animation, and you can start one right after the other in the Timeline.

For best results, tween one shape at a time in your Flash movie. Doing so gives you greater control over the object and the tween effect.

When defining a shape tween, the Frame panel has a blending option to help you create just the right look for your effect. You can apply two types of blends to your shape: Distributive or Angular. If you apply a Distributive blend, Flash smoothes out the straight lines and sharp corners as your shape morphs. If you choose an Angular blend, Flash keeps all the sharp angles and lines intact during the tween.

CREATE A SHAPE TWEEN (CONTINUED)

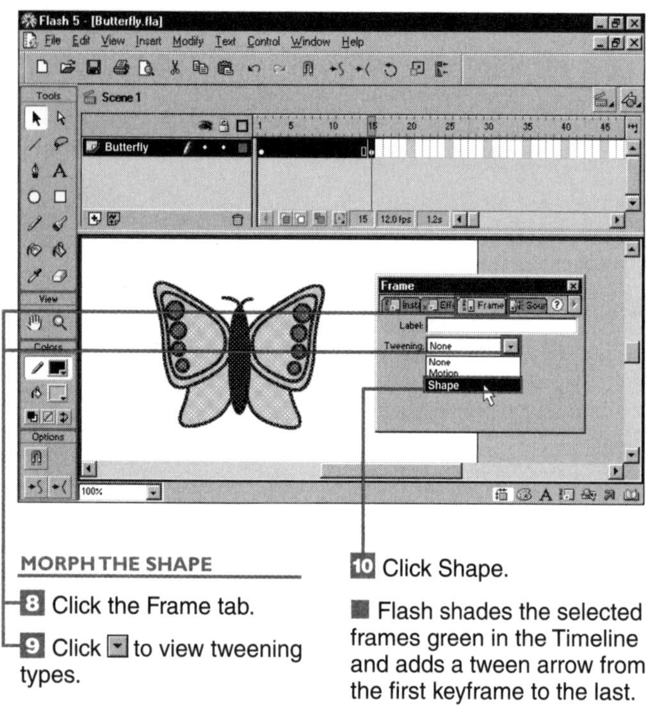

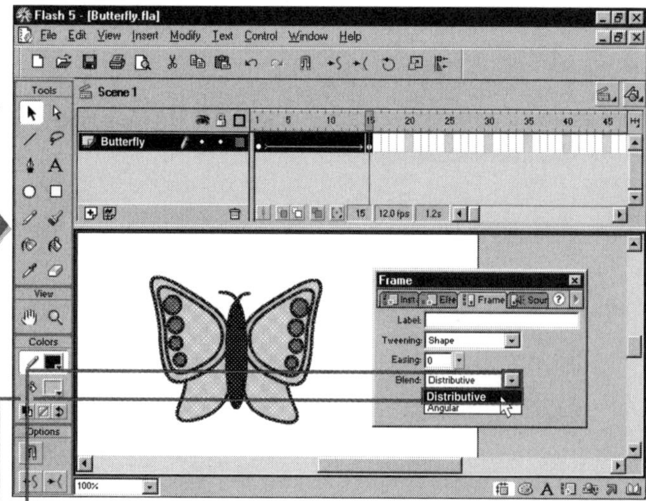

MORPH THE SHAPE

8 Click the Frame tab.

9 Click ▾ to view tweening types.

10 Click Shape.

■ Flash shades the selected frames green in the Timeline and adds a tween arrow from the first keyframe to the last.

11 Click ▾ to view blend types.

12 Click a blend type.

■ You can use the Distributive blend to smooth out lines in the in-between frames.

■ You can use the Angular blend to keep the sharp corners and straight lines that occur during the morph effect.

Can I use a symbol from my movie's Library?

✔ Yes, but you must convert it first. You cannot shape tween symbols, but you can take a symbol and break it apart into objects that the shape tween effect can morph. To turn a symbol into an object, place the symbol on the Stage (see Chapter 22), click Modify, and click Break Apart.

Depending on how many groups of objects comprise the symbol, you may need to select the command several times to reach the last level of ungrouped objects.

Can I tween multiple shapes on the Stage?

✔ Yes. However, all the shapes must be on the same layer. Remember, Flash cannot tween symbols or grouped shapes.

Can I quickly lengthen my shape tween?

✔ Yes. Just drag the end keyframe to lengthen the tween effect. Flash automatically recalculates the new in-between frames for you.

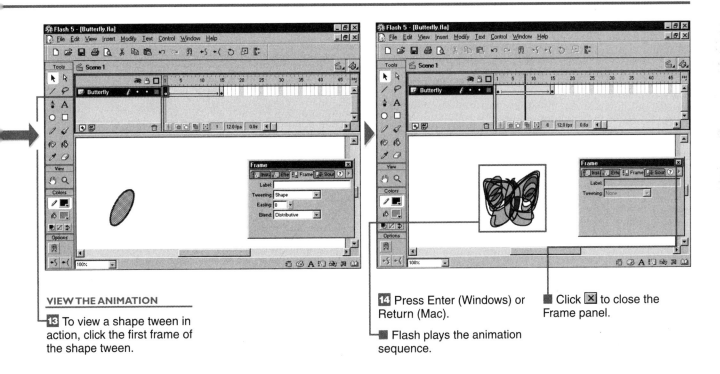

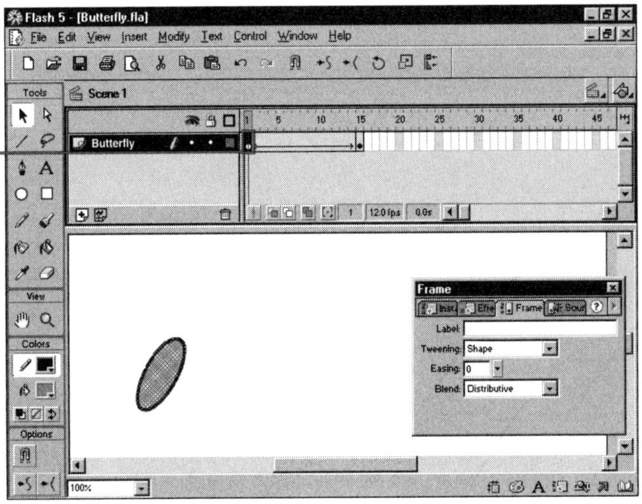

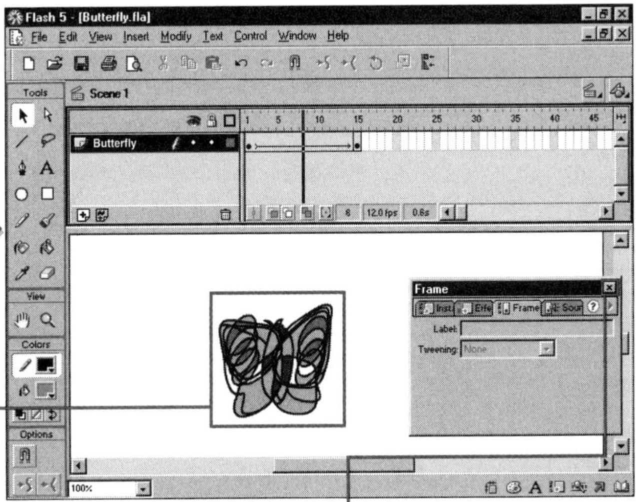

VIEW THE ANIMATION

13 To view a shape tween in action, click the first frame of the shape tween.

14 Press Enter (Windows) or Return (Mac).

■ Flash plays the animation sequence.

■ Click ☒ to close the Frame panel.

USING SHAPE HINTS

You can help Flash determine how to morph shapes during a shape tween by adding *shape hints.* A shape hint is a marker that identifies areas on the original shape that match up with areas on the final shape and mark crucial points of change. Shape hints are labeled *a* through *z*, which means you can use up to 26 shape hints in a shape tween.

Use shape hints when you are morphing a particularly complex shape. For example, perhaps you are shape tweening a company logo and turning it into a picture of your top-selling product, or perhaps you are shape tweening a cartoon character into a completely different character for a Web page. By assigning shape hints to the object you are morphing, you can help Flash figure out points of change.

Shape hints appear as tiny numbers in a circle icon, starting out yellow in the first keyframe of the sequence and turning green in the end keyframe. Shape hints are placed along the edges of the shape you are morphing, and must be placed in alphabetical order.

USING SHAPE HINTS

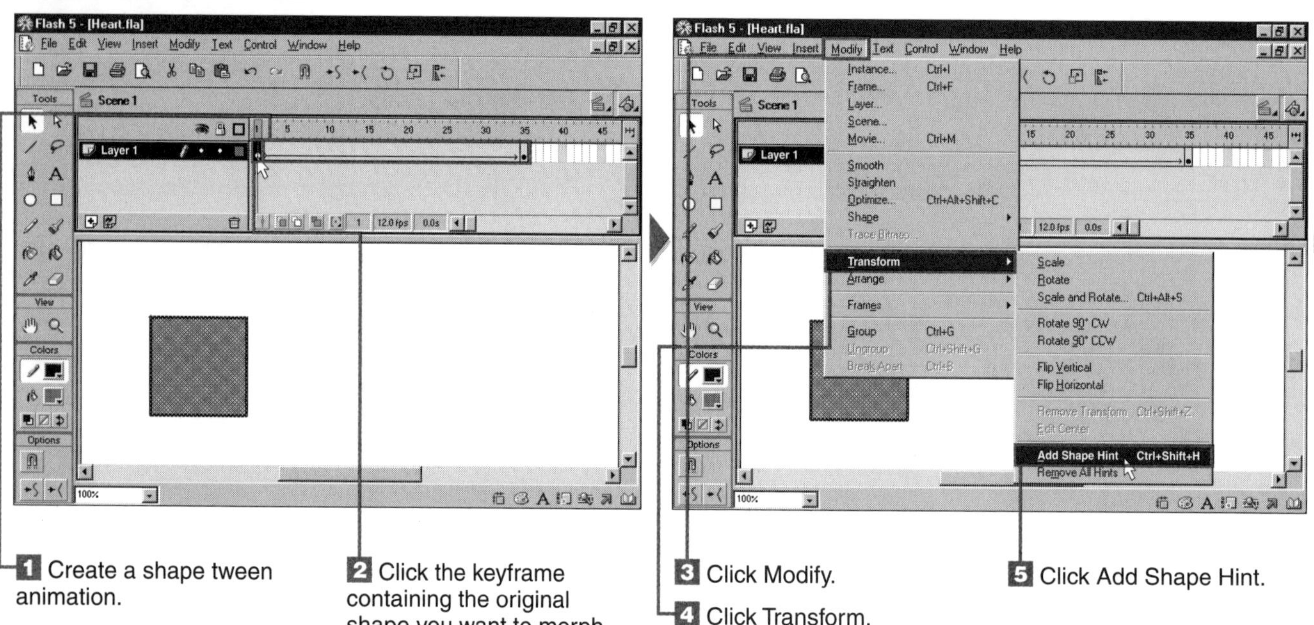

1 Create a shape tween animation.

Note: See "Create a Shape Tween" earlier in this chapter for details.

2 Click the keyframe containing the original shape you want to morph.

3 Click Modify.

4 Click Transform.

5 Click Add Shape Hint.

What can I do if my shape hints vary their positions between the first keyframe and the last?

✔ Seeing exactly where you place shape hints around an object is not always easy. To help you, first make sure you have magnified your view so that you can see where you place the hints. Use the View drop-down list at the bottom of the Stage area to set a magnification. Next, turn on the onion-skinning feature and move the onion-skinning markers to show all the frames within the shape tween. Click ▣ to turn on the outlining feature. See Chapter 8 to learn more about onion skinning.

What if shape hints still do not help create the morphing effect I am looking for?

✔ If this happens, you may want to try creating a few intermediate shapes to assist Flash in determining how to morph the shape. For example, if you are shape-tweening a complex shape that includes lots of details around the edges, you can add a few keyframes that contain key changes in the shape rather than relying on just a starting keyframe and an ending keyframe to complete the tween.

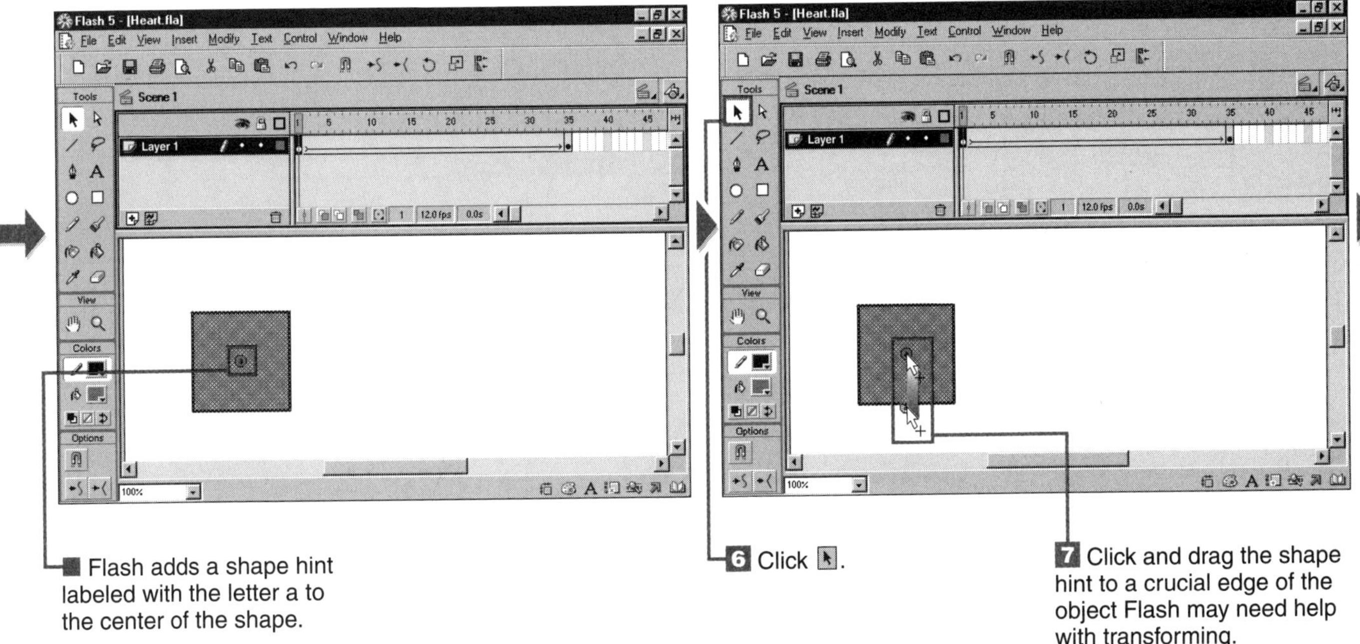

■ Flash adds a shape hint labeled with the letter a to the center of the shape.

6 Click ▶.

7 Click and drag the shape hint to a crucial edge of the object Flash may need help with transforming.

CONTINUED

USING SHAPE HINTS (CONTINUED)

The more shape hints you add to the shape tween, the smoother the morphing transformation will be. You can use as many as 26 hints on your shape. When determining where to place your shape hints, position them at key areas of change around the edges of the shape. For example, to morph a heart into a star shape, you can place shape hints at all the edges where the points of the star appear as well as where points are recessed to create the star shape.

You must also make sure that the shape hints you place around the object in the second keyframe correspond with the same order of shape hints on the object in the first keyframe. If you do not use the order that you used in the first keyframe, the effect does not work properly.

For best results, assign shape hints counterclockwise around the edges of the shape, starting with the upper-left corner of the shape. Use the onion-skinning feature to help you see how the shape changes across the animation sequence. See Chapter 24 to learn more about the onion skin feature.

USING SHAPE HINTS (CONTINUED)

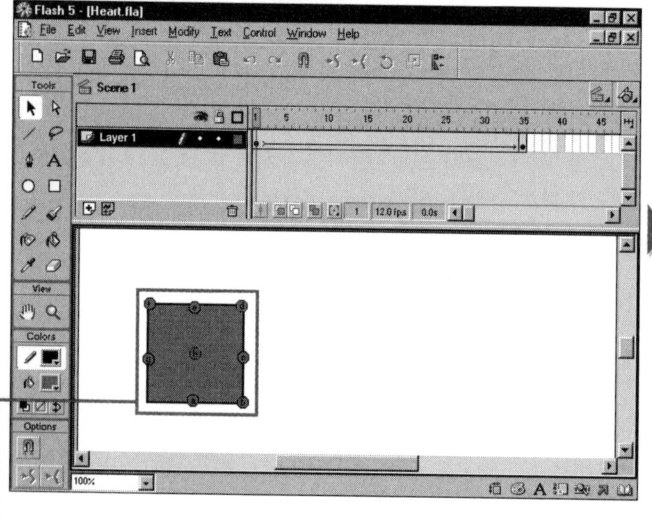

8 Repeat steps 3 through 7 to continue adding shape hints to other areas on the shape that can assist Flash with morphing the final shape design.

Note: You must arrange shape hints around the shape's edge in alphabetical order going clockwise or counterclockwise.

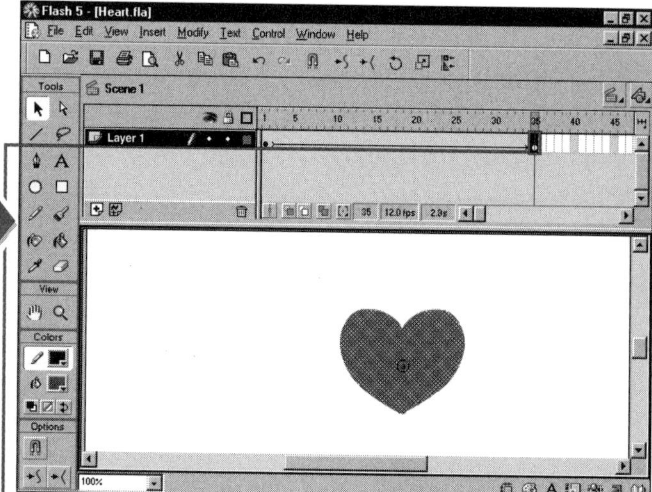

9 Click the last keyframe in the shape tween.

■ In this example, shape hints have been added to the final shape and stacked in the middle of the shape.

How do I remove a shape hint?

✔ To delete a shape hint, click and drag the shape hint completely off the Stage area. To rid the keyframe of all the shape hints, click the Modify menu, click Transform, and then click Remove All Hints.

Can I see all the shape hints for my shape tween effect?

✔ Yes. Make sure that you are currently viewing the layer containing the tween effect. Click the View menu and click Show Shape Hints.

I am having trouble making sure I place the hints in the right place. What can I do?

✔ Although it is tedious, one way to keep your shape hints straight is to switch back and forth between the two keyframes as you add them. This way you can be sure that you placed both hints in the same spot.

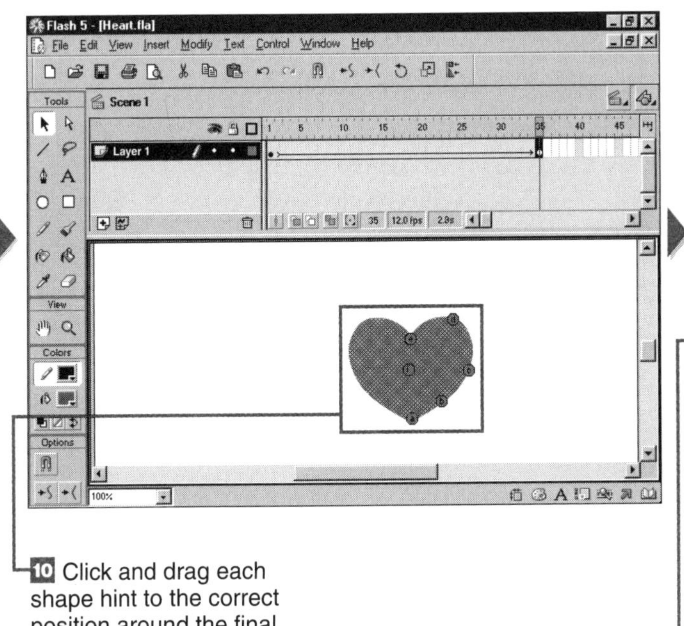

10 Click and drag each shape hint to the correct position around the final shape.

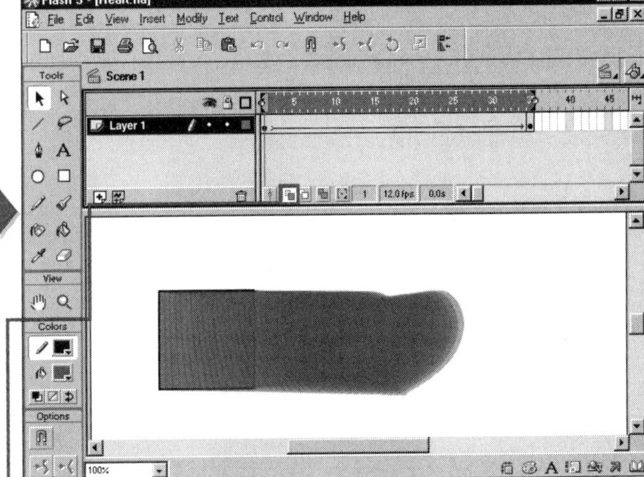

■ You can adjust the shape hints in the final frame as needed.

■ Clicking ▣ lets you see how the in-between frames morph the shape as directed by the shape hints.

■ You can play the movie to see the animation on the Stage.

Note: See "Create a Shape Tween" earlier in this chapter to learn about viewing animations on the Stage.

USING REVERSE FRAMES

You can save some animating time by reusing frames in your movie. For example, if you create a motion tween that makes a symbol grow in size, you can reverse the frame sequence to create the opposite effect in the second half of the animation. All it takes is an application of the Reverse Frames command.

Use the Reverse Frames feature to quickly repeat an animation sequence in the opposite order. For example, perhaps you have a flag logo that waves or a candle symbol that has a flickering flame. You can copy the sequence and make it play in its reverse. This saves you from having to create another animation sequence for the backwards effect.

You can also apply the Reverse Frames command any time you want to reorder the frames to play the other way around.

USING REVERSE FRAMES

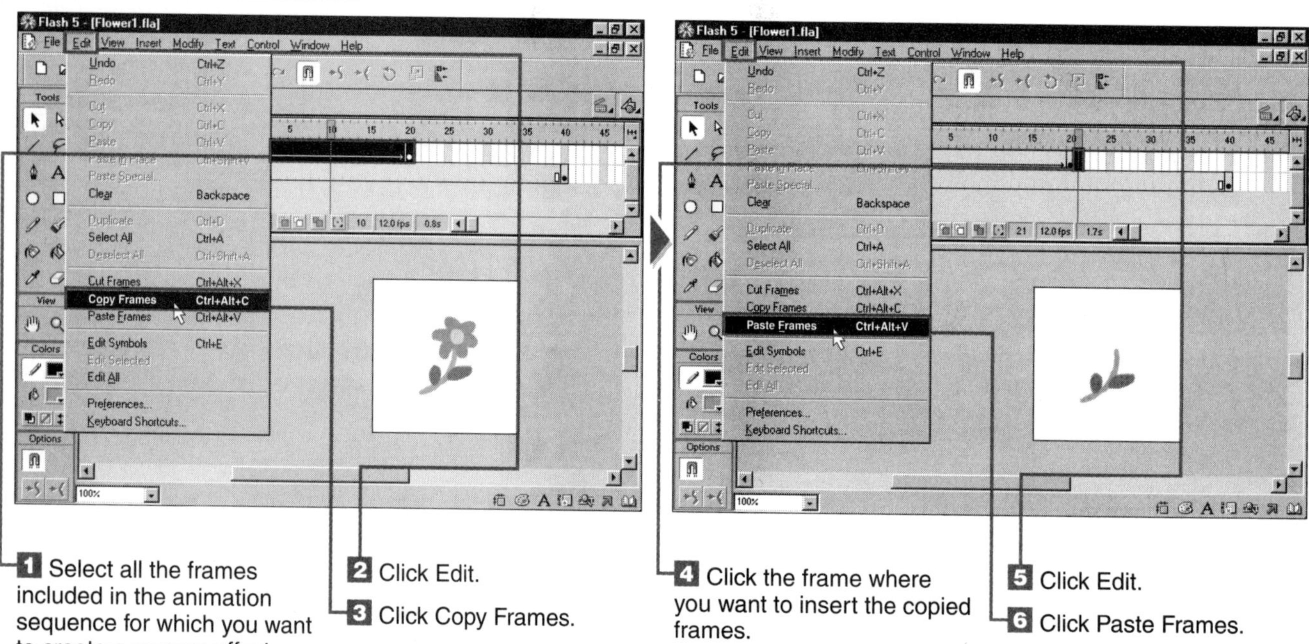

1 Select all the frames included in the animation sequence for which you want to create a reverse effect.

2 Click Edit.

3 Click Copy Frames.

4 Click the frame where you want to insert the copied frames.

5 Click Edit.

6 Click Paste Frames.

How do I check to see whether the reverse frames work?

✔ One way to check is to open the Flash Player window and test the movie. Click the Control menu and click Test Movie. The Flash Player window opens and plays the sequence. To stop the movie, press Enter. To close the Player window, click ☒.

How else can I activate the Reverse Frames command?

✔ Right click the frames and a pop-up menu appears with frame-related commands, including the Reverse Frames, Copy Frames, and Paste Frames commands.

How do I reverse a reverse?

✔ You can immediately undo the Reverse Frames command if you click the Undo button (↶) on the Main toolbar. Make sure that you do this immediately after that you realize you are not happy with the animation results.

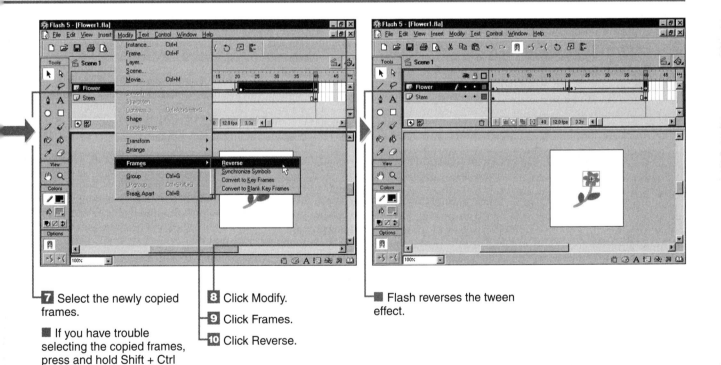

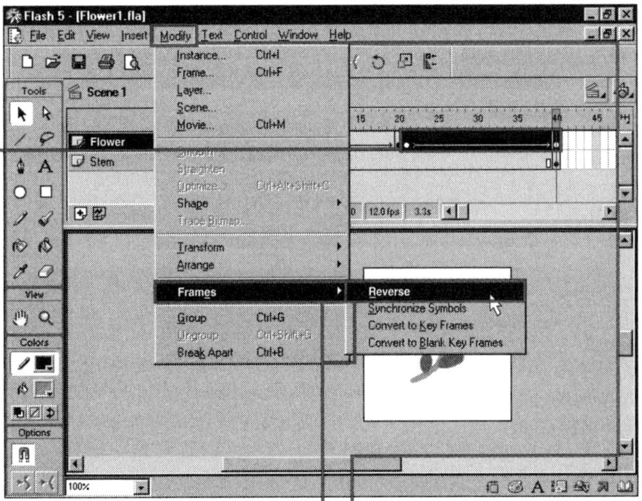

7 Select the newly copied frames.

■ If you have trouble selecting the copied frames, press and hold Shift + Ctrl while clicking the frames.

8 Click Modify.

9 Click Frames.

10 Click Reverse.

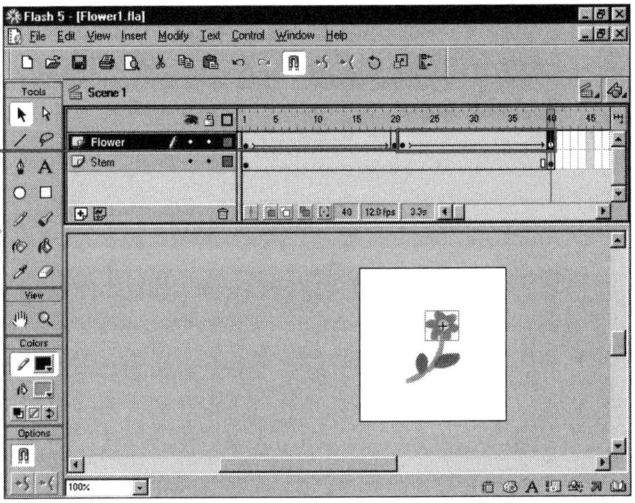

■ Flash reverses the tween effect.

UNDERSTANDING FLASH BUTTONS

A popular way to enable users to interact with your Flash movies is through the use of *rollover buttons*. You can create a simple button that changes in appearance when the user rolls the mouse pointer over it, and changes appearance again when the user clicks it. Buttons are commonly employed on Web pages. You can create buttons in Flash that are static (still) or animated (seem to be moving).

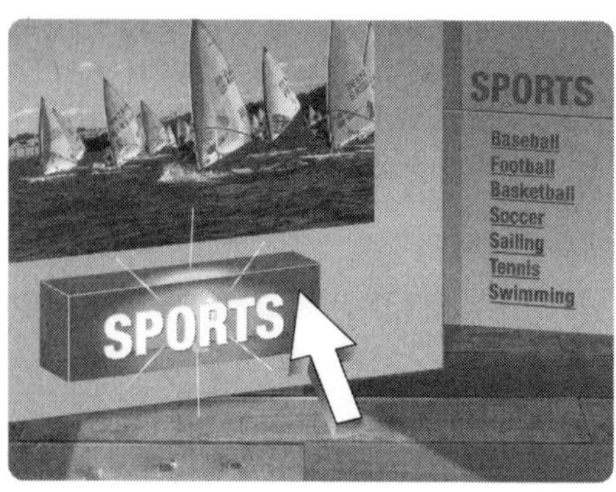

Buttons are Symbols

Buttons are a type of symbol to which Flash assigns *behaviors*. The behaviors are based on what happens when the mouse pointer interacts with the button. You can assign Flash actions to a button that trigger an action such as Get URL or Load Movie. See Chapter 28 to learn more about assigning Flash actions.

You can turn any symbol you create in Flash into a button symbol or you can create a new button from scratch. You can custom-make a button shape that includes text specific to the interactive task the user performs. Flash even comes with a few pre-drawn buttons you can use, found in the Buttons Library. You can also use different symbols for different stages of the button. For example, the button, labeled "Click Here," may appear as a gray box when it is inactive, but it may become a cartoon character when the user moves the mouse over the button.

When you create a button, you need to think about how you want the button to behave when the user interacts with it. Do you want it static or animated? Do you want it to make a sound? What do you want to happen when the user rolls over the button, clicks the button, and releases the button? You can make buttons as complex or as simple as you want. You must also determine the button's purpose. When you activate the button, what happens? Does it play a movie, stop a movie, or open a form?

Button Frames

There are four stages to a button: inactive, rollover, click, and release. The inactive stage is what the button looks like when not in use. For example, it may be an oval shape with the text "Submit" or "Stop." The rollover stage is what the button looks like when the user rolls over it with the mouse. The click stage is what the button looks like when the user clicks on it. The release stage is what the button looks like after the user has performed a click action. You can choose to make the button look the same for all four stages, or you can use different symbols for some or all of the stages.

When you create a button in Flash, it comes with its own Timeline and four distinct frames: Up, Over, Down, and Hit. The four frames make up a mini-movie clip of the button's behavior. A button's timeline does not actually play like other Flash timelines, but rather jumps to the appropriate frame directed by the user's mouse action.

You decide what symbol to use in each frame of a button's Timeline. If you use different symbols in each frame (with the exception of the Hit frame), the button appears animated.

Up Frame

You use the Up frame to display the inactive button. This is the frame the user sees when the mouse pointer is not hovering over the button. By default, the Up frame has a keyframe added already in the button's timeline.

Over Frame

The Over frame displays what the button looks like when the mouse pointer moves, or "rolls" over the button. For example, you can make the button turn bright red or emit a sound when the user places the mouse pointer over it to indicate that the button is active.

Down Frame

The Down frame displays what the button looks like when a user clicks it.

Hit Frame

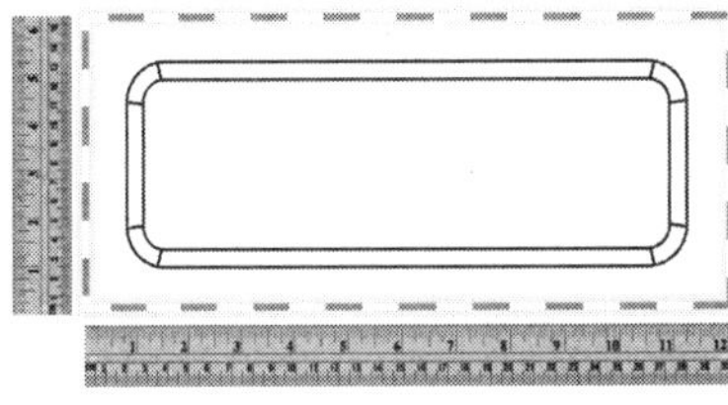

The Hit frame defines the button area or boundary as a whole. This frame is often the same size and shape as the image in the Over and Down frames. The Hit frame differs from the other button frames in that the user does not actually see it.

CREATE A BUTTON SYMBOL

You can turn any symbol into a button symbol in Flash. By assigning a button behavior to a symbol, you are turning it into an interactive element. You can then use the button in a movie frame, a Web page, or any other area where you want users to interact with your project. See the section "Understanding Flash Buttons" to learn more about button basics.

When you create a button, it includes a Timeline with four frames: Up, Over, Down, and Hit. You must assign an image or action to each of the four button states. You can make the image the same in each frame, or you can vary it to create the illusion of movement. You can make any object or drawing, such as a simple geometric shape, into a button that the user can easily identify and click. You may want to include a text block on the button shape that identifies the button or its purpose. See Chapters 18, 19, and 20 to learn more about creating drawings and text blocks in Flash.

CREATE A BUTTON SYMBOL

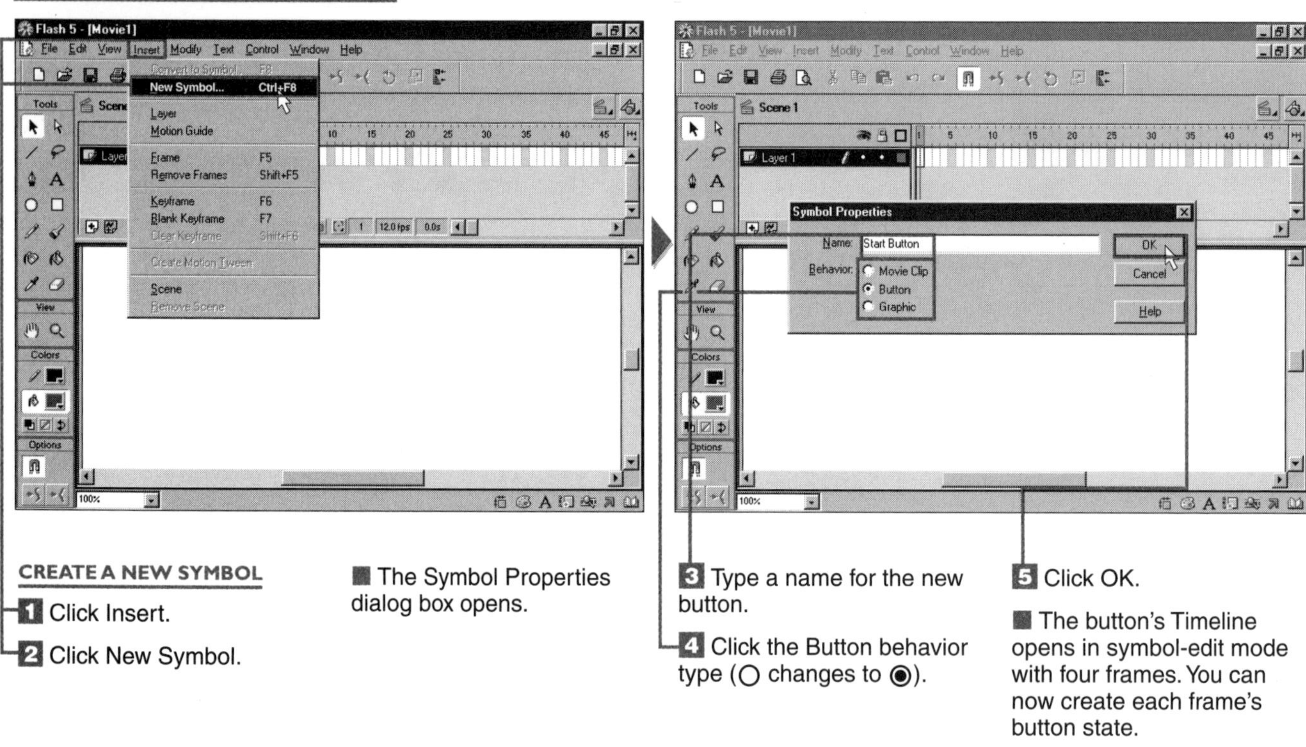

CREATE A NEW SYMBOL

1 Click Insert.

2 Click New Symbol.

■ The Symbol Properties dialog box opens.

3 Type a name for the new button.

4 Click the Button behavior type (○ changes to ◉).

5 Click OK.

■ The button's Timeline opens in symbol-edit mode with four frames. You can now create each frame's button state.

Does Flash have pre-made buttons I can use?

✔ Yes. Flash has several common libraries, including sounds, movie clips, and buttons. To display the button library, click Windows, Common Libraries, Buttons. The Buttons Library window appears. The Buttons Library works like the regular Library window See Chapter 22 to learn more about using the Library. Double-click a folder name to see a list of button types. You can preview a button by clicking its name. You can use a button from the library simply by dragging it off the Library window onto the Stage.

Can I use a button from another Flash file?

✔ Yes. If you have stored a button symbol in another Flash project, you can open the other file's Library window and place an instance of the symbol on the Stage. Click the File menu and click Open As Shared Library. This displays the Open As Shared Library dialog box. Double-click the Flash file you want to utilize. The associated Library window opens onscreen. You can now use any button symbol you have stored in the Library.

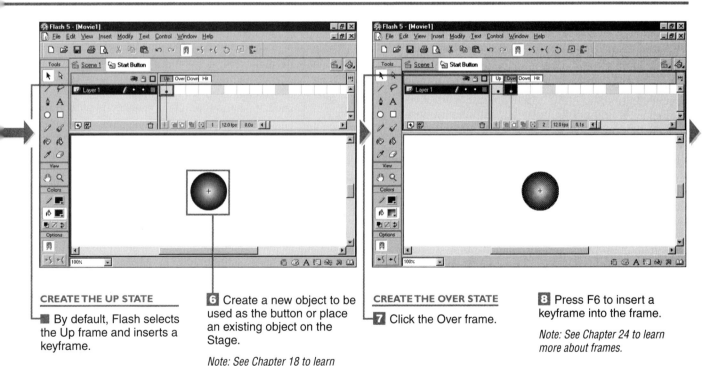

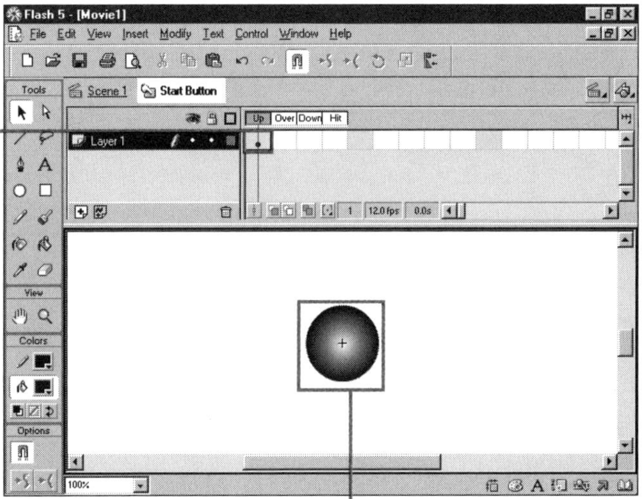

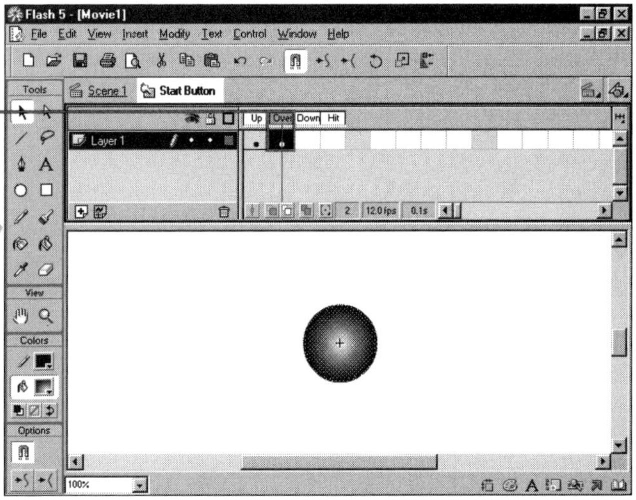

CREATE THE UP STATE

■ By default, Flash selects the Up frame and inserts a keyframe.

6 Create a new object to be used as the button or place an existing object on the Stage.

Note: See Chapter 18 to learn more about using the Flash drawing tools.

CREATE THE OVER STATE

7 Click the Over frame.

8 Press F6 to insert a keyframe into the frame.

Note: See Chapter 24 to learn more about frames.

CONTINUED

CREATE A BUTTON SYMBOL (CONTINUED)

When deciding what you want your button to look like, consider your audience. Are they technologically savvy enough to recognize the image you use as a button onscreen, or do you need to keep the button simple and easy to understand? Although it is sometimes tempting to use detailed drawings as buttons, simple geometric shapes are always reliable for a general audience. You can draw a new object to use as a button using any of the Flash drawing tools, or you can use an imported graphic as a button.

You can make even the simplest of buttons more exciting with a few variations. For example, if you duplicate the same object in each button frame, you can make minor changes so that the button appears different in each state. Or, you can change the color, scale, or shape for each keyframe.

CREATE A BUTTON SYMBOL (CONTINUED)

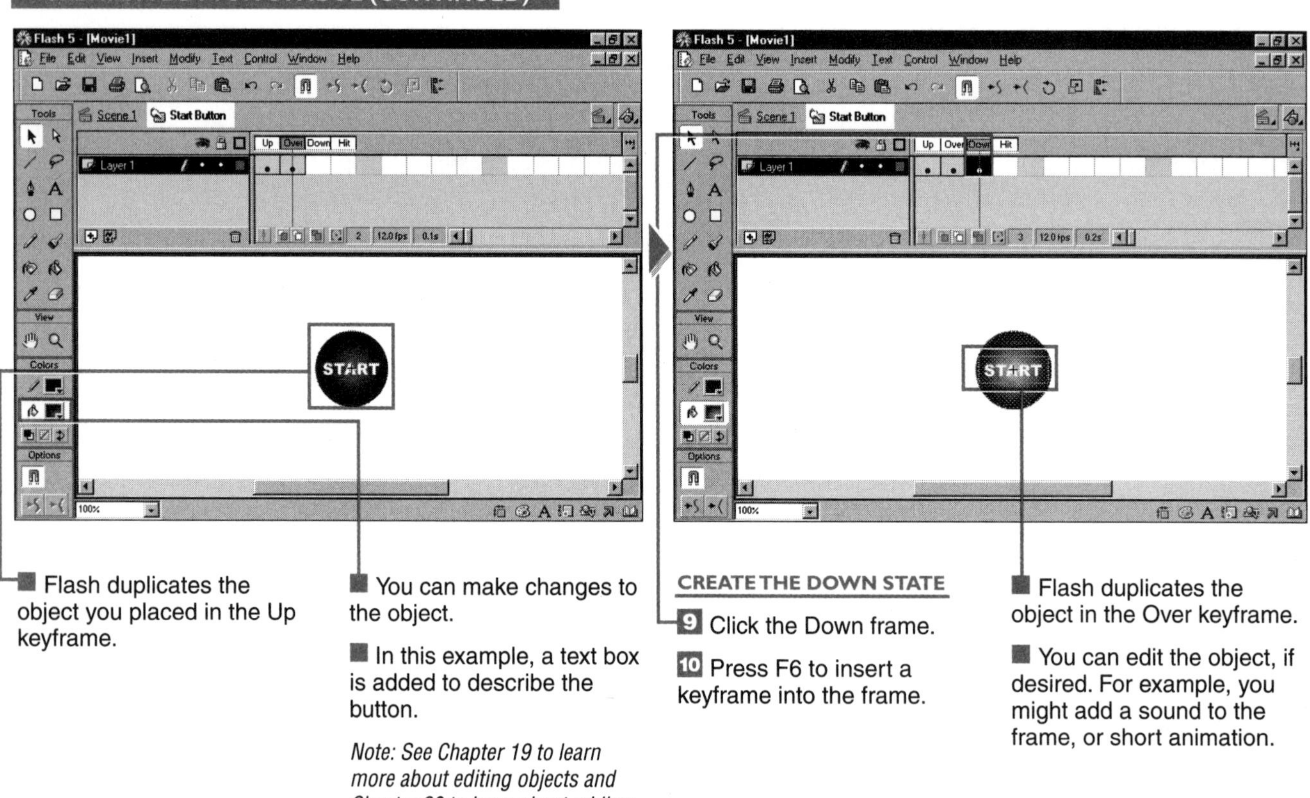

■ Flash duplicates the object you placed in the Up keyframe.

■ You can make changes to the object.

■ In this example, a text box is added to describe the button.

Note: See Chapter 19 to learn more about editing objects and Chapter 20 to learn about adding text.

CREATE THE DOWN STATE

9 Click the Down frame.

10 Press F6 to insert a keyframe into the frame.

■ Flash duplicates the object in the Over keyframe.

■ You can edit the object, if desired. For example, you might add a sound to the frame, or short animation.

What edit mode am I in?

✔ There are two edit modes in Flash: movie-edit mode and symbol-edit mode. Flash switches you to symbol-edit mode when you create a button. You can always tell when you are in symbol-edit mode if you see the name of the symbol to the right of the scene name at the top of the Timeline. To exit symbol-edit mode at any time, just click the scene name link. You can also exit symbol-edit mode by pressing Ctrl+E (Windows) or Command+E (Mac).

How do I close the Library window?

✔ Click the Show Library button (📖) to close the Library window, or simply click the window's Close button (☒).

How do I preview a button?

✔ In symbol-edit mode, click the button's Up frame, and then press Enter (Windows) or Return (Mac). Watch the Stage as Flash plays through the four button frames. Any changes made to frames appear during playback.

✔ You can preview the button in movie-edit mode by pressing Ctrl+Alt+B to activate the button on the Stage and moving the mouse pointer over the button and clicking it to see the rollover capabilities.

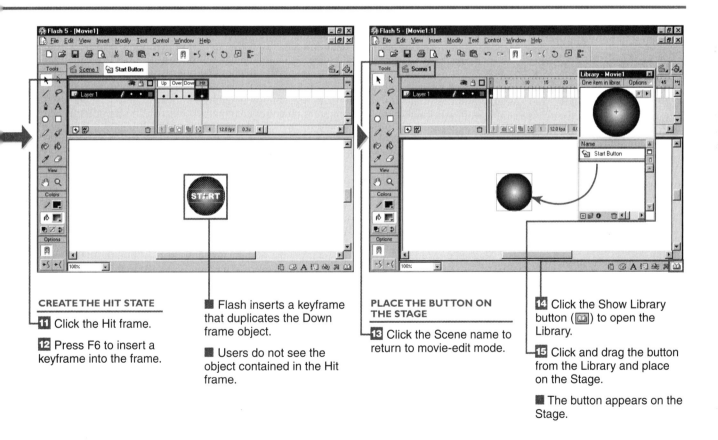

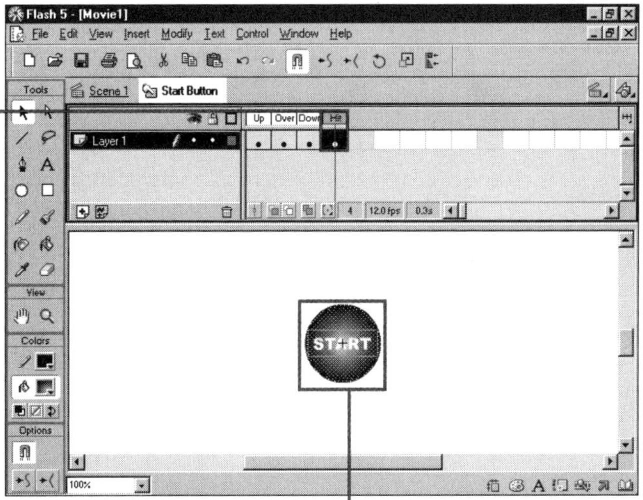

CREATE THE HIT STATE

11 Click the Hit frame.

12 Press F6 to insert a keyframe into the frame.

■ Flash inserts a keyframe that duplicates the Down frame object.

■ Users do not see the object contained in the Hit frame.

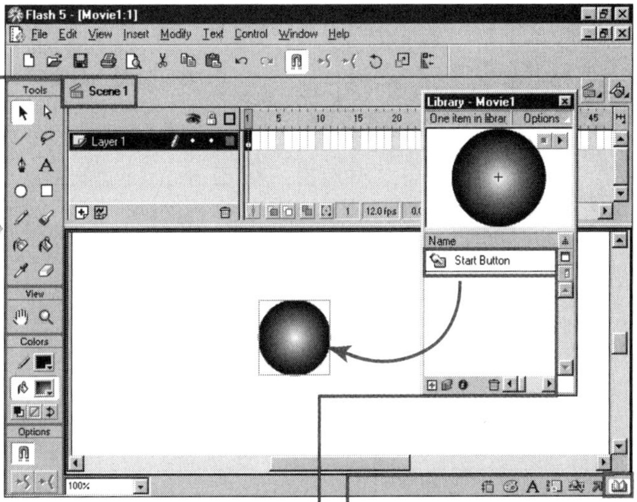

PLACE THE BUTTON ON THE STAGE

13 Click the Scene name to return to movie-edit mode.

14 Click the Show Library button (📖) to open the Library.

15 Click and drag the button from the Library and place on the Stage.

■ The button appears on the Stage.

CREATE SHAPE-CHANGING BUTTONS

Although a simple geometric shape makes a good button, you may want something a bit more exciting. One way to jazz up an interactive button is to create the illusion of changing shapes. To do this, you can change the object you use for each button state. For example, an ordinary circle shape button can become a flower when the user rolls over it with the mouse. It can change into an entire bouquet when the user clicks on it with the mouse.

Creating a shape-changing button requires four different shapes. The Up, Over, and Down frames can each have a different shape, but the Hit frame needs a shape that encompasses all three of the other shapes. Although a user does not view the Hit frame, it defines a button's size. See the section "Create a Button Symbol" to learn more about creating buttons.

CREATE SHAPE-CHANGING BUTTONS

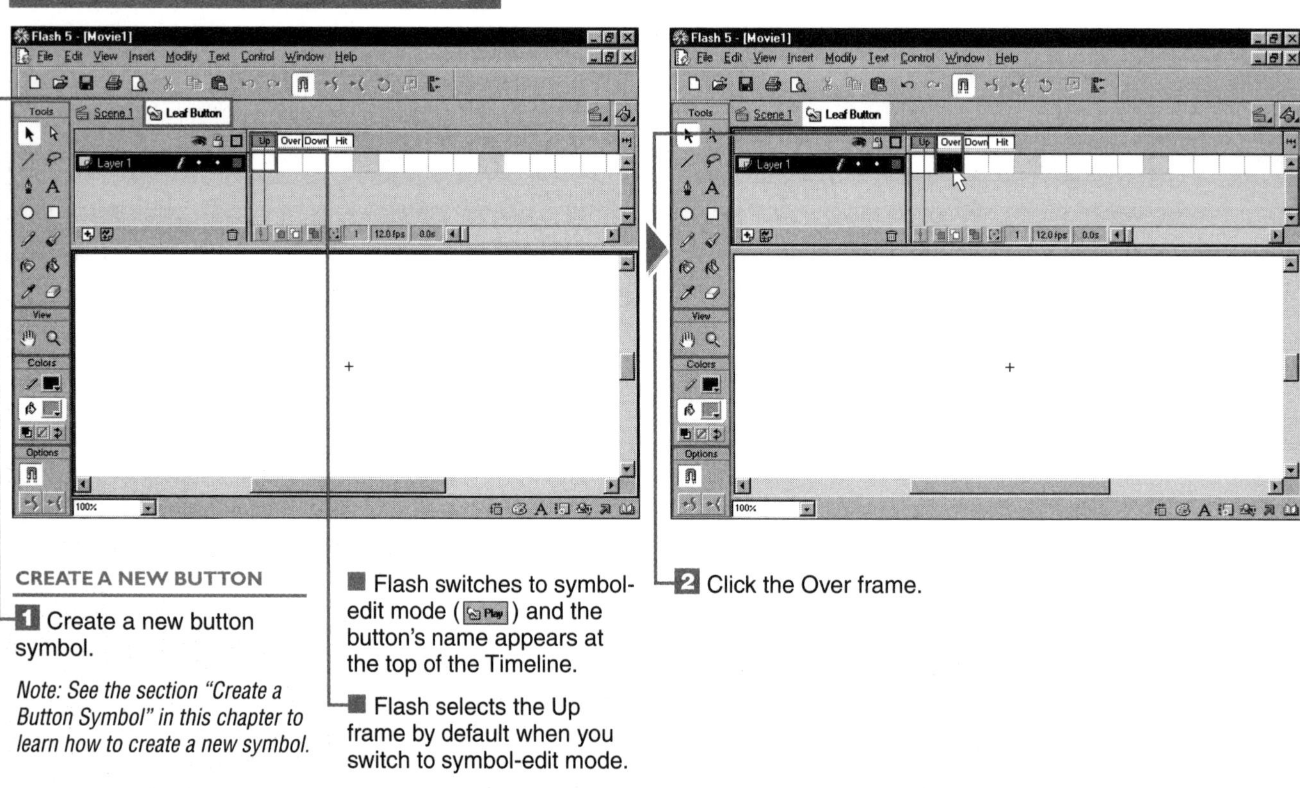

CREATE A NEW BUTTON

1 Create a new button symbol.

Note: See the section "Create a Button Symbol" in this chapter to learn how to create a new symbol.

■ Flash switches to symbol-edit mode (Play) and the button's name appears at the top of the Timeline.

■ Flash selects the Up frame by default when you switch to symbol-edit mode.

2 Click the Over frame.

Can I use layers in my button?

✔ Yes. The button's timeline works just like the main Timeline in movie-edit mode. You can add different layers to your button to organize various objects. For example, if your button includes a text block, you may want to place the text on another layer, or if your button uses a sound, place the sound clip on a separate layer from the graphic. You can add, delete, and rename layers in symbol-edit mode just as you do in movie-edit mode. See Chapter 21 to learn more about using layers in Flash.

How do I view a newly created button in movie-edit mode?

✔ You create buttons in symbol-edit mode. When you finish, and return to movie-edit mode, you do not see the button symbol unless you place an instance of the button symbol onto the Flash Stage. Click 📖 to open the Library window and drag the button onto the Stage.

How do I toggle between symbol-edit and movie-edit mode?

✔ You can quickly toggle back and forth between editing modes using a keyboard shortcut. Press Ctrl+E (Windows) or Command+E (Mac).

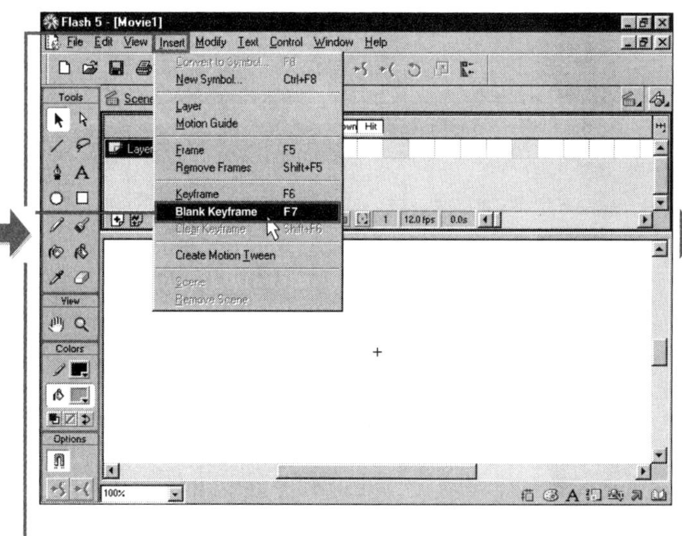

3 Click Insert.

4 Click Blank Keyframe.

■ Flash inserts a blank keyframe.

5 Repeat steps 3 and 4 to add blank keyframes to the Down and Hit frames.

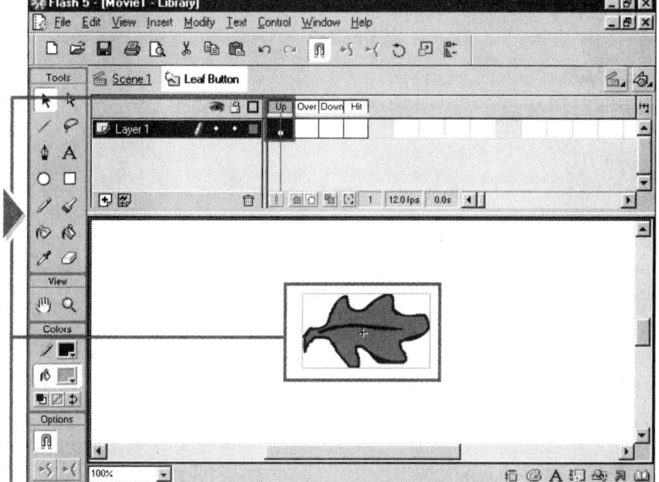

CREATE THE UP STATE

6 Click the Up frame to select it.

7 Create a new object or place an existing object on the Stage.

Note: See Chapter 18 to learn more about using the Flash drawing tools or see Chapter 22 to learn how to use symbols and instances.

CONTINUED

CREATE SHAPE-CHANGING BUTTONS (CONTINUED)

If a button's image stays the same for all four frames in the button's timeline, users cannot distinguish between its active and inactive states. Changing the button's image for each state gives users some idea of the button's status. They can see a difference when the mouse pointer hovers over a live button or when they click the button.

Shape-changing buttons can add pizzazz to Web pages. For example, you can create a button that blends in with the page, only to come alive with a different shape as soon as the user rolls over it with the mouse. This type of button becomes a *hotspot* — an area for which the user must hunt in order to activate the control.

Common switches also make good shape-changing buttons. For example, in its inactive state, a button can look like a common light switch resembling the Off setting, but when the user clicks the button, it changes to resemble the On setting of the toggle. You can come up with all sorts of interesting shapes to use as buttons in Flash.

CREATE SHAPE-CHANGING BUTTONS (CONTINUED)

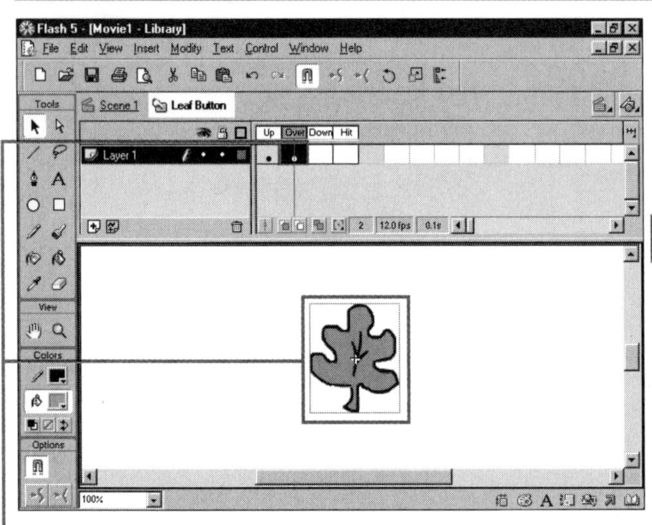

CREATE THE OVER STATE

8 Click the Over frame to select it.

9 Create a new object or place an existing object on the Stage to use as the active button state.

■ The object must differ from the object placed in the Up frame.

Note: See Chapter 18 to learn more about using the Flash drawing tools or see Chapter 22 to learn how to use symbols and instances.

CREATE THE DOWN STATE

10 Click the Down frame to select it.

11 Create another new object or place an existing object on the Stage.

■ Make this object differ from the other two objects used in the previous frames.

Why do I need to draw a shape in the Hit frame?

✔ Although the Hit frame is invisible to the user, it defines the active area of the button making it essential to the button's operation. You must make the object you draw big enough to encompass the largest object in the other button frames. If you do not, a user can click an area of the button that does not activate. If you have trouble guessing how large of an area to define, click ▣ to see outlines of the shapes on all the other frames. Click ▣ again to turn the feature off.

How do I make changes to a button?

✔ Double-click the button symbol to return to symbol-edit mode and make changes to the objects in each button timeline frame. For example, you may decide to use a different shape in your shape-changing button. After modifying your button, remember to check the Hit frame to make sure the defining shape size encompasses any new shapes in the other frames.

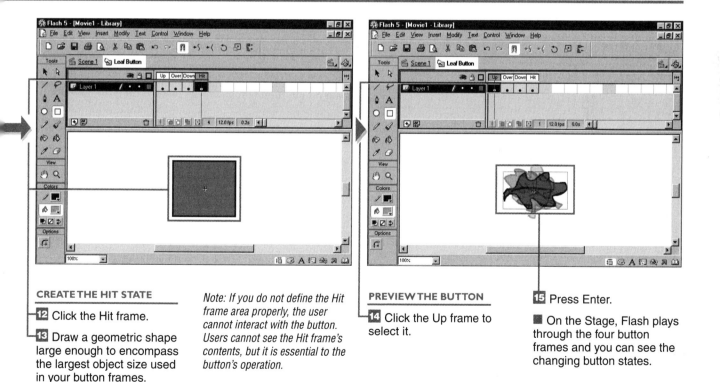

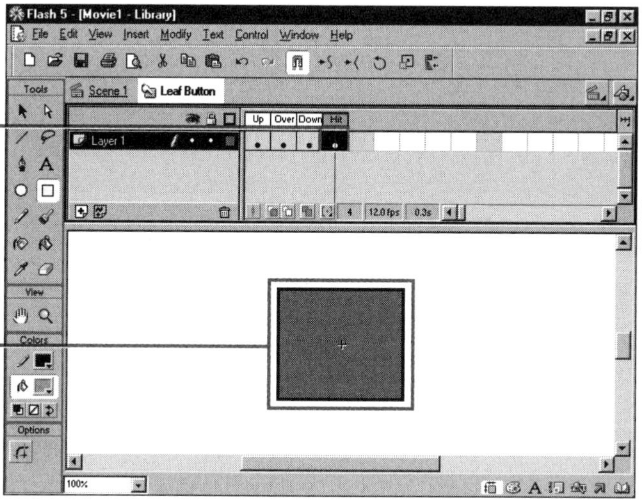

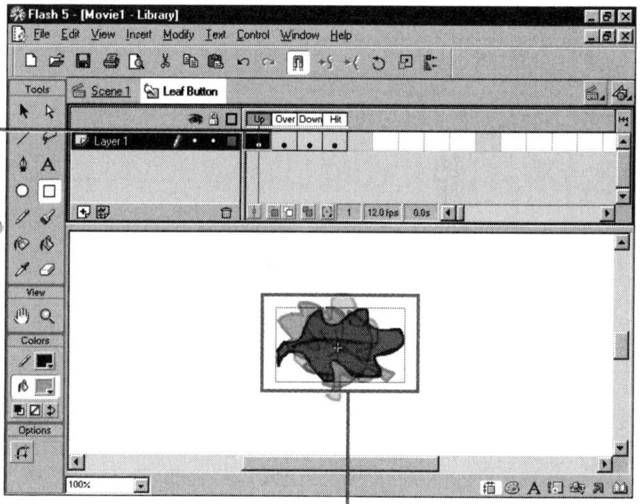

CREATE THE HIT STATE

12 Click the Hit frame.

13 Draw a geometric shape large enough to encompass the largest object size used in your button frames.

Note: If you do not define the Hit frame area properly, the user cannot interact with the button. Users cannot see the Hit frame's contents, but it is essential to the button's operation.

PREVIEW THE BUTTON

14 Click the Up frame to select it.

15 Press Enter.

■ On the Stage, Flash plays through the four button frames and you can see the changing button states.

CREATE AN ANIMATED BUTTON

You can create impressive animation effects for buttons. For example, you can make a button seem to glow when the mouse pointer hovers over it, or animate the button with a cartoon that includes sound, such as a character dancing around and singing. Spinning buttons, jumping buttons, and flashing buttons are all good examples of animation effects you can apply to help draw the user's attention to interactive buttons.

Flash makes it easy to place movie clips into your button frames. Movie clips add far more animation to a button versus shape-changing buttons. You must first create a movie clip or import one and then assign it to a button state. Movie clips utilize their own timelines, which means that they play at their own pace. The button remains animated as long as the clip plays. See Chapters 24 and 25 to learn how to create animations and movie clips in Flash.

CREATE AN ANIMATED BUTTON

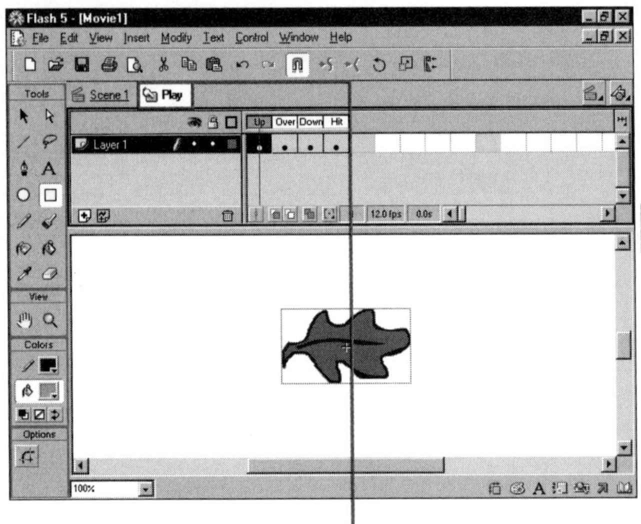

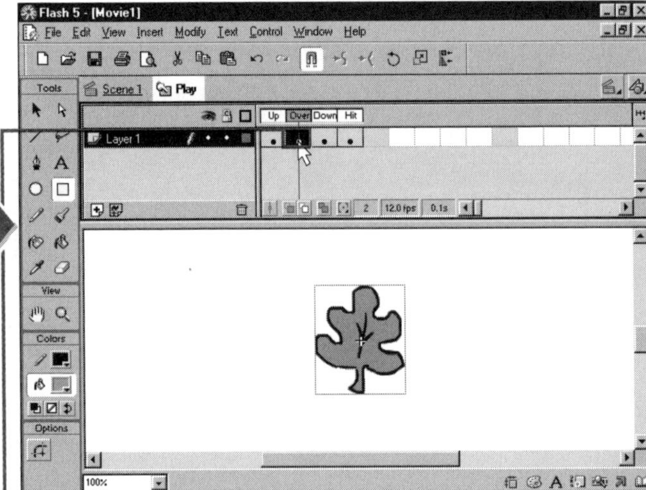

INSERT A MOVIE CLIP

1 Double-click the button to which you want to add an animation.

■ Flash switches you to the symbol-edit mode.

■ The button's name appears above the Timeline.

Note: See the Section "Create a Button Symbol" in this chapter to learn how to create a button.

2 Click the frame to which you want to add an animation, such as the Up, Over, or Down frame.

Note: The Hit frame is not seen by the user, so it is not useful to animate the frame.

Can I use an animation clip from another Flash file?

✔ Yes. Click the File menu and click Open as Shared Library. Locate the Flash file containing the clip you want to use, and then double-click the filename. This opens the other file's Library on-screen and you can drag the clip you want to use onto the Stage.

Does Flash come with any premade animation clips I can use?

✔ Yes. You can find animation clips to study, use, or help you complete the steps in this section. To find the Flash animation clips, click the Window menu and click Common Libraries, and then click Movie Clips. The Movie Clips Library window opens. You can then drag a clip onto a button frame.

Is there a limit to the length of a button animation?

✔ No. However, remember that the purpose of your button is for user interaction. When you add a long animation sequence to a button state, you keep the user waiting to complete the action. It is a good idea to keep animation sequences short when applying them to buttons.

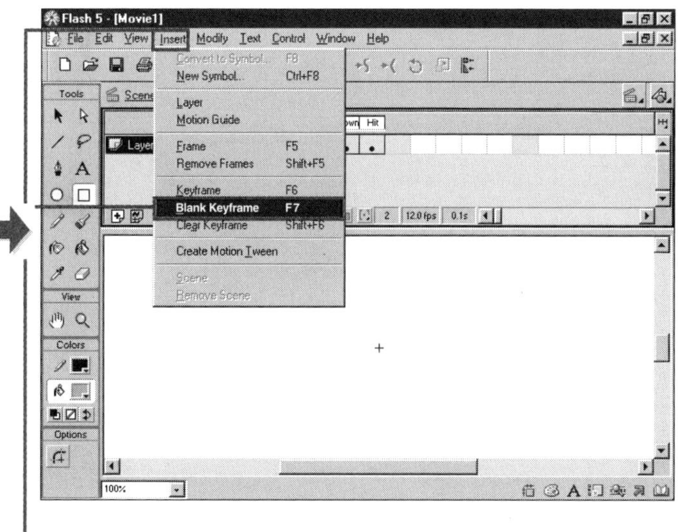

3 Click Insert.

4 Click Blank Keyframe.

■ Flash inserts a blank keyframe.

Note: If the frame already has an object, press Shift+F6 to clear the existing keyframe and object.

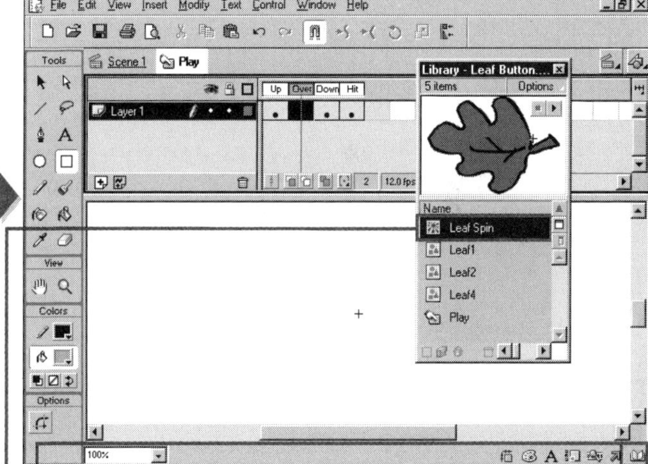

5 Click the Show Library button (📖) to open the Library window.

6 Click the movie clip that you want to insert.

Note: See Chapter 22 to learn how to use the Flash Library. See Chapters 24 and 25 to learn how to create animations and movie clips in Flash.

CONTINUED

CREATE AN ANIMATED BUTTON (CONTINUED)

You can add an animation to any button state. For example, you may want the user to see a spinning leaf when the button is inactive, or you may want the leaf object to spin only when the user rolls over the button with the mouse. You can play the animation when the user actually clicks the mouse button. The only frame you do not want to animate is the Hit frame because its contents are not visible to the user.

You can use animation sequences you create in Flash or animations authored in other programs. Be sure to test your movie clips to make sure they work the way you want before importing them into a Flash button frame. Testing beforehand may save you some time and effort later.

Avoid using animations that play too long. The user may not be patient enough to wait through a long animation sequence, especially upon repeat use of a button.

CREATE AN ANIMATED BUTTON (CONTINUED)

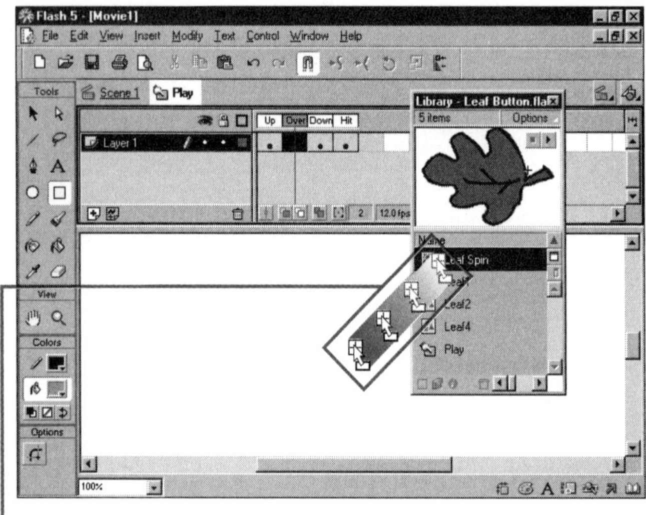

7 Click and drag the movie clip from the Library window and place it on the Stage where the button appears.

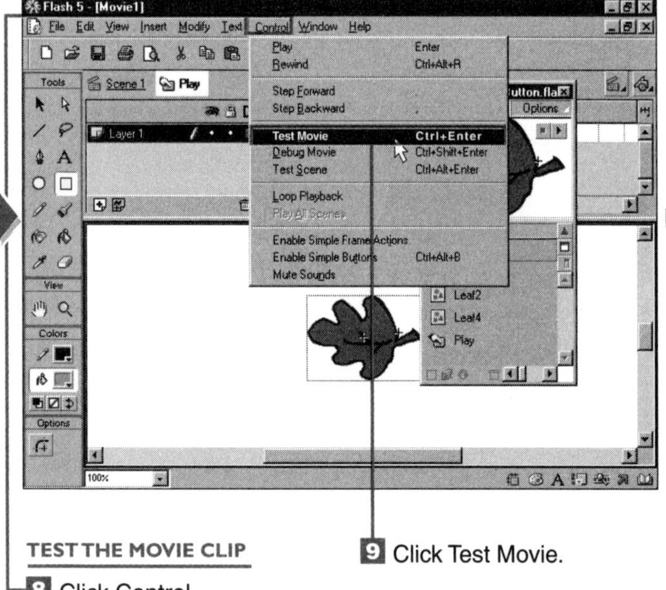

TEST THE MOVIE CLIP

8 Click Control.

9 Click Test Movie.

Can I add sounds to button frames?

✔ You can add sound clips to button frames the same way you add movie clips. Try adding a sound from Flash's Sound Library. Start by clicking on a frame. Next, click the Window menu, click Common Libraries, and then Sounds. The Sounds Library opens. In the Sounds Library window, click the sound clip and drag it to the button area on the Stage. A sound wave appears in the frame. You can press Enter (Windows) or Return (Mac) to test the button sequence. See Chapter 27 to learn more about adding sounds to frames.

How do I preview the animated button in movie-edit mode?

✔ When you press Ctrl+Alt+B in Windows (Command+Alt+B on a Mac) to preview a button's rollover capabilities in movie-edit mode, any movie clips you added to button frames do not run. Instead, you see the first frame of the movie clip. To see the fully animated button, click Control and then click Test Movie. This opens up the Flash Player window inside the Flash program window and plays the animation. Click the Player window's ☒ to exit and return to the Flash Stage.

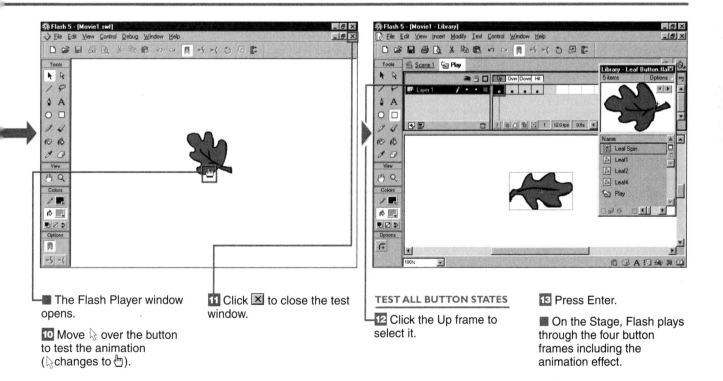

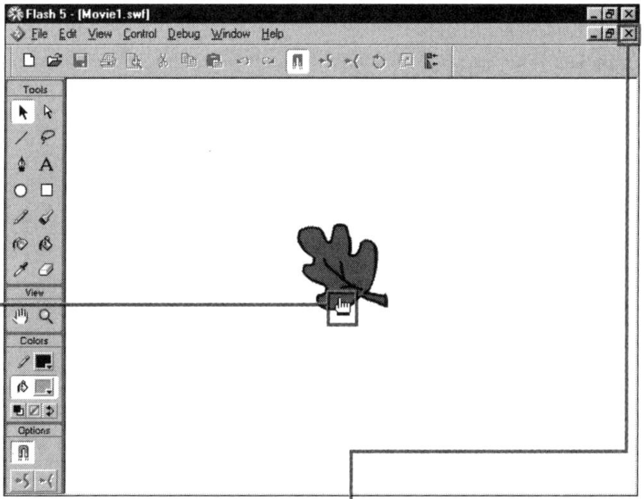

■ The Flash Player window opens.

10 Move ⇖ over the button to test the animation (⇖ changes to ☝).

11 Click ☒ to close the test window.

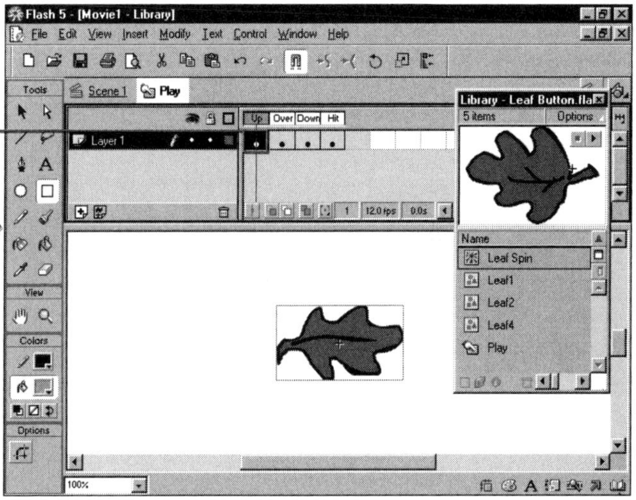

TEST ALL BUTTON STATES

12 Click the Up frame to select it.

13 Press Enter.

■ On the Stage, Flash plays through the four button frames including the animation effect.

ASSIGN A BUTTON ACTION

You can assign all kinds of actions to buttons you create in Flash. Buttons already utilize built-in actions, such as moving immediately to the Down frame when a user clicks the button. You can add other Flash actions to your buttons. For example, you can add a Play action to a button so that a movie clip starts playing when the user clicks the button, or a Stop action that enables the user to stop a movie that is in progress.

You assign actions, also called *frame actions*, to individual frames in your movie's Timeline. An action is a behavior, such as stopping a movie, and is triggered by an *event*, such as a mouse click. See Chapter 28 to learn more about assigning actions. In the case of buttons, you can assign frame actions that determine how the user interacts with the button. You add frame actions in movie-edit mode, not symbol-edit mode, and you add them to the frame containing the button. Always test any actions you assign to make sure they work as expected.

ASSIGN A BUTTON ACTION

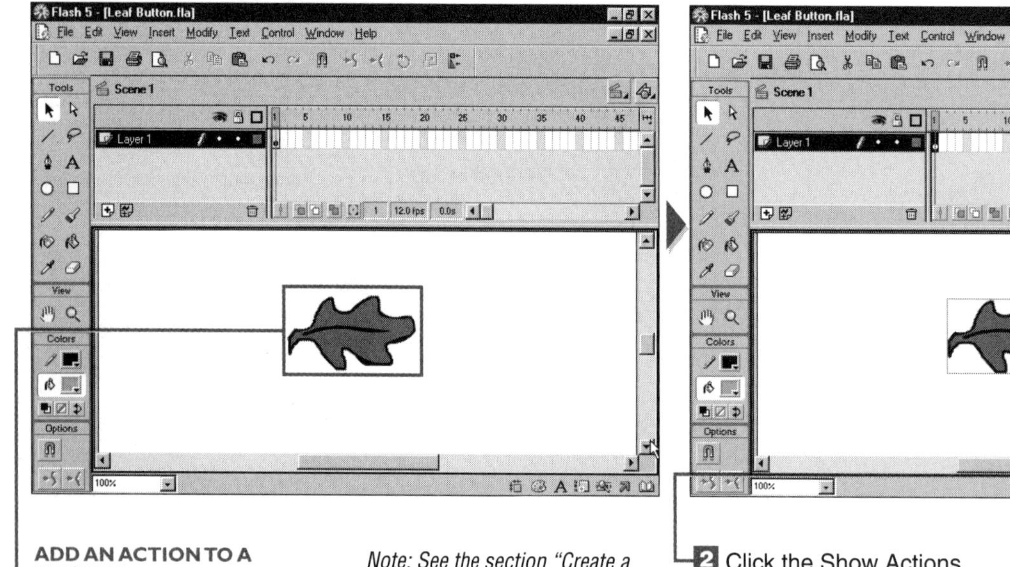

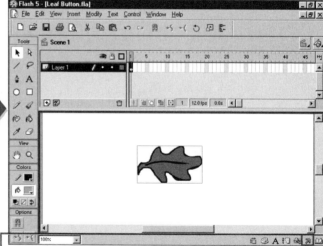

ADD AN ACTION TO A BUTTON

1 Click the button symbol to which you want to add an action.

Note: See the section "Create a Button Symbol" to learn how to create a button.

2 Click the Show Actions button ( ).

■ The Object Actions dialog box opens.

What types of actions are good for buttons?

✔ The Go To action jumps the user to a particular frame or scene in your movie. The Play action starts playing a specified movie clip. The Stop action stops a movie in progress. You can use this action in a presentation to allow users to stop and read the screen or ask questions.

What is an event handler?

✔ An event handler, such as the `On Mouse-Event`, manages the action. You can recognize the `On Mouse Event` in the Object Actions dialog box by the words "on," such as "on release." The words following the word "on" set the parameters for the event. Click the appropriate check boxes in the Object Actions dialog box to specify which event you want.

I cannot select my button on the Flash Stage. Why?

✔ If Flash displays the button animation sequence when you move your ⇱ over the button, you have the Enable Simple Buttons feature active. Press Ctrl+Alt+B to disable the feature and then click the button to select it.

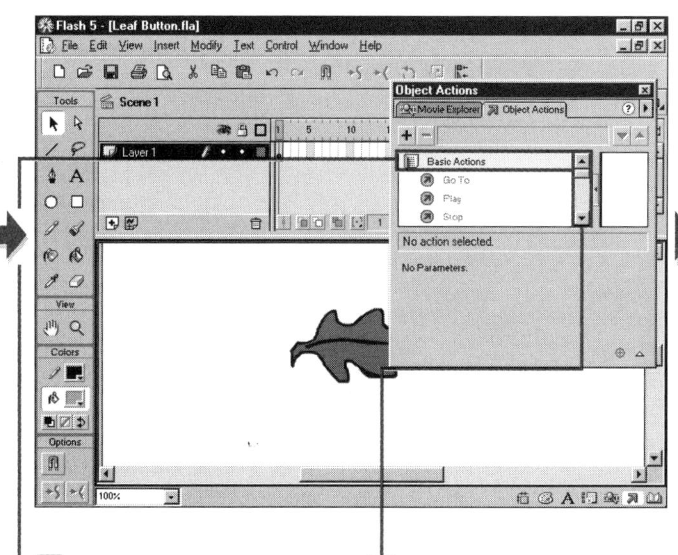

3 From the Object Actions Toolbox list, click Basic Actions.

4 Scroll through the list of actions and locate the one you want to apply.

Note: See Chapter 28 to learn how to work with Flash actions.

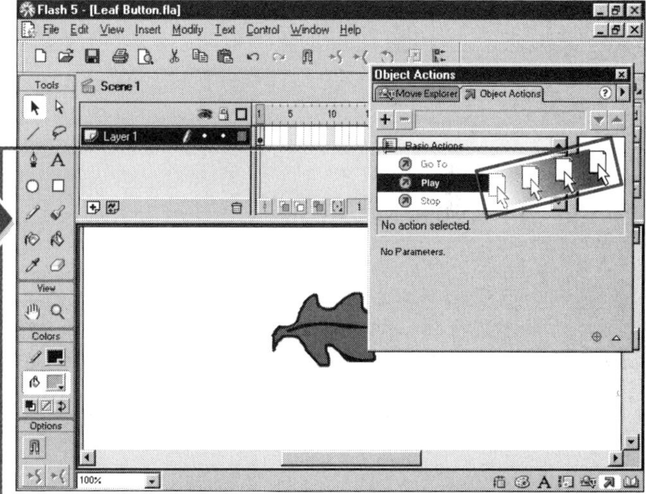

5 Click and drag the action from the list and drop it in the Actions list box.

■ You can also double-click the action name to immediately place it in the Actions list box.

CONTINUED

ASSIGN A BUTTON ACTION (CONTINUED)

Flash actions are simplified programming scripts that instruct Flash how to perform a certain task, such as loading a movie or stopping a sound clip. Using a basic programming language, actions include command strings to spell out exactly what action Flash must perform. Most button actions require input from the user, such as moving the mouse over the button, or clicking the button. You do not have to know programming in order to use Flash actions.

In addition to the action you assign, Flash also automatically assigns a special event handler, called the `On Mouse Event` action, to the button. The `On Mouse Event` action acts as a manager to make sure whatever action you assign works properly with the button actions that are already built-in to the symbol type.

See Chapter 28 to learn more about Flash actions and how you can put them to use.

ASSIGN A BUTTON ACTION (CONTINUED)

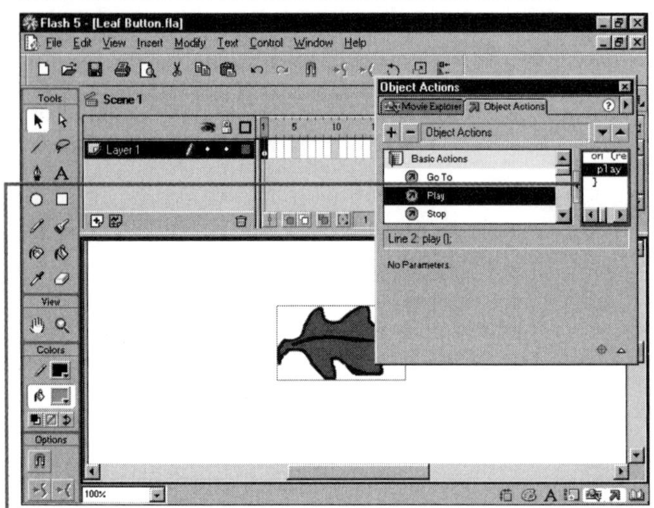

■ Flash adds the necessary action components to the Actions list.

Note: See Chapter 28 to learn how to work with Flash actions.

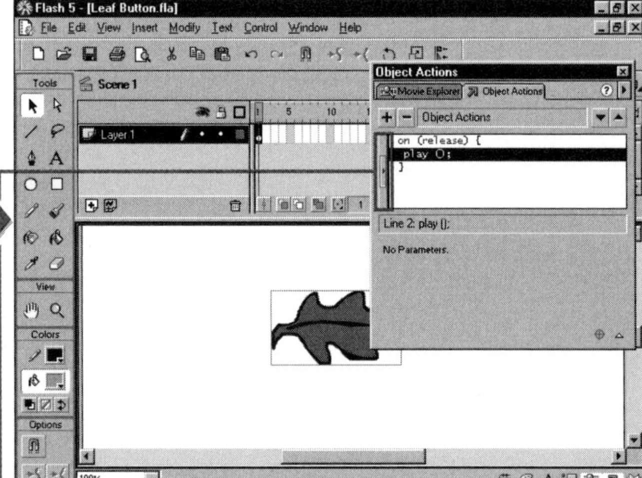

■ To see the Actions list in full size, you can click the Widen button (▯).

Can I add multiple actions to a button?

✔ Yes. You can use the Actions Toolbox to add more actions to a button, either before or after an existing action. For example, you can add multiple actions to occur within one set of On/End actions, and Flash triggers all of the actions by a single mouse event.

How do I edit an action assigned to a button?

✔ You can perform edits to your button actions in the Object Actions panel. Click the line you want to edit in the Actions list. Depending on the action, a variety of parameters appear at the bottom of the panel. You can make changes to those parameters, if necessary. To remove an action component from the Actions list, click the line you want to delete and then click ⊟. To add an action, click ⊞ and then click another action.

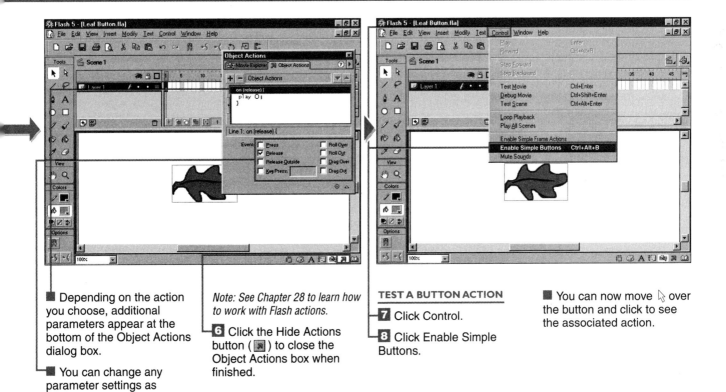

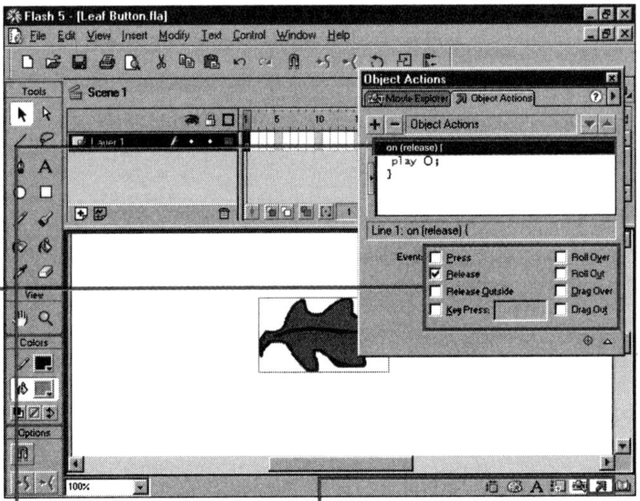

■ Depending on the action you choose, additional parameters appear at the bottom of the Object Actions dialog box.

■ You can change any parameter settings as necessary.

Note: See Chapter 28 to learn how to work with Flash actions.

6 Click the Hide Actions button (▣) to close the Object Actions box when finished.

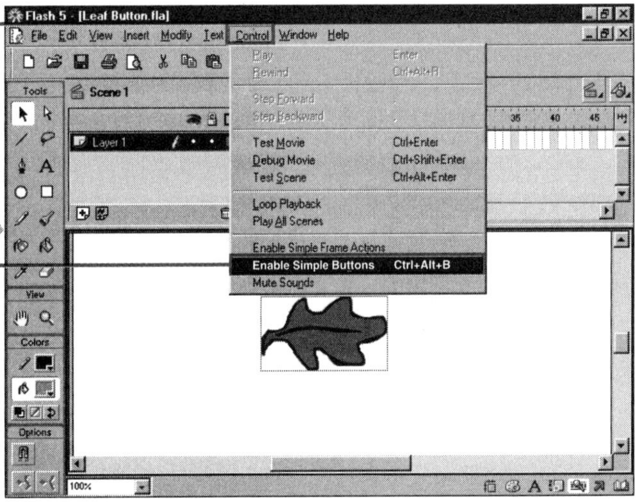

TEST A BUTTON ACTION

7 Click Control.

8 Click Enable Simple Buttons.

■ You can now move ⇖ over the button and click to see the associated action.

AN INTRODUCTION TO FLASH SOUNDS

Adding sound to your Flash projects is like adding icing to a cake. With sounds, you can help convey your message and give your movies a polished edge. You can make your sounds as simple as short sound effect clips, or as complex as coordinating background music. Sounds can include voice narrations, musical scores, and sound effects, such as a doorbell ringing or a lightning strike.

You can assign a sound that continues to play throughout your Flash movie, or synchronize a sound to play with specific frames. You can assign sound clips to buttons to make them even more interactive. You can apply sounds to enhance your Flash presentations, movies, cartoons, and other projects in seemingly endless ways.

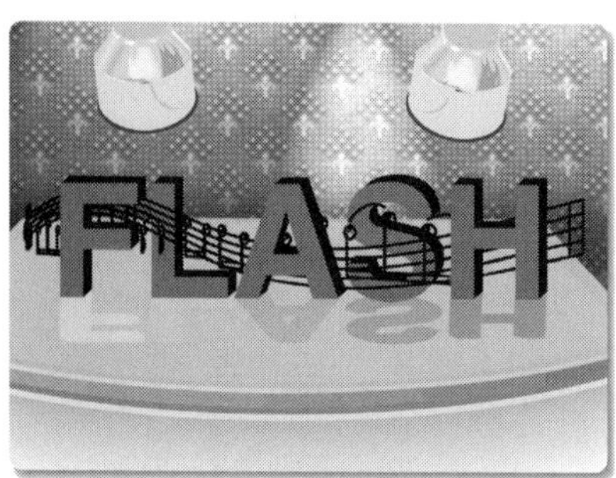

Flash Sounds and Layers

You can add sounds to your Flash movie frames in the same way that you add other frame content, such as graphics and buttons. Although you can only add one sound per frame in Flash, you can use multiple layers for different sounds. For example, to play multiple sounds at the same time, you can add new sounds to the same movie frame, but assign them to different layers.

Flash Sound Symbols and Libraries

Flash treats sound clips as symbols and stores them in the Library. You can use copies of a sound clip as many times as you want throughout your movie. You can also use sound clips saved in other Flash files.

Working with Digital Sounds

Although invisible, sounds are made of waves that vary in frequency and amplitude. Digital sounds are visually represented as *waveforms*. Waveforms appear as vertically stacked lines of varying heights resembling the output from a geological measurement of an earthquake. The more intense the sound, the taller and denser the waveform line measurement.

For computer usage, sounds are transformed into mathematical equations called *digital sampling*. Digital quality is measured by how many samples exist in a single second of the sound, called the *sampling rate*. Sampling rates are expressed in *kilohertz* (kHz). The higher the rate, the larger the file size, and the clearer the sound. Typically, sampling size is measured in 8, 16, or 24 bits. A smaller sampling rate results in a smaller file size. When planning sounds for your Flash movie, remember that larger sound clips take longer to download.

Types of Sounds

All sounds you add in Flash, whether music, narration, or sound effects, fall into two categories: *event driven* and *streamed*. An action in your movie triggers event driven sounds and they must be download completely before playing. You assign an event sound to start play on a specific keyframe and it continues to play independently of your movie's Timeline. If the event sound is longer than your movie, it continues to play even when your movie stops. You can use event sounds when you do not want to synchronize a sound clip with frames in your movie.

Streamed sounds download as they are needed, and start playing even if the rest of the clip has not yet loaded. Flash synchronizes streamed sounds with your movie's frames, and in fact, attempts to keep any created animation in sync with the streamed sound. Streaming sound works great for sounds you intend to play over the Internet.

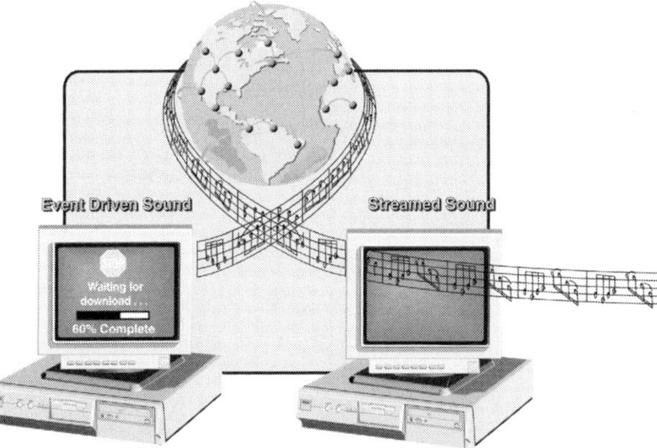

When assigning event or streamed sounds, you can use the options in the Sound panel to specify the sound type. Flash offers four sync options — event, stream, start, stop — based on what you want the sound to do, such as make an animation sequence play along with a sound track.

Sound File Formats

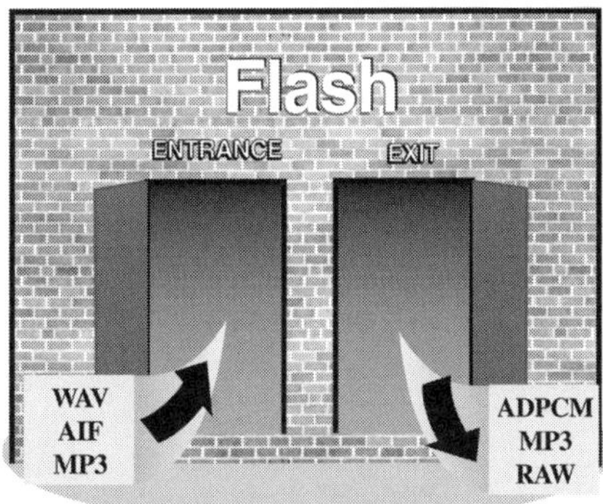

Flash recognizes a large variety of sound file formats. You can import WAV, AIFF, MP3, and QuickTime file formats into your movies. If you have QuickTime 4 or later, you can also import a few additional sound file formats, including Sun AU and Sound Designer II formats. When importing sound effects, Flash works best with 16-bit sounds.

You can export the audio you use in your Flash movies as MP3 format, or you can compress it as ADPCM, MP3, or RAW. You can find compression options for sounds available in the Publish Settings dialog box. See Chapter 30 to learn more about using this feature to export your Flash movies.

IMPORT A SOUND CLIP

Although you cannot record sounds in Flash, you can import sounds from other sources for use with movies and other projects. For example, you can download an MP3 file from the Internet and add it to a movie, or import a saved recording to play with a Flash button. Flash supports popular sound file formats, such as WAV and AIFF.

When assigning sounds in Flash, you add them to keyframes the same way you add graphics and buttons. Before you can add a sound to a frame, you must first import it into your movie's Library. When you import a sound file, it remains in the Library where you can add it to various portions of your movie as many times as you like. See Chapter 22 to learn more about using the Flash Library window.

The Import command enables you to import all kinds of file types, including graphic and sound files.

IMPORT A SOUND CLIP

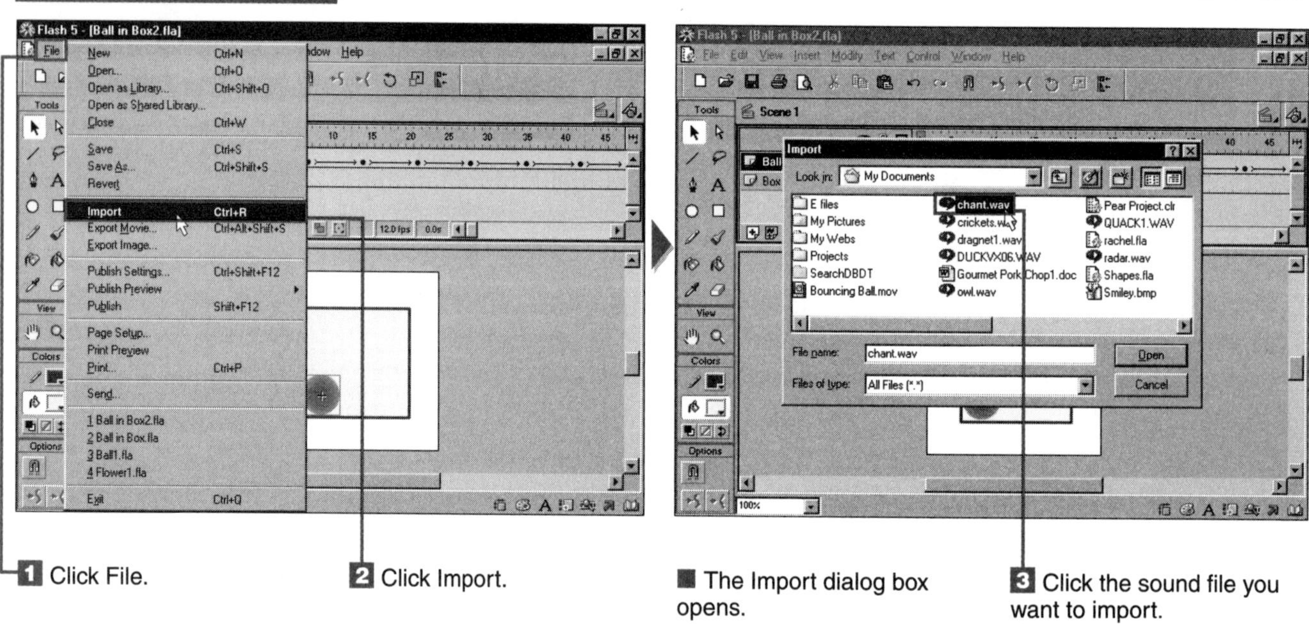

1 Click File.

2 Click Import.

■ The Import dialog box opens.

3 Click the sound file you want to import.

Does Flash have any sounds I can use?

✔ Flash has several common libraries from which you can borrow items, and one includes sounds. To display the sound library, click Windows, click Common Libraries and then click Sounds. Double-click a folder name in the Sounds Library window to see a list of sounds. You can preview a sound by clicking the sound's name and then clicking ▶. You can drag the sound off the library window onto the Stage to use it.

Do I need to worry about the size of my sound file?

✔ Yes. You can make sound files very large, particularly if you are importing a sound file to use as background music for your movie. However, lengthy sound files also take longer to download when users are accessing Flash files from your Web site. For all of these reasons, it is a good idea to make sure that your sound files are as short as you can possibly make them. Trim off excess parts of the file or plan to use an audio clip that loops in your movie.

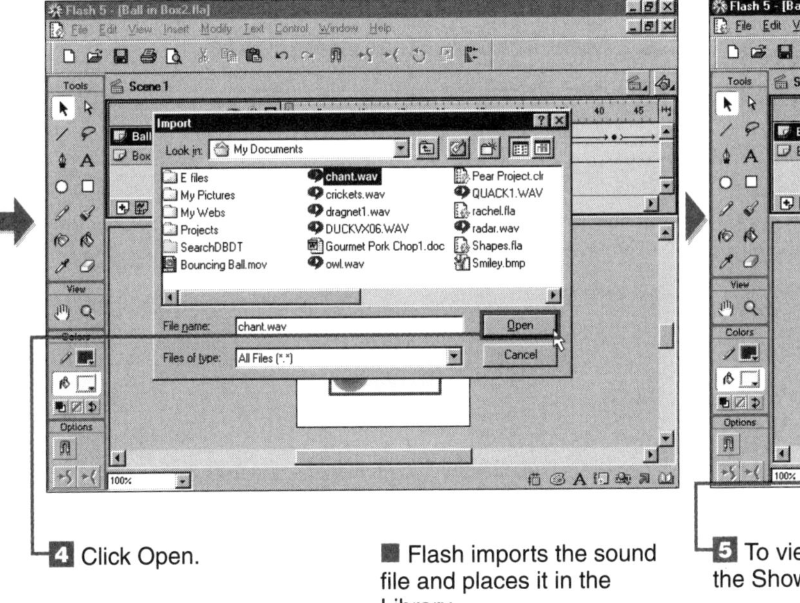

4 Click Open.

■ Flash imports the sound file and places it in the Library.

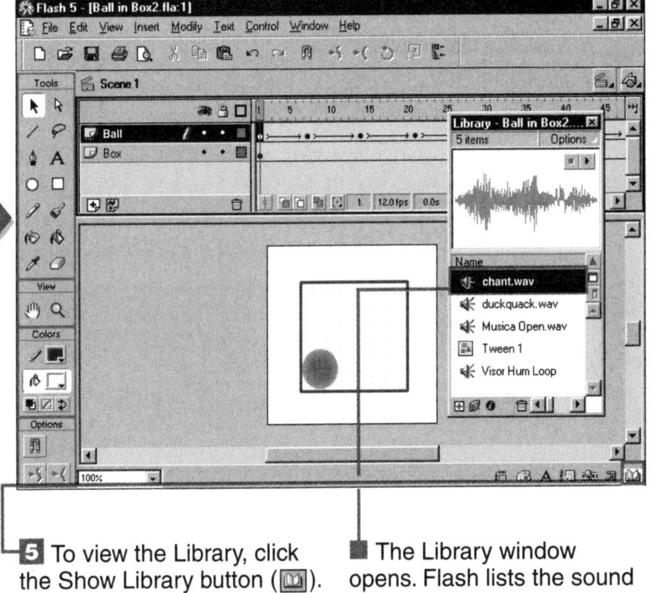

5 To view the Library, click the Show Library button (📖).

■ The Library window opens. Flash lists the sound file in the window.

ADD A SOUND LAYER

You can organize various elements, including sounds, in your movie using Flash *layers.* Layers appear in the Flash Timeline and you use them to hold graphics, animations, and sounds. Like graphics, you assign sounds to frames in the Timeline.

By keeping your sound clips on a separate layer, you can more easily locate the sounds in your Flash movie and see how they relate to items in other layers. Placing sounds in separate layers also lets you more easily edit them later. When you place sounds on separate layers, you can treat the layers as audio channels in your Flash movie, and the various layers play together during playback. You can also name a sound layer with a distinct name so that you immediately recognize its contents.

Flash allows for multiple sound layers in your movie. For example, your movie may use a layer for special-effects sounds, like a doorbell ringing, and another layer for music, like a background song or arrangement.

See Chapter 21 to learn more about working with Flash layers.

ADD A SOUND LAYER

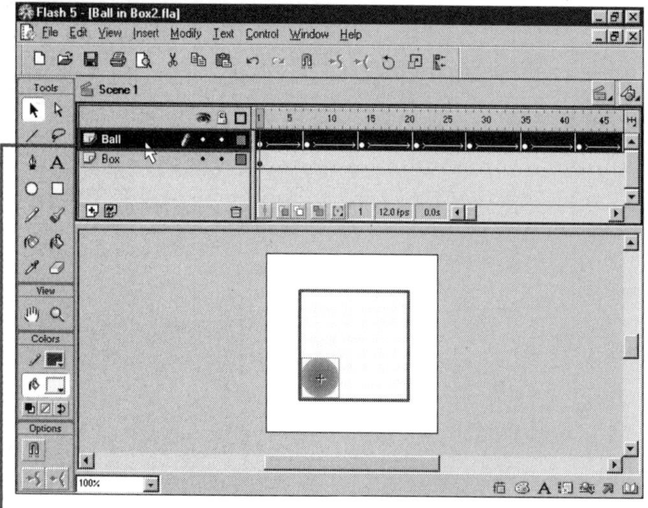

1 Click the layer below where you want to insert a new layer.

■ Flash always adds a new layer to the Timeline directly above the active layer.

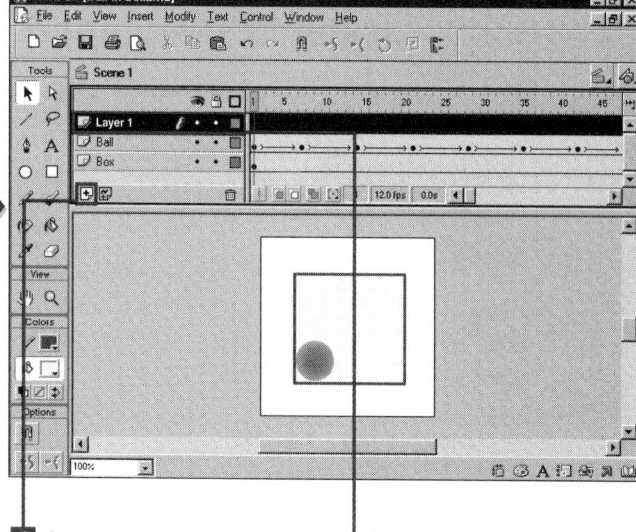

2 Click the Insert Layer button ( ).

■ A new layer appears on top of the active layer.

Can I make a soundtrack layer?

✔ Although Flash uses no official soundtrack layer, you can organize multiple sound layers and place them visually under a mask layer and name the mask layer "Soundtrack." By placing all of your sound layers beneath a labeled mask layer, you can quickly see the organization of sound files in your Flash movie.

How can I tell which object is on which layer?

✔ You can choose to view your layer contents as outlines on the Stage. Click the colored square button whose ToolTip reads "Show All Layers As Outlines" (■) under the square icon column in the Timeline (■ changes to □). Flash outlines all objects on the layer in the same color as the square you clicked.

Can I enlarge the size of my sound layer?

✔ Yes. Enlarging a layer that contains a sound clip enables you to more easily view its waveform image in the Timeline. To enlarge the layer height, right-click the layer name and click Properties. This opens the Layer Properties dialog box. Click the Layer Height drop-down arrow and choose a percentage. Click OK to close the dialog box and apply the new size.

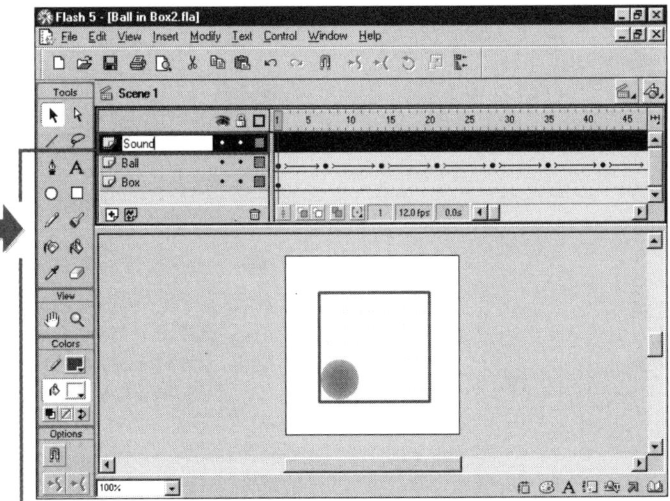

3 To give the layer a distinct name, double-click the default layer name.

4 Type a name that identifies this layer as a sound layer.

5 Press Enter.

■ Flash saves the new layer name.

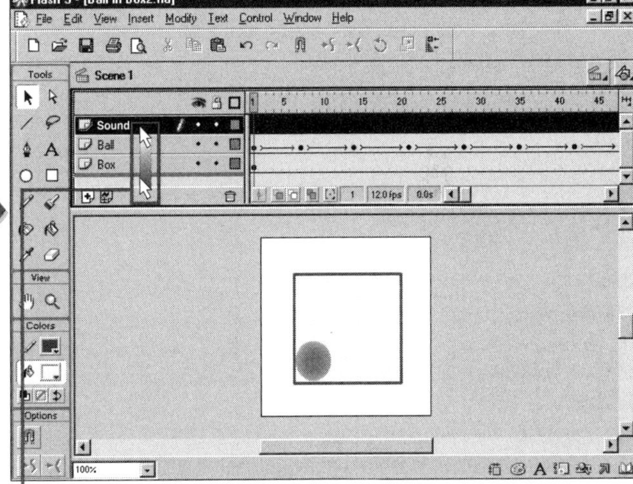

■ To make the sound layer easy to find, you can drag the layer to the top or bottom of the Timeline layer stack.

ASSIGN SOUND TO A FRAME

You can enliven any animation sequence with a sound clip whether you add a single sound effect or an entire soundtrack. You save sound files as instances that you can insert into frames on the Timeline and use throughout your movie. Flash represents sounds as waveforms in Flash frames. See Chapter 21 to learn more about frames.

Sound files appear as symbols when you save them in the Flash Library. You can drag a sound clip from the Library out onto the Stage to assign it to any frame in your movie. Once on the stage, Flash gives no visual representation of the sound. Instead, a *waveform* — an image of vertical lines representing the digital sampling of the sound — appears in the Timeline frame.

Depending on the length of the sound file, the sound may play through several frames of your movie. Unlike a graphic or button symbol, however, sound clips appear as outlines on the Stage and the waveform for the sound appears in the designated layer and frame in the Timeline.

ASSIGN SOUND TO A FRAME

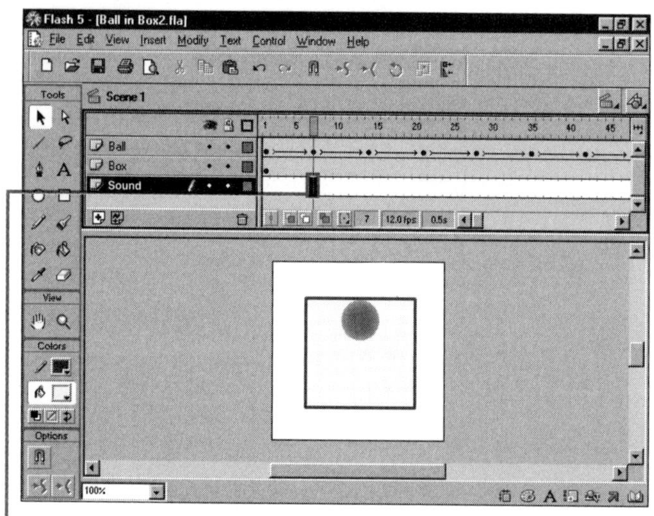

1 Click the frame to which you want to add a sound.

■ To organize your sounds, you can add the sound to a specially named layer dedicated to sound clips.

Note: See the section "Add a Sound Layer" for more information.

2 Press F6 to insert a keyframe.

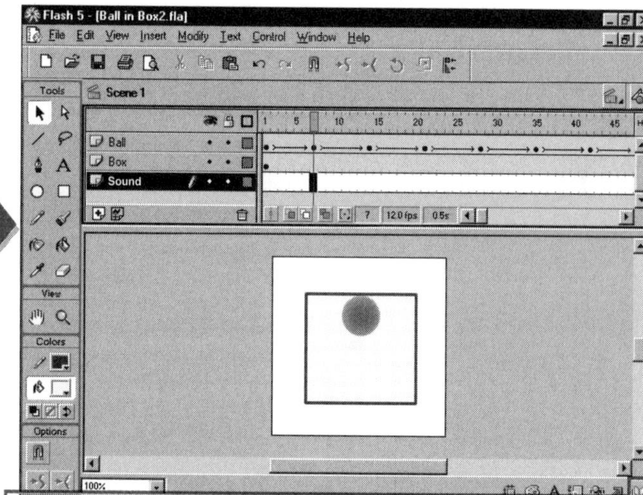

3 Click the Show Library button (📖).

■ The Library window opens.

How do I know which sound is which?

✔ Because sounds appear as waveforms in the Timeline, it is not always easy to determine exactly which sound is which. One way you can quickly tell is to hover your mouse pointer directly over the waveform. A ToolTip appears with the sound's name.

Can I use sound clips from another movie's Library?

✔ Yes. You can easily insert sounds from another file's library. Click the File menu and click Open as Library. The Open as Library dialog box appears. Click the filename and then click Open. The Library window opens listing the other file's symbols. Drag the sound clip you want to use out onto the Stage.

Why does my sound's waveform appear squished into one frame?

✔ If you assign a sound file to a keyframe that appears at the end of your movie, or if you have yet to add additional frames or keyframes to your movie, the sound's waveform appears only in the frame in which you assigned it. This makes the waveform appear very squished in the frame.

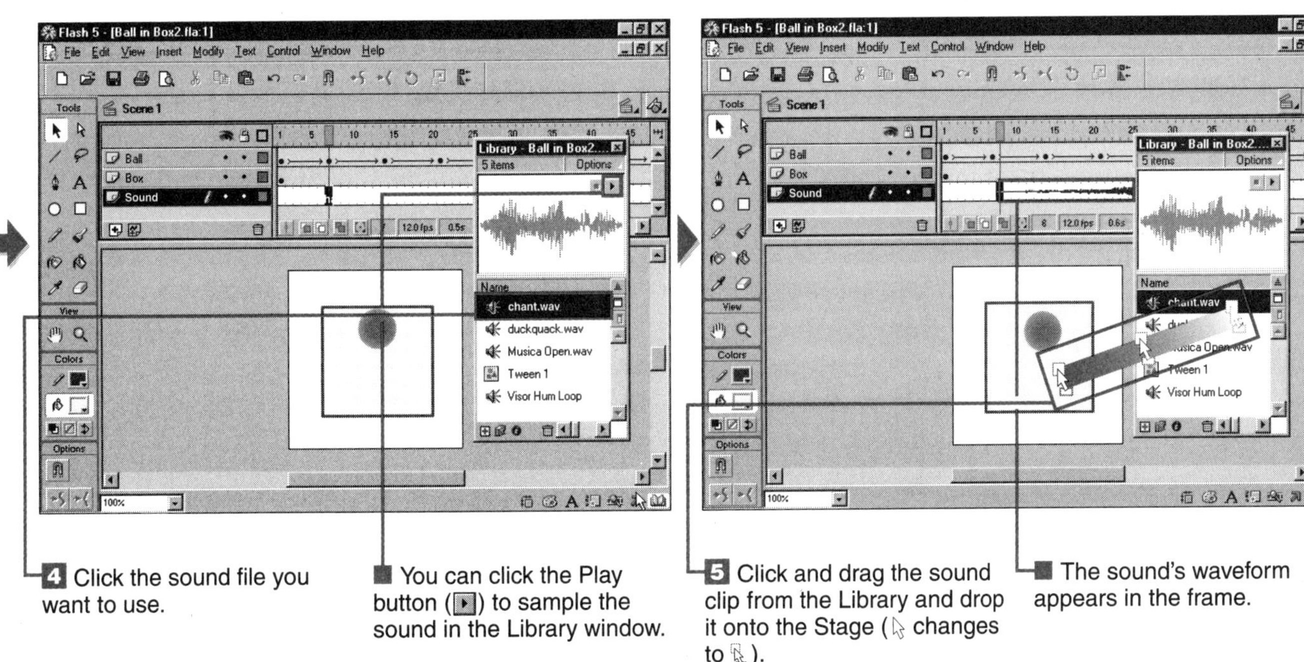

4 Click the sound file you want to use.

■ You can click the Play button (▶) to sample the sound in the Library window.

5 Click and drag the sound clip from the Library and drop it onto the Stage (↖ changes to ↖).

■ The sound's waveform appears in the frame.

ASSIGN SOUNDS TO BUTTONS

One of the best ways you can use sound on your Web page is to apply it to buttons. You can add sounds to buttons to help people know how to interact with the buttons or just to give the buttons added flair. For example, you can add a clicking sound that the user hears when he or she clicks a button. If your buttons are part of a graphic or page background, adding a sound to the button's rollover state helps users find the buttons on the page. See Chapter 26 to learn more about creating interactive buttons in Flash.

Sounds can make your buttons more interactive and realistic. You can add a different sound to each button state, such as a chime effect that plays when the user rolls over the button with the mouse and a click effect when the user actually clicks the button. It is not necessary to add a sound to the Hit state because the user never sees or interacts with this button state.

ASSIGN SOUNDS TO BUTTONS

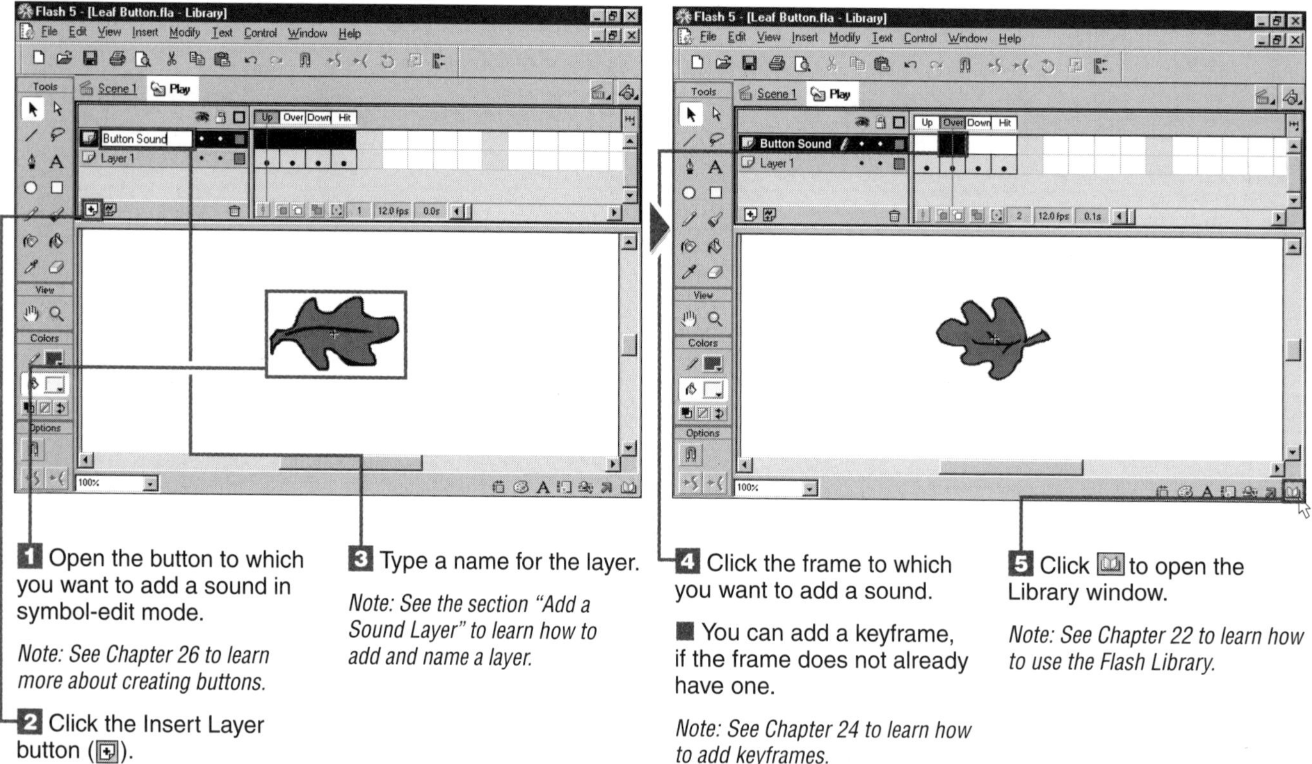

1 Open the button to which you want to add a sound in symbol-edit mode.

Note: See Chapter 26 to learn more about creating buttons.

2 Click the Insert Layer button ( ).

3 Type a name for the layer.

Note: See the section "Add a Sound Layer" to learn how to add and name a layer.

4 Click the frame to which you want to add a sound.

■ You can add a keyframe, if the frame does not already have one.

Note: See Chapter 24 to learn how to add keyframes.

5 Click to open the Library window.

Note: See Chapter 22 to learn how to use the Flash Library.

To which button frame should I assign a sound?

✔ The most practical frames to use when assigning sounds are the Over and Down frames, but you can assign sounds to any button frame. For example, you may want the button to beep when the user rolls over the button with the mouse pointer. This alerts the users to the button. To do this, assign a sound to the Over frame. You may also want the button to make another type of sound when the user actually clicks it; assign a sound to the Down frame.

Why do I need a separate layer for sound?

✔ When adding sounds to buttons, it is a good idea to create a separate layer for the sound in the button's Timeline. This helps you distinguish the sound from any animation or graphics effects you assign to the button's various frames. You can have numerous layers in a button's Timeline, and, regardless of how many layers you add, you do not affect the overall file size. The sound clip size, however, does affect the file size.

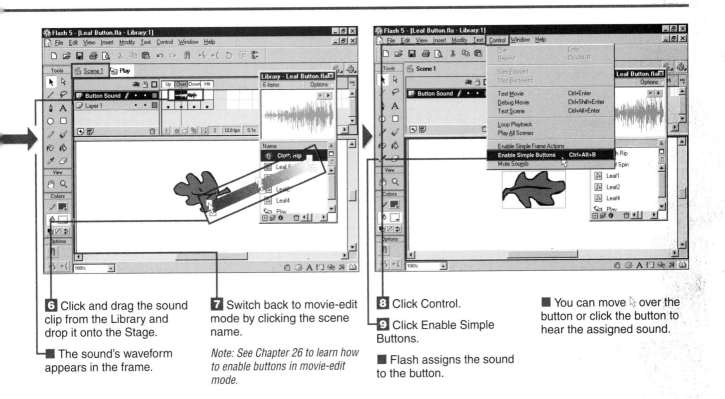

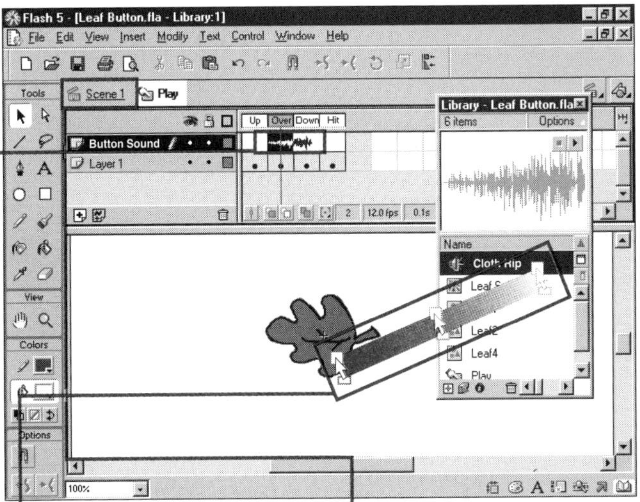

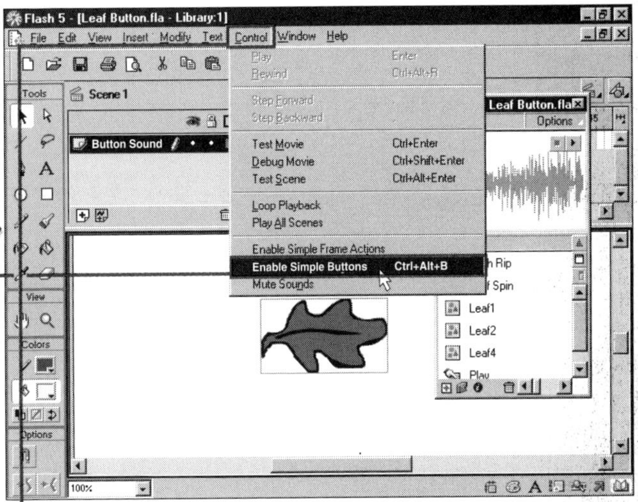

6 Click and drag the sound clip from the Library and drop it onto the Stage.

■ The sound's waveform appears in the frame.

7 Switch back to movie-edit mode by clicking the scene name.

Note: See Chapter 26 to learn how to enable buttons in movie-edit mode.

8 Click Control.

9 Click Enable Simple Buttons.

■ Flash assigns the sound to the button.

■ You can move over the button or click the button to hear the assigned sound.

CREATE EVENT SOUNDS

You can assign an event-driven sound in your Flash project, which an action triggers. *Event* sounds play in their entirety and in their own Timeline. The user must completely download the sound before they can play it. By default, Flash treats all sounds that you add as event sounds unless you specify another type. See the section "Assign Sound to a Frame" to learn more about assigning sounds.

You can use event sounds to include background music for your movie. Keep in mind, however, that if the sound file is longer than your movie, the sound keeps playing until it ends or encounters a Stop command. If your movie happens to loop and the event sound does not stop by the time the movie reaches its starting point again, Flash plays two instances of the sound at the same time. This overlapping of sounds does not create a very harmonious effect in the movie, so be sure to time the length of your event sound before setting your movie to loop status.

CREATE EVENT SOUNDS

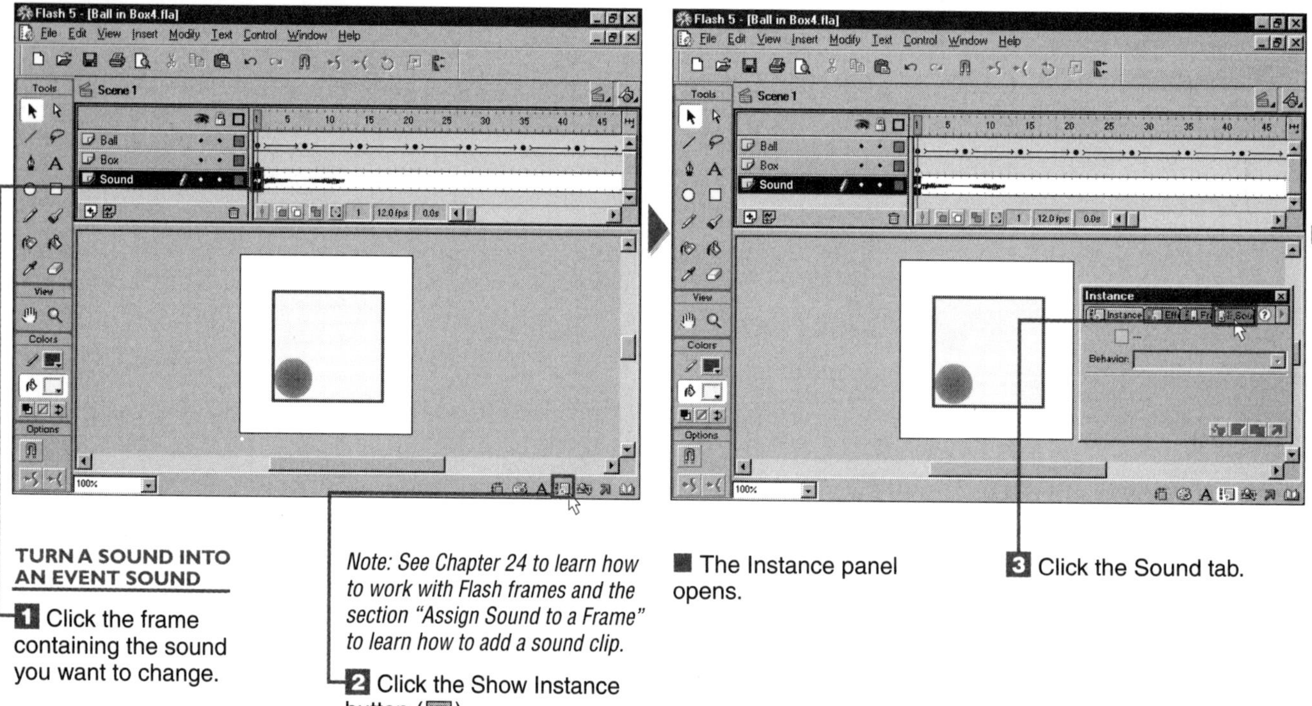

TURN A SOUND INTO AN EVENT SOUND

1 Click the frame containing the sound you want to change.

Note: See Chapter 24 to learn how to work with Flash frames and the section "Assign Sound to a Frame" to learn how to add a sound clip.

2 Click the Show Instance button (▣).

■ The Instance panel opens.

3 Click the Sound tab.

Can I overlap event sounds, or start two sounds simultaneously?

✔ By default, any sound you assign to a frame is an event sound until you change it to something else. Although you can only insert one sound per frame, you can use multiple layers to play sounds at the same time or to overlap them. For example, you can place one event sound in a sound layer labeled Sound 1 and assign the sound to frame 1. You can create a second layer and name it Sound 2, and place yet another sound in frame 5. Both sounds play together when you start the movie.

What types of sounds work best as event sounds?

✔ For best results in Flash, assign event sounds to short sound clips. Sound effects, like a hand clap or a bell ringing, work well as event sounds. Long clips, such as an entire song, work best as streamed sounds.

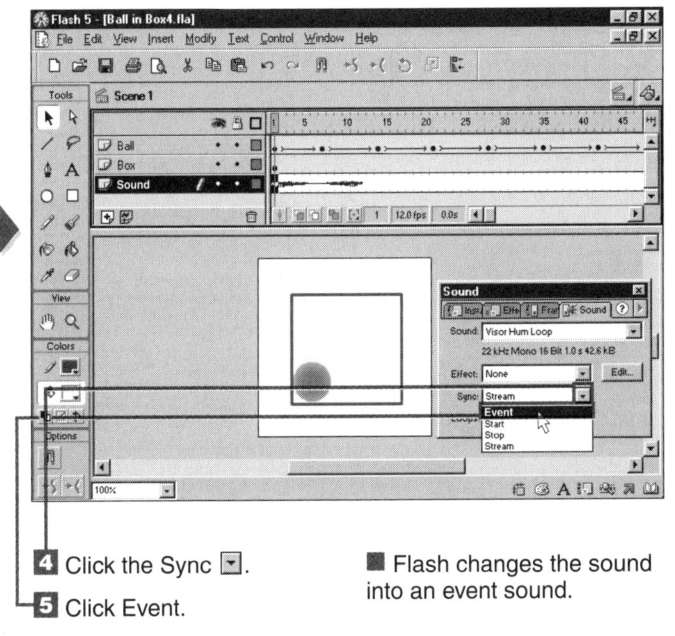

4 Click the Sync ▾.

5 Click Event.

■ Flash changes the sound into an event sound.

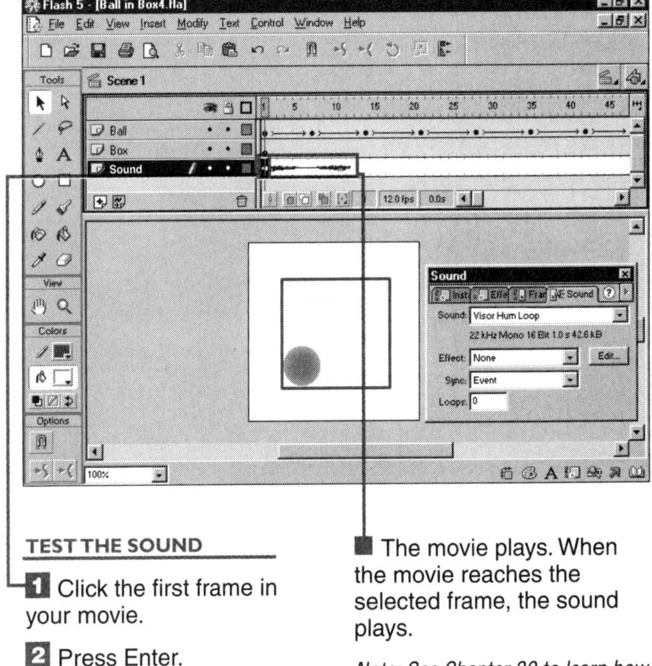

TEST THE SOUND

1 Click the first frame in your movie.

2 Press Enter.

■ The movie plays. When the movie reaches the selected frame, the sound plays.

Note: See Chapter 30 to learn how to play Flash movies.

ASSIGN START SOUNDS

You can use the Flash *start* sound control to start a new instance of a sound even if it is already playing from an earlier instance in your movie. The start sound command is handy when you want to synchronize a sound with your animation. See the section "An Introduction to Flash Sounds" to learn more about sound types.

The tricky thing to remember about start sounds is that they act just like event sounds with the exception of one important difference. If an instance of the sound happens to be playing already, which can happen if your movie loops, the start sound does not restart itself. In the case of event sounds, a second instance of the sound starts playing regardless of whether a current instance plays, which can mean that you have two or more instances of the same sound playing at different stages. Needless to say, this does not always sound harmonious. When you assign the start sound, this does not happen. You hear only one instance of the sound, not a doubling of the same sound.

ASSIGN START SOUNDS

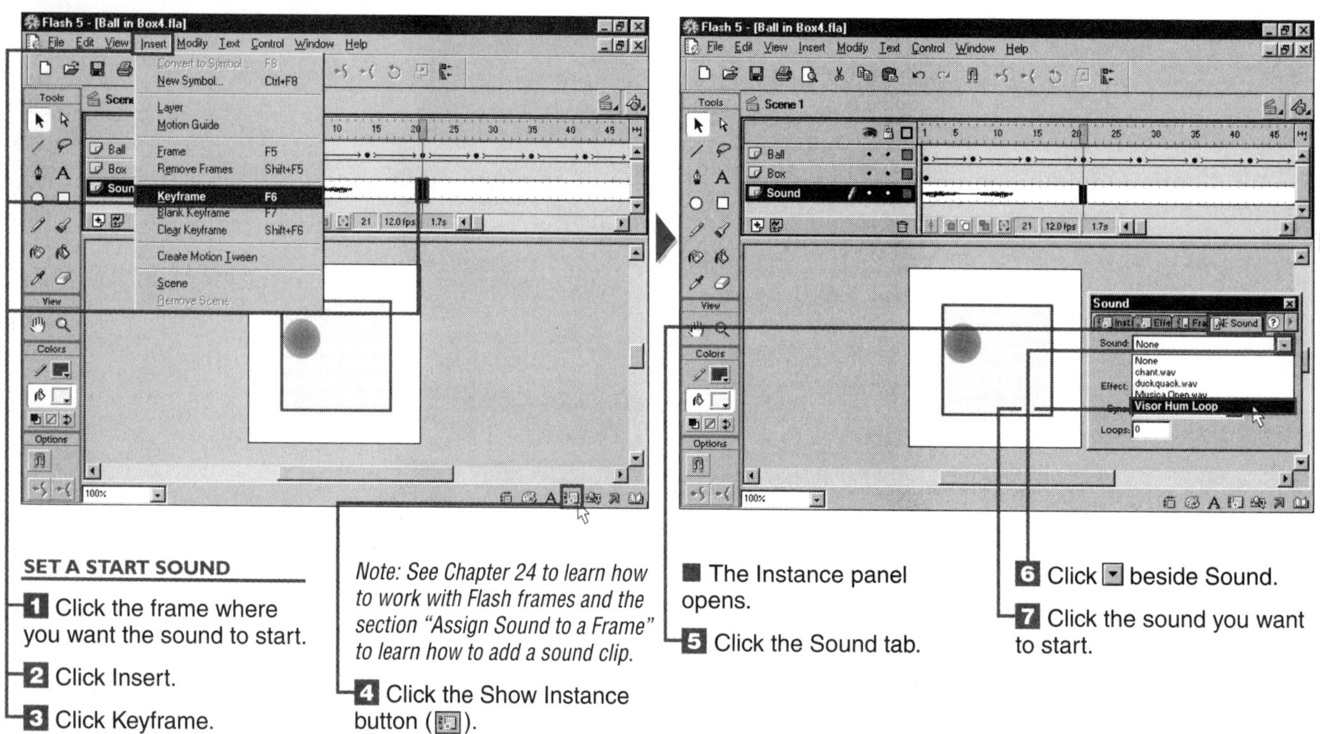

SET A START SOUND

1 Click the frame where you want the sound to start.

2 Click Insert.

3 Click Keyframe.

Note: See Chapter 24 to learn how to work with Flash frames and the section "Assign Sound to a Frame" to learn how to add a sound clip.

4 Click the Show Instance button (▣).

■ The Instance panel opens.

5 Click the Sound tab.

6 Click ▾ beside Sound.

7 Click the sound you want to start.

How can I control the sound's volume?

✔ You can find volume effects controls in the Sound panel. Click ▼ in the Effects box to view the available settings. For example, to make the sound fade in, click the Fade In setting. Learn more about editing sounds in the section "Edit Sounds."

Can I reassign a sound's sync type?

✔ Yes. You can easily redesignate a sync type for any sound in your movie. Simply open the Sound panel and apply another sync type to the selected frame containing the sound you want to change.

What does the Loop option do?

✔ You can set your sound clip to loop by typing the number of times you want the loop to occur in the Loop text box located in the Sound panel. For example, if you want the clip to keep playing indefinitely, try setting a large number, such as 50 or 75.

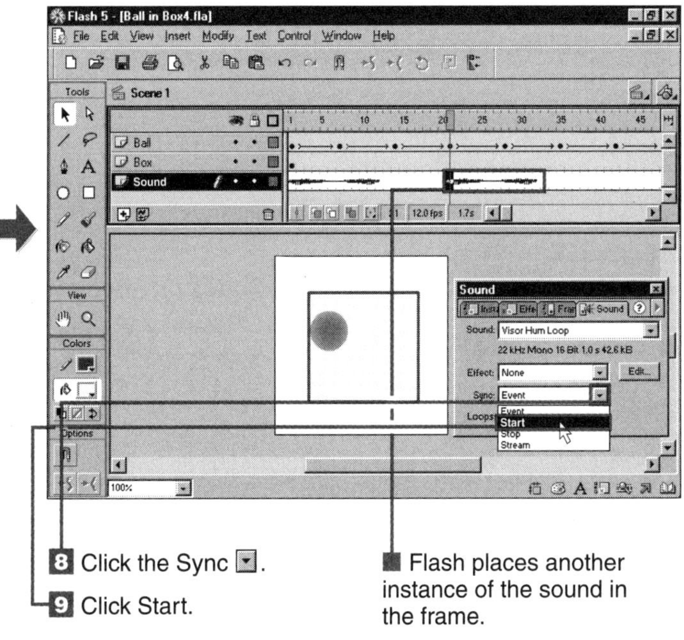

8 Click the Sync ▼.

9 Click Start.

■ Flash places another instance of the sound in the frame.

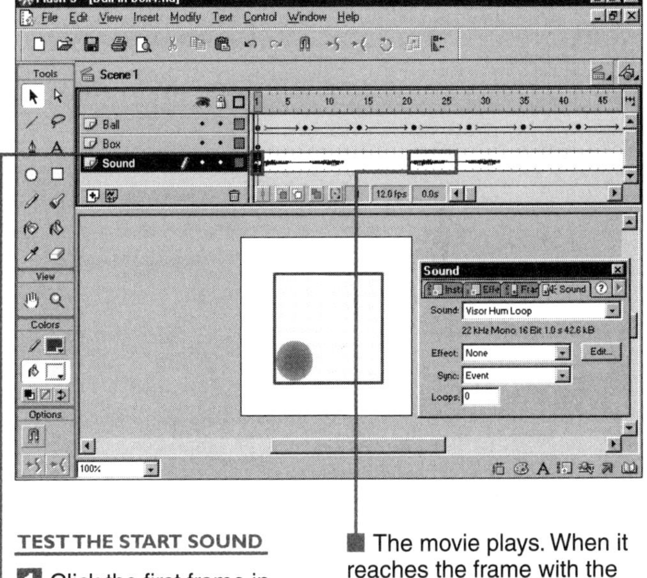

TEST THE START SOUND

1 Click the first frame in your movie.

2 Press Enter.

■ The movie plays. When it reaches the frame with the start sound, the sound plays again.

Note: See Chapter 30 to learn how to play Flash movies.

ASSIGN STOP SOUNDS

If you want to stop a sound before it reaches the end, you can insert a *stop* sound. For example, if your animation ends on a particular frame, but your sound clip goes on much longer, you can put a stop sound in the frame to end the sound.

You use stop sounds in conjunction with event sounds. If you have a long sound clip playing as a background in your movie, you can stop it at a certain point in your movie by placing a stop sound in the frame where you want the sound to end. A stop sound is simply an instruction that tells Flash to quit playing a specific event sound.

See the section "Assign Start Sounds" to learn how to add a start sound to your movie.

ASSIGN STOP SOUNDS

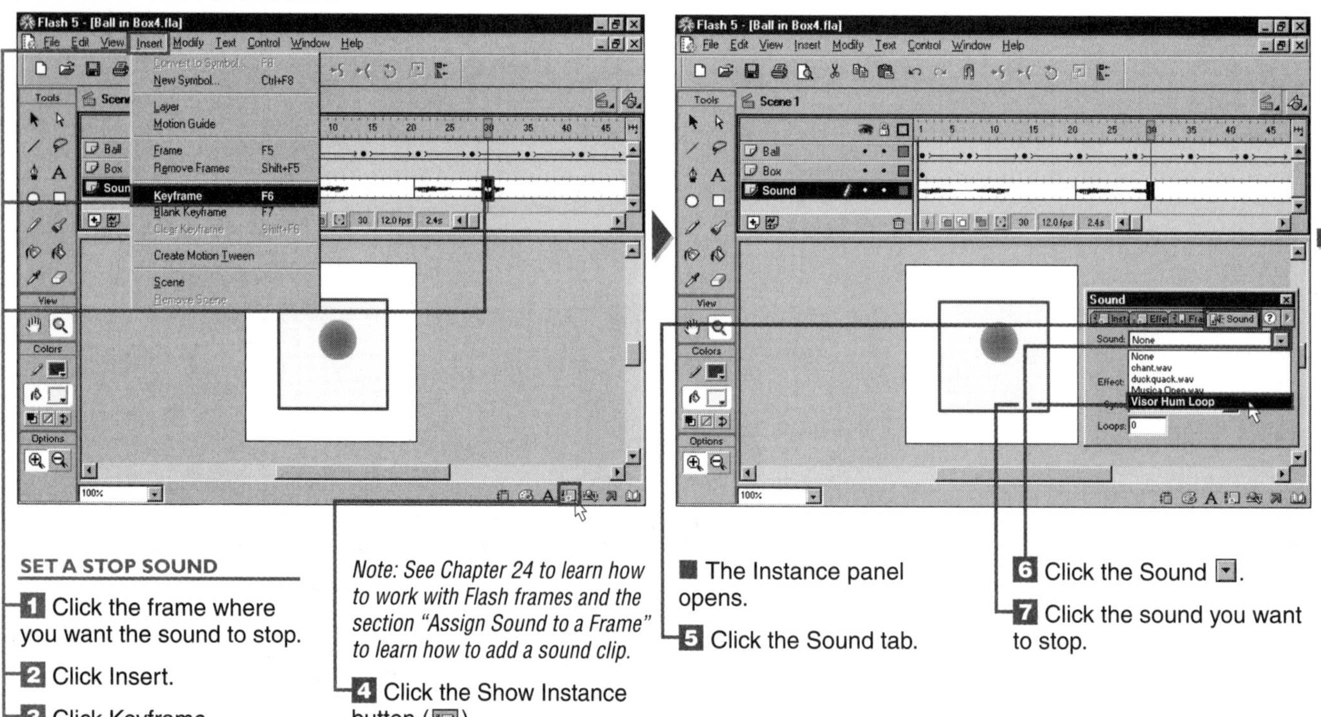

SET A STOP SOUND

1 Click the frame where you want the sound to stop.

2 Click Insert.

3 Click Keyframe.

Note: See Chapter 24 to learn how to work with Flash frames and the section "Assign Sound to a Frame" to learn how to add a sound clip.

4 Click the Show Instance button (▢).

■ The Instance panel opens.

5 Click the Sound tab.

6 Click the Sound ▾.

7 Click the sound you want to stop.

Do I have to have the stop sound in the same layer as the sound I am stopping?

✔ You do not have to assign a Stop command to the same layer containing the sound you want to stop. The command immediately stops any playback of the sound regardless of where you assign the sound.

How do I stop a streaming sound?

✔ Insert a blank keyframe in the sound layer at the point in your movie where you want the audio to end. See Chapter 24 to learn more about inserting keyframes into your movie's Timeline.

Can I stop all the sounds playing in my movie?

✔ Yes. First select the frame in which you want to add the action. Click the Show Actions button (◙) to display the Frame Actions panel. View the Basic Actions list and select Stop All Sound. Flash adds the command to the actions list box. Click the Hide Actions button (◙) to close the Frame Actions panel. When you test your movie, all sounds stops when Flash reaches the frame containing the action.

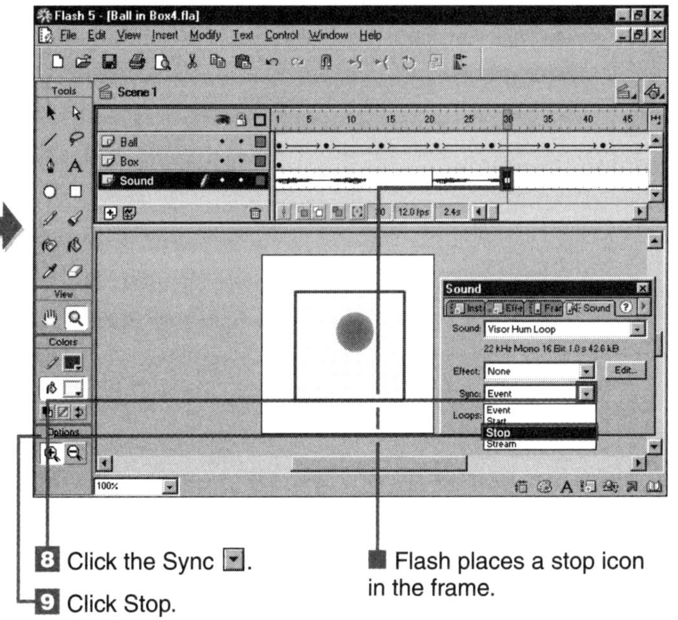

8 Click the Sync ▾.

9 Click Stop.

■ Flash places a stop icon in the frame.

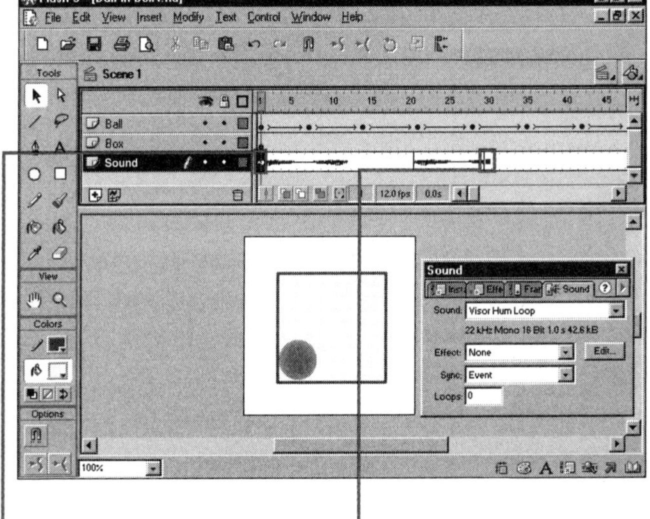

TEST THE STOP SOUND

1 Click the first frame in your movie.

2 Press Enter.

■ The movie plays. When it reaches the frame with the stop sound, the sound stops playing.

Note: See Chapter 30 to learn how to play Flash movies.

ASSIGN STREAMING SOUNDS

You can use *streaming* sounds for Flash movies you place on Web pages. Streaming sounds are good for long sound files, such as a musical sound track. The sound starts streaming as the page downloads, so the user does not have to wait for the entire file to finish downloading. Users can hear the sound as soon as the streaming or downloading starts. This happens because Flash breaks the sound into smaller units for easier downloading.

With streaming sound, Flash synchronizes the frames in your movie with the sound clip. If your sound is a bit slow when downloading, the frames slow down as well. The synchronization forces Flash to keep your animation at the same pace as the sounds. Occasionally the sound may play much faster than Flash can display the individual frames, resulting in skipped frames. When your animation ends, the streaming sound stops.

ASSIGN STREAMING SOUNDS

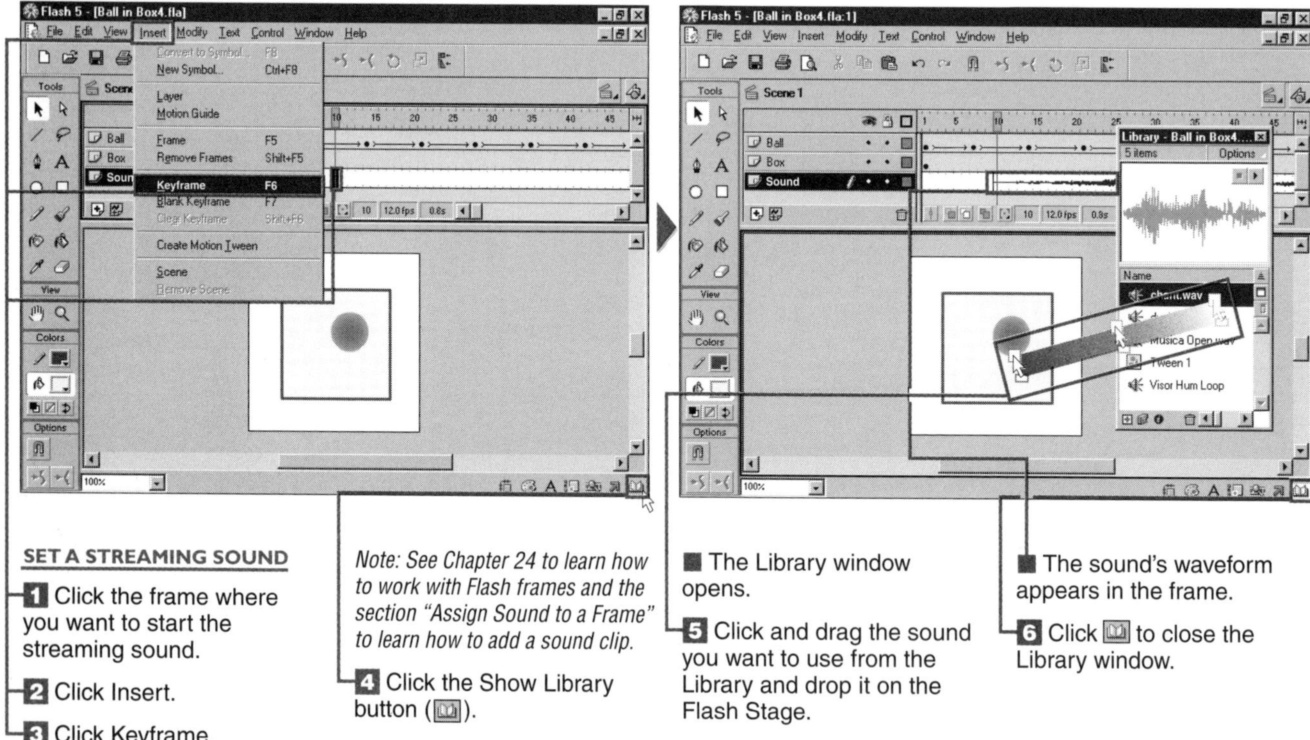

SET A STREAMING SOUND

1 Click the frame where you want to start the streaming sound.

2 Click Insert.

3 Click Keyframe.

Note: See Chapter 24 to learn how to work with Flash frames and the section "Assign Sound to a Frame" to learn how to add a sound clip.

4 Click the Show Library button (📖).

■ The Library window opens.

5 Click and drag the sound you want to use from the Library and drop it on the Flash Stage.

■ The sound's waveform appears in the frame.

6 Click 📖 to close the Library window.

What do I do if my streaming sound gets cut off too soon?

✔ You can try switching the units from seconds to frames. To do so, click Edit in the Sound panel. The Edit Envelope dialog box opens to reveal the sound file. Click ▤ to set the unit scale to Frames and click ☒ to close the dialog box. Play the movie again to test it.

Does my movie's frame rate affect my sounds?

✔ Yes, particularly for longer-playing sounds. For example, if your movie uses the default frame rate of 12 frames per second (fps), a 30-second sound consumes 360 frames in your movie. If you change the frame rate to 18 fps, the sound uses 540 frames. The frame rate and the length of your sound factor into how your movie plays. To change your movie's frame rate, click the Modify menu and click Movie. This opens the Movie Properties dialog box where you can change the frame rate for your movie.

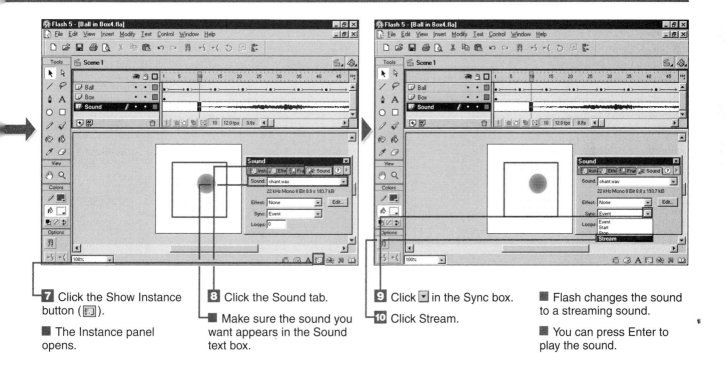

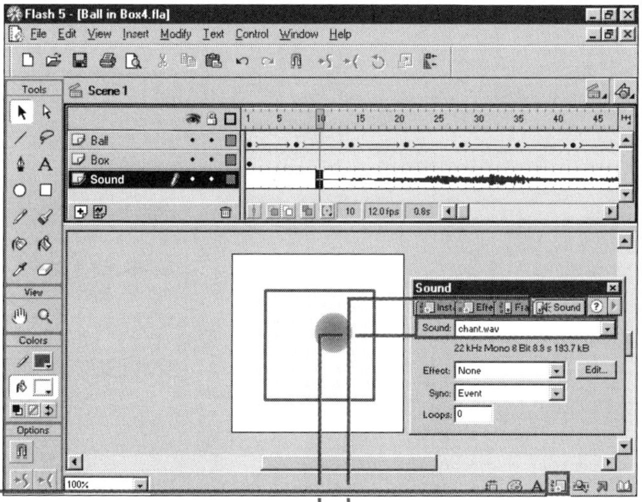

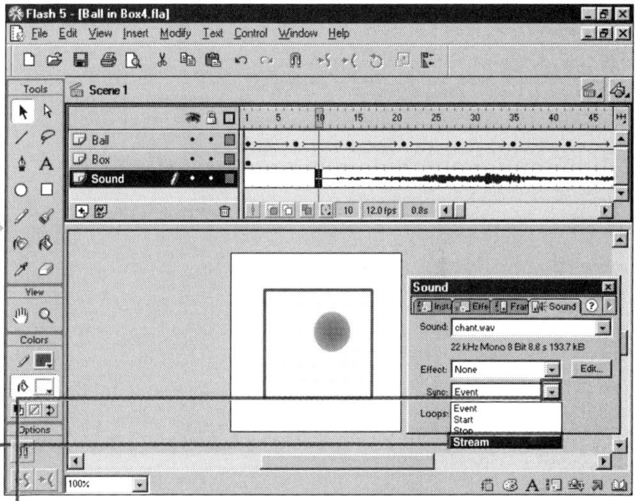

7 Click the Show Instance button (▤).

■ The Instance panel opens.

8 Click the Sound tab.

■ Make sure the sound you want appears in the Sound text box.

9 Click ▾ in the Sync box.

10 Click Stream.

■ Flash changes the sound to a streaming sound.

■ You can press Enter to play the sound.

LOOP A SOUND

You can make a sound play over and over again with the Loop command. *Looping* means to play the sound repeatedly, as many times as you like. You can choose to loop event and streaming sounds in your Flash movies.

When you loop a sound, you are only using one instance of the sound throughout your movie. To set the number of times you want a sound to repeat, use the Loop field in the Sound panel. The number you type dictates how often the sound plays. For example, if you type a setting of 5, Flash loops the sound five times from start to finish. If you specify a loop setting that exceeds the length of your movie and the sound is an event sound, the sound continues to play even after your movie stops. For that reason, it is important to test any loop setting you type to make sure it works in the timing of your movie's playback.

LOOP A SOUND

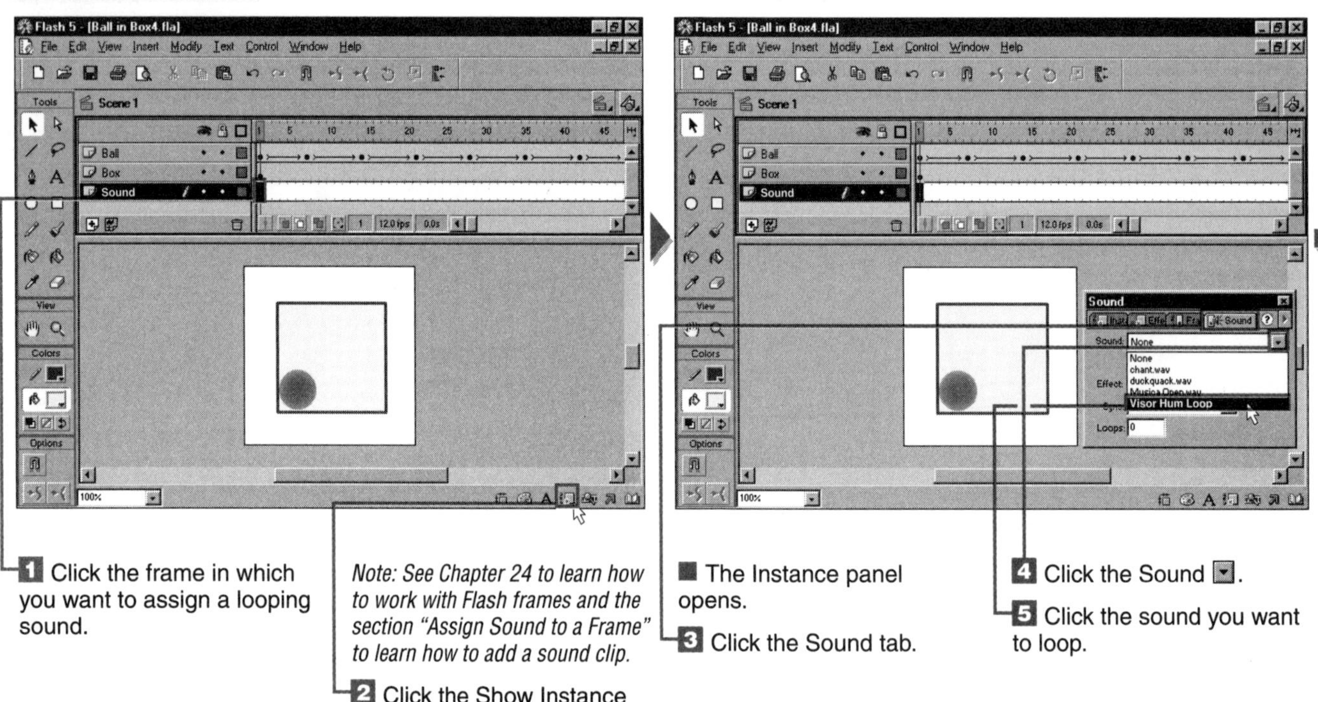

1 Click the frame in which you want to assign a looping sound.

2 Click the Show Instance button.

Note: See Chapter 24 to learn how to work with Flash frames and the section "Assign Sound to a Frame" to learn how to add a sound clip.

■ The Instance panel opens.

3 Click the Sound tab.

4 Click the Sound ▼.

5 Click the sound you want to loop.

What if I want the sound to loop forever?

✔ If you have set a streaming sound, you can set the loop to a high number, like 30 or 40. Flash does not loop the sound that many times, but the sound keeps looping until the end of the movie.

How do I change a sound's properties?

✔ You can change any sound's properties through the Library window. Display the Library and click the sound you want to change. Click ⓘ to open the Sound Properties dialog box. Here you can view information about the sound file and set export compression for the sound.

How do I update a sound I use throughout my movie?

✔ Perhaps upon testing your movie you need to edit a sound you use frequently throughout the movie. From the Library window, click the sound you want to edit, and then click the Options menu. Choose Edit With or Edit With QuickTime Player. You can then edit the sound with the sound editing program you choose. Save the sound file and Flash updates every instance of it throughout your movie.

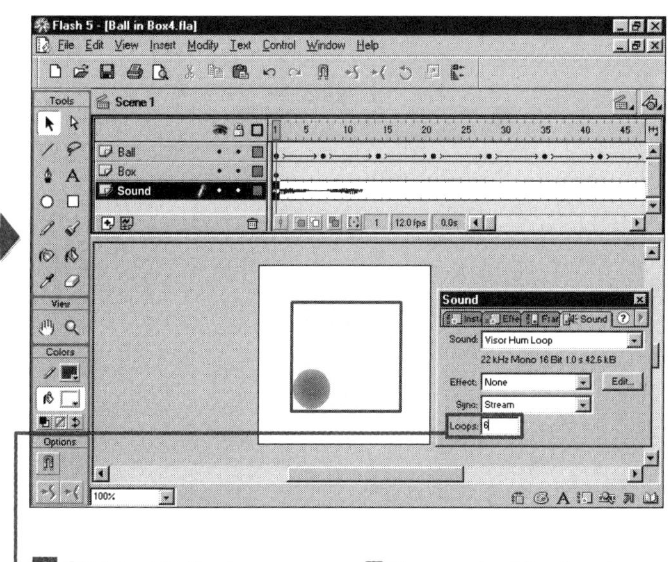

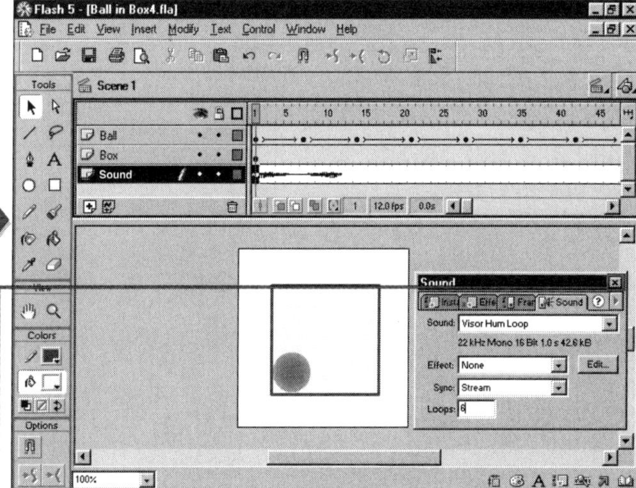

6 Click inside the Loops box.

7 Type the number of times you want the sound to loop.

■ You can test the looping effect by pressing Enter to play the movie.

Note: See Chapter 30 to learn how to play Flash movies.

8 To close the Sound panel, click ☒.

EDIT SOUNDS

Flash comes with some handy volume controls to fade sounds in or out, or make sounds move from one speaker to another in a stereo setup. For applying simple sound effects such as these, use the Effects drop-down list in the Sound panel. For additional editing controls, open the Edit Envelope dialog box.

When you import a sound into Flash, its file includes information about the sound's length, volume, and stereo settings. You can fine-tune these settings using the Edit Envelope dialog box. Flash's sound-editing controls enable you to define start and end points for sounds, or to adjust the volume at different points in the sound. For example, you can make your sound files smaller in size if you define the exact point at which a sound starts to play, or define the point where the sound ends.

The Edit Envelope dialog box displays your sound as a waveform with both left and right audio channels. You can click the waveform in either channel and drag edit points, called *envelope handles*, to adjust the volume and length of a sound.

EDIT SOUNDS

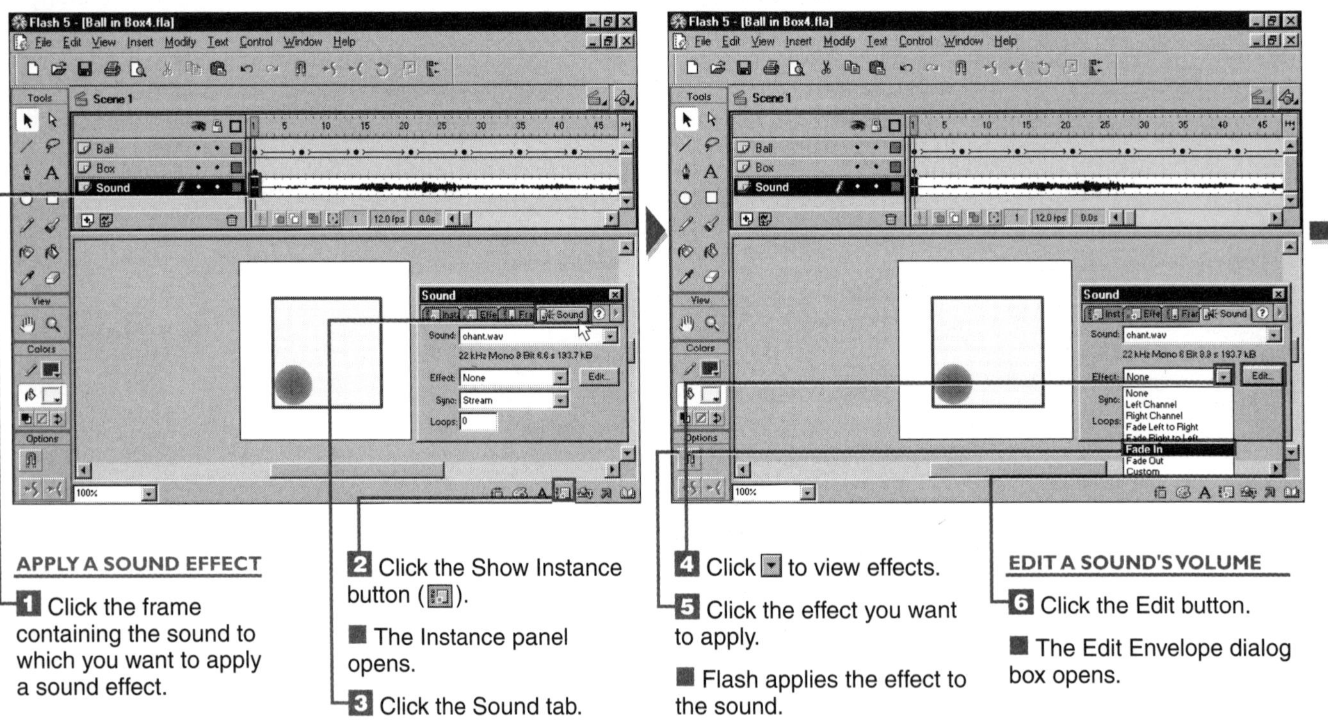

APPLY A SOUND EFFECT

1 Click the frame containing the sound to which you want to apply a sound effect.

2 Click the Show Instance button (▣).

■ The Instance panel opens.

3 Click the Sound tab.

4 Click ▼ to view effects.

5 Click the effect you want to apply.

■ Flash applies the effect to the sound.

EDIT A SOUND'S VOLUME

6 Click the Edit button.

■ The Edit Envelope dialog box opens.

How do I create start and end points for my sound?

✔ Drag the Time In control marker, located at the far left side of the Sound Timeline bar separating the two channels in the Edit Envelope dialog box, to create a new start point for your sound. To create a new end point, drag the Time Out control marker, located at the far right side of the Sound Timeline bar separating the two channels.

Can I change the panning for a sound channel?

✔ Yes. *Panning* refers to the stereo effects of a sound, adjusting the left and right audio channels. You can adjust the volume by dragging envelope handles in either audio channel in the Edit Envelope dialog box to create panning effects for your movie.

How many envelope handles can I use on a channel?

✔ You can add up to eight envelope handles to either channel and drag them up or down to adjust sound volume.

How do I remove an envelope handle?

✔ Click and drag the handle (□) off the channel to remove it from the sound.

What are audio channels?

✔ Flash audio channels simulate stereo audio channels that make sounds move from one speaker to the other. The top waveform box in the Edit Envelope dialog box represents the right channel, the bottom box represents the left channel.

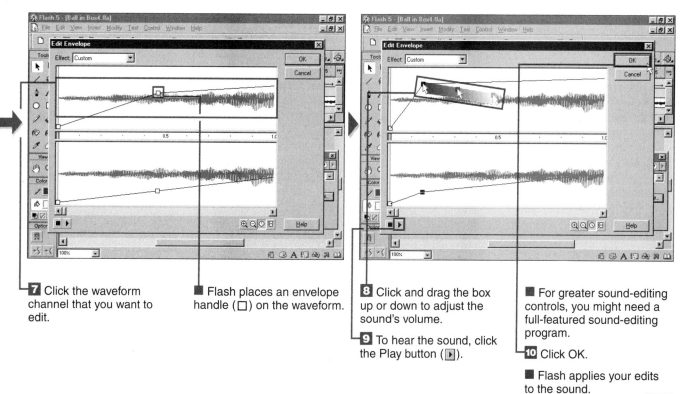

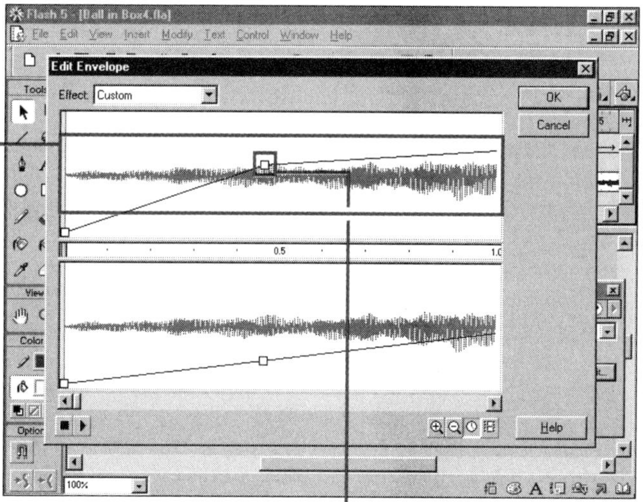

7 Click the waveform channel that you want to edit.

■ Flash places an envelope handle (□) on the waveform.

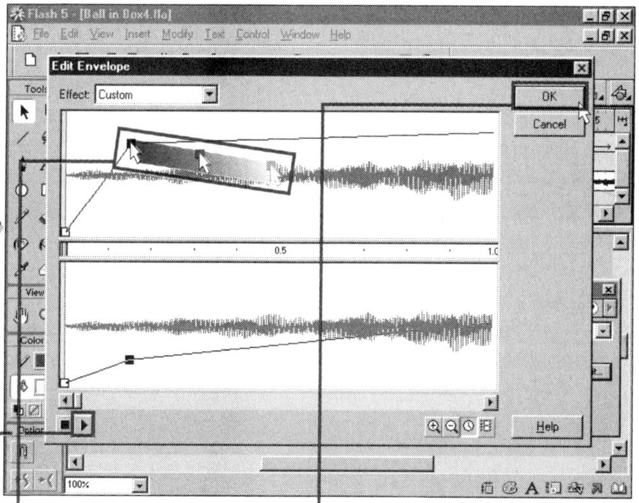

8 Click and drag the box up or down to adjust the sound's volume.

9 To hear the sound, click the Play button (▶).

■ For greater sound-editing controls, you might need a full-featured sound-editing program.

10 Click OK.

■ Flash applies your edits to the sound.

SET AUDIO OUTPUT FOR EXPORT

You can control how you export sounds in your Flash files. You can find options for optimizing your sound files for export in the Publish Settings dialog box. Options include settings for compressing your sounds in ADPCM, MP3, or RAW format. By default, Flash exports sounds in MP3 format using a bit rate of 16 Kbps. MP3 is the emerging standard for distributing audio on the Internet.

The Publish Settings dialog box has options for controlling both Event and Streaming sounds. You can specify exactly how you want to compress your movie's sounds for export. You can also change the settings for bit rate and quality. If you do not reset any sound options in the Publish Settings dialog box, Flash exports the file using the default settings. To learn more about publishing your Flash movies, see Chapter 30.

SET AUDIO OUTPUT FOR EXPORT

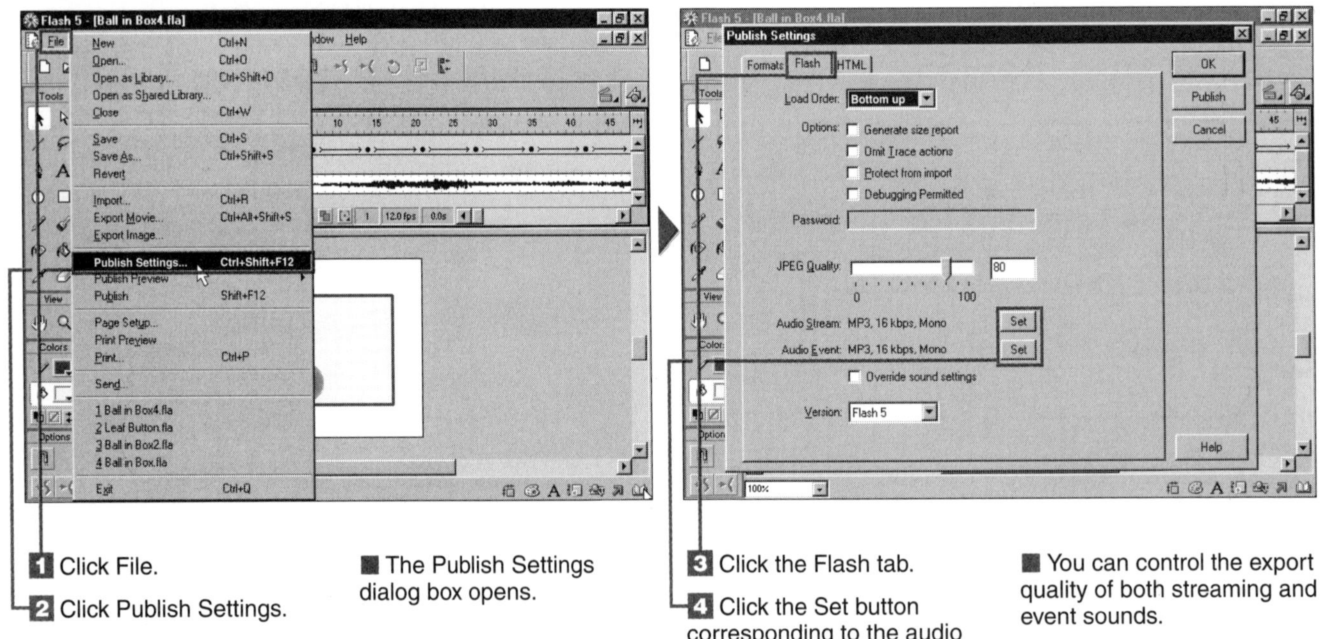

1 Click File.

2 Click Publish Settings.

■ The Publish Settings dialog box opens.

3 Click the Flash tab.

4 Click the Set button corresponding to the audio type you want to control.

■ You can control the export quality of both streaming and event sounds.

■ Clicking either Set button opens the Sound Settings dialog box.

What is a good bit rate for MP3?

✓ MP3 efficiently compresses audio files, resulting in high bit rates — therefore better quality — and small file sizes. This is why MP3 is emerging as the standard for distributing sounds on the Internet, especially on Web pages. For large music files, try a setting of 64 Kbps. For speech or voice files, try 24 or 32 Kbps. To set near CD quality, use a setting of 112 or 128 Kbps. Use 16 Kbps settings for simple button sounds, or larger audio sounds where quality is not crucial.

What can I do to minimize my movie's file size?

✓ You can do several things, particularly for sound portions of your file. If you loop event sounds, use short sound clips. Avoid making streaming sounds loop. You can get more out of the same sounds in a movie if you apply some editing techniques, such as fading sound in or out at different keyframes. You can experiment with the editing options in the section "Edit Sounds."

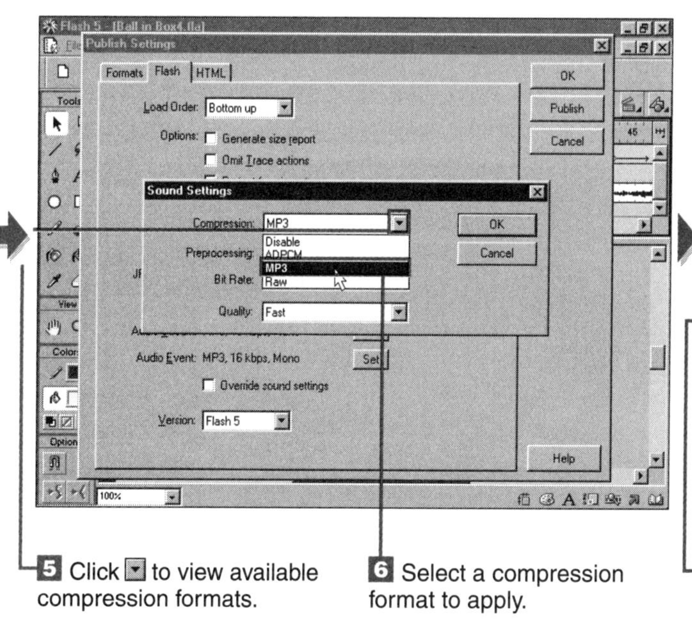

5 Click ▾ to view available compression formats.

6 Select a compression format to apply.

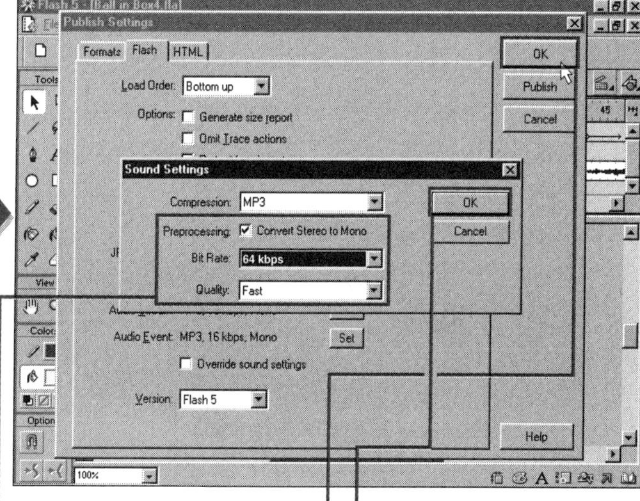

■ Depending on the format you select, the remaining options in the Sound Settings dialog box reflect settings associated with your selection.

■ You can make changes to the remaining settings.

7 Click OK to close the Sound Settings dialog box.

8 Click OK.

■ The Publish Settings dialog box closes and Flash saves your settings.

AN INTRODUCTION TO FLASH ACTIONS

You can add interactivity to your Flash movies by assigning an *action*, or behavior, to a frame or button. The occurrence that triggers the action is an *event*. The result of the action is the *target*.

You can add Flash actions in different levels of complexity. You add *frame actions* to give you greater control over how a movie plays. You add *button actions* to enable users to interact via a button. Or you can add *complex actions* that require parameters for users to interact with elements in your movie. This chapter discusses frame and button actions. To learn more about complex actions that involve parameters, see Chapter 29.

Although Flash has many actions, you use the Stop All Sounds, the Go To, and the Navigation actions more commonly.

Stop All Sounds Actions

The Stop All Sounds action tells Flash to cancel any sounds that are currently playing in the movie. You can use this action to stop a looping background soundtrack for a particular frame or frames. You can also assign this action to a button that enables users to stop the sounds from playing, in which case the action becomes a button action that enables input. The Stop All Sounds action is a frame action that does not necessarily require any input from the user.

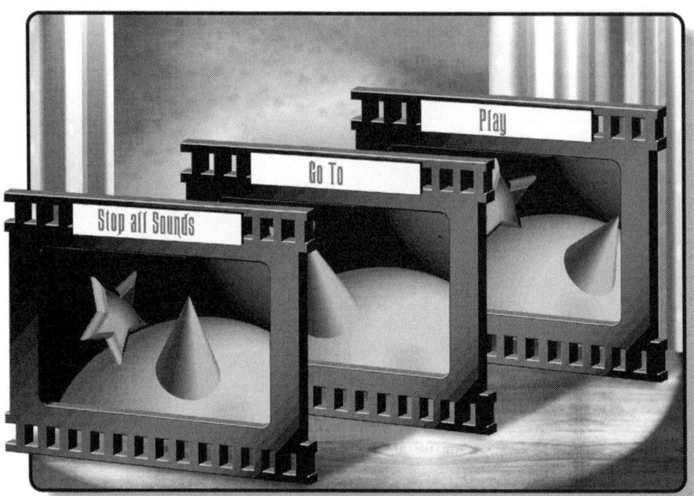

Go To Actions

Another example of a frame action that requires no user input is the Go To action. The Go To action tells Flash to jump to a specified frame in the movie's Timeline and start playing that frame. When assigning the Go To action to a frame, you tell Flash to change the current frame by jumping to a new targeted frame in the movie. You determine the frame to which the movie jumps.

Navigation Actions

You can use navigation actions, common in Flash movies, to place a button in your movie that users can click to stop the movie. By assigning a button with the Stop action in the movie frame containing a large amount of text, you enable users to stop the movie to read the text. You can assign a Play action to another button in the same frame so that users can click the Play button to continue with the presentation.

Using Actions in Flash

You use actions to tell Flash how to perform certain tasks in a movie. Actions are based on principles of cause and effect. For example, the action of clicking a button is a cause, while stopping a movie is the efffect, or the behavior, of the action.

Although Flash actions work like macros and scripting commands in programming languages, you do not need to know a scripting language to use them. When you assign an action, Flash adds it to an *action list* for that particular frame. Flash then executes the actions in the order they appear in the list.

Using Events in Flash

Anything that causes an action is called an *event*. In Flash terminology, an event triggers an action in your movie. Flash recognizes three types of events: *mouse events,* or button actions, *keyboard events,* and *frame events,* also called frame actions. For example, a mouse event occurs when a user interacts with a button, See Chapter 26 to learn about creating Flash buttons. Keyboard events occur when a user presses a keyboard key, to which you assign an action. You place frame events in keyframes in your movie and trigger actions that occur at certain points in the movie's Timeline.

Event Handlers

Event handlers, which manage events, tell Flash when to perform an action and make sure the action carries out the task. When you assign an action, Flash automatically includes an event handler. If you assign a button action, Flash includes the On Mouse Event handler. If you assign a frame action, Flash includes the On Clip Event handler. You can recognize an event handler in the actions list by the word "on" followed by the type of event.

Targets

A *target* is the object which the action affects. You direct Targets toward the current, or *default,* movie, other movies, also called the *Tell Target,* or a browser application, also called an *external target*. For example, you can place a button in your movie that, when clicked, opens a Web page. You direct most of your frame actions toward the current movie, which is the default target.

ADD ACTIONS TO FRAMES

You can use the Frame Actions panel to add actions to your movie. Frames can include multiple actions, but you can only assign an action one frame at a time. You add actions to the frame's *action script,* a list of actions associated with the frame. Flash performs the actions in the order they appear in the list.

Flash groups the types of actions in categories in the Frame Actions panel. The Basic Actions category includes all the commonly used actions, such as Go To, Play, Stop, and Get URL. Complex actions are listed among the other categories and include ActionScript operators, functions, and properties.

When you assign an action, it appears in the actions list on the right side of the Frame Actions panel. By default, you cannot see the actions list in its entirety. You can expand the list with the Widen button to view the action notation and set any additional parameters that are associated with the action.

ADD ACTIONS TO FRAMES

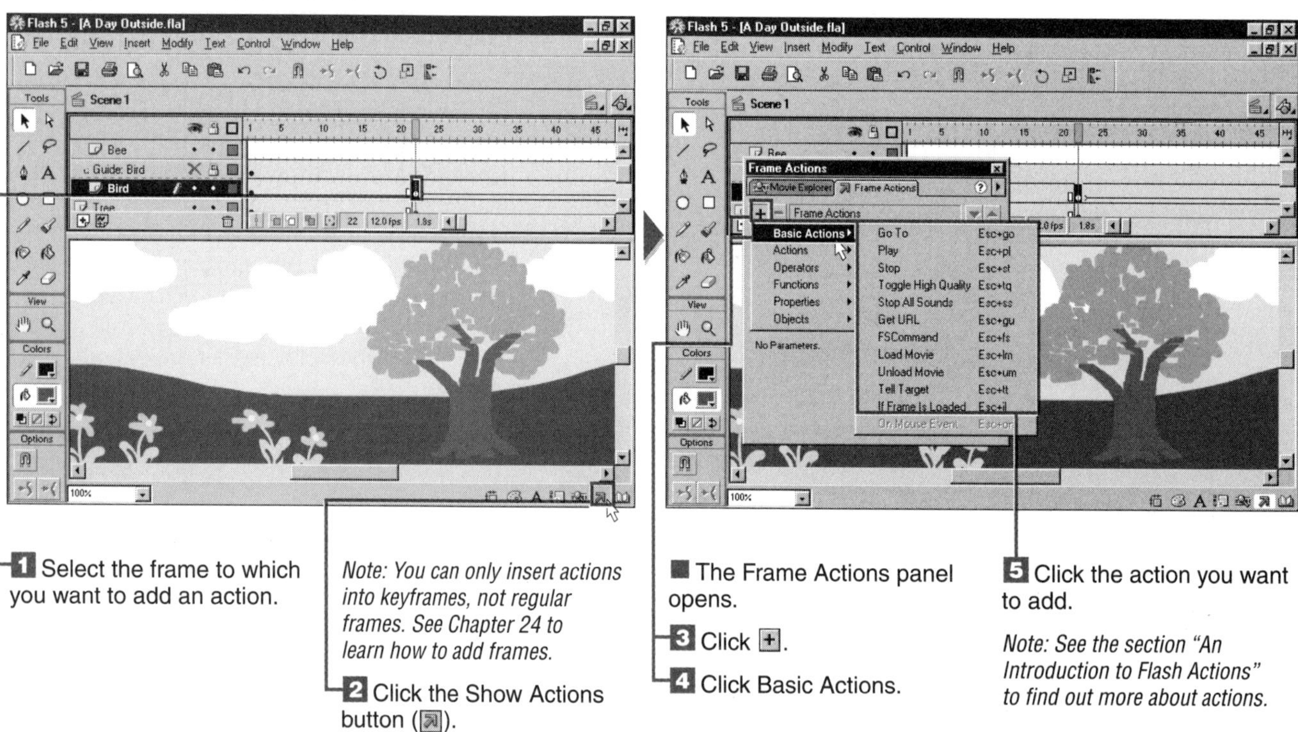

1 Select the frame to which you want to add an action.

Note: You can only insert actions into keyframes, not regular frames. See Chapter 24 to learn how to add frames.

2 Click the Show Actions button (▣).

■ The Frame Actions panel opens.

3 Click ⊞.

4 Click Basic Actions.

5 Click the action you want to add.

Note: See the section "An Introduction to Flash Actions" to find out more about actions.

How do I organize actions in my movie?

✔ To help you clearly identify actions you assign to frames, consider creating a layer specifically for actions in your movie. This technique simplifies the process of finding the action you want to edit. To add a layer to the Timeline, click the Insert Layer button (). A new layer appears above the current layer. You can rename the layer or move it to another position in the layer stack. See Chapter 21 to find out more about moving and positioning Flash layers.

How do I remove an action from my movie?

✔ Select the frame containing the action you want to delete and then click Show Actions button () to open the Frame Actions panel. From the actions list, select the action statement you want to remove. Click . The action is removed from the list.

Can I edit an action?

✔ Yes. To make changes to an action's parameters, open the Frame Actions panel and select the action statement for the action you want to modify. The associated parameters appear at the bottom of the Frame Actions panel. You can make changes to the parameters as needed.

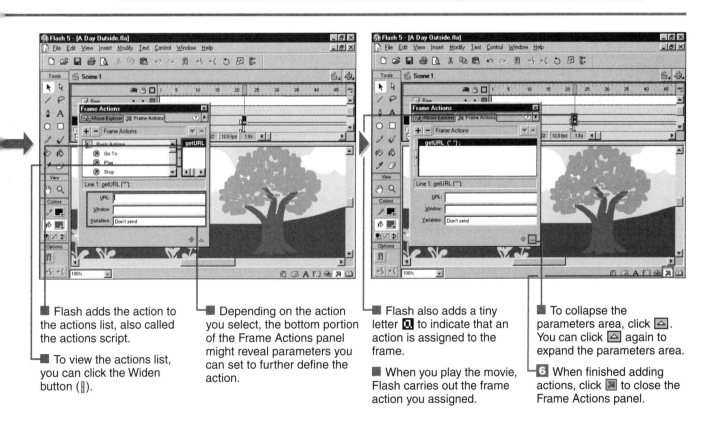

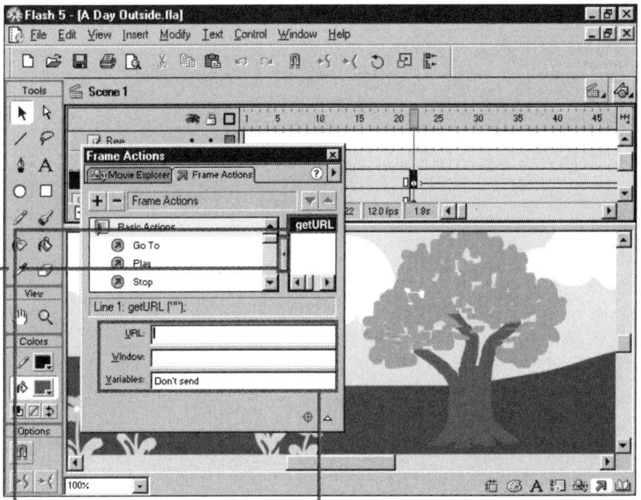

■ Flash adds the action to the actions list, also called the actions script.

■ To view the actions list, you can click the Widen button ().

■ Depending on the action you select, the bottom portion of the Frame Actions panel might reveal parameters you can set to further define the action.

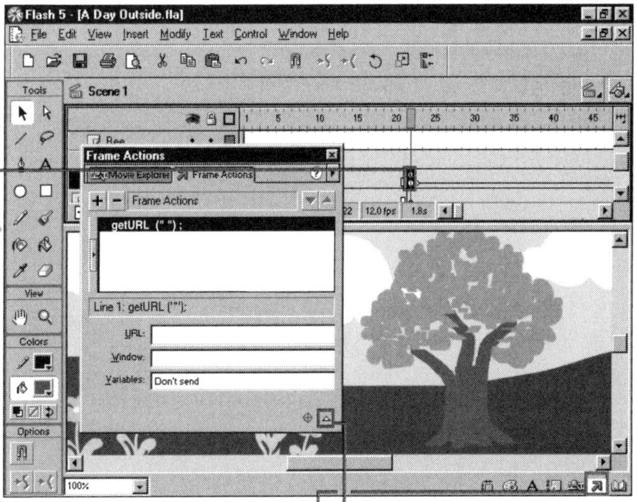

■ Flash also adds a tiny letter to indicate that an action is assigned to the frame.

■ When you play the movie, Flash carries out the frame action you assigned.

■ To collapse the parameters area, click . You can click again to expand the parameters area.

6 When finished adding actions, click to close the Frame Actions panel.

ASSIGN GO TO ACTIONS

You can assign a Go To action that tells Flash to start playing a particular frame in your movie. You can use the Go To action with frames or buttons. When Flash follows a Go To action, it jumps to, or "goes to," a specified target frame.

The Go To action includes parameters you can define to play a specific frame. You can enter a frame number as the target frame, or if your frames are organized with labels, you can enter the label of the target frame. (See "Assign Frame Labels" later in this chapter, to learn more about labeling frames.)

The Go To action has two variations: Go To and Play, or Go To and Stop. The Go To and Play parameter is used by default. With the play parameter active, Flash goes to the frame you specify and immediately starts playing the movie from there. If you deselect the Go To and Play check box, the action statement reads Go To and Stop. This means Flash will stop playing the movie when it jumps to the designated frame.

ASSIGN GO TO ACTIONS

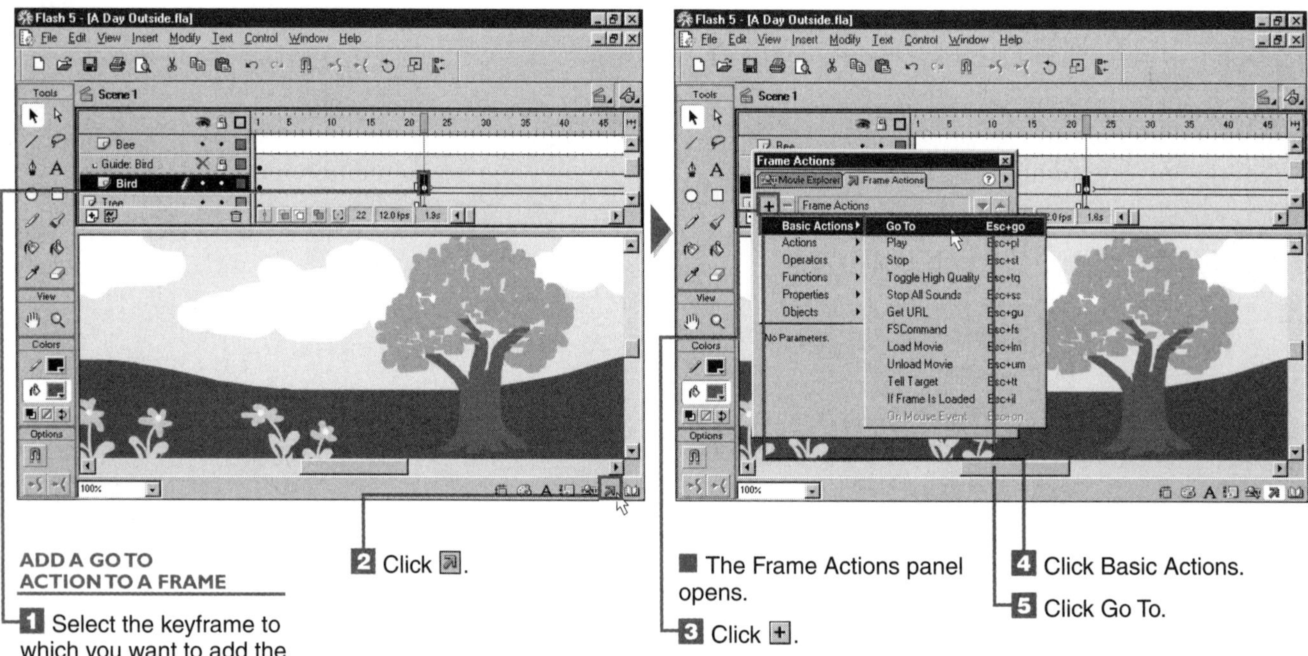

ADD A GO TO ACTION TO A FRAME

1 Select the keyframe to which you want to add the action.

2 Click .

■ The Frame Actions panel opens.

3 Click .

4 Click Basic Actions.

5 Click Go To.

Can I reference a scene in the Go To parameters that I have not created yet?

✔ Yes. You can plan ahead and reference scenes you have not yet created in your movie. If the scene still is not available when you play the movie, Flash ignores the Go To command because it does not reference a legitimate frame in your movie.

Do I need to label my frames?

✔ Although you can certainly refer to any frame by its number, you have an opportunity to label frames with distinct titles that more readily tell you about the frame's content. Labeling frames is particularly helpful with longer Flash movies. You can use labels to tell you when a key change occurs in an animation, or to indicate a new element that appears in the movie. Labeling is an organizational tool and can help you with keeping your actions organized as well. To learn more about assigning labels to frames, see the section "Assign Frame Labels," later in this chapter.

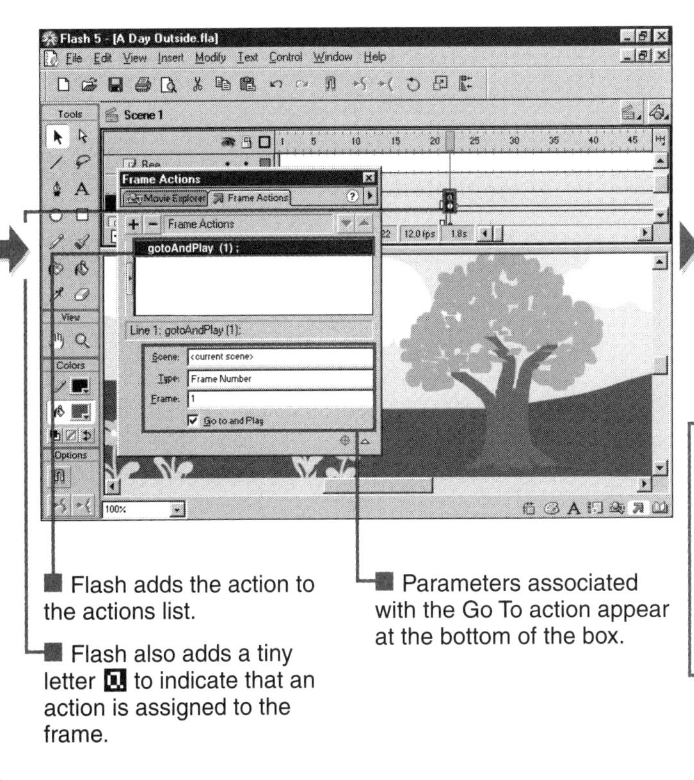

■ Flash adds the action to the actions list.

■ Flash also adds a tiny letter a to indicate that an action is assigned to the frame.

■ Parameters associated with the Go To action appear at the bottom of the box.

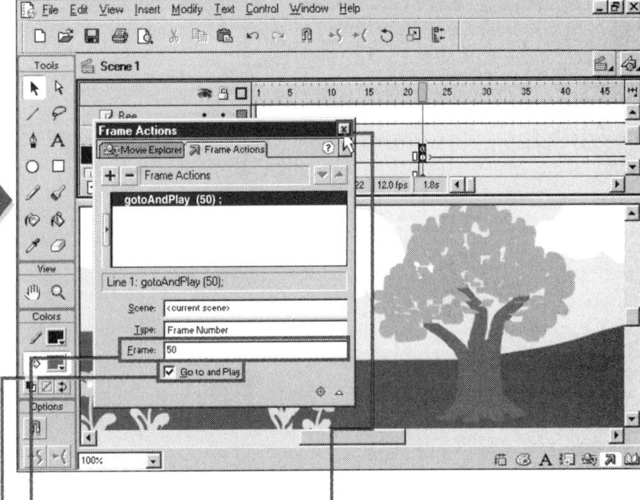

6 Type the number of the frame to which you want to go.

■ You can click Go to and Play to make the movie continue playing when it jumps to the designated frame (☐ changes to ☑).

■ You can uncheck Go to and Play to go to the designated frame and stop.

7 To close the Frame Actions panel, click ☒.

■ When you play the movie, Flash follows the frame action you assigned.

CONTINUED

ASSIGN GO TO ACTIONS (CONTINUED)

You can also reference scenes in a Go To action. Scenes are simply organized sections of your Flash movie. You can specify a scene name in the Go To action parameters. When you assign a Go To action, Flash follows the instruction during the course of playing the movie and jumps to the scene you referenced.

If you edit your movie later, such as add or delete frames or entire scenes, be sure to update any Go To actions to reference the correct frames or scenes. If you fail to update the Go To action, the action may not "go to" the correct frame.

Always test your movies after you add an action to any frame or button. Testing the action helps you determine if you have set the correct parameters.

See the section "Assign Frame Labels" to find out more about labels, or see Chapter 24 to discover how to create scenes.

ASSIGN GO TO ACTIONS (CONTINUED)

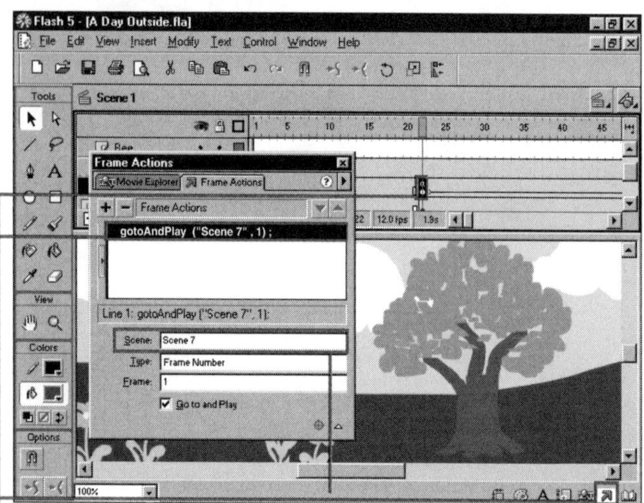

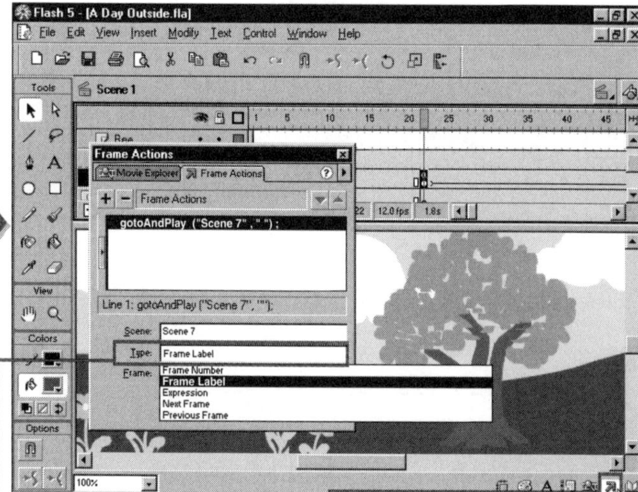

ADD A GO TO ACTION TO A SCENE

1 Select the keyframe to which you want to add the action.

2 Click .

3 Add a Go To action to the actions list.

Note: See the subsection "Add a Go To Action to a Frame."

4 Type the scene name.

■ Flash fills in the parameters in the actions list.

■ To go to a specific frame label instead of a frame number, you can select Frame Label in the Type text box.

5 Click Frame Label, then type the label into the Frame text box.

Note: See the section "Assign Frame Labels" to find out more about organizing action frames.

■ When you play the movie, Flash follows the frame action you assigned.

6 To close the Frame Actions panel, click .

Can I test my action out on the Stage?

✔ Yes, if you turn on the Enable Frame Actions feature. Click the Control menu and then click Enable Simple Frame Actions. A check mark next to the command name means the feature is on; no check mark means the feature is off. You should turn the feature off when not in use, or Flash will engage the Go To command as you work with your movie's frames on the Timeline.

Can I go to a specific frame in another scene?

✔ Yes. First type the name of the scene in the Scene text box, then click the Type box and choose a Frame Number or Frame Label. If you choose a Frame Number type, you must then enter the frame number. If you choose a Frame Label type, you must enter the label.

How do I jump to the previous frame?

✔ Click the Type drop-down parameter and choose Previous Frame. This causes the movie timeline to jump back to the frame preceding the frame in which you added this action.

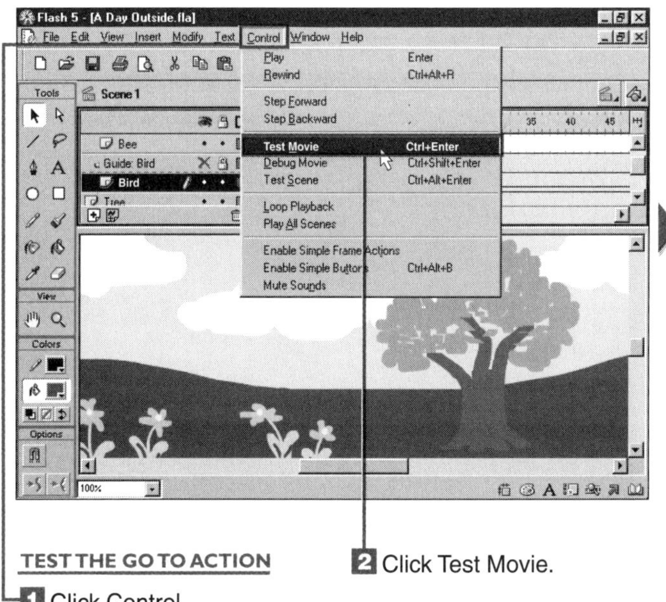

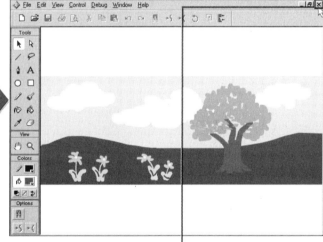

TEST THE GO TO ACTION

1 Click Control.

2 Click Test Movie.

■ Flash opens the Flash Player window and plays the movie.

3 Click ☒ to exit the Player window.

ASSIGN STOP AND PLAY ACTIONS

You can assign a Stop action to stop a movie from playing, or you can assign a Play action to play it again. See the section "Introducing Flash Actions" to find out more about frame actions.

For example, perhaps one of the keyframes in your movie is text heavy and you want to enable the user to pause and read the text. You can create a button and assign a Stop action that enables the user to stop the movie and assign a Play action to another button that lets the user play the movie again.

Stop and Play actions are two of the basic Flash navigation and interaction buttons. The Stop and Play actions are commonly used with buttons. See Chapter 26 to learn more about creating buttons in Flash. If you add a Stop action to a frame, you must add a Play action to start the movie playing again. The steps in this example demonstrate how to add a Stop action and a Play action to two different buttons in a movie.

ASSIGN STOP AND PLAY ACTIONS

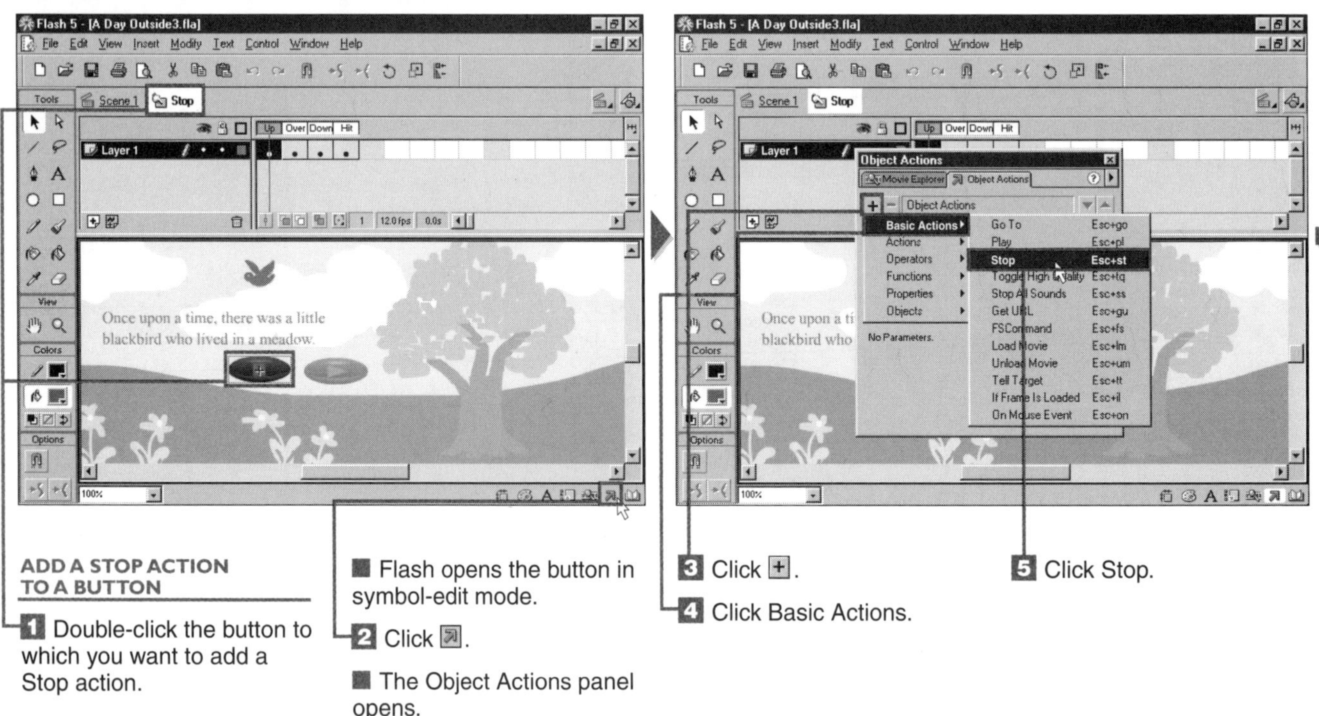

ADD A STOP ACTION TO A BUTTON

1 Double-click the button to which you want to add a Stop action.

■ Flash opens the button in symbol-edit mode.

2 Click ⧉.

■ The Object Actions panel opens.

3 Click +.

4 Click Basic Actions.

5 Click Stop.

What is the difference between frame actions and object actions?

✔ Actions can be applied to frames or buttons. Frame actions are assigned to frames and control how a movie plays. Button actions, as demonstrated in the steps below, are assigned to buttons and require input from the user. For example, a Stop action assigned to a button enables the user to stop a movie by clicking the button to which the action is assigned. You can assign Stop and Play actions to frames or buttons, but remember that button actions require user input in order to carry out the action.

How do I assign a Stop action to a frame?

✔ To assign a Stop action to a frame rather than a button, simply click the frame to which you want the action assigned and follow steps 2 through 5 of the "Add a Stop Action to a Button" section. To assign a Play action to a frame, follow steps 9 through 12 in the "Add a Play Action to a Button" section. To learn more about assigning frame actions, see the "Add Actions to Frames" section.

Does a Play action in a scene affect the rest of the movie's Timeline?

✔ A scene has its own independent timeline separate from the rest of the movie's Timeline. If you add a Play action to a frame in that scene, it does not effect the main movie's Timeline.

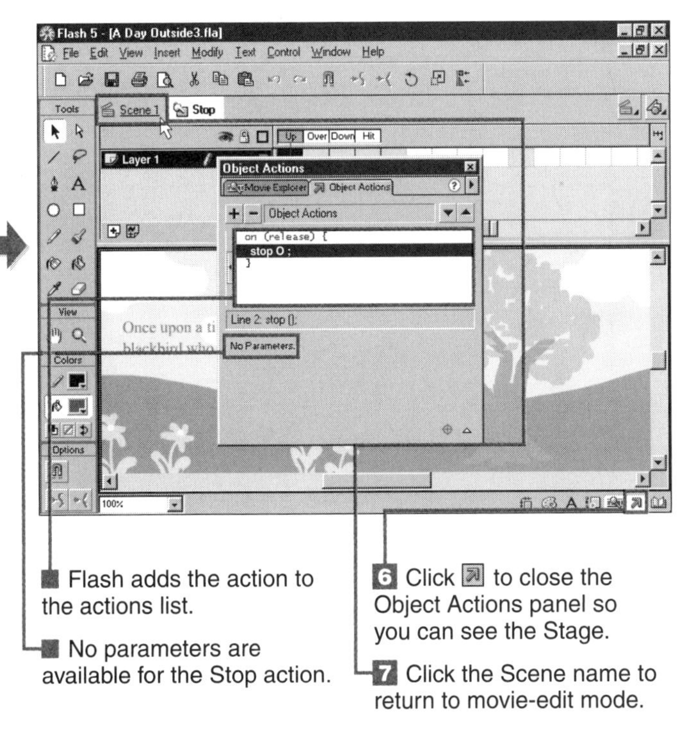

■ Flash adds the action to the actions list.

■ No parameters are available for the Stop action.

6 Click ⧉ to close the Object Actions panel so you can see the Stage.

7 Click the Scene name to return to movie-edit mode.

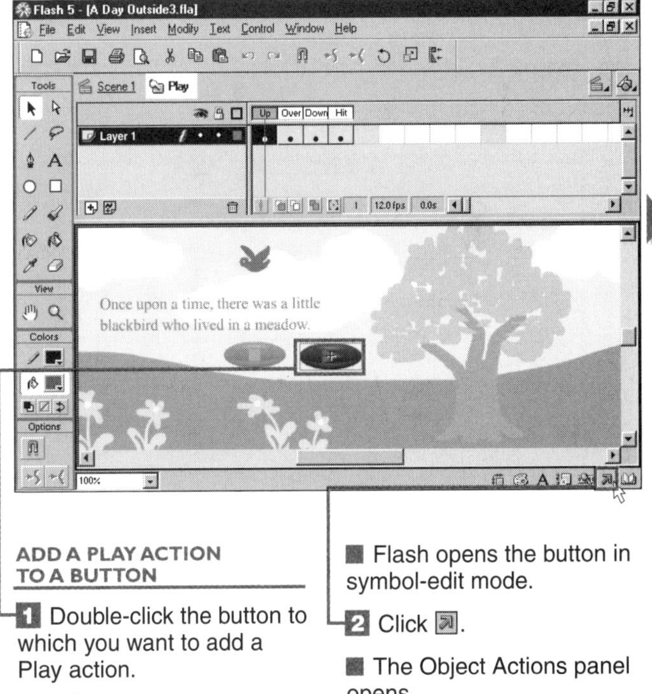

ADD A PLAY ACTION TO A BUTTON

1 Double-click the button to which you want to add a Play action.

■ Flash opens the button in symbol-edit mode.

2 Click ⧉.

■ The Object Actions panel opens.

CONTINUED

ASSIGN STOP AND PLAY ACTIONS (CONTINUED)

Assign the Stop and Play actions to give users control over the movie's playback. Stop and Play actions act much like the controls found on a VCR or CD player. In many cases, you will want to use the two commands together because the Stop action ceases the movie from playing while the Play action starts a movie previously stopped with the Stop action.

The Play action plays the movie based on the assigned frame rate, measured in frames per second. (To learn more about setting the frame rate for playback, see Chapter 24.)

Like other actions you assign in Flash, a tiny letter *a* appears in the frame in which a Stop or Play action is assigned. This icon, which stands for action, lets you know you have an action assigned to the frame as you view the Timeline.

ASSIGN STOP AND PLAY ACTIONS (CONTINUED)

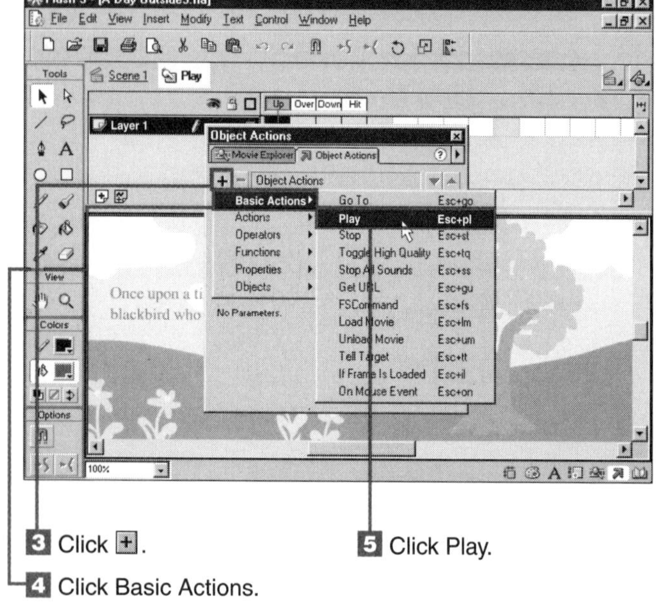

3 Click ⊞.

4 Click Basic Actions.

5 Click Play.

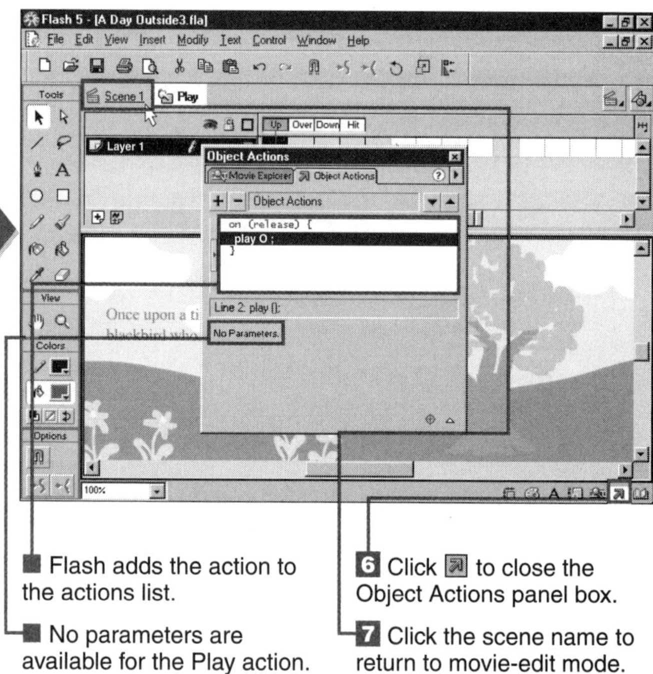

■ Flash adds the action to the actions list.

■ No parameters are available for the Play action.

6 Click ⊠ to close the Object Actions panel box.

7 Click the scene name to return to movie-edit mode.

Can I resize the type in the actions list?

✔ If you have trouble reading the small type in the actions list, you can resize it. To do so, click ▶ to display a pop-up menu. Click Font Size. Select Small, Medium, or Large font sizes. Flash then resizes the action list text.

To which layer should I add an action?

✔ Although you can add actions to the current layer along with your animation, you may want to employ a separate layer just for actions. A separate layer, named Actions, can help keep actions organized.

Does Flash support a Pause action?

✔ No. However, a Stop action acts like a pause action in that your movie stops playing and rests on the frame to which the Stop action is activated. You can place a Stop action at the start of a movie to keep the movie from playing automatically when opened as a self-playing projector file. To learn more about distributing your Flash movies, see Chapter 30.

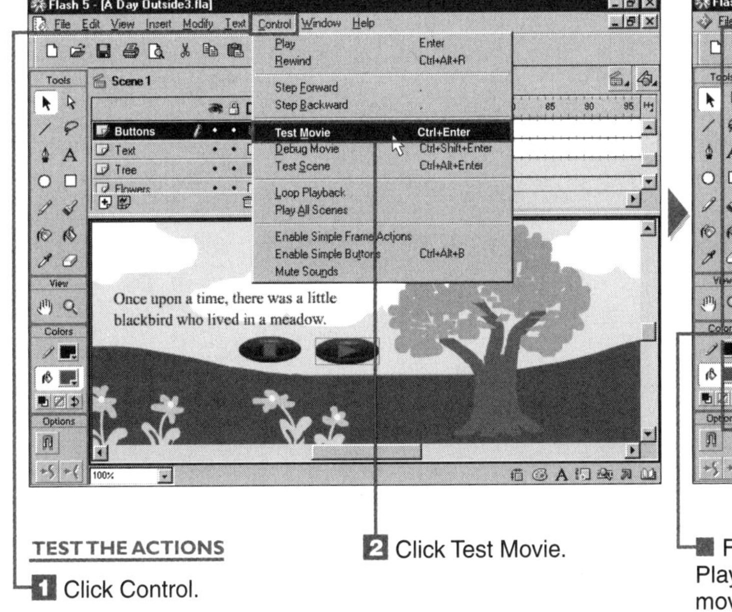

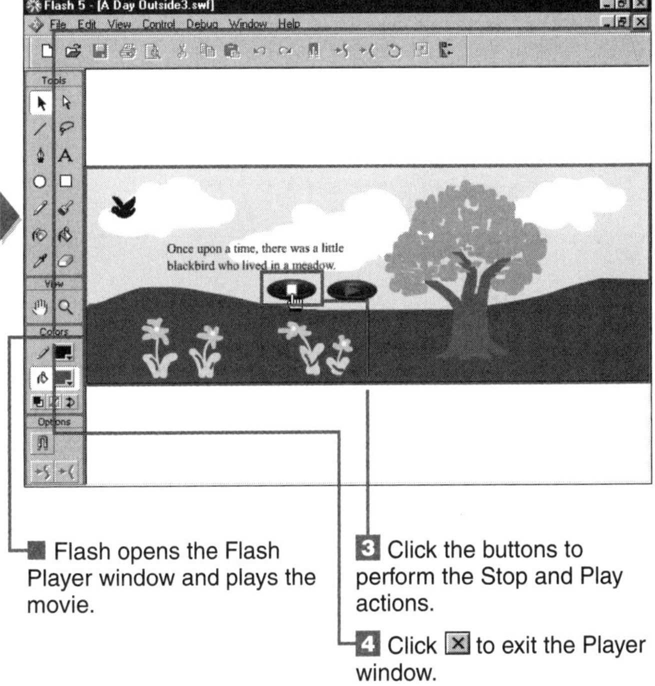

TEST THE ACTIONS

1 Click Control.

2 Click Test Movie.

■ Flash opens the Flash Player window and plays the movie.

3 Click the buttons to perform the Stop and Play actions.

4 Click ☒ to exit the Player window.

LOAD A NEW MOVIE

You can use the Load Movie action to start a movie file within your current movie. Use this action to replace the current movie with another, or play the loaded movie on top of the current movie as if it were another layer.

The Load Movie action can help you create "layered" animation action. Suppose that you create a movie of a wooded background. In the middle of the movie, you can load a movie of a man walking. By loading the walking man in the middle of the woods movie, you can combine both movies to make it look as if the man is walking through the woods.

The Load Movie action is also handy for downloading issues. For example, you can have a long movie comprised of four sections. If a user wants to skip the first three sections and view only the fourth, he or she would normally have to wait for all the sections to download. The Load Movie action provides the user a way of accessing the section he or she wants to view.

LOAD A NEW MOVIE

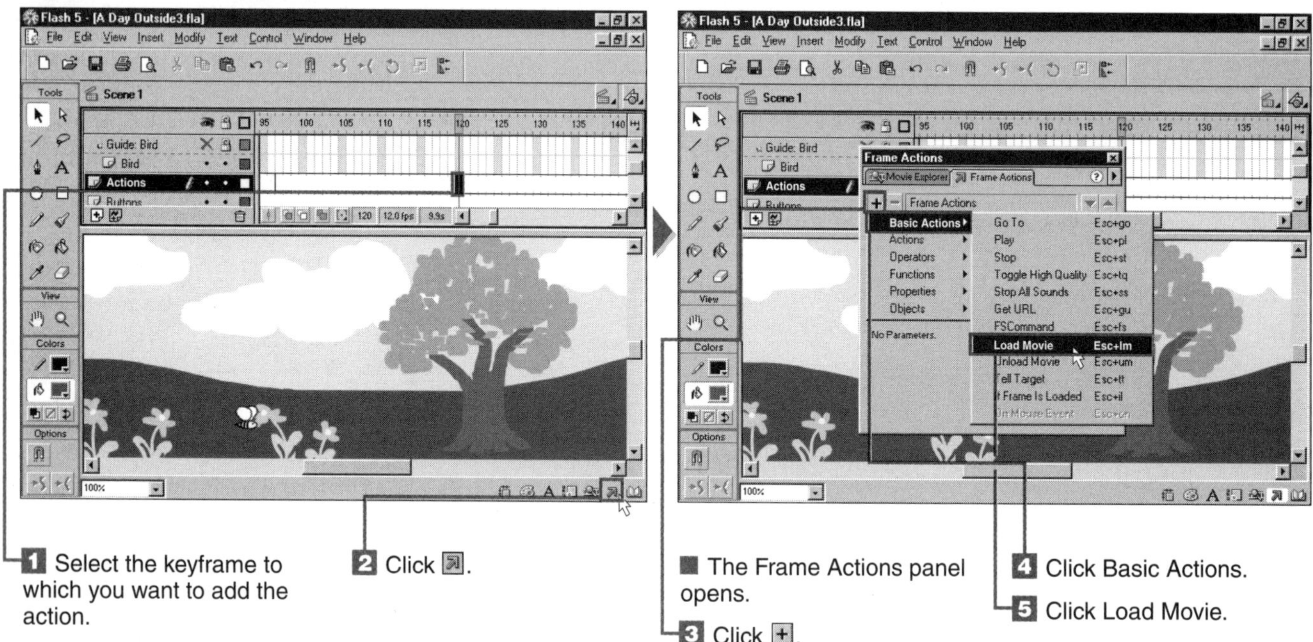

1 Select the keyframe to which you want to add the action.

2 Click [icon].

■ The Frame Actions panel opens.

3 Click [+].

4 Click Basic Actions.

5 Click Load Movie.

Can I open the movie in a separate browser window?

✔ Another way you can load a new movie file to play is to use the Get URL action. This action opens the new movie in a separate browser window. Follow the same steps shown in this section, but select the Get URL action instead of the Load Movie action. In the parameters, type the path to the movie file you want to load in the URL text box. In the Window text box, type **_blank**. Leave the Variables text box in the default state (do not send).

What are movie levels?

✔ Flash handles the playing of multiple movies as levels. The current movie is always playing at level 0. When you play a second movie with the Load Movie action, it plays at the level you designate, starting with level 1 or higher. Like stacking, movies play on top of the bottom level, so a movie set to play at level 2 visually appears on top of movies at levels 1 and 0. If you specify level 0 for the location level with the Load Movie action, the new movie replaces the existing movie. If you assign another level, the new movie plays on top of the existing movie.

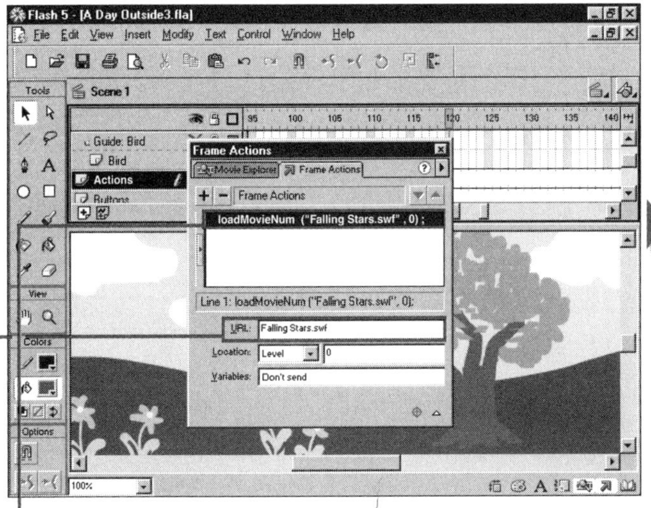

■ Flash adds the action to the actions list.

6 Click in the URL box and type the name of the movie file you want to load.

■ You can type a relative path, which includes just the filename and extension, or you can type an absolute path to the movie. An absolute path includes the drive and folder where the file is located.

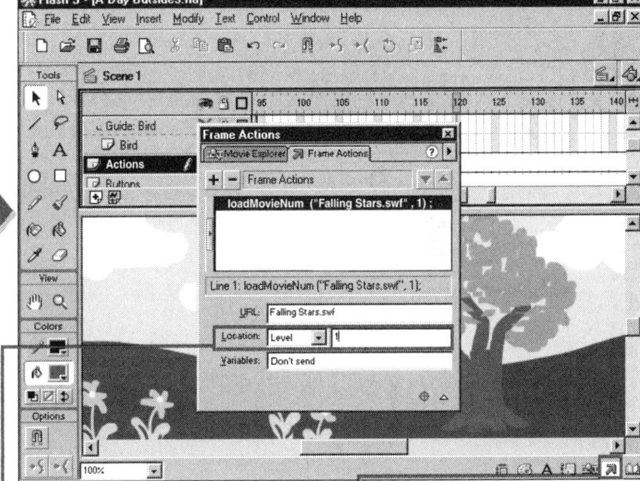

7 Select a location parameter for your movie.

■ You can leave the level at 0 to replace the current movie with the new movie. To make the new movie play on top of the current movie, type **1** or higher in the box.

■ To close the Frame Actions panel, click ⧉.

■ You can test the action by playing the movie in the Flash Player window.

Note: See the section "Assign Go To Actions" to test an action.

CHANGE ACTION ORDER

You can have more than one action assigned to a frame or button. All actions are listed in the actions list in the Actions panel, whether it is the Frame Actions panel used to assign frame actions or the Object Actions panel used to assign button actions. (See the section "Add Actions to Frames" to learn more about displaying the Actions panel.) Although you can only add one action at a time, you can change the order of your actions list at any time.

When you add more than one action to a frame, Flash executes the actions in the order they appear in the actions list. You can reorder the actions as necessary. For example, you may want to move a Stop action before a Play action. Using the arrow buttons in the panel, you can reorder the two actions.

See the section "Add Actions to Frames" to find out more about assigning actions.

CHANGE ACTION ORDER

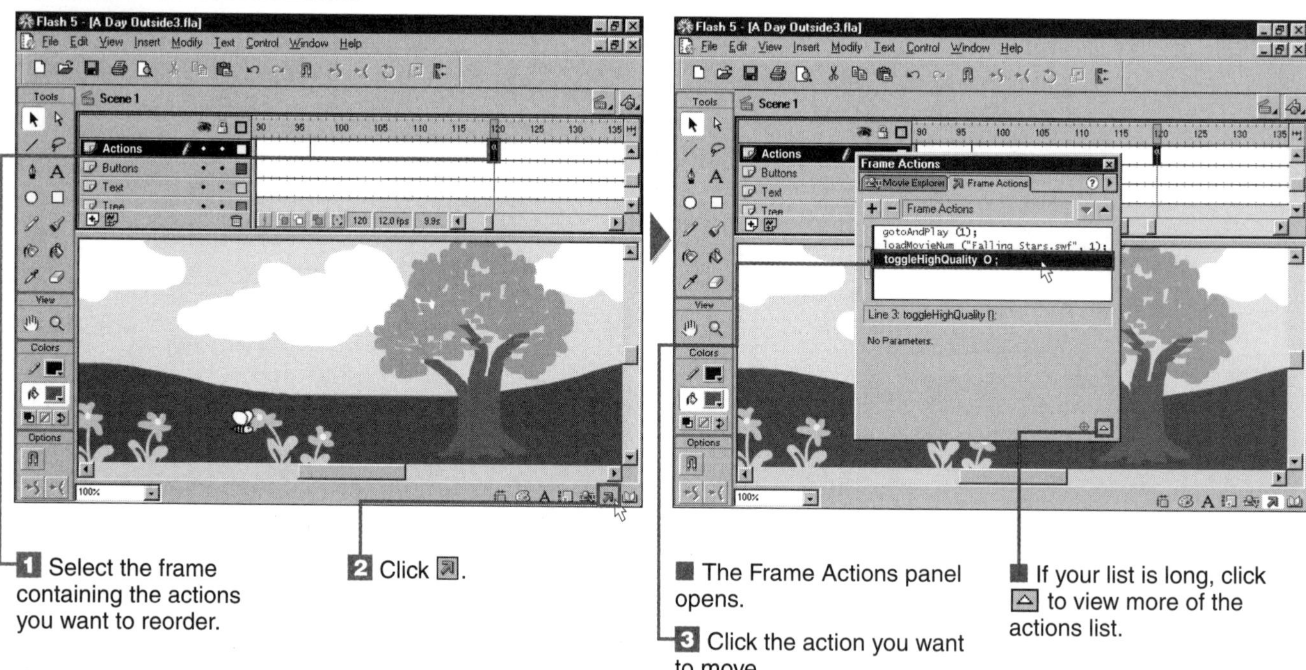

1 Select the frame containing the actions you want to reorder.

2 Click ⧉.

■ The Frame Actions panel opens.

3 Click the action you want to move.

■ If your list is long, click △ to view more of the actions list.

Can I delete an action I no longer want?

✔ Yes. You can quickly remove an action from the actions list in the Frame Actions panel that you no longer need in your movie. First select the action statement in the actions list. Next, click the − button. Flash removes the action from the list and the action is no longer a part of the frame or button.

Is there a faster way to open the Actions panel?

✔ Yes. You can double-click the frame containing the action (look for a tiny letter *a* icon to indicate the frame has an action assigned), and the Frame Actions panel opens immediately and you can edit or add actions.

Can I drag and drop action statements?

✔ Yes. Another way to edit the action order is to drag a selected action statement up or down in the actions list and drop the action statement when it reaches the desired location. You can also drag a new action onto the list, or remove actions you no longer want by dragging them off the list.

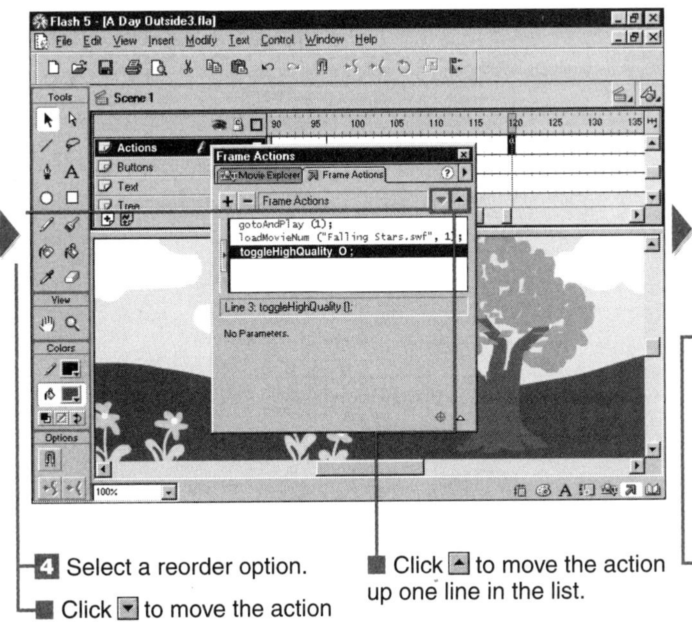

4 Select a reorder option.

■ Click ▼ to move the action down one line in the list.

■ Click ▲ to move the action up one line in the list.

■ Flash moves the action up or down as directed.

■ You can click ▼ or ▲ as many times as needed to move the action line.

5 Click ↗ to close the Frame Actions panel.

ASSIGN FRAME LABELS

You can keep your frames and actions organized if you use labels. If you assign a label to a keyframe, the label appears when you move the mouse pointer over the label flag. If you assign a label to a keyframe that starts tween animation, the label appears across the in-between frames in the Timeline. You can also use the label name in action parameters, such as the Go To action. See the section "Add Actions to Frames" to find out more about assigning actions.

Labeling a frame gives you an opportunity to clearly define the frame's contents. For example, you can label a frame in which your company logo appears or you can use a label to note where a new animation sequence begins in your movie. Once you have labeled important frames in your movie, you can reference them by their labels rather than frame numbers. You will find it much easier to remember a label name versus a frame number.

ASSIGN FRAME LABELS

1 Click the frame to which you want to add a label.

2 Click the Show Instance button (▣).

■ The Instance panel opens.

3 Click the Frame tab.

4 Click the Label box and type a descriptive label for the frame.

■ Keep your labels brief and to the point.

5 Press the Enter key.

What if I cannot see my label flags?

✔ You can resize the frames in your Timeline to make them easier to see. Click the Timeline Menu button (▤), then click Large. Flash resizes your Timeline to show large frames.

What is the difference between a label and a comment?

✔ A comment is typically a longer notation than a label. Labels are used to identify frames, while comments are used to create notes to yourself or to others working on the Flash file. When adding labels, you have an opportunity to create a simple label or a comment. Labels show up as little red flags on the Timeline, and comments appear with two slash marks on the Timeline. Labels are exported with the movie file while comments are not.

Can a frame have both a label and a comment?

✔ No, you cannot assign both a label and a comment to a frame, you can only use one.

How do I assign a comment?

✔ To assign a comment instead of a label, simply precede the label text with two slash marks (//). Add the slash marks to each line in your comment.

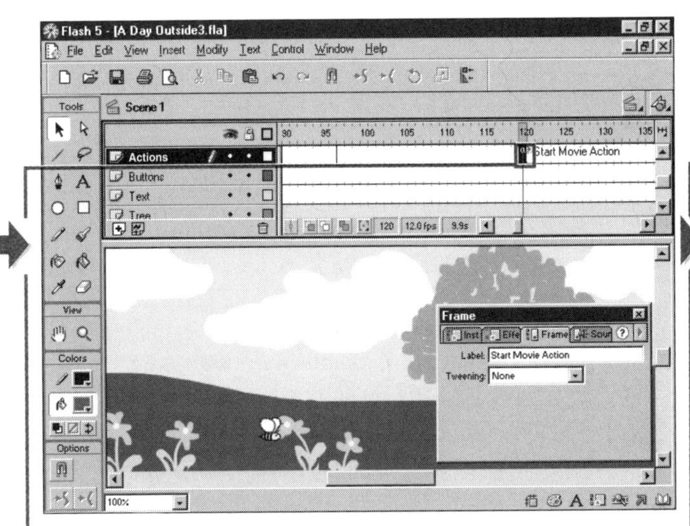

■ Flash inserts a label flag in the frame.

■ If there is room, Flash displays the label across the frames.

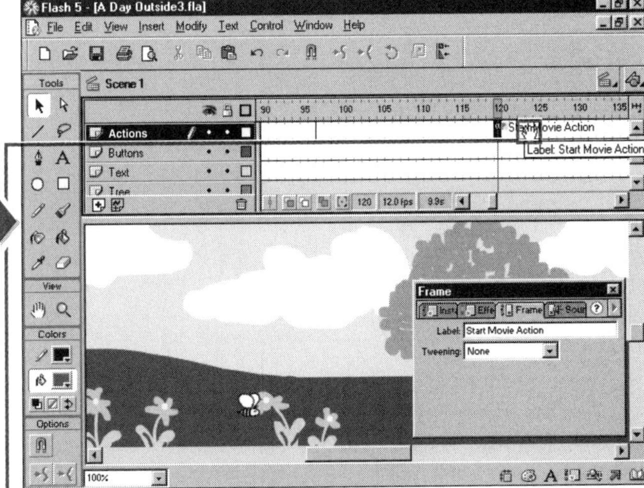

■ If you cannot see the label text, move the ↖ over the label flag and pause (↖ changes to ☝).

■ Flash displays the label name.

UNDERSTAND COMPLEX ACTIONS

You can add complex interactivity to your Flash projects that enable users to manipulate objects, type input, and access files that are not part of the original movie. Interactive movies utilize Flash *actions*, sets of instructions that tell the movie what to do if a certain event occurs. Depending on the complexity of the action, you can also define parameters that set up controls for the action.

For example, you can have an interactive action that uses a

dynamic text box in your Flash movie that enables a user to enter his or her name and generate a message using the name, such as "Hello, Dave. Welcome to my Web site."

You can break down actions into several levels of complexity in Flash. ***Frame actions*** give you greater control of how a movie plays. ***Button actions*** enable users to interact with your movie via a button. ***Complex actions***, which you learn about in this chapter, use parameters that enable others to interact with elements in your movie. To learn more about assigning frame and button actions, see Chapter 28.

A Word about ActionScript

Flash actions are written in *ActionScript*. This programming language, similar to JavaScript, uses object-oriented scripting. Though technically not a true programming language, ActionScript is an assortment of scripting commands, which add interactivity to objects in your Flash movies. Simply put, you can use Flash's ActionScript programming language as a tool to define how your movie behaves and how other users interact with the movie.

You do not need to know ActionScript or any other programming language in order to create actions in Flash. If you are well versed in scripting languages, such as JavaScript, you can certainly employ your knowledge to write scripts in Flash. If you are new to writing scripts, you can still create simple scripts that add interactivity to your project based on action commands available in the Actions panel.

Enter Scripting Code

Scripting languages are based on codes, as shown in this example:

```
on (release) { setProperty
("myMovieClip", _visible, 0);
```

This code example changes the visibility of a movie clip, named myMovieClip, when the user presses the associated button in the Flash movie. The setProperty action has parameters for setting a level of visibility, in this case a setting of zero (0), which makes the clip invisible.

Script coding, such as the script used in the example, are written in the Object Actions panel in the actions list box, also called the ***script window***. You use the Object Actions panel when you assign an action to an object in your movie, such as a button or symbol. The same panel becomes the Frame Actions panel when you assign an action to a frame in your movie.

Types of Flash Actions

The Actions panel categorizes Flash actions into several groups: Basic Actions, Actions, Operators, Functions, Properties, and Objects. All the basic actions, such as those you use for navigating in the movie, are found in the Basic Actions category. You can find all the necessary elements for building scripts in the remaining groups of actions in the Actions panel. The Actions group lists all the ActionScript actions such as ***setProperty*** and ***set variable,*** and also includes the same actions found in the Basic Actions group.

The Operators group lists operators for comparing and combining values, such as mathematical operators. The Functions group lists built-in functions such as True, False, and Random. The Properties group lists characteristics you can set for your movies, such as dimensions (width and height). The Objects group offers several predefined objects for manipulating objects or working with information entered by the user.

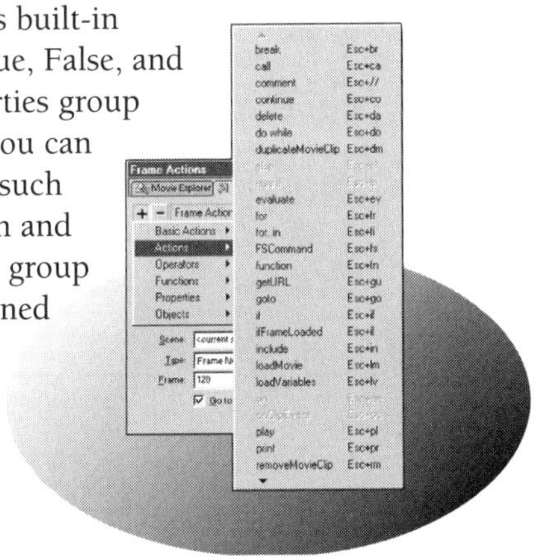

Using Expressions and Variables

When assigning actions in Flash, you can create formulas for manipulating data, called ***expressions,*** and holding places for changeable pieces of data, called ***variables***. Expressions are any part of your Flash action that results in a value. Quite simply, an expression is a phrase that represents a result or evaluation.

Variables are containers that hold values. Variable values can include numbers, test strings, and Boolean values.

Here is an example of an expression that evaluates which frame number to go to in a Flash movie:

```
on (release){
gotoAndPlay (5 + 10);
}
```

In this script expression, Flash evaluates 5 + 10 to arrive at frame number 15 and jumps to that particular frame in the movie.

When you plug in variables, the expression looks like this:

```
on (release){
luckyNumber = 5
secondLuckyNumber = 10
gotoAndPlay (luckyNumber +
secondLuckyNumber);
}
```

The variables in this script, luckyNumber and secondLuckyNumber, are used to accomplish the same thing as the first script example, jumping to a particular frame in the movie. Variable names always begin with a character and should describe the value you are collecting. The variables you define for an action determine the type of information a user types.

The sections in this chapter touch on a few of the more complex actions you can assign. You can learn more about scripting actions studying the sections in Parts 3 and 4 of this book or by consulting the Flash Help files. See Chapter 17 to learn more about accessing these files.

ADD A VARIABLE TEXT FIELD

You can use a variable text field to collect information from a user. Editable text fields appear in your Flash project and enable users to click inside and enter data. For example, you can use an input text box to enable users to type data in a form or survey. You can also use text fields to return ActionScript output, such as a message.

When you create an input text box for variable information, you assign a variable name to the box. This name describes the value that the user types into the box, such as **`name`**, **`favoriteColor`**, or **`luckyNumber`**. You can then use the variable text field value in your Flash actions. For example, you can have a text field that collects the user's age. You can name the variable `age`.

Variable names always begin with a character and are case sensitive. To help you identify variable names in script coding, use a lowercase letter to start the name.

You can assign variable names to text fields you create using the Text tool in Flash rather then assign a variable in the Actions panel.

ADD A VARIABLE TEXT FIELD

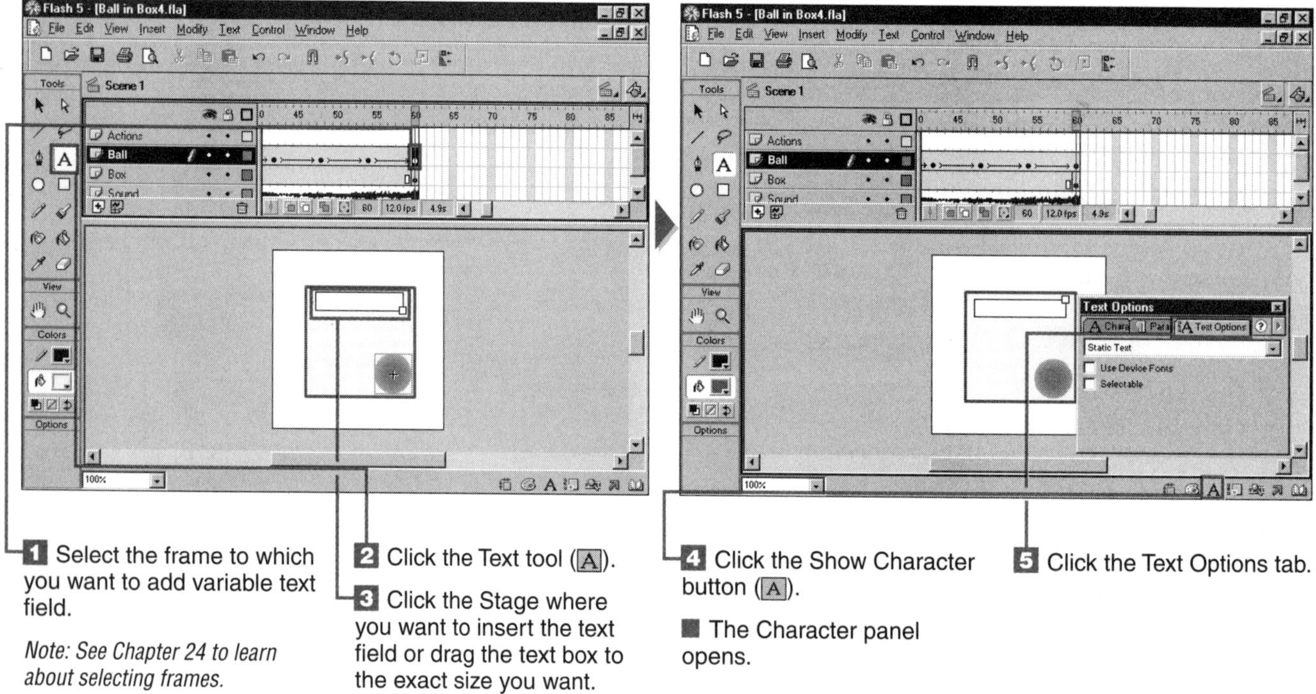

1 Select the frame to which you want to add variable text field.

Note: See Chapter 24 to learn about selecting frames.

2 Click the Text tool (A).

3 Click the Stage where you want to insert the text field or drag the text box to the exact size you want.

4 Click the Show Character button (A).

■ The Character panel opens.

5 Click the Text Options tab.

What types of text boxes I can use in Flash?

✔ Flash utilizes three types of text boxes: static, dynamic, and input. Use *static* text boxes to include text as part of your movie, such as a logo or product name. Use *dynamic* text boxes to display data that updates, such as stock quotes or basketball scores. Use *input* text boxes to collect interactive information from the user. See Chapter 20 to learn more about creating text boxes in Flash.

Can I format the text box for user input?

✔ Yes. Any formatting you apply to the text box is what the user sees when they type data into the box. You can specify font, font size, font color, and more. See Chapter 20 to learn more about applying formatting to text boxes.

How do I add a border around my text box?

✔ From the Text Options tab, click the Border/Bg check box (❑ changes to ☑). This places a border around the text field.

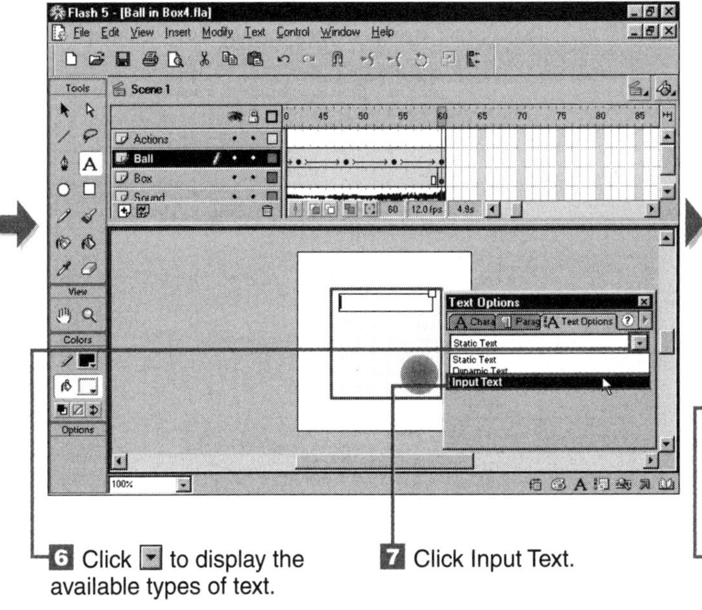

6 Click ▾ to display the available types of text.

7 Click Input Text.

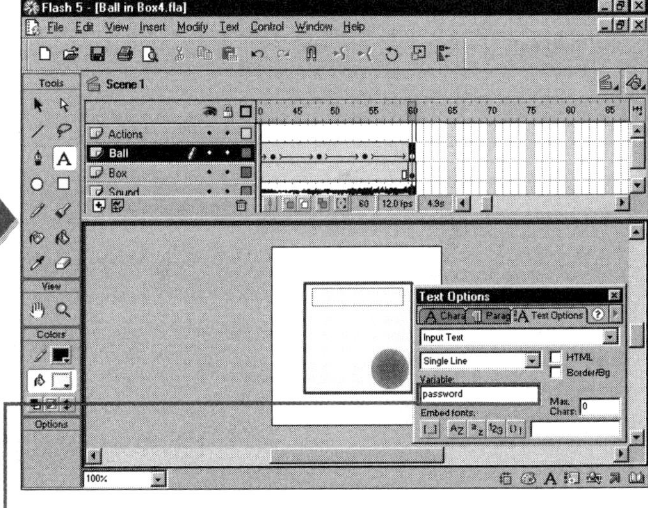

8 Click in the Variable box and type a name for the variable.

■ You can now use the variable name in your Flash actions for this particular text box and any values typed within it.

ASSIGN AN IF FRAME IS LOADED ACTION

You can use *conditional actions* in Flash to ask questions of your users. For example, with an *If/Then statement,* if a certain condition is met, such as the user typing a name, an action takes place, such as jumping to a frame in the movie. If the condition is not met, Flash moves on to the next line in the script. Conditional actions include If, Else, If Frame Is Loaded, and Loop.

An *If Frame Is Loaded* statement tests whether a particular frame is loaded yet. Web designers use the If Frame Is Loaded condition to create a mini-movie, called a *preloader,* that tells the user to hold while the main movie downloads. Although the steps in this section demonstrate how to apply the If Frame is Loaded action, you can follow these steps to practice other If/Then conditions in your Flash movie.

The If Frame Is Loaded action is available in the Actions panel in the Basic Actions category, or in the Actions category.

ASSIGN AN IF FRAME IS LOADED ACTION

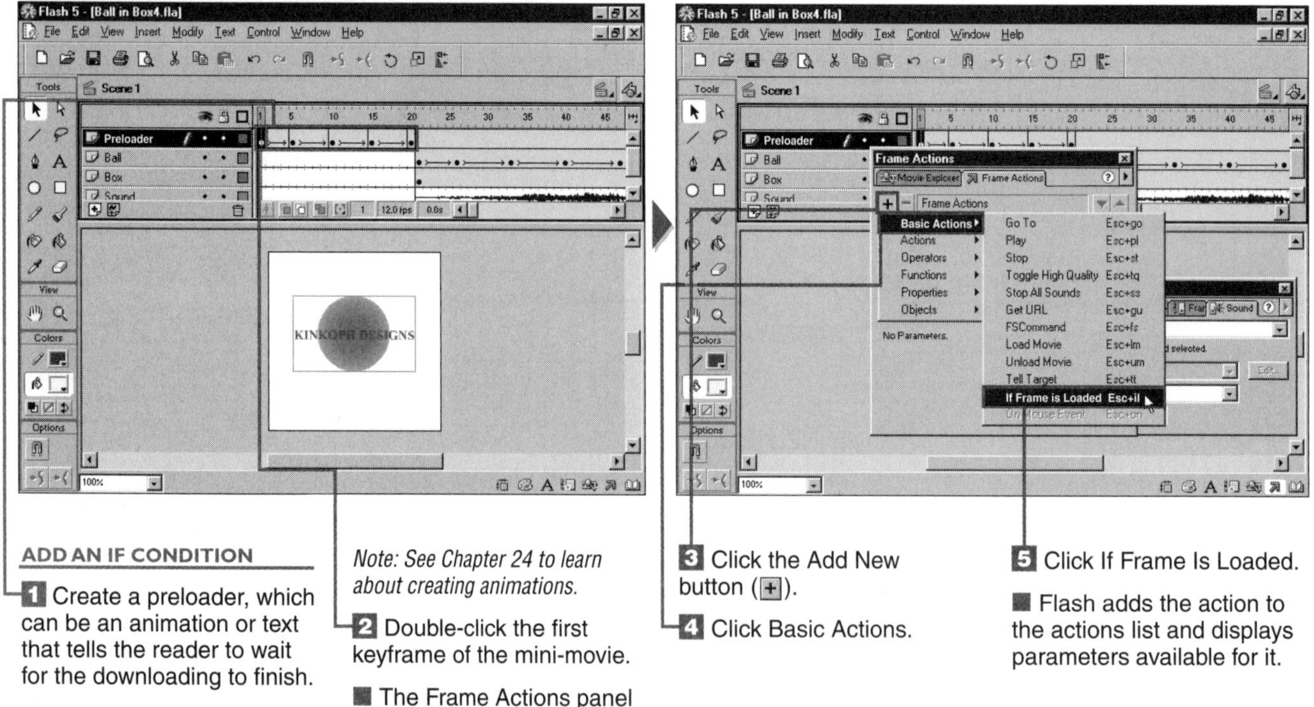

ADD AN IF CONDITION

1 Create a preloader, which can be an animation or text that tells the reader to wait for the downloading to finish.

Note: See Chapter 24 to learn about creating animations.

2 Double-click the first keyframe of the mini-movie.

■ The Frame Actions panel appears.

3 Click the Add New button (+).

4 Click Basic Actions.

5 Click If Frame Is Loaded.

■ Flash adds the action to the actions list and displays parameters available for it.

What exactly is a condition?

✔ A *condition* is simply a container for a statement (or statements) that executes if a value is true. A condition is comprised of three parts: the prerequisite or condition that must be met, the statement that executes if the prerequisite is met, and a termination of the statement, or End If.

Can I use comparison operators in my If statements?

✔ Yes. You can add comparison operators, such as <, >, >=, to your action statements. They are particularly useful with some conditional actions. You can find a full menu of operators you can use by clicking [+] in the Actions panel and then clicking Operators. Select an operator from the menu list to add it to your statement.

Should I place my actions in a separate layer?

✔ Yes. It is a good idea to keep your actions organized in a separate layer from your other movie layers. You do not have to do this, but it can help. For example, you can name the layer "Actions" so you know exactly where to look when you need to edit actions associated with your movie. To learn more about using layers in Flash, see Chapter 21.

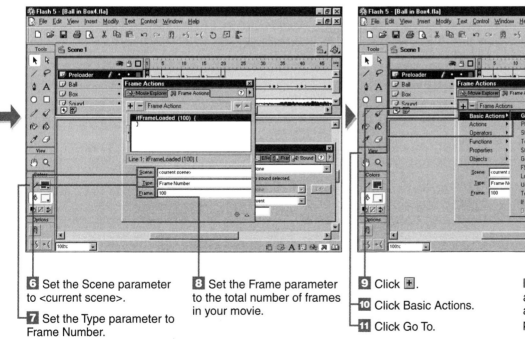

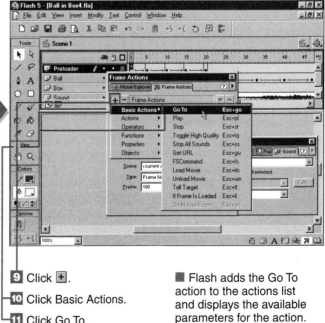

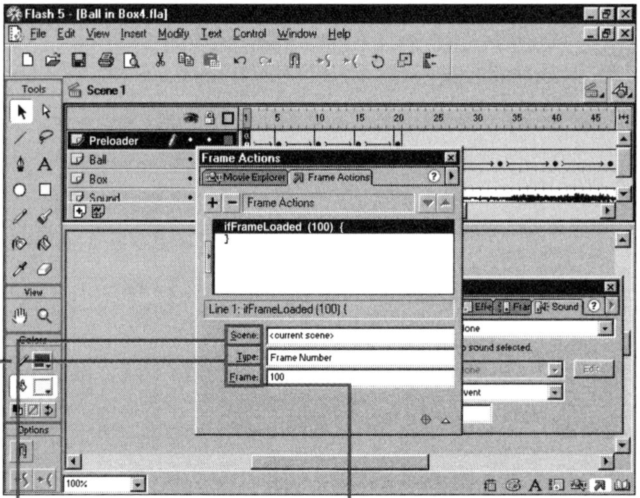

6 Set the Scene parameter to <current scene>.

7 Set the Type parameter to Frame Number.

8 Set the Frame parameter to the total number of frames in your movie.

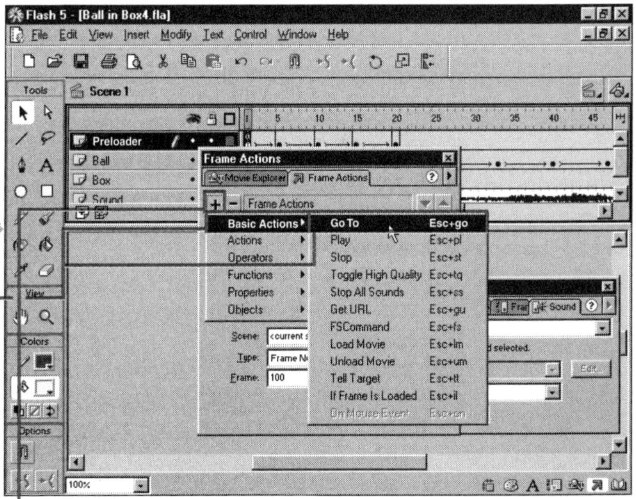

9 Click [+].

10 Click Basic Actions.

11 Click Go To.

■ Flash adds the Go To action to the actions list and displays the available parameters for the action.

CONTINUED

ASSIGN AN IF FRAME IS LOADED ACTION (CONTINUED)

The If Frame Is Loaded action tests whether the user's computer has downloaded a certain frame in your movie. If the frame is downloaded, the condition is met. If the frame is not yet downloaded, Flash continues to the next action if there is one, or in this case, the next frame of your preloader movie.

A *preloader* is a teaser movie that plays while the user waits for the rest of the file to download. You can make the preloader animated cartoon, such as a clock with whirring hands, or a message box that says, "Please wait." A 20-frame preloader is a good mini-movie length because it downloads quickly itself. You can even set up the preloader to repeat until the condition of your action is met.

See Chapter 28 to learn more about using the Actions panel to add actions in Flash.

ASSIGN AN IF FRAME IS LOADED ACTION (CONTINUED)

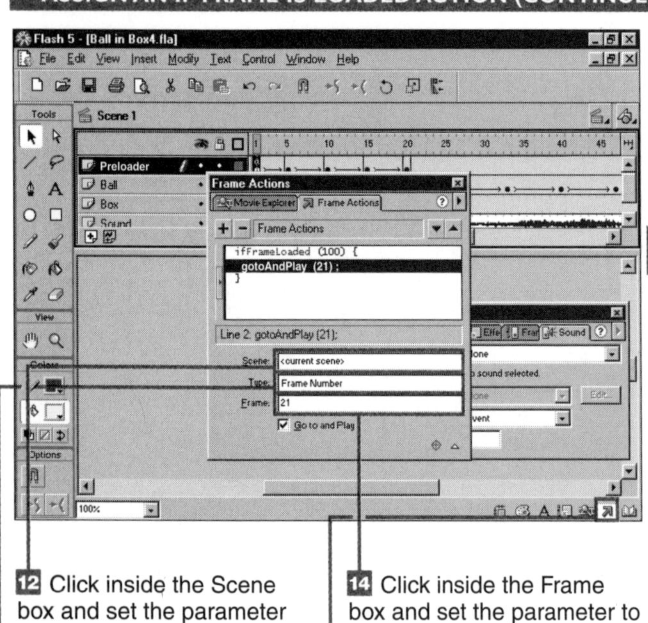

12 Click inside the Scene box and set the parameter to <current scene>.

13 Click inside the Type box and set the Type parameter to Frame Number.

14 Click inside the Frame box and set the parameter to the first frame that starts your movie.

15 Click ▣ to close the Frame Actions panel.

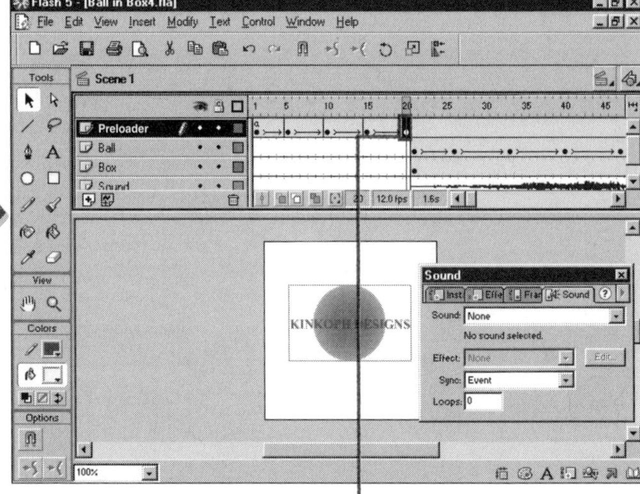

LOOP THE PRELOADER MOVIE

■ To make your preloader movie loop, add another Go To action to your mini-movie.

16 Double-click in the last frame of your mini-movie.

■ Flash opens the Frame Actions panel.

Can I preview the movie to see if the action works or not?

✔ You can always test your movies in the Flash Player window. To test if the If Frame Is Loaded action works properly, click the Control menu and click Test Scene. In the player window, click the View menu and then click Show Streaming. This simulates the streaming condition encountered on the Web.

What if my main movie downloads quickly?

✔ When you test your movie on the Web, it may download quicker than anticipated, and you may not need a preloader. If you do use a preloader and you think that the user may wait through it to start the main movie, you can always add the If Frame Is Loaded action to every frame in the preloader movie. This makes Flash test to see if the downloading condition is met before advancing to each frame in the preloader.

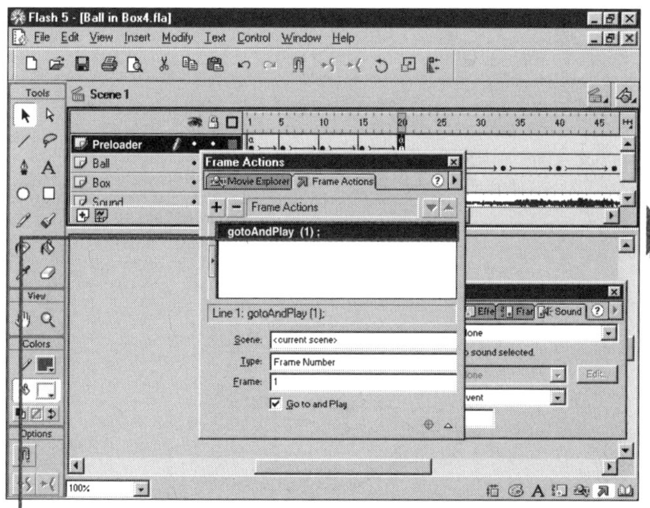

17 Add another Go To action, this time setting the action to Go To and Play the first frame of the preloader movie.

Note: See steps 9 through 14 to add a Go To action.

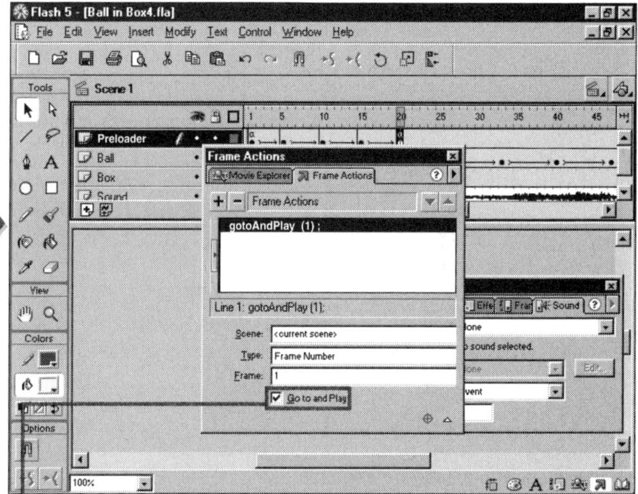

18 Make sure the Go To and Play check box is selected in the action parameters area.

■ Your movie is now set to loop unless the conditional action is met in frame 1 and the entire file is downloaded.

USING THE GET URL ACTION

You can use the Get URL action to take users to other files or Web pages. You can also use this action to open a file or movie in a new browser window. For example, you can insert a Get URL action in a standalone Flash Player projector movie, which, when activated, opens a browser window and downloads the specified HTML page.

There are four different targets you can specify in the action's parameters. `_self` opens the designated HTML page in the current frame of the current browser window. `_blank` opens the designated file in a completely new browser window `_parent` opens the page in the parent of the current browser, and `_top` opens the page in the top-level frame of the current window.

In the steps demonstrated in this section, you learn how to assign a Get URL action to a button in your Flash movie that opens a file in a new browser window. See Chapter 28 to learn more about using the Actions panel.

USING THE GET URL ACTION

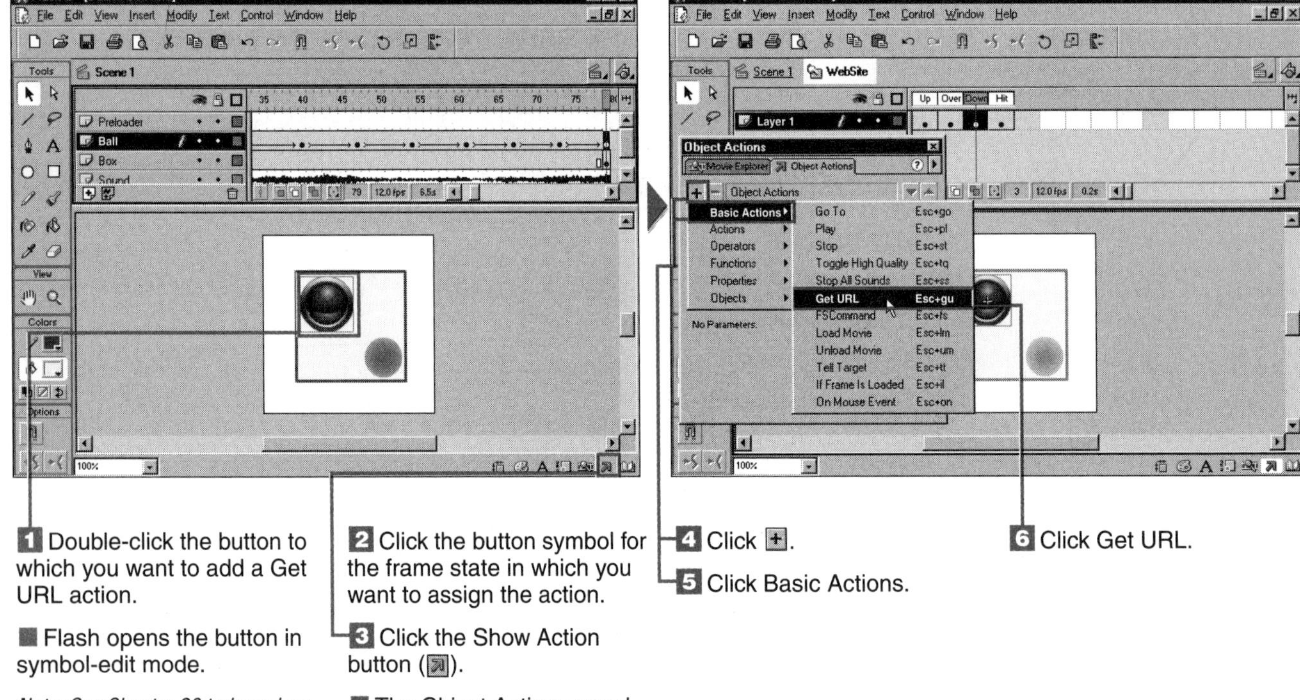

1 Double-click the button to which you want to add a Get URL action.

■ Flash opens the button in symbol-edit mode.

Note: See Chapter 26 to learn how to create buttons.

2 Click the button symbol for the frame state in which you want to assign the action.

3 Click the Show Action button.

■ The Object Actions panel opens.

4 Click +.

5 Click Basic Actions.

6 Click Get URL.

What do I need to know about using URLs with the Get URL action?

✔ *URL* stands for "Uniform Resource Locator," the standard way of addressing files on the Internet. There are two types of URLs: absolute and relative. An *absolute* URL is a complete address, including the protocol needed to open the file, such as http://www.hungryminds.com. A *relative* URL is a shorthand version of the address, such as mymovieclip.swf. With a relative address, you are telling Flash to look for the file in a relative location, such as the current folder.

How does a statement's syntax work?

✔ Scripting statements work a certain way in the actions list window. Most statements start with a keyword that identifies the action, such as `if` or `gotoAndPlay`. Data between curly brackets ({}) lists the action and parameters that need to be carried out. If you have more than one action, a semicolon separates each action in your actions list. Quotation marks appear around values in your action statement, while parentheses encompass any unusual aspects of the script.

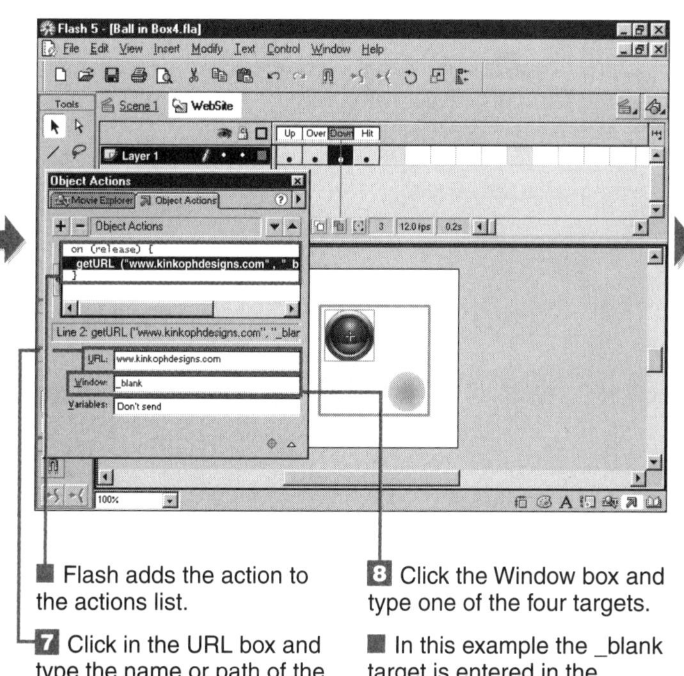

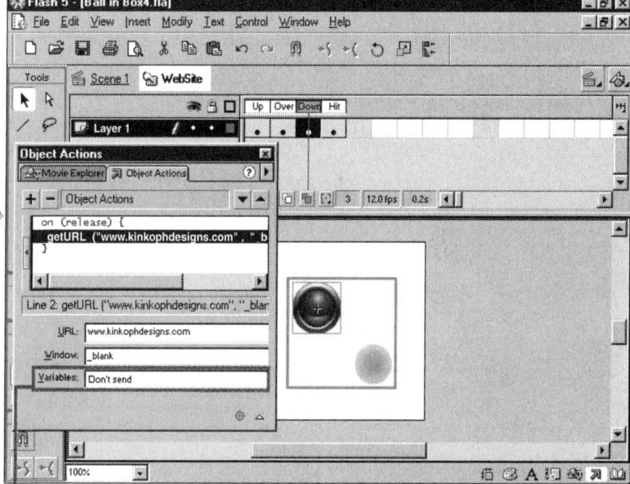

■ Flash adds the action to the actions list.

7 Click in the URL box and type the name or path of the file you want to open.

8 Click the Window box and type one of the four targets.

■ In this example the _blank target is entered in the parameter to open the file in another browser window.

■ Click the Variable parameter and set to Don't send if you do not want to pass any variables to the target.

■ You can now test the action and Flash loads the URL you specified when you click the button.

USING THE TELL TARGET ACTION

You can use the Tell Target action to control and manipulate the individual timelines of your movie clips. In other words, you can control the timelines of movies within your movie without having to assign the action to a specific timeline. You just have to target the timeline you want to control. The more complex your movies, the more likely they are to utilize separate interactive segments.

Movie clips are mini-movies that use their own timelines, and act like any other symbol you place on the Stage, such as graphics or buttons, and you can manipulate them as such. You can learn how to save animation sequences as movie clip symbols in Chapter 24.

When referencing targets, you use a directory structure. If a clip resides within another clip, you must indicate this in the target path, such as `tellTarget ("Big Clip/MyClip1") {`.

USING THE TELL TARGET ACTION

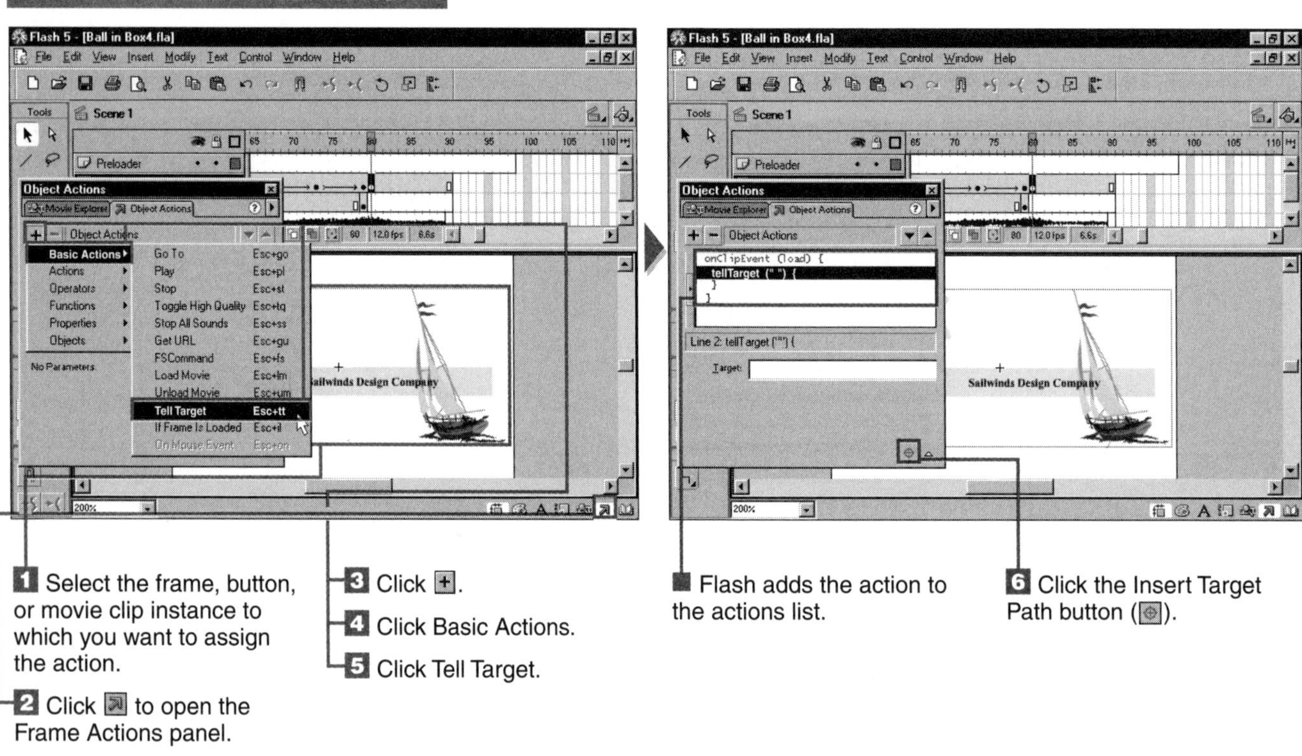

1 Select the frame, button, or movie clip instance to which you want to assign the action.

2 Click to open the Frame Actions panel.

3 Click +.

4 Click Basic Actions.

5 Click Tell Target.

■ Flash adds the action to the actions list.

6 Click the Insert Target Path button.

Which Target option settings should I use?

✔ There are two option types at the bottom of the Insert Target Path dialog box. The default setting of Dots is fine for most movies. The Dots notation mode is similar to JavaScript. The Mode setting controls how movie clips display in your directory tree list. Relative displays only clips found in the current frame. Absolute displays every movie clip instance in your file.

Can I nest actions in Flash?

✔ Yes. Nesting actions within other actions is quite common for all programming languages. You can nest actions for a movie clip within the Tell Target statement that tell the action what to do. Nesting is when you place an action inside another action. Nested actions are indented in the actions list box in the Actions panel.

How do I remove an action from the actions list?

✔ Select the action statement, then click ▭ at the top of the Actions panel. This removes the statement from the list box.

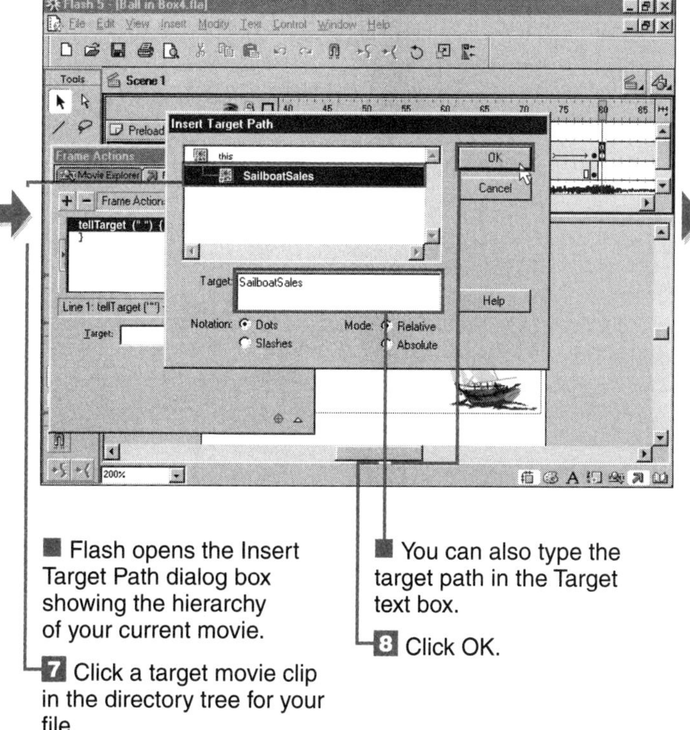

■ Flash opens the Insert Target Path dialog box showing the hierarchy of your current movie.

7 Click a target movie clip in the directory tree for your file.

■ You can also type the target path in the Target text box.

8 Click OK.

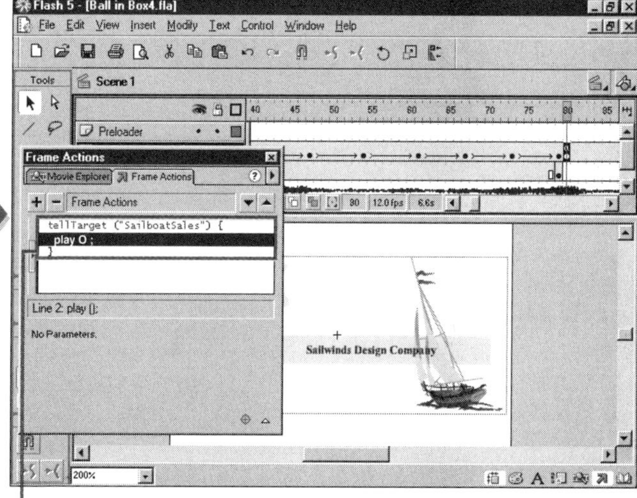

■ Flash adds the target path to your actions list.

■ You can now add any additional actions to tell the movie clip what to do, such as Play or Stop.

Note: See Chapter 28 to learn more about using the Actions panel.

CONTROL THE FLASH PLAYER WITH THE FS COMMAND

You can use the FS Command to make your Flash movie communicate with a browser or with other programs that run Flash movies, including the standalone Flash Player. The FS Command is an action that enables you to code your movie to interact with JavaScript used with HTML pages. See Chapter 30 to learn more about using the Flash Player.

For example, you can add an FS Command that tells the Flash Player to make the movie fill the screen or hide the player's menu bar. You can define two parameters when assigning the FS Command: ***command*** and ***arguments***. Commands include FullScreen, AllowScale, ShowMenu, Exec, and Quit. Arguments include True/False conditions.

If you use the FullScreen command with your FS Command action, a true argument sets the player window to full-screen mode without a menu bar. If you assign this action to a button, your action statement may look like this:

```
on(release) {
fscommand ("fullscreen",
"true");
}
```

If a false argument is used, the player window shows the movie in the size specified in the Flash Movie Properties dialog box.

CONTROL THE FLASH PLAYER WITH THE FS COMMAND

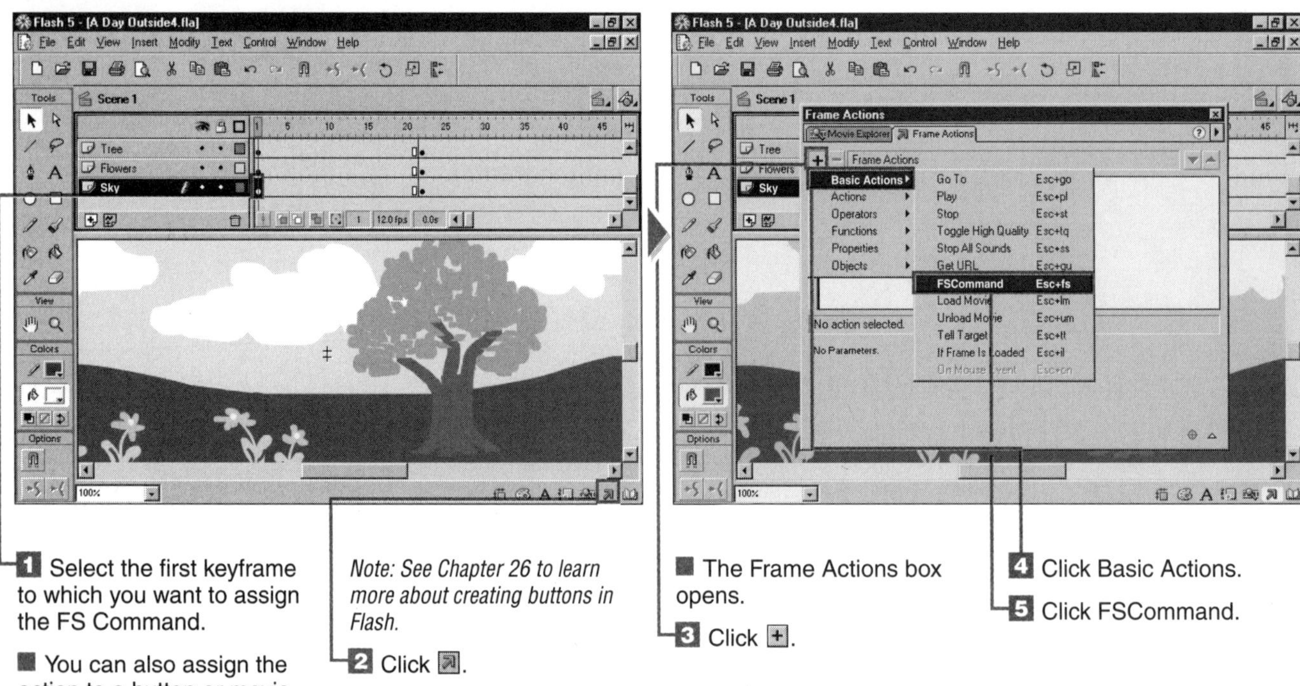

1 Select the first keyframe to which you want to assign the FS Command.

■ You can also assign the action to a button or movie clip instance.

2 Click ⬚.

Note: See Chapter 26 to learn more about creating buttons in Flash.

■ The Frame Actions box opens.

3 Click ⊞.

4 Click Basic Actions.

5 Click FSCommand.

What do the other FS Commands do?

✔ The steps in this section show how to use the FullScreen FS Command. There are four other commands you can specify. Use the AllowScale command to enable users to scale your Flash movie. A false value for this command keeps the movie to the sizes you set up in the Movie Properties dialog box. The user can still resize the standalone player, but not the movie playing inside the player window. Use the ShowMenu command to toggle the menu bar on or off in the player window. Use the Exec command to open another executable file inside the player window. Use the Quit command to close the player window.

Can I play my movies on alternative players besides the Flash Player?

✔ Your Flash movies plays best with Macromedia's Flash Player, but you can also play them in other players. For example, you can use the Java edition of the Flash Player if you are using any Java-compatible browser. You can also play your Flash files as RealFlash (the makers of RealPlayer) presentations on the Web. QuickTime also supports Flash files.

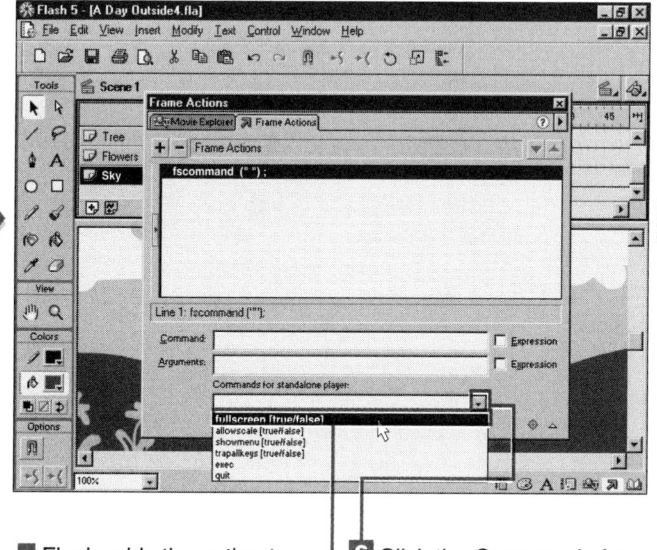

■ Flash adds the action to the actions list.

6 Click the Commands for Standalone Player box to display a list of options.

7 Click an FS Command. In this example, fullscreen [true/false], is selected.

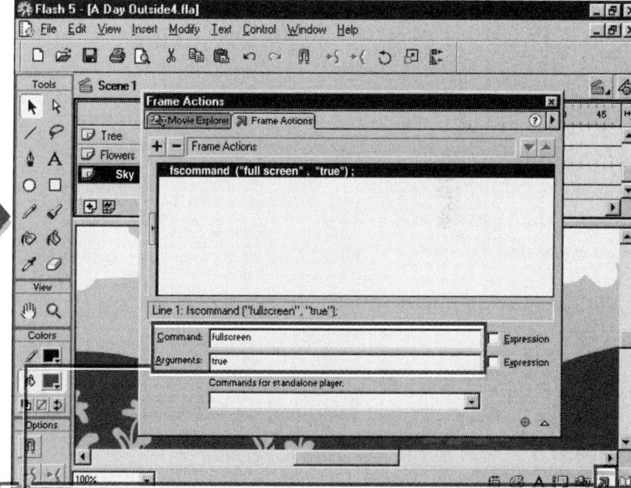

■ Flash adds the parameters to the actions list box.

8 Click ⧉ to close the Actions panel.

■ You can now publish your movie as a standalone player projector and test the action.

Note: See Chapter 30 to learn more about publishing movies and using the projector.

UNDERSTAND DISTRIBUTION METHODS

You can distribute your Flash projects to an audience in several ways. You may publish a Flash movie to a Web page, save it as a QuickTime movie to send to another user via e-mail, or deliver the movie as a self-playing file. You can assign a distribution method using the Publish Settings dialog box, or you can export your movie as another file type using the Export Movie dialog box.

Start with an Authoring File

When you create content in Flash, you start by creating an *authoring file*. The authoring file is where you draw and animate your movie's content. This file contains all the elements that make up your movie, such as bitmap objects, sounds, symbols, buttons, text, and so on. For this reason, may create an authoring file that is quite large in file size.

Any time you start a file in Flash, you are working with the authoring file for your movie. Authoring files use the .fla file extension. When you publish or export the movie, Flash creates another file type, such as an SWF or HTML file.

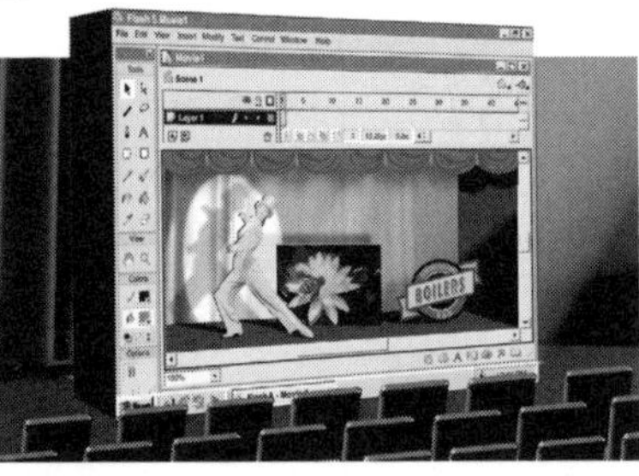

Create an Export File

After you create the authoring file and get it working just the way you want, you can turn it into an *export file*. When you create an export file, you are creating a file that is separate from the authoring file. Flash offers two exporting features: Export Movie, and Publish. The feature you select depends on what you want to do with your Flash content. When you export a movie using the Export Movie feature, you export your file as a specific file type for another program, such as QuickTime, to use.

When you publish a file, you are turning your content into a file type viewable from the Web. The process of publishing compresses the file contents, making it easier for others to view the file. The resulting file is uneditable, so you cannot change its contents. Published Flash movie files use the .swf file extension.

Export Formats

The Export feature enables you to save the file as another file format, such as a series of still images or an animated sequence. You can use more than a dozen different file formats when exporting a Flash movie. See the table "Flash Export File Formats" for a complete listing. You can even export your movie as a series of GIF or PNG images. When exporting a Flash authoring file, keep in mind that you may lose all the vector-based information for the file, unless you choose to export to a vector-based format, such as Macromedia Freehand.

Flash Export File Formats

File Format	Extension
Adobe Illustrator	.ai
Animated GIF, GIF image	.gif
Bitmap	.bmp
DXF Sequence/AutoCad DXF Image	.dxf
Enhanced Metafile	.emf
EPS	.eps
FutureSplash Player	.spl
Generator Template	.swt
JPEG Sequence/JPEG image	.jpg
PICT Sequence	.pct
PNG Sequence/PNG Image	.png
QuickTime	.mov
WAV Audio	.wav
Windows AVI	.avi
Windows Metafile	.wmf

Publish in Flash Player Format

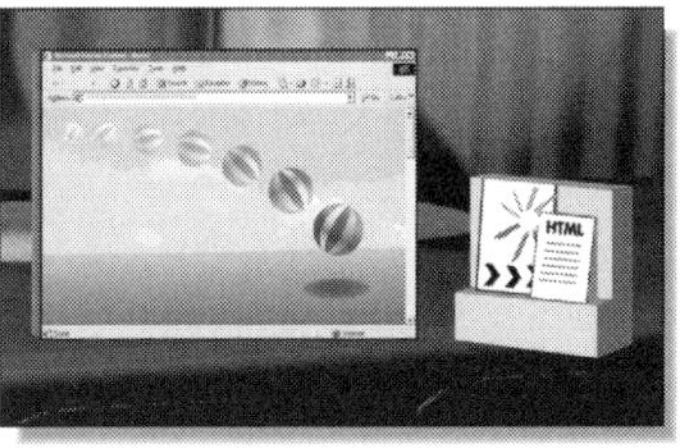

Your Flash creations really shine when you publish them in the original program format — Flash Player format. When you distribute a movie as a movie file, Flash saves it in the SWF file format, which requires users to have the Flash Player application or plug-in to view it. The Flash Player is the most widely used player on the Web and comes preinstalled with most computers and all Web browsers today.

You use the Publish feature to quickly turn any Flash authoring file into SWF format for use on the Web. The Publish feature also generates the HTML code you need to make your movie or interactive creation ready for the Web.

Publish as a Projector

Another way to distribute your movie is to turn it into a *projector*. A projector is a standalone player that runs the movie without the need of another application. Use the Projector feature to distribute your Flash creations to users who do not have access to the Flash Player or plug-in.

Using the Bandwidth Profiler

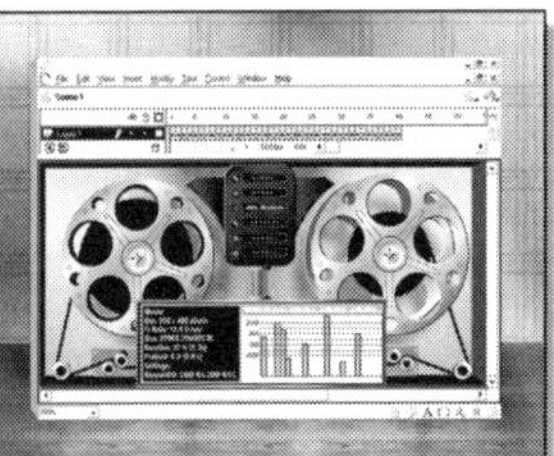

When preparing a movie for publishing, Flash offers a handy tool to help you check for quality and optimal playback. The Bandwidth Profiler is a valuable tool that can help you fix problem areas that hold up your movie while downloading into the browser window. Use the Profiler to help you fix problems before you post the Flash file on a Web page.

Print Movie Content

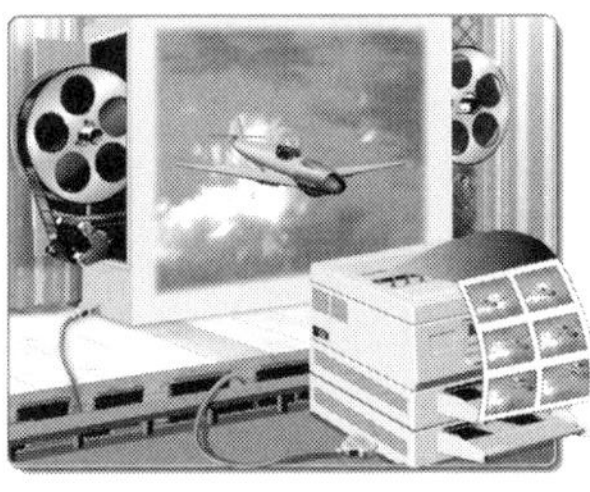

Yet another option to consider when distributing movie content is to simply print out your movie frames. Although this certainly is not a dynamic way to present your movie to others, you may find it useful to print out portions of your movie to distribute to members of a project team or to show to your boss. Flash comes with several options for preparing your movie frames for printing, all of which you find in the Page Setup dialog box (Windows) or the Print Margins dialog box (Mac).

PLAY A FLASH MOVIE IN FLASH

You can use the Flash Player to play your Flash movies. You can play movies from within Flash 5, or outside the confines of the Flash 5 program window by using the Flash Player window. The Flash Player is installed when you install Flash 5 onto your computer.

Flash Players are also readily available with today's Web browsers, such as Microsoft Internet Explorer and Netscape Navigator. Computer manufacturers now ship many new machines with the Flash Player preinstalled for your convenience. The Flash Player is an open standard widely used on the Internet today. It is also the most popular player technology, ranking above Java and Windows Media Player. Macromedia offers free Flash Player downloads available on their Web site.

The Flash Player is a separate application for viewing Flash multimedia files. As such, when you download a Flash file, it opens into its own window along with several menu commands for controlling how a movie plays.

PLAY A FLASH MOVIE IN FLASH

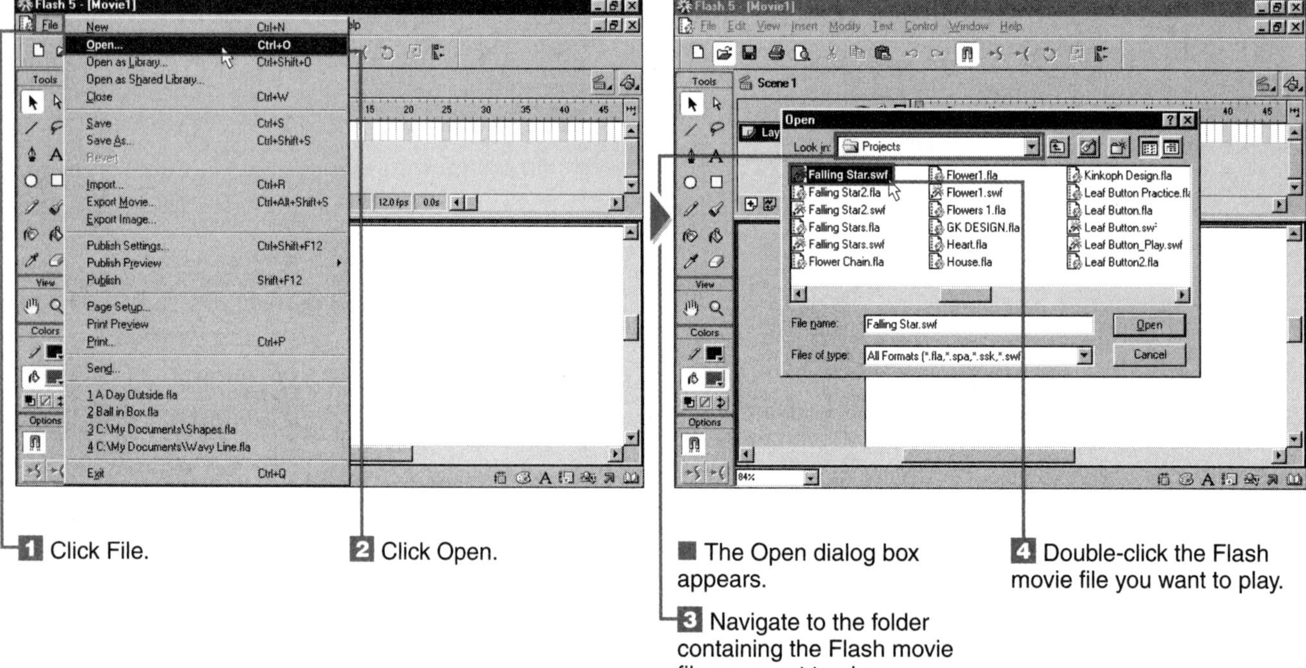

1 Click File.

2 Click Open.

■ The Open dialog box appears.

3 Navigate to the folder containing the Flash movie file you want to play.

4 Double-click the Flash movie file you want to play.

How do I stop the movie from looping?

✔ The Flash Player window has a few tools you can use to control how the movie plays. Click the Control menu to see the available commands. The Loop command is turned on by default. To deactivate the command, click Loop. To stop the movie from playing, click Stop or just press Enter.

How does the Player window differ from the test movie window?

✔ The Flash Player window and text movie window are one and the same. You can also open the Flash Player window by clicking the Control menu on the Flash menu bar and then selecting Test Movie. The Flash Player window opens and displays the current movie.

How do I open another movie to play in the Flash Player window?

✔ As long as you have the Flash Player window open, you can view other Flash movies as well. To view another movie, click the File menu, then click Open. Click the Browse button. Navigate to the next movie file you want to play. Double-click the movie filename. When you click OK, the movie starts playing.

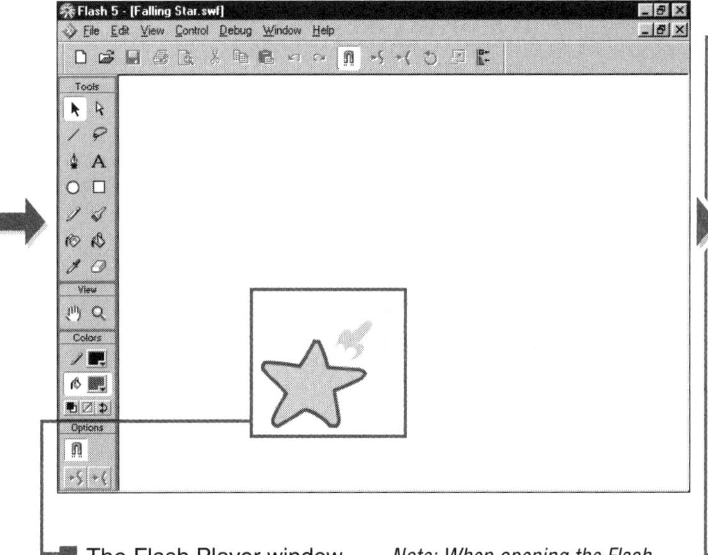

■ The Flash Player window opens and plays the movie.

Note: When opening the Flash Player from within the Flash 5 program, the Player fits inside the Flash program window and has a separate set of window controls and menu commands.

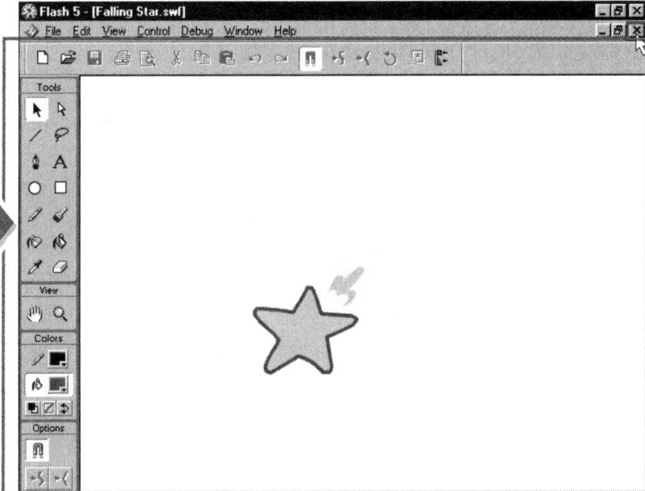

■ To close the movie, you can click ☒.

PLAY A FLASH MOVIE IN A BROWSER

You can play a Flash movie using the browser's Flash plug-in. Most browsers, such as Microsoft Internet Explorer and Netscape Navigator, include the Flash Player plug-in program for playing SWF files. Most Internet users can access Flash Web content without downloading the Flash Player application separately, which makes the Flash Player the most widely used player on the Internet. Today's browsers and computer systems come with the Flash Player preinstalled.

If you place your Flash animations on a Web page, users are able to see them automatically, unless they are using a very old version of a browser. When you surf the Web, you encounter hundreds of Web pages that include Flash animations. Flash effects such as animated banners, interactive menus, and multimedia clips play automatically on the Web page. In this section, you learn how to play a Flash movie utilizing the built-in player in your browser.

PLAY A FLASH MOVIE IN A BROWSER

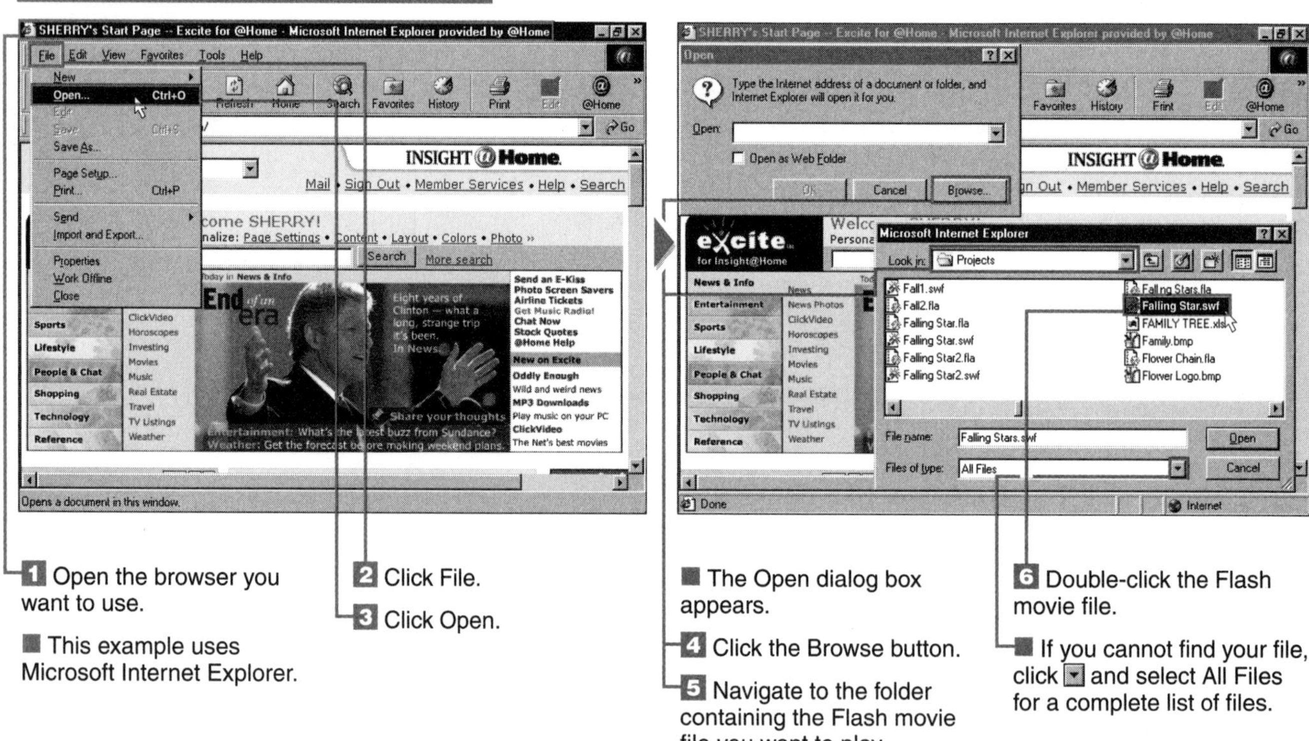

1 Open the browser you want to use.

■ This example uses Microsoft Internet Explorer.

2 Click File.

3 Click Open.

■ The Open dialog box appears.

4 Click the Browse button.

5 Navigate to the folder containing the Flash movie file you want to play.

6 Double-click the Flash movie file.

■ If you cannot find your file, click ▾ and select All Files for a complete list of files.

Can older browser versions view Flash movies?

✔ It depends on how old the version of the browser program is. The Flash Player plug-in is available with Netscape Navigator 3 or later, or Microsoft Internet Explorer 3 or later. Earlier versions of these browsers do not include the Flash Player plug-in.

Do I have to view all Flash elements using the Flash Player window?

✔ No. Flash embeds many of the interactive Web page elements, such as animated banners, interactive menus and buttons, in the Web page. These elements do not open a separate player window, but are a part of the Web page itself.

How do I control the movie's screen size?

✔ The movie's screen size is set when you define the Stage area measurements. To learn how to set the Stage size, see Chapter 17. You can also control the size of the movie display window that appears inside the browser window when a Flash movie plays. You can find movie-display controls in the Publish Settings dialog box. Learn more about these controls in the section "Publish a Movie in HTML Format."

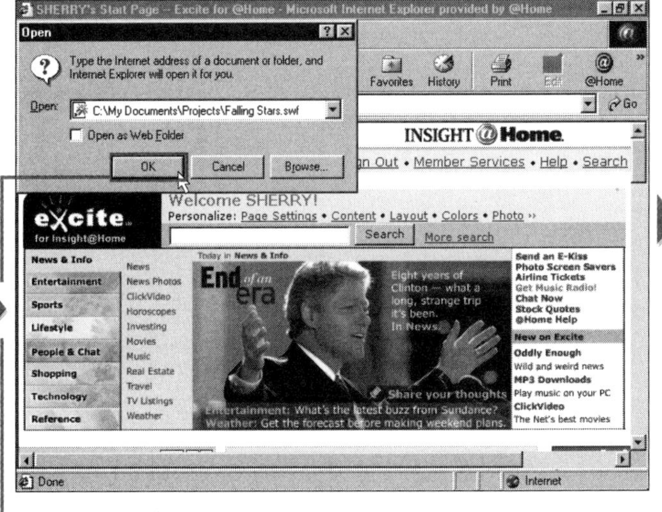

7 Click OK.

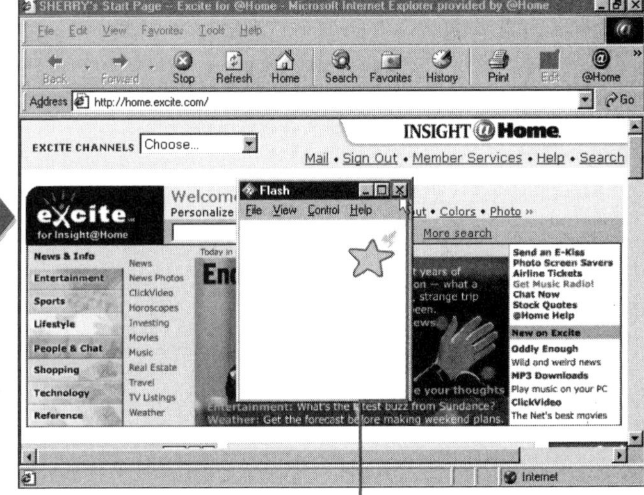

■ The Flash Player window opens and the movie begins playing.

■ To close the movie, click ☒.

TEST MOVIE BANDWIDTH

You can use the Flash Bandwidth Profiler to help you determine which movie frames can cause problems during playback on the Web. File size and the user's data-transfer rate affect how smoothly and quickly your movie downloads and plays.

With the Bandwidth Profiler you can test six different modem speeds, and gauge which frames in your movie use the most bytes. This information helps you to see exactly where your movie may slow down during playback. For example, you can use the Bandwidth Profiler to simulate different modem speeds such as comparing how long a movie takes to download at 28.8 Kbps versus 36.6 Kbps.

When you activate the Bandwidth Profiler, it opens as a window at the top of the screen. The left section of the Profiler displays the different status areas you can check, such as the movie's dimensions and speed or the frame state. The right section displays a timeline and a graph detailing frame data.

TEST MOVIE BANDWIDTH

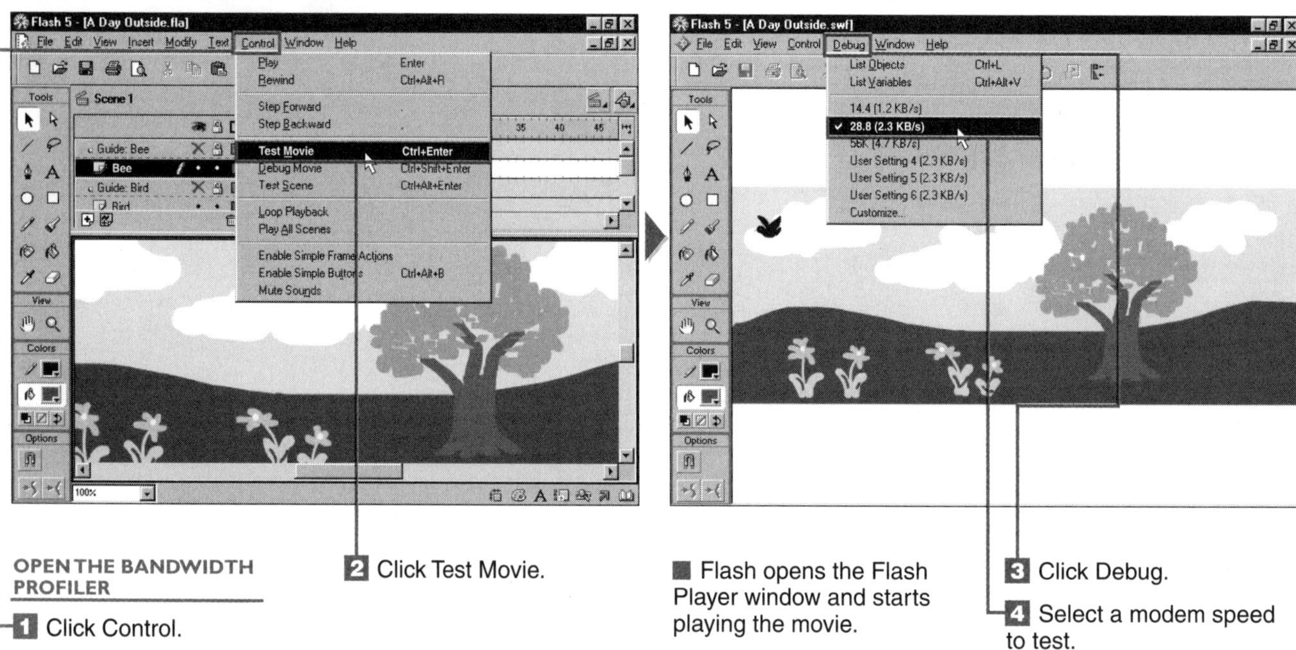

OPEN THE BANDWIDTH PROFILER

1 Click Control.

2 Click Test Movie.

■ Flash opens the Flash Player window and starts playing the movie.

3 Click Debug.

4 Select a modem speed to test.

Can I customize the download speed I want to test?

✔ Yes. To customize the modem speed, click the Debug menu in the Flash Player window. Click Customize. Flash opens the Custom Modem Settings dialog box. Set a speed to simulate in the test. For example, you can change an existing speed settings' bit rate by typing in another bit rate. Or you can enter a custom speed in a User Setting box and a bit rate to test for that speed. Click OK to save your changes.

Can I save the test settings for use with another movie?

✔ Yes. Just leave the Bandwidth Profiler open in the Flash Player window. You can open another movie from the player window, or you can return to the player window at a later time and use the same Profiler settings. To open another movie without leaving the player window, click File, then click Open. Double-click the movie you want to view and it begins playing in the player window.

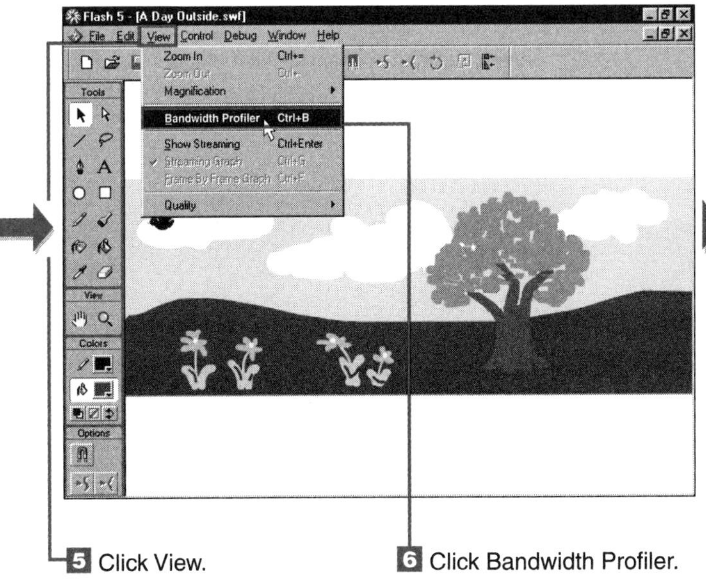

5 Click View.

6 Click Bandwidth Profiler.

■ Flash displays the Bandwidth Profiler at the top of the window.

■ The left side of the Profiler shows information about the movie, such as file size and dimensions.

■ The bars on the right represent individual frames and the total size, in bytes, of data in the frame.

CONTINUED

TEST MOVIE BANDWIDTH (CONTINUED)

You can use two different views in the Flash Bandwidth Profiler to see how the frames play in your movie: Streaming Graph mode or Frame by Frame Graph mode. The default view is Streaming Graph mode. Depending on the view you select, the right section of the Profiler displays data differently.

A vertical bar on the graph represents a single frame in the movie. The bars correspond with the frame number shown in the timeline. In Streaming Graph mode, the alternating blocks of light and dark gray show relative byte size of each frame and the stack indicates how much data must download, or *stream*, into a browser window. Streaming Graph mode shows you the real-time performance of your Flash movie.

In Frame by Frame Graph mode, Flash profiles each frame side by side. If a frame's bar extends above the bottom red line of the graph, the Flash movie pauses to download the frame's data. Frame by Frame Graph mode shows you which frames are causing delays during movie downloads.

TEST MOVIE BANDWIDTH (CONTINUED)

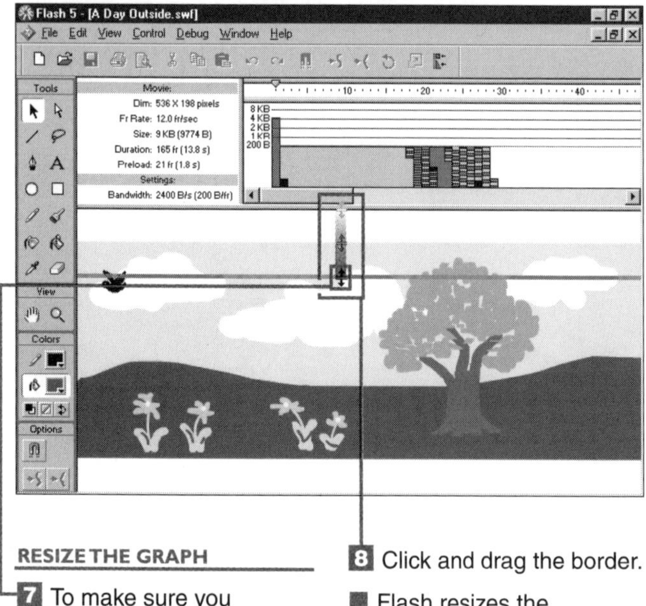

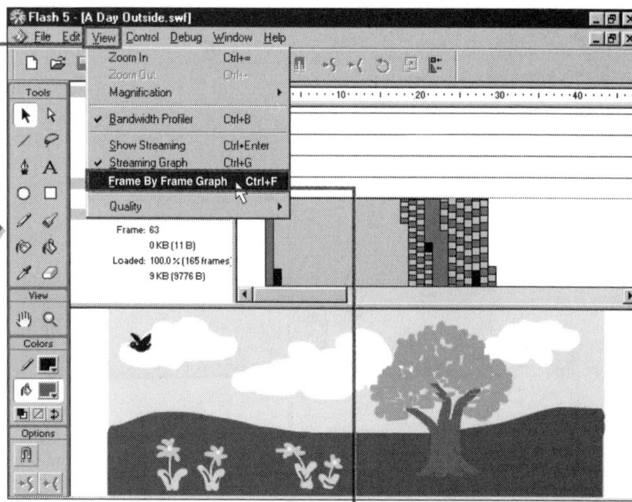

RESIZE THE GRAPH

7 To make sure you are viewing all the movie's information on the left side of the Profiler, move the pointer over the bottom border until the pointer turns into ↕.

8 Click and drag the border.

■ Flash resizes the Bandwidth Profiler.

CHANGE THE GRAPH VIEW

9 To check which frames might be causing a slow down, switch to Frame by Frame Graph mode by clicking View.

10 Click Frame by Frame Graph.

How do I view a specific frame in the Profiler?

✔ Use the scroll bar arrows ◀ ▶ to move left or right in the Profiler Timeline at the top of the Profiler graph. To view a specific frame, drag the playhead to the frame, or click the playhead where you want it to go.

Does the Bandwidth Profiler test the exact modem speed?

✔ No. The Profiler estimates typical Internet connection speeds to estimate downloading time. Modem speeds are typically never full strength. For example, a 28.8 Kbps modem can download 3.5 kilobytes of data per second under perfect conditions, there are no perfect conditions when connecting to the Internet. In real life conditions, a 28.8 Kbps modem is lucky to download 2.3 kilobytes of data per second. Flash gears each modem test speed setting in the Profiler towards real-life connection speeds.

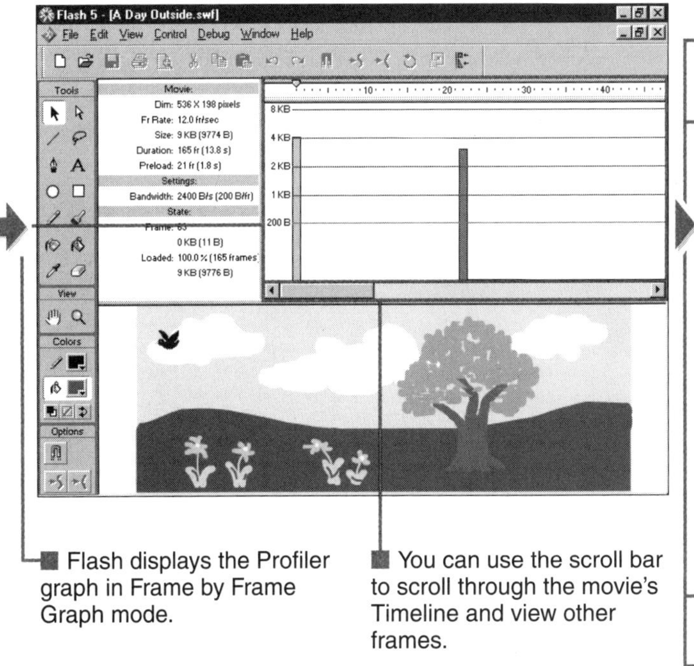

■ Flash displays the Profiler graph in Frame by Frame Graph mode.

■ You can use the scroll bar to scroll through the movie's Timeline and view other frames.

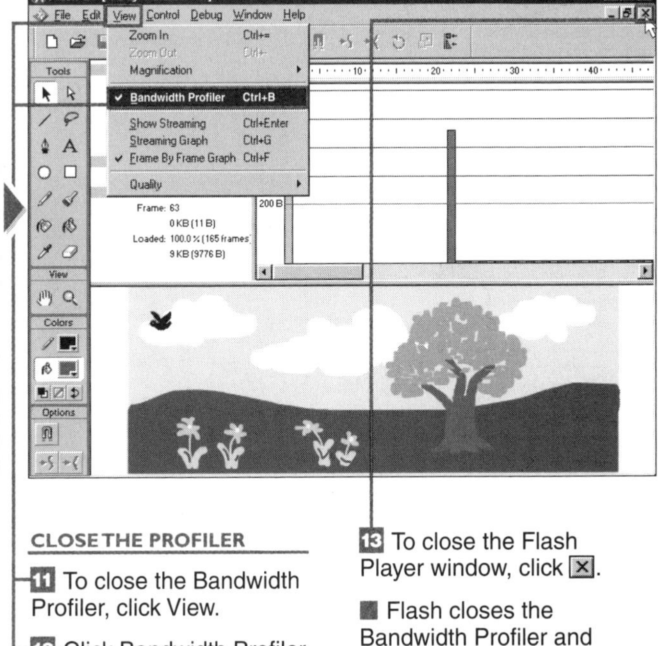

CLOSE THE PROFILER

11 To close the Bandwidth Profiler, click View.

12 Click Bandwidth Profiler.

13 To close the Flash Player window, click ☒.

■ Flash closes the Bandwidth Profiler and the Player window.

PUBLISH A MOVIE

You use two phases to publish your Flash movie. First you prepare the files for publishing using the Publish Settings dialog box, and then you publish the movie using the Flash Publish command.

By default, Flash is set up to publish your movie as an SWF file for the Web, but you can choose to publish in other formats. For example, you can publish your movie as a GIF, JPEG, or PNG image, or as a self-playing Windows or Mac file, or as a QuickTime movie.

In addition to choosing a format, the Publish Settings dialog box also offers you a chance to give the file a distinct name. The Publish Settings dialog box is set up to assign default names, but you can override the settings and type your own unique filenames.

Depending on the format you select, you may find additional publishing options among the other tabs in the Publish Settings dialog box. Learn more about setting additional publishing options in the section "Publish a Movie in HTML Format."

PUBLISH A MOVIE

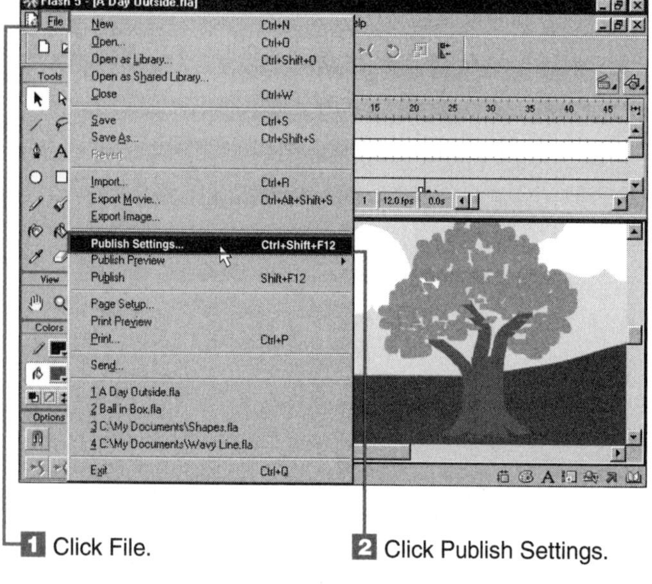

1 Click File.

2 Click Publish Settings.

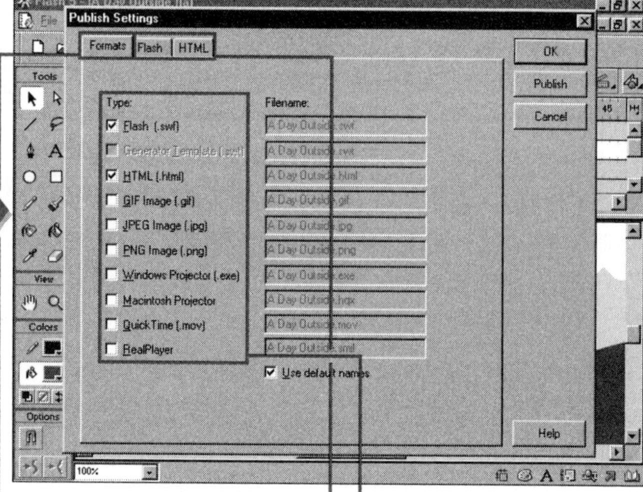

■ The Publish Settings dialog box appears.

Note: If you have already published your file, tabs from your last changes appear in the dialog box.

3 Click the Formats tab.

4 Click the Format option you want to use (☐ changes to ☑).

■ Depending on which format you select, additional tabs appear with options related to that format.

Can I preview a movie before I publish it?

✔ Yes. Testing your movie to check how it plays, especially in a browser, often is a good idea. Flash has a feature that lets you preview a movie in a browser window before you publish the movie. Click File. Click Publish Preview. Click Default. Flash opens the movie in your default Web browser.

How does the Publish feature differ from the Export Movie feature?

✔ You use Publish feature specifically for publishing your work for use on the Web. The Export Movie feature enables you to save your Flash project as another file type, so you can use it in another program. To learn more about these features, see the section "Understand Distribution Methods."

Do I always have to publish a movie through the Publish Settings dialog box?

✔ No. If you want to publish the movie using the previous settings you set up in the Publish Settings dialog box, you can click the File menu and then click Publish. Flash does not give you a chance to name the file if you choose to publish directly and bypass the Publish Settings dialog box.

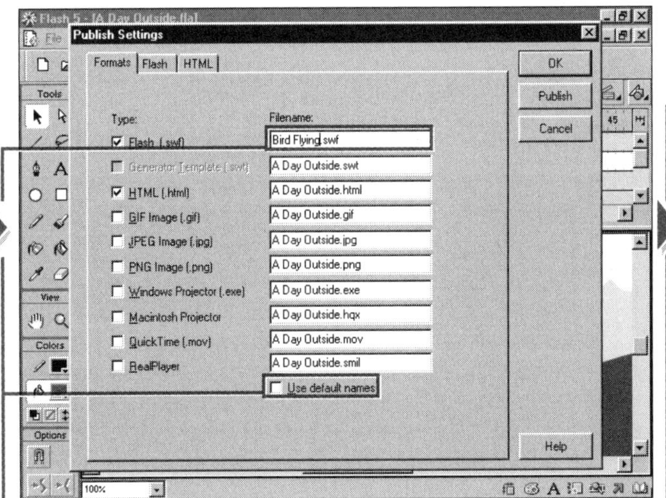

■ To assign a different filename other than the default supplied by Flash, you can click Use Default Names (☑ changes to ☐) and type a new filename in the format's textbox.

■ Flash publishes your files to the My Documents folder unless you specify another folder and filename path in the Filename box.

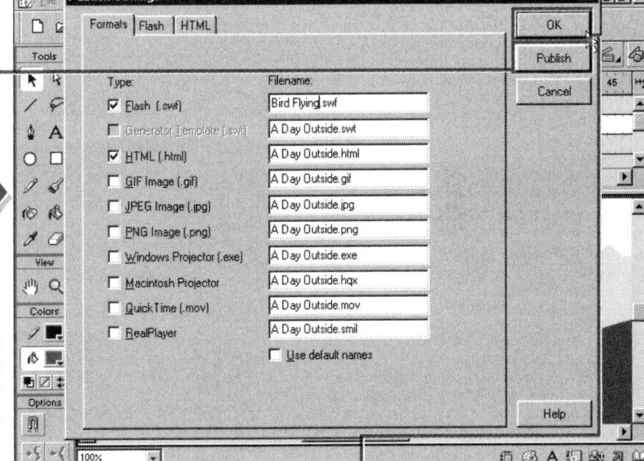

5 When you are ready to publish the movie using the settings you selected, click Publish.

■ Flash generates the necessary files for the movie.

6 Click OK.

■ Flash saves the settings and closes the Publish Settings dialog box.

PUBLISH A MOVIE IN HTML FORMAT

You can save a movie in HTML format, which is the most widely used format on the Web. In response, Flash creates an HTML page that displays your movie along with the SWF movie file. In other words, the HTML document sets up browser settings and activates the movie.

When publishing to HTML format, Flash generates all the necessary HTML code for you, including the tags you need to view your page in both Microsoft Internet Explorer and Netscape Navigator. The HTML markup tags utilize the browser's built-in Flash Player. You can then upload the HTML document to your Web server.

Flash bases the HTML document you create on a template that contains basic HTML coding. By default, Flash assigns the Flash Only template, which is the simplest template you can use to create an HTML document. You can choose from other templates, such as an image map, or if you know HTML code, you can customize the template. The steps in this section show you how to publish your movie to the default template.

PUBLISH A MOVIE IN HTML FORMAT

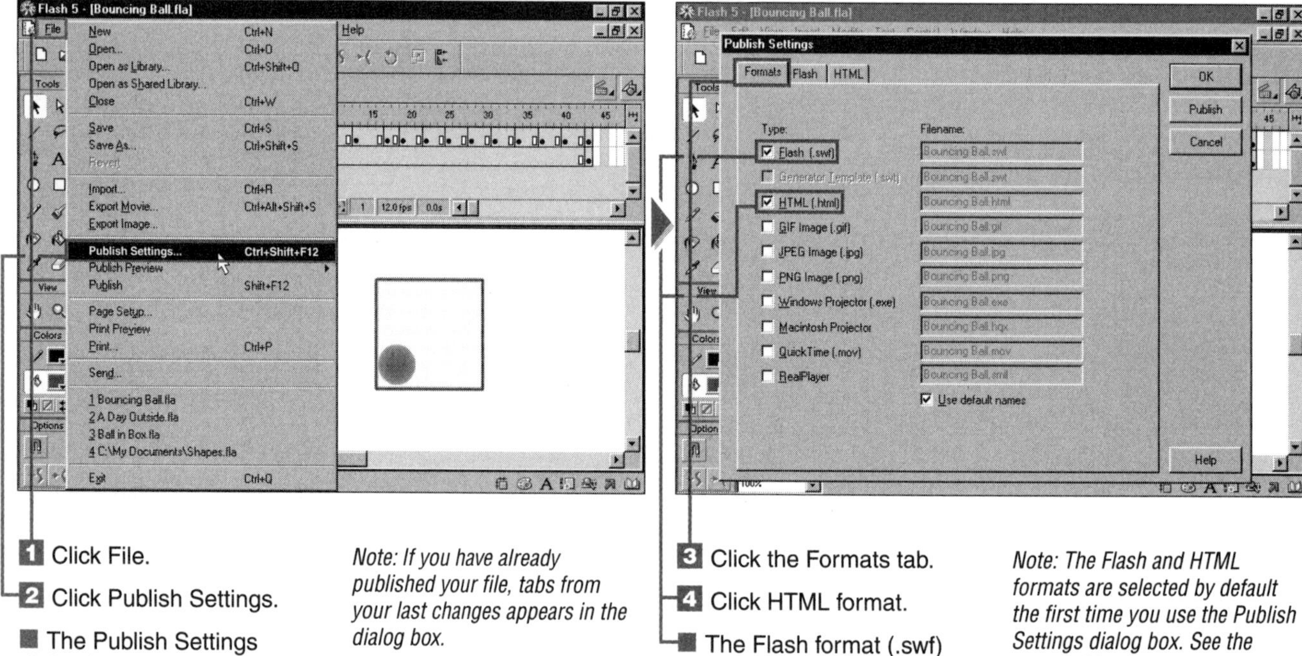

1 Click File.

2 Click Publish Settings.

■ The Publish Settings dialog box appears.

Note: If you have already published your file, tabs from your last changes appears in the dialog box.

3 Click the Formats tab.

4 Click HTML format.

■ The Flash format (.swf) is selected by default.

Note: The Flash and HTML formats are selected by default the first time you use the Publish Settings dialog box. See the section "Publish a Movie" to find out more about publishing Flash movies.

What HTML tags does Flash insert into the HTML document?

✔ The Publish feature inserts the tags necessary for playing a Flash movie file in the browser window, including the `OBJECT` tag for Microsoft's Internet Explorer browser and the `EMBED` tag for Netscape's Navigator browser. Flash also inserts the `IMG` tag for displaying the movie file in another format, such as animated GIF or JPEG. The `OBJECT`, `EMBED`, and `IMG` tags create the movie display window Flash uses to play the Flash movie.

Can I make my own HTML templates for Flash?

✔ Yes. You can set up your own HTML templates or customize existing ones. Be sure to save any HTML templates in the HTML subfolder within the Flash application folder on your computer system. Flash looks for all HTML templates in the HTML folder. The template must also include a title that starts with the recognized HTML title code $TT, such as $TTMy Template.

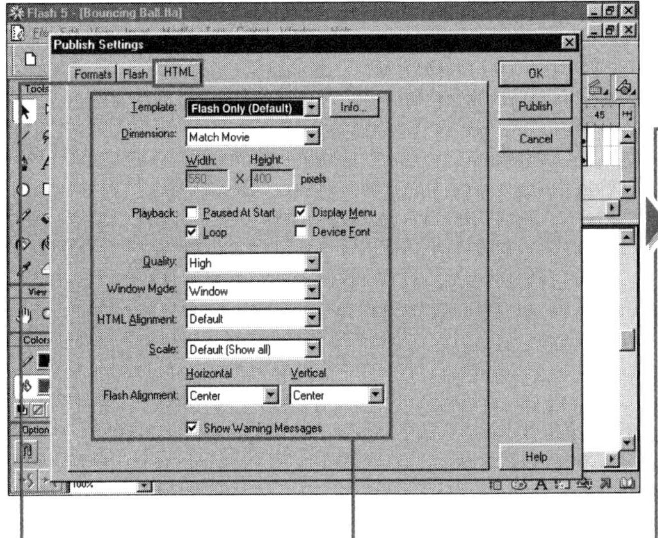

5 Click the HTML tab.

■ Flash displays options associated with generating a Web page, such as playback options and movie dimensions.

6 Select any options you want to apply.

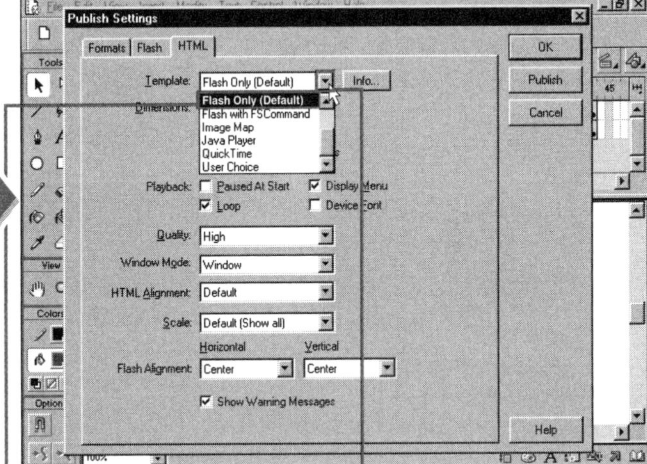

■ The default Flash Only template allows other Flash users to view your movie. Users without the Flash plug-in cannot view the movie.

■ You can click the ▼ in the Template box and select another template from the list.

CONTINUED

PUBLISH A MOVIE IN HTML FORMAT (CONTINUED)

The HTML tab in the Publish Settings dialog box has a variety of options for controlling how your movie plays in the browser window. You can set alignment, dimensions, and even playback options. Any changes you make to the settings overrides any previous settings for the file.

For example, you can specify an alignment placement for the movie on the Web page, such as Left, Center, or Right. You can also define the movie display window's dimensions. You can control exactly how a movie starts, indicating whether the user starts the movie manually or if the movie loops continuously.

You can also specify new movie dimensions that differ from the movie's original screen size dimensions. If you do specify a size other than the default movie size, you must indicate how you want to scale the movie to fit in the dimensions you specify.

PUBLISH A MOVIE IN HTML FORMAT (CONTINUED)

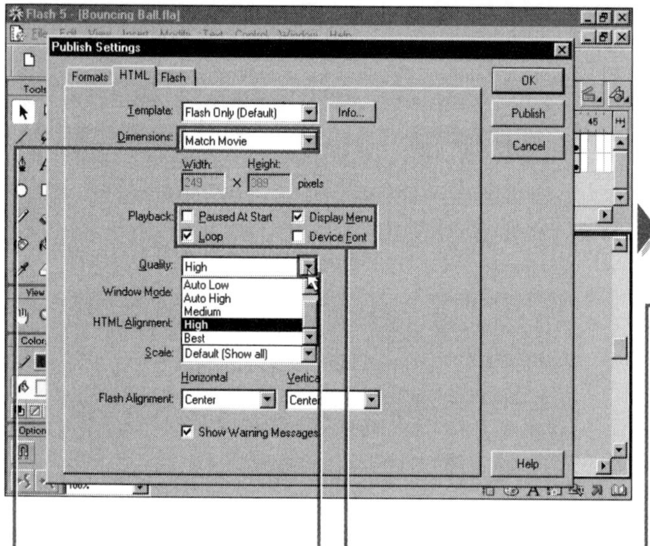

■ You can click the ▼ to set width and height attribute values for the movie display window — the area where the Flash plug-in plays the movie.

■ You can click a Playback option to control how the movie plays on the Web page (☐ changes to ☑).

■ You can click the ▼ and select options for controlling the image quality during playback.

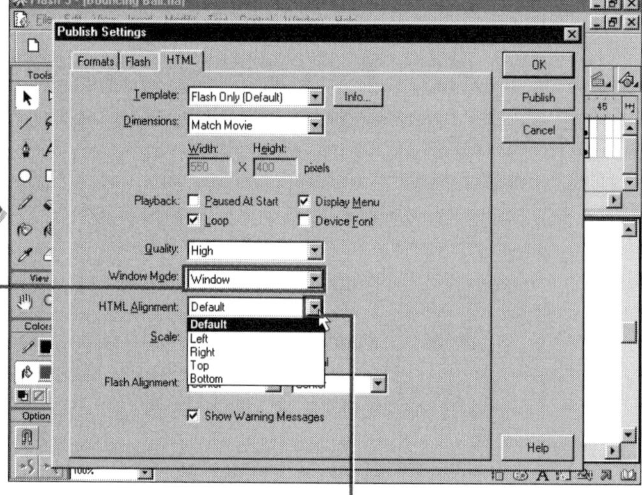

■ You can click the Window Mode ▼ and select options for playing your movie on a regular, opaque, or transparent background (Windows browsers only).

■ You can click the ▼ in the HTML Alignment box and change the alignment of your movie as it relates to other Web page elements.

How do I make my movie full-size in the browser window?

✔ To make your Flash movie appear full-screen size in the browser window, click the ▾ in the Dimensions box . Select Percent. Type 100 as the percent values in the Width and Height text boxes.

How can I tell which HTML template does what?

✔ Select the template you want to know more about, then click the Info button in the Publish Settings dialog box to see a description of the selected template.

How do I view the source code for a Flash template?

✔ Open the template file, which Flash stores in the HTML subfolder within the Flash application folder, in SimpleText (Mac) or Notepad (Windows) to see the source code.

Can I see elements of my authoring file in the SWF file for my movie?

✔ No. When you publish your movie as a SWF file, you do not see any of your authoring elements even if you open the .swf file in the Flash program window. You can only see your authoring elements in the FLA file.

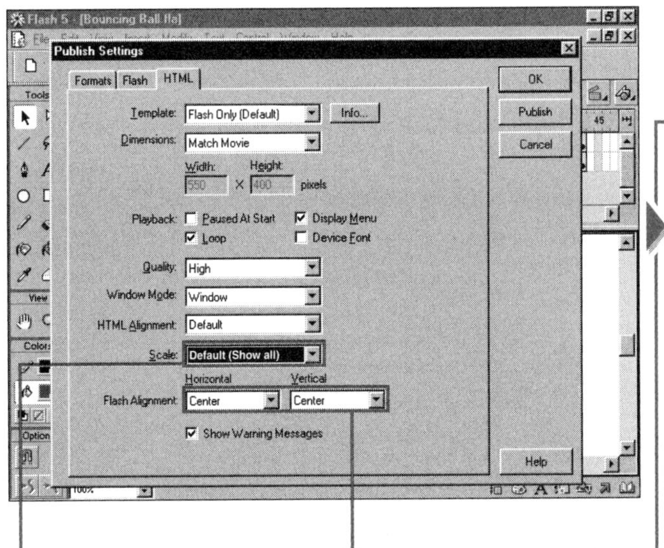

■ If you choose to set new dimensions for the movie, you can click the Scale ▾ to rescale movie elements to fit the new size.

■ You can click the Flash Alignment ▾ and designate how the movie aligns in the movie window area.

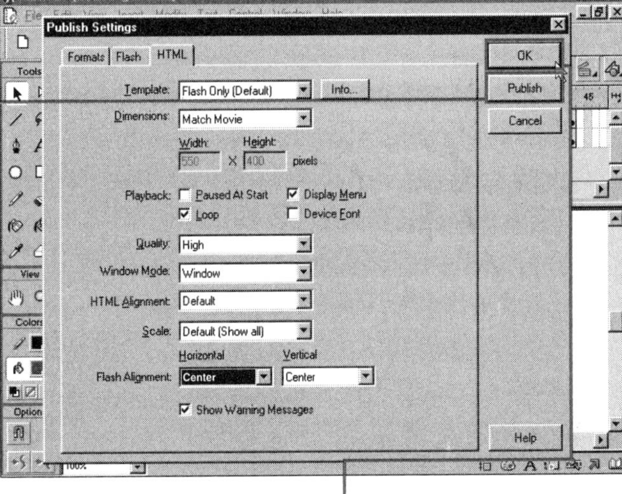

7 When you are ready to publish the movie using your settings, click the Publish button.

■ Flash generates the necessary files for the HTML document.

8 Click OK.

■ The Publish Settings dialog box closes and Flash saves your settings.

CREATE A FLASH PROJECTOR

You can create a Flash movie that plays in its own Flash Player window without the benefit of another application, which means that anyone receiving the file does not need to install the Flash Player application. When you publish the movie as a Windows Projector or Macintosh Projector format, Flash publishes the movie as an executable file with an .exe extension.

Flash projectors are simply self-extracting, self-sufficient mini-applications designed to play movies in real time. Because the projector files are self-sufficient, you can easily place the files on disks to give directly to friends and colleagues, or send them as e-mail file attachments. The only catch is that you must publish the projector file to a format appropriate to the computer platform the end user needs. For example, if you want to send a Flash movie projector file to a friend who uses a Mac, make sure you publish the file to a Mac projector format (HQX) and not a Windows projector format (EXE).

CREATE A FLASH PROJECTOR

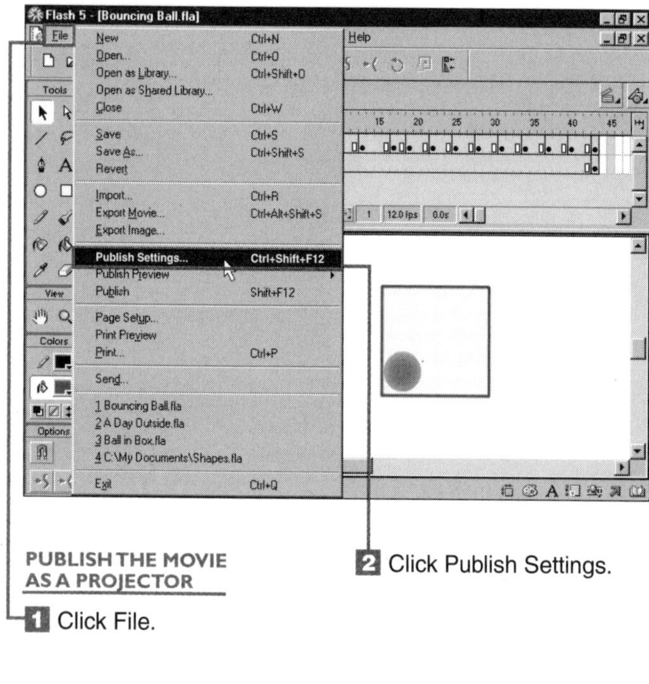

PUBLISH THE MOVIE AS A PROJECTOR

1 Click File.

2 Click Publish Settings.

■ Flash opens the Publish Settings dialog box.

Note: If you have previously published your file, tabs from your last changes appear in the dialog box.

3 Click the Formats tab.

4 Select a projector format (☐ changes to ☑).

■ If you do not want to publish your movie for the Web, you can deselect the Flash and HTML format check boxes (☑ changes to ☐).

Can I rename the movie file?

✔ Yes. If you want a different name for the movie, deselect the Use Default Names check box (☑ changes to ☐) in the Publish Settings dialog box, and then type another name next to the movie format to which you are saving.

What is the difference between a standalone player and a projector?

✔ When you save a file as a Projector file, you are making an executable copy of your Flash movie. This file does not require a player or plug-in. It comes with everything necessary to run the movie. A regular SWF file packs only the movie data, not the player. Regular SWF files require the Flash Player in order to view the movie.

Do I need to worry about licensing my projector file?

✔ Macromedia allows free distribution of its Flash Player and Projector product. If you are distributing your movie for commercial purposes, however, you need to check the Macromedia Web site for information about crediting Macromedia. Visit www.macromedia.com/support/programs/mwm. You need to include the "Made with Macromedia" logo on your packaging and give proper credits on your credit screen.

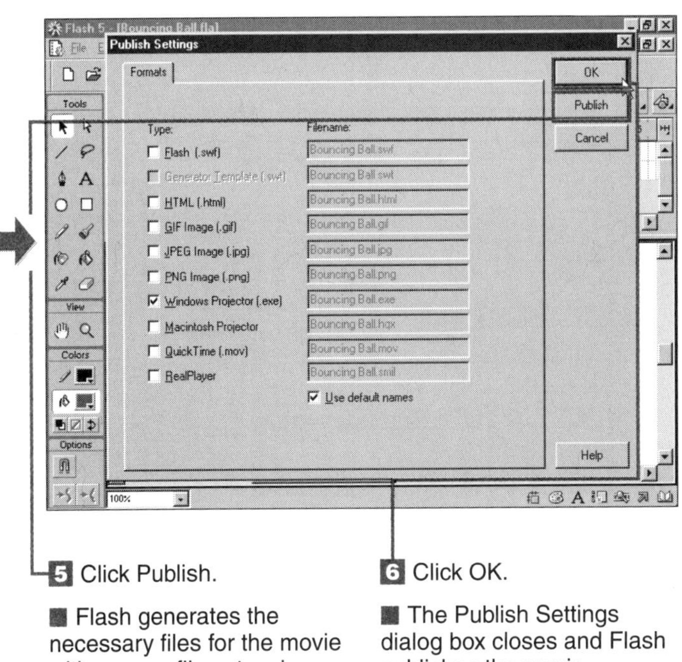

5 Click Publish.

■ Flash generates the necessary files for the movie with an .exe file extension.

6 Click OK.

■ The Publish Settings dialog box closes and Flash publishes the movie.

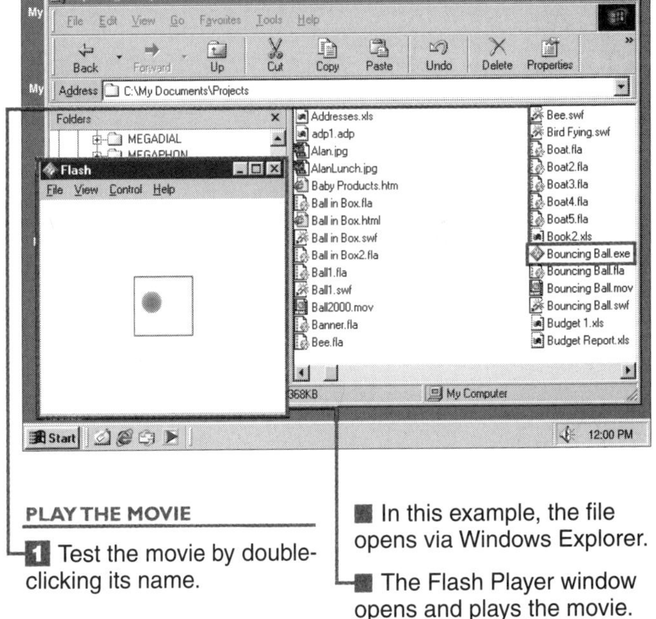

PLAY THE MOVIE

1 Test the movie by double-clicking its name.

■ In this example, the file opens via Windows Explorer.

■ The Flash Player window opens and plays the movie.

EXPORT TO ANOTHER FORMAT

You can easily export a Flash movie into another file format for use with other applications. For example, you can save your movie as a Windows AVI file or as a QuickTime file, or perhaps you want to save each frame as a bitmap sequence. Flash can export over a dozen different file formats in both Windows and Mac platforms.

The Export feature of Flash differs from the Publish feature in that it creates editable Flash content. You use the Publish feature when you want to generate Web-based content See the section "Publish a Movie in HTML Format" for more information. Unlike the Publish feature, Export savings are not saved with the movie file.

When exporting to other file formats, you can choose to export the entire Flash movie as an animated sequence or as still images. Depending on the file format, exporting may cause the loss of the Flash vector information, unless you export to a vector-based file format, such as Adobe Illustrator.

EXPORT TO ANOTHER FORMAT

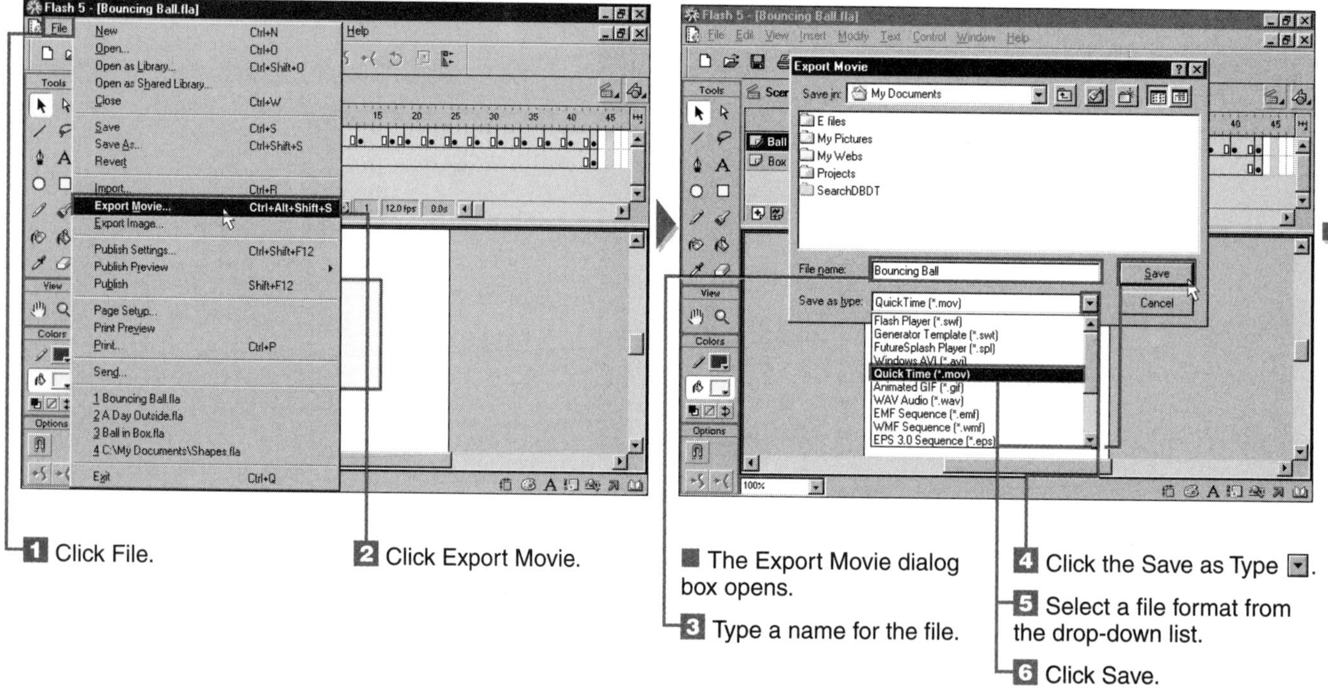

1 Click File.

2 Click Export Movie.

■ The Export Movie dialog box opens.

3 Type a name for the file.

4 Click the Save as Type ▼.

5 Select a file format from the drop-down list.

6 Click Save.

What is the difference between exporting a movie and publishing a movie?

✔ When you publish a movie, you can publish to Flash (SWF), Generator Template, HTML, GIF, JPEG, PNG, Windows Projector, Macintosh Projector, QuickTime, and RealPlayer formats. When you export a movie, you can save the file in over a dozen different file formats, such as Windows AVI or Animated GIF. The two features share some of the formats and options, but when you publish a movie as opposed to exporting it, Flash saves information about the movie's Publish settings along with the movie file. When you export a movie, you are saving it to a single format.

Can I export a single frame rather than an entire movie?

✔ Yes. First select the frame you want to save as an export file. Then click the File menu and click Export Image. This opens the Export Image dialog box. Give the file a distinct name, and format type, then click Save. Depending on the format you select, additional parameters may appear for you to set.

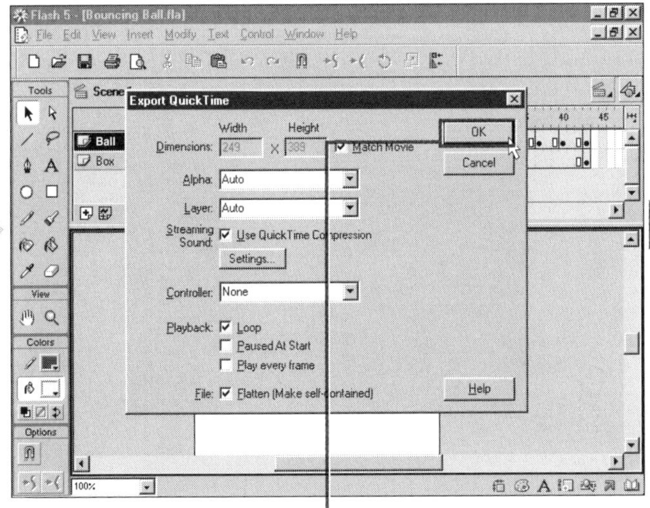

■ Depending on the file type you selected, an additional Export dialog box opens with options for size, sound, and video format.

■ You can make any selections necessary.

7 Click OK.

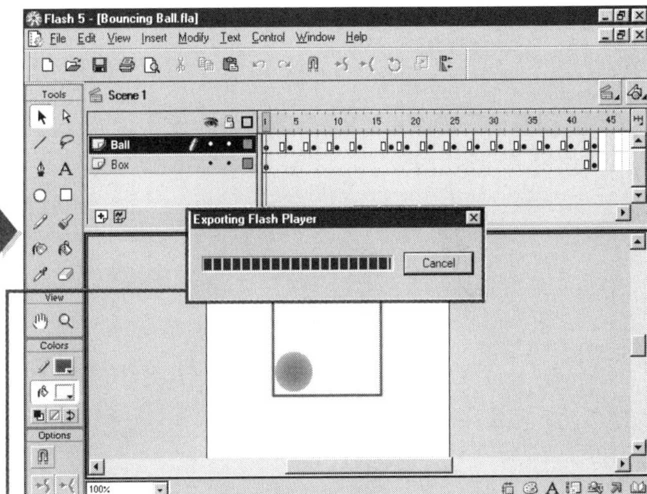

■ Flash exports the movie to the designated file type.

Note: Depending on the file type, another dialog box can open first. Make any selections necessary, and click OK to continue exporting.

Note: Interactive elements you include in your Flash movies may not export to other file formats properly.

PRINT MOVIE FRAMES

Some Flash projects may require you to print out a frame or series of frames. For example, you may print out frame content to show a storyboard of the movie. You can use the Page Setup dialog box (Windows) or Print Margins dialog box (Mac) to specify a layout for the storyboard, then use the Print dialog box to specify which pages to print.

You can specify a variety of printing options for frames. You can print a single frame and designate margins, alignment, page orientation and paper size for the printout. You can print thumbnails — miniatures of your movie's frames — and print them as boxes or in a grid, or fit them all onto a single page of paper.

You can find frame and storyboarding options in the Page Setup dialog box (Windows) or Print Margins dialog box (Mac). The options in this dialog box can help you set up your frames for printing. To actually print the pages, you must activate the Print command by opening the Print dialog box and printing from there, or by clicking the Print button.

PRINT MOVIE FRAMES

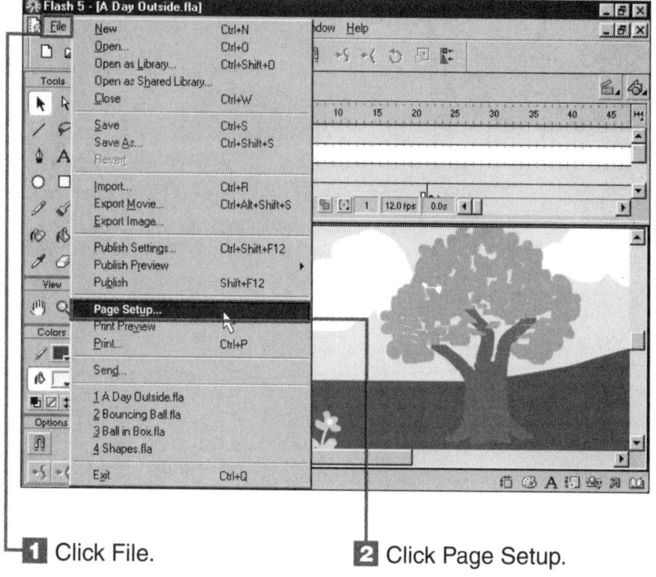

1 Click File.

2 Click Page Setup.

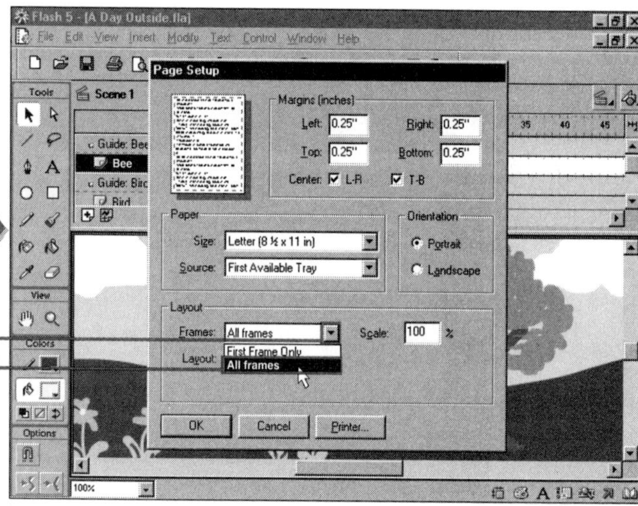

■ The Page Setup dialog box opens.

3 Click the Frames ▼.

4 Click All frames.

■ You can use the First Frame Only option if you want to print just the first frame of the movie.

Can I preview before I print?

✔ You can preview exactly how the frames and layout appear on the printed page using the Flash Print Preview feature. Click [Print Preview icon] to open the Print Preview window. Click the Print button to print the frames, or click the Close button to return to the Flash window.

Can I add labels to each printed frame?

✔ Yes. If you select one of the storyboard layout options in the Print dialog box, a Label frames check box appears. Click this check box (❑ changes to ☑) to print the scene and frame number for each frame you print out in the storyboard.

Will Flash print any symbols I have placed in the work area off of the Stage?

✔ No. Flash prints only the symbols and objects found on the Stage area of any given frame. If you move a symbol off the Stage to place in a later frame or insert later, the symbol does not display in your printout.

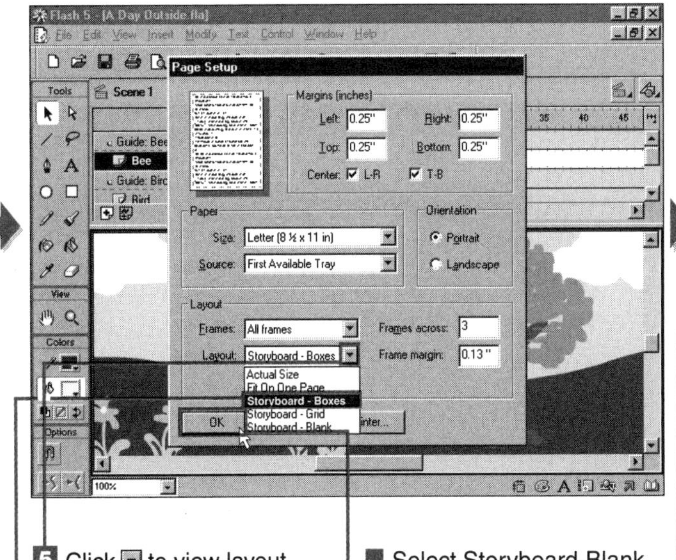

5 Click [▼] to view layout options.

6 Click an option.

■ Select Storyboard-Boxes to print in storyboard boxes.

■ Select Storyboard-Grid to print in a grid pattern.

■ Select Storyboard-Blank to print only the graphic items of each frame.

7 Click OK.

■ The Page Setup dialog box closes.

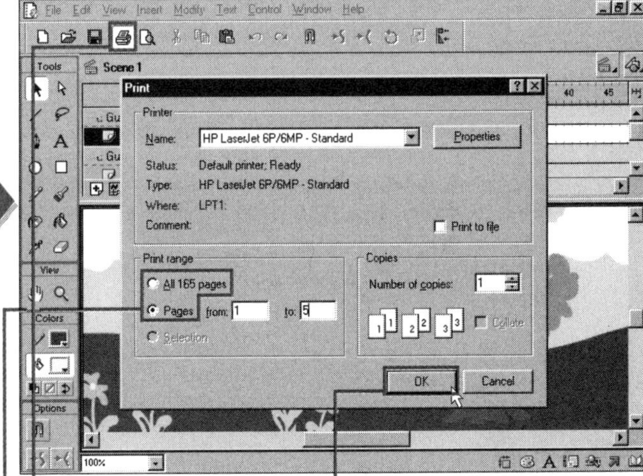

8 Click the Print button ([Print icon]).

■ The Print dialog box opens.

9 Select a Print Range option (○ changes to ◉).

■ You can click All pages to print the entire movie.

■ Alternately, you can click Pages and type a range of pages you want to print.

10 Click OK.

■ Flash prints the specified pages and layout.

SECTION III

31) BUILDING A WEB SITE

Combine Dreamweaver and Flash 544
Sample Site Planning Considerations 546
Create a Sample Flash Interface 547
Create a Simple Preloader 548
Add a Skip Intro Button 550
Create an Intro Text Effect 552
Create a Laser-Writing Animation Effect 554
Create a Welcome Page 560
Add Hot Buttons 562
Create a Drop-Down Menu 564
Use the Root Property Action Statement 570
Enable Testing Options 571
Create Button Animations 572
Create a Tool Tip 574
Create a Chat Feature 576

32) BUILDING WEB SITE FORMS WITH FLASH

Create a Simple Flash Form 582
Create a Clear Button 584
Create a Submit Button 586
Create a Scrolling Text Box 588
Edit a User Profile 590
Create a User Login Screen 592
Create a User Log Out Option 596
Use the Mail To Command 598
Add a Search Tool 600

BUILDING A WEB SITE WITH DREAMWEAVER AND FLASH

33) ENHANCING THE WEB SITE

Integrate a Flash Banner 606
Create a Link with the Get URL Action 608
Call a Server-Side Script 610
Control Windows with Get URL Options 612
Control Windows with JavaScript 614
Make Your Files Downloadable 616
Optimize Web Site Graphics 618
Optimize a Large Movie 620
Flag a User Error 622

COMBINE DREAMWEAVER AND FLASH

You can combine the power of both Macromedia's Dreamweaver and Flash to create a dynamic Web site that is sure to grab the attention of anyone who visits. Because the Flash and Dreamweaver software are produced by the same company, integrating the two is quite easy.

When using Dreamweaver, inserting a Flash movie is as simple as clicking a button and selecting the movie to insert. Dreamweaver also gives you the ability to manipulate your Flash movie after you have inserted it on your Web page. You can change the size, background color, and placement of your Flash movie.

If you are new to Web page building, you should review Part I of this book, which shows how to use the Dreamweaver program. If you are new to creating animations, buttons, and other Web-based elements in Flash, visit Part II. After you have a general understanding how both of these programs work, you are ready to tackle this part of the book.

Build a Sample Web Site

This part shows you step-by-step how to plan for your own Web site, develop goals, design an introduction, and add Flash techniques that are sure to give your own site pizzazz. You can combine techniques such as creating a drop-down menu, using special effects, utilizing JavaScript, and creating search tools for your site along with your other Web designing experiences to create a dynamic site that you can publish on the Web. Mastering these techniques gives you a good foundation to build your own Web site, whether your site is purely for fun or profit.

To demonstrate how you can combine Dreamweaver and Flash to create a dynamic Web site, the CD-ROM at the back of this book includes a sample Web site you can study. Note that some of the site elements, such as the search and chat features, do not run properly unless the site is published on a Web server because the scripts that provide the functionality reside and run on the computer hosting the site. You should take this into consideration when using such scripts on your own site. Most server-side scripts offering advanced functionality (for example, chat applications, message boards, search engines, Web cams, credit card validation, and so on) require a specific type of server or server configurations depending on the language the script is written in.

The sample site is a simple e-commerce site focusing on selling books. Although creating an e-commerce site warrants greater coverage than room allows in this book, the sample site gives you a glimpse into some of the strategies that go into such a site. This part focuses on the techniques used to create the sample site.

How Does the Site Use Dreamweaver and Flash?

Flash is used to create the user interface for the sample site. The term *user interface* refers to the part of a Web site or software program with which users interact, usually through buttons, menu bars, scroll bars, and other graphical elements. When the Flash interface is complete and ready to be published online, the movie must be embedded in an HTML file. Dreamweaver provides a graphic user interface for programming HTML and simplifies the process of embedding a Flash movie and setting its specifications.

How Do I Publish My Site After It Is Finished?

When you have created a combined Dreamweaver/Flash site, you have a couple of options to publish your pages. One option is to register with an online Web page publishing community such as Tripod or Geo Cities. Their services are usually free, but they add advertisements to your page. If having ads on your Web site strikes you as unseemly, just remember that if it were not for the ads, your page would not be published for free.

Another option is to contact your local ISP (Internet service provider). They can give you information on their publishing services and direct you on how to have your own live Web site on the Internet. One note of caution: ISPs usually charge a fee for publishing a Web site, so shop around to see what is offered in your area.

Getting Started

Always consider your users above all else when developing a Flash-based site. Flash sites are continuously criticized for usability issues when designers neglect to consider the user (for example, using buttons that do not appear to be a clickable item). Paying specific attention to usability and navigation issues before you begin building your site lends to a more user-friendly site. To do so, you need to determine your audience, their bandwidth, the primary goals of the site, the navigation, and any other special criteria before Flash is even opened. Flow charting and storyboarding are both examples of ways to organize your thoughts and ensure that you have taken usability issues into consideration. Planning and defining your site's criteria and layout are essential to the success of the site as a whole. The following sections help you take the first steps in determining your site's requirements and navigation.

SAMPLE SITE PLANNING CONSIDERATIONS

The difference between building a good Web site and a great Web site is planning. As discussed in Chapter 1, the right planning includes organizing your ideas, gathering your content, and defining your audience.

During your planning phase, think about your site's requirements and how you want users to navigate around your site. Also, think through your site's introduction.

Determine Site Requirements

Start your planning by listing the requirements for your site. Listing items in categories of wants versus needs is a good idea. This helps you to prioritize tasks. Some of the requirements considered for the sample Web site created for this chapter included easy navigation; a searchable database of products; a registration form for visitors; a flashy, attention-getting introduction; and some animations to keep the user's attention throughout the presentation of information.

After you have listed your requirements, write down some potential solutions. For example, a solution for the example site's searchable catalog of products is to use ASP (Active Server Pages) and a product database.

Determine Site Navigation

The importance of sketching out a site map is discussed in Chapter 1. For the sample Web site, we used a flow chart to help pin down the navigational details as well.

Start your navigational flow chart with a welcome page, and then add any additional pages that you need. Trace paths of links from the welcome page to subordinate pages.

Do not forget to include what buttons should be present on each screen. Including a global navigation menu, or elements of navigation, on every page to ensure the user does not get lost is a good practice.

Storyboard Your Site Intro

Many Flash sites include an introduction animation following the welcome page (containing site requirements, plugin detection, welcome text, and so on), which serves as a preview or advertisement for the site. To create your own Flash introduction, first start with a bit of planning, using a technique called storyboarding. *Storyboarding* is a technique used by developers of cartoons, commercials, movies, and many other media types that involves simply sketching or writing out what each scene or sequence entails.

Putting together the intro animation is not too difficult — you can employ the animation techniques covered in Chapters 24 and 25. In the demo Web site, the intro consists of everything the user sees until they view the Flash interface containing the menu bar. The beginning of the intro starts with the preloader (see "Create a Simple Preloader") and ends with the laser-writing effect.

CREATE A SAMPLE FLASH INTERFACE

An *interface* is the part of a program or Web site with which the user interacts. Buttons, menus, input text boxes, and so on, are all basic parts of an interface. You can create an interface to use for your Web site using Flash.

A Flash interface allows you to combine user interactions and animation to give the user an interactive experience.

Creating the interface should be one of your first steps, because resizing and modifying the interface later is difficult. If you have accurately defined the site navigation taking usability issues into consideration, you should need to modify only page-level content in future revisions. Keep in mind that any modifications to navigational elements should be applied to the site as a whole to ensure that the flow of the site remains consistent.

Begin designing your Flash interface using *placeholders*. Placeholders are just simple shapes (circle, square, triangle) used in place of buttons and graphics. You can add the real buttons and graphics later. Using placeholders for interface elements can allow you to play around with the design and layout of your site. After you get everything positioned as you like, you can publish your Flash file to see how the elements look as an HTML page. To make changes, simply return to the original Flash file and edit the elements.

CREATE A SAMPLE FLASH INTERFACE

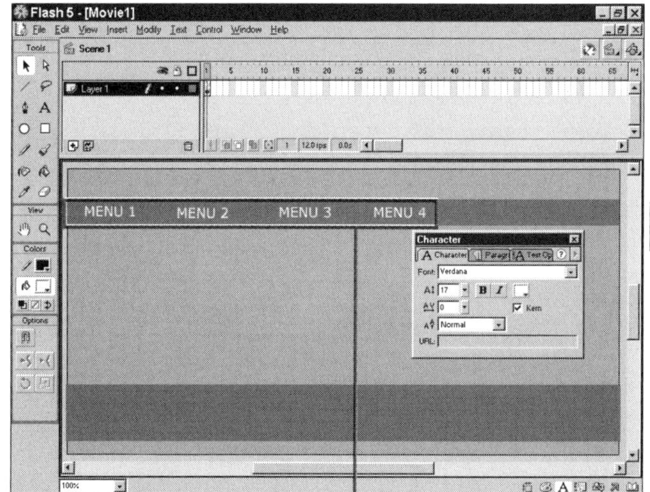

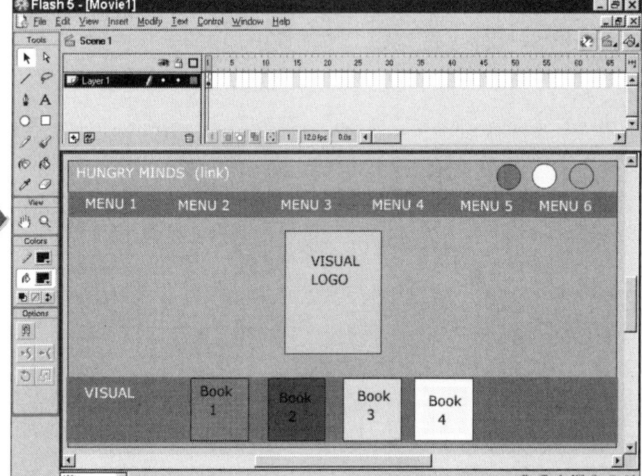

1 Open a new Flash file and set the movie properties to desired values.

■ In this example, the movie width is set to 728 and the height is set to 350.

2 Determine the basic look of your interface and add placeholders for important elements.

Note: See Chapter 18 to learn more about creating shapes in Flash.

3 Add functionality to any placeholder buttons to ensure that the site flows according to the flow chart.

4 Save your file so you can add your visual elements following the storyboard stage.

■ Use placeholders to approximate the same dimensions as intended buttons or graphics.

■ You can publish the file as an HTML page or use Test Movie (Control menu) to see how it looks.

CREATE A SIMPLE PRELOADER

You can add a preloader to your site's intro page to keep a visitor's interest while the remainder of your Web site downloads. A *preloader* mainly consists of a small animation and information concerning the state of the Web site.

When working with a Flash-driven site, a preloader is very important. If a Web user visits your site and has to wait too long for the Web pages to download, chances are the visitor will leave your site. A general statement declaring that the site is loading informs visitors that the site is not broken or down, but just taking a moment to load. In many instances, a loading statement includes a percentage graphic showing how much of the download has occurred.

You may have seen examples of preloaders at other Web sites you have visited. When planning your preloader, keep in mind that a preloader's main purpose is to show loading progress. Whether you choose to accurately represent the amount of data loaded is up to your discretion, but it is important that the animation sequence represent progress. The following example explains how to display a preloader movie clip before moving onto the actual site content.

CREATE A SIMPLE PRELOADER

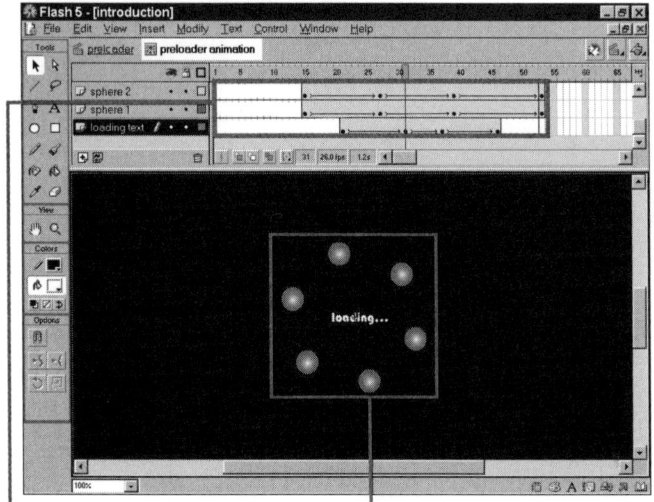

1 Create an animation sequence to use as your preloader and save it as a movie clip symbol.

Note: See Chapter 24 to learn about creating animation effects and saving them as movie clips.

2 Develop a simple animation with a message that your site is loading.

■ Keep graphics and number of frames to a minimum to prevent the user from waiting for the preloader to download.

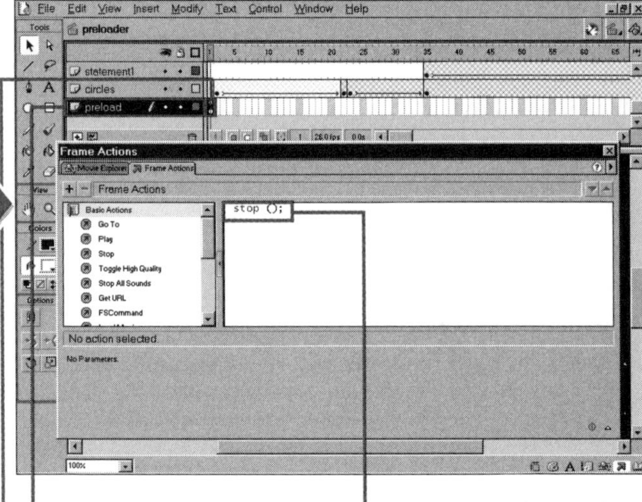

3 Add two layers to the main movie and name them **actions** and **preload**.

Note: See Chapter 21 to learn how to add layers.

4 Insert the preloader movie clip into frame 1 of the preloader layer.

5 Assign a `Stop` action to the first frame of the actions layer.

Note: See Chapter 28 to learn how to add actions.

I do not see my preloader when testing my movie. Why?

✔ The rest of your Flash movie must be complete in order to test your preloader. If you have not created anything beyond frame 1, there is nothing to preload. If you test your preloader by viewing the published HTML document of your Flash file, you see the preloader only for a moment because loading a Flash movie directly from your computer takes less than a second, depending on the speed of your computer.

How long should my preloader run?

✔ The speed at which the visitor connects to the Internet and the size of the Flash movie you are loading are the main factors determining the length of time your preloader runs. The typical user will wait 10 seconds for a site to load. The amount of data that can be loaded in 10 seconds (about 100K on a 56K modem) depends on the user's bandwidth, so it is important that you determine the connection speed of your audience. Consider separating your site into individual SWF files or using multiple preloader sequences if your entire site cannot be loaded in this timeframe.

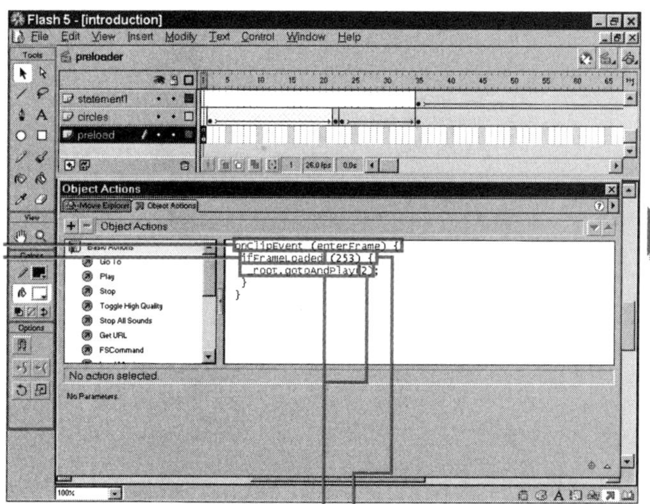

6 With the preloader clip selected in frame 1, assign an `onClipEvent` action.

7 Click EnterFrame.

8 Add an `ifFrameLoaded` action.

9 Type **253** in the Frame field or the number of the last frame in your movie.

10 Add a `Go To` action.

11 Type **2** in the Frame field.

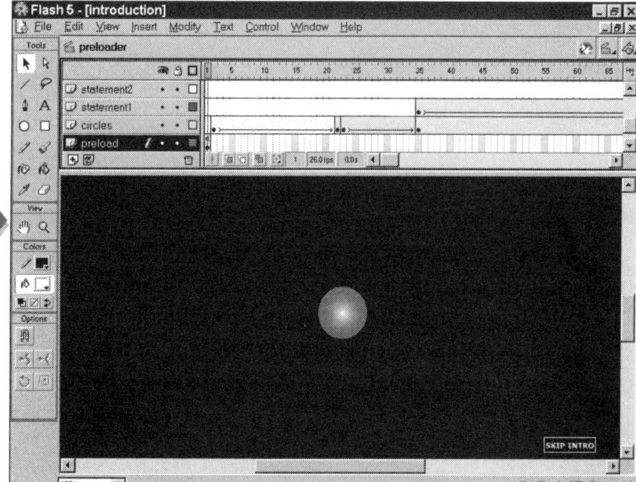

12 Switch to Expert mode in the Actions panel.

13 Add `_root` before the `gotoAndPlay` statement.

Note: See "Using the Root Property Action Statement" for more information.

■ You can now test your preloader and see how it works.

Note: See Chapter 30 to learn more about testing Flash movies.

ADD A SKIP INTRO BUTTON

You can give users who revisit your site the option to skip the introduction page by adding a skip intro button. Visitors do not typically enjoy sitting through a minute of downloading and a 20-second introduction to a site that they have already seen. You can add a skip intro button as a courteous way to allow visitors to bypass the introduction and go straight to the interface.

In most cases, you need to make the skip intro button viewable only during the movie preloader, the simple animation that plays while your movie loads. If the preloader takes 20 seconds, the user has 20 seconds to activate the skip intro button in order to bypass the introduction movie. If they fail to activate the button in time, they must sit through the site introduction. See "Create a Simple Preloader," earlier in this chapter, for more information on preloaders.

The steps in this section demonstrate how to assign a skip intro button and assign a `GetURL` action to the button. The `GetURL` action used in this example calls a new HTML page containing the Flash user interface. You may wish to use the `gotoAndPlay` frame action to take the user to another frame or scene if the intro animation is in the same Flash file, or the `loadMovie` action if you want to load a new SWF file (containing the user interface) into the current movie instead.

ADD A SKIP INTRO BUTTON

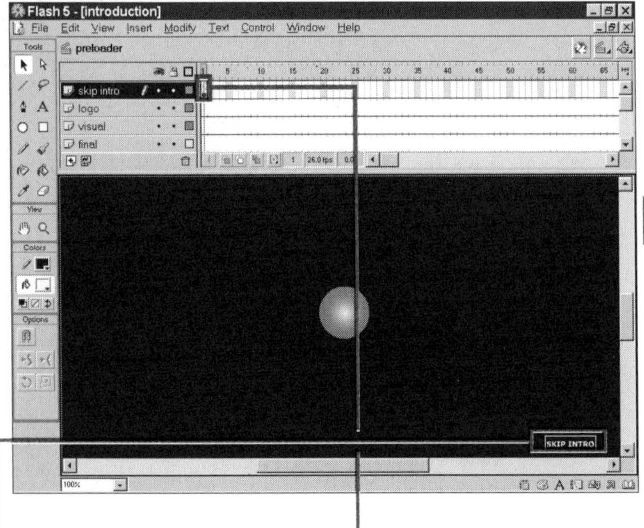

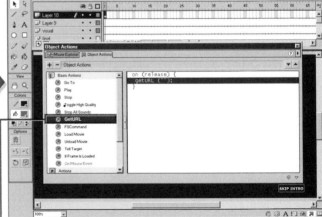

1 Create a simple skip intro button.

Note: See Chapter 26 to learn more about creating buttons.

Note: Make sure that you create a button that downloads quickly.

2 Insert the button into frame 1 of your intro movie.

3 Assign the `GetURL` action to frame 1.

Note: See Chapter 28 to learn more about assigning actions.

Why do I select `_top` in the Window field for step 5? What does this parameter refer to?

✔ The Window parameter of the `GetURL` action according to the ActionScript dictionary is "an optional argument specifying the window or HTML frame that the document should be loaded into." The definitions of each parameter are listed below:

`_self` specifies the current frame in the current window.

`_blank` specifies a new window.

`_parent` specifies the parent of the current frame.

`_top` specifies the top-level frame in the current window.

When loading the user interface, when are each of the following used appropriately: `GetURL`, `loadMovie`, or `gotoAndPlay`?

✔ `GetURL` is used when you want to load a new page, external script, or URL. `LoadMovie` is used if you have a bandwidth-heavy site that needs to be separated into multiple SWFs. Use the `gotoAndPlay` frame action if your site is small enough to keep in one SWF file.

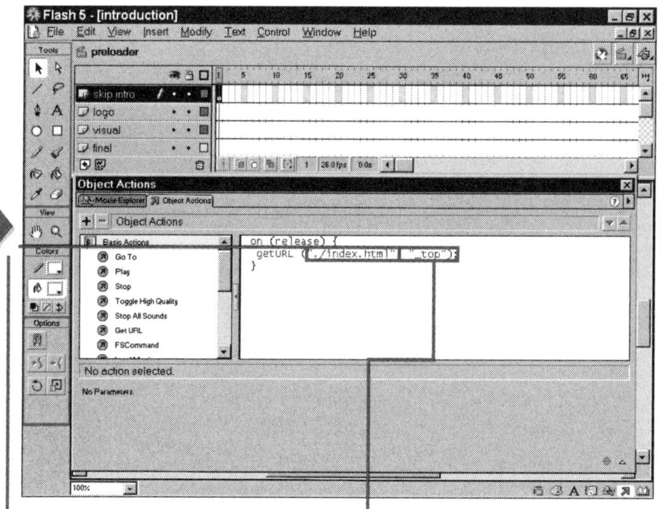

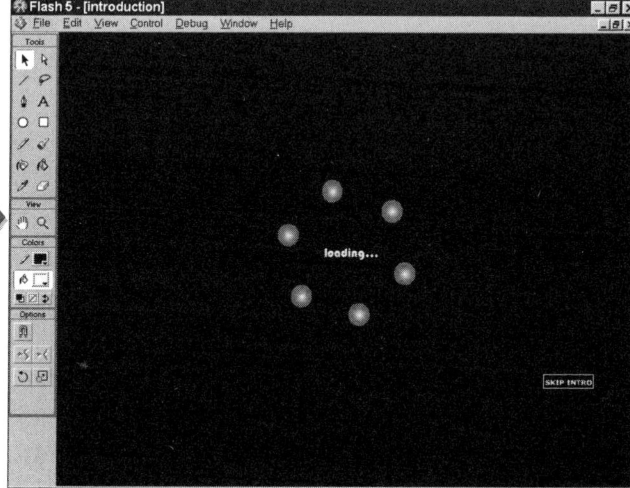

4 In the URL field type the path of the page holding your interface.

5 In the Window field select `_top`.

Note: Assign the `GetURL` action to the last frame in the intro animation movie as well. This action loads the user interface if the user chooses to watch the intro animation.

6 Test the button.

Note: See Chapter 28 to learn more about testing buttons.

■ The button loads your main interface when testing the movie using the Test Movie command.

■ Testing the button in a published HTML page launches your default browser to load the main movie.

CREATE AN INTRO TEXT EFFECT

Text effects include any special treatments to text including changing the alpha channel (opacity), tint, scale, or rotation of a letter or group of letters and adding motion, sound, or animation. Generally, text effects are used when the designer's intent is to focus the user's attention on a specific word or phrase. Although text effects can add a great deal of visual stimuli to a presentation, be careful not to overuse or complicate the presentation. If used in excess, text effects can detract from the message and quickly increase file size. However, if used sparingly and in good taste, they can add a great deal to the overall aesthetic value of a statement.

In the Web site example demonstrated in this chapter, a simple text effect is used as an intro animation that appears as the transition between the welcome page and the main page. The effect allows users plenty of time to read key marketing points. This particular text effect fades as it grows, and after it hits a certain point, fades out again. The steps below show you how to create this effect using 30 frames.

CREATE AN INTRO TEXT EFFECT

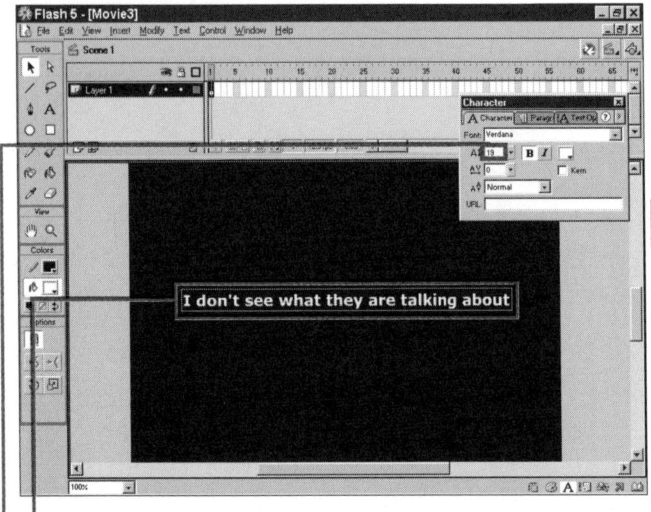

1 Open a new Flash file and add a static text block to the Flash Stage.

2 Format the text in a medium-sized font.

Note: See Chapter 20 to learn more about working with text in Flash.

3 Convert the text to a graphic symbol.

Note: See Chapter 22 to learn more about converting objects to symbols in Flash.

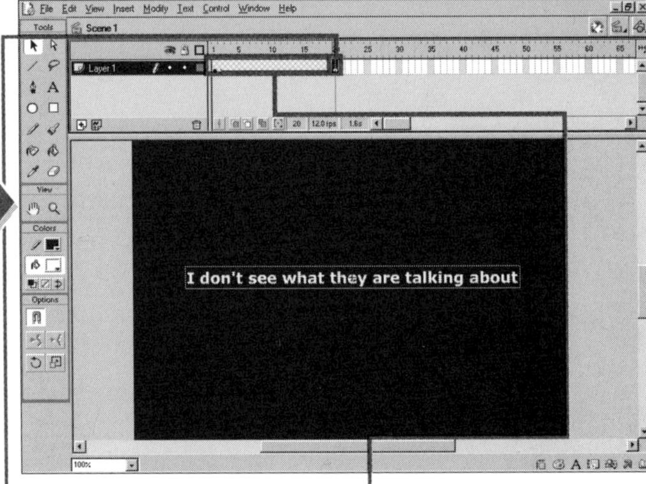

4 Insert a keyframe into frame 20.

Note: See Chapter 24 to learn more about Flash frames.

5 Create a motion tween between frames 1 and 20.

Note: See Chapter 25 to learn how to create a motion tween.

What is the difference between a static and a dynamic text box?

✔ A static text box is an inactive block of text, whereas a dynamic text box is assigned a variable and the text can be changed through the use of an ActionScript. A dynamic text box might be used on the interface movie to personalize the site after a user has signed in.

What it easing?

✔ Easing is a property you can change for a motion tween that allows you to speed up or slow down the appearance of the effect. Easing in, represented by number values –1 through –100, slowly accelerates the animation and picks up speed towards the end of the sequence. Easing out, represented by number values 1 through 100, accelerates your animation in the beginning and slows it towards the end. In the demo Web site intro effect, easing is added to the text effect to produce a pausing effect. To change the easing value for your motion tween effect, open the Frame panel and adjust the Easing slider.

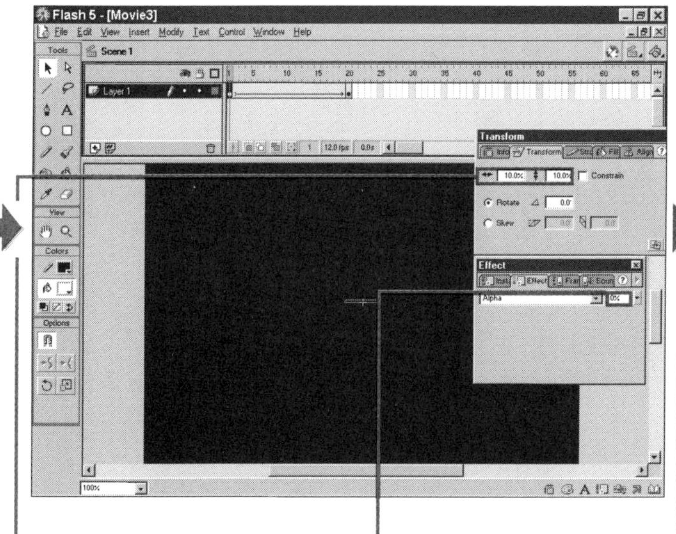

6 In frame 1, use the Scale command to decrease the instance size to about 10% of the original size.

Note: See Chapter 19 to learn how to resize objects.

7 Also in frame 1, change the alpha value of symbol instance to 0%.

Note: See Chapter 22 to learn how to change the alpha value for symbols.

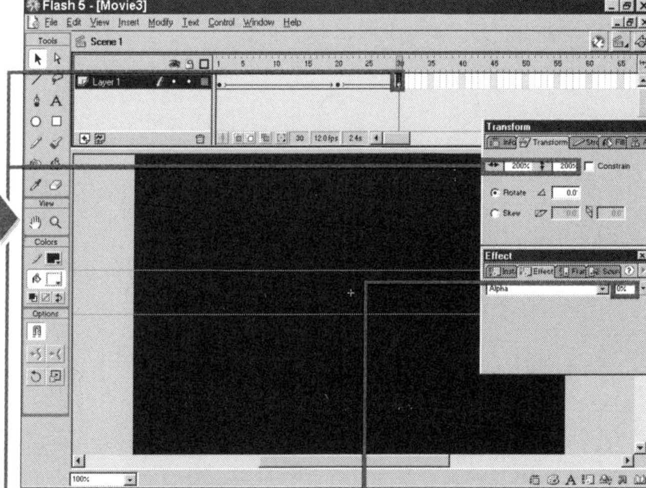

8 Insert a keyframe in frame 30.

9 Create a motion tween between frame 20 and frame 30.

10 In frame 30, scale the instance size to 200-300% of the original size.

11 In frame 30, change the alpha value of symbol to 0%.

■ Repeat these steps for as many statements as you want to animate for your own Intro.

■ The demo site's Intro ends on a static text block.

CREATE A LASER-WRITING ANIMATION EFFECT

You can use Flash to create amazing special effects to wow your Web site visitors and increase traffic to your site. The laser-writing animation effect illustrated here can be used to simulate writing text or the illustration of a graphic element. Laser-writing is best used on a single character or illustration. Remember, you want the effect to be something that the user is intrigued by. Like text effects, it is important to remember that effects such as these can increase file size and slow down playback if used in excess.

The following steps explain how to give the illusion that the animation sequence is writing the character. However, you are actually creating an animation sequence over the top of portions of the character that are revealed at the time the laser point passes over the given section. In this section, you create the special effect of laser-writing as demonstrated on the sample site included in this book. This effect can be seen at the end of the site introduction as the laser-writes the "V" part of the Visual logo. For simplicity's sake, this example uses a circle instead of a V for the laser writing effect.

CREATE A LASER-WRITING ANIMATION EFFECT

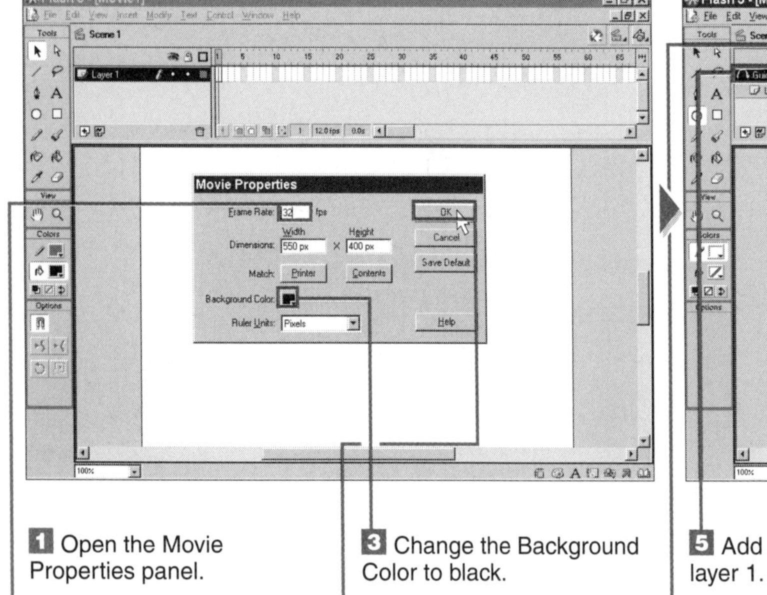

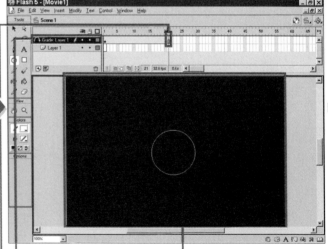

1 Open the Movie Properties panel.

Note: See Chapter 24 to learn how to set movie properties.

2 Change the Frame Rate to **32** fps.

3 Change the Background Color to black.

■ You may decide to change these settings depending on how you want your effect to look.

4 Click OK to apply the new settings.

5 Add a guide layer to layer 1.

Note: See Chapter 21 to learn about guide layers.

6 Add a regular frame to frame 21 of the guide layer.

7 Using white as the outline color, draw a medium-sized circle without a fill on the Stage.

■ When using text, be sure to choose a heavy, large font for the effect to be visible.

Should I lock my guide layer?

✔ Yes. Locking layers to prevent unnecessary changes — especially guide layers — is a good idea. To lock a layer, simply click the Lock icon bullet to the right of the layer name. A Lock icon appears over the bullet indicating the layer is now locked. You can not edit anything on the layer unless you unlock it again. See Chapter 21 to learn more about working with Flash layers.

Can I make the laser light point appear to blink?

✔ Yes. You can adjust instance tint to make the effect appear to blink, resulting in a unique effect. To do this you would convert your laser source to a symbol and modify each instance. For example, in frame 2 of your laser movie, you can insert a keyframe and change the tint of the light source instance to make it darker. Continue alternating tints, light and dark, for each instance of the light source. When you play back your movie, a blinking effect is created as your laser appears to write.

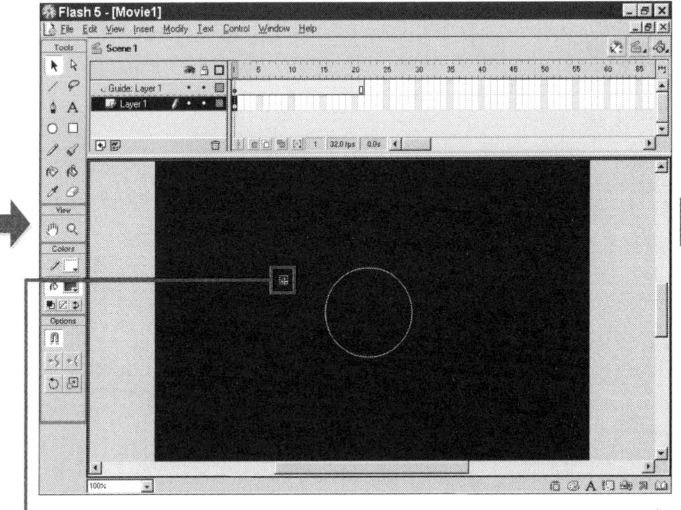

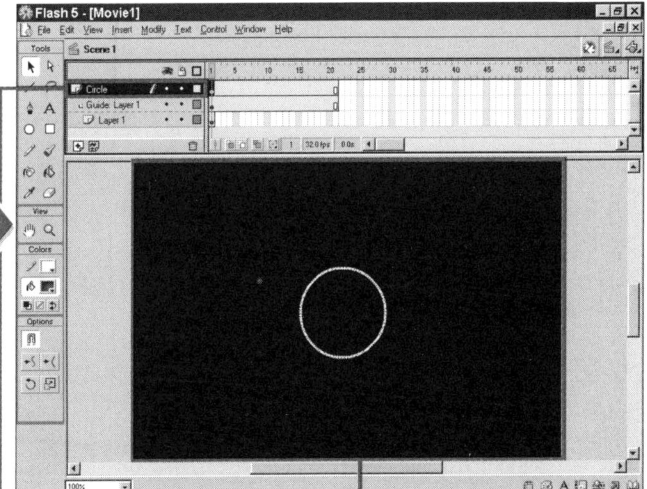

8 In layer 1, frame 1, create a circle shape to use as the laser light point.

■ In this example, the light point uses a gradient fill. The size of the point is about 10 by 10 pixels.

Note: See Chapter 19 to learn about gradient fills.

9 Select the laser light point and convert it into a graphic symbol.

■ In this example the symbol is named light point.

Note: See Chapter 22 to learn to convert symbols.

10 Add a new layer to the Timeline and name it **Circle**.

Note: See Chapter 21 to learn how to add layers.

11 Copy and paste the circle from the guide layer and place it in the circle layer.

Note: See Chapter 19 to learn how to copy objects.

CONTINUED

CREATE A LASER-WRITING ANIMATION EFFECT (CONTINUED)

So far, you have created the guide layer for the light point animation and set the stage for the effect. In the following steps you animate the light point symbol in a revolution around the circle while revealing three additional circles simultaneously. As mentioned, the illusion of the "writing" is created with four independently layered elements. The effect is accomplished by revealing portions of the image in each position the light point passes over. In the remaining steps, you are asked to erase portions of the circle in correspondence with the light point's position. Upon completion of a full revolution, the frame order of a given erased circle is reversed to represent the laser-writing. A keyframe is inserted in every frame of the Circle layer in order that portions of the circle appear at the same rate as the animation of the light point located one layer up from the revealed circle. The sequence on the circle layer is then duplicated and displaced on the timeline in two additional layers for use with different colored circles. The staggered animations of the three circles illustrate the "burning" effect of the laser.

CREATE A LASER-WRITING ANIMATION EFFECT (CONTINUED)

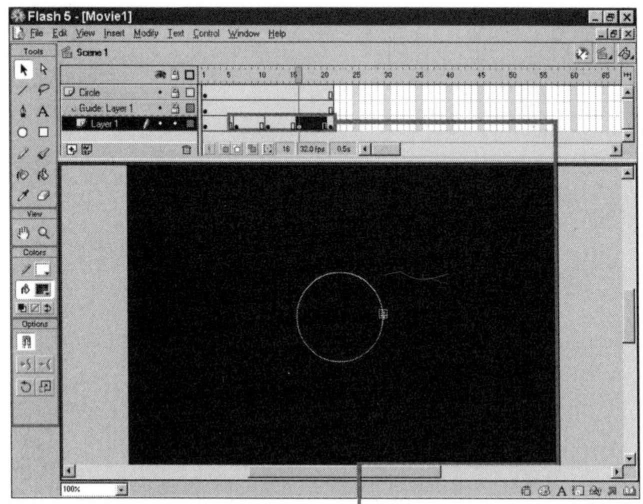

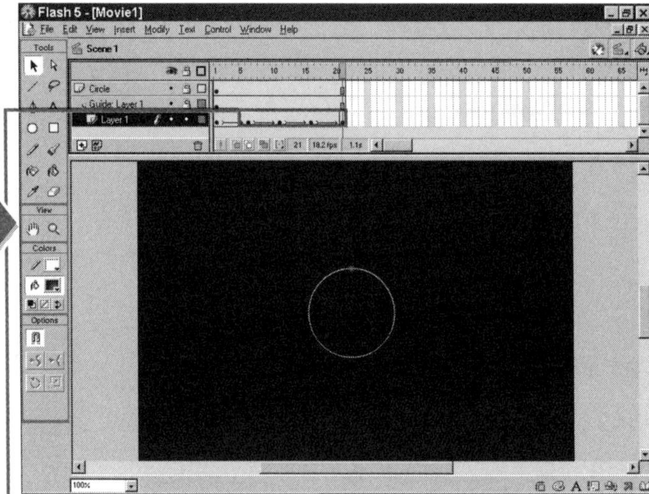

12 In layer 1, frame 1, place an instance of the laser light point on the top part of the circle.

Note: See Chapter 22 to learn how to insert an instance.

13 Add keyframes to frames 6, 11,16, and 21, and move the laser light point in quarter increments around the circle in each keyframe.

■ For example, in frame 6, move the laser point a quarter around the circle, clockwise.

14 Create a motion tween between each keyframe, starting with frame 1 and ending on frame 21.

Note: See Chapter 25 to learn how to create a motion tween.

■ This creates the effect of the laser point making one revolution around the circle.

How precise can I get with positioning content in Flash?

✔ The Info panel contains an X and Y coordinate field that allows you to enter exactly what coordinate you want to place your object on the Stage. On the Info panel next to the X and Y fields is a diagram allowing you to pick whether the upper-left corner of the object is placed at the coordinates specified or whether the center of the object is placed at the coordinates. The X and Y coordinate reading of where the cursor is on the Stage is also shown at the bottom of the Info panel. If you have a hard time placing objects exactly where you want them using a mouse, this feature can be of great use to you.

Does it matter which way I erase the circle parts?

✔ No. You can use any method you prefer to erase parts of the circle in step 16. You can use the Eraser tool or any of its modifiers to erase the lines. To learn more about the available tools for erasing parts of your drawings, see Chapter 19.

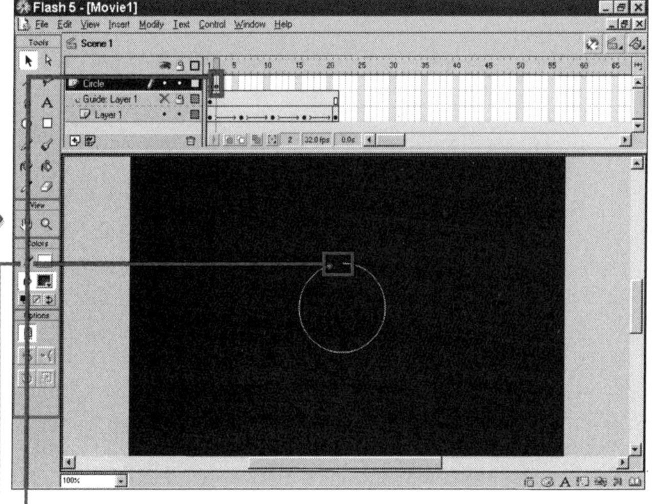

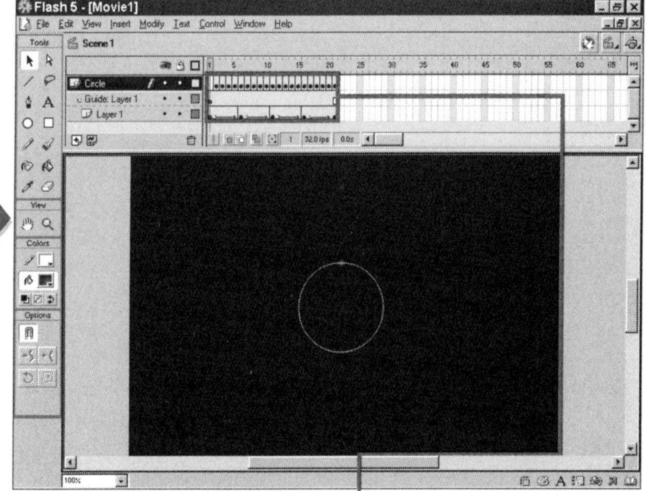

15 In the circle layer, add a new keyframe to frame 2.

Note: See Chapter 24 to learn how to add frames.

16 Select part of circle in which the laser pointer moved over and erased it.

■ The easiest way to remove a portion of the circle outline is to use the Arrow tool to create a box around the part of the circle needing to be deleted, and delete it.

17 Repeat steps 15 and 16 to continue removing parts of the circle until you reach frame 21.

18 Select all frames and reverse them.

Note: See Chapter 25 to learn how to reverse frames.

■ This creates the effect of the laser point drawing the circle.

CONTINUED

CREATE A LASER-WRITING ANIMATION EFFECT (CONTINUED)

The laser-writing technique can be used in other ways besides writing a text character. For example, you can use this method to laser-write any two dimensional shape or illustration, such as a logo outline. After it is perfected, the laser-writing technique is a really neat effect that is sure to catch the eye of anyone visiting your Web site.

If you plan to apply this effect to multiple characters or words, however, be aware of what a time-consuming process this might be. You may want to think twice before using laser-writing on a wordy project. In this example, instead of writing out the entire word *visual*, only the V in the Visual logo was written. Assigning the effect to just one letter saves time you can spend elsewhere in creating your Web site. However, if you are not under any type of deadline, try this effect to write out shapes, graphic images, and anything else you can think of.

CREATE A LASER-WRITING ANIMATION EFFECT (CONTINUED)

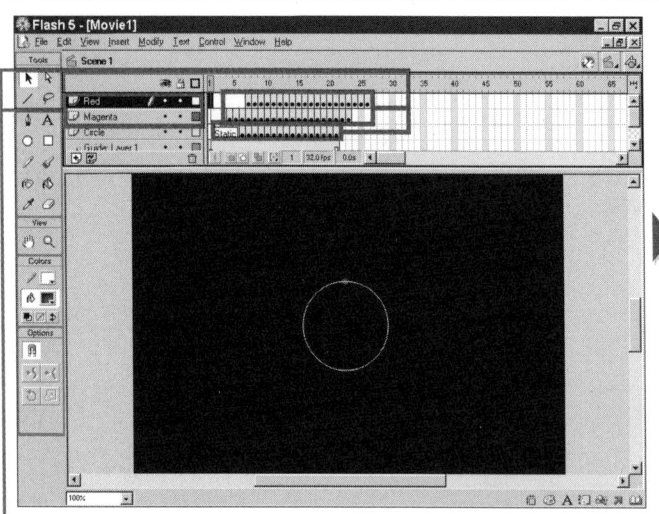

19 Add two new layers, named magenta and red, to the top of the Timeline.

20 Select all frames in the circle layer and copy them.

21 Paste the frames into the red and magenta layers.

■ When pasting the frames, stagger them 2-3 frames down the Timeline. For example, in the magenta layer paste the frames 2-3 frames down from where the content starts in the circle layer.

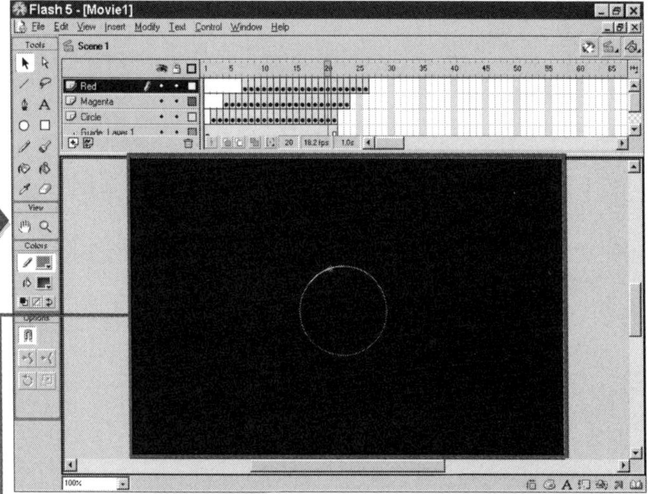

22 For each keyframe in the magenta layer, select the circle content and change its color from white to magenta.

23 Repeat step 22 for the red layer, changing the color from white to red.

■ This creates the effect of a laser writing a circle.

Can I stagger the different colored layers more than two frames?

✔ Yes. You can stagger the colored layers of the laser effect to more or less than two frames. You may want to test out different amounts until you find the effect that you like the best. If you stagger them too much, the time between the "burn" and the "glow" stage is very long and it might lead away from the laser effect.

Can I use a different color besides red for my laser-writing effect?

✔ Yes. Although a red gradient fill color is used in this section, you can certainly assign another color for the effect. The general rule behind the colors is that the first layer stays white, the second layer should be white mixed with the color you want as a final result, and the last color is the color you want as your final result. By sticking to that general rule you should be able to have your laser write in any color you choose.

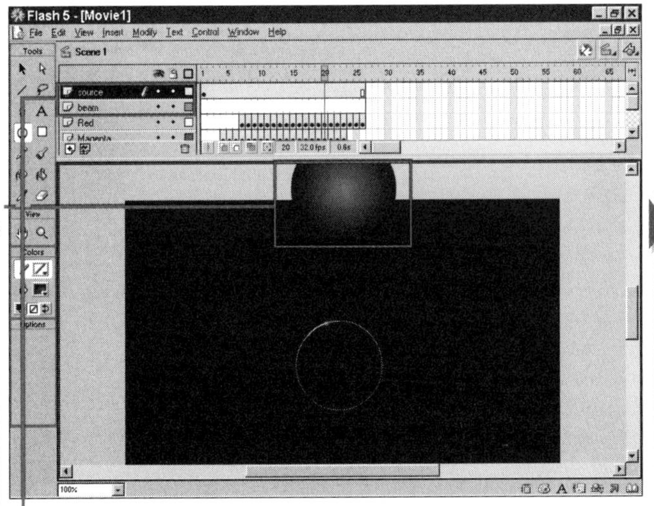

24 Add two more layers named **beam** and **source**.

■ Place the source layer at the top.

25 In the source layer, create the laser light source.

■ In this example, a large sphere was created with a red, radial gradient fill.

Note: See Chapter 19 to learn more about gradients.

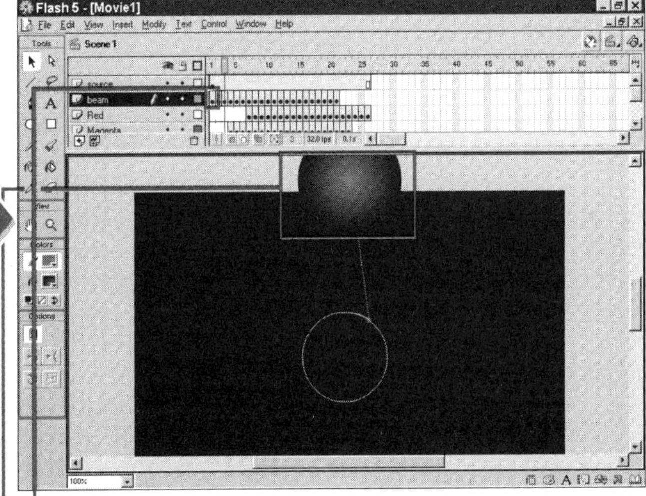

26 Add a blank keyframe to frame 1 of the beam layer.

27 Use the Line tool to connect the middle of the laser source to the laser point.

Note: See Chapter 18 to learn about the Line tool.

28 Continue adding blank keyframes to the beam layer that connect the source to the laser point until you have reached frame 21.

■ You can now test the effect.

CREATE A WELCOME PAGE

You can create a welcome page using Dreamweaver that greets visitors accessing your Web site. A welcome page is a visitor's first impression of your site. For that reason, include a brief description of your site and a list of any browser requirements the visitor might need to view the site properly. By listing requirements up front, you can help visitors avoid viewing problems when they enter your site if they are not using a compatible browser.

You can also include a Flash movie or JavaScript function which tests for the Flash plug-in on the welcome page. Such detection generally is done at this point to notify the user whether they need to update or obtain the latest version of the Flash plug-in. Multiple versions are available online and can be obtained in the Flash support section of the Macromedia Web site. The welcome page demonstrated in this section uses three horizontal frames. The overall design is clean and simple, because a welcome page should not overwhelm a visitor with too much information or visual elements at once. Rather, a simple design like this one appears inviting and yet gives the visitor the appropriate information for getting the most out of your Web site.

CREATE A WELCOME PAGE

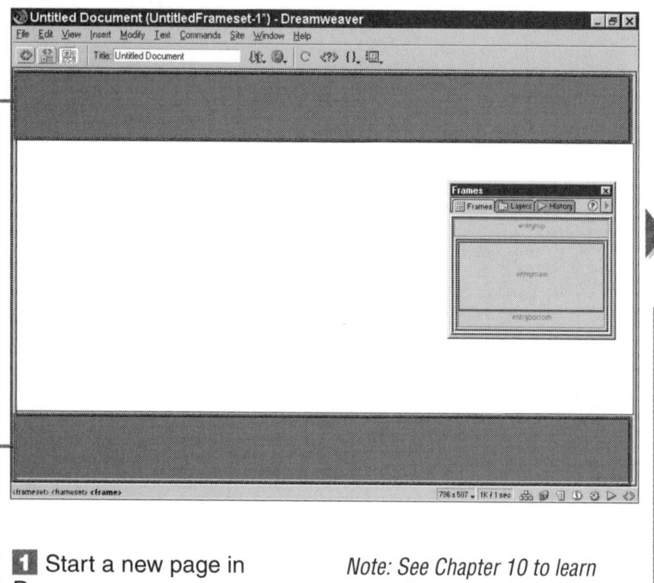

1 Start a new page in Dreamweaver.

2 Insert a top frame.

3 Add a bottom frame.

4 Name the top frame **entrytop**, the middle frame **entrymain**, and the bottom frame **entrybottom**.

Note: See Chapter 10 to learn more about frames.

5 Set the background colors.

Note: See Chapter 6 to learn how to change background colors.

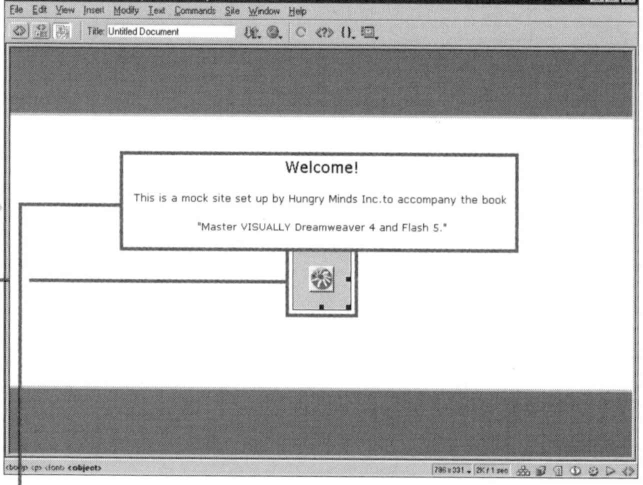

6 In the entrymain frame type a brief description of your site and format as you like.

7 Insert a simple movie clip animation to serve as a Flash detector.

■ If the user sees the animation when viewing the page, they have the necessary plug-in.

Note: See Chapters 24 and 25 to learn how to create animations in Flash.

Where can I find additional methods for detecting the Flash plug-in and redirecting the user accordingly?

✔ The following sites offer plug-in detection techniques as well as known issues with particular browsers. Keep in mind that Flash content is displayed in some browsers if *any* version of the plug-in is detected, so, if you have Flash 4 or 5 functionality in your site, your site can still be displayed with the Flash 3 plug-in, but Flash ignores the functionality not compatible with the older version of the plug-in that the user has installed. For this reason, you should test for the appropriate version of the plug-in.

www.macromedia.com/support/flash/
www.moock.org/
www.flashkit.com/

If I detect for the appropriate version of the plug-in and browser in the welcome screen, do I need to display the requirements for my site?

✔ If you are confident in your detection methods and have tested your site on multiple browsers with and without the correct version of the plug-in, you can opt to redirect the user accordingly. Oftentimes, developers choose to forward the user directly to the Flash content if the appropriate plug-in is detected, or redirect the user to a page that notifies that an upgrade of the plug-in is necessary. Also note that later versions of IE downloads and installs the plug-in automatically using IE's ActiveX component.

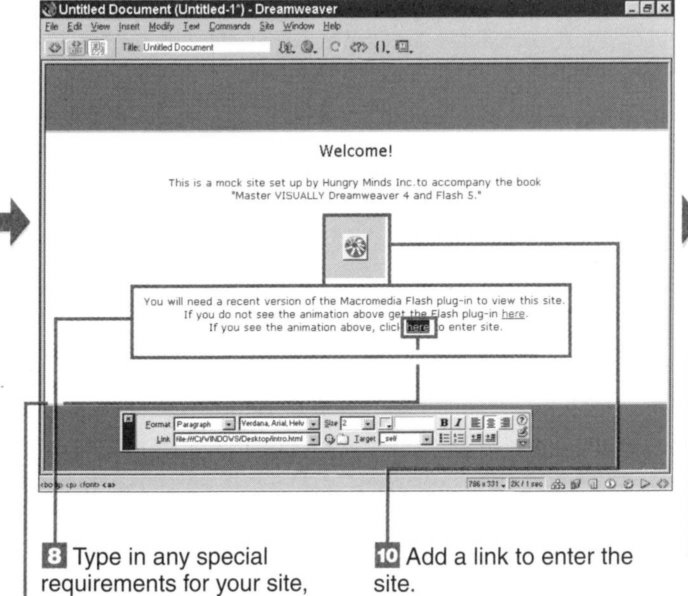

8 Type in any special requirements for your site, such as the need for the Flash plug-in.

9 Add a link to allow visitors to download the Flash plug-in.

Note: See Chapter 7 to learn how to add links.

10 Add a link to enter the site.

■ In this example, the target is `_self` to make the Flash intro play inside the entrymain frame.

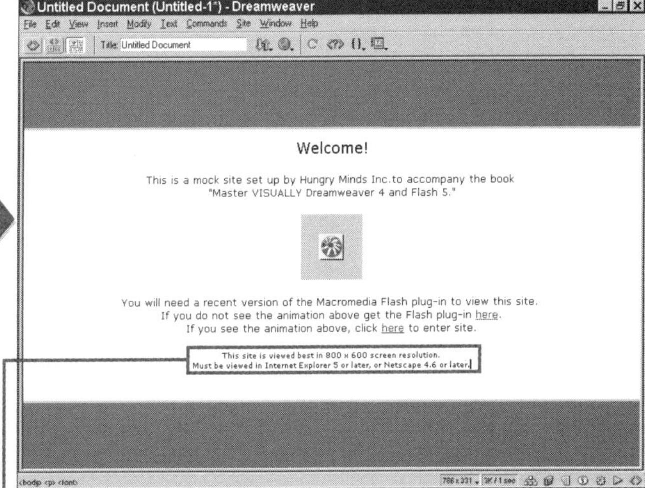

11 List any browser requirements or additional screen settings needed to view your site.

■ You can now save the welcome page.

Note: See Chapter 4 to learn more about saving Web pages.

■ Add this page to the folder containing your published Web.

■ You can preview this page in a browser to be sure it looks like you want it.

ADD HOT BUTTONS

You can create *hot buttons* that quickly take visitors to certain parts of your Web site. Hot buttons are simply shortcuts to a specified location on your site. The user clicks the hot button to immediately jump to a designated area on your site, whether that location is a different page entirely or just another area on the same page.

The sample Web site demonstrated in this chapter employs three hot buttons located in the upper-right corner. The buttons provide quick and easy navigation to the parts of the Web site that are anticipated to be the most visited or used. When creating your own hot buttons, consider using them to direct visitors to important areas of your site, such as the home page or contact page.

The steps in this section illustrate how to create the hot buttons used in the sample Web site. You can utilize these same steps but add customized touches to make the buttons unique to your own Web site.

ADD HOT BUTTONS

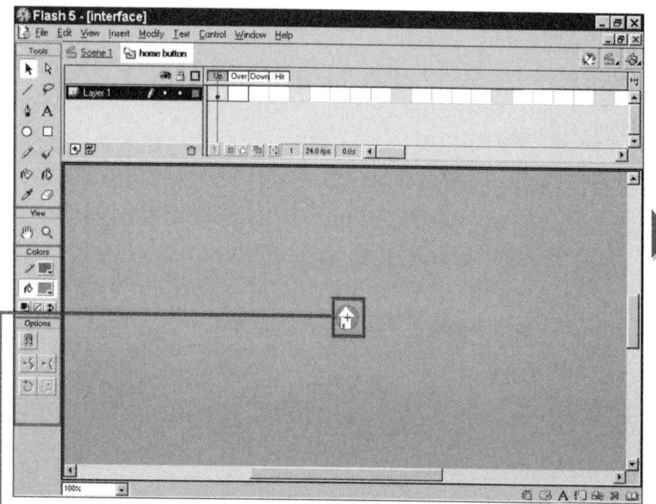

1 Create a new button symbol to use as your hot button.

■ In this example, a picture representing "home" is used to create a home page button.

Note: See Chapter 26 to learn more about creating button symbols in Flash.

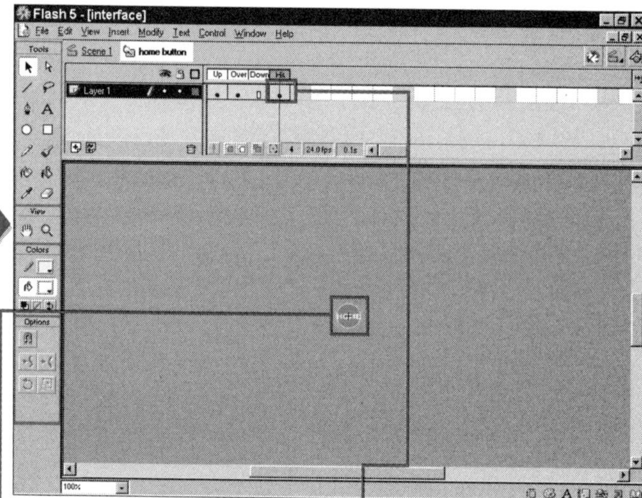

2 Create a rollover button image or text block in the Over frame.

■ In this example, the word *HOME* is the rollover image, and the outline of the button changes to another color.

3 Insert a keyframe into the Hit frame.

4 Add a fill shape or object that encompasses the button as well as any text box in the rollover state.

Note: See Chapter 26 to learn about button frame states.

Must the hot buttons be rollover buttons?

✔ No, but you may want the buttons to have some sort of action to indicate that they are in fact buttons. In the sample Web site, the button pictures clearly give a clue as to where the user is directed if they click a button. In addition, the buttons are rollover buttons so that when the user moves his or her mouse over a button, the rollover text assigned in step 2 reveals exactly where they are directed to if they click the button.

How do I use a text link in the same manner as a hot button (with an action triggered on a rollover)?

✔ When using text as a link in Flash, first be sure to use a solid-filled box in the hit state of the button. Otherwise, the user has to roll over the text itself and the spaces between the characters are not considered part of the link. Although the text is not represented as a graphical button, Flash treats it as any other button and the same actions can be applied.

How can I test the buttons without using the Player window?

✔ Click the Control menu and select Enable Simple Buttons. With this feature activated, you can move your mouse pointer over the button on the Stage and engage the button to test its effects.

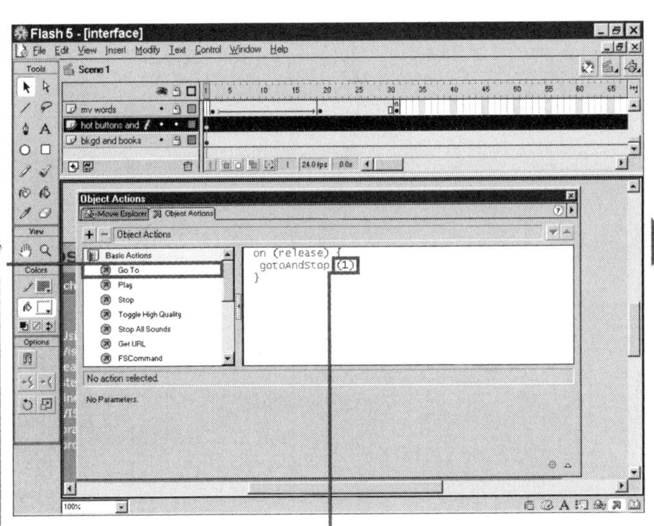

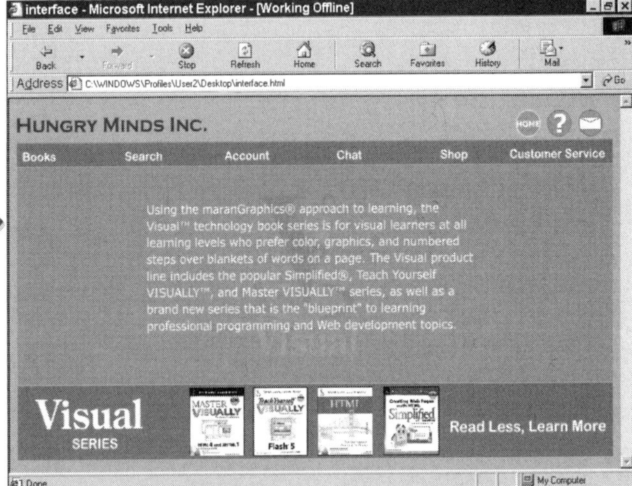

5 Exit symbol-edit mode and return to the main movie.

6 With the button selected on the Stage, open the Object Actions panel.

7 Assign a `Go To` action.

8 Uncheck the Go To and Play check box.

9 In the Frame field type the frame number that corresponds with the beginning or home page of your site.

■ You can now test the button by enabling buttons, testing the movie in the Flash Player window, or by viewing the HTML page containing your movie.

Note: See Chapter 30 to learn more about testing your Flash movies.

CREATE A DROP-DOWN MENU

You can create a drop-down menu in Flash to incorporate in your Web site interface. A drop-down menu consists of a button labeled with a category title, and a list of options that appear to drop down below the button when the button is clicked.

A drop-down menu is a simple, handy way to allow users to navigate through your site.

Creating a drop-down menu is not a simple task, but a drop-down menu has many benefits. A drop-down menu is an intuitive feature with which most users are fairly comfortable, so site visitors readily know how to use one on your page. Also, after you have created one drop-down menu, duplicating and customizing it for additional drop-down menus is fairly simple.

Each drop-down menu is actually a separate movie clip. On the sample Web site, the clips are lined up on the navigation bar. After you get the main concepts down behind the formation and execution of a drop-down menu, there are all sorts of opportunities to be creative and invent new types of drop-down menus.

CREATE A DROP-DOWN MENU

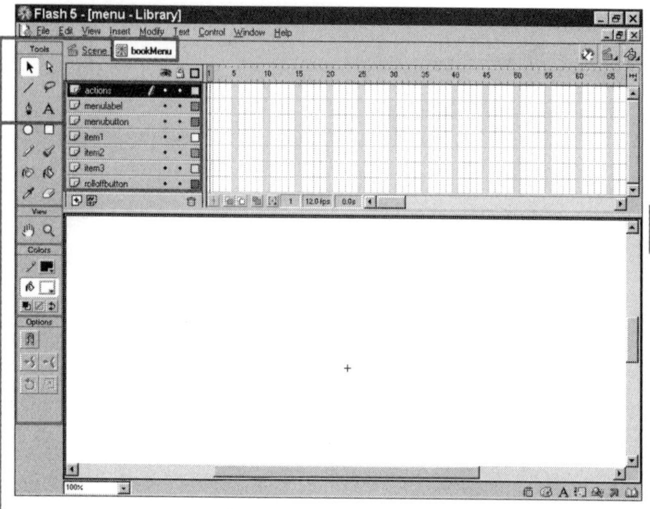

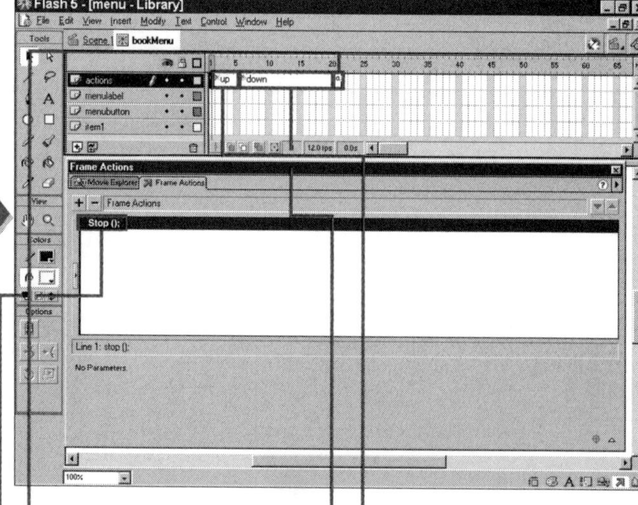

1 Create a movie clip symbol named bookMenu.

2 Add six layers to the symbol's timeline for a total of seven layers and name them actions, **menulabel**, **menubutton**, **item1**, **item2**, **item3**, and **rolloffbutton**.

■ Seven layers are needed to make a drop-down menu with three options. Add or delete layers based on the number of options you want.

Note: See Chapter 21 to learn more about layers.

3 In the actions layer, insert a keyframe into frames 6 and 21.

Note: See Chapter 24 to learn how to add frames.

4 Assign a `Stop` action to frame 1 and frame 21.

5 Select frames 1 through 5 in the actions layer and label them up.

Note: See Chapter 28 to learn how to add actions and labels.

6 Select frames 6 through 20 and label them down.

What if I have a large quantity of items to display on my drop-down menu?

✔ If you have many items for your drop-down menu, you may want to categorize the items and then create submenus. For example, instead of having item 1, item 2, and item 3 drop down from the menu, you might have category 1, category 2, and category 3. The sub-category menus can then appear to the right of the current drop-down menu using the same functionality added to the button triggering the initial drop-down. This results in nested menus or submenus.

What if I want my menus to expand another way?

✔ You can apply any type of Flash technique to make your menu expand or drop any way you want. For example, instead of dropping down you might make it pop up or come out of the right or left. The menu in this section is created strictly for functionality, but your menu can serve two purposes; it can act as an attention getter and as a means of navigation. However, make sure that it is clear that the menu is associated with the current selection. Keep the menu system close to the button used to trigger the menu.

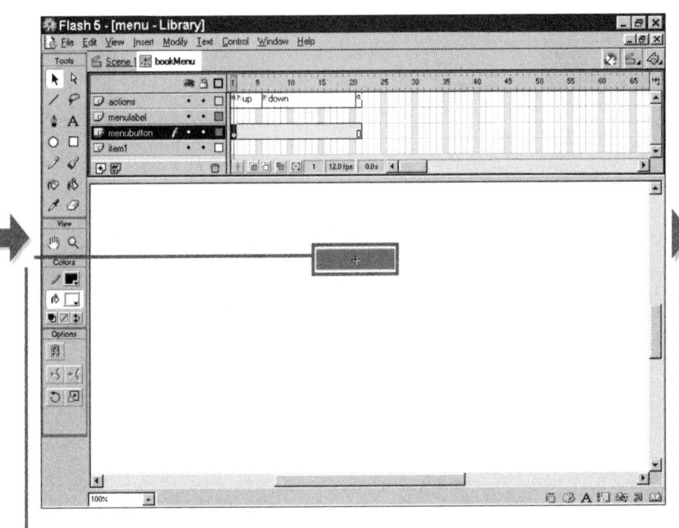

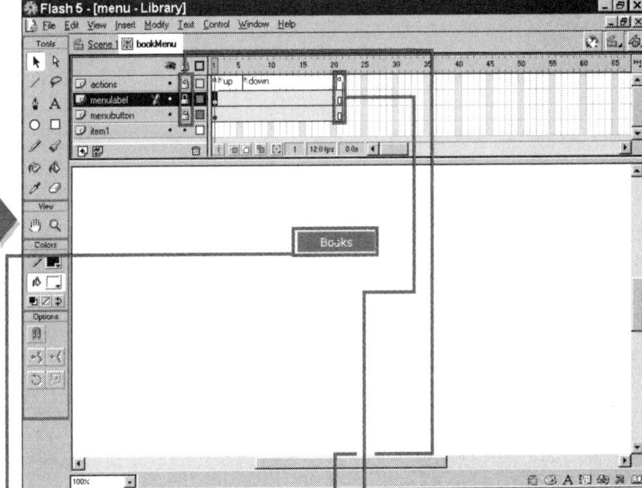

7 In the menubutton layer, add a button.

■ In this example, a rectangle was drawn and converted into a button.

Note: See Chapter 26 to learn how to create buttons.

8 Assign the `Go To` action to the button.

9 Set the Type field to Frame Label.

10 In the Frame field, type **down**.

11 In the menulabel layer, add a text box that contains the name of the menu and place it over the button created in step 8.

Note: See Chapter 20 to learn how to add text.

12 Insert a regular frame into frame 21 in both the menubutton and menulabel layers.

13 Lock the actions, menulabel, and menubutton layers.

Note: See Chapter 21 to learn how to lock layers.

CONTINUED

CREATE A DROP-DOWN MENU (CONTINUED)

To create the dropping down of the menu, the buttons move down and fade in. This effect is achieved by using a motion tween. In the first frame, the button is set to have an Alpha value of zero. As the button moves down, the Alpha value increases giving the appearance of a fade in as the button falls.

To create the finished menu bar, all menu movie clips are placed in a line and spaced out evenly. Adding or dropping menus is as simple as removing or adding another menu clip and distributing the space between the clips. One thing to be careful of is the size of the menu clips. As you add more menus to the menu bar, the size of the menu clips should get somewhat smaller to accommodate the added menus.

After reading through this section, you can apply other Flash techniques to it and create innovative, eye-popping menus to use as navigational tools on your Web site.

CREATE A DROP-DOWN MENU (CONTINUED)

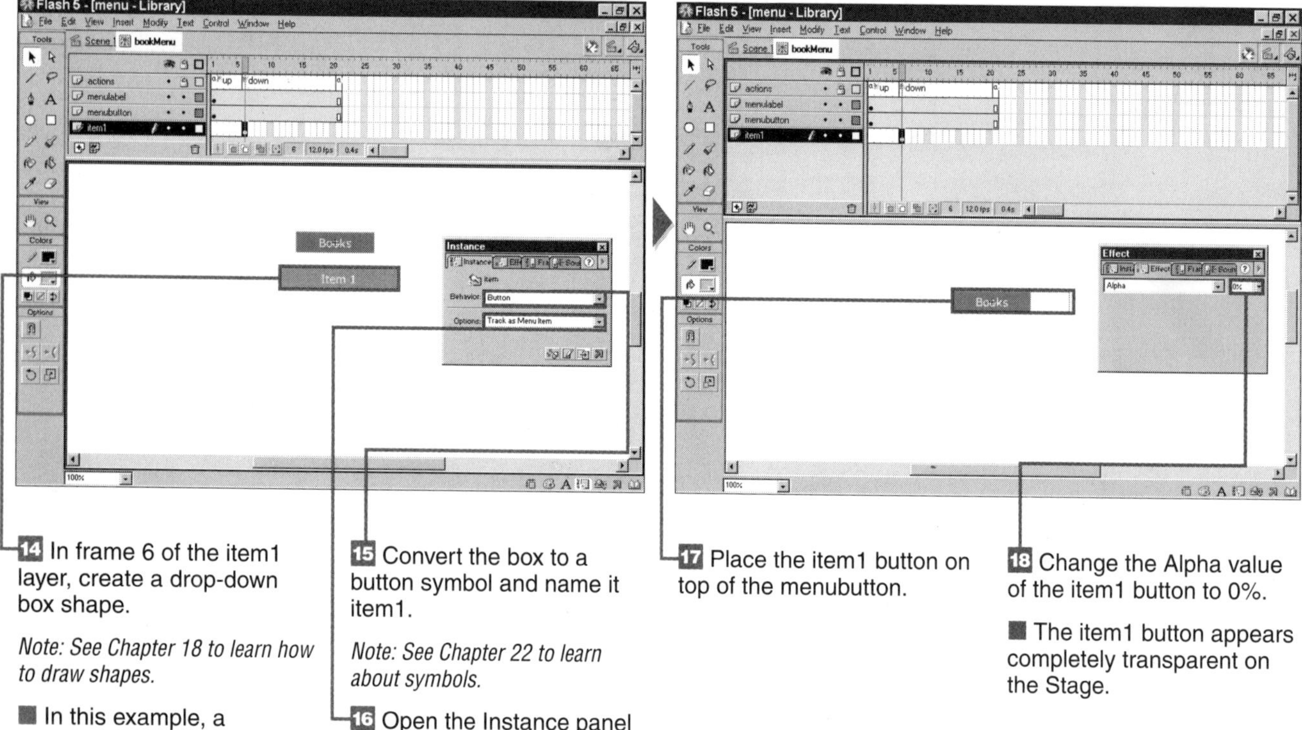

14 In frame 6 of the item1 layer, create a drop-down box shape.

Note: See Chapter 18 to learn how to draw shapes.

■ In this example, a rectangle is used as the box, slightly wider than the menu button width.

15 Convert the box to a button symbol and name it item1.

Note: See Chapter 22 to learn about symbols.

16 Open the Instance panel and set the Options drop-down list to Track as Menu Item.

17 Place the item1 button on top of the menubutton.

18 Change the Alpha value of the item1 button to 0%.

■ The item1 button appears completely transparent on the Stage.

What is the Alpha value?

✔ The Alpha option used in the steps in this section makes an object transparent. You can find the Alpha option in the Effect panel: Click the Show Instance button, and then click the Effect tab. Choose Alpha from the Effect drop-down list, and then adjust the Alpha slider by dragging it up or down. A value of 0% makes the object completely transparent. A value of 100% makes the object totally visible.

What is an invisible button and why would I use it?

✔ An invisible button is a button that contains content only in the Hit frame and not the other three button frame states. The result is a button that is not seen in the Flash movie, but can be clicked on or appears when the user's mouse is over it. There are various uses of invisible buttons. They can be placed behind blocks of text or behind graphics — they can actually be placed behind anything on the Flash Stage. When an invisible button is placed on a Stage it appears as a translucent aqua-colored object so you can easily place it where you want it, but when your Flash movie is tested or viewed, it is invisible.

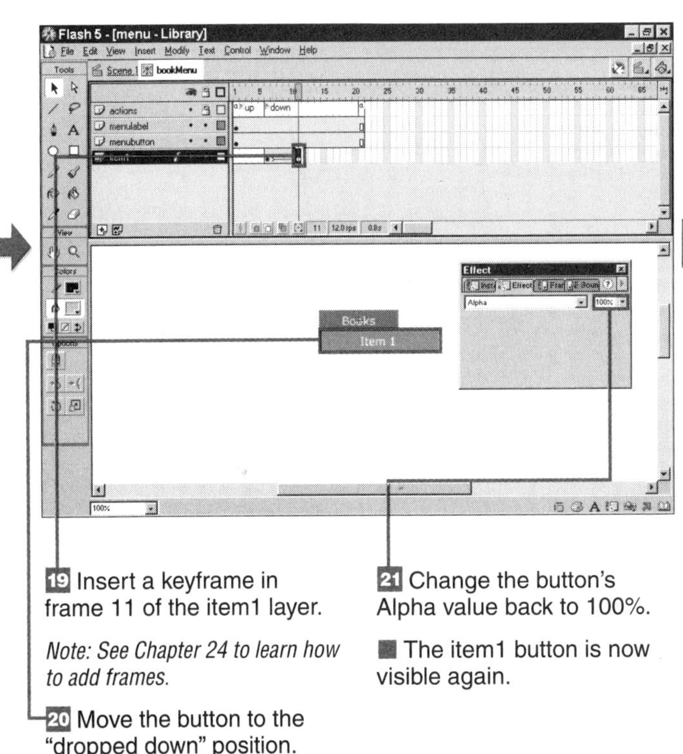

19 Insert a keyframe in frame 11 of the item1 layer.

Note: See Chapter 24 to learn how to add frames.

20 Move the button to the “dropped down” position.

21 Change the button's Alpha value back to 100%.

■ The item1 button is now visible again.

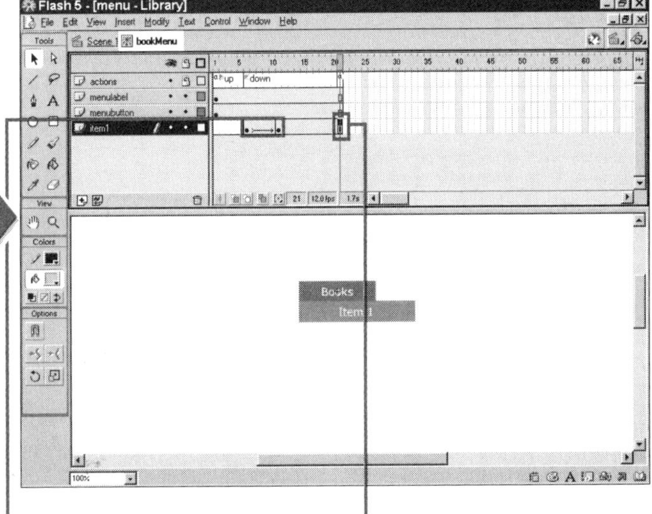

22 Create a motion tween in frames 6 through 11.

■ This creates the effect of the button changing from invisible to visible on the Stage.

Note: See Chapter 15 to learn more about motion tweens.

23 Insert a regular frame in frame 21 of the item1 layer.

Note: See Chapter 24 to learn how to add frames.

CONTINUED

CREATE A DROP-DOWN MENU (CONTINUED)

In steps 1 through 23 of this section, you have created the functionality for making the menu appear when the button triggering the menu is clicked. Next, you add functionality to make the menu disappear when the user rolls off the drop-down menu or the button triggering the menu to open. This is accomplished with the use of an invisible button that is placed underneath of the drop-down menu and associated button, sized slightly larger than the menu itself. The menu is triggered off when the user rolls off the invisible button. Keep in mind there exist a number of variations to this menu system that allow you to customize your menu. After you understand the concepts of opening and closing a menu based on button actions, you can develop different transitions for opening and collapsing the menus.

CREATE A DROP-DOWN MENU (CONTINUED)

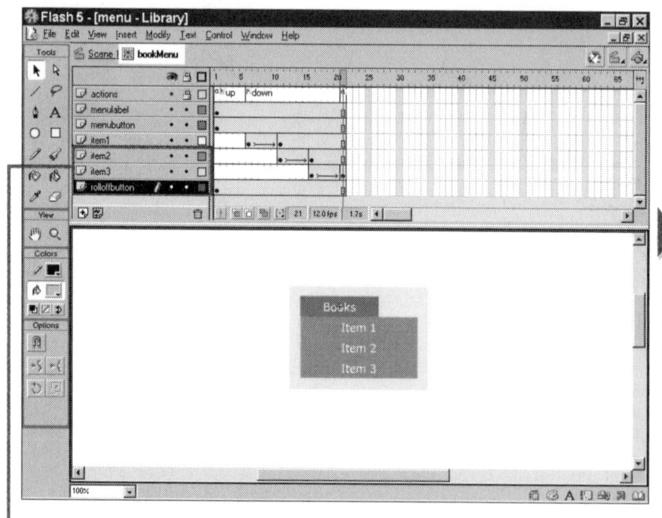

24 Repeat steps 14 through 22 to create additional buttons for the other menus included on the page, changing the frame numbers where applicable.

■ Your movie timeline should look something like this when finished.

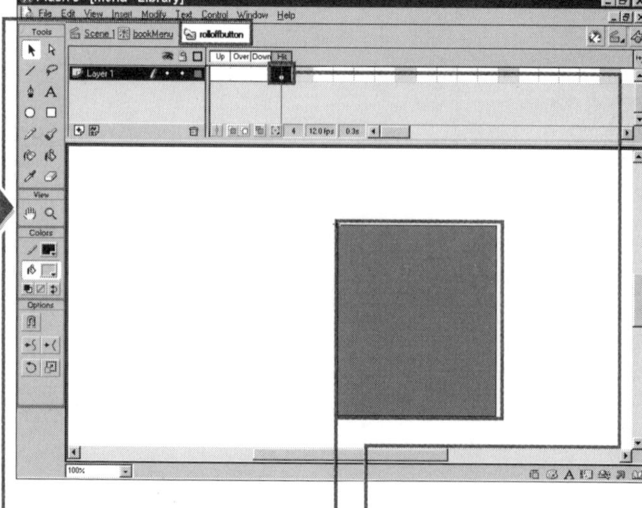

25 Create a new button symbol named rolloffbutton.

■ This will be an invisible button to detect when the user moves their mouse pointer off of the drop-down menu.

Note: See Chapter 26 to learn how to create buttons.

26 With the button in symbol-edit mode, add a keyframe to the Hit frame.

27 Draw a medium-sized square.

Note: See Chapter 18 to learn how to draw shapes.

Can I add sounds to menus and buttons?

✔ Yes. For example, you can add a sound to the buttons when the user clicks them, or you can add a sound to enhance the dropping down of the menu options. You can add sound to your drop-down menu the same way in which you add sounds to other Flash movie elements. For more about using sounds in Flash, see Chapter 27.

Was anything special done to the item buttons?

✔ Nothing is special about the item buttons. In the button's Over frames the colors are lightened to indicate the mouse is hovering over the item. When dealing with menus it is important that the user is always aware of what they are going to choose.

How can I minimize the space between my menu buttons (Books, Search, Account, etc.)?

✔ The invisible rolloff buttons for your menu buttons (steps 30 and 31) may overlap if you move your menu buttons closer together, preventing menus from closing when the user rolls off a given menu button used to trigger a menu on and off. You can resolve this issue by modifying the hit state of the invisible buttons. Open a given menu's rolloff button in Symbol Edit mode and delete a portion of the upper right-hand corner, minimizing the button's area to the right of the menu button.

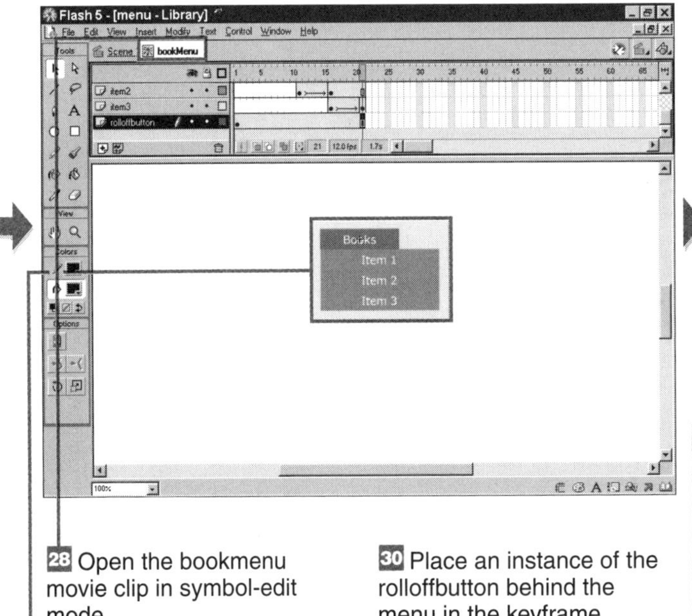

28 Open the bookmenu movie clip in symbol-edit mode.

29 Create a new layer in the lowest level of the bookmenu movieclip and insert a keyframe in frame 27.

30 Place an instance of the rolloffbutton behind the menu in the keyframe created in step 29.

31 Resize the rolloffbutton slightly larger than the expanded menu and Books button on all sides.

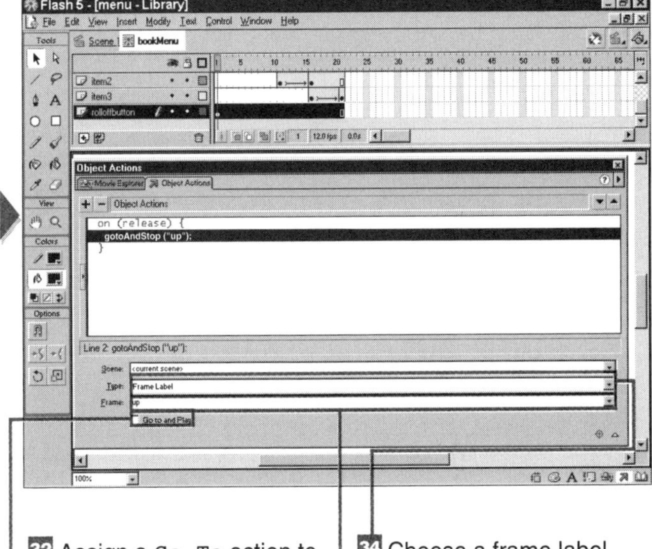

32 Assign a `Go To` action to the rolloffbutton.

Note: See Chapter 28 to learn how to add actions.

33 Uncheck the Go to and Play check box (☑ changes to ☐).

34 Choose a frame label.

35 Choose up.

■ You can now test the menu effect.

Note: See Chapter 30 to learn how to test movies.

USING THE ROOT PROPERTY ACTION STATEMENT

Flash movie clips utilize their own timelines independent of your main movie's timeline. When you assign actions concerning frame numbers inside a movie clip they refer to the frame numbers of the movie clip's timeline. However, you may need to reference a frame in the main movie's timeline from within a movie clip. To do this, you can use a Root Property action statement.

For example, if you want to go to frame 25 in the main movie timeline from your movie clip, you would attach the following action to the symbol that references the root movie timeline:

```
_root.gotoAndStop(25).
```

Without the Root Property statement, the movie clip would jump to frame 25 in the movie clip's timeline rather than the intended frame in the main timeline.

In the sample Web site, the Root Property statement is used to go to frames in the main timeline when the user selects one of the options from the drop-down menu movie clip.

USING THE ROOT PROPERTY ACTION STATEMENT

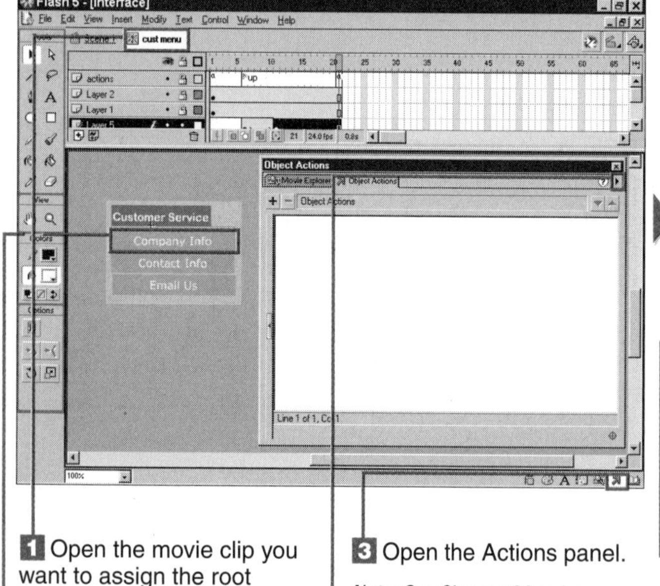

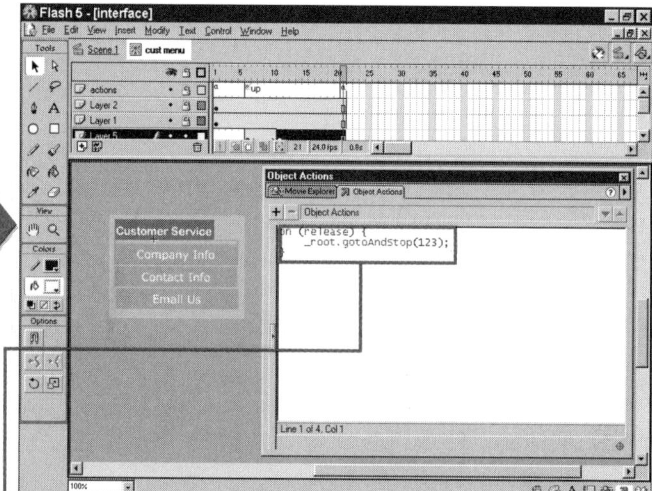

1 Open the movie clip you want to assign the root property action to in symbol-edit mode.

2 Choose the symbol that contains the action referencing the root of the movie.

3 Open the Actions panel.

Note: See Chapter 28 to learn more about actions.

4 Click ▸ and click Expert mode.

■ Flash switches you to Expert mode.

5 Type **On (release) {_root.gotoAndStop(123);}**.

■ This statement tells the Flash movie to go to the root movie and stop in frame 123.

■ In the sample site, this statement is assigned in the drop-down menu movie clip.

ENABLE TESTING OPTIONS

You can enable the Simple Frame Actions and Simple Buttons features in Flash to test your movie actions and buttons without having to view your movie in the Flash Player window to see how things work. When you enable the Simple Frame Actions and Simple Buttons commands, Flash makes your actions and buttons operable from the Stage.

For example, perhaps you have a button to which you have assigned a `Go To and Stop` action telling the playhead to go to frame 1 in your movie and stop. If you enable the Simple Frame Actions and Simple Buttons commands, you can click the button on the Stage and see Flash carry out the actions in the movie's Timeline.

Enabling button actions is useful when you wish to quickly test a button's behavior, such as rollover effects and simple button actions. Generally speaking, it is best to work with this feature disabled, as you cannot move or transform a button when it is active.

ENABLE TESTING OPTIONS

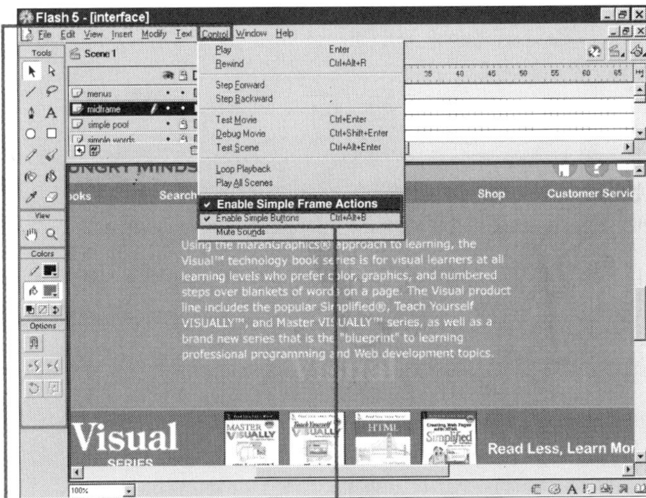

1 In Flash, click Control.

2 Click Enable Simple Frame Actions.

■ Flash enables frame actions on the Stage.

3 Click Control.

4 Click Enable Simple Buttons.

■ Flash enables buttons on the Stage.

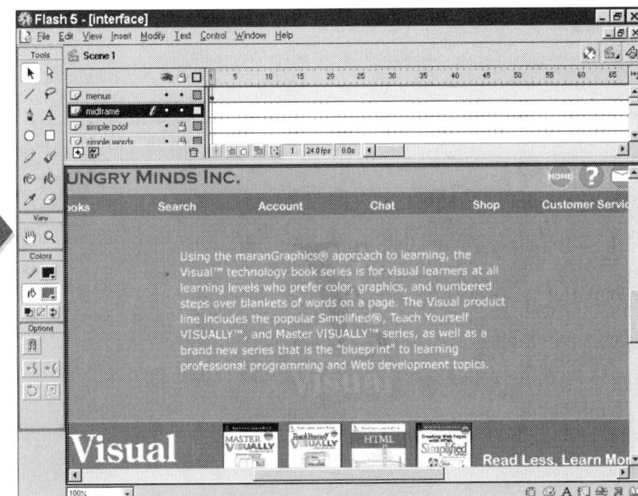

■ With both features on, any buttons and associated actions are operable from the Stage.

■ In this example, the Home button rollover effect displays when the mouse rolls over the button.

CREATE BUTTON ANIMATIONS

You can turn regular button links into simple animations that are sure to grab the attention of anyone browsing your site. Instead of static graphical buttons, turn your buttons into mini-animations that jump into action as soon as the user hovers over or clicks the buttons.

On the sample Web site, an animation starts when a visitor clicks a graphic of a book cover for a particular series. The effect is an enlarged image of the book cover that moves to the right side of the screen while the series title animates into view and text detailing the series appears beneath the title.

By presenting this simple animation, the Web site visitor hopefully stays interested in the page, reads about the series, and finds a book series that fits their technology skill level. In turn, they might move on to the series page, possibly finding a book containing a subject about which they want to learn more, and hopefully purchase the book online.

The steps in this section use Flash animation skills and buttons along with a `Go To` action.

CREATE BUTTON ANIMATIONS

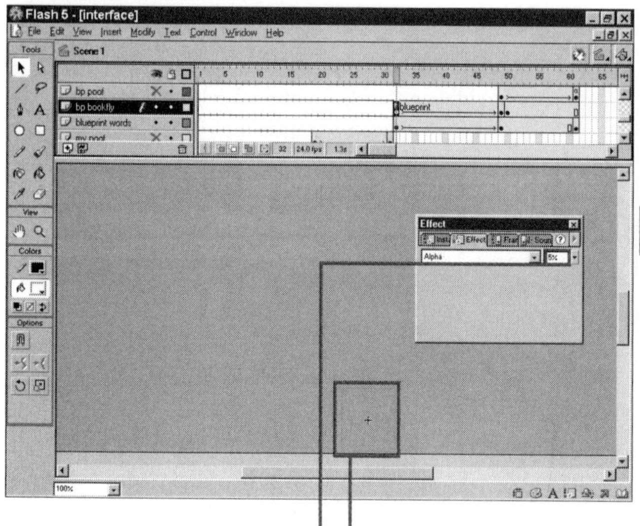

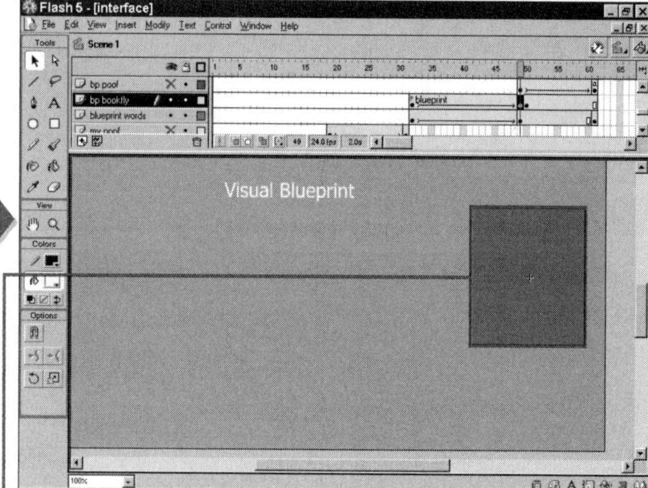

1 In your Flash interface movie, create a rectangle shape the same size as the book cover graphic.

2 Convert the rectangle to a graphic symbol.

3 Place an instance of the rectangle shape over the book cover.

4 Use the Effect panel to change the Alpha setting of the rectangle symbol to 5%.

5 Insert a keyframe into frame 21.

Note: See Chapter 24 to learn how to add frames.

6 Move the rectangle symbol to its new position.

7 Use the Effect panel to change the Alpha value to 100%.

8 Use the Scale button to increase the symbol size to about 300%.

Can I do anything else with this animation effect?

✔ You do not have to use the same movement for your button animation. You may prefer to make your product spin to the side, zig-zag, grow wings and fly, whatever you like. Remember, the purpose of the animation is to get the user's attention. You also can use this technique in a different location on your page. Any type of simple animation anywhere on the page is most likely to get the user's attention while they browse your site.

Can I make a button animation a movie clip and use it that way?

✔ Yes. You can make this animation a movie clip and have it set up to play when the user clicks your button. Make sure, however, that the movie clip loads into the right level of your movie, and that it is set up to disappear when the user clicks something else.

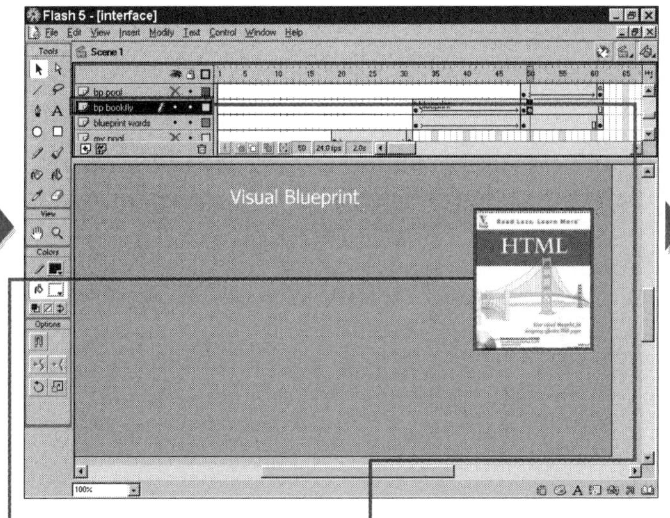

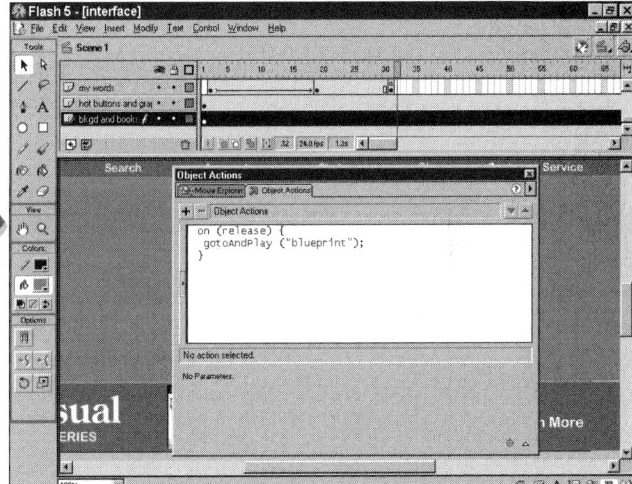

9 In frame 22, insert a picture of the book cover.

■ The book cover image in this movie is a JPEG saved as a symbol.

■ The book cover image should be the same size and position of the big rectangle shape.

10 Label it **frames**.

■ In this example, the frames were labeled according to book series.

Note: See Chapter 28 to learn how to label frames.

11 Assign a `Go To` action.

Note: See Chapter 28 to learn how to add actions.

12 Change the type to Frame Label.

13 In the frame field, type in the Frame Label.

■ Test the animation by enabling buttons, testing the movie, or viewing the HTML page.

Note: See Chapter 30 to learn how to test movies.

CREATE A TOOLTIP

A ToolTip is a little message box that pops up while a user's mouse hovers over a button or graphic. You can add a ToolTip to buttons or graphics on your Web site to give users more information about the item.

ToolTips are fairly simple to add and are common practice on most Web sites. ToolTips are very useful when you want to give a user more information about a feature without cluttering up the design of the interface.

In the example shown in this section, a ToolTip is added to the clickable graphic button of a book. The ToolTip gives the user more information about the product series. Ordinarily, the text "Click here for more information" would be needed to instruct the user. By adding a ToolTip instead, the information appears only when the user's mouse hovers over the image of the book. The ToolTip reduces the need for extra text, which in turn clutters the page.

CREATE A TOOLTIP

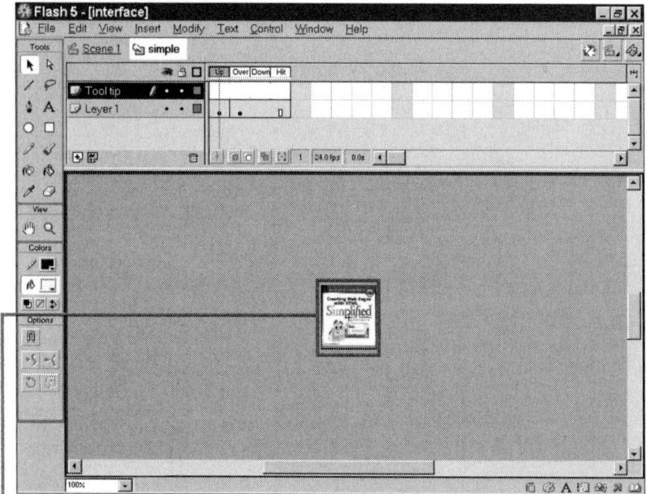

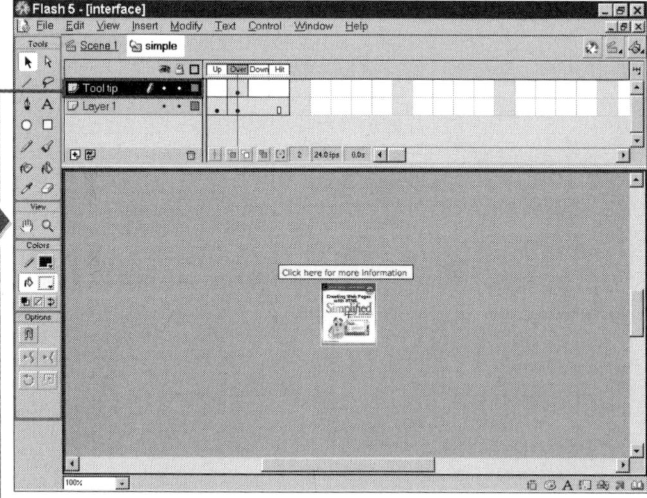

1 Select the button or graphic to which you wish to add a ToolTip.

■ In this example, the graphic image of the book is actually a button.

2 Switch to symbol-edit mode.

Note: See Chapter 22 to learn more about editing symbols.

3 Insert a new layer.

■ You create the ToolTip in the new layer; you may want to label the new layer **ToolTip**.

Note: See Chapter 21 to learn about layers.

4 Insert blank keyframes into the Over and Hit frames of layer 2.

Note: See Chapter 24 to learn about inserting keyframes.

Can I change the look of the ToolTip?

✔ Yes. The ToolTip in the example is merely a standard look. You can make the ToolTip a triangle, have the tool tip fade in rather than appear, or you can have an animation for a ToolTip. Basically, anything you can create in Flash can be added as a ToolTip. Do not go overboard though: You do not want your ToolTip too complex, because it may take a second or two to load, and the user's mouse may just be over an image for a second or so.

Can I use ToolTips elsewhere?

✔ Yes. You can add ToolTip all sorts of places, leaving it to your discretion what is over labeling. ToolTips can be added to images, to inform the user that they are seeing "Master Visually Book" or they can be added to links informing the user where they will be redirected to if they click the button.

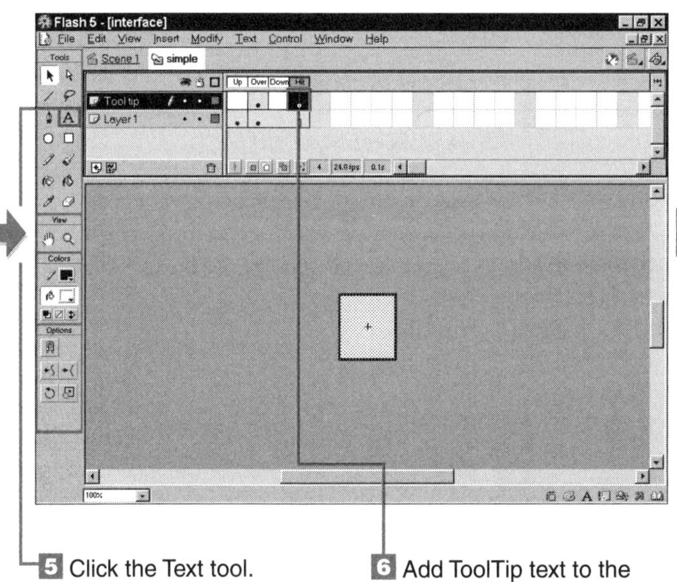

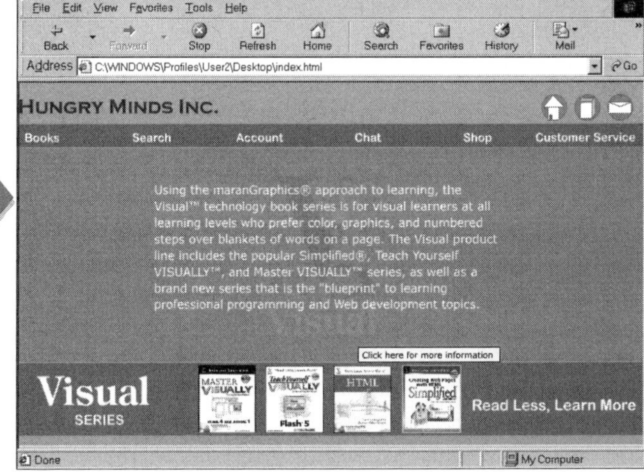

5 Click the Text tool.

6 Add ToolTip text to the Over frame in ToolTip layer.

■ Font size for ToolTip text is set to 10.

7 In the Hit frame of layer 2 add a shape that is the same size of the button.

Note: Objects added to the Hit frame do not appear in your Flash project.

Note: See Chapter 26 to learn about creating buttons.

■ You can now test your movie to see the ToolTip.

CREATE A CHAT FEATURE

You can create a Flash movie that enables your site's visitors to "chat" or talk to each other. Using such a feature on your own Web site can increase visitor interest and repeat traffic.

Chat is one of the most popular forums for communicating on the Internet, and many Web sites offer chat features to visitors. If you are not already familiar with chatting, this form of Internet communication enables users to converse by typing in messages that are immediately posted on the host Web server and read by everyone else in the corresponding chat window. By typing conversational messages back and forth, users simulate talking face to face.

The steps in this section outline how to create a chat feature similar to the one found on the sample Web site included in this book.

Next, you modify the Flash interface, or the presentation of what the user sees when using the chat application, for use in your site. Any customization of the actual chat application needs to be done in PHP and is not discussed in this book. Note that in order for this application to run, the server hosting your site must have the PHP interpreter installed.

CREATE A CHAT FEATURE

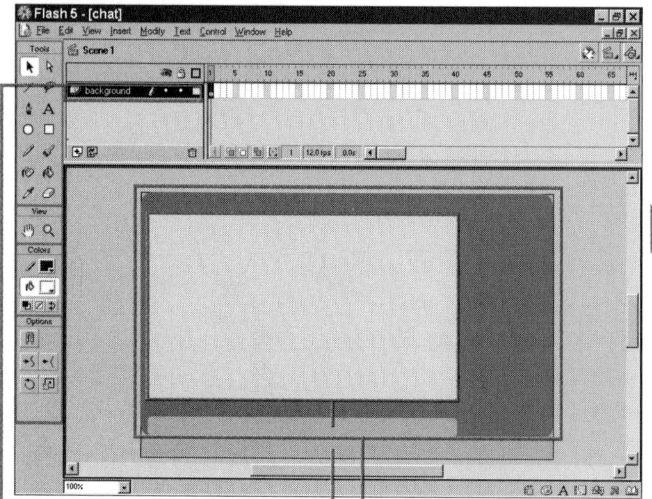

1 Create a new Flash movie named chat.

2 Rename layer 1 to background.

Note: See Chapter 21 to learn how to name layers.

3 Create a rectangle fill shape to use as the chat feature's background.

Note: See Chapter 18 to learn how to draw shapes.

4 Draw another rectangle shape on top of the first shape.

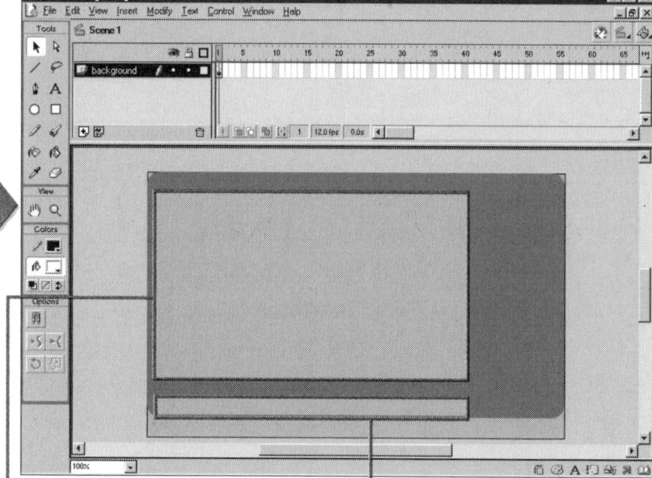

5 Select the new shape and delete it, leaving a white open square on the Stage.

■ The white square becomes the chat area where the conversation appears.

6 Repeat steps 4 and 5 to create a smaller message text box at the bottom of the chat feature.

■ This area is where users type their messages.

Why should I use the Embed Fonts option for dynamic text as shown in step 11?

✔ Embedding fonts ensures that dynamic text appears in the selected font on a given user's machine. Flash converts static text to scalable vector graphics on export to ensure the font you selected is used regardless of whether the user has the font installed. Because dynamic text is based on variable values and can be dynamically updated, Flash does not convert the text to vector graphics. In order for dynamic fonts to appear in the font specified, you must embed the font in the SWF file when the movie is published. Use this feature sparingly, however, because a single font can add up to 12K on export.

How can I customize my chat?

✔ You can customize the chat feature in many different ways. The easiest way of customization is to change the color scheme of the chat movie. The chat feature illustrated in these steps is made up of blues to match the blues in the Flash interface. You might customize your own chat feature by modifying the reposition and size of the chat window, and reformatting the text boxes.

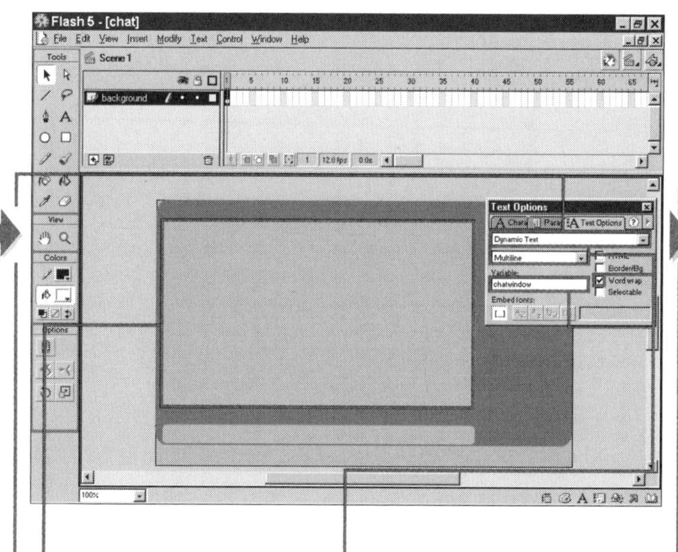

7 Add a text box to the chat area in place of the deleted square in step 5.

Note: See Chapter 20 to learn how to add text.

8 Open the Text Options panel and set the Text Type to Dynamic.

9 Set the Line Type to Multiline.

10 Type **chatwindow** as the Variable name.

11 Enable the Word Wrap and Embed Fonts options.

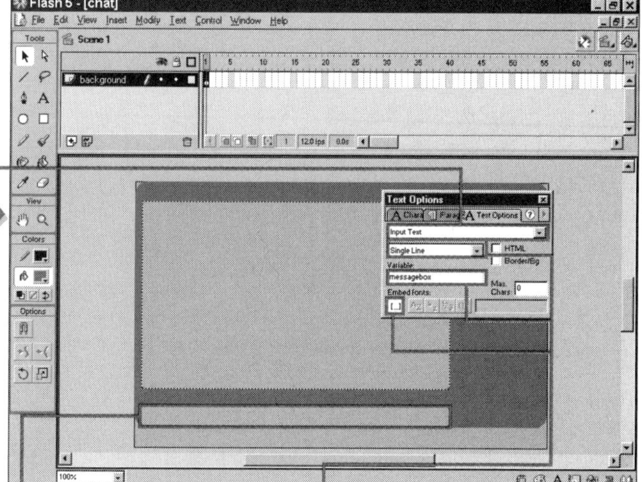

12 Add a second text box to the message text area.

13 Open the Text Options panel and set the Text Type to Input.

14 Set the Line Type to Single Line.

15 Type **messagebox** as the Variable name.

16 Enable the Embed Fonts option.

CONTINUED

CREATE A CHAT FEATURE (CONTINUED)

The real work in this chat feature is being handled by the PHP scripts that are called by the Flash movie you create. The PHP scripts are what actually run the chat feature. What happens behind the scenes is that information from a visitor's browser, say the chat message typed in, gets passed via the PHP script to the hosting server which in return passes information back to the user's browser. The information passed back in this case is the updated chat text, and the updated chat text is displayed by the Flash movie in a dynamic text box.

This section shows a good example of how a dynamic text box can be employed. In the chat feature, a constant update of a text variable is required, so a dynamic text box is used. A static text box allows for no changes to the text, while a dynamic text box is used to reflect changes.

CREATE A CHAT FEATURE (CONTINUED)

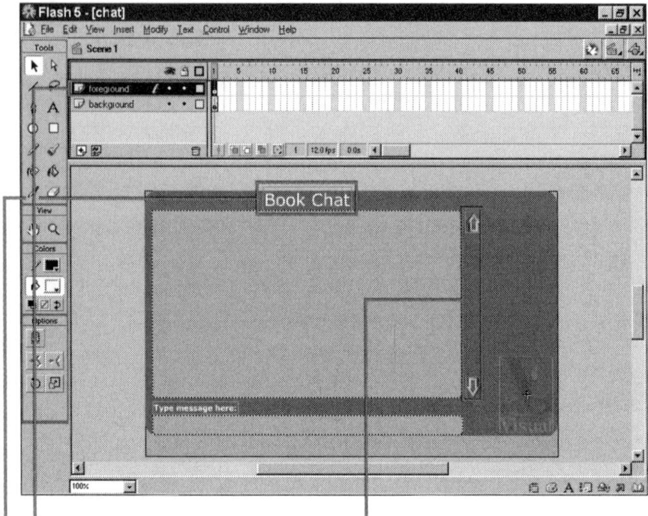

17 Create a new layer and name it foreground.

18 Add title text over the chat area and the message box.

■ You can customize the look of the chat feature in this layer, such as adding a logo.

19 Add scroll arrows to the right of chat area.

Note: See Chapter 32 for more information about adding scroll arrows.

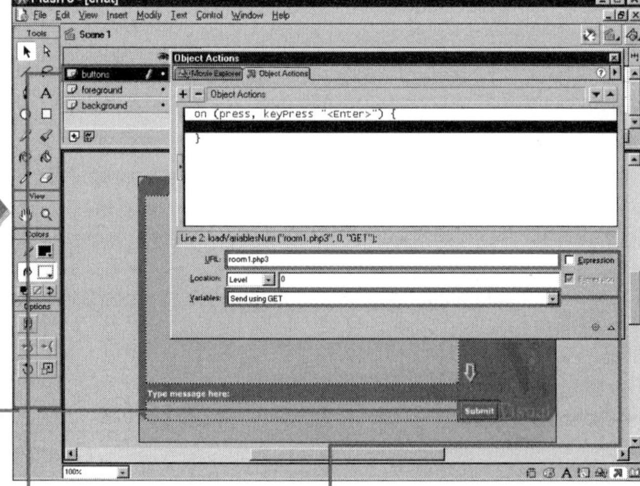

20 Add a submit button to the right of the message box on a new layer named buttons.

Note: See Chapter 32 to learn about adding a submit button.

21 Assign a `loadVariables` action to the submit button.

Note: See Chapter 28 to learn how to assign actions.

22 In the URL field type the name of PHP file handling the message text.

23 Choose Send using GET.

What is a PHP script?

✔ PHP is an abbreviation for *Hypertext Preprocessor*. PHP is a cross-platform, server-side HTML embedded scripting language comparable to ASP. When a script is said to be server-side, it means that the script runs on the server hosting the Web page rather than running on the person's computer viewing the Web page. The script executes on the server and the information is relayed back to the viewer's browser.

Where do I get PHP and how do I use it?

✔ PHP is open source software, meaning that it is free to download and use as long as you do not distribute it as your own. You can visit www.PHP.net to find out more information on PHP. The site has downloads available and tutorials if you are new to PHP and interested in learning it. There is nothing special needed to create PHP files — a basic text editor will do. The file extension for PHP files is .php.

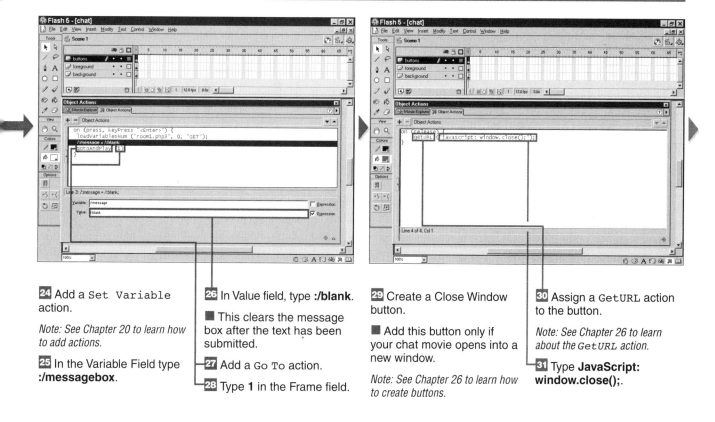

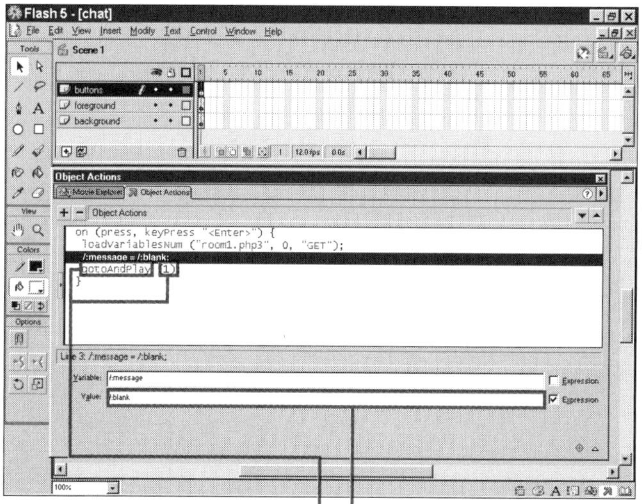

24 Add a `Set Variable` action.

Note: See Chapter 20 to learn how to add actions.

25 In the Variable Field type **:/messagebox**.

26 In Value field, type **:/blank**.

■ This clears the message box after the text has been submitted.

27 Add a `Go To` action.

28 Type **1** in the Frame field.

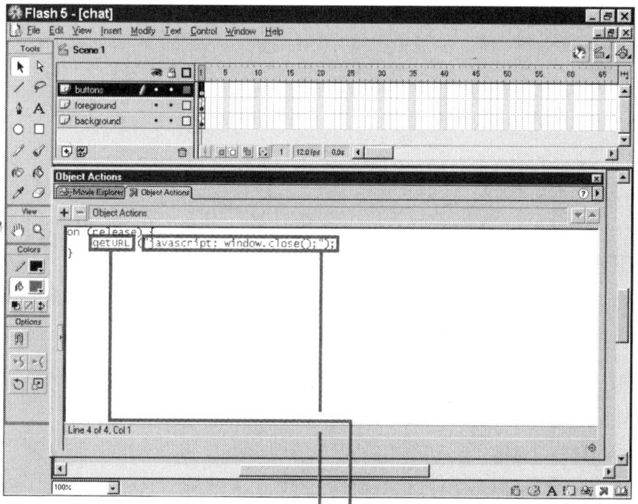

29 Create a Close Window button.

■ Add this button only if your chat movie opens into a new window.

Note: See Chapter 26 to learn how to create buttons.

30 Assign a `GetURL` action to the button.

Note: See Chapter 26 to learn about the `GetURL` action.

31 Type **JavaScript: window.close();**.

CONTINUED

CREATE A CHAT FEATURE (CONTINUED)

So far, you have put the required elements in place for the user to input and submit information to the chat application. In the following steps, you add functionality that provides the means of communication between the Flash movie and the PHP application running on the server. After a user has entered the text to be sent to the chat application, a string variable is saved and sent to the PHP script using the `Load Variables` action. Finally, a call action is used to erase the local variables and restart the script. This event, which is triggered each time the playhead encounters the frame action, is what tells the chat text file to update every couple of seconds. When the file is updated, its contents (the chat conversation) are inserted into the dynamic text box assigned the messagebox variable value. The `gotoAndPlay` action inserted in steps 41 and 42 tell the Flash playhead to continuously loop and run the call frame action, updating the file.

CREATE A CHAT FEATURE (CONTINUED)

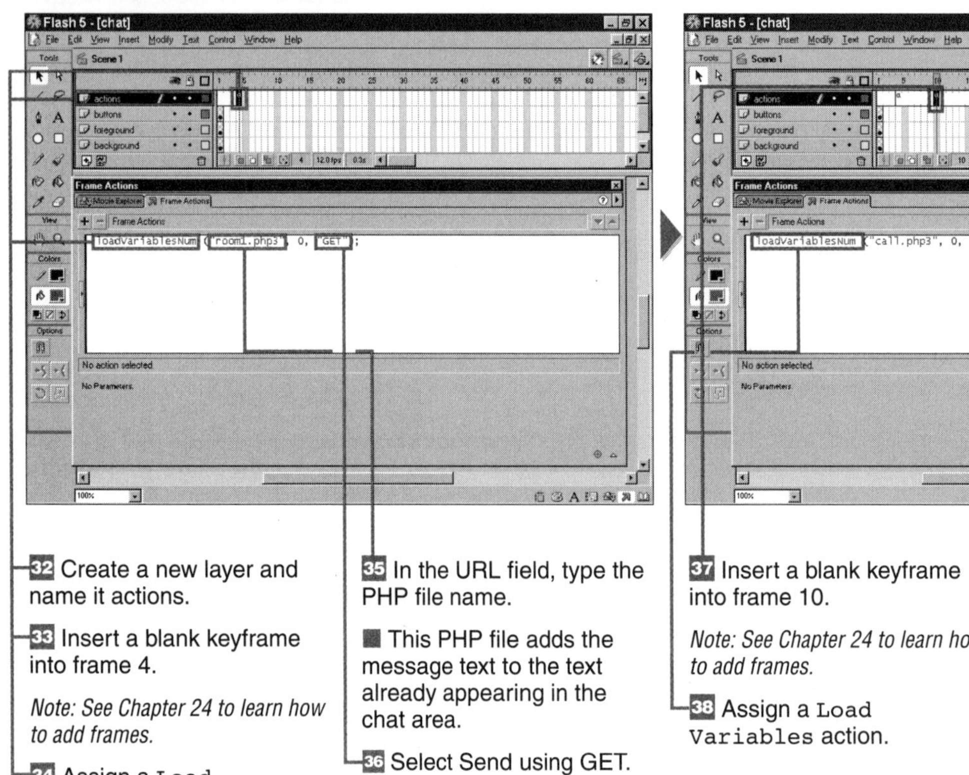

32 Create a new layer and name it actions.

33 Insert a blank keyframe into frame 4.

Note: See Chapter 24 to learn how to add frames.

34 Assign a `Load Variables` action.

35 In the URL field, type the PHP file name.

■ This PHP file adds the message text to the text already appearing in the chat area.

36 Select Send using GET.

37 Insert a blank keyframe into frame 10.

Note: See Chapter 24 to learn how to add frames.

38 Assign a `Load Variables` action.

39 In the URL field, type the PHP filename.

■ This PHP file displays the chat area text.

40 Select Send using GET.

Why should I label my frames?

✔ Label your frames on a dedicated layer to keep track of where key animations or frame actions occur. After a keyframe is labeled, the label, along with a small red flag icon, appears on the Timeline. To label a frame, first insert a keyframe in the desired layer and frame number. Open the Frame panel; click the Show Instance button and then click the Frame tab. In the Label field, type the name you wish to assign the frame. You can now reference the frame by its label as you would when specifying a frame number.

What other features can I add to customize the chat movie?

✔ You can add all kinds of features seen in today's modern top end chat rooms. Some features that you may want to add are displaying the visitor's user name next to his or her message, a list of all users currently in the chat room, or the ability to select one user and chat directly. As mentioned earlier, any changes to the actual chat application must be made in PHP. Refer to www.php.com and www.phpbuilder.com to learn more about coding in PHP.

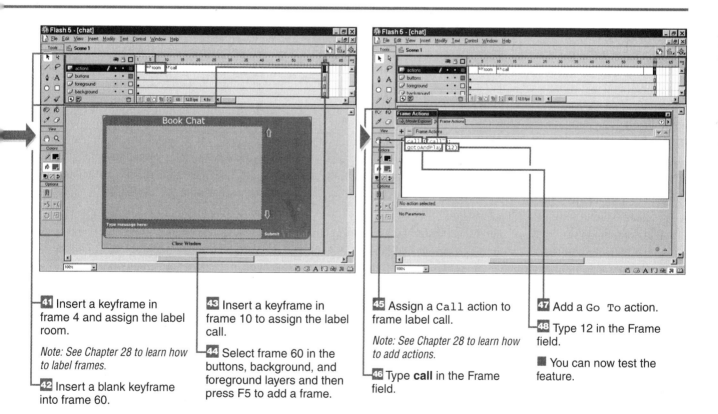

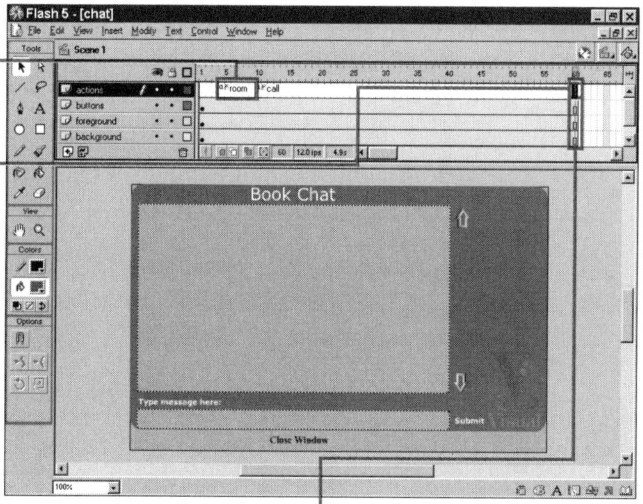

41 Insert a keyframe in frame 4 and assign the label room.

Note: See Chapter 28 to learn how to label frames.

42 Insert a blank keyframe into frame 60.

43 Insert a keyframe in frame 10 to assign the label call.

44 Select frame 60 in the buttons, background, and foreground layers and then press F5 to add a frame.

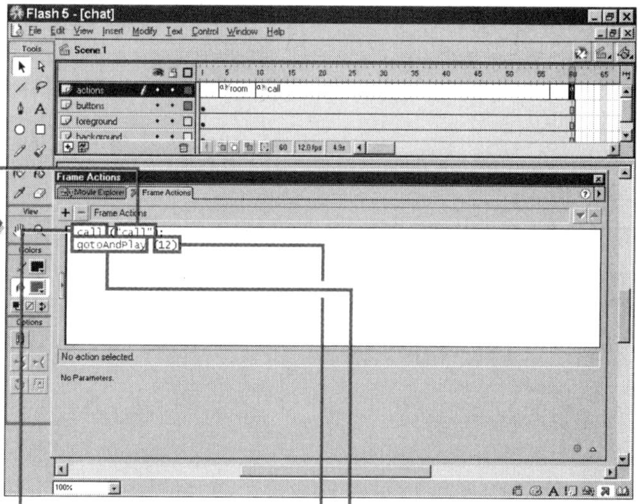

45 Assign a `Call` action to frame label call.

Note: See Chapter 28 to learn how to add actions.

46 Type **call** in the Frame field.

47 Add a `Go To` action.

48 Type 12 in the Frame field.

■ You can now test the feature.

CREATE A SIMPLE FLASH FORM

You can create a basic form in Flash to gather data from visitors who stop by your Web site. Forms are a very important element to feature on any Web site, especially an e-commerce site. The data you collect from a form can range from personal information, such as name or e-mail address, to detailed questions such as, "How did you hear about our site?"

You can use the data you collect with your form to create a database of visitor information, which can provide numerous benefits to an e-commerce site. For example, if your form requires users to list their city and state, you can determine which areas of the country are generating the most sales from your Web site.

The steps in this section demonstrate how to create a simple form comprised of text boxes and buttons. You can find this same form on the sample Web site when you click the Account drop-down menu and choose Registration. In essence, this form is used to set up a user profile. If you have experience creating forms in HTML, creating forms in Flash is just as easy, if not easier.

CREATE A SIMPLE FLASH FORM

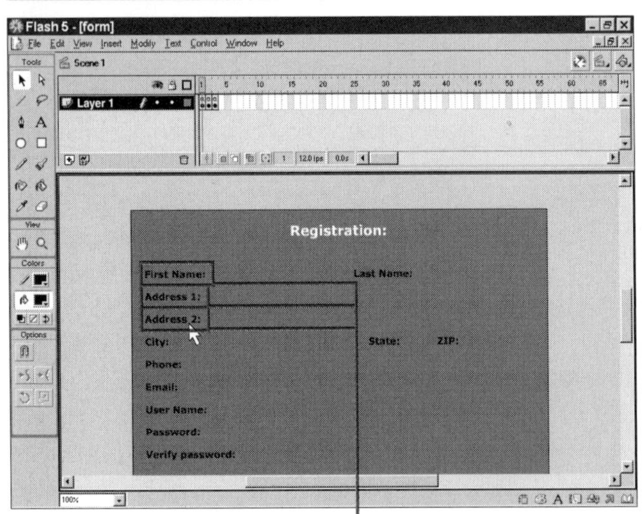

1 Create a new movie file to use as your form, specifying a design and background.

2 Add text boxes to label each field you want to use in the form.

Note: See Chapter 20 to learn how to add text.

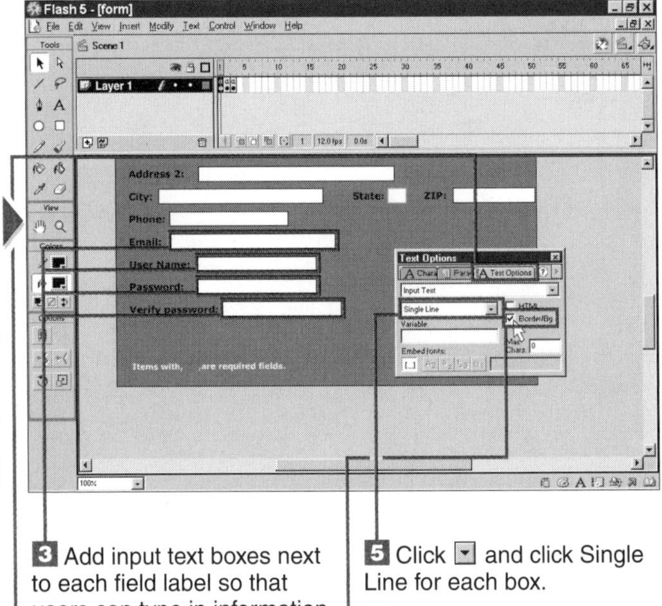

3 Add input text boxes next to each field label so that users can type in information.

4 Click the Text Options tab.

Note: To learn more about text boxes, see Chapter 20.

5 Click ▾ and click Single Line for each box.

6 Click Border/Bg to include a border for each box (☐ changes to ☑).

Are there other features I can include on my form?

✔ Yes. You can add common form features such as radio buttons, check boxes, and drop-down lists, all of which you can create in Flash. The type of form elements you add depends on the type of information you are collecting. For example, you may use radio buttons when you want to allow users to select one choice out of many. Like other parts of a Web site, good planning is necessary when designing a form. Think about how you want to present information and the ways in which you want to collect the data.

Is there a way to check if the information that my visitors enter is correct?

✔ Yes and no. You can use form validation to check for things such as making sure that a user enters numbers in number fields, that text is in text fields, and that the user enters five or nine digits into a zip code field. However, there is no check to make sure John Smith is actually John Smith.

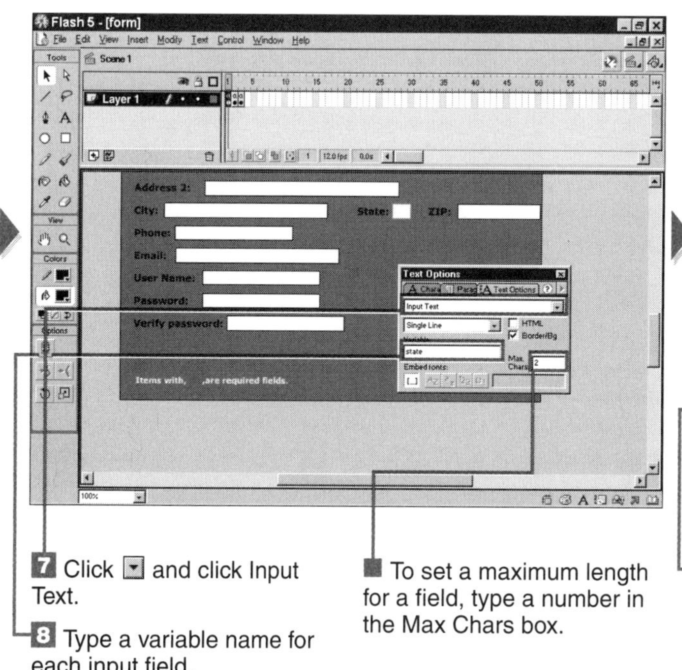

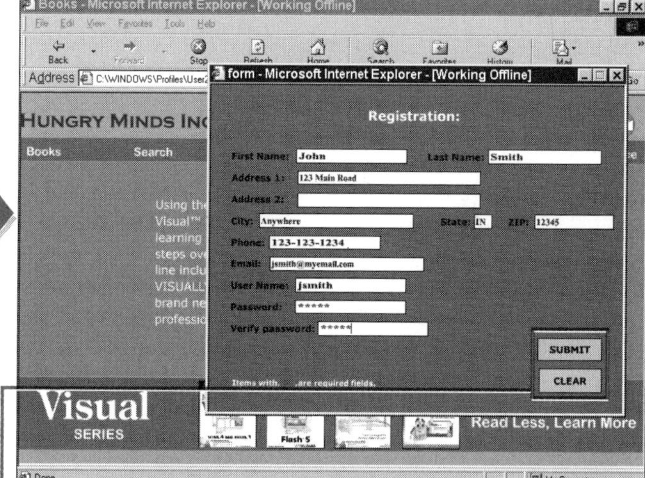

7 Click ▾ and click Input Text.

8 Type a variable name for each input field.

■ To set a maximum length for a field, type a number in the Max Chars box.

■ You can create a Submit button and Clear button for your form.

Note: See the sections "Create a Submit Button" and "Create a Clear Button" to learn more about adding these features to your form.

■ Your form is now ready to publish.

Note: To publish a page in Flash, see Chapter 30.

CREATE A CLEAR BUTTON

You can create a Clear button for your Flash form that allows a visitor a quick and simple way to erase all the information that they type into the form. Without a Clear button the only way a visitor can clear his or her entries is to go back to each field and manually delete the information. Needless to say, users may find this quite tedious.

When creating a Clear button remember to keep your button proportional to the rest of your form's elements and label your button appropriately. For example, you can label your button Reset or Clear Form to Start Over.

In the sample Web site, a Clear button is used on a form for collecting user information. The steps in this section show you how to create the same kind of button, assigning actions to set every variable on the page equal to `:/blank`, which, essentially, is a null value.

CREATE A CLEAR BUTTON

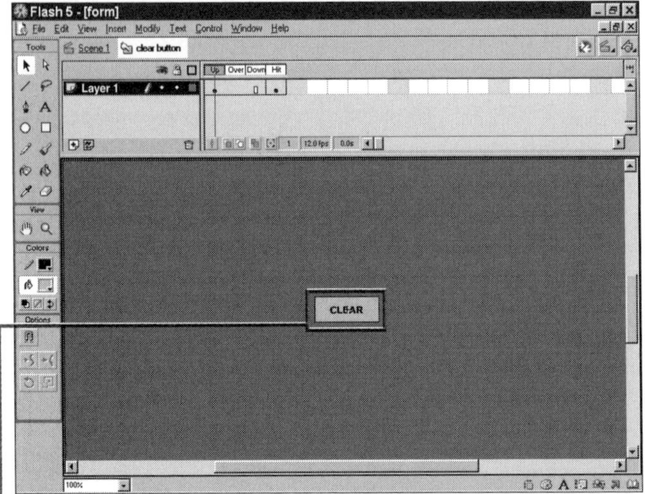

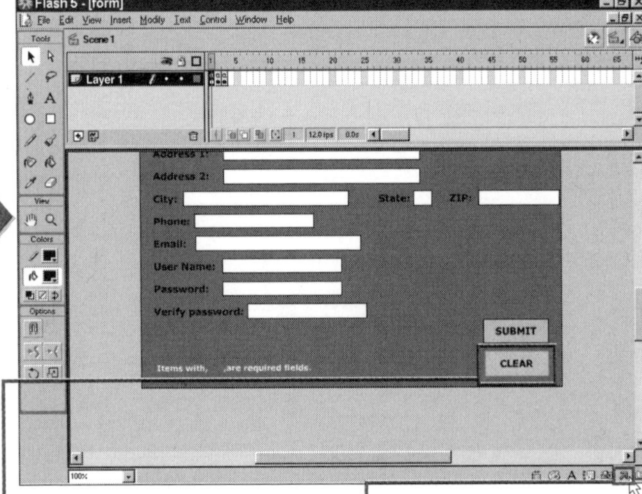

1 Create a Flash form movie.

Note: See the section "Create a Simple Flash Form" for more information.

2 Create a new button symbol labeled Clear or Reset.

Note: See Chapter 22 to learn how to create symbols, and see Chapter 26 to learn how to create buttons.

■ When designing the button, include an object in the Hit frame.

3 Add your button to your form.

Note: See Chapter 22 to learn how to add symbols to the Stage.

4 Click the button to select it.

5 Click the Show Actions button (![]).

Note: See Chapter 28 to learn how to add actions.

Can I add Clear buttons in other Flash movies?

✔ You can use this technique anywhere on your site where the user enters information. For example, you may want to include a Clear button in your Chat movie that enables users to clear their message before sending it to the chat area.

When I press the Clear button, nothing clears. What did I do wrong?

✔ Be sure to check that you set each text box variable to **:/blank**. This command statement basically resets all the text fields to "blank" text fields. Setting the text field variables equal to "" may also work; however, if you have a space in the text field and do not have a check for it, a user can submit your form with nothing but spaces in the text fields. Although you cannot see a space, it takes up a character position, and the text box containing it is not entirely empty.

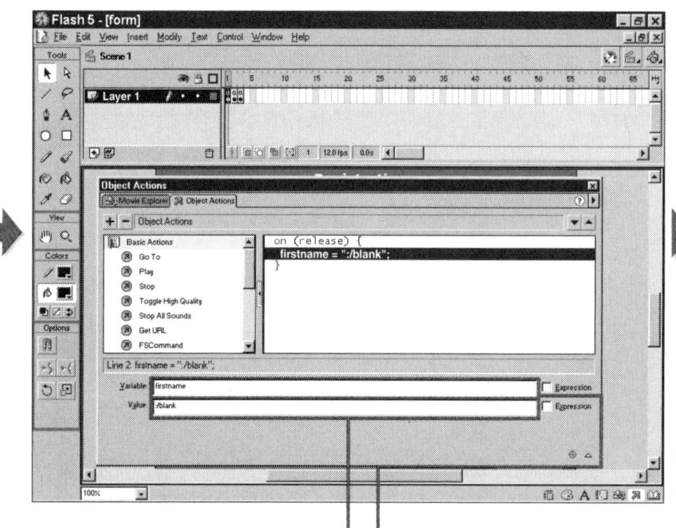

■ The Object Actions dialog box appears.

6 Assign a `Set Variable` action to the button.

Note: To learn how to assign variables to actions, see Chapter 29.

7 Type a unique name for the first field on your form.

8 In the Value field type **:/blank**.

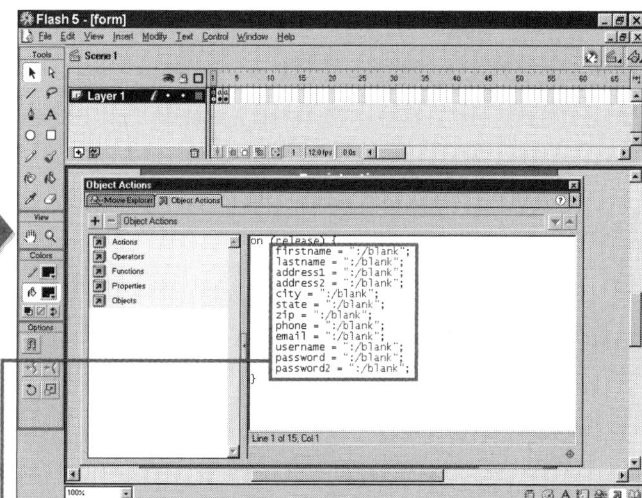

9 Repeat steps 6 through 8, changing the variable name for each field on your form.

■ Check that the panel lists all text field variables with `:/blank` as the value for each.

■ You can now test your button.

Note: See Chapter 30 to learn how to add actions.

CREATE A SUBMIT BUTTON

You can add a Submit button to your Flash forms so that users can send their information to your database. Your form uses the Submit button to signal that it is complete and to trigger a validation, calling an ASP server-side script and using the POST method to create a new record in your database.

You can make your validation simple or complex depending on your needs and wants. The validation in this example checks to see if the required fields are filled in. The information does not have to be correct or the right type of information, as long as something was entered. You can add actions to the Submit button to check and make sure all the required fields have a value. You can use more complicated error checks. For example, you can check to make sure a user types in the proper format or if a user name is already in use. In the sample Web site, the Submit form is fairly simple; however, it provides you with the necessary skills to create more complex Submit buttons of your own.

CREATE A SUBMIT BUTTON

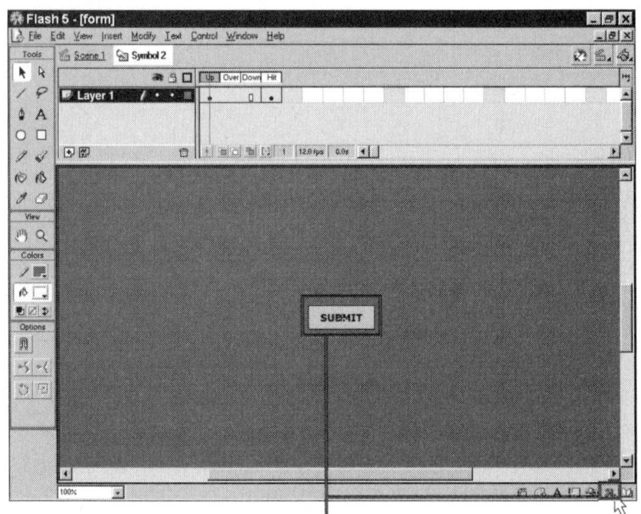

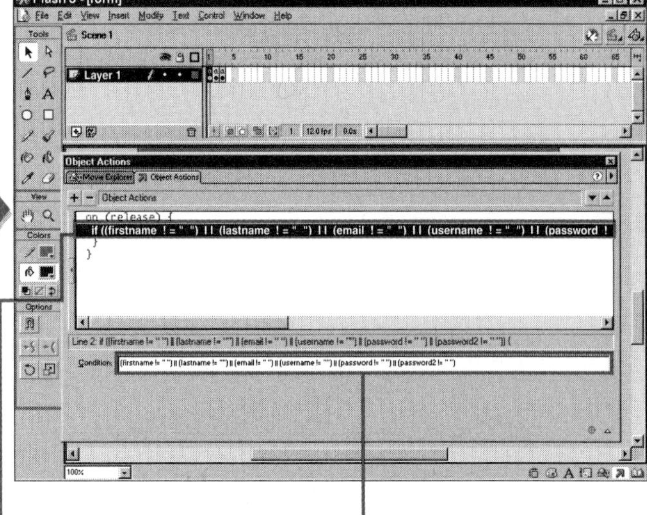

1 Create a Flash form movie.

Note: See the section "Create a Simple Flash Form" for more information.

2 Create a new button symbol and add it to the form.

Note: See Chapter 26 to learn how to create buttons, and see Chapter 22 to learn how to use symbols.

3 Click the button symbol.

4 Click .

■ The Object Actions dialog box appears.

5 Add an `If` action.

Note: See Chapter 28 to learn how to assign actions.

6 Type a condition that checks for the validation parameters you require.

7 Add form validations if desired.

Do I need to validate everything the user types?

✔ No. You may choose to validate certain fields. Validate the fields that are important to you. You can validate only that the information is entered in the correct format. Remember, a user can type false information in the correct format allowing the user to move on and enter the site, sending the false information to your database.

How do I test a movie that uses an ASP script?

✔ You cannot test the movie without running the script on a Web server. You can, however, remove the `Load Variables` action and test the movie without running a Web server. If you do this, no information writes to your database.

What is a confirmation page?

✔ A confirmation page is just a message that appears letting the user know that they have indeed filled out the form correctly and are ready to move on. The conformation page in this example is located in the third frame of the form movie and is shown after the user has completed the form correctly.

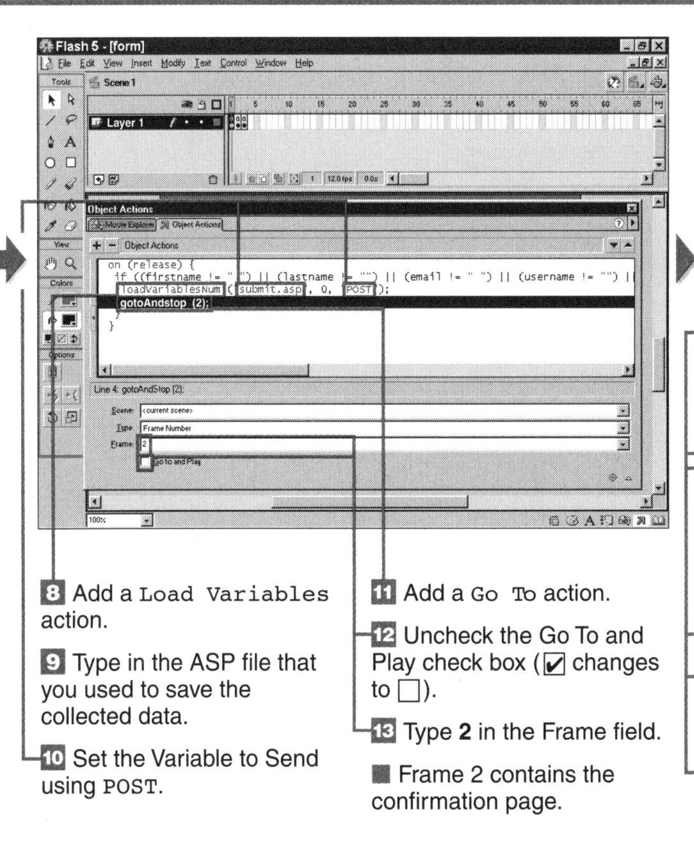

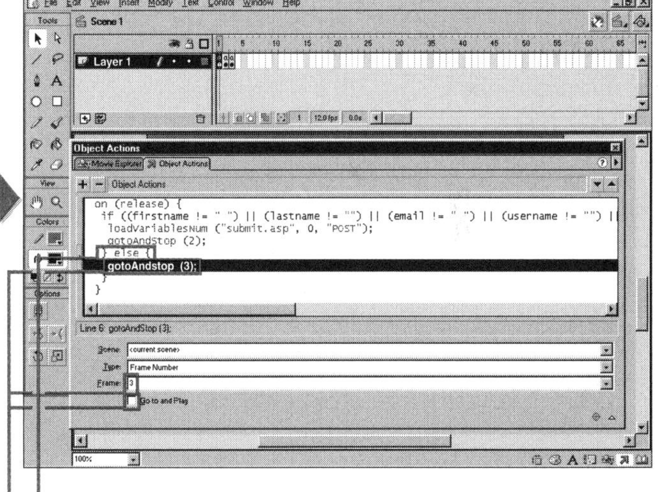

8 Add a `Load Variables` action.

9 Type in the ASP file that you used to save the collected data.

10 Set the Variable to Send using `POST`.

11 Add a `Go To` action.

12 Uncheck the Go To and Play check box (☑ changes to ☐).

13 Type **2** in the Frame field.

■ Frame 2 contains the confirmation page.

14 Add an `else` action.

15 Add a `goto` action.

16 Uncheck the Go To and Play check box (☑ changes to ☐).

17 Type **3** in the Frame field.

■ Frame 3 contains a message informing the user that they need to go back and correct fields.

■ You are now ready to test your Submit button. You can test ASP only while running a Web server.

CREATE A SCROLLING TEXT BOX

You can create a multiline input text box that allows for scrolling. You can use this type of text box on your Flash form to allow users to type comments or give other input. You can control the size of the text box to keep it proportionate to the rest of your form.

In the Web page example used in this chapter, a multiline input box is added to the Flash form movie. The input box allows visitors to leave comments after registering. It allows for about 4 or 5 lines of text to be visible at one time. With only 4 or 5 lines of text visible at one time, buttons are added to the text box that enable the user to scroll up and down.

You do not have to add the scroll buttons; the user can use the up and down arrow keys on their keyboard to maneuver inside the text box, but it is a good idea to include the buttons as a courtesy.

CREATE A SCROLLING TEXT BOX

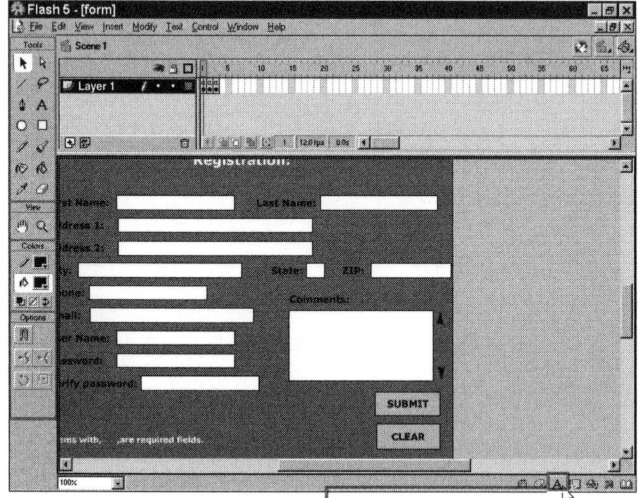

1 Create a Flash form movie.

Note: See the section "Create a Simple Flash Form" for more information.

2 Click the Show Character button (A).

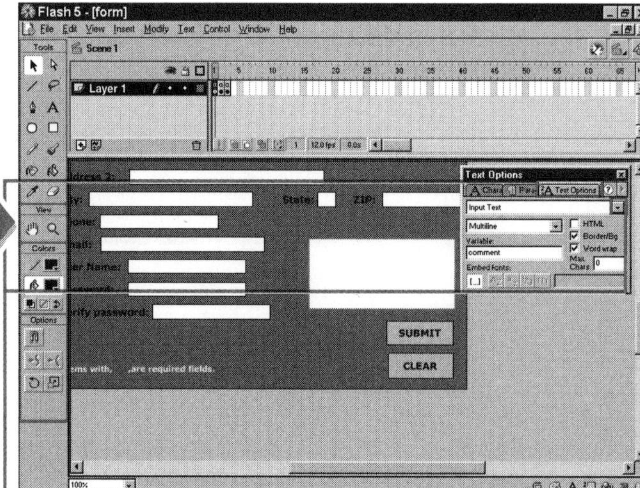

■ The Text Options box appears.

3 Click the Text Options tab.

4 Click ▾ and select Input Text.

■ You can click ▾ and click Multiline to make your box more than one line.

■ You can click Border/Bg or Word wrap to create a border or wrap the words of your box (☐ changes to ☑).

When creating my text box, how do I know how many lines it will display?

✔ When creating your text box, click the Stage where you want your input text box and press Enter for the number of lines you want displayed. Each time you press the Enter key, the text box increases in height, reflecting the amount of lines that you want to be visible at one time.

My text does not scroll. Why not?

✔ You can start by checking your code to make sure that the up button is subtracting an amount, and that the down button is adding an amount. Also check to see if you mistyped the name of your text box variable in your code. Be sure that the variable names in the code match the actual names of the variables.

Can I make the box scroll more than one line at a time?

✔ Yes. In the example shown, 1 is added or subtracted from the `InputText.scroll` variable. If you want your movie to scroll more or less, change the 1 to a larger or smaller number. The larger you make the number, the higher the amount of lines that scroll. The smaller you make the number, the less it scrolls.

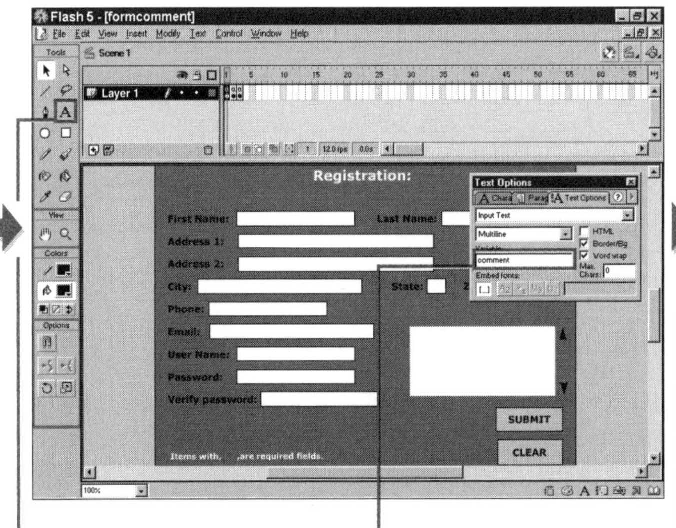

■ Specify the maximum number of characters in the box by typing a number.

5 Click the Text tool button (A).

6 Click and drag to create a text box.

7 Type a variable name for the text box.

8 Create two scroll buttons.

9 Assign an `On Mouse Event` action to the up scroll button.

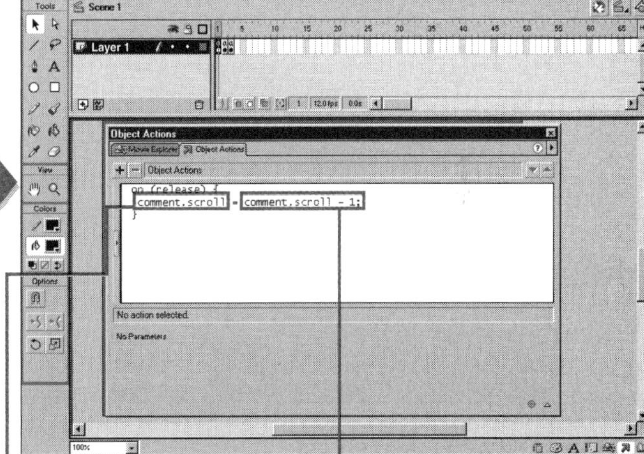

10 Set the event option to Press.

11 Add a `Set Variable` action.

12 In the Variable field type **comment.scroll**.

13 In the Value field type **comment.scroll-1**.

14 Check the Expression check box.

■ Repeat steps 11 through 14 for the down scroll arrow, but change the text to **comment.scroll+1**.

EDIT A USER PROFILE

If you are using forms on your site to register users and compile user profiles, you can also offer your visitors a way to update their profiles. A user profile consists of the personal information gathered from a form included on your Web site. If, for example, a user changes address or marries, the user can update the profile. Without such an option, the user may register again with the new information creating a duplicate entry in your database.

To add an edit profile feature, you must first create a Flash form to collect user information, to which you add an ASP script and GET actions to retrieve user data. When a user types in data, all the necessary text fields fill with the user's old information allowing the user to edit the data as needed and resubmit it. You can use this same technique with search engines; you use an ASP script to retrieve the variables that match the keyword the user types. To learn how to create a Flash form, see the section "Create a Simple Flash Form."

EDIT A USER PROFILE

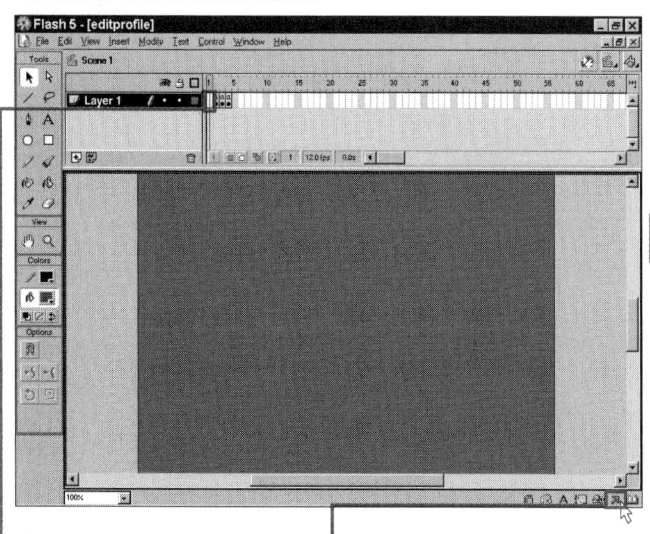

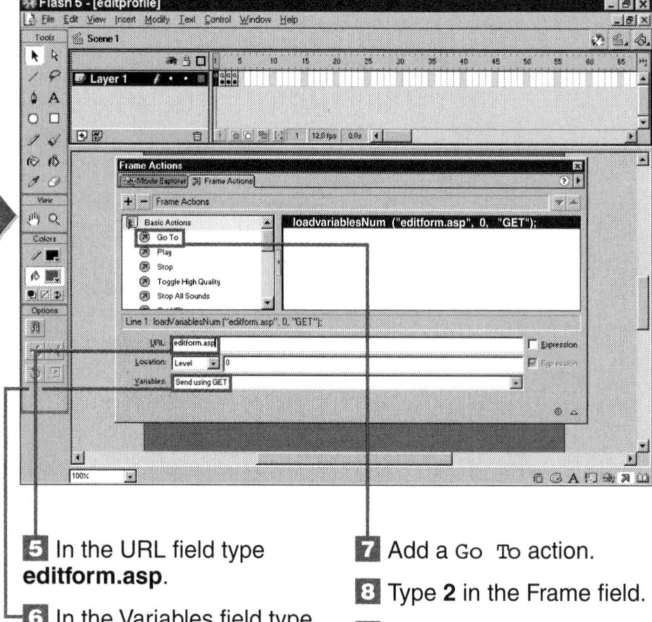

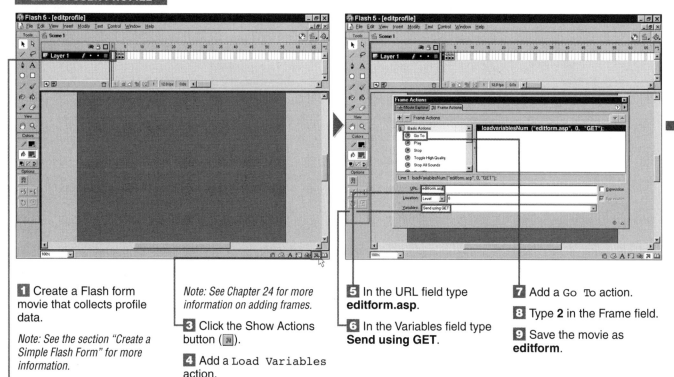

1 Create a Flash form movie that collects profile data.

Note: See the section "Create a Simple Flash Form" for more information.

2 Insert a regular frame into frame 1.

Note: See Chapter 24 for more information on adding frames.

3 Click the Show Actions button (▣).

4 Add a `Load Variables` action.

■ The Frame Actions dialog box appears.

5 In the URL field type **editform.asp**.

6 In the Variables field type **Send using GET**.

7 Add a `Go To` action.

8 Type **2** in the Frame field.

9 Save the movie as **editform**.

What are GET and POST methods?

✔ GET and POST are both methods for passing information on to a Web page. In this example and other examples on your site, you use them to pass information to and from your Flash movie and your Active Server Pages.

What is the difference between the GET and POST methods?

✔ The GET method sends data by appending the data to the URL of the page. You may have seen an example of this if you have ever looked at that long URL on the results page of a search engine site. The POST method sends the data and the URL separately. The GET method is faster and is good for small forms. The POST method takes a little longer but can handle sending large quantities of information. This form is pretty small, so you may want to opt to use the GET method to receive your information.

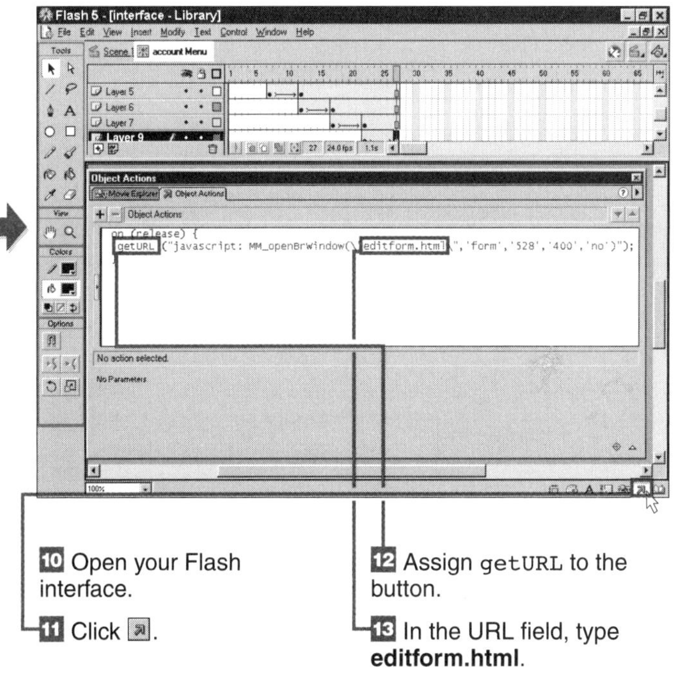

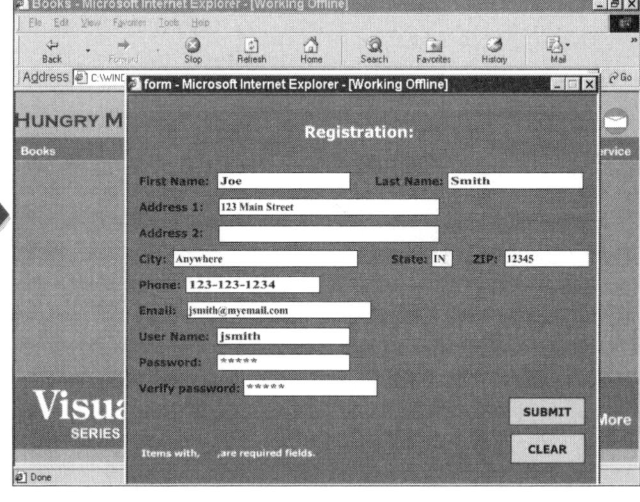

10 Open your Flash interface.

11 Click [icon].

12 Assign getURL to the button.

13 In the URL field, type **editform.html**.

■ When the edit form movie is called from interface, the ASP file displays filled-in form fields.

■ After the user edits the information and submits the new form, it is saved and replaces the old form.

CREATE A USER LOGIN SCREEN

You can create a screen that allows visitors to log in to your site with their user name and password. You might also use this feature if you want only registered users to access restricted areas of your site. Also, a user login screen can make your Web site more personable by addressing the user by name.

To make your own login screen, you must first create a Flash movie that consists of input text fields for the user to type their name and password. To log in, the user first must register in your database. This requires the user to fill out and submit a registration form that creates a user profile. See the section "Create a Simple Flash Form" to learn more about making forms in Flash.

After you create the login screen, you use ASP and the POST scripts to pull the user name and password from your database and compare the login information with the user's profile information in your database. If everything checks out the user can continue into your site. If not, the form clears and the user must retype their name and password information.

CREATE A USER LOGIN SCREEN

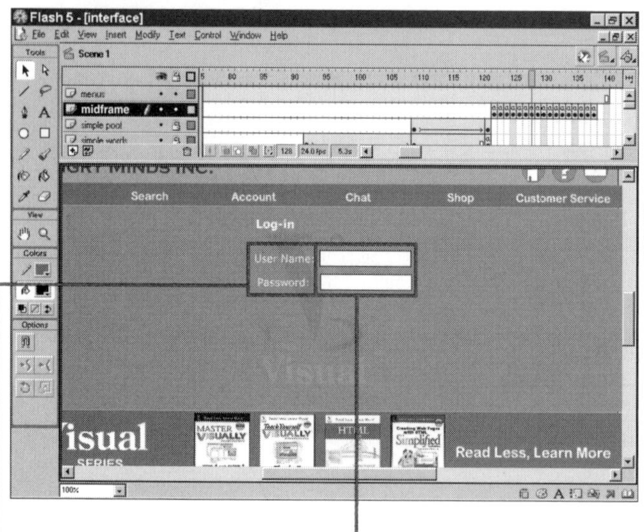

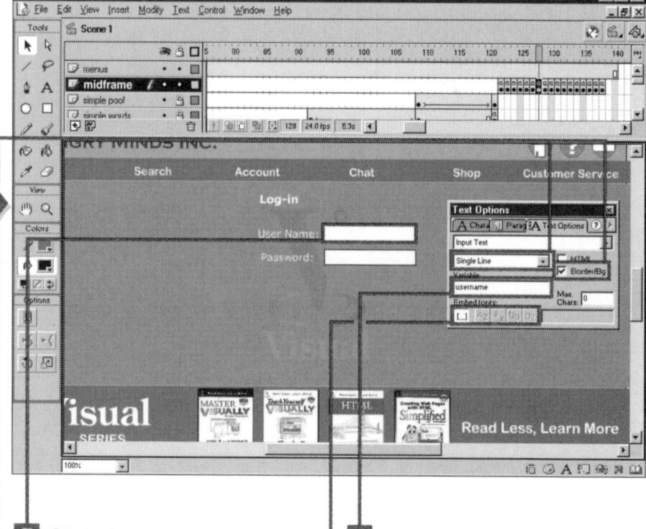

1 Open an existing interface movie.

■ Choose the layer that you want to create the login feature in.

2 Create two text boxes to use as field labels, one for the user name, the other for the password.

3 Create two input text boxes.

Note: See Chapter 20 to learn how to add text.

4 Use the Text Options panel to set the Text Type of both to Input.

5 Click the user name text box.

6 Click ▼ and click Single Line.

■ You can click Border/Bg to create a border for the box (☐ changes to ☑).

7 Type **username** in the Variable box.

■ You can click an Embed fonts option or type a number for the maximum characters in your box.

Can I limit the number of times a user attempts to log in?

✔ Yes, you can create a variable to keep track of how many times a person attempts to log in. You can even temporarily lock out a user if they consecutively fail to log in properly. To create a variable to keep track of how many times a user attempts to log in, simply use the `Set Variable` action to set a variable to zero. Whenever a user fails to log in, use the `Set Variable` action to increment the variable by one.

Is my site completely safe now that it has the password protection?

✔ No. Nothing is completely safe on the Internet. Password protection provides security from the general user, but it does not stop a hacker from gaining access to your site by using someone else's password.

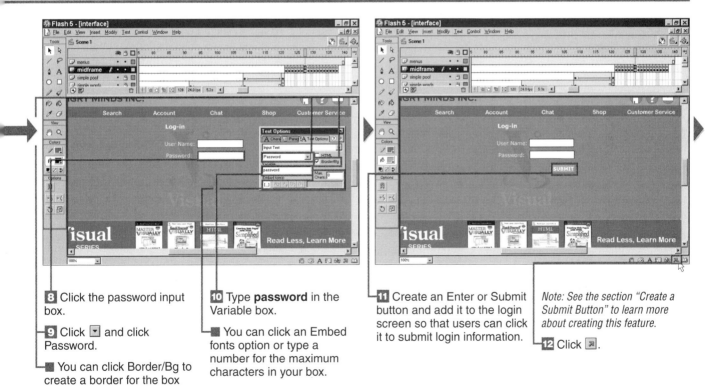

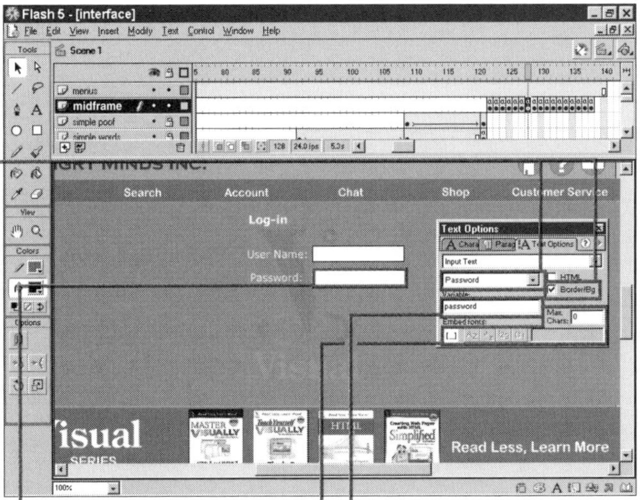

8 Click the password input box.

9 Click ▾ and click Password.

■ You can click Border/Bg to create a border for the box (☐ changes to ☑).

10 Type **password** in the Variable box.

■ You can click an Embed fonts option or type a number for the maximum characters in your box.

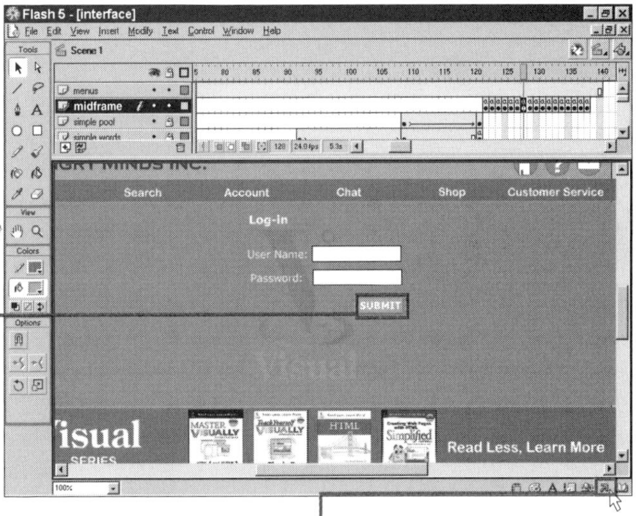

11 Create an Enter or Submit button and add it to the login screen so that users can click it to submit login information.

Note: See the section "Create a Submit Button" to learn more about creating this feature.

12 Click ▣.

CONTINUED

CREATE A USER LOGIN SCREEN (CONTINUED)

The welcome used in this section is basically a type of confirmation screen informing the user that they have successfully logged in. In the welcome screen you insert the user's name into a greeting to create a personalized feeling for your user. You create a variable to be set to the first name of the user in which you determine after your ASP script runs. After your ASP script runs, the variable is set to the user's first name and a dynamic text box displays the variable containing the user's first name in the greeting.

After a user successfully logs in, you assign a `Go To` action telling your Flash movie where the welcome screen is located. In the example file, the welcome screen is located in the layer containing all content between the drop-down menus and the bar with book covers.

CREATE A USER LOGIN SCREEN (CONTINUED)

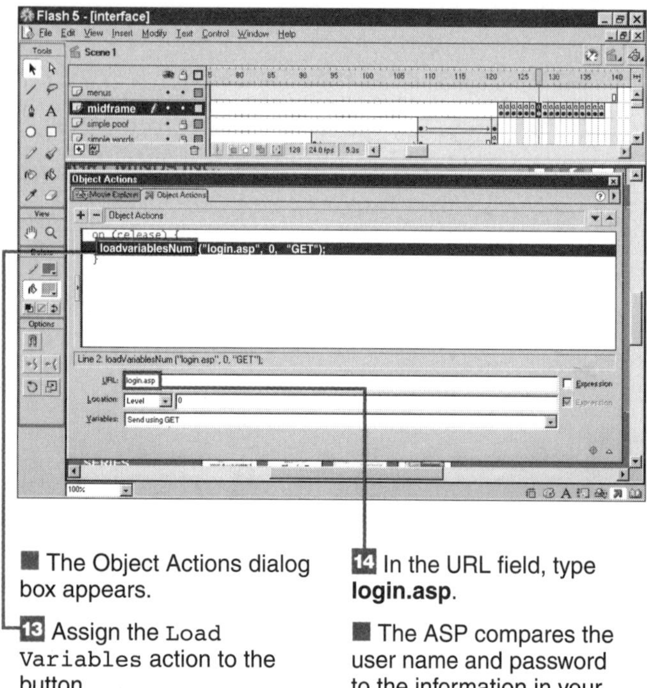

■ The Object Actions dialog box appears.

13 Assign the `Load Variables` action to the button.

Note: See Chapter 28 to learn how to assign actions.

14 In the URL field, type **login.asp**.

■ The ASP compares the user name and password to the information in your database, and determines whether they match.

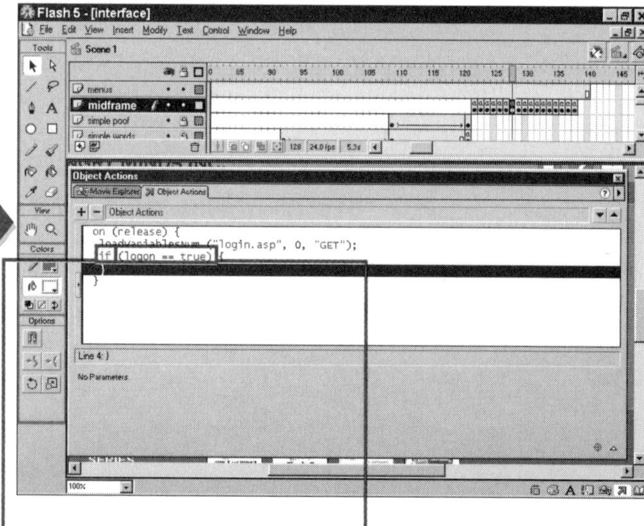

15 Add an `If` action.

Note: See Chapter 28 to learn how to assign actions.

16 Create a condition if `logon` equals `true`.

How can I test my login screen?

✔ To test your login screen, you can follow the steps to register as a normal user would. After you have created your screen name and password, you can attempt to log in. Because this feature makes use of ASP, the files must be located on a Web server in order to run properly. If you log in correctly you should be taken to the welcome page with a greeting. Try logging in incorrectly to be sure that the appropriate actions that you have in place function when a user fails to login properly.

How do I know whether a user is logged on?

✔ You can create a system to check a variable containing either a yes or no. The variable containing the login status is initially set at no, but at the time of a successful log in, the variable is set to yes. When the user logs out, the variable is changed back to no.

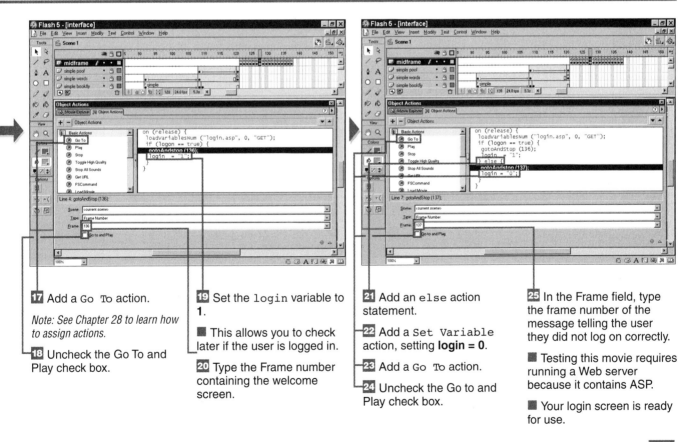

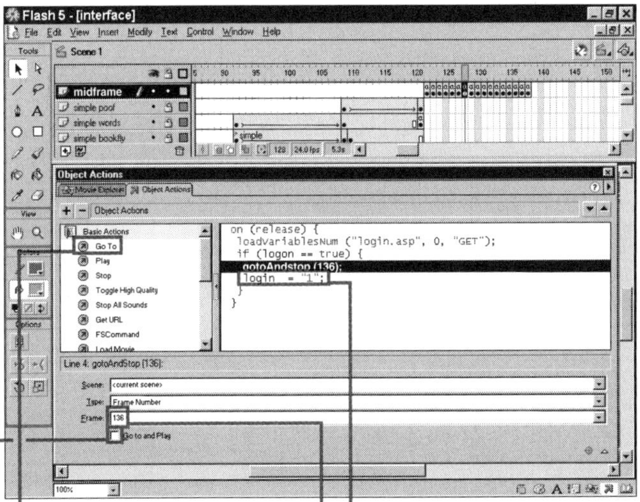

17 Add a `Go To` action.

Note: See Chapter 28 to learn how to assign actions.

18 Uncheck the Go To and Play check box.

19 Set the `login` variable to **1**.

■ This allows you to check later if the user is logged in.

20 Type the Frame number containing the welcome screen.

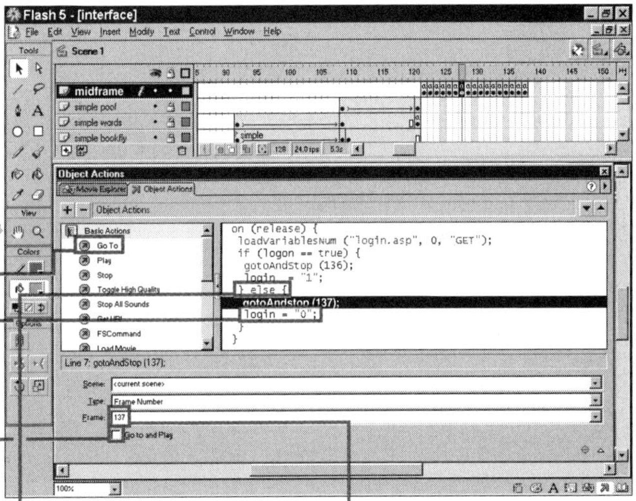

21 Add an `else` action statement.

22 Add a `Set Variable` action, setting **login = 0**.

23 Add a `Go To` action.

24 Uncheck the Go to and Play check box.

25 In the Frame field, type the frame number of the message telling the user they did not log on correctly.

■ Testing this movie requires running a Web server because it contains ASP.

■ Your login screen is ready for use.

CREATE A USER LOG OUT OPTION

You can provide users with an option of logging out of your Web site. When the user clicks on the Log out button, a confirmation message appears. If they choose to log out, Flash clears all variables concerning their visit.

It may not seem important to provide a log out option, but if you have a site with numerous purchasing selections that utilize information such as credit card numbers and other confidential data, having a log out option is a safety feature. Such a feature prevents another user from accessing the previous user's data, particularly if the computer is in a public place, such as a library.

To help you understand how such a feature works, this section shows you how to clear login variables set when the user logs in to your site, utilizing the same feature found on the sample Web site included with this book. See the section "Create a User Login Screen" to learn more about creating a login variable.

CREATE A USER LOG OUT OPTION

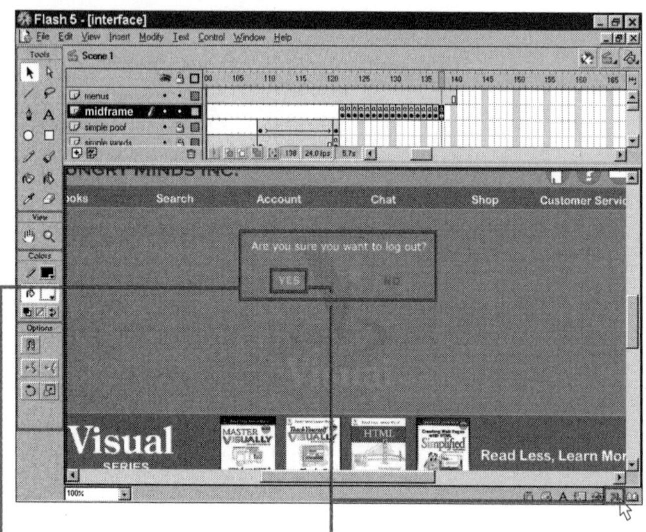

1 Create a confirmation page in your Flash interface movie consisting of a message asking the user if they really want to log off.

2 Add response buttons on the page.

Note: To learn more about adding buttons, see Chapter 26.

3 Click a response button.

4 Click [icon].

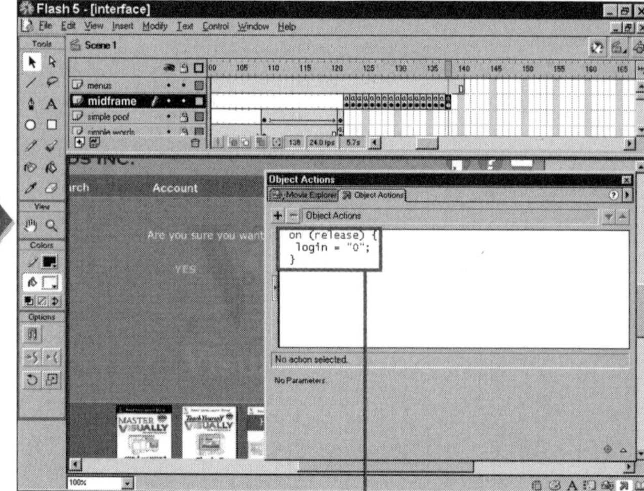

■ The Object Action panel appears.

5 Assign a `Set Variables` action.

Note: See Chapter 28 to learn how to add actions.

6 List variables that you want to clear and set them equal to "".

■ Although this example clears the `login` variable, you can use the steps in this section to clear any variables you want.

What actions might I assign to a No button on the confirmation page?

✔ Depending on the flow and design of your Web site, you might have the user go to a number of places after clicking a No button. For example, you might redirect the user back to the last place on your site where they encountered the log out option, or you could take them to an information page telling them that they did not log out and that they are still able to use the site features.

Why should I have the log out feature if the user can just close the browser window?

✔ It is true that closing the browser window technically logs the user out. However, if the user is on a public computer and they shut down the browser window containing the Flash interface, but forget to shut down the form window or chat window, another user may access the computer and chat under the other user's name or change the other user's information on the form.

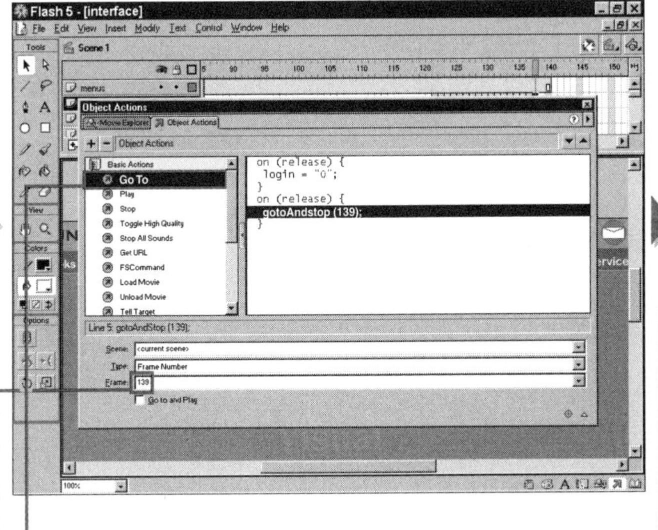

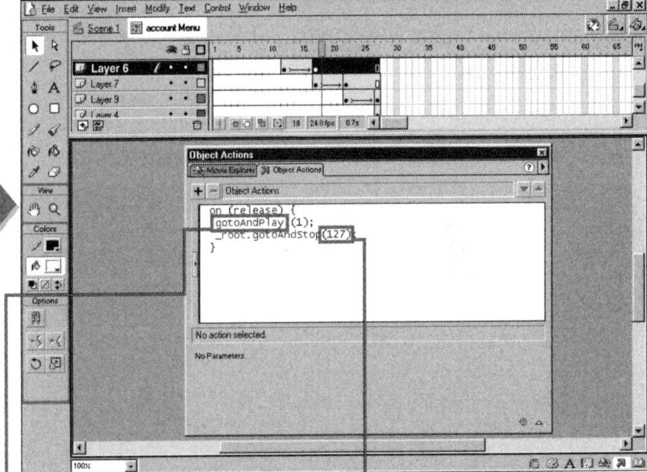

7 Add a Go To action.

Note: See Chapter 28 to learn how to add actions.

8 Type the frame number containing the log out confirmation page created in step 1.

■ The No button in this example has no actions attached to it, allowing the user to navigate from the confirmation screen.

9 Select the Log out button on the drop-down menu.

10 Assign a Go To action.

11 Uncheck the Go to and Play check box (☑ changes to ☐).

12 Type the frame number in which you created a log out confirmation page.

■ Your log out option is ready to use.

■ You can test the movie by logging out and logging in again.

USE THE MAILTO COMMAND

You can use the `mailto` command to allow users to contact you from your Web site with a simple click of a button. One of the requirements most users have for a Web site is a quick and simple way for visitors to contact them with any comments or questions. When you combine the `GetURL` action with the `mailto` command statement, you can meet this requirement with relatively little effort.

When you assign a `GetURL` action and a `mailto` command, the combination triggers the user's default e-mail program when the user clicks a button. Flash opens a new message window and pre-addresses it with any address you specify. This Web site feature enables your visitors to contact you with any questions or comments with the click of a button. In addition, this feature saves users the trouble of writing down or trying to remember an e-mail address. You can view and use an example of this option on the CD-ROM included with this book.

USE THE MAILTO COMMAND

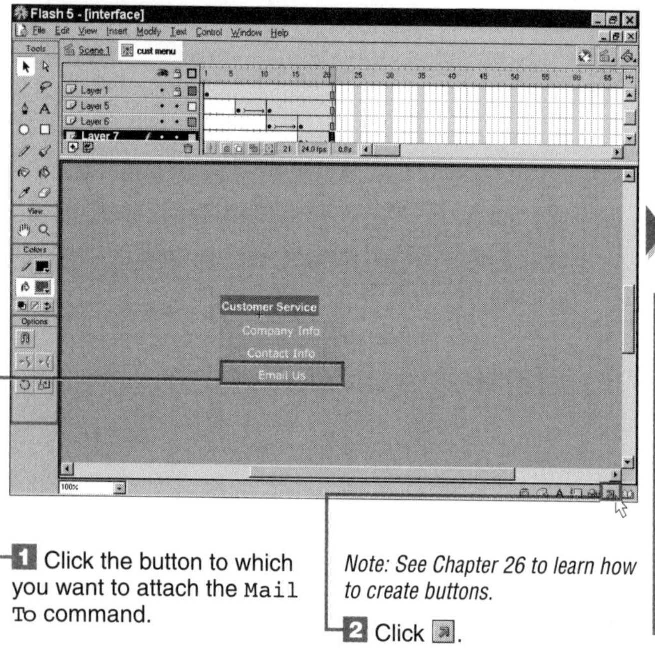

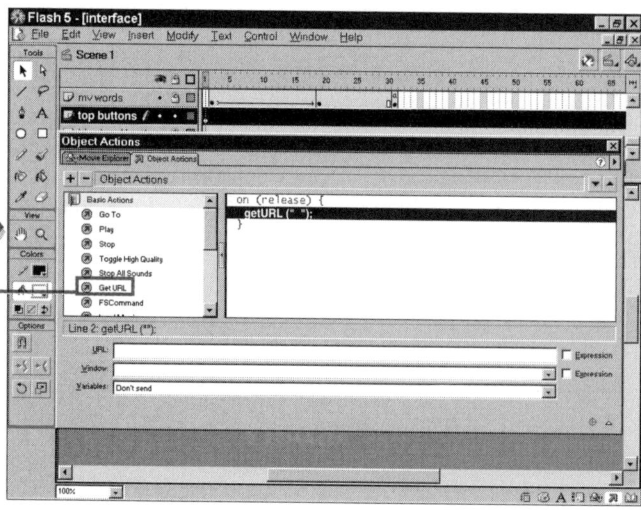

1 Click the button to which you want to attach the `Mail To` command.

Note: See Chapter 26 to learn how to create buttons.

2 Click .

■ The Object Actions dialog box appears.

Note: See Chapter 28 to learn how to assign actions.

3 Assign the `Get URL` action.

Why not list my e-mail address on the page instead?

✔ The more features you can add to your site to save visitors time and effort keeps users coming back to your Web site. It is much easier for a visitor to use this feature rather than having to write down your e-mail address and then manually open their e-mail program later and type the address in. The `mailto` command bypasses all of this and saves the user time and effort.

What if they do not want to launch their e-mail program?

✔ For that reason, you should clearly label the button you attach the `mailto` command to. Give the user some idea of what is going to happen if they click the button. In case they do not wish to launch their e-mail program, they can choose not to click the button.

What if my e-mail address changes?

✔ You have to reopen the file and the Actions panel and correct the action statement for the `mailto` command to include your new e-mail address. Save your changes and republish the Web.

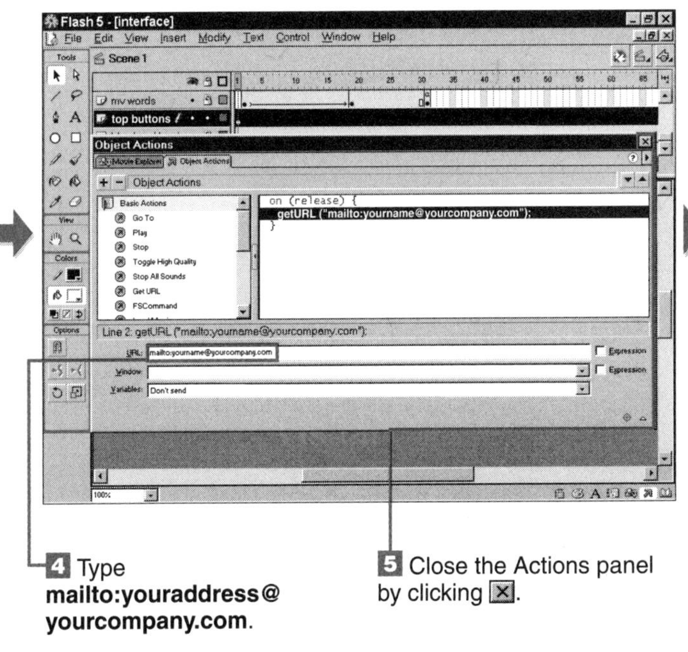

4 Type **mailto:youraddress@yourcompany.com**.

5 Close the Actions panel by clicking ☒.

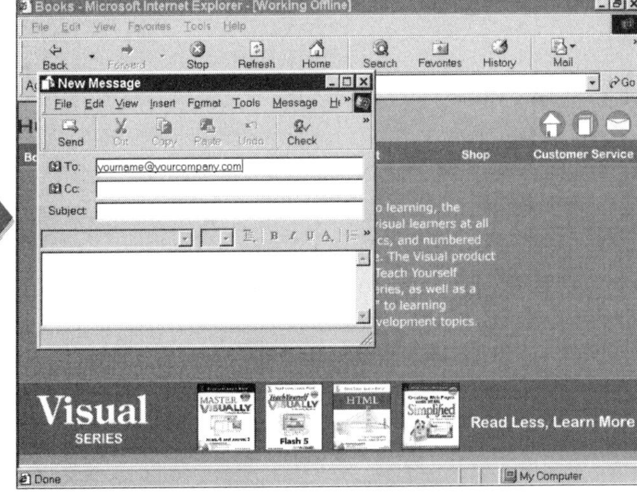

■ Flash assigns the actions to the selected button.

■ You can test the movie and click on the button. When activated, it should trigger a new message window.

ADD A SEARCH TOOL

You can create a Flash movie to use as a search tool to access data on your Web server. A search tool feature enables visitors to search your site for specific information. Without such a feature, visitors may not find what they want and may exit your site in frustration. Using a form you create in Flash, a user can submit a query to your database that generates a response from the server.

In the sample Web site included with this book, a search tool enables users to find books based on author, title, or subject. Book data, such as author name, subject, and title, is stored as variable information, and an ASP script conducts the actual database search.

For example, if a visitor searches by subject and enters the keyword **Dreamweaver** into the search form, the Flash interface calls an ASP code that looks through the subject field of the database and pulls all records containing "Dreamweaver."

ADD A SEARCH TOOL

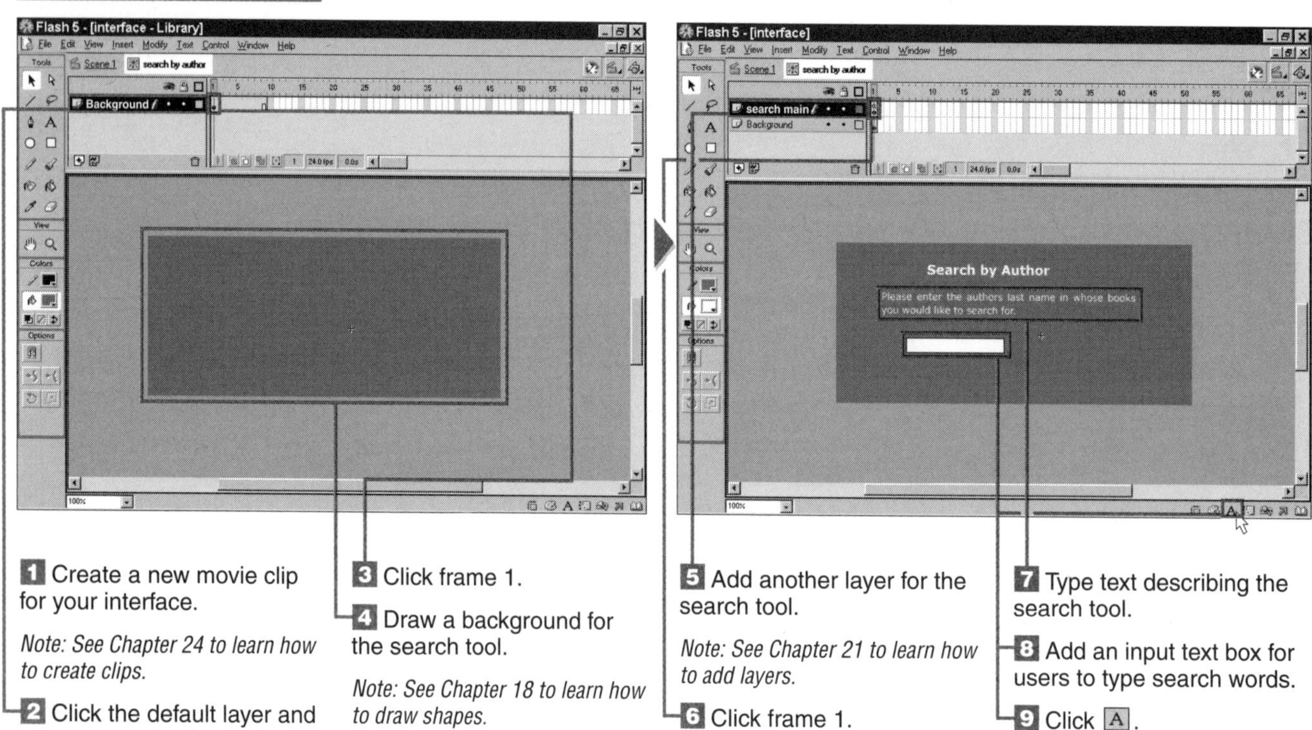

1 Create a new movie clip for your interface.

Note: See Chapter 24 to learn how to create clips.

2 Click the default layer and type a name for it.

3 Click frame 1.

4 Draw a background for the search tool.

Note: See Chapter 18 to learn how to draw shapes.

5 Add another layer for the search tool.

Note: See Chapter 21 to learn how to add layers.

6 Click frame 1.

7 Type text describing the search tool.

8 Add an input text box for users to type search words.

9 Click A.

How do I create my database?

✔ It would take another book to relay instructions on how to create a database for your products. There are different database strategies and many different types of database software from which to pick. Depending on your needs and budget, it is hard to say what software you should use. For the sample Web site, a simple database was created in Microsoft Access.

What exactly is ASP?

✔ ASP, short for Active Server Pages, is a technology developed by Microsoft to create dynamic, powerful Web pages. One important feature of ASP that directly relates to this section is ASP's ability to connect to a database. ASP can be used to make information in a database readily available to visitors of your site. Not only do users have access to information in your database through your Web site, but they can also manipulate data in your database. You can use an ASP page to update, add, or delete records in your database.

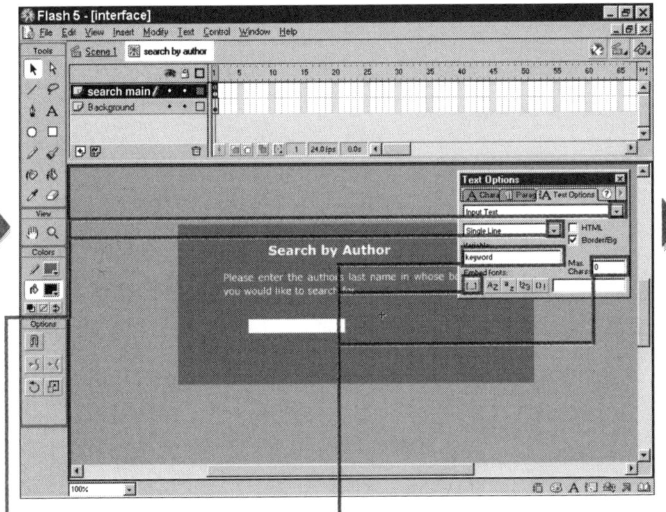

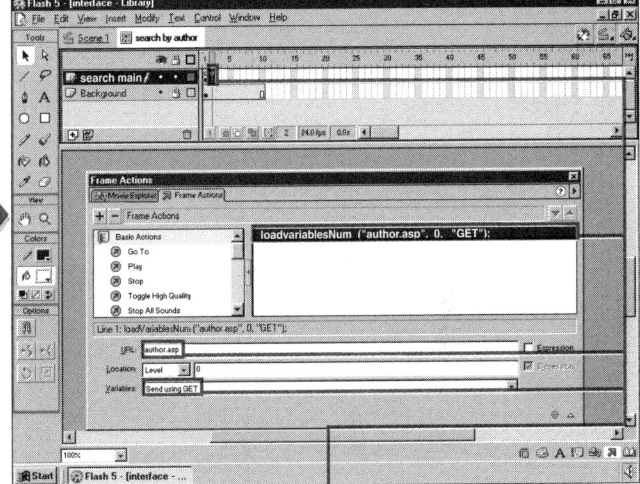

■ The Text Options box appears.

10 Click ▾ and click Input Text.

11 Click ▾ and click Single Line.

■ You can create a border by clicking Border/Bg.

12 Type the maximum characters you want.

13 Type a name for the box.

14 Click the first Embed fonts button.

15 Add the text **Enter** to the right of input text box.

16 Convert the new text to a button symbol.

17 Assign a `Go To` action to the button symbol.

18 Type **2** in the Frame field.

19 Select frame 1 and add a `Stop` action.

20 Insert a blank keyframe into frame 2.

21 Assign the `Load Variables` action.

22 Type the ASP page.

23 Select Send using GET.

CONTINUED

ADD A SEARCH TOOL (CONTINUED)

You can create different types of searches for your Web site. In the sample Web site, users can not only search by author, but also by book title and subject. This section focuses on a subject search, but you can adapt these same steps to add other types of searches, creating search forms for each type.

For example, after you have completed a movie clip for one search type, you can make a few edits to adapt the clip to another search type.

An important part of designing the search tool movie clip is inserting extra frames to allow for the actual search to occur. In this example, several frames are added to display a message alerting the user that the search is in progress. You may need to add more frames after testing the feature if your server response is slow.

ADD A SEARCH TOOL (CONTINUED)

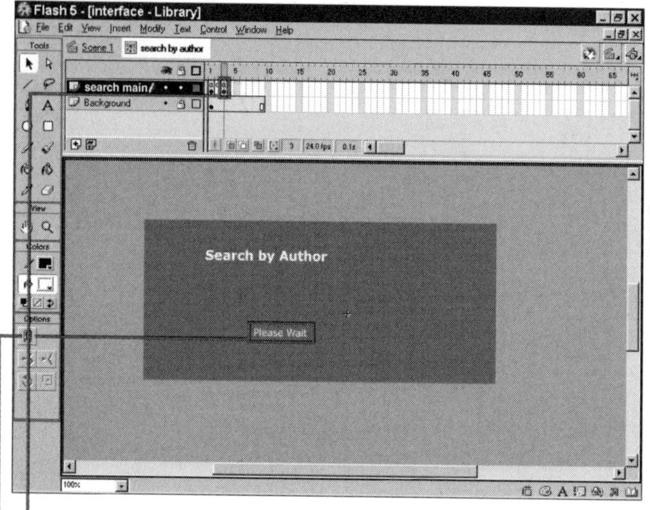

24 Insert a blank keyframe in frame 3.

25 Create another set of text boxes, this time conveying a message that informs the user that the search tool is processing the search.

■ In this example the message reads Please Wait. You can use another message or a picture, such as an hourglass.

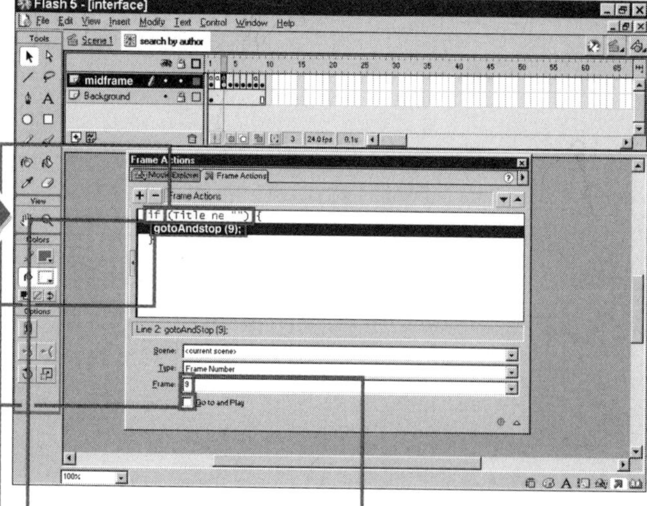

26 Add an `If` action to frame 3.

27 In Condition field type **Title ne ""**.

28 Add a `Go To` action.

29 Uncheck the Go to and Play check box option.

30 In the Frame field, type **9**.

■ These actions check to see if there are search results. If yes, the movie returns to frame 9; if not, it keeps playing the wait message.

■ Your own frame numbers may vary.

How do I program the ASP code used in this example?

✔ Going into the details of Active Server Pages is beyond the scope of this book. If you are indeed a visual learner, you may want to read the book *Active Server Pages 3.0: Your visual blueprint for developing interactive Web sites* (Hungry Minds, Inc., 2000).

Can I allow a user to search for multiple items?

✔ Yes. You can alter your search movie to allow users to enter multiple keywords when they are searching. However, creating a multiple-keyword search is a little more complicated. A multiple-keyword search does not require any changes to your Flash movie other than a different set of directions, but it does require some code changes in your ASP. Although it may be a little more difficult, the multiple-keyword search can prove to be very beneficial to your users, especially if you have a large amount of information that they may be searching through.

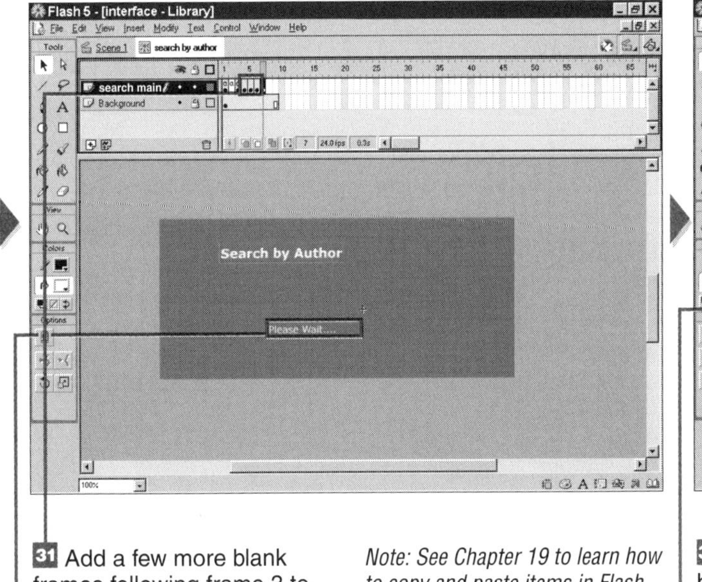

31 Add a few more blank frames following frame 3 to allow time for the search.

32 Copy and paste the objects from frame 3 into the new frames.

Note: See Chapter 19 to learn how to copy and paste items in Flash.

■ You can vary the objects slightly to create interest. In this example, periods were added one frame at a time to the words Please Wait.

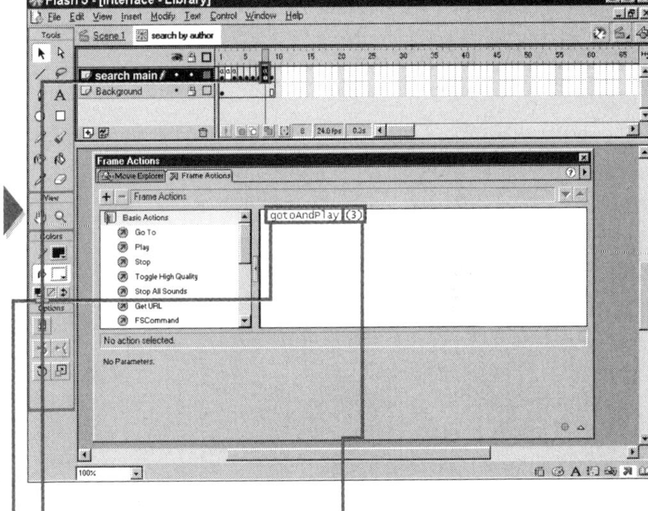

33 Add another regular blank frame and copy and paste the search box title at the top of the search area.

34 Assign a Go To action.

Note: See Chapter 28 to learn how to add actions.

35 Type **3** in the Frame field.

CONTINUED

ADD A SEARCH TOOL (CONTINUED)

You do not necessarily have to have a searchable database for all information that you wish to make available to your users. There are certain times in which this technique can be applied and certain times in which it is too much to have a searchable database.

For example, if you are posting a 20-game schedule for your son or daughter's soccer team on your Web site, you do not need to have ASP or a database; simply posting the schedule on your site is an efficient way to get the information to your visitors.

However, perhaps you prefer to post the schedule for a major league baseball team. Although the schedule can be posted without this technique, it can be a nice feature to add to the searchable database in case a visitor would like the dates of when their favorite team plays another team. The visitor can filter the schedule to show only games involving two teams. If you sell tickets to sporting events, this might be a great feature to add to your site.

ADD A SEARCH TOOL (CONTINUED)

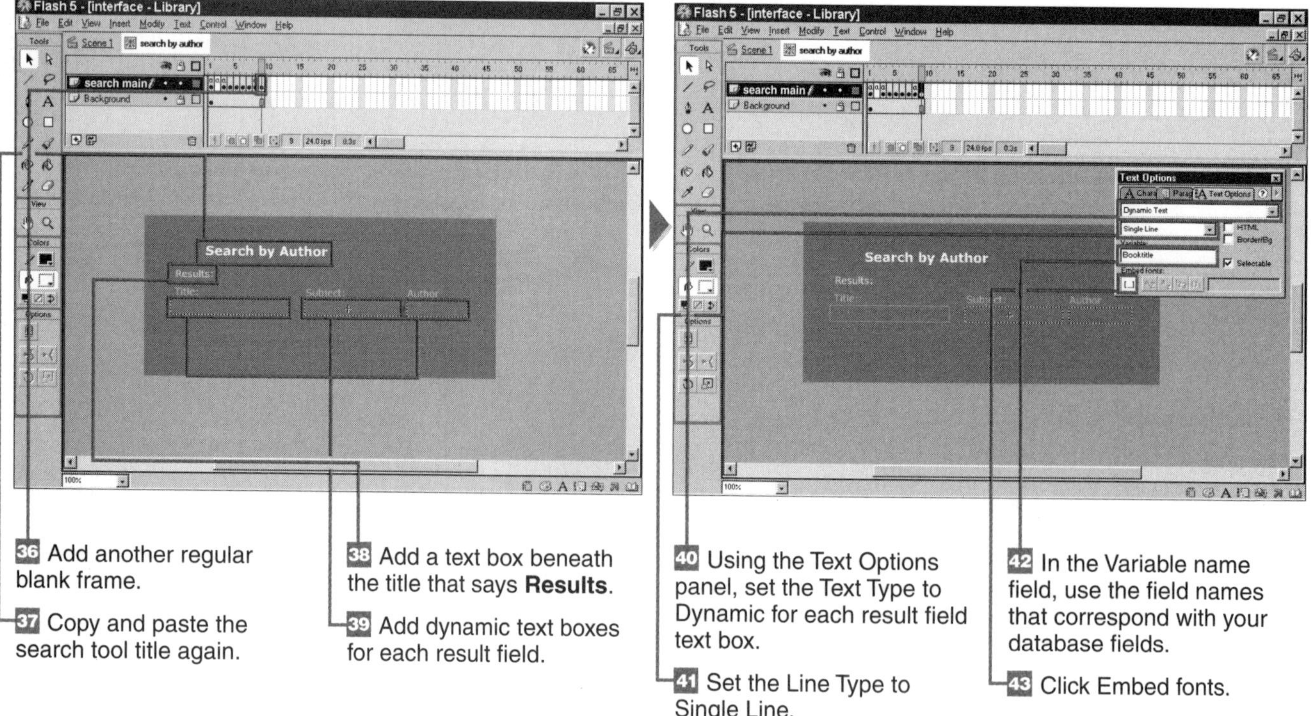

36 Add another regular blank frame.

37 Copy and paste the search tool title again.

38 Add a text box beneath the title that says **Results**.

39 Add dynamic text boxes for each result field.

40 Using the Text Options panel, set the Text Type to Dynamic for each result field text box.

41 Set the Line Type to Single Line.

42 In the Variable name field, use the field names that correspond with your database fields.

43 Click Embed fonts.

What if I am selling some other product besides books?

✔ The database used in the sample Web site was set up with fields containing title, author, subject, and ISBN. The ISBN is a number that uniquely identifies books; it is similar to a social security number. If you are selling tools, you may want fields containing manufacturers, type of tool (screwdriver, hammer, and so on), product description, and model number. The model number would serve as a unique identifier for each tool. You may want users to be able to search for the type of tool or the manufacturer, possibly both. For example, a visitor may want to search for screwdrivers made by Stanley.

When should I use the lock layer option?

✔ When working with a multi-layer Flash movie with symbols in different layers overlapping, it is good practice to employ the lock layer option. When a layer is locked, all items on that layer are viewable, but they cannot be selected; therefore, they cannot be moved, deleted, or edited in any way.

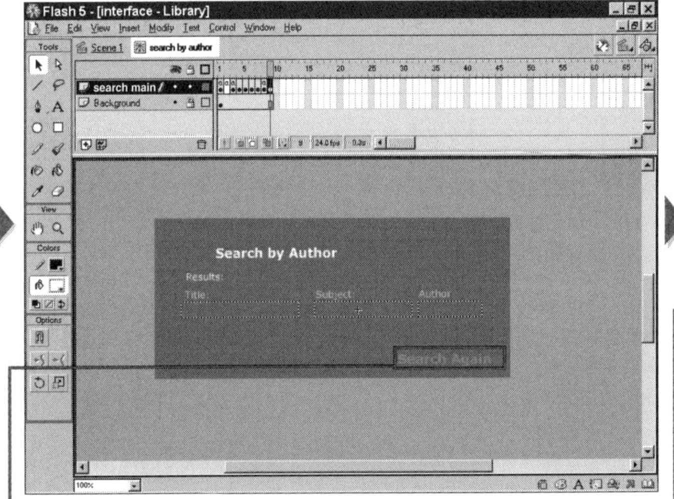

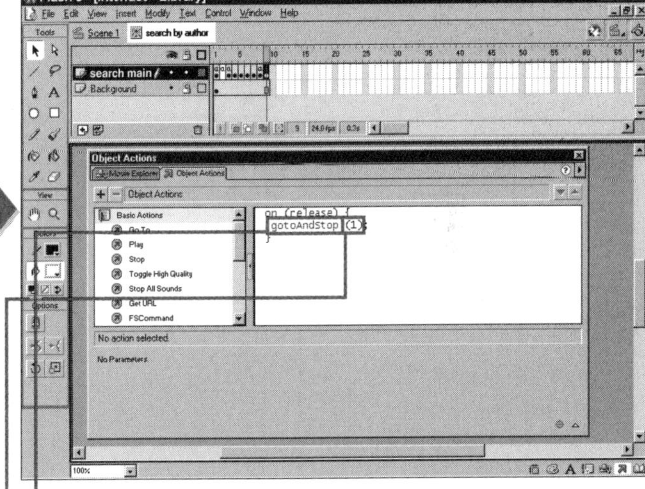

44 Add a text box to the bottom of the search area and type **Search Again**.

45 Convert the new text into a button symbol.

Note: See Chapter 22 to learn how to convert symbols.

46 Assign a `Go To` action to the button symbol.

47 Type **1** in the Frame field.

■ Because this section involves an ASP script, it can be tested only when running through a Web server.

INTEGRATE A FLASH BANNER

You can create a Flash banner to advertise services for your Web site. *Banners* are mini-commercials that advertise a product or service for your company, or another company, on a Web site. You can create such an animated banner in Flash and place it on a Web page created in Dreamweaver.

When designing a banner, you must consider the dimensional and file sizes. *Dimensional size* refers to the height and width of the banner as it appears on a Web page. The standard size of a full banner should be 468 x 60 (pixels). Although ads range in size, the most common variation being 230 x 33, the full banner is the most popular and universal ad on the Internet today. *File size*, measured in kilobytes (K), refers to the amount of storage space the banner requires, which determines the length of time it takes to download on a Web page. As a good rule of thumb, try to keep your banner under 15K for loading quickly on a Web page.

INTEGRATE A FLASH BANNER

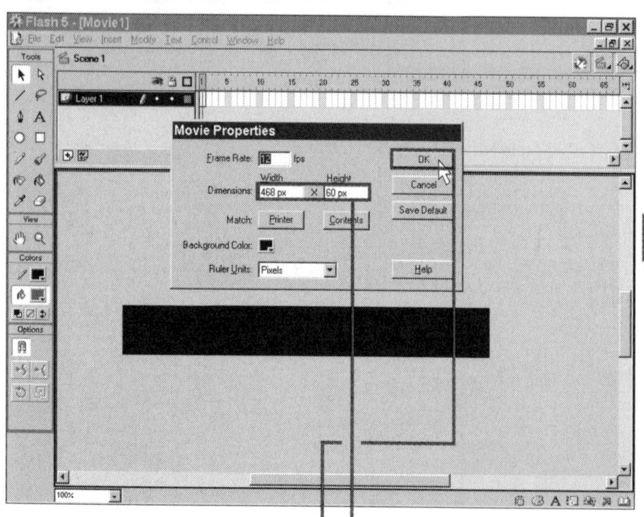

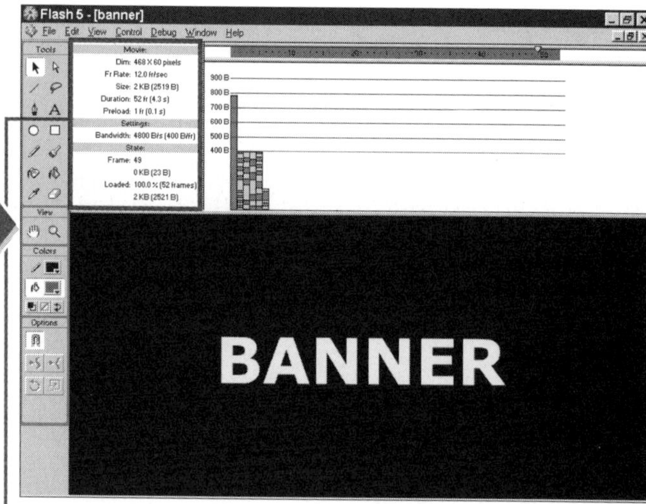

CREATE A FLASH BANNER

1 From the File menu, select New to create a new Flash movie.

2 Open the Movie Properties dialog box.

Note: See Chapter 17 to learn more about movie properties.

3 Change the dimensions to banner size by setting the width to 468 pixels and the height to 60 pixels.

4 Click OK.

5 Create a simple animation advertising your site.

6 Test your movie with the Bandwidth Profiler enabled to check that the movie's size is under 15K.

Note: See Chapter 30 for more information on the Bandwidth Profiler.

7 Publish your Flash file.

Note: See Chapter 30 for information on publishing Flash files.

What if the user does not have the Flash plug-in?

✔ It is important that you test for the appropriate version of the Flash plug-in (see the tips in Chapter 31 for more information) if your ad is published in Flash format. Because you are unlikely to use any advanced features of Flash in a banner ad, you should consider exporting your movie in Flash 3 format to increase the likelihood of the user having the plug-in. Flash also enables you to publish your movie to an animated GIF if you wish to avoid plug-in detection. Finally, keep in mind that you should have an alternate, non-Flash ad to use in place of your Flash banner for users who do not have the plug-in.

How do I get my banner on someone else's site?

✔ To get more traffic flowing to your site, you may want to use a banner to advertise your site on other Web pages. Some companies have banners informing visitors that they are accepting ads. Other companies have a link to information about advertising. You can also contact the Webmaster and ask for information. Usually, the Webmaster's e-mail link is listed at the bottom of a company's home page. Also, depending on the traffic flow on your site, you may want to open your site up to banner advertising from other companies.

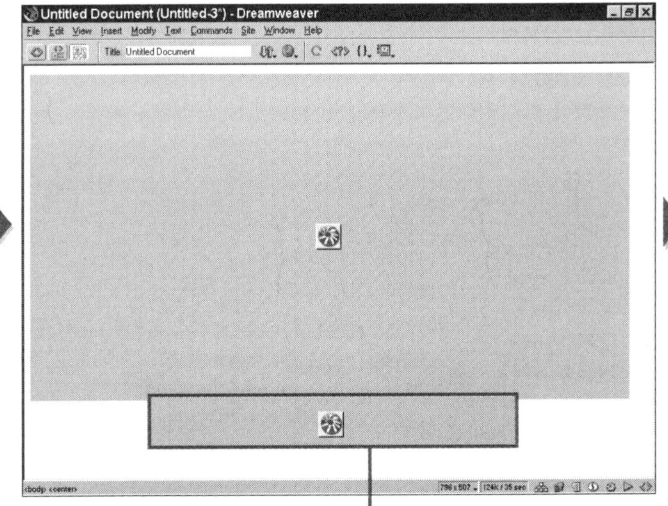

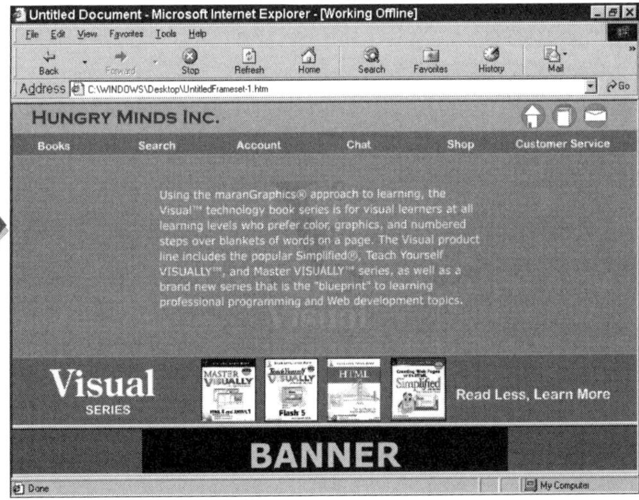

ADD A FLASH BANNER TO YOUR WEB PAGE

8 In Dreamweaver, open the page you wish to incorporate your banner ad.

9 Place your Flash banner ad in the desired location on the page.

Note: See Chapter 30 to learn how to add Flash movies to your page in Dreamweaver.

10 Preview the page in an external browser.

Note: See Chapter 4 to learn about previewing Web pages in a browser.

CREATE A LINK WITH THE GET URL ACTION

You can call an external file, address, or script that resides outside your Flash movie using the `getURL` action. (See Chapter 28 to learn more about assigning actions in Flash.) Because of the incorporation of Flash's ability to store variable values with the release of Flash 4, Flash is not considered the closed system it once was. Incorporation of external functions in coordination with Flash ActionScripting enables a developer the freedom of communicating outside the Flash movie. Before this functionality was incorporated (Flash Versions 1 through 3), Flash was considered a relatively closed system, meaning any interaction and functionality was accomplished within Flash only. The `getURL` action plays a key factor in Flash's ability to communicate with external files and functions.

The concepts of using the action are in direct relation to the way you would call the desired file, address, or script in HTML. Relative (../directory/file) and absolute addressing (http://www.yoursite.com) of files, as well as some of the general syntax of calling script functions remains consistent between HTML and Flash. In addition, each use of the `getURL` action provides the option to specify the window or frame you target and how variables are sent.

CREATE A LINK WITH THE GET URL ACTION

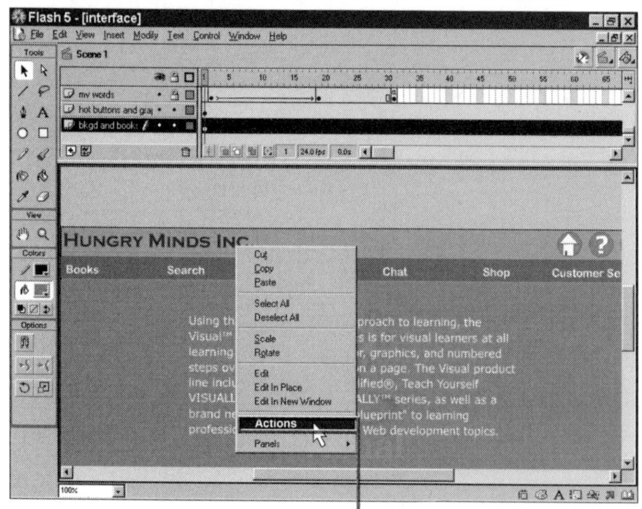

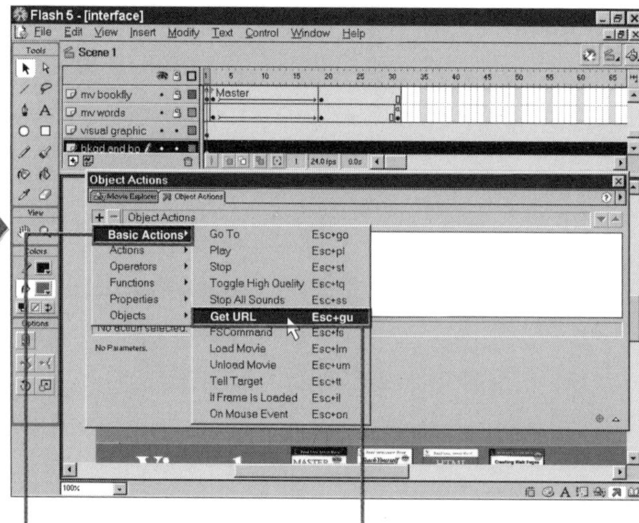

1 Convert the desired text or graphic you wish to link to a button symbol.

Note: See Chapter 22 to learn how to convert to a symbol.

■ In this example, text is converted into a button.

2 Open the Object Actions panel by right-clicking the button created in step 1 and then clicking Actions.

3 Click Basic Actions to add the `Get URL` action to the button.

4 Click Get URL to assign the action to the button.

What are other uses for the `getURL` action?

✔ Do not let its name deceive you; `getURL` can get, or call, many things other than a URL, such as JavaScripts, HTML documents that reside locally, other Flash movies, and files offered to visitors for download. `getURL` can also send and receive variables with the use of the `GET` and `POST` methods.

How can you use `getURL` to load a local file in a different directory?

✔ If you want to load local files that reside in a directory on the same level as the Flash movie, type **./directory name/filename.html** in the URL field. To go up a level to retrieve a local file, type **./../directoryname/ filename.html** in the URL field. This line tells Flash to go up a directory level and to look for the file in the specific directory.

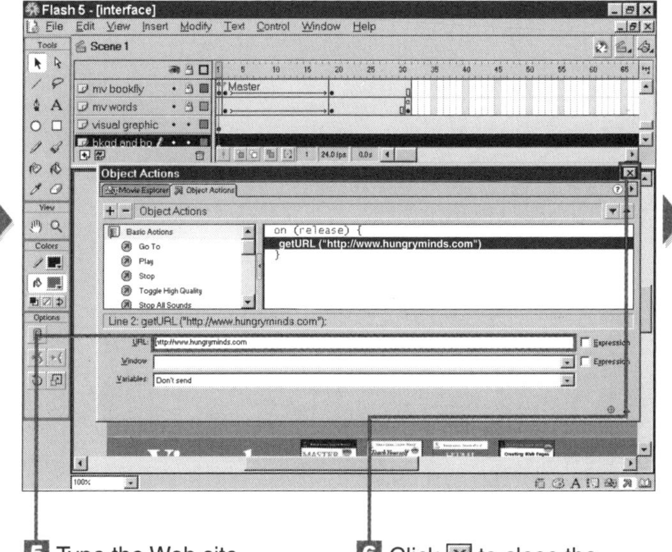

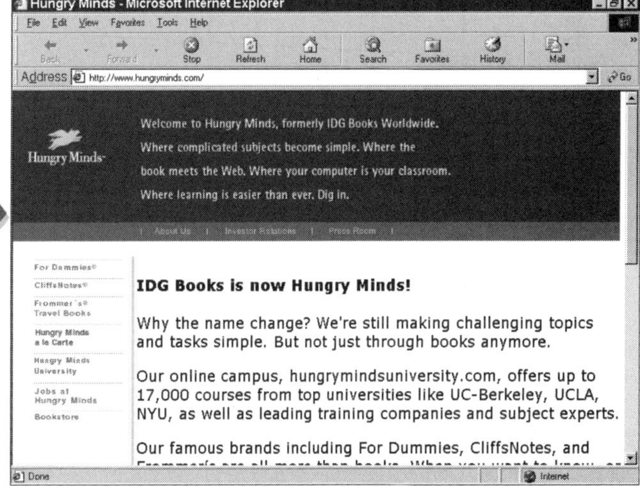

5 Type the Web site address or HTML page you want to open.

■ To open an HTML document or other type of document in the same directory as the current Web page, type **./filename.html**.

6 Click ☒ to close the Object Actions panel.

■ The button now loads the assigned URL you added in step 5 when the user clicks the button.

CALL A SERVER-SIDE SCRIPT

You can call server-side scripts written in languages such as ASP, PHP, or Java from your Flash movie to offer advanced interactivity. With server-side scripts, you can allow users to utilize scripts that reside on the server from the Flash interface that they are viewing in their browser window. The ability to call other scripts from the Web server where your site is published adds interactivity between your site and your visitor.

Server-side scripts perform a variety of tasks, including searching a database, entering user records to create a profile, editing user records to change the user profile, or changing the user's logon and password.

For example, a Flash chat application can be driven with a PHP script that provides the functionality for the Flash interface the user interacts with. Calling server-side scripts can be accomplished by attaching the `Loadvariables` action to a Submit button in a Flash form.

CALL A SERVER-SIDE SCRIPT

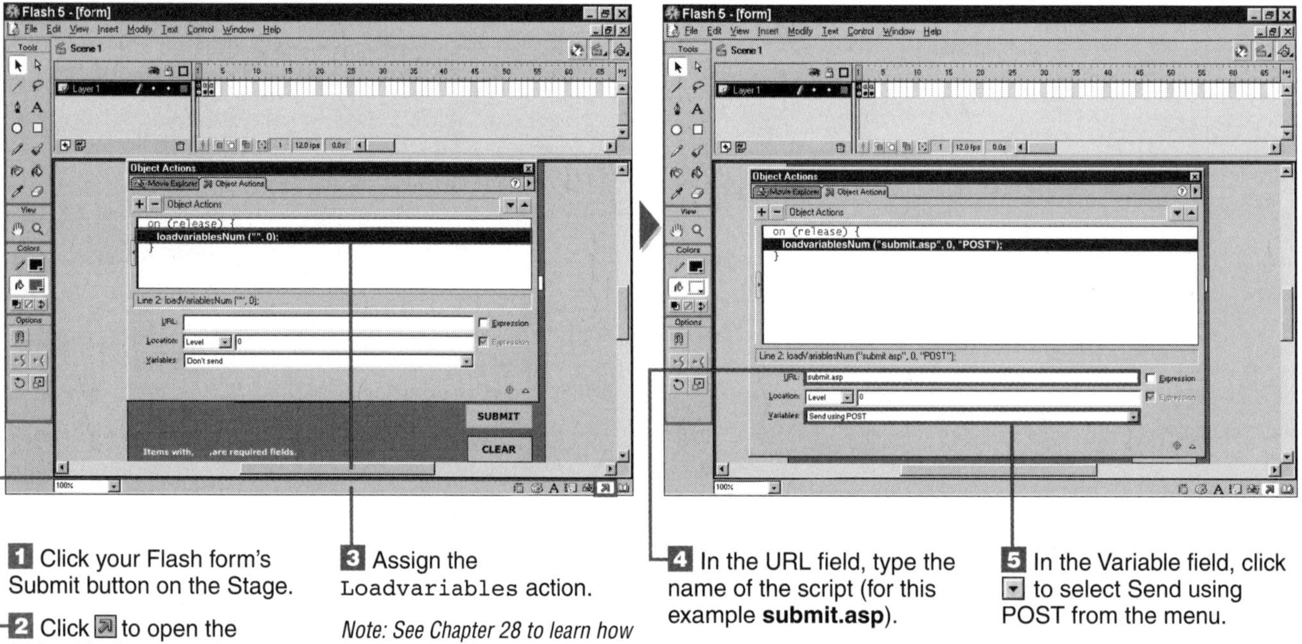

1 Click your Flash form's Submit button on the Stage.

2 Click [icon] to open the Object Actions panel.

3 Assign the `Loadvariables` action.

Note: See Chapter 28 to learn how to add actions.

4 In the URL field, type the name of the script (for this example **submit.asp**).

5 In the Variable field, click [icon] to select Send using POST from the menu.

How do I make an acceptance message?

✔ An acceptance message is simply a text box you place in one of your movie frames to validate the execution of your script. Generally a validation occurs in the server-side script after the user submits the entered information. This validation should check if all required fields are entered. Following validation, the script should then send a value back to the Flash movie that directs the movie to a frame notifying the user that the information was received successfully or not.

Why are my ASP scripts not executing?

✔ To test a call to an ASP page, you must have Internet Information Server (IIS) or Personal Web Server (PWS). IIS servers are used to host and read ASP pages. PWS is a program that resides on your local computer for testing before uploading your files to the IIS server hosting your site. If you are running your files from an IIS server or PWS and still have problems, make sure the Flash and ASP pages are in the correct Web directory. It is also possible that you have an error in your ASP or script code. For more information about Active Server Pages, refer to *Active Server Pages 3.0: Your visual blueprint for developing interactive Web sites* (Hungry Minds, Inc., 2000).

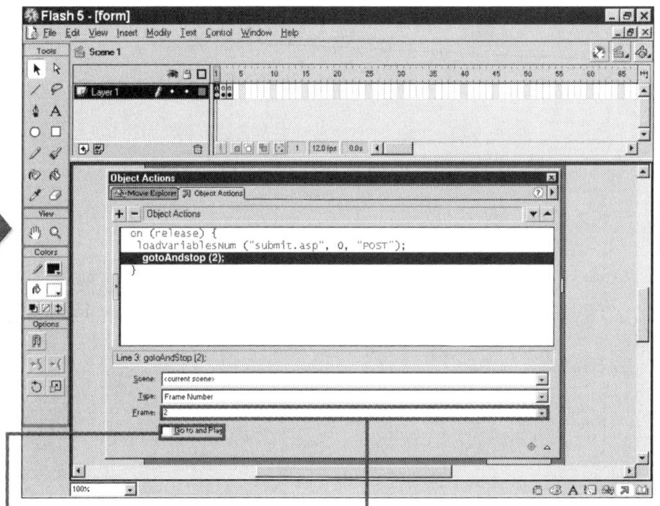

6 Add a Go To action following the `Load Variables` action assigned in step 3.

7 Click to uncheck the Go to and Play check box (☑ changes to ☐).

8 In the Frame field, type the Frame number of your acceptance message.

■ An acceptance message tells the user that the form was successfully submitted after the information is processed by the server-side script.

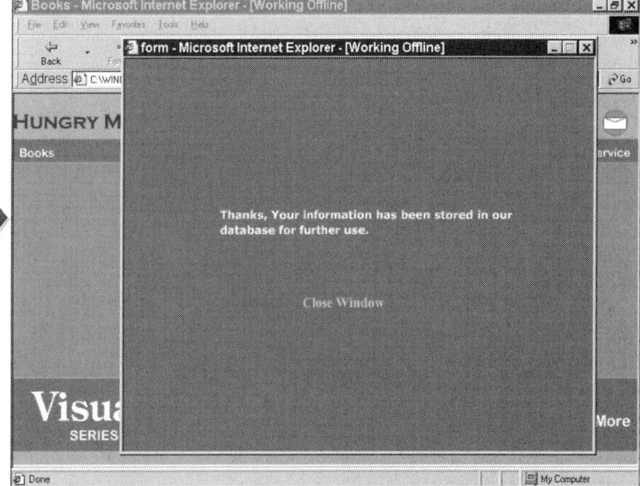

■ You can now publish and test your movie calling the script.

Note: Please refer to Chapter 30 for more information on publishing your movies.

■ When a user clicks the Submit button, submit.asp loads and the user is directed to the acceptance message.

CONTROL WINDOWS WITH GET URL OPTIONS

You can target different window areas when redirecting a visitor to another Web site or displaying new content. You can also add links to your Flash interface using the getURL action and control what the user sees when they follow the link. The getURL action offers four different options for controlling the window type. These four options are _self, _top, _blank, and _parent. Each option targets a different window reference for loading new content.

If your HTML pages reside in multiple frames, window options are very important. Choosing _top targets the top-level frame of the current window for the content to be loaded into. _Parent targets the parent of the current frame for the new content to be loaded into.

If you are not using frames, the only two you have to worry about are _blank and _self. When you specify _self, you are telling the new content to be loaded into the current frame of the Flash movie. When you use _blank, a new browser window opens for the new content.

You can use the getURL window options to load a Flash interface into the top-level frame of the Web page once your Intro animation has finished playing or the Skip Intro button has been clicked.

CONTROL WINDOWS WITH GET URL OPTIONS

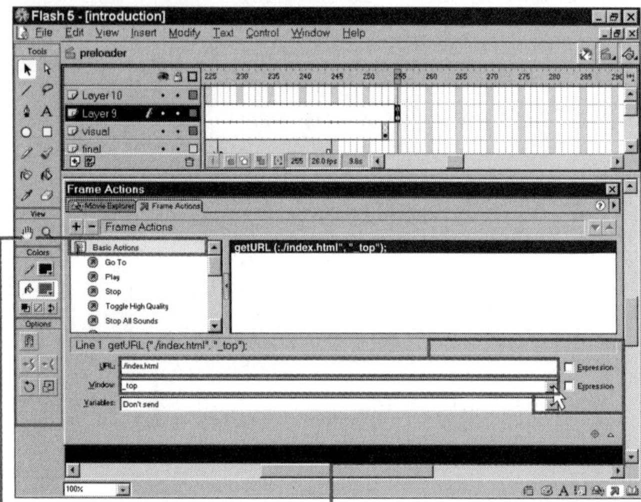

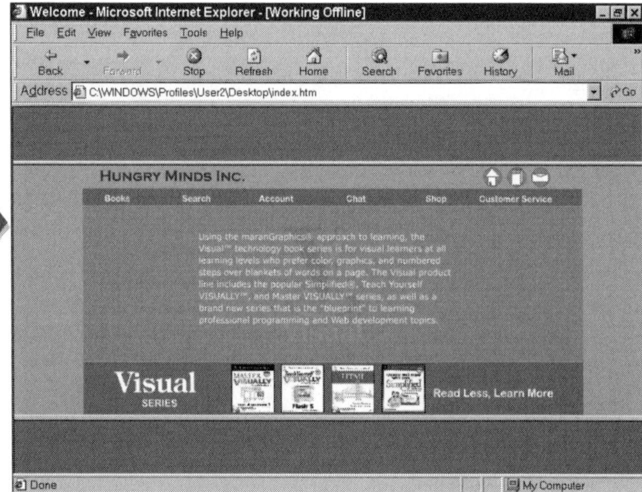

1 Open your Intro movie Flash file (.fla).

2 Double-click the last frame to open the Frame Actions panel.

3 Click Basic Actions to add the Get URL action to the button.

4 Click Get URL to assign the action to the button.

5 In URL field, type the name of the page that contains the interface movie.

6 Click ▾ to select _top in the Window field.

_TOP

■ The URL loads into the full document window.

Can I set window features when I choose _blank to open the URL in its own window?

✔ Yes. You can use a JavaScript function to control the size and position of a new window as it appears with the `_blank` tag. JavaScript functions can set the properties of features such as scrollbars, toolbars, the status bar, and others as well. You can learn how to use a JavaScript function in the section "Control Windows with JavaScript" later in this chapter.

Why does the content load in the same manner when I target _top and _parent?

✔ You will not see a difference in the way the two targeting mechanisms work unless you are using nested frames. A *nested* frame is one that resides within a frame held in a parent frameset. Targeting using `_top` opens the link in the current browser window on top of the current frameset. In other words, it does not load the targeted page in the current frame. Targeting using `_parent` opens the desired link in the current browser window, using the current frameset. It uses the frameset, the file that lays out the individual frames, not the current frame.

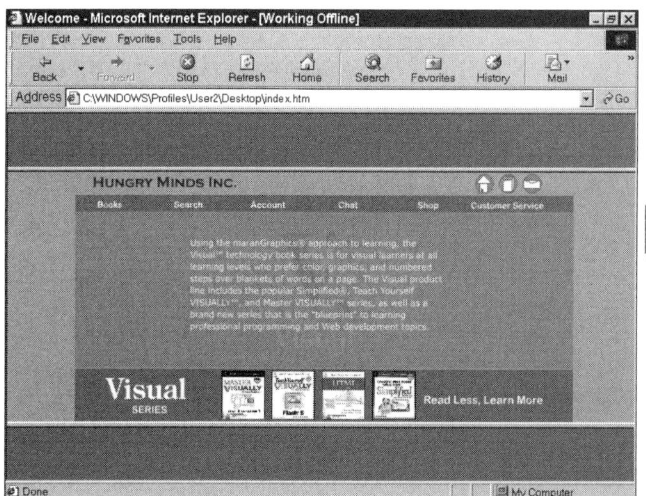

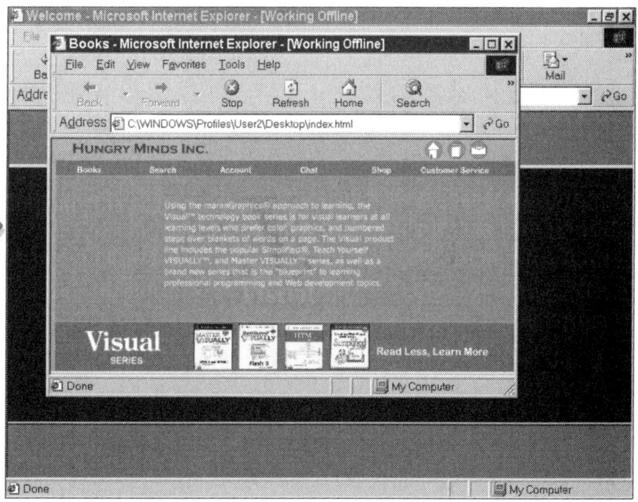

_SELF

■ The Flash interface loads into the same frame it was called from by the intro movie if you use the `_self` tag in step 6.

Note: Using the `_parent` tag would produce a result identical to the `_self` tag because the middle frame is considered to be the parent window in this example.

_BLANK

■ To open the link in a new window, use the `_blank` tag in step 6.

CONTROL WINDOWS WITH JAVASCRIPT

JavaScript is a client-side scripting language that enables users to control virtually any aspect or feature of the browser window. You can use JavaScript to specify the size and properties of new open windows in your Flash movie. Whether it is a pop-up window, a page displaying another Flash movie, or a link to another site, you nay need to open a new browser window. You can use JavaScript code that, when called, automatically opens a new window according to the size and display properties that you choose in advance. You can even control whether the new window has browser features such as scroll bars, a toolbar, and a status bar.

JavaScript can launch a URL in a new window, where you can set width and height as well as position. In addition, features such as scrollbars, toolbars, and the status bar can be turned on or off.

CONTROL WINDOWS WITH JAVASCRIPT

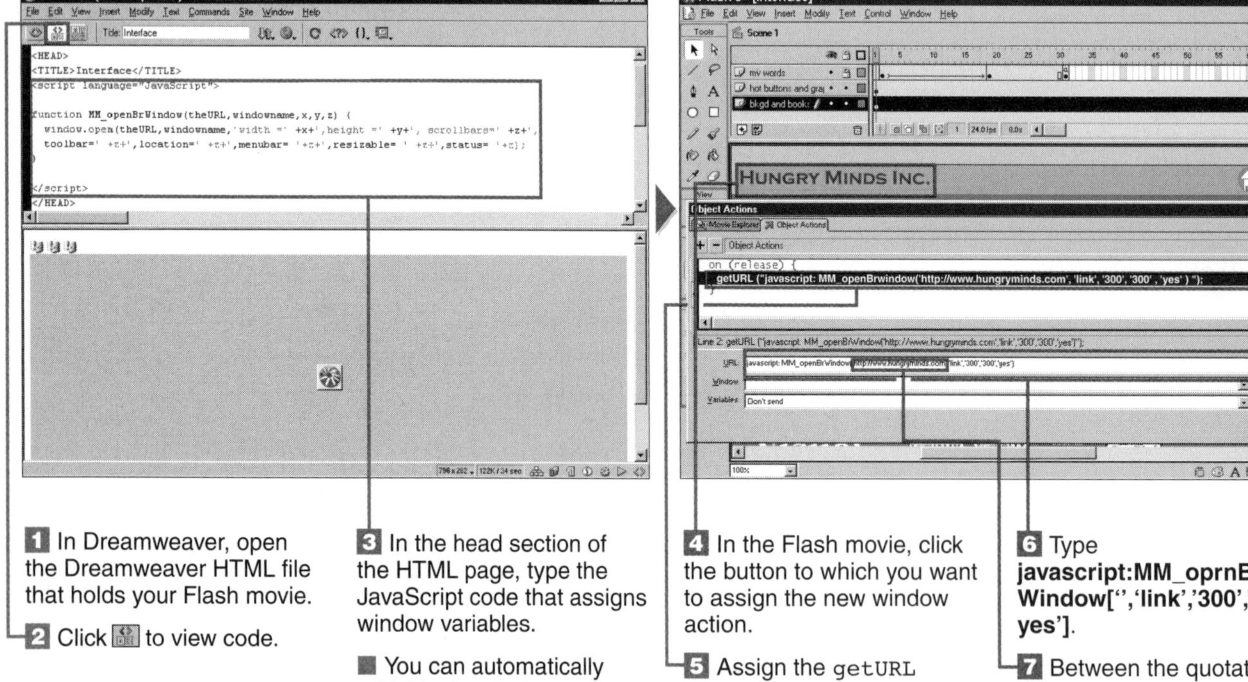

1 In Dreamweaver, open the Dreamweaver HTML file that holds your Flash movie.

2 Click [icon] to view code.

3 In the head section of the HTML page, type the JavaScript code that assigns window variables.

■ You can automatically add this JavaScript code by applying the Open Browser Window behavior to the Flash movie. See Chapter 13 for details.

4 In the Flash movie, click the button to which you want to assign the new window action.

5 Assign the `getURL` action.

Note: See Chapter 28 to learn how to add actions.

6 Type **javascript:MM_oprnBr Window['','link','300','300','yes']**.

7 Between the quotation marks, type the URL you wish to open.

How can I adjust the JavaScript variables to resize my windows?

✔ In step 3 of the example below, variables `x`, `y`, and `z` control the window's size and the appearance of interface controls, such as scroll bars. When you call the function and assign the `getURL` action, you can assign different values to the variables in the code to change the appearance of the opening window. The `x` variable controls the height of the window, and the `y` variable controls the width. Both dimensions are measured in pixels. The `z` variable controls the presence of interface controls, such as the menu bar, toolbar, and scrollbars. You must assign a `yes` or `no` value for `z`. `yes` includes the window's extra features, and `no` hides them, as shown in the fourth figure below.

Can I close a window using JavaScript?

✔ Yes. Closing a window is similar to opening a window. To close a window, use JavaScript's `window.close( )` function. You can call this, and any other JavaScript function, from the `getURL` button action in Flash.

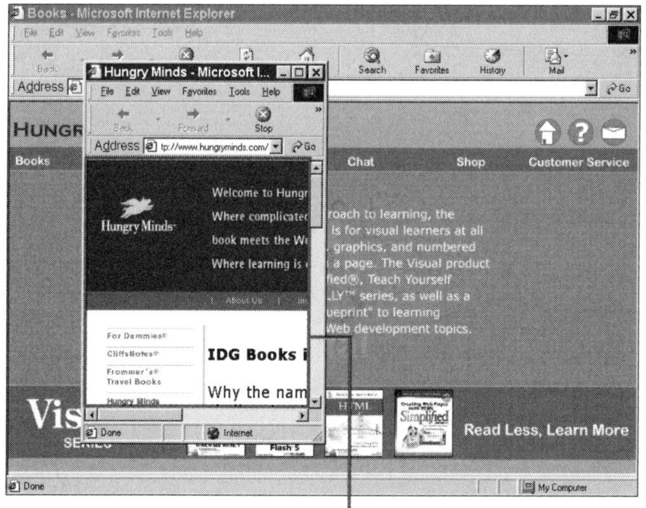

8 Click the button to which you assigned the action.

■ The target URL opens in a window sized according to the JavaScript code you assigned.

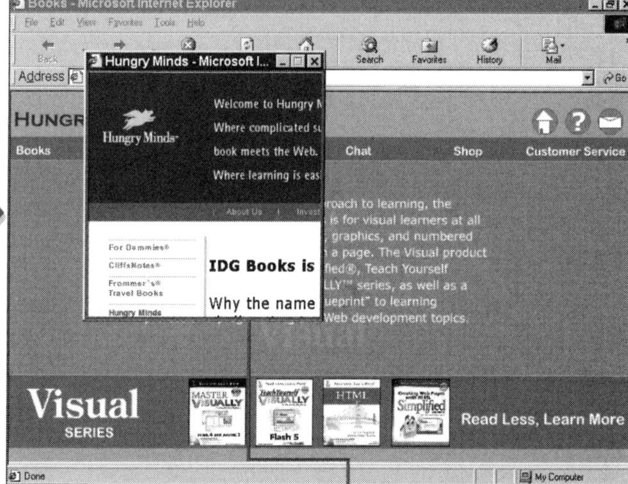

■ You can experiment with the variables in step 3 to reshape and resize the window.

■ You can change the `z` value from `yes` to `no` to hide the new window's scrollbars, toolbars, and main menu.

MAKE YOUR FILES DOWNLOADABLE

You can enable users to download files from your Flash interface. You may have files that you want to share with the general public. Downloading files from Web sites is quite common. For example, many software companies have demos of their programs that you can download from their Web sites and try for free.

If you have a product that you can provide electronic information about, whether it is software demos, house blueprints, or book excerpts, it may be a good idea to offer a sample to your visitors. If one out of every ten visitors checks out your sample, likes it, and buys it, you have already increased sales 10 percent.

Virtually any file type unrecognized as a default for the browser gives the user the option to either open the file from the current location or save it to disk before opening when the user clicks on an associated link. However, keep in mind that some files, such as Acrobat PDFs or Microsoft Office formats open within the browser if the browser you are using is equipped with the appropriate add-in or plug-in.

MAKE YOUR FILES DOWNLOADABLE

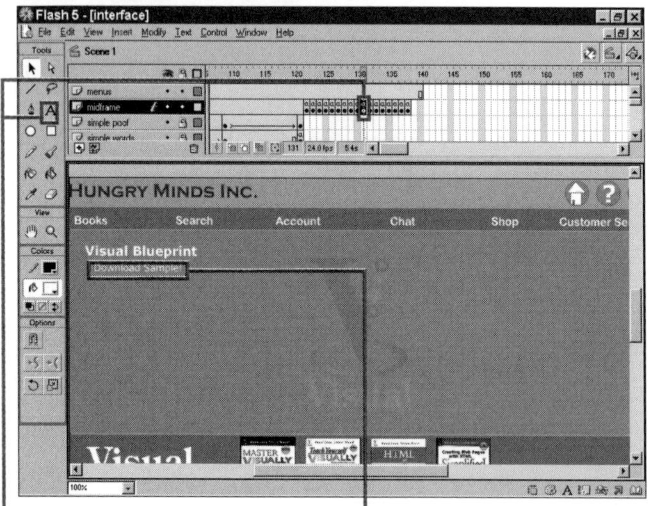

1 Open a new or existing Flash movie.

2 Click the frame that will contain the Download button.

3 Click A.

4 Add a text box to the Stage.

5 Type a name for the Download button in the text box.

6 Select the text box and convert it into a button symbol.

Note: See Chapter 22 for more about symbols.

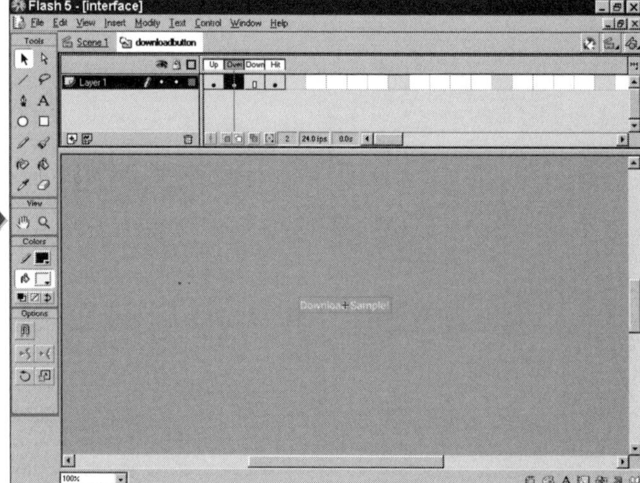

■ You can edit the button's features, if desired. In this example, the button changes text color when the mouse rolls over it.

Can I make other file types available for download?

✔ Yes. You can make almost any file type downloadable from your site. Some of the files that you can make downloadable are Acrobat Reader (PDF) files, executable (EXE) files, Microsoft Word (DOC) files, Text (TXT) files, and many other types. Due to the nature of the `getURL` action, some files do not download, but execute when entering them into the `getURL` command line. If you enter a JavaScript (.js extension) file, the script executes rather than downloads. Also, if you enter an HTML (.html or .htm extension) document, the HTML document loads into the browser window rather than downloads as a file.

Are there any risks to my visitors or myself with file downloads?

✔ There are no real threats to making files downloadable from your site. One of the files that you make available for download could be infected by a virus, which would make everyone who downloads it from your site very unhappy. But the chances of that happening are pretty slim if you perform frequent maintenance on your site and regularly run a virus check on your files.

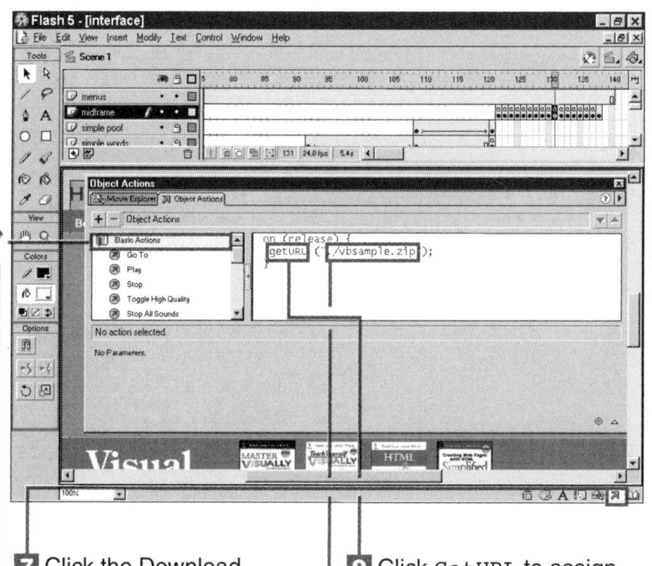

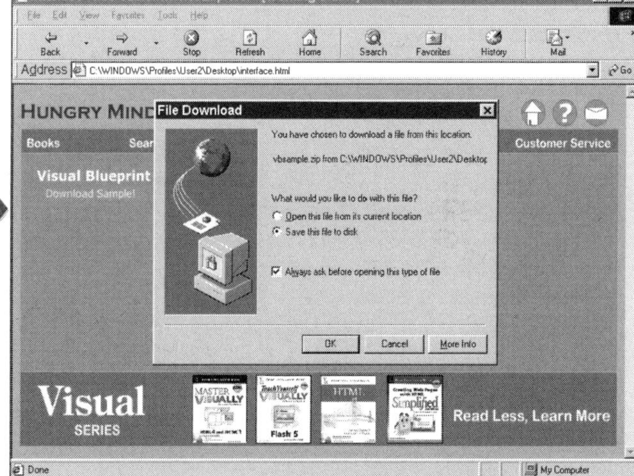

7 Click the Download button you just created, then click [icon] to open the Object Actions panel.

Note: See Chapter 28 to learn more using the Object Actions panel.

8 Click Basic Actions to add a button action.

9 Click `GetURL` to assign the action to the button.

10 Type the path of file to be downloaded.

11 Publish and test your movie in a browser to verify the file is correctly linked.

Note: See Chapter 30 to learn more about publishing your movie.

■ When you click the button in a browser, a Download dialog box appears, giving the user the option to either open the file from its current location or save the file to a local location.

COMPRESS WEB SITE GRAPHICS

You can reduce the downloading time that your site requires by editing your graphics. Large, high-quality graphics can really add to your file size and to the time it takes to download your site. By using a graphical editing program, you can give up resolution without giving up quality, and resize graphics to a common denominator. For example, why import an image measuring 300 x 300 if you are going to scale it down 25 percent when you place it on the Flash Stage?

Cover graphic appears when the cover is clicked and displayed in the middle of interface. Using the graphic editor, the JPEG files are resized to the largest setting needed for the movie, then imported. Each JPEG file takes up about 8K. In GIF format, the size doubles to 17K. As a Web designer, you need to be aware of what file type your images are saved as, because this is another way to optimize your graphics. This task shows how to optimize a JPEG graphic.

COMPRESS WEB SITE GRAPHICS

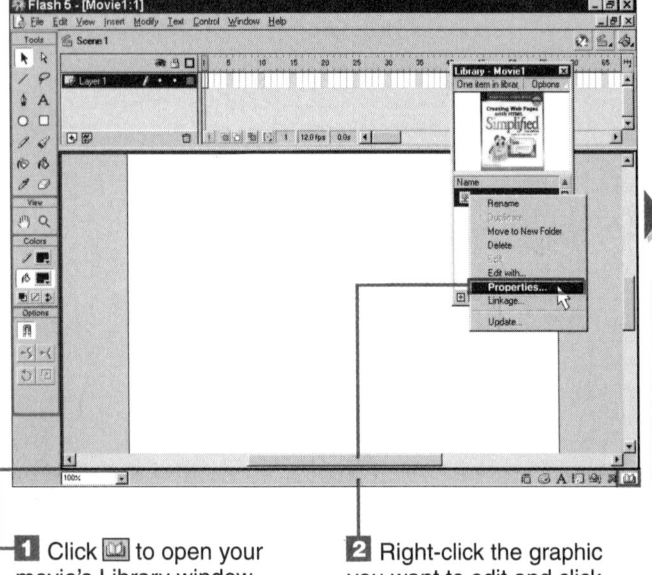

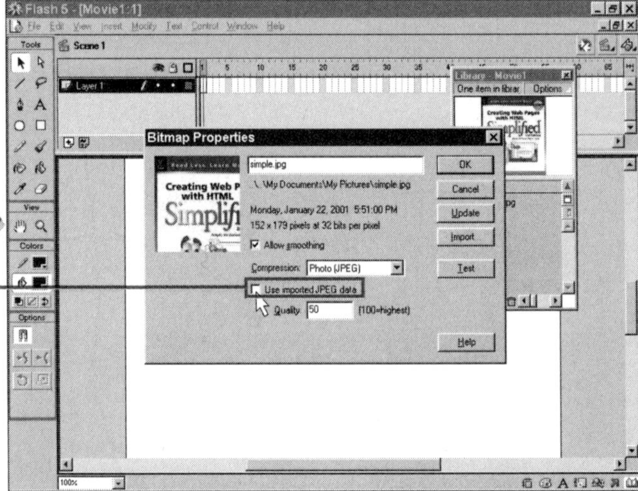

1 Click [icon] to open your movie's Library window.

Note: See Chapter 22 to learn how to use the Library.

2 Right-click the graphic you want to edit and click Properties.

■ Flash opens the Bitmap Properties dialog box.

■ This example uses a JPEG graphic.

3 Click to uncheck the Use imported JPEG data check box (☑ changes to ☐).

What other graphics can be used in Flash?

✔ Flash supports a wide variety of image types. GIF and JPEG are some of the more commonly used image types. Bitmaps are also another popular image type. Some other types of images that Flash is able to import are Adobe Illustrator files, TIFF files, PICT images, PNG images, and Adobe Photoshop images.

How can I save an image in Flash as something other than a Flash movie?

✔ Flash is a wonderful application that can not only be used to create animations for the Web, but can be used as a graphical tool as well. Some people prefer to create images in Flash and save them as image files rather than Flash movies so they can use the images elsewhere. To do this you need to export the image from Flash into another file format. You can learn how to use Flash's image export feature in Chapter 30.

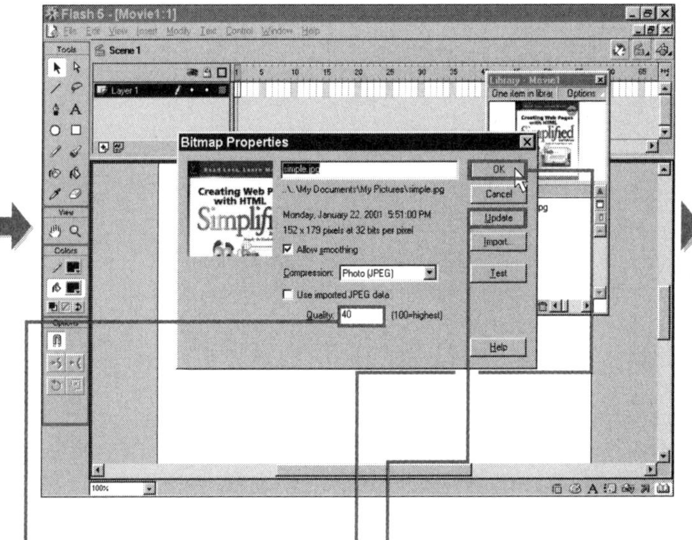

4 Type a value in the Quality field.

■ This value refers to the amount of compression. The lower the number, the more compression and the lower the quality and size.

5 Click Update.

■ Flash optimizes the graphic and displays information at the bottom of the Properties dialog box about the compression size.

6 Click OK to close the dialog box.

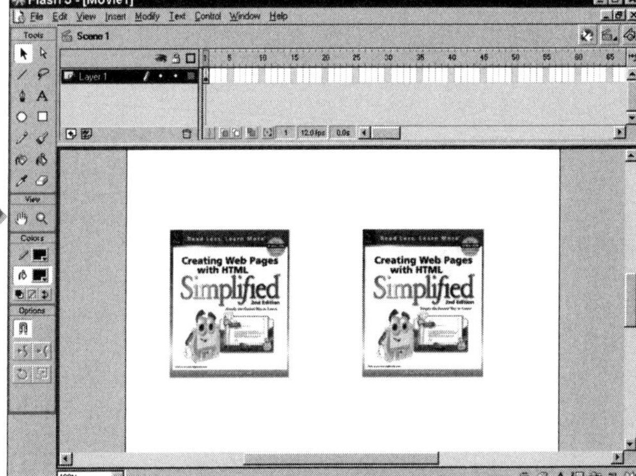

■ Two graphic images appear side by side here with little noticeable difference in quality.

■ The right image is optimized with a quality value of 40. The left image is not optimized.

■ Compression has reduced the file size of the SWF in this example from 24.5K to 18.7K.

REDUCE DOWNLOAD TIME FOR A LARGE MOVIE

You can optimize your movies by breaking up a large Flash movie into more manageable chunks. Instead of one big movie, you can create multiple smaller movies that load upon a visitor's request. This can cut down on file size and download time.

For example, there is no reason to keep your Web site visitors waiting for the chat portion of the site's Flash interface movie to load when all they want to do is buy a book. By making the chat feature a separate movie and only loading it when a visitor requests it from the chat menu, you can cut back on the time a user has to wait for the entire interface to load.

You do not lose any functionality by breaking up a large movie. However, do not make the mistake of allowing a smaller movie segment to become an additional big movie, too. When a visitor does request a smaller movie, you can choose to make it load into your main movie's interface or have it appear in a new window.

REDUCE DOWNLOAD TIME FOR A LARGE MOVIE

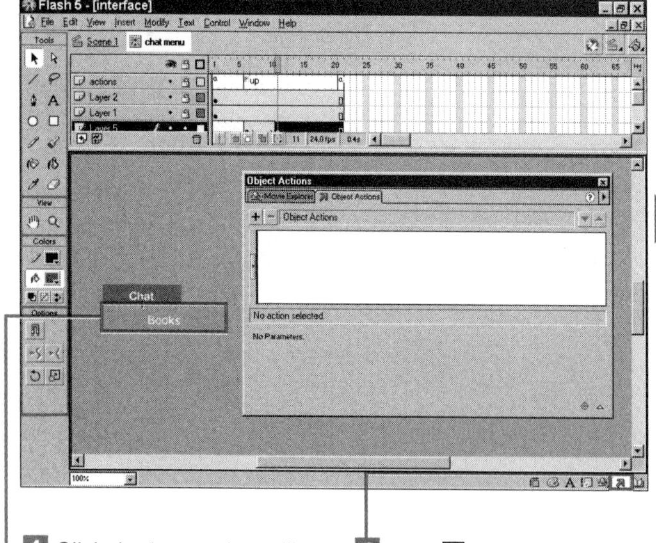

1 Click the button that will call the separate Flash movie.

2 Click [icon] to open the Object Actions panel.

Note: See Chapter 28 to learn how to add actions.

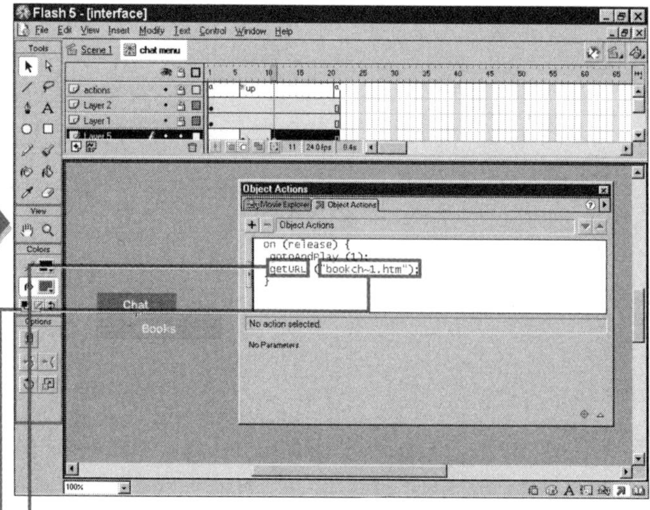

3 Assign the `GetURL` action by double-clicking Get URL from the Basic Actions list in the Object Actions panel.

4 In the URL field, type the path of the file you want to open in a new window.

■ In this example, a `gotoAndPlay(1)` button action was added to close the drop-down menu.

Can I control the properties of the new window opened?

✔ Yes. By using JavaScript, you can control many aspects of the new window containing the smaller Flash movie. JavaScript enables you to specify the size, position, and features included on the new window. Greater detail on using JavaScript to control windows is discussed in "Control Windows with JavaScript," earlier in this chapter.

Can I load movie clips in external files to reduce file size for use with a thumbnail gallery?

✔ Yes. You can use optimized small pictures for a thumbnail gallery and store the full-size pictures as separate clips. This can save your visitors a lot of download time. With this technique visitors can load only the pictures they want to see. Use this optimizing technique to open pictures in a new window displaying the full-sized, high-quality image. You do not have to save your full-size images as movie clips; they can be regular HTML files.

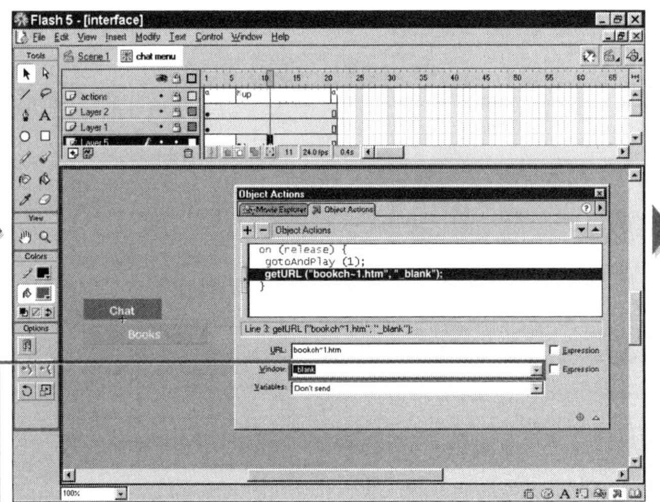

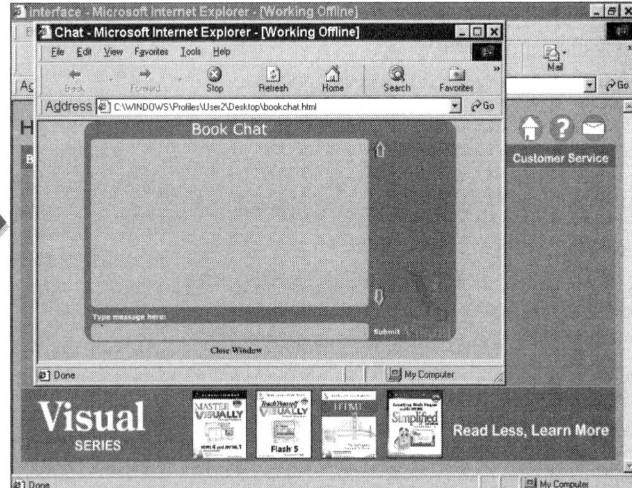

5 Type _**blank** in the Window field to open the link in a new window.

■ You can use JavaScript to open the file in a new window of desired size.

■ After publishing and testing this example, the targeted file is loaded into a new window separate from the interface file when the user clicks the Books button.

FLAG A USER ERROR

You can use the JavaScript `alert()` method to quickly inform your user of errors. The `alert()` method from Flash is especially easy because it requires only one line of code and no scripting in the actual HTML document.

Although `alert()` is an easy tool to use, it is not a good idea to employ it too often. If it is overused it can be very disruptive to the flow of your Web site.

The `alert()` method produces a small window with a statement or error message flag that you designate in advance and an OK button for the user to accept. When the alert window is activated, all other windows become inactive and nothing can be done until the user clicks OK.

In this example, you can use the `alert()` method to inform users that they cannot use the Flash chat without first logging on to the Web server.

FLAG A USER ERROR

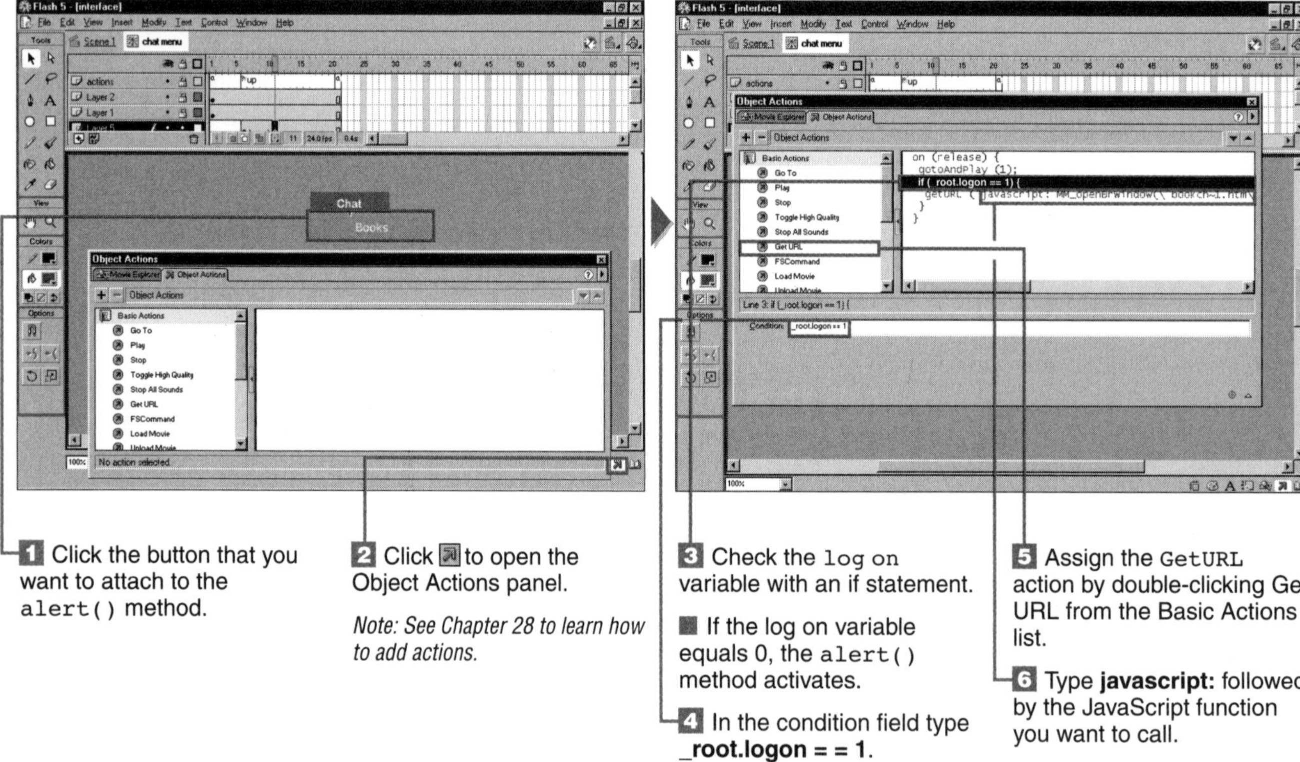

1 Click the button that you want to attach to the `alert()` method.

2 Click [icon] to open the Object Actions panel.

Note: See Chapter 28 to learn how to add actions.

3 Check the `log on` variable with an if statement.

■ If the log on variable equals 0, the `alert()` method activates.

4 In the condition field type **_root.logon = = 1**.

5 Assign the `GetURL` action by double-clicking Get URL from the Basic Actions list.

6 Type **javascript:** followed by the JavaScript function you want to call.

What can I use in place of an alert?

✔ There are a couple of alternate solutions other than using the `alert()` method. You can re-create the alert window by opening a new window using an `open window` script. You would need to create a simple Web page containing the error information you want to relay to your users and display it in the new window. Another possible solution for using the `alert()` method is to redirect your users to a frame in your Flash movie containing the information you want your user to know.

Where would be a good place to use the `alert()` method?

✔ There are no defined applications for this method. It is used frequently to inform users that they are entering or leaving a secure Internet site. Alert boxes are commonly used for error messages, which point out why something is not working. Because you cannot count on your visitors reading everything, an error message flag lets them know what they need to do.

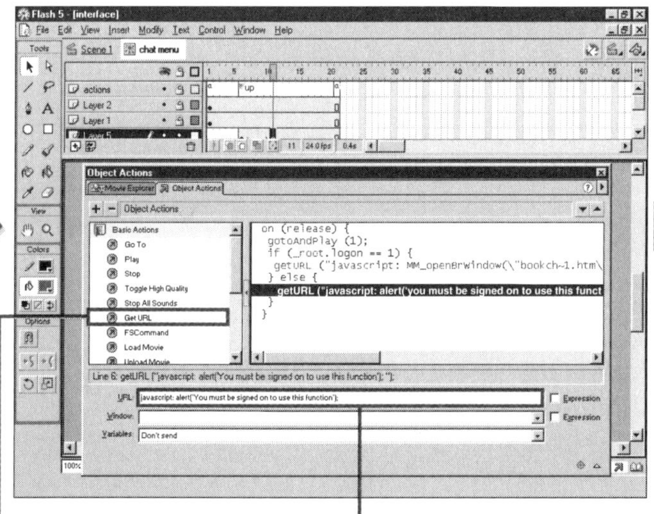

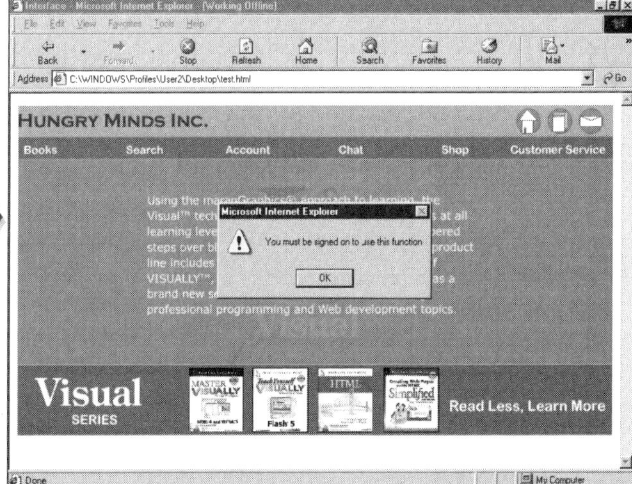

7 Assign the `else` action by double-clicking else.

8 Assign the `GetURL` action by double-clicking Get URL.

9 In URL field type **javascript: alert('You must be signed on to use this function');**.

■ Inside the parenthesis is the statement that is relayed to the user. You can customize this to fit your needs.

10 Click Control in the main menu, and then select Test Movie.

11 Click the Chat and then the Book button without logging in.

■ The alert box is activated as a result of when a user attempts to use the chat feature without signing in.

SECTION IV

34) BUILDING INTERFACE CONTROLS WITH FLASH

Create an Animated Menu 626
Adjust Sound Clip Volume 632
Create an Advanced Preloader 638
Set Property of a Movie Clip 644
Track Cursor Position 648
Create a Window Hierarchy 652

35) ENHANCING INTERACTIVITY IN FLASH

Create a Password Identification Box 656
Park a Movie Clip 660
Emulate an Array 664
Combine Strings Given by a User 668
Send a Form Using a CGI Script 676
Make a Movie Clip Act Like a Button 680

36) CREATING SPECIAL EFFECTS IN FLASH

Create a Gravity Effect 682
Create a Magnifying Glass Effect 686
Create a Dragable Menu 692
Create a Filmstrip Effect 696

ADVANCED FLASH TECHNIQUES

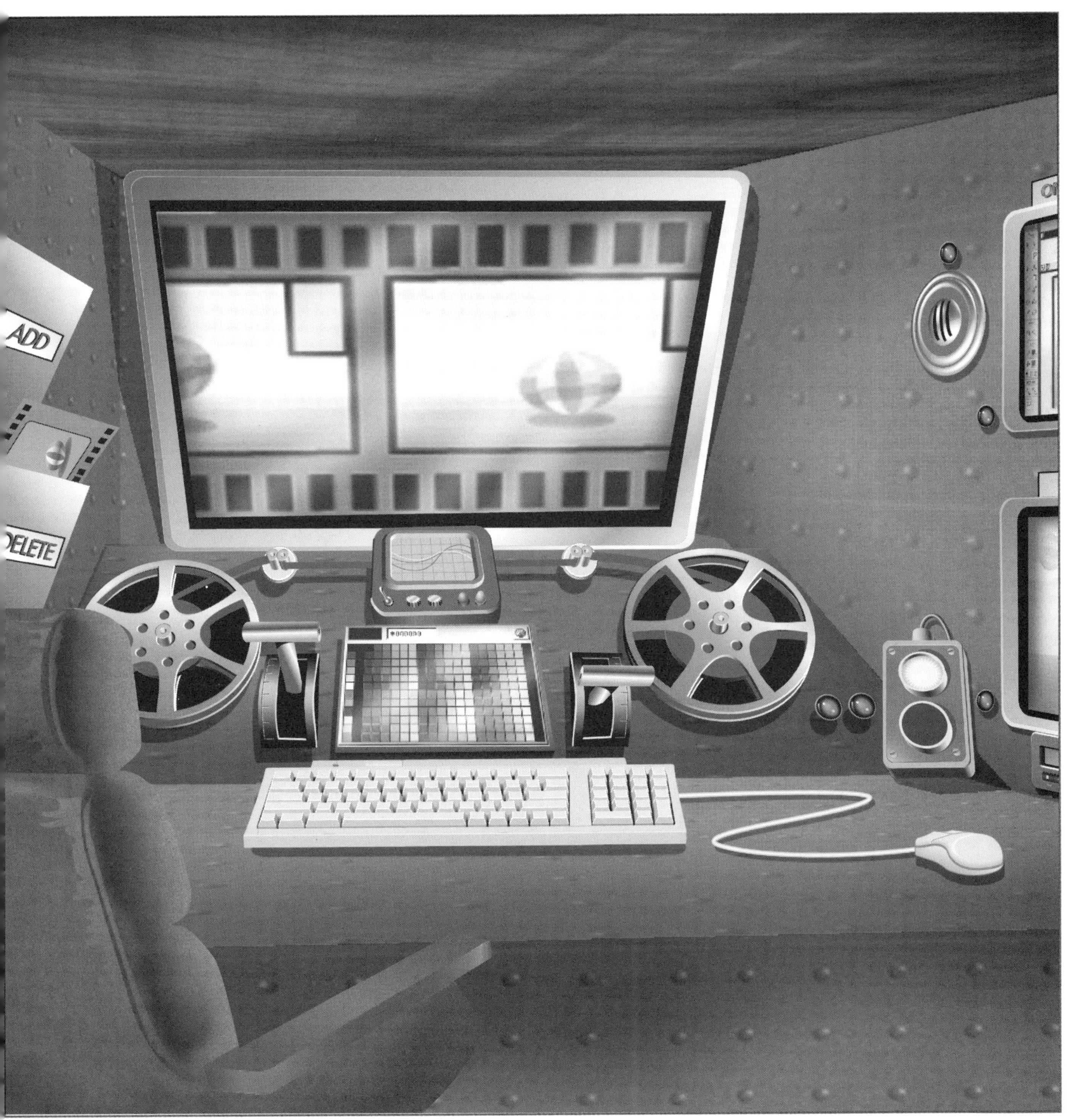

CREATE AN ANIMATED MENU

You can create an animated menu system that animates buttons or links in your Flash project.

Generally, such a menu animates only when the user interacts with the menu and closes when the user is not interacting directly.

You can set the menu up with a timer that tells the menu to close if the user does not return to the menu.

The steps in this section show an animation sequence with multiple stages. The animation presents three buttons in a very direct fashion. Your own animated menu may include buttons that are part of a larger graphic, such as the menu found on some Web sites.

Flash EXE filename:

AnimatedMenu.exe

Flash filenames:

AnimatedMenu.fla

AnimatedMenu.swf

AnimatedMenu.hqx

CREATE AN ANIMATED MENU

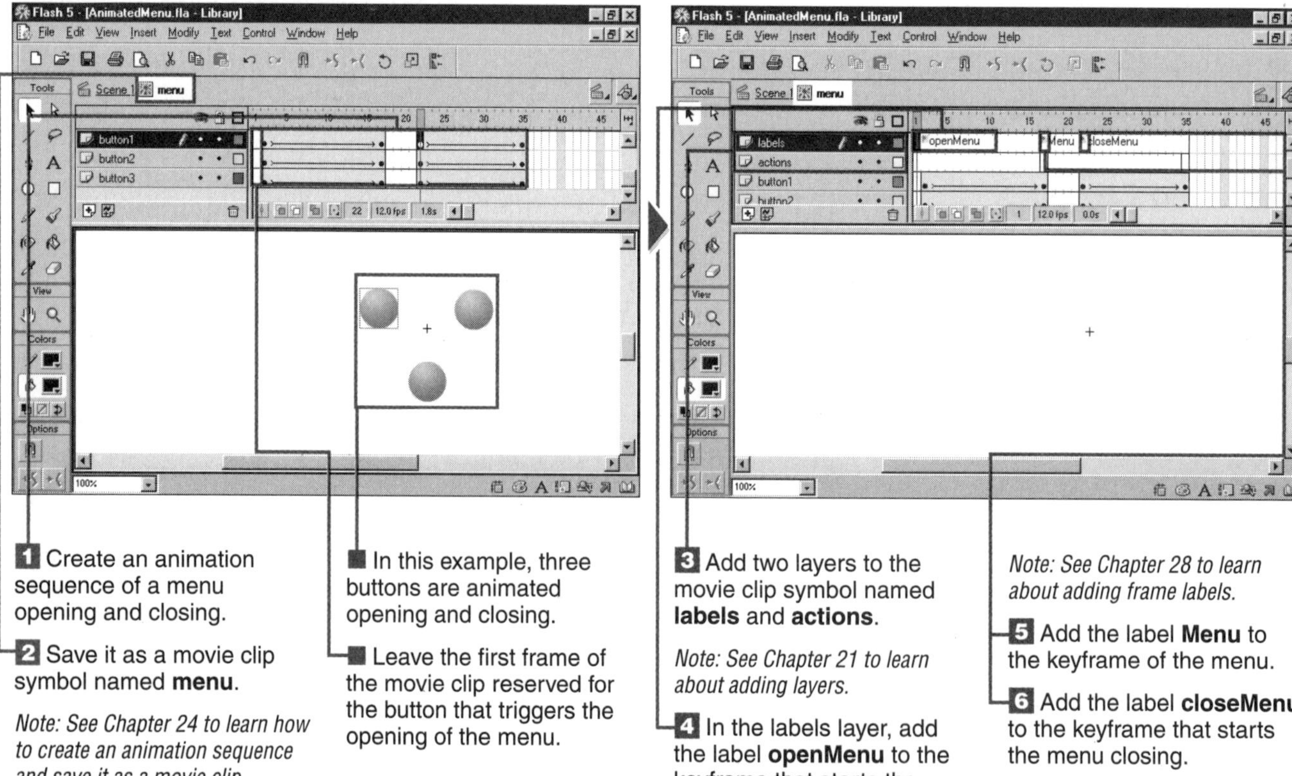

1 Create an animation sequence of a menu opening and closing.

2 Save it as a movie clip symbol named **menu**.

Note: See Chapter 24 to learn how to create an animation sequence and save it as a movie clip.

■ In this example, three buttons are animated opening and closing.

■ Leave the first frame of the movie clip reserved for the button that triggers the opening of the menu.

3 Add two layers to the movie clip symbol named **labels** and **actions**.

Note: See Chapter 21 to learn about adding layers.

4 In the labels layer, add the label **openMenu** to the keyframe that starts the opening of the menu.

Note: See Chapter 28 to learn about adding frame labels.

5 Add the label **Menu** to the keyframe of the menu.

6 Add the label **closeMenu** to the keyframe that starts the menu closing.

Can I use animated graphic symbols as buttons?

✔ Yes. Depending on the complexity of how the buttons are animated onto the Stage, you may wish to animate graphic symbols (identical in appearance to the functional buttons) and swap them with the actual buttons when they are in place.

What makes the menu close?

✔ Each time the Playhead enters frame 2 of the counter timeline, Flash checks to see if the value of n is 5. If n is 5, or 5 seconds have passed where the user has not interacted with any of the menu buttons, the action script tells the menu movieclip to go to and play frame 22:

```
if (n==5) {
  with (_root.menu) {
    gotoAndPlay (22);
  }
}
```

In the example shown in this task, the Playhead in the menu timeline is stopped on frame 15, where the menu has completed opening and the counter movie clip is introduced.

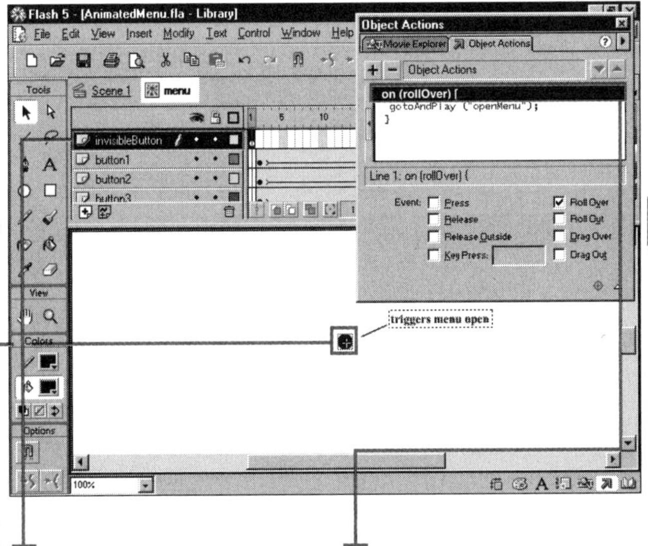

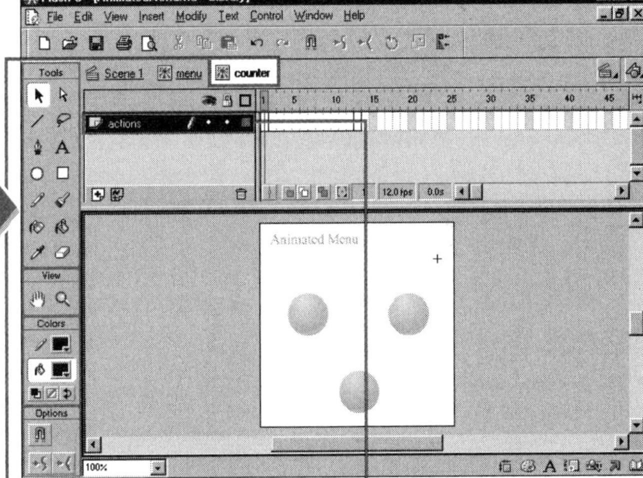

7 Add another layer, named **invisibleButton**.

8 Place a button in the first frame of the new layer that triggers the opening of the menu.

Note: See Chapter 26 to learn more about creating buttons.

9 Add a mouse event action to the button that tells the movie to play when either pressed or hovered over, triggering the opening of the menu.

Note: See Chapter 28 to learn more about adding actions.

10 Create a new movie clip symbol within the menu movie clip and name it **counter**.

Note: See Chapter 22 to learn more about symbols.

11 Add a layer to the counter movie clip and name it **actions**.

Note: See Chapter 21 to learn about adding layers.

CONTINUED

CREATE AN ANIMATED MENU (CONTINUED)

So far in this section, you created an animated sequence for opening and closing the menu, as well as a movie clip named counter, which tells the menu to close when the user ceases interaction with the menu system. Next, you add functionality to your movie clip that tracks the number of seconds the user is not in contact with the menu system.

Because your frame rate is 12 frames per second by default, the counter movie clip needs to add 1 to the value of *n* (or once every second) after the variable checks for the desired timeout limit.

By including timeout functionality for a menu, you ensure that the user can concentrate on the movie clip rather than the opened menu. This is especially important for sites that include multiple menus. You can also tell one menu system to close when another is opened.

CREATE AN ANIMATED MENU (CONTINUED)

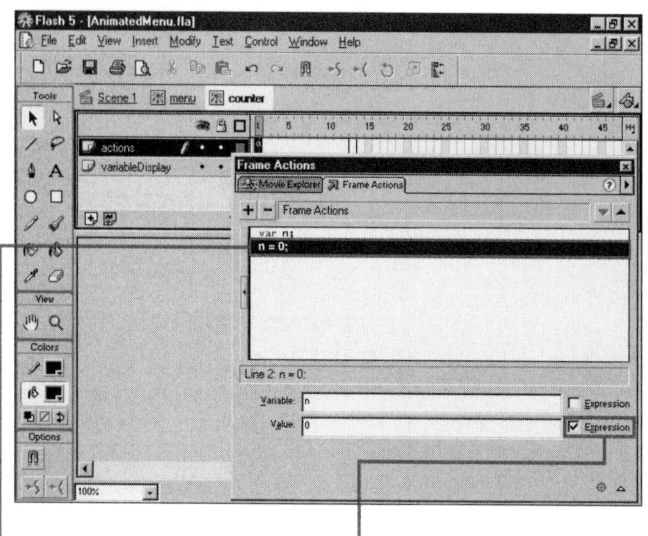

12 Insert the `var` frame action in the first frame of the actions layer, setting a variable entitled `n` to an initial value of 0.

Note: See Chapter 28 and 29 to learn about adding actions in Flash.

■ Leave the Expression check box selected for the Value parameter.

Note: You may need to resize the Frame Actions panel to see the Expression check boxes.

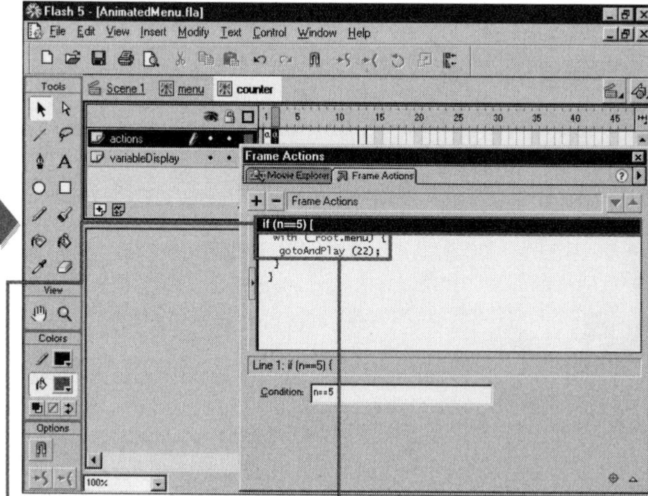

13 In frame 2 of the actions layer, add an `if` action to check if `n` is the number of seconds you want to leave the menu open if the user stops interacting with the menu.

Note: See Chapter 28 and 29 to learn about adding actions in Flash.

■ If the time limit has been reached, instruct the menu to close.

I do not want to use a button to open my menu. How can I trigger a menu to open from the first frame of my animation?

✔ You can use an invisible button in cases where you do not want to display a visible Menu Open button. For example, a developer might stop the Playhead on the first frame of the animation that opens the menu system. An invisible button (a button containing only a `Hit` state) is placed over the top of the first frame of the animation. The button tells the menu to open when the user rolls over the desired area of the graphic.

Can I animate the buttons used in the menu?

✔ Yes. You can have animated rollovers for a button by placing a movie clip in the button's `Over` state. To learn more about animating techniques, see Chapters 24 and 25.

How do I switch Action panel modes?

✔ You can switch back and forth between Normal and Expert modes using the panel's pop-up menu. Click ▸ in the upper-right corner of the Actions panel and then click Expert or Normal mode.

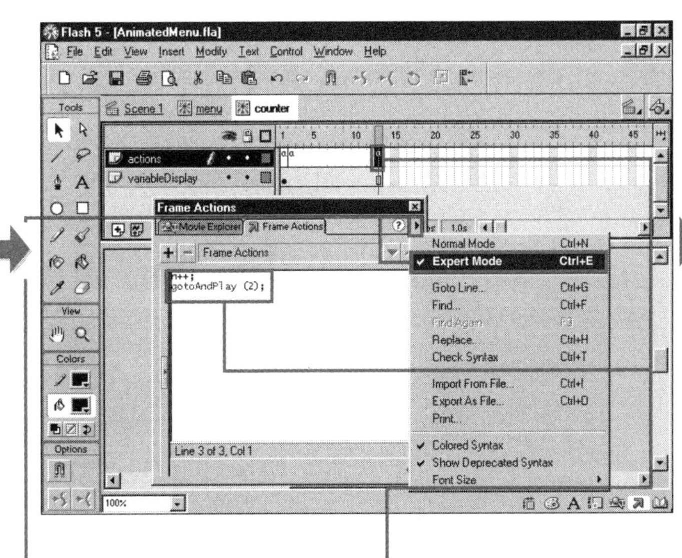

14 Click ▸ and then click Expert mode.

■ The Actions panel switches to Expert mode.

15 Add a frame action `n++` to frame 13 of the actions layer, which first adds 1 to `n` and then sends the playhead back to frame 2, where the variable is checked for timeout again.

Note: See Chapter 28 to learn about adding actions.

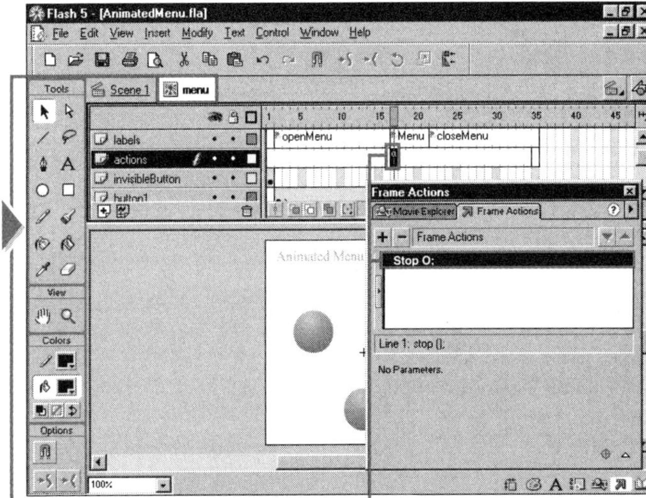

16 Return to the menu movie clip timeline.

Note: See Chapter 22 to learn about switching editing modes.

17 Add a `Stop` frame action in frame 17 where the menu completes the opening animation sequence.

Note: See Chapter 28 to learn about adding actions.

CONTINUED

CREATE AN ANIMATED MENU (CONTINUED)

Finally, you add an object action to the buttons in the animated menu that resets the value of *n* when the user is in contact with them. This ensures that the menu does not close while the user is reading or using the menu system.

This example closes the menu after the user ceases interaction with the menu and only allows the user to open the menu again after the menu is completely closed. You can add advanced functionality, as seen on the Xbox site, that opens the menu if the user rolls over the closing sequence while the menu is in the process of closing. In order to do this with your own menu system, you must add tracking methodology where the menu knows the stage of closing and opens the menu from the specified point and not from the beginning of the opening sequence.

CREATE AN ANIMATED MENU (CONTINUED)

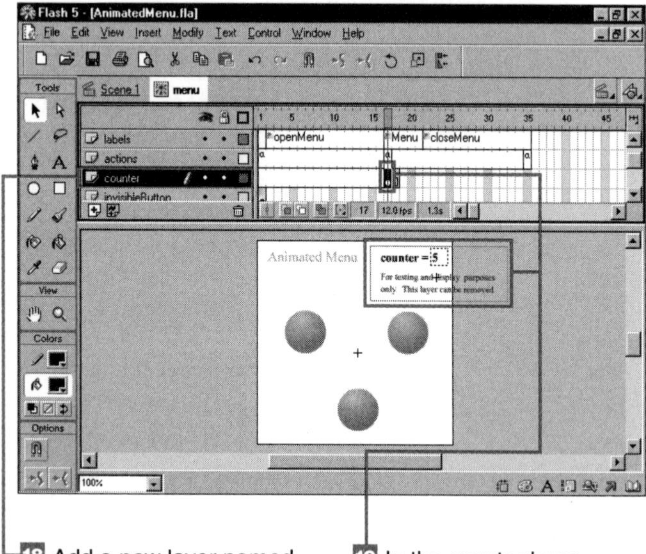

18 Add a new layer named **counter** to the menu movie clip.

Note: See Chapter 21 to learn about adding layers.

19 In the counter layer, insert an instance of the counter movie clip in the same frame number as the `Stop` action.

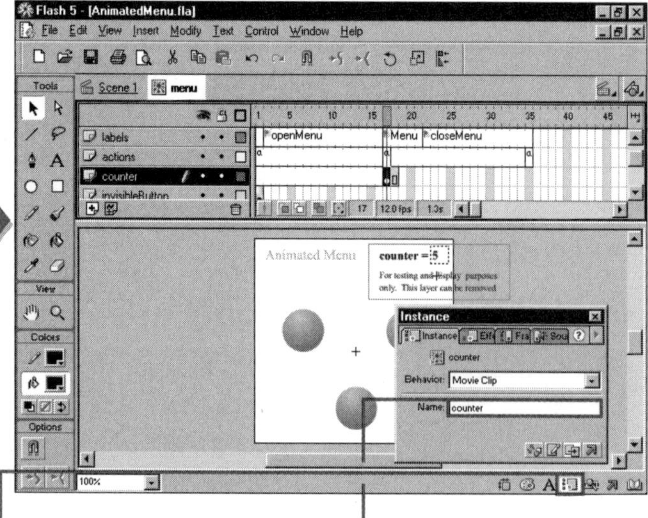

20 Click [icon] to open the Instance panel.

21 Click in the Name text box and name the instance **counter**.

■ You can click [icon] to close the panel again and get it out of the way.

Are button actions different from frame actions?

✔ Any actions you assign to objects in your Flash movies, including buttons, are considered object actions. For example, mouse events are a subset of the on action located in the Actions list. You can perform actions when a user rolls over (`on (rollOver)`) or rolls off (`on (rollOut)`) a button. An action assigned to a particular frame in your movie is a frame action. Either type of action can be assigned from the action panel.

In step 22, what does the "with (`_root.menu.counter`)" object action do?

✔ The `with` object action (Actions menu) in Flash 5 is comparable to the `Tell Target` action used in Flash 4. The `with` action specifies that you are performing actions using the counter movie clip instance (step 18) located within the menu movie clip.

In step 22, what does the "`_root.menu.counter.n = 0;`" action do?

✔ In this action, you set the variable *n* of the counter movie clip instance (step 17), located in the menu movie clip in the main timeline (`_root`). See Chapter 28 to learn more about setting action variables.

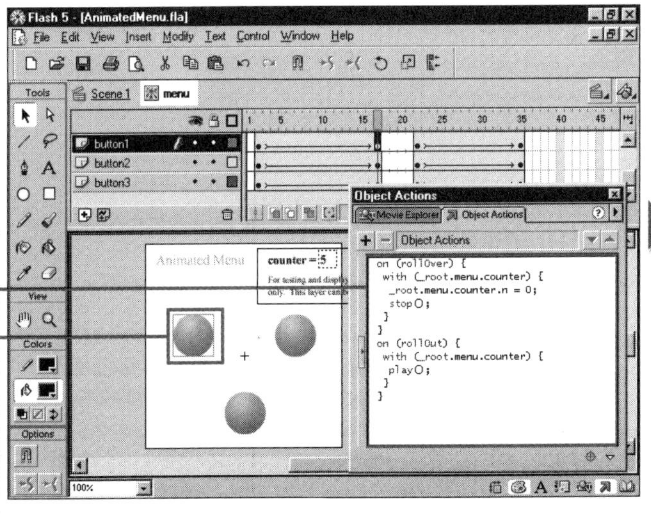

22 Add an object action for each button in your menu which resets the value of `n` when the user rolls over a button.

Note: See the Tips section for explanation of this step.

Note: The stop action is included in the button `on (rollover)` action to stop the counter while the user is interacting with the button.

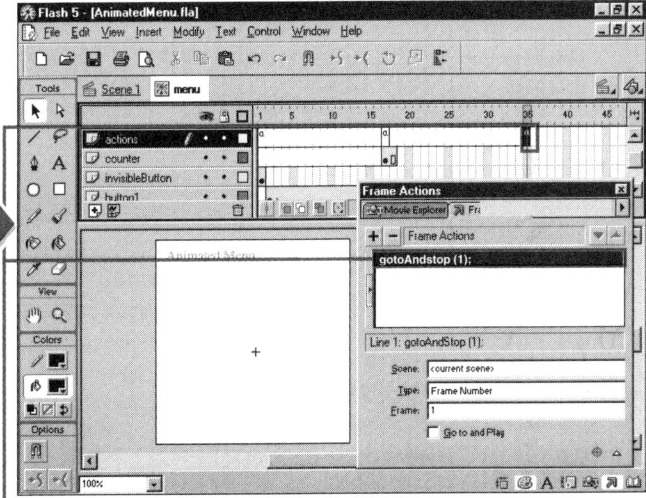

23 Add a `gotoAndStop(1)` frame action in frame 35 (the conclusion of the menu's closing sequence) which sends the playhead back to frame 1 in the menu timeline.

■ You can now test the actions using the Test Movie feature.

Note: The playhead remains in frame 1 of the menu timeline until the user interacts with the button that triggers the opening of the menu again.

ADJUST SOUND CLIP VOLUME

You can add controls to your Flash project that enable users to adjust the volume of a sound clip using the `getVolume` and `setVolume` actions. Because users generally have their sound levels set differently, it can be beneficial to provide functionality that lets them turn the volume of background music or a particular sound clip up or down. Flash 5 also enables the user to set the balance of a sound clip or transform a sound (a combination of adjusting the pan and volume simultaneously).

The steps in this example use buttons to demonstrate how the volume settings are applied and adjusted. Such functionality can also be applied to slide bars as well.

Flash EXE filename:

AdjustVolume.exe

Flash filenames:

AdjustVolume.fla

AdjustVolume.swf

AdjustVolume.hqx

sample.wav

ADJUST SOUND CLIP VOLUME

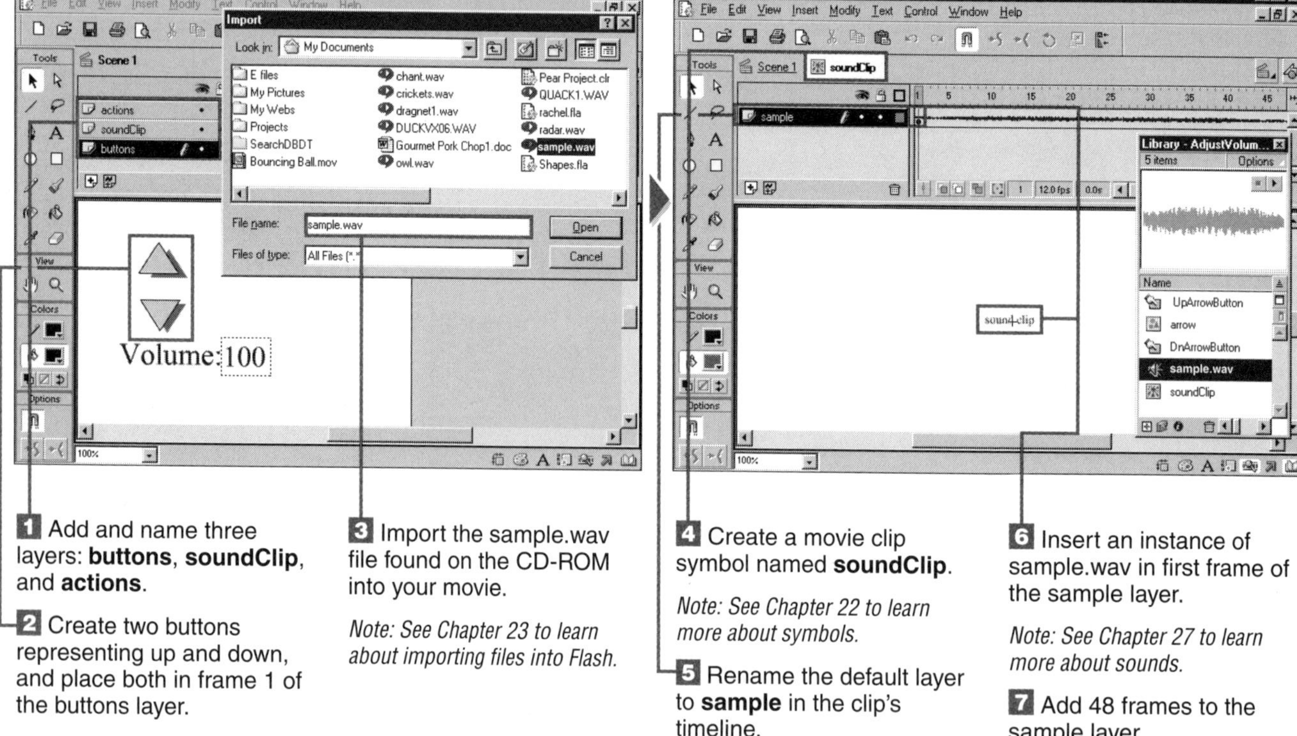

1 Add and name three layers: **buttons**, **soundClip**, and **actions**.

2 Create two buttons representing up and down, and place both in frame 1 of the buttons layer.

3 Import the sample.wav file found on the CD-ROM into your movie.

Note: See Chapter 23 to learn about importing files into Flash.

4 Create a movie clip symbol named **soundClip**.

Note: See Chapter 22 to learn more about symbols.

5 Rename the default layer to **sample** in the clip's timeline.

6 Insert an instance of sample.wav in first frame of the sample layer.

Note: See Chapter 27 to learn more about sounds.

7 Add 48 frames to the sample layer.

How do I check my sound clip's properties?

✔ To check the properties of any sound file you have imported into Flash, first open the Library window and select the sound file. Next, right-click the clip's name and click Properties in the pop-up menu. Flash opens the Sound Properties dialog box detailing information about the sound. To learn more about working with sound clips in Flash, see Chapter 27.

Do I have to create new buttons for this task?

✔ No. You can find suitable volume control buttons in the Buttons Library. Click the Window menu and click Common Libraries, Buttons.

In step 7, why do I add 48 frames to the sample layer?

✔ Adding frames to the layer containing a sound clip allows you to see the duration of the clip in respect to the number of frames at the set frame rate. If you run into problems with sound clips looping, it is often easier to debug your problems when you can see a full visual representation of a sound. See Chapter 27 to learn more about working with sounds in Flash.

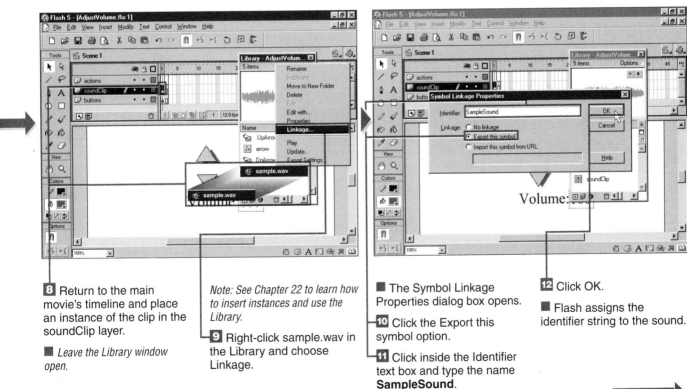

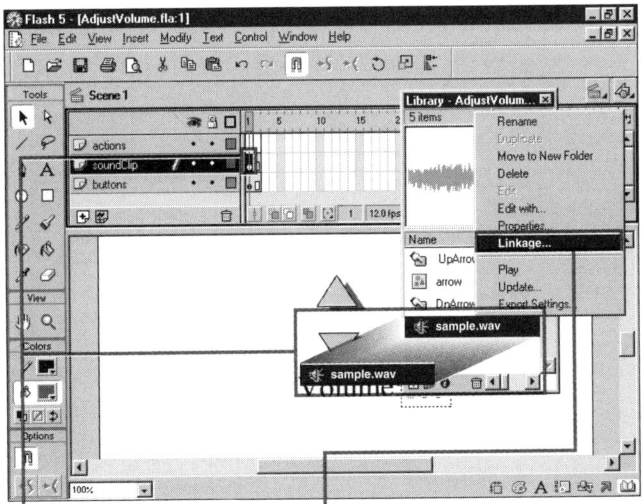

8 Return to the main movie's timeline and place an instance of the clip in the soundClip layer.

■ *Leave the Library window open.*

Note: See Chapter 22 to learn how to insert instances and use the Library.

9 Right-click sample.wav in the Library and choose Linkage.

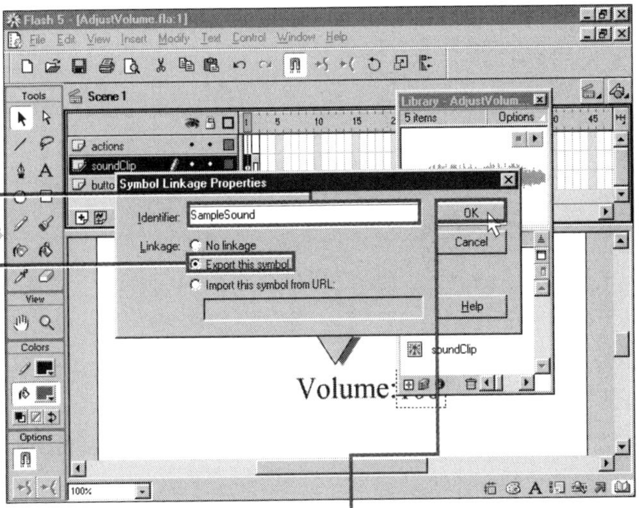

■ The Symbol Linkage Properties dialog box opens.

10 Click the Export this symbol option.

11 Click inside the Identifier text box and type the name **SampleSound**.

12 Click OK.

■ Flash assigns the identifier string to the sound.

CONTINUED

ADJUST SOUND CLIP VOLUME (CONTINUED)

After you create the buttons for controlling the volume, and you assign an Indentifier to the sound file in the Library, you are ready for the next phase in adding volume controls.

In the remaining steps in this section, you assign Flash actions and set parameters to give your buttons actual control over the volume. When assigning a variable value to the buttons, it is a good idea to set the value equal to the volume of the clip and then adjust the value to manipulate the clip's volume setting.

In addition, you add functionality to the buttons that not only adds or subtracts from the volume variable value, but also verifies that the user does not set the volume to a value less than 0% or greater than 100%.

ADJUST SOUND CLIP VOLUME (CONTINUED)

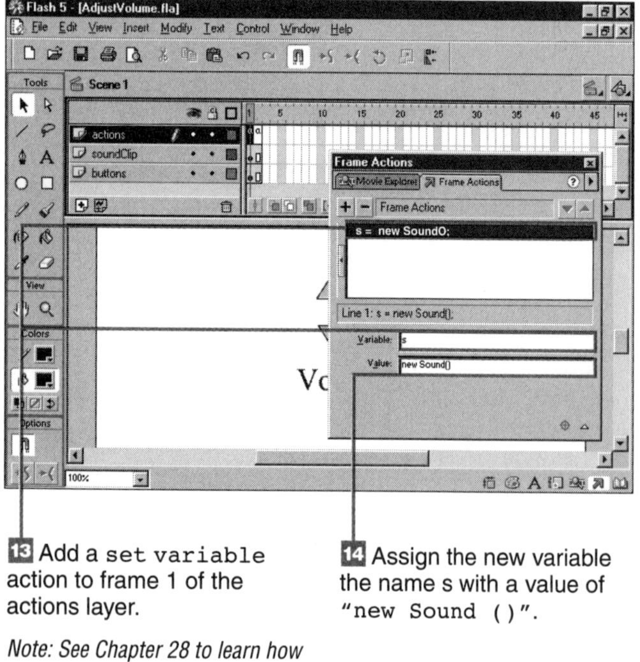

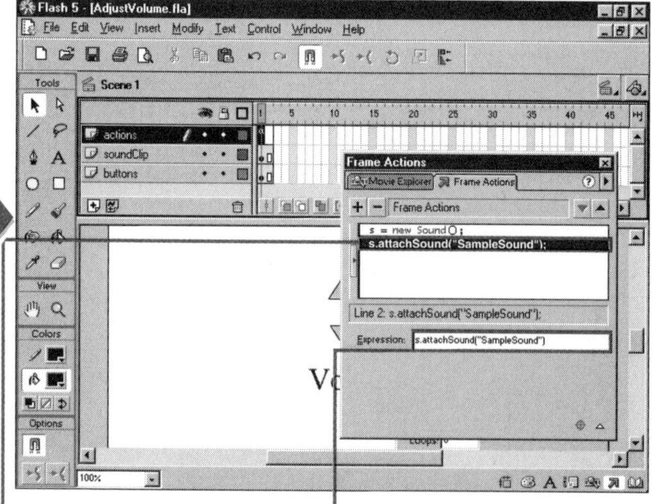

13 Add a `set variable` action to frame 1 of the actions layer.

Note: See Chapter 28 to learn how to assign actions.

14 Assign the new variable the name s with a value of `"new Sound ()"`.

15 Add the `attachSound` object action.

■ You can find this action listed in the Objects category under the heading Sounds in the Actions toolbox list.

Note: See Chapter 28 to learn more about how actions are listed in the Actions panel.

16 Prefix the action with the variable s and assign the idName "**SampleSound**".

Can I pan (set balance of) a sound clip?

✔ Yes. You can move the sound output from the left to right speaker and vice versa using `getPan` and `setPan` actions, found in the Sound Objects actions category. Advanced users can also manipulate both the balance and volume simultaneously using the `soundTransformObject` action.

Can I control playback using the Sound Object?

✔ Yes. You can start playback from either the beginning or from a selected point in the clip using the `start` method of the Sound Object. Additionally, the `stop` method offers the capability to stop a particular clip or all sounds currently playing.

How do I use a slide controller for setting my volume or balance?

✔ You can constrain a slider within a movie clip to a bounding box that constrains the slider button to a specified range of motion. Next, add or subtract a value from the volume setting based on the slider's current position. See Flash's ActionScript Reference in the Flash help files on creating sound controls for more details. See Chapter 17 to learn more about accessing the Help files.

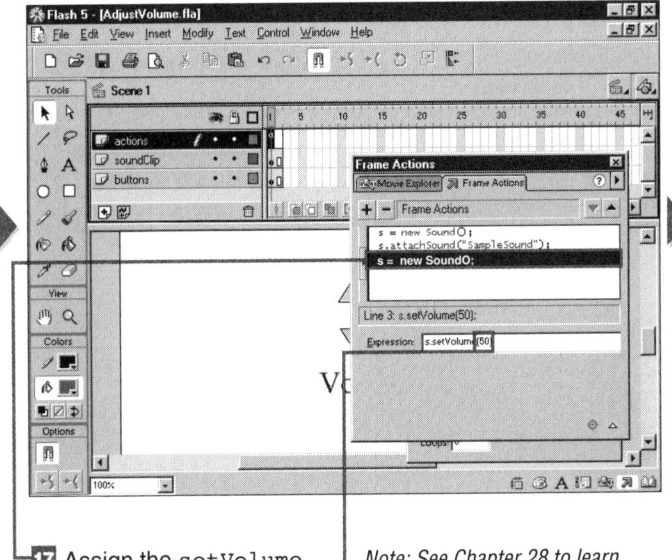

17 Assign the `setVolume` object action.

Note: See Chapter 29 to learn about advanced actions.

■ This action is listed in the Objects category under the heading Sounds in the Actions toolbox list.

Note: See Chapter 28 to learn more about how actions are listed in the Actions panel.

18 Set the initial volume level to `50` (maximum volume is 100).

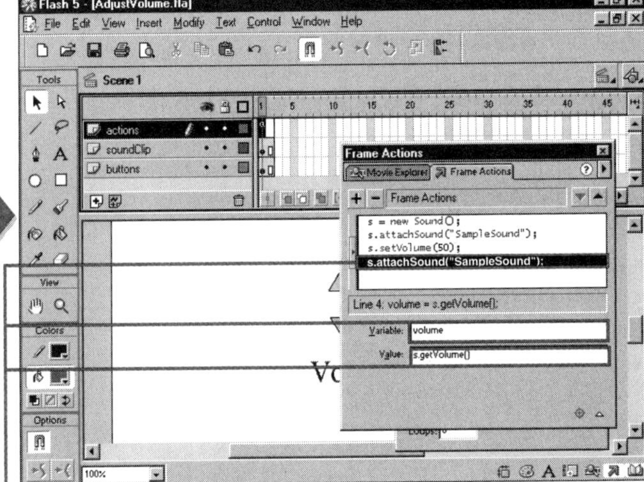

19 Assign a new variable volume the value of the current volume level set.

Note: See Chapter 29 to learn about variables in actions.

CONTINUED

ADJUST SOUND CLIP VOLUME (CONTINUED)

As you add the actions outlined in this task, an action statement is added for each action and listed in the Actions panel. When entering variables, the variable name is followed by an equals sign (=) and a value, where applicable.

There are a couple of rules to be aware of when assigning variable names to your scripts. First, scripts must begin with a letter character, not a number or special character. You can compose the rest of the name using letters, numbers, or underscores. You cannot use spaces. Variable names are not case-sensitive, so whether you enter *SampleSound* or *samplesound*, Flash handles the name in the same way in carrying out the statements.

You should use variable names that clearly define what the variable is. This helps you recognize the variable in your action statements.

ADJUST SOUND CLIP VOLUME (CONTINUED)

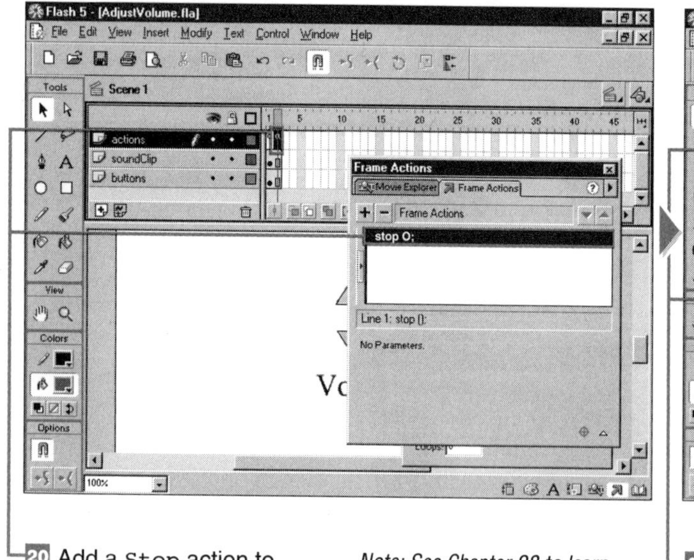

20 Add a `Stop` action to frame 2 of the actions layer.

Note: See Chapter 28 to learn more about adding actions in Flash.

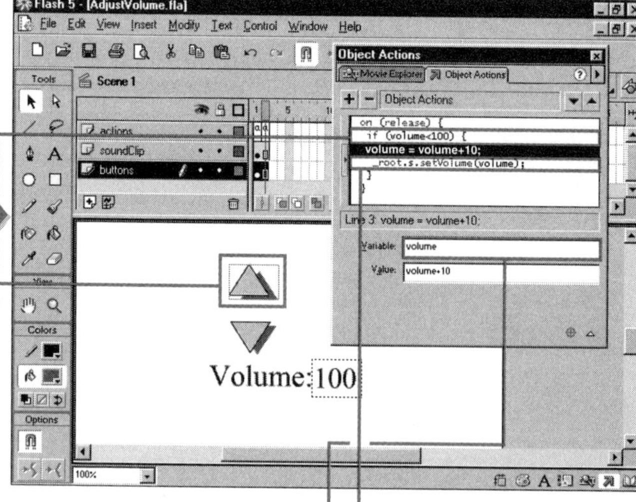

21 Select the Up button and verify in the Actions panel that the volume has a setting of less than 100 when the user releases the mouse button.

22 Set the `volume` variable equal to its current value plus 10.

23 Assign the volume of the `s` variable's attached sound the current value of volume.

Why is the sound attached to a variable?

✔ The sound is attached to a variable in order to create an object with adjustable attributes. You cannot directly manipulate the volume of an imported sound file.

Can I specify different compressions for each sound file?

✔ Yes. You can choose to compress all files in the same manner, or individually. It is possible to save the file by customizing files independently of one another. To do so, right-click the sound file, and choose either Properties or Export Settings.

Can I edit a sound before adding it to my movie?

✔ Yes. Flash has some rudimentary editing controls for adjusting sounds used in your movies. To access the Edit Envelope feature, open the Sound panel, select the sound you wish to edit, and then click the Edit button. To learn more about this feature, see Chapter 27.

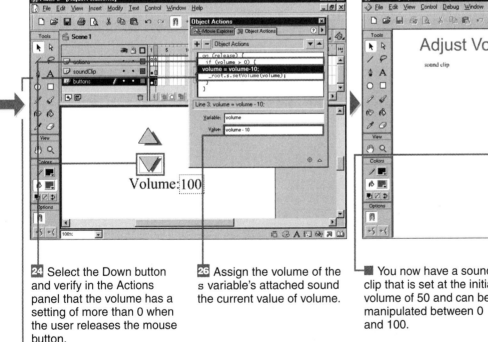

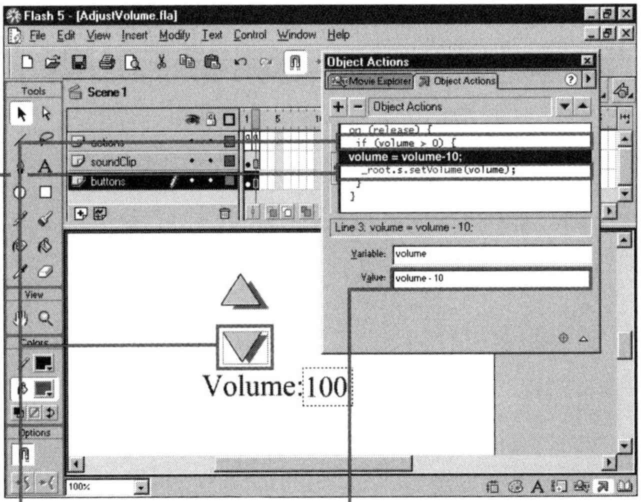

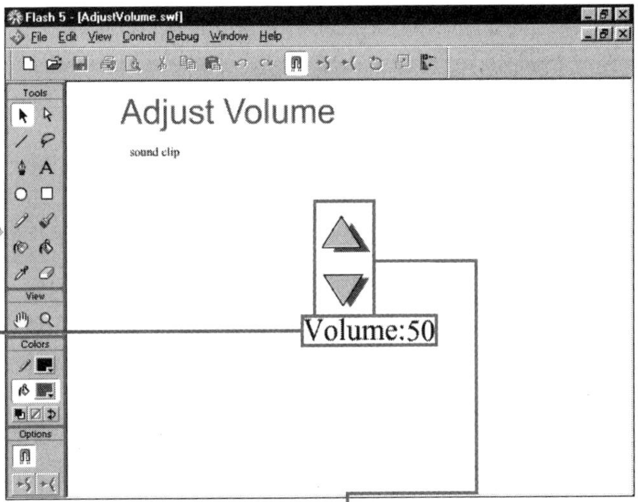

24 Select the Down button and verify in the Actions panel that the volume has a setting of more than 0 when the user releases the mouse button.

25 Set the `volume` variable equal to its current value minus 10.

26 Assign the volume of the s variable's attached sound the current value of volume.

■ You now have a sound clip that is set at the initial volume of 50 and can be manipulated between 0 and 100.

■ You can test the movie in the player window and see how the controls work.

Note: See Chapter 30 to learn how to test Flash movies.

CREATE AN ADVANCED PRELOADER

You can create an animated progress bar and display the percentage of how much of your Web site has downloaded to the user's machine using a Preloader. A *Preloader* is an animation that plays while the user waits for a specific amount of information to load. Preloaders are commonly used on the Web today. You can find a nice example of a Preloader at the Chrysalis Retail Entertainment Web site, www.cre.co.uk/main.htm.

In this task, you learn how to set up both a progress bar and the actions necessary for determining downloaded content. This task example uses a combination of a graphic symbol (named PreloaderBar) scaled in width from 0 to 100% and a movie clip (named getPercentage) that dynamically displays the actual percent of site loaded.

Flash EXE filename:

AdvancedPreloader.exe

Flash filenames:

AdvancedPreloader.fla

AdvancedPreloader.swf

AdvancedPreloader.hqx

CREATE AN ADVANCED PRELOADER

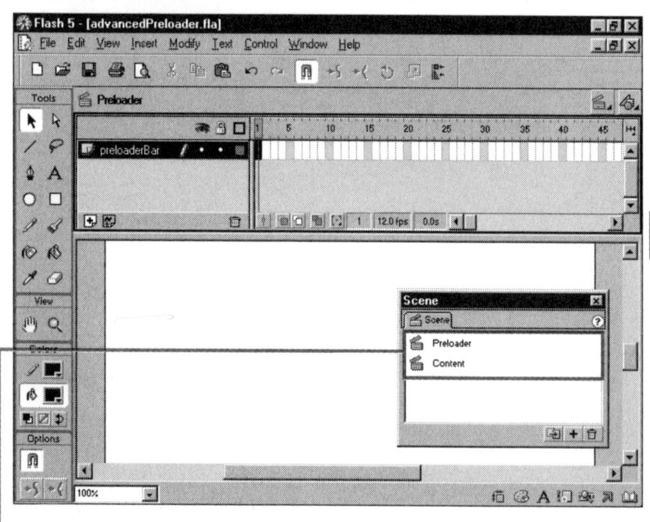

1 Create two scenes in your Flash movie: one for the Preloader animation, named **Preloader**, and another for your primary movie, named **Content**.

Note: See Chapter 24 to learn how to create scenes.

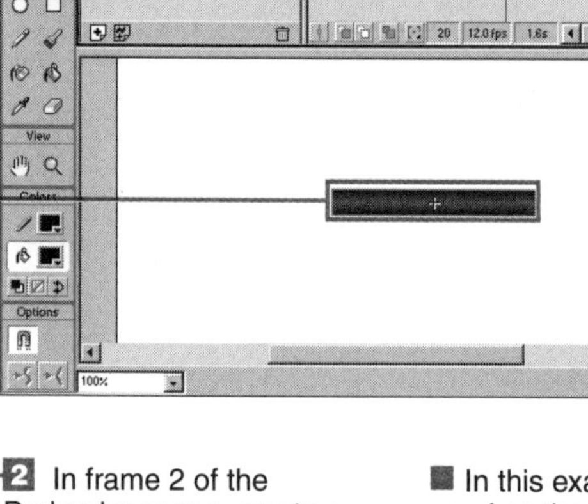

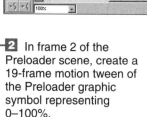

2 In frame 2 of the Preloader scene, create a 19-frame motion tween of the Preloader graphic symbol representing 0–100%.

Note: See Chapter 25 to learn how to create a motion tween animation.

■ In this example, a bar is used as the Preloader graphic.

■ Be sure to place new movie elements on different layers and give the layers distinct names. In this example, the tween layer is named preloaderBar.

What types of graphics make good Preloaders?

✔ The graphic symbol used to illustrate this task is a bar that is animated with a motion tween to show a 0% state that grows to a 100% state. The bar starts out short and increases in length to signify the percentage of downloaded content. You can use similar graphic symbols in your own Preloader. Any animation illustrating a beginning and ending point (indicating progress) works. To learn more about the Flash drawing tools, see Chapters 18 and 19. To learn how to save a graphic object as a symbol to reuse in your Flash project, see Chapter 22.

What is the ideal approach to loading large amounts of content?

✔ The most ideal way to load large amounts of content is to separate your movie into individual SWF files Flash Player files. Although this can also be done by separating your movie into different sections which are targeted on individual HTML pages, loading and unloading swfs within Flash provides for smoother transitions and faster processing. See Chapters 28 and 29 to learn more about Flash actions, including the Load Movie and Unload Movie actions.

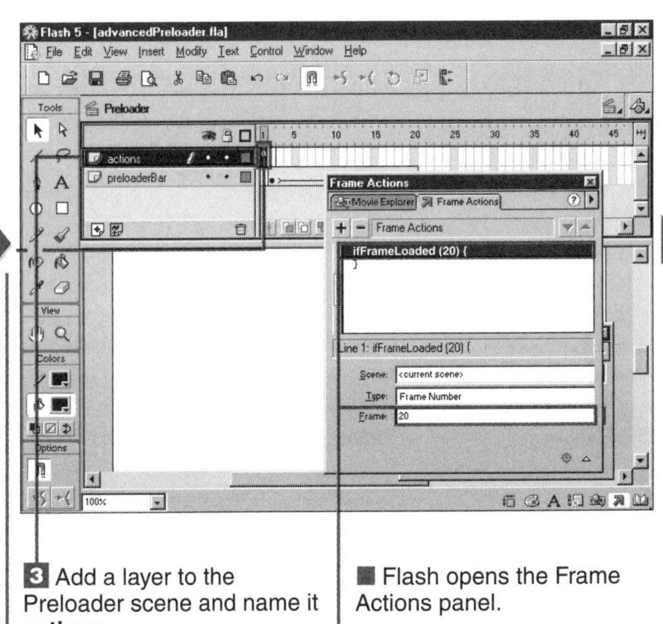

3 Add a layer to the Preloader scene and name it **actions**.

Note: See Chapter 21 to learn about adding layers.

4 Double-click frame 1 of the actions layer to add a frame action.

■ Flash opens the Frame Actions panel.

5 Add an `If Frame Is Loaded` action and set the Frame field value to 20.

Note: See Chapter 28 to learn about adding frame actions.

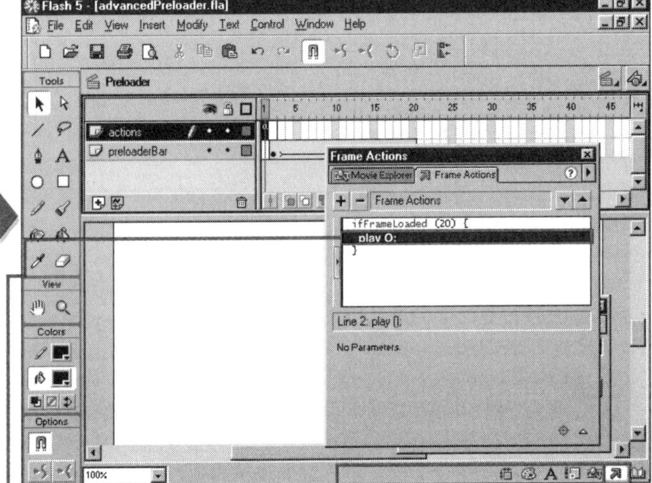

6 Add a `Play` action to the same frame, below the `If Frame Is Loaded` action.

Note: See Chapter 28 to learn about adding frame actions.

■ Leave the Actions panel open to add more actions.

■ To close the Actions panel any time, just click ⧉.

CONTINUED

CREATE AN ADVANCED PRELOADER (CONTINUED)

There are numerous variations of Preloader animations and techniques on the Web, the best of which include some indication of the actual content downloaded. The indicator may be a bar or clock that shows the user how much content has downloaded onto their computer. You have probably encountered numerous Preloaders during the course of your Web sessions without paying much notice.

Although Flash is a streaming technology, a Preloader ensures that playback of your movie is not stopped due to bandwidth restrictions when your movie is played over the Web. In order to preview the Preloader technique on your own computer, make sure the Show Streaming option is selected in the View menu of the Flash Player window; otherwise, the animation may play too quickly for viewing. See Chapter 30 to learn more about testing your Flash movies in the Flash Player window.

CREATE AN ADVANCED PRELOADER (CONTINUED)

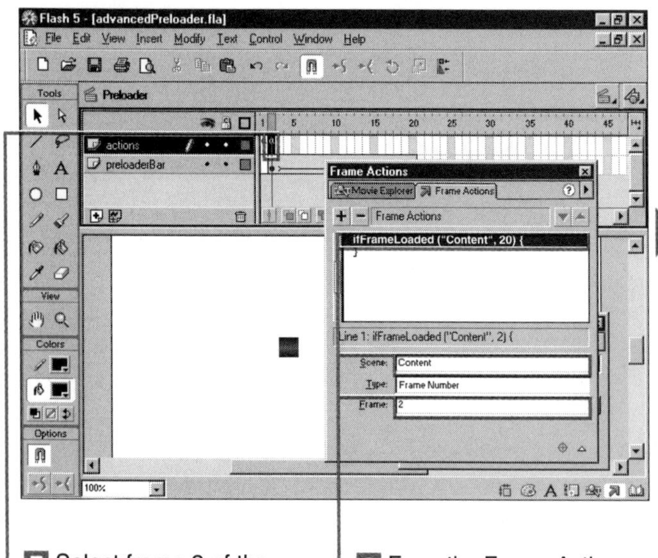

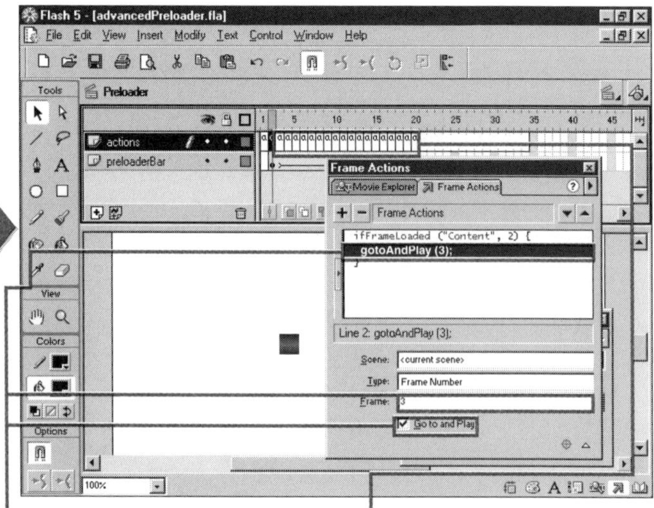

7 Select frame 2 of the actions layer.

8 From the Frame Actions panel, add an `If Frame Is Loaded` action, setting the Scene to `Content` and the Frame to 2.

Note: See Chapter 28 to learn about adding actions.

9 Add a `Go To` action, setting the Frame value to 3 and selecting the Go to and Play check box.

Note: The frames you check against should be relative to the total number of frames in the Content scene.

10 Repeat steps 8 through 9 for frames 3 through 19 of the Preloader scene using respective frame numbers in each action.

Why should I check my frame value against the relative number of frames?

✔ The Preloader's progress in this example is based on the number of frames loaded in the Content scene, which in this example is 20 frames total. You can also base this on the frames in your movie where the file size is increased by graphic elements. Divide your total number of frames by 100 to determine the increment of frames you check against in step 9. For example, if your Content scene is 200 frames in length, you want to verify that 2 frames are loaded for every percent the Preloader progress bar advances.

Why does the movie skip directly to my Content scene when I test the movie?

✔ For you to see the Preloader animate locally, first place a considerable amount of media elements in your Content scene. Next, when testing the movie with Flash's Test Movie command, click the View menu on the player window and select Show Streaming. Then choose an appropriate modem speed from the Debug menu to ensure bandwidth is taken into consideration. To learn more about testing your movie's bandwidth, see Chapter 30.

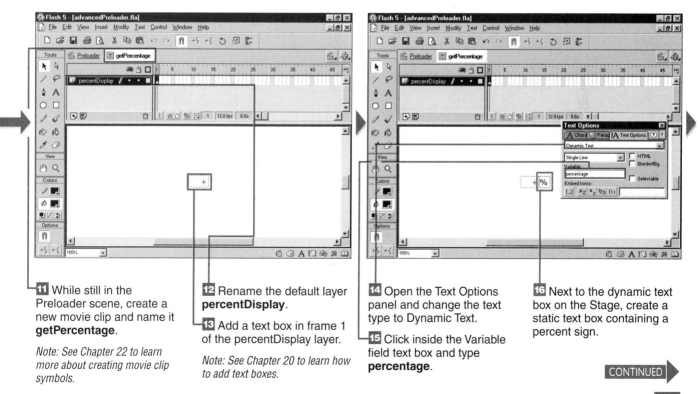

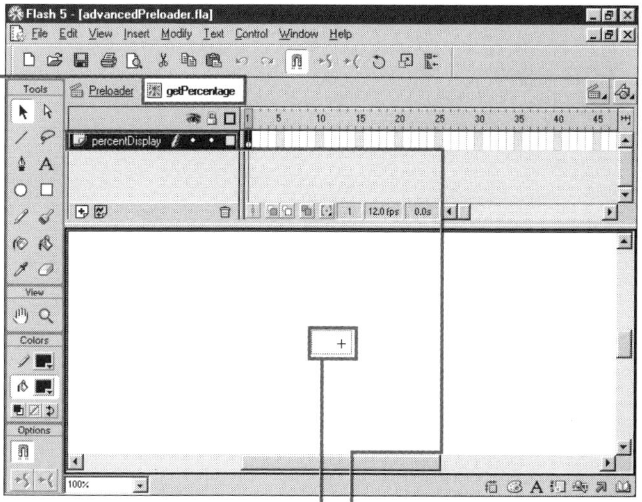

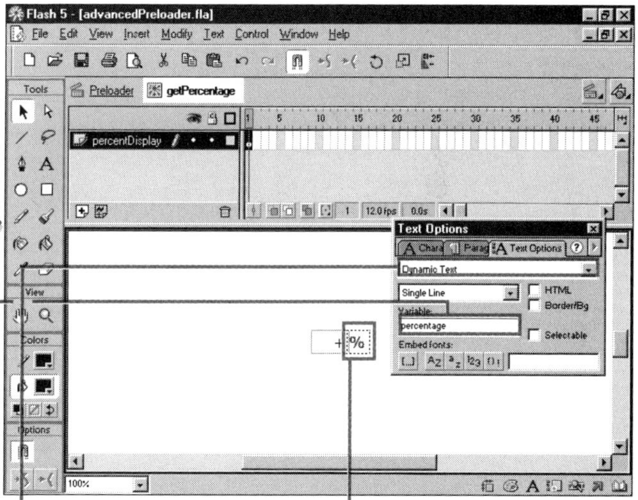

11 While still in the Preloader scene, create a new movie clip and name it **getPercentage**.

Note: See Chapter 22 to learn more about creating movie clip symbols.

12 Rename the default layer **percentDisplay**.

13 Add a text box in frame 1 of the percentDisplay layer.

Note: See Chapter 20 to learn how to add text boxes.

14 Open the Text Options panel and change the text type to Dynamic Text.

15 Click inside the Variable field text box and type **percentage**.

16 Next to the dynamic text box on the Stage, create a static text box containing a percent sign.

CONTINUED

CREATE AN ADVANCED PRELOADER (CONTINUED)

Keep in mind that there are numerous ways of using a Preloader in your Flash projects. Progress bars, percentages, and custom animations are only a few variations of this powerful technique. Verifying if a certain number of frames or bytes is loaded is important to maintain smooth playback.

Determining how much information you want loaded before playback continues should be based on your audience's bandwidth. Use the Bandwidth Profiler to show where your movie is the "heaviest" and control the playback accordingly. Otherwise, your movie may stall during playback while it waits to download content. To learn more about the Bandwidth Profiler, see Chapter 30.

Sound clips and bitmap images are two of the heaviest media elements used in a Flash movie; be sure to use each sparingly. If you find that preloading your movie elements still hinders playback, try dividing your movie into separate SWF files and use the `loadMovie` and `unloadMovie` actions to keep only currently used elements on the Stage at a given time.

CREATE AN ADVANCED PRELOADER (CONTINUED)

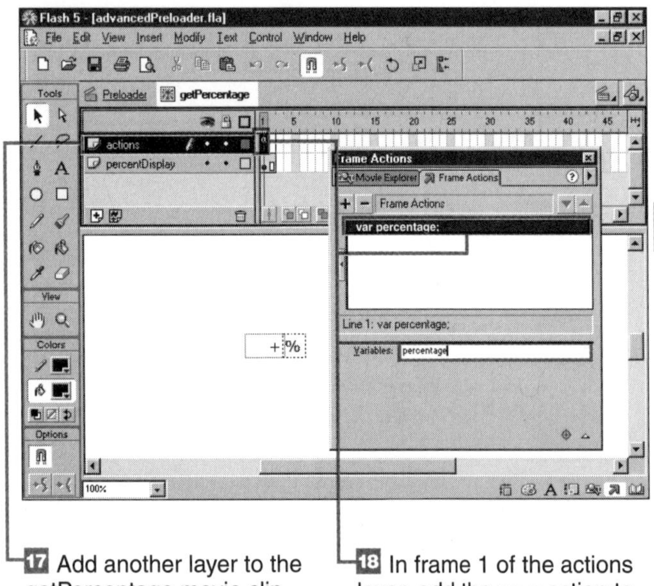

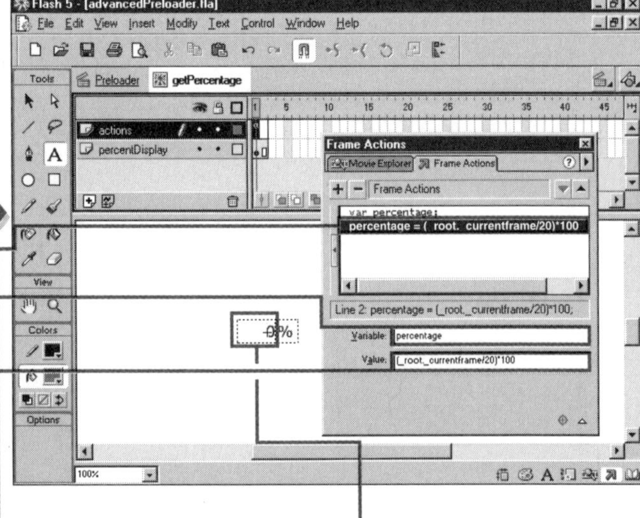

17 Add another layer to the getPercentage movie clip and name it **actions**.

Note: See Chapter 21 to learn how to add layers.

18 In frame 1 of the actions layer, add the `var` action to the actions list with the value percentage assigned to the Variables field.

Note: See Chapter 28 to learn how to add actions.

19 Set a new variable `percentage` to the value of the current frame of the Preloader scene timeline, divided by the total number of frames in the Content scene, multiplied by 100.

■ The value `percentage` is displayed in the dynamic text box.

How do I show the actual number of bytes loaded (as shown on the Chrysalis Retail Entertainment site)?

✔ You can obtain the number of bytes loaded (streamed) of a particular movie clip using the `getBytesLoaded` action. The `getBytesTotal` action returns the total number bytes for an external movie that you are loading. If your movie is not evenly weighted, you may want to base the Preloader's progress on the total number of bytes loaded instead of the number of frames loaded.

How do I limit the percentage to whole numbers only?

✔ The actual size of your text field displaying the `Percentage` variable in the getPercentage movie clip determines how many characters are displayed at a time (decimals included). Decrease the field width to prevent decimal points from being displayed by dragging the text field's bottom-right corner.

Where can I learn more about adding actions in Flash?

✔ You can consult the Flash help files to learn more about using and constructing actions in your Flash projects. You can also find help with more complex action scripts in the ActionScript Reference Help files. To learn more about using the Help files, see Chapter 17.

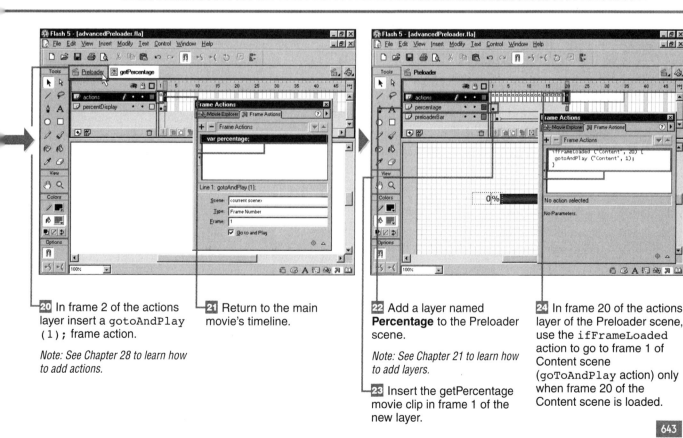

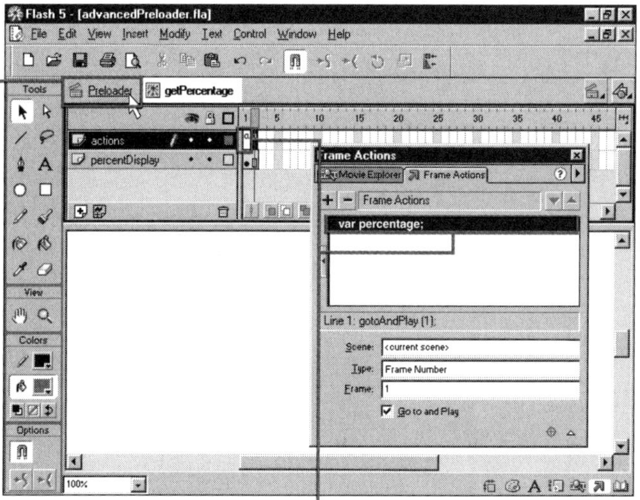

20 In frame 2 of the actions layer insert a `gotoAndPlay (1);` frame action.

Note: See Chapter 28 to learn how to add actions.

21 Return to the main movie's timeline.

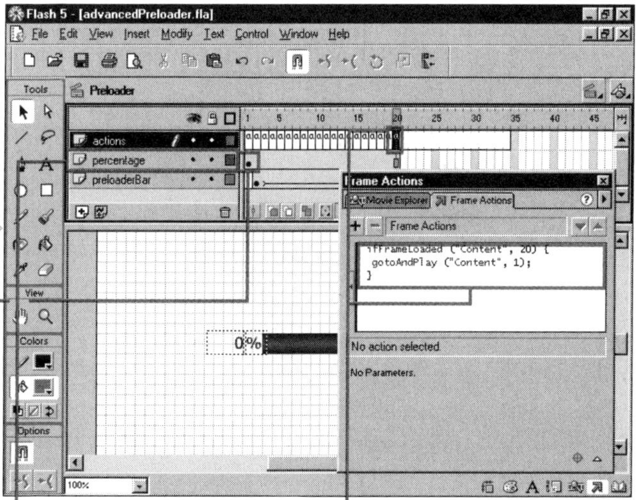

22 Add a layer named **Percentage** to the Preloader scene.

Note: See Chapter 21 to learn how to add layers.

23 Insert the getPercentage movie clip in frame 1 of the new layer.

24 In frame 20 of the actions layer of the Preloader scene, use the `ifFrameLoaded` action to go to frame 1 of Content scene (`goToAndPlay` action) only when frame 20 of the Content scene is loaded.

SET PROPERTY OF A MOVIE CLIP

You can use the `setProperty` action to dynamically change the *x* and *y* scale or position, alpha channel (transparency), quality, rotation, visibility, or instance name of a movie clip. The steps in this section change the *x* and *y* scale of the movie clip named **mc** based on button actions.

Properties can be dynamically manipulated on frame actions as well and are not limited to those already mentioned. Changing a movie's properties dynamically makes for a more scalable application, because the properties are stored in designated variable values. Purdue University's Virtual Visit (www.tech.purdue.edu/resources/map/mapv2/), has an interactive 3D map that uses Flash's ability to change the scale and position of a movie clip on a button action.

Flash EXE filename:

SetPropertyOfMC.exe

Flash filenames:

SetPropertyOfMC.fla

SetPropertyOfMC.swf

SetPropertyOfMC.hqx

UpButtonAction.txt

DownButtonAction.txt

SET PROPERTY OF A MOVIE CLIP

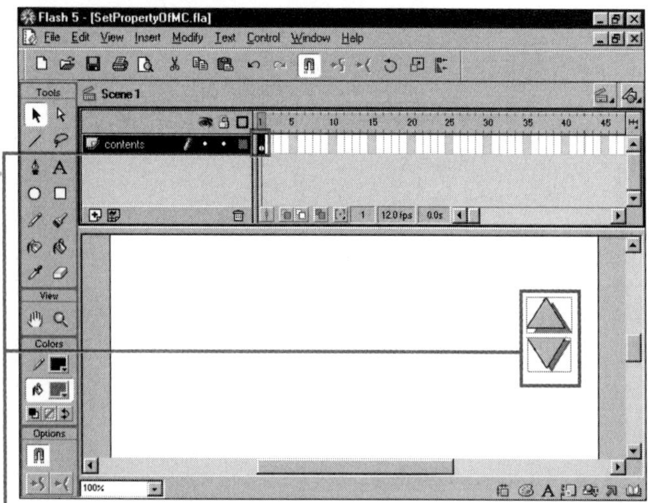

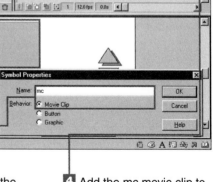

1 Create an Up button (**upbutton**) and a Down button (**downbutton**) and add the buttons to frame 1 in your movie's main timeline.

Note: See Chapter 26 to learn how to create buttons in Flash.

■ In this example, an arrow graphic symbol was created and used for both buttons.

2 Add a graphic to the Stage.

■ The graphic can be anything pertaining to your movie.

3 Convert the graphic into a movie clip symbol named **mc**.

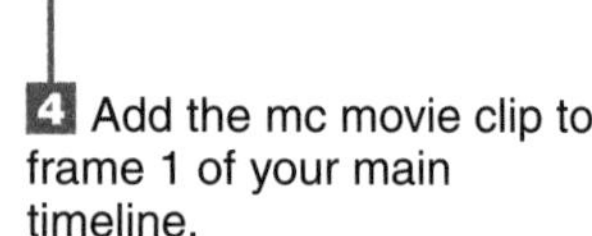

4 Add the mc movie clip to frame 1 of your main timeline.

Note: See Chapter 18 to learn more about using the drawing tools and see Chapter 22 to learn about symbols.

What is the difference between Normal mode and Expert mode?

✔ When assigning actions in Flash, you can set parameters using Normal mode, which is the default mode, or enter script statements in Expert mode. Expert mode is more like a text editor, where you can type in action script statements and edit them as needed. However, you cannot delete or reorder your statements in Expert mode or select from parameter options for a particular action. You can switch back and forth between modes using the ▶ button in the upper-right corner of the Actions panel. Simply click the button and choose which mode you want to use.

Can I set the button actions in Normal mode instead of Expert mode?

✔ Yes. So long as you have entered the code correctly, you can return the editing mode to Normal and view each action's parameters. The menus that provide the actions used are listed below:

`on (press)`: Basic Actions – On Mouse Event

`getProperty`: Functions

`If` and `setProperty`: Actions

`<=` : Operators

`_xscale` and `_yscale`: Properties

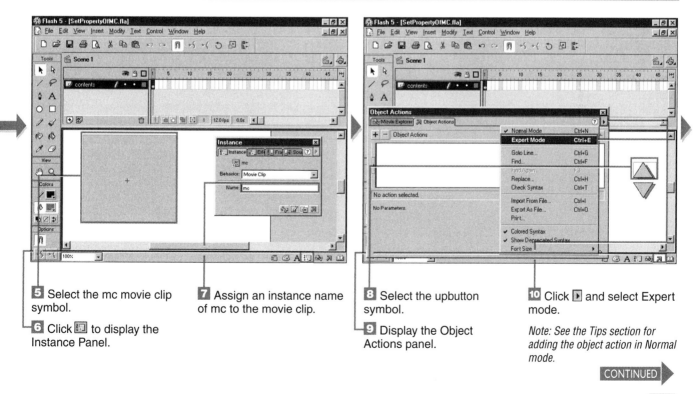

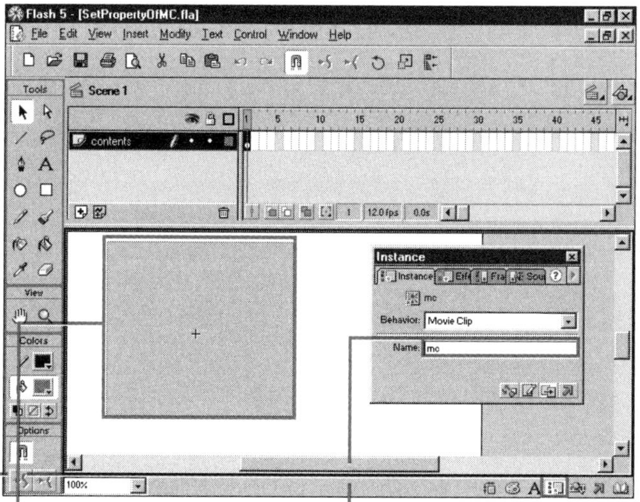

5 Select the mc movie clip symbol.

6 Click ▣ to display the Instance Panel.

7 Assign an instance name of mc to the movie clip.

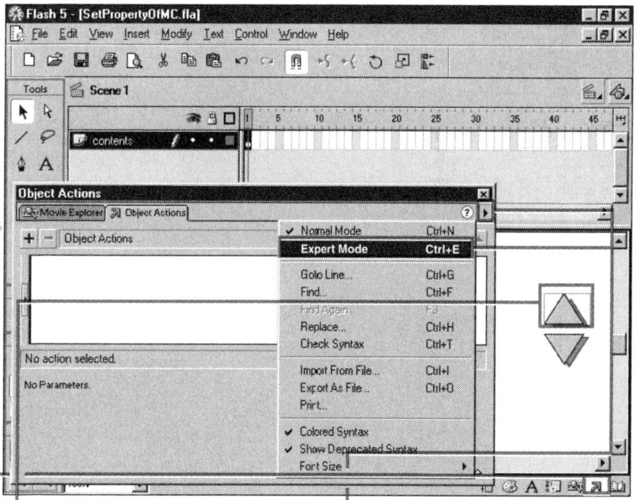

8 Select the upbutton symbol.

9 Display the Object Actions panel.

10 Click ▶ and select Expert mode.

Note: See the Tips section for adding the object action in Normal mode.

CONTINUED

SET PROPERTY OF A MOVIE CLIP (CONTINUED)

The `setProperty` action enables you to change how a movie clip plays. Keep in mind that if you take time to assign values to a movie clip's properties and then load the movie clip into a target, such as another movie clip, the loaded clip takes on all the properties of the targeted clip.

In this task example, you define the x-scale and y-scale properties of the movie clip. The *x-scale* property represents how much of the clip has been scaled from its original size, horizontally. The *y-scale* property represents the same scaling, only measured vertically. By assigning the properties to buttons, other users can click the buttons and scale the designated clip based on the percentage value you determine in the actions parameters.

To test how the actions work, view the movie in the Flash Player window and click the buttons to see the scaling effect work.

SET PROPERTY OF A MOVIE CLIP (CONTINUED)

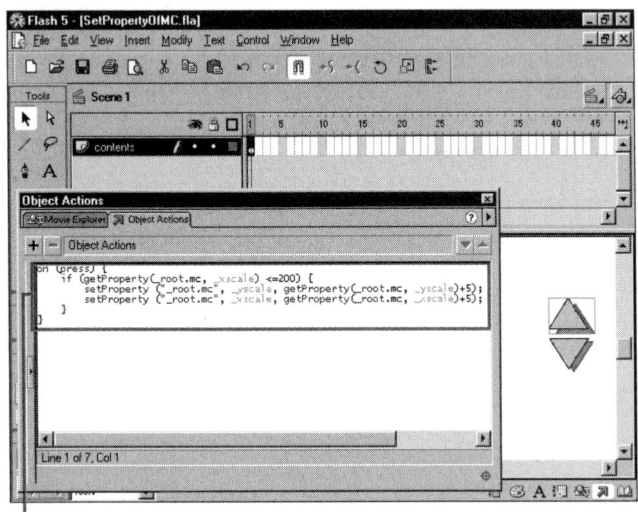

11 Copy and paste the `upbutton` action from the UpButtonAction.txt file found on the CD-ROM included with this book and add it to the actions list box.

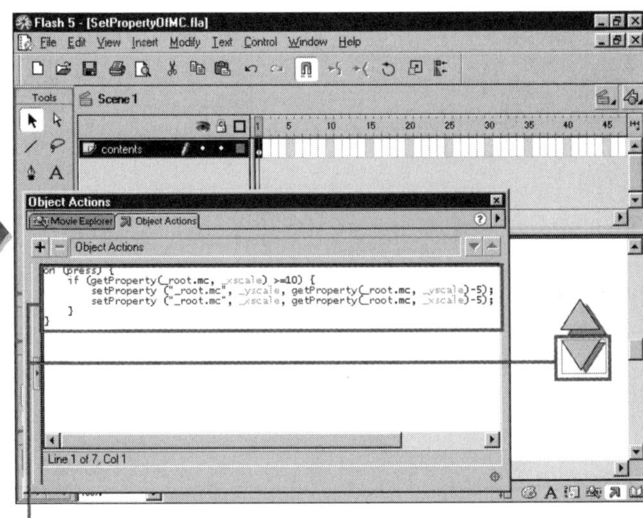

12 Repeat steps 8 through 11 for the `downbutton` action using the DownButtonAction.txt file.

Why do I verify the x-scale of my movie clip only when I set both the x- and y-scale properties?

✔ Note that you are subtracting the same increment from both the x- and y-scale proportions in steps 12 and 13. Because the ratio of the horizontal and vertical scale is proportional, you only need to verify one or the other.

Why is tint not an option in the list of properties I am allowed to set?

✔ Tint is not a property that you can manipulate directly with setProperty. The Color object, however, allows you to obtain and manipulate the RGB color value of movie clips. See the following methods: `getRGB`, `getTransform`, `setRGB`, and `setTransform`. Use the Flash help documentation to learn more about these methods.

How do I resize my Actions panel?

✔ You can resize the Actions panel to make it easier to see the statements you enter. To do so, simply move your mouse pointer over the left or right border edge of the panel and the pointer takes the shape of a double-sided arrow. Click and drag the border to a new size.

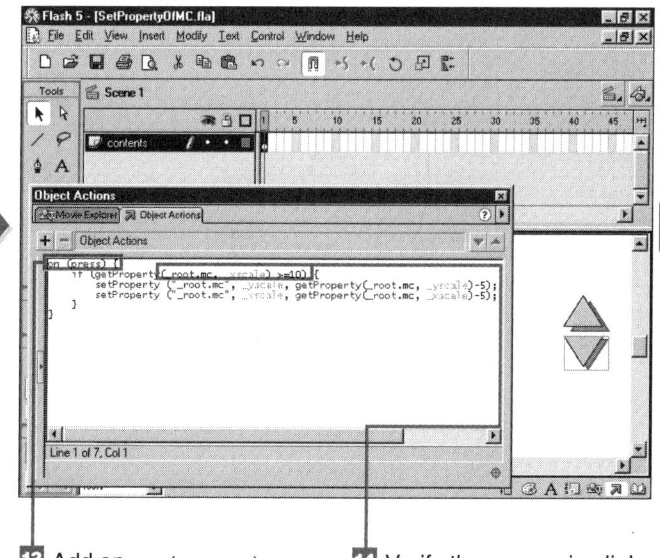

13 Add an `on (press)` mouse event.

Note: See Chapter 28 to learn more about Flash actions.

14 Verify the mc movie clip's x-scale is 10% or more of its original size (100%).

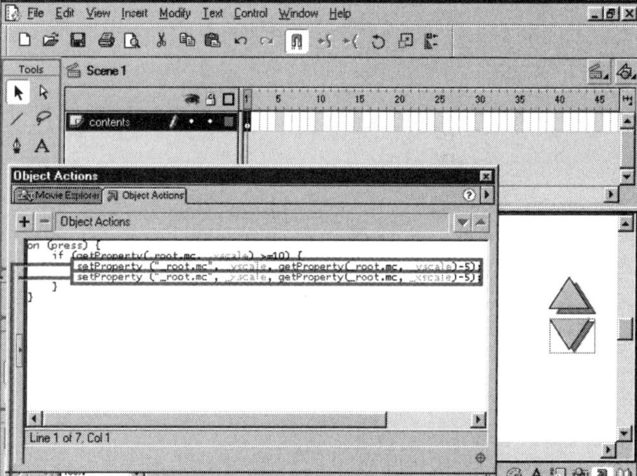

15 Set the y-scale of the mc movie clip to the current y-scale minus 5%.

16 Set the x-scale of the mc movie clip to the current x-scale minus 5%.

■ You can now test the actions using the `Test Movie` command.

Note: See Chapter 30 to learn how to test movies.

TRACK CURSOR POSITION

You can track the user's cursor position within a Flash project using *x, y* coordinates. Although this is a relatively simple task, *x* and *y* coordinates can be used for creating a number of advanced techniques other than visual appeal alone. Designers often display the cursor coordinates as part of the interface layout, while developers use them extensively for advanced functionality. Examples include triggering animation playback, dynamically relocating movie clips on the Stage, or manipulating movie properties, such as opacity or color tint.

The example outlined in this section is used only for displaying the cursor coordinates. In many advanced uses, however, the coordinates are obtained and stored in hidden values either for the precise location or displacement of a particular symbol.

You can find a great example of this same technique at the Yigal-Azrouel fashion line Web site (www.yigal-azrouel.com/flashpage.htm). The alpha channels of the background images on this site are tuned relative to the user's cursor position in the browser window.

Flash EXE filename:

TrackCursorPosition.exe

Flash filenames:

TrackCursorPosition.fla

TrackCursorPosition.swf

TrackCursorPosition.hqx

TRACK CURSOR POSITION

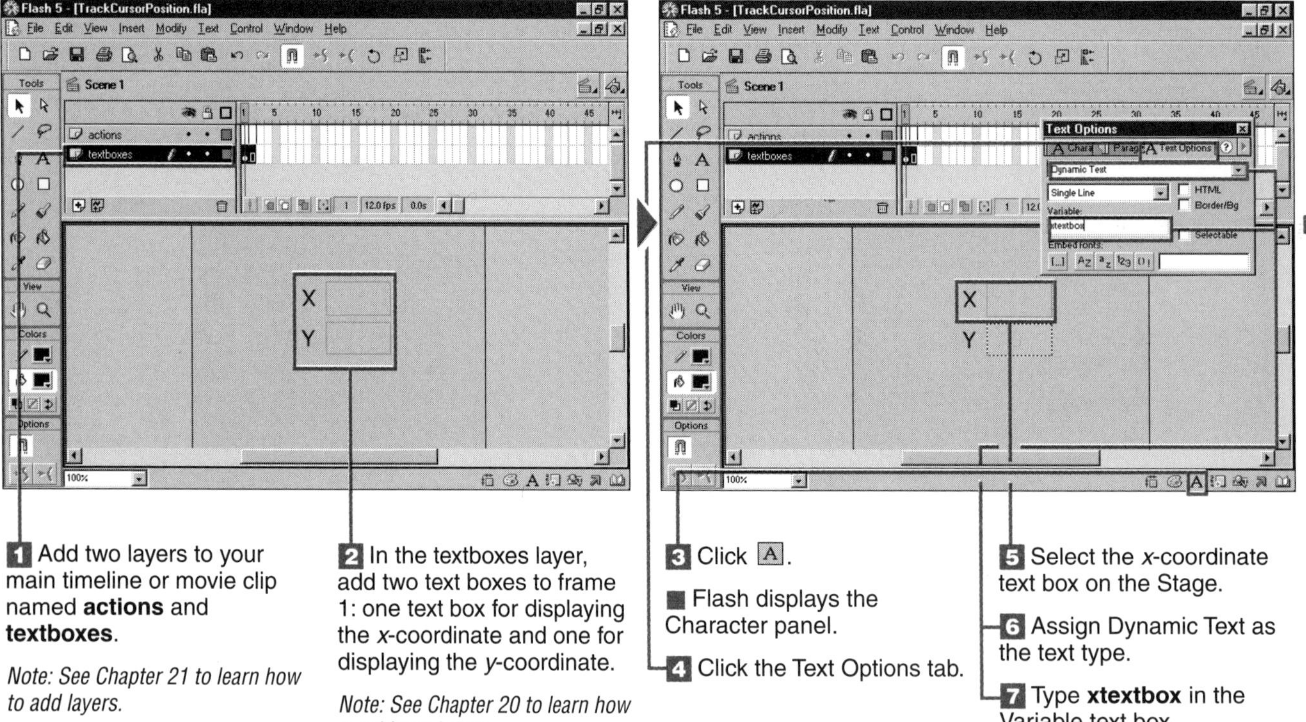

1 Add two layers to your main timeline or movie clip named **actions** and **textboxes**.

Note: See Chapter 21 to learn how to add layers.

2 In the textboxes layer, add two text boxes to frame 1: one text box for displaying the *x*-coordinate and one for displaying the *y*-coordinate.

Note: See Chapter 20 to learn how to add text boxes.

3 Click A.

■ Flash displays the Character panel.

4 Click the Text Options tab.

5 Select the *x*-coordinate text box on the Stage.

6 Assign Dynamic Text as the text type.

7 Type **xtextbox** in the Variable text box.

What is the difference between a static text box and a dynamic text box?

✔ A static text box is used for text that remains constant on the Stage, such as body copy, page titles, or navigation instructions. A dynamic text box is used for displaying dynamically updating text, such as user input boxes, text retrieved from a database, or a variable value obtained either from a function within your movie or an external script.

Can I add a border to a text box?

✔ Yes. With the Text Options panel open, click the Border/Bg check box. This adds a border around the text box. You cannot see this option if the text box is a static text box. The option is available only for dynamic or input text boxes.

Can I obtain the mouse coordinates within a movie clip independent of the main Stage?

✔ Mouse coordinates can be obtained for either the main Stage or a specific movie clip. Coordinates are referenced from the upper-left corner of the Stage or movie clip as the origin (0,0). See Flash's ActionScript help files to "Getting the mouse position" for more details.

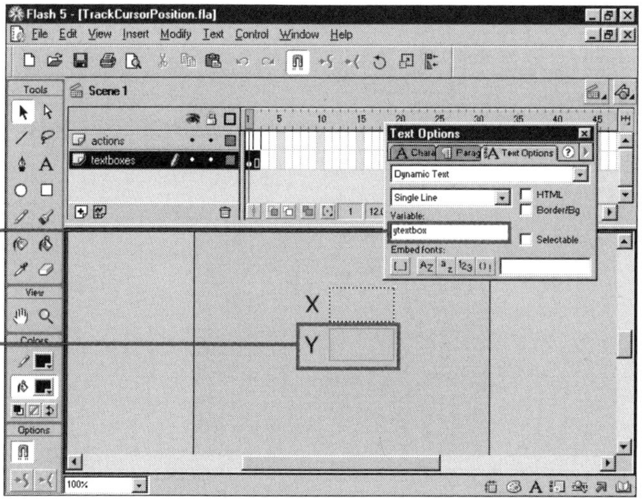

8 Repeat steps 5 through 7 for the *y*-coordinate text box, but type **ytextbox** in the Variable text box.

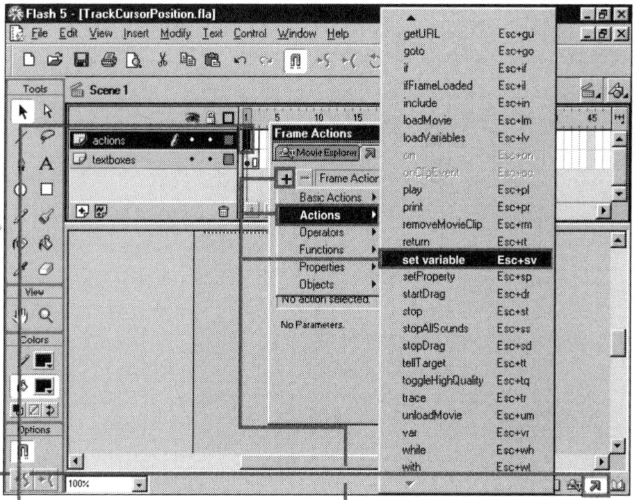

9 Click in frame 1 of the actions layer.

10 Click ⧉.

■ Flash opens the Frame Actions panel.

11 Click + and click Actions, Set Variable.

Note: See Chapter 28 to learn how to add frame actions.

CONTINUED

TRACK CURSOR POSITION (CONTINUED)

In the first phase of creating the track cursor position technique in your own Flash file, as shown in the previous steps, you established two dynamic text boxes for displaying the mouse coordinates. You then assigned each text box as a variable value. These steps are not necessary for *using* the acquired coordinates in advanced scripting, but they are good for testing your scripts and for visual appeal when used as part of the interface design.

The next phase in creating this technique is to add functionality to the mouse coordinates by assigning variable values. You do this by assigning the variable values to the text boxes you created in the previous steps.

The last phase in applying this technique to your own Flash movie is to tell the main movie's Timeline to loop and continue to check for new mouse coordinates to ensure that they are continuously updated. In a real-world application of this script, you would include the functionality in a movie clip that loops independently of the main Flash Timeline.

TRACK CURSOR POSITION (CONTINUED)

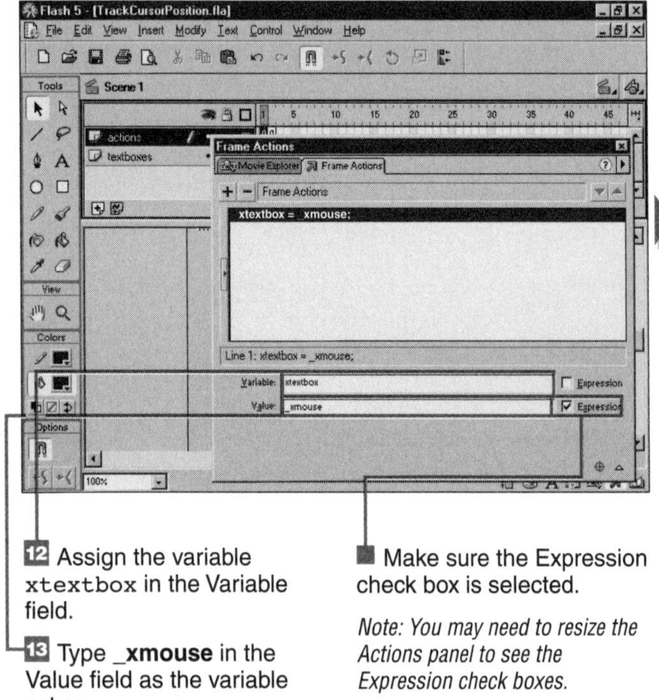

12 Assign the variable `xtextbox` in the Variable field.

13 Type **_xmouse** in the Value field as the variable value.

■ Make sure the Expression check box is selected.

Note: You may need to resize the Actions panel to see the Expression check boxes.

14 Repeat steps 11 through 13 for the ytextbox variable, but enter **_ymouse** in the variable Value field.

■ Make sure the Expression check box is selected.

Note: You may need to resize the Actions panel to see the Expression check boxes.

What exactly is considered a Property?

✔ Properties are defined by the Flash ActionScript reference as parameters you set to define an object in your movie. Properties can be set for any movie clip instance and altered indefinitely while the instance is present and defined on the Stage.

Do I need to click the Expression box following a variable name or value?

✔ Only if you want the value to be treated as a number, Boolean, or expression. By selecting the Expression check box, you are telling Flash that the text entered is part of a statement that produces a value. For example, the text value "200+200" maintains the text verbatim if the Expression check box is *not* selected, but returns the value 400 if it *is* selected.

Where are the `_xmouse` and `_ymouse` properties found in the Action menu?

✔ Both `_xmouse` and `_ymouse` can be found in the Properties action list in the Action panel's toolbox. They are properties of the *mouse cursor position*, not the position of a movie clip or other instance of a symbol on the Stage. If you want to obtain the position of a symbol on the Stage, use the `_x` and `_y` properties, found in the same menu.

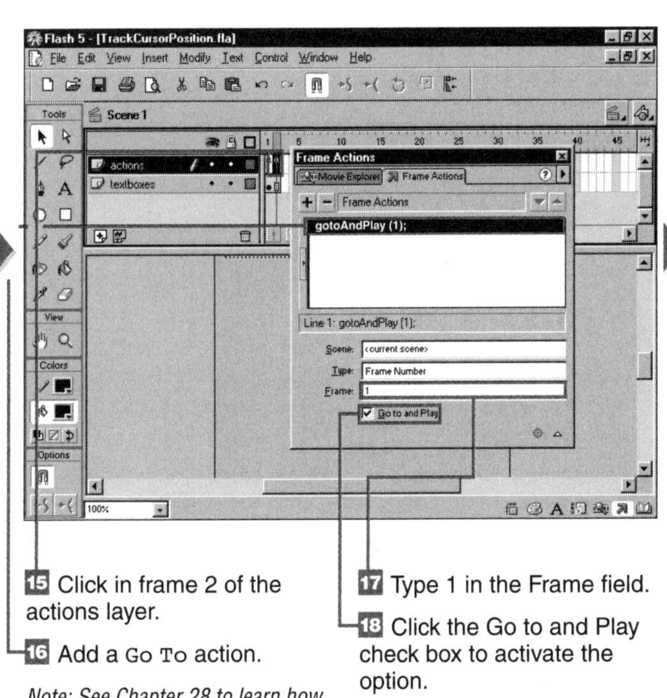

15 Click in frame 2 of the actions layer.

16 Add a Go To action.

Note: See Chapter 28 to learn how to add actions.

17 Type 1 in the Frame field.

18 Click the Go to and Play check box to activate the option.

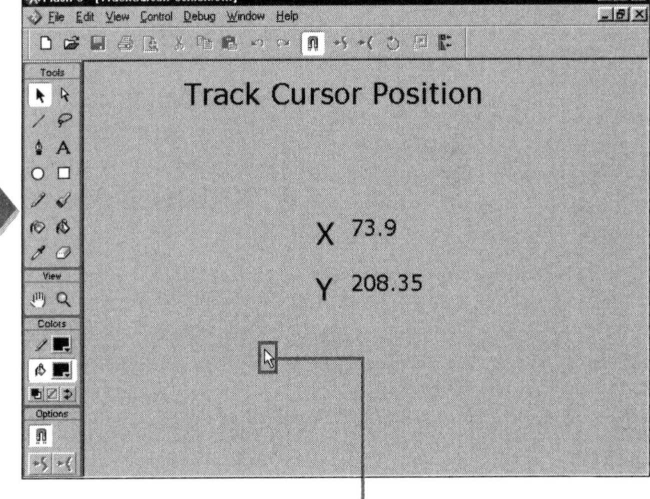

■ You can now test the actions in your movie in the Flash Player window.

Note: See Chapter 30 to learn how to test movies.

■ Notice that everywhere you move the mouse on-screen while testing the movie, the coordinates appear in the text boxes.

CREATE A WINDOW HIERARCHY

You can create a window hierarchy in your Flash project using a combination of two object actions: `swapDepths` and `startDrag`. A window hierarchy refers to the placement or precedence of overlapping windows on the Flash movie Stage. In a window hierarchy, one window appears "on top" if two or more windows are open.

Window systems are often used for offering navigation, menus, and sound controls to users. Additional functionality, such as a Close or Minimize option, are often added as well. The steps in this section show you how to create a window hierarchy using two windows.

Flash EXE filename:
WindowHierarchy.exe

Flash filenames:
WindowHierarchy.fla
WindowHierarchy.swf
WindowHierarchy.hqx

CREATE A WINDOW HIERARCHY

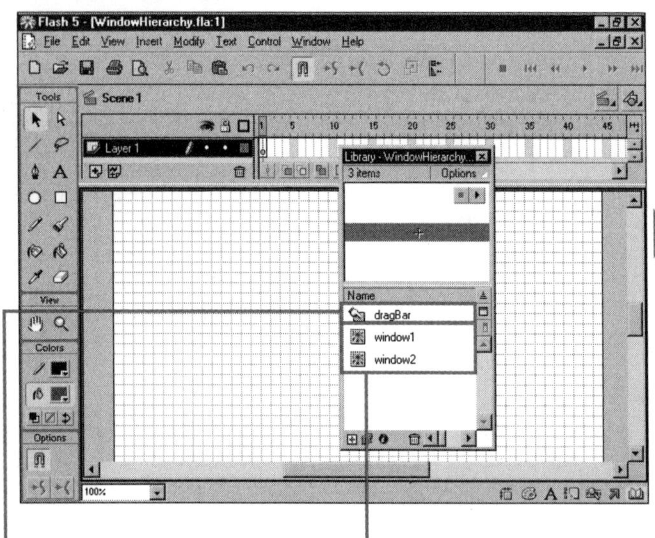

1 Create a button symbol named **dragBar** to use for both windows.

Note: See Chapter 26 to learn how to create buttons.

■ In this example, the button is a red bar.

2 Create two movie clip symbols named **window1** and **window2**.

Note: See Chapter 24 to learn about movie clips.

■ Use the dragBar button symbol as each window's title bar and use a box fill shape as the window.

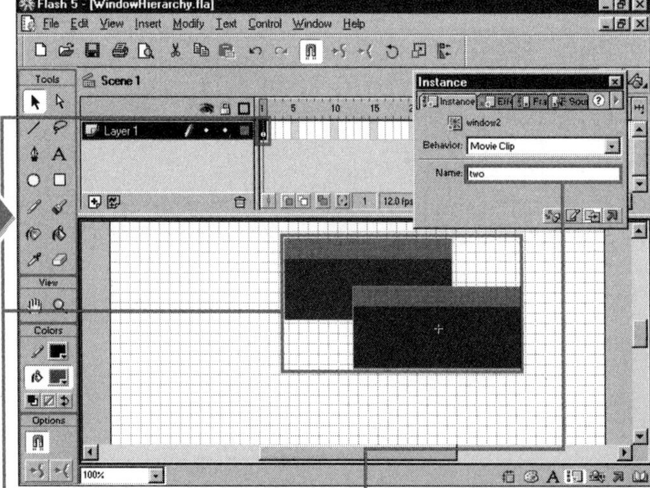

3 Place both window1 and window2 clips in frame 1 of the main Timeline.

Note: See Chapter 22 to learn more about adding symbols to the Stage.

4 Assign window1 an instance name of `one` and window2 an instance name of `two`.

Note: See Chapter 22 to learn more about adding instances in Flash.

Why should I reuse the dragBar button in both window1 and window2?

✔ Both menu title bars have the same appearance, and because multiple uses of the same symbol do not increase file size. steps 6 through 13 add functionality to each instance of the dragBar button (in window1 and window2) that brings the selected window to the front of the unselected window and allows the window to be dragged to another location on the Stage.

How do I assign an instance name to a movie clip?

✔ Select the movie clip on the Stage, then click [icon] to open the Instance panel. Click in the Name text box and type the desired name for the instance. You can then use the name in your action statements to specify the movie clip.

How do I collapse a window?

✔ You can hide the contents of a window and display only the dragBar button by creating a frame in your movie clip that shows only the bar. Use a Restore button or link to send the Playhead to a frame where the window contents are again displayed.

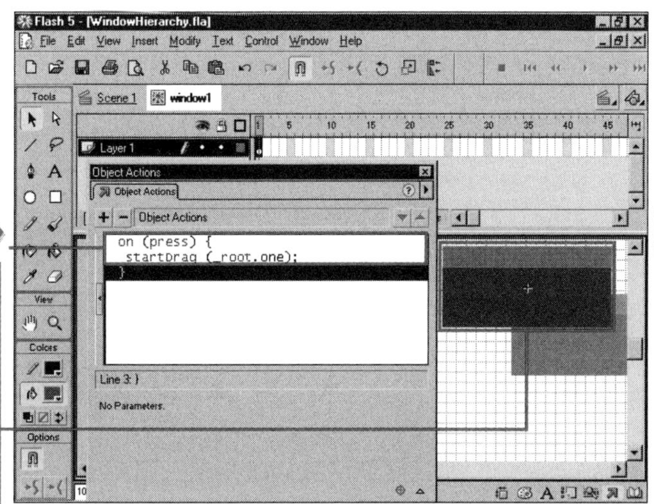

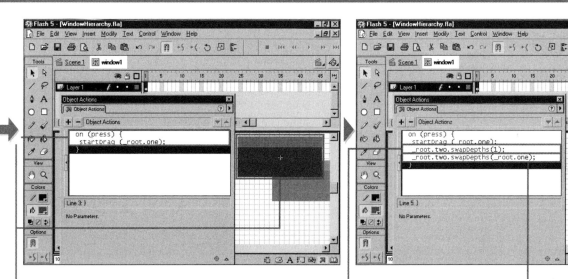

5 Open the window1 clip in symbol-edit mode and add a `startDrag` action that drags on the press of the dragBar button.

Note: See Chapters 28 and 29 to learn how to add Flash actions.

■ In this example, the statement `startDrag (_root.one);` enables the drag.

6 Set the depth value of window2 to 1 by adding the `swapDepths` action.

■ In this example, the statement `_root.two.swapDepths (1);` sets the depth value.

7 Add another `swapDepths` action to swap the depth level of window2 with window1.

■ In this example, the statement `_root.two.swapDepths (_root.one);` sets the depth level.

CONTINUED

CREATE A WINDOW HIERARCHY (CONTINUED)

The swapDepths action swaps the stacking order, also called the depth level, of one movie with another. The startDrag action enables you to click and drag a movie clip to another location. The steps in this example show you how to simulate a hierarchical window environment that places the selected window in front of another window and enables the user to move the window to another location.

The startDrag action is added to a movie clip of your window. Only one movie clip can be dragged at a time in your Flash project. Your movie clip remains draggable until it encounters a stopDrag action, or until it encounters another movie clip.

You can use draggable windows, such as the type demonstrated in these steps, in games you create in Flash, or as part of a Web site interface you design in Flash.

CREATE A WINDOW HIERARCHY (CONTINUED)

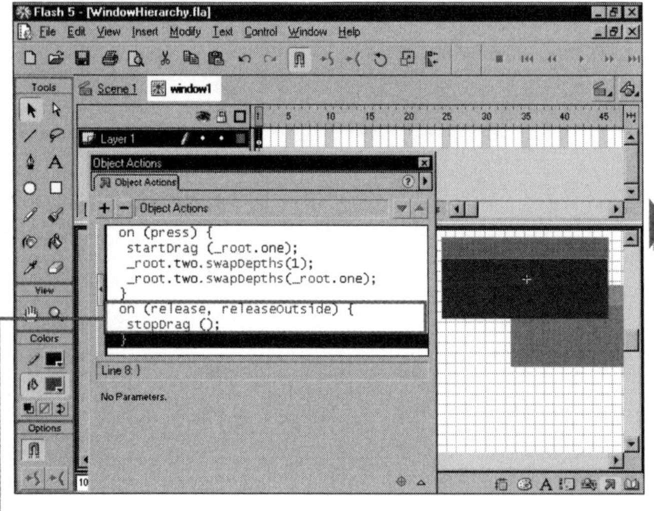

8 On the release of the dragBar button in the window1 movie clip, add a stopDrag action to stop dragging the movie clip.

Note: See Chapters 28 and 29 to learn how to add Flash actions.

■ In this example, the statement on (release, releaseOutside) {stopDrag (); } sets the end of the drag.

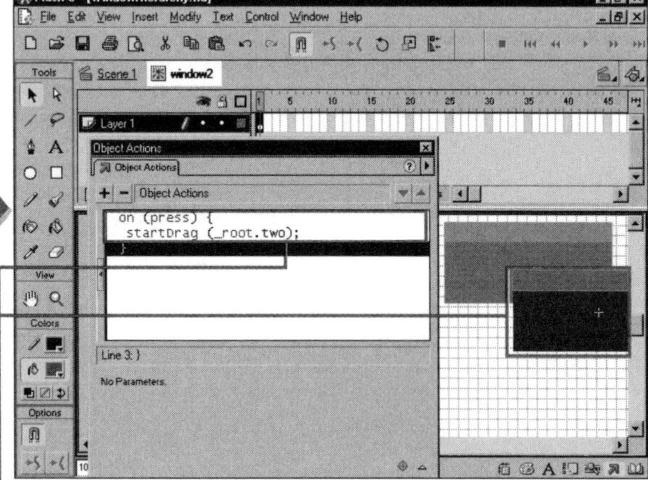

9 Open the window2 clip in symbol-edit mode and add a startDrag action that drags on the press of the dragBar button.

Note: See Chapters 28 and 29 to learn how to add Flash actions.

■ In this example, the statement startDrag (_root.two); enables the drag.

How do I create a window hierarchy when using more than two windows?

✔ For instances when you have multiple windows, you need to have a method that tracks what depth level a given window is on. Remember the `swapDepths` action only exchanges the current depth of a movie clip with a specified depth level. In order to have complex hierarchy of multiple movie clips, set variable values that keep track of depth levels and use the `swapDepths` action to exchange a movie clip's depth with the value of a given variable depth.

How do I close a window?

✔ So long as you have a means of opening the window after it is closed, you can use the instance `_visible` property to show and hide a movie clip.

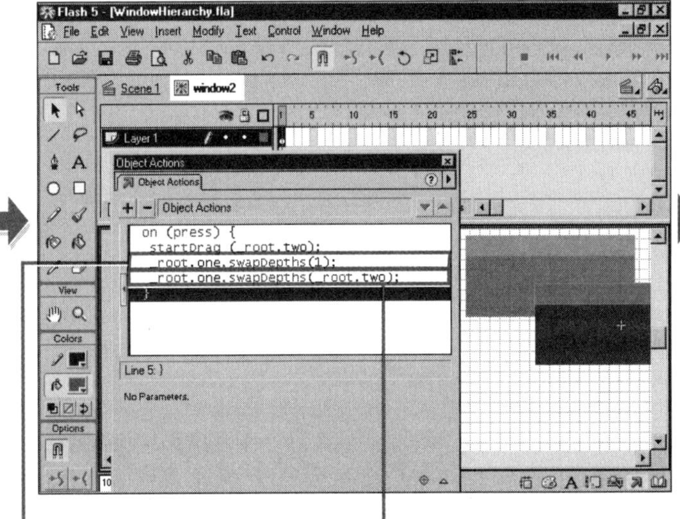

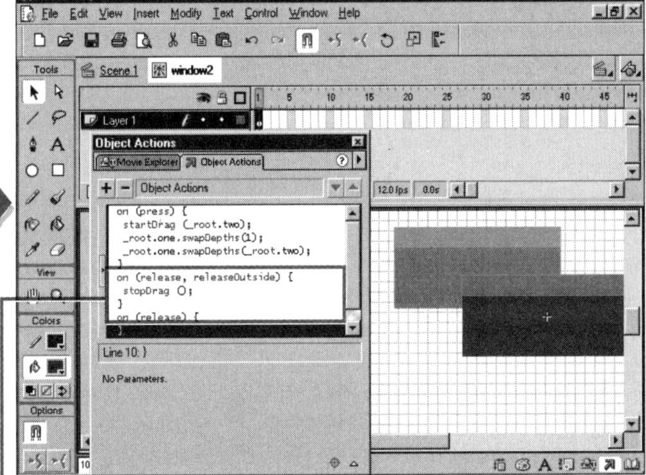

10 Set the depth value of window1 to 1 by adding the `swapDepths` action.

■ In this example, the statement `_root.one.swapDepths(1);` sets the depth value.

11 Add another swapDepths action to swap the depth level of window2 with window1.

■ In this example, the statement `_root.one.swapDepths(_root.two);` sets the depth level.

12 On the release of the dragBar button in the window2 movie clip, add a `stopDrag` action to stop dragging the movie clip.

Note: See Chapters 28 and 29 to learn how to add Flash actions.

■ The selected window is placed in front of the non-selected window and is draggable until the mouse button is released.

■ You can now test the effect in the Flash Player window.

CREATE A PASSWORD IDENTIFICATION BOX

You can add a Password Identification box to your Flash movie that prompts users for a password in order to proceed. A Password Identification box uses a password text field and the `if` and `else` actions. When the user encounters this box in a Flash file, they are prompted for a password. Depending on the string entered in the text field, the user is directed to various options you determine in advance.

The steps in this section demonstrate how to add a Password Identification field to your movie, along with a submit button the user can click after typing the password into the field.

Flash EXE filename:

Password.exe

Flash filenames:

Password.fla

Password.swf

Password.hqx

CREATE A PASSWORD IDENTIFICATION BOX

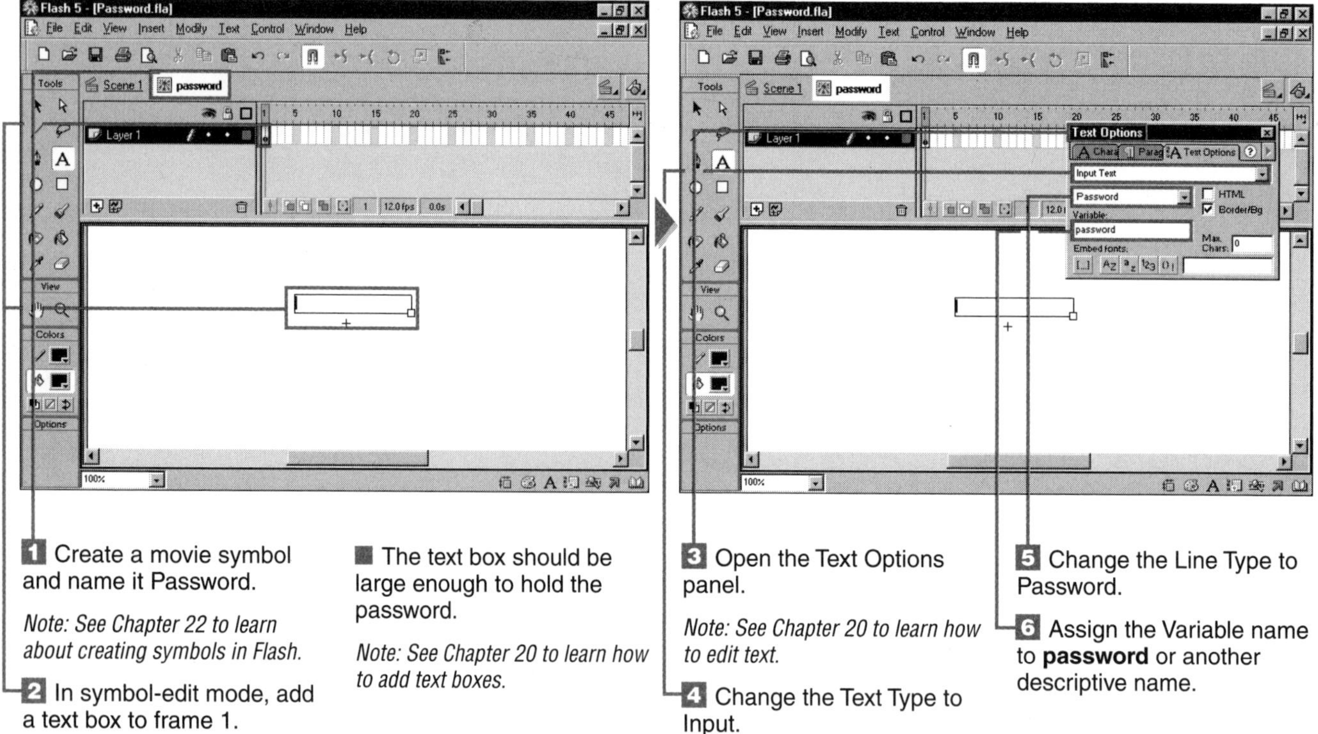

1 Create a movie symbol and name it Password.

Note: See Chapter 22 to learn about creating symbols in Flash.

2 In symbol-edit mode, add a text box to frame 1.

■ The text box should be large enough to hold the password.

Note: See Chapter 20 to learn how to add text boxes.

3 Open the Text Options panel.

Note: See Chapter 20 to learn how to edit text.

4 Change the Text Type to Input.

5 Change the Line Type to Password.

6 Assign the Variable name to **password** or another descriptive name.

Is the password protection 100% secure?

✔ No. A user can play through a Flash movie and disregard the stop actions. If you want to be completely secure, introduce a separate movie with the secret information and tell it to play during the `If` statement in the password movie. This way, if the user has disregarded the stop action, he still needs the password to start the movie.

Can I create a password without making it an *additional* movie symbol?

✔ Yes. However, assigning the Password Identification box as a movie symbol enables the designer more flexibility and protection.

Does Flash have any premade buttons I can use?

✔ Yes. You do not have to create your own buttons to use in your Flash projects. You can use the buttons available in the Buttons Library. Click the Window menu and select Common Libraries, Buttons. This opens the Buttons Library and you can choose a button to assign.

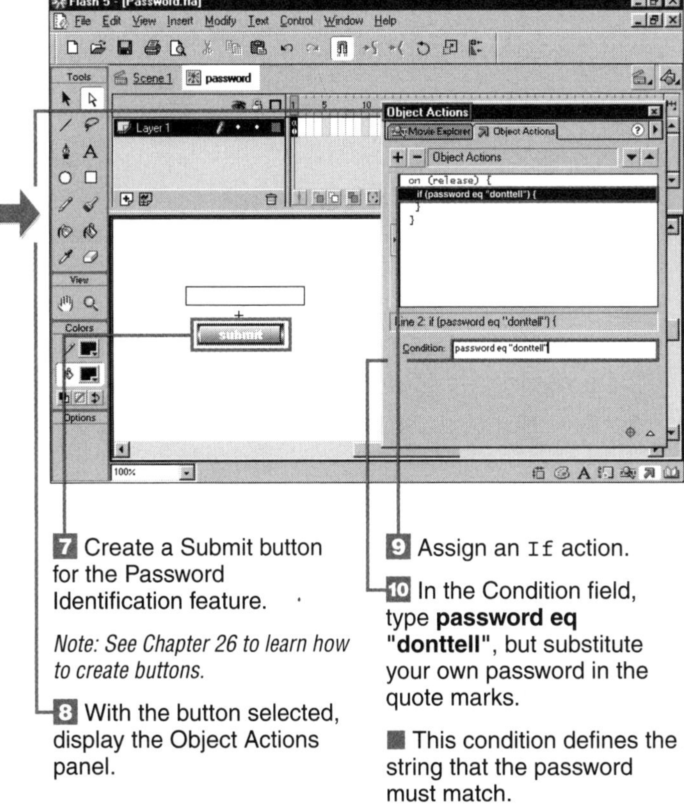

7 Create a Submit button for the Password Identification feature.

Note: See Chapter 26 to learn how to create buttons.

8 With the button selected, display the Object Actions panel.

9 Assign an `If` action.

10 In the Condition field, type **password eq "donttell"**, but substitute your own password in the quote marks.

■ This condition defines the string that the password must match.

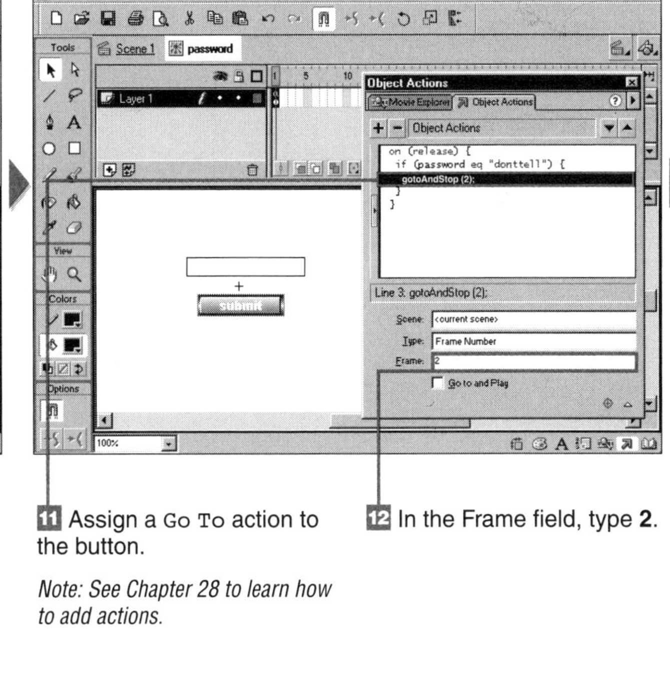

11 Assign a `Go To` action to the button.

Note: See Chapter 28 to learn how to add actions.

12 In the Frame field, type **2**.

CONTINUED

CREATE A PASSWORD IDENTIFICATION BOX (CONTINUED)

You can use the Password Identification feature in any number of ways, including as an entry password to a Web page or Flash movie, as a question/answer field in a trivia game, and in certain limited strings.

For example, you may have the user enter the city in which they live in the Identification field, and if it does not match the criteria you establish as the password, the user is restricted from entering. Such a limited entry string would restrict users from other cities but would not restrict users who match the criteria you define as the password.

When creating a Password Identification box, be sure to include some sort of text statement that tells the user whether the password has been accepted. This lets the user know what happened after they typed in the password. You should probably devote some time to thinking about what you want the user to know when they type an incorrect password, be it is as simple as, "Try again," or, "Incorrect password," or even one of these messages along with information about how to obtain the correct password.

CREATE A PASSWORD IDENTIFICATION BOX (CONTINUED)

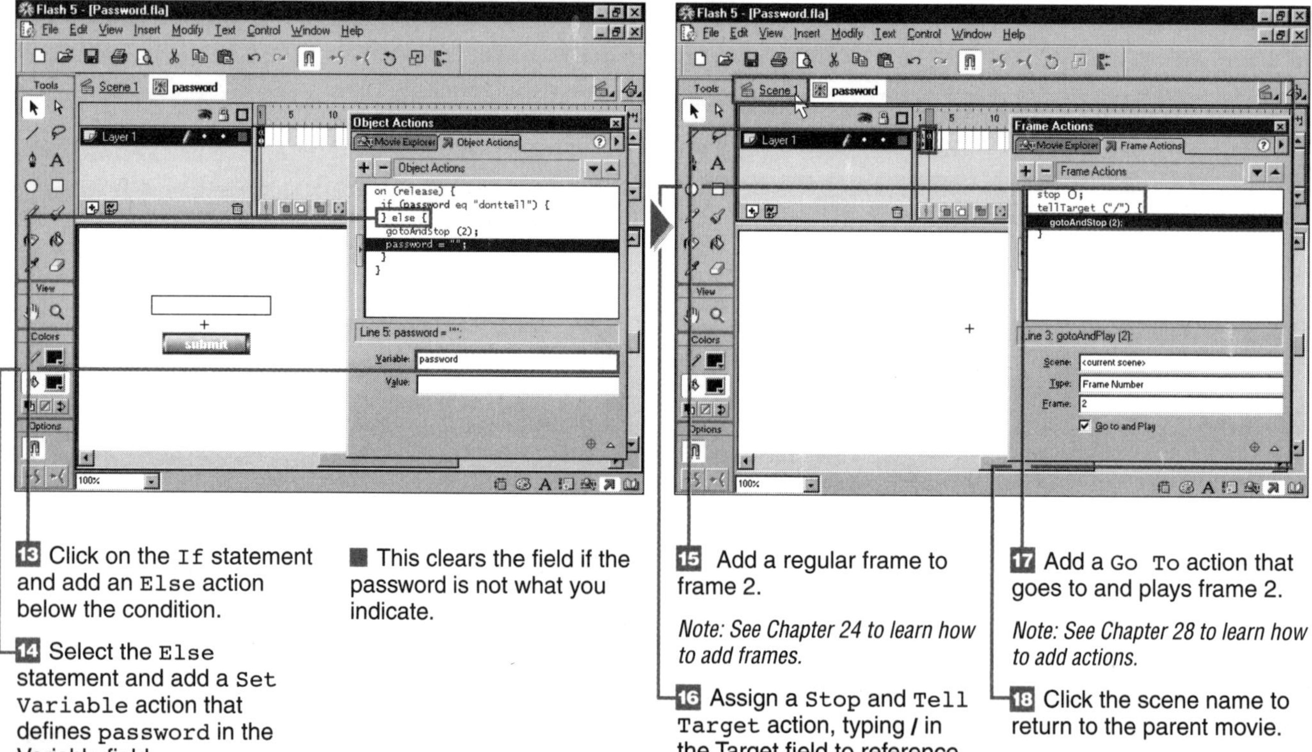

13 Click on the `If` statement and add an `Else` action below the condition.

14 Select the `Else` statement and add a `Set Variable` action that defines `password` in the Variable field.

■ This clears the field if the password is not what you indicate.

15 Add a regular frame to frame 2.

Note: See Chapter 24 to learn how to add frames.

16 Assign a `Stop` and `Tell Target` action, typing **/** in the Target field to reference the parent movie.

17 Add a `Go To` action that goes to and plays frame 2.

Note: See Chapter 28 to learn how to add actions.

18 Click the scene name to return to the parent movie.

How do I debug my actions?

✔ When you work with actions, it is not always easy to tell what action is creating a hang-up during playback. You can use Flash's debugging feature to help determine bugs in your movies. With the Flash file open, click the Control menu and choose Debug Movie. Flash opens your movie in the player window and displays the Debugger panel. From here you can check how your movie plays, how the actions and their variables work, and so on. Any changes you make to variables in the Debugger panel are immediately changed in the movie as it plays in the player window.

Can I password-protect my movie in any other way?

✔ Yes. You can use the Flash publishing feature to set a password for your Flash movie file. Click the File menu and choose Publish Settings. Click the Flash tab, choose an Options check box, such as Protect from Import or Debugging Permitted, and then type a password in the Password text box. Click OK when finished.

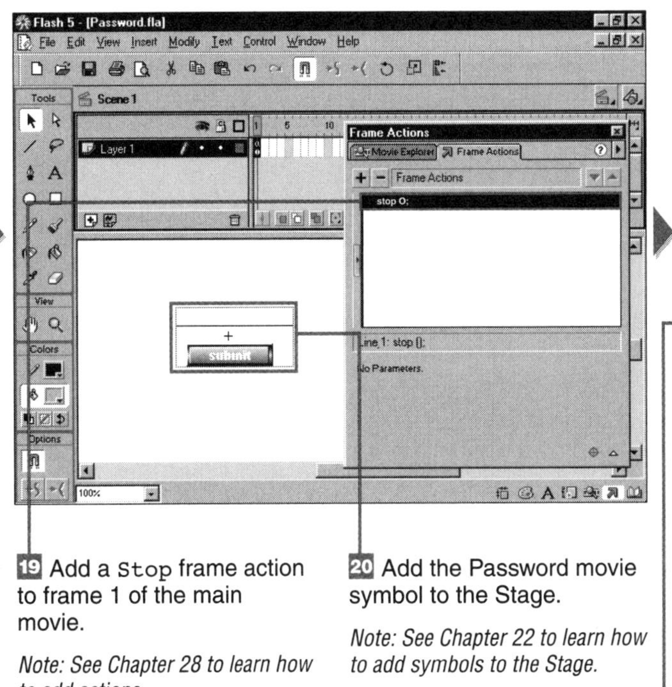

19 Add a `Stop` frame action to frame 1 of the main movie.

Note: See Chapter 28 to learn how to add actions.

20 Add the Password movie symbol to the Stage.

Note: See Chapter 22 to learn how to add symbols to the Stage.

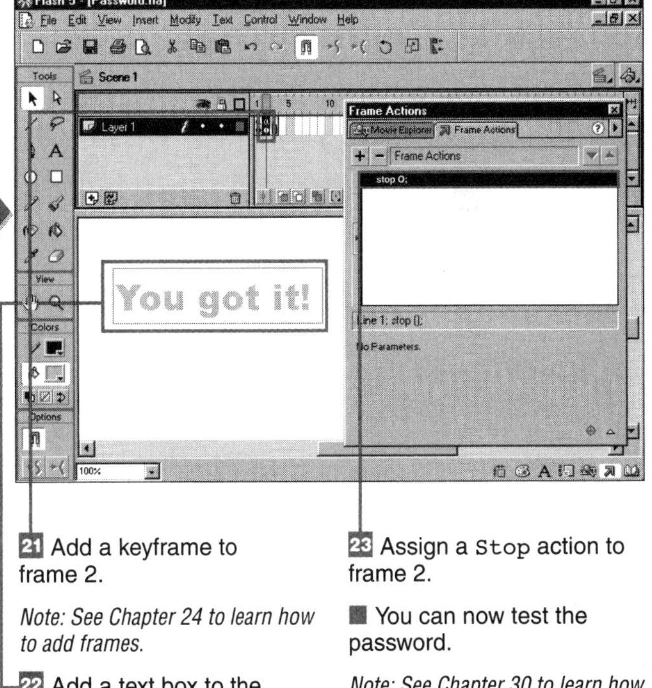

21 Add a keyframe to frame 2.

Note: See Chapter 24 to learn how to add frames.

22 Add a text box to the Stage that tells the user that they have entered the correct password and now have access.

23 Assign a `Stop` action to frame 2.

■ You can now test the password.

Note: See Chapter 30 to learn how to test movies.

PARK A MOVIE CLIP

You can park, or place, a movie clip inside a parent movie. As in preloading in JavaScript, this technique enables the designer to load a movie and reuse it again at any time.

This technique hides a movie clip inside a movie and uses the Tell Target action to play the movie. If the Flash movie is published from the bottom layer up in the Publish Settings dialog box, the clip is there for the designer or user's use at any time during the movie. See Chapter 30 to learn more about publishing your Flash movies.

The steps in this section show you how to use a button to initiate a movie. However, keep in mind that anything can start the movie, including another movie, a certain frame, and so on.

Flash EXE filename:
ParkClip.exe

Flash filenames:
ParkClip.fla
ParkClip.swf
ParkClip.hqx

PARK A MOVIE CLIP

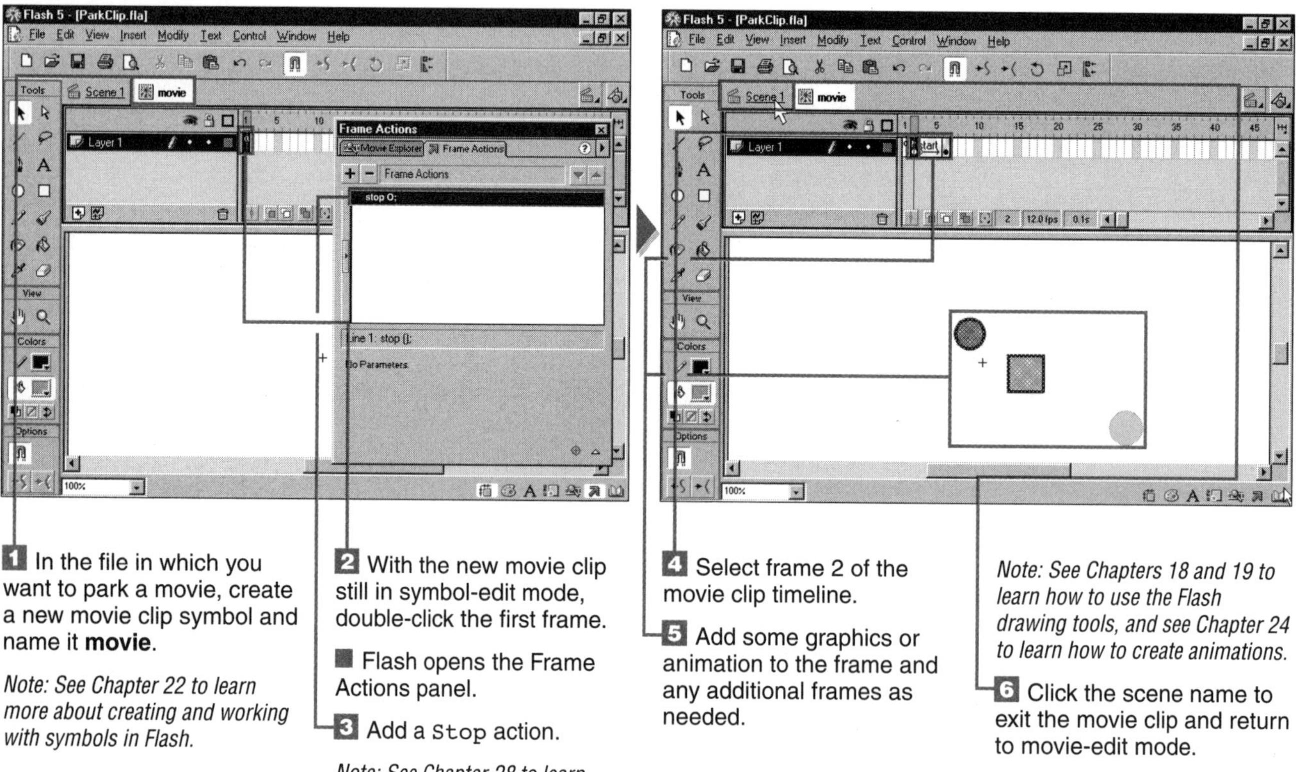

1 In the file in which you want to park a movie, create a new movie clip symbol and name it **movie**.

Note: See Chapter 22 to learn more about creating and working with symbols in Flash.

2 With the new movie clip still in symbol-edit mode, double-click the first frame.

■ Flash opens the Frame Actions panel.

3 Add a `Stop` action.

Note: See Chapter 28 to learn about adding actions.

4 Select frame 2 of the movie clip timeline.

5 Add some graphics or animation to the frame and any additional frames as needed.

Note: See Chapters 18 and 19 to learn how to use the Flash drawing tools, and see Chapter 24 to learn how to create animations.

6 Click the scene name to exit the movie clip and return to movie-edit mode.

Does the movie play over anything when I click the button?

✔ You need the movie to load first, so be sure to place it on layer 1. If the movie is on the bottom layer, anything on the layers above it appear in front of the movie. You can, however, change the publish settings to load from the top layer down and place the movie in frame 1 of the top layer in your main movie Timeline. It obstructs nothing while stopped (because there is nothing in frame 1) but appears on top of everything when played. To learn more about the Flash Publish Settings options, see Chapter 30.

If I have a really big clip to load, does it delay the rest of the movie while it loads?

✔ Yes. That is why many designers use a preloading mini-movie, called a *Preloader*. Unless you have an `If Frame Is Loaded` action statement, the movie plays immediately and may cause some stopping during the movie. You can learn more about creating a Preloader in Chapter 31.

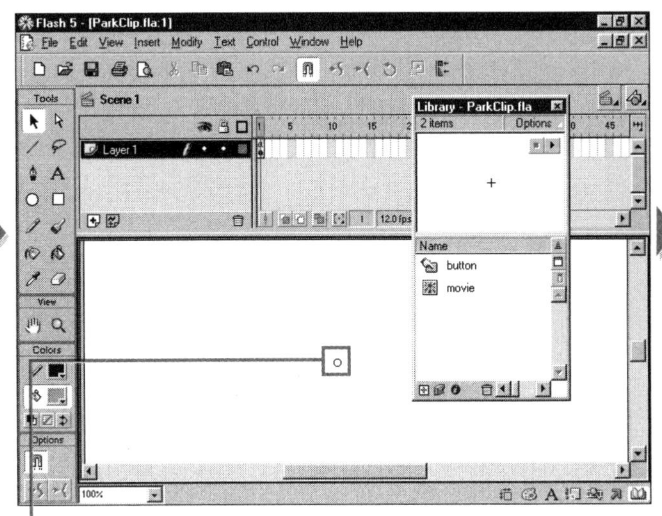

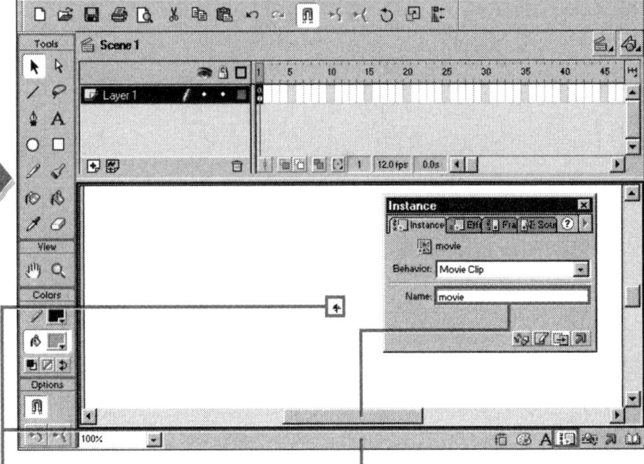

7 In frame 1 of layer 1, insert an instance of the **movie** movie clip.

Note: See Chapter 22 to learn about adding instances to the Stage using the Library window.

■ The movie clip is not visible on the Stage because nothing is in the first frame, but you should see a circular marker to indicate its position.

8 With the movie-clip instance selected, click the Show Instance button ( ).

■ Flash opens the Instance panel.

Note: See Chapter 22 to learn how to edit instances.

9 In the Name field text box, name the instance **movie**.

Note: You can close any open panels you are no longer using to clear your view of the Stage.

CONTINUED

PARK A MOVIE CLIP (CONTINUED)

One of the main reasons you may prefer to park a movie clip rather than load the movie another way is the ability to reuse the clip whenever it is needed throughout your project. The regular method of loading a movie can sometimes involve stalling due to downloading issues.

By parking a movie clip instead, you can alleviate any concerns over stalled downloading time any time you want to present the clip again in your main movie.

When parking a movie, the clip has to load only once and it is ready to play instantaneously at your command. When employing this technique, Flash treats the clip as part of the frame where the clip is inserted. This means Flash reads the entire movie clip symbol when the Playhead reaches the frame containing the clip and not the entire contents of the movie clip as another item to be downloaded.

PARK A MOVIE CLIP (CONTINUED)

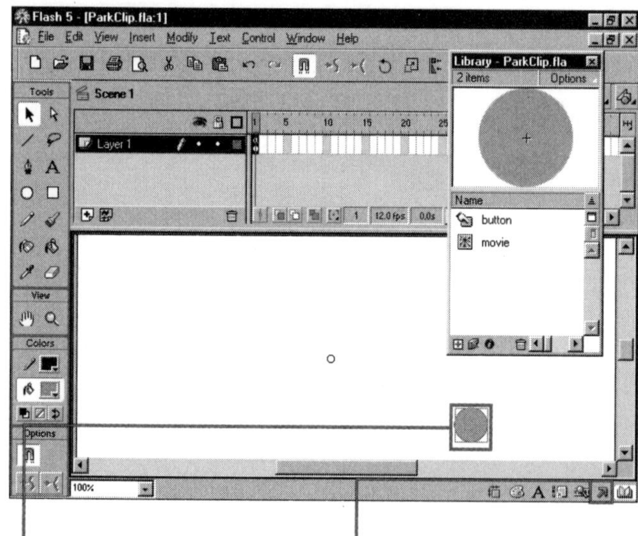

10 Create a new button or use a button from the Buttons library and place it in frame 1.

Note: See Chapter 26 to learn about creating buttons.

11 With the button selected, click the Show Actions button (⧉).

■ Flash opens the Object Actions panel.

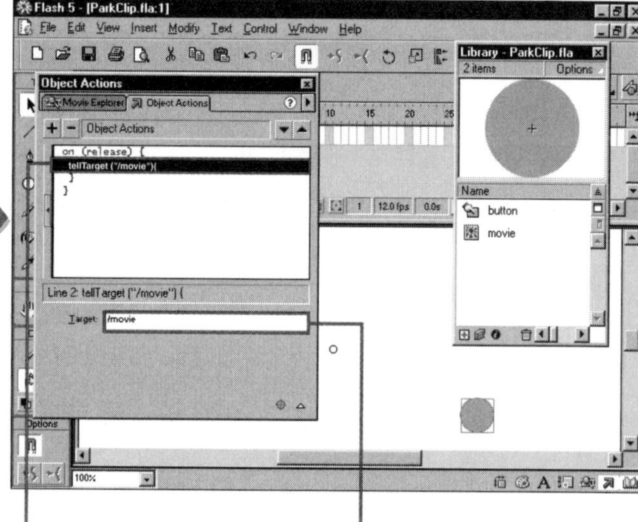

12 Add a `Tell Target` action.

13 Assign the **movie** movie clip as the Variable.

Note: See Chapter 28 to learn more about assigning actions.

If I have a long movie, how do I stop it?

✔ You can create another Tell Target button or frame and tell the same movie to Go to and Stop at frame 1. This effectively stops the movie and makes it disappear.

Should I add labels to my movie?

✔ Yes. When possible, you should add labels to your frames to help you know what keyframes hold, where important content appears, or when an important animation sequence occurs. Labeling is a great organizational help, particularly with long movies. You can learn more about adding frame labels in Chapter 28.

Can I change the `Tell Target` event?

✔ Yes. When you assign the **`Tell Target`** action to the button in step 12, **`On (Release)`** appears directly above the action statement, indicating the movie plays when the user releases the mouse button after a press. If you want to change it to something different, such as **`On Press`** or **`Rollover`**, select the **`On (Release)`** statement and choose the appropriate event variable.

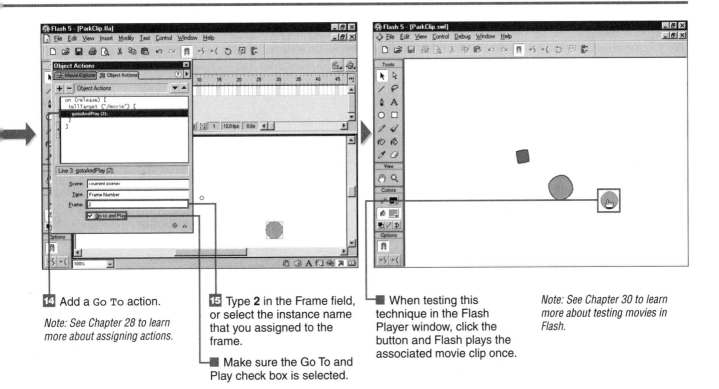

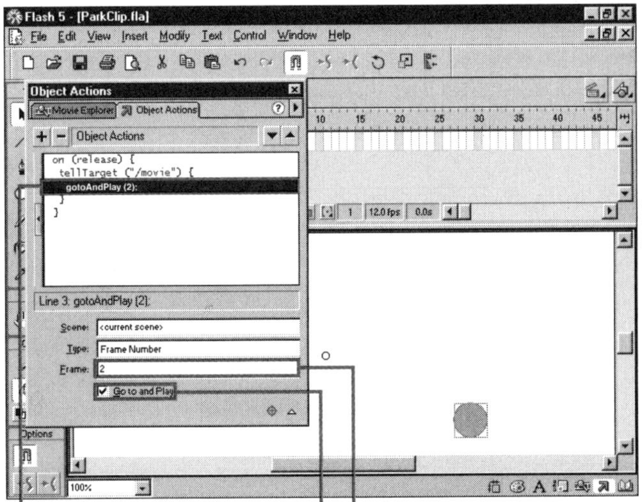

14 Add a `Go To` action.

Note: See Chapter 28 to learn more about assigning actions.

15 Type **2** in the Frame field, or select the instance name that you assigned to the frame.

■ Make sure the Go To and Play check box is selected.

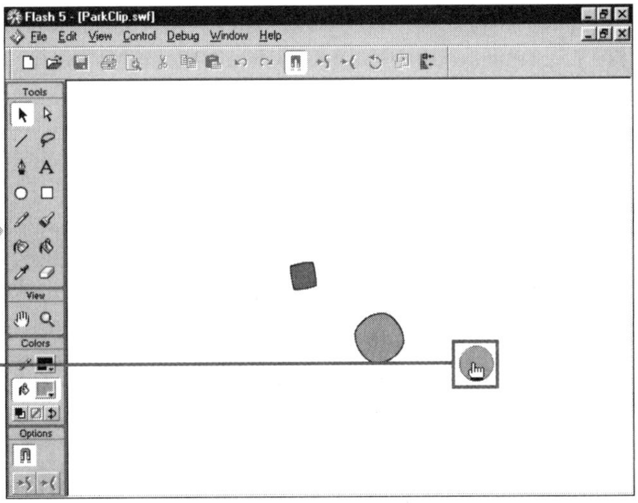

■ When testing this technique in the Flash Player window, click the button and Flash plays the associated movie clip once.

Note: See Chapter 30 to learn more about testing movies in Flash.

EMULATE AN ARRAY

You can create an array with ten random numbers and output them in an output box on playback. Quite simply, an array is a big block of information set in a specific order. Arrays are used in many different scripts, such as JavaScript, to assign names and values based on a movie in Flash. Some of the more simple uses for arrays include placement of buttons or movies, random order of events, and decoding. Variations can include a wider range of possible numbers, a different number of values in the array, and of course what is done with the values.

The steps in this section demonstrate a looping program that determines a value for ten different and random variables.

Flash EXE filename:
EmulateArray.exe

Flash filenames:
EmulateArray.fla
EmulateArray.swf
EmulateArray.hqx

EMULATE AN ARRAY

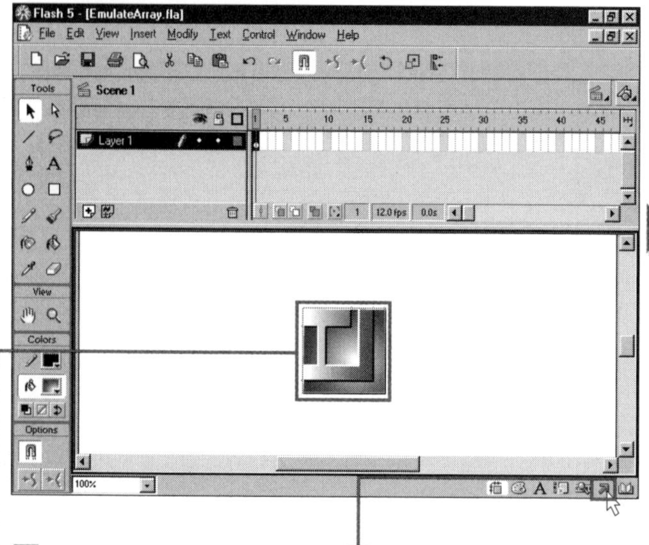

1 Add a button to the Stage in the file you want to use for this technique.

■ You can create a new button, or add one from the Buttons Library.

Note: See Chapter 26 to learn more about creating buttons in Flash.

2 With the button selected, click the Show Actions button ( ).

■ Flash opens the Object Actions panel.

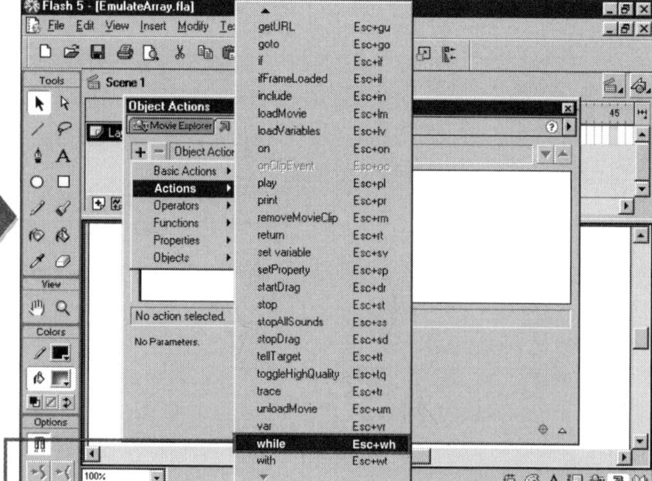

3 Add a `While` action to use as the looping statement.

■ When you add this type of Loop action, Flash automatically includes the `On (Release)` and `End On` statements.

What is a looping statement?

✔ Use a looping statement to repeat a set of actions. For example, the `While` statement is a classic example of a loop. The `While` statement performs a series of actions you designate as long as a condition is true. If you do not specify a way to make the condition false, the looping statement is endless. Always include a condition for a false value to stop the looping statement.

Can I make it so that I can get multiple numbers from the same button?

✔ Yes. When you declare the number `10` in step 4, you are declaring the number of variables that are given a value. You can change this number to increase the number of variables given or write an additional action that clears the value for `x` and resets the process. This can be done by adding a `set Variable` action in another `On mouseEvent (Release)` statement and making the variable `x` and the value `0`. This, however, changes the values of all the variables assigned. If all you want is more numbers, change the `x<10` statement.

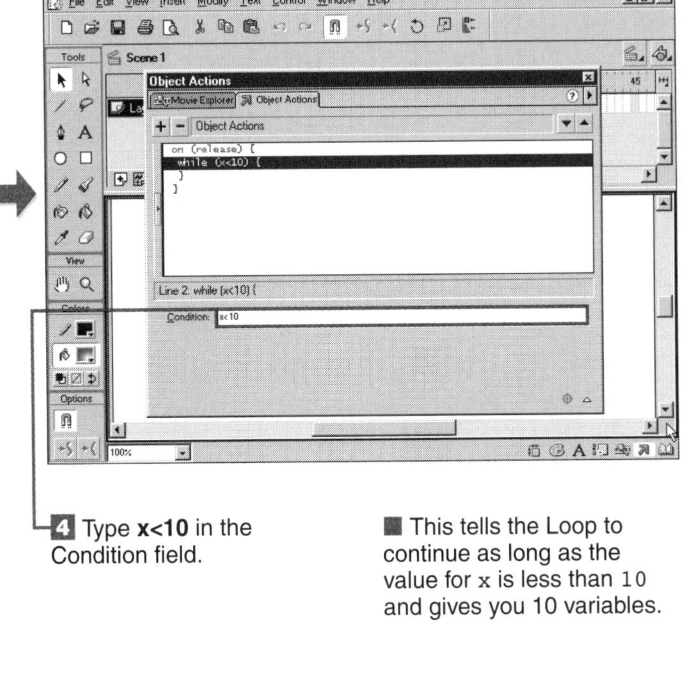

4 Type **x<10** in the Condition field.

■ This tells the Loop to continue as long as the value for `x` is less than `10` and gives you 10 variables.

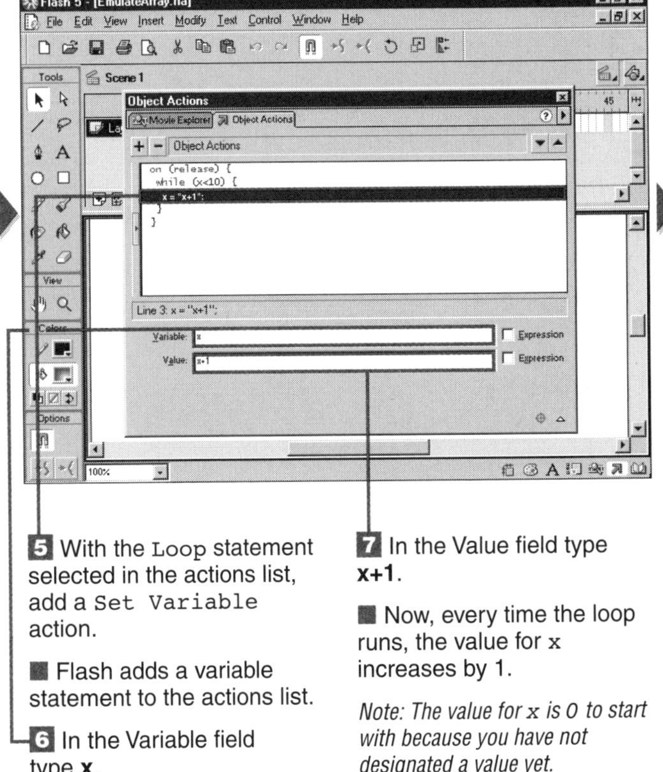

5 With the `Loop` statement selected in the actions list, add a `Set Variable` action.

■ Flash adds a variable statement to the actions list.

6 In the Variable field type **x**.

7 In the Value field type **x+1**.

■ Now, every time the loop runs, the value for `x` increases by 1.

Note: The value for x is 0 to start with because you have not designated a value yet.

CONTINUED

EMULATE AN ARRAY (CONTINUED)

An array can include many different types of *variables* (specific bits of information that comprise an array) such as text strings, numbers, or anything else, really. While a variable is comprised of a single value, an array object can contain multiple values. By allowing you to group stored data, arrays make it easier to work with the data.

In the example demonstrated in this section, the array uses ten random variables. An array's use is strictly up to the designer or user, but some uses include a specific set of numbers for a certain name, a lottery combination, or an identification name or serial number.

EMULATE AN ARRAY (CONTINUED)

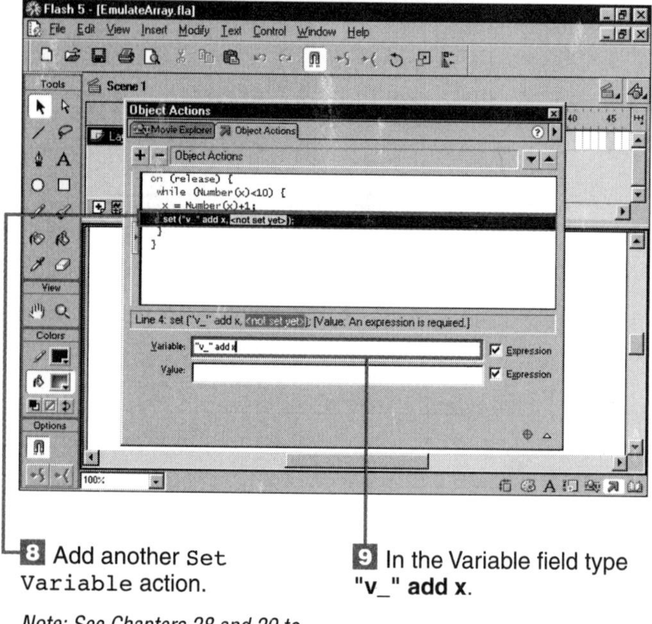

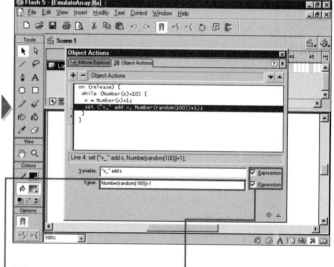

8 Add another `Set Variable` action.

Note: See Chapters 28 and 29 to learn how to add and set variables.

9 In the Variable field type **"v_" add x**.

10 In the Value field type **Number(random(100))+1**.

■ This gives a random number (1 to 100) to the variable being selected during this loop cycle.

■ Make sure the Expression check box is selected for both parameters.

Why are array properties identified by numbers?

✔ Array object properties are identified by numbers to represent their position in the array. The identifying numbers, also called an index, allow you more flexibility to access and manipulate the array. The first property of an array starts with 0, the second property is 1, and the sequence continues for the number of variables you want to identify.

Why must the Expression check box be selected?

✔ The Expression check box, when selected, tells Flash that the variable is not a literal text string, but a description.

What is the fastest way to test my array?

✔ Press Ctrl+Enter (Windows) or Command+Return (Mac) to switch to the built-in Flash Player window and see your movie.

Does the user see the numbers in the output box?

✔ No. The output box is for the use of the playback option in Flash only. It is used for reporting problems such as missing or incorrect statements in a program to the designer. It is not available in any Internet browser or in a standalone projector or movie.

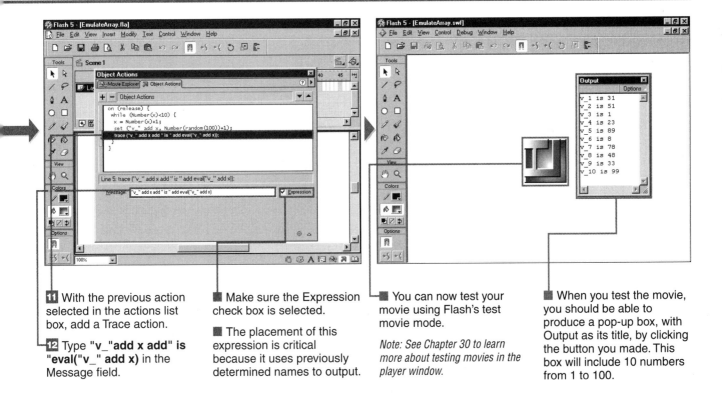

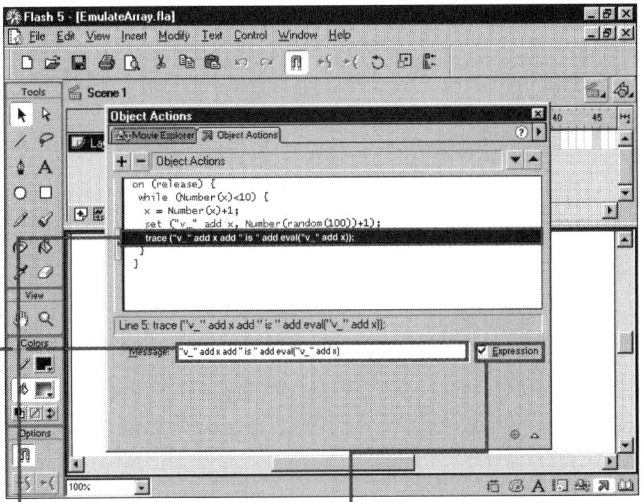

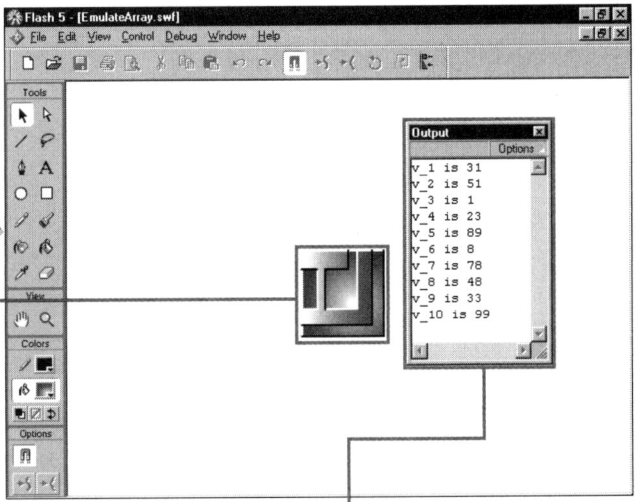

11 With the previous action selected in the actions list box, add a Trace action.

12 Type **"v_"add x add" is "eval("v_" add x)** in the Message field.

■ Make sure the Expression check box is selected.

■ The placement of this expression is critical because it uses previously determined names to output.

■ You can now test your movie using Flash's test movie mode.

Note: See Chapter 30 to learn more about testing movies in the player window.

■ When you test the movie, you should be able to produce a pop-up box, with Output as its title, by clicking the button you made. This box will include 10 numbers from 1 to 100.

COMBINE STRINGS GIVEN BY A USER

You can gather strings of data entered by the user and combine them to create a uniform statement. In the example in this section, you produce a variation of the family favorite *Mad Libs* and prompt the user for an adjective, a number, and a planet name, and display a sentence using those words in it. This technique has an infinite amount of variations, including user identification and simplification of information.

The steps in this section involve the use of editable text fields and the `Set variable` action.

Flash EXE filename:

CombineStrings.exe

Flash filenames:

CombineStrings.fla

CombineStrings.swf

CombineStrings.hqx

COMBINE STRINGS GIVEN BY A USER

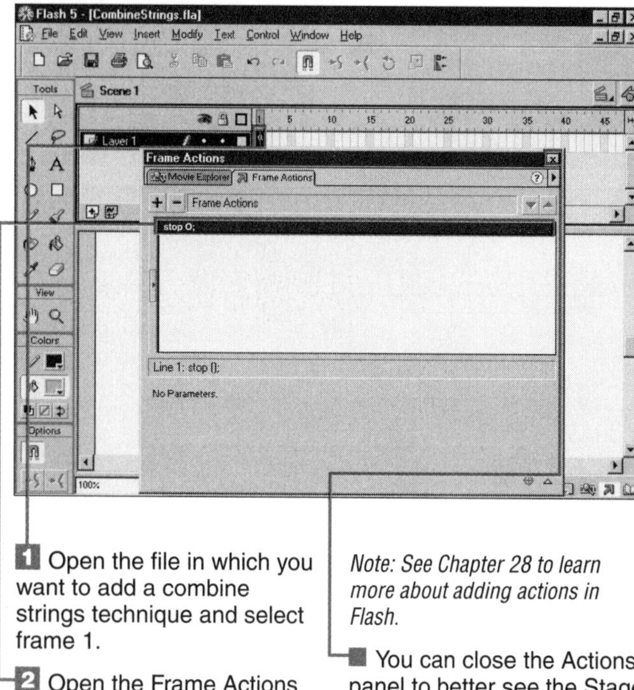

1 Open the file in which you want to add a combine strings technique and select frame 1.

2 Open the Frame Actions panel and add a `Stop` action.

Note: See Chapter 28 to learn more about adding actions in Flash.

■ You can close the Actions panel to better see the Stage for the next steps.

3 Create a box shape with a fill color (choose a color other than white) on one half of the Stage.

Note: See Chapter 18 to learn how to draw shapes.

4 Create a static text box near the top of the fill shape and type **Please enter the following:** in the text box.

Note: See Chapter 20 to learn how to add text.

Why must I set text box types?

✔ Assign text types to your text boxes to tell Flash how to treat the boxes. You can choose from three different text types: static, dynamic, or input. Use static text for text that does not change in your movie. Use dynamic and input boxes for text boxes that reflect input or action statement results. You can change text box type using the drop-down list in the Text Options panel.

How long can the sentence be?

✔ There is no limit to the amount of text that goes into the expression, but you have to look out for two things: The punctuation is more difficult to troubleshoot as the expression gets longer, and the text field that holds the value has to correspond to the length of the expression or else text is cut off.

What can the user input into the text fields?

✔ In most cases, users can put anything into the text fields. If you want to limit the possibilities that they can input, you must include an `if` action in the button statements telling them to insert a different value (for example, a number if they did not enter a number).

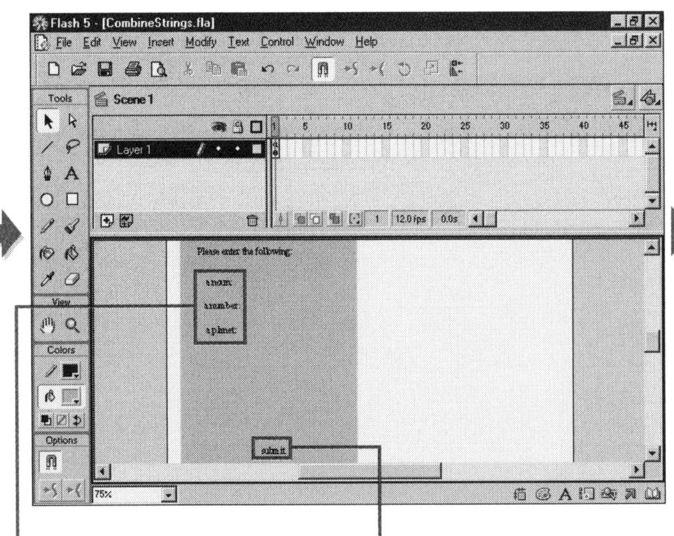

5 To the left side of the box, add three static text boxes containing these variable names: **a noun, a number, a planet**.

■ Leave enough space for editable text fields to the right of the variable names.

6 Add a static text box at the very bottom of the box and type **submit**.

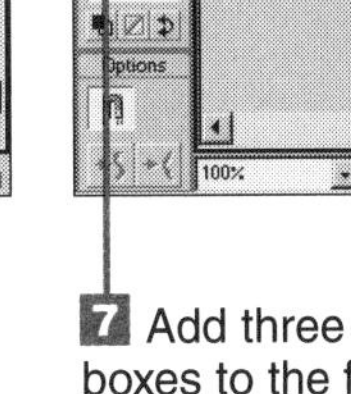

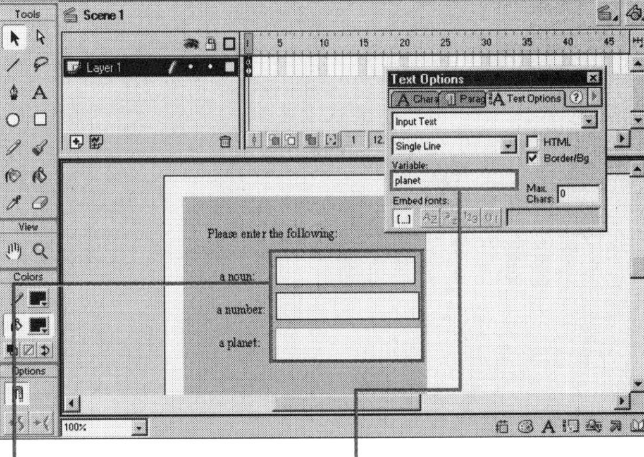

7 Add three input text boxes to the fill shape box, one beside each variable name, and use the Text Options panel to assign each box Input text type status.

8 Using the Text Options panel, assign Variable names for each input text box, using the names you assigned in step 5: noun, number, and planet.

CONTINUED

COMBINE STRINGS GIVEN BY A USER (CONTINUED)

Text strings are a common type of variable value used in Flash actions. The term *string* is used in many programming languages, including Flash's ActionScript, to specify text values. Text strings can use letters, spaces, punctuation, and numbers. For example, you may have a text string that asks the user something like, "How are you today?" or, "What is your favorite color?" You must enclose string values in quote marks, such as

```
lucky number = "7";
```

You can use the + operator to join strings. In the following statement, a personal greeting is generated:

greeting = "Hello, " + firstName;

Although lowercase and uppercase characters are not an issue in variable names, they are important in text strings. Text strings are literal, so if you type *HELLO*, the user sees all caps, but if you type *Hello*, the user sees an initial cap.

COMBINE STRINGS GIVEN BY A USER (CONTINUED)

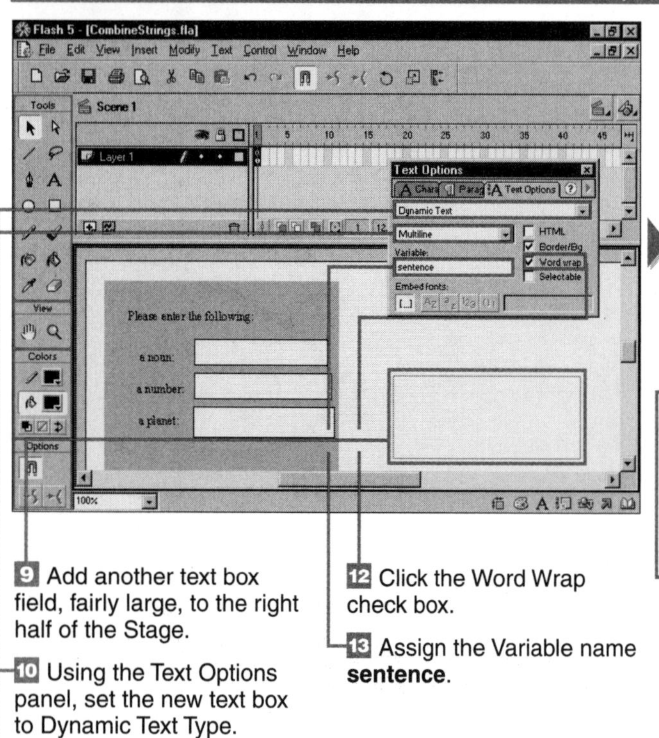

9 Add another text box field, fairly large, to the right half of the Stage.

10 Using the Text Options panel, set the new text box to Dynamic Text Type.

11 Set the Line Type to Multiline.

12 Click the Word Wrap check box.

13 Assign the Variable name **sentence**.

14 Create a new button or insert a button from the Buttons Library, and place it right above the text box containing the word submit.

Note: See Chapter 26 to learn how to create buttons in Flash.

15 Add the `Set Variable` action to the button.

Note: See Chapter 28 to learn how to add actions.

■ Flash automatically adds the `On (Release)` and `End On` statements.

Can the user change the variables in the sentence after it is printed?

✔ Yes. After the Submit button has been pressed, the user can input different answers into the fields to change the sentence. Also the designer can clear the text boxes after the Submit button had been pushed by adding the `Set Variable` action after the first one in the button for every variable you want cleared. Leave the value for these blank.

Can I allow users to copy and paste my poetic masterpieces?

✔ Yes. In the dynamic text box created in step 9, you can click the Selectable check box in the Text Options panel. This allows users to select the text in your movie.

What if I include punctuation in my sentence that does not appear in the SWF file?

✔ This can happen if you have not selected the Include Font option. At the very bottom of the Text Options panel are options for embedding fonts, including letters, numbers, and punctuation. Click the Include Everything button to make sure your punctuation is included in the published file. See Chapter 30 to learn more about publishing your movies.

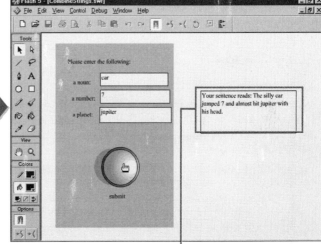

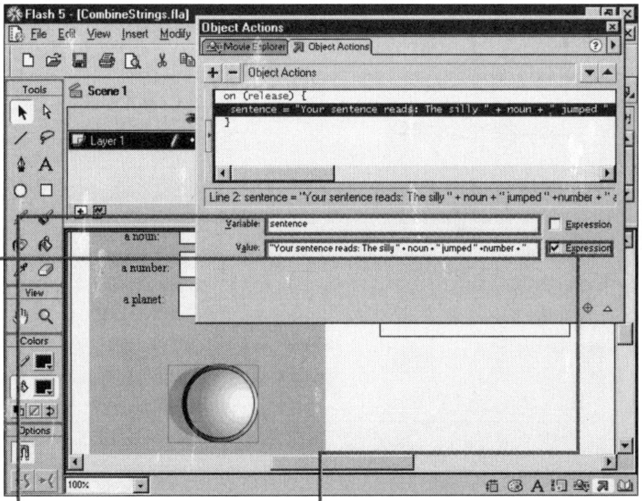

16 Type the word **sentence**.

17 Type the following expression: **Your sentence reads: The silly "+noun+" jumped"+number" feet and almost hit "+planet+" with his head**.

■ Make sure that the punctuation and placement is correct or else it may not read correctly.

18 Make this field an expression.

19 Test your movie.

Note: See Chapter 30 to learn how to use the Flash Player window.

■ When you type variable text into the text boxes and click the button, the text string should result in a silly sentence.

REPLICATE A MOVIE RANDOMLY OR BY COMMAND

You can replicate a movie clip in a Flash movie to replay automatically in random areas on the Stage or by command. *Replicate* means to duplicate the movie either by a preprogrammed control or by a control activated by the user, such as a click of a button. One of the most common uses for this technique is in games you create in Flash. With a little imagination, you might come up with some other ways to employ this technique on a Web site or in a standalone Flash presentation.

A replicating movie plays in random positions on the Flash Stage. For example, when the user clicks the designated button, the clip seems to duplicate itself and start playing again in another area of the Stage while the first clip continues playing on its own.

Flash EXE filename:

ReplicateMovie.exe

Flash filenames:

ReplicateMovie.fla

ReplicateMovie.swf

ReplicateMovie.hqx

REPLICATE A MOVIE RANDOMLY OR BY COMMAND

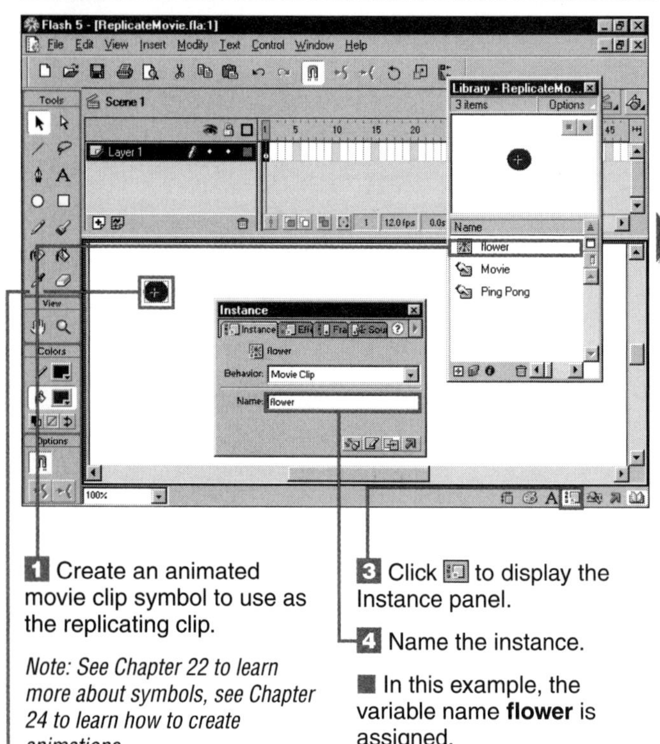

1 Create an animated movie clip symbol to use as the replicating clip.

Note: See Chapter 22 to learn more about symbols, see Chapter 24 to learn how to create animations.

2 Place an instance of the movie clip on the Stage.

3 Click to display the Instance panel.

4 Name the instance.

■ In this example, the variable name **flower** is assigned.

5 Create a new button or use one from the Buttons Library and place it on the Stage.

Note: See Chapter 26 to learn how to create buttons, see Chapter 22 to learn how to add symbols to the Stage.

6 With the button instance selected, click .

■ Flash opens the Object Actions panel.

Can I delete each of the movie clips after I add them?

✔ No. You cannot select specific clips to remove. You can, however, delete all of them. Add a new button, assign it the instance **delete**, and then add this loop to the actions list:

```
On (Release)
  Loop While (remove <= var)
  Remove Movie Clip ("new" &
    remove)
  Set Variable: "remove" =
    remove + 10
  End Loop
  Set Variable: "var" = "0"
  Set Variable: "remove" = "0"
  End On
```

This deletes the movie clips one at a time until the new variable, `remove`, is equal to the variable `var`.

How do I resize the Actions panel?

✔ You can resize the Actions panel any time you need to see statements in the actions list area. To resize the panel, move the mouse pointer over the right or left edge of the panel, click and drag to a new size. Resizing does not affect the statements in any way.

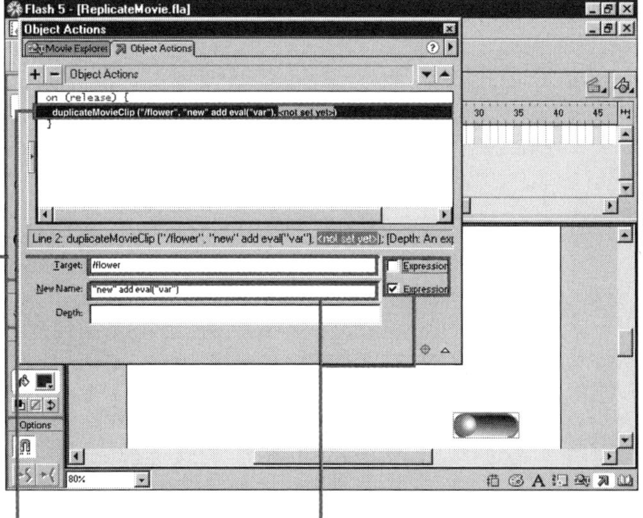

7 Assign the `duplicateMovieClip` action.

Note: See Chapter 28 to learn more about assigning actions.

8 Click in the Target field and type the name of your movie clip preceded by a "/".

■ This parameter tells the movie where the clip is located.

9 Type the name of the new clip inside of quotes. Add an ampersand and a variable name of your choice.

■ Make sure the Expression box is checked.

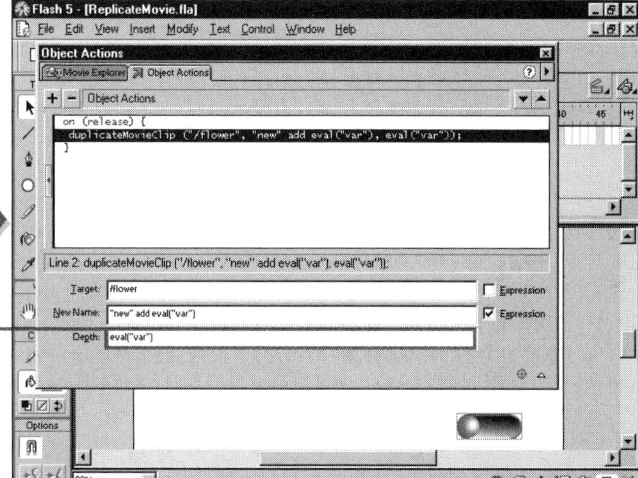

10 In the Depth field, type the same variable that was used in the new name field.

Note: This parameter allows the movie to create new layers in which to add the new movies.

■ You may need to enlarge the Actions panel to see the complete action statement.

CONTINUED

REPLICATE A MOVIE RANDOMLY OR BY COMMAND (CONTINUED)

Replicating a movie randomly or by command is a useful technique if you are creating a game using Flash. For example, if you have a movie clip that relates to another object in the Flash movie, you can increase the probability that that movie clip touches the object by replicating the movie clip.

For example, in a game scenario where the user must click on animated amoeba targets in order to "kill" them, a replicating movie clip can be used for the amoebas. The movie clip would include a short animation of an amoeba object seeming to move or undulate slightly. If the clip is replicating randomly, the task of clicking on it becomes more difficult for the user, increasing the challenge of the game. It is also possible to count the clips that have been eliminated using the Set Variable action.

REPLICATE A MOVIE RANDOMLY OR BY COMMAND (CONTINUED)

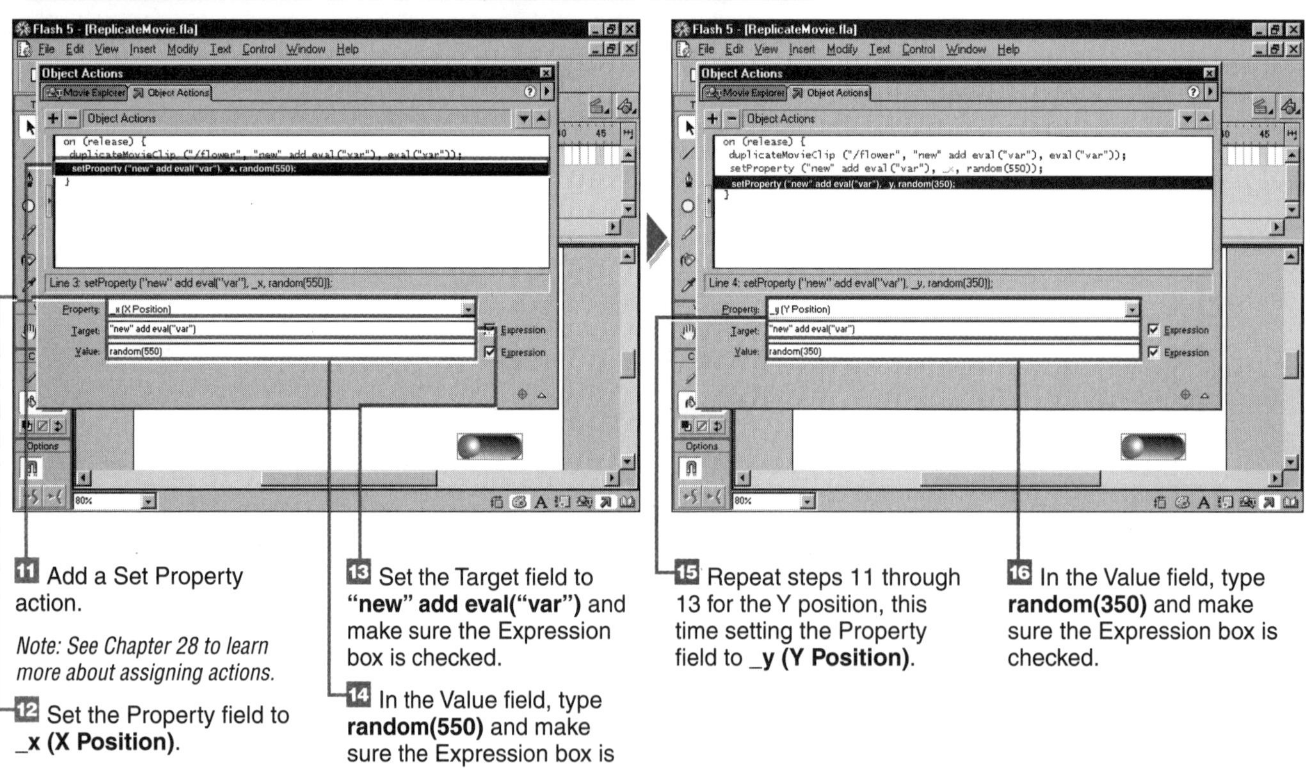

11 Add a Set Property action.

Note: See Chapter 28 to learn more about assigning actions.

12 Set the Property field to **_x (X Position)**.

13 Set the Target field to **"new" add eval("var")** and make sure the Expression box is checked.

14 In the Value field, type **random(550)** and make sure the Expression box is checked.

15 Repeat steps 11 through 13 for the Y position, this time setting the Property field to **_y (Y Position)**.

16 In the Value field, type **random(350)** and make sure the Expression box is checked.

Can I set a limit on the number of movie clips that the user can add?

✔ Yes, if you include an `if` statement before the duplicate statement and set the condition to `var<=[specific number]` you can limit the number of duplicated movie clips.

Can I change other properties, too?

✔ Yes. You can change any of the properties (alpha, rotation, and so on) and randomize them as well, just by adding the set property value.

What do the numbers in the random statements mean?

✔ They are numbers that the random program can select between 0 and one less than the number you specify. 550 and 350 were selected because they were the dimensions of the default movie. You can make this number whatever you would like. If you want to make a range not including 0, use this expression: `Random(400)+75`. This creates a range between 75 and 475 to duplicate it in.

Where can I learn more about writing ActionScript statements?

✔ Flash installs with help files dedicated to ActionScript. To access these files, click the Help menu and click ActionScript Reference.

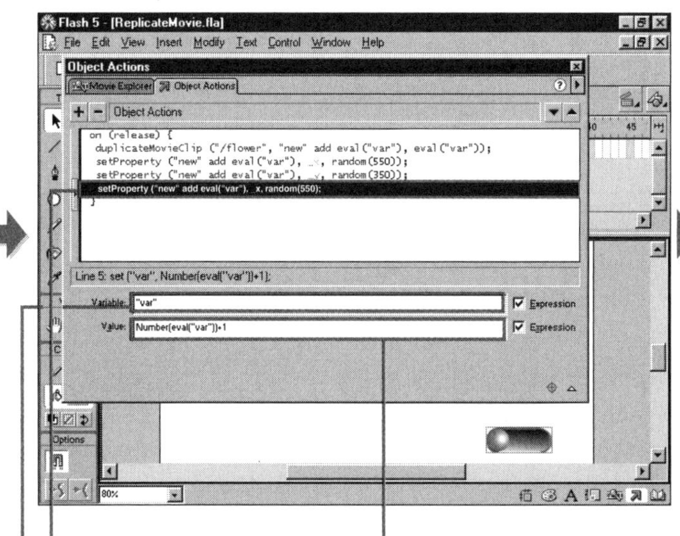

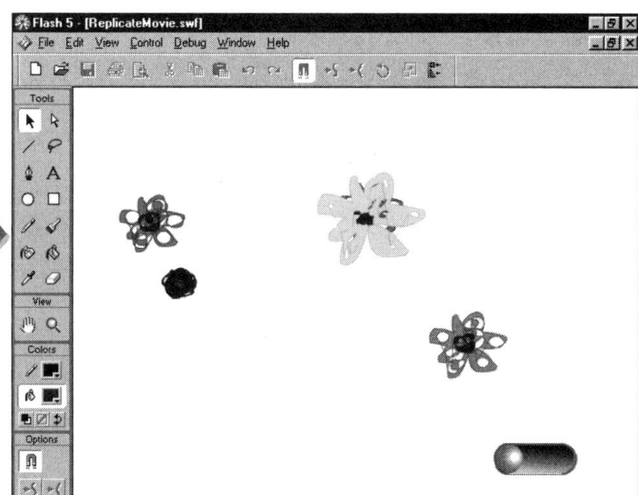

17 Add a `Set Variable` action.

Note: See Chapter 28 to learn how to add actions.

18 In the Variable field, type your variable name surrounded by quotes and make sure the Expression box is checked.

19 In the Value field, type **Number(eval("var"))+1"** and make sure the Expression box is checked.

20 Test your movie in the player window.

Note: See Chapter 30 to learn more about testing movies in the player window.

■ Each time you click the button, the movie clip replicates and loops continuously onscreen.

SEND A FORM USING A CGI SCRIPT

You can create a form in Flash that sends information to an unspecified user using a destination specified by the person filling out the form. For example, perhaps you want to allow your Web site visitors the ability to send their name and e-mail address along with a message to the Web designer's e-mail account. You can use a form, such as the one you create in this section, to do the job.

Note: The companion CD-ROM does not contain the Perl script necessary to make this technique work. You can download these scripts for free from sites like www.worldwidemart.com/scripts/ (Matt's Script Archive). This file should be placed in an accessible folder (most likely called `cgi-bin`) on your server and is accessed directly from the Flash file.

Developers use this technique is used to get information to an unspecified recipient (or specified if that variable is set). This example uses the dynamic text field options with the `GetURL` action assigned to the form button that carries out the action.

Flash EXE filename:

SendForm.exe

Flash filenames:

SendForm.fla

SendForm.swf

SendForm.hqx

SEND A FORM USING A CGI SCRIPT

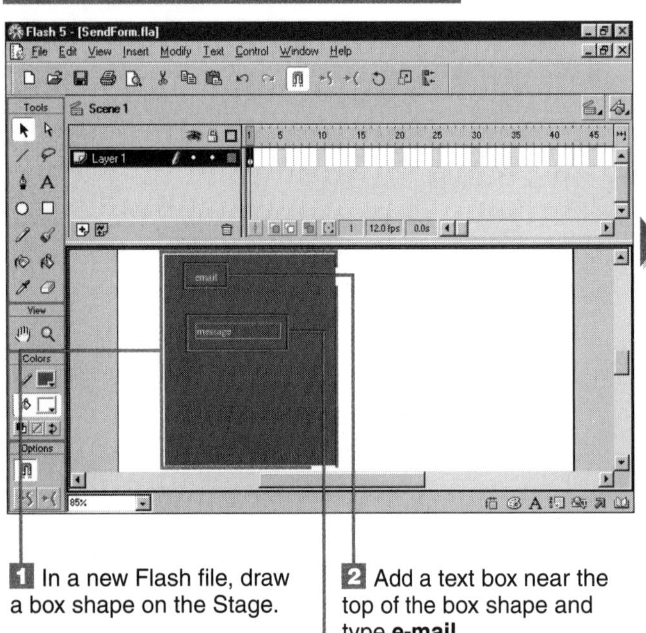

1 In a new Flash file, draw a box shape on the Stage.

■ Use any fill color for the box.

Note: See Chapters 18 and 19 to learn more about using the Flash drawing tools.

2 Add a text box near the top of the box shape and type **e-mail**.

Note: See Chapter 20 to learn more about adding text boxes.

3 Add another text box an inch below the first and type **message**.

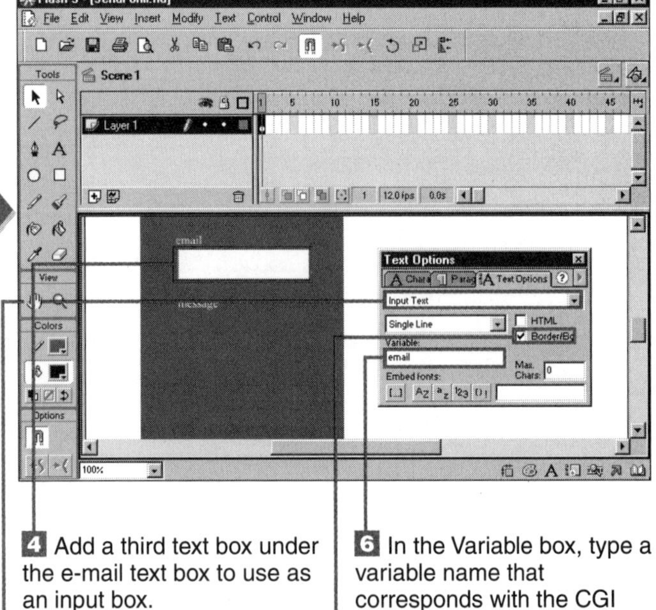

4 Add a third text box under the e-mail text box to use as an input box.

5 Open the Text Options panel and set the Text Type to Input.

Note: See Chapter 20 to learn how to set text options.

6 In the Variable box, type a variable name that corresponds with the CGI script, such as **e-mail**.

7 Select the Border/Bg check box.

What is Perl?

✔ If you are new to Web design, you may not be familiar with all the scripting languages used on the Internet. Perl, which stands for Practical Extraction and Report Language, is a high-level programming language that has been adopted as the language of choice among Web developers. For that reason, you can find numerous CGI interfaces and libraries of Perl scripts on the Web that relate to Web page creation. As you explore such libraries on the Internet, you find that most Perl scripts are stored as text source files.

Can I have hidden strings sent with the form?

✔ If you want to specify the recipient, for example, and would not like to display it, Flash can do this very effectively by setting the variable. In the first frame, perhaps with the background box selected, select the action set variable. Set the variable to the recipient and the value to the e-mail address.

How many strings can I prompt the user to enter?

✔ You can prompt the user for as many strings as you want, as long as they match up with variables in the CGI script.

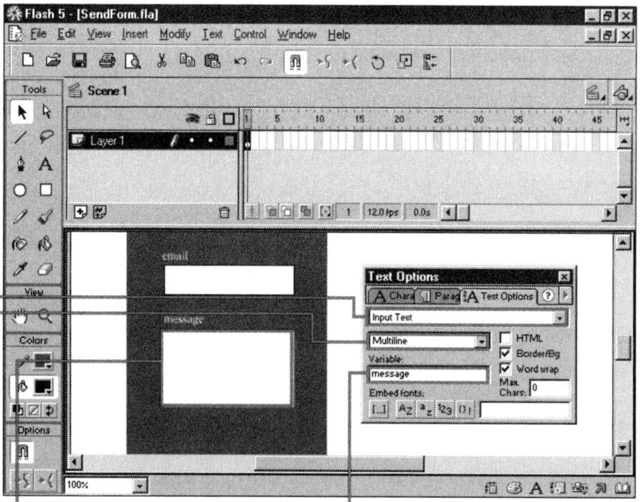

8 Add another input text box beneath the message text box.

9 Assign the new text box Input status.

10 Set the Line Type to Multiline and select the Word Wrap check box.

11 Enter the Variable name that corresponds to the CGI script.

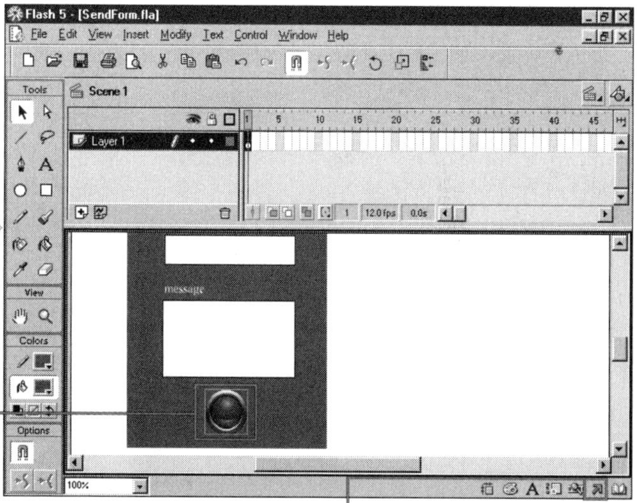

12 Insert a button symbol of your design or from the common Buttons library.

Note: See Chapter 26 to learn how to create buttons.

13 With the button selected, click [icon] to open the Object Actions panel.

Note: See Chapter 28 to learn how to add actions.

CONTINUED

SEND A FORM USING A CGI SCRIPT (CONTINUED)

CGI, which stands for Common Gateway Interface, is a standard method of sending information to a Web server. CGI programs, when running on a server, produce dynamic content, such as an HTML page, per a user's request. Most CGI programs are written in a scripting language, such as Perl, and as such that is where they acquire the name "CGI script."

CGI scripts can perform a variety of tasks. Some of the more popular CGI scripts you may have encountered on Web sites include site searches, text counters, Web page counters, and timers. CGI scripts are also used with form e-mail, which is demonstrated in this section.

CGI scripts take certain variables, in this example a user's name and message, and sends them to a specified person. CGI scripts are mainly used with HTML documents such as forms, but can be very useful in Flash.

SEND A FORM USING A CGI SCRIPT (CONTINUED)

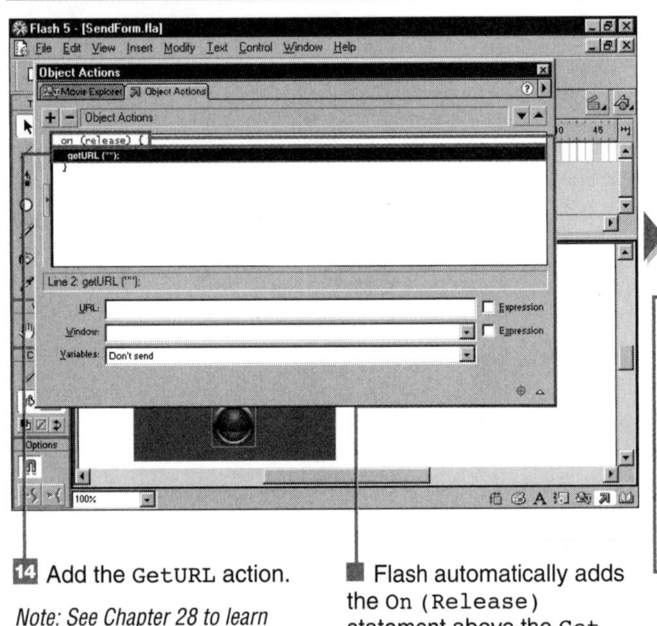

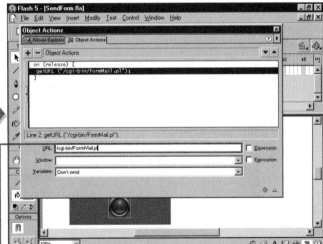

14 Add the GetURL action.

Note: See Chapter 28 to learn more about actions.

■ Flash automatically adds the `On (Release)` statement above the `Get URL` statement in the actions list.

15 In the URL parameter, enter a relative URL (/cgi-bin) or an absolute URL (http://yoursite/cgi-bin).

Every time I send the e-mail, I get an error on my browser saying that it could not find the filename /cgi-bin/FormMail.pl.

✔ You did not accurately set the URL of the CGI script. You should use an absolute URL. An absolute URL identifies a complete address on the Web, while a relative URL is a partial address that describes a file's location relative to another file.

Other troubleshooting

✔ The Perl script you download should include a readme file. The readme file contains all of the specifications for the Perl script you use, including the variable names and other locations of certain interpreters. Be sure to consult the readme file before tackling this technique.

Where can I find other instructions for creating Web page forms?

✔ See Chapter 31 to learn how to add all kinds of Web page elements to your Web site, including forms. The Create a Simple Form section walks you through the necessary steps to building your first Web page form in Flash. You can customize this form for all kinds of uses, such as creating account profiles, e-commerce, and e-mailing.

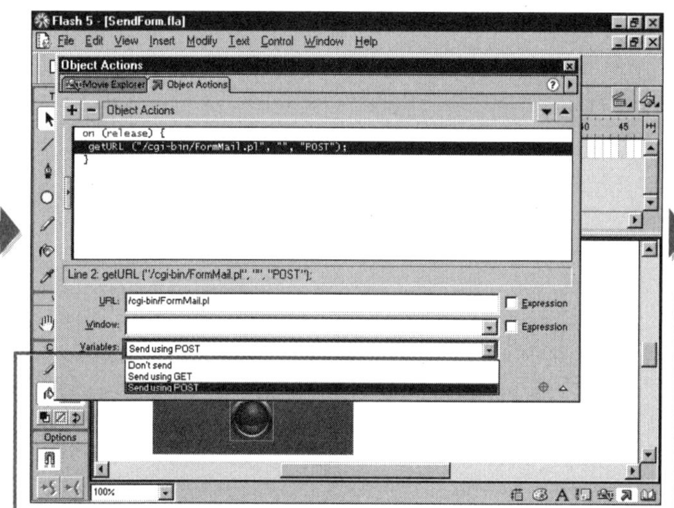

16 Click the Variables box and select either Send Using GET or Send Using POST from the drop-down list.

Note: Send Using GET is mainly used for short terms whereas Send Using POST is better for longer strings — this is important if you want to create an e-mail form.

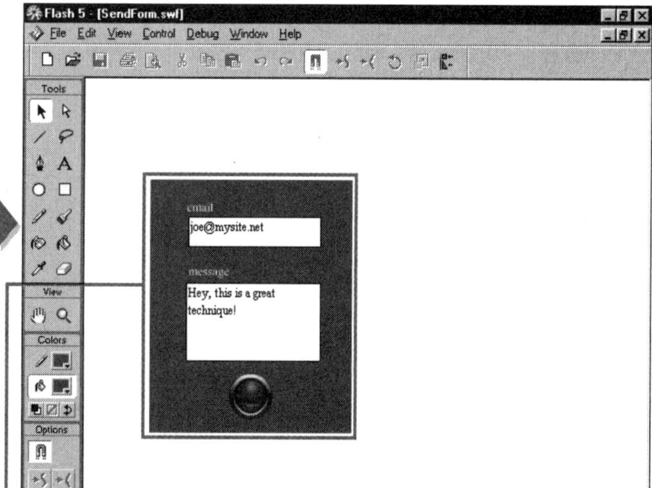

17 Test the form to make sure the action and scripts work properly.

Note: See Chapter 30 to learn more about testing Flash movies.

MAKE A MOVIE CLIP ACT LIKE A BUTTON

You can make a movie clip act like a button for a variety of uses. You can use this technique in a number of ways, one of which is in a game scenario. For example, perhaps your Flash game uses a moving target that, when clicked, changes the action of the movie or adds to a list of "hits."

You could also make the clip act like a button for a stoppable movie embedded in another movie.

The trick to this technique is to cover the entire movie with an invisible button. The Tell Target action is assigned to stop the movie or do whatever you, as the designer, want.

Flash EXE filename:

ButtonMovieClip.exe

Flash filenames:

ButtonMovieClip.fla

ButtonMovieClip.swf

ButtonMovieClip.hqx

MAKE A MOVIE CLIP ACT LIKE A BUTTON

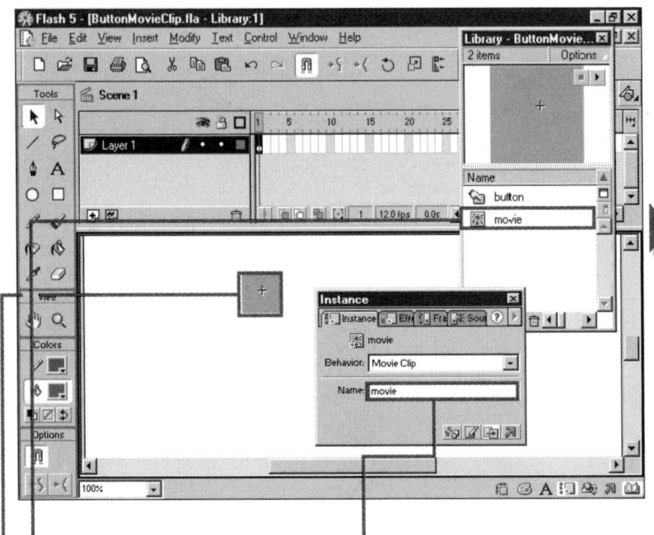

1 Create a movie clip symbol, named **movie**, containing the animation you want to use as a button.

Note: See Chapter 24 to learn to create movie clips.

2 Return to the main movie and add the clip to the Stage.

3 Use the Instance panel to assign the instance the variable name **movie**.

Note: See Chapter 22 to learn more about instances.

4 After assigning a name, double-click the instance to open the movie clip in symbol-edit mode.

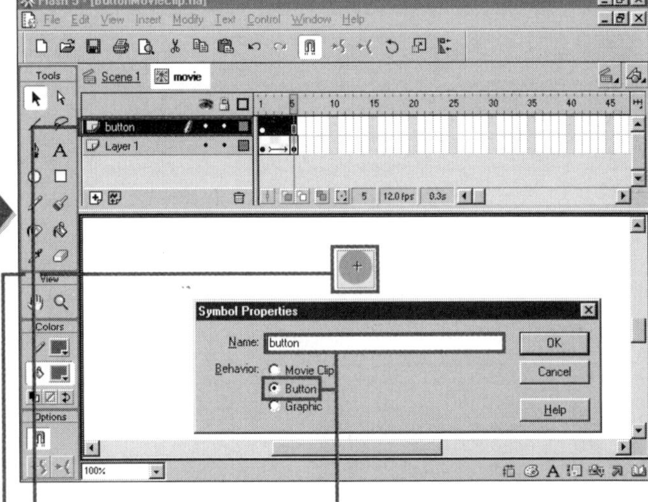

5 Add a new layer and name it **button**.

Note: See Chapter 21 to learn more about layers.

6 Encompass the clip's entire animation area on the Stage with a fill shape of any color.

Note: See Chapter 18 to learn more about the Flash drawing tools.

7 Convert the fill shape into a button symbol named **button**.

Note: See Chapter 22 to learn about turning graphics into symbols.

If I have a very dynamic movie that changes dimensions, how do I create a button for that?

✔ The size of the button cannot change. Your best bet is to create a separate button for the drastically different parts of the movie.

My movie moves around within the main movie. How can I keep the button on the movie clip?

✔ Because the button is embedded in the actual movie clip, it follows wherever the actual movie clip goes.

Can I use another way to make the button invisible in step 8?

✔ Yes. You can create the button, then decrease its Alpha percentage setting in the Effect panel. See Chapter 19 to learn about modifying Alpha properties.

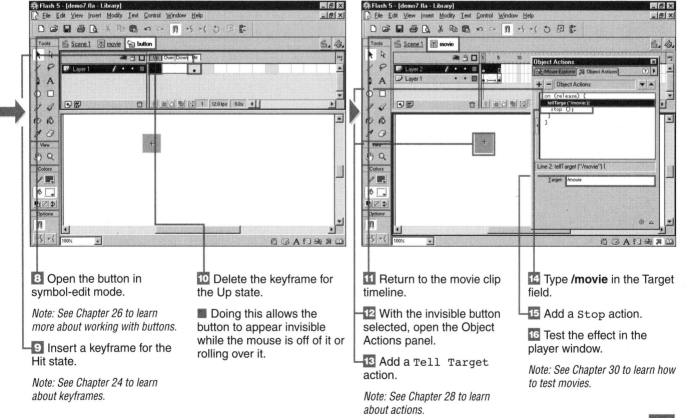

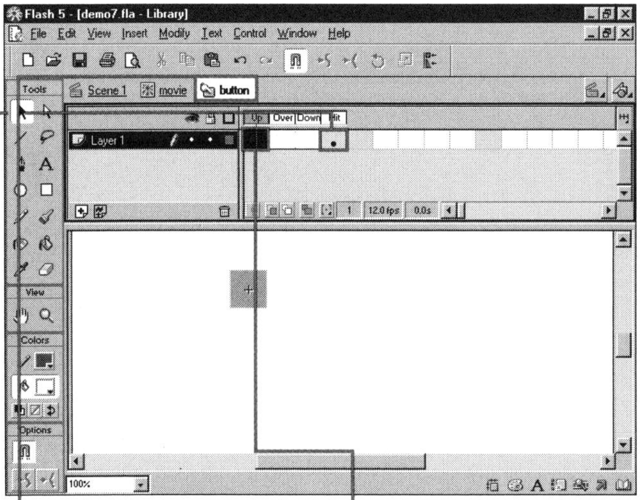

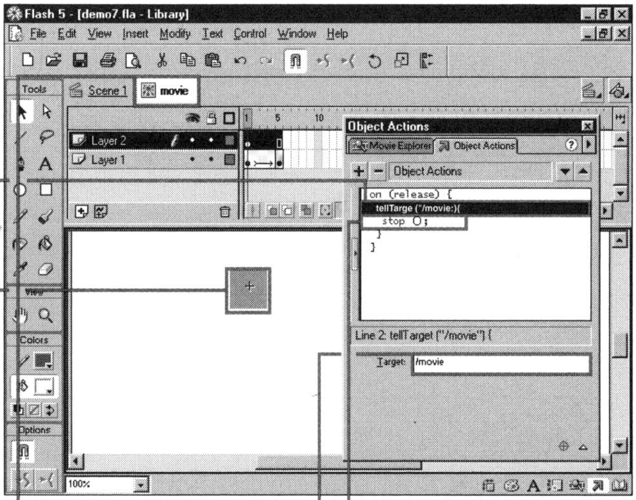

8 Open the button in symbol-edit mode.

Note: See Chapter 26 to learn more about working with buttons.

9 Insert a keyframe for the Hit state.

Note: See Chapter 24 to learn about keyframes.

10 Delete the keyframe for the Up state.

■ Doing this allows the button to appear invisible while the mouse is off of it or rolling over it.

11 Return to the movie clip timeline.

12 With the invisible button selected, open the Object Actions panel.

13 Add a `Tell Target` action.

Note: See Chapter 28 to learn about actions.

14 Type **/movie** in the Target field.

15 Add a `Stop` action.

16 Test the effect in the player window.

Note: See Chapter 30 to learn how to test movies.

CREATE A GRAVITY EFFECT

You can create a gravity effect and attach it to an object or objects in your Flash movie. This is a great effect that you may wish to add to a game in which you want objects to appear to be affected by gravity. Not only can you use this technique in games, you can add this technique to objects in your Flash movie for the Web.

For example, perhaps you are creating a Flash animation advertising an athletic store. You can attach the gravity effect to a basketball and have it bounce across the screen.

Flash EXE filename:
Gravity.exe

Flash filename:
Gravity.fla

CREATE A GRAVITY EFFECT

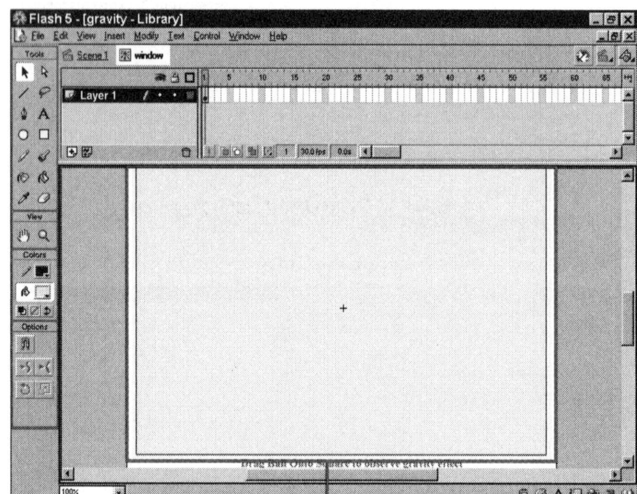

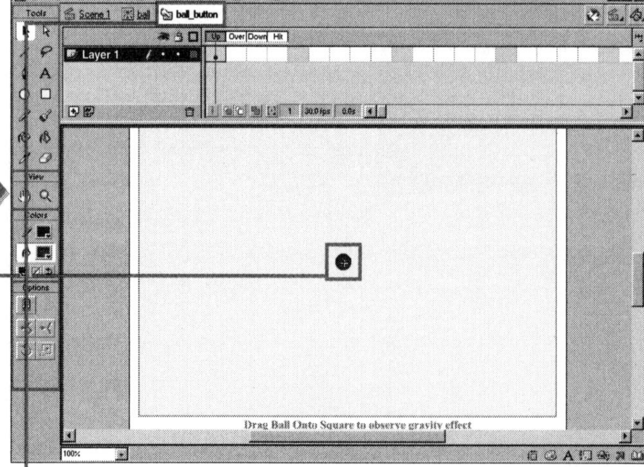

1 Create 3 layers in a new movie and name them **ballplane**, **ball**, and **actions**.

Note: See Chapter 21 to learn how to add layers.

2 Create a new movie clip named **ballplane**.

Note: See Chapter 22 to learn about symbols.

3 In frame 1 of the movie clip, draw a rectangle.

Note: See Chapter 18 to learn how to draw in Flash.

4 Return to the main movie and create a new button named **ball button**.

Note: See Chapter 26 to learn how to create buttons.

5 Create a ball object in the Up frame.

■ This example shows a 20 by 20 pixel circle with a blue radial gradient fill.

Note: See Chapter 18 to learn how to draw in Flash.

Can I change the way gravity affects the objects in my movie?

✔ Yes. By changing certain variable values you can change the way gravity affects your objects. You can change the gravity effect by increasing the gravity so the ball does not bounce nearly as much or not at all. You could also decrease the gravity effect so the ball is almost experiencing weightlessness. By making the gravity variable negative, you would make the ball bounce on the top part of the window rather than the bottom.

Where can I find the gravity constant?

✔ The gravity constant is found in frame 1 of the actions layer. By looking at the code used in this example, you discover that the gravity constant is 4. Another variable that affects the way the gravity works is the bounce variable. The closer the bounce variable gets to the value of 1, the more bounces you get before the ball stops. If the bounce variable is set to 1, the ball continuously bounces; if it is set to 0, the ball does not bounce at all.

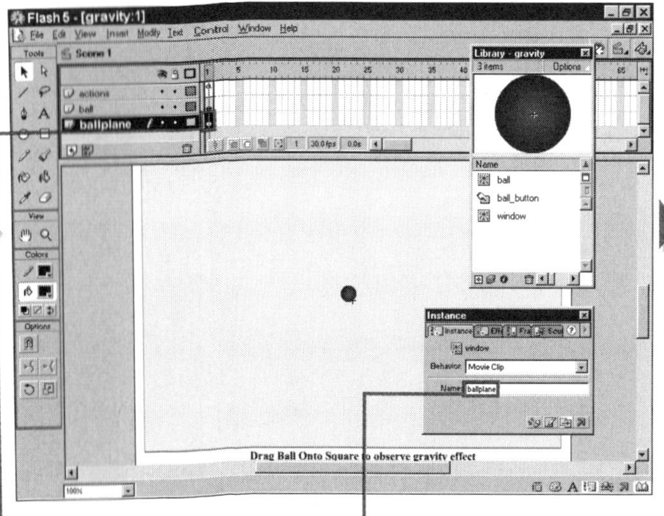

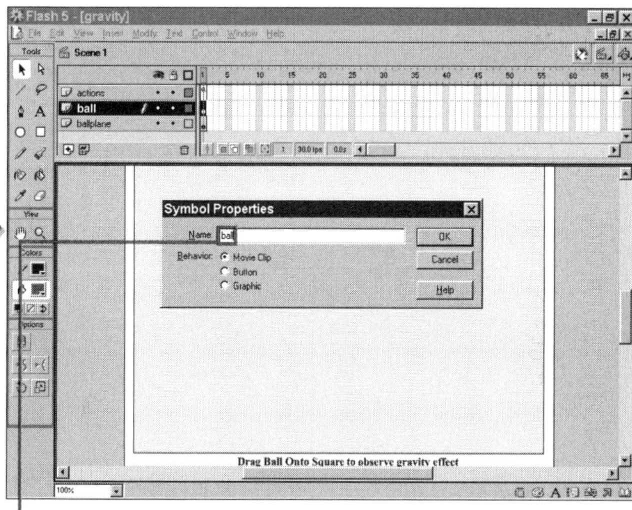

6 Return to the main movie and place an instance of the movie clip into frame 1 of the ballplane layer.

Note: See Chapter 22 to learn how to insert instances.

7 Use the Instance panel to name the clip **ballplane**.

8 Place an instance of the ball button in frame 1 of the ball layer.

9 Convert the ball button to a movie clip symbol and name it **ball**.

Note: See Chapter 22 to learn how to work with symbols and instances.

CONTINUED

CREATE A GRAVITY EFFECT (CONTINUED)

In this example, you use an ActionScript to develop a gravity effect and then attach it to an object shaped like a racquetball. When the racquetball is moved onto the window, the ball bounces up and down, eventually coming to a stop on the bottom as if it were adhering to the laws of gravity. You can alter the ActionScript controlling the gravity effect to create your own custom gravity effect. Maybe you want your gravity to work by attracting things to the left of a screen, or maybe you want your gravity to affect things in a diagonal motion — the number of effects you can achieve is endless.

If you want to get really creative and advanced, you can take this movie and manipulate it into a miniature basketball or ball toss game. If you are into creating games, this is an important technique to learn because gravity affects everything.

CREATE A GRAVITY EFFECT (CONTINUED)

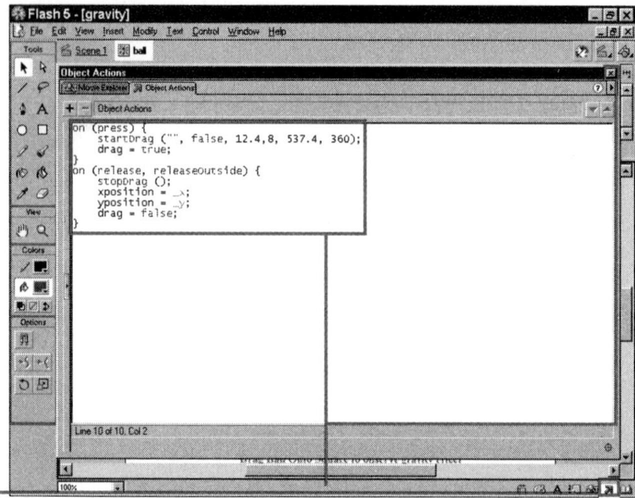

10 With the ball movie clip in symbol-edit mode, click the Show Actions button (▣) to open the Actions panel.

Note: See Chapter 28 to learn about Flash actions.

11 Enter the ActionScript shown in this figure.

Note: See Chapter 29 to learn about ActionScripts.

12 Click the Close button (☒) to close the Actions panel.

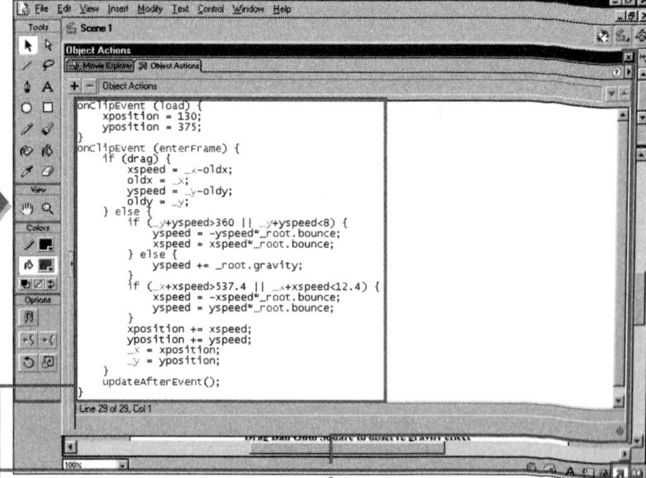

13 Return to the main movie and select the ball movie clip.

14 Click ▣ to open the Actions panel.

15 Enter the ActionScript shown in this figure.

Note: See Chapter 29 to learn about ActionScripts.

16 Click ☒ to close the Actions panel.

How come the ball does not bounce when I test my movie?

✔ Obviously, something is wrong if the ball does not bounce when testing your movie. Most likely, you should check your code thoroughly. This technique contains many variables; a typo may appear in the code. The Flash debugger is a great tool for checking code. If your code checks out okay, check the symbols; perhaps one of the symbols is mislabeled or maybe the proper actions did not get assigned to the symbol.

Can I test ActionScripts on smaller test movies before adding them to my main movie?

✔ Yes. To save yourself a lot of frustration, you may want to develop a small movie to test little pieces of your ActionScript on while developing the main movie. Experiment with the ActionScript on the small movie until you are comfortable adding it to your main movie. Chances are that you will discover syntax errors as you test individual pieces of code on smaller movies before implementing them in your main movie.

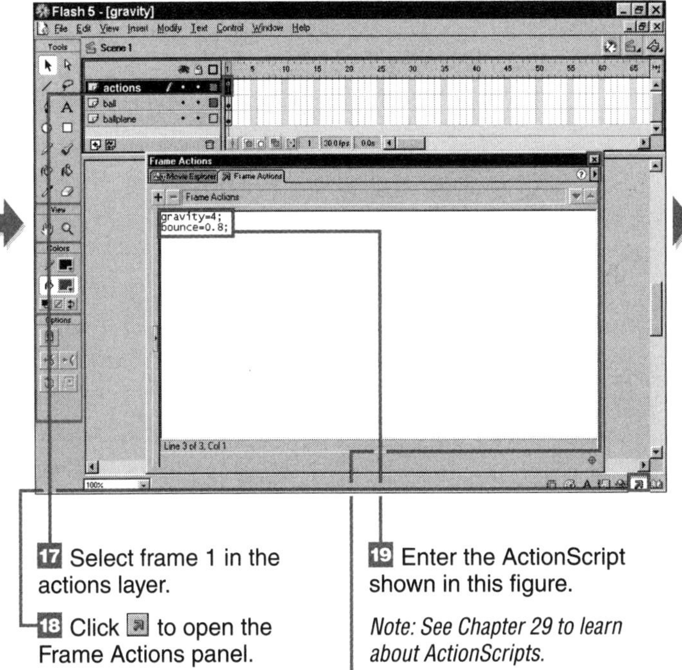

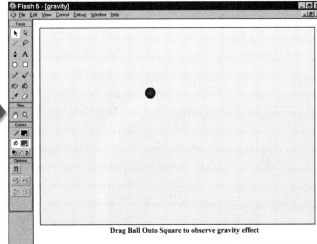

17 Select frame 1 in the actions layer.

18 Click ▣ to open the Frame Actions panel.

Note: See Chapter 28 to learn how to use the Frame Actions panel.

19 Enter the ActionScript shown in this figure.

Note: See Chapter 29 to learn about ActionScripts.

20 Click ☒ to close the Actions panel.

Flash 5 - [gravity]

Drag Ball Onto Square to observe gravity effect

21 Test the effect.

Note: See Chapter 30 to learn how to test movies.

CREATE A MAGNIFYING GLASS EFFECT

You can use the technique of masking layers to create a magnifying glass effect. The masking feature enables you to hide certain parts of your movie and make certain parts visible at a given time. You can learn more about masking layers in Chapter 21.

In this example, you create a magnifying glass and drag it over an image, enlarging the part of the image under the magnifying glass. For the example, we make use of the masking effect, applying it to the enlarged image. The only portion of the enlarged image that will be viewable is the part seen through the magnifying glass.

Flash EXE filename:
magnify.exe

Flash filename:
magnify.fla

CREATE A MAGNIFYING GLASS EFFECT

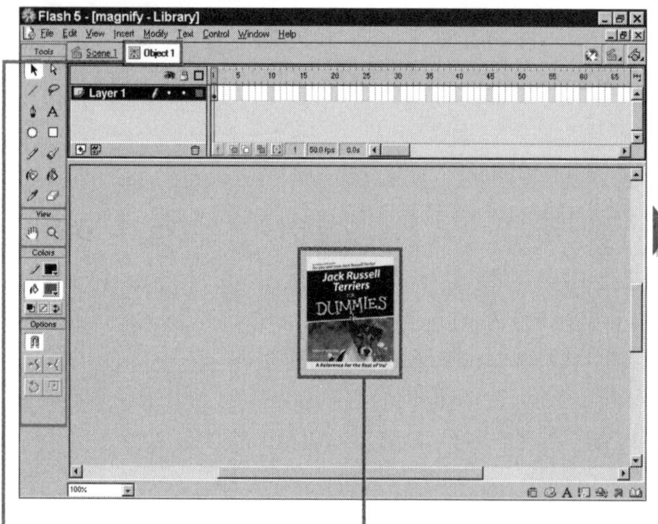

1 Create a new movie clip symbol and name it **Object 1**.

Note: See Chapter 22 to learn how to create symbols.

2 Insert the image to be used as the magnified view into frame 1 of the movie clip's timeline.

Note: See Chapter 23 for more information on importing images into Flash.

3 Return to the main movie and create three layers named **symbol**, **magnifier**, and **actions**.

Note: See Chapter 21 to learn how to add and name layers.

4 Place an instance of the Object 1 clip into frame 1 of the symbol layer.

Note: See Chapter 22 to learn how to add instances.

5 Insert a regular frame into frame 3 of the symbol layer.

What is the importance of naming the layers?

✔ When working with small, simple Flash movies, you may not see the importance of labeling layers. When you start working with larger, more complex Flash movies, having layers labeled becomes very important. When editing symbols, figuring out what layer the symbol is in may be difficult without labeling. Labeling layers is more of an organizational tool for the creator. Labeling layers can also help others who may work on your Flash movies.

How do I order my layers?

✔ Ordering your layers depends on what you are creating. Remember that any object you place in the top layer covers everything under it. There is no set of rules to how you order your layers, although the background layer should be on the bottom, and action layers are usually found on top. Because action layers do not contain any objects, they do not cover anything, so they are fine in the top layer.

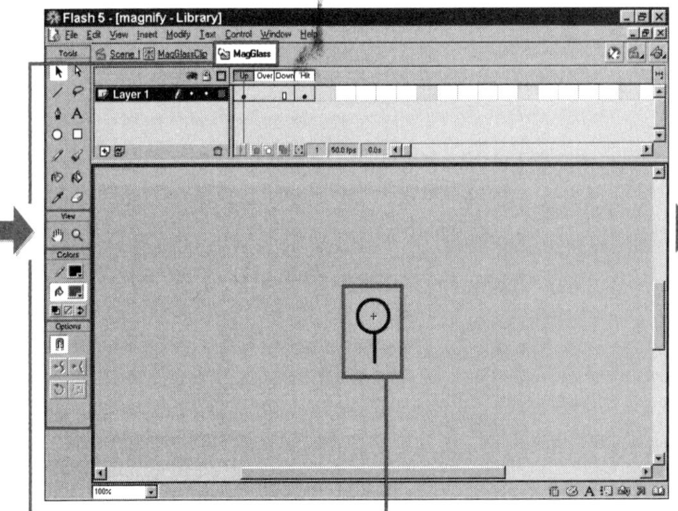

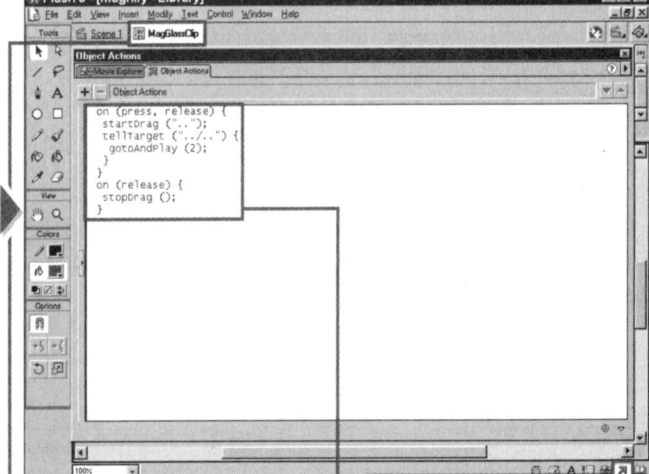

6 Create a new button symbol and name it **MagGlass**.

Note: See Chapter 26 to learn how to create buttons.

7 In the button timeline, create the magnifying glass to use as the button.

■ In this example, a 40 x 40 pixel circle with a line on the bottom simulates a magnifying glass. The circle must not have a fill.

8 Return to the main movie and create a new movie clip symbol named **MagGlass clip**.

9 Place an instance of the **MagGlass** button into frame 1 of the **MagGlass** movie clip timeline.

10 With the MagGlass button selected, click [icon] to open the Object Actions panel.

11 Add the ActionScript shown in this figure.

Note: See Chapter 29 to learn about ActionScripts.

CONTINUED

CREATE A MAGNIFYING GLASS EFFECT (CONTINUED)

You use the masking layers feature of Flash to create the magnifying effect. Masking layers may be difficult at first to grasp, but after you work with it for a while, you may find it pretty simple to use and you may want to use in other Flash movies.

Basically, two layers are involved when masking: the *content layer* and the *mask layer*. You use the mask layer to hide the content layer. In order to see what is in the content layer, you need to create a "window" in your mask layer. Any shape, image, or content placed in the mask layer acts as a window to the content layer beneath it.

In this example, the image of a magnified book cover is in the content layer, and the mask layer contains the circle inside the magnifying glass. The image in the mask layer is dragable so that a user can drag the magnifying glass around and view the entire image in the content layer.

CREATE A MAGNIFYING GLASS EFFECT (CONTINUED)

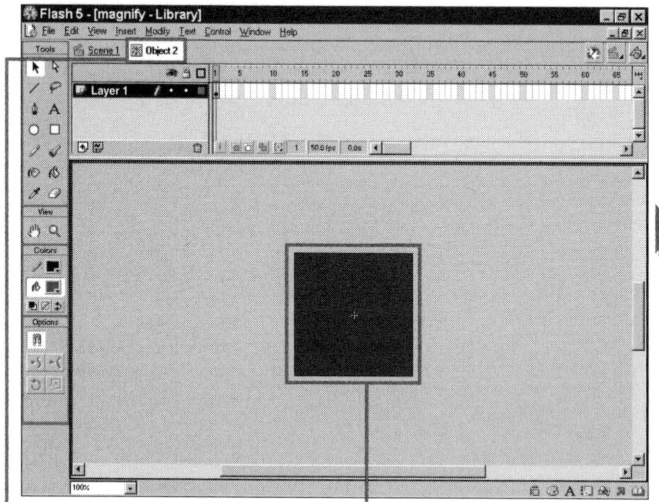

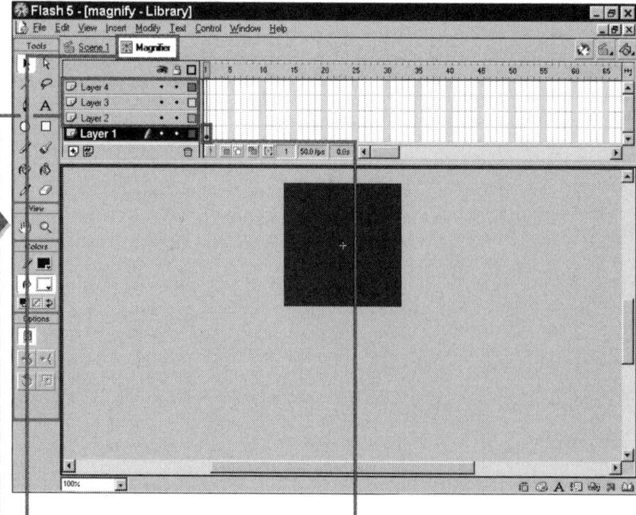

12 Return to the main movie and create a new movie clip symbol named **Object 2**.

Note: See Chapter 22 to learn how to create symbols.

13 Use the Rectangle tool to draw a square on the Stage.

■ This square must be at least as big as the magnify image. Color does not matter.

Note: See Chapter 18 to learn how to use the drawing tools.

14 Return to the main movie and create a new movie clip symbol named **Magnifier**.

15 Insert three more layers in the **Magnifier** clip timeline to bring the total number of layers to four.

16 Place an instance of **Object 2** into frame 1 of layer 1.

How can I find out the image size in pixels?

✔ To find out the image's width and height in pixels, open the Info panel by clicking [icon]. The Info panel gives you the width and height in pixels and the *x* and *y* coordinates of your image. You may want to edit the numbers in the Info panel for exact positioning or to create shapes of an exact size. In this example, a circle 20 pixels wide by 20 pixels high is created in the mask layer. Rather than selecting the circle tool and estimating what 20 by 20 pixels would be, you can simply select the Oval tool, draw a circle of any size or shape, and in the Info panel type in 20 for the width and type in 20 for the height. This gives you a circle of exactly 20 by 20 pixels.

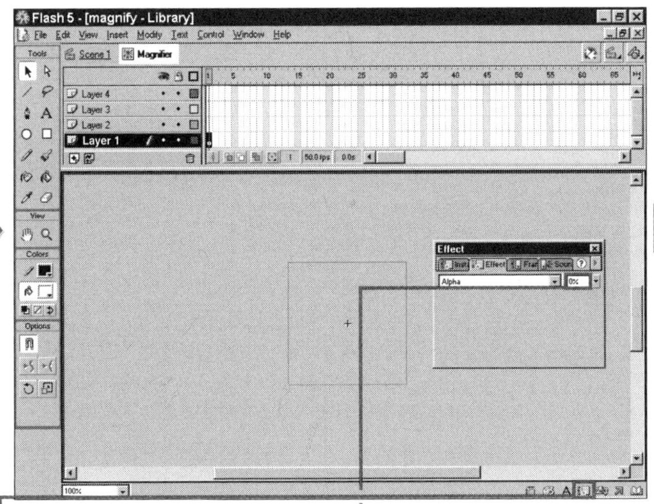

17 Click the Show Instances button ([icon]) to open the Instance panel.

18 Use the Instance panel to name the instance **picture**.

19 Change the alpha value to 0%.

■ This makes the graphic transparent.

Note: See Chapter 22 to learn how to modify an instance.

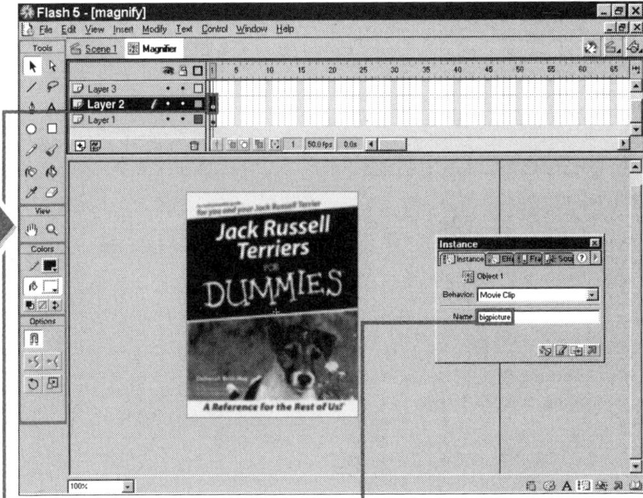

20 Place an instance of **Object 1** into frame 1 of layer 2.

21 Scale the image to 200% width and 200% height.

Note: See Chapter 19 to learn how to resize objects.

22 Use the Instance panel to name the instance **bigpicture**.

Note: See Chapter 22 to learn how to modify an instance.

CONTINUED

CREATE A MAGNIFYING GLASS EFFECT (CONTINUED)

You can use the magnifying technique in many ways. You can apply it to an educational presentation for children in which, for example, a child moves the cursor over a leaf to simulate how the leaf looks under a microscope.

You can use a picture of a leaf as your top picture and a picture of plant cells as your magnified layer. If you want to get really scientific and creative, you can show how the leaf looks through different types of microscopic lenses.

This technique is not limited to educational tools — you can also apply it to games or to create a cool effect for your Web site's introduction.

CREATE A MAGNIFYING GLASS EFFECT (CONTINUED)

23 In layer 3, with the circle tool, create the center of the magnifying glass.

■ This should be the same size as the circle used in the **MagGlass** button.

24 Change the layer properties for layer 3 to Mask.

Note: See Chapter 21 to learn more about masking layers.

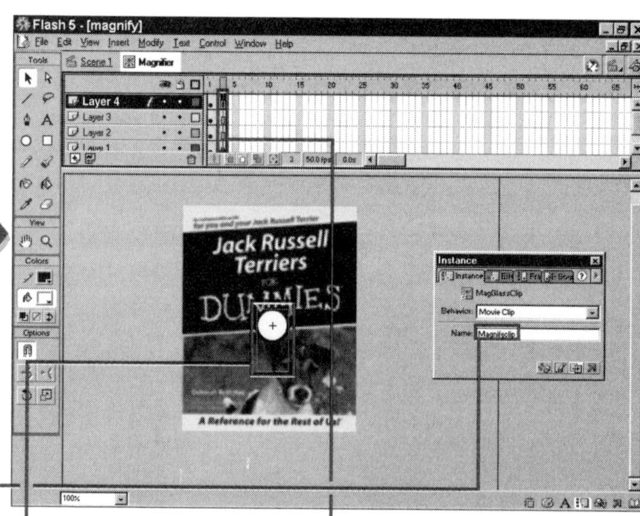

25 Place an instance of the **MagGlassClip** onto the Stage into frame 1 of layer 4.

26 Position the instance so that the magnifying glass circle is directly over the circle in layer 3.

27 Use the Instance panel to name the instance **Magnifyclip**.

Note: See Chapter 22 to learn how to modify an instance.

28 Insert a regular frame into frame 3 of each layer.

Note: See Chapter 24 to learn how to add frames.

Why have actions in a separate layer?

✔ Creating a layer specifically for assigning actions to frames can help to organize your work better. With all the motion tweens and other things going on in the timeline, a layer devoted just to actions makes finding and editing specific actions easier.

What if I want to increase the magnification?

✔ In this example, the image is magnified by 200%; you may wish to increase the power of your magnifying glass. To increase the power of your magnifying glass, change the variables in step 21 from 200% to a higher number. Be aware that when you increase the size of an image, the viewer may not be able to recognize the object anymore. Instead of increasing the size of the image to be magnified, you may want to externally edit the image so that the image quality remains decent.

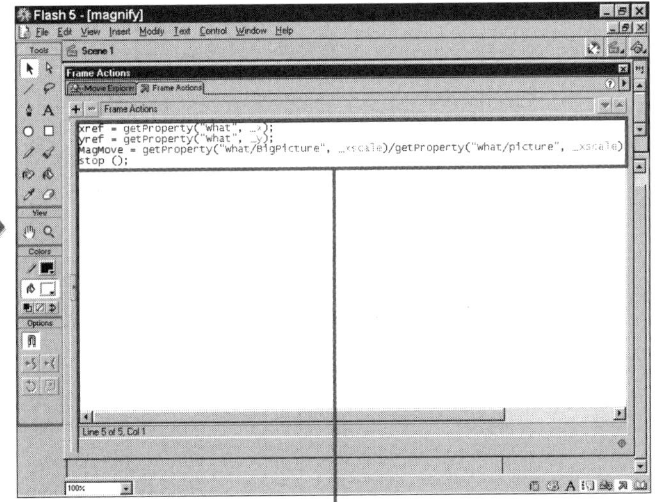

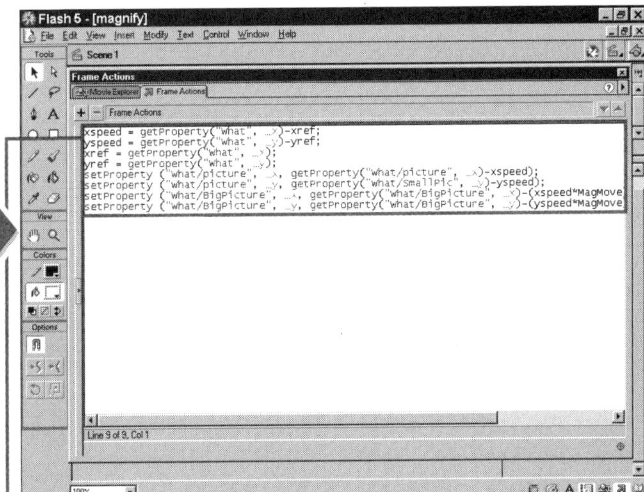

29 Return to the main movie and drag the magnifier movie clip onto the Stage in the magnifier layer.

30 Open the Instance panel and label the magnifier movie clip **what**.

31 Insert a regular frame into frame 3 of the magnifier layer.

32 In frame 1 of the actions layer, add the ActionScript shown in this figure.

Note: See Chapter 29 to learn how to add ActionScripts.

33 Insert blank keyframes into frames 2 and 3 of the actions layer.

34 Add the ActionScript shown in this figure to frame 2.

35 Add a GoTo action to frame 3.

36 In the frame field enter **2**.

37 Test the movie by launching the Flash player.

Note: See Chapter 30 for more information about testing Flash movies.

CREATE A DRAGABLE MENU

You can use Flash ActionScripts to create a dragable menu. This effect can come in very handy if you use Flash to create a game or want to have more user interaction with your Web site. You can make Flash objects, in this case a menu, dragable using the `startDrag` and `stopDrag` actions.

When you make an object dragable, the user can click on the object and, while holding down the mouse button, reposition the object somewhere else in the window. All functionality of the menu remains even though the menu changes its position.

To follow the steps in this example, use a previously created menu, such as the drop-down menu created in Part III, and add the drag property to it. You can also apply the drag property to a different object, but you cannot follow along step by step.

Flash EXE filename:

dragmenu.exe

Flash filename:

dragmenu.fla

CREATE A DRAGABLE MENU

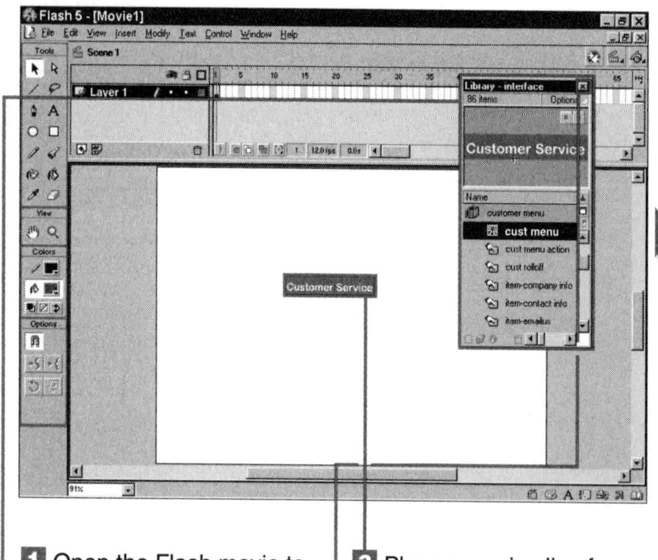

1 Open the Flash movie to which you want to add this effect.

2 Open the interface movie as a library.

3 Place a movie clip of any drop-down menu onto the Stage.

■ This example uses the Customer Service menu created in Chapter 31.

4 Click ☒ to close the library.

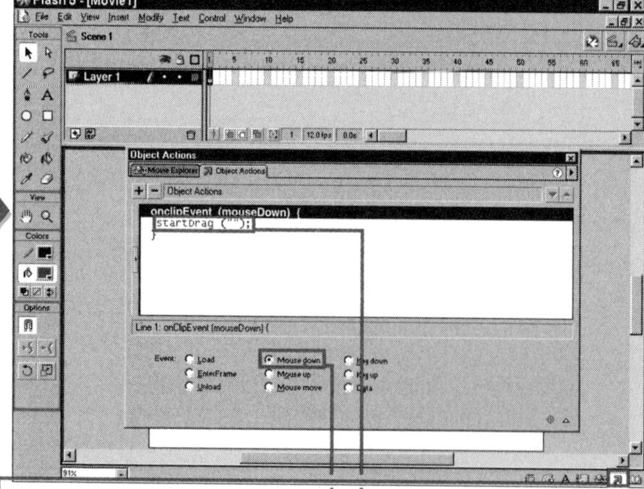

5 Click [icon] to open the Actions panel for the movie clip.

Note: See Chapter 28 to learn how to add actions in Flash.

6 Add a `startDrag` action.

7 Click `onclipEvent` and choose Mouse Down.

What do the other options for `startDrag` mean?

✔ There is a Target field, a check box for Constrain to rectangle, and another check box for Lock mouse to center. The Target field is where you enter the target path of the movie clip that you are adding the drag option to. The check box for Constrain to rectangle does exactly what it sounds like it would perform. The four fields to the right of the check box become active when it is checked. These fields are for entering the variable names or numbers for the rectangle that bound your movie clip — L stands for left, R stands for right, *T* stands for top, and B stands for bottom. If the check box for Lock to center is checked, the mouse pointer locks to the center of the movie clip when you click the movie clip to drag it. Otherwise the mouse pointer is locked on the part of the movie clip that was clicked on initially.

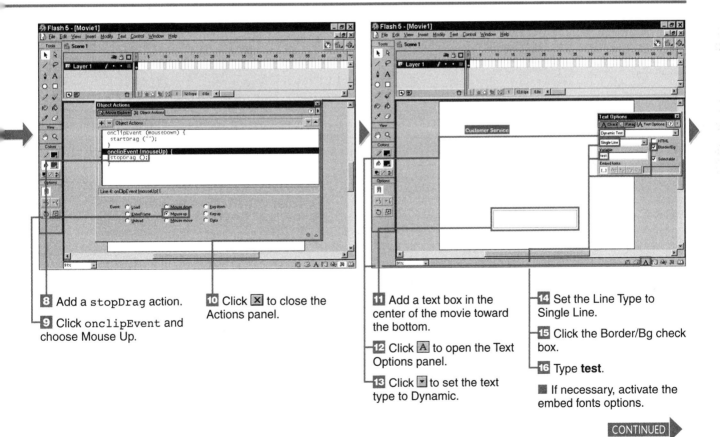

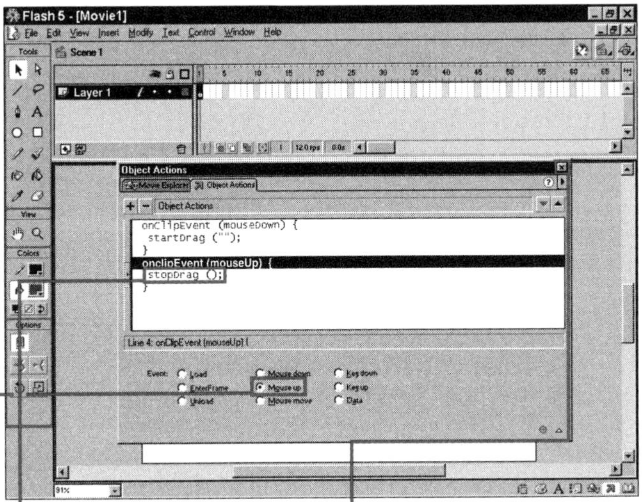

8 Add a `stopDrag` action.

9 Click `onclipEvent` and choose Mouse Up.

10 Click ☒ to close the Actions panel.

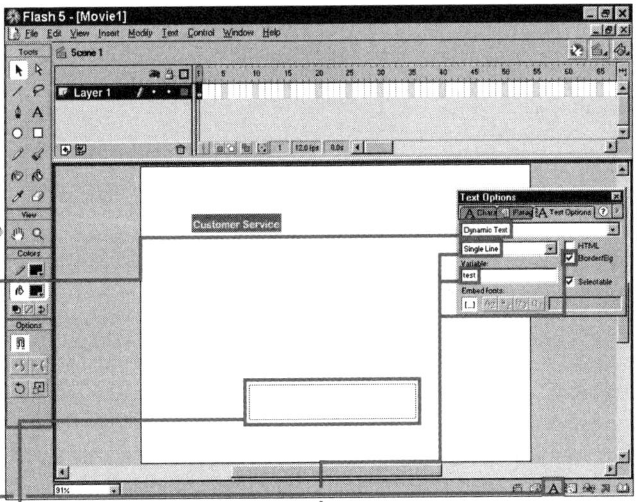

11 Add a text box in the center of the movie toward the bottom.

12 Click A to open the Text Options panel.

13 Click ▾ to set the text type to Dynamic.

14 Set the Line Type to Single Line.

15 Click the Border/Bg check box.

16 Type **test**.

■ If necessary, activate the embed fonts options.

CONTINUED

CREATE A DRAGABLE MENU (CONTINUED)

To test the functionality of this technique, you can assign actions to the menu items. The actions that you assign are set variable actions. You create a dynamic text box in the center of your movie and when the menu item button is clicked, it sets the variable of the text box to whatever you assigned to it. In this example, each menu item button sets the dynamic text box variable equal to the name of the item button. For example, the Contact us button inserts the text "Contact us" into the dynamic text box. All other buttons have the same actions, each assigning the text of their names to the dynamic text box. Now when you test this movie, the actions assigned to the item buttons are performed regardless of the location of the menu.

CREATE A DRAGABLE MENU (CONTINUED)

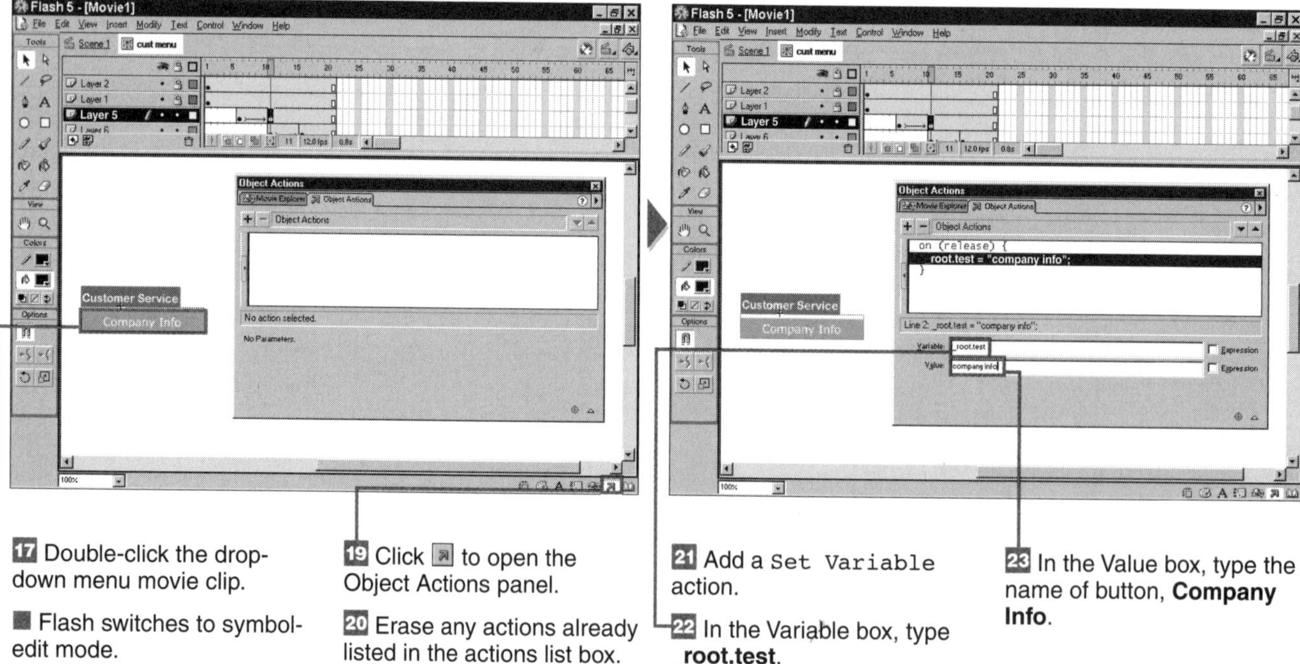

17 Double-click the drop-down menu movie clip.

■ Flash switches to symbol-edit mode.

18 Click the first item, Company Info.

19 Click the icon to open the Object Actions panel.

20 Erase any actions already listed in the actions list box.

Note: Refer to Chapter 29 for more information on working with actions.

21 Add a `Set Variable` action.

22 In the Variable box, type **_root.test**.

23 In the Value box, type the name of button, **Company Info**.

How can I modify this technique to create a dragable window?

✔ You create a dragable window much the same way. To start, you need to have a movie clip of the window that you want to make dragable. Then simply follow the same steps of applying the ActionScript to the movie clip.

Can only movie clips be dragable?

✔ No. You can give any symbol the drag property. You add the drag property to any object the same way you add it in this example.

How do dragable objects benefit my site?

✔ Enabling users to drag certain objects creates more interactivity between your visitors and your site. Visitors may get bored and leave your site if it lacks interactivity. In this example, the drag property attached to the menu gives users some customization ability over what they see. If they prefer the menu to be on the left, they can move it there.

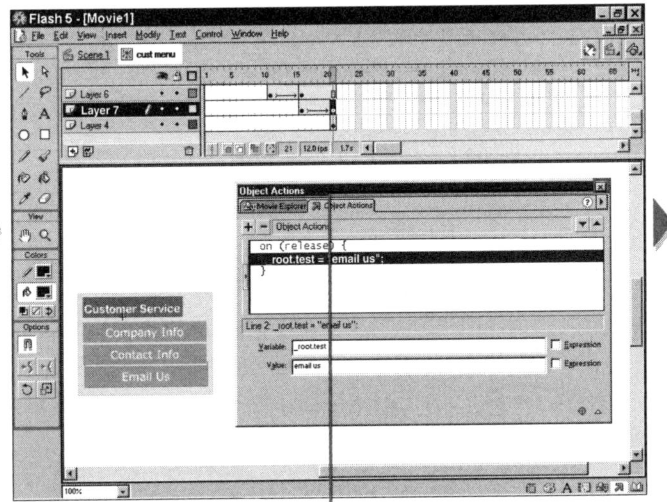

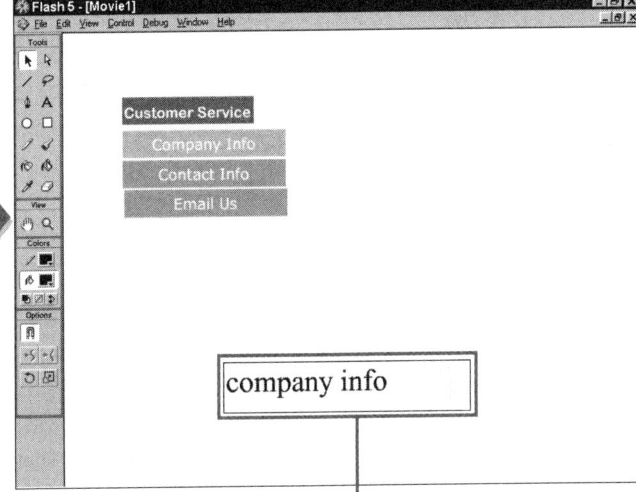

24 Repeat steps 17 through 23 until the actions for all items are changed.

25 Click ☒ to close the Actions panel and exit symbol-edit mode.

26 Test the movie; the menu should be dragable.

■ When a menu item is clicked, its text should appear in the input text box.

CREATE A FILMSTRIP EFFECT

You can create a bar with scrolling images on it to simulate an animated filmstrip. With a couple of quick ActionScript sequences, the steps in this example transform a static bar with book cover images into a moving, eye-catching, effective method to get a visitor's attention. With a couple of additional steps, the moving book bar can become an interactive menu.

This effect works by showing an image and attaching a duplicate of the image to itself in a different level of the Flash movie. At any given time, you actually see the original picture and the duplicate of the picture. You cannot tell which image is the real image and which image is the duplicate. By duplicating itself and attaching itself to either end, a seamless, constant flow of images parade across the screen, creating the filmstrip effect.

Flash EXE filename:
filmstrip.exe

Flash filename:
filmstrip.fla

CREATE A FILMSTRIP EFFECT

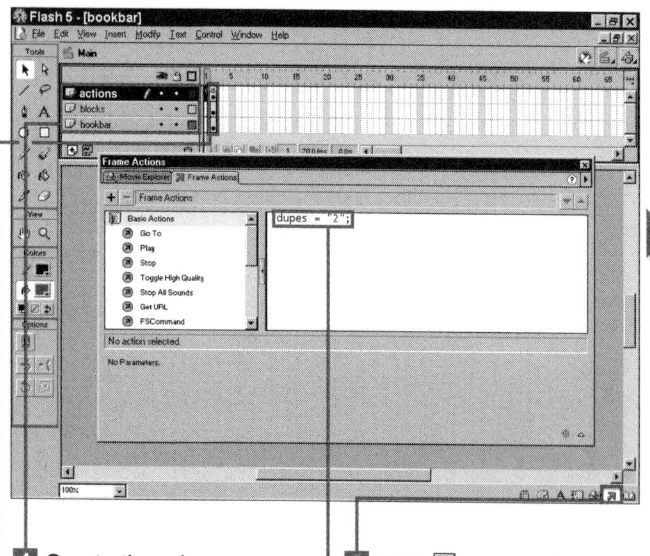

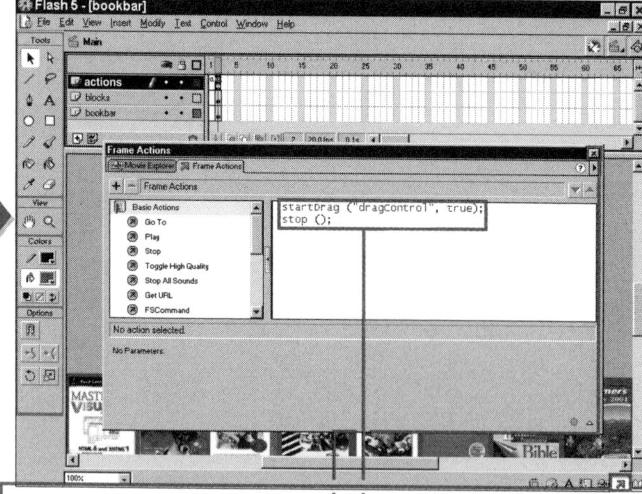

1 Create three layers named **bookbar**, **blocks**, and **actions**.

Note: See Chapter 21 to learn how to add and name layers.

2 Insert blank keyframes into frames 1 and 2 of each layer.

3 Click [icon] to open the Actions panel for frame 1 of the actions layer.

Note: See Chapter 28 to learn how to add actions.

4 Enter the ActionScript shown in this figure.

5 Click [icon] to open the Actions panel for frame 2 of the actions layer.

6 Enter the ActionScript shown in this figure.

7 Click [X] to close the Actions panel.

What types of images are good to use for this effect?

✔ You can use almost any type of image for the filmstrip effect. If your images are small, as in the example shown here, be sure to use many images. The effect does not work right with only two or three images when using small pictures. If you do not have as many images as demonstrated in this example, you can expand the blocks on the side of the filmstrip to show less. Although this example does not work with two or three small pictures, it works with panoramic images. Other things to keep in mind are general graphic manipulation techniques. Scaling a large image down 10 percent is going to affect the quality of the image when it is smaller. Using many images may drastically increase the loading time of your movie. Refer to optimizing your Flash movie with graphics discussed in Chapter 33.

```
speed = 50;
drag = "/dragControl";
/:w = getProperty("/nav", _width);
/:xPos = getProperty(drag, _x);
/:yPos = getProperty(drag, _y);
/:xPos = /:xPos-(720/2);
setProperty ("/nav", _x, getProperty("/nav", _x)-(/:xPos/speed));
if (Number(getProperty("/nav", _x))<Number(-(/:w/2))) {
 setProperty ("/nav", _x, 0.01);
} else if (Number(getProperty("/nav", _x))>0) {
 setProperty ("/nav", _x, -/:w/2);
}
```

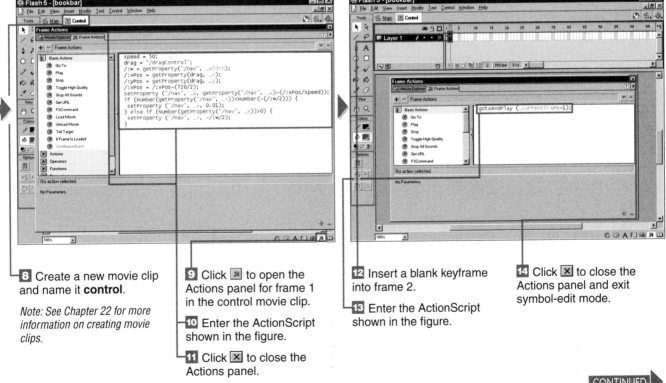

8 Create a new movie clip and name it **control**.

Note: See Chapter 22 for more information on creating movie clips.

9 Click ⧉ to open the Actions panel for frame 1 in the control movie clip.

10 Enter the ActionScript shown in the figure.

11 Click ☒ to close the Actions panel.

```
gotoAndPlay (_currentframe-1);
```

12 Insert a blank keyframe into frame 2.

13 Enter the ActionScript shown in the figure.

14 Click ☒ to close the Actions panel and exit symbol-edit mode.

CONTINUED

CREATE A FILMSTRIP EFFECT (CONTINUED)

You can turn the filmstrip effect into an interactive menu. Instead of inserting static graphics into your bar, you can insert buttons to create an interactive menu.

To convert the filmstrip example demonstrated in this example into a menu, you must take all the book cover images and convert them into buttons. After converting them into buttons, you can assign actions to them. After you finish creating the buttons and assigning actions, you have a navigation menu with a filmstrip effect.

If you want the filmstrip to move up and down instead of left and right, go into the ActionScript and change all the _x variables to _y and all of the _y to _x. After changing the code, you have to create a bar that consists of images stacked on top of each other instead of being side by side.

CREATE A FILMSTRIP EFFECT (CONTINUED)

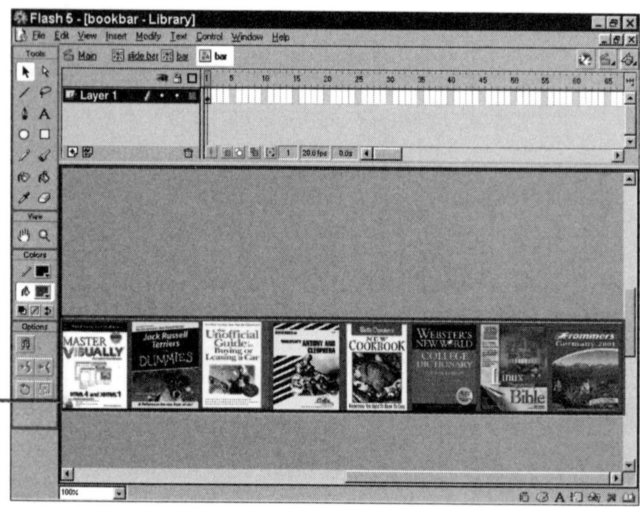

15 Create new graphic symbol and name it **bar images**.

Note: Refer to Chapter 22 for more information on creating symbols in Flash.

■ This graphic is the image bar that scrolls across the screen.

16 Return to the main movie and create a new movie clip symbol named **bar**.

17 Place an instance of the bar image's graphic onto the bar movie clip's stage.

■ Frame 1 in layer 1 is fine.

18 In the main movie, place an instance of the bar movie clip onto the Stage in frame 2 of the bookbar layer.

19 Select the bar movie clip and convert it to a movie clip named **slide bar**.

20 In symbol-edit mode, use the Instance panel to name the movie clip **bar**.

How do I slow down the speed of this effect?

✔ You can change a variable that controls the speed of your scrolling filmstrip effect. In the set of actions attached to frame 1 of the control movie clip, you find the variable controlling the speed. In this example, the variable is set to 50. Remember that the higher you make the speed variable the slower your movie scrolls. The lower you make the variable, the faster your movie scrolls.

The center of the movie clip controlling the direction of scroll seems off. Why?

✔ There is a spot in the code where you need to enter the length, in pixels, of the bar you are scrolling. In frame 1 of the control movie clip there is a line: `/:xPos = /:xPos-(720/2);` The number 720 is the width of the bar in pixels. You need to change this number to have the correct center point for scrolling.

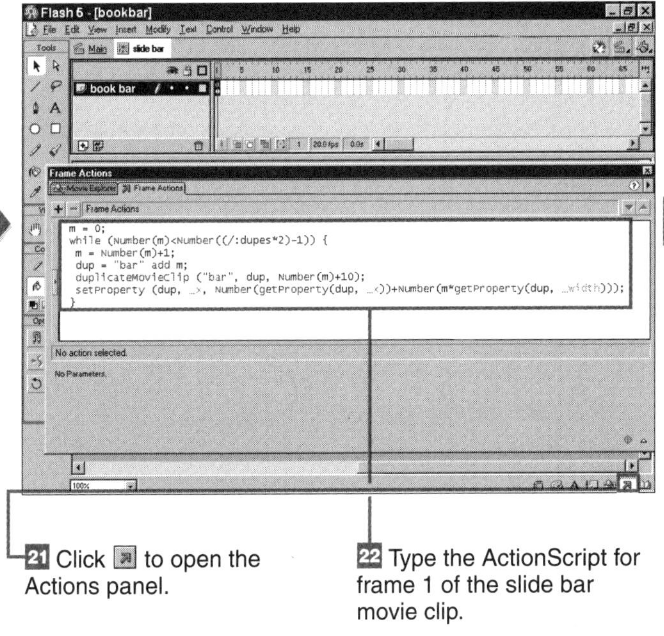

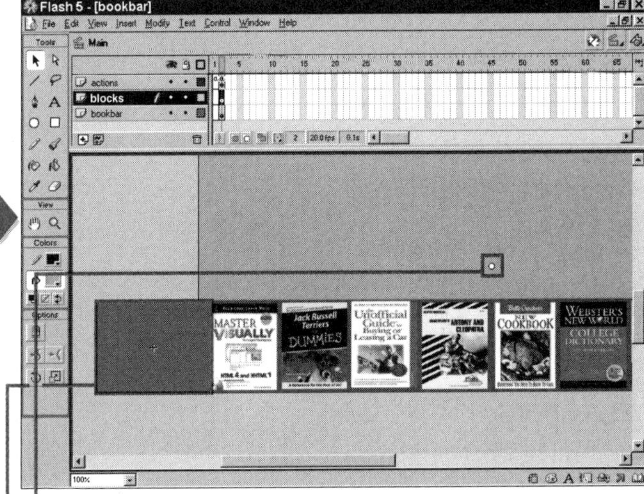

21 Click [icon] to open the Actions panel.

22 Type the ActionScript for frame 1 of the slide bar movie clip.

23 Return to the main movie and add the control movie clip to the Stage in frame 2 of the actions layer.

24 In the blocks layer, create shape boxes to control how much of the bar is shown at one time.

■ The size of the blocks vary depending on how many images and the size of the images. In this example, the blocks prevent two book covers from being on the screen at the same time.

25 Test the movie by viewing in Flash player.

WHAT'S ON THE CD-ROM

The CD-ROM included in this book contains many useful files and programs. Before installing any of the programs on the disc, make sure that a newer version of the program is not already installed on your computer. For information on installing different versions of the same program, contact the program's manufacturer.

SYSTEM REQUIREMENTS

To use the contents of the CD-ROM, your computer must be equipped with the following hardware and software:

- A PC with a 486 or faster processor and a sound card, or a Mac OS computer with a 68030 or faster processor
- Microsoft Windows 95 or later, or Mac OS 7.5 or later
- At least 16MB of total RAM installed on your computer
- At least 135MB of hard drive space
- A double-speed (2x) or faster CD-ROM drive
- A monitor capable of displaying at least 256 colors
- A modem with a speed of at least 14,400 bps

ACROBAT VERSION

The CD-ROM contains an e-version of this book that you can view and search using Adobe Acrobat Reader. You can also use the hyperlinks provided in the text to access all Web pages and Internet references in the book. You cannot print the pages or copy text from the Acrobat files.

WEB LINKS

Dreamweaver Tips

(www.thatguy.com/dreamweaver)

Additional information about Dreamweaver and Web design at Mike Wooldridge's personal site.

INSTALLING AND USING THE SOFTWARE

For your convenience, the software titles appearing on the CD-ROM are listed alphabetically.

Acrobat Reader

For Microsoft Windows 95/98/NT/2000. Evaluation version. This disc contains an evaluation version of Acrobat Reader from Adobe Systems, Inc. You will need this program to access the e-version of the book also included on this disc.

Author's sample files

For Mac and Windows 95/98/NT. These files contain all the sample code from the book. You can browse these files directly from the CD-ROM, or you can copy them to your hard drive and use them as the basis for your own projects. To find the files on the CD-ROM, open the D:\SAMPLE folder. To copy the files to your hard drive, run the installation program D:\SAMPLES.EXE. The files will be placed on your hard drive at C:\QMFD.

BBEdit Lite v4.6

For Macintosh. By Bare Bones Software. BBEdit is a popular text-based HTML editor. You can use BBEdit to edit the HTML documents that you create in Dreamweaver. This Lite version lacks some of the features available in the full version (BBEdit 6.0.1) but does not expire. For more information, visit www.bbedit.com.

BBEdit v6.0.1

For Macintosh. By Bare Bones Software. BBEdit is a popular text-based HTML editor that you can use to edit the HTML documents that you create in Dreamweaver. This demo version is identical to the retail version but expires after 24 launches. For more information, visit www.bbedit.com

CSE HTML Validator Professional v4.50

For Win 95/98/NT/2000/Me. By AI Internet Solutions. CSE HTML Validator Professional is an HTML syntax checker that you can use to validate the HTML documents that you create in Dreamweaver. This trial version expires after 50 uses. For more information, visit www.htmlvalidator.com.

CSE HTML Validator Lite v2.01

For Win 95/98/NT/2000/Me. By AI Internet Solutions. CSE HTML Validator Lite is an HTML syntax checker that you can use to validate the HTML documents that you create in Dreamweaver. This Lite version has fewer features than the professional version and includes advertising, but does not expire. For more information, visit www.htmlvalidator.com.

CuteFTP v4.0

For Win 95/98/NT/2000/Me. By GlobalSCAPE. CuteFTP is a popular Internet file-transfer application. You can use CuteFTP to transfer the pages that you create in Dreamweaver to and from a Web server. This shareware version expires after 30 days. For more information, visit www.cuteftp.com.

Dreamweaver v4.0

For Win 95/98/NT/2000/Me and Macintosh. By Macromedia. Dreamweaver is a full-featured application for designing, publishing, and maintaining Web pages. This trial version expires after 30 days. For more information, visit www.macromedia.com/dreamweaver.

Dreamweaver JavaScript Integration Kit for Macromedia Flash 5

For Win 95/98/NT and Macintosh. By Macromedia. Use this kit to help you create Flash interfaces to use with your Dreamweaver Web site and set controls for the Flash Player window. For more information, visit www.macromedia.com/downloads.

Fireworks v4.0

For Win 95/98/NT/2000/Me and Macintosh. By Macromedia. Fireworks lets you create, edit, and optimize images for use on your Web pages. You can create images in Fireworks and then add them to the pages that you build in Dreamweaver. This trial version expires after 30 days. For more information, visit www.macromedia.com/fireworks.

Flash v5.0

For Win 95/98/NT/2000/Me and Macintosh. By Macromedia. Flash is the leading Web application development software. This trial version expires after 30 days. For more information, visit www.macromedia.com/flash.

Flash CorelDRAW Exporter

For Win 95/98/NT. By Macromedia. Use this add-on to bring CorelDRAW files into Flash with ease. For more information, visit www.macromedia.com/downloads.

Flash Deployment Kit

For Win 95/98/NT and Mac. By Macromedia. This kit helps you to implement Flash content onto existing or new Web sites. For more information, visit www.macromedia.com/downloads.

Flash Player v5

For Win 95/98/NT/2000/Me and Macintosh. By Macromedia. The Flash Player is a free Web player application for viewing Flash content on the Web. For more information, visit www.macromedia.com/software/flashplayer.

Flash Writer for Adobe

For Win 95/98/NT/2000/Me and Macintosh. By Macromedia. Use this handy plug-in to help you export your Adobe Illustrator files into Flash or directly onto the Web. For more information, visit www.macromedia.com/downloads.

HomeSite v4.5

For Win 95/98/NT/2000/Me. By Allaire. HomeSite is a popular text-based HTML editor that you can use to edit the HTML documents that you create in Dreamweaver. This evaluation version expires after 60 days. For more information, visit www.allaire.com/homesite.

Paint Shop Pro v7

For Win 95/98/NT/2000/Me. By Jasc Software. Paint Shop Pro lets you create, edit, and optimize images for use on your Web pages. You can create images in Paint Shop Pro and then add them to the pages that you build in Dreamweaver. This evaluation version expires after 30 days. For more information, visit www.jasc.com.

TROUBLESHOOTING

We tried our best to compile programs that work on most computers with the minimum system requirements. Your computer, however, may differ and some programs may not work properly for some reason.

The two most likely problems are that you do not have enough memory (RAM) for the programs you want to use, or you have other programs running that are affecting the installation or running of a program. If you get error messages such as `Not enough memory` or `Setup cannot continue`, try one or more of these methods and then try using the software again:

- Turn off any anti-virus software.
- Close all running programs.
- In Windows, close the CD-ROM interface and run demos or installations directly from Windows Explorer.
- Have your local computer store add more RAM to your computer.

If you still have trouble installing the items from the CD-ROM, please call the Hungry Minds Customer Care phone number, 800-762-2974 (outside the U.S.: 317-572-3993). You can also e-mail Hungry Minds technical support at techsupdum@hungryminds.com.

MASTER VISUALLY DREAMWEAVER 4 & FLASH 5 ON THE CD-ROM

You can view *Master VISUALLY Dreamweaver 4 & Flash 5* on your screen using the CD-ROM included at the back of this book. The CD-ROM allows you to search the contents of the book for a specific word or phrase. The CD-ROM also provides a convenient way of keeping the book handy while traveling.

You must install Acrobat Reader on your computer before you can view the book on the CD-ROM. This program is provided on the disc. Acrobat Reader allows you to view Portable Document Format, or PDF, files. These files can display books and magazines on your screen exactly as they appear in printed form.

To view the contents of the book using Acrobat Reader, display the contents of the disc. Open the PDF folder. Then double-click the chapter you want to view.

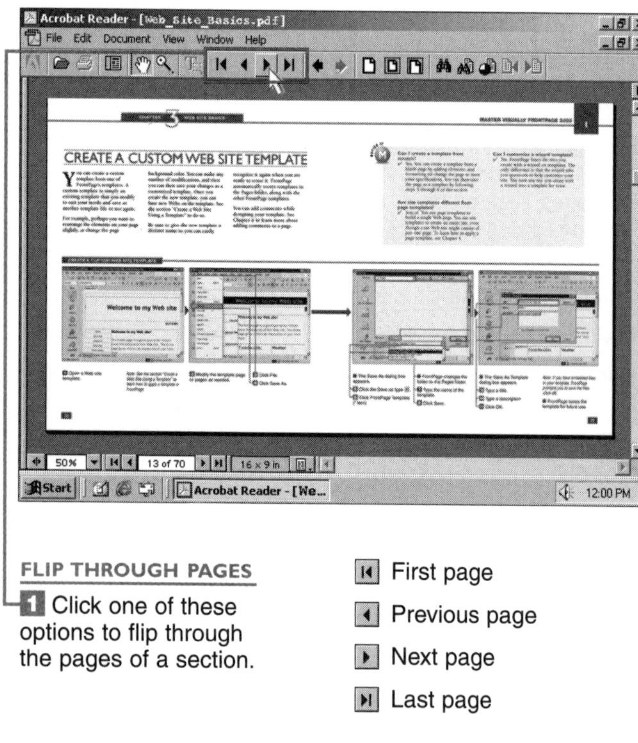

FLIP THROUGH PAGES

1 Click one of these options to flip through the pages of a section.

- First page
- Previous page
- Next page
- Last page

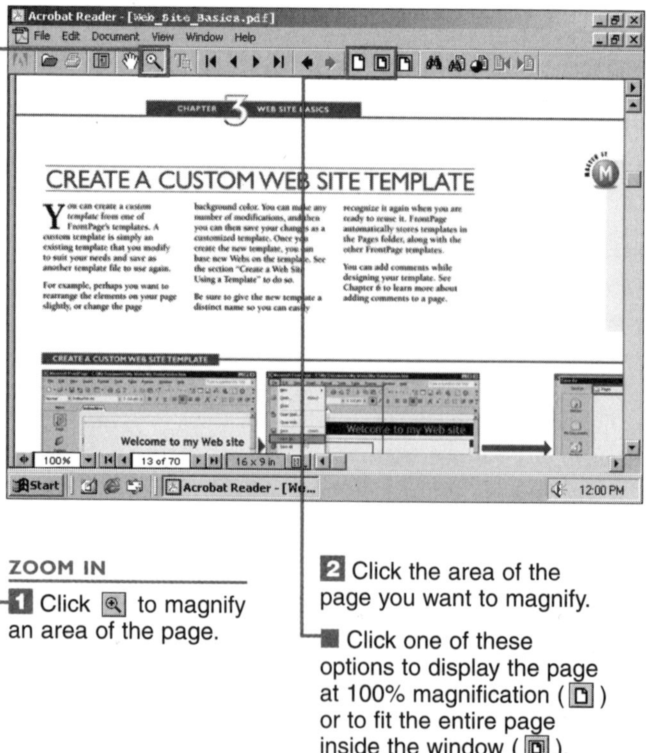

ZOOM IN

1 Click to magnify an area of the page.

2 Click the area of the page you want to magnify.

■ Click one of these options to display the page at 100% magnification ( ) or to fit the entire page inside the window ( ).

How do I install Acrobat Reader?

✔ Open the `Software\Reader` folder on the CD-ROM disc. Double-click the `AR405eng.exe` file and then follow the instructions on your screen. Or, you can use the visual interface to install Acrobat Reader. (Begin by clicking the idg.exe icon.)

How do I search all the sections of the book at once?

✔ You must first locate the index. While viewing the contents of the book, click [icon] in the Acrobat Reader window. Click Indexes and then click Add. Locate and click the index.pdx file, click Open and then click OK. You need to locate the index only once. After locating the index, you can click [icon] to search all the sections.

How can I make searching the book more convenient?

✔ Copy the Acrobat Files folder from the CD-ROM disc to your hard drive. This enables you to easily access the contents of the book at any time.

Can I use Acrobat Reader for anything else?

✔ Acrobat Reader is a popular and useful program. There are many files available on the Web that are designed to be viewed using Acrobat Reader. Look for files with the `.pdf` extension.

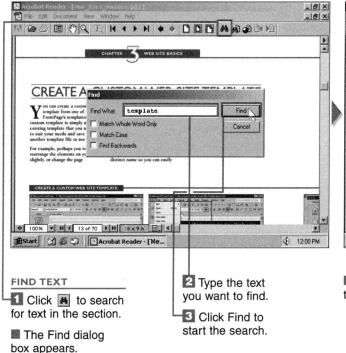

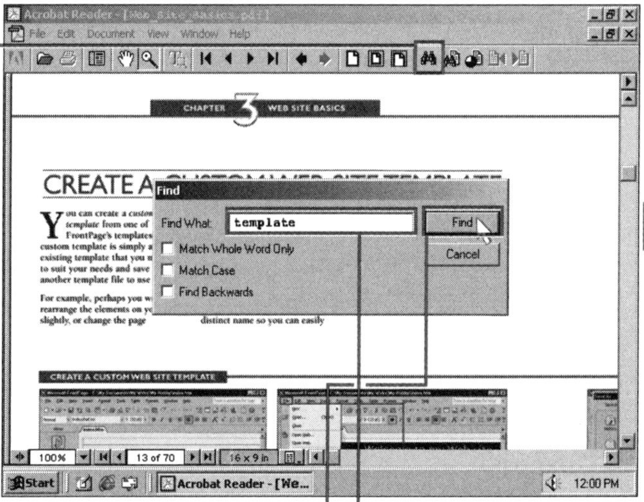

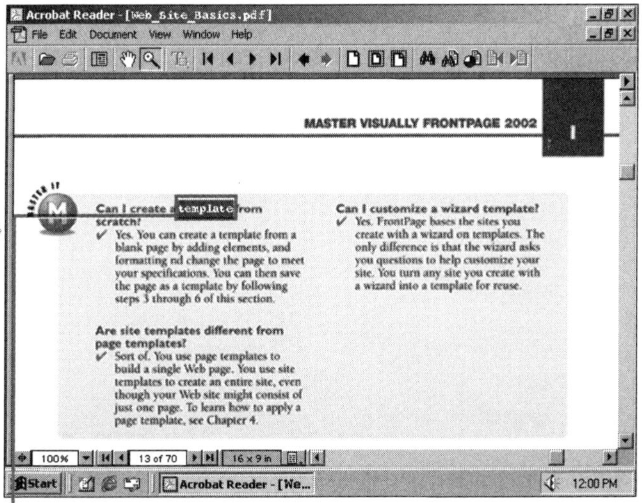

FIND TEXT

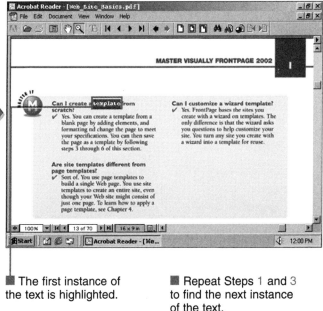

1 Click [icon] to search for text in the section.

■ The Find dialog box appears.

2 Type the text you want to find.

3 Click Find to start the search.

■ The first instance of the text is highlighted.

■ Repeat Steps 1 and 3 to find the next instance of the text.

APPENDIX

Hungry Minds, Inc.
End-User License Agreement

READ THIS. You should carefully read these terms and conditions before opening the software packet(s) included with this book ("Book"). This is a license agreement ("Agreement") between you and Hungry Minds, Inc. ("HMI"). By opening the accompanying software packet(s), you acknowledge that you have read and accept the following terms and conditions. If you do not agree and do not want to be bound by such terms and conditions, promptly return the Book and the unopened software packet(s) to the place you obtained them for a full refund.

1. **License Grant.** HMI grants to you (either an individual or entity) a nonexclusive license to use one copy of the enclosed software program(s) (collectively, the "Software") solely for your own personal or business purposes on a single computer (whether a standard computer or a workstation component of a multi-user network). The Software is in use on a computer when it is loaded into temporary memory (RAM) or installed into permanent memory (hard disk, CD-ROM, or other storage device). HMI reserves all rights not expressly granted herein.

2. **Ownership.** HMI is the owner of all right, title, and interest, including copyright, in and to the compilation of the Software recorded on the disk(s) or CD-ROM ("Software Media"). Copyright to the individual programs recorded on the Software Media is owned by the author or other authorized copyright owner of each program. Ownership of the Software and all proprietary rights relating thereto remain with HMI and its licensers.

3. **Restrictions On Use and Transfer.**

   (a) You may only (i) make one copy of the Software for backup or archival purposes, or (ii) transfer the Software to a single hard disk, provided that you keep the original for backup or archival purposes. You may not (i) rent or lease the Software, (ii) copy or reproduce the Software through a LAN or other network system or through any computer subscriber system or bulletin-board system, or (iii) modify, adapt, or create derivative works based on the Software.

   (b) You may not reverse engineer, decompile, or disassemble the Software. You may transfer the Software and user documentation on a permanent basis, provided that the transferee agrees to accept the terms and conditions of this Agreement and you retain no copies. If the Software is an update or has been updated, any transfer must include the most recent update and all prior versions.

4. **Restrictions on Use of Individual Programs.** You must follow the individual requirements and restrictions detailed for each individual program in the appendix of this Book. These limitations are also contained in the individual license agreements recorded on the Software Media. These limitations may include a requirement that after using the program for a specified period of time, the user must pay a registration fee or discontinue use. By opening the Software packet(s), you will be agreeing to abide by the licenses and restrictions for these individual programs that are detailed in the appendix and on the Software Media. None of the material on this Software Media or listed in this Book may ever be redistributed, in original or modified form, for commercial purposes.

5. **Limited Warranty.**

   (a) HMI warrants that the Software and Software Media are free from defects in materials and workmanship under normal use for a period of sixty (60) days from the date of purchase of this Book. If HMI receives notification within the warranty period of defects in materials or workmanship, HMI will replace the defective Software Media.

   (b) HMI AND THE AUTHOR OF THE BOOK DISCLAIM ALL OTHER WARRANTIES, EXPRESS OR IMPLIED, INCLUDING WITHOUT LIMITATION IMPLIED WARRANTIES OF MERCHANTABILITY AND FITNESS FOR A PARTICULAR PURPOSE, WITH RESPECT TO THE SOFTWARE, THE PROGRAMS, THE SOURCE CODE CONTAINED THEREIN, AND/OR THE

TECHNIQUES DESCRIBED IN THIS BOOK. HMI DOES NOT WARRANT THAT THE FUNCTIONS CONTAINED IN THE SOFTWARE WILL MEET YOUR REQUIREMENTS OR THAT THE OPERATION OF THE SOFTWARE WILL BE ERROR FREE.

(c) This limited warranty gives you specific legal rights, and you may have other rights that vary from jurisdiction to jurisdiction.

6. **Remedies.**

(a) HMI's entire liability and your exclusive remedy for defects in materials and workmanship shall be limited to replacement of the Software Media, which may be returned to HMI with a copy of your receipt at the following address: Software Media Fulfillment Department, Attn.: *Master VISUALLY Dreamweaver 4 and Flash 5*, Hungry Minds, Inc., 10475 Crosspoint Blvd., Indianapolis, IN 46256, or call 1-800-762-2974. Please allow four to six weeks for delivery. This Limited Warranty is void if failure of the Software Media has resulted from accident, abuse, or misapplication. Any replacement Software Media will be warranted for the remainder of the original warranty period or thirty (30) days, whichever is longer.

(b) In no event shall HMI or the author be liable for any damages whatsoever (including without limitation damages for loss of business profits, business interruption, loss of business information, or any other pecuniary loss) arising from the use of or inability to use the Book or the Software, even if HMI has been advised of the possibility of such damages.

(c) Because some jurisdictions do not allow the exclusion or limitation of liability for consequential or incidental damages, the above limitation or exclusion may not apply to you.

7. **U.S. Government Restricted Rights.** Use, duplication, or disclosure of the Software for or on behalf of the United States of America, its agencies and/or instrumentalities (the "U.S. Government") is subject to restrictions as stated in paragraph (c)(1)(ii) of the Rights in Technical Data and Computer Software clause of DFARS 252.227-7013, or subparagraphs (c) (1) and (2) of the Commercial Computer Software - Restricted Rights clause at FAR 52.227-19, and in similar clauses in the NASA FAR supplement, as applicable.

8. **General.** This Agreement constitutes the entire understanding of the parties and revokes and supersedes all prior agreements, oral or written, between them and may not be modified or amended except in a writing signed by both parties hereto that specifically refers to this Agreement. This Agreement shall take precedence over any other documents that may be in conflict herewith. If any one or more provisions contained in this Agreement are held by any court or tribunal to be invalid, illegal, or otherwise unenforceable, each and every other provision shall remain in full force and effect.

INDEX

A

absolute addressing, 91
absolute text size, 68
acceptance message, 611
Acrobat Reader, 700
Action panel, 629
actions
- actions list, resizing type in, 499
- button actions, 460–463, 488
- debugging, 659
- deleting, 491, 503
- described, 460, 462, 488
- editing, 463, 491
- event handlers. *See* event handlers
- events. *See* events
- frame actions, 488, 490–491, 497
- getURL action, 608–609, 612–613
- goto action, 488, 492–495
- layers, 499
- Load Movie action, 500–501
- multiple actions added to buttons, 463
- Navigation action, 488–489
- order of, changing, 502–503
- organizing, 491
- Play action, 496–499
- in separate layers, 691
- Stop action, 496–499
- Stop All Sounds action, 488
- targets, 488, 489
- testing, 463, 499
- types of actions good for buttons, 461
- using, 489

Actions group, 507
ActionScript
- described, 506
- gravity effect, used to create, 684–685

advanced features of Dreamweaver, 7
alert ( ) method, 622–623
aligning
- objects, 330–331
- ordered lists, 61
- paragraphs, 53
- tables, 111
- text, 338–339
- vertical alignment, 331

alternate text, 87
animated buttons
- another file, clip from, 457
- creating, 572–573
- described, 456, 458
- Dreamweaver and Flash combined to create Web site, 572–573
- length of, 457
- movie clip, changed into, 573
- movie clip, inserting, 456–458
- premade animation clips, 457
- previewing, 459
- sounds, adding, 459
- testing, 459
- testing movie clip, 458–459
- using effect, 573

animated menu
- buttons, animated graphic symbols as, 627
- buttons used in menu, animating, 629
- closing, 627
- creating, 626–631
- described, 626
- opening from first frame, 629
- switching Action panel modes, 629

animation
- Animation Row, 221
- animation speed, 228–229
- behavior, triggering animation with, 230–231

buttons. *See* animated buttons
deleting scenes, 407
dragging a path, creating an animation by, 224–225
frame-by-frame animation. *See* frame-by-frame animation
frame rate, 384–385
how it works, 380–381
menus. *See* animated menu
movie clip, saving as, 408–409
Movie Explorer, 410–411
new scene, adding, 406
onion-skinning, 398–401
opening scene panel, 406
premade movie clips, 409
previewing, 402
reordering scenes, 407
by rotating a symbol, 418–421
scenes, creating, 406–407
setting movie dimensions and speed, 384–385
speed, 228–229, 403
stopping movie after particular scene, 407
straight-line animation, 222–223
switching between scenes, 407
trigger applied to animation, removing, 231
tweened animation, 381
with tweened frames, 383
types of, 381
using, 380
Animation Row, 221
array, emulating, 664–667
ASP scripts
forms, 587
testing, 611
Assets panel
applying assets, 249
content, adding, 248–249
copying assets from one site to another, 249
described, 246
editing assets, 249
finding items, 247
inserting assets, 248
multimedia, viewing, 247
nicknaming favorite asset, 251
refreshing lists, 247
removing assets from Favorites, 251
removing items from, 251
specifying favorite assets, 250–251
attributes, copying, 324–325
audience, defining, 9
audio channels, 485
authoring file, 520
author's sample files on CD, 700
Auto rotate setting, 425
automated rotation, 419
Autoplay, 221

B

Back button, 221
background color
changing, 86
layers, 204
Stage, 279
Bandwidth Profiler
changing graphview, 528–529
closing, 529
download speed, customizing, 527
Frame by Frame Graph mode, 528
opening, 526–527
Preloader and, 642
resizing graph, 528
specific frame, viewing, 529
Streaming Graph mode, 528

(continued)

Bandwidth Profiler *(continued)*
- test settings, saving, 527
- testing movie bandwidth, 526–529
- views, 528

banners
- adding to your Web page, 607
- creating, 606
- described, 606
- dimensional size, 606
- file size, 606
- Flash plug-in, when user does not have, 607
- on someone else's site, 607

BBEdit Lite v4.6, 700

BBEdit Lite v6.0.1, 700

behaviors
- browser versions, checking, 207
- browsers and, 206–207
- buttons, 446
- customized browser window, opening, 214–215
- described, 206
- form validation, 207, 212–213
- JavaScript, debugging, 218–219
- JavaScript used to create, 206
- rollover images, creating, 207, 208–209
- status bar message, creating, 210–211
- triggering animation with, 230–231
- user's browser, checking, 216–217

bitmap graphics
- described, 372
- edits on bitmap fill, 379
- fills, turning bitmaps into, 378–379
- formats, 373
- pixels, 372
- reusing, 375
- as tiled pattern, 379
- tracing, 376–377
- vector graphics, conversion to, 376–377

blank keyframes, 388

blank spaces, 57

block text box, 335

body of page, applying classes to, 193

bold text, 66–67, 336

borders
- added to text box, 649
- frames, 164–165

brightness, 368

browsers
- attributes, not specifying window, 215
- consistent appearance of pages in, 51
- customized browser window, opening, 214–215
- described, 5
- list of, 217
- naming the window, 215
- plug-ins, checking for, 217
- previewing Web pages in, 50–51
- Primary Browser, 51
- and style sheets, 187
- used to distribute movies, 524–525
- user's browser, checking, 216–217

Brush tool
- drawing objects with, 298–299
- modes, 299
- one direction, brushing in, 299
- pressure-sensitive tablets and, 299
- selecting brush size, 298

button actions, 460–463, 488

button animations. *See* animated buttons

button symbols, 359

buttons
- actions, 460–463, 488
- animated buttons. *See* animated buttons
- animated graphic symbols as, 627

in animated menu, 629
appearance of, 450
assigning sounds to, 472–473
behaviors, 446
described, 446
Down frame, 447
editing, 455
frames, 447
Hit frame, 447
layers, 453
movie clip acting like, 680–681
movie-edit mode, 453
Over frame, 447
premade buttons, 449, 657
previewing, 451, 455
rollover buttons, 446
shape-changing buttons, 452–455
stages of, 446–447
stored button from another file, using, 449
symbol converted to, 448–451
symbol-edit mode, 451, 453
Up frame, 447
viewing, 453

C

cache, 43
Caption style, 72
Cascading Style Sheets. *See* style sheets
CD-ROM
Acrobat Reader, 700
Acrobat version, 700
author's sample files, 700
BBEdit Lite v4.6, 700
BBEdit Lite v6.0.1, 700
CSE HTML Validator Lite v2.01, 700
CSE HTML Validator Professional v4.50, 700
CuteFTP v4.0, 701
Dreamweaver JavaScript Integration Kit for Macromedia Flash 5, 701
Dreamweaver v4.0, 701
Fireworks v4.0, 701
Flash CorelDRAW Exporter, 701
Flash Deployment Kit, 701
Flash Player v5, 701
Flash v5.0, 701
Flash Writer for Adobe, 701
HomeSite v4.5, 701
Paint Shop Pro v7, 701
software on, 700–701
system requirements, 700
troubleshooting, 701–702
Web links, 700
centering images, 79
CGI script, sending form using, 676–679
Change Link Sitewide command, 257
Character panel, 336–337
chat feature
creating, 576–581
customizing, 577, 581
described, 576
Dreamweaver and Flash combined to create Web site, 576–581
embedding fonts for dynamic text, 577
features, adding, 581
labeling frames, 581
PHP scripts, 578–579
check boxes, adding to forms, 138–139

Check In/Check Out system
- check in a file, 253
- check out a file, 253
- described, 252
- enable Check In/Check Out, 252

checking entered information on forms, 583
classes, creating, 190–191
Clean Up HTML command, 34–35
Clean Up Word command, 35
Clear button, 584–585
code, hyperlink, 90
color
- background color. *See* background color
- coding HTML, 33
- columns, 115
- effects, 368–369
- gradient effects, 320
- line segments, 289, 307
- swatches, 322

color set
- color swatches, removing, 322
- described, 322
- editing, 322–323
- loading, 323
- saving, 323

columns
- color, 115
- deleting, 119
- dimensions, changing, 123
- inserting, 118

complex actions
- Actions group, 507
- conditional actions, 510–513
- described, 506
- expressions, 507
- FS Command, 518–519
- getURL action, 514–515
- If Frame Is Loaded action, 510–513
- layers, 511
- Operators group, 507
- preloader, 512–513
- Tell Target action, 516–517
- types of, 507
- variable text field, 508–509
- variables, 507

compression of graphics, 618–619
conditional actions, 510–513
confirmation page, 587
content
- gathering, 8
- library items, 173

continuous rotation, 419
copying
- assets, 249
- attributes, 324–325
- frames, 404–405
- graphics, 375
- layers, 353
- objects, 304–305

Copyright style, 72
creating
- advanced Preloader, 638–643
- animated menu, 626–631
- external style sheets, 198–199
- filmstrip effect, 696–699
- forms, 130, 582–583
- frame-by-frame animation, 394–397
- frames, 150
- gradient effects, 319–320
- gravity effect, 682–685
- hyperlinks, 90–91
- layers, 200–201

library items, 170–171
motion tween, 412–415
new folder, 235
new HTML styles, 73
Password Identification box, 656–659
shape tween, 436–439
symbols, 364–365
templates, 178–179
Web pages, 46
windows hierarchy, 652–655
CSE HTML Validator Lite v2.01, 701
CSE HTML Validator Professional v4.50, 700
CSS selectors used to modify links, 196–197
Current Frame, 221
cursor position, tracking, 648–651
curved lines
degree of curvature, 293
drawing with Pen tool, 292–293
points, editing, 293
rough appearance of, 295
straightening, 289
custom line, drawing, 290–291
customizing HTML tags, 188–189
customizing strokes, 313
CuteFTP v4.0, 701

D

data, handling form, 130
dead pages, removing, 243
deleting
actions, 491, 503
external style sheets, 199
file in Site window, 235
frames, 158, 392–393
gradient effects, 321
images, 77
instances, 367
layers, 346–347
library items, 171
scenes, 407
symbols, 371
templates, 179
demoting a keyframe, 393
deprecated tags, 41
depth added with layers, 345
Design Notes
adding to object on Web page, 255
creating, 254–255
described, 254
remote sites, specifying Design Notes not be uploaded to, 255
storing, 255
viewing, 255
designing forms, 130
detaching library content for editing, 176–177
detaching page from templates, 183
digital sampling, 464
dimensions of layer, 226
direction of rotation, 419
direction of spin, 423
distribution methods
authoring file, 520
Bandwidth Profiler, 521, 526–529
browsers, 524–525
described, 520
export file, 520
export file formats, 520–521
exporting movie to another format, 538–539
Flash Player, 522–523
Flash Player format, publishing in, 521
full-size, viewing movie as, 535

(continued)

distribution methods *(continued)*
- previewing movies before publishing, 531
- printing movie content, 521
- printing movie frames, 540–541
- projector, creating, 536–537
- Projector feature used to distribute movie, 521
- Publish Settings dialog box, 530–531
- publishing a movie in HTML format, 532–535
- publishing movies, 530–531
- source code for Flash template, viewing, 535
- testing movie bandwidth, 526–529

Document window
- Code and Design view, 18
- Code view, 18
- customizing view, 19
- described, 10
- overview, 18
- using, 18–19
- views, 18
- Web page features not appearing in, 19
- WYSIWYG view, 18

Down frame, 447

download time, reducing, 620–621

downloadable files, 616–617

downloading files, 240–241

drag and drop used to copy frames, 405

draggable menu
- creating, 692–695
- described, 692
- functionality, testing, 694
- startDrag, 693

dragging a path, creating an animation by, 224–225

dragging layers to Trash button, 347

drawing
- Brush tool, drawing objects with, 298–299
- curves with Pen tool, 292–293
- custom line, drawing, 290–291
- with fill color, 296–297
- freeform lines, drawing, 287
- line segments, 286–287
- lines, 286–287
- motion path, 431–432
- ovals, 296
- rectangles, 296–297
- ruler used to help draw lines, 287
- in Smooth mode, 295
- straight lines, drawing, 286
- in Straighten mode, 295

Drawing tool used to define motion path, 431

Drawing toolbar
- Arrow, 284
- Brush, 284
- Color tools, 285
- Dropper, 284
- Eraser, 284
- Ink Bottle, 284
- Lasso, 284
- Line, 284
- Option tools, 285
- Oval, 284
- overview, 284
- Paint Bucket, 284
- Pen, 284
- Pencil, 284
- Rectangle, 284
- Subselect, 284
- Text, 284
- View tools, 285

Dreamweaver
advanced features, 7
described, 4
help documentation, 14–15
interface. *See* Dreamweaver interface
starting, 12–13
Dreamweaver Exchange, 15
Dreamweaver interface
Document window, 10, 11
Launcher bar, 10, 11
on Macintosh, 11
menus, 10, 11
Objects panel, 10, 11
panel, 10, 11
Property Inspector, 10, 11
toolbar, 10, 11
on Windows PC, 10
Dreamweaver JavaScript Integration Kit for Macromedia Flash 5, 701
Dreamweaver v4.0, 701
drop-down menu
Alpha value, 567
creating, 564–569
expanding other ways, 565
invisible buttons, 567
item buttons, 569
items displayed on, large quantity of, 565
minimizing space between menu buttons, 569
sounds, adding, 569
Dropper tool, 324–325
duplicate symbol, creating, 365
duplicating Web pages, 49

E

easing, 553
editable regions, setting, 180–181
editing
actions, 463, 491
buttons, 455
color set, 322–323
fills, 308–309
library items, 174–175
line segments, 306–307
sounds, 484–485
source code, 32–33
style sheet class, 194–195
symbols, 369, 370–371
templates, 184–185
elements, choosing form, 130
embedded style sheets, 187
empty tags, 35
Eraser tool
described, 316
modifiers, 317
using, 316–317
white fill compared, 317
errors, displaying, 33
event handlers, 489
event sounds, 465, 474–475
events
described, 489
frame events, 489
keyboard events, 489
mouse events, 489
export, setting audio output for, 486–487
export file, 520
export file formats, 520–521

exporting movie to another format, 538–539
expressions, 507
external style sheets
- attaching, 198–199
- creating, 198–199
- deleting, 199
- embedded styles, 199
- example of, 199
- linking to, 199

F

features to include on forms, 583
file formats
- export file formats, 520–521
- sounds, 465

file uploading, adding to forms, 146
files
- closing files, 273
- compressions for sound files, specifying, 637
- downloadable files, 240–241, 616–617
- formats, saving files in different, 273
- graphics, saving as image files, 619
- group of files, searching through, 259
- hyperlinks to other files, 100–101
- loading local files in different directories, 609
- naming files, 273
- new files, opening, 271
- opening, 270–271
- organizing files and folders, 234–235
- rearranging site files, 234
- recent files, determining which are, 243
- risks for downloadable files, 617
- saving files, 272–273
- size of files, 467
- types of files available for download, 617
- unhiding files, 245
- uploading files, 240–241

Fill Color dialog box, 297
fills
- adjusting edit points on fill outline, 309
- color, editing, 309
- editing, 308–309
- Fill Color palette, 308
- reshaping, 308–309
- turning bitmaps into, 378–379

filmstrip effect
- creating, 696–699
- described, 696
- images for, 697
- interactive menu, turning filmstrip effect into, 698
- speed of, 699

firewalls, 237
Fireworks v4.0, 701
Fixed-width style, 72
flagging user error, 622–623
Flash
- advantages of, 264
- animation with, 265
- closing files, 273
- Dashboard feature, 281
- drawing levels, 283
- Drawing toolbar, 266, 267, 284–285
- files, opening, 270–271
- formats, saving files in different, 273
- Help features, 280–281
- history of, 264
- importing graphics, 283
- interactivity, adding, 265

keyboard, navigation with, 268
line segments, drawing. *See* line segments
on Macintosh, 267
main toolbar, 266
menu bar (Macintosh), 267
menu bar (Windows), 266
mini-windows, 269
mouse, navigation with, 268
naming files, 273
new files, opening, 271
objects, 282–283
overlay level, 283
overview, 264
saved file, opening, 270
saving files, 272–273
segments, 282
shape recognition, 282
sound, adding, 265
stage level, 283
Stage or Movie Area (Macintosh), 267
Stage or Movie Area (Windows), 266
Timeline (Macintosh), 267
Timeline (Windows), 266
title bar (Macintosh), 267
title bar (Windows), 266
tutorials, 281
window, program, 266–268
on Windows, 266
Work Area (Macintosh), 267
Work Area (Windows), 266
Flash CorelDRAW Exporter, 701
Flash Deployment Kit, 701
Flash Player, 522–523
Flash Player format, publishing in, 521
Flash Player v5, 701
Flash v5.0, 701
Flash Writer for Adobe, 701
flipping objects, 314–315
fonts
changing, 64–65
color, 70–71
monospaced font style, 65
sans serif, 65
serif, 65
size, 68–69
text, 337
formatting
bitmap graphics, 373
line segments, 288–289
text, 336–337
forms
Anything option, 213
ASP script, 587
browser events triggering validation, 213
CGI script, sending form using, 676–679
check boxes, adding, 138–139
checking entered information, 583
Clear button, creating, 584–585
client-side validation, 212
confirmation page, 587
creating, 130, 582–583
data, handling form, 130
described, 7, 582
designing, 130
e-mail address in field, determining, 213
elements, choosing, 130
features to include on, 583
file uploading, adding, 146
GET method, 591
hidden information, adding, 147
(continued)

forms *(continued)*
- hidden strings sent with, 677
- jump menus, creating, 144–145
- lists, adding, 142–143
- mailto command, 598–599
- menus, adding, 142–143
- multiline text fields, adding, 134–135
- numbers in field, determining, 213
- other instructions for creating, 679
- overview, 130
- password field, adding, 136–137
- POST method, 591
- processing form information, 130
- radio buttons, adding, 140–141
- reset button, adding, 149
- scrolling text box, creating, 588–589
- search tool, adding, 600–605
- server-side validation, 212
- setting up, 131
- Submit button, 148, 586–587
- text fields, adding, 132–133
- user log out screen, creating, 596–597
- user login screen, creating, 592–595
- user profile, editing, 590–591
- validating, 212–213, 587
- wrapping behavior, 134–135

frame actions, 488, 497

frame-by-frame animation
- animation, 381
- creating, 394–397
- described, 394
- in-between frames, adding, 395
- motion tween compared, 413
- Snap To Objects feature, 397
- Stage, repositioning objects on, 397
- symbols, editing, 395

frame labels, 504–505

frame links, 91

Frame panel, 419

frame rate, 228–229, 384–385

framed sites, 156–157

frames
- actions, added to, 490–491
- adding, 386–389
- blank keyframes, adding, 388
- borders, 164–165
- buttons, 447
- changing number of, 229
- content, adding, 154–155
- copying, 404–405
- creating, 150, 220
- deleting, 158, 392–393
- demoting a keyframe, 393
- described, 7
- dimensions, changing, 162–163
- dividing a page into, 151
- drag and drop used to copy, 405
- HTML tags for, 155
- hyperlinks, 160–161
- images loaded into, 155
- keyboard shortcuts for adding, 387
- keyframe, 382–383, 387
- motion tween, 413
- moving, 404–405
- multiple frames, adding, 389
- multiple frames, selecting, 390
- naming, 159
- nested frames, 153
- opening pages in, 154–155

overview, 150
placeholder frame, 382
predefined framesets, 152
properties, modifying, 391
regular frame, adding, 386–387
resizing, 167
reversing the order of a segment of frames, 393
saving framed sites, 156–157
scroll bars, 166
selecting, 390
single frame, selecting, 390
sizing, 389
sounds, adding, 470–471
static frames, 383
status of frames, changing, 392–393
time and movement controlled by, 382
in Timeline, 387
types of, 382–383
undoing deletion, 393

freeform lines, drawing, 287
FS Command, 518–519
FTP, 238
full-size, viewing movie as, 535

G

GET method, 591
getURL action
_blank tag, 613
described, 514–515
links created with, 608–609
loading local files in different directories, 609
other uses for, 609
_parent tag, 613
_self tag, 613
_top tag, 613
windows controlled with, 612–613

GIF images, 74
goto action
assigning, 492–495
described, 492
labeling frames, 493
referencing not yet created scene, 493
testing, 494–495

gradient effects
assigning, 320
as Brush color, 321
color, 320
creating, 320–323
deleting, 324
described, 301, 318
existing gradients, changing, 321
radial gradients, 321
saving, 321

graphic symbols, 359, 639
graphics. *See* images
gravity constant, 683
gravity effect
ActionScript used to create, 684–685
creating, 682–685
described, 682
gravity constant, 683
objects, changing way gravity affects, 683

group of files, searching through, 259
grouping objects, 326–327
guide layers, 345
Guided Tour, 14

H

head content
- described, 38
- description information, 39
- inserting, 38–39
- keyword information, 39
- meta tags, 38
- refreshing pages, 39
- viewing, 38

headings
- colors, 55
- creating, 54–55
- fonts, 55
- levels of, 54–55

Headline style, 72

help documentation
- Dreamweaver Exchange, 15
- extending Dreamweaver's capabilities, 15
- Guided Tour, 14
- online help, 15
- printed copy of, 15
- using, 14–15

hexadecimal codes, 71

hidden information, adding to forms, 147

hiding layers, 347

hierarchy, creating window, 652–655

History panel
- applying commands, 25
- creating commands, 24–25
- Document window, copying information into, 25
- overview, 22
- reducing number of recorded steps, 25
- undo commands, 22

Hit frame, 447

HomeSite v4.5, 701

horizontal lines
- described, 287
- drawing, 307

host director, 239

hosting Web sites, 9

hot buttons, 562–563

HTML
- attributes, 30
- Clean Up HTML command, 34–35
- Clean Up Word command, 35
- color coding, 33
- combining nested font tags, 35
- creating Web pages without knowing code, 31
- described, 4, 30
- direct access to code, 31
- documents, 31
- editing source code, 32–33
- empty tags, 35
- errors, displaying, 33
- head content, 38–39
- optimizing, 34–35
- Quick Tag Editor. *See* Quick Tag Editor
- Reference panel, 40–41
- standard, 30
- tags. *See* HTML tags
- viewing source code, 32
- wrap, making code, 33

HTML attributes, finding and replacing, 259

HTML Styles panel, 72–73

HTML tags
- deprecated tags, 41
- described, 30
- frames, 155

HTTP, 238

hyperlinks
absolute addressing, 91
to another page within site, 92–93
to another Web site, 94–95
automatic testing of external sites, 95
checking, 109
code, 90
color and, 106–107
colored border, adding, 97
creating, 90–91, 185
deleting external page, 95
described, 6
disappearing, 107
e-mail hyperlink, creating, 108
to external style sheets, 199
frame links, 91
getURL action, created with, 608–609
hotspots, 102–103
image hyperlinks, creating, 96–97
image maps, 102–103
to information on same page, 98–99
link changed sitewide, 257
link created using Site Map, 245
multiple hyperlinks within image, creating, 102–103
named anchors, 98–99
opening linked page, 93
opening new window with, 104
organizing, 93
to other files, 100–101
overview, 92
relative addressing, 90
removing external hyperlinks, 95
removing hyperlinks from image, 97
renaming external page, 95
renaming pages and, 93
root-relative addressing, 91
row of hyperlinks, distinguishing, 93
site window, hyperlink by using, 105
underlining and, 107
viewing, 101
HyperText Markup Language. *See* HTML

I

ideas, organizing, 8
If Frame Is Loaded action, 510–513
images
alternate text, adding, 87
background images, 84–85
centering, 79
compression, 618–619
copying, 375
deleting, 77
described, 6, 74
download time, 75
enlarging, 80–81
filmstrip effect, 697
frames, 155
GIF images, 74
horizontal rule, adding, 83
importing, 373–375
inserting into Web pages, 76–77
JPEG images, 75
pasting, 375
pixels, size in, 689
PNG images, 75
resizing, 80–81
retrieving, 74
saving as image files, 619
series of images, importing, 375

(continued)

images *(continued)*
  shrinking, 80–81
  sizing, 77, 80–81
  space around, adding, 82
  storing, 77
  support for, 375, 619
  text wrapped around, 78
importing
  graphics, 373–375
  sound clips, 466–467
in-between frames, adding, 395
incremental changes, viewing, 415
indents, text, 340–341
inserting
  assets, 248
  columns, 118
  head content, 38–39
  images, 76–77
  instances, 366–367
  library items, 172–173
  movie clip, 456–458
inspectors
  combining, 23
  described, 16
instances
  brightness, 368
  color effects, modifying, 368–369
  deleting, 367
  described, 358
  editing symbol instead of, 369
  inserting, 366–367
  Library. *See* Library
  modifying, 368–369
  naming, 369
  replacing, 367
  testing edits, 369
  tint, 368
  transparency, 368, 369
interactive menu, turning filmstrip effect into, 698
interactivity
  array, emulating, 664–667
  button, making movie clip act like, 680–681
  CGI script, sending form using, 676–679
  movie clip, parking, 660–663
  movie clip acting like button, 680–681
  Password Identification box, creating, 656–659
  replicating a movie, 672–675
  strings given by a user, combining, 668–671
interface controls
  animated menu, creating, 626–631
  cursor position, tracking, 648–651
  movie clip, setting property of, 644–647
  Preloader, creating advanced, 638–643
  sound clip volume, adjusting, 632–637
  window hierarchy, creating, 652–655
ISPs, 9, 232
italic text, 66–67, 336

J

JavaScript
  breakpoints, 219
  closing windows with, 615
  code one statement, 219
  debugging, 218–219
  described, 31
  execution of code, stopping, 219
  variables, adjusting, 615
  windows, used to control, 614–615
JPEG images, 75
jump menus, creating, 144–145

K

kerning text, 338–339
keyboard shortcuts
- creating, 26–27
- frames, 387
- preinstalled shortcuts, 27
- printing, 27
- reassigning, 27
- Web pages, used to save, 49

Keyboard Shortcuts Editor, 26
keyframes
- adding, 417
- demoting, 393
- described, 382–383, 387
- selecting, 412–413

L

label text box, 334–335
labels, adding to movie clip, 663
laser-writing animation effect
- blink, making laser light point appear to, 555
- colors and, 559
- creating, 554–559
- described, 554, 556
- erasing circle parts, 557
- guide layers, locking, 555
- positioning content, 557
- staggering different colored layers, 559

lassoing objects, 302
Launcher
- customizing, 17
- described, 16
- icons, 17
- orientation of, 17
- using, 16–17

Launcher bar
- described, 10, 11
- displaying, 17
- icons, 17
- using, 16

Layer Properties dialog box, 348–349
layers
- actions, 499, 691
- adding, 346–347
- background color, 204
- buttons, 453
- complex actions, 511
- copying, 353
- creating, 200–201
- deleting, 346–347
- depth added with, 345
- dragging layers to Trash button, 347
- guide layers, 345
- hiding, 347, 350–351
- Layer Properties dialog box, 348–349
- locking, 351
- mask layers, 345, 356–357
- motion guide layer, 354–355
- naming, 687
- nested layers, 201
- ordering, 687
- organization with, 344
- outline color, 349
- overview, 344–345
- plain guide layer, 354–355
- plain layer, 345
- properties of, changing, 203
- renaming, 350
- repositioning, 202–203
- resizing, 202–203, 351

(continued)

layers *(continued)*
- rotating, 225
- setting layer properties, 348–349
- sounds, 464, 468–469
- stacking, 352–353
- stacking order, 205
- Timeline, working with layers in, 350–351
- types of, 345, 349
- viewing, 351, 353
- visibility of, 203

layout tables
- content, adding, 127
- creating, 124–125
- deleting, 127
- formatting, 127
- rearranging, 126–127
- spacer images, 128–129
- width of, adjusting, 128–129

length of animated buttons, 457

lengthening, shape tween, 439

Library
- closing Library window, 361
- deleting folders, 363
- described, 358
- folders, 362–363
- moving a symbol to another folder, 363
- new folder, creating, 362–363
- opening Library window, 360–361
- renaming folders, 363
- sounds, 464
- Stage, placing symbol from Library on, 361
- symbols from another Library, using, 361
- using, 360–363
- widening Library window, 363

library items
- content, 173
- creating, 170–171
- deleting, 171
- described, 168
- detaching library content for editing, 176–177
- editing, 174–175
- inserting, 172–173
- re-creating, 171
- reverting detached library item back to undetached state, 177
- searching for instances of, 173
- update process, keeping instances of library items from being changed during, 175
- updating, 174–175
- viewing, 169

line breaks, 56

line color, motion path, 431

line segments
- color, 289, 307
- custom line, drawing, 290–291
- drawing, 286–287
- editing, 306–307
- formatting, 288–289
- freeform lines, drawing, 287
- horizontal lines, 287, 307
- length of, 306
- Line Style dialog box, 290–291
- mistakes, fixing, 291
- precise editing of points on, 307
- ruler used to help draw, 287
- shape of, 307
- shape recognition feature, 291
- smoothing, 291, 294–295
- straight lines, drawing, 286

straightening, 289, 294–295
thickness, 287, 307
vertical lines, 287, 307
Line Spacing slider, 341
Line Style dialog box, 290–291
links. *See* hyperlinks
lists, adding to forms, 142–143
Load Movie action, 500–501
loading color set, 323
local sites
cache, 43
described, 42
naming, 43
setting up, 42–43
locking layers, 351
logging errors during file transfers, 241
login screen. *See* user login screen
Loop, 221
Loop option, 477
looping sounds, 482–483
looping spin effect, 425
looping statement, 665

M

Macintosh, 13, 267
Magic Wand modifier, 303
magnifying glass effect
creating, 686–691
described, 686
increasing magnification, 691
masking layers used to create, 688
using, 690
mailto command, 598–599
margins, text, 340–341
mask layer, 345, 356–357
menus
adding to forms, 142–143
animated menus. *See* animated menu
draggable menus. *See* draggable menu
Dreamweaver interface, 10, 11
drop-down menus. *See* drop-down menu
jump menus, creating, 144–145
minimizing sound file size, 487
modifying instances, 368–369
motion guide layer, 354–355, 430
motion path
animating symbols along a, 430–433
drawing, 431–432
Drawing tool used to define, 431
line color, 431
thickness, 431
motion tween, 437
animating by rotating a symbol, 418–421
Auto rotate setting, 425
automated rotation, 419
continuous rotation, 419
creating, 412–415
described, 412, 414
direction of rotation, 419
direction of spin, 423
frame-by-frame animation compared, 413
Frame panel, accessing, 419
frames, adding, 413
incremental changes, viewing, 415
keyframe, adding, 417
keyframes, selecting, 412–413
looping spin effect, 425
motion guide layer, 430
path, animating symbols along a, 430–433
resizing symbol, 427–428

(continued)

motion tween *(continued)*
- Scale option, 428
- shape tween compared, 413
- speed of spinning effect, 423, 425
- spin rotation, selecting, 424
- spinning a symbol to create animation effect, 422–425
- stopping, 416
- symbol size, animation by changing, 426–429
- symbols, selecting, 412–413
- testing tween effect, 415
- tween effect, creating, 414, 422–423
- viewing spin, 425

movie clip
- acting like button, 680–681
- animation, saving as, 408–409
- deleting, 673
- download time, reducing, 620–621
- inserting, 456–458
- instance name, assigning, 653
- labels, adding, 663
- limiting number of clips user can add, 675
- parking, 660–663
- replicating a movie, 672–675
- setProperty action, 644–647
- setting property of, 644–647
- stopping, 663
- symbols, 359
- Tell Target action, 663
- thumbnail gallery, 621
- x-scale, verifying, 647

movie-edit mode, 453

Movie Explorer, 410–411

movie levels, 501

MP3, 487

multiline text fields, adding to forms, 134–135

multimedia
- customizing, 89
- downloading, 89
- inserting, 88–89
- sound file, inserting, 89

multiple actions added to buttons, 463

multiple frames
- adding, 389
- selecting, 390

multiple objects, selecting, 301

multiple strokes, 313

N

naming
- files, 273
- frames, 159
- instances, 369
- layers, 687
- local sites, 43

Navigation action, 488–489

nested font tags, 35

nested frames, 153

nested layers, 201

new animation scene, adding, 406

Normal style, 72

notes on templates, 179

O

objects
- aligning, 330–331
- applying classes to, 192
- center point, changing, 315
- changing way gravity affects, 683
- complex shapes, selecting, 303

copying, 304–305
dragging used to select, 301
fill, selecting only, 301
flipping, 314–315
grouping, 326–327
lassoing, 302
Magic Wand modifier, 303
moving, 304–305
multiple objects, selecting, 301
part of object, selecting, 303
precise degree of rotation, 315
precise positioning of, 305
precise sizing, 311
resizing, 310–311
resizing item beyond Stage, 311
rotating, 314–315
scaling, 310–311
selecting, 300–303
skewing, 315
stacking, 328–329
symbols, converted to, 364–365
ungrouping, 327
unselecting a selected object, 301
vertical alignment, 331
Objects panel
dialog box, 21
Dreamweaver interface, 10, 11
overview, 21
using, 21
onion-skinning, 398–401
online help, 15
opening file from Site window, 235
opening scene panel, 406
opening Web pages, 44–45
Operators group, 507
ordered lists
aligning, 61
creating, 60–61
modifying numerals, 61
nested ordered lists, 61
ordering layers, 687
organizing
actions, 491
files and folders, 234–235
layers, 344
outline color, 349
outline stroke, adding, 312–313
outlines, deleting, 313
ovals, drawing, 296
Over frame, 447
overlapping sounds, 475
overlining links, 197

P

Paint Bucket tool
adding a fill, 300
adding a gradient fill, 301
filling objects with, 300–301
Gap Size modifier, 301
Paint Shop Pro v7, 701
panels
Action panel, 629
Assets panel. *See* Assets panel
Character panel, 336–337
combining, 23
described, 16
Dreamweaver interface, 10, 11
Frame panel, 419

(continued)

panels *(continued)*
- History panel. *See* History panel
- HTML Styles panel, 72–73
- moving, 17
- Objects panel. *See* Objects panel
- Reference panel, 40–41
- resizing, 17

panning effects, 485
paragraphs
- aligning, 53
- applying classes to, 193
- creating, 52–53
- images in, 53
- removing formatting, 53
- width of, 53

part of object, selecting, 303
password field, adding to forms, 136–137
Password Identification box, creating, 656–659
passwords
- additional movie symbol, creating password without making it a, 657
- Password Identification box, creating, 656–659
- security of password protection, 657

pasting graphics, 375
path, animating symbols along a, 430–433
PC, 12
Pen tool
- curves, drawing with, 292–293
- customizing, 293

Perl, 677
Personal Web Server, 611
pixels
- described, 372
- size, 689

placeholder frame, 382
plain guide layer, 354–355
plain layer, 345
Play action
- actions, 496–499
- button, adding to, 497–498

Play button, 221
Playback Rate, 221
Playhead, 221
PNG images, 75
pop-up labels, 227
POST method, 591
pre-existing sounds, 467
pre-made buttons, 449
precise degree of rotation, 315
precise editing of points on, 307
precise positioning of objects, 305
precise sizing of objects, 311
predefined framesets, 152
predefined styles, 72
preferences
- code options, 29
- customizing information in Document window status bar, 29
- font styles, 29
- setting, 28–29

Preferences dialog box, 28–29
Preloader
- Bandwidth Profiler and, 642
- bytes loaded, showing, 643
- content, loading large amounts of, 639
- creating advanced, 638–643
- frame value checked against relative number of frames, 641
- graphic symbol used as, 639
- percentage limited to whole numbers, 643
- viewing Preloader animate locally, 641

preloader, 512–513, 548–549

premade animation clips, 457
premade movie clips, 409
premature disconnection from Web server, 239
Preview in Browser command, 50–51
previewing
- animated buttons, 459
- animations, 402
- buttons, 451, 455
- movies before publishing, 531
- symbols, 365

Primary Browser, 51
printed copy of Dreamweaver help documentation, 15
printing
- movie content, 521
- movie frames, 540–541

processing form information, 130
projector
- creating, 536–537
- playing movie, 537
- renaming movie file, 537
- standalone player compared, 537

Projector feature used to distribute movie, 521
properties
- changing, 203
- defined, 651
- modifying, 391

Property Inspector
- Dreamweaver interface, 10, 11
- expanded mode, 20
- help documentation, 20
- overview, 20
- standard mode, 20
- switching between modes, 20
- using, 20

Publish Settings dialog box, 530–531
publishing a movie in HTML format, 532–535
publishing movies, 530–531
publishing site, 545
PWS, 611

Q

Quick Tag Editor
- customizing, 37
- described, 36
- Edit Tag mode, 36, 37
- exiting, 37
- incorrect HTML, entering, 37
- Insert HTML mode, 36, 37
- Wrap Tag mode, 36

R

radial gradients, 318
radio buttons, adding to forms, 140–141
raster graphics. *See* bitmap graphics
re-creating library items, 171
rearranging site files, 234
recent files, determining which are, 243
rectangles, drawing, 296–297
Reference panel, 40–41
regular frame, 386–387
relative addressing, 90
relative text size, 69
remote sites, 236–239
renaming layers, 350
reordering animation scenes, 407
replacing instances, 367
replicating a movie, 672–675
repositioning layers, 202–203

reset button, adding to forms, 149
reshaping fills, 308–309
resizing
  frames, 167
  images, 80–81
  layers, 202–203, 351
  objects, 310–311
  text boxes, 342–343
  Timeline, 389
retrieving images, 74
reusing bitmap graphics, 375
Reverse Frames command, 444–445
reversing the order of a segment of frames, 393
reverting detached library item back to undetached state, 177
Rewind button, 221
rollover buttons, 446
Root Property action statement, 570
root-relative addressing, 91
rotating objects, 314–315
rotating text boxes, 343
rows
  deleting, 119
  dimensions, changing, 123
  inserting, 118
  single table row or column, changing color of, 115
ruler used to help draw lines, 287

S

sample Web site, building, 544
sampling rate, 464
Scale option, 428
scaling objects, 310–311
scenes, creating animation, 406–407
script coding, 506
scripts, assigning variable names to, 636
scroll bars, 166
scrolling text box, 588–589
search patterns, saving, 261
search tool
  adding, 600–605
  ASP, 601
  database, when to have, 604
  database creation, 601
  described, 600
  forms, adding to, 600–605
  lock layer option, 605
  multiple items, searching for, 603
  product specificity, 605
  types of searches, 602
searching for instances of library items, 173
selecting
  frames, 390
  objects, 300–303
series of images, importing, 375
server, moving site to different, 241
server-side scripts, 610–611
setting layer properties, 348–349
setting movie dimensions and speed, 384–385
setting up local sites, 42–43
shape-changing buttons, 452–455
shape hints, 440–443
shape of line segments, 307
shape tween
  creating, 436 439
  lengthening, 439
  motion tween compared, 413, 437
  shape hints, 440–443
  speed of, 437

shapes
  customizing strokes, 313
  multiple strokes, 313
  outline stroke, adding, 312–313
  outlines, deleting, 313
  strokes, adding, 312–313
shrinking images, 80–81
single frame, selecting, 390
site maintenance
  Assets panel, 246–247
  Change Link Sitewide command, 257
  Check In/Check Out system, 252–253
  Design Notes, 254–255
  group of files, searching through, 259
  HTML attributes, finding and replacing, 259
  link changed sitewide, 257
  link created using Site Map, 245
  search patterns, saving, 261
  Site map, 244–245
  site report, 256
  source code searches, 259
  text, finding and replacing, 258–259
  text patterns, searching for, 260–261
  white space in regular expression, specifying, 261
Site map
  link created using, 245
  subset, viewing, 245
  temporarily hiding part of, 245
  unhiding files, 245
  using, 244–245
Site Map view, 244–245
site navigation, 546
site planning considerations, sample, 546
site report, 256
Site window, 233–235
size of sound files, 467
sizing images, 80–81
skewing objects, 315
skip intro button, 550–551
smoothing lines, 291, 294–295
Snap To Objects feature, 397
software on CD, 700–701
sound
  adding sound layer, 468–469
  animated buttons, adding, 459
  audio channels, 485
  buttons, assigning sounds to, 472–473
  buttons for controlling volume, 633–634
  compressions for sound files, specifying, 637
  described, 464
  digital sampling, 464
  editing, 484–485, 637
  event driven sounds, 465
  event sounds, creating, 474–475
  export, setting audio output for, 486–487
  file formats, 465
  frames, adding sound to, 470–471
  importing sound clips, 466–467
  layers, 464, 468–469
  Library, 464
  Loop option, 477
  looping, 482–483
  minimizing file size, 487
  MP3, 487
  overlapping, 475
  pan clips, 635
  panning effects, 485
  playback, 635
  pre-existing sounds, 467
  properties of sound clip, 633
  sampling rate, 464

(continued)

sound *(continued)*
- setting balance of clips, 635
- size of files, 467
- slide controller used to set volume/balance, 635
- soundtrack layer, 469
- start sounds, assigning, 476–477
- stop sounds, assigning, 478–479
- streaming sounds, 465, 480–481
- symbols, 464
- sync type, reassigning, 477
- types of, 465
- variable, attached to, 637
- volume, 477, 632–637
- waveforms, 464, 471

soundtrack layer, 469
source code for Flash template, viewing, 535
source code searches, 259
SourceSafe, 237
space added around images, 82
spacer images, 128–129
special characters, 62–63
special effects
- draggable menu, 692–695
- filmstrip effect, 696–699
- gravity effect, 682–685
- magnifying glass effect, 686–691

speed
- animations, 403
- shape tween, 437
- of spinning effect, 423

spin rotation, 424
spinning a symbol to create animation effect, 422–425
stacking
- layers, 352–353
- objects, 328–329

stacking order of layers, 205
Stage
- background color, 279
- repositioning objects on, 397
- settings, saving, 279
- sizing, 278–279
- units of measurement for, 279

stages of buttons, 446–447
start sounds, 476–477
startDrag action, 654
starting Dreamweaver, 12–13
starting Web site, 545
static frames, 383
status bar message
- creating, 210–211
- disappear, causing message to, 211
- length of message, 211
- special information in, 211

status of frames, 392–393
Stop action
- actions, 496–499
- assigning, 496–499
- button, adding to, 496–497
- frame, assigning to, 497

Stop All Sounds action, 488
stop sounds, 478–479
stopDrag action, 654
stopping
- file transfers, 241
- motion tween, 416
- movie after particular scene, 407

stored button from another file, using, 449
storing images, 77
storyboard, 546

straight-line animation, 222–223
straight lines, drawing, 286
straightening curved lines, 289
straightening line segments, 294–295
streaming sounds, 465, 480–481
strings given by a user, combining, 668–671
strokes
- adding, 312–313
- customizing strokes, 313
- multiple strokes, 313
- outline stroke, adding, 312–313

style sheets
- applying classes, 192–193
- body of page, applying classes to, 193
- classes, creating, 190–191
- CSS selectors used to modify links, 196–197
- customizing HTML tags, 188–189
- described, 31
- editing a style sheet class, 194–195
- embedded style sheets, 187
- external style sheets, 187, 198–199
- layers. *See* layers
- objects, applying classes to, 192
- options, 191
- overlining links, 197
- overview, 186–187
- paragraphs, applying classes to, 193
- underlining links, 197
- Web browsers and, 187

Submit button, 148, 586–587
support for graphics, 375
swapDepths action, 654
switching between animation scenes, 407
symbol-edit mode, 451, 453
symbols
- button symbols, 359
- converted to buttons, 448–451
- creating, 364–365
- deleting, 371
- described, 358
- duplicate symbol, creating, 365
- editing, 370–371, 395
- graphic symbols, 359
- Library. *See* Library
- movie clip symbols, 359
- objects converted to, 364–365
- previewing, 365
- selecting, 412–413
- sounds, 464
- types of, 359

sync type, reassigning, 477
synchronizing local and remote sites, 242–243
system requirements for CD, 700

T

tables
- aligning, 111
- alignment of table content, changing, 117
- another table, inserting, 113
- background, changing, 114–115
- borders, changing color of, 115
- captions added to images with, 113
- cell dimensions, changing, 122
- cell spacing, changing, 116
- color, changing background, 114
- column, deleting, 119

(continued)

tables *(continued)*
- column, inserting, 118
- column dimensions, changing, 123
- content, inserting, 112–113
- described, 7
- dimensions, changing, 122–123
- duplicating, 111
- editable, defined as, 181
- forms, organizing, 113
- HTML tags for, 111
- image, adding background, 115
- layout table. *See* layout tables
- Layout View, creating layout table in, 124–125
- merging cells, 120–121
- overview, 110
- padding, changing, 116
- row, deleting, 119
- row, inserting, 118
- row dimensions, changing, 123
- single table row or column, changing color of, 115
- splitting cells, 120–121
- table dimensions, changing, 123
- text, inserting, 112–113
- Web page, inserting tables into, 110–111

targets, 488, 489

Tell Target action, 516–517, 663

templates
- applying template to page based on different template, 183
- creating, 178–179
- deleting, 179
- described, 168
- detaching page from, 183
- editable regions, setting, 180–181
- editing, 184–185
- layer made editable, 181
- links, creating, 185
- notes on, storing, 179
- page created using, 182–183
- table defined as editable, 181
- viewing, 169

testing
- actions, 463, 499
- animated buttons, 459
- instances, 369
- movie bandwidth, 526–529
- movie clip, 458–459
- options, 571
- tween effect, 415

text
- adding, 334–335
- aligning, 338–339
- alternate text, 87
- block text box, adding, 335
- bold, applying, 336
- border added to text box, 649
- Character panel, 336–337
- described, 6
- finding and replacing, 258–259
- fonts, 337
- formatting. *See* text formatting
- images, wrapped around, 78
- indents, 340–341
- italics, applying, 336
- kerning, 338–339
- label text box, adding, 334–335
- Line Spacing slider, 341
- margins, 340–341
- moving text boxes, 342–343

resizing text boxes, 342–343
rotating text boxes, 343
static text box, dynamic text box compared, 649
Text tool, 334–335

text boxes, 669

text fields, adding to forms, 132–133

text formatting
absolute text size, 68
applying HTML styles, 72
blank spaces, 57
bold, 66–67
Caption style, 72
Copyright style, 72
creating new HTML styles, 73
Fixed-width style, 72
font color, changing, 70–71
font size, changing, 68–69
fonts, changing, 64–65
headings, 54–55
Headline style, 72
hexadecimal codes, 71
HTML Styles panel, 72–73
italic, 66–67
line breaks, 56
Normal style, 72
ordered lists, 60–61
paragraphs, creating, 52–53
predefined styles, 72
relative text size, 69
special characters, 62–63
unordered lists, 58–59

text patterns, searching for, 260–261

text strings, 670

Text tool, 334–335

thickness
of lines, 287, 307
motion path, 431

thumbnail gallery, 621

tiled pattern, bitmap graphics as, 379

time and movement controlled by frames, 382

Timeline
buttons, 274
Current Frame Indicator, 275
Current Scene, 274
customizing options, 275
docking, 276–277
Frame Numbers, 274
Frames, 274
frames, sizing, 389
hiding, 277
layer buttons, 275
Layers, 274
layers, 275, 350–351
moving, 276–277
Playhead, 275
resizing to view more layers, 389

timelines
Animation Row, 221
animation speed, 228–229
Autoplay, 221
Back button, 221
behavior, triggering animation with, 230–231
Current Frame, 221
described, 220
dimensions of layer, 226
dragging a path, creating an animation by, 224–225
frame rate, changing, 228–229

(continued)

timelines *(continued)*
- frames, changing number of, 229
- frames, creating, 220
- Keyframes, 221
- keyframes, 220
- layers, rotating, 225
- Loop, 221
- Play button, 221
- Playback Rate, 221
- Playhead, 221
- pop-up labels, 227
- Rewind button, 221
- speed of animations, 225
- straight-line animation, 222–223
- Timelines Inspector, 221
- Timelines Menu, 221
- trigger applied to animation, removing, 231
- visibility of layer, 226
- Z-index, 226–227

Timelines Inspector, 221
Timelines Menu, 221
tint, 368
tool tips, 574–575
toolbar
- Drawing toolbar. *See* Drawing toolbar
- Dreamweaver interface, 10, 11
- main toolbar, 266

tracing bitmap graphics, 376–377
transparency, 368, 369
trigger applied to animation, removing, 231
troubleshooting CD, 701–702
tween effect, creating, 414
tween speed, 434–435
tweened animation, 381

U

underlining links, 197
undoing deletions, 393
ungrouping objects, 327
unordered lists
- colored bullets, 59
- creating, 58–59
- items, extra space between, 59
- modifying bullets, 59
- nested unordered list, 59

unselecting a selected object, 301
Up frame, 447
update process, keeping instances of library items from being changed during, 175
updating
- library items, 174–175
- Web sites, 174–175, 184–185

uploading files, 240–241
user error, flagging, 622–623
user log out screen, 596–597
user login screen
- creating, 592–595
- described, 592
- limiting number of login attempts, 593
- login status, 595
- password protection, 593
- testing, 595
- welcome screen, 594

user profile, editing, 590–591

V

validating information, 587
variable text field, 508–509
variables, complex actions, 507

vector graphics
  bitmap graphics, conversion to, 376–377
  described, 264, 372
  formats, 373
vertical alignment, 331
vertical lines, 287, 307
viewing
  buttons, 453
  Design Notes, 255
  head content, 38
  hyperlinks, 101
  incremental changes, 415
  layers, 351, 353
  library items, 169
  source code, 32
  templates, 169
visibility of layers, 203, 226
volume, 477

W

waveforms, 464, 471
Web browsers. *See* browsers
Web links on CD-ROM, 700
Web pages
  creating, 46
  duplicating, 49
  keyboard shortcut used to save, 49
  opening, 44–45
  Preview in Browser command, 50–51
  previewing Web page in browser, 50–51
  saving, 48–49
  titles, adding, 47
Web servers, 5, 232
Web site building
  button animations, 572–573
  chat feature, 576–581
  drop-down menu, creating, 564–569
  hot buttons, adding, 562–563
  interface, creating sample Flash, 547
  intro text effect, creating, 552–553
  laser-writing animation effect, creating, 554–559
  overview, 544
  preloader, creating simple, 548–549
  publishing site, 545
  Root Property action statement, 570
  sample Web site, building, 544
  site navigation, 546
  site planning considerations, sample, 546
  site requirements, 546
  skip intro button, adding, 550–551
  starting Web site, 545
  storyboard, 546
  testing options, 571
  tool tips, 574–575
  welcome page, creating, 560–561
Web site publishing
  creating new folder, 235
  dead pages, removing, 243
  deleting file in Site window, 235
  downloading files, 240–241
  firewalls, 237
  FTP, 238
  host director, 239
  HTTP, 238
  ISPs, 232
  logging errors during file transfers, 241

(continued)

Web site publishing *(continued)*

opening file from Site window, 235
organizing files and folders, 234–235
premature disconnection from Web server, 239
rearranging site files, 234
recent files, determining which are, 243
remote sites, 236–239
server, moving site to different, 241
Site window, 233–235
SourceSafe, 237
steps for, 232
stopping file transfers, 241
synchronizing local and remote sites, 242–243
uploading files, 240–241
Web servers, 232
WebDAV, 237

Web sites

audience, defining, 9
building. *See* Web site building
content, gathering, 8
described, 5
hosting, 9
ideas, organizing, 8
ISPs, 9
planning, 8–9
publishing. *See* Web site publishing
site maintenance, 244–261
updating, 174–175, 184–185

WebDAV, 237
welcome page, 560–561
white space in regular expression, specifying, 261
windows
- closing, 653
- collapsing, 653
- draggable windows, 695
- getURL action used to control, 612–613
- hierarchy, creating, 652–655
- JavaScript used to control, 614–615
- moving, 17
- resizing, 17

wrap, making code, 33
wrapping behavior in forms, 134–135

X

_xmouse property, 651

Y

_ymouse property, 651

Z

Z-index, 226–227

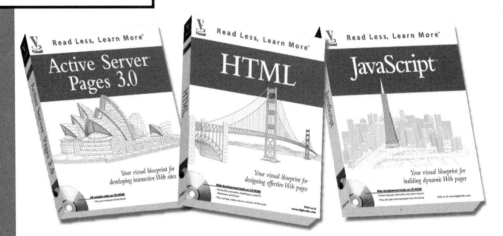

ORDER FORM

TRADE & INDIVIDUAL ORDERS

Phone: **(800) 762-2974**
or **(317) 572-3993**
(8 a.m.–6 p.m., CST, weekdays)
FAX : **(800) 550-2747**
or **(317) 572-4002**

EDUCATIONAL ORDERS & DISCOUNTS

Phone: **(800) 434-2086**
(8:30 a.m.–5:00 p.m., CST, weekdays)
FAX : **(317) 572-4005**

CORPORATE ORDERS FOR VISUAL™ SERIES

Phone: **(800) 469-6616**
(8 a.m.–5 p.m., EST, weekdays)
FAX : **(905) 890-9434**

Qty	ISBN	Title	Price	Total

Shipping & Handling Charges

	Description	First book	Each add'l. book	Total
Domestic	Normal	$4.50	$1.50	$
	Two Day Air	$8.50	$2.50	$
	Overnight	$18.00	$3.00	$
International	Surface	$8.00	$8.00	$
	Airmail	$16.00	$16.00	$
	DHL Air	$17.00	$17.00	$

Subtotal ______________

CA residents add applicable sales tax ______________

IN, MA and MD residents add 5% sales tax ______________

IL residents add 6.25% sales tax ______________

RI residents add 7% sales tax ______________

TX residents add 8.25% sales tax ______________

Shipping ______________

Total ______________

Ship to:

Name ______________________________

Address ______________________________

Company ______________________________

City/State/Zip ______________________________

Daytime Phone ______________________________

Payment: ☐ Check to Hungry Minds (US Funds Only)
☐ Visa ☐ Mastercard ☐ American Express

Card # ______________ Exp. __________ Signature ______________